DESIGN LAW

ELGAR INTELLECTUAL PROPERTY LAW AND PRACTICE

Series Editors: Trevor Cook, *Partner, WilmerHale* and Johanna Gibson, *Herchel Smith Professor of Intellectual Property Law, Queen Mary University of London*

The Elgar Intellectual Property Law and Practice series is a library of works by leading practitioners and scholars covering discrete areas of law in the field of intellectual property. Each title will describe the law in detail, but will also be deeply analytical, highlighting and unpicking the legal issues that are most critical and relevant to practice. Designed to be detailed, focused reference works, the books in this series aim to offer an authoritative statement on the law and practice in key topics within the field, from *Trade Marks* to *Pharmaceuticals*, from *Patent Standards* to *Trade Secrecy* and from *IP Licensing* to *IP Valuation*.

For a full list of Edward Elgar published titles, including the titles in this series, visit our website at www.e-elgar.com.

DESIGN LAW

DESIGN LAW

Global Law and Practice

Edited by

DANA BELDIMAN

Professor, Bucerius Law School, Hamburg, Germany, Professor-in-Residence, University of California Law San Francisco and Partner, Squire Patton Boggs LLP, San Francisco, USA

ELGAR INTELLECTUAL PROPERTY LAW AND PRACTICE

Cheltenham, UK • Northampton, MA, USA

© Editor and Contributing Authors Severally 2024

All rights reserved. No part of this publication may be reproduced, stored in a retrieval system or transmitted in any form or by any means, electronic, mechanical or photocopying, recording, or otherwise without the prior permission of the publisher.

Published by
Edward Elgar Publishing Limited
The Lypiatts
15 Lansdown Road
Cheltenham
Glos GL50 2JA
UK

Edward Elgar Publishing, Inc.
William Pratt House
9 Dewey Court
Northampton
Massachusetts 01060
USA

A catalogue record for this book
is available from the British Library

Library of Congress Control Number: 2024941204

This book is available electronically in the **Elgar**online
Law subject collection
https://dx.doi.org/10.4337/9781800886520

ISBN 978 1 80088 651 3 (cased)
ISBN 978 1 80088 652 0 (eBook)

Printed and bound by CPI Group (UK) Ltd, Croydon, CR0 4YY

CONTENTS

Extended contents	vii
List of figures	xxii
List of tables	xxiii
List of contributors	xxiv
Preface	xxvii
Table of cases	xxviii
Table of legislation	xlviii

Introduction to *Design Law* *Dana Beldiman*		1

PART I DESIGN LAWS AROUND THE WORLD COUNTRY-BY-COUNTRY

1	Overview of industrial design protection in Australia *Stuart Irvine and Carl Harrap*	30
2	Industrial design law in Canada – 2024 *Robert B. Storey, Adam Bobker, Matthew J. Graff and James Raakman*	80
3	Design law in China *Paolo Beconcini*	111
4	Industrial design law in France *Catherine Mateu*	159
5	Industrial design law in Italy *Marco F. Francetti and Matteo Mozzi*	184
6	Industrial design law in India *Shwetasree Majumder and Eva Bishwal*	209
7	Industrial design law in Japan *Taketo Nasu*	234
8	Design protection in the Nordic countries (Denmark, Finland and Sweden) *Teemu Matikainen, Jens Schovsbo and Marcus Norrgård*	265
9	Design patent law in the United States *Elizabeth Ferrill, Kelly Horn, William Neer and Troy Viger*	293
10	Design law at the crossroads – a post-Brexit review of design protection in the UK *Jane Cornwell and Lynne Chave*	337

| 11 | Design prosecution before the EUIPO and the Court of Justice of the EU
Henning Hartwig | 378 |

PART II INTERNATIONAL TREATIES AND JURISDICTION

12	The functioning of the African Regional Intellectual Property Organisation (ARIPO) for industrial design registration: realities and possibilities *Chijioke Okorie*	427
13	The Draft Design Law Treaty's forbidden words *Margo A. Bagley*	441
14	Multistate infringement of design rights: jurisdiction and applicable law – the European approach *Alexander von Mühlendahl*	455

PART III PRESENT-DAY AND FUTURE TRENDS IN DESIGN LAW

15	Redesigning design protection: the problem of overlap *Shubha Ghosh*	484
16	Prior art in EU design law and its worldwide implications – taking advantage of flexibilities or being obstructed by ambiguities *Lavinia Brancusi*	503
17	The concept of aesthetic creative freedom in design, copyright, and trademark law – a European perspective *Henning Hartwig*	541
18	Fashion and design law *Ulrika Wennersten, Laurent Manderieux and Patricia Covarrubia*	582

PART IV THE WAY FORWARD – A LOOK AT THE FUTURE

| 19 | Artificial intelligence and EU design law
Mikko Antikainen and Heidi Härkönen | 612 |
| 20 | Designing for the European Green Deal – a supplementary protection regime for circular designs in the EU
Dana Beldiman, Stina Teilmann-Lock and Anna Tischner | 651 |

| Index | 678 |

EXTENDED CONTENTS

List of figures	xxii
List of tables	xxiii
List of contributors	xxiv
Preface	xxvii
Table of cases	xxviii
Table of legislation	xlviii

INTRODUCTION TO *DESIGN LAW*

- A. INTRODUCTION — I.001
- B. HIGHLIGHTS OF SALIENT DESIGN LAW TOPICS — I.005
    1. Cumulative Protection — I.006
        - (a) The expansion of copyright protection — I.008
        - (b) Curtailing the effect of copyright protection — I.014
    2. Functionality — I.017
    3. Spare Parts and the Right to Repair — I.027
        - (a) The repair clause in the EU — I.029
        - (b) Repair clauses in other jurisdictions — I.033
        - (c) Jurisdictions without repair clauses — I.034
    4. Visibility — I.038
        - (a) EU present and proposed law on visibility — I.039
        - (b) Attenuated visibility requirement in some jurisdictions — I.042
        - (c) Jurisdictions maintaining visibility as a requirement — I.045
    5. Emerging Technologies — I.046
        - (a) The challenge of new technologies — I.046
        - (b) Workarounds — I.049
        - (c) Legal reform — I.050
        - (d) Artificial intelligence and design — I.052
- C. PRESENT-DAY TRENDS AND CHALLENGES IN DESIGN LAW — I.053
- D. THE WAY FORWARD – A LOOK AT THE FUTURE OF DESIGN LAW — I.062
- E. EU DESIGN LAW REFORM — I.066
    1. Design Regulation — I.068
        - (a) Definitions — I.068
        - (b) Visibility — I.070
        - (c) Repair clause — I.071
        - (d) Expanded digital infringement — I.072
        - (e) Additional defences — I.073
    2. Design Directive — I.074
        - (a) Elimination of unregistered designs at national level — I.075
        - (b) Repair clause transition period — I.076
        - (c) Cultural heritage — I.077
    3. Timeline for Adoption and Implementation — I.078

EXTENDED CONTENTS

PART I   DESIGN LAWS AROUND THE WORLD COUNTRY-BY-COUNTRY

1   OVERVIEW OF INDUSTRIAL DESIGN PROTECTION IN AUSTRALIA

A.	OVERVIEW OF INDUSTRIAL DESIGN PROTECTION IN AUSTRALIA	1.001
	1. Registered Designs in Australia	1.001
	2. Other Mechanisms for Protecting Industrial Designs in Australia	1.004
	(a) Protection of industrial designs via copyright	1.005
	(b) Protection of industrial designs via trade mark	1.011
	(c) Protection of industrial designs via consumer protection laws	1.014
	3. Sources of Law	1.016
	4. What is a Design	1.021
	(a) A 'product'	1.023
	(b) 'Visual features'	1.030
	(i) 'Visual features' vis-à-vis virtual designs	1.034
	5. Prior Art	1.041
	6. Grace Period and Prior Disclosure	1.046
	(a) Prior disclosure of a design on/after 10 March 2022	1.047
	(b) Prior disclosure of a design before 10 March 2022	1.052
	(c) Prior use of a 'corresponding design' that has not been applied industrially	1.054
	7. Exclusions from Protection	1.059
	8. Rights Granted	1.060
	9. Infringement	1.063
	(a) Infringing conduct	1.063
	10. Infringement Exemptions	1.067
	(a) Prior use	1.067
	(b) Spare parts exemption to infringement	1.072
	11. Substantial Similarity in Overall Impression	1.079
	12. The 'Familiar Person'	1.086
	13. Ownership and Entitlement	1.090
	(a) Rights of co-owners	1.096
	14. Term	1.099
B.	PROCEDURE	1.101
	1. Applications and Priority Date	1.101
	(a) Filing date and the minimum filing requirements	1.103
	(b) Multi-design applications	1.105
	(c) Further (or 'divisional') design applications	1.108
	(d) Priority date	1.113
	(e) Statements of Newness and Distinctiveness	1.119
	(f) Request for registration	1.123
	(g) Publication of design applications	1.126
	2. Registration Procedure	1.129
	(a) Notifications under section 41 and amendment	1.132
	(b) Formalities check	1.134
	(c) Designs that must be refused	1.138
	(d) A common design in relation to more than one product	1.139
	3. Post-registration Rights and Renewal	1.142
	4. Examination and Certification Procedure	1.146
	(a) Responses to notifications and amendment	1.149
	(b) Certificate of examination	1.153
	5. Amendments	1.155
	(a) Applications	1.155
	(b) Registered designs	1.160
	(c) Correction of the Register	1.166
	6. Challenges to Validity	1.168
	(a) Requesting examination	1.168
	(b) Providing information	1.170

			(c) Revocation proceedings before the Commissioner	1.173
			(d) Revocation and rectification proceedings before the Court	1.175
		7.	Extensions of Time	1.179
	C.	DISPUTES		1.185
		1.	Invalidity	1.185
		2.	Infringement	1.186
			(a) Infringement proceedings	1.186
			(b) Remedies for infringement	1.191
			(c) 'Innocent' infringement	1.193
			(d) Unjustified threats of infringement	1.196
	D.	SIGNIFICANT JUDICIAL DECISIONS IN THE JURISDICTION		1.201
		1.	Substantial Similarity in Overall Impression	1.201
			(a) *Review 2 Pty Ltd v Redberry Enterprise Pty Ltd* [2008] FCA 1588	1.201
			(b) *LED Technologies Pty Ltd v Roadvision Pty Ltd* [2012] FCAFC 3	1.209
			(c) *World of Technologies (Aust) Pty Ltd v Tempo (Aust) Pty Ltd* [2007] FCA 114	1.211
		2.	The Standard of the Informed User	1.214
			(a) *Multisteps Pty Ltd v Source and Sell Pty Ltd* [2013] FCA 743	1.214
			(b) *Astrazeneca AB* [2007] ADO 4	1.216
		3.	Clarity of the Design	1.219
			(a) *Keller v LED Technologies Pty Ltd* [2010] FCAFC 55	1.219
		4.	Evaluating the Validity of a Design over the Prior Art Base	1.222
			(a) *LED Technologies Pty Ltd v Elecspess Pty Ltd* [2008] FCA 1941	1.222
			(b) *Keller v LED Technologies Pty Ltd* [2010] FCAFC 55	1.224
		5.	Fonts and Graphical User Interfaces	1.225
			(a) *Microsoft Corporation* [2008] ADO 2	1.225
			(b) *Apple Inc* [2017] ADO 6	1.227
		6.	Repair Defence	1.229
			(a) *GM Global Technology Operations LLC v S.S.S. Auto Parts Pty Ltd* [2019] FCA 97	1.229
	E.	PRACTICAL ASPECTS OF DESIGN LAW		1.238
		1.	Australian Design Filings, Registrations, and Certifications	1.238
		2.	Court Cases	1.240
		3.	Assignment of Registered Designs	1.246
		4.	Compulsory Licences	1.249
	F.	COMMENTS, ANALYSIS, EVALUATION		1.252
		1.	Design Law Reform *de lege ferenda*	1.252
			(a) Protecting virtual or non-physical designs	1.255
			(b) Protecting partial designs	1.263
			(c) Protection for incremental improvements of designs	1.273
2	INDUSTRIAL DESIGN LAW IN CANADA – 2024			
	A.	FUNDAMENTALS OF CANADIAN DESIGN LAW		2.001
		1.	Relevant Legislation and Administration	2.001
			(a) Legislation	2.001
			(b) Administration	2.005
		2.	Protecting a Design	2.006
			(a) Subject matter	2.006
			(b) Required information	2.011
			(c) Application procedure	2.012
			(d) Design representation	2.014
			(e) Articles protected	2.015
			(f) Grace period	2.016
			(g) Geographic scope	2.017
			(h) Ownership rights	2.018
			(i) Period of examination	2.019
			(j) Typical costs	2.020
			(k) Alternative application mechanisms	2.021

		(l) Formalities	2.023
		(m) Priority	2.024
		(n) Deferred publication	2.026
	3.	Application Refusal	2.027
		(a) Grounds of objection	2.027
		(b) Response	2.028
		(c) Appeal of refusal	2.029
	4.	Third-party Oppositions	2.031
	5.	Registration	2.032
		(a) Effect of registration	2.032
		(b) Term	2.036
		(c) Renewal	2.038
	6.	Registrable Transactions	2.040
		(a) Assignments	2.040
		(b) Licences	2.042
		(c) Security interests	2.046
	7.	Invalidity	2.047
		(a) Grounds	2.047
		(b) Procedure	2.048
	8.	Design Enforcement	2.051
		(a) Jurisdiction	2.051
		(b) Infringement	2.052
		(c) Procedure	2.055
		(d) Injunctive relief	2.059
		(e) Stays	2.060
		(f) Expedited proceedings	2.061
		(g) Representation	2.064
		(h) Limitation period	2.065
		(i) Criminal liability	2.066
		(j) Unauthorised threats of infringement	2.067
	9.	Defences	2.068
		(a) Non-infringement	2.068
		(b) Additional grounds	2.070
	10.	Relief	2.071
		(a) Remedies	2.071
		(b) Recovery of costs	2.074
	11.	Appeal	2.075
		(a) Border control measures	2.077
	12.	Other Related Rights	2.078
	13.	Hague Agreement – International Protection for Canadian Applicants	2.080
		(a) Application procedure	2.081
		(b) Fees	2.085
		(c) Examination	2.088
		(d) Registration	2.091
		(e) Publication	2.092
	14.	Hague Agreement – Treatment of International Applications in Canada	2.095
		(a) Basic procedure	2.095
		(b) Examination	2.097
		(c) Unity of design	2.098
		(d) Novelty	2.100
		(e) Grant	2.101
		(f) Term and renewal	2.102
		(g) Transfers	2.106
B.		PRACTICAL ASPECTS OF CANADIAN DESIGN LAW	2.108
	1.	Effective Protection Strategies	2.108
		(a) Background	2.108

		(b) Protection under the Industrial Design Act	2.111
		(c) Copyright protection for designs	2.115
		(d) Trademark protection for designs	2.119
	2.	Statistics and Trends	2.124
		(a) Design applications filed and registrations granted	2.124
C.	COMMENTS ON CANADIAN DESIGN LAW		2.125
	1.	Legislative Reform	2.125
		(a) Legislative history	2.125
		(b) Novelty provision	2.128
		(c) Application requirements	2.133
		(d) Applications with multiple design variations	2.134
		(e) Amendments to applications	2.139
		(f) Recent policy and practice changes	2.143
		(g) Fee increase	2.148
		(h) Other issues	2.149
		(i) Final comment	2.154

3 DESIGN LAW IN CHINA

A.	SUBSTANTIVE ASPECTS OF DESIGN PROTECTION IN CHINA		3.001
	1.	Overview	3.001
	2.	Eligibility Requirements	3.005
		(a) Novelty	3.007
		(i) Disclosure by publication	3.008
		(ii) Disclosure by use	3.011
		(iii) Grace period	3.013
		(b) Distinctiveness	3.014
		(i) Visibility	3.016
		(c) Fit for industrial use	3.019
		(d) Good faith	3.021
	3.	Scope of Protection	3.022
		(a) Object of the comparison	3.025
		(b) The ordinary user test	3.028
		(c) Examination of the identity/similarity comparison	3.030
		(i) The evaluation process and the observation method	3.031
		(ii) Determination of the scope of protection and infringement in particular design cases	3.036
		(d) Examination of the scope of protection and designer's freedom	3.039
		(e) Functionality as a limit to the scope of protection	3.043
		(f) Ownership and terms	3.045
		(i) Ownership and service inventions	3.046
		(ii) Co-ownership	3.048
B.	PROCEDURAL ASPECTS OF DESIGN PROTECTION IN CHINA		3.049
	1.	National Registration	3.049
		(a) Granting authority	3.050
		(b) Priority	3.051
		(c) Application procedure	3.056
		(d) Drawings	3.062
		(e) Partial design	3.069
		(f) Examination procedure	3.080
		(g) Publication, registration and renewal	3.084
	2.	International Registrations	3.087
C.	DISPUTING DESIGN RIGHTS		3.090
	1.	Invalidation	3.090
	2.	Design Infringement	3.096
	3.	Civil Enforcement	3.098
		(a) Civil claims	3.102

				(b) Remedies	3.103
				(i) Damages	3.104
				(c) Most common defences	3.107
		4.	Administrative Enforcement		3.108
	D.	SIGNIFICANT JUDICIAL DECISIONS IN THE JURISDICTION			3.111
		1.	Scope of Protection and Designer Freedom		3.112
	E.	PRACTICAL ASPECTS OF DESIGN LAW			3.119
		1.	Business Aspects: Transferability/Licensing		3.119
			(a) Transfer of design patent rights and technology transfer		3.120
			(b) License of design patent rights		3.121
		2.	Specific Interesting Application of Design Patents		3.124
			(a) Auto parts		3.124
			(b) Design patents and the metaverse		3.125
	F.	CONCLUSION			3.127

4 INDUSTRIAL DESIGN LAW IN FRANCE

A.	SUBSTANTIVE			4.002
	1.	Legal Framework		4.003
	2.	Rights Granted, Ownership, Term		4.008
	3.	Conditions for Protection		4.012
		(a) The appearance of the product		4.016
		(b) Novelty		4.021
		(c) Individual character		4.027
		(d) Public policy and morality		4.032
		(e) Lack of functionality		4.034
		(f) Interconnectability		4.035
		(g) Harm to prior copyrights, designs and distinctive rights		4.036
		(h) Repair clause		4.037
B.	PROSECUTION			4.038
	1.	Duration		4.044
	2.	Priority		4.047
	3.	Grounds for Refusal		4.048
	4.	International Option		4.051
C.	DISPUTES			4.052
	1.	Invalidity Actions		4.052
	2.	Litigation		4.058
	3.	Remedies		4.064
	4.	Customs Measures		4.068
D.	PRACTICAL ASPECTS OF DESIGN LAW			4.070
	1.	A Few Figures		4.070
	2.	Business Aspects of Design Law		4.072
		(a) Exploitation of designs		4.073
		(b) Scope of the right		4.078
		(c) Limits of the right		4.083
E.	IMPORTANT JUDGMENTS RECENTLY ISSUED IN THE DESIGNS SPHERE			4.091
	1.	Comments, Analysis, Evaluation		4.101
	2.	Current Legal Framework		4.104
		(a) In France		4.104
		(b) In Europe		4.106
F.	THE EU LEGISLATION REFORM PROJECT			4.115
G.	FUTURE OUTLOOK RELATED TO 3D PRINTING			4.120

5 INDUSTRIAL DESIGN LAW IN ITALY

A.	PROTECTION OF INDUSTRIAL DESIGN	5.001
B.	THE LEGAL FRAMEWORK	5.005

C.	REQUIREMENTS FOR PROTECTION	5.011
D.	THE EXCLUSION OF PROTECTION DUE TO TECHNICAL CHARACTERISTICS	5.026
E.	REGISTRATION PROCEDURE	5.030
F.	THE RIGHTS CONFERRED BY THE REGISTRATION	5.041
G.	NULLITY OF THE REGISTRATION	5.048
H.	EXHAUSTION OF RIGHTS	5.051
I.	PROTECTION UNDER COPYRIGHT LAW	5.053
J.	ENFORCEMENT OF RIGHTS	5.065
K.	TECHNICAL EXPERTISE	5.097
L.	COMPENSATION FOR DAMAGES AND OTHER SANCTIONS	5.101
M.	CUSTOMS ENFORCEMENT	5.108
N.	ADMINISTRATIVE DATA	5.119

6 INDUSTRIAL DESIGN LAW IN INDIA

- A. SUBSTANTIVE AND PROCEDURAL LAW — 6.001
  1. Brief Overview of Industrial Design Protection in India and Applicable Legislations — 6.001
  2. Scheme of the Act — 6.006
     - (a) What is a design? — 6.006
     - (b) What is an article? — 6.009
     - (c) Functionality — 6.012
     - (d) Industrial process or means — 6.015
     - (e) What is 'new' and 'original'? — 6.016
     - (f) Grace period for 'exhibitions' — 6.022
     - (g) Reciprocity arrangement and priority — 6.024
     - (h) Classification of articles — 6.025
     - (i) Rights granted and term — 6.026
     - (j) Lapsed design — 6.029
  3. Procedure — 6.030
     - (a) Registration — 6.030
       - (i) Summary of steps — 6.030
       - (ii) Formality — 6.038
       - (iii) Substantive examination — 6.040
         - NEW OR ORIGINAL — 6.041
         - HAS BEEN DISCLOSED TO THE PUBLIC IN INDIA OR IN ANY OTHER COUNTRY — 6.043
         - IS NOT SIGNIFICANTLY DISTINGUISHABLE FROM A KNOWN DESIGN — 6.044
         - COMPRISES CONTAINS SCANDALOUS OR OBSCENE MATERIAL — 6.047
  4. Other IP laws that Protect the Two- and Three-dimensional Appearance of Products — 6.048
     - (a) Trademarks — 6.048
     - (b) Copyrights — 6.054
     - (c) Patents — 6.058
  5. Disputes — 6.060
     - (a) Cancellation — 6.061
       - (i) Prior-registered designs — 6.062
       - (ii) Prior publication — 6.063
         - PUBLICATION IN PRIOR DOCUMENTS — 6.065
         - PUBLICATION BY PRIOR USE — 6.066
       - (iii) Not new or original — 6.067
       - (iv) Not registerable under this Act — 6.068
       - (v) Not a design defined under section 2 (d) — 6.069
     - (b) Piracy — 6.070
- B. PRACTICAL ASPECTS OF DESIGN LAW — 6.073
  1. Licensing of Design Rights — 6.073
  2. Assignment — 6.076
- C. EVALUATION, ANALYSIS, COMMENTS — 6.078

7 INDUSTRIAL DESIGN LAW IN JAPAN

- A. DESCRIPTIVE PART — 7.001
  - 1. Substantive — 7.001
    - (a) Brief overview of industrial design protection in the jurisdiction — 7.001
      - (i) Design — 7.002
      - (ii) Trademark — 7.007
      - (iii) Copyright — 7.008
      - (iv) Unfair competition — 7.009
    - (b) Legal framework for registered and non-registered industrial design in effect in Japan — 7.010
      - (i) Industrially applicable — 7.012
      - (ii) Novel — 7.013
      - (iii) Not easily creatable — 7.015
      - (iv) Not identical or similar to a part of design in earlier applications — 7.016
      - (v) First-to-file rule — 7.017
      - (vi) Unregistrable items — 7.019
  - 2. Registration Procedure — 7.020
    - (a) National registration — 7.020
      - (i) Enjoyment of rights — 7.020
      - (ii) Application procedure — 7.022
      - (iii) Appeal trial — 7.028
      - (iv) Post registration — 7.030
      - (v) Remedies in cases of inconsistent views, etc. — 7.034
      - (vi) Priority claim — 7.036
    - (b) International registration — 7.037
  - 3. Disputes — 7.040
    - (a) Prosecution — 7.040
      - (i) Grounds for invalidity — 7.040
      - (ii) Procedure – invalidation trial — 7.042
      - (iii) Procedure – action against trial decision — 7.045
    - (b) Litigation — 7.048
      - (i) Scope of protection — 7.048
      - (ii) Finding infringement in view of the specific scope of protection — 7.051
      - (iii) Defences — 7.052
      - (iv) Enforcement (injunction, damages) — 7.057
    - (c) Other dispute resolution — 7.063
      - (i) Customs measures — 7.063
      - (ii) Criminal penalty — 7.064
  - 4. Significant Judicial Decisions in the Jurisdiction — 7.065
    - (a) *Flexible and Elastic Hose* case — 7.065
    - (b) *Carabiner* case — 7.066
- B. PRACTICAL ASPECTS OF DESIGN LAW — 7.067
  - 1. Statistics/Trends — 7.067
    - (a) Number of filings — 7.067
    - (b) Number of court cases — 7.068
    - (c) Rate of success; etc. — 7.069
  - 2. Business Aspects — 7.070
    - (a) Transferability — 7.070
    - (b) Licensing — 7.072
  - 3. Specific Interesting Applications or Case Studies — 7.075
- C. COMMENTS, ANALYSIS, EVALUATION — 7.076
  - 1. Comments on Present Legal Framework (Legislation and Case Law) — 7.076
  - 2. Design Law Reform *de lege ferenda* — 7.077
  - 3. Future Outlook in Light of New Technologies — 7.078

EXTENDED CONTENTS

8 DESIGN PROTECTION IN THE NORDIC COUNTRIES (DENMARK, FINLAND AND SWEDEN)

- A. DESCRIPTIVE PART — 8.001
  1. Substantive — 8.001
     - (a) Brief history of industrial design protection in the Nordic countries — 8.001
     - (b) Overview of the current situation — 8.010
     - (c) A closer look at the (national) design right system in the Nordic countries — 8.018
  2. Procedural Aspects — 8.030
  3. Disputes — 8.037
     - (a) Grounds for invalidity — 8.037
     - (b) Litigation — 8.040
  4. Significant Judicial Decisions in the Jurisdiction — 8.049
- B. PRACTICAL ASPECTS OF DESIGN LAW — 8.057
- C. COMMENTS, ANALYSIS, EVALUATION — 8.064

9 DESIGN PATENT LAW IN THE UNITED STATES

- A. DESCRIPTIVE PART — 9.001
  1. Substantive Aspects of U.S. Design Patent Law — 9.001
     - (a) Sources of design patent law — 9.003
     - (b) Protectable subject matter — 9.006
     - (c) Design disclosure requirements — 9.008
     - (d) Novelty (anticipation) — 9.011
     - (e) Obviousness (inventive step) — 9.013
     - (f) Additional considerations — 9.014
     - (g) Related IP laws and comparison to design protection — 9.017
       - (i) Utility patents — 9.018
       - (ii) Copyright — 9.019
       - (iii) Trademarks/trade dress — 9.021
       - (iv) Unfair Competition Prevention Acts — 9.023
  2. Procedural — 9.024
     - (a) Registration procedure — 9.024
     - (b) Overview — 9.025
     - (c) Application requirements — 9.027
     - (d) Priority — 9.035
     - (e) Expedited examination — 9.036
     - (f) Amendments — 9.037
     - (g) International registration — 9.038
  3. Disputes — 9.039
     - (a) Prosecution — 9.039
       - (i) Administrative body — 9.039
       - (ii) Legal grounds — 9.041
       - (iii) Challenges — 9.043
       - (iv) Timing — 9.046
       - (v) Fees — 9.047
     - (b) Litigation — 9.048
       - (i) Related enforcement proceedings to prosecution — 9.048
       - (ii) Infringement — 9.049
       - (iii) Direct infringement — 9.053
       - (iv) Indirect infringement — 9.057
       - (v) Defences to infringement — 9.059
       - (vi) Remedies for infringement — 9.063
  4. Significant Judicial Decisions in the United States — 9.071
     - (a) *Egyptian Goddess, Inc. v. Swisa, Inc.*, 543 F.3d 665 (Fed. Cir. 2008) (en banc) — 9.071
     - (b) *International Seaway Trading Corp. v. Walgreens Corp.*, 589 F.3d 1233 (Fed. Cir. 2009) — 9.072

EXTENDED CONTENTS

			(c) *In re SurgiSil, L.L.P.*, 14 F.4th 1380 (Fed. Cir. 2021)	9.074
			(d) *In re Maatita*, 900 F.3d 1369 (Fed. Cir. 2018)	9.078
			(e) *In re Daniels*, 144 F.3d 1452 (Fed. Cir. 1998)	9.081
			(f) *In re Owens*, 710 F.3d 1362 (Fed. Cir. 2013)	9.084
			(g) *Hoop v. Hoop*, 279 F.3d 1004 (Fed. Cir. 2002)	9.088
			(h) *Pacific Coast Marine Windshields Ltd. v. Malibu Boats, LLC*, 739 F.3d 694 (Fed. Cir. 2014)	9.089
			(i) *Samsung Electronics Co. v. Apple Inc.*, 137 S. Ct. 429 (2016)	9.091
			(j) *Columbia Sportswear N. Am., Inc. v. Seirus Innovative Accessories, Inc.*, 80 F.4th 1363 (Fed. Cir. 2023)	9.092
	B.	PRACTICAL ASPECTS OF DESIGN LAW		9.095
		1.	Statistics/Trends	9.095
		2.	Business Aspects: Transferability/Licensing	9.104
		3.	Case Studies	9.107
	C.	COMMENTS, ANALYSIS, AND EVALUATION		9.116
		1.	Comments on Present Legal Framework (Legislation and Case Law)	9.116
			(a) Design patent enforcement in district court	9.116
			(b) Design patent enforcement at the International Trade Commission	9.117
		2.	Design Law Reform De Lege Ferenda	9.119
			(a) Conflict between product life cycle and design patent pendency at the USPTO	9.119
		3.	Areas in Which Improvement/Amendment Is Required (e.g., Inconsistencies, Gaps, and Insufficiencies), and How They Should Be Corrected	9.122
			(a) Damages for design patent infringement	9.122
			(b) Multi-component products under the total profits rule	9.124
		4.	Future Outlook in Light of New Technologies	9.128

10 DESIGN LAW AT THE CROSSROADS – A POST-BREXIT REVIEW OF DESIGN PROTECTION IN THE UK

	A.	OVERVIEW		10.001
	B.	UK REGISTERED DESIGNS		10.004
		1.	Introduction	10.004
		2.	Requirements for Valid UK Design Registration	10.007
			(a) 'Design'	10.007
			(b) Novelty and individual character	10.011
			(c) Exclusions from protection	10.023
		3.	Ownership, Duration and Post-grant Invalidation	10.027
		4.	Infringement and Defences	10.031
	C.	UK UNREGISTERED DESIGN RIGHTS		10.035
		1.	UK Unregistered Design Right	10.035
			(a) Introduction	10.035
			(b) Qualification	10.039
			(c) Protectable UKUDR 'designs'	10.041
			(d) Exclusions from UKUDR	10.045
			(e) Originality	10.050
			(f) Ownership and duration	10.053
			(g) Infringement and defences	10.055
		2.	New Post-Brexit Forms of UK Unregistered Design	10.059
	D.	OTHER IP RIGHTS PROTECTING DESIGNS		10.064
		1.	Copyright	10.065
		2.	Registered Trade Marks and Passing Off	10.068
	E.	PROCEDURE AND ENFORCEMENT		10.070
		1.	UK Design Registration Procedure	10.070
			(a) Introduction	10.070
			(b) Filing basics	10.071
			(c) Examination	10.075
			(d) Publication, registration and post-grant matters	10.077

		2.	Enforcement of Design Rights	10.079
			(a) Introduction	10.079
			(b) Choice of forum	10.080
			(c) Pre-action communications, 'threats' and standing to sue	10.083
			(d) The English courts' approach to design cases	10.085
			(e) Remedies	10.088
			(f) Criminal enforcement	10.093
	F.	CONCLUSION		10.095

11 DESIGN PROSECUTION BEFORE THE EUIPO AND THE COURT OF JUSTICE OF THE EU

	A.	INTRODUCTION TO THE COMMUNITY DESIGN SYSTEM		11.001
	B.	FACTS, EVIDENCE, AND ARGUMENTS		11.006
		1.	EUIPO Case Law and Practice	11.009
		2.	General Court and CJEU	11.011
	C.	DISCLOSURE OF PRIOR ART		11.016
		1.	Relevant Prior Art	11.018
		2.	Disclosure of Obscure Prior Art	11.023
		3.	Disclosure of Own Prior Art	11.026
		4.	Disclosure of Confidential Prior Art	11.028
		5.	Disclosure of Prior Art as a Consequence of an Abuse	11.031
		6.	Burden of Submission and Proof in a Case of Unauthorised Disclosure	11.035
	D.	NOVELTY OF THE COMMUNITY DESIGN		11.038
	E.	INDIVIDUAL CHARACTER OF THE COMMUNITY DESIGN		11.045
		1.	Degree of Freedom of the Designer	11.051
		2.	Informed User	11.053
		3.	Overall Impression	11.057
	F.	LACK OF CONSISTENCY OF THE COMMUNITY DESIGN		11.061
		1.	Lack of Unity in Invalidity Proceedings	11.066
		2.	Lack of Unity in Registration Proceedings	11.070
	G.	OTHER GROUNDS OF INHERENT INVALIDITY OF THE COMMUNITY DESIGN		11.073
		1.	Features of Community Design Solely Dictated by Technical Function	11.074
		2.	Features of Community Design Necessarily Reproduced to Permit Interconnectivity	11.080
		3.	Exception in Case of Modular System	11.083
		4.	Visible During Normal Use	11.088
	H.	CONFLICT BETWEEN EARLIER TRADEMARK AND LATER COMMUNITY DESIGN		11.095
		1.	Trademark Standards	11.096
		2.	Distinctive Sign (Earlier Mark)	11.098
		3.	Genuine Use of the Earlier Mark	11.100
		4.	Use of the Earlier Mark in the Later Design as a Mark	11.101
		5.	Use of the Earlier Mark in the Later Design for Similar or Identical Goods and Services	11.102
		6.	Similarity of Signs	11.106
		7.	Likelihood of Confusion	11.107
		8.	Maintenance of the Later Design in an Amended Form?	11.108
	I.	CONFLICT BETWEEN EARLIER COPYRIGHT AND LATER COMMUNITY DESIGN		11.112
		1.	Copyright Standards	11.113
		2.	Work Protected Under National Copyright Law	11.115
		3.	Unauthorised Use of the Work	11.118
	J.	CONFLICT BETWEEN EARLIER DESIGN AND LATER COMMUNITY DESIGN		11.121
		1.	Design Infringement Standards	11.122
		2.	Degree of Freedom of the Designer of the Earlier Design	11.124
		3.	Scope of Protection of the Earlier Design	11.130
		4.	Infringing Use of the Earlier Design by the Later Community Design	11.131
	K.	CONCLUSIONS		11.133

PART II INTERNATIONAL TREATIES AND JURISDICTION

12 THE FUNCTIONING OF THE AFRICAN REGIONAL INTELLECTUAL PROPERTY ORGANISATION (ARIPO) FOR INDUSTRIAL DESIGN REGISTRATION: REALITIES AND POSSIBILITIES

A.	INTRODUCTION	12.001
B.	THE LEGAL FRAMEWORK OF ARIPO'S INDUSTRIAL DESIGN SYSTEM	12.006
	1. The Registration Procedure at ARIPO	12.009
	2. The Formal Examination	12.013
	3. 'Opposition' by Member States	12.017
	4. Substantive Examination	12.021
	5. Appeals	12.028
C.	THE HARARE PROTOCOL: REALITIES AND FILING TRENDS	12.029
D.	FUTURE POSSIBILITIES: ARIPO AND THE AFRICAN CONTINENTAL FREE TRADE AREA AGREEMENT	12.031
E.	CONCLUSION	12.036

13 THE DRAFT DESIGN LAW TREATY'S FORBIDDEN WORDS

A.	INTRODUCTION	13.001
B.	THE AFRICAN GROUP DISCLOSURE OF ORIGIN PROPOSAL	13.007
C.	THE NEED FOR POLICY SPACE AND EXPERIMENTATION IN DESIGN LAW	13.017
D.	THE DRAFT DESIGN LAW TREATY AND THE WIPO IGC	13.026
E.	CONCLUSION	13.032

14 MULTISTATE INFRINGEMENT OF DESIGN RIGHTS: JURISDICTION AND APPLICABLE LAW – THE EUROPEAN APPROACH

A.	INTRODUCTION	14.001
B.	EUROPEAN UNION	14.004
	1. IP Rights in the EU	14.004
	2. Enforcement of IP Rights in the EU	14.006
	3. Infringement of National Design Rights	14.010
	(a) Design right protected in a single Member State	14.010
	(b) Multiple parallel national design rights	14.019
	(c) Applicable law to the infringement of national design rights	14.024
	4. Unitary IP Rights	14.025
	(a) Competent courts	14.026
	(b) Jurisdiction	14.030
	(i) Subject-matter jurisdiction	14.031
	(ii) International jurisdiction	14.034
	(AA) COMMUNITY DESIGN COURTS WITH EU-WIDE JURISDICTION	14.035
	(BB) COMMUNITY DESIGN COURTS WITH LIMITED JURISDICTION	14.038
	(iii) Multiple defendants – involuntary joinder of several parties	14.040
	(iv) Jurisdictions for provisional measures and remedies	14.043
	(c) Defences	14.044
	(d) Applicable law	14.045
	(e) Related actions	14.053
C.	THE EUROPEAN UNION AND THE LUGANO CONVENTION	14.057
D.	SOLUTIONS AT THE INTERNATIONAL LEVEL	14.063
	1. Hague Conference on Private International Law	14.063
	2. Academic Studies and Proposals	14.065
	(a) CLIP Principles	14.067
	(i) Jurisdiction	14.069
	(ii) Applicable law	14.070
	(b) Kyoto Guidelines	14.072

		(i) Jurisdiction		14.074
		(ii) Applicable law		14.077

PART III PRESENT-DAY AND FUTURE TRENDS IN DESIGN LAW

15 REDESIGNING DESIGN PROTECTION: THE PROBLEM OF OVERLAP
A.	INTRODUCTION	15.001
B.	MEANING OF DESIGN	15.010
	1. Industrial Design	15.018
	2. Ornamental Design	15.028
	3. Functional Design	15.042
C.	CRITICAL CONCERNS OF OVERLAPPING REGIMES	15.043
	1. Design Patent in US with Some Comparison with Japanese Design Registration	15.043
	2. The Problem of Overlap	15.049
D.	CONCLUSION	15.052

16 PRIOR ART IN EU DESIGN LAW AND ITS WORLDWIDE IMPLICATIONS – TAKING ADVANTAGE OF FLEXIBILITIES OR BEING OBSTRUCTED BY AMBIGUITIES
A.	INTRODUCTION	16.001
B.	DEFINING PRIOR ART IN THE EU DESIGN LAW	16.005
	1. Setting the Scene	16.006
	(a) EU prior art matching the model of relative novelty	16.007
	(b) Presumptive knowledge of disclosure established by administrative or judicial body	16.011
	2. What Constitutes Disclosure, What Does Not?	16.015
	(a) Rules of disclosure	16.017
	(b) The safeguard clause – the general exception	16.023
	(c) First disclosure of an unregistered Community design	16.028
	3. Additional Normative Exceptions	16.032
	(a) Confidential disclosure	16.033
	(b) Disclosure within 'grace period'	16.034
	(c) Abusive disclosure	16.039
C.	ISSUES OF THE SUBJECT-MATTER DISCLOSED UNDER THE EU DESIGN LAW	16.042
	1. The Subject-matter of a Relevant Piece of Prior Art	16.043
	(a) EU concepts of 'design' and 'product'	16.044
	(b) Earlier disclosure and IPRs	16.048
	2. Comparing a Contested Design with an Earlier Disclosure	16.051
	(a) The significance of the representation of 'design features' vis-à-vis wording	16.052
	(b) Relevant subject-matter for the comparison of two designs when testing novelty or individual character	16.057
	(c) Subject-matter of self-disclosure and grace period	16.062
D.	THE INTERSECTION BETWEEN EU PRIOR ART AND FOREIGN STANDARDS – REMARKS FROM GLOBAL PERSPECTIVE	16.065
	1. Divergent Standards of Prior Art – Absolute Novelty and Different Models of Grace Period	16.067
	2. Divergent Notions of a Protectable Design	16.073
	3. Concluding Remarks	16.080

17 THE CONCEPT OF AESTHETIC CREATIVE FREEDOM IN DESIGN, COPYRIGHT, AND TRADEMARK LAW – A EUROPEAN PERSPECTIVE
A.	INTRODUCTION	17.001
B.	THE LEGAL CONCEPT OF AESTHETIC CREATIVE FREEDOM	17.002

	C.	AESTHETIC CREATIVE FREEDOM IN DESIGN, COPYRIGHT, AND TRADEMARK LAW	17.007
		1. Aesthetic Creative Freedom in Design Law	17.008
		2. Aesthetic Creative Freedom in Copyright Law	17.014
		3. Aesthetic Creative Freedom in Trademark Law	17.044
	D.	LIMITS TO AESTHETIC CREATIVE FREEDOM IN DESIGN, COPYRIGHT, AND TRADEMARK LAW	17.046
		1. Limits to Aesthetic Creative Freedom in Design Law	17.047
		(a) Aesthetic limits	17.047
		(b) Technical limits	17.050
		(c) Statutory limits	17.057
		2. Limits to Aesthetic Creative Freedom in Copyright Law	17.064
		(a) Aesthetic limits	17.064
		(b) Technical limits	17.067
		(c) Statutory limits	17.074
		3. Limits to Aesthetic Creative Freedom in Trademark Law	17.076
		(a) Aesthetic limits	17.076
		(b) Technical limits	17.078
		(c) Statutory limits	17.085
	E.	COMPARABLE STANDARDS UNDER DESIGN, COPYRIGHT, AND TRADEMARK LAW?	17.088
		1. Commonalities	17.089
		2. Differences	17.092
		3. Too Much Cumulation?	17.096

18 FASHION AND DESIGN LAW

	A.	GLOBAL PERSPECTIVE ON THE PROTECTION OF FASHION BY DESIGN LAW	18.001
		1. Introduction	18.001
	B.	THE PROTECTION OF FASHION BY EU DESIGN LAW	18.011
		1. Fashion and the Concept of Design	18.011
		2. Community and National Registered Design	18.016
		(a) Novelty and individual character	18.021
		(b) Grounds for refusal	18.028
		3. Unregistered Community Designs	18.032
		4. Ownership of Design in the Fashion Industry	18.038
		5. Infringement in the Fashion Industry	18.041
	C.	CONTEMPORARY ISSUES IN THE FASHION INDUSTRY	18.052
		1. Artificial Intelligence, Fashion and Design Law	18.052
		2. 3D and 4D Printing in Fashion and Design Law	18.057
		3. Fashion and Traditional Knowledge	18.061
		4. Fashion, Design Law, and Circular Economy	18.066
		5. Overlapping IP Protections for Fashion in EU Law	18.075

PART IV   THE WAY FORWARD – A LOOK AT THE FUTURE

19 ARTIFICIAL INTELLIGENCE AND EU DESIGN LAW

	A.	INTRODUCTION	19.001
	B.	DESIGN AND DESIGN LAW IN THE DIGITAL AGE	19.007
		1. The Roots of the Design Regime and the Digital Revolution of Design	19.007
		2. Virtual/Digital Designs According to EU Design Law	19.011
	C.	AI-DRIVEN DESIGN IN THE IP REGIME	19.022
		1. AI and IP in General	19.022
		2. AI-generated Output as Artistic Works: The Conflict with Copyright	19.026
		3. AI and EU Design Law: The Issues of 'Designership' and Design Development	19.030
		(a) 'Designership'	19.034
		(b) The concept of 'design development' in EU design law	19.045

			(c) Practical implications	19.059
	D.	TAILORING EU DESIGN LAW FOR THE DIGITAL AGE?		19.068
		1.	Design-based Approach in the Age of AI	19.068
		2.	Issues to Consider in Terms of Protecting Purely AI-generated Designs	19.079
	E.	CONCLUSIONS		19.083

20 DESIGNING FOR THE EUROPEAN GREEN DEAL – A SUPPLEMENTARY PROTECTION REGIME FOR CIRCULAR DESIGNS IN THE EU

	A.	INTRODUCTION		20.001
	B.	BACKGROUND – THE CIRCULAR ECONOMY'S DESIGN MANDATES		20.007
		1.	Circularity in the Design Industry	20.008
		2.	Circular Business Models for Design: Gerrard Street and Skagarak	20.013
	C.	DESIGN LAW IN LIGHT OF CIRCULAR DESIGN POLICY GOALS		20.017
		1.	Design Law Policies in a Linear Economy	20.017
		2.	Design Law in a Circular Economy	20.023
	D.	THE OBJECT OF PROTECTION		20.028
		1.	Trapped by the Concept of a Product's Appearance	20.029
		2.	Is There a Way Ahead?	20.032
	E.	CONSIDERATIONS FOR A NEW DESIGN LAW MODEL		20.036
		1.	Introduction	20.036
		2.	Access and Incentive	20.041
			(a) Two models	20.043
			(i) Compensatory liability regime	20.044
			(ii) The unregistered design regime	20.050
			(b) The envisioned circular design protection regime	20.055
			(c) Does the proposed model provide an adequate balance between early and broad access and incentive to be attractive to circular designers?	20.059
	F.	CONCLUSION		20.065

Index   678

FIGURES

9.1	Drawing of SurgiSil lip implant	314
9.2	Drawing of Blick art tool 'Stump'	314
9.3	Drawing of shoe bottom	315
9.4	Drawing of 'leecher' with and without leaf	316
9.5	Drawings of the mouthwash bottle of the '709 application	317
9.6	Drawings of the mouthwash bottle of the '172 application	318
9.7	Drawing of Fig. 2 in Design Patent No. D435,332	325
9.8	Drawing of Fig. 1 of the D542,211 patent	326
9.9	Product sold by Defendants on eBay with part number MBZ-610–19-MB	327
9.10	Drawing of Fig. 1 of Design Patent D593,087	328
9.11	Drawing of Fig. 1 of Design Patent D618,677	328
9.12	Drawing of Fig. 1 of Design Patent D504,889	328
9.13	Drawing of Fig. 1 of Design Patent D604,305	328

TABLES

1.1	Australian design filings, registrations, and certifications	73
2.1	Canadian industrial design applications filed	104
2.2	Canadian industrial design registrations granted	105
6.1	Comparison of visual features protected by design law and functional features protected by patent law	226
7.1	The JPO Status Report 2023	260
7.2	Number of civil cases involving design rights before the District Court	261
7.3	Number of civil cases involving design rights before the High Court	261
7.4	Number of actions against the JPO's trial decision involving design rights before the intellectual property high court	261
8.1	The number of direct national design right applications in Denmark, Finland and Sweden (1980–2020)	287
9.1	U.S. design patent applications filed (USPTO, U.S. patent statistics chart calendar years 1963–2020, USPTO, design data August 2023)	322
15.1	Breakdown of patent and design applications and grants in 2017	500
15.2	Top recipients of design patents, 2017	500
15.3	Overlapping design protection in furniture	502
15.4	Overlapping design protection in jewellery	502

CONTRIBUTORS

Mikko Antikainen, Senior Lecturer in Commercial Law, Jyväskylä University School of Business and Economics, Finland.

Margo A. Bagley, Vice Dean and Asa Griggs Candler Professor of Law, Emory University School of Law, USA.

Paolo Beconcini, Head of the China Intellectual Property Team at Squire Patton Boggs LLP, China/USA.

Dana Beldiman, Dr. jur., M.A., J.D., L.L.M., Professor of Law and Academic Director of Transnational Center of Technology, IP and Media Law, Bucerius Law School, Hamburg, Germany; Professor in Residence, University of California Law San Francisco, USA, Partner, Squire Patton Boggs LLP, San Francisco, USA.

Eva Bishwal, Associate, Fidus Chambers, India.

Adam Bobker, Barrister and Solicitor, Registered Trademark Agent, Partner, Bereskin & Parr LLP, Toronto, Canada.

Lavinia Brancusi, Dr. iur., Institute of Law Studies, Polish Academy of Sciences, New Technologies Law Centre, Warsaw, Poland.

Lynne Chave, UCL Institute of Brand and Innovation Law, University College London, UK.

Jane Cornwell, Senior Lecturer in Intellectual Property Law, University of Edinburgh, UK.

Patricia Covarrubia, Reader in Intellectual Property Law, School of Law, University of Buckingham, UK.

Elizabeth Ferrill, Attorney-at-Law, Finnegan LLP, Washington DC, USA.

Marco F. Francetti, Attorney-at-Law admitted before the Supreme Court, Studio Legale Jacobacci & Associati, Milan, Italy.

Shubha Ghosh, Ph.D., J.D., Crandall Melvin Professor of Law, Syracuse University College of Law, USA.

Matthew J. Graff, Barrister and Solicitor, Registered Patent and Trademark Agent, Partner, Bereskin & Parr LLP, Mississauga, Canada.

Carl Harrap, Patent Attorney, Principal at FPA Patent Attorneys Pty Ltd, Australia.

Heidi Härkönen, LL.D. (trained on the bench), Postdoctoral researcher, Faculty of Law, University of Turku, Finland.

Henning Hartwig, Dr. jur., Attorney-at-Law, Partner, BARDEHLE PAGENBERG, Munich, Germany.

Kelly Horn, Attorney-at-Law, Finnegan LLP, Washington DC, USA.

Stuart Irvine, Patent Attorney, Principal at FPA Patent Attorneys Pty Ltd, Australia.

Shwetasree Majumder, Attorney-at-Law, Managing Partner, Fidus Chambers, India.

Laurent Manderieux, Professor of Intellectual Property Law, Member of the Directorate Board, L.L.M. in Law of Internet Technology, Law Department, Bocconi University, Milan, Italy.

Catherine Mateu, Lawyer Specialised in Intellectual Property, partner at ARMENGAUD GUERLAIN, Paris, France.

Teemu Matikainen, Doctor of Laws (LL.D.), University of Helsinki, Finland.

Matteo Mozzi, Italian and European Patent Attorney, Jacobacci & Partners SpA firm, Milan, Italy.

Alexander von Mühlendahl, Dr.Iur.; J.D., LL.M. (Northwestern Univ.); Attorney-at-Law and Senior Counsel, BARDEHLE PAGENBERG, Munich, Germany; Visiting Professor, Centre for Commercial Law Studies (CCLS), Queen Mary University of London, UK.

Taketo Nasu, Attorney-at-Law, Blakemore & Mitsuki, Tokyo, Japan.

Marcus Norrgård, Dr.jur., Professor of Law, Faculty of Law/Vaasa Unit, University of Helsinki, Finland.

William Neer, Attorney-at-Law, Finnegan LLP, Washington DC, USA.

Chijioke Okorie, Ph.D, Lecturer in Intellectual property law and Chief Researcher/Founder, Data Science Law Lab, Faculty of Law, University of Pretoria, South Africa.

CONTRIBUTORS

James Raakman, Barrister and Solicitor, Registered Patent and Trademark Agent, Partner, Bereskin & Parr LLP, Mississauga, Canada.

Jens Schovsbo, Dr.jur., Ph.D, Professor of intellectual property law, Center for Information and Innovation Law (CIIR), University of Copenhagen, Denmark.

Robert B. Storey, Barrister and Solicitor, Registered Patent and Trademark Agent, Partner, Bereskin & Parr LLP, Montréal, Canada.

Stina Teilmann-Lock, Ph.D, Associate Professor and Research Director of Governance, Culture and Learning; Department of Business Humanities & Law; Copenhagen Business School, Denmark.

Anna Tischner, Dr hab., Professor, Intellectual Property Law Chair, Faculty of Law, Jagiellonian University, Krakow, Poland.

Troy Viger, Attorney-at-Law, Finnegan LLP, Washington DC, USA.

Ulrika Wennersten, Associate Professor in Private Law, Faculty of Law, Lund University, Sweden.

PREFACE

This will extend my heartfelt appreciation to Edward Elgar Publishing for their invaluable support and facilitation in bringing this publication to fruition. Special recognition goes to Stephanie Tytherleigh for her unwavering encouragement and assistance throughout the process of developing this book.

The guidance and insights provided by Anna Tischner and Henning Hartwig have been of immeasurable value in shaping this project. I am indebted to Ramya Singh for her essential contribution in editing chapters of this book with thoroughness and meticulous attention to detail.

Above all, I wish to express my profound gratitude to our esteemed contributors hailing from diverse corners of the globe. Their dedication in sharing their extensive knowledge have greatly enriched this book with profound insights and intellectual depth. I am confident that the book's chapters will serve as windows to new cultures and fresh perspectives on design law for our readers.

Finally, I extend my heartfelt thanks to my husband, Justs Karlsons, for his unwavering support and understanding, and having displayed the patience of Job throughout the duration of this extensive project.

Dana Beldiman

TABLE OF CASES

EUROPEAN UNION (EU)

Activa v Targa [Grilling apparatus], EUIPO (Board of Appeal), 4 October 2021, R 1651/2020–3   **11.017**

Actona v Inter Link [Coffee tables], EUIPO (Board of Appeal), 5 February 2015, R 1496/2013–3   **11.019**

Beverly Hills Teddy Bear Co v PMS International Group Plc [2020] FSR 11   **10.063**

Biscuits Poult v Banketbakkerij Merva Case T-494/12 EU:T2014757   **18.022**

Blake [Outer portion of a tyre], EUIPO (Board of Appeal), 29 August 2022, R 197/2021–5   **17.044**

Blažek Glass v Šindelařova [Nail files], EUIPO (Board of Appeal), 28 July 2009, R 921/2008–3   **11.041**

BoA dec. in cases R 0151/2017–3 9 (European patent)   **16.048**

BoA dec. in cases R 0414/2018–3   **16.048**

BoA dec. in cases R 609/2006–3 (logo Midas)   **16.050**

BoA dec. in cases R 931/2018–3 (Taiwanese patent)   **16.048**

BoA dec. in cases R 1008/2018–3 (European Patent application)   **16.048**

BoA dec. in cases R 1060/2017–3 (US design patents)   **16.048**

BoA dec. in cases R 1243/2017–3   **16.048**

BoA dec. in cases R 1283/2018–3   **16.048**

BoA dec. in cases R 1586/2017–3 (Polish utility model)   **16.048**

BoA dec. in cases R 1827/2019–3   **16.048**

BoA dec. in cases R 1928/2018–3 (German utility model)   **16.048**

Building blocks from a toy building set, Board of Appeal (EUIPO), 30 May 2022, R 1524/2021–3   **11.087**

Burberry Limited, EUTM No 017911858   **18.077**

C-4/03, *Gesellschaft fur Antriebstechnik mbH & Co. KG v. Lamellen und Kupplungsbau Beteiligungs KG*, CJEU 13.7.2006   **14.016**

C-5/08 *Infopaq International A/S v Danske Dagblades Forening* [2009] ECLI:EU:C:2009:465   **8.014, 10.051, 17.022, 19.028, 19.048**

TABLE OF CASES

C-21/76, *Handelskwekerij G. J. Bier BV v. Mines de potasse d'Alsace SA*, 30.11.1976   **14.013**

C-24/16 and C-25/16 *Nintendo Co Ltd v BigBen Interactive GmbH* ECLI:EU:C:2017:724   **4.085, 10.034, 14.041, 14.049–14.051, 18.050**

C-30/15 P *Rubik's cube* ECLI:EU:C:2016:849   **17.079**

C-32/08 *Fundacion Espanola para la Innovacion de la Artesania (FEIA) v Cul de Sac Espacio Creativo SL and Acierta Product & Position SA* [2009] ECLI:EU:C:2009:418   **8.026, 18.038, 18.039**

C-39/97 *Canon* ECLI:EU:C:1998:442   **11.107**

C-48/09 P, *Lego*, EU:C:2010:516   **18.081**

C-53/87 *CICRA et al. v Renault* [1988] ECLI:EU:C:1988:472   **8.025**

C-101/11 P and C-102/11 P *Neumann, Galdeano del Sel v. Baena Grupo*, EU:C:2012:641   **11.013, 16.014, 16.050, 17.061, 17.062**

C-123/20 *Ferrari SpA v Mansory Design Holding GmbH*, ECLI:EU:C:2021:889   **11.060, 16.046, 18.035, 20.030**

C-145/10 *Eva-Maria Painer v Standard Verlags GmbH and Others* [2011] ECLI:EU:C:2011:798   **8.014, 14.022, 17.022, 17.039–17.041, 18.075, 19.028, 19.044**

C-163/16, *Louboutin*, EU:C:2018:423   **18.079**

C-169/08 *Flos SpA v Semeraro Casa e Famiglia SpA*, ECLI:EU:C:2011:29   **10.066**

C-172/18, *AMS Neve Ltd v. Heritage Audio SL*, CJEU, 5.9.2019   **14.039**

C-199/20 P *Gamma-A v EUIPO/Zivju* ECLI:EU:C:2020:662   **11.135–11.137**

C-205/13, *Hauk*, EU:C:2014:2233   **18.080, 18.083, 18.078**

C-231/16, *Merck KGaA v. Merck & Co. Inc*, CJEU 19.10.2017   **14.056**

C-235/09, *DHL Express France SAS v. Chronopost SA*, CJEU 12.4.2011 **14.037**

C-237/19 *Gomboc v Szellemi Tulajdon Nemzeti Hivatala* ECLI:EU:C:2020:296   **17.088, 17.103, 18.075, 18.082, 18.084**

C-238/87 *AB Volvo v Erik Veng (UK) Ltd* [1988] ECLI:EU:C:1988:477   **8.025**

C-251/95 *Sabel v Puma* EU:C:1997:528   **17.043**

C-281/10 *PepsiCo Inc v Grupo Promer Mon-Graphic SA* ECLI:EU:C:2011:679   **10.015, 10.030, 16.014, 17.061, 19.046**

C-299/99 *Koninklijke Philips Electronics NV/Remington Consumer Products Ltd* ECLI:EU:C:2002:377   **17.086, 18.081**

C-310/17 *Levola Hengelo BV v Smilde Foods BV* [2018] ECLI:EU:C:2018:899   **8.014, 10.067, 18.075**

C-342/97 *Lloyd Schuhfabrik Meyer vs Klijsen Handel* ECLI:EU:C:1999:323   **17.043**

C-345/13 *Karen Millen Fashions Ltd v Dunnes Stores* ECLI:EU:C:2014:2013
               10.022, 16.060, 17.093, 18.047
C-358/23 P *Tinnus v EUIPO/Mystic* ECLI:EU:C:2023:809 11.135
C-360/12, *Coty Germany GmbH v. First Note Perfumes NV*, CJEU, 5.6.2014
                       14.039
C-361/15 P and C-405/15 P *Easy Sanitary Solution v. Group Nivelles*, EU:C:2017:720 10.022, 11.022, 11.044, 11.050, 16.027, 16.061, 17.104
C-382/21 P *EUIPO v KaiKai* ECLI:EU:C:2021:1050 11.137
C-393/09, *Bezpečnostní softwarová asociace — Svaz softwarové ochrany v Ministerstvo kultury* ECLI:EU:C:2010:816 19.013
C-395/16 *DOCERAM GmbH v CeramTec GmbH* [2018] ECLI:EU:C:2018:172
  I.020, 8.055, 10.024, 11.075, 18.028, 18.029, 19.049, 19.052–19.054, 19.056, 19.057
C-397/16 *Acacia Srl v Pneusgarda Srl and Audi AG and Acacia Srl and Rolando D'Amato v Dr. Ing. h.c.F. Porsche AG* [2017] ECLI:EU:C:2017:992 I.031, I.033, 8.050, 10.034, 18.069
C-421/20, *Acacia Srl v. Bayerische Motoren Werke Aktiengesellschaft*, CJEU 3.3.2022 14.051
C-472/21 *Monz Handelsgesellschaft International mbH & Co. KG v Buchel GmbH & Co. Fahrzeugtechnik KG* ECLI:EU:C:2023:105 I.040, I.041, 11.092
C-479/12 *Gautzsch v Munchener Boulevard Mobel Joseph Duna* ECLI:EU:C:2014:75 11.017, 11.021, 11.022, 14.047, 16.024, 16.025, 18.044
C-523/10, *Wintersteiger AG v. Products 4U Sondermaschinenbau GmbH*, CJEU 19.4.2012 14.013
C-539/03, *Roche Nederland BV v. Primus*, CJEU 13.7.2006 14.017, 14.022
C-616/10, *Solvay SA v. Honeywell Fluorine Products Europe BV*, CJEU 12.7.2012 14.016
C-683/17 *Cofemel – Sociedade de Vestuario SA v G-Star RawCV* [2019] ECLI:EU:C:2019:721 I.010–I.012, 5.004, 5.060, 5.061, 5.064, 8.014, 8.015, 8.072, 10.067, 17.001, 17.005, 17.014, 17.016–17.019, 17.023, 17.026, 17.039, 17.040, 17.042, 17.064, 17.068, 17.072, 17.074, 17.088, 17.096–17.098, 17.101, 18.004, 19.026, 19.088
C-684/21 *Papierfabriek Doetinchem BV v Sprick GmbH Bielefelder Papier- und Wellpappenwerk & Co.* ECLI:EU:C:2023:141 I.020, 11.079, 17.052, 18.028
C-783/18 P *EUIPO/Wajos* ECLI:EU:C:2019:1073 17.044
C-833/18 *SI and Brompton Bicycle Ltd v Chedech / Get2Get* [2020] ECLI:EU:C:2020:461 I.010, 8.014, 10.067, 17.014, 17.031, 17.033, 17.036, 17.069, 17.072, 17.092, 17.097, 18.075
Caresyntax v EIZO [Computer screens], EUIPO (Board of Appeal), 17 February 2017, R 755/2016–3 11.067

Caresyntax v EIZO [Computer screens], EUIPO (Board of Appeal), 17 February 2017, R 755/2016–3   **11.062**

Case Comment on Herbert Neuman v EUIPO/Jose Manuel Baena [2013] IIC 249–254   **17.061, 17.062**

Case G 1/21 *Videoconference* ECLI:EP:BA:2021:G000121.20210716   **11.138**

CASTROL v NORMANPLAST [Cans], EUIPO (Board of Appeal), 7 July 2008, R 1516/2007–3   **11.025**

CENTREX v ISOGONA [Coffee pot], EUIPO (Board of Appeal), 8 November 2006, R 216/2005–3   **11.041**

Cutelarias Cristema v Francisco do Carmo Silva Mota [Hatchets], EUIPO (Board of Appeal), 18 May 2021, R 2019/2020–3   **11.019**

DAKS Simpson Limited, EUTM No 008134405   **18.077**

Device of a gummy bear, EUIPO (Board of Appeal), 11 October 2023, R 872/2023–4   **17.044**

Essity v The Procter & Gamble [Part of sanitary napkin], EUIPO (Board of Appeal), 25 October 2011, R 978/2010–3   **11.041**

Greiner Packaging v Vrhovski [Plastic spoon, foldable], EUIPO (Board of Appeal), 1 October 2013, R 505/2012–3   **11.040**

G-Star Raw CV v Rhodi Ltd and others [2015] EWHC 216 (Ch)   **10.036**

Haverkamp v Sissel [Pebble beach surface pattern], EUIPO (Board of Appeal), 26 February 2016, R 2619/2014–3   **11.040**

Hee Jung Kim v Zellweger, EUIPO (Invalidity Division), 1 March 2006, ICD 1477   **11.098, 11.103, 11.104**

Hypertherm v B & Bartoni [Welding torches (part of -)], EUIPO (Board of Appeal), 16 July 2021, R 2843/2019–3   **11.091**

ING-DiBa v Banca Monte, EUIPO (Board of Appeal), 26 November 2015, Joined cases R 113/2015–2 and R 174/2015–2   **11.010**

Karen Millen Fashion Ltd v Dunnes Stores C-345/13 EU:C:2014:2013   **18.026**

Karen Millen Ltd v Dunnes Stores Ltd [2008] ECDR 11   **1.223**

King.com v TeamLava [Animated Icons], EUIPO (Board of Appeal), 1 December 2016, R 1951/2015–3   **11.047**

Lafner v Abart [Adornment], EUIPO (Board of Appeal), 19 November 2020, R 1213/2019–3   **11.020**

Linak v ChangZhou Kaidi [Electrically operated lifting column, in particular for tables], EUIPO (Board of Appeal), 21 March 2017, R 1412/2015–3, **11.019**

Linder Recycling Tech GmbH v Franssons Verkstader AB (R 690/2007–3)   **I.019, I.020, 10.024**

L'Oreal SA v Bellure NV [2008] ETMR 1   **10.069**

L'Oreal SA v RN Ventures Ltd [2018] ECDR 14; [2018] EWHC 173 (Pat)   **10.018, 10.022 11.128**

TABLE OF CASES

Normann v Paton Calvert [Colanders], EUIPO (Board of Appeal), 11 August 2009, R 887/2008   **11.042, 11.043**

R 690/2007–3 *Linder Recyclingtech GmbH v. Franssons Verkstader AB* [2009] Decision of the Third Board of Appeal   **19.054, 19.057**

R 1003/2005–3 *Pepsico v. Grupo Promer Mon-Graphic* [2006] Decision of the Third Board of Appeal   **19.055**

Roll4you v Kesselman [Cigarette paper], EUIPO (Board of Appeal), 19 July 2017, R 691/2016–3   **11.040**

Rothy's Inc v Giesswein Walkwaren AG [2020] EWHC 3391 (IPEC), 16 December 2020, Case No IP 2019–000084   **18.015, 20.031**

Rothy's Inc v Giesswein Walkwaren AG [2021] FSR 18   **10.010, 10.018, 10.020, 10.033, 10.086**

Stenman [Safety locks for bicycles], EUIPO (Board of Appeal), 21 September 2004, R 351/2004–3   **11.009**

T-9/07 *Grupo Promer v EUIPO/PepsiCo* ECLI:EU:T:2010:96   **10.015, 17.050, 17.057, 17.060, 17.086, 19.051**

T-9/15 *Ball Beverage v EUIPO and Crown Hellas* ECLI:EU:T:2017:386   **11.046, 11.068, 11.065, 11.094, 16.058**

T-10/08 *Kwang Yang Motor Co. Ltd. v Honda Giken Kogyo Kabushiki Kaisha* ECLI:EU:T:2011:446   **17.011, 19.051**

T-11/08 *Kwang Yang v. Honda Giken*, EU:T:2011:447   **16.048**

T-15/13 *Group Nivelles v EUIPO and Easy Sanitary Solutions* ECLI:EU:T:2015:281   **11.010, 11.022, 16.027, 17.104**

T-19/22 *Piaggio v EUIPO/ Zhejiang Zhongneng* ECLI:EU:T:2023:763 **17.103**

T-22/13 *Senz Technologies v OHIM* ECLI:EU:T:2015:310   **10.020, 16.048**

T-39/13 *Skirting boards* ECLI:EU:T:2014:852   **11.048, 11.049**

T-41/14 *Argo v EUIPO and Clapbanner* ECLI:EU:T:2015:53   **11.038, 16.048**

T-55/12 *Su-Shan Chen v. AM Denmark*, EU:T:2013:219   **16.050**

T-68/10 *Watches* ECLI:EU:T:2011:269   **11.010, 11.049, 16.018**

T-68/11 *Kastenholz v EUIPO/Qwatchme* ECLI:EU:T:2013:298   **11.041, 11.112, 11.115, 16.048, 17.100, 19.045**

T-74/18 *Visi/one v. EasyFix*, EU:T:2019:417   **16.018**

T-83/11 & T-84/11 *Antrax v. Heating Company*, EU:T:2012:592   **16.048**

T-84/16 *Banca Monte v EUIPO/ING-DiBa* ECLI:EU:T:2017:661   **11.010**

T-84/21 *Doll's heads* ECLI:EU:T:2021:844   **11.047**

T-90/16 *Thomas Murphy/EUIPO and Nike Innovate CV* ECLI:EU:T:2017:464   **11.046, 11.049, 17.011**

T-148/08 *Beifa Group v OHIM* ECLI:EU:T:2010:190   **16.048, 17.092**

T-153/08 *Shenzhen Taiden Industrial Co Ltd v OHIM* ECLI:EU:T:2010:248   **10.015, 10.020, 16.026**

T-169/19 *Style & Taste v EUIPO and Polo/ Lauren* ECLI:EU:T:2021:318
11.095
T-191/18 *Rietze/ EUIPO and Volkswagen* ECLI:EU:T:2019:378 **11.020**
T-192/18 *Rietze v EUIPO and Volkswagen* ECLI:EU:T:2019:379 **11.020, 11.053**
T-193/20 *Eternit v EUIPO/Eternit* ECLI:EU:T:2021:782 **17.095**
T-209/18 *Porsche v EUIPO and Autec* ECLI:EU:T:2019:377 **11.055, 11.058, 11.059, 16.062, 17.011, 17.049, 17.058, 19.046**
T-219/18 *Piaggio v EUIPO and Zhejiang Zhongneng* ECLI:EU:T:2019:681
11.057, 17.103
T-228/16 *Haverkamp v EUIPO and Sissel* ECLI:EU:T:2018:369 **11.039**
T-286/16 *Toilet seats [part of -]* ECLI:EU:T:2017:411 **11.046**
T-296/17 *Buck-Chemie/EUIPO and Henkel* ECLI:EU:T:2018:823 **17.051**
T-357/12 *Sachi Premium-Outdoor Furniture Lda v OHIM* ECLI:EU:T:2014:55
10.017
T-367/17 *Linak v EUIPO and ChangZhou Kaidi* ECLI:EU:T:2018:694
11.054
T-368/17 *Linak v. ChangZhou* EU:T:2018:695 **16.050**
T-450/09 *Rubik's Cube* ECLI:EU:T:2014:983 **17.079, 17.084**
T-483/20 *Tecnica v EUIPO and Zeitneu* ECLI:EU:T:2022:11 **11.097**
T-488/20 *Guerlain/EUIPO* ECLI:EU:T:2021:443 **17.044**
T-489/20 *Eos v EUIPO* ECLI:EU:T:2021:547 **17.044**
T-494/12 *Biscuits Poult SAS v OHIM*, EU:T:2014:757 **20.030**
T-515/19 *Lego* ECLI:EU:T:2021:155 **11.015, 11.075–11.077, 11.081**
T-525/13 *H&M Hennes & Mauritz BV & Co KG v OHIM* ECLI:EU:T:2015:617
10.019
T-532/18 *Aroma Essence v EUIPO and Refan Bulgaria* ECLI:EU:T:2019:609
11.039
T-560/18 *Atos v EUIPO and Andreas Fahl* ECLI:EU:T:2019:767 **11.051, 17.050, 17.057**
T-566/11 and T-567/11 *Viejo Valle v. Etablissements Coquet* EU:T:2013:549
11.112, 11.117, 16.050
T-601/17 *Rubik's Cube* ECLI:EU:T:2019:765 **17.079–17.083**
T-608/11 *Beifa v. Schwan Stabilo* EU:T:2013:334 **16.048**
T-617/21 *B & Bartoni* ECLI:EU:T:2023:152 **11.091**
T-651/16 *Crocs v EUIPO and Gifi* ECLI:EU:T:2018:137 **11.025, 16.026, 16.027**
T-651/17 *Hours/EUIPO and Zhejiang Auarita* ECLI:EU:T:2018:855 **17.051**
T-666/11 *Danuta Budziewska v. Puma SE*, EU:T:2013:584 **16.048**

TABLE OF CASES

T-684/20 *Legero v EUIPO/Rieker* ECLI:EU:T:2021:912   **11.043, 17.013, 17.050, 17.095**

T-748/18 *Glimarpol v EUIPO/Metar* ECLI:EU:T:2020:321   **11.037**

T-760/16 *Basil/EUIPO and Artex* ECLI:EU:T:2018:277   **17.051**

T-767/17 *Eglo v EUIPO and Briloner* ECLI:EU:T:2019:67   **11.047, 11.050, 11.052, 11.054, 17.049**

T-862/19 *Brasserie St Avold v EUIPO* ECLI:EU:T:2020:561   **17.044**

T 2125/16 *Doherty Amplifier* ECLI:EP:BA:2021:T212516.20210916   **11.138**

Thane International Group's Application [2006] ECDR 8   **16.030**

THD Acoustic v HARRON [MP3 players and recorders], EUIPO (Board of Appeal), 25 July 2009, R 552/2008–3   **11.037**

Ur & Penn v Bell & Ross [Watches], EUIPO (Board of Appeal), 27 October 2009, R 1267/2008–3   **11.025**

Vasco [Radiators for heating], EUIPO (Board of Appeal), 17 March 2008, R 592/2007–3   **11.066**

Vasco v ANTRAX [Radiators for heating], EUIPO (Board of Appeal), 2 November 2010, R 1451/2009–03   **11.040**

Volkswagen v European Flipper, EUIPO (Board of Appeal), 15 December 2021, R 609/2021–2   **11.097**

WebTuner [Adapter], EUIPO (Board of Appeal), 3 December 2013, R 1332/2013–3   **11.064**

Xeltys v Cavius [Smoke alarms (part of -)], EUIPO (Board of Appeal), 13 July 2016, R 277/2016–3   **11.023**

OTHER JURISDICTIONS

Australia

Apple Inc [2017] ADO 6 (14 June 2017); [2017] ADO 7   **1.036, 1.137, 1.227–1.228**

Aristocrat Technologies Australia Pty Limited [2021] ADO 1   **1.137**

Astrazeneca AB [2007] ADO 4   **1.216–1.218**

Caroma Industries Ltd [1991] ADO 3   **1.140**

GM Global Technology Operations LLC v S.S.S. Auto Parts Pty Ltd [2019] FCA 97   **1.229–1.237**

GM Global Technology Operations LLC v S.S.S. Auto Parts Pty Ltd (No 2) (Costs) [2019] FCA 1813.   **1.237**

Keller v LED Technologies Pty Ltd [2010] FCAFC 55 **1.177, 1.219–1.221, 1.224**

Kimberly-Clark Ltd v Commissioner of Patents (No 3) (1988) 13 IPR 569 **1.182, 1.214–1.215**

TABLE OF CASES

LED Technologies Pty Ltd v Elecspess Pty Ltd [2008] FCA 1941   **1.222–1.223**
Microsoft Corporation [2008] ADO 2   **1.029, 1.136, 1.225–1.226**
Pyrrha Design Inc. v Plum and Posey Inc., 2022 FCA 7   **17.104**
Reckitt Benckiser Inc [2008] ADO 1   **1.165**
Review 2 Pty Ltd v Redberry Enterprise Pty Ltd [2008] FCA 1588   **1.223**
Safe Sport v Puma [1985] 4 IPR 120   **1.008, 1.057**

Belgium

Savic NV v Plana D.O.O., Brussels District Court, 19 October 2023, A/22/02872   **17.100**

Canada

Crocs Canada, Inc v. Double Diamond Distribution Ltd [2022] FC 1443.   **2.053**
Pyrrha Design Inc. v Plum and Posey Inc. [2019] FC 129   **17.104**

China

Guiding Case No. 158 Shenzhen Weibang Technology Co Ltd v Li Jianyi & Shenzhen Yuancheng Intelligence Equipment Co. Ltd Supreme People's Court Case No. 6342/2019   **3.046**
Jaguar Land Rover v. JMC decision of 2018   **3.044**
Shanghai Zhonghan Chenguang Stationery Manufacturing Co, Ltd v. Ningbo Weiyada Pen Co, Lt,. Ningbo Weiyada Stationery Co., Ltd. and Shanghai Chengshuo Industry and Trade Co, Ltd [2010] Min Ti Zi No. 16   **3.085**
Triangle v. Bridgestone and Patent Reexamination Board [2016]   **3.043**
Zhejiang Jianlong Sanitary Ware Co Ltd v Grohe Co Ltd and Zhejiang Jianlong Sanitary Ware Co Ltd and Grohe Co Ltd. Supreme People's Court [2015] Min Ti Zi No. 2   **3.023, 3.040, 3.112**

Denmark

Ilse Jacobsen Rubber Boots, Danish Supreme Court, 10 June 2020, BS-7741/2019-HJR, [2021] IIC 228   **17.025**
Judgment from the Maritime and Commercial Court of 30 March 2021, BS-9628/2020-SHR   **8.056**
Judgment of the Supreme Court reported in Ugeskrift for Retsvasen U 2015.2011   **8.050**

Finland

Code of Judicial Procedure [Oikeudenkäymiskaari, 1.1.1734/4, 1.7.2021/642] (Finland)	**8.041**
Finnish Supreme Administrative Court Judgment of 13 November 2012 in KHO 2012:94	**8.056**
Finnish Supreme Court in KKO 2005:105 (Fiskars)	**8.040**
Finnish Supreme Court Judgment from 2007 in KKO 2007:103	**8.043**
Judgment of 26 April 2018 in KKO 2018:36	**8.053**
Judgment of 31 December 2007 in KKO 2007:103	**8.051, 8.052**
Market Court judgment of 16 February 2015 in MAO:110/15	**8.062**

France

Appeals Court of Paris, Pole 5, Chamber 1, November 16, 2021	**4.025**
Commercial Chamber, Court of Cassation, March 26th, 2008, No. 06–22.013	**4.080**
Criminal Chamber of the Supreme Court, June 27, 2018, Parisac Sarl v. C (Christophe), case n° 2016–86478, PIBD 2018, 1102, IIID-640	**4.005**
Gal v Yves St Laurent CA Paris, 18 September 2002	**18.013**
Paris Appeals Court, Pole 5, 2nd chamber, October 13, 2017, Association Expressions de France v. INPI case n° 2016/23487	**4.033**
Paris Appeals Court, Pole 5 chamber 2, October 18, 2019, Maisons du Monde France SAS v Billiet Vanlaere BVT SA (Belgique)	**4.026**
Paris Appeals Court, Pole 5, 2nd chamber, June 19, 2020, Olivia Garden (Belgique) v Coiff'idis SAS, case n° 2018/20559, PIBD 2020, 1143, IIID-8	**4.031**
Paris Appeals Court, Pole 5, 2nd chamber, June 18, 2021, Clee Sasu / Sensas SA; C, case n°2019/20119	**4.034**
Paris Civil Court of Appeal, May 26th, 2017, Telekom Slovenije (Slovénie) v Générale de Téléphone SA n°15/10204	**4.059**
Paris, Court of Appeal, November 24th, 2020, No. 18/23477	**4.080**
Paris Court of Appeal, 23 March 2021, no 18/28435 *APM Monaco v Swarosvski Crystal Online*	**18.036**
Paris Court of Appeal, 25 June 2021, no 19/05464	**18.036**
Paris Court of First Instance, January 22, 2008, Beauté Prestige International SA / Tissus Manal SARL, case n°2006/14593	**4.006**
Paris Judicial Court, February 8, 2022, F v Akis Technology Sarl; O, case n°2019/14142, PIBD 2022, 1183, IIID-8	**4.055**
Save Willy Sarl (Belgique); Saint Herblain Distribution SAS, case n°2018/09091, PIBD 2020, 1132, IIID-101	**4.026**

Supreme Court, December 19th, 2013, No. 12/29499   **4.062**
Supreme Court, Social Chamber, September 22, 2015, G (Pierrette G) / Lalique SA; Lalique Parfums SAS; D, case n°2013–18803, PIBD 2015, 1039, IIID-800   **4.011**

Germany

Access right of the architect, German Federal Supreme Court, 29 April 2021, I ZR 193/20   **17.034**
Ballerina, German Federal Supreme Court, 11 January 2018, I ZR 187/16   **11.126, 17.092**
Bathing Shoe, Dusseldorf Appeal Court, 25 April 2019, I-20 U 103/18 **11.020, 11.039**
Beetle, Braunschweig Appeal Court, 10 March 2022, 2 U 47/19   **17.026**
BGH I ZR 126/06, GRUR 2009   **16.030**
BGH judgement dated 20 December 2018 – I ZB 26/18   **18.025**
Birthday Train, German Federal Supreme Court, 13 November 2013, I ZR 143/12   **17.001, 17.005, 17.020, 17.034, 17.067**
Bogner B/Barbie B, German Federal Supreme Court, 2 February 2012, I ZR 50/11   **17.045**
Cabinet Lamp, German Federal Supreme Court, 15 December 2022, I ZR 173/21   **17.027**
Car Body, German Federal Patent Court, 13 October 2004, 28 W (pat) 98/00   **17.072, 17.078**
Climbing Spider, German Federal Supreme Court, 12 May 2011, I ZR 53/10   **17.001, 17.019, 17.068**
Crib, Dusseldorf District Court, 17 September 2019, 14c O 225/17   **17.065, 17.104**
Cutting Board, German Federal Supreme Court, 24 March 2022, I ZR 16/21   **11.069**
Dog Figure, German Federal Supreme Court, 8 July 2004, I ZR 25/02 **17.022, 17.096**
Dusseldorf Appeal Court, 25 November 2014, I-20 U 193/13   **11.010**
Frankfurt Appeal Court, 17 November 2014, 6 W 96/14   **11.010**
Fun Glasses, Dusseldorf Appeal Court, 1 September 2020, I-20 U 27/19   **17.089**
Furniture, Hamburg Appeal Court, 11 January 2018, 5 U 98/16   **11.043**
German Federal Supreme Court, judgment of June 2, 2016, I ZR 226/14   **14.036**
Higher Regional Court of Dusserldorf, judgement dated 24 April 2019 – I-20 U 103/18   **18.023**

ICE, German Federal Supreme Court, 7 April 2011, I ZR 56/09   **11.125, 11.132**

IPS/ISP, German Federal Supreme Court, 5 March 2015, I ZR 161/13 **17.094**

Le Corbusier, German Federal Supreme Court, 10 December 1986, I ZR 15/85   **17.092**

Lego Mini Figure, Dusseldorf District Court, 8 December 2022, 14c O 46/21   **17.026**

Magnetic Jewellery, Frankfurt Appeal Court, 15 September 2020, 11 U 76/19   **17.026**

Marcel Breuer II, German Federal Supreme Court, 5 November 2015, I ZR 91/11   **17.097**

Meda Gate, German Federal Supreme Court, 24 January 2019, I ZR 164/17   **11.132**

Milla, German Federal Supreme Court, 23 February 2012, I ZR 68/11   **11.125, 17.013**

Paper Dispenser, German Federal Supreme Court, 7 October 2020, I ZR 137/19   **17.052, 17.053**

Paper Dispenser, German Federal Supreme Court [2022] 53 IIC 278   **11.076, 17.005, 17.052**

Porsche 911, German Federal Supreme Court, 7 April 2022, I ZR 222/20   **17.026, 17.094, 17.096, 17.098**

Porsche 911, German Federal Supreme Court, 17 April 2022, I ZR 222/20   **17.027–17.029**

Porsche 911, Stuttgart Appeal Court, 20 November 2020, 5 U 125/19   **17.026, 17.071, 17.072, 17.093**

Pram I, German Federal Supreme Court, 28 September 2011, I ZR 23/10   **11.125**

Pram II, German Federal Supreme Court, 12 July 2012, I ZR 102/11   **11.125, 11.126, 11.132, 17.001, 17.010, 17.013, 17.047, 17.054**

Radiator Grille, German Federal Patent Court, 11 July 2019, 30 W (pat) 812/16   **11.056**

Raupentin, German Federal Supreme Court, 2 April 1971, 1 ZB 3/70   **17.045**

Saddle bottom view I, German Federal Supreme Court, 1 July 2021, I ZB 31/20   **11.090**

Saddle bottom view II, German Federal Supreme Court, 15 June 2023, I ZB 31/20   **11.093**

Saint Gottfried, German Federal Supreme Court, 19 March 2008, I ZR 166/05   **17.093**

Sports Helmet, German Federal Supreme Court, 20 December 2018, I ZB 25/18   **11.062, 11.069, 17.021**

Stretch-Limousine, German Federal Court of Justice, 22 April 2010, I ZR 89/08   **17.024, 17.096**

Table Mat, German Federal Supreme Court, 19 May 2010, I ZR 71/08   **11.125, 17.012, 17.013, 17.023, 17.092**

Tubular Steel Chair I, German Federal Supreme Court, 27 February 1961, I ZR 127/59   **17.036**

USM Haller, Dusseldorf District Court, 14 July 2020, 14c O 57/19   **17.026**

Variable Figurative Mark, German Federal Supreme Court, 6 February 2013, I ZB 85/11   **17.021**

Wheel Cap, German Federal Patent Court, 18 February 2021, 30 W (pat) 806/18   **11.020**

Wristwatch, German Federal Supreme Court, 28 January 2016, I ZR 40/14   **11.132, 17.013, 17.024, 17.094**

Writing Utensil, German Federal Supreme Court, 24 March 2011, I ZR 211/08   **11.051, 11.125, 17.001, 17.008, 17.012**

India

Add Print (India) Enterprises Pvt. Ltd. v Mohan Impressions Pvt. Ltd. 2013 (53) PTC 485 (Mad)   **6.063**

Alert India v Naveen Plastic 1997 (17) PTC 15 (Del)   **6.070**

Apollo Tyres v Pioneer Trading Corporation and Ors 2017 (72) PTC 253 (Del)   **6.012**

Bharat Glass Tube Ltd v Gopal Glass Works Ltd. 2008 (37) PTC 1 (SC)   **6.016, 6.079, 6.081**

Carlsberg Breweries A/S v Som Distilleries and Breweries Ltd. ('Carlsberg') 2019 (77) PTC 1 (Del)   **6.052, 6.053**

Crocs Inc. USA v Aqualite India Ltd. 2019 (79) PTC 75; 2019 (78) PTC 100 (Del)   **6.053**

Dabur India Ltd. V Amit Jain 2009 (39) PTC 104 (Del) (DB)   **6.070**

Dart Industries Inc. and Ors v Polyset Plastics Pvt. Ltd. and Ors 2018(75) PTC495(Del)   **6.012, 6.013, 6.070**

Dart Industries Inc. v Techno Plast and Ors 2016 (67) PTC 457; *Ritika Pvt Ltd v Biba Apparels Pvt. Ltd.* MANU/DE/0784/2016   **6.057**

Escorts Construction Equipment Ltd. v Action Construction Equipment Pvt. Ltd. 1999 PTC 36 (Del)   **6.014**

Faber- Castell Aktiengesellschaf and Anr v Pikpoen Pvt. Ltd. 2003 (27) PTC 538 (Bom)   **6.062**

GlaxoSmithKline Consumer Healthcare GmbH& Co. vs Anchor Health and Beautycare Pvt. Ltd. 2004 (29) PTC 72 (Del)   **6.067**

Hindustan Lever Ltd. v Nirma Pvt. Ltd. AIR 1992 Bom 195   **6.008**

TABLE OF CASES

J.N. Electricals v President Electrical (1980) ILR 1 Delhi 215   **6.070**
Microfibers Inc. v Girdhar & Co. and Another 2009 (40) PTC (Del) **I.015, 6.057**
Microlube India Ltd. v Rakesh Kumar Trading and Ors 2012 (50) PTC 161 (Del)   **6.072**
Mohan Lal and Ors v Sona Paints and Hardwares and Ors 2013 (55) PTC 61 (Del)   **6.049, 6.051, 6.053**
Pentel Kabushiki Kaisha v M/s Arora Stationers (2019) 79 PTC 42 (Del)   **6.078**
Reckitt Benckiser India Ltd. v Wyeth Ltd. ('Reckitt Benckiser') 2013 (54) PTC 90 (Del)   **6.020, 6.066**
Smithkline Beecham plc. and Ors v Hindustan Lever Ltd. and Ors 2000 (20) PTC 83 (Del)   **6.049**
The Wimco Ltd. v Meena Match Industries AIR 1983 Del 537   **6.066**
Vega Auto Accessories Pvt Ltd v S.K. Jain (2018) 75 PTC 59 (Del)   **6.078**
Whirlpool of India Ltd. v Videocon Industries Ltd 2014 (60) PTC 155 (Bom)   **6.078**

Italy

Court of Bologna – May 5, 2011, Giurisprudenza Annotata Diritto Industriale no. 5728   **5.029**
Court of Milan – IP Specialized Section – November 22, 2017   **5.046, 5.058**
Court of Turin – IP Specialized Section, January 12, 2018   **5.045**
Court of Turin – June 25, 2009; Giurisprudenza Annotata di Diritto Industriale, no. 5441   **5.029**
Court of Venice – IP Specializes Section, August 10, 2015   **5.047**
Court of Venice, July 5, 2021 – case 2052/2021 Am s.r.l. + Officina Murano s.r.l. *vs.* New Murano Gallery s.r.l. + New Murano Gallery Production s.r.l.   **5.064**
Italian Supreme Court, 28 November 2023, Sentenza 19136/2019 RG No. 33100/2023   **17.101**
Supreme Court, January, 21, 2009, no. 1570   **5.013**
Supreme Court, March 23, 2017, no. 7477   **5.057**
Thun, Italian Supreme Court, 14 October 2022, 30331/2022   **17.036**
Zhejiang Zhongneng v Piaggio, Turin District Court, 17 March 2017, Sentenza No. 1900/2017 RG No. 13811/2014   **17.101**
Zhejiang Zhongneng v Piaggio, Turin Appeal Court, 12 December 2018, Sentenza No. 677/2019 RG No. 1628/2017   **17.101**

TABLE OF CASES

Japan

IP High Court, Heisei 17-nen (ne) 10079, decided on October 31, 2005
    7.066

Osaka District Court, Heisei 25-nen (wa) 1074, decided on September 24, 2015
    7.077

Spain

Spanish Supreme Court, *Original Buff, SA v The owner of the Spanish industrial design No 514810–01 and No 514810–02*, decision No 608/2021, 16 September 2021
    18.023

Sweden

Code of Judicial Procedure [Rättegangsbalk (1942:740) (i ändrad lydelse upp till Lag (2021:1107)
    8.041

Jetson Chair, Swedish Patent and Market Court, 2 November 2022, PMT 16530–21
    17.091

Judgment of 8 June 2010 in T 3469–09 (Drawbar) by the Court of Appeal for Western Sweden
    8.055

Judgment of 16 May 2013 in T 1519–12
    8.054

Mio and Others v Galleri Mikael & Thomas Asplund Aktiebolag, Swedish Patent and Market Court of Appeal, 21 September 2023, PMT 13496–22 **17.029, 17.031–17.039, 17.042, 17.043**

Stockholm District Court judgment of 25 February 2009 in T 27373–06 **8.062**

Stockholm District Court judgment of 16 December 2009 in T 10454–08
    8.062

Switzerland

Barbecue grill, Aargau Commercial Court, 3 August 2021, HOR.2019.16
    17.025

Barbecue grill, Swiss Federal Supreme Court, 17 June 2022, 4A_472/2021 and 4A_482/2021
    17.025, 17.041, 17.104

United Kingdom

A Fulton Co Ltd v Grant Barnett & Co Ltd [2001] RPC 16
    10.048

Action Storage Systems Ltd v G-Force Europe.com Ltd [2017] FSR 18 (IPEC)
    10.048, 10.051, 10.052, 10.087

TABLE OF CASES

Ahmet Erol v Sumaira Javaid, 18 May 2017, O-253–17 **11.024**
Albert Packaging Ltd v Nampak Cartons & Healthcare Ltd [2011] FSR 32 **10.052**
AMP Inc v Utilux Pty Ltd [1971] FSR 572 **I.020, 10.024, 10.082**
Bailey (t/a Elite Anglian Products) v Haynes (t/a RAGS) [2007] FSR 10 **10.047**
Bayerische Motoren Werke Aktiengesellschaft v Round & Metal Ltd [2012] ECC 28 **10.034**
Cantel Medical (UK) Ltd v Arc Medical Design Ltd [2018] EWHC 345 (Pat) **10.017–10.020, 10.024, 10.036**
C&H Engineering v F Klucznik & Sons Ltd (No.1) [1992] FSR 421 **10.036**
Coca-Cola Co, In re [1986] 1 WLR 695 **10.068**
The Distillers Co Ltd's Application (1953) 70 RPC 221 **1.163**
Dyson Ltd v Qualtex (UK) Ltd [2006] RPC 31 **10.042**
Dyson Ltd v Vax Ltd [2010] ECDR 18; [2012] FSR 4 **10.014, 10.017, 10.021, 10.024, 10.085**
Electronic Techniques (Anglia) Ltd v Critchley Components Ltd [1997] FSR 401 **10.056**
Fairfax & Favor Ltd v The House of Bruar Ltd [2022] ECDR 12 **10.033, 10.036**
Farmers Build Ltd (In Liquidation) v Carier Bulk Materials Handling Ltd [2000] ECDR 42 **10.036, 10.042, 10.050, 10.056**
Ferrero's Design [1978] RPC 473 **1.033**
Freddy SPA v Hugz Clothing Ltd [2021] ECDR 8 **10.069**
GBL UK Trading Ltd v H&S Alliance Ltd [2022] RPC 3 **10.009**
George East Housewares Ltd v Fackelmann GMBH & Co KG [2017] ETMR 4 **10.069**
George Hensher Ltd v Restawile Upholstery (Lancs) Ltd [1976] AC 64 **10.065**
Gimex International Groupe Import Export v Chill Bag Company Ltd and Others [2012] ECDR 25; [2012] EWPCC 31 **10.008, 10.018, 10.022, 16.027**
Gramophone Company Limited v Magazine Holder Company [1910] 27 RPC 152 **I.042, 1.033**
Green Lane Products Ltd v PMS International Group plc [2008] ECDR 15; [2008] EWCA Civ 358 **10.012, 10.021, 16.027**
Jaguar Land Rover Ltd v Ineos Industries Holdings Ltd [2020] ETMR 56 **10.068**
Kohler Mira Ltd v Bristan Group Ltd [2014] FSR 1 **10.010**
Kohler Mira Ltd v Bristan Group Ltd (No2) [2015] FSR 9 **10.090**
L Woolley Jewellers Ltd v A and A Jewellery Ltd [2003] FSR 15 **10.056**
Lambretta Clothing Co Ltd v Teddy Smith (UK) Ltd [2005] RPC 6, **10.042, 10.052**

TABLE OF CASES

Landor & Hawa International Ltd v Azure Designs Ltd [2006] ECDR 31; [2006] EWCA 1285   10.024, 18.029

London Taxi Corp Ltd (t/a London Taxi Co) v Frazer-Nash Research Ltd [2018] ETMR 7   10.068

Louver-Lite Ltd v Harris Parts Ltd (t/a Harris Engineering) [2012] EWPCC 53   10.016

Lucasfilm Ltd v Ainsworth [2011] ECDR 21   10.065

Lutec (UK) Ltd v Cascade Holdings Ltd [2022] FSR 6   10.010, 10.020, 10.033, 10.086

Mackie Designs Inc v Behringer Specialised Studio Equipment (UK) Ltd [1999] RPC 717   10.042

Magmatic Ltd v PMS International Group Plc [2013] ECC 29; [2014] ECDR 20; [2016] ECDR 15   10.010, 10.017, 10.018, 10.033, 10.037, 10.073, 10.082

Magmatic v PMS International (2015) 37 EIPR 180, 185   10.033

Magmatic v. PMS International [2014] EWCA 181 and [2016] UKSC 12 by contrast to [2013] EWHC 1925   16.059

Mark Wilkinson Furniture Ltd v Woodcraft Designs (Radcliffe) Ltd [1998] FSR 63   10.046

Marks and Spencer Plc v Aldi Stores Limited [2023] FSR 17   10.022, 10.033

Neptune (Europe) Ltd v Devol Kitchens Ltd [2017] ECDR 25   10.044, 10.056

Numatic International Ltd v Qualtex UK Ltd [2010] RPC 25   10.069

Ocular Sciences Ltd v Aspect Vision Care Ltd [1997] RPC 289, 421   10.035, 10.044, 10.048, 10.052

Original Beauty Technology Co Ltd v G4K Fashion Ltd [2021] FSR 20; [2022] ECDR 18   10.021, 10.036, 10.069, 10.091

PMS International Group Plc v Magmatic Ltd [2016] UKSC 12   I.025

Procter & Gamble Co v Reckitt Benckiser (UK) Ltd [2007] ECDR 4; [2008] ECDR 3   10.010, 10.011, 10.017, 10.018, 10.021, 10.033, 10.085

Procter & Gamble Company v Reckitt Benckiser (UK) Ltd [2007] EWCA Civ 936   18.027

Procter &Gamble v. Reckitt Benckiser, [2006] EWHC 3154 (Ch)   16.059

PulseOn OY v Garmin (Europe) Ltd [2019] ECDR 8   10.021, 10.022

Raft Ltd v Freestyle of Newhaven Ltd and Others [2016] EWHC 1711 (IPEC)   10.051

Reckitt & Colman Products Ltd v Borden Inc [1990] RPC 341   10.069

Red Spider Technology v Omega Completions Technology [2010] EWHC 59 (Ch)   10.047

Response Clothing Ltd v Edinburgh Woollen Mill Ltd [2020] ECDR 11   10.067

Rolawn Ltd v Turfmech Machinery Ltd [2008] ECDR 13   10.0047

TABLE OF CASES

Samsung Electronics (UK) Ltd v Apple Inc [2013] ECDR 1; [2013] ECDR 2
    10.010, 10.015, 10.017, 10.019, 10.021, 10.024, 10.032, 10.033, 10.086
Samsung Electronics (UK) Ltd v Apple Inc [2013] FSR 9; [2013] FSR 10 **10.089**
Samsung v. Apple, [2012] EWHC 1882 (Pat)   **16.059**
Scholes Windows Ltd v Magnet Ltd [2002] FSR 10   **10.052**
Scomadi Ltd v RA Engineering Co Ltd [2018] FSR 14   **10.017**
Sealed Air Ltd v Sharp Interpack Ltd [2013] EWPCC 23   **10.010**
Shnuggle Ltd v Munchkin Inc [2020] FSR 22   **10.012, 10.043, 10.044, 10.051**
Societe des Produits Nestle SA v Cadbury UK Ltd [2017] ETMR 31   **10.068**
Spin Master Ltd v PMS International Ltd [2018] ECDR 22   **10.086**
TuneIn Inc v Warner Music UK Ltd and Sony Music Entertainment UK Ltd
    [2021] EWCA Civ 441   **10.006**
The University Court of The University of St Andrews v Student Gowns Ltd
    [2020] ETMR 17   **10.080**
Vetco Gray UK Ltd v FMC Technologies Inc [2007] EWHC 540 (Pat)   **10.080**
Virgin Atlantic Airways Ltd v Premium Aircraft Interiors Group Ltd [2009]
    ECDR 11   **10.044**
WaterRower (UK) Ltd v Liking Ltd (T/A Topiom) [2022] EWHC 2084
    (IPEC) 5 August 2022; [2023] ECDR 1   **10.067, 17.091**
Whitby Specialist Vehicles Ltd v Yorkshire Specialist Vehicles Ltd [2015] ECDR
    11   **10.017, 10.022, 10.051**
Whitby Specialist Vehicles Ltd v Yorkshire Vehicles Ltd and Ors [2014] EWHC
    4242 (Pat)   **11.127**
Woodhouse UK plc v Architectural Lighting Systems (trading as Acquila Design)
    [2006] ECDR 11   **10.015**

United States

Apple, Inc. v. Samsung Elecs. Co., 678 F.3d 1314 (Fed. Cir. 2012)   **9.009**
Apple Inc. v. Samsung Elecs. Co., 786 F.3d 983 (Fed. Cir. 2015)   **9.113, 9.114,**
    9.124
Apple, Inc. v. Samsung Elecs. Co., 920 F. Supp. 2d 1079 (N.D. Cal. 2013)
    9.113, 9.114
Apple, Inc. v. Samsung Elecs. Co., No. 11-CV-01846-LHK, 2011 WL 7036077
    9.113
Apple Inc. v. Samsung Elecs. Co., No. 11-CV-01846-LHK, 2017 WL 4776443
    9.126
Ariad Pharms., Inc. v. Eli Lilly & Co., 598 F.3d 1336, 1351 (Fed. Cir. 2010)
    9.087
Arminak & Assocs., Inc. v. Saint-Gobain Calmar, Inc., 501 F.3d 1314, 1323
    (Fed. Cir. 2007)   **9.054**

TABLE OF CASES

Automotive Body Parts Association v. Ford Global Technologies, LLC, No. 18–1613 (Fed. Cir. 2019) **1.036**
Bard, Inc. v. M3 Sys., Inc., 157 F.3d 1340 (Fed. Cir. 1998) **9.088**
Campbell Soup Co. v. Gamon Plus, Inc., 10 F.4th 1268 (Fed. Cir. 2021) **9.013**
Catalina Lighting, Inc. v. Lamps Plus, Inc., 295 F.3d 1277 (Fed. Cir. 2002) **9.063, 9.065**
Cleveland Clinic Found. v. True Health Diagnostics LLC, 760 F. App'x 1013, 1020–21 (Fed. Cir. 2019) **9.004**
Columbia Sportswear N. Am., Inc. v. Seirus Innovative Accessories, Inc., 80 F.4th 1363 (Fed. Cir. 2023) **9.053, 9.092–9.094**
Columbia Sportswear N. Am., Inc. v. Seirus Innovative Accessories, Inc., No. 3:17-cv-01781-HZ, 2017 WL 5494999 **9.127**
Contessa Food Prods., Inc. v. Conagra, Inc., 282 F.3d 1370 (Fed. Cir. 2002) **9.051, 9.053, 9.109**
Converse, Inc. v. ITC, 909 F.3d 1110, 1116–17 (Fed. Cir. 2018) **9.022**
Cuozzo Speed Techs., LLC v. Lee, 579 U.S. 261, 276 (2016) **9.004**
Curver Luxembourg, SARL, v Home Expressions, Inc., 938 F.3d 1334 (Fed. Cir. 2019) **9.077, 11.022**
Daimler AG v. A-Z Wheels LLC, 334 F. Supp. 3d 1087 (2018) **9.110**
Daniels, In re, 144 F.3d 1452 (Fed. Cir. 1998) **9.081–9.083**
eBay Inc. v. MercExchange, L.L.C., 547 U.S. 388 **9.067**
Egyptian Goddess, Inc. v. Swisa, Inc., 543 F.3d 665 (Fed. Cir. 2008) **9.012, 9.051–9.054, 9.071, 9.073, , 9.112**
Elmer v. ICC Fabricating, Inc., 67 F.3d 1571, 1577 (Fed. Cir. 1995) **9.053**
Ethicon Endo-Surgery, Inc. v. Covidien, Inc., 796 F.3d 1312 (Fed. Cir. 2015) **9.052, 9.055**
Ex parte Donaldson, 26 U.S.P.Q.2d 1250, 1251 (B.P.A.I. 1992) **9.006**
Ex parte Strijland, 26 U.S.P.Q.2d 1259 (B.P.A.I. 1992) **9.129**
Feist Publ'ns, Inc. v. Rural Tel. Serv. Co., 499 U.S. 340, 345 (1991) **9.019**
Festo Corp. v. Shoketsu Kinzoku Kogyo Kabushiki Co., 535 U.S. 722 **9.090**
Finch, In re, 535 F.2d 70 (C.C.P.A. 1976) **9.003**
Fourth Est. Pub. Benefit Corp. v. Wall-Street.com, LLC, 139 S. Ct. 881, 889 (2019) **9.019**
Geiger, In re, 425 F.2d 1276 (C.C.P.A. 1970) **9.016**
Georgia-Pacific Corp. v. U.S. Plywood Corp., 318 F. Supp. 1116, 1121 (S.D.N.Y. 1970) **9.064**
Georgia-Pacific Corp. v. U.S. Plywood-Champion Papers, Inc., 446 F.2d 295 (2d Cir. 1971) **9.064**
Goodyear Tire & Rubber Co. v. Hercules Tire & Rubber Co., 162 F.3d 1113, 1116 (Fed. Cir. 1998) **9.052, 9.054**

TABLE OF CASES

Gorham Co. v. White, 81 U.S. 511, 528, 20 L. Ed. 731 (1871) **9.006, 9.109**

Grain Processing Corp. v. Am. Maize-Prods. Co., 185 F.3d 1341, 1350 (Fed. Cir. 1999) **9.064**

Halo Elecs., Inc. v. Pulse Elecs., Inc., 579 U.S. 93 **9.066**

High Point Design LLC v. Buyers Direct, Inc., 730 F.3d 1301 (Fed. Cir. 2013) **9.013**

Hoop v. Hoop, 279 F.3d 1004 (Fed. Cir. 2002) **9.088**

Hupp v. Siroflex of Am., Inc., 122 F.3d 1456, 1460 (Fed. Cir. 1997) **9.007**

Int'l Seaway Trading Corp. v. Walgreens Corp., 589 F.3d 1233 (Fed. Cir. 2009) **9.012, 9.015, 9.072**

Jack Schwartz Shoes v. Skechers U.S.A., 2002 U.S. Dist. LEXIS 25699 **9.108**

Kimberly-Clark Corp. v. Procter & Gamble Distrib. Co., 973 F.2d 911 **9.031**

L.A. Gear, Inc. v. Thom McAn Shoe Co., 988 F.2d 1117, 1124 (Fed. Cir. 1993) **9.049**

LKQ Corp. v. GM Glob. Tech. Operations LLC., 102 F.4th 1280, 1298 (Fed. Cir. 2024) **9.013**

Maatita, In re, 900 F.3d 1369 (Fed. Cir. 2018) **9.008, 9.078–9.080**

Markman v. Westview Instruments, Inc., 52 F.3d 967, 976–79 (Fed. Cir. 1995) (en banc), *aff'd*, 517 U.S. 370 (1996) **9.050**

Mazer v. Stein, 347 U.S. 201 (1954) **15.006, 15.031, 15.033**

Nordock, Inc. v. Systems Inc., 803 F.3d 1344, 1355 (C.A.Fed.2015) **9.127, 15.043**

Oakley, Inc. v. Sunglass Hut Int'l, 316 F.3d 1331, 1338–39 (Fed. Cir. 2003) **9.068**

Octane Fitness, LLC v. ICON Health & Fitness, Inc., 572 U.S. 545 **9.070**

Owens, In re, 710 F.3d 1362 (Fed. Cir. 2013) **9.009, 9.084–9.087**

Pacific Coast Marine Windshields Ltd. v. Malibu Boats, LLC, 739 F.3d 694 (Fed. Cir. 2014) **9.052, 9.089–9.090**

Progme Corp. v. Comcast Cable Commc'ns LLC, No. 17–1488, 2017 WL 5070723 **9.058**

Quanta Comput., Inc. v. LG Elecs., Inc., 553 U.S. 617, 625 (2008) **9.061**

Richardson v. Stanley Works, Inc., 597 F.3d 1288, 1295 (Fed. Cir. 2010) **9.049**

Rubik's Brand Limited v Flambeau, Inc., et al, No. 17CV6559PGGKHP, 2021 WL 363704 (S.D.N.Y. 31 Jan 2021) **17.006**

Samsung Electronics, Ltd. v. Apple, Inc., 137 Sup. Ct. 429 (2016) **9.091, 9.101, 9.102, 9.113, 9.114, 9.123, 9.125, , 9.130, 15.005, 15.007, 15.043**

SCA Hygiene Prods. Aktiebolag v. First Quality Baby Prods., LLC, 137 S. Ct. 954 **9.062**

Schnell, In re, 46 F.2d 203 (C.C.P.A. 1931) **9.006**

SmithKline Diagnostics, Inc. v. Helena Lab'ys Corp., 926 F.2d 1161, 1164 (Fed. Cir. 1991) **9.064**

Sport Dimension, Inc. v. Coleman Co., 820 F.3d 1316, 1320 (Fed. Cir. 2016) **I.024, 9.007**

Star Athletica, L.L.C. v. Varsity Brands, Inc., 137 S. Ct. 1002 (2017) **I.016, 9.020, 15.005, 15.006**

SurgiSil, L.L.P., In re, 14 F.4th 1380 (Fed. Cir. 2021) **9.006, 9.074–9.077, 11.022**

Therasense, Inc. v. Becton, Dickinson & Co., 649 F.3d 1276, 1287 (Fed. Cir. 2011) **9.060**

Todd v. Montana Silversmiths, Inc., 379 F. Supp. 2d 1110 **17.105**

TrafFix Devices, Inc. v. Mktg. Displays, Inc., 532 U.S. 23, 29–30 (2001) **9.021**

Two Pesos, Inc. v. Taco Cabana, Inc., 505 U.S. 763, 769 (1992) **9.022**

Wal-Mart Stores, Inc. v. Samara Bros., 529 U.S. 205, 213 (2000) **15.026**

Webb, In re, 916 F.2d 1553, 1557–58 (Fed. Cir. 1990) **9.006**

Wine Enthusiast v Vinotemp International, 317 F.Supp.3d 795, 801 (S.D.N.Y. 2018) **11.127**

Wing Shing Prods. (BVI), Ltd. v. Simatelex Manufactory Co., 479 F. Supp. 2d 388 **9.057, 9.058**

ZUP, LLC v. Nash Mfg., Inc., 229 F. Supp. 3d 430, 454 (E.D. Va. 2017), *aff'd*, 896 F.3d 1365 (Fed. Cir. 2018) **9.058**

TABLE OF LEGISLATION

INTERNATIONAL TREATIES, CONVENTIONS, PROTOCOL AND AGREEMENTS

African Union's (AU) African Continental Free Trade Area (AfCFTA) Agreement **12.004**
Agreement on Trade Related Aspects of Intellectual Property Law (TRIPS) **1.019, 15.011, 18.007**
    art 2 **15.013**
    art 3(1) **16.031**
    art 9.1 **15.013**
    art 9.2 **15.013**
    art 18 **16.031**
    art 25 **15.011, 15.017**
    art 25(1) **16.060**
    art 25.2 **15.013, 15.016, 18.007**
    art 26 **15.011, 15.017, 15.013, 15.014, 15.017, 18.007**
    art 31 **20.042, 20.063**
Agreement on the Withdrawal of the United Kingdom of Great Britain and Northern Ireland from the European Union and the European Atomic Energy Community [2019] OJ C384I/17
    art 54 **10.005**
    art 55 **10.005**
    art 56 **10.005**
    art 59 **10.005**
Bern Convention of the Protection of Literary and Artistic Works of September 9, 1886, as implemented by Law no. 399 of June 20, 1978 **5.055, 19.007, 19.027**
    art 2(7) **18.004**
    art 7(1) **19.027**
Convention on Biological Diversity 1993 (aka the Biodiversity Convention) **18.065**
CLIP Principles
    art 2:101 **14.069**
    art 2:202 **14.069**
    art 2:203 **14.069**
    art 2:206 **14.069**
    art 2:401 (1) **14.069**
    art 2:401 (2) **14.069**
    art 3:101 **14.070**
    art 3:102 **14.070**
Design Law Treaty (DLT) **I.055, 13.002, 16.019**
    art 1bis **13.028**
    art 3 **13.003, 13.014, 13.023, 13.028**
    art 23(4) **13.014**
European Patent Convention (EPC)
    art 52.1 **18.076**
    art 52.2b **18.076**
EU-UK-Trade and Cooperation Agreement **4.107**
Exit Agreement **4.111**
Hague Agreement of 1960 (as implemented in Italy by the Law no. 744 of October 24, 1980) **1.020, 5.036**
Hague Treaty (1960) **18.005**
Harare Protocol
    s 1 **12.009**
    s 1(3) **12.009**
    s 1bis **12.010**
    s 1bis(3) **12.019**
    s 2(5) **12.010**
    s 2(6) **12.011**
    s 2(8)(c) **12.011**
    s 4(1) **12.010**
    s 4(2) **12.013**
    s 4(2)(b) **12.014**
    s 4(3) **12.021**
    s 4(3)(a) **12.017**
    s 4(3)(d) **12.019**
    s 4(4) **12.017, 12.020**
    s 4(5) **12.028**

s 4(6)	**12.016, 12.026**	art 267 (3)	**17.027**
s 4(7)	**12.016**	Vienna Convention on the Law of Treaties	
s 4bis	**12.028**	art 18	**13.013**
s 5bis	**12.015**	Withdrawal Agreement	**4.107, 4.108**
s 22	**12.025**	art 57	**10.060**
Harare Protocol Regulations		WIPO Patent Law Treaty (PLT)	**13.002**
Rule 2(1)	**12.007**		
Rule 2(4)	**12.007**		
Rule 3(1)	**12.007**	## EU LEGISLATION	
Rule 3(2)(a)	**12.007**		
Rule 3(2)(b)	**12.007**	Brussels I Regulation	**14.009,**
Rule 5bis	**12.010**	**14.012–14.014**	
Rule 8	**12.011**	art 4	**14.012, 14.020, 14.074**
Rule 9	**12.010**	art 6 (1)	**14.060**
Rule 10	**12.010**	art 7	**14.013**
Rule 13	**12.010**	art 7 (1)	**14.039**
Rule 15	**12.014**	art 8	**14.060**
Rule 15bis(2)	**12.028**	art 8 (1)	**14.017, 14.040, 14.041,**
Rule 18*quater*	**12.021**	**14.069, 14.075**	
Rule 20bis	**12.007**	art 24	**14.060, 14.076**
Rule 22bis	**12.008**	art 24 (4)	**14.016**
Locarno Agreement of October 10, 1968		art 29	**14.055**
	5.034, 18.006	art 30	**14.055**
London Treaty (1934)	**18.005**	art 31(2)	**14.055**
Lugano II Convention	**14.058**	Brussels Regulation	
art 22	**14.060, 14.076**	art 8 (1)	**14.021**
art 69(5)	**14.058**	Civil Jurisdiction and Judgments Act 1982	
Lusaka Agreement of December 9, 1976			**10.080**
	12.001	s 16	**10.080**
Nagoya Protocol 2010	**18.065**	sch 4	**10.080**
Paris Convention in Lisbon in 1958		Civil Procedure Rules	
art 5*quinquies*	**8.005, 8.068**	Part 63	**10.081, 10.085**
Paris Convention of 1883		Rule 63.2	**10.081**
art 4.C	**18.003**	Rule 63.13	**10.081**
art 6-*ter*	**5.023, 5.048, 5.0450**	Community Designs Implementing	
art 11	**5.018**	Regulation (CDIR)	
Swakopmund Protocol		art 1(1)	**16.055**
s 10	**13.019**	art 1(2)	**19.013**
s 19	**13.020**	art 6	**4.029**
s 19.2	**13.020**	art 11	**11.064**
s 19.3	**13.020**	art 11 (1)	**11.071**
Treaty on the Functioning of the European Union (TFEU)		art 11 (2)	**11.071**
		art 14 (1)	**16.055**
art 114	**14.005**	art 14(1)(d)	**16.055**
art 118	**14.004**	art 14 (2)	**16.055**
art 267	**14.026, 16.014, 17.029**		

TABLE OF LEGISLATION

Community Designs Regulation (CDR) 4.003, 5.030, 5.110, 8.001, 10.002, 11.001, 11.050, 11.133, 14.004, 14.028, 16.002, 18.009, 18.010, 18.014, 18.016, 18.054, 19.007, 19.014, 20.015

art 3   4.016, 11.050, 11.062, 11.065–11.069, 11.071, 17.004, 20.028, 20.050

art 3(1)   16.044, 19.015
art 3(2)   16.045, 19.017
art 3(a) 16.043, 19.011, 19.012, 20.032
art 3(b) 16.045, 19.012, 19.013, 20.028
art 3.8   18.013
art 3b   18.011
art 3c   18.012
art 4   16.050, 18.021, 19.067, 20.050
art 4(1)   19.045
art 4 (2)   11.048, 11.088–11.091, 20.030, 20.032
art 4 (3)   11.089, 11.090
art 4.1(a)(b)   18.022
art 4.2   18.012
art 4.3   I.039
art 5   11.002, 11.010, 11.043, 16.043, 16.050, 20.050
art 5 (1)   11.038, 11.040, 11.044
art 5(1)(a)   16.043
art 5(1)(b)   16.043
art 5(2)   11.038, 11.040, 11.072, 16.063, 19.045
art 5.1   18.023
art 5.1(b)   18.023
art 6   11.002, 11.010, 11.042, 11.043, 11.045, 11.055, 16.043, 16.050, 18.047, 18.054, 20.050
art 6(1)   11.129, 19.053
art 6(1)(a)   16.043
art 6(1)(b)   16.043
art 6 (2)   11.12916.063,, 17.001, 17.003, 17.006, 17.050, 17.053, 17.055, 17.057, 19.044, 19.048, 19.050, 19.051
art 6.1   18.024
art 6.1(b)   18.024

art 7   4.026, 11.010, 11.016, 16.011, 16.024, 16.027, 16.048–16.050, 18.023, 20.050
art 7(1)   10.022, 11.016, 11.018, 11.021, 11.022, 11.025, 11.028, 11.030, 11.037, 16.007–16.009, 16.020, 16.027, 16.028, 16.033, 16.043
art 7(2)   11.026, 11.033, 11.034, 16.009, 16.031, 16.034, 16.040, 16.063, 19.067
art 7(2)(a)   16.037
art 7(3)   11.031, 11.032, 16.009, 16.031, 16.037, 16.039, 16.040
art 7.2   18.043
art 7.2(b)   3.013
art 8   4.094, 20.032, 20.050
art 8 (1)   8.055, 11.074–11.079, 11.081, 11.082, 11.085–11.087, 17.052–17.055, 19.053
art 8 (2)   11.080–11.083, 11.085–11.087, 14.047
art 8 (3)   11.083–11.087
art 8.1   I.018, 18.028
art 8.3   18.028
art 9   18.030, 20.050
art 10   11.123, 16.027, 19.048, 20.050
art 10 (1)   16.053, 19.053, 11.129, 17.054, 17.055, 17.094
art 10 (2)   11.129, 17.001, 17.003, 17.010, 17.053, 17.055, 19.044
art 10.1   4.078, 18.041
art 10.2   4.078, 18.024, 18.041
art 11   10.059, 10.063, 11.004, 19.067, 20.043, 20.050
art 11(1)   8.016, 16.028, 16.031
art 11(2)   11.022, 16.028, 16.029, 16.031
art 12   11.050, 18.019, 20.050
art 13   20.050
art 14   4.011, 8.026, 19.037, 19.048, 19.071
art 14(1)   19.036, 19.037, 19.058, 19.071
art 14(2)   19.044
art 14(3) 8.027, 8.028, 19.037, 19.038, 19.042, 19.044, 19.071

art 14.1	**18.038, 18.040**	art 79 (3) (c)	**14.041**
art 14.2	**18.038**	art 80	**8.039**
art 14.3	**18.039, 18.040**	art 80 (1)	**14.028**
art 18	**19.039, 19.040, 19.073**	art 81	**8.039, 14.031**
art 18(a)	**I.041, 16.046**	art 81 (1) (d)	**14.048**
art 19	**16.027, 18.071**	art 82	**14.034**
art 19(1)	**19.020**	art 82 (5)	**14.049, 14.051**
art 19(2)	**8.043, 10.059, 16.028,**	art 85	**14.044, 16.011**
	19.067, 20.043, 20.050	art 85 (1)	**11.124, 17.093**
art 19.1	**18.041**	art 85 (2)	**14.044, 16.028, 17.093**
art 19.2	**5.030, 18.043**	art 85.1	**18.045**
art 19(2)d	**19.019**	art 85.2	**18.046, 18.047**
art 20	**20.042**	art 86	**14.044, 16.011**
art 20(1)(b)	**20.038**	art 88 (1)	**14.045**
art 20(c)	**19.041**	art 88 (2)	**14.046, 14.047, 14.051**
art 20 (1)	**11.101**	art 89	**14.046**
art 20.1 a–b	**18.048**	art 89 (1)(a)	**14.046**
art 20.1 c	**18.049**	art 89 (1)(b)	**14.046**
art 21	**18.051, 18.071**	art 89 (1)(c)	**14.046**
art 22	**4.089, 8.024**	art 89 (1)(d)	**14.047, 14.051**
art 25(1)	**16.051**	art 90 (1)	**14.043**
art 25(1)(b)	**18.030**	art 90 (3)	**14.043**
art 25(1)(e)	**16.050**	art 93	**14.032**
art 25(1)(f)	**16.050**	art 95	**14.056**
art 25 (1)	**11.061,**	art 96 (2)	**17.097**
	11.064–11.066, 11.068, 11.069,	art 110	**8.050**
	11.095–11.098, 11.111, 11.112,	art 110(1)	**18.069**
	11.114, 11.121–11.122, 11.125,	art 110a	**11.004, 16.030**
	11.130, 11.131, 17.092	art 110a(5)	**10.063, 16.030, 16.031**
art 25 (2)	**17.103**	rec 7	**19.048, 19.074, 19.085, 20.019**
art 25 (6)	**11.109**	rec 20	**16.035, 16.040, 18.043**
art 27	**4.077**	Copyright, Designs and Patents Act 1988	
art 32	**8.028**	(CDPA)	**I.026**
art 32(3)	**10.084**	s 4	**10.065**
art 36 (1)	**20.031**	s 51	**10.065**
art 36 (6)	**10.010, 11.022, 11.094,**	s 52	**10.065**
	11.110, 16.027, 16.053, 20.031	s 213(1)	**10.050**
art 41(1)	**16.017**	s 213(2)	**10.041, 10.044**
art 43	**16.017**	s 213(3)(a)	**10.047**
art 44(1)	**16.017**	s 213(3)(b)	**10.048**
art 47	**11.064**	s 213(3)(b)(i)	**10.048**
art 50(1)	**10.077**	s 213(3)(b)(ii)	**10.048**
art 52	**14.044, 16.011**	s 213(3)(c)	**10.046**
art 60 (1)	**11.011**	s 213(4)	**10.050**
art 61 (2)	**11.011**	s 213(5)	**10.039**
art 63	**11.008**	s 213(6)	**10.041**
art 79	**14.034**	s 214(1)	**10.053**

s 214(2)	10.053	art 3 (3)	11.090, 11.092, 20.030
s 215(1)	10.053	art 3 (4)	11.090, 11.092
s 215(3)	10.053	art 3.1	I.075
s 215(4)	10.053	art 3. 4	I.039
s 216(1)(a)	10.054	art 4	4.029, 5.014, 8.062, 16.050
s 216(1)(b)	10.054	art 4(2)	16.063
s 217	10.039	art 5	5.020, 8.062, 16.050
s 217(1)	10.039	art 5 (2)	16.063, 17.001, 17.003
s 217(3)	10.040	art 5.2	18.024
s 218	10.039	art 6	8.062, 11.010, 16.011, 16.050, 18.023
s 219	10.039		
s 220	10.039	art 6(1)	10.022, 16.007–16.009, 16.020, 16.033, 16.043
s 220(1)(b)	10.040		
s 222	10.053	art 6(2)	**16.009, 16.034, 16.040, 16.063**
s 226(1)	10.055	art 6(2)(a)	16.037
s 226(2)	10.056	art 6(3)	16.009, 16.037, 16.039
s 226(3)	10.055	art 7	8.062
s 226(4)	10.056	art 7.1	18.028
s 227	10.057	art 8	4.032, 8.062
s 229(1)	10.084	art 9	8.062, 11.123
s 229(3)	10.091	art 9(1)	16.053
s 233	10.090	art 9 (2)	11.127, 17.001, 17.003
s 234	10.084	art 9.1	18.041
s 235(1)	10.084	art 9.2	4.078, 18.041
s 236	10.058	art 10	8.062, 18.019
s 237	10.054, 20.051	art 11	8.062
s 239	10.092	art 11(1)	16.051
s 244A	10.058	art 11(2)	16.051
s 244B	10.058	art 11(2)(a)	16.050
s 253–253E	10.083	art 11(2)(b)	16.050
s 263(1)	10.041, 10.053	art 12	8.062, 18.071
Council Regulation (EC) No 2100/94 of 27 July 1994 on Community plant variety rights (OJ 1994 L 227 p. 1) **14.004**		art 13	8.062, 20.042
		art 13.1a–b	18.048
		art 13.1c	18.049
Design Directive (DDir) **4.015, 4.027, 5.056, 8.001, 10.002, 11.001, 11.133, 14.005, 16.002, 17.023, 18.008, 18.016, 19.007, 20.015**		art 14	I.029, I.036, 8.020, 8.050, 18.069
		art 14 1 a	I.077
		art 15	8.062, 18.051, 18.071
art 1	8.062, 17.004	art 16	17.103, 18.019
art 1(a)	16.043, 20.028	art 17	5.003
art 1(b)	16.045	art 17 (2)	17.091, 17.097
art 1a	18.013	art 19	I.032
art 2	8.062	art 19.3	I.076
art 2(3)	16.044, 19.015	rec 11	20.030, 20.031
art 2(4)	16.045, 19.017	rec 13	11.127
art 2(b)	20.028	Design law in the European Union ('EU') 11.001	
art 3	4.020, 4.027, 8.062, 18.022		

TABLE OF LEGISLATION

Designs and International Trade Marks (Amendment etc) (EU Exit) Regulations 2019/638
r 3	**10.061**
r 4	**10.060**
sch 1	**10.061**
sch 1, para 27	**10.084**
sch 1, para 33	**10.081**
sch 1, para 59	**10.083**
sch 1, para 60	**10.083**
sch 1, para 61	**10.083**
sch 2	**10.060**
sch 2, para 25	**10.084**
sch 2, para 29	**10.081**
sch 2, para 54	**10.083**
sch 2, para 55	**10.083**
sch 2, para 56	**10.083**

Directive 2001/29/EC of the European Parliament and of the Council of May 22, 2001 **17.023, 17.027, 17.029, 17.040**
art 2	**17.014, 17.029**
art 2(a)	**4.091**
art 4	**17.029**
art 5	**17.014**

Directive 2004/48/EC of the European Parliament and of the Council of 29 April 2004 on the enforcement of intellectual property rights (IPRED Directive) **4.065, 8.045, 10.088, 18.008**

Directive 2009/24/EC of the European Parliament and of the Council of 23 April 2009
art 2(3)	**19.038**

Directive (EU) 2015/2436 of the European Parliament and of the Council of 16 December 2015 to approximate the laws of the Member States relating to trade marks (OJ 2015 L 336 p. 1) **14.005**
art 4	**8.017**

EU Directive 71/1998 **1.033, 5.028**

EUDR
art 3 (1)	**1.068**
art 3 (2)	**1.068**
art 3 (2) b	**1.069**
art 9(2) (d)	**1.072**
art 18(a)	**1.041**
art 18 a	**1.070**
art 20 (1) (e)	**1.073**
art 20 a (1)	**1.071**
art 20a	**1.032**
art 20a (2)	**1.071**
art 96(2)	**1.010**
rec 18	**1.070**

EU Trademark Regulation **14.030**

European Commission Proposal of 30 March 2022 for a Regulation of the European Parliament and the Council establishing a framework for setting ecodesign requirements for sustainable products and repealing Directive 2009/125/EC (COM/2022/142 final)
art 5	**20.008**

European Union (Withdrawal) Act 2018
s 6	**10.006**

European Union (Withdrawal Agreement) Act 2020
s 1	**10.002**
s 39(1)	**10.002**

European Union trade mark Regulation
art 9	**8.017**

EUTMIR
art 3(3)(e)	**18.077**
art 7(1)(e)(i–iii)	**18.078**

EUTMR
art 25 (1)	**11.101**
art 130 (2)	**14.048**

Intellectual Property Act 2014
s 1(1)	**10.044**
s 1(3)	**10.050**
s 1(4)	**10.050**

Intellectual Property (Enforcement etc) Regulations 2006 (SI 1028/1006)
r 3	**10.091**

Proposal for a Directive of the European Parliament and of the Council on the legal protection of designs (recast), Brussels, 28 November.2022, COM(2022) 667 final, 2022/0392(COD) **19.014**

Registered Designs Act 1949 ('RDA 1949') **10.004**
s 1(2)	**10.007**
s 1(3)	**10.008**
s 1B(1)	**10.011**
s 1B(2)	**10.012**
s 1B(3)	**10.013**

s 1B(5)	10.022	s 24F	10.084
s 1B(6)(a)	10.022	s 24F(4)	10.084
s 1B(6)(b)	10.022	s 26–26E	10.083
s 1B(6)(c)	10.022	s 35ZA(1)	10.093
s 1B(6)(d)	10.022	s 35ZA(3)	10.093
s 1B(6)(e)	10.022	s 35ZA(4)	10.093
s 1B(8)	I.045, 10.011	s 35ZA(5)	10.093
s 1C(1)	10.024	s 35ZA(8)	10.093
s 1C(2)	10.025	sch 1A	10.005
s 1C(3)	10.025	sch 1A, para 3	10.005
s 1D	10.026	sch 1A, para 6	10.005
s 2(1)	10.027	sch 1A, para 7	10.005
s 2(1B)	10.027	sch 1A, para 8	10.005
s 2(3)	10.027	sch 1A, para 9	10.005
s 2(4)	I.048, 10.028	sch 1A, para 10	10.005
s 3A	10.075	sch 1B	10.005
s 5	10.077	Registered Designs Rules 2006, SI 2006/1974 ('RDR')	
s 7(1)	10.031		
s 7(3)	10.031	r 4(1)	10.072
s 7(4)	10.031	r 4(5)	10.074
s 7A(1)	10.031	r 4(7)	10.073
s 7A(2)(a)	10.034	r 5(2)	10.072, 10.073
s 7A(2)(b)	10.034	r 5(5)	10.073
s 7A(2)(c)	10.034	r 6	10.074
s 7A(3)	10.034	r 9(1)	10.072
s 7A(4)	10.034	r 42(1)(a)	10.072
s 7A(5)	10.034	r 42(4)	10.072
s 7B	10.034	r 43	10.072
s 8	10.029	Regulation (EC) 1891/2006	4.003
s 8(3)	10.078	Regulation 2017/1001 of 14 June 2017 on the European Union trade mark [2017] OJ L154/1	14.004
s 8(4)	10.078		
s 8A	10.078		
s 11ZA(1)(a)	10.030	art 4	18.077
s 11ZA(1)(b)	10.030	art 7	8.017
s 11ZA(1A)	10.030	art 123	14.028
s 11ZA(2)	10.027, 10.030	Regulation (EC) No 40/94	
s 11ZA(3)	10.030	art 7 (1)	17.079, 17.080
s 11ZA(4)	10.030	art 95	14.028
s 11ZB	10.030	Regulation No 207/2009	
s 12A	10.005	art 109(1)(a)	14.056
s 14	10.074	Regulation (EU) No 608/2013 of the European Parliament and of the Council of 12 June 2013 concerning customs enforcement of intellectual property rights and repealing Council Regulation (EC) No 1383/2003	4.069, 5.108, 8.048
s 15B	10.029		
s 19	10.029		
s 20(1)	10.027		
s 20(1A)(c)	10.027		
s 24A(1)	10.084		
s 24B	10.090	art 2	5.110

art 3	5.109	s 75	1.007, 1.009
art 17	5.111	s 77	1.009

Rome II Regulation **14.009, 14.024**
   art 8   **14.024**
   art 8 (2)   **14.048–14.049, 14.051**
Statute of the CJEU
   art 58a (1)   **11.134**
Trade Mark Act (1994)
   s 3(1)(b)   **10.068**
   s 3(2)   **10.068**
Trade Mark Directive
   art 10   **8.017**
UK Unregistered Design Right (UDR) Intellectual Property Act 2014   **20.043**
UK Registered Designs Rules 2006   **10.074**
United Kingdom the Patents and Designs Act   **6.001**

NATIONAL LEGISLATION

Africa

Botswana's Industrial Property Act 2010   **12.024**
   s 45(4)   **12.018, 12.023**
Ghana's Industrial Designs Act, 2003
   s 2(4)   **12.023**
Intellectual Property Laws Amendment Act 2013   **13.021**
   s 28B(4)(b)   **13.021**
   s 43B(6)(b)   **13.021**
   s 53B(3)(b)   **13.021**
Kenya's Industrial Property Act, 2001
   s 84(2)   **12.024**
   s 86(4)   **12.023**
Namibia's Industrial Property Act 2012   **12.024**
Namibia's Industrial Property Act No. 1 of 2012
   s 93(3)   **12.024**
   s 93(4)   **12.023**

Australia

Australian Copyright Act 1968   **1.006**
   s 74(1)   **1.006, 1.055**

Australian Designs Act 2003 (the Designs Act) **I.042, 1.001, 1.016, 1.018, 1.242**
   Pt 4   **1.223**
   s 1(xi)   **12.024**
   s 5   **1.002, 1.021, 1.024, 1.055, 1.177, 1.189**

s 5A	1.113
s 6(1)	1.023
s 6(2)	1.025
s 6(3)	1.027
s 7(1)	1.030
s 7(2)	1.031
s 7(3)	1.032
s 8	1.002
s 10(1)	1.248
s 10(1)(f)	1.060
s 10(2)	1.060, 1.063
s 10(1)(a)-(e)	1.060
s 11(1)	1.246
s 11(2)	1.246
s 13(1)	1.091
s 14(2)(a)	1.096
s 14(2)(b)	1.097
s 14(2)(c)	1.097, 1.247
s 14(4)	1.098
s 15	1.041, 1.147, 1.177
s 15(1)	1.080, 1.223
s 15(2)(a)	1.044
s 15(2)(b)	1.044
s 15(2)(c)	1.045
s 16	1.223
s 16(1)	1.042, 1.148, 1.223
s 16(2)	1.043, 1.080, 1.148, 1.223
s 17(1)	1.048
s 17(1)(a)	1.048
s 17(1)(b)	1.048, 1.053
s 17(1A)	1.048
s 17(1B)	1.051
s 17(1C)	1.050
s 17(1D)	1.049
s 18	1.054–1.056, 1.058
s 18(2)	1.056
s 19	1.082–1.084, 1.224
s 19(1)	1.083, 1.204–1.206, 1.223
s 19(2)	1.205, 1.206, 1.223

TABLE OF LEGISLATION

s 19(2)(a)	1.083, 1.204, 1.206	s 71A(3)	1.070
s 19(2)(b)	1.083, 1.119	s 71A(4)	1.071
s 19(2)(c)	1.083, 1.204, 1.206	s 72	1.072, 1.231, 1.232
s 19(2)(d)	1.083, 1.084, 1.204, 1.206	s 72(1)	1.073
s 19(3)	1.204, 1.206, 1.213	s 72(1)(a)	1.232
s 19(4)	1.086, 1.087, 1.206, 1.214, 1.215	s 72(1)(b)	1.232
		s 72(1)(c)	1.232
s 21	1.118	s 72(2)	1.077
s 21(1)	1.092	s 72(5)	1.073, 1.074
s 21(2)(a)	1.103	s 73	1.143
s 21(2)(b)	1.103	s 73(1)	1.188
s 22(1)	1.106	s 73(3)	1.187
s 22(2)	1.105	s 75(1)	1.191
s 23	1.112, 1.118	s 75(1A)	1.194
s 25	1.126	s 75(2)	1.194
s 26	1.104	s 75(3)	1.192
s 27(2)	1.117	s 75(4)	1.195
s 28(3)	1.156	s 77	1.144, 1.196
s 33	1.123, 1.133, 1.151	s 77(1)	1.197
s 37	1.124	s 77(1A)	1.198
s 39	1.129, 1.130	s 77(3)	1.199
s 40	1.130, 1.131	s 80	1.200
s 41	1.132, 1.133, 1.151, 1.155	s 90	1.249
s 43(1)	1.059, 1.138	s 90(3)	1.250
s 46(1)	1.099	s 91(4)	1.251
s 46(b)	1.100	s 93	1.167, 1.175, 1.178
s 47	1.100	s 93(3)(b)	1.094
s 47(2)	1.100	s 93(3)(c)	1.094
s 60	1.128	s 111	1.128
s 63	1.146	s 118(1)	1.248
s 64(2)	1.146	s 137(1)	1.179
s 65	1.147	s 137(2)(a)	1.179
s 65(1)	1.168	s 137(2)(b)	1.183
s 66	1.150	s 137(3)	1.184
s 66(1)	1.160	s 137(4)	1.184
s 66(6)	1.162	s 137(5)	1.184
s 67	1.153	s 139	1.145
s 67(3)	1.152	Australian Designs Regulations 2004 (the Designs Regulations)	1.001, 1.016
s 68	1.152		
s 68(5)	1.174	r 1.05	1.113
s 69	1.170	r 2.01	1.053
s 71	1.164	r 3.01(a)	1.103
s 71(1)	1.063	r 3.01(b)	1.103
s 71(1)(a)	1.081	r 3.01(c)	1.103
s 71(2)	1.065	r 3.05	1.104
s 71(4)	1.190	r 3.06(2)	1.093, 1.113
s 71A(1)	1.068, 1.069	r 3.06(5)	1.116

r 3.07	**1.116**	Canada	
r 3.14	**1.133, 1.151**		
r 4.01	**1.123**	Copyright Act	**2.002**
r 4.04	**1.134**	Industrial Design Act	**2.001, 2.007, 2.109,**
r 4.05	**1.134**	**2.111–2.114, 2.116, 2.125–2.128**	
r 4.05(1)(g)	**1.137**	s 2	**2.006**
r 4.06	**1.059**	s 4	**2.150, 2.152**
r 4.09	**1.100**	s 7	**2.152**
r 5.02	**1.147**	s 7(c)	**2.151**
r 5.03	**1.150**	s 8.2	**2.010, 2.128**
r 5.04	**1.150**	s 8.2(1)(c)	**2.131**
r 9.05 (1)	**1.166**	s 10(1)	**2.036**
r 9.05 (2)	**1.166**	s 11	**2.129, 2.138**
r 9.05 (4)	**1.166**	s 11(1)(a)	**2.034**
r 9.05 (5)	**1.166**	s 11(2)	**2.034**
r 11.18	**1.135**	s 12	**2.150**
Australian Trade Marks Act 1995	**1.011, 1.012**	s 18	**2.065**
		s 22(1)	**2.049**
Australia's Competition and Consumer Act 2010		Industrial Design Regulations	**2.001, 2.007, 2.125, 2.127, 2.128, 2.147**
s 18	**1.015**	s 14	**2.142**
sch 2	**1.015**	s 17	**2.133**
Copyright Regulations 1969		s 25(2)	**2.139**
r 17	**1.008, 1.057**	s 25(2)(b)	**2.142**
Designs Act 1906	**1.240**	s 25(3)	**2.141**
Designs Amendment (Advisory Council on Intellectual Property Response) Act 2021	**1.018, 1.125, 1.259**	s 31	**2.131**
		s 33(2)	**2.038**
		s 33(3)	**2.038**
sch 1	**1.046**	s 47(1)	**2.037**
sch 2	**1.067**	s 47(2)	**2.037**
Designs Amendment (Advisory Council on Intellectual Property Response) Regulations 2021	**1.053**	s 50(4)	**2.049**
		Trademarks Act	**2.003, 2.067, 2.123**
Designs Bill 2020	**1.259**	China	
Explanatory Memorandum to the Designs Amendment (Advisory Council on Intellectual Property Response) Bill 2020	**1.088**	China Patent Examination Guidelines 2021	**3.077**
		pt I, ch 3, art 3.1	**3.081**
IP Australia, Designs Examiners' Manual of Practice and Procedure		pt I, ch 3, art 3.2	**3.081**
		pt I, ch 3, art 3.3	**3.081**
s 8.12	**1.169, 1.174**	pt I, ch 3, art 3.4	**3.081**
s 9.4.	**1.036**	pt I, ch 3, art 3.5	**3.081**
s 13.7.	**1.033**	pt I, ch 3, art 4.2.1	**3.065**
s 22.3	**1.161**	pt I, ch 3, art 4.2.2	**3.065**
s 22.5	**1.163**	pt I, ch 3, art 4.2.3	**3.066**
Trade Marks Act 1995		pt I, ch 3, art 4.2.4	**3.067**
s 6	**1.011**	pt I, ch 3, art 4.4	**3.072, 3.073**
s 17	**1.011**		

pt I, ch 3, art 4.4.2	3.074	art 18	3.057
pt I, ch 3, art 4.4.3.1	3.074	art 20	3.021
pt I, ch 3, art 8.3	3.083	art 23.2	3.014
pt I, ch 3, art 9.1.2.3	3.059	art 24	3.013
pt I, ch 3, art 9.4.2	3.077	art 27	3.058
pt I, ch 3, art 74	3.020	art 28	3.057
pt II, ch 3, art 2.1.2.1	3.008	art 29.1	3.051
pt II, ch 3, art 2.1.2.2	3.011	art 29.2	3.052
pt IV, ch 3, art 3.3.5	3.091	art 30.2	3.053
pt IV, ch 3, art 3.4	3.091	art 31.2	3.059
pt IV, ch 3, art 3.5	3.091	art 32	3.061
pt IV, ch 3, art 3.7.3	3.091	art 40	3.081
pt IV, ch 3, art 3.7.5	3.091	art 41.1	3.082
pt IV, ch 3, art 4.1.1	3.091–3.093	art 41.2	3.082
pt IV, ch 3, art 4.1.1.	3.091	art 42	3.061, 3.085
pt IV, ch 3, art 4.1.(1)	3.092	art 45	3.090
pt IV, ch 3, art 4.2.1	3.092	art 46.2	3.095
pt IV, ch 3, art 4.2.2	3.092	art 47.1	3.094
pt IV, ch 3, art 4.3.1.1	3.092	art 47.2	3.094
pt IV, ch 3, art 4.3.1.2 (i)	3.092	art 50	3.123
pt IV, ch 3, art 4.3.1.2 (ii)	3.092	art 53	3.123
pt IV, ch 3, art 4.3.2	3.092	art 64	3.062
pt IV, ch 3, art 4.4.1	3.091	art 64.2	3.022
pt IV, ch 3, art 4.4.2	3.093	art 65	3.096, 3.098, 3.108
pt IV, ch 3, art 7	3.093	art 67	3.107
pt IV, ch 5, art 3	3.022	art 68	3.108
pt IV, ch 5, art 4	3.029	art 70	3.108
pt IV, ch 5, art 5.1.1	3.026	art 71	3.104, 3.106
pt IV, ch 5, art 5.1.1.3	3.014, 3.026	art 71.2	3.105
pt IV, ch 5, art 5.1.2	3.026	art 74	3.099
pt IV, ch 5, art 5.1.2.1	3.032	art 77	3.107
pt IV, ch 5, art 5.1.2.1.2	3.017	Civil Code	
pt IV, ch 5, art 5.2.1	3.034	art 179	3.103
pt IV, ch 5, art 5.2.2	3.033	Civil Procedure Law of the People's Republic of China 2017	
China Patent Law 2020	I.049	art 6	3.099
art 2.4	3.019	art 14	3.099
art 3.1	3.050	art 20(1)	3.101
art 5	3.080	art 20(2)	3.101
art 6.1	3.046	art 40	3.100
art 6.3	3.047	art 120	3.098
art 10.1	3.120	art 149	3.099
art 10.2	3.120	art 153	3.100
art 11.2	3.045, 3.102	art 155	3.101
art 12	3.121	art 166	3.100
art 14	3.048	art 175	3.100
art 15	3.047	art 176	3.100
art 16.1	3.047		

art 199	**3.101**
art 200	**3.101**
Design Act 2020	
art 2.1	**3.125**
Draft Implementing Regulations of the Patent Law 2020	**3.054**
art 1	**3.057**
art 12	**3.046**
art 27	**3.068**
art 30.2	**3.074**
art 32	**3.054**
art 76	**3.047**
Guidelines for Patent Infringement Determination issued by Beijing Higher People's Court 2017	
art 65	**3.023**
art 65.2	**3.023**
Implementation Regulation of the Patent Law (2021)	
art 27	**3.068**
Implementing Regulations 2010	
art 16.3	**3.047**
art 76	**3.047**
Implementing Regulations of the China Patent Law 2014	
art 1	**3.057**
art 2	**3.057**
art 12	**3.046**
art 14.2	**3.122**
art 15.3	**3.057**
art 16	**3.057**
art 31.2	**3.069**
art 35.1	**3.059**
art 35.2	**3.059**
art 56	**3.086**
art 65	**3.091**
art 66	**3.091**
art 66.2	**3.094**
art 67	**3.092**
art 68	**3.091**
art 70	**3.093**
art 70.3	**3.093**
art 72.1	**3.093**
art 72.2	**3.093**
art 76	**3.047**
art 77	**3.047**
Industrial Design Protection Act 2020	**I.047, 3.125**
Interpretation on Several Issues Concerning the Application of Law in the Trial of Patent Infringement Cases(II) adopted by the Supreme People's Court on March 21, 2016 ('2016 Interpretation')	
art 14	**3.041**
art 15	**3.036**
art 16.1	**3.036**
art 16.2	**3.036**
art 17	**3.038**
Measures for Patent Administrative Law Enforcement 2015	
art 12	**3.109**
art 13	**3.109**
art 16	**3.109**
art 21	**3.109**
art 46	**3.110**
art 48	**3.110**
Order of the State Intellectual Property Office of the People's Republic of China, No. 62/2011	
art 11	**3.122**
art 14	**3.122**
art 16	**3.122**
Patent Administrative Law Enforcement Measures, Promulgated by order no 60 of the State IP office on December 29, 2010, according to order no 71 of the State IP Office on May 29, 2015	
art 10	**3.109**
The Patent Law of the People's Republic of China ('China Patent Law/Patent Law')	**3.001**
art 2.4	**3.070**
art 3.1	**3.050**
art 6	**3.046**
art 11.2	**3.096**
art 15	**3.047**
art 16	**3.047**
art 23	**3.005, 3.007, 3.009, 3.083**
art 27	**3.068**
art 29.1	**3.051**
art 29.2	**3.052**
art 30.2	**3.053**
art 31.2	**3.059**
Registered Designs (Amendment) Act (no 29 of 2017) 2017	
art 2(c)	**3.125**

lix

Supreme People's Court Interpretation of 2009	
art 9	3.022, 3.023, 3.033
art 10	3.028
art 11	3.018, 3.031

Denmark

The Consolidate Designs Act (Consolidate Act No. 89 of January 29, 2019) (Denmark)	8.010
Consolidate Trade Marks Act (Denmark)	
s 3	8.017
s 4	8.017
Danish Administration of Justice Act	
Chapter 29a	8.042
Chapter 40	8.041
Chapter 57a	8.042
Denmark (Design Act ([Lov om monstre]) No. 218 of 27 May 1970)	8.007
Part 5	8.037
Part 7	8.045
s 1	8.018, 8.026
s 1(1)	8.007
s 2	8.019
s 2(1)	8.007
s 2(2)	8.007
s 4	8.019
s 5	8.007
s 5-6	8.021
s 6	8.024
s 6-7	8.007
s 7	8.021
s 8	8.021
s 9	8.022
s 10(3)	8.008
s 10-11	8.022
s 12	8.023
s 13	8.031
s 17	8.032
s 18	8.008, 8.031, 8.034
s 18a	8.034
s 19	8.034
s 20	8.034
s 23	8.029
s 24	8.008, 8.035
s 28	8.007
s 36	8.047
s 51	8.063
Design Act in 1905	8.002
Design Act of 1899	8.002
Marketing Practices Act (Markedsforingsloven, LBK nr 1216 af 25/09/2013)	
s 3	8.016

Finland

Code of Judicial Procedure [Oikeudenkäymiskaari, 1.1.1734/4, 1.7.2021/642](Finland)	8.041
Finland (Design Act [Mönsterrätt- slag] No. 221/1971 of 12 March 1971)	8.007
s 1	8.026
s 4-4a	8.021
s 4b	8.021
s 5-5a	8.022
s 5b	8.022
s 5c	8.023
s 10	8.031
s 12	8.031
s 17	8.032
s 18	8.031
s 24	8.029, 8.035
s 27	8.063
s 28–30	8.025
s 35b	8.047
The Finnish Government Bill	8.024
Finnish Registered Designs Decree	
s 2	8.031
s 13	8.032
s 13(2)	8.033
Registered Designs Act (Act No. 221 of March 12, 1971, as amended up to Act No. 551 of April 26, 2019) (Finland)	8.010
Trade Marks Act (Tavaramerkkilaki, 26.4.2019/544)	
s 4	8.017
s 5	8.017
s 11–12	8.017
Unfair Business Practices Act	
s 1	8.040
s 1(1)	8.016
s 2	8.040

France

CPI
- art L.511-7 — **4.032**

French Code of Civil Procedure
- art 768 — **4.060**

French Intellectual Property Code (IPC)
- art L.122-5 — **4.037, 4.085**
- art L.123-1 — **4.046**
- art L.511-1 — **4.016**
- art L.511-2 — **4.027**
- art L.511-3 — **4.022**
- art L.511-5 — **4.020, 4.035**
- art L.511-6 — **4.026**
- art L.511-8 — **4.034**
- art L.511-9 — **4.011**
- art L.512-4 — **4.036, 4.052**
- art L.513-1 — **4.037, 4.046**
- art L.513-6 — **4.037**
- art L.513–1 — **4.105**
- art L.513–2 — **4.073**
- art L.513–3 — **4.076**
- art L.513–4 — **4.081**
- art L.513–5 — **4.078**
- art L.513–6 — **4.085**
- art L.513–7 — **4.086**
- art L.513–8 — **4.090**
- art L.521-3-2 — **4.055**
- art L.521–7 — **4.065**
- art R. 512–15 — **4.076**

Highway Code
- art L. 110–1 — **4.087**

RDMC
- art 4 — **4.020, 4.027**
- art 9 — **4.029**

Germany

German Designs Act
- s 1 — **11.069**
- s 33 (1) — **11.069**
- s 39 — **17.093**

India

Code of Civil Procedure, 1908
- Order I Rule 3 — **6.052**

Copyright Act, 1957
- s 2 — **6.006**
- s 2 (c) — **6.007, 6.054**
- s 2 (c) (i) — **6.055**
- s 2 (c) (ii) — **6.055**
- s 2 (c) (iii) — **6.055**
- s 14 (c) — **6.026**
- s 15 (2) — **6.028, 6.056**

Designs Act, 1911
- s 2 (5) — **6.008**

Designs Act, 2000 ('the Act') — **I.015, 6.003**
- s 2 (a) — **6.009**
- s 2 (d) — **6.006, 6.040, 6.069**
- s 2 (g) — **6.040**
- s 4 — **6.016, 6.040, 6.068**
- s 5(1) — **6.040**
- s 5 (1) — **6.040**
- s 6(3) — **6.044**
- s 6(6) — **6.044**
- s 6 (1) — **6.025**
- s 11 — **6.026**
- s 11 (1) — **6.026**
- s 11 (2) — **6.023**
- s 19 — **6.061, 6.072**
- s 19 (1) (a) — **6.062**
- s 21 — **6.022**
- s 22 — **6.070**
- s 22 (3) — **6.072**
- s 30 — **6.076**
- s 44 — **6.024**
- s 44 (1) — **6.024, 6.062**

Designs Rules
- Rule 32 — **6.076**
- Rule 33 — **6.076**
- Rule 34 — **6.076**
- Rule 35 — **6.076**

Indian Designs Act
- art 2 — **16.078**
- art 21 — **16.071**

Indian Patents & Designs Act, 1911 (1911 Act) — **6.001, 6.002**

Indian Patents Act, 1970 — **6.058**
- s 2 (1) (j) — **6.058**

Indian Penal Code, 1860
- s 479 — **6.006, 6.008**

Invention and Designs Act, 1888 — **6.001**

TABLE OF LEGISLATION

Manual of Designs Practice and Procedure
    6.008
Paris Convention for the Protection of Industrial Property, 1883 **6.001**
Patents and Designs Act, 1907 **6.001**
Patterns and Designs Protection Act **6.001**
Trade and Merchandise Marks Act, 1958
  s 2 **6.006, 6.008**
  s 2 (1) (v) **6.006**
Trade Marks Act, 1999 **6.048**
  s 2 (m) **6.048**
  s 2 (zb) **6.048**
  s 2 (1) (zb) **6.006**
  s 3 (2) **17.078**
  s 25 (1) **6.048**
  s 25 (2) **6.048**
  s 27 (2) **6.048**

Italy

Copyright Law by Italian Legislative Decree no. 95 of February 2, 2001 **I.008, 5.056**
Industrial Property Code (IP Code) **5.007**
  art 5 **5.051**
  art 9 **5.009**
  art 31 **5.011, 5.012, 5.048**
  art 31.1 **5.007**
  art 32 **5.014, 5.048**
  art 33 **5.020, 5.022, 5.048**
  art 33.2 **5.022**
  art 33-*bis* **5.023, 5.048**
  art 34 **5.015, 5.048**
  art 34.3 **5.016**
  art 35 **5.048**
  art 36 **5.026, 5.048**
  art 38.1 **5.030**
  art 38.2 **5.031**
  art 38.3 **5.031**
  art 39.4 **5.049**
  art 41 **5.041**
  art 41.2 **5.042**
  art 43 **5.048**
  art 44 **5.054**
  art 118 **5.048**
  art 120 **5.067**
  art 120.6 **5.069**
  art 121.2 **5.071**
  art 124 **5.105**
  art 125 **5.103**
  art 126 **5.107**
  art 129 **5.079, 5.081**
  art 129(3) **5.082**
  art 129.3 **5.082**
  art 130 **5.079, 5.081**
  art 131 **5.083**
  art 131–1-*bis* **5.085**
  art 167 **5.032**
  art 241 **5.028**
Intellectual Property Code
  art 66 **5.031**
  art 241 **I.033**
Italian Civil Code
  art 1223 **5.103**
  art 1226 **5.103**
  art 1227 **5.103**
  art 2593 **5.006**
  art 2598 **5.010, 5.104**
Italian Code of Civil Procedure
  art 669-*bis* **5.073**
  art 669-*quaterdecies* **5.073**
  art 669-*sexies*. 2 **5.074**
  art 669-*undecies* **5.076**
Italian Copyright Act
  art 2 (10) **17.005**
Italian Copyright Law
  art 2 **5.008, 5.053**
  art 2(10) **5.057**
  art 25 **5.054**
  art 56 **5.054**
Legislative Decree no. 15 of February 20, 2019
  art 2.1 **5.009**
Legislative Decree no. 145 of 2013 **5.068**

Japan

Administrative Case Litigation Act **7.046**
  art 33, para 1 **7.046**
Civil Act
  art 709 **7.058**
Code of Civil Procedure
  art 6, para 1 **7.069**
  art 285 **7.047**
  art 312 **7.047**

art 313	7.047	art 9-2	7.034
art 318, para 1	7.047	art 10	7.041
art 318, para 4	7.047	art 10, para 1	7.005, 7.033
Copyright Act	7.001	art 10, para 4	7.005
Customs Act		art 10-2, para 1	7.035
art 69-2, para 1, Item 3	7.063	art 14, para 1	7.006, 7.031, 7.057
art 69-2, para 2	7.063	art 15, para 1	7.036
art 69-3	7.063	art 16	7.025
art 69-4	7.063	art 17	7.025
art 69-11, para 1, Item 9	7.063	art 17, Item 3	7.035
art 69-11, para 2	7.063	art 17, para 1	7.040
art 69-12	7.063	art 17-2	7.026
art 69-13	7.063	art 17-3, para 1	7.034
Design Act	7.001, 7.002	art 18	7.026
art 1	15.019	art 19	7.026
art 2	7.002, 15.019	art 20, para 1	7.010, 7.027, 7.029
art 2, para 1	7.011	art 20, para 2	7.010, 7.027, 7.029
art 2, para 2	7.049, 7.057	art 20, para 3	7.006, 7.030, 7.057
art 2.1	I.045	art 20, para 4	7.031
art 3	15.019–15.021	art 21, para 1	7.010, 15.015
art 3, para 1	7.010, 7.012, 7.025, 7.056, 7.065	art 21, para 2	7.010
		art 22, para 1	7.071
art 3, para 1, Item 1	7.013, 7.025	art 22, para 2	7.071
art 3, para 1, Item 2	7.013	art 23	7.048, 7.065
art 3, para 1, Item 3	7.013, 7.065	art 23 *proviso*	7.073
art 3, para 2	7.015, 7.025, 7.065	art 24, para 1	7.048
art 3-2	7.016	art 24, para 2	7.051
art 3-2 *proviso*	7.016	art 27, para 1	7.073
art 4, para 1	7.014	art 27, para 2	7.073
art 4, para 2	7.014	art 28, para 3	7.074
art 5	15.022	art 29	7.055
art 5, Item 1	7.019	art 29-2	7.056
art 5, Item 2	7.019	art 36	7.052
art 5, Item 3	7.019	art 37, para 1	7.057
art 6, para 1	7.010, 7.022	art 37, para 2	7.057
art 6, para 1, Item 1	7.022	art 37, para 3	7.057
art 6, para 1, Item 2	7.022	art 38	7.057, 7.064
art 6, para 1, Item 3	7.022, 7.066	art 38, Item 1	7.050
art 6, para 2	7.023	art 38, Item 2	7.050
art 7	7.004, 7.025, 7.035, 7.038, 7.041, 7.078	art 38, Item 3	7.050
		art 38, Item 4	7.050
art 8	7.004, 7.025, 7.041	art 38, Item 5	7.050
art 8-2	7.004, 7.025	art 38, Item 6	7.050
art 8–2	7.041	art 38, Item 7	7.050
art 9	7.025	art 38, Item 8	7.050
art 9, para 1	7.005, 7.017	art 38, Item 9	7.050
art 9, para 2	7.018	art 39	7.059

TABLE OF LEGISLATION

art 39, para 1	**7.061**	art 60-22	**7.037**
art 39, para 2	**7.062**	art 60-23	**7.037**
art 39, para 3	**7.062**	art 60-24	**7.026, 7.028, 7.034**
art 40	**7.059**	art 68, para 2	**7.021, 7.024, 7.027**
art 41	**7.054**	art 68, para 3	**7.020**
art 42	**7.039**	art 69	**7.064**
art 42, para 1	**7.027, 7.029, 7.032**	art 69-2	**7.064**
art 43, para 1	**7.027, 7.029**	s 1(a)(i)	**7.033**
art 43, para 2	**7.032**	International Registration of Industrial Designs ('Geneva Act') in 2015	**3.087, 7.037**
art 44, para 1	**7.032**		
art 44, para 2	**7.032**		
art 46, para 1	**7.028**	art 1 (vi)	**7.038**
art 47, para 1	**7.034**	art 1 (vii)	**7.038**
art 47, para 1 *proviso*	**7.034**	art 1 (xix)	**7.038**
art 48, para 1	**7.040**	art 1 (xxviii)	**7.038**
art 48, para 2	**7.042**	art 5, para (1)(vi)	**7.039**
art 48, para 3	**7.043**	art 7, para (2)	**7.039**
art 49	**7.044**	art 10 (2)	**7.038**
art 50, para 1	**7.028**	art 10 (3)(a)	**7.038**
art 50, para 2	**7.029**	Patent Act	**I.047, 9.003**
art 50, para 3	**7.029**	art 8	**7.021**
art 52	**7.028, 7.029, 7.042–7.044**	art 17, para 3	**7.024**
art 59, para 1	**7.045**	art 18, para 1	**7.024, 7.027**
art 59, para 2	**7.045, 7.046**	art 18-2	**7.024**
art 60-3	**7.037, 7.038**	art 25	**7.020**
art 60-4	**7.037**	art 27, para 4	**7.073**
art 60-5	**7.037**	art 42	**7.036**
art 60-6	**7.037**	art 42-3, para 1	**7.036**
art 60-6, para 1	**7.038**	art 42-3, para 2	**7.036**
art 60-6, para 2	**7.038**	art 42-3, para 3	**7.036**
art 60-7	**7.037**	art 50	**7.026**
art 60-8	**7.037**	art 52, para 1	**7.026**
art 60-9	**7.037**	art 52, para 2	**7.026**
art 60-10	**7.037**	art 69, para 1	**7.052**
art 60-11	**7.037**	art 69, para 2	**7.052**
art 60-12	**7.037**	art 73, para 1	**7.071**
art 60-13	**7.037, 7.039**	art 98, para 1, Item 1	**7.070**
art 60-14	**7.037**	art 98, para 1, Item 2	**7.073**
art 60-15	**7.037**	art 98, para 2	**7.070**
art 60-16	**7.037**	art 99	**7.074**
art 60-17	**7.037**	art 104-3	**7.054**
art 60-18	**7.037**	art 113	**7.042**
art 60-19	**7.037**	art 132, para 1	**7.042**
art 60-20	**7.037**	art 134, para 1	**7.044**
art 60-21	**7.037**	art 134, para 3	**7.044**
art 60-21, para 1	**7.039**	art 134, para 4	**7.044**
art 60-21, para 3	**7.039**	art 136, para 1	**7.028, 7.043**

art 137, para 1	**7.028, 7.043**	s 14	**8.016**
art 145, para 1	**7.044**	Swedish Design Act	
art 150, para 1	**7.029**	s 1	**8.019**
art 153, para 1	**7.029**	s 1a	**8.018, 8.026**
art 156, para 1	**7.044**	s 2	**8.019**
art 157, para 2	**7.044**	s 2a	**8.019**
art 158	**7.028**	s 3-3a	**8.021**
art 160, para 1	**7.029**	s 4	**8.021**
art 178, para 3	**7.045**	s 4a	**8.021**
art 178, para 4	**7.045**	s 5	**8.022**
art 178, para 5	**7.045**	s 7-7a	**8.022**
art 181, para 1	**7.046**	s 7b	**8.023**
art 181, para 2	**7.046**	s 10	**8.031**
Penal Code		s 17	**8.032**
art 38, para 1	**7.064**	s 19	**8.031**
Regulations for the Enforcement of the Design Act		s 24	**8.029, 8.035**
		s 27	**8.063**
art 2, para 1	**7.066**	s 31	**8.037**
art 6, para 1	**7.066**	s 35	**8.045, 8.047**
Trademark Act	**7.001, 7.007**	s 35b	**8.041**
art 3, para 1, Item 3	**7.007**	Swedish Design Protection Regulation	
art 3, para 2	**7.007**	s 2	**8.031**
Unfair Competition Prevention Act	**7.001, 7.009**	s 13	**8.032**
		Trademarks Act (Varumärkeslag, 2010:1877 i ändrad lydelse upp till Lag 2021:561)	
art 2, para 1, Item 3	**7.009**	s 5	**8.017**
art 19, para 1, Item 5(a)	**7.009**	s 7	**8.017**
		s 9	**8.017**
		s 10	**8.017**

Portugal

Lei no 9.279 de 14/05/1996 (Lei da Propriedade Industrial alterada pela Lei no 14.200 de 2/09/2021)
art 95 **16.076**

Sweden

Code of Judicial Procedure [Rättegangsbalk (1942:740) (i ändrad lydelse upp till Lag (2021:1107)]
s 3 **8.041**
Design Protection Act (1970:485) (as amended up to Act (2020:542) (Sweden) **8.010**
Marketing Act (Marknadsföringslag, 2008:486 i ändrad lydelse upp till Lag 2020:542)
s 5 **8.016**
s 6 **8.016**

United States

15 U.S.C.	
§ 1052	**9.021, 9.022**
§ 1127	**9.021, 15.025**
17 U.S.C.	
§ 101	**15.033**
§ 102	**9.019**
§ 302	**9.019**
19 U.S.C.	
§ 1337(a)(1)(B)	**9.117**
§ 1337(b)(1)	**9.118**
28 U.S.C.	
§ 1295	**9.005**
§ 1331	**9.005**
§ 1338(a)	**9.005, 9.116**
35 U.S. Code	

TABLE OF LEGISLATION

§ 6(a)	9.039	§ 1.3	9.004
§ 6(b)(1)–(4)	9.039	§ 1.53(f)	9.031
§ 101	9.003, 9.018	§ 1.63	9.004, 9.031
§ 102	9.003, 9.025, 9.041, 9.072, 9.073	§ 1.76	9.004
§ 102(a)(1)	9.011, 16.071	§ 1.76(b)(1)	9.032
§ 102(a)(2)	9.011	§ 1.84	9.004, 9.009
§ 102(b)(1)	9.011, 16.071	§ 1.84(m)	9.009
§ 102(b)(2)	16.071	§ 1.121	9.004
§ 103	9.003, 9.013, 9.025, 9.041	§ 1.152	9.004
§ 112	9.003, 9.008, 9.025, 9.079, 9.080, 9.082, 9.083	§ 1.153	9.004
		§ 1.154	9.004, 9.027
§ 115	9.032	§ 1.155	9.004
§ 116(a)	9.031	§ 2.181	9.021
§ 119	9.003	§ 42.15(a)(1)	9.047
§ 119(e)	9.003, 9.011	§ 42.15(a)(2)	9.047
§ 119(a)–(d)	9.035	§ 42.15(b)(1)	9.047
§ 120	9.083, 9.085	§ 42.15(b)(2)	9.047
§ 122(b)	9.011	§ 42.101	9.043
§ 154	9.018	§ 42.102	9.046
§ 154(d)	9.038	§ 42.104	9.041
§ 171	9.003, 9.015, 9.018, 9.025, 15.024, 16.069	§ 42.201	9.044
		Copyright Act of 1976	15.033, 15.037
§ 171(a)	9.001, 9.006, 9.128	art 2(2)	15.039
§ 171(b)	9.003, 9.122	Leahy-Smith America Invents Act ('AIA')	
§ 171(a)–(b)	16.079	s 3(n)(1)	9.046
§ 172	9.003, 9.011, 9.035	Manual of Patent Examining Procedure (MPEP)	
§ 173	9.001, 9.003, 9.034		
§ 251	9.040	§ 301.IV	9.033
§ 255	9.040	§ 607	9.026
§ 261	9.033	§ 714.14	9.026
§ 271	9.049	§ 804.02.II	9.016
§ 271(a)	9.001, 9.056	§ 1502	9.006
§ 271(b)	9.057, 9.058	§ 1503.01	9.027, 9.028
§ 271(c)	9.057, 9.058	§ 1503.02	9.009, 9.029
§ 284	9.063, 9.064, 9.066, 9.122, 9.123	§ 1503.02.III	9.037
§ 285	9.070	§ 1504.01	9.006, 9.128
§ 286	9.062	§ 1504.01(d)	9.015
§ 289	9.003, 9.049, 9.063, 9.065, 9.066, 9.091, 9.122, 9.124–9.127, 9.130, 15.043	§ 1504.01(a).I	9.129
		§ 1504.01(a).I.A.	9.006
		§ 1504.01(a).IV	9.129
§ 311(c)(1)	9.046	§ 1504.02	9.008
§ 315(a)(2)	9.048	§ 1504.04	9.037
§ 315(e)	9.045	§ 1504.04.I	9.008
§ 321	9.046	§ 1504.06.II	9.016
§ 325(a)(2)	9.048	§ 1504.10	9.035
§ 325(e)	9.045	§ 1504.30(a)	9.099
Code of Federal Regulations ('C.F.R.')		§ 2109	9.031

§ 2109.01		**9.031**	United States Patent Code	**I.051**
Tariff Act of 1930			U.S. Const	
s 337		**9.117**	art. III § 2	**9.005**

INTRODUCTION TO *DESIGN LAW*

Dana Beldiman

A.	INTRODUCTION	I.001		(a) The challenge of new technologies	I.046
B.	HIGHLIGHTS OF SALIENT DESIGN LAW TOPICS	I.005		(b) Workarounds	I.049
	1. Cumulative Protection	I.006		(c) Legal reform	I.050
	(a) The expansion of copyright protection	I.008		(d) Artificial intelligence and design	I.052
	(b) Curtailing the effect of copyright protection	I.014	C.	PRESENT-DAY TRENDS AND CHALLENGES IN DESIGN LAW	I.053
	2. Functionality	I.017	D.	THE WAY FORWARD – A LOOK AT THE FUTURE OF DESIGN LAW	I.062
	3. Spare Parts and the Right to Repair	I.027	E.	EU DESIGN LAW REFORM	I.066
	(a) The repair clause in the EU	I.029		1. Design Regulation	I.068
	(b) Repair clauses in other jurisdictions	I.033		(a) Definitions	I.068
				(b) Visibility	I.070
	(c) Jurisdictions without repair clauses	I.034		(c) Repair clause	I.071
				(d) Expanded digital infringement	I.072
	4. Visibility	I.038		(e) Additional defences	I.073
	(a) EU present and proposed law on visibility	I.039		2. Design Directive	I.074
				(a) Elimination of unregistered designs at national level	I.075
	(b) Attenuated visibility requirement in some jurisdictions	I.042		(b) Repair clause transition period	I.076
	(c) Jurisdictions maintaining visibility as a requirement	I.045		(c) Cultural heritage	I.077
				3. Timeline for Adoption and Implementation	I.078
	5. Emerging Technologies	I.046			

A. INTRODUCTION

The rapid pace of change in our society subjects the traditional structure of design laws to considerable strain. Technological development has resulted in creation of 'designs' that transcend the brick-and-mortar concept of a design object, manifest in virtual designs, NFTs, various metaverse applications, and more. Environmental concerns dictate a shift in the economy towards circularity, meant to conserve finite resources and curbing waste. At the same time, design law grapples with long-standing inherent controversies, which create uncertainty and impede its effectiveness, such as issues surrounding cumulative protection, functionality, spare parts, etc. **I.001**

I.002 This book addresses some of the afore-mentioned concerns. It is authored by an international group of distinguished academics and experienced practitioners, who all contribute a wealth of knowledge and a diversity of perspectives. Its target is a broad audience interested in global design law. Practitioners as well as scholars, right holders as well as aspiring designers, policymakers as well as students, will all find knowledge and inspiration in the book's chapters.

I.003 Within its conceptual framework, the book is divided into two segments. In the first segment, a compilation of country-by country chapters, we have strived to showcase representative jurisdictions, with rich and diverse design traditions and laws. These chapters cover the existing positive law and prevailing case law of Australia, Canada, China, France, Italy, India, Japan, the Nordic countries (Denmark, Finland, and Sweden), the United States, the United Kingdom, and the European Union. The second segment offers in-depth analysis and critical assessment of several theoretical aspects of international design law. These chapters include jurisdictional issues, the status of selected treaties,[1] a comparative treatment of prior art in the European Union and beyond, the concept of aesthetic creative freedom, cumulative protection, protection of AI generated works and considerations for reframing design law to align with the goals of the circular economy.

I.004 The present introduction is meant to give the reader a more detailed understanding of some of the issues explored in this book. It will start by offering highlights of selected substantive topics, which find different resolutions among jurisdictions, before proceeding to provide an overview of the theoretical chapters.

B. HIGHLIGHTS OF SALIENT DESIGN LAW TOPICS

I.005 The following will address a few 'wicked' issues raised by the chapters of the book, which continue to cause controversy in design law around the world. Specifically, we will address cumulative protection, functionality, spare parts/right to repair, visibility and emerging technologies. Following a brief synopsis of each topic, we have summarised observations on the respective topic from the featured jurisdictions.

---

1 Harare Protocol on Patents and Industrial Designs within the Framework of the African Regional Intellectual Property Organization (ARIPO) and the upcoming Design Law Treaty (DLT).

INTRODUCTION

1. Cumulative Protection

Policing the border between copyright law and design law, is becoming an increasingly difficult task for national courts and legislators.[2] Cumulative protection arises from the dual nature of industrial designs as both functional and aesthetic creations, allowing protection under multiple IP regimes. Most frequently, cumulation appears in connection with copyright,[3] as the blend of aesthetic and functional features in applied art permitting courts to find copyrightable aesthetic features in objects, which are also protected under design law.

I.006

Cumulative protection is mostly not doctrinally sanctioned, but arises, fully or partially, as a *de facto* situation, resulting from the change of standards for protectability in another regime, in most instances, copyright. Its practical implications, however, are considerable. On the one side, for right holders, access to multiple regimes offers 'attractive alternatives or supplements to protection by design law'.[4] Because copyright, unfair competition and, in some jurisdictions, trademark law are not subject to registration requirements, they provide a convenient fallback in the event design protection fails. Furthermore, the short duration of design protection facilitates strategies for sequential protection under multiple regimes whose duration of protection exceeds that of design law.[5] On the other side, opponents of cumulative protection argue that appropriation for periods well beyond a design product's normal lifespan risks stifling innovation and competition. It further leads to evisceration of the limitations and exceptions built into the design regime. If for instance, as pointed out in Chapter 8 (Nordic), auto 'spare parts can gain protection via copyright or unfair competition, then the limitations in design law in this respect are being undermined.'[6] Finally, cumulative protection also raises the issue of double recovery.[7]

I.007

---

2 Jens Schovsbo, Teemu Matikainen, and Marcus Norrgård, Design Protection in the Nordic Countries, Chapter 8, Section C.
3 Shubha Ghosh, Redesigning Design Protection: The Problem of Overlap, Chapter 15, Section C (2). However, design features are also protectable under trademark and unfair competition law. While in theory each regime applies to a different aspect of design products, in practice it is hard to impossible to draw precise demarcation lines. This leads to divergent jurisprudence in the field.
4 Schovsbo (et al.), (n. 2), Chapter 8, Section C.
5 See Holger Ernst, Intellectual Property as a Management Discipline, Technology and Innovation, Vol. 19, pp. 481–492, 2017. For instance, an initial period of design protection offers a convenient means of gaining secondary meaning for purposes of trademark law.
6 Schovsbo (et al.), (n. 2), Chapter 8, Section C; *see also* Annette Kur, Tobias Endrich, Laimboeck, Marck Huckschlag, Substantive Law Aspects of the 'Design Package', (2023) 72(6) GRUR International 557–565.
7 Ghosh (et al.), (n. 3), Chapter 15, Section A.

(a) The expansion of copyright protection

I.008 Historically, some jurisdictions have developed doctrines of strict separability between regimes, such as the concept of '*scindibilita*' in Italy.[8] The more recent trend, however, is to recognise an increasingly capacious sphere of copyright law, which leads to automatic concomitant protection under both regimes.

I.009 Even in Italy, the country of '*scindibilita*', 'some authors and court decisions admitted the protection of aesthetically separable features of a mass product according to the provisions of the copyright law, if these features were not subservient to its industrial or utilitarian nature, namely if it was in theory possible to imagine the work as an aesthetic project, separated from its function ('*scindibilità concettuale*')'.[9] Officially, this expansion of copyright law was enabled by the Legislative Decree no. 95 in February 2, 2001 and provided that copyright protection may be granted to works of industrial design on condition that they have an artistic value.[10]

I.010 The concept of cumulation, at least regarding copyright law, seems now being firmly embedded, not only in practice, but also in the law. Articles 96(2) EUDR and 23 DDir of the EU Design Reform Package[11] essentially confirm cumulative protectability of designs by endorsing the approach taken by the CJEU in the *Cofemel* and *Brompton Bike*[12] cases, by declaring as 'requirements of Union copyright law' – that the 'uniform European concept of work now undeniably applies to the area of applied art' applicable in determining cumu-

---

8   Traditionally, a work of industrial design was not entitled to copyright protection under Italian law, based on the consideration that where the only function of the shape is to provide a particular aesthetic or ornamental quality to a product, it remains closely linked to the purpose of the product itself and may only be protected as an ornamental design, by obtaining a design registration. Marco F. Francetti and Matteo Mozzi, Industrial Design Law in Italy, Chapter 5, Section I. The principle of 'dissociation' ('*scindibilita*') essentially prohibited copyright protection for industrial designs. Copyright Law of Italy (Law No. 633 of April 22, 1941, as amended by Decree Law No. 154 of May 26, 1997). Art 2(4) provided that protection is available for 'works of sculpture, painting, drawing, engraving and similar figurative arts [...], even where such works are applied to industrial products, if their artistic value is distinct from the industrial character of the product with which they are associated'. WIPO, Standing Committee on the Law Of Trademarks, Industrial Designs and Geographical Indications Ninth Session, Doc. SCT/9/6, Geneva, November 11 to 15, 2002.
9   Francetti (et al.), (n. 8), Chapter 5, Section I.
10 Ibid.
11 The final form of the EU Design Package of 2022 appears as follows: Proposal for a Directive of the European Parliament and of the CounciL on the legal protection of designs (recast), https://data.consilium.europa.eu/doc/document/ST-12714-2023-ADD-1/en/pdf (DDir or PDDir) and Proposal for a Regulation of the European Parliament and of the Council amending Council Regulation (EC) No 6/2002 on Community designs and repealing Commission Regulation (EC) No 2246/2002 (EUDReg or PEUDRef) https://data.consilium.europa.eu/doc/document/ST-12714-2023-ADD-2/en/pdf.
12 Case C-683/17 *Cofemel v G-Star* ECLI:EU:C:2019:721; Case C-833/18 *Brompton v Chedech/Get2Get* ECLI:EU:C:2020:461.

lative protectability of designs.¹³ Combined, these decisions, as aptly summarised in the Nordic chapter, require EU countries to grant copyright protection to works of applied art which are 'the result of the author's free and creative choices; not determined by technical constraints or by following rules; stamped with the author's 'personal touch'; and expressed in a manner which makes it identifiable with sufficient precision and objectivity.'¹⁴

The result is that, in EU case law, copyright's reach has expanded, and now covers many of design law's traditional fields, causing increasing overlap problems.¹⁵ For instance, a decision by the Danish Supreme Court made it clear that 'fashion items, as such, may acquire copyright protection according to the same principles as other types of works'.¹⁶ The authors express concern that this 'may open copyright's doors to fashion items such as clothing, footwear and accessories which have hitherto not been protected by copyright law in Denmark.¹⁷ In Finland, any design object was in principle protectable by copyright even before *Cofemel*.¹⁸ Whether the Court will alter its position in upcoming cases is doubtful.¹⁹   **I.011**

Admittedly, the notion of extensive cumulation may have caused the *Cofemel* Court certain unease, given its statement that the risk of cumulation exists 'only in certain situations'.²⁰ However, the Court did not go on to clarify the nature of such 'certain situations', nor did the EU Design Reform Package. As a result, cumulation is *de facto* endorsed, while the specifics of 'certain situations' remain legally uncertain.   **I.012**

Cumulation of rights is particularly acute in the UK where (at the time of writing) the law provides for three forms of unregistered design protection, as well as (to a greater or lesser degree) the possibility of protecting designs via copyright, registered trademarks, and passing off.²¹ The authors express   **I.013**

---

13 Kur et al., (n. 6), 563; *Cofemel v G Star*, (n. 12).
14 Schovsbo (et al.), (n. 2), Chapter 8, Section A (1) (b).
15 Ibid.
16 Ibid.
17 Ibid.
18 Ibid., citing judgment reported in Ugeskrift for Retsvæsen 2020, 2817. See also Jens Schovsbo, 'Danish Supreme Court Denies Copyright in Rubber Boots' (2020) 15(9) *Journal of Intellectual Property Law & Practice* 679.
19 At the time of this writing two referrals are pending before the CJEU: Case C-580/23 Mio and Others and a Federal Court of Germany referral, involving USM Haller.
20 [A]lthough the protection of designs and the protection associated with copyright may, under EU law, be granted cumulatively to the same subject matter, that concurrent protection can be envisaged only in certain situations', *Cofemel* (n. 12), Judgment, paragraph 11; see also Kur (et al.) (n. 13), p. 563.
21 The UK chapter signals a 'particularly egregious case study in overlap and complexity in relation to designs.' Jane Cornwell and Lynne Chave, Design law at the crossroads-a post-Brexit review of design protection in the UK, Chapter 10, Section F.

the hope that the UKIPO's review of UK design protection will take at least some steps to address and simplify the position, which cause uncertainty and challenges to designers and other stakeholders.[22]

(b) Curtailing the effect of copyright protection

I.014 Some jurisdictions have sought to curtail the effect of copyright protection, by implementing more precise lines of demarcation. Jurisdictions, such as Canada, India, and Australia, cut off copyright protection once the design is 'applied industrially'. In other words, if the design is applied to articles that have a utilitarian function, copyright is rendered unenforceable, once more than 50 articles embodying the design have been made.[23] However, in some jurisdictions, such as Australia and India, the rule does not apply to two-dimensional artistic work. In Australia, an image of the artistic work printed on a surface of the product, will not be considered a protectable 'corresponding design'. However, copyright in the artistic work is retained, whether or not a design is registered under the Designs Act or not. In the specific case of India, the intent falls prey to the ambiguity of the Copyright Act. The phrase in the Copyright Act ('any other work of artistic craftsmanship') provides no clarity on the specific type of three-dimensional products that would qualify for copyright protection but would be disqualified for design protection.'[24] Similarly, in Australia, an image of the artistic work printed on a surface of the product, will not be considered a 'corresponding design'. However, copyright in the artistic work is retained, whether a design is registered under the Designs Act or not.[25]

I.015 In these jurisdictions, the intent seems to be to reduce overlap as much as possible, by clearly differentiating between the protection provided by copyright law, as opposed to that provided by design law. In India, for instance, case law makes 'a clear distinction between an original artistic work, and the design derived from it for industrial application on an article', whereby 'the Designs Act 2000 intended a shorter term for copyright when from the copyright a design is created which is applied for commercial purposes.'[26]

---

22 Cornwell (et al.), (n. 21), Chapter 10, Section F.
23 Robert Storey, Adam Bobker, Matthew Graff, and James Raakman, Industrial Design in Canada, Chapter 2, Section A (1) (a); Shwetasree Majumder and Eva Bishwal, India, Chapter 6, Section A (4) (b); Stuart Irvine and Carl Harrap, Overview of Industrial Design Protection in Australia, Chapter 1, Section A (2) (a).
24 Majumder (et al.), (n. 23), Chapter 6, Section A (4) (b), citing Section 2 (c) (iii) of the Indian Copyright Act.
25 Irvine (et al.), (n. 23), Chapter 1, Section A (2) (a).
26 Majumder (et al.), (n. 23), Chapter 6, Section A (4) (b), citing *Microfibers Inc. v. Girdhar & Co. & Anr.* 2009 (40) PTC (Del).

US design patent law has in effect fashioned its own version of demarcation. In **I.016** the US, copyright protection may coexist with design patent protection, to the extent that the expression is 'ornamental'.²⁷ However obtaining copyright protection for designs which display both aesthetic and functional features, faces the hurdle of essentially requiring separability of aesthetic from functional features. According to the most recent pronouncement of the US Supreme Court in *Star Athletica, L.L.C. v. Varsity Brands*, protectability of an element depends on whether the element is perceived as a two- or three-dimensional work of art separate from the underlying useful article, and whether it can be imagined separately from the useful article into which it is incorporated.²⁸ Under this test, as long as a design can be 'imaginatively' separated from the useful article, that separated feature is copyright protectable. This test, in theory, limits overlap, however its outcome predictability is not high.

2. Functionality

Most countries' design laws exclude functional features from protection in **I.017** order to prevent technological inventions from being appropriated without meeting the stringent requirements of patentability.²⁹

These 'functionality' exceptions generally provide that features of a product's **I.018** appearance which are dictated by its technical function are exempt from design protection.³⁰ As the authors of Chapter 10 (UK) correctly observe, 'interpretation of this exclusion has proved notoriously controversial'.³¹ Apart from the inherent difficulty of determining when a feature is in fact functional, courts have been challenged by having to determine the quantum of functional features which leads to loss of protection. Therefore, views on the applicable methodology diverge.

The applicable standard under the EU Design Regulation is that 'a Community **I.019** design shall not subsist in features of appearance of a product which are solely

---

27   Elizabeth Ferrill, Kelly Horn, William Neer, Troy Viger, Design Patent Laws in United States, Chapter 9, Section A (1) (g) (ii).
28   To determine whether an aesthetic element of a useful article falls under copyright protection, the US Supreme Court has articulated the standard that the element must (1) 'be perceived as a two- or three-dimensional work of art separate from the useful article' and (2) 'qualify as a protectable pictorial, graphic, or sculptural work—either on its own or fixed in some other tangible medium of expression—if it were imagined separately from the useful article into which it is incorporated. Ferrill (et al.), (n. 27), Chapter 9, Section A (1) (g) (ii); *Star Athletica, L.L.C. v. Varsity Brands, Inc.*, 137 S. Ct. 1002, 1007 (2017).
29   TRIPS Art. 26.
30   For instance, the wording of CDReg provides that a design right 'shall not subsist in features of appearance of a product which are solely dictated by its technical function.' CDReg Art.8.1.
31   Cornwell (et al.), (n. 21), Chapter 10, Section B (2) (c).

dictated by its technical function.'³² However, the methodology for determining whether specific features are 'solely dictated by function' has been in dispute. For years, courts have adjudicated following the so called 'multiplicity of forms' approach, which holds that a design is protectable 'only if the technical function cannot be achieved by any other configuration'.³³ In other words, the availability of design alternatives indicates that the design is not solely dictated by function, and the feature is therefore protectable. This approach was strongly criticised by the EUIPO's Board of Appeal,³⁴ on the ground that it applies only in 'highly exceptional circumstances' and therefore excludes 'too few designs'.³⁵ Consequently, it results in potential innovation-stifling overprotection, which hollows out the functionality exception.

I.020 A different standard, the 'causative' test, was proposed, which focuses on whether technical reasons underlie the choice of a feature's appearance.³⁶ This approach was ultimately endorsed by the CJEU in 2017 in *Doceram*³⁷ and subsequently confirmed by the CJEU in *Papierfabriek Doetinchem*.³⁸ The absence of aesthetic considerations in development of a design would render it unprotectable. Otherwise stated, a product's configuration is solely dictated by its technical function and therefore unprotectable, if every feature of the design is solely determined by technical considerations.³⁹

I.021 Outside the EU, the standards applied range from strict exclusion of any functional feature to equivalents of the above-described 'multiplicity of forms' or 'causation' approaches, to absence of a functionality exclusion altogether.

I.022 Similar to courts in the EU, China has rejected the 'no alternative design' approach to the functionality exclusion. The Beijing IP Court stated in this regard that 'the decision on functional design elements does not depend on whether the design has no alternative due to functional or technical constraints, rather it depends on whether the ordinary consumers of the products

---

32 CDReg Art. 8(1).
33 *Linder Recycling Tech GmbH v Franssons Verkstäder AB* (R 690/2007-3).
34 Ibid.
35 Ibid.; Schovsbo, Jens and Dinwoodie, Graeme B., Design Protection for Products that are 'Dictated by Function' (April 18, 2018), in Kur, M. Levin and J. Schovsbo (eds), *The EU Design Approach – A Global Appraisal* (Edward Elgar) available at SSRN: https://ssrn.com/abstract=3164916 or http://dx.doi.org/10.2139/ssrn.3164916.
36 *Lindner Recycling Tech GmbH v Franssons* (n. 33).
37 C-395/16 *Doceram GmbH v CeramTec GmbH* ECLI:EU:C:2018:172.
38 Case C-684/21 (*Papierfabriek Doetinchem*), ECLI:EU:C:2023:141.
39 *Amp Inc v Utilux Pty Ltd* [1971] F.S.R. 572; Schovsbo (et al.), (n. 2), Chapter 8, SectionA (4); Doceram, (n. 37).

see that the design is determined only by a specific function and does not need to consider whether the design is aesthetic'.[40]

India, on the other hand, has preserved a defence that is akin to the 'multi- **I.023** plicity of forms' method. According to the Delhi High Court, 'if a particular function can be achieved through a number of different forms, then a defence of functionality must fail. For the defence of functionality to succeed, it is essential for the defendant to establish that the design applied for is the only mode/option which was possible considering the functional requirements of the products. Even otherwise, assuming that the shape also performs a certain function, that, by itself, is not determinative of the fact that the design is functional, if that is not the only shape in which the function could be performed'.[41]

The US, whose design law is patterned on the patent regime, grants protection **I.024** to designs that are 'new, original and ornamental'.[42] Peculiarly, the term 'functionality' appears nowhere in the law. Instead, it is treated as the converse of the 'ornamentality' requirement, while the ornamentality requirement receives mere lip service.[43] However, in general, case law holds that a design patent does not protect a design that is purely functional, meaning a design that is 'dictated by' its function and completely lacking in ornamentality.[44] Nonetheless, courts continue to vacillate between a categorical exclusion, i.e. 'purely functional', requiring complete absence of ornamentality, on the one hand, and a balancing approach, i.e., 'primarily functional', on the other.[45] Either standard seems to apply a four-factor test, in which the core factor is the existence of alternative designs. The central idea is that a design should not be deemed functional if there are alternative (substitute) designs that would carry out the function equally well.[46] In short, the US approach to functionality aligns with that of India, but not with the EU and China.

Whether a feature is functional, is relevant not only to determine validity of **I.025** a design, as outlined above, but may also impact determination of the scope

---

40 *Triangle v. Bridgestone and Patent Reexamination Board* (2016), Jing Xing Zhong, the Beijing IP Court, evaluated the validity of a design patent for a tire thread design.
41 Majumder (et al.), (n. 23), Chapter 6, Section A (2) (c).
42 'Whoever invents any new, original and ornamental design for an article of manufacture may obtain a patent therefor, subject to the conditions and requirements of this title.' 35 US Code 171.
43 Jason J Du Mont and Mark David Janis, Functionality in Design Protection Systems (2012) 19 *Journal of Intellectual Property Law* p. 261, 2012, Indiana Legal Studies Research Paper No. 210, SSRN: https://ssrn.com/abstract=2147996.
44 Ferrill (et al.), (n. 27), Chapter 9, Section A (1) (b); *Sport Dimension, Inc. v. Coleman Co.*, 820 F.3d 1316, 1320 (Fed. Cir. 2016).
45 Du Mont, et al. (n. 43), p. 282.
46 Ibid.

of protection.[47] The underlying principle is that unprotectable features should not be taken into consideration when assessing the overall appearance of a design. Accordingly, in evaluating infringement, features dictated by technical function should be discounted.[48] For instance, in Australian law a feature's functionality is relevant in determining the scope of protection, even though there is no explicit 'technical functionality' type exclusion.[49] In assessing the scope of protection when functional features are present, courts often struggle, as demonstrated by some US cases. If, as required, functional features must not be considered in determining the scope of protection, they must be 'discounted' or 'factored out'. If the rule is interpreted too literally, the scope is effectively assessed only based on the aesthetic features that remain after 'factoring out' the functional ones. In that case, the design will inevitably produce a different overall impression from the allegedly infringing device.[50] A better approach was used by UK courts in *Magmatic Ltd v PMS International*.[51] There, the court emphasised the importance of having a narrow feature-by-feature analysis, followed by a final global assessment of the overall impression.[52]

I.026 Finally, some design regimes are functionality-neutral, in that they do not feature a functionality exclusion at all. For instance, Australian law does not have an explicit 'technical functionality' type exclusion. Similarly, the authors of the Nordic design chapter point out that prior to the adoption of the EU Directive and Regulation, former Nordic design law featured a functionality-neutral definition of the object of protection. Under former sec. 1(1), protection was simply available for the appearance of the products, regardless of whether the appearance was determined by aesthetic or functional considerations, while the function itself could not be protected by the Design Act.[53] The UK unregistered design right (UKUDR) presents another instance in which functional features are protected by a design law. The UKUDR was introduced by the Copyright, Designs and Patents Act 1988 (CDPA),[54] as a form of limited design protection intended particularly for functional designs. In contrast with UK registered designs, it does not exclude purely

---

47 Du Mont and Janis, (n. 43) differentiating between 'validity functionality' and 'scope functionality'.
48 Cornwell (et al.), (n. 21), Chapter 10, Section B (2) (b). See also Irvine (et al.), (n. 23), Chapter 1, Section A (4) (b).
49 Irvine (et al.), (n. 23), Chapter 1, Section A 4 (b).
50 *Richardson v Stanley Works*, 543 F3d 1288 (Fed Cir 2010); *OddzOn Prods. v. Just Toys, Inc* 122 F.3d 1396 (Fed.Cir.1997).
51 *PMS International Group Plc v Magmatic Ltd* [2016] UKSC 12.
52 Ibid.
53 Schovsbo (et al.), (n. 2), Chapter 8, Section A (1) (a).
54 CDPA 1988, para 3.2.

functional designs[55] and the object of protection is defined neutrally in terms of functionality or aesthetics.'[56]

3. Spare Parts and the Right to Repair

A long-time controversial issue in design law is the tension relating to control over the secondary market for component parts of a complex product.[57] This issue arises most prominently in the automotive area,[58] because collision damage creates a regular demand for spare parts. Thus, a lucrative, but hotly disputed, market for spare parts is established. Automotive manufacturers assert their design right to component parts against competitors. In turn, service providers demand an exception to design rights that would allow them to service the spare parts market. **I.027**

An exception to design law in the form of a 'right-to-repair' would indeed reduce the tension by opening up the spare parts market to non-design right holders.[59] Following extended and heated debates, some, but not all, jurisdictions have enacted 'repair clauses'.[60] Their general tenor is to exempt component parts of a complex product from design protection, on the condition that they are used for the purpose of the repair, so as to restore the original appearance of the product.[61] A brief overview of how some the jurisdictions featured in this book have dealt with the spare parts issue follows. **I.028**

(a) The repair clause in the EU

The situation in the EU well illustrates the tensions underlying the spare parts issue. Because member states could not agree on a repair clause at the time the Design Directive 98/71 was passed, a compromise solution, also referred **I.029**

---

55 Cornwell (et al.), (n. 21), Chapter 10, Section C (1) (d), citing CDPA 3.14.
56 The UKUDR can subsist in 'articles' of all kinds, including component parts and has been invoked in cases 'from pig fenders and slurry separators to contact lenses and medical devices' but also 'in cases involving aesthetic designs including clothing and footwear. –Cornwell (et al.), (n. 21), Chapter 10, Section C (1) (c).
57 From a legal standpoint, the issue arises out of introduction by most jurisdictions of separate protection for component parts, results in creation of a captive market of spare parts. Dana Beldiman, Constantin Blanke-Roeser, *An International Perspective on Design Protection of Visible Spare Parts*, Springer, 2017.
58 However, design right issues relating to spare parts also arise for other items which require periodic replacement such as razor blades, printer cartridges, coffee machine capsules, etc.
59 *See generally,* Beldiman (et al.), (n. 57). For clarification, design protection applies to 'must match' parts (parts whose appearance must match the appearance of the product), but not to 'must fit' parts, which are excluded from design protection due to their functional characteristics.
60 As of the date of this writing Austria, Bulgaria, Cyprus, the Czech Republic, Denmark, Estonia, Finland, Croatia, Malta, Portugal, Romania, Sweden, Slovakia and Slovenia had not adopted a repair clause.
61 For instance, CDReg Art. 110 is worded: 'protection as a Community design shall not exist for a design which constitutes a component part of a complex product used within the meaning of Article 19(1) for the purpose of the repair of that complex product so as to restore its original appearance'.

to as 'freeze-plus' was adopted in Article 14, which provided for a 'status quo', requiring member states to maintain in force their national regulations and not to increase the level of protection pending a further proposal by the Commission.[62] In contrast, the subsequently adopted Community Design Regulation (CDReg), passed in 2001 did include a repair clause as a transitional provision.[63] As a result, for many years, EU Community Design rights have been subject to the repair clause of Article 110 CDReg, while at national level the solution was largely left to national legislatures, which may or may not have enacted a repair exception.[64]

I.030 In the jurisdictions in which a repair clause is in effect,[65] the controversy has now moved to interpreting the scope of the clause. The repair exception applies to parts meant to 'restore the original appearance of the product'. The debate relates to whether dual use parts, in other words, parts that can be used both for repair purposes and to upgrade the appearance of a vehicle, such as wheel trims, would fall within this exception, regardless of the purpose of the use. If the provision is interpreted as applying only for repair purposes, the scope of the repair clause would be considerably narrowed.[66] In a 2015 decision, the Danish Supreme Court, for instance, differentiated between must-match parts (such as body parts whose shape depends on the appearance of the car) and parts, such as wheel trims, whose shape is independent of the appearance of the car, and which could therefore serve to upgrade the vehicle.[67] The Court effectively reduced the scope of the exemption, by holding the repair clause not applicable to parts such as wheel trims, which fall under protection of the Design Directive.[68]

I.031 The CJEU's *Acacia*[69] decision made it clear, that the issue of dual use parts presents an evidentiary dilemma: in order to decide whether a dual use part falls under the repair exception, the court must receive credible evidence of how the part is used. In other words, the parts provider must show that the part in question is in fact used to 'restore the original appearance of the product'. The CJEU resolved this issue' by imposing extensive due diligence obligations of

---

62 DDir, Art. 14; Schovsbo (et al.), (n. 2), Chapter 8, Section A (1) (c); *Kur*, Annette, GRUR 2002, 661, 669.
63 *See e.g.* CD Reg Art 110.
64 Schovsbo (et al.), (n. 2), Chapter 8, Section A (4).
65 See n 60.
66 Schovsbo (et al.), (n. 2), Chapter 8, Section A (4).
67 Ibid.
68 Ibid.
69 CJEU Cases C-397/16 and C-435/16 *Acacia*, an infringement case between BMW and Acacia, an Italian supplier of, inter alia, wheel rims.

the beneficiaries of the provision'.[70] Thus, a diligent manufacturer or supplier is obliged to refrain from selling component parts if it possesses knowledge or is on notice of the fact, that parts will be used by downstream users disregarding the conditions of the repair clause. The intended effect would be to exclude from the right to repair, parts such as wheel trims, which might serve to upgrade, rather than for repair of the product. In doing so, however, the Court's solution places on spare part providers an excessively high burden of proof,[71] which cannot necessarily be met. In addition, the decision has drawn criticism for limiting the scope of the repair clause.[72]

Finally, after 'three decades of quarrel', EU law on spare parts repair is being harmonised,[73] in the expectation that it will open up and increase competition, especially in the automotive spare parts market. In EUDR Article 20a and DDir Article 19 of the EU Design Package, member states have agreed on the introduction of a new EU repair clause.[74] Its tenor differs somewhat from the transitional provision of Article 110 CDReg. First, the exemption applies to 'a component part of a complex product, upon whose appearance the design of the component part is dependent, and which is used … for the sole purpose of the repair of that complex product so as to restore its original appearance'.[75] In other words, the form of the relevant component parts must depend on the appearance of the complex product ('form-dependent parts'). Second, to benefit from the exemption, the manufacturer or seller must duly inform the consumers about the origin of the product to be used for the purpose of the repair of the complex product.[76] **I.032**

(b) Repair clauses in other jurisdictions

Other jurisdictions, including EU member countries, enacted their own flavour of repair clauses, ranging from no clause at all, to different variations thereof. Australia has adopted an equivalent of the EU repair clause. Its law provides **I.033**

---

70 Ibid., para 88. These obligations 'cover information duties (i.e., clear and visible information on the product, on the packaging, in catalogues or commercial documents, that the product reproduces the protected design of another entity and is intended only for the purpose of repairing a complex product in order to restore its initial appearance) and contractual instruments to ensure the strict compliance of its downstream users with the conditions of the repair clause'.
71 Dana Beldiman, Constantin Blanke-Roeser and Anna Tischner, Spare Parts and Design Protection – Different Approaches to a Common Problem - Recent Developments from the EU and US Perspective, (2020) 69(7) *GRUR International*.
72 Schovsbo (et al.), (n. 2), Chapter 8, Section A (4).
73 On 25 September 2023, the Council of the EU adopted its General Approach on the revision of the Design Directive ('DD', 2022/0392 COD) and the Design Regulation ('DR', 2022/0391 COD).
74 DDir, Art. 19 DD, EUDR, Art. 20a.
75 Ibid.
76 Ibid.

that repairs relating to the design of a component part of a complex product, will not infringe a registered design, if used for the purpose of repairing a complex product so as to restore its overall appearance.[77] 'Repair of a complex product' includes restoring or replacing a decayed or damaged component of the complex product to a good or sound condition.[78] The French legislator has introduced a repair clause which entered into force on January 1st, 2023, for products intended to restore a vehicle to its initial appearance. Its applicability is however limited to parts of motor vehicles or trailers.[79] Regarding all other operations, the exception for repair purposes applies only to parts related to glazing.[80] Germany adopted a repair clause in 2020.[81] Departing from the tenor of Article 110(1) CDReg, a part falls within the purview of the clause, if it is 'form-dependent' (*formgebunden*), i.e., its appearance is dictated by the appearance of the original, as for instance hoods or fenders. In contrast, parts which are not dependent on the appearance of the vehicle (e.g., wheel rims) are not exempt.[82] This makes the scope of the German repair clause significantly narrower than Article 110(1) CDReg. Italy, enacted a repair clause as transitional rule based on the provisions of the EU Directive no. 71/1998.[83] The law distinguishes between spare parts and accessories (mainly in the automotive world). The former are aimed at restoring the original appearance of a complex products. As such, they fall under the repair clause and may freely circulate in the market. Accessories (products intended to modify or improve the original aspect of a product) may be protected as registered designs and enforced by the registrant. The UK design law features a repair defence that permits use of a design for the purpose of the repair of a complex product so as to restore its original appearance.[84] The equivalent defence for Community designs did receive detailed consideration from Arnold J in *BMW v Round & Metal*, in which he notably took the opposite approach to that later taken by the ECJ in *Acacia*.[85]

---

77 Irvine (et al.), (n. 23), Chapter 1, Section A (10) (b).
78 Ibid.
79 As defined in the French Highway Code L. 110-1; Catherine Mateu, Industrial Design Law in France, Chapter 4, Section B (3).
80 Ibid.
81 § 40a DesignG.
82 Würtenberger and Freischem (2019) GRUR 55, 58 ff.
83 Art 241 of the Italian IP Code provides that exclusive rights on a component of a complex product may not be enforced to prevent the manufacture and trade of said components, when intended to restore the original appearance of the complex product. Francetti (et al.), (n. 8), Chapter 5, Section D.
84 Cornwell (et al.), (n. 21), Chapter 10, Section B (4).
85 CJEU Cases C-397/16 and C-435/16 *Acacia*, (n. 69); *Bayerische Motoren Werke Aktiengesellschaft (BMW) v Round and Metal Ltd*, England and Wales High Court (Patents Court) 2012; Cornwell (et al.), (n. 21), Chapter 10, Section B (4).

(c) Jurisdictions without repair clauses

I.034 A number of countries outside the EU do not feature repair clauses in their design laws and, accordingly, the secondary market for spare parts remains disputed. In Canada, no specific rules for design protection of spare parts have been introduced. However, the Canadian Act 'contemplates kits consisting of a complete or substantially complete number of parts that can be assembled to construct a finished article. Carrying out any of the actions in relation to the kit that would constitute an infringement if done in relation to an article assembled from the kit is an infringement'.[86]

I.035 Chinese design patent law has similarly not adopted a repair clause in its legislation. Moreover, under the new Chinese Amended Patent Law of 2020, unlike under the prior law, eligibility of the partial designs is determined independently from that of the overall product, which makes their protection and enforcement easier. However, this facilitation of spare parts protection has raised concern about the increase of junk design patents, against the background that China's system is based on formal examination only and its history is known as a' hotbed of patent squatting'.[87]

I.036 The Design Acts of Denmark, Finland and Sweden have not adopted the 'repair clause' and consequently component parts are not excluded from design protection. According to the "freeze plus' compromise of DDir Article 14, protection for 'must match' parts (notably 'crash parts' of automobiles such as fenders) is limited to a maximum of 15 years.'[88] From the design patent law of the US a repair clause is also absent. Automotive manufacturers therefore enjoy exclusivity in the market and are free to enforce design patents for collision parts against spare parts manufacturers. Repeated proposals for adoption of a repair clause at federal level have been unsuccessful.[89] Any challenges to design patent protection of component parts, must therefore be based on the intrinsic limitations of the US design patent law, notably, the functionality doctrine.[90]

---

86 Storey, (et al.), (n. 23), Chapter 2, Section A (9) (a).
87 Paolo Beconcini, Design Law in China, Chapter 3, Section B (1) (e).
88 Schovsbo (et al.), (n. 2), Chapter 8, Section A (1) (c)_This is the maximum period under the national Designs Acts adopted in the 1970s.
89 Nonetheless, laws regulating various aspects of the right to repair have been adopted by many US states, including California, New York, Connecticut, Delaware, Massachussetts.
90 *Automotive Body Parts Association v. Ford Global Technologies, LLC*, No. 18-1613 (Fed. Cir. 2019) in which the court held Ford's design patent nonfunctional and enforceable on the basis of evidence of actual alternative designs.

I.037 To conclude, although the EU is now enacting a uniform spare parts rule, the treatment of spare parts around the world remains rather spotty.

4. Visibility

I.038 The concept of visibility plays multiple different roles in design law. Visibility derives from the fact that design law protects appearance, which is perceived by the eye. It further provides a clear and precise identification of the design to be protected and it is therefore linked to the overall impression formed by the informed user. Visibility is an express requirement for protection only as regards component parts of complex products. The following will present the treatment of visibility under EU law, followed by a review of its status in some other jurisdictions.

(a) EU present and proposed law on visibility

I.039 Prior to revision of the EU design law by way of the EU Design Package proposal 2022,[91] visibility appeared only in the context of component parts, which are denied protection if not visible during the normal use of a product. According to CDReg Recital 12, as well as CDReg Article 4(2)(a) and DDir Article 3(3)(a), a design could only have individual character if the component part remains visible during normal use, once it has been incorporated into the complex product.[92] Normal use is defined as 'use by the end user, excluding maintenance, servicing or repair work'.[93] Therefore, visibility appeared to be a condition of eligibility only in case of component parts, but not of others. Furthermore, the last sentence of Recital 12 suggests that non-visible component parts 'should not be taken into consideration for the purpose of assessing whether other features of the design fulfil the requirements for protection'.[94]

I.040 Visibility of component parts has most recently been interpreted by the CJEU's *Monz* case[95] involving visibility of the underside of a bicycle saddle during 'normal use'. The Court broadened the concept of visibility, by holding

---

[91] EU Design Package (n. 11).
[92] CDReg Art. 4(2)(a) and DDir Art. 3(3)(a).
A design applied to or incorporated in a product which constitutes a component part of a complex product shall only be considered to be new and to have individual character: (a) if the component part, once it has been incorporated into the complex product, remains visible during normal use of the latter; and (b) to the extent that those visible features of the component part fulfil in themselves the requirements as to novelty and individual character. 3. 'Normal use' within the meaning of paragraph (2)(a) shall mean use by the end user, excluding maintenance, servicing or repair work.
[93] CDReg Art. 4.3; DDir Art. 3. 4.
[94] CDReg Recital 12.
[95] Case C-472/21, *Monz Handelsgesellschaft International mbH & Co. KG v Büchel GmbH & Co. Fahrzeugtechnik KG*.

that normal use covers 'acts relating to the customary use of a product, as well as other acts which may reasonably be carried out during such use and which are customary from the perspective of the end user, including those which may be performed before or after the product has fulfilled its principal function, such as the storage and transportation of that product'.[96] The legal uncertainty following *Monz*, if left unchecked, is likely to open the door to future attempts of reinterpretation.

The revisions of the EU Design Package re-direct the focus of the analysis proposed in *Monz*, by emphasising the role of visibility as yardstick in defining the 'object of protection'. Article 18a CDReg defines visibility exclusively in terms of its appearance as 'shown visibly in an application for a registered EU design and made available to the public'.[97] Scholars have welcomed this solution as it 'prevents any additional recourse to a (preconceived, real-life) product to ascertain the protected appearance of the design. It is not possible, by way of imagination or interpretation, to complete or contradict the design with a specific product in mind'.[98] Accordingly, whether features of appearance are visible at any particular time is irrelevant to whether a part benefits from protection.[99] Therefore, 'the case law developed or approved by the CJEU in which the "actual" visibility of design elements in the respective product is decisive is no longer tenable'.[100] Furthermore, it would be reasonable to conclude that the scope of Article 18(a) CDR is not restricted only to 'parts of a product' or 'parts of a complex product' and that it would apply to any kind

I.041

---

96   Id.
97   The Recitals to this effect preceding the Regulation set forth in the EU Design Package provide as follows:
     In order to ensure legal certainty, it is appropriate to clarify that protection is conferred upon the right holder for those design features of a product, in whole or in part, which are shown visibly in an application for a registered EU design and made available to the public by way of publication. (Recital 10)
     Apart from being shown visibly in an application, design features of a given product do not need to be visible at any particular time or in any particular situation of use in order to attract design protection. An exception should apply to the design protection of component parts of a complex product that need to remain visible during normal use of that product. (Recital 11)
     Further the Object of protection has been defined as follows: 'Protection shall be conferred for those features of the appearance of a registered EU design which are shown visibly in the application for registration.' EUDR Art. 18(a); *see also* Kur et al (n. 6).
98   Annette Kur, Tobias Endrich-Laimböck, and Marc Huckschlag, Position Statement of the Max Planck Institute for Innovation and Competition of 23 January 2023 on the 'Design Package' (Amendment of the Design Regulation and Recast of the Design Directive) (January 23, 2023). Max Planck Institute for Innovation & Competition Research Paper No. 23-05, https://ssrn.com/abstract=4344539 or http://dx.doi.org/10.2139/ssrn.4344539.
99   Ibid.
100 Kur et al., (n. 6).

of design.[101] In making the changes referred to, EU design is at the forefront of modernising design law in terms of visibility.

(b) Attenuated visibility requirement in some jurisdictions

I.042 Nonetheless, other jurisdictions have also made some progress in this regard. For instance, the Australian Designs Act does also not explicitly define whether a 'visual feature' of a product must be visible or not. According to case law however, 'if a feature (e.g., an internal feature of a product) is not apparent during "normal" use of a product, the prevailing view is that such a feature cannot contribute to the overall impression'.[102] Conversely, if a feature is visible during normal use then it can contribute to the overall impression.[103]

I.043 In China, visibility of design features is not an eligibility requirement, but a corollary of the distinctiveness requirement, and will come up during the identity/similarity comparison of the design patent with comparative prior art, in invalidation or infringement proceedings. Here, visibility is relevant in determining the cognitive level of the 'ordinary person'.[104]

> For instance, in cases of special designs such as spare parts, the knowledge should be that of both the buyer and user of the product. This could be the case of a car tire rim. Here, cognitive level of the normal consumer should be determined with reference to both those who assemble or repair vehicles (qualified user) and the users of the vehicles on the road. However, if the spare part is not visible to the end user when the product is in use, but it is visible to the mechanic when he buys it and installs it in the vehicle, in this case the ordinary person is only the qualified user.[105]

I.044 The UKUDR presents an even stronger approach to reducing the role of visibility. As pointed out in section 2 above, the law was introduced to primarily provide protection for functional three-dimensional designs. As a corollary to this, a 'UKUDR can subsist in elements of shape or configuration which are wholly internal to the relevant article, unlike UK registered designs which cannot protect features of component parts of complex products not visible in normal use.'[106]

---

101 Lavinia Brancusi, Prior Art in EU design law and its worldwide implications – Taking advantage of flexibilities or being obstructed by ambiguities, Chapter 16, Section C (1) (a).
102 Irvine (et al.), (n. 23), Chapter 1, Section A (4) (b), See, e.g., *Gramophone Company Limited v Magazine Holder Company* (1910) 27 RPC 152 and Ferrero's Design [1978] RPC 473.
103 Irvine (et al.), (n. 23), Chapter 1, Section A (4) (b).
104 This should be determined with reference to both those who assemble or repair vehicles (qualified user) and the users of the vehicles on the road. 'However, if the spare part is not visible to the end user when the product is in use, but it is visible to the mechanic when he buys it and installs it in the vehicle, in this case the ordinary person is only the qualified user.' Beconcini, (n. 87), Chapter 3, Section A 3 (b).
105 Beconcini (et al.), (n. 87), Chapter 3, Section A (3) (b).
106 Cornwell (et al.), (n. 21), Chapter 10, Section C (1) (c) (see Section B.2.(b)).

(c) Jurisdictions maintaining visibility as a requirement

I.045 UK registered design law, on the other hand, maintains the rule that component parts of complex products, once incorporated, must remain visible during normal use of the complex product and the visible features of the component must be new and have individual character.[107] Visibility is furthermore relevant in assessing infringement, which depends on how the design is used: the informed user is taken as likely to pay more attention to parts of the design that are visible when using the product.[108]

5. Emerging Technologies

(a) The challenge of new technologies

I.046 Traditionally, design law was conceived to protect physical objects, i.e., design products which belong to the world of atoms. As we are rapidly moving into a virtual world, much of the economic value is created virtually, in the world of bits. Potential virtual design objects range from such as GUIs, computer-generated icons, to holographic projections and games, to various metaverse applications, such as NFTs, and to designs authored by AI. Pressure is increasing to protect these virtual designs.

I.047 A few jurisdictions have already taken steps towards adapting to these new realities, by expanding the definition of the object of protection to non-physical products or virtual products. Singapore was one of the first countries to change its design law. The Singapore Registered Designs Act has included non-physical products (virtual) products in the scope of products protectable by a design patent since 2017.[109] In April 2020, Japan's 'Craftsmanship Law' expanded its design protection to include projected graphic images and other designs used by virtual reality technology.[110] Similarly, Korea added graphic images to the definition of design under their Design Patent Act in October, providing that these images can be protected without including a display screen in the drawings.[111]

I.048 In rare instances, the existing design law allows protection of virtual designs which may be computer-generated. In the UK, the Registered Designs

---

107 Cornwell (et al.), ibid., Section B (2) (b); RDA 1949, s1B(8).
108 Ibid.
109 Singapore Registered Designs (Amendment) Act (no 29 of 2017) 2017, Art 2(c). (https://sso.agc.gov.sg/Acts-Supp/29-2017/Published/20170615170000?DocDate=20170615170000), introducing the category of 'non-physical product' in Section 2 to provide protection for certain kinds of virtual designs.
110 Japan Design Act 2020, Art 2.1, https://wipolex.wipo.int/en/text/581568.
111 Industrial Design Protection Act 2020, https://wipolex.wipo.int/en/legislation/details/20927.

Act of 1949 already contains a provision on computer-generated designs.[112] According to this law, in circumstances in which a design is generated by computer, absent a human author, 'the person by whom the arrangements necessary for the creation of the design are made, shall be taken to be the author'.[113]

(b) Workarounds

I.049 However, in many countries, virtual designs are still not protectable. In that case, workarounds are used to provide owners with some protection. For instance, in Australia, a virtual 'design' such as a graphical user interface (GUI), is not validly registrable, because the Australian design office considers the elements of a GUI not to be visual 'features'. Therefore, it requires another device, such as a display screen, to actively generate the visual features of the design. In the US, virtual designs are not protectable because they fail to meet the 'article of manufacture' requirement.[114] Nonetheless, they may receive protection by claiming a computer-generated design shown on a computer screen, monitor, other display panel. This includes moving computer-generated icons, specifically 'images that change in appearance during viewing', whereby only the beginning and end images, but not the intermediary images, qualify for protection.[115] In China the debate about expanding design protection to non-physical products is ongoing, but to date no specific regulation has been implemented, since virtual products may not be considered 'industrial products', as required by the China Patent Law. At this stage, GUIs for instance, are only eligible for protection if they are attached to 'a physical product' as a carrier of the design which is for instance a display panel terminal such as computer screens.[116] Nonetheless, applications have been filed and even successfully registered in China for 'metaverse' focused designs. For example, an application for a virtual (metaverse) streetlamp was filed referring to 'Smart Street Lamp (Metaverse)', out of concern that using the words 'metaverse' or 'virtual' would likely have led to a rejection. As filed, the application passed the formal test for registration. Of course, whether enforcement of this registration in a game or Metaverse context will be successful, remains to be seen.[117]

---

112 Cornwell (et al.), (n. 21), Chapter 10, Section B (3).
113 Ibid.; RDA 1949, s2(4).
114 Ferrill (et al.), (n. 27), Chapter 9, Section C (3) (c).
115 Ibid.
116 Beconcini (et al.), (n. 87), Chapter 3, Section E (2) (b).
117 Ibid.

(c) Legal reform

Reform of design laws to include virtual designs in the object of protection is currently ongoing in several countries. The EU Design Package proposes to define a protectable product as any product that 'is embodied in a physical object or materialises in a digital form'.[118] Furthermore, 'graphic works or symbols, logos, surface patterns, typographic typefaces, and graphical user interfaces' are specifically added to the list of protected products.[119] Somewhat surprising in this definition is the explicit exclusion of 'computer programs'. Scholars have described this provision, absent further clarification, as vague, as well as ineffective and possibly even confusing.[120]   **I.050**

The Australian government is also in the process of reviewing the issue of virtual designs, as discussed in further detail in Chapter 1.[121] Finally, public consultations have started at the US Patent and Trademark Office (USPTO)[122] on whether its interpretation of the 'article of manufacture' requirement in the United States Patent Code should be revised to protect digital designs that encompass new and emerging technologies. Under consideration are 'projections, holographic imagery, or virtual/augmented reality [that] do not require a physical display screen or other tangible article to be viewable'.[123] It has been suggested that the term 'article of manufacture' should be construed broadly to encompass this new technology and make it eligible for design patent protection.   **I.051**

(d) Artificial intelligence and design

Finally, artificial intelligence (AI) is possibly the largest looming issue in IP protection, including design law. Chapter 19 'Artificial Intelligence and EU Design Law' is dedicated to whether AI-driven design can be protectable under existing design laws, notably the EU law. A more detailed description can be found below, in Section D of this Introduction.   **I.052**

---

118 PDEUDReg Art. 3(2) and PDDir Art. 2(4).
119 Ibid.; see also Mikko Antikainen and Heidi Härkönen, Artificial Intelligence and EU Design Law, Chapter 19, Section B (2).
120 Kur (et al.), Position Statement of the Max Planck Institute for Innovation and Competition of 23 January 2023, (n. 98).
121 Irvine (et al.), (n. 23), Chapter 1, Section F 1(a).
122 Ferrill (et al.), (n. 27), Chapter 9, Section C (3) (c). USPTO, 'Summary of public views on the article of manufacture requirement of 35 U.S.C. § 171' (2022) United States Patent and Trademark Office Working Paper, online: https://www.uspto.gov/sites/default/files/documents/USPTO-Articles-of-Manufacture-April2022.pd.
123 Ferrill (et al.), (n. 27), Chapter 9, Section C (3) (c).

C. PRESENT-DAY TRENDS AND CHALLENGES IN DESIGN LAW

I.053 The following remarks will provide a short overview of the chapters in Parts II and III, which are meant to offer in-depth critical examination of various substantive and procedural issues topical in present-day design law. Part II is dedicated to procedural matters relating to international treaties and jurisdiction.

I.054 The African Regional Intellectual Property Organisation (ARIPO) covers all intellectual property rights, for the 20 Contracting States who are parties to the Harare Protocol.[124] In Chapter 12, Chijokie Okorie explains how the industrial design system currently functions under ARIPO and explores its possibilities of future development under this treaty.

I.055 Margo Bagley delves into the puzzling situation of the 'forbidden words' of the WIPO Design Law Treaty (DLT) in Chapter 13. This treaty is mainly directed toward increasing the efficiency and effectiveness of the cross-border acquisition and protection of industrial design rights. However, a mere 'eight words': 'traditional knowledge, traditional cultural expressions, and biological/genetic resources', proposed by the African Group, have held back negotiations of this treaty draft for eight years. The author explains why. She remains nonetheless optimistic as to the ultimate outcome.

I.056 In Chapter 14, Alexander von Mühlendahl tackles the thorny procedural aspects of jurisdiction, applicable law, and choice of forum in design right litigation. These jurisdictional disputes arise when a design right is valid in more than one country, such as the EU unitary design rights, as well as in instances in which more than one court is competent to decide design infringement cases. Choices in this regard may have significant legal and strategic ramifications.

I.057 Next, Henning Hartwig signals the far-reaching implications of a new procedural rule relating to the prosecution of Community designs in Chapter 11. Starting with May 1, 2019, an appeal brought against a decision of the General Court concerning an EUIPO decision shall not proceed unless allowed by the CJEU. Under the CJEU's new practice, future cases will hardly be reviewed, as it is extremely difficult to meet the CJEU's strict standards. Consequently, the importance and impact of the case law of the General Court and the EUIPO with respect to Community design matters is expected to increase.

---

124 The 20 Contracting States are Botswana, Cape Verde, Kingdom of Eswatini, The Gambia, Ghana, Kenya, Kingdom of Lesotho, Liberia, Malawi, Mozambique, Namibia, Rwanda, Sao Tome and Principe, Seychelles, Sierra Leone, Sudan, Tanzania, Uganda, Zambia and Zimbabwe.

This unique, highly topical chapter offers a fascinating window into the world of design prosecution in the EU, including thought-provoking positions taken from both a conceptual and practical perspective.

Part III features chapters on substantive design law issues. It starts with Chapter 15 by Shubha Ghosh, which considers the problem of cumulative protection through multiple IP regimes from a doubly comparative perspective. The first perspective compares different areas of intellectual property (design patent and sui generis design law) as to their respective policies, subject matter, and doctrinal boundaries. The second perspective, by exploring how different states, Japan, and the US, legislate to protect design within a set of intellectual property laws. **I.058**

In Chapter 16, Lavinia Brancusi contributes a thorough examination of prior art in design law, viewed from an international perspective. The author delves deeply into the concepts of relevant disclosure, normative exceptions to disclosure and disclosure of unregistered designs, under the EU model of relative novelty. Thereafter, the interaction between EU and non-EU design systems is examined, emphasising distinctive features of non-EU design laws. **I.059**

In Chapter 17, Henning Hartwig points to the well-established adage in European design, copyright, and trademark law that the scope of protection of the design, work, or trademark correlates with the degree of departure from the existing design corpus or variety of forms, or as put by the CJEU the 'degree of creative freedom exercised'. This chapter, which, to some extent, provides an overarching concept for the evergreen issue of cumulation of different IP laws (see above B 1 and below Part I), delves into the question of whether there are limits to aesthetic creative freedom and, if so, what they are. It discusses the most recent case law and the referral to the CJEU (C-580/23),[125] which has the potential to re-shape EU copyright law. In light of these recent developments, the author poses intriguing questions: Do boundaries differ depending on the underlying IP right? Might there be even more similarities than differences? In short: Where do design, copyright, and trademark law eventually meet? **I.060**

Chapter 18 which deals with Fashion in Design Law, the final chapter of Part III, is authored by Ulrika Wennersten, Laurent Manderieux and Patricia Covarrubia. It features an in-depth examination of the treatment of fashion in design law, with a focus on EU Law. At the outset, the relationship between fashion and the concept of design and the requirements for protection and **I.061**

---

125 Referral by the Swedish court Case C-580/23 (Mio and Others, 21 Sep 2023).

registration, as well as the concept of Unregistered Community Design, are presented. The authors then address the issue of design ownership within the fashion industry and infringement, a significant concern in the fashion industry. The chapter next explores contemporary issues in the fashion industry, such as the intersection of artificial intelligence and design law in fashion, the implications of 3D printing technology in fashion and design law, as well as the relationship between fashion law and the circular economy, with a focus on sustainability in fashion. A discussion of the relationship between fashion and traditional knowledge, sheds light on the conflict between modern fashion trends and age-old traditional designs. The chapter concludes with a look at overlapping intellectual property protections for fashion under EU law.

D. THE WAY FORWARD – A LOOK AT THE FUTURE OF DESIGN LAW

I.062 Part IV concludes the book with two forward-looking chapters. The first chapter considers the possibility of protecting designs generated (in part) by AI, the second explores the role design law may play in the circular economy, a new economic paradigm responsive to environmental challenges.

I.063 In Chapter 19, Mikko Antikainen and Heidi Härkönen shed light on the scarcely researched topic of the treatment by design law of AI-driven designs. The stumbling block in terms of protection of AI generated designs is the act of 'design development'. While the act of 'design development' necessitates human contribution, the required level of human intervention is not very high. Consequently, the authors conclude that a large number of AI-assisted designs are potentially protectable, assuming they meet the requirements for protection.

I.064 In Chapter 20, Dana Beldiman, Stina Teilman-Lock, and Anna Tischner ask whether design law can be better aligned with the goals of the circular economy. The incentive structure of design law, arguable more than that of other IP laws, tends to encourage overconsumption, resource depletion and waste. It materialises in shorter product lifespans and rapid, possibly even planned, product obsolescence, characteristic of the 'take, make, dispose' economic model, which contributes to environmental degradation. In sharp contrast thereto, the values of the circular economy aim to maintain product components and materials at their highest utility for the maximum period of time and at terminating in end-of-life reutilisation.[126] Whether products follow a linear or circular path is a choice made during the design phase of product. Statistics show that 80 per cent of the environmental impact of a product is determined at the design stage.[127]

This prompts the question whether design law can be reframed to better align with the values of the circular economy. If so, design law could serve designers' interests while avoiding a negative environmental externality, and at the same time heighten its relevance as a legal instrument. In Chapter 20, the authors consider how current design law might be modified in the direction of sustainability and circularity. Specifically, two key elements of design law are investigated. The first asks whether the definition of the 'object and protection' is sufficiently capacious to include circular features. The second element considers the incentive-access balance of a reframed law and examines if a purely economic-driven law can make concessions to social/environmental interests, without sacrificing its ability to act as an incentive to create. The authors outline a possible structure, doctrinally based both on the principle of liability rules and the provisions of the European and UK unregistered design system. **I.065**

E. EU DESIGN LAW REFORM

At the time this book is being published, reform of EU design law is ongoing. Both the Design Regulation and the Design Directive will be modernized and adapted to the needs of the digital age and of environmental considerations. **I.066**

Procedurally, the main points have been agreed upon among the co-legislators, however, the final version of the reform package is still outstanding. Therefore, the following will provide a brief overview of a few of the most significant proposed changes to be expected in the revised design law.[128] **I.067**

---

126 Beldiman, Teilman-Lock, Tischner, Chapter 20; E. Macarthur, Towards the Circular Economy, Journal of Industrial Ecology, 10, pp. 4–8. (2012).
127 Malahat Ghoreishi and Ari Happonen, New promises AI brings into circular economy accelerated product design: a review on supporting literature, E3S Web of Conferences 158, 06002 (2020) https://doi.org/10.1051/e3sconf/202015806002 ICEPP 2019.
128 Article numbers are based on a draft version.

1. Design Regulation

(a) Definitions

I.068 Some of the key changes of the reform package involve the definition of "design" and "product". "Design" is defined, as previously, as the appearance of a product resulting from certain features, which are listed with particularity.[129] Significantly, however, the following phrase is added to the existing definition: "*including the movement, transition or any other sort of animation of those features.*"[130] This change enables design protection to function in a virtual world, covering animation and digital designs.

I.069 The definition of "product", previously limited to industrial or handicraft items other than computer programs, is expanded to include any product: "*regardless of whether it is embodied in a physical object or materialises in a digital form*".[131] The definition further lists new forms of covered products, including "*graphic works or symbols, logos, surface patterns, typographic typefaces, and graphical user interfaces*"[132], thus aligning design law with current technological advances by extending protection to digital-only products of the virtual world, such as NFTs or the metaverse.

(b) Visibility

I.070 The visibility requirement has acquired new emphasis by becoming a requirement of protectability. The new law provides that "*Protection shall be conferred for those features of the appearance of a registered EU design which are shown visibly in the application for registration.*"[133] Whether design features are visible at any particular time or situation is irrelevant to their protectability.[134]

(c) Repair clause

I.071 The scope of the clause has been narrowed, compared to its prior instantiation. In essence, it now provides in essence, the following:

- first, the clause narrowly applies to "form-dependent" parts. In other words, protection is granted only to parts whose appearance depends on the design

---

129 EUDR Article 3 (1) and (2).
130 Ibid.
131 Ibid.
132 EUDR Article 3 (2) b
133 EUDR Article 18 a.
134 EUDR Recital 18; Dana Beldiman, Introduction to Design Law, Section A 4.

of the complex product ("*a component part of a complex product, upon whose appearance the design of the component part is dependent*");[135]
- second, to be protectable, a part must be used for purposes of repair only ("*for the sole purpose of the repair of that complex product so as to restore its original appearance*");[136]
- third, in order to benefit from the exemption, the manufacturer or seller of the part must inform consumers about the part's origin, so as to allow an informed choice between competing parts to be used for repair.[137]

(d) Expanded digital infringement

In order to effectively prevent illegitimate copying of protected designs, the scope of design protection was expanded to include products created by digital and 3D printing technologies. Thus, "*creating, downloading, copying and sharing or distributing to others any medium or software recording the design*" will be subject to the rightholder's consent.[138] **I.072**

(e) Additional defences

The list of defenses to design rights has been expanded to include "comment, critique or parody."[139] **I.073**

2. Design Directive

The recast Directive mirrors the changes to the Regulation, and in addition, features further proposals which apply to the national design laws of member states. **I.074**

(a) Elimination of unregistered designs at national level

National unregistered design protection will be eliminated, with the result that design protection under the national laws of member states can be obtained only by way of registration. Unregistered design protection will continue to exist only at pan-EU level, in the form of the EU Unregistered Design protection.[140] **I.075**

---

135 EUDR Article 20 a (1).
136 Ibid.
137 EUDR Article 20a (2); Dana Beldiman, Introduction to Design Law, Section A 3.
138 EUDR Article 9(2) (d).
139 EUDR Article 20 (1) (e)
140 DDir Article 3.1.

(b) Repair clause transition period

I.076 The Directive's repair clause contains the same wording as the Regulation. However, to safeguard the interests of existing right holders, it proposes a transition period of 8 years, from the effective date the Directive.[141]

(c) Cultural heritage

I.077 Member States will be entitled to prevent misappropriation of cultural heritage elements of national interest, by provisions basing denial on improper registration and by way of invalidation. "Cultural Heritage" will be defined in line with UNESCO'S definition and includes monuments, buildings, artefacts, handicrafts, and costumes.[142]

3. Timeline for Adoption and Implementation

I.078 Both the Design Regulation and the Directive have been agreed upon in principle by the Council in December 2023 and approved by the European Parliament in March 2024. The instruments will enter into force on the twentieth day following publication in the Official Journal. The regulation will become effective 4 months thereafter, and the EU Member States will have 36 months to transpose the directive into their national systems.

---

141 DDir Article 19.3.
142 DDir Article 14 1 a.

PART I

DESIGN LAWS AROUND THE WORLD COUNTRY-BY-COUNTRY

1

OVERVIEW OF INDUSTRIAL DESIGN PROTECTION IN AUSTRALIA

Stuart Irvine and Carl Harrap

A. OVERVIEW OF INDUSTRIAL DESIGN PROTECTION IN AUSTRALIA	1.001
1. Registered Designs in Australia	1.001
2. Other Mechanisms for Protecting Industrial Designs in Australia	1.004
(a) Protection of industrial designs via copyright	1.005
(b) Protection of industrial designs via trade mark	1.011
(c) Protection of industrial designs via consumer protection laws	1.014
3. Sources of Law	1.016
4. What is a Design	1.021
(a) A 'product'	1.023
(b) 'Visual features'	1.030
(i) 'Visual features' vis-à-vis virtual designs	1.034
5. Prior Art	1.041
6. Grace Period and Prior Disclosure	1.046
(a) Prior disclosure of a design on/after 10 March 2022	1.047
(b) Prior disclosure of a design before 10 March 2022	1.052
(c) Prior use of a 'corresponding design' that has not been applied industrially	1.054
7. Exclusions from Protection	1.059
8. Rights Granted	1.060
9. Infringement	1.063
(a) Infringing conduct	1.063
10. Infringement Exemptions	1.067
(a) Prior use	1.067
(b) Spare parts exemption to infringement	1.072
11. Substantial Similarity in Overall Impression	1.079
12. The 'Familiar Person'	1.086
13. Ownership and Entitlement	1.090
(a) Rights of co-owners	1.096
14. Term	1.099
B. PROCEDURE	1.101
1. Applications and Priority Date	1.101
(a) Filing date and the minimum filing requirements	1.103
(b) Multi-design applications	1.105
(c) Further (or 'divisional') design applications	1.108
(d) Priority date	1.113
(e) Statements of Newness and Distinctiveness	1.119
(f) Request for registration	1.123
(g) Publication of design applications	1.126
2. Registration Procedure	1.129
(a) Notifications under section 41 and amendment	1.132
(b) Formalities check	1.134
(c) Designs that must be refused	1.138
(d) A common design in relation to more than one product	1.139
3. Post-registration Rights and Renewal	1.142
4. Examination and Certification Procedure	1.146
(a) Responses to notifications and amendment	1.149
(b) Certificate of examination	1.153
5. Amendments	1.155
(a) Applications	1.155
(b) Registered designs	1.160
(c) Correction of the Register	1.166
6. Challenges to Validity	1.168
(a) Requesting examination	1.168
(b) Providing information	1.170

	(c) Revocation proceedings before the Commissioner	1.173		(a) *Keller v LED Technologies Pty Ltd* [2010] FCAFC 55	1.219
	(d) Revocation and rectification proceedings before the Court	1.175	4.	Evaluating the Validity of a Design over the Prior Art Base	1.222
7.	Extensions of Time	1.179		(a) *LED Technologies Pty Ltd v Elecspess Pty Ltd* [2008] FCA 1941	
C.	DISPUTES	1.185			1.222
1.	Invalidity	1.185		(b) *Keller v LED Technologies Pty Ltd*	
2.	Infringement	1.186		[2010] FCAFC 55	1.224
	(a) Infringement proceedings	1.186	5.	Fonts and Graphical User Interfaces	1.225
	(b) Remedies for infringement	1.191		(a) *Microsoft Corporation* [2008] ADO 2	1.225
	(c) 'Innocent' infringement	1.193			
	(d) Unjustified threats of infringement	1.196		(b) *Apple Inc* [2017] ADO 6	1.227
D.	SIGNIFICANT JUDICIAL DECISIONS IN THE JURISDICTION	1.201	6.	Repair Defence	1.229
				(a) *GM Global Technology Operations LLC v S.S.S. Auto Parts Pty Ltd* [2019] FCA 97	1.229
1.	Substantial Similarity in Overall Impression	1.201			
	(a) *Review 2 Pty Ltd v Redberry Enterprise Pty Ltd* [2008] FCA 1588		E.	PRACTICAL ASPECTS OF DESIGN LAW	1.238
		1.201	1.	Australian Design Filings, Registrations, and Certifications	1.238
	(b) *LED Technologies Pty Ltd v Roadvision Pty Ltd* [2012] FCAFC 3		2.	Court Cases	1.240
		1.209	3.	Assignment of Registered Designs	1.246
	(c) *World of Technologies (Aust) Pty Ltd v Tempo (Aust) Pty Ltd* [2007] FCA 114		4.	Compulsory Licences	1.249
			F.	COMMENTS, ANALYSIS, EVALUATION	1.252
		1.211	1.	Design Law Reform *de lege ferenda*	1.252
2.	The Standard of the Informed User	1.214		(a) Protecting virtual or non-physical designs	1.255
	(a) *Multisteps Pty Ltd v Source and Sell Pty Ltd* [2013] FCA 743	1.214			
				(b) Protecting partial designs	1.263
	(b) *Astrazeneca AB* [2007] ADO 4	1.216		(c) Protection for incremental improvements of designs	1.273
3.	Clarity of the Design	1.219			

A. OVERVIEW OF INDUSTRIAL DESIGN PROTECTION IN AUSTRALIA

1. Registered Designs in Australia

The primary mechanism for protecting industrial designs in Australia is via a hybrid registration/examination system. This system is governed by the Australian *Designs Act 2003* (**the Designs Act**) and the Australian *Designs Regulations 2004* (**the Designs Regulations**). **1.001**

The Designs Act requires a design to be in relation to a product[1] and defines a design as the overall appearance of the product relating from one or more visual features thereof.[2] **1.002**

---

1 Designs Act 2003; s 8.
2 Designs Act 2003; s 5.

1.003 Australian design applications are registered on the strength of a formalities check only. Substantive examination of a registered design is optional, however substantive examination must be requested and a design certified before enforcement is possible.

2. Other Mechanisms for Protecting Industrial Designs in Australia

1.004 Australian law does not provide for an unregistered designs right. In certain cases, though, it may be possible to obtain some protection for industrial designs via copyright protection, trade mark protection, and/or consumer protection law.

(a) Protection of industrial designs via copyright

1.005 The overlap of Australian registered design and copyright laws is an area of significant complexity.

1.006 The Australian *Copyright Act* 1968 defines the concept of a 'corresponding design' in relation to an artistic work:

> [A] corresponding design, in relation to an artistic work, means visual features of shape or configuration which, when embodied in a product, result in a reproduction of that work, whether or not the visual features constitute a design that is capable of being registered under the Designs Act.[3]

1.007 As a general proposition, where a 'corresponding design' in relation to an artistic work has been industrially applied, reproducing the artistic work by embodying the corresponding design in a product will not be an infringement of the copyright in that artistic work. This is regardless of whether the design in respect of the corresponding design has been registered under the Designs Act or not.[4]

1.008 A design is deemed to have been applied industrially if it is applied to more than 50 articles.[5] That said, depending on its nature a design may be found to have been applied industrially even if applied to fewer than 50 articles.[6]

---

[3] Copyright Act 1968; s 74(1).
[4] Copyright Act 1968; s 75.
[5] Copyright Regulations 1969; Reg 17.
[6] IP Australia, Designs Examiners' Manual of Practice and Procedure; s 18.5(4), citing *Safe Sport v Puma* (1985) 4 IPR 120.

1.009 An exception to this, however, is where the artistic work is a building, a model of a building, or a work of artistic craftsmanship. In this case, copyright protection in the artistic work is retained unless a corresponding design is registered under the Designs Act.[7]

1.010 In addition, the definition of 'corresponding design' (above) is defined as visual features of shape and configuration that are embodied in a product. Accordingly, where an artistic work is embodied in a product in two dimensions (e.g. by printing an image of the artistic work on a surface of the product), that embodiment will not be considered a 'corresponding design'. In this case copyright in the artistic work is retained, whether or not a design is registered under the Designs Act or not.

(b) Protection of industrial designs via trade mark

1.011 The Australian *Trade Marks Act* 1995 defines a trade mark to be 'a sign used, or intended to be used, to distinguish goods and services'.[8] A 'sign' is further defined to include (inter alia) devices and shapes.[9]

1.012 Accordingly, provided the other requirements for trade mark protection are met, two- and three-dimensional industrial designs can potentially be protected as trade marks under the Australian Trade Marks Act.

1.013 If trade mark protection can be obtained there is no preclusion to trade mark and design protection co-existing.

(c) Protection of industrial designs via consumer protection laws

1.014 Australian consumer protection laws do not provide any specific protection for industrial designs.

1.015 If use of a design amounts to misleading or deceptive conduct, however, such use may fall within the scope of the Australian Consumer Law which provides that 'a person must not, in trade or commerce, engage in conduct that is misleading or deceptive or is likely to mislead or deceive'.[10]

---

7   Copyright Act 1968; ss 75, 77.
8   Trade Marks Act 1995; s 17.
9   Trade Marks Act 1995; s 6.
10 Australia's Competition and Consumer Act 2010, Schedule 2; s 18.

3. Sources of Law

1.016 Registered design protection in Australia is governed by the Australian *Designs Act 2003* (**the Designs Act**) and the Australian *Designs Regulations 2004* (**the Designs Regulations**).

1.017 Both the Designs Act and the Designs Regulations are available online via the Australian Government Federal Register of Legislation: https://www.legislation.gov.au/.

1.018 In 2021 the Designs Act was amended by the Designs Amendment (Advisory Council on Intellectual Property Response) Act 2021. Unless otherwise stated, reference to the Designs Act in this chapter is reference to the *Designs Act 2003* as amended by the *Designs Amendment (Advisory Council on Intellectual Property Response) Act 2021*.

1.019 Australia is a party to the Paris Convention for the Protection of Industrial Property. Australia is also a member of the World Trade Organization and, accordingly, party to the Agreement of Trade-Related Aspects of Intellectual Property Rights (TRIPS).

1.020 Australia is not currently a party to the Hague Agreement Concerning the International Registration of Industrial Designs. Investigation into the implications of becoming a party to the Hague Agreement has been flagged by the relevant government agency (IP Australia) for future consideration.

4. What is a Design

1.021 In Australia, a registered design must be in relation to a product and is defined as the overall appearance of the product relating from one or more visual features thereof.[11]

1.022 As outlined at section A.7, the Designs Act prohibits registration of certain designs.

  (a) A 'product'

1.023 The Designs Act provides that anything that is manufactured or handmade is a product.[12]

---

11 Designs Act 2003; s 5.
12 Designs Act 2003; s 6(1).

1.024 A product may be a 'complex product', which is defined as a product comprising at least two replaceable component parts which permit disassembly/reassembly of the product.[13]

1.025 A product may also be a component part of complex product. This will only be the case, however, if the component part is made separately.[14]

1.026 Relevantly, a part or portion of a product which is not separately made and/or cannot be non-destructively separated from a broader product is not considered a 'product' under the Designs Act. To illustrate this, consider the common example of a cup with a handle:

- If the cup and handle are integrally formed (e.g. a ceramic cup), only the cup (complete with the handle) as a whole will be considered a product under Australian law. The handle of such a cup would not, by itself, be considered a product.
- Alternatively, if the handle was made separately to and removable from the cup, Australian law would consider: the cup part to be a product; the handle part to be a product; and the assembled cup and handle to be a product.

1.027 An object with one or more indefinite dimensions may be considered a product, but only if one or more of the following criteria apply:[15]

- a cross-section taken across any indefinite dimension is fixed or varies according to a regular pattern;
- all the dimensions remain in proportion;
- the cross-sectional shape remains the same throughout, whether or not the dimensions of that shape vary according to a ratio or series of ratios;
- it has a pattern or ornamentation that repeats itself.

1.028 Common examples of products with indefinite dimensions are extrusions that have a constant cross-section, but an indefinite length and sheet products that have a repeating pattern.

1.029 The Australian Designs Office has held that there must be a product that is separately identifiable to the design. In other words, they cannot merge into a common entity. Accordingly, a type font in and of itself is not registrable.[16]

---

13 Designs Act 2003; s 5.
14 Designs Act 2003; s 6(2).
15 Designs Act 2003; s 6(3).
16 *Microsoft Corporation* [2008] ADO 2.

(b) 'Visual features'

1.030 The visual features of a product are defined to include shape, configuration, pattern, and ornamentation.[17]

1.031 There is no prohibition against a visual feature serving a functional purpose and visual features are not excluded merely because they are dictated solely by technical function.[18] Visual features serving a functional purpose are evaluated in the same manner as all other visual features.

1.032 The feel of a product is not a visual feature, and nor are the materials used in a product.[19] While a product's materials are not themselves visual features, they may of course contribute to the product's visual features. For example, glass would not be a visual feature, however the transparent/translucent appearance provided by the use of glass may be a visual feature.

1.033 Where an internal feature of a product is or becomes visible during normal use of the product, those features are capable of contributing to overall impression of a design in relation to that product.[20] If a feature is not apparent during 'normal' use of a product, however, the prevailing view is that such a feature cannot contribute to overall impression.[21]

(i) 'Visual features' vis-à-vis virtual designs

1.034 Special mention of 'visual features' and their relevance to 'virtual designs' is warranted. An example of a virtual design is a design in respect of a graphical user interface (GUI) or the like, which requires another device, such as a display screen, to actively generate the visual features of the design.

1.035 The Australian Designs Office is of the view that virtual designs are not validly registrable.

1.036 This view is based on two alternative interpretations of 'visual features' that the Australian Designs office has adopted:

- In one interpretation, the Designs Office forms the view that a visual feature must be assessed when a product is 'at rest'.[22]

---

17 Designs Act 2003; s 7(1).
18 Designs Act 2003; s 7(2).
19 Designs Act 2003; s 7(3).
20 See e.g. *Gramophone Company Ltd v Magazine Holder Company* (1910) 27 RPC 152 and *Ferrero's Design* [1978] RPC 473.
21 IP Australia, Designs Examiners' Manual of Practice and Procedure; s 13.7.
22 IP Australia, Designs Examiners' Manual of Practice and Procedure; s 9.4.

- In another interpretation, a Hearing Officer of the Design Office formed the view that images generated on a device (e.g. a display) by software are not visual features *of* such a device.[23]

Under both of these interpretations, when an electronic device with a GUI is substantively examined, the Designs Office takes the view that any GUI elements are not visual features. These features are, therefore, ignored when considering whether the design is new and distinctive. Accordingly, unless the device (or other 'product' on which the GUI is displayed) is itself distinctive, the design is found invalid. **1.037**

It should be noted that neither of these interpretations of 'visual features' as they relate to GUIs (or other virtual designs) has been considered by the Australian courts. **1.038**

Further, the approach of the Designs Office in considering products in an 'at rest' state has been subject to criticism, including by the Australian Government's Advisory Council on Intellectual Property which, in a Review of the Australian Designs System, stated 'There is nothing in the legislation which requires that visual features be observable in the "resting" state or when unconnected to electricity.'[24] **1.039**

The issue of virtual designs is a subject of review the by the Australian Government, as discussed in section F.1. **1.040**

5. Prior Art

In order to be registrable, a design in Australia must be new and distinctive when compared to the prior art base.[25] **1.041**

A design will be considered new, unless it is identical to a prior art design.[26] **1.042**

A design will be considered distinctive unless it is substantially similar in overall impression to a prior art design.[27] Substantial similarity in overall impression is discussed further at section A.11. **1.043**

---

23 *Apple Inc* [2017] ADO 6 (14 June 2017) at [35].
24 Advisory Council on Intellectual Property, Review of the Designs System. Final Report. March 2015. Section 2.5.2.
25 Designs Act 2003; s 15.
26 Designs Act 2003; s 16(1).
27 Designs Act 2003; s 16(2).

1.044 The prior art base for a registered Australian design includes designs publicly used in Australia and designs published in a document anywhere in the world.[28]

1.045 The prior art base can also include designs that were disclosed in an Australian design application, but were not published until after the priority date of a design in question. For such designs to qualify as prior art they must:[29]

- be disclosed in an Australian design application (disclosure in a foreign application is not sufficient);
- be entitled to an earlier priority date than the design in question; and
- be published (or made available for public inspection) after the priority date of the design in question.

6. Grace Period and Prior Disclosure

1.046 Australian law with respect to prior disclosure and grace periods changed as of 10 March 2022.[30]

(a) Prior disclosure of a design on/after 10 March 2022

1.047 Where prior disclosure of a design occurred on or after 10 March 2022, Australian law provides general grace period provisions that may apply.

1.048 Generally speaking, these provisions provide that disclosure of a design in the 12 months preceding a registered design's priority date[31] is to be ignored if that disclosure was:

- on or after 10 March 2022[32]; and
- by a 'relevant entity'[33] or another party that derived or obtained the design from a 'relevant entity'[34].

1.049 A 'relevant entity' is defined as the registered owner of the design, any predecessor in title of the registered owner, or the person who created the design.[35]

---

28 Designs Act 2003; s 15(2)(a), (b).
29 Designs Act 2003; s 15(2)(c).
30 This is due to amendments made to the Designs Act by Schedule 1 of the Designs Amendment (Advisory Council on Intellectual Property Response) Act 2021.
31 Designs Act 2003; s 17(1).
32 Designs Act 2003; s 17(1A).
33 Designs Act 2003; s 17(1)(a).
34 Designs Act 2003; s 17(1)(b).
35 Designs Act 2003; s 17(1D).

When a relevant entity publishes a design, or authorises the publication of a design, then disclosure by another party after the date of publication of the same design, or a design substantially similar in overall impression to the design, is presumed to be derived or obtained from the relevant entity for the purposes of the grace period provisions. This presumption can be rebutted by establishing that the other party independently created the design.[36] **1.050**

The grace period does not apply to publication by the Australian Designs Office or a Designs Office (or similar body) of another country, if that publication is under the relevant law or international agreement relating to designs.[37] For example and in particular, publication before the priority date of a design application or registered design by a Designs Office or equivalent in accordance with their authorised functions will be prior art not covered by the grace period. **1.051**

(b) Prior disclosure of a design before 10 March 2022

Where prior publication of a design occurred before 10 March 2022, the general grace period provisions described above (section A.6(a)) do not apply. **1.052**

In this case, the prior disclosure can be disregarded if an Australian design application (note, not the priority application) is filed within six months of the prior disclosure and: **1.053**

- the prior disclosure was by a person who derived the design from the owner (or the owner's predecessor in title) and who disclosed the design without the consent of the owner (or the owner's predecessor in title);[38] or
- the prior disclosure was at an official or officially recognised exhibition.[39]

(c) Prior use of a 'corresponding design' that has not been applied industrially

In addition to the provisions discussed above, Section 18 of the Designs Act provides one further mechanism by which a prior disclosure can be disregarded. **1.054**

---

36   Designs Act 2003, s 17(1C).
37   Designs Act 2003; s 17(1B).
38   Designs Act 2003; s 17(1)(b), prior to amendment by the Designs Amendment (Advisory Council on Intellectual Property Response) Act 2021 (which includes in s 3 a saving provision for ss 17(1)).
39   Designs Regulations 2004; Reg 2.01, prior to amendment by the Designs Amendment (Advisory Council on Intellectual Property Response) Regulations 2021. An official or officially recognised exhibition includes exhibitions: within the meaning of Art 11 of the Paris Convention for the Protection of Industrial Property done at Paris on 20 March 1883; within the meaning of Article 1 of the Convention relating to International Exhibitions done at Paris on 22 November 1928; and/or international exhibitions recognised by the Australian Registrar of Designs.

1.055 Section 18 of the Designs Act is concerned with 'corresponding designs'. As discussed at section A.2(a) (in relation to design/copyright overlap), a corresponding design, in relation to an artistic work, is defined as visual features of shape or configuration which, when embodied in a product, result in a reproduction of that work.[40]

1.056 Section 18 provides that a corresponding design (in relation to an artistic work) is not to be treated as other than new and distinctive by any use previously made of the artistic work unless:[41]

- the previous use involved selling (or other similar commercial activities) products to which the design has been industrially applied; and
- the previous use was by, or with consent of, the owner of the copyright in the artistic work.

1.057 A design is deemed to have been applied industrially, if it is applied to more than 50 articles.[42] That said, depending on its nature a design may be found to have been applied industrially even if applied to fewer than 50 articles.[43]

1.058 If Section 18 of the Designs Act applies, no time limit imposed for filing a design application.

7. Exclusions from Protection

1.059 The Designs Act requires the Registrar to refuse to register certain designs.[44] These include:

- Designs for medals, designs including the word 'ANZAC', designs resembling paper money or a prescribed security, scandalous designs, and the Arms, flags, emblems and other signs of Australia or another country.
- Any design that is or incorporates a protected design under the Olympic Insignia Protection act 1987 (Cth), including refusing designs that differ from a protected design only in immaterial details, in features commonly used in a relevant trade or which is an obvious adaptation of a protected design.

---

40 Designs Act 2003; s 5. Copyright Act 1968; s 74(1).
41 Designs Act 2003; s 18(2).
42 Copyright Regulations 1969; Reg 17.
43 IP Australia, Designs Examiners' Manual of Practice and Procedure; s 18.5(4), citing *Safe Sport v Puma* (1985) 4 IPR 120.
44 Designs Act 2003; s 43(1). Designs Regulations 2004; Reg. 4.06.

- Any design for a product that is an integrated circuit, part of an integrated circuit or a mask used to make an integrated circuit.

8. Rights Granted

During the term of registration of a design, the exclusive rights provided to the registered owner of the registered design are to:[45] **1.060**

- make or offer to make a product, in relation to which the design is registered, which embodies the design;
- to import such a product into Australia for sale, or for use for the purposes of any trade or business;
- to sell, hire or otherwise dispose of, or offer to sell, hire or otherwise dispose of, such a product (or to keep such a product for the purpose of doing so); and
- to use such a product in any way for the purposes of any trade or business (or to keep such a product for the purpose of doing so).

In addition, the registered owner also has the exclusive right to authorise another person to do any of these things.[46] **1.061**

The exclusive rights of a registered design owner are personal property and capable of assignment and devolution by will or operation of law.[47] **1.062**

9. Infringement

(a) Infringing conduct

A person infringes a registered Australian design if, during the term of registration and without the license or authority of the owner of the registered design[48] or the exclusive licensee,[49] the person performs certain actions with respect to a product that:[50] **1.063**

- is a product in relation to which the design is registered; and
- embodies a design that is identical to, or substantially similar in overall impression to, the registered design. Substantial similarity in overall impression is discussed at section A.11.

---

45 Designs Act 2003; s 10(1)(a)-(e).
46 Designs Act 2003; s 10(1)(f).
47 Designs Act 2003; s 10(2).
48 Designs Act 2003; s 71(1).
49 Designs Act 2003; s 71(1).
50 Designs Act 2003; s 71(1).

1.064 Infringing conduct is:

- making or offering to make such a product;
- importing such a product into Australia for sale, or for use for the purposes of any trade or business;
- selling, hiring or otherwise disposing of such a product (or offering to do);
- using such a product in any way for the purposes of any trade or business (or keeping such a product for this purpose); or
- keeping a product for the purpose of the immediately preceding two points.

1.065 It is not an infringement of a registered Australian design to import products that were authorised by the registered owner in another country.[51] In other words, parallel importation of a product is not an infringement of a registered design covering the design of the product.

1.066 Infringement proceedings are discussed further at section C.2.

10. Infringement Exemptions

(a) Prior use

1.067 On 10 March 2022, amendments to the Designs Act that introduced an infringement exemption for prior use came into force.[52] This exemption was introduced to balance the additional rights given to design owners by the introduction of the 12-month grace period (discussed at section A.6(a)).

1.068 The prior use infringement exemption is available in relation to any registered design with a priority date on or after 10 March 2022.[53]

1.069 The prior use exemption is available to a person:

- Who performed conduct before the priority date of the registered design that would infringe the registered design if performed during the term of registration, or taken definite steps (contractually or otherwise and whether or not in Australia) towards such conduct;[54] and
- The conduct or definite steps was/were immediately before the priority date or only temporarily stopped at the priority date.

---

51 Designs Act 2003; s 71(2).
52 Designs Amendment (Advisory Council on Intellectual Property Response) Act 2021; Schedule 2.
53 Designs Act 2003; s 71A(1).
54 Designs Act 2003; s 71A(1).

The person may have independently created the design or obtained the design 1.070
from publicly available material, including from a publication by the design
owner or a publication authorised by the design owner. However, the infringement exemption will not apply if the person derived the design from the design
owner (or predecessor in title or design creator) from information that was not
publicly available.[55]

When the prior use exemption applies, the exemption can continue to apply 1.071
for the life of the registered design. Further, if a person is entitled to the
infringement exemption they may dispose of this exemption to another person,
who receives the benefit of the exemption.[56]

(b) Spare parts exemption to infringement

The Designs Act provides that certain repairs will not infringe a registered 1.072
design.[57]

In particular, where a design is in respect of a component part of a complex 1.073
product, a person will not infringe that design if they use (or authorise use of)
a product for the purpose of the repair of a complex product so as to restore
its overall appearance.[58] The use referred to for the purposes of the spare parts
exemption covers all five limbs of infringing conduct discussed in section
A.9(a).[59]

Repair of a complex product is defined to include restoring or replacing 1.074
a decayed or damaged component of the complex product to a good or sound
condition.[60]

To illustrate, consider a registered design in respect of a spoiler for a car. In this 1.075
case the product (the spoiler) is a component part of a complex product (the
car). A party providing a new spoiler embodying the registered design:

- Would not infringe the registered design if the spoiler was provided for
  repair purposes – i.e. to restore the car to its original appearance. This may
  occur, for example, as part of a standard crash repair.
- Would infringe the registered design if the spoiler was provided for the
  purpose of changing a car from its original appearance to a different

---

55   Designs Act 2003; s 71A(3).
56   Designs Act 2003; s 71A(4).
57   Designs Act 2003; s 72.
58   Designs Act 2003; s 72(1).
59   Designs Act 2003; s 72(5).
60   Designs Act 2003; s 72(5).

appearance. This may occur, for example, if a person was trying to modify an original car to look like a higher end variant thereof (by adding a spoiler that was not part of the original car).
- Would infringe the registered design if the spoiler was fitted to a brand-new car.

1.076 While most examples of the spare parts exemption to infringement are automotive based, it is important to note that the exemption is not limited to automotive spare parts. The language of the statute requires only that the product be a component part of a complex product and the use is to repair the complex product to restore its overall appearance.

1.077 The registered owner bears the burden of proving that the use or authorisation by the person alleged to infringe was not for a repair purpose or that the person out reasonable to have known that the use or authorisation was not for a repair purpose.[61]

1.078 A case discussing the requirements of the repair defence and the requirements of an owner of a registered design to establish the repair defence does not apply is discussed at section D.6.

11. Substantial Similarity in Overall Impression

1.079 In Australia, determining whether one design is substantially similar in overall impression to another design can arise in the contexts of both validity and infringement.

1.080 In the context of validity, a design will not be a registrable design if it is substantially similar in overall impression to a prior art design.[62]

1.081 In the context of infringement, a product that embodies a design that is substantially similar in overall impression to a registered design may infringe that registered design.[63]

1.082 Section 19 of the Designs Act outlines the factors that need to be considered when determining whether one design is substantially similar in overall impression to another design.

---

61 Designs Act 2003; s 72(2).
62 Designs Act 2003; ss 15(1), s 16(2).
63 Designs Act 2003; s 71(1)(a).

Specifically, Section 19 of the Designs Act provides that if a person (or court) **1.083** is required to determine whether one design is substantially similar in overall impression to another design, the person must:

- Give greater weight to similarities than to differences.[64]
- Have regard to the state of development of the prior art base for the design.[65]
- If applicable, have regard to any particular visual features identified in a statement of newness and distinctiveness filed with the design application (see section B.1(e)). At the same time, however, the person must have regard to such features in the context of the design as a whole.[66]
- If the design application was not filed with a statement of newness and distinctiveness, have regard to the appearance of the design as a whole.[67]
- If only part of the design is substantially similar to another design, have regard to the amount, quality and importance of that part in the context of the design as a whole.[68]
- Have regard to the freedom of the creator of the design to innovate.[69]

Section 19 of the Designs Act further provides that when considering the **1.084** defined factors, the person (or court) must apply the standard of a user who is familiar with the product to which the design relates (or similar products).[70] This is discussed next in section A.12.

Case law concerning substantial similarity in overall impression is discussed **1.085** further at section D.1.

12.   The 'Familiar Person'

As noted above, where a person is required to determine whether one design is **1.086** substantially similar in overall impression to another design, the Designs Act requires that person to apply the standard of the 'familiar person'.[71]

Specifically, when deciding whether a design is substantially similar in overall **1.087** impression (by consideration of the factors outlined above), a person or court:

---

64   Designs Act 2003; s 19(1).
65   Designs Act 2003; s 19(2)(a).
66   Designs Act 2003; s 19(2)(b).
67   Designs Act 2003; s 19(3).
68   Designs Act 2003; s 19(2)(c).
69   Designs Act 2003; s 19(2)(d).
70   Designs Act 2003; s 19(4).
71   Designs Act 2003; s 19(4).

... must apply the standard of a person (the *familiar person*) who is familiar with the product to which the design relates, or products similar to the product to which the design relates (whether or not the familiar person is a user of the product to which the design relates or of products similar to the product to which the design relates).[72]

1.088 Prior to March 2022, the 'standard of the informed user' was employed for questions of substantial similarity in overall impression and the case law referenced different approaches on the issue of whether the standard required the person to be a user of the relevant products. The amendment to refer to the 'familiar person' was introduced to clarify that:

> ... the standard does not require that the person be a user of the products in question.... Instead, the standard is that of a person who is familiar with the product, or products similar to that product. The changes emphasise that the standard imposed is not higher than familiarity or limited by how that familiarity is acquired. Familiarity may be gained through use, but the standard does not require that the notional person be a user of the products in question. The changes make it clear that the intended standard is to be flexible enough to incorporate where relevant the views of consumers, experts, specialists, and skilled tradespersons.[73]

1.089 Case law regarding the current standard of the 'informed user' (which remains relevant when applying the replacement standard of the 'familiar person') is discussed at section D.2.

13. Ownership and Entitlement

1.090 Entitlement to an Australian registered design must, ultimately, stem from the designer(s).

1.091 Specifically, the Designs Act provides that any of the following may be registered as the owner of a registered design:[74]

- the person who created the design (i.e. the designer) or a person deriving title therefrom;
- where the design was created in the course of employment or a contract with another party, the employer/other party (unless there is agreement to the contrary) or a person deriving title therefrom.

---

72 Designs Act 2003; s 19(4).
73 Explanatory Memorandum to the Designs Amendment (Advisory Council on Intellectual Property Response) Bill 2020; paragraph 223.
74 Designs Act 2003; s 13(1).

1.092 The Designs Act provides that any person (entitled or otherwise) may be the applicant of an Australian design application.[75] Careful consideration of the applicant is, however, required. Filing an application with the wrong applicant may compromise any priority claim and/or give rise to a ground of revocation if the design is subsequently registered in the wrong name.

1.093 In order to benefit from the priority date of a basic application, Australian law requires that a convention application must be made by the applicant of the basic application or the assignee of the applicant of the basic application (or the legal personal representative of the applicant or applicant's assignee).[76] Filing with an alternative applicant may, therefore, compromise the priority claim.

1.094 Further, the Designs Act provides that a court may revoke registration of a design where:

- the original registered owner was not an entitled person in relation to the design when the design was first registered;[77] and/or
- the original registered owner was an entitled person but another (unlisted) person was also entitled.[78]

1.095 As discussed below, Australian designs can be registered quickly after filing. If an application is filed naming an applicant that is not the entitled (and solely entitled) owner, and the design proceeds to registration before this is corrected, it may prove fatal to validity.

(a) Rights of co-owners

1.096 Where there are two or more registered owners of a registered design, each owner is entitled to an equal and undivided share in the exclusive rights in that design.[79]

1.097 Further, each owner is entitled to exercise the exclusive rights in the design without accounting to other owners.[80] However, granting a licence or assigning an interest in the design requires the consent of all owners.[81]

---

75 Designs Act 2003; s 21(1).
76 Designs Regulations 2004; Reg 3.06(2).
77 Designs Act 2003; s 93(3)(b).
78 Designs Act 2003; s 93(3)(c).
79 Designs Act 2003; s 14(2)(a).
80 Designs Act 2003; s 14(2)(b).
81 Designs Act 2003; s 14(2)(c).

1.098 The standing provisions regarding co-ownership may be varied by contrary agreement between the registered owners.[82]

14. Term

1.099 A registered Australian design can be maintained for up to ten years from the filing date of the Australian application that first disclosed the design.[83]

1.100 An Australian design is initially registered for a period of five years. At the end of that five-year period the registration can be renewed for a further five years (on payment of a single renewal fee).[84] The renewal can also be completed within the period of six months following the expiration of the five-year term.[85] Payment in this period incurs an additional fee.

B. PROCEDURE

1. Applications and Priority Date

1.101 An application for registration of a design is governed by Chapter 3 of the Designs Act. Registration of a design that is the subject of an application is governed by Chapter 4 of the Designs Act.

1.102 Design applications are filed with IP Australia, an agency within the Department of Industry, Science, Energy and resources of the Australian Government. IP Australia provides an online portal through which design applications may be filed and through which applicants can manage their design rights. IP Australia's homepage is at https://www.ipaustralia.gov.au/.

(a) Filing date and the minimum filing requirements

1.103 To meet the minimum filing requirements, the application must include a representation of each design;[86] and information that:

- indicates an intent to file a design application;
- identifies the applicant; and

---

82 Designs Act 2003; s 14(4).
83 Designs Act 2003; s 46(1).
84 Designs Act 2003; ss 47, 46(b).
85 Designs Act 2003; s 47(2); Designs Regulations 2004; r 4.09.
86 Designs Act 2003; s 21(2)(a); Designs Regulations 2004; r 3.01(c), which also contemplate the filing of information that appears to be a representation, although how this will be applied in practice is unclear.

- allows the applicant to be contacted, which is typically met by providing an address for service.[87]

An application is given a filing date of the day when the application meets the minimum filing requirements.[88] **1.104**

(b) Multi-design applications

Australian law does provide for multi-design applications – i.e. a single design application that includes multiple designs. In this case, the designs must be connected (see below) and the person entitled to be recorded as the owner of the registered designs must be the same for each design.[89] **1.105**

The connection between the designs required for two or more designs to be pursued in a single, multi-design application is one of: **1.106**

- The design is a common design in relation to two or more products; or
- The designs are in relation to the same product; or
- The designs are in relation to different products, with each product belonging to the same Locarno Agreement class.[90]

Each design in a multi-design application will be registered with a unique registration number. Issues of infringement and validity are determined with respect to each design. **1.107**

(c) Further (or 'divisional') design applications

In some cases a Design Application may include multiple designs that cannot be included in a single application. This may be due to insufficient official fees being paid and/or the multiple designs not being connected as described at section B.1(b). **1.108**

In this case an objection will be raised by the Designs office. **1.109**

If the sole issue is that insufficient fees have been paid, this can be addressed by paying additional fees or excluding one or more designs from the initial application. **1.110**

If the designs are not properly connected, the only option is to exclude one or more designs from the initial application. **1.111**

---

87   Designs Act 2003; s 21(2)(b); Designs Regulations 2004; rr 3.01(a) and (b).
88   Designs Act 2003; s 26; Designs Regulations 2004; r 3.05.
89   Designs Act 2003; s 22(2).
90   Designs Act 2003; s 22(1).

1.112 Where a design is excluded from an initial application, it can be pursued in a 'further' application – effectively a divisional application.[91] A further application can, however, only be filed provided the initial application has not lapsed or been withdrawn, and no design(s) in the initial application have been registered or published.[92]

(d) Priority date

1.113 Applications with a filing date may claim a priority date up to six months earlier than the filing date, based on the date that an application for protection in respect of the design was made in a Convention country ('the basic application').[93] The Convention countries are a signatory to the Paris Convention for the Protection of Industrial Property of 20 March 1883 and members of the World Trade Organization.[94]

1.114 There is no requirement to file a copy of the basic application with IP Australia. However, the Registrar may request a copy of the basic application, for example to enable an examiner to determine whether the design is entitled to the claimed priority date. If a request is made and a copy of the basic application is not filed within two months from the request, then the priority date will revert to the Australian filing date.

1.115 Applications under the Hague Agreement Concerning the International Deposit of Industrial Designs, under the Benelux Designs Convention or under Treaty Establishing the European Community that applied for protection in a Convention country may be basic applications for a claim of priority.

1.116 The basic application is the first application in a Convention country.[95] However, in line with Article 4C of the Paris Convention, the applicant may request a later application by the same applicant be the basic application for the purposes of claiming priority. For the request to be granted and the earlier application disregarded, the earlier application must have been withdrawn, abandoned or refused without becoming open for public inspection and the earlier application must not have been used as the basis for a priority claim in a Convention country.[96]

---

91   Designs Act 2003; s 23.
92   Designs Act 2003; s 23.
93   Designs Regulations 2004; r 3.06(2).
94   Designs Act 2003; s5A; Designs Regulations 2004; r 1.05.
95   Designs Regulations 2004; r 3.06(5).
96   Designs Regulations 2004; r 3.07.

Each design in a design application or in a registered design may have a different priority date.[97] **1.117**

If a design is excluded from an initial application (see also section B.1(c)) and pursued in a further application under sections 23 and 21 of the Designs Act, then the design has the priority date it had under the initial application. **1.118**

(e) Statements of Newness and Distinctiveness

An Australian Design application may, though need not, be accompanied by a Statement of Newness and Distinctiveness. This Statement can be used by an applicant to identify particular visual features of the design that are new and distinctive.[98] **1.119**

If a Statement of Newness and Distinctiveness is filed with a design it becomes relevant when both validity and infringement are considered. Specifically, and as discussed at section A.11, when determining whether one design is substantially similar in overall impression to another design, particular regard must be had to any feature identified in the subject design's Statement of Newness and Distinctiveness. **1.120**

Although a Statement of Newness and Distinctiveness can be used to emphasise particular visual features (and, as a corollary, de-emphasise other features) it cannot be used to have any visual features of a design disregarded entirely. The emphasised features are still considered in the context of the design as a whole, including the de-emphasised features. For example, if the product is shown in solid lines for the emphasised features and broken lines for the de-emphasised features, the features shown in broken lines are still considered for providing the context of the design as a whole. **1.121**

Designs with different statements of newness and distinctiveness will be considered by the Australian Designs Office as distinct designs. As one example, if design application includes a first set of figures illustrating a product with a particular feature in broken line, and a second set of figures that illustrates the same product excepting that feature is in solid line, these two sets of figures will be considered separate designs. Accordingly, if multiple 'embodiments' are to be protected in Australia they must ultimately be filed as distinct designs. This may be done initially (via a single multi-design application or separate applications) or by filing 'further' applications as discussed at section B.1(c). **1.122**

---

97 Designs Act 2003; s 27(2).
98 Designs Act 2003; s 19(2)(b).

(f) Request for registration

1.123 An applicant must request registration of a design on filing or within six months of the priority date of the design.[99] Failure to request registration, within this period, of each design disclosed in an application that has not been excluded or withdrawn from the application, results in the design application lapsing.[100]

1.124 A design application for a design excluded from an initial application (see section B.1(c)) must include a request for registration.[101]

1.125 For applications filed prior to the commencement of the Designs Amendment (Advisory Council on Intellectual Property Response) Act 2021, it was possible to request publication of a design disclosed in an application instead of registration. Under this option, a design application would be published without being registered (the option further foreclosing the possibility of registration). After commencement, the publication option is no longer available.

(g) Publication of design applications

1.126 The Registrar of Designs is required to publish bibliographic details of an application that meets the minimum filing requirements.[102] These include the name of the applicant, the name of the product or products to which the design relates, the filing date and the details of any basic application to which Convention priority is claimed.

1.127 When a design application is registered, the representations showing the design or designs are entered in the register of designs and published.

1.128 Any statement of newness and distinctiveness filed for the application is also published, but is not entered into the register.[103] A consequence of this is that the Statement of Newness and Distinctiveness cannot be amended once a design application has been registered.

---

99 Designs Regulations 2004; r 4.01.
100 Designs Act 2003; s 33.
101 Designs Act 2003; s 37.
102 Designs Act 2003; s 25.
103 Designs Act 2003; ss 60, 111.

2. Registration Procedure

The Registrar is required to register the design of a design application for a single design in relation to a single product after a request for registration has been filed if: **1.129**

- satisfied that the design application satisfied a formalities check; and
- the design does not require to be refused under subsection 43(1) (see section A.7).[104]

If the design application is purportedly a common design in relation to more than one product, there is an additional requirement for registration: **1.130**

- The design is a common design in relation to each product (see section B.2(d));[105]

If the design application discloses more than one design, an additional requirement for registration is: **1.131**

- Each product belongs to the same Locarno Agreement class.[106]

(a) Notifications under section 41 and amendment

If the Registrar is not satisfied that the requirements for registration are met, the applicant is notified and provided an opportunity to amend the application.[107] (See section B.5(a) regarding amendments to design applications.) **1.132**

In response, the applicant must amend the application and/or respond in writing within a prescribed period, which is currently two months, to satisfy the Registrar that the design or designs of the application are registrable. The application lapses at the end of the prescribed period if the amendment or response does not satisfy the Registrar that each design is registrable.[108] The applicant may respond more than once within the prescribed period, if required to satisfy the Registrar. **1.133**

(b) Formalities check

The Registrar is required to confirm a range of matters as part of the formalities check of a design application. These include that the design application is in the approved form and in English, that the product or products are sufficiently **1.134**

---

104 Designs Act 2003; s 39.
105 Designs Act 2003; ss 39, 40.
106 Designs Act 2003; s 40.
107 Designs Ac 2003t; s 41.
108 Designs Act 2003; ss 33, 41; Designs Regulations 2004; r 3.14.

identified to enable classification in accordance with the Locarno Agreement, and that the representations or any specimen filed as a representation meet quality and reproducibility requirements.[109]

1.135 The approved form must be in English and any text in a filed document, other than text forming part of a design, must be in English or accompanied by a translation of the document into English, together with a certificate of verification of the translation.[110]

1.136 The identified product or products must each be a product within the meaning of the Designs Act.[111] Commentary on what is and what is not a product is in section A.4(a).

1.137 Additionally, the number of designs disclosed in the design application must match the number of designs identified, by the applicant, as being separate designs disclosed in application.[112] Claiming a single product and showing different configurations of a reconfigurable product, for example a container with its lid in open or on and closed or off positions respectably, is acceptable. In contrast showing screen shots of an animation on a display screen have been found to relate to separate designs, not a single design.[113] Similarly, showing a bank of gaming machines as individual gaming machines situated in close proximity, but without a physical join or connection, has been found to show four discrete products, not a single product of a bank of gaming machines.[114]

(c) Designs that must be refused

1.138 Under subsection 43(1) of the Designs Act, the Registrar is required to refuse certain designs (see section A.7).

(d) A common design in relation to more than one product

1.139 A single design may be in relation to multiple products, provided it is a common design in relation to those products.

1.140 In determining whether a single design is a common design, the Registrar will consider what design features across the range of products in question can be

---

109 Designs Regulations 2004; rr 4.04, 4.05.
110 Designs Regulations 2004; r 11.18.
111 *Microsoft Corporation* [2008] ADO 2.
112 Designs Regulations 2004; r 4.05(1)(g).
113 *Apple Inc* [2017] ADO 7.
114 *Aristocrat Technologies Australia Pty Limited* [2021] ADO 1.

and are common. For example, tap handles and spouts with common upstands may constitute a common design.[115]

If there is a common design, there is no need for the products to be classifiable in the same Locarno Agreement class. **1.141**

3. Post-registration Rights and Renewal

As discussed at section A.14, a registered design has a maximum term of ten years. **1.142**

Whilst the exclusive rights provided under the Designs Act are granted for a registered design, infringement proceedings can only be brought against a person if the design has been examined and a certificate of examination has been issued.[116] In other words, infringement proceedings can only be brought in relation to a certified design. **1.143**

In addition, a threat to bring infringement proceedings in respect of a design that has not been certified is deemed an unjustified threat. Making an unjustified threat entitles the person to whom the threat was made apply to a court for relief.[117] **1.144**

If the registration of a design ceases to be in force due to a failure to meet a requirement of the Designs Act, then there are provisions for the protection of third parties who took definite steps to use the design commercially in the period whilst the registration was ceased.[118] **1.145**

4. Examination and Certification Procedure

The owner or any other person or a court may request examination of a registered design.[119] Material relating to the newness and distinctiveness of the design may be included with the request for examination.[120] This allows the owner or, more typically, a third party, to place material before the Registrar for consideration during examination. **1.146**

---

115 For example, *Caroma Industries Ltd* [1991] ADO 3, considering whether a set of articles has 'commonality of design' under the Designs Act 1906.
116 Designs Act 2003; s 73.
117 Designs Act 2003; s 77.
118 Designs Act 2003; s 139.
119 Designs Act 2003; s 63.
120 Designs Act 2003; s 64(2).

1.147 When examining a registered design, the Registrar considers whether the design should not have been registered and whether the design is new and distinctive when compared to the prior art base for the design as it existed before the priority date of the design.[121]

1.148 A design will be considered new unless it is identical to a design that forms part of the prior art base,[122] and distinctive unless it is substantially similar in overall impression to a design that forms part of the prior art base.[123] The prior art base for a design is discussed at section A.5, and substantial similarity in overall impression is discussed at section A.11.

(a) Responses to notifications and amendment

1.149 If the Registrar is satisfied that a ground of revocation of the registered design exists, the applicant is notified and provided an opportunity to amend the design (see section B.5(b)).

1.150 The registered owner must either contest the ground for revocation in writing or request amendment of the Register within a prescribed period so as to satisfy the Registrar that the design should not be revoked.[124] The prescribed period is six months from the first notification of a ground of revocation or, if a new ground of revocation is raised responsive to material filed by a person, the later of this six month period or three months after the notification first raising the new ground of revocation.[125]

1.151 The registration of the design ceases at the end of the prescribed period if the amendment or response does not satisfy the Registrar that there is not a ground of revocation.[126] The applicant may respond more than once within the prescribed period if required to satisfy the Registrar of this.

1.152 The registration of the design is revoked if the Registrar is satisfied that a ground of revocation remains made out despite an amendment proposed by the registered owner. The registered owner, and if applicable the person who requested examination, must be given a reasonable opportunity to be heard before the design is revoked and an appeal of the decision of the Registrar

---

121 Designs Act 2003; ss 65, 15; Designs Regulations 2004; r 5.02.
122 Designs Act 2003; s 16(1).
123 Designs Act 2003; s 16(2).
124 Designs Act 2003; s 66; Designs Regulations 2004; r 5.03.
125 Designs Regulations 2004; r 5.04.
126 Designs Act 2003; ss 33, 41; Designs Regulations 2004; r 3.14.

may be made to the Federal Court or the Federal Circuit and Family Court of Australia (Division 2).[127]

(b) Certificate of examination

If the Registrar is satisfied that there is no ground of revocation of the design and there is no appeal of this decision, the Registrar issues a certificate of examination.[128] 1.153

A registered design for which a certificate of examination has issued is enforceable (see section B.3). 1.154

5.   Amendments

(a) Applications

An applicant may amend a design application while it remains pending, either voluntarily or in response to a notification under section 41 (see section B.5(a)). 1.155

An amendment of a design application must not alter the scope of the application by the inclusion of matter that was not in substance disclosed in the documents of the original design application.[129] 1.156

Amendments to the bibliographic details of the application, including amending an applicant name or address or amending the designer details are allowable. 1.157

Amendments to the representations are also allowable, provided the design of the amended representation was in substance disclosed in the original documents. This allows, for example, inconsistency between representations to be corrected. 1.158

Prior to registration, the statement of newness and distinctiveness may also be amended, including by the addition of a statement or the deletion of a statement. 1.159

---

127   Designs Act 2003; ss 67(3), 68.
128   Designs Act 2003; s 67.
129   Designs Act 2003; s 28(3).

(b) Registered designs

1.160 If the Registrar is satisfied, in the course of examining a registered design, that a ground for revocation of the registered design exists, then the owner may request amendment of the design to remove the ground for revocation.[130]

1.161 Where the amendment is not responsive to an examiner's communication, then an issue arises as to how the Registrar is to be satisfied that a ground for revocation has been made out. The Registrar takes the view that the owner believes there is a ground of revocation and assumes that one has been made out.[131]

1.162 An amendment filed during examination must not increase the scope of the design registration or alter the scope of the registration by the inclusion of matter that was not in substance disclosed in the documents of the original design application.[132] The restriction on new matter is the same as the restriction for amending a design application.

1.163 When examining a request for amendment against the requirement of not increasing the scope of the design registration, the Designs Office considers the 'Distillers Test': 'Would the amendment make anything an infringement which would not have been an infringement before the amendment?'.[133]

1.164 Applying the Distillers Test requires an evaluation of the overall impression of the design, since under section 71 of the Designs Act infringement is concerned with whether a product which embodies a design that is identical to, or substantially similar in overall impression to, the registered design.

1.165 Any statement of newness and distinctiveness for the application when it was registered cannot be amended, as it is not entered into the register.[134]

(c) Correction of the Register

1.166 The Registrar may correct a clerical error or an obvious mistake in the Register, either of their own motion or on request.[135] Unlike amendments during examination, the correction can materially alter the scope of the registered design

---

130 Designs Act 2003; s 66(1).
131 IP Australia, Designs Examiners' Manual of Practice and Procedure; s 22.3.
132 Designs Act 2003; s 66(6).
133 IP Australia, Designs Examiners' Manual of Practice and Procedure; s 22.5, citing *The Distillers Co Ltd's Application* (1953) 70 RPC 221 at 223.
134 *Reckitt Benckiser Inc* [2008] ADO 1.
135 Designs Regulations 2004; r 9.05 (1), (2).

and if so, the Registrar publishes, in the Official Journal a notice of the correction request and a person may oppose the amendment.[136]

1.167 The owner of a registered design may apply to a court for rectification of the Register in relation to the registered design, but only if a certificate of examination has issued for the registered design.[137]

6. Challenges to Validity

(a) Requesting examination

1.168 As discussed at section B.4, any person can request examination of a design that has been registered.[138]

1.169 Relevantly, examination of the same design may be requested multiple times, by the same or different parties. In this regard, IP Australia provides that issue estoppel does not apply to examination.[139]

(b) Providing information

1.170 Any person may provide to the Registrar material relating to whether a registered design is new or distinctive.[140] Such material can be provided without requesting examination and may be accompanied by a declaration providing evidence of the publication of the material.

1.171 If material is filed under this provision, the Registrar will provide the material to the owner of the registered design. The material will also be open to public inspection.

1.172 Where such materials are provided without requesting examination, however, there is no requirement for the Registrar to examine the registered design and consider whether the material establishes a ground of revocation of the design.

(c) Revocation proceedings before the Commissioner

1.173 A registered design may be revoked through the examination process described in section B.4.

---

136 Designs Regulations 2004; r 9.05(4), (5).
137 Designs Act; s 93.
138 Designs Act 2003; s 65(1).
139 IP Australia, Designs Examiners' Manual of Practice and Procedure; s 8.12.
140 Designs Act 2003; s 69.

1.174 Examination may be requested and the Registrar will perform examination whether or not a certificate of examination issued arising from a previous examination.[141] If there are infringement or revocation proceedings before a court, the Registrar is barred from revoking the design.[142]

(d) Revocation and rectification proceedings before the Court

1.175 A person may apply to a court for revocation of a registered design, but only if a certificate of examination has issued for the design.[143]

1.176 The grounds on which a court may revoke the registration of the design are:

- that the design is not a registrable design;
- that one or more of the original registered owners was not an entitled person in relation to the design when the design was first registered, or that one or more other persons were entitled when the design was first registered, if it is just and equitable in all the circumstances to revoke the design;
- that the registration of the design, or the certificate of examination, was obtained by fraud, false suggestion or misrepresentation; or
- that the design is a corresponding design to an artistic work, and copyright in the artistic work has ceased.

1.177 A registrable design is a design that is new and distinctive over the prior art base.[144] A corresponding design to an artistic work means visual features of shape or configuration which, when embodied in a product, result in a reproduction of that work.[145] Although not explicit in the Act, a registered design may be revoked if it is not reasonably clear and succinct.[146] A case referring to this requirement is discussed at section D.3(a).

1.178 A person may apply to a court for rectification of the Register in relation to a registered design, but only if a certificate of examination has issued for the registered design.[147] An applicant for rectification must a person aggrieved by the state of the Register they are seeking to rectify.

---

141 IP Australia, Designs Examiners' Manual of Practice and Procedure; s 8.12.
142 Designs Act 2003; s 68(5).
143 Designs Act 2003; s 93.
144 Designs Act 2003; ss 5, 15.
145 Designs Act 2003; s 5; Copyright Act 1968; s 74.
146 *Keller v LED Technologies Pty Ltd* [2010] FCAFC 55.
147 Designs Act 2003; s 93.

7. Extensions of Time

Deadlines for action in relation to an application for a registered design, a registered design, or proceedings under the Designs Act may be extended where the failure to perform the action was due to an error or omission.[148] **1.179**

Where the failure to perform the action was due to an error or omission by the Registrar, a Deputy Registrar, a Designs Office employee, or a person providing services to the Designs Office, then an extension of time is available as of right – the Registrar must extend the time for doing the relevant act. **1.180**

Where the failure to perform the action was due to an error or omission by the applicant or registered owner or their agent, then the Registrar has a discretion to grant an extension of time. **1.181**

In both cases it is necessary to show an error or omission. These words are interpreted broadly, to include both inadvertence and accidental steps and errors resulting from faulty reflection. However, in all cases there must be causal link between the error or omission and the failure to meet the deadline.[149] **1.182**

An extension of time is also available if the failure to perform the action was due to circumstances beyond the control of the relevant person, a force majeure provision.[150] **1.183**

An extension of time may be requested and allowed after the deadline.[151] If the extension of time is for more than three months, the Registrar will advertise the extension and an opposition process is available.[152] **1.184**

C. DISPUTES

1. Invalidity

Avenues for challenging the validity of a registered design before both the Designs Office and Courts are described at section B.6. **1.185**

---

[148] Designs Act 2003; ss 137(1), (2)(a).
[149] *Kimberly-Clark Ltd v Commissioner of Patents* (No 3) (1988) 13 IPR 569.
[150] Designs Act 2003; s 137(2)(b).
[151] Designs Act 2003; s 137(3).
[152] Designs Act 2003; ss 137(4), (5).

2. Infringement

(a) Infringement proceedings

1.186 As discussed at sections B.2 and B.4, Australian designs are registered on the strength of a formalities check only and requesting examination is optional.

1.187 Before infringement proceedings can be brought, however, a registered design must be examined and certified.[153]

1.188 Infringement proceedings may be bought by the registered owner of a registered design[154] or by an exclusive licensee.[155]

1.189 Infringement proceedings must be bought before a prescribed court. Various Australian Courts are prescribed, including the Federal Court of Australia.[156]

1.190 Infringement proceedings must be started within six years from the day on which the alleged infringement occurred.[157]

(b) Remedies for infringement

1.191 Where infringement of a registered design is found, the court has a discretion to grant an injunction and (at the option of the plaintiff) either damages or an account of profits.[158]

1.192 A court also has a discretion to award additional damages, having regard to the flagrancy of the infringement and all other relevant matters.[159]

(c) 'Innocent' infringement

1.193 A court may refuse to award damages, reduce the damages that would otherwise be awarded, or refuse to make an order for an account of profits in certain circumstances.

---

153 Designs Act 2003; s 73(3).
154 Designs Act 2003; s 73(1).
155 Designs Act 2003; s 73(1).
156 Designs Act 2003; s 5.
157 Designs Act 2003; s 71(4).
158 Designs Act 2003; s 75(1).
159 Designs Act 2003; s 75(3).

Once such circumstance in which this discretion may be exercised is where **1.194**
a defendant satisfies the court that, at the time of infringement:

- it was not aware that a design application had been filed;[160] and/or
- it was not aware that the design was registered and had taken all reasonable steps to ascertain whether the design was registered.[161]

Marking a product or its packaging to indicate registration of a design is **1.195**
considered prima facie evidence that a defendant was aware of the design
registration.[162]

(d) Unjustified threats of infringement

Section 77 of the Designs Act provides that a person to apply to a prescribed **1.196**
court for relief from unjustified threats of infringement.[163]

Where threats are found to be unjustified, a court may declare the threats to **1.197**
be unjustified, award an injunction against the continuation of the threats, and
award damages.[164]

The court may also award additional amount in an assessment of damages **1.198**
having regard to any factors considered by the court to be relevant, including
(inter alia) the flagrancy of the threats and the need to deter similar threats.[165]

A threat to bring infringement proceedings in respect of a registered design **1.199**
that has not been certified is explicitly defined to be an unjustified threat.[166]

Mere notification of the existence of a registered design does not, however, **1.200**
constitute a threat of infringement proceedings.[167]

---

160 Designs Act 2003; s 75(1A).
161 Designs Act 2003; s 75(2).
162 Designs Act 2003; s 75(4).
163 Designs Act 2003; s 77.
164 Designs Act 2003; s 77(1).
165 Designs Act 2003; s 77(1A).
166 Designs Act 2003; s 77(3).
167 Designs Act 2003; s 80.

D. SIGNIFICANT JUDICIAL DECISIONS IN THE JURISDICTION

1. Substantial Similarity in Overall Impression

(a) *Review 2 Pty Ltd v Redberry Enterprise Pty Ltd* [2008] FCA 1588

1.201　In this Federal Court case, the plaintiff (**Review**) alleged infringement of their registered design for a dress by Redberry Enterprise (**Redberry**).

1.202　The product name in the registered design was 'Ladies garments' and a set of representations in colour depicted the shape of the dress and the colour and pattern of the material. Redberry claimed that the design was invalid, as not distinctive over the prior art base.

1.203　The design of the alleged infringing dress was not identical to the registered design and therefore the Court considered whether it was substantially similar in overall impression to the registered design. The similarities included the shape of the bodice, neck and waist, including a satin ribbon tie. The differences included shape of the skirt part of the dress and the pattern, including the colour, of the designs.

1.204　The Court summarised the inquiry at paragraph 35:

> Considered by reference to the standard of the informed user, in deciding whether the design embodied in the Redberry garment is substantially similar in overall impression to the Review Design, the Court must: (1) give more weight to similarities between the designs in question than to differences (s 19(1)); (2) have regard to the state of development of the prior art base for the Review Design (s 19(2)(a)); (3) have regard to the freedom of the designer to innovate (s 19(2)(d)); and (4) since only part of the Redberry design is substantially similar to the Review Design, have regard to the amount, quality and importance of that part in the context of the design considered as a whole (s 19(2)(c)). Further, since the design application for the Review Design did not include a statement of newness and distinctiveness, the Court must have regard to the appearance of the Review Design as a whole (s 19(3)).

1.205　The Court considered the interaction between, on the one hand, the requirement of section 19(1) to give more weight to similarities, and on the other hand, the required considerations of section 19(2). Referring to the clear similarities between the registered design and the Redberry garment, the Court stated at paragraph 38: 'If this were all, a finding of infringement might be readily made, since the similarities between the designs are to be given greater weight than the differences (s 19(1)). As noted already, however, the inquiry under the Designs Act is more complex and sophisticated than this.'

The Court concluded at that section 19(2) modified the effect of section 19(1), so as to result in a finding that the Redberry garment was not substantially similar in overall impression, stating at paragraph 45: **1.206**

> Notwithstanding the direction in s 19(1) and the clear similarities between the Review Design and the design embodied in the Redberry garment, having regard to the directions in ss 19(2)(a), (c) and (d), 19(3) and (4), the informed user would conclude that the design embodied in the Redberry dress creates a different overall impression to the Review Design considered as a whole, principally because of the difference in the shape of the skirts, combined with the differences in pattern (including colour). That is, in this case, s 19(2)(c), considered in light of s 19(2)(a) and (d), operates to modify the effect of s 19(1) of the Designs Act.

Similarly, none of the items of prior art were identical to the registered design and therefore the Court considered whether the registered design is substantially similar in overall impression to any of the designs in the prior art base. The Court stated at paragraph 59: **1.207**

> As previously noted, having regard to the prior art to which reference has already been made and to the Review Design, and taking into account the freedom of the designer to innovate, the informed user would be aware that there is limited freedom to design a cross-over or wrap dress (or similar ladies' garment) and that, for the most part, what gives the Review Design its different overall impression from the prior art, from the perspective of the informed user, is the shape and configuration of the skirt, combined with differences in pattern…

The coincidence of the features that gave the Review Design its different overall impression with the features that distinguished the Redberry garment from the registered design led to the result of a finding that the Review Design was valid and not infringed. **1.208**

(b) *LED Technologies Pty Ltd v Roadvision Pty Ltd* [2012] FCAFC 3

This Full Federal Court case was an appeal of a decision of a single judge of the Federal Court rejecting LED Technologies claim of infringement of its registered designs. **1.209**

In considering infringement and the issue of substantial similarity in overall impression, Justice Besanko commented: **1.210**

> It seems to me that in terms of infringement, one of the most significant matters is that the registered designs appeared in a crowded field of prior art. As the trial judge noted, many of the features of similarity between the registered designs and the respondents' lights were features that were common in the prior art. Even if less weight is placed on the difference in the underside of the base it is still a relevant visual feature and, with the other features identified by the trial judge, leads me to conclude that the trial judge

DESIGN LAW

did not err in deciding that the design embodied in the respondents' lights was not substantially similar in overall impression to the registered design.

(c) *World of Technologies (Aust) Pty Ltd v Tempo (Aust) Pty Ltd* [2007] FCA 114

1.211 This Federal Court case included a claim that a registered design for a vacuum cleaner was invalid due to a prior publication of the vacuum cleaner in a brochure.

1.212 The brochure in question showed only a single perspective view of the vacuum cleaner, leaving a number of visual features of the product undisclosed. In contrast, the registered design included a full set of views showing all details of the product to which the design was to be applied.

1.213 In finding the registered design invalid, Justice Jessup held at paragraph 61:

> Although shown on the brochure in front perspective view only, the impression obtained from that angle permits the viewer to make a reasonable assessment not only of the side, but also of the front, of the vacuum cleaner. Assuming, as I do, that the product is symmetrical, I take it that the other front perspective view would convey the same impression. Further, the item is displayed on the brochure in such a way as to permit the viewer to gain a reasonably good impression of the appearance of the product from the top. The only faces of the product which it is impossible to perceive from the brochure are those of the rear and of the underside. Notwithstanding these omissions, I consider that the vacuum cleaner is sufficiently represented on the Suzhou Fak brochure to give a good impression of the appearance of the design of the product as a whole, as required by s 19(3) of the Designs Act. Taking that approach, I find that the design for which the applicant applied for, and subsequently secured, registration is substantially similar in overall impression to that which appeared on the printed brochure for the MC-801 vacuum cleaner distributed at the Canton Fair in April 2005. The latter was a design published in a document outside Australia and was, accordingly, part of the prior art base for the purposes of registrability.

2. The Standard of the Informed User

(a) *Multisteps Pty Ltd v Source and Sell Pty Ltd* [2013] FCA 743

1.214 This Federal Court case concerned a claim of infringement of registered designs to produce containers. Justice Yates of the Federal Court considered the standard of the informed user for the task of evaluating substantial similarity in overall impression. He considered the secondary materials[168] to the Designs Act, noted comments that the informed user is flexible enough to

---

168 The Australian Law Reform Commission Report No. 74, *Designs* (Sydney, 1995).

incorporate where relevant the views of consumers, experts, specialists and skilled tradespersons and commented at paragraphs 66 and 67:

> The test in s 19(4) of the Designs Act reflects this more general approach. Apart from the tag 'the informed user', the standard prescribed by s 19(4) appears to be indifferent as to how and in what circumstances familiarity is acquired. In my respectful view, the standard does not proceed on the requirement that the notional person be a user of the products in question – although, obviously, familiarity can be gained through use. Similarly, it does not proceed on the distinctions that the United Kingdom and European cases draw about who can and who cannot be a user.
>
> Importantly, however, s 19(4) does not impose a standard higher than familiarity. The standard fixes the appropriate level of generality (or particularity) at which a design is to be assessed… This may be a reason for saying that the notional person is not a design expert, lest it be thought that a standard of design evaluation more rigorous or exacting than familiarity is involved. However, in my view, it is not a reason for excluding, necessarily, a design expert from being a person having the required familiarity.

1.215 Justice Yates found that there was no need to confine the standard of the informed user to any particular user. Instead, finding at paragraph 70 'However, in all cases, the necessary and only qualification is that the person be familiar with produce or similar containers.' As to the perceptions of the general body of consumers, he found at paragraph 71 that these were not relevant in the present case:

> I do not regard the perceptions of the general body of consumers who purchase packaged products at retail to be indicative of the standard of the informed user in the present case. It is entirely possible, of course, that some consumers, for whatever reason, might have a particular interest in produce containers and, because of particular circumstances, possess the requisite familiarity to meet the standard under s 19(4). However, as a matter of general approach, I would regard this to be the exception rather than the rule.

(b) *Astrazeneca AB* [2007] ADO 4

1.216 This Designs Office decision concerned a design for an inhalation device, of a type used for asthma inhalers. The inhalation device of the design in question was identical to a prior art design, except that it included an indicator on an end that had the appearance of a dial or gauge marked with numbers.

1.217 The Deputy Registrar considered on the one hand that a device that indicated the number of puffs remaining would likely be of great significance to user. On the other hand the Deputy Registrar was cognisant that the question was one of appearance, not function and if the indicator were not functional, then the user may have a different view of the product.

1.218 The Deputy Registrar found that, in this case, an expectation of functionality would affect the significance of the indicator, stating:

> If the informed user's assessment is affected by an expectation of functionality, the fact that such functionality may not actually exist is not relevant. In this case, the question is: would the informed user's attention be drawn to the indicator on the end? If the user would look there in the expectation that there is a useful indicator present, that is sufficient. In particular, it does not matter whether or not the indicator would function. If the user's attention is particularly drawn to that feature, that fact alone is sufficient to indicate the feature as being one of importance (in the Designs context).

3. Clarity of the Design

(a) *Keller v LED Technologies Pty Ltd* [2010] FCAFC 55

1.219 In this case, Australia's Full Federal Court confirmed that although there is not an explicit ground of revocation based on lack of clarity, this requirement is inferred from the requirement to file representations.

1.220 At paragraph 39, Emmett J stated:

> The relevant test is whether the Designs are reasonably clear and succinct. The Designs Act requires representations embodying the relevant design. A design is the overall appearance of a product resulting from one or more visual features of a product. No assessment of distinctiveness for the purposes of validity, or for the purposes of infringement, can be made without knowledge of the overall appearance of a product resulting from one or more visual features of the product.

1.221 At paragraph 43, Emmett J went on to agree with the primary Judge that while the drawings filed with the designs in question were not perfect and could have been clearer they were 'reasonably clear and succinct' and, therefore, the lack of clarity was not fatal to the designs.

4. Evaluating the Validity of a Design over the Prior Art Base

(a) *LED Technologies Pty Ltd v Elecspess Pty Ltd* [2008] FCA 1941

1.222 In this case, the Federal Court considered how to assess distinctiveness of a design in comparison to the prior art base.

1.223 From paragraph 55, Gordon J stated:

> Secondly, contrary to the Respondents' submissions, distinctiveness is to be assessed not by comparing the design in question to the prior art base as a whole but by comparing it individually to each relevant piece of prior art: s 15(1) read with ss 16(1) and (2). Part 4 of Chapter 2 of the 2003 Designs Act must be read as a whole. The Respondents

cannot, as they do, simply selectively choose ss 15(1) and 19(2) to support their contention that a comparison is made of the design with the totality of the entire relevant prior art base for that design whilst ignoring the express words of the rest of Pt 4 including ss 16 and 19(1). It is those sections which expressly provide that a design is distinctive unless it is substantially similar in overall impression to a design that forms part of the prior art base for the design. As a result, a design that combines various features, each of which can be found in the prior art base when considered as a whole but not in any one particular piece of prior art, is capable of being distinctive: Review 2 Pty Ltd v Redberry Enterprise Pty Ltd [2008] FCA 1588 at [60]; Karen Millen Ltd v Dunnes Stores Ltd [2008] ECDR 11 at [82]–[84] (stating that the registered design must be assessed with regard to particular prior designs rather than a hypothetical amalgam of a number of prior designs). See also Lockwood Security Products Pty Ltd v Doric Products Pty Ltd (2007) 235 ALR 202 (upholding the validity in the patent context of a combination of features known collectively in the prior art).

(b) *Keller v LED Technologies Pty Ltd* [2010] FCAFC 55

In this case, the Full Federal Court noted that there was an interaction between the scope of a registered design and the prior art base, commenting at paragraph 53 in the context of evaluating the validity of the designs in issue: **1.224**

> The task of the Court is to compare each of the Designs with each relevant piece of prior art. Section 19 does not refer simply to the prior art base, but to the state of development of the prior art base. The primary judge observed, albeit in the context of infringement, that the extent of difference required to make a design distinctive will depend on the state of development of the relevant prior art base. A more developed prior art base will mean that smaller differences will be sufficient to result in a finding that there is no substantial similarity (see par 5.23 of Australian Law Reform Commission Report No 74, Designs (1995)).

5.   Fonts and Graphical User Interfaces

(a) *Microsoft Corporation* [2008] ADO 2

In this Designs Office decision, an application for design that specified a product name of 'Type Font' was considered. The representations set out the letters A to Z in upper and lower cases, the numbers 0 to 9 and several special characters that appear on a keyboard. **1.225**

In finding the design application did not meet the formalities requirements for a design application, the Deputy Registrar stated at paragraph 14: **1.226**

> The present design is for a font. It is not a hammer for a typewriter; it is not a type element for use in type-setting with metal blocks; it is not a rubber stamp. It is the shape of characters that might be applied to any of these things – as well as any other medium – be that paper, computer screen, light projection etc. Indeed, in the computer environment a type font exists as a binary file (in the Windows® environment, usually as

a .TTF or .FON file), with that file being used to control how information is presented on computer output – whatever that output might be (monitor, printer, etc). I do not think that the present design shows a product bearing visual features. Rather, the representations show a collection of visual features intended to be applied to unspecified products in unspecified arrangements.

(b) *Apple Inc* [2017] ADO 6

1.227 In this Designs Office decision, an application for a design that specified a product name of 'Display Screen' was considered. The sole representation included a stylised radio bounded by a dashed rectangular box. The Deputy Registrar found that a display screen was a product within the meaning of the Designs Act.

1.228 However, the Deputy Registrar found that the stylised radio was not a visual feature of the product, and therefore found the design not new or distinctive over prior art with similarly shaped displays, despite the displays not showing anything resembling the stylised radio.

6. Repair Defence

(a) *GM Global Technology Operations LLC v S.S.S. Auto Parts Pty Ltd* [2019] FCA 97

1.229 This Federal Court case considered the applicant's claim that the respondent, an importer and supplier of parts for motor vehicles, infringed its registered design rights.

1.230 The parts in question were capable of being used to repair relatively high-specification vehicles that originally included parts of the same appearance. The parts in question were also capable of being used – and in some instances were used – to replace parts on relatively low-specification vehicles, so as to make them appear like the high-specification vehicles.

1.231 The respondent relied on the repair defence provisions of section 72 of the Designs Act, stating that the repair defence provided a complete answer to the claim of infringement. Justice Burley noted that the operation of the repair defence had not been tested by the Court to date, and its terms opened up rich opportunities for dispute.

1.232 As to the requirement section 72(1)(c) for 'the [alleged infringing] use or authorisation [to use] is for the purpose of the repair of the complex product so as to restore its overall appearance in whole or part', it was explained that it is the knowledge of the respondent supplier that is relevant, stating at paragraphs 79–83 and 86–87:

The starting point is that a product that falls within sub-sections 72(1)(a) and (b) will be capable of being used for more than one purpose; a permitted repair purpose within sub-section 72(1)(c), and a prohibited purpose, such as that alleged in the present context, the enhancement of a vehicle. It is the knowledge of the person who has imported, offered for sale or sold the product that separates the two. If in infringement proceedings an alleged infringer asserts that it had the repair purpose within sub-section 72(1)(c), then it is to be assumed that it had that purpose, unless the registered owner proves otherwise.

In the present case, witnesses for SSS asserted on oath that SSS has a policy of selling parts for repair only and that its conduct in importing, keeping, offering for sale and selling the parts was guided by that purpose. GMH seeks to dislodge that evidence by pointing to factors which, it submits, indicate that the evidence of the witnesses is not to be accepted.

The parties agreed that the following formula assists in considering the question (emphasis added):

At the point just prior to the relevant use, the Customer's non-repair use was actually known or a reasonable person in [SSS'] position would consider that the circumstances were such as to create in that person's mind a belief that he or she knew that the Customer's intended use was not for repair, such that if [SSS] proceeds with the proposed use, **its use became that of the Customer**.

GMH submits that the concession by some of the SSS witnesses in cross-examination that some parts that they sell might not be used for repair is decisive. However, s 72 focuses on the intention of SSS. It does not require that SSS maintain control over the part after its importation, sale or keeping to make sure that it is ultimately applied to a vehicle for repair or to track the progress of goods it sells through the supply chain. The task that the Court is asked to determine is whether, on the basis of all of the evidence, including the positive evidence that SSS did have the repair purpose, GMH has established that SSS knew or ought reasonably to have known that the importation, sale or keeping was not for that purpose. The concession that a part may ultimately not be used for that purpose was, in most cases, an acknowledgement of the simple fact that SSS did not retain control over its parts and that, being a part that might be used for two purposes, there is a prospect that it will not be used for a repair purpose.

In this regard, the immediate question is the purpose of the importer or seller, not of the person who acquires the part from them....

A manufacturer is highly unlikely to know, at the point that the part comes off the production line, what will ultimately become of it. In the normal flow of commerce, the manufacturer will no doubt sell to a wholesaler, which in turn will sell to a retailer, which in turn will sell to a user. There is no direct link between the infringing act and its ultimate use (the remoteness problem). When the act of making is complete, the manufacturer is unlikely to have any real idea of its ultimate fate. But that is unimportant. The defence is not concerned with the actual use of the part, but the purpose of the manufacture (or other use). What did the manufacturer intend by manufacturing the part? The same observations may be made in relation to other acts of use, although the remoteness problem is more acute at the point of manufacture of a part, and less acute at the retail sale point when the seller is more likely to be dealing directly with the ultimate user.

A question raised in the debate between the parties is whether an alleged infringer has a duty to enquire as to what a purchaser may use a product for. This, it seems to me, also distracts from the statutory question. The question is really; on the existing facts, what do the circumstances indicate the alleged infringer knew or ought reasonably to have known based on the facts as proved? In the present case, GMH provides particulars of the Knowledge Factors which form the basis for its contention that SSS knew (for the purpose of its case of actual knowledge) or ought reasonably to have known (for constructive knowledge) that its use was not for the repair purpose. It is by reference to these, in the context of the circumstances of the individuals named, that the question of repair purpose is to be considered.

1.233 As the respondent parties were corporations, the requisite knowledge to prove infringement is that of a human actor within each company. This knowledge cannot be eschewed by authorising individuals with a wide discretion (see paragraphs 92, 94 and 101). However, having implemented policies reflecting an earnest desire to ensure parts were sold for repair only, senior management was entitled to assume that their employees would follow company policy (see paragraphs 371, 430). The knowledge cannot be formed as an aggregate of the knowledge of two or more people (see paragraphs 100, 101).

1.234 Justice Burley held that each alleged exploitation of the registered design alleged to infringe needed to be considered. He confirmed that it was for the registered design owner to prove that a repair purpose was not held (see paragraphs 60, 61, 436).

1.235 In relation to the act of importation he considered the correct time for assessing the relevant purpose is the date on which each act of importation took place, having regard to all of the relevant surrounding circumstances leading to that point.

1.236 Justice Burley also considered the actual and constructive knowledge of the respondent supplier when considering other exclusive design rights, including the policies in place by the respondent supplier at the time. The right to sell was considered in relation to 26 wholesale transactions by the respondent supplier. He found that the applicant had discharged its onus to prove the requisite knowledge of the supplier in relation to eight of them. The name of the purchaser, information in email footers of the purchaser and information on their website (when it was established that the responsible person in the seller had a practice of reviewing a customer's website), were relevant, as were the size of the sales transaction.

The Court declared that the respondents ought reasonably to have known that the sales of ten products across the eight transactions were not for the purpose of repair and therefore they infringed the registered design rights of eight designs of the applicant.[169]

1.237

E. PRACTICAL ASPECTS OF DESIGN LAW

1. Australian Design Filings, Registrations, and Certifications

The figures in Table 1.1 below are based on IP Australia's 2021 Intellectual Property Report.[170]

1.238

Table 1.1   Australian design filings, registrations, and certifications

	Calendar year 2020	Average over 2011–2020
Australian design filings	7165	7067
Australian design registrations	6332	6660
Australian design certifications	998	1064

Source: Australian Intellectual Property Report 2021 https://www.ipaustralia.gov.au/tools-and-research/professional-resources/data-research-and-reports/publications-and-reports/australian-intellectual-property-report-2021.

Of the 7,165 Australian design applications filed in 2020, approximately 36 per cent were filed in the name of Australian entities and approximately 64 per cent were filed in the name of non-Australian entities.

1.239

2. Court Cases

The Designs Act 2003 replaced the Designs Act 1906. The Explanatory Memorandum to the 2003 Act explains that in part, the current Act was passed to:

1.240

- Address industry concern that the designs system provided ineffective protection, with the requirement for registration that a design be only new or original resulting in registration being too easy to obtain. The distinctiveness threshold for registration was intended to require greater differentiation over prior art designs.
- Address industry concern that infringement was too difficult to prove. The 2003 Act aligned the tests for distinctiveness and infringement.

---

169   *GM Global Technology Operations LLC v S.S.S. Auto Parts Pty Ltd (No 2) (Costs)* [2019] FCA 1813.
170   Australian Government, IP Australia. *Australian Intellectual Property Report 2021*; Chapter 4. https://www.ipaustralia.gov.au/ip-report-2021 at 14 March 2022.

1.241 The 2003 Act was described in the Minister's second reading as a 'fundamental change to the registration and protection of industrial designs in Australia', with key features including 'a higher threshold test for gaining rights and a broader infringement test, which will make a design registration harder to obtain but easier to enforce'.

1.242 For the purposes of this section only published decisions on cases concerning a claim of infringement of one or more registered designs, with or without a cross-claim for invalidity of a design registered under the Designs Act have been considered. Some cases have been excluded, for example when the outcome was based on the design owner being found to have authorised the alleged infringing conduct or whether the outcome rested on a defence to infringement other than revocation. Under the Designs Act 2003 there have been about ten such cases considering alleged infringement of one or more registered designs. The authors are not aware of the number of cases alleging design infringement that have been commenced, but did not result in a published decision, for example due to being settled during the course of the matter.

1.243 Infringement was found in seven of the ten cases. In some cases infringement was conceded. In those seven cases:

- in three cases the respondent made an unsuccessful claim for revocation;
- in two cases there was no cross-claim for invalidity;
- in one case the registered designs were found invalid over prior publication or use by the owner of the registered designs.

1.244 Of the three cases in which infringement was not found, cross-claims for invalidity were filed. The designs were found valid in two cases and invalid in one.

1.245 Accordingly, the registered owner was successful in about 60 per cent of the cases overall, although the small number of cases means that the utility of this statistic may be limited. However, from the reasoning of the court in the cases to date, it appears that the two concerns of the 1906 Act have been addressed or at least reduced.

3. Assignment of Registered Designs

1.246 An assignment of a registered design (or interest therein) must be in writing and be signed by (or on behalf of) both the assignor and assignee.[171]

---

171 Designs Act 2003; s 11(1) and (2).

Where there are multiple registered owners of a registered design, assignment of an interest in the design requires the consent of all owners.[172] **1.247**

Any change in ownership of a registered design should be promptly recorded in the Register of Designs. This is due to: **1.248**

- the exclusive rights that attach to a registered design attach to the registered owner thereof;[173] and
- the Register of Designs is prima facie evidence of the particulars (which include the owner of a registered design) that are maintained therein.[174]

4. Compulsory Licences

The Designs Act includes provisions which provide a court with the ability to grant a compulsory license in respect of a registered design.[175] **1.249**

Generally speaking, in order to grant a compulsory license a court must be satisfied that:[176] **1.250**

- products embodying the design have (unreasonably) not been made in Australia;
- the registered owner has provided no satisfactory reason for failing to exercise the exclusive rights in the design; and
- the party applying for the compulsory licence has made reasonable attempts to obtain a licence on reasonable terms and conditions.

Where a court grants a compulsory license, and the registered design owner and licensee cannot agree on an amount, the court may determine an amount for the licence that is just and reasonable having regard to the economic value of the licence.[177] **1.251**

---

172 Designs Act 2003; s 14(2)(c).
173 Designs Act 2003; s 10(1).
174 Designs Act 2003; s 118(1).
175 Designs Act 2003; s 90.
176 Designs Act 2003; s 90(3).
177 Designs Act 2003; s 91(4).

F. COMMENTS, ANALYSIS, EVALUATION

1. Design Law Reform *de lege ferenda*

1.252 The Designs Act was most recently amended by a 2021 amendment Act.[178]

1.253 While these amendments made a number of significant changes (including, e.g. the introduction of a grace period), IP Australia is continuing exploration of additional areas that may require change.

1.254 At the time of writing, IP Australia is exploring further legislative reform, in particular with a view to providing protection for non-physical or virtual products (e.g. graphical user interfaces), select parts of products (e.g. partial designs), and providing flexibility for the protection of designs as they evolve.[179]

(a) Protecting virtual or non-physical designs

1.255 At the time of writing, the view of the Australian Designs office is that virtual or non-physical designs (such as graphical user interfaces) cannot be protected by registered designs.

1.256 If an application for a virtual design identifies a valid product (e.g. a device or display on which the virtual design is displayed), there is no ground on which registration of the application can be refused. Accordingly, such applications will (absent any other formalities flaw) proceed to registration.

1.257 If certification of a virtual design is requested, however, the Designs Office will typically revoke the registered design. As discussed above at section A.4(b)(1), this is due to the view of the Designs Office that 'virtual' features are not visual features of the product in question, and ignores those features when determining whether the design is new and distinctive over the prior art.

1.258 Notably, the refusal to certify virtual designs is:

- based on the Designs Office interpretation of the legislation rather than any explicit exclusion for such subject matter; and
- has not been considered by the Australian courts.

1.259 From October to December 2019, IP Australia conducted a public consultation on policy issues that were being considered for inclusion in the Designs

---

[178] Designs Amendment (Advisory Council on Intellectual Property Response) Act 2021.
[179] IP Australia. 'Designs Initiatives'. https://www.ipaustralia.gov.au/about-us/our-agency/our-research/design-initiatives accessed on 10 October 2023.

Bill 2020 (which, in due course, became the Designs Amendment (Advisory Council on Intellectual Property Response) Act 2021.

Virtual designs were one area included in this consultation, with IP Australia reporting that 17 of 19 participants who provided feedback were in favour or providing registered design protection for virtual designs in some form.[180] **1.260**

Despite this, no amendments relevant to protecting virtual designs were included in the 2021 Amendment Act. **1.261**

Between 13 June 2023 and 13 August 2023, IP Australia held a further public consultation around how virtual and non-physical designs should be protected.[181] At the time of writing, IP Australia reports that the next steps are to refine the proposal and report to the Government, which will then decide whether to proceed with legislation and/or further consultation.[182] **1.262**

(b) Protecting partial designs

Another area of Australian Law that has been flagged for further consideration is the protection of partial designs. **1.263**

In this context, a partial design refers to a design in respect of an integral part of a broader product that cannot be removed/separated (non-destructively) from the broader product. **1.264**

Protecting partial designs is a somewhat vexed issue under Australian designs law. **1.265**

As discussed above at section A.4(a), the definition of 'product' in the Designs Act does not include integral parts of larger products. In order for a design to be valid, therefore, it must be in respect of (and the representations must depict) a product that is manufactured separately. **1.266**

---

180 IP Australia. Response to public consultation: Implementing accepted recommendations from the Advisory Council on Intellectual Property Review of the Designs System. May 2020. Section 1.
181 A copy of the 'Protect Virtual Designs' consultation paper is available at https://consultation.ipaustralia.gov.au/policy/enhancing-australian-design-protection/user_uploads/designs-consultation---protect-virtual-designs.pdf, and published responses to the consultation are at https://consultation.ipaustralia.gov.au/policy/enhancing-australian-design-protection/consultation/published_select_respondent, both accessed 10 October 2023.
182 https://consultation.ipaustralia.gov.au/policy/enhancing-australian-design-protection/ accessed 10 October 2023.

1.267 In the example of the ceramic cup with an integral handle, this means that even if the desire was to protect the appearance of the handle alone (i.e. a partial design) the entire cup would need to be shown.

1.268 As also discussed above, however, both validity and infringement of an Australian design require consideration of the *overall* appearance of that design. While a Statement of Newness and Distinctiveness can, effectively, be used to de-emphasise certain features there is no mechanism to have a feature of the design representations disregarded entirely.

1.269 As a result, protecting partial designs in Australia is difficult. At best the visual features of the part of the design that are of interest can be emphasised, but even then those features are considered in the context of the broader product's overall appearance.

1.270 In the 2019 public consultation conducted by IP Australia, 18 of 20 participants who provided feedback were in favour of providing for the protection of partial designs.[183]

1.271 Once again, however, despite this feedback in favour of providing a mechanism to protect partial designs, no relevant amendments were included in the 2021 Amendment Act.

1.272 Partial designs were also considered in IP Australia's recent public consultation (discussed at section F.1(a) above) so this too is an area that may see legislative reform in the relatively near future (e.g. 2024–2025).[184]

(c) Protection for incremental improvements of designs

1.273 The public consultation discussed at section F.1(a) above also considered options for protecting incremental improvements of designs.[185]

1.274 This area of consultation was focused on options for (and the desirability of) protecting designs that are developed 'using an incremental process involving rounds of ideation, prototyping and testing'.

---

183 IP Australia. Response to public consultation: Implementing accepted recommendations from the Advisory Council on Intellectual Property Review of the Designs System. May 2020. Section 1.
184 A copy of the 'Protect Partial Designs' consultation paper is available at https://consultation.ipaustralia.gov.au/policy/enhancing-australian-design-protection/user_uploads/designs-consultation---protect-partial-designs.pdf accessed 10 October 2023.
185 A copy of the 'Protection for Incremental Improvements of Designs' consultation paper is available at https://consultation.ipaustralia.gov.au/policy/enhancing-australian-design-protection/user_uploads/designs-consultation---protect-incremental-improvements.pdf accessed 10 October 2023.

1.275 As stated in the Public Consultation paper: 'This proposal would permit a designer to file a preliminary design at an early stage to obtain a priority date, and then convert it to a main design application later, incorporating any incremental design features. The main design has priority from the preliminary design.'

1.276 The detailed proposal put forward in respect of incremental designs does appear to raise some complexities, and as a general proposition appeared to receive less support than the proposals in respect of virtual and partial designs discussed above.[186] Nonetheless, this area is also under consideration and may see legislative reform.

---

186 See the published responses to the consultation are at https://consultation.ipaustralia.gov.au/policy/enhancing-australian-design-protection/consultation/published_select_respondent accessed 10 October 2023.

2

INDUSTRIAL DESIGN LAW IN CANADA – 2024

Robert B. Storey, Adam Bobker, Matthew J. Graff and James Raakman

A. FUNDAMENTALS OF CANADIAN DESIGN LAW		2.001	(a) Grounds	2.047
			(b) Procedure	2.048
	1. Relevant Legislation and Administration	2.001	8. Design Enforcement	2.051
			(a) Jurisdiction	2.051
	(a) Legislation	2.001	(b) Infringement	2.052
	(b) Administration	2.005	(c) Procedure	2.055
	2. Protecting a Design	2.006	(d) Injunctive relief	2.059
	(a) Subject matter	2.006	(e) Stays	2.060
	(b) Required information	2.011	(f) Expedited proceedings	2.061
	(c) Application procedure	2.012	(g) Representation	2.064
	(d) Design representation	2.014	(h) Limitation period	2.065
	(e) Articles protected	2.015	(i) Criminal liability	2.066
	(f) Grace period	2.016	(j) Unauthorised threats of infringement	2.067
	(g) Geographic scope	2.017		
	(h) Ownership rights	2.018	9. Defences	2.068
	(i) Period of examination	2.019	(a) Non-infringement	2.068
	(j) Typical costs	2.020	(b) Additional grounds	2.070
	(k) Alternative application mechanisms	2.021	10. Relief	2.071
			(a) Remedies	2.071
	(l) Formalities	2.023	(b) Recovery of costs	2.074
	(m) Priority	2.024	11. Appeal	2.075
	(n) Deferred publication	2.026	(a) Border control measures	2.077
	3. Application Refusal	2.027	12. Other Related Rights	2.078
	(a) Grounds of objection	2.027	13. Hague Agreement – International Protection for Canadian Applicants	2.080
	(b) Response	2.028		
	(c) Appeal of refusal	2.029	(a) Application procedure	2.081
	4. Third-party Oppositions	2.031	(b) Fees	2.085
	5. Registration	2.032	(c) Examination	2.088
	(a) Effect of registration	2.032	(d) Registration	2.091
	(b) Term	2.036	(e) Publication	2.092
	(c) Renewal	2.038	14. Hague Agreement – Treatment of International Applications in Canada	2.095
	6. Registrable Transactions	2.040		
	(a) Assignments	2.040		
	(b) Licences	2.042	(a) Basic procedure	2.095
	(c) Security interests	2.046	(b) Examination	2.097
	7. Invalidity	2.047	(c) Unity of design	2.098

	(d) Novelty	2.100		registrations granted	2.124
	(e) Grant	2.101	C.	COMMENTS ON CANADIAN DESIGN LAW	
	(f) Term and renewal	2.102			2.125
	(g) Transfers	2.106	1.	Legislative Reform	2.125
B.	PRACTICAL ASPECTS OF CANADIAN			(a) Legislative history	2.125
	DESIGN LAW	2.108		(b) Novelty provision	2.128
1.	Effective Protection Strategies	2.108		(c) Application requirements	2.133
	(a) Background	2.108		(d) Applications with multiple design	
	(b) Protection under the Industrial			variations	2.134
	Design Act	2.111		(e) Amendments to applications	2.139
	(c) Copyright protection for designs			(f) Recent policy and practice	
		2.115		changes	2.143
	(d) Trademark protection for designs			(g) Fee increase	2.148
		2.119		(h) Other issues	2.149
2.	Statistics and Trends	2.124		(i) Final comment	2.154
	(a) Design applications filed and				

A. FUNDAMENTALS OF CANADIAN DESIGN LAW

1. Relevant Legislation and Administration

(a) Legislation

Registration of industrial designs is governed by the *Industrial Design Act*[1] and the *Industrial Design Regulations*[2] (the '*Act*' and '*Regulations*', respectively). However, in some cases, the *Copyright Act* and/or the *Trademarks Act* can also provide protection for designs. **2.001**

The *Copyright Act*[3] expressly excludes protection for industrial designs applied to an article having a utilitarian function that has been reproduced in more than 50 items. However, there are exceptions to this exclusion, including graphic or photographic representations applied to the face of an article, and designs that are representations of a real or fictitious being or event or place. **2.002**

The *Trademarks Act*[4] recognises that designs such as figurative elements and three-dimensional shapes of products and modes of packaging can identify the source of goods and services and can therefore also be registered as trademarks. However, the Trademarks Office will require an applicant to provide evidence that such designs have become distinctive as of the filing date of the application for registration. **2.003**

---

1 https://laws-lois.justice.gc.ca/eng/acts/I-9/.
2 https://laws-lois.justice.gc.ca/eng/regulations/SOR-2018-120/index.html.
3 https://laws-lois.justice.gc.ca/eng/acts/c-42/.
4 https://laws-lois.justice.gc.ca/eng/acts/t-13/.

2.004 Design owners should consider all forms of protection, and consider the scope and term of protection provided, as well as the costs. More details are provided in Part B.

(b) Administration

2.005 The primary design authority in Canada is the Industrial Design Office, which is a part of the Trademarks and Industrial Design Branch of the Canadian Intellectual Property Office ('CIPO').[5]

2. Protecting a Design

(a) Subject matter

2.006 An application to register a design under the *Act* must relate to features of shape, configuration, pattern or ornament in a finished article, or a combination of those features, that appeal to and are judged solely by the eye.[6]

2.007 Colour may be claimed as a feature of a design provided that the accompanying drawings or photographs are in colour. Computer generated icons, including animated icons, may also qualify for design protection.[7]

2.008 A single application can cover two or more variants of a design, provided that all of the included variants do not differ substantially from one another. A single application can also relate to designs for a set of articles ordinarily used or sold together to which the same design or variants thereof have been applied.

2.009 Designs that consist only of features that are dictated solely by a utilitarian function of the finished article cannot be registered, nor can designs that are contrary to public morality or order.

2.010 A design must be novel to be registrable. An application to register a design must be filed, or have a Convention priority date, earlier than any third-party public disclosure of the design or a design not differing substantially from it, applied to the same article or an analogous article, anywhere in the world, or in a Canadian design application having an earlier filing date or priority date.[8] As

---

5   https://ised-isde.canada.ca/site/canadian-intellectual-property-office/en/trademarks/trademarks-opposition-board/correspondence-procedures.
6   *Act*, s 2.
7   https://ised-isde.canada.ca/site/canadian-intellectual-property-office/en/industrial-design-office-practice-changes-fact-sheet.
8   *Act*, s 8.2.

noted below, there is a one-year grace period for disclosures by the applicant and related parties, and as also noted below, a Canadian design application can claim priority to a foreign application under the Paris Convention.

(b) Required information

An application to register a design under the *Act* requires the name and contact information for the applicant as well as one or more drawings and/or photographs that fully disclose the design. To complete the application, the applicant must provide its full postal address, the title of the design (being the name of the finished article), the name and address of its agent (if applicable), optional descriptive or limitation statements (if applicable), a Convention priority claim (if applicable), an indication of divisional status (if applicable) and payment of the filing fee. **2.011**

(c) Application procedure

An application for registration of an industrial design can be filed either in writing by mail or by fax, or electronically using CIPO's electronic filing interface. **2.012**

Industrial design protection may also be pursued in Canada through the Hague System. A Hague application designating Canada must comply with certain provisions of Canadian national law. For example, a Canadian divisional application resulting from a Hague application is treated as a national application. **2.013**

(d) Design representation

A design application requires a representation of the design in the form of one or more photographs, drawings, or other reproductions that include at least one view that shows the finished article to which the design is applied in isolation. **2.014**

(e) Articles protected

An application to register a design under the *Act* must include a title, which is essentially the name of the finished article to which the design relates. A design cannot be registered in the abstract, and subject matter in Locarno Class 32 (graphic symbols and logos, surface patterns, ornamentation) is generally not acceptable in Canada. **2.015**

(f) Grace period

A design application must be filed, or have a Convention priority date, earlier than any third-party public disclosure of the design anywhere in the world, or **2.016** in a Canadian design application having an earlier filing date or priority date. The application must also be filed in Canada, or have a Convention priority date, within one year of the first publication of the same design, or a design not differing substantially from it, applied to the same article or an analogous article anywhere in the world, by the applicant, or a predecessor, or a person who obtained knowledge of the design from the applicant or a predecessor.

(g) Geographic scope

2.017 The *Act* is federal legislation and applies throughout Canada.

(h) Ownership rights

2.018 An application to register a design can be filed only by the 'proprietor' of the design. The author, i.e. the creator(s), is the first proprietor unless the author was paid by another party to make the design (e.g. an employer), in which case the other party is the first proprietor. The rights in the design may be assigned to a subsequent proprietor, either before or after filing an application. An applicant should ensure that it can demonstrate that it is the proprietor and that it can identify the author(s) of the design and any earlier proprietor(s), and has appropriate assignments to establish its chain of title.

(i) Period of examination

2.019 Canadian design applications are typically examined within about 21 months to two years. If the examiner raises no objections, the application will issue to registration soon thereafter. It is possible to request advanced examination upon payment of a fee of about $500 CAD. If objections are raised, prosecution of the application will be extended.

(j) Typical costs

2.020 Obtaining a Canadian industrial design registration typically costs in the order of $2,500 to $4,000 CAD, depending on whether objections are raised by the examiner and, if so, the nature of the objections. The government fee for filing an application in 2023 is $430.30 CAD, but as of 2024 will be $567.00 CAD. An extra fee is charged for multiple drawings: as of 2023, the extra fee is $10.75 CAD per each sheet of drawings over ten; as of 2024, the extra fee is $14.00 CAD per each drawing over ten. The government fee for maintaining a registration in effect beyond five years costs $376.50 CAD as of 2023; this will increase to $496.00 CAD in 2024.

(k) Alternative application mechanisms

2.021 A Canadian national design application can be filed in paper form with the Industrial Design Office. However, it has become an efficient alternative to file Canadian design applications electronically using CIPO's electronic filing interface.

2.022 It is also possible to obtain industrial design protection in Canada under the Hague System by filing an international application designating Canada with World Intellectual Property Organization's ('WIPO') International Bureau.

(l) Formalities

2.023 No Power of Attorney is needed.

(m) Priority

2.024 A Canadian design application can include a claim to Convention priority based on a foreign application for the same design. The request for priority must be made while the Canadian application is pending and within the six-month priority period. A request for priority may be included in the application or in a separate document and must set out the foreign filing date and the name of the foreign country or office where the priority application was filed. (Although it is not mandatory, it is common to include the foreign application number as well.) While a priority request can be corrected during the pendency of the application, the priority date cannot be changed after the six-month priority deadline. It is generally not necessary to file a copy of the priority application unless requested by CIPO.

2.025 Prior to a legislative change that came into effect on November 5, 2018, Convention priority had little practical effect because the one-year grace period was measured to the actual Canadian filing date. However, now the one-year grace period is measured to the priority date, which can effectively extend the permissible period of prior publication for the applicant by up to 18 months.

(n) Deferred publication

2.026 Pending Canadian design applications are not made available to the public until 30 months after the filing date or the earliest priority date, or when the application issues to registration. An applicant may request delay of registration up to 30 months after the filing date or the earliest priority date. Such a request requires payment of a government fee of approximately $100 CAD. The applicant may subsequently withdraw the request for delay of registration.

3. Application Refusal

(a) Grounds of objection

2.027 A Canadian industrial design application is examined for both formal and substantive compliance with the *Act* and *Regulations*. Examiners can raise objections based on a number of grounds including: lack of novelty; unregistrable subject matter; multiple designs that do not qualify as variants or designs for sets; insufficient quality of the drawings and/or photographs; and inconsistencies in the views of the drawings and/or photographs.

(b) Response

2.028 Objections raised in examiner's reports can be addressed either by written arguments that refute the objection, or amendments that address and overcome the objection. It should be noted, however, that applications may not be amended to substantially change the design, including changing the name of the finished article to one that is substantially different.

(c) Appeal of refusal

2.029 CIPO recently changed the examination refusal and review process. If objections raised in an examiner's report are not overcome, CIPO will issue a Final Examination Report. Thereafter, if an applicant's response is insufficient to overcome all the examiner's objections, the file will automatically be transferred for review by a 'subject-matter expert' from the policy and legislation group of the Trademarks and Industrial Designs Branch. Unlike the previous appeals procedure, an applicant is not able to request an oral hearing.

2.030 A final refusal by the Industrial Design Office can be appealed to the Federal Court.

4. Third-party Oppositions

2.031 The *Act* and *Regulations* do not provide for third-party oppositions.

5. Registration

(a) Effect of registration

2.032 Upon approval by the Office, a Canadian design application issues to registration. The Office sends the proprietor a Notice of Industrial Design Registration that details the relevant information and includes copies of the design drawings and/or photographs.

When a Hague application is determined to be registrable in Canada, CIPO will send a statement of grant of protection in respect of the design to the International Bureau of WIPO.   **2.033**

The proprietor of an issued design registration has the exclusive right to make, sell, and import an article in respect of which the design is registered and to which the design, or a design not different substantially from it, has been applied.[9] In considering whether differences are substantial, the extent to which the registered design differs from any previously published design may be taken into account.[10]   **2.034**

The exclusive rights of a proprietor of a registered industrial design commence on the date of issuance of the registration.   **2.035**

(b) Term

A Canadian design registration has a term of ten years after the issuance of the registration or 15 years from the application filing date, whichever is later, subject to renewal as of the fifth anniversary.[11]   **2.036**

A Canadian Hague registration has a term of ten years from the date of issuance or 15 years from the international registration date, whichever is later, subject to renewal of the international registration in respect of Canada on the fifth and tenth anniversary.[12]   **2.037**

(c) Renewal

To maintain the exclusive right, the owner must pay a renewal fee within five years of the registration date.[13] There is a six-month grace period beyond the five years with payment of an additional late fee.[14]   **2.038**

In the case of a Hague registration, the international registration is valid for an initial period of five years from the international registration date and can be renewed for two additional five-year terms. Before expiry of the first five-year term, the renewal fee in respect of Canada must be paid to the International Bureau of WIPO. (Note that although there is a fee due at the fifth anniversary, there is no fee due at the tenth anniversary. Also note that the renewal   **2.039**

---

9   *Act*, s 11(1)(a).
10   *Act*, s 11(2).
11   *Act*, s 10(1).
12   *Regulations*, s 47(1) and (2).
13   *Regulations*, s 33(2).
14   *Regulations*, s 33(3).

of the international registration in respect of Canada on the fifth anniversary must be effected even if the Canadian Hague application has not yet issued to registration.)

6. Registrable Transactions

(a) Assignments

2.040 The Canadian rights in an industrial design, whether already registered or not yet registered, are transferable. The rights in a design may be transferred in whole or in part, for example, with geographic or market limitations. Mergers involving the applicant or registrant are generally treated as a transfer.

2.041 A transfer in respect of a registered design or design that is the subject of a pending application can be registered in the Industrial Design Office. CIPO will register a transfer upon request and with payment of a fee. Evidence of the transfer (e.g. a copy of the written assignment agreement) is required when the request is filed by the transferee, but is generally not required when filed by the transferor. It is recommended that transfers of design rights be registered with CIPO promptly, because a transfer of a registered design that has not been registered is void against a subsequent transferee if the transfer to the subsequent transferee has already been registered.

(b) Licences

2.042 The parties to an industrial design licence are generally free to negotiate the terms of the licence. Licence agreements can be negotiated with various terms and conditions, including exclusive and non-exclusive licences, and with time limits and restrictions on territory. There is no requirement for quality control provisions in the term of a Canadian industrial design licence.

2.043 The *Act* and *Regulations* do not expressly address recordal of licences concerning a registered Canadian design or a design that is the subject of a Canadian design application. However, it is CIPO's practice to record such licences and make those records available to the public upon publication.

2.044 An exclusive licensee of a registered design can bring an infringement action, but the proprietor must be made a party to the action.

2.045 Canadian industrial designs are not subject to compulsory licensing.

(c) Security interests

As with licences, the *Act* and *Regulations* do not provide for the recordal of security interests, but a person may provide CIPO with copies of such documents that relates to a registration or application.

2.046

7. Invalidity

(a) Grounds

Grounds for invalidity of a registration include: the design lacks novelty (e.g. the design was published more than 12 months before the application date); improper subject matter (e.g. the design consists only of features that are dictated solely by a utilitarian function of the finished article); the entity named as the proprietor was not in fact or in law the proprietor; and the declaration accompanying the application was false.

2.047

(b) Procedure

Invalidation of a registration can be sought through an action or application to the Federal Court. The Federal Court has exclusive jurisdiction to hear and determine proceedings concerning Hague registrations. Appeals can be brought to the Federal Court of Appeal without leave, and to the Supreme Court of Canada with leave.

2.048

Standing is required to commence invalidation proceedings, with the *Act* requiring a 'person aggrieved' to institute proceedings, or an 'interested person' in the case of a Hague registration.[15]

2.049

In invalidation proceedings, the burden of proof is on the party seeking expungement, but once an allegation of invalidity is raised and supported by some evidence, the registrant must meet each ground of invalidity. For example, if it is alleged that the design was disclosed more than 12 months before the application date, and there is evidence of a disclosure, the registrant could show that the circumstances of the disclosure gave rise to duty of confidence and therefore the disclosure did not make the design available to the public.

2.050

---

15   *Act*, s 22(1) and *Regulations*, s 50(4).

8. Design Enforcement

(a) Jurisdiction

2.051 The Federal Court of Canada has concurrent jurisdiction with provincial/territorial superior courts to hear intellectual property disputes. While provincial courts have concurrent jurisdiction for enforcement, the country-wide jurisdiction of the Federal Court gives it the ability to grant relief throughout Canada in a single proceeding, in addition to having the exclusive jurisdiction to expunge invalid registrations.

(b) Infringement

2.052 In defining the exclusive right, the *Act* provides that no person may, without the licence of the proprietor of the design, make, import for the purpose of trade or business, or sell, rent, or offer or expose for sale or rent, any article in respect of which the design is registered and to which the design or a design not differing substantially therefrom has been applied.

2.053 The question as to whether an alleged infringing article differs substantially from a registered design requires applying a four-part analysis from the perspective of an 'informed consumer', with the steps of: (i) examining the prior art and the extent to which the registered design differs from any previously published designs; (ii) assessing the design for any utilitarian function, or any method or principle of manufacture or construction (as such features of the design are not protectable under the *Act*); (iii) examining the design itself to determine the scope of protection based on the figures and accompanying description in the registration; and (iv) conducting a comparative analysis of the registered design and alleged infringing article, taking the first three factors into account.[16] The closer the prior art is to the registered design, the narrower will be the protection that is afforded to the design. The further the prior art is from the registered design, the broader will the protection that is afforded to the design.

2.054 The comparison between the design of an allegedly infringing article and the registered design must consider the designs in their entirety, though the relevant designs may relate to only portions of the articles. The same holds true when comparing any prior art designs with the registered design.

---

16 See *Crocs Canada, Inc v. Double Diamond Distribution Ltd*, 2022 FC 1443.

(c) Procedure

2.055 The key pre-trial procedural stages are pleadings, discovery, expert reports, and trial. It typically takes two years or more to reach trial from commencement of the proceedings.

2.056 In actions, the rules of the Federal Court and the provincial/territorial superior courts provide the right of pre-trial discovery of relevant documents and materials, as well as the right to a pre-trial examination of a representative of each party.

2.057 At the trial of an action, evidence is typically presented, and witnesses are cross-examined, in Court, orally. In an application, evidence is submitted in the form of written affidavit, with cross-examination out of Court. In both types of proceeding, submissions are typically made both in writing and orally.

2.058 Issues of validity and infringement are heard in the same proceeding.

(d) Injunctive relief

2.059 Preliminary (interlocutory) injunctions are available only if the moving party shows: (i) there is a serious issue to be tried; (ii) they would suffer irreparable harm pending the decision on the merits; and (iii) the balance of convenience favours an injunction. This test can be difficult to satisfy since clear and non-speculative evidence of irreparable harm is required. Therefore, preliminary (interlocutory) injunctions are relatively uncommon in intellectual property disputes in Canada. However, final injunctions are typically available after the case has been decided on the merits, unless there are extenuating circumstances.

(e) Stays

2.060 Stays are available at the discretion of the court if there is an invalidity claim in another court or jurisdiction if it would be in interests of justice. A party may also bring a motion to stay a proceeding on the basis of *forum non conveniens*. The party seeking the stay must demonstrate that continuance of the proceeding would cause prejudice or injustice to that party and would not cause an injustice to the other party or parties to the proceeding.

(f) Expedited proceedings

2.061 Rules of court allow for applications (paper trial) where facts can be established with affidavit evidence alone. Applications tend to be faster and less costly than full actions with discovery and trials with live witnesses, but the moving party has to do more work up front to initiate the proceeding. Decisions are generally reached within a year.

2.062 Another option is a summary trial, which can be decided based on a paper record, potentially supplemented with some live witnesses, which are being used increasingly in Canada to decide even technical issues in intellectual property disputes, particularly if there is a discrete issue dispositive of the case. Timing of a summary trial can also be within a year.

2.063 In addition, there are simplified actions on affidavit evidence available within the Federal Court where only monetary relief is sought less than $100,000 CAD, and provincial/territorial small claims courts can be an option to recover damages (no injunction) within certain claim limits (e.g. $35,000 CAD in Ontario).

(g) Representation

2.064 Lawyers of any provincial or territorial jurisdiction in Canada may represent parties at the Federal Court. There are some restrictions for lawyers of one province/territory to practice in another province/territory.

(h) Limitation period

2.065 Under the *Act*, there is a limitation period pursuant to which no remedy is available for an act of infringement committed more than three years before commencement of the court action for infringement.[17]

(i) Criminal liability

2.066 There are no criminal liabilities for design infringement.

(j) Unauthorised threats of infringement

2.067 A false or misleading statement tending to discredit the business, goods or services of a competitor can give rise to claim of trade libel under the *Trademarks Act*. There can also be liability for the tort of intentional interference with economic relations.

---

17   *Act*, s 18.

9. Defences

(a) Non-infringement

2.068 It is a defence to infringement if it can be shown that the defendant did not engage in at least one of the activities defining the exclusive right. Furthermore, a design registration must relate to a specific finished article, and application of the same features to other articles will not be an infringement of the registered design. Moreover, the defendant's article must be compared to the registered design to determine if it differs substantially therefrom.

2.069 Canada does not have any specific considerations for design protection of spare parts. However, the *Act* contemplates kits consisting of a complete or substantially complete number of parts that can be assembled to construct a finished article. Carrying out any of the actions in relation to the kit that would constitute an infringement if done in relation to an article assembled from the kit is an infringement.

(b) Additional grounds

2.070 The *Act* provides a limited defence for an innocent infringer that was not aware that a design was registered, in which case only injunctive relief shall be awarded, but the defence is not available if the registered articles are marked. Proper marking consists of the capital letter 'D' in a circle and the name, or abbreviation of the name, of the proprietor, placed on the registered articles distributed in Canada or the associated labels/packaging.

10. Relief

(a) Remedies

2.071 If infringement is found, the remedies that are available are similar to that of other intellectual property regimes and include damages, accounting of profits, injunctive relief, delivery up or destruction, and punitive damages.

2.072 Damages are assessed based on the plaintiff's lost profits, if the plaintiff lost sales, or reasonable royalty, to the extent the plaintiff did not lose sales. Damages are awarded to restore the plaintiff to the position they would have been in 'but for' the infringement. An accounting of profits is assessed based on all of the defendant's profits (revenues less allowable expenses) caused, directly and indirectly, by the infringement. Punitive damages are available if the conduct of the defendant was reprehensible and deserving of censure by the court.

2.073 All issues are usually raised in one proceeding, but the parties may request and the court may choose to bifurcate issues relating to liability from issues relating to the quantum of monetary relief.

(b) Recovery of costs

2.074 Costs follow the event and are usually recoverable from the losing party, at the discretion of the court. The amount of the costs can be determined either by a tariff in the court's rules, or on a lump sum basis at the discretion of the court. Where sophisticated parties are involved, the lump sum that can be recovered by the winning party may be 25–50 per cent of legal fees, plus disbursements.

11. Appeal

2.075 The right of appeal from a first instance judgment is subject to the review standards of palpable and overriding error for questions of fact or questions of mixed fact/law, and correctness on points of law.

2.076 Special circumstances are required before new evidence will be admitted at the appeal stage. The new evidence must not have been discoverable, with due diligence, prior to the first hearing, and the new evidence must be material.

(a) Border control measures

2.077 The Canada Border Services Agency's Request for Assistance programme can be used to identify and detain shipments suspected of containing counterfeit trademark goods or pirated copyright goods, but industrial design registrations are not included in the programme.

12. Other Related Rights

2.078 In certain cases, as noted above, a design may qualify for overlapping protection under Canadian copyright or trademark laws, which may not require registration.

2.079 Canada does not recognise unregistered design rights.

13. Hague Agreement – International Protection for Canadian Applicants

2.080 Canada joined the Hague Agreement (Geneva '1999' *Act*) effective as of Nov. 5, 2018. Under this system, Canadians can file a single international application to pursue industrial design protection in any of the member countries (96 countries at the time of writing). As well, Canada can be designated in an international application to pursue protection of the subject matter of the international application in Canada.

(a) Application procedure

2.081 The process for seeking protection via the Hague system begins by preparing and filing an Application for International Registration of a Design. The international application must be presented in the prescribed form. This requirement can be met by using WIPO's 'eHague' online filing system, which is recommended, as this tool proceeds step-by-step through the application process, requesting input or upload of the relevant information at each step. Alternatively, the official Form DM/1 (available as a pdf on WIPO's website) can be used.

2.082 The international application must be filed directly with WIPO. Canada has formally notified WIPO that CIPO will not serve as an office of indirect filing, so international applications from Canada cannot be filed with CIPO.

2.083 The international application can claim convention priority to an earlier application filed in a contracting party to the Paris Convention, provided the earlier application was filed not more than six months prior to the international application.

2.084 The content of the international application includes some familiar subject matter as well as some additional requirements when compared to a national Canadian industrial design application. Details of these requirements are set out in the relevant legislation (e.g. Chapter 2 of the 'Common Regulations' under the Hague Agreement), as well as the 'Administrative Instructions for the Application of the Hague Agreement'. Some notable points include the following:

- Multiple Designs: multiple designs may be included in a single international application, up to a maximum of 100, provided they belong to the same Locarno class. The designs may lead to refusals by member countries (including Canada) that have local unity requirements; this is discussed in greater detail below.
- Design Count: each distinct set of figures is counted as a distinct design. So, for example, regardless whether two sets of figures are considered by the Applicant to pertain to a single design (e.g. differing only in certain features shown in solid vs. broken line), the two sets of figures are counted as two separate 'designs'.

- Figure Labels: instead of labelling the figures as 'Fig.1', 'Fig. 2', etc., text such as 'Fig.' or 'Figure' should be omitted, and the numbering should follow the format of using two numerals separated by a decimal point, with the numeral in front of the decimal point identifying a specific set of figures (specific design) and the numeral after the decimal portion identifying each unique view within the set (e.g. 1.1, 1.2, 1.3, etc. for the first design, 2.1, 2.2, 2.3, etc. for the second design, and so on). Text indicated the view (e.g. 'Perspective', 'Front', 'Right', etc.) may be included with the figure numbering.
- Disclaimed Portions: the official form provides a description field for each design to identify disclaimed subject matter (e.g. 'The broken lines in the reproductions represent portions that form no part of the design'). An explanation of the omission of certain views (e.g. as symmetrical to another shown view) and a brief description of characteristic features of the design can also be included in this field.
- Designation: the Applicant must designate the countries (contacting parties) where protection of the design is desired.
- Applicant Email Address: the international application must include an email address for the Applicant; this needs to be distinct from, and in addition to, an email address for the Applicant's representative (if Applicant has appointed a representative).
- Product Indication/Class: the international application must provide, for each 'design', a 'Product Indication' that identifies the product which constitutes the design or in relation to which the design is to be used. The Locarno class to which each design belongs must also be identified.
- Designation-dependent Content: depending on which jurisdictions have been designated, the international application may need to include additional content. For example, the United States requires that the international application include a claim, as required to obtain a filing date in a local US design patent application. Contracting parties have an obligation to bring such requirements to the attention of WIPO by way of a formal declaration, and these requirements are expressly accommodated in the official filing form.

(b) Fees

2.085 All fees associated with an international application are charged in Swiss Francs (CHF). The fees for filing the application (with current amounts) include the following:

- Basic fee: 397 CHF for the first design; plus 19 CHF for each additional design;

- Publication fee: 17 CHF per view, plus if filing by paper, 150 CHF per page;
- Designation fee: depends on which countries are chosen, e.g. GB fee is 42 CHF for first design plus 2 CHF for each additional design; Canada is 303 CHF per design; Japan is 682 CHF per design.

2.086 In addition, there is an Excess length description fee of 2 CHF /word in the description section exceeding 100 words.

2.087 Regarding timing, the fees are considered due at the time of filing, but filing with no payment or insufficient payment of fees does not affect the filing date. If payment has not been received by the time the application is examined, then the first examination report will include a requirement for payment.

(c) Examination

2.088 The international application will be picked up by an Examiner at WIPO and reviewed for compliance with formalities. If there are any defects, the Examiner will issue a report in the form of an 'invitation to correct irregularities'. This can be expected soon after the filing date, often within two weeks. The invitation will set a three-month due date to make the necessary corrections.

2.089 Most irregularities will not affect the filing date. However, the filing date will be postponed if any of the follow requirements are not met:

- application filed in one of the prescribed languages (English, French, Spanish);
- includes an indication (express or implied) that registration under Hague is sought;
- includes identification of the applicant;
- includes sufficient information allowing the applicant or representative, if any, to be contacted;
- includes a reproduction (drawing) of each design for which protection is sought;
- includes the designation of at least one contracting party.

2.090 If the response fails to remedy the identified deficiencies, then the application may be considered abandoned. In some cases, particularly if the response raises new issues, WIPO can issue another invitation to correct defects, setting a new three-month period within which a response is due.

(d) Registration

2.091 Once the application complies with all requirements, WIPO will issue an International Registration Certificate. The certificate will include a copy of the application (including all the drawings) as well as the usual bibliographic information. The date of international registration will generally be same as the filing date of the application, even in cases where changes in response to invitations to correct irregularities were submitted well after the filing date.

(e) Publication

2.092 The international registration will be published in the International Designs Bulletin, normally 12 months after the international registration date or as soon as possible thereafter. It is possible to request earlier publication, for example, immediately upon registration. It is also possible to defer publication upon request, to 30 months after the earlier of the filing date or the priority date.

2.093 Publication in the Bulletin serves as notice to the designated countries that the application is ready to be examined for compliance with local requirements. If local requirements are not satisfied, a notice of refusal must be sent within a specified time period of six months or 12 months, depending on the country. The notice of refusal will be sent by the local office to WIPO, published in the International Designs Bulletin, and a copy shall be transmitted to the holder. The holder will then be given the same opportunities to respond to the rejection as would be the case for rejections in locally filed applications.

2.094 If the registration complies, or is amended to comply, with local requirements, then the local office will issue a Statement of Grant of Protection to WIPO, which will be published in the Bulletin, and a copy will be sent to the holder.

14. Hague Agreement – Treatment of International Applications in Canada

(a) Basic procedure

2.095 As mentioned above, publication of the international registration certificate in the Bulletin triggers the start of the time period within which the industrial designs branch of CIPO must issue a notice of refusal if it intends to oppose effectiveness of the international registration in Canada. That time period in Canada is 12 months. If a notice of refusal is not sent within this time period, the design will be deemed to be registered in Canada, with effect from the day after the expiry of the 12-month period.

The international registration is deemed to be a 'Hague application' under **2.096**
Canadian industrial design law, with an effective filing date equal to the international registration date. CIPO will assign the Hague application a Canadian design application number, and the application will be added to the Canadian Industrial Designs Database. If the international registration contains more than one design, then CIPO will assign a distinct Canadian design application number to each design.

(b) Examination

If upon examination CIPO determines that the Hague application fails to **2.097**
comply with Canadian requirements, CIPO will send a notice of refusal to WIPO and will also send a courtesy copy to the holder or representative, if any. The notice of refusal will have the same effect as an examination report issued in local applications, and will set a three-month due date for reply. The notice of refusal must set out the grounds on which the refusal is based. There are some limitations on the objections that can be raised. For example, CIPO cannot raise formality objections in a refusal, since CIPO is deemed to have acknowledged compliance with formalities by virtue of the examination conducted by WIPO. However, CIPO could raise objections based on other grounds, notably including unity of design and novelty.

(c) Unity of design

Even though the Hague systems permits inclusion of up to 100 designs in **2.098**
a single application, Canadian design law requires that an application be limited to one design applied to a single finished article or set. The one design can include variants, which is defined to mean 'designs applied to the same article or set and not differing substantially from one another'. Guidelines provided by CIPO further explain that 'Generally, to be accepted as variants, the designs must be very similar and possess the described features without substantial variation.'

The Hague system permits contracting parties to refuse the effects of the international registration, pending compliance with the requirement of unity of **2.099**
design, provided the contracting party has given notice to that effect to WIPO via formal declaration. CIPO has not submitted such a declaration to WIPO, and so it cannot issue refusals based on unity requirements. Instead, CIPO ensures compliance with Canadian unity of design requirements by separating each of the designs in an international registration into separate Canadian applications, each bearing a unique Canadian serial number. These are not

considered 'divisional' cases but are treated as a bundle of rights corresponding to the protection sought in the international registration.

(d) Novelty

2.100 CIPO will also conduct a substantive examination to assess novelty of the design presented in the international registration. This involves CIPO making a determination of the features of the design, and comparing the design to the relevant prior art. How much a design needs to differ from the prior art in order to be considered novel is fact-dependent and determined on a case-by-case basis.

(e) Grant

2.101 Once CIPO is satisfied that the Hague application complies with Canadian requirements, it will issue a Notice of Grant of Protection to WIPO. The Statement of Grant of Protection, when issued by CIPO for an international application containing multiple designs, will list all of the Canadian registration numbers corresponding to the designs of the international application. It will also update the Canadian database to indicate the applications have been registered in Canada, and provide the Canadian registration date.

(f) Term and renewal

2.102 The initial term for an international registration is five years from the registration date. This term must be renewable for a minimum of two additional five-year periods, so that a minimum duration of protection of 15 years is made available. Some contracting parties provide longer terms, for example Europe provides a term of protection up to 25 years.

2.103 Maintenance fees for international applications and local (national) rights granted therefrom are payable directly to WIPO. WIPO will send a notice to the holder of the design and the representative, if any, six months before the expiry of the current term. The total fee due for renewal includes:

- Basic renewal fee: 200 CHF, plus 17 CHF for each design in excess of the first design.
- Designation renewal fee: either standard renewal fee set by WIPO, or Individual renewal designation fee for those countries that have submitted an individual fee declaration.

2.104 Canada has made such declaration, and the designation renewal fee for renewing a design that designates Canada is currently set at 265 CHF for the first renewal, and 0 CHF for subsequent renewals. More particularly, the designation renewal fee due at the fifth anniversary of the registration date is considered to cover the first designation renewal (years five–ten) as well as the second designation renewal (years ten–15). Even though no second designation fee is due, the applicant must nevertheless make a second renewal by the tenth anniversary of the registration date to maintain the registration for years ten–15 of the term.

It is notable that national design protection based on an international registration can be renewed fully or partially. For example, renewal can be limited to only some of the designated contracting parties, and renewal can be limited to only some of the designs, if more than one design is included in the registration. **2.105**

(g) Transfers

Transfers of ownership of any international registrations or local protection granted therefrom must be recorded through WIPO. The Hague system does not distinguish between underlying reasons for a transfer, such as assignment, bankruptcy, or change of name, etc., nor does it investigate the validity of any assertion of a change in ownership. Recordal of a transfer is effective to change the 'holder' of record from the previous owner to the new owner. **2.106**

To be entitled to be recorded as holder, the new owner (transferee) must meet the requirements for entitlement to engage the Hague system, i.e. by virtue of connection with a contracting party. The requests for recording the transfer are expected to be presented and signed by the current holder. Requests presented by the new owner will be accepted if they are signed by current holder, or if they are signed by the new owner and supported by documentation establishing that the new owner is the successor in title to the holder. **2.107**

B. PRACTICAL ASPECTS OF CANADIAN DESIGN LAW

1. Effective Protection Strategies

(a) Background

In the context of Canadian intellectual property law, the terms 'design' and 'industrial design' refer to visual features that give a manufactured article a specific appearance. The specific features mentioned in the statutory definition of a design are shape, configuration, pattern and ornament. Most manufactured goods display at least some design features, and in many fields, designs play a critical role in whether a product is commercially successful or not. Examples include clothing and fashion accessories, automobiles, home furnishings and **2.108** housewares, as well as many forms of packaging, such as perfume bottles. Designs derive their value from making manufactured articles appear attractive or distinctive.

2.109 Designs are fundamentally visual works of art, and one might therefore expect industrial designers to be entitled to claim copyright protection for their creations just as other artists can. However, for certain designs applied to utilitarian articles, copyright provides little or no protection. Implicitly, the legislative rationale is that the extensive term of copyright would undesirably interfere with competition in the development and supply of utilitarian products. Therefore, an alternative less enduring form of legal protection has been provided for designs in the *Industrial Design Act*.

2.110 In many cases protection for industrial designs may nonetheless still be found through copyright. In some situations, moreover, protection for designs can also be found within the law of trademarks. It is therefore important to understand the advantages and limitations of all forms of design protection.

(b) Protection under the Industrial Design Act

2.111 As set out in detail in Part A, specific legal protection for designs in Canada is provided in the *Industrial Design Act* and the *Industrial Design Regulations*. The statute establishes a registration system that includes a substantive examination of design applications. An application to register a design must be filed within one year of its first publication anywhere in the world. The design must be novel to be registrable, and it must be original and sufficiently different from previous designs. Originality must be assessed from the perspective of the informed consumer who is familiar with the relevant market. Registration gives the design owner the exclusive right to use the design during the term of the registration.

2.112 Most other countries also provide a special form of legal protection for industrial designs, though in many cases the term of protection is significantly longer. In many countries, the protection is obtained through a registration scheme similar to that found in Canada, either with or without substantive examination.

2.113 The protection provided by registration under the *Industrial Design Act* is an exclusive right or monopoly, not merely the right to prevent copying. Thus, even where copyright exists, obtaining a design registration may provide a broader effective scope of protection than would be provided by copyright alone.

While copyright and trademark law both have significant roles to play in the protection of some types of designs in Canada, industrial design registrations are undoubtedly the most important means of protecting designs for mass produced utilitarian objects.

2.114

(c) Copyright protection for designs

Although industrial designs may involve structural considerations derived from an article's utilitarian function, designs may nonetheless qualify for copyright protection as artistic works. To the extent that copyright is available, it provides a number of advantages over other forms of legal protection for designs. In particular, copyright protection arises automatically when an original work is created, and the term of protection in most cases lasts throughout the life of the author, plus an additional 50 years (soon to be extended to 70 years). Moreover, a work may qualify for copyright protection even if it is not novel or significantly different from earlier works, as long as it was not itself copied.

2.115

Therefore, it is usually desirable to rely on copyright to protect industrial designs wherever possible, even if protection is also applied for under the *Industrial Design Act*. However, copyright is not always available to protect designs.

2.116

In Canada, the limitations in using copyright to protect designs depend on when the design was created. For designs created prior to a statutory amendment that came into effect in 1988, copyright in industrial designs is not recognised at all, except for designs that are not used or intended to be used as models or patterns to be multiplied by an industrial process; a design is deemed to be used as a model or pattern to be multiplied by an industrial process if the design is applied to wallpaper, carpeting, textiles or lace, or if it is reproduced or intended to be reproduced in more than 50 articles.

2.117

For designs created after the 1988 amendment, there is no general denial of copyright in any original industrial design. However, copyright may become unenforceable once more than 50 articles embodying the design have been made if the design is applied to articles that have a utilitarian function. For such designs, copyright remains enforceable only where the design is one of certain specified types, such as representations of a real or fictitious being, place or event, and graphic or photographic matter applied to the face of the article. For designs applied to non-utilitarian articles, that is, articles that merely serve as a substrate for artistic or literary matter, copyright also continues to be enforceable regardless of the number of articles made.

2.118

(d) Trademark protection for designs

2.119 Designs are applied to articles to give them a specific appearance and thereby make them visually distinct. The ability to distinguish one trader's goods from those of others is the essential role of a trademark. Accordingly, trademark law also comes into play in protecting industrial designs.

2.120 Trademark protection for designs has the advantage of potentially lasting indefinitely. Moreover, trademark rights do not depend on having a chain of title extending back to the design creator. However, they are dependent on establishing that the public associates the design with a single source.

2.121 The main problem with relying on trademark law to protect product shapes is that it generally requires a significant amount of time and marketing expense before the shape of a product or its packaging becomes recognised by the public as distinguishing origin and is associated with a single source. How long it may take depends on many factors, including how distinctive the product shape is.

2.122 In Canada and in certain other countries, trademark rights are recognised in unregistered trademarks as well as registered trademarks. Registration though, provides a number of advantages and product shapes can be registered as trademarks in both Canada and the US upon a showing of actual distinctiveness.

2.123 One strategy that has been recognised in trying to obtain both short- and long-term protection for product and package configurations is first to apply for and obtain protection under the *Industrial Design Act*, and later to apply for and obtain a registration under the *Trademarks Act* after the design has become distinctive.

2. Statistics and Trends

(a) Design applications filed and registrations granted

2.124 Set out in Tables 2.1 and 2.2 below are statistics for Canadian industrial design applications from 2018 to 2023, as provided by the Canadian Intellectual Property Office (CIPO). These include both national applications and Hague applications.

Table 2.1   Canadian industrial design applications filed

	2018 to 2019	2019 to 2020	2020 to 2021	2021 to 2022	2022 to 2023
Industrial design applications	6,139	7,408	8,161	9,067	8,895

Table 2.2   Canadian industrial design registrations granted

	2018 to 2019	2019 to 2020	2020 to 2021	2021 to 2022	2022 to 2023
Industrial design registration	5,542	5,343	5,095	6,700	9,307

C. COMMENTS ON CANADIAN DESIGN LAW

1.   Legislative Reform

(a) Legislative history

2.125 Canada's first statute dealing with industrial designs was passed in 1868. It was badly drafted, to the point that it received judicial criticism for being seriously in need of amendment. Nevertheless, it took the Canadian Parliament 120 years before it started to address some of the deficiencies in the legislation. In the late 1980s and early and mid-1990s, a series of revisions were introduced that helped fix some of the major problems with the *Industrial Design Act* and *Regulations*. However, many problems persisted until the coming into force of the current versions of the *Act* and *Regulations* on November 5, 2018.

2.126 Among other things, the current *Act* has a complete overhaul of the novelty requirements for registrable designs. The current *Act* also added a provision to address the anomalous lack of an automatic extension to address deadlines arising on a day when the Industrial Design Office is closed. Perhaps most significantly, the amendments that came into force in 2018 enabled Canada to accede to the Hague Agreement, which provides a system for filing international design applications designating any of over 90 member countries.

2.127 The changes set out in the current *Act* and *Regulations*, and the Industrial Design Office Practice Manual that was adopted at the same time, are generally seen as steps in the right direction. Nevertheless, there remain several troubling aspects that should be addressed by further legislative amendment.

(b) Novelty provision

2.128 The *Act* defines novelty based on no prior disclosure of 'the same design, or a design not differing substantially from it'.[18] It also indicates that such a design destroys novelty if it is applied to the same finished article or an 'analogous' finished article. Unfortunately, neither the *Act* nor the *Regulations* provide any objective criteria for assessing whether a previously disclosed design does or

---

18   *Act*, s 8.2.

does not 'differ substantially' from a design in an application, or whether a previous design was applied to an article that is 'analogous' to the article identified in the application.

2.129   Whereas section 11 of the *Act*, dealing with infringement, expressly indicates that 'in considering whether differences are substantial, the extent to which the registered design differs from any previously published design may be taken into account', the novelty definition has no such provision.

2.130   Interestingly, and some would say unfairly, whereas prior art designs applied to so-called 'analogous' articles can destroy novelty, the rights in a registered design do not extend to analogous articles. They are limited to the 'article in respect of which the design is registered'.

2.131   The novelty requirement of the *Act* also requires, in section 8.2(1)(c), that the same design or a design not differing substantially from it may not have been disclosed in an earlier filed Canadian design application. Section 31 of the *Regulations* adds the limitation that disclosure in an earlier Canadian design application does not destroy novelty if the earlier application was filed within 12 months by the same applicant or a predecessor in title.

2.132   This is intended to prevent so-called 'self-collision' by an applicant who files applications for similar designs on different dates. However, it also appears to allow an applicant to file two or more applications for the same design and potentially obtain multiple registrations that together would extend the term of protection beyond the maximum period contemplated by the *Act*.

(c)   Application requirements

2.133   Section 17 of the *Regulations* now establishes a presumption that 'an application is deemed to relate to *all of the features* of shape, configuration, pattern or ornament' shown in the representation of the design, as well as setting out exceptions to the presumption. However, assuming it is intended that the presumption and the exceptions will also apply to an issued registration, this should be made clearer, for example, the presumption could refer to 'the design contained in an application' instead of just 'an application'.

(d)   Applications with multiple design variations

2.134   One of the significant changes in CIPO's Industrial Design Office Practice Manual adopted in 2018 relates to the treatment of so-called 'variants'. A Canadian design application can include two or more designs, but only if they qualify as variants, meaning designs that do not differ 'substantially'.

Traditionally, the Canadian Design Office has interpreted this strictly – and somewhat arbitrarily.

2.135 One aspect of variants relates to multiple designs that differ from each other as to which portions of the article are included as defining the design.

2.136 In many other jurisdictions, it is common practice to protect a design with a varying scope by depicting multiple embodiments in which portions of the article are shown in different combinations of solid and stippled lines. However, historically this was not considered acceptable by the Canadian Design Office.

2.137 In an unexpected reversal of longstanding policy, the new Practice Manual presents an example of acceptable variants that includes two embodiments of a design with different portions shown in solid and stippled lines. This has the potential for providing much more flexibility to Canadian design applicants.

2.138 Unfortunately, similar to the test for novelty, a long-recognised problem remains that neither the *Act* nor the *Regulations* nor the Manual provide any objective criteria for assessing whether two designs differ 'substantially' for the purpose of qualifying as variants, which can be included in a single application. As noted above, whereas section 11 of the *Act*, dealing with infringement, expressly indicates that 'in considering whether differences are substantial, the extent to which the registered design differs from any previously published design may be taken into account', the definition of 'variants' has no similar provision.

(e) Amendments to applications

2.139 Section 25(2) of the *Regulations* preserves the long-recognised principle that an application can be amended before it has issued to registration, provided that the amendment does not 'substantially' alter the design. Unfortunately, the *Regulations* also preserve the problem of not having any objective standard for assessing whether an amendment 'substantially' changes the design.

2.140 This problem is similar to the problem mentioned above relating to novelty, and it is also found in the definition of 'variants'.

2.141 Another related problem exists in section 25(3) of the *Regulations* with respect to changing the name of the article to which a design application pertains to a 'substantially different article' if the application has been published.

2.142 Another problematic area is found in section 25(2)(b), which prohibits an application from being amended 'to add a representation of a design'. This limitation may prohibit an applicant from adding an additional view, or changing photographs to drawings or *vice versa, even when no matter would be added*. Both practices were previously permitted. Although CIPO's consultation document indicates that the intent of this provision may be only to prevent the addition of a representation that shows a different design or features, the text of section 14 of the *Regulations* does not appear to be consistent with this.

(f) Recent policy and practice changes

2.143 In another major departure from over a century of design practice in Canada, written descriptions are optional in design applications under the new regime. The *Regulations* now establish a presumption that 'an application is deemed to relate to all of the features of shape, configuration, pattern or ornament shown in the representation of the design', except where the representation includes features shown in stippled lines which will be presumed not to be part of the design. These presumptions can be overcome by an appropriate written statement.

2.144 The Practice Manual now provides that any written statement 'must clearly describe which features are claimed and must not create alternatives that may lead to ambiguity…'. Surprisingly, the Manual states that the following statement would not be acceptable: 'The design is the visual features of the entire article shown in the reproductions, whether those features are features of one of shape, configuration, ornament or pattern or are a combination of any of these features.'

2.145 Prohibiting such a statement is surprising because for many years the Office's previous Practice Manual indicated expressly that such a description statement was acceptable, based on the definition in the *Act* and a decision of the Patent Appeal Board in 1999.

2.146 The following additional changes provided in the current Manual offer greater flexibility than the previous policies and practices of the Canadian Design Office:

- photographs and drawings are acceptable together in the same application;
- more than one environmental view may be included, as long as there is at least one view showing the article in isolation;
- an article that opens and closes or extends and retracts can be shown in intermediate positions as well as fully open/extended and fully closed/

retracted positions, provided that the article is normally seen and used in all such positions;
- it is permissible to show electronic icons in isolation, that is, without any need for a display screen depicted in stippled lines;
- further guidance is provided with respect to the Office's relatively recent acceptance of computer-generated animated designs and colour as a design feature;
- the Office will also accept contrasting colour tones, and stippled or coloured boundary lines, and also partial blurring to distinguish design and non-design portions of an article, all of which can be particularly useful in dealing with CAD images. (Note though that the presumption in the *Regulations* mentioned above regarding stippled lines does not apply in respect of these drawing techniques.)

Interestingly, the Practice Manual addresses the drafting problem noted above that the *Regulations* prohibit an application from being amended 'to add a representation of a design'. A straightforward reading of this limitation would prevent an applicant from adding an additional view, or changing photographs to drawings or vice versa, even when no new matter would be added – in contrast to prior Office practice. However, notwithstanding the language of the *Regulations*, the Manual sets out expressly that: 'The addition of a photograph or reproduction of the design in the application is acceptable provided that it does not add new subject matter.' 2.147

(g) Fee increase

CIPO regularly raises the government fees associated with applying to register industrial designs, and also to maintain design registrations. Most years, relatively small increases have been implemented annually, reflecting Canada's overall rate of inflation. However, in 2024, fee increases of about 30% are being implemented. 2.148

(h) Other issues

It has also been noted that there appears to be a significant drafting inconsistency within the *Act*. 2.149

Section 4 of the *Act* sets out that it is the 'proprietor of a design' who may apply to register the design, and section 12 of the *Act* establishes that the 'author' is the first proprietor, unless he has executed the design for another person for good and valuable consideration in which case the other person is the first proprietor. 2.150

2.151 However, section 7(c) of the *Act* indicates that a design is registrable only if it was 'created by the applicant or the applicant's predecessor in title'.

2.152 New designs are commonly created by employees or by contract designers, and the first proprietor of the design is the company for whom they work or by whom they were hired on contract. Absent a transfer, it is that company who has the right to apply to register the design under section 4 of the *Act*. However, that company did not create the design itself, nor was the design created by a predecessor in title of that company. Therefore, it appears that such a design is unregistrable under section 7 of the *Act* to the only possible applicant who may register the design.

2.153 The problem would appear to arise whenever a design has been created by someone who is not the first proprietor.

(i) Final comment

2.154 Hopefully, these remaining problem areas will be addressed by the Canadian government in the near future.

3

DESIGN LAW IN CHINA

Paolo Beconcini

A.	SUBSTANTIVE ASPECTS OF DESIGN PROTECTION IN CHINA	3.001	(a) Granting authority	3.050
			(b) Priority	3.051
	1. Overview	3.001	(c) Application procedure	3.056
	2. Eligibility Requirements	3.005	(d) Drawings	3.062
	(a) Novelty	3.007	(e) Partial design	3.069
	(i) Disclosure by publication	3.008	(f) Examination procedure	3.080
	(ii) Disclosure by use	3.011	(g) Publication, registration and renewal	3.084
	(iii) Grace period	3.013	2. International Registrations	3.087
	(b) Distinctiveness	3.014	C. DISPUTING DESIGN RIGHTS	3.090
	(i) Visibility	3.016	1. Invalidation	3.090
	(c) Fit for industrial use	3.019	2. Design Infringement	3.096
	(d) Good faith	3.021	3. Civil Enforcement	3.098
	3. Scope of Protection	3.022	(a) Civil claims	3.102
	(a) Object of the comparison	3.025	(b) Remedies	3.103
	(b) The ordinary user test	3.028	(i) Damages	3.104
	(c) Examination of the identity/similarity comparison	3.030	(c) Most common defences	3.107
	(i) The evaluation process and the observation method	3.031	4. Administrative Enforcement	3.108
			D. SIGNIFICANT JUDICIAL DECISIONS IN THE JURISDICTION	3.111
	(ii) Determination of the scope of protection and infringement in particular design cases	3.036	1. Scope of Protection and Designer Freedom	3.112
	(d) Examination of the scope of protection and designer's freedom	3.039	E. PRACTICAL ASPECTS OF DESIGN LAW	3.119
			1. Business Aspects: Transferability/Licensing	3.119
	(e) Functionality as a limit to the scope of protection	3.043	(a) Transfer of design patent rights and technology transfer	3.120
	(f) Ownership and terms	3.045	(b) License of design patent rights	3.121
	(i) Ownership and service inventions	3.046	2. Specific Interesting Application of Design Patents	3.124
	(ii) Co-ownership	3.048	(a) Auto parts	3.124
B.	PROCEDURAL ASPECTS OF DESIGN PROTECTION IN CHINA	3.049	(b) Design patents and the metaverse	3.125
	1. National Registration	3.049	F. CONCLUSION	3.127

A. SUBSTANTIVE ASPECTS OF DESIGN PROTECTION IN CHINA

1. Overview

3.001 The Patent Law of the People's Republic of China ('China Patent Law/Patent Law') in its current version[1] defines a design as: '(…) a new design for the overall or partial shape, pattern, or combination of a product, as well as the combination of its colors, shapes, and patterns that is aesthetically pleasing and suitable for industrial applications'.[2]

3.002 In order to enjoy design protection in China, an industrial product does not need to be beautiful, but only aesthetically original and different from the common design adopted by the market for that type of product.[3] It is this aesthetic originality of the product that determines its value and commercial success. The colour of a product alone cannot constitute a design, unless it constitutes a pattern.

3.003 Therefore, a Chinese design patent aims at protecting the original aesthetic value and visual effect of an everyday industrial and consumer product as the key factor that enables the right holder to secure a successful positioning of its product in the Chinese market.[4]

3.004 China only recognizes protection to registered design patents. Unregistered designs find no protection in China unless they may be part of a copyright or a trade dress. Trade dress protection of a design is possible only as long as the design and its decorative parts have acquired a high reputation among the relevant Chinese consumers as a source of product origin.[5]

---

1   中华人民共和国专利法 Patent Law of the People's Republic of China. It was promulgated by the Standing Committee of the National People's Congress on December 27, 2008, and amended in 2020 by Decision of the Standing Committee of the National People's Congress on Amending the 'Patent Law of the People's Republic of China', Adopted at the 22nd Meeting of the Standing Committee of the 13th National People's Congress on October 17, 2020版, see https://www.lawinfochina.com/display.aspx?id=34138&lib=law accessed on May 15, 2023. In this chapter we will cite it as the Patent Law version of 2020.
2   Patent Law of the People's Republic of China 2020, art 2.4.
3   Paolo Beconcini and Margherita Farina, 'Design Patent Protection for Automotive Spare Parts in China: A Comparative Analysis with the US and EU Laws and Legal Practice', (2016) Vol. 8 Bocconi Legal Papers, 59; Paolo Beconcini, *Design Rights, Functionality and Scope of Protection*, Christofer Carani (ed.), Vol. 3 AIPPI Law Series 2017 Wolters Kluwer, 193.
4   Ibid.
5   中华人民共和国反不正当竞争法（2019年修订）（律商网整理）Anti-Unfair Competition Law of the People's Republic of China 2019.

2. Eligibility Requirements

3.005 The China Patent Law under Article 23 states a first set of patentability requirements. According to this provision, a design to be eligible for patent protection must be:

- novel, that is not known to the public through publication or disclosure by use at home and abroad before the filing date
- obviously different from the existing design or the combination of existing design features and
- shall not conflict with the legal rights that others have obtained before the filing date.

3.006 Although the above provision is considered the key norm on design eligibility, additional requirements are also to be found in other provisions such as Article 2.4 which provides the definition of a design patent.

(a) Novelty

3.007 A design is patentable and valid if it is 'novel'. This means that at the time of filing, the design: (a) is not known to the public in or outside China; (b) it has not been already applied for in China by others or (c) has not been recorded or published after the later application in other patent-related filings by others.[6] The requirement of novelty reflects the decision of the Chinese legislator to incorporate design in the patent system. Therefore, the rules on novelty set forth for invention patents and utility models apply to design patents as well. In particular, the design will lack novelty if it has been disclosed either by use or publication in China or abroad before the date of filing.

(i) Disclosure by publication

3.008 Publication in this context means that carriers who independently disseminate technical or design content which contains the invention can prove the date of their publication. Publications can be typed paper documents such as patent documents, scientific and technological articles, books, magazines and newspapers, textbooks, manuals, product catalogues, brochures, etc. Publications in the sense of the China Patent Law also include audio and video materials made by electric, optic, magnetic or photographic means, as well as materials in digital form such as those on the internet, and on other online databases.[7] The determination of whether a document is to be considered a publication in the

---

6   China Patent Law 2020, art 23.
7   China Patent Examination Guidelines 2021, pt II, ch 3, art 2.1.2.1.

sense of the China Patent Law is not affected by the language or the place of publication, the amount of distribution or whether it has been read. A novelty destroying application will occur when the public is at least theoretically able to know of it, if it wishes to do so.[8]

3.009 On the other hand, publications containing wording such as 'confidential', 'internal materials', 'restricted publication', will not be considered publications if they were originally distributed to a restricted group of qualified people and were considered confidential. Even if disclosed to a larger public by accident or in breach of the confidentiality clause, these will not be regarded as publications in the sense of Article 23 of the Patent Law.[9]

3.010 The printing date of the publication is considered to be the date of disclosure. If there is no publication date, other external means of proof can be used as evidence. Where only a month or a year is indicated as the publication date, the last date of the month or year is considered to be the date of disclosure.[10]

(ii) Disclosure by use

3.011 Disclosure by use means that, by use the design is disclosed or placed in the state of being available to the public.[11] Means of disclosure by use include making, using, selling, importing, exchanging, presenting, demonstrating, exhibiting and the like, which can make the technical content available to the public, so long as the relevant technical content is placed in such state that the public can gain the knowledge for it, if they wish so, and it has no relevance whether the public has actual knowledge of the design. It is important that through such means of use, the design is clearly disclosed and made available to the public, no matter whether the public has concretely known of the use.[12] On the other hand, if a disclosure at an exhibition or a demonstration does not disclose the full content of the design, then such use will not destroy the novelty of the design. The date on which the design and product are available to the public is regarded as the date of disclosure.[13]

3.012 Disclosure made in a speech at a symposium or a class, or when disclosure is done through talking, broadcasting, televising, or streaming is considered a form of disclosure by other means other than publication and use according

---

8 Ibid.
9 Ibid.
10 Ibid.
11 China Patent Examination Guidelines 2021, pt II, ch 3, art 2.1.2.2.
12 Ibid.
13 Ibid.

to the law. The date of the action in this case is considered to be the date of disclosure.[14]

(iii) Grace period

A disclosure by use or publication can be excused in certain specific cases. In particular, the China Patent Law provides a grace period of six months prior to the filing that cures certain types of disclosures: (a) when the design is disclosed for the first time at an international exhibition sponsored by the Chinese government; (b) when published for the first time in a specific academic technological conference; (c) when the design is disclosed by others as an error or against the consent of the right holder. The 2020 fourth amendment ('2020 amendment') to the China Patent Law has added a fourth and new exception: (d) it is disclosed to the public for the first time in the public interest, when a state of emergency or any extraordinary circumstance occurs in the country. This latter addition was obviously prompted by the need to get quick market use approval for vaccines and therapeutics related to the Covid-19 pandemic.[15] Here it is important to note that the grace period of the China Patent Law does not align with corresponding rules in the EU[16] and the US.[17] The latter allow for 12 months' voluntary disclosures while voluntary disclosure in China is limited to state-sanctioned exhibitions or academic events. This can cause confusion and the ultimate loss of rights in China. Foreign right holders are therefore advised to file a design patent in China before they plan to disclose and test their new designs in the EU and in the USA or refrain from disclosure at all before filing the design in the country of origin.

3.013

(b) Distinctiveness

For a design patent to be valid it must be 'distinctively different' from the prior art designs in the same category of goods,[18] and must not conflict with any

3.014

---

14 Ibid.
15 China Patent Law 2020, art 24.
16 Council Regulation EC 6/2002, on Community Design Regulation, art 7.2(b). This Regulation provides that a disclosure is not novelty destroying if a design for which protection is claimed has been made available to the public during the 12-month period preceding the date of filing of the application or, if a priority is claimed, the date of priority.
17 35 USC 102(b)(1) provides that a disclosure made one year or less before the effective filing date of a claimed invention shall not be prior art under 35 USC 102(a)(1) with respect to the claimed invention if: (1) the disclosure was made by the inventor or joint inventor or by another who obtained the subject matter disclosed directly or indirectly from the inventor or a joint inventor; or (2) the subject matter disclosed had, before such disclosure, been publicly disclosed by the inventor or a joint inventor or by another who obtained the subject matter disclosed directly or indirectly from the inventor or a joint inventor.
18 China Patent Law 2020, art 23.2. Given that like novelty, the distinctiveness of a design will only be examined in case of an invalidation lawsuit, the issue of classification of designs, will also be raised in that context. China Patent Examination Guidelines 2021, pt IV, ch 5, art 5.1.1.3 provides that whether two designs belong to the same class of products:

existing rights lawfully obtained by another party before the filing date (i.e., trademarks, copyright and trade dress).

The requirement of distinctiveness means that the product shape and/or patterns and colours and their combinations must clearly distinguish the product from the standard appearance of other products in the same category. Distinctive design features must also be readily identifiable. It is this distinctiveness that makes the patented design innovative and compliant with the patentability requirements stipulated in Article 23 of the Patent Law.[19]

3.015 The Supreme People's Court in '*Provisions on Several Issues relating to Hearing Administrative Cases on Patent Granting and Validity (I)*' published on April 28, 2020, further stipulated that designs obtained by the recombination of other known designs are not distinctively different when their recombination is obvious or easy to be perceived by the ordinary consumer, unless the recombination produces a substantially different and unique visual effect.[20] In summary, a product needs to be aesthetically original and different from the common design used for that product in the market in order to enjoy design protection in China.[21]

(i) Visibility

3.016 Visibility of design features is not an eligibility requirement, but a corollary of the distinctiveness requirement. The issue of the visibility of aesthetic design features will come up during the identity/similarity comparison of the design patent with a comparative prior art, within an invalidation procedure or during the same phase in an infringement proceeding before a People's Court ('people's court/ court').

3.017 The Patent Examination Guidelines provide that, when making a similarity comparison, a patent examiner or a judge in an administrative proceeding for a patent validity determination, shall conclude that design differences between the patent and the comparative prior art do not take away the overall impres-

---

In determining the category of products, reference shall be made to the title, the international classification for designs and the shelf classification of the product when it is on sale. However, the determination of whether two products belong to the same category shall be based on whether the uses of the two products are identical (…).

19 孔玮与吉安宇之源光电科技有限公司侵害外观设计专利权纠纷一案再审民事判决书（2018）最高法民再86号 (Kong Wei and Ji'an Yuzhiyuan Optoelectronics Technology Co., Ltd. Retrial Civil Judgment in the Case of Infringement of Design Patent Right, Supreme People's Court, Fa Min Zai No. 86/2018).

20 最高人民法院公布《关于审理专利授权确权行政案件若干问题的规定（一）》（征求意见稿）向社会公众公开征求意见, 2020-28-04 (Supreme People's Court Provisions on Several Issues relating to Hearing Administrative Cases on Patent Granting and Validity (I) of April 28, 2020, art 22.).

21 Beconcini and Farina (n 3), 53–83.

sion of similarity when there are just 'slight changes in some fine details which cannot be noticed by paying normal attention' (e.g., the different number of slats in a venetian blind), 'exist in parts that cannot be seen easily or cannot be seen at all when the product is in use'.[22]

As to the similarity examination in an infringement case, Article 11 of the 2009 Supreme Court's Interpretation on Certain Legal Issues relating to Patent Infringement Cases ('Supreme People's Court Interpretation of 2009')[23] provides in particular that when determining infringement, a judge should consider only parts that can be easily or directly seen when the product is in use, compared to the parts that are not visible, when determining the scope of protection (i.e., the overall visual effect) of the design.

3.018

(c) Fit for industrial use

Article 2 section 4 of the Patent Law also requires that the product in question is fit for industrial use, which means that the product can be mass produced. Handicrafts, agricultural products, livestock products and natural products which cannot be mass produced do not meet this requirement.

3.019

However, design protection is not available for several products due to the difficulties related to production or nature, like fixed buildings, bridges, etc. that cannot be reproduced depending on specific geographical conditions, products whose shapes, patterns, and colours are not fixed because they contain substances with no fixed shapes such as gases, liquids, and powders. Moreover, objects that cannot act on vision or are difficult to determine with the naked eye, and require special tools to distinguish their shapes, patterns, and colours, etc., cannot be given design protection.[24]

3.020

(d) Good faith

A new requirement has been added by Article 20 of the fourth amendment of 2020 to the China Patent Law. When applying for patents and exercising patent rights the patentee must abide by the principle of good faith. The patent rights shall not be abused to harm public interests or the legitimate rights and interests of others. Any misuse of patent rights, elimination, or restriction of competition, which constitutes monopolistic behaviour, shall be dealt with in

3.021

---

22   China Patent Examination Guidelines 2021, pt IV, ch 5, art 5.1.2.1.2.
23   最高人民法院关于审理侵犯专利权纠纷案件应用法律若干问题的解释，法释[2009]21号，发文日期: 2009-12-28,生效日期: 2010-01-01 (Interpretations of the Supreme People's Court Concerning Certain Issues on the Application of Law for the Trial of Cases on Disputes over Infringement on Patent Rights, Fa Shi 2009 no. 21 of December 28, 2009, effective on January 1, 2010 art 11).
24   China Patent Examination Guidelines 2021, pt I, ch 3, art 74.

accordance with the Anti-Monopoly Law of the People's Republic of China. Given the fact that China adopts a 'first to file' system and formalities-only examination with no declaration or oath requirement in place, the introduction of this good-faith requirement could serve as a guiding law for the current bad faith practice of securing patents to obtain tax advantages and government subsidies, blackmail and free-ride the profit of rightful owner, etc.

3. Scope of Protection

3.022 The scope of protection of a design patent is determined by the drawings or photographs in the patent application.[25] This applies to both invalidation[26] and infringement proceedings.[27] Therefore, the following section will be relevant for both design invalidation and infringement proceedings, given that the rules and principles governing the determination of a design scope of protection and similarity with another design are substantially the same in both cases, although they may be enunciated in different regulations or court decisions.

3.023 Both the Patent Examination Guidelines in relation to design validity, as well as the jurisprudence of the Supreme People's Court[28] and of the Beijing Higher Court[29] with respect to design infringement, agree that the brief description of the figures may be used to explain the views depicted in the design patent's drawings or photographs. More recently, the Supreme People's Court has allowed the observations filed by the patentee in the proceeding of invalidation and the proceeding of litigation thereof, to be considered, to understand the protection scope of the design patent. However, the case law has given a more limited weight to this parameter for several reasons.[30] Therefore, the scope of protection will be reflected by the drawings in the patented design and not in its physical embodiments. The patented product may serve as a reference for

---

25 China Patent Law 2020, art 64.2.
26 China Patent Examination Guidelines 2021, pt IV, ch V, art 3.
27 Supreme People's Court Interpretation of 2009, art 9 (Note 24).
28 Ibid.
29 Guidelines for Patent Infringement Determination issued by Beijing Higher People's Court 2017, art 65 https://bjgy.chinacourt.gov.cn/article/detail/2017/04/id/2825592.shtml accessed May 7, 2023. This provision states that:
> In the trial of a case of dispute over infringement of a design patent, the protection scope of the patent shall be determined first. The protection scope of a design patent shall be determined by the design incorporated in the patented product illustrated in the drawings or photographs, and the brief description and essential features of the design, as well as observations filed by the patentee in the procedure of invalidation and the procedure of litigation thereof, may be used for understanding the protection scope of the patent for design.
30 *Zhejiang Jianlong Sanitary Ware Co Ltd v Grohe Co Ltd and Zhejiang Jianlong Sanitary Ware Co Ltd and Grohe Co Ltd.* Supreme People's Court (2015) Min Ti Zi No. 2. https://cgc.law.stanford.edu/zh-hans/judgments/spc-2015-min-ti-zi-23-civil-judgment/ accessed May 7 2023.

helping the judge or examiner to understand the design but cannot be the basis for the determination of the design's scope of protection.[31]

3.024 Determination of a design patent's scope of protection comes into question either during an invalidation proceeding or an enforcement of the design patent against an alleged infringing product. In both situations, the design patent invalidation examiner and judge, or the civil court will have to first determine the design's scope of protection[32] and then conduct an analysis of the identity/similarity of the patented design and the claimed prior art or infringing physical embodiment respectively. However, such determination is not separable, both logically and practically from the process of evaluation of identity and similarity between the design patent and the claimed prior art in an invalidation action and the alleged infringing product designs in an infringement proceeding. In fact, the scope of protection will be the first initial step of the identity/similarity evaluation process, where the examiner or the civil judge will determine the aesthetic features having novel and original effect that will have to be compared with the prior art or infringing design physical embodiments. The key steps of this evaluation process are: (a) determining the object of comparison; (b) determining the standard user by whose point of view the protection scope and comparison are to be conducted; (c) the identity/similarity comparison; (d) the limits of the scope of protection (e.g. designer's freedom, functional features etc.). We shall consider below these steps of the evaluation process, and understand that its principles and rules apply in the same way to identity/similarity comparisons in both invalidation and infringement proceedings.

(a) Object of the comparison

3.025 The law provides that a civil judge in a design patent infringement or the examiner in an invalidation procedure, will have to compare the infringing products or the prior art against the drawings or photos contained in the design patent under evaluation and not its physical embodiment. It is generally not appropriate to compare the alleged infringing product with the actual product of the patented design.[33]

3.026 The comparison will proceed further, once it is also confirmed that the design under comparison and the prior art or infringing product belong to the same or approximate class of products. Two designs will be considered identical or

---

31 Beijing Higher Peoples Court Guidelines year 2017, (n 29) art 65.2.
32 *Grohe* (n 30).
33 Ibid.

similar, only if they belong to the same category of products. When determining the category of the product, the examiner, or the civil judge, cannot limit themselves to the declared Locarno classification. Although this classification constitutes an important reference, attention must also be paid to the title of the design patent, the shelf classification of the corresponding product when on sale, and, most importantly the usage of the products.[34] If the products under comparison have identical use (e.g., a mechanical and an electronic watch, a towel and a carpet), they belong to the same category. If they have similar use, the products under comparison belong to an approximate category.[35] A toy and a tiny ornament can be considered products of the same category. However, a toy car and a real car are not to be considered as belonging to the same or approximate class.[36] Nonetheless, the Supreme People's Court found that the scale model of a bus disclosed to preview the design of the real luxury coach to be launched at a world-famous exhibition a few days later, was considered to belong to the same class of the luxury coach.[37] It is evident that the scale model was not considered to be a toy car. When a product has multiple uses, whereby only some of the uses are the same as those in a claimed design patent, the two designs should still be deemed as belonging to similar types of products. For example, watches with MP3 and watches without MP3 features, both have timekeeping purposes, and they belong to similar types of products.[38]

3.027 If the design and the prior art or the alleged infringing products belong to neither the same or approximate product class, then the respective invalidation and/or infringement complaints should be dismissed.

(b) The ordinary user test

3.028 The determination of the scope of protection of a design and its comparison with the prior art in an invalidation proceeding or an alleged infringing product in a civil lawsuit for the violation of a design patent, must be conducted based on the knowledge level and cognitive ability of the general consumers of the design patent product.[39] This 'ordinary user' test refers to an imaginary subject whose knowledge level and cognitive ability are objectively determined, in

---

34 China Patent Examination Guidelines 2021, pt IV, ch 5, art 5.1.1. The same identical provision for the case of infringement evaluation is contained in art 9 of the Interpretation of the Supreme People's Court Interpretation on the Law in the Trial of Patent Infringement Disputes (n 27).
35 China Patent Examination Guidelines 2021, pt IV, ch 5, art 5.1.2.
36 Ibid.
37 中华人民共和国国家知识产权局专利复审委员会效宣告审查决定（第14484号） (The Patent Reexamination Board of the State Intellectual Property Office of the People's Republic of China announced the review decision (No. 14484).
38 China Patent Examination Guidelines 2021, pt IV, ch 5, art 5.1.1.3.
39 Supreme People's Court Interpretation of 2009, art 10 (n 23).

order to reduce the risk of subjective judgments, in order to achieve a fair decision in a legal dispute. The Chinese regulators know that different types of products have different consumers. For this reason, the consumer for a certain type of design product must be selected by keeping in mind the real shelf and purchase cycles of a product as well as its common usages.[40] For instance, in cases of special designs such as spare parts, the knowledge should be that of both the buyer and user of the product. This could be the case of a car tire rim. Here, the cognitive level of the normal consumer should be determined with reference to both those who assemble or repair vehicles (qualified user) and the users of the vehicles on the road. However, if the spare part is not visible to the end user when the product is in use, but it is visible to the mechanic when he buys it and installs it in the vehicle, in this case the ordinary person is only the qualified user.[41]

3.029 The general criteria and characteristics that an 'ordinary user' shall possess to be used as a test in each specific case are (a) common knowledge of the designs and commonly used design methods for the same or similar products. For instance, an ordinary user of cars, shall know about the cars on the market through advertisement, media, real life presence on the roads, or by purchasing cars; (b) the capability to recognize differences in shapes, patterns and colours between design patent products, without necessarily having the ability to notice minor or tiny differences.[42] More recently, the Supreme People's Court has also pointed out how the knowledge and cognitive ability of the ordinary user may vary depending on the available design space and designer's freedom. To suffice, the cognitive ability to identify smaller changes decrease when the design offers space for large variations and increase when the designer's freedom is limited by necessitated technical features.

(c) Examination of the identity/similarity comparison

3.030 As stated above, an examiner or a civil judge will have to define the scope of protection once involved in a design patent dispute. They will then need to identify the relevant features that create the protectable overall visual effect of the design patent and give them the appropriate protection during the identity/

---

40 厦门市市场监督管理局与被申请人福建顺昌虹润精密仪器有限公司专利行政裁决纠纷案（2020）最高法行申516号(*Xiamen Hickory Automation Technology Co., Ltd., Xiamen City Market Supervisory Authority and the respondent Fujian Shunchang Rainbow Run Precision Instrument Co., Ltd*. Patent Reexamination Board, Patent Dispute Administrative Rulings (2020) Supreme Law Xingshen No. 516.
41 申请再审人国家知识产权局专利复审委员会、浙江今飞机械集团有限公司与被申请人浙江万丰摩轮有限公司专利无效行政纠纷案, (2010) 行提字第5号 (*Patent Reexamination Board of SIPO v. Zhejiang Wanfeng Motorcycle Wheel Corp*. Patent Reexamination Board, Case No. 5/2010).
42 China Patent Examination Guidelines 2021, pt IV, ch 5, art 4.

similarity comparison. This process will be affected by the selected user test, by the method of observation of the ordinary user, which in turn will be affected by the designer's freedom in respect to the specific class of design products.

(i) The evaluation process and the observation method

3.031 Article 11 of the Supreme People's Court Interpretation no. 2009/21 on Several Issues Concerning the Application of the Law in the Trial of Patent Infringement Disputes, contains the general rules for the comparison process in a design patent infringement proceeding, by which a civil judge will both identify the design patent scope of protection and evaluate its infringement by a comparable design. This norm provides that:

> The people's court shall make a comprehensive judgment in view of the overall visual effects of the design based on the design feature(s) of the patented design and the accused infringing product when determining the identity or similarity of designs. The design features that are mainly determined by the technical function and the features that do not affect the overall visual effects such as product material, internal structure and so on shall not be considered.
>
> The following situations usually have a greater impact on the overall visual effect of the design:
>
> (1) The parts that are easily directly observed during normal use of the product are relative to other parts (...).'[43]

3.032 The judge will therefore start by identifying the overall visual effect of the design patent based on its drawings and supported by the brief description, its title and product classification. The features and visual effect identification process, shall be conducted based on the knowledge and cognitive capabilities of the ordinary user, taking into consideration the designer's freedom, excluding the design features dictated solely by functional necessity or which are not visible. The latter includes changes in fine details, like the number of slats of a venetian blind. Also, the size of the product designs is not to be considered when determining the visual features of the design scope of protection and in the following comparison.[44] The court or the patent examiner will then consider all these features together and determine whether the alleged infringing design or the prior art produce an overall different visual effect compared to the patented design. Therefore, when conducting the comparison, the judge or examiner will first identify such features in the design patent and then in the compared product design. Afterwards, the judge or examiner will look at the differences and take stock of all the rules and exceptions indicated above to

---

43 Supreme People's Court Interpretation of 2009, art 11 (n 23).
44 China Patent Examination Guidelines 2021, pt IV, ch 5, art 5.1.2.1.

determine the weight of such differences on the overall visual effect of the two designs under comparison.

The evaluation of the overall visual effect of the patented design and the ensuing identity/similarity comparison must be conducted through the ordinary user's direct and overall observation and comprehensive judgment.[45] In the process of comprehensive observation the ordinary user will generally be more influenced by the design features that are easily directly observed during normal use of the product, and those that are different from the existing design.[46] 3.033

During the overall observation and comprehensive determination process and in addition to the already mentioned limitations, the ordinary user will have to observe another set of rules affecting the observation process itself. In particular, the concerned design patent is to be compared only with one prior art at a time and not with a combination of cited prior arts.[47] This is particularly important in invalidation cases or to determine the admissibility of a prior art defence in an infringement lawsuit. 3.034

At the end of the comparison, the judge or the examiner, will have to reach a conclusion. If there is no difference between the alleged infringing design and the authorized design in terms of overall visual effects, the people's court shall determine that the two are the same. If there is no substantial difference in overall visual effects, they shall be deemed similar. 3.035

(ii) Determination of the scope of protection and infringement in particular design cases

Particular provisions apply to special design patents. For instance, Article 15 of the 'Interpretation on Several Issues Concerning the Application of Law in the Trial of Patent Infringement Cases(II)', adopted by the Supreme People's Court on March 21, 2016 ('**2016 Interpretation**'), deals with the determination of the scope of protection of designs for products in set: when the alleged 3.036

---

45 The observation is direct in that it is not allowed to observe with magnifying glasses, microscope, chemical analysis, other instruments or means as stipulated by the China Patent Examination Guidelines 2021, pt IV, ch 5, art 5.2.2.

46 Supreme People's Court Interpretation of 2009, art 9 (n 23). See also 孔玮与吉安宇之源光电科技有限公司侵害外观设计专利权纠纷一案再审民事判决书（2018）最高法民再86号 (*Kong Wei v. Ji'an Yuzhiyuan Optoelectronics Technology Co, Ltd*, Infringement of Appearance Design Patent Dispute Retrial Civil Judgment (2018) Supreme Court Min Zai No. 86. In this case concerning the infringement of a streetlamp's outer design, the Supreme People's Court re-stated that only the features on the shell and the bottom view of the design are visible to the common user when looking up from the street. All other features on the upper surface of the lamp will not be visible when the product is in use and therefore will not form part of the design scope of protection and therefore of its distinctiveness requirement.

47 China Patent Examination Guidelines 2021, pt IV, ch 5, art 5.2.1.

infringing design is identical with or similar to one of the designs, the people's court shall determine that the accused design falls within the scope of protection of the patent.[48] This provision reflects the logic behind the determination of the scope of protection of designs products in set, where multiple designs coexist in one patent and whether one or more are not valid or have a limited scope of protection, does not automatically affect all the others. Article 16.1 of the 2016 Interpretation stipulates that for a design patent of a complicated product with a unique way of assembling the individual components, where the accused design is identical with or similar to the design of the complicated product in its assembled state, the people's court shall determine that the accused design falls within the protection scope of the patent.[49] Article 16.1 and Article 16.2 of the 2016 Interpretation add that for a design patent of a complicated product with no assembly relation or with no unique assembly relation among the individual components, where the accused design is identical with or similar to the designs of all the individual components of the complicated product, the people's court shall determine that the accused design falls within the protection scope of the patent; where the accused design lacks the design of one individual component of the complicated product or is neither identical with nor similar to the design of one individual component, the people's court shall determine that the accused design does not fall within the scope of protection of the patent.[50]

3.037 A practical example of a complex product design with a unique assembly relation is that of a blender with the upper blending bowl, blades and the lower motor and base. In this case the above provision will recognize infringement only if the comparative design encompasses both complex elements in exclusive relation. Therefore, only the assembled state of the design will be given protection. A complex product with no exclusive assembly relation, such as toy building blocks, the protection will encompass all the elements of the design.

3.038 For those design of products in variant states Article 17 of the 2016 Interpretation provides that where the accused design is identical with or similar to the patented design in all its user states as shown in the relevant views, the people's court shall determine that the accused design falls within the scope of protection of the patent; where the accused design lacks or is

---

48 最高人民法院关于审理侵犯专利权纠纷案件应用法律若干问题的解释（二），法释〔2016〕1号] (Interpretation on Several issues Concerning The Application of Law to the Trial of Patent Infringement Disputes (II), Law interpretation of the Supreme People's Court No. 2016/1 http://gongbao.court.gov.cn/Details/409a66a5e85613e92594a31b410220.html accessed May 7, 2023.
49 Ibid.
50 Ibid.

neither identical with nor similar to the design in at least one of its use states, the people's court shall determine that the accused design doesn't fall within the scope of protection of the patent.[51]

(d) Examination of the scope of protection and designer's freedom

The designer's freedom is an important criterion that affects the determination of the knowledge of the ordinary user, and therefore will affect the design's scope of protection and the determination of the weight different features hold in the identity/similarity comparison process. The first legal elaboration of the concept of designer's freedom was contained in 2010 Supreme People's Court judgment in a case concerning the invalidation of a design patent for the shape of the spikes of a motorbike tire rim.[52]

3.039

In its decision the Supreme People's Court introduced the concept of 'design space' as one of the criteria to determine the level of knowledge of the ordinary user test. The Supreme People's Court concluded that in products with developed designs there will always be a lower degree of design freedom. In such cases, even a small change of the designs could affect the overall visual impression on an ordinary user. For newer products, there will instead be a higher degree of design freedom because in such cases, there will be a larger number of choices and availability of design formats and styles. Small changes may therefore attract less attention from the ordinary user. The Supreme People's Court concluded that such distinction would impact the scope of protection of the two different classes of designs, with the former enjoying a lesser and the latter a broader protection. However, this case ignored the fact that every design of an industrial product is functional and thus did not consider the relevance of functional features. In fact, designer freedom lies between the folds of functionality, meaning that the designers have carve their creative shapes and forms from otherwise functional features. A confirmation and a further elaboration on the concept of designer's freedom was contained in the 2015 Supreme People's Court decision in the *Grohe* case.[53] In this judgment the Supreme People's Court articulated that:

3.040

> When judging whether there is a clear difference between the two designs, consider the design space or the creative freedom of the designer, which is helpful to accurately determine the level of the general consumer's cognitive ability. Generally speaking, if the design space is large, it is not easy for the average consumer to notice the subtle differences between different designs (...). Because the size of the design space is a relative

---

51 Ibid.
52 *Wanfeng Motorcycle Wheel Corp* (n 41).
53 *Grohe* (n 30).

concept, it is generally limited by the technical function of the product, the necessity of adopting common features of such products, and the existing design. Factors such as the degree of design congestion should be considered from the above aspects when weighing the design space of the relevant design features, especially paying attention to the status of the existing design.

3.041 Article 14 of the 2016 Interpretation of the Supreme People's Court, codified the above jurisprudence:

> When determining the level of knowledge and discriminability of an ordinary consumer to a design, the people's court shall normally consider the design space of the products in the same or similar category as the patented design at the time of infringement. Where the design space is relatively large, the people's court may determine that it is usually unlikely for an ordinary consumer to notice the minor differences between the compared designs; where the design space is relatively small, the people's court may determine that it is usually more likely for an ordinary consumer to notice the minor differences between two compared designs.[54]

3.042 Therefore, based on these judgments and provisions, the designer's freedom will be used by the court or the CNIPA examiner to objectively divide the patented design into relevant features and assess them against the prior designs, giving greater protection to the identified features wherever there is a limited degree of design freedom. Therefore, there is now not only a comparison between the design patent overall visual effect and that of the comparative design, but before that, there will be a comparison of the patented design's discrete features with the prior art in order to weigh in their scope of protection.[55] From the above judgments and provisions it is also clear that designer's freedom in China is used mostly as a criterion to identify the relevant design features of the patent rather than determining the overall visual effect of the compared designs.

(e) Functionality as a limit to the scope of protection

3.043 Functionality is not directly regulated by the law as a patentability requirement and is defined only in relation to the determination of a design patent's scope of protection. In this context some authors have argued that functionality should be understood as a negative patentability requirement and perhaps complementary, or even equivalent, to the requirement of aesthetic appeal. However, this is not the direction taken by the case law that has now achieved consensus in defining functionality or non-functionality as a complementary

---

54 Supreme People's Court Interpretation of 2016, (n 48).
55 Xiaojun Guo, Weiwei Han, 'China's New Patent Infringement Trial Rules Become Effective-Introduction to the Judicial Interpretation(II) Regarding Patent Infringement of the China's SPC(Part I)', 2016 CCPIT News & Articles https://www.ccpit-patent.com.cn/node/3663 accessed May 7, 2023.

and independent eligibility requirement. In *Triangle v. Bridgestone and Patent Reexamination Board* (2016), Jing Xing Zhong, the Beijing IP Court, called upon to determine the validity of a design patent for a tire thread design and clarified that:

> The decision on functional design elements does not depend on whether the design has no alternative due to functional or technical constraints, rather it depends on whether the ordinary consumers of the products sees that the design is determined only by a specific function and does not need to consider whether the design is aesthetic.[56]

Later, in the *Jaguar Land Rover v. JMC* decision of 2018, the Beijing Higher Court took the opportunity to better define the eligibility requirement of aesthetic value and to detach it from a generic definition of the same as a matter of subjective taste.[57] In particular, the Beijing High Court concluded that aesthetic appeal of a design is defined through a balanced determination between the decorativeness and the natural functionality embodied in each design feature, whereby the degree of decorativeness is determined by the designer's freedom for the feature or product under examination.[58] It is obvious that a design which is solely defined by functional features, will lack aesthetic appeal, while the protectable scope of a design's aesthetic feature will have to be determined on a product-by-product basis, taking into consideration the degree of freedom that the designer possesses in adding decorative elements to the functionally defined features of each design under examination. **3.044**

(f) Ownership and terms

A design patent grants to the registrant an exclusive right to the economic exploitation of the design, including the right of producing, manufacturing, using, offering for sale, selling and exporting. Moreover, the economic exploitation can also be carried by licensing or transfer. However, these activities cannot be conducted without the owner's consent for production and business purposes.[59] The exclusivity granted to the owner of the Chinese **3.045**

---

56 株式会社普利司通、三角集团有限公司与国家知识产权局专利复审委员会二审，(2016, 京行终 3233号) (*Bridgestone Co., Ltd., Triangle Group Co., Ltd. and the Patent Reexamination Board* of the State Intellectual Property Office for the second instance, Beijing Higher Court Judgment No. 3233/2016).
57 (捷豹路虎有限公司等与江铃控股有限公司二审，(2018)京行终4169号). (*Jaguar Land Rover Co., Ltd. v. Jiangling Holdings Co., Ltd.* second instance, Beijing Higher Court Judgment No. 4169/2018).
58 Ibid. In this decision the Court stated that:
(...) the design of a product is usually composed of two basic factors: function and aesthetics, (...), as far as a specific design feature of a design product is concerned, the dual requirements of functionality and aesthetics need to be considered at the same time, which is a compromise between technical and decorative characteristics. The functional or decorative characteristics of product design features are usually relative, and to make an absolute distinction between functional design features and decorative design features is unrealistic in most cases.
59 China Patent Law 2020, art 11.2.

design only extends to the original visual effect of the design product and does not cover or concern any technically necessary forms and functions which do not contain the protected aesthetic effects.

(i) Ownership and service inventions

3.046 If a design is created by a person in the execution of tasks of the entity employing her or mainly by mainly using the employer's material and technical conditions, this is a service invention-creation and the right to apply for a patent on that design belongs to the employing entity by operation of law.[60] Service invention-creation 'made by a person in execution of the tasks of the entity to which he belongs' in Article 6 of the Patent Law means any invention-creation made: (a) in the course of performing his own duty; (b) in execution of any task, other than his own duty, which was delivered to him by the entity to which he belongs; (c) within one year of his retirement, removal from office, or termination of the employee or personnel relationship, provided that the invention-creation relates to his own duty in the entity where he worked or relates to a task assigned to him by the entity.[61] The latter provision is particularly important and aims at reducing acts of unfair competition. In 2019, a leading judgment of the Supreme People's Court has set additional standards for a former employee that failed to comply with the provisions of law, ushering in a friendlier system for the patentee that has been criticized by some scholars as a stifling innovation.[62]

3.047 Unlike the US, there is no need of a specific written transfer agreement from the inventor to the entity employing him. The right automatically belongs to the entity by operation of law, while the employee maintains the right to be named as the inventor in the patent documents.[63] In practice, it is still recommendable to have short agreements in place with the employee that will insulate the employer from any risk of later claims by current or former employees.

60　China Patent Law 2020, art 6.1. Implementing Regulations of the China Patent Law 2014, art 12 (confirmed also in the Draft Implementing Regulations 2020 provides that service invention-creation 'made by a person in execution of the tasks of the entity to which he belongs' mentioned in art 6 of the Patent Law means any invention-creation made: (a) in the course of performing his own duty; (b) In execution of any task, other than his own duty, which was delivered to him by the entity to which he belongs; (c) inventions and creations made within one year after retirement or transfer from the original unit or the termination of labor or personnel relations, and related to the work performed by the original unit or the tasks assigned by the original unit.

61　Draft Implementing Regulations to the Patent Law 2020, art 12.

62　指导案例158号：深圳市卫邦科技有限公司诉李坚毅、深圳市远程智能设备有限公司专利权权属纠纷案, (2019最高法民申6342号) *(Guiding Case No. 158 Shenzhen Weibang Technology Co Ltd v Li Jianyi & Shenzhen Yuancheng Intelligence Equipment Co. Ltd*, Supreme People's Court Case No. 6342/2019). Jennifer Che, Sally Yu, 'How Far Can an Employer Reach to Own Employee-made 'Service Inventions'?, 2020 China Patent Strategy https://chinapatentstrategy.com/how-far-can-an-employer-reach-to-own-employee-made-service-inventions/ accessed on May 7, 2023.

63　China Patent Law 2020, art 16.1 and Implementing Regulations 2010, art 16.3.

The entity is also free to dispose of this right and may agree to transfer it to the employee.⁶⁴ In that case the contract prevails over the provisions of the law. For any non-service invention, the right to apply for a patent shall remain with the inventor or designer, which could be also an employee as long as the invention was not part of his job duties and he did not use means of the employer to achieve it. Eventually, the inventor/employee will have to be paid a reasonable remuneration based on the scope of commercialization and implementation of the design, as well as the economic benefits yielded, unless is otherwise agreed by the parties.⁶⁵ This provision supersedes the previous regulation that left the employer free to provide for remuneration in a contract (e.g., the employment agreement) or in its bylaws. This change is more favourable to the employee/inventor.⁶⁶ If no specific agreement is concluded by the party, the law itself will provide the base to calculate such a remuneration.⁶⁷

(ii) Co-ownership

3.048 The China Patent Law provides that, unless provided otherwise by the parties in a written agreement, patent co-ownership is a 'joint ownership', meaning that both co-owners enjoy the rights and assume the obligations towards the joint property in its entirety (not by shares). If the co-owners wanted a co-ownership by shares and the free assignability of such shares, they would have to provide so in a written agreement.⁶⁸ Also, and unless regulated otherwise by a written agreement, the same provision allows each co-owner to give a non-exclusive license of the application or the registered patent to any third party without the consent of the other co-owners, provided that the royalties thereby collected are equally distributed among the co-owners.⁶⁹ The situation of co-ownership, especially when not regulated by an ad hoc agreement, presents risks especially when the relation between the foreign right holders with its Chinese business partners deteriorate. Consequently, conflicts with respect to sub-licensing and enforcement will emerge which may be difficult to resolve.

---

64 China Patent Law 2020, art 6.3.
65 China Patent Law 2020, art 15 and Implementing Regulations 2010, art 76.
66 Implementing Regulations 2014, art 76. This norm provides that: 'An entity which has been granted a patent can reach an agreement with the inventor or designer or stipulate in its legally formed bylaws with regard to the form and amount of rewards remunerations as mentioned in Article 16 of the Patent Law.' This provision has been fully amended by the same art 76 of the 2020 Draft Implementing Regulations to the Patent Law that reads: 'Unless otherwise agreed, the inventor or designer shall pay rewards and remunerations in accordance with Article 15 of the Patent Law when the service invention is completed.'
67 Implementing Regulations of the China Patent Law 2014, art 77.
68 China Patent Law 2020, art 14.
69 Ibid.

B. PROCEDURAL ASPECTS OF DESIGN PROTECTION IN CHINA

1. National Registration

3.049 The 2020 amendment to the Patent Law ('2020 amendment') entered into force on June 1, 2021, is the fourth amendment since the adoption of the law in 1985, which regulates the process of registration of national patents. The China Patent Law is complemented by the 2014 Implementing Regulations of the China Patent Law.[70]

(a) Granting authority

3.050 Under the China Patent Law, design is protected as a form of patent along with invention patents and utility models. According to Article 3.1 of the Patent Law[71] currently in force, designs are filed with and granted by the China National Intellectual Property Administration ('**CNIPA**'), a governmental agency under the direct control and responsibility of the State Council. CNIPA uniformly accepts and reviews patent applications, and grants design patent rights in accordance with the law.

(b) Priority

3.051 China has adopted the 'first to file' system. According to Article 29.1 of the Patent Law, a design applicant can enjoy a foreign priority within six months from the date when the design is filed for the first time in a foreign country. Where a design patent application on the same subject is filed in China, the right of priority may be enjoyed in accordance with the agreement signed between the foreign country and China or the international treaty both countries are members of, or in accordance with the principle of reciprocal recognition of priority.[72]

3.052 The 2020 amendment also added a specific regulation about the claim of domestic priority. Article 29.2 of the Patent Law provides that, if the applicant of a design in China, files another application with CNIPA for the same subject matter within six months from the date of the first application, this applicant may enjoy the right of priority.'[73] Before the China Patent Law was amended in 2020, design applicants were in no position to amend the domes-

---

[70] The 2020 Draft Implementing Regulations that should fully implement the 2020 Fourth Amendment to the Patent Law has not been approved as yet. When will generally refer to the 2014 Implementing Regulations currently in force unless we cite the 2020 Draft Implementing Regulations.
[71] China Patent Law 2020, art 3.1.
[72] China Patent Law 2020, art 29.1.
[73] China Patent Law 2020, art 29.2.

tically filed designs after they had submitted the application, while this was possible when claiming a foreign priority. A slightly amended design would have been the object of a completely new application. With the introduction of domestic priority, the design applicant can adjust the content of the relevant design while retaining the earlier application date. This amendment aligns the treatment of domestic to that of foreign priority and finally adapts the priority system to the necessity of adequately implementing the newly introduced protection of partial designs in China, as we shall see later.[74]

Article 30.2 of the Patent Law requires that priority must be claimed with a written statement at the time of the application, while a copy of the first patent application is to be filed within three months from the filing date of the application. If the applicant fails to submit a written statement with the application or to submit a copy of the first patent application document within the deadline, the CNIPA will consider that no priority has been claimed.[75] **3.053**

The 2020 Draft Implementation Regulation of the Patent Law now adds that: **3.054**

> the design applicant that has previously applied for utility model or invention patent, in claiming domestic priority, may file an application for design patent on the same subject matter as shown in its drawings; if the prior application is a design patent application, he may file an application on the same subject matter.[76]

In both cases, novelty can be preserved, and disclosure excused if priority is claimed within the deadlines provided by the law. **3.055**

(c) Application procedure

While in Europe industrial designs are protected also when unregistered, even if for a limited period, in China, the design of an industrial product enjoys protection and can be enforced against infringers only after a successful registration with CNIPA. **3.056**

The application procedure for a design patent registration can be done in traditional written form and mail delivery, or by using other prescribed forms,[77] **3.057**

---

74 In practice, it could be now possible to use the domestic priority claim rules to file a second design claiming priority of the first application in China and using the second one to protect a portion of the previous design that was not specifically protected, i.e., in dotted lines. This assuming that dotted lines that are now allowed by the draft of the new Implementing Rules to the Patent Law will be finally approved.
75 China Patent Law 2020, art 30.2.
76 Draft Implementing Regulations to the Patent law 2020, art 32. There is no such provision in the 2010 Implementing Regulations that are currently in force.
77 Implementing Regulations 2014, art 16. This provision requires that the applicant must fill the required forms indicating the following items: (1) The name/title of the design; (2) If the applicant is a Chinese

like the available online filing system.⁷⁸ Foreigners, foreign enterprises or other foreign organizations that do not have a habitual residence or place of business in China shall entrust a patent agency established according to law to apply for patents and handle other patent affairs in China.⁷⁹ The power of attorney given to the Chinese agent will not need to be notarized and can be simply executed with the signature by the right holder's legal representative or a proxy.⁸⁰ The language of the filings is Chinese.⁸¹ The filing date of the design will be the date of receipt of the patent application documents by the CNIPA. If the application documents are sent by mail, the date stamped on the postmark date shall be the application date.⁸²

3.058 When filing the design application, the right holder will have to provide, in addition to the relevant filing forms in Chinese, a written request, the title of the design, the drawings or pictures of the design that clearly shows the design of the product (normally six views of the product) and a brief description of the design.⁸³

3.059 It is important to note that a design application shall be limited to one design. However, two or more similar designs for the same product, or two or more designs for products that are used in the same category and sold or used in sets, may be filed as one application.⁸⁴ The provision identifies two types of mul-

---

    entity or individual, its name or name, address, postal code, organization code or resident ID number; if the applicant is a foreigner, foreign enterprise or other foreign organization, its name or name, Nationality or registered country or region (in Chinese); (3) The name of the designer; (4) If the applicant entrusts a patent agency, the name and agency code of the trustee agency, as well as the name, practice certificate number, and contact phone number of the patent agent designated by the agency; (5) Where priority is claimed, the application date, application number, and name of the original receiving agency when the applicant filed a patent application for the first time (the earliest application); (6) Signature or seal of the applicant or the patent agency; (7) List of application documents; (8) A list of additional documents; (9) Other related matters that need to be stated. The same provisions are contained in the 2020 draft version of the Implementing Rules that is in the process of being approved.

78 Patent Law Implementing Regulations 2014, art 1. The new article 1 of the Draft Implementing Regulations not yet in force, makes a more explicit statement about off and online filings, including design application filings:

    The various procedures stipulated in the Patent Law and these Regulations shall be handled in written form or other forms prescribed by the Patent Administration Department of the State Council. The written form includes electronic form and paper form.

    Various documents submitted in paper form are converted into electronic form by the patent administration department of the State Council and recorded in the electronic system database, which has the same effect as the original paper form documents, and the parties have evidence to prove that there are errors in the records of the electronic system database of the patent administration department of the State Council.

79 China Patent Law 2020, art 18.
80 Implementing Regulations of the China Patent Law 2014, art 15.3.
81 Implementing Regulations of the China Patent Law 2014, art 2.
82 China Patent Law 2020, art 28.
83 China Patent Law 2020, art 27.
84 China Patent Law 2020, art 31.2.

tiple designs. The first is the case of 'two or more similar designs of the same product'. The provision allows the filing of variations of a main design concept in one application. The law provides that the other designs of the product shall be similar to the main design indicated in the brief description and the number of similar designs contained in an application for design shall not exceed ten variations.[85] Furthermore, the Patent Examination Guidelines provide that two or more such designs will be considered similar if they only differ in fine details, features commonly found in the products in question, the repeated and continuous arrangement of a design unit, or mere differences in colours.[86] However, such definition does not include the case of designs of the same product in variable states, like for example of a toy car that can be unfolded into a robot. In such cases, each state of the product must be protected by a separate design application. The second case of designs eligible of multiple filings involves the classic example of the design of a teapot and the design of the teacups. The expression 'Two or more designs' which are incorporated in products belonging to the same class and being sold or used in set in Article 31.2 of the Patent Law, means not only that the products design belongs to the same class in the Locarno Classification, but also that they embody the same design concept and are customarily sold or used at the same time.[87]

3.060 The title and classification of the design are also important because they will affect later comparisons with prior art or with infringing designs in invalidation and infringement proceedings respectively. As we shall see in more detail, only designs of the same class or product category are to be compared. For instance, it will be important to make sure that the design is a 'car' and not a 'toy car', 'tableware' and not 'sticker for tableware'[88] and so on.

3.061 Upon receiving the required patent application documents, CNIPA will notify the applicant of the date of application and release the application number. For applications sent by mail, an acceptance notice from CNIPA shall generally be received within one to two months. Design applications are normally granted within 18 months from the filing date and offer a 15-year, non-renewable exclusive right of use and exploitation to the registrant, subject to payment of

---

85 Implementing Regulations of the China Patent Law 2014, art 35.1.
86 China Patent Examination Guidelines 2021, pt I, ch 3, art 9.1.2.3.
87 Implementing Regulations of the China Patent Law 2014, art 35.2.
88 Leknow Sun Min, 'Case Analysis of Design Patent Protection Scope: Name Limitation Leads to Non-infringement', 2020 Patent Talk https://zhuanlan.zhihu.com/p/56426932 accessed on May 15, 2023.

renewal fees.⁸⁹ An applicant may withdraw his or its application for a patent at any time before the patent right is granted.⁹⁰

(d) Drawings

3.062 The scope of protection of a design patent is determined by the product incorporating the patented design as shown in the drawings or photographs, while the brief description of the design features required with the application, may be used to explain the design as shown in the drawings or pictures.⁹¹ Therefore, the drawings or photographs are the most important features defining the scope of protection of the design patent.

3.063 The submitted drawing or picture should clearly show the design of the product that requires patent protection. The applicant shall submit a coloured picture or photograph in an application for a design patent for colour protection. For a design patent application containing the request for protection of colours, the colour of the picture should be firm and not fade easily.

3.064 In a three-dimensional design in which the essential features involve six sides, the applicant must file orthographic projections of the six side views. If the essential features involve less than six views, the applicant must provide an explanation as to why views are omitted in the design description.

3.065 In addition, the applicant can file reference views, normally used to provide context of the intended use of the product incorporating the design. Colours can be included, and the applicant may choose whether to specifically claim colours as an essential design feature.⁹²

3.066 If the product design involves only one surface, only the orthographic view of that side shall be submitted.⁹³ Whereas, if the product design key involves both sides, the two-sided orthographic view should be submitted. Multiple views can be arranged on the same drawing. The layout direction of each view should be consistent, and the views should be clearly separated from each other. Vertical or horizontal typesetting can be used. If necessary, the applicant should also submit the expanded view, cross-sectional view, enlarged view, and

---

89   China Patent Law 2020, art 42. The new 15-year duration for a design patent in China has been adopted by the latest amendment of the Patent Law in 2020. Previously, design patents had a duration of ten years.
90   China Patent Law 2020, art 32.
91   China Patent Law 2020, art 64.
92   China Patent Examination Guidelines 2021, pt I, ch 3, art 4.2.1, 4.2.2.
93   Classic example of plane or two-dimensional design that enjoys protection of the law is the GUIs, that can now be protected by design patents in China.

phase diagram of the design product. In addition, the applicant may submit reference drawings, which are usually used to indicate the purpose, method of use, or place of use of the design product.[94]

The applicant in such cases must also provide at least an orthographic projection of the involved design.[95] **3.067**

Article 27 of the 2021 Implementation Regulation of the Patent Law now allows full use of dotted and dashed lines together to disclaim portions of the design. However, the use of shading is not included and may not be allowed.[96] This will help when filing partial design applications. In fact, a partial design application, as any design application, will have to first comply with the requirement of Article 27 of the Patent Law by including a view of the overall product. At the same time, the overall product will have to be disclaimed from the scope and this will have to be done by using dotted or dashed lines. **3.068**

(e) Partial design

Until the 2020 amendment, protection for partial design was available in China only for limited exceptions.[97] At most, partial designs could be highlighted in the description of the whole design. **3.069**

The amended Patent Law now allows partial designs. Article 2.4 of the Patent Law reads: 'Designs mean any new design of the shape, the pattern, or their combination, or the combination of the color with shape or pattern, of a product *in whole or in part*, which creates an aesthetic appeal and is fit for industrial application.'[98] **3.070**

Such an amendment places the China Patent Law closer to the US and the EU design systems, enabling applicants to protect their designs and innovations more comprehensively. With the introduction of the partial design, there is no longer a need for applicants to delete or modify the dotted line from their prior **3.071**

---

94 Patent Examination Guidelines 2021, pt I, ch 3, art 4.2.3.
95 Patent Examination Guidelines 2021, pt I, ch 3, art 4.2.4.
96 Draft Implementing Regulations of the Patent Law 2020, art 27. The provision stipulates that: 'Whoever applies for a partial design patent shall submit a view of the overall product and use a combination of dashed and solid lines or other means to indicate the content that needs to be protected.'
97 2014 China Patent Law, art. 31.2 provided that the law protects the design of any parts of a product that can be used and sold separately from the main product. This provision made protection dependent on the part relation to the whole.
98 Until the fourth amendment to the Patent Law in 2020, partial designs were protectable if the parts of product they referred to, could be sold, or used separately from the main product.

application into solid lines when submitting applications in China based on the priority of a partial design application in the US or the EU.

3.072 A more detailed definition of partial design is now provided by the amended Patent Examination Guidelines:

> Partial design refers to a new design that is aesthetically pleasing and suitable for industrial applications based on the partial shape, pattern, or combination of products, as well as the combination of color, shape, and pattern. Where the protection of an indivisible part of a product is required, the application shall be submitted in the form of a partial design. For example, 'carved seat backrest', 'automobile tire tread', etc.[99]

3.073 As to the design description required by the Patent Law when filing the application, the draft of the 2021 Patent Examination Guidelines provides that the part to be protected and the whole product should be described in the product name.[100]

3.074 As to drawings, the outline of the part to be protected will have to be represented by a solid line, while dotted or dashed lines will be used to represent the rest of the product.[101] In addition, a partial enlarged view may also be used, that is, the content to be protected is the content displayed in the enlarged view described, in conjunction with the brief description. Alternative ways to separate the solid line of the partial design from the rest, like for example shading, seems to be allowed by the amended examination guidelines.[102] However, in such latter case, the description must provide supporting explanation.[103]

3.075 Although partial designs can be represented by pictures instead of drawings, in practice it may be more difficult to use the photo format to reflect the partial design to be protected, as it is often difficult to distinguish partial designs through pictures or photos.[104] Although the applicant may be able to supplement the picture or photo with a brief description, the textual explanation is not as direct and clear as the visual presentation, and this could cause difficulties to the applicant in later invalidation or infringement proceedings.

3.076 The eligibility requirements will be determined on the features of the partial design independently from the overall design product, thereby increasing

---

99 Patent Examination Guidelines 2021, pt I, ch 3, art 4.4.
100 Ibid.
101 Draft Implementing Regulations 2020, art 30.2.
102 Patent Examination Guidelines 2021, pt I, ch 3, art 4.4.2.
103 Patent Examination Guidelines 2021, pt I, ch 3, art 4.4.3.1.
104 Pictures can be also another type of reproduction of the design that is neither a photo or a technical drawing: e.g., pictures of CAD simulations.

the probability of surviving validity challenges and to effectively enforce the design against infringers. On the other hand, the partial design will have to remain visible once incorporated into the main product, to continue enjoying protection.

Partial design applications will not likely be obtainable by filing a divisional application following the rejection of a whole design application. The 2021 Draft Amendment to the Patent Examination Guidelines provides that if the original application is a design relating to the entire product, part of it is not allowed to be submitted as a divisional application. In case the original application is just a partial design, the applicant is not allowed to submit the entire product or other parts as a divisional application.[105] **3.077**

At present, although the CNIPA currently allows the submission of partial design application documents, no examination will be performed due to the lack of an approved version of the implementing regulations to the China Patent Law and the amendment of the Patent Examination Guidelines, to address all these practical questions. **3.078**

Although the admission of partial design protection in China is a sign of modernization of the Chinese Patent Law, challenges will remain in a system that provides only formal examination of design applications and for decades that has been the hotbed of patent squatting. Amendments to the examination procedures and the use of new technologies boosted by artificial intelligence, may reduce the risk of rising junk partial designs, thus reducing the cost and risk of legitimate prior right holders. **3.079**

(f) Examination procedure

Design patents in China are not examined as to their substantive eligibility requirements such as novelty, originality, and aesthetic effect. Lack of any eligibility requirement will have to be normally raised after the registration of the design by means of filing an administrative proceeding for design patent invalidation. Therefore, the CNIPA will generally examine a design patent application only as to its formal requirements. In accordance with Article 40 of the Patent Law, the patent examination department of CNIPA will perform a preliminary examination for design applications. This includes the determination of whether the grant of the design patent would violate the laws of the state, is contrary to the socialist morality, or is detrimental to public interest.[106] **3.080**

---

105 Patent Examination Guidelines 2021, pt I, ch 3, art 9.4.2.
106 China Patent Law 2020, art 5.

3.081 During the preliminary examination process, the examiner will issue a notice of rectification in case of formal problems that can be corrected by the applicant. This is often the case of correcting bibliographic data in the filed forms or errors in filling in the required forms.[107] The applicant can make corrections and supplement whatever is required in accordance with the notice. In case of obvious defects (e.g., defects in the supplied drawings or pictures), the examiner at CNIPA will issue an office action in which he will also express his opinion and recommendations and will invite the applicant to file a response within a given deadline.[108] In case the applicant fails to respond to the notice of rectification by the Office or the Office action, CNIPA will issue a Notice that the application is deemed to be withdrawn.[109] A non-rectifiable defect in an application shall lead to a direct decision to reject the application.[110] However, if no such defects are found, or any rectifications and corrections have been made and accepted by the Office, the Office must immediately issue the relevant patent certificate, and register and announce it with a Notice of Grant. The design patent right shall become effective as on the date of announcement.[111] The whole process may presently last between eight to 12 months, of which, three to six months are taken up by the formal examination phase.

3.082 Against a rejection decision, the applicant can file a request for re-examination with the patent division of CNIPA. The review procedure must be filed with a written complaint within three months from the date of receipt of the rejection notification.[112] Against an unfavourable review decision, the applicant can file an administrative appeal with the Beijing IP Court within three months from receiving notification of the review decision.[113]

3.083 In the most recent effort to reduce the rise of invalid filings, the Patent Examination Guidelines has introduced the possibility that an examiner may conduct a substantive examination of the element of distinctiveness of the filed design patent in partial and limited derogation of the principle of sole formal examination of design patent applications. In particular, it provides that during the preliminary examination, the patent examiner can verify whether the application is 'obviously' not in compliance with the requirement of distinctiveness

---

107 Patent Examination Guidelines 2021, pt I, ch 3, art 3.2.
108 Patent Examination Guidelines 2021, pt I, ch 3, art 3.3.
109 Patent Examination Guidelines 2021, pt I, ch 3, art 3.4. It provides an extension to file a response in case the applicant can prove he was not able to respond by the original deadline for good reasons.
110 Patent Examination Guidelines 2021, pt I, ch 3, art 3.5.
111 China Patent Law 2020, art 40 and Patent Examination Guidelines 2021, pt I, ch 3, art 3.1.
112 China Patent Law 2020, art 41.1.
113 China Patent Law 2020, art 41.2.

set forth in Article 23 of the Patent Law. In practice, the examiner could decide to compare the existing designs with the application.[114] While previous attempts at curbing malicious filings focused on verifying cases of obvious lack of novelty, the new provision extends the check to the other requirement of distinctiveness.

(g) Publication, registration and renewal

Following the preliminary examination, the design is published. A design patent is enforceable immediately after the grant. 3.084

After the publication of the design patent, a registration certificate will be issued by CNIPA. The design patent will be valid for 15 years from the date of filing.[115] A Chinese design patent is not renewable. Any further development of a design patent will have to be filed as a new application. An expired design patent, although not renewable, can still be protected in China by copyright, 3D marks or trade dress,[116] if the conditions and requirements for these parallel protections are met. 3.085

After a design patent grant is announced, the patentee or any interested party may request the CNIPA to make a patent right evaluation report.[117] Given that the patent is granted without substantive examination, such report can be used to evaluate the strength of the design just granted and prepare for its future defence against invalidations, or to be enforced against infringers. 3.086

2. International Registrations

On February 5, 2022, China acceded to the Hague Agreement Concerning the International Registration of Industrial Designs ('Hague Convention').[118] China has been negotiating such accession for a few years, and it was partly anticipated by certain measures of harmonization introduced with the latest amendment to the Patent Law in 2019, such as, the extension of a design patent duration from ten to 15 years. 3.087

---

114 Patent Examination Guidelines 2021, pt I, ch 3, art 8.3.
115 China Patent Law 2020, art 42.
116 Trade dress protection of an expired design patent was recognized for the first time in 2010 In 上海中韩晨光文具制造有限公司诉宁波微亚达制笔有限公司宁波微亚达文具有限公司、上海成硕工贸有限公司擅自使用知名商品特有装潢纠纷再审案（2010）民提字第16号 (*Shanghai Zhonghan Chenguang Stationery Manufacturing Co, Ltd v. Ningbo Weiyada Pen Co, Lt,. Ningbo Weiyada Stationery Co., Ltd. and Shanghai Chengshuo Industry and Trade Co, Ltd* (2010) Min Ti Zi No. 16).
117 Implementing Regulations of the China Patent Law 2014, art 56.
118 The Geneva Act 1999 of the Hague Agreement Concerning the International Registration of Industrial Designs was adopted on July 2, 1999. The Geneva Act 1999 entered into force on December 23, 2003.

3.088 The Hague Convention allows right holders to secure design protection simultaneously in multiple countries or regions through a single international application, in a single language with a single set of fees and, unlike the Madrid Convention for trademarks, there is no requirement to file a national application first. Inventors in China will thus be able to use the International Design System to file and protect their designs overseas with one procedure which will help them save time and money. At the same time, foreign right holders will be able to cover China with one application filed in their language and English with one set of fees.

3.089 Under the Hague Convention, the international application filed with WIPO is examined only as to formalities and published within 12 months from the filing date. Each country designated by the applicant has the right to perform a substantive examination of the application. Given that China does not provide for substantive examination of design applications, the WIPO examination and publication will complete the examination formalities. China may still reject the application on other grounds and has six to 12 months to do that. Such rejections may centre mostly on certain differences in the design formalities and drawing standards still existing between China and the US or Europe. Despite the recent reforms in China concerning design technical standards and drawings requirements, we may expect rejections by the China IPO (CNIPA) based on such grounds.

C. DISPUTING DESIGN RIGHTS

1. Invalidation

3.090 As design applications are not examined as to substance, challenges to the patent validity will have to be raised through an administrative complaint with the competent patent authority under CNIPA.[119] It is important to highlight the fact that in cases where a design patent under invalidation is also the object of an infringement lawsuit, the validity claims will not be heard and decided by the infringement judge, but by the CNIPA in a parallel proceeding.

3.091 An invalidation procedure is initiated by filing a formal complaint to the patent administrative department of the CNIPA[120] and by paying the required

---

119   China Patent Law 2020, art 45.
120   Patent Examination Guidelines 2021, pt IV, ch 3, art 3.4.

administrative fees.[121] The complaint must be in written form and contain the grounds for requesting invalidation as well as the supporting evidence.[122] Failure to comply with these legal requirements will result in the rejection of the invalidation complaint.[123] The initial phase of case acceptance may last three to four months and will be concluded with a formal notification by CNIPA that the petitioner's invalidation complaint has been accepted. In cases where the design patent under invalidation is also involved in an infringement lawsuit, the CNIPA will also send a notification of pending invalidation to the civil court.[124] The infringement judge may then decide to suspend the civil litigation pending the invalidation proceeding. The invalidation petitioner has the right to request this suspension in the civil lawsuit. The invalidation complaint will then be notified to the respondent with a summon to file rebuttal and counterevidence within a deadline. The patentee/respondent will have a month from the notification of the complaint to file its defences and provide supporting counterevidence.[125] Once the CNIPA receives the response from the patentee, it will send it to the invalidation petitioner with a new deadline, normally 30 days, to make additional rebuttals and provide rebutting evidence. If one of the parties does not respond to the transferred documents within the given deadline, said party will be deemed to have knowledge of the facts, causes and evidence contained in the notified documents and to have waived its right to respond.[126]

3.092 In this initial phase of defence and evidence exchanges, the invalidation petitioner can modify or add causes of action to its original complaint, but will have to do this within 30 days from the filing of the original invalidation petition or will otherwise lose the right.[127] The only exception concerns cases

---

121 Patent Examination Guidelines 2021, pt IV, ch 3, art 3.5. This norm provides that the fees must be paid within one month from the filing date of the appeal.
122 Implementing Regulations of the China Patent Law 2014, art 65. Patent Examination Guidelines 2021, pt IV, ch 3, art 3.3.5 provides in particular that the petitioner must explain the causes of invalidation in a concrete manner, that is not in an abstract sentence stating general principles or facts, while reference must be made to the supporting evidence. In the comparison section of the complaint the petitioner must explain the design and all its features and conduct a comparison based on the examination principles established by the law.
123 Implementing Regulations of the China Patent Law 2014, art 66.
124 Patent Examination Guidelines 2021, pt IV, ch 3, art 3.7.5., 4.1.1. s.
125 Implementing Regulations of the China Patent Law 2014, art 68 and 2021 Patent Examination Guidelines 2021, pt IV, ch3, art 3.7.3. It is worth noticing that while art 69 of the Patent Law allows the owner of a patent or a utility model to make amendments to the claims within the original scope of protection of the patent, such an option of modifying the design is not available to the design holder.
126 Implementing Regulations of the China Patent Law 2014, art 68 and Patent Examination Guidelines 2021, pt IV, ch 3, art 4.4.1 in combination with of the Patent Examination Guidelines 2021, pt IV, ch 3, art 4.1.1.
127 Implementing Regulations of the China Patent Law 2014, art 67 and Patent Examination Guidelines 2021, pt IV, ch 3, art 4.2.1.

of amending the causes of invalidation that are obviously irrelevant to the submitted evidence, so as to avoid a rejection of the invalidation ex officio.[128] The same general principle applies to the submission of additional evidence. Additional evidence by the petitioner must be submitted within a month from the filing of the original complaint and the petitioner must explain how such additional evidence is relevant to the claims.[129] Late filings will be rejected. One important exception concerns the late filing of new evidence. The law provides that evidence, that is in common knowledge of the person skilled in the art, or is complementary for meeting legal requirements or to complete required formalities (e.g., notarizations and legalizations) is admissible.[130] The same provisions apply for the additional evidence filed by the patentee.[131]

3.093 Once the exchange of defences and rebuttals is completed, the CNIPA will arrange for an oral hearing. Although not mandatory, it is normal practice to call such oral hearing.[132] Normally, it may take place within three to four months from the evidence exchange phase. During the hearing the evidence and defences will be cross-examined.[133] A decision can be issued at the oral hearing, but it is rarely, or, more commonly given within a couple of months from the hearing. The decision must be delivered in written form and is appealable. It is important to note that, if the petitioner fails to appear at the hearing, the CNIPA will dismiss the case as the non-participation is equated to a request for withdrawal.[134] The petitioner has the right to withdraw its invalidation complaint at any time before the CNIPA decision is issued and notified.[135] However, the CNIPA retains discretion in deciding whether a withdrawal will be accepted. CNIPA retains the right to issue a full or partial invalidation decision even in cases of withdrawal by the petitioner.[136] This is an important point to consider especially if the parties to the dispute decide to settle the case and make the withdrawal one of the settlement conditions. It

---

128 Patent Examination Guidelines 2021, pt IV, ch 3, art 4.2.2 (ii) and Patent Examination Guidelines 2021, pt IV, ch 3, art 4.1.1.
129 Implementing Regulations of the China Patent Law 2014, art 67 and Patent Examination Guidelines 2021, pt IV, ch 3, art 4.3.1.1 and Patent Examination Guidelines 2021, pt IV, ch 3, art 4.1.(1).
130 Patent Examination Guidelines 2021, pt IV, ch 3, art 4.3.1.2 (i) and (ii), 4.1.1.
131 Patent Examination Guidelines 2021, pt IV, ch 3, art 4.3.2, 4.1.1.
132 Implementing Regulations of the China Patent Law 2014, art 70 and Patent Examination Guidelines 2021, pt IV, ch 3, art 4.4.2, 4.1.1.
133 The Patent Examination Guidelines dedicate the whole of Chapter 4 of Part IV to describe in detail the formalities and procedure of the oral hearing.
134 Implementing Regulations of the China Patent Law 2014, art 70.3 and Patent Examination Guidelines 2021, pt IV, ch 3, art 7 and Patent Examination Guidelines 2021, pt IV, ch 3, art 4.1.1.
135 Implementing Regulations of the China Patent Law 2014, art 72.1.
136 Implementing Regulations of the China Patent Law 2014, art 72.2

would defy the agreement's consideration if, despite the withdrawal, the owner would still lose the patent.

Any patent declared invalid, is deemed as it never existed. Therefore, the invalidation retroacts to the time of the design patent first filing.[137] The decision on invalidating a patent shall, prior to the invalidation of the patent, have no retroactive effect on any judgment or mediation document on patent infringement which has been made and enforced by the people's court, on any implemented or compulsorily enforced decision concerning the settlement of a dispute over patent infringement, or on any performed contract for licensing a patent exploitation or for assignment of patent right. However, the patentee shall compensate for the damages it has maliciously caused to others.[138] In cases where no appeal is filed by the patentee within the appeal deadline, the decision is final. In case of rejection of the invalidation petition, the petitioner will be barred from refiling an invalidation petition on the same reasons and evidence, in application of the general legal principle of '*ne bis in idem*' (no two judgments on the same demand).[139]

3.094

A party dissatisfied with the CNIPA decision can file an administrative appeal with the Beijing IP Court within three months from the receipt of the notification of the decision.[140] The appealed party will be the CNIPA, while the non-appealing party has the right to attend the proceedings and file supportive arguments as a third party.[141] If no appeal of the decision is filed within the deadline, the decision is final and will be announced by CNIPA.

3.095

2. Design Infringement

According to Article 11.2 of the Patent Law after the granting of a patent for a design, no entity or individual shall, without permission of the patentee, exploit the patent, that is to say, they shall not make, promise to sell, sell, or import the product incorporating its or his patented design, for production and business purposes. Based on China's dual enforcement system, design patent holders can file either an administrative or a civil suit to enforce their exclusive design rights against unauthorized use.[142] Administrative enforcement includes summary administrative proceedings and custom border protection.

3.096

---

137 China Patent Law 2020, art 47.1.
138 China Patent Law 2020, art 47.2.
139 Implementing Regulations of the China Patent Law 2014, art 66.2.
140 China Patent Law 2020, art 46.2.
141 Ibid.
142 China Patent Law 2020, art 65.

Administrative proceedings aim at stopping the infringement through an administrative fine and injunctions, but do not allow damage compensation claims, which are in the exclusive jurisdiction of civil judges of the people's courts. Administrative enforcement must be given precedence over a civil lawsuit when the design patent is already being litigated in a civil court.

3.097 In the following section, we will present a detailed description of both administrative and civil proceedings for the enforcement of IP rights and in particular, design patents.

3. Civil Enforcement

3.098 Civil proceedings are initiated with the filing of a lawsuit or a pre-trial motion for injunction or evidence preservation with a people's court.[143] The lawsuit can be filed by the patent holder or the exclusive licensee. The non-exclusive licensee can be a plaintiff only with the consent of the right holder.[144]

3.099 People's Courts are entrusted by the law to hear IP cases.[145] Cases involving foreign parties, like a foreign plaintiff or defendant, are filed with the People's Intermediate Court, or IP Courts depending on the rules of territorial jurisdiction as we shall see in the following paragraph.[146] The statute of limitations of actions for patent infringement cases is three years, calculated from the date when the patentee or interested parties became aware of or should have become aware of the infringement.[147] There are three degrees of jurisdiction in Chinese civil litigation: A first instance trial can last between 12 to 18 months[148] depending on the case complexity and whether the court decides to suspend

---

143 Civil Procedure Law of the People's Republic of China 2017, art 120 (中华人民共和国民事诉讼法 http://www.legaldaily.com.cn/zt/content/2020-07/07/content_8239108.html).
144 China Patent Law 2020, art 65.
145 Civil Procedure Law 2017, art 6. However, civil courts, even the Supreme People's Court, are subject to the supervision of the criminal prosecution system. In fact, the Civil Procedure Law 2017, art 14 provides that the People's Procuratorate has the right of supervision over civil litigation. This explains why, even after a retrial decision by the Supreme People's Court, a party could still file a petition with the People's Procuratorate in Beijing to complain of any alleged violation of the law by the civil or administrative courts.
146 最高人民法院关于审理专利纠纷案件适用法律问题的若干规定，法释〔2015〕4号 2015年2月1日起施行，第二条 (Several Provisions of the Supreme People's Court on Applicable Legal Issues in the Trial of Patent Dispute Cases, issued by the Supreme People's Court, No.4/2015, art. 2). Based on this provision, Intermediate Courts are now in charge of hearing patent disputes cases even without foreign elements, thus eliminating the jurisdiction of the grass root courts over patent infringement disputes.
147 China Patent Law 2020, art 74.
148 Civil Procedure Law 2017, art 149 provides strict terms for the conclusion of a first instance case:
Cases tried by the people's court using ordinary procedures shall be concluded within six months from the date of filing the case. If there are special circumstances that need to be extended, it can be extended for six months with the approval of the president of this court; if it needs to be extended, it should be reported to the higher people's court for approval.

the case following the filing of a parallel design patent invalidation suite by the defendant in the infringement case. A first instance judgment will become final and effective if the other party does not file appeal within the assigned deadline.

Appeals are filed through the court of first instance which then transfer the case to the people's court of second instance.[149] This transfer takes place within a few days, but delays are common, sometimes stretching for several weeks or even months. The appellate panel is composed of three to five judges[150] and decisions are taken by majority. After hearing an appellate case, the people's court of second instance can: (1) reject the appeal and sustain the first instance judgment if the facts were clearly found and the law was correctly applied in the original judgment; (2) amend the judgment if the law was incorrectly applied in the original judgment; (3) overrule the first instance judgment and send the case back to the court of first instance for retrial if in the original judgment the facts were incorrectly found or were not clearly found and the evidence was inconclusive. The people's court of second instance may also decide to amend the judgment directly after investigating and clarifying the facts; (4) overrule the first instance judgment and send the case back for retrial if in the original judgment there were violations of the prescribed procedure that may have affected its correctness.[151] A judgment of appeal is immediately effective and enforceable.[152] Appellate proceedings should last no more than three months.[153] In practice this deadline can be extended as needed. **3.100**

It is still possible for any party in the procedure to apply to the Supreme People's Court or the court of higher instance for the retrial of the case, when the party believes the final appellate judgment is wrong.[154] Retrial is possible only under special circumstances categorically provided by the Civil Procedure[155] **3.101**

In practice, courts retains discretion as to duration depending on the case complexity. However, judges will tend to close a case within the same year when it was filed if the lawsuit was initiated in the first part of the year. This has a lot to do with the internal regulations and management guidelines of each court, including assignment of promotion and bonuses to judges and management of court resources.

149 Civil Procedure Law 2017, art 166.
150 Civil Procedure Law 2017, art 40.
151 Civil Procedure Law 2017, art 153.
152 Civil Procedure Law 2017, art 175.
153 Civil Procedure Law 2017, art 176.
154 Civil Procedure Law 2017, art 199.
155 Civil Procedure Law 2017, art 200. This norm provides that: (1) There is new evidence sufficient to overturn the original judgment or ruling; (2) The basic facts found in the original judgment or ruling lack evidence to prove; (3) The main evidence for the facts found in the original judgment or ruling is forged; (4) The main evidence for the facts found in the original judgment or ruling has not been cross-examined; (5) For the main evidence needed for the trial of the case, the parties cannot obtain by themselves due to objective reasons, and apply to the people's court in writing for investigation and collection, but the people's court has not investi-

and the Supreme People's Court has clear discretion (*certiorari*) in determining such circumstances and the acceptance of a request for retrial.[156] The Supreme People's Court also has the right to advocate jurisdiction on cases that have a countrywide impact.[157] The Supreme People's Court exercises sole discretion to evaluate this impact and this does not need to be of legal nature. The judgments of the Supreme People's Court are final and not appealable.[158]

(a) Civil claims

3.102 Infringement claims can be filed against the acts of manufacturing, selling, offering for sale and importing products infringing a design patent.[159] Unlike invention patents and utility models, only the use of a design functions and technical benefit for production and business purposes without consent of the right holder is prohibited by the law. Therefore, the mere use of a design without any intent of economic exploitation would not qualify as an infringement and would not rise to an actionable claim.

(b) Remedies

3.103 According to Article 179 of the Civil Code the following remedies are available to a right holder, including the owner of a design patent against an infringer: (1) cessation of the infringement; (2) removal of the nuisance; (3) elimination of the danger; (4) restitution; (5) restoration; (6) repair, redoing or replacement; (7) continuance of performance; (8) compensation for losses; (9) payment of liquidated damages; (10) elimination of adverse effects and rehabilitation of reputation; and (11) extension of apologies. Where punitive damages are provided by law, such provisions shall be followed. Below we elaborate the remedy of damages as compensation.

---

gated and collected it; (6) The application of the law in the original judgment or ruling is indeed wrong; (7) The composition of the trial organization is illegal or the judges who should be recused in accordance with the law have not recused; (8) A person with no capacity for litigation does not participate in the litigation without a legally-designated representative or a party who should participate in the litigation because of reasons that cannot be attributable to him or his litigation representative; (9) Violating the law and depriving the parties of the right to debate; (10) Judgment in absentia without being summoned by a subpoena; (11) The original judgment or ruling omitted or exceeded the litigation request; (12) The legal document on which the original judgment or ruling was made has been revoked or changed; (13) The judges committed embezzlement and acceptance of bribes, practiced malpractice for personal gains, or violated the law in the trial of the case.

156 Civil Procedure Law 2017, art 20(2).
157 Civil Procedure Law 2017, art 20(1).
158 Civil Procedure Law 2017, art 155.
159 China Patent Law 2020, art 11.2. In practice, also claims against the act of export are actionable in a Chinese court as a form of unauthorized use of the patent right.

(i) Damages

3.104 The damages for a patent infringement shall be determined according to the actual loss suffered by the right holder due to the infringement or the profit obtained by the infringer from the infringement. If it is difficult to determine the loss suffered by the right holder or the profit obtained by the infringer, the damages shall be reasonably determined by reference to the multiple of the royalty for the enforced patent. Where it is difficult to determine the loss suffered by the right holder, the benefits obtained by the infringer, and the patent royalty, the people's court may, by taking into account factors such as the type of the patent and the nature and circumstances of the infringement, determine the damages as neither less than 30,000 Chinese Yuan (also referred to as RMB) nor more than five million Yuan.[160]

3.105 It is important to note that the amount of compensation determined by one of the above methods, or by resorting to the statutory range, will also have to include the reasonable expenses the plaintiff has incurred to stop the infringement. The law includes the investigation and attorney cost.[161]

3.106 The 2020 fourth amendment of the Patent Law introduced punitive damages into patent litigation in China. The China Patent Law provides that in case of an intentional patent infringement with serious circumstances, the damages may be determined as no less than one, nor more than five times, the amount determined based on the already mentioned calculation methods.[162]

(c) Most common defences

3.107 Within the time limits established by the infringement procedure, a defendant in a design patent infringement lawsuit has a number of key defences: (a) defendant can file a motion to object the court jurisdiction; (b) defendant can file a parallel invalidation proceeding against the enforced patent and request suspension of the infringement proceedings; (c) the user or seller of a patented product can prove he obtained the product legitimately and without knowing that the product was produced and sold without permission of the patentee;[163] (d) defendant can counterclaim that its product does not infringe the design patent (different class of products, different visual effect); (e) defendant can counterclaim it has an identical right (e.g., Design, 3D mark, copyright, trade dress). Most commonly, the defendant may have applied for a later design

---

160 China Patent Law 2020, art 71.
161 China Patent Law 2020, art 71.2.
162 China Patent Law 2020, art 71.
163 China Patent Law 2020, art 77.

patent or utility model for the same product. The court shall always grant protection to the prior register right;[164] (f) defendant can counterclaim that the design was already known to the prior art before the date of filing of the plaintiff's patent (prior art defence);[165] (g) defendant can counterclaim estoppel, which bars a patentee who has withdrawn certain subject matter from the scope of protection during the patent application process or invalidation proceeding (by making a narrowing amendment or making a statement to the patent office that narrowly interpreted a claim term) from reclaiming it in an infringement proceeding.[166]

4. Administrative Enforcement

3.108 The patent administrative department of the State Council may handle patent infringement disputes at the request of the patentee or interested party.[167] Although Administrative bodies are not entitled to settle claims for damage compensation, the law still provides that the patent administrative department, upon request of the parties may hold a mediation regarding the compensation amount for infringement of the patent right. This could be a good strategic tool to seek a quick settlement and case resolution with an infringer, especially in cases of lesser economic value.[168] If the defendant is eventually found guilty of infringement, the patent administrative department will issue a judgment where it can order confiscation of any illegal income, and may fine the infringer no more than five times the illegal income or if there is no illegal income or the illegal income is no more than 50,000 Yuan, issue a fine of not more than 250,000 Yuan. If the infringement reaches the threshold for criminal liability, the case will be transferred to the criminal authorities.[169] This rarely happens, especially in case of design patent infringements, given also the very vague thresholds to determine criminal liability and the often-conflicting interests of different administrations with overlapping competence over the same cases.

---

164 Several Provisions of the Supreme People's Court on Applicable Legal Issues in the Trial of Patent Dispute cases of January 2015, No. 4/2015, art 15 (n 146).
165 China Patent Law 2020, art 67 and 最高人民法院关于审理侵犯专利权纠纷案件应用法律若干问题的解释, 法释[2009]21号, 发文日期: 2009-12-28,生效日期: 第十四条 (Interpretations of the Supreme People's Court Concerning Certain Issues on the Application of Law for the Trial of Cases on Disputes over Infringement on Patent Rights, Fa Shi 2009 no 21 of December 28, 2009, effective on January 1, 2010 art 14.2).
166 最高人民法院关于审理侵犯专利权纠纷案件应用法律若干问题的解释, 法释[2009]21号, 发文日期: 2009-12-28,生效日期: 第六条 (Interpretations of the Supreme People's Court Concerning Certain Issues on the Application of Law for the Trial of Cases on Disputes over Infringement on Patent Rights, Fa Shi 2009 no 21 of December 28, 2009, effective on January 1, 2010, art 6).
167 China Patent Law 2020, arts 65, 70.
168 China Patent Law 2020, art 65.
169 China Patent Law 2020, art 68.

Similar to the procedure before the people's court, the plaintiff must be the patent holder, his/her heirs or the exclusive licensee. The non-exclusive licensee can be a plaintiff only with the consent of the right holder.[170] Proceedings for infringement disputes are filed with a Letter of Request containing the facts of the case and the supporting evidence, as well as any other requests such as evidence investigation or evidence preservation.[171] The case must be docketed within five days.[172] The procedure is faster compared to court proceedings where the same initial phase may last a couple of months or more. In fact, the procedure must be wrapped up within three months from the date of filing and an extension of maximum 30 days is allowed only in extremely complicated cases.[173] However, the time of a suspension, for example in case of suspension pending an invalidation of the actioned design patent, will not be computed in the three months' deadline. The same applies to the time required for an expert appraisal where one is appointed.[174] Eventually, the patent administration officials in charge of a case have the discretion to decide whether the case can be decided with or without an oral hearing. An oral hearing can also be requested by one or both parties and must be approved by the officials in charge of the case.[175]

3.109

The judgment with the cease-and-desist injunction will be published within 20 days from its issuance[176] and can be appealed before the territorially competent administrative court or an administrative review can be initiated with the administration supervising the local patent bureau.[177] The judgment will not be halted by the appeal or review procedure.[178]

3.110

D. SIGNIFICANT JUDICIAL DECISIONS IN THE JURISDICTION

Unlike common law system jurisdictions, China's interpretation of the laws is normally provided in a statutory form. However, Opinions and Interpretations of the law by the Supreme People's Court are binding on all civil and admin-

3.111

---

170 专利行政执法办 – 2010年12月29日国家知识产权局令第60号发布 根据2015年5月29日发布的国家知识产权局令第七十一号，第十条 (Patent Administrative Law Enforcement Measures, Promulgated by order no 60 of the State IP office on December 29, 2010, according to order no 71 of the State IP Office on May 29, 2015, art 10).
171 Measures for Patent Administrative Law Enforcement 2015, art 12.
172 Measures for Patent Administrative Law Enforcement 2015, art 13.
173 Measures for Patent Administrative Law Enforcement 2015, art 21.
174 Measures for Patent Administrative Law Enforcement 2015, art 21.
175 Measures for Patent Administrative Law Enforcement 2015, art 16.
176 Measures for Patent Administrative Law Enforcement 2015, art 46.
177 Measures for Patent Administrative Law Enforcement 2015, art 48.
178 Ibid.

istrative judges and patent examiners. Furthermore, since the creation of specialized IP courts, judicial precedence and their citation in design patents' infringement or invalidation proceedings have become more common and the decisions of some courts, like the Beijing and Shanghai IP courts have become very authoritative. In this section, we will provide an example of a leading judicial decision in the field of Design patent that applies many of the rules described in the preceding sections of this chapter.

1. Scope of Protection and Designer Freedom

3.112 To provide a concrete and schematic example of the process leading to the determination of a design patent's scope of protection and the identity/similarity analysis, we will break down the Supreme People's Court steps that led to the judgment in the retrial of the Grohe decision by the Supreme People's Court in 2015.[179]

3.113 The case concerned the infringement and the parallel invalidation proceedings of a patent for the outer design of a shower head owned by the German company Grohe AG by the Chinese company Zhejiang Jianlong Sanitary Ware Co, Ltd. Grohe sued Jianlong in 2012 before the Taizhou Intermediate Court, which rejected Grohe's claims and found that the differences between the two products were sufficient to take the overall similarity of their visual effects. In the appeal proceedings the Higher Court of Zhejiang province criticized the reasoning process of the first instance court. The appellate court noted that the infringement comparison conducted by the trial court was a simple listing and accumulation of the differences between the design and a one-on-one comparison. The appellate court instead, after introducing the method of designer freedom to guide the ordinary user test in the determination of the scope of protection and similarity comparison of the designs in question, concluded that the Jianlong's product indeed infringed Grohe's design patent. In particular, the appellate court went on to compare the selected aesthetic visual features of the design patent with the prior art and concluded that the runway-shaped sprinkler outlet surface should be considered as the design feature of the authorized design that is different from the existing design. The accused infringement design adopted a highly similar outlet surface design. All the other differences were minor decorative or minor visible elements that did not take away the feeling of overall visual similarity of the compared designs. Jianlong, dissatisfied with the decision, filed a request for retrial with the Supreme People's Court in 2015. The Supreme People's

---

179 *Grohe* (n 31).

Court granted *certiorari*, and issued a judgment in August 2015 that revoked the appellate judgment and confirmed the judgment of first instance against Grohe's infringement claim.

The following are the steps undertaken by the Supreme People's Court in determining the scope of protection of the Grohe's patent and conducting the similarity analysis of the design with Jianlong's allegedly infringing product. 3.114

Step 1: Evaluation of the designs' classification 3.115

The Supreme People's Court reviewed whether the designs in dispute belonged to the same class. They are both shower heads and certainly belong to the same class of products.

Step 2: Determination of the design patent scope of protection 3.116

The design features of the design patent that give to it the protectable aesthetic visual effect was determined and selected. In making this determination the Supreme People's Court considered that 'For existing products, the patented design generally has part of the content of the existing design, and also has design content that is different or similar to the existing design. It is this part of the design content that makes the authorized design innovative.' To determine this the Supreme People's Court did two things:

(a) It evaluated the design features based on: (i) the drawings and whatever was recorded by the patentee in the brief description; (ii) the statements by Grohe about the design features made in the patent authorization confirmation before the patent re-examination Board or infringement proceedings (including search reports); (iii) Jianlong's counter-statements and supporting evidence. In this case, Grohe, claimed that the runway-shaped water surface was a design feature of the authorized design involved in the case, while Jianlong disputed such a claim by stating that also the handle and other components of the showerhead are relevant. However, Jianlong did not provide evidence to support its counterclaim. The Supreme People's Court, after reviewing the search report in the parallel invalidation proceedings containing references to prior designs as well, concluded that the runway-shaped water surface is indeed one of the relevant design features in this case, compared to the prior art.
(b) Next, the Supreme People's Court proceeded to identify the parts of the design and the related class of product that are easily and directly observable during normal use of the registered design products involved in the

case. In particular, the Court set out to identify: '(…) the parts that are easy to be directly observed during normal use of an authorized design product (…) from the perspective of the general consumer, according to the use of the product, and comprehensive consideration of the various use conditions of the product'. Shower heads normally consist of nozzles and handles and the portion of space they occupy compared to the entire product structure is generally the same. Furthermore, the shower nozzle product can be hand-held or hung on the wall for use. In its normal use state, the nozzle, the handle and their connection are the parts most easily and directly observable by the ordinary user.

(c) Further, the Supreme People's Court considered whether the design also contained solely functional features. In particular, the Court considered whether the button on the handle of the Grohe design patent was a design feature solely dictated by technical necessity, and therefore excluded from the design scope of protection, or whether it allowed room for aesthetic factors and was therefore to be included in the overall visual effect of the design patent. In this respect the Court concluded that:

> The function of the push button is to control the water flow switch. Whether to set the push button is determined by whether the function of controlling the water flow switch needs to be implemented on the final shower head product. However, the shape of the push button can have a variety of designs. When ordinary consumers see the push button on the shower head handle, they will naturally pay attention to its decoration and consider whether the design of the push button is aesthetically pleasing, rather than just considering whether the push button can realize the function of controlling the water flow switch.

Therefore, there is still freedom for the designer to add aesthetic visual elements. The Supreme People's Court included the push button in the design scope of protection's relevant features.

In light of the above, the Supreme People's Court clearly stated, that based on the design patent drawings and additional relevant documents and evidence, the scope of protection included the new shape of the nozzle with the runway-shaped water surface (over Jianlong's objection), that of the handle and its connection to the nozzle (over Grohe's objections), as well as the switch button on the handle (again over Grohe's objection) were the relevant design features that distinguished this design from the prior art and defined its scope of protection. All these features will be generally more influential to the overall visual effect of the design patent than other design features of the same.

3.117 Step 3: Comparison of the design patent with the alleged infringing product

The Supreme People's Court first looked at whether any features in the Jianlong design product were substantially similar to the selected features of the design patent. In this respect, the Court observed that the allegedly infringing design adopts a runway-shaped water surface design, that was highly similar to the authorized design involved in the case. Then the Court moved on to review the design features of the Jianlong design and listed the differences between the features of the two designs under comparison. In addition, the distinctive design features of the alleged infringing product design compared with the authorized design involved in the case other than non-design features should also be considered, as long as they are sufficient to make a significant difference between the two in terms of overall visual effects. Here is how the Court detailed the examination and analysis of the differences:

> In addition to the design feature of the sprinkler's water surface shape, design features such as the shape of the sprinkler and its transitions, the ratio of the width of the sprinkler to the diameter of the handle, and other design features also have a significant impact on the overall visual effect of the product. Although the design of the alleged infringing product adopts a runway-shaped water surface that is highly similar to the authorized design involved, the feature of the sprinkler and the transitional shape of each surface, as well as the sprinkler, handle and connection in the involved design patent are in a circular arc transition, while the sprinkler, handle and connection surfaces of the alleged infringing product design are all in an inclined transitions, which makes the overall design style of the two appear obviously different. In addition, the distinctive design features of the alleged infringing product design compared with the authorized design involved in the case other than non-design features should also be considered as long as they are sufficient to make a significant difference between the two in terms of overall visual effects. Secondly, the nozzles, handles and joints of shower nozzle products are all parts that are easily directly observed during normal use. Therefore, when comprehensively judging the overall visual effect of a design, these features must also be taken into account. Specifically, there is a racetrack-shaped push button on the handle of the involved design patents, whereby the alleged infringing product does not have this feature (...). (Furthermore) The bevel angle generated by the connection between the nozzle and the handle of the involved design patent is relatively small, while that of the alleged infringing product is larger. These are clear differences.

Step 4: Weighing the differences and reaching a conclusion   3.118

Considering the above and the degree of freedom allowed by this type of product to a designer, the Supreme People's Court concluded that, although the design of the alleged infringing product adopts a runway-shaped water surface that is highly similar to the authorized design involved, there were significant differences in various features that are easily observable and affecting the overall visual effect of the two designs:

It is precisely because the design of the alleged infringing product does not contain all the design features of the authorized design involved in the case, and the different design features of the design of the accused product and the authorized design involved in the case, such as the handle, the design of the nozzle and the joint of the handle, etc., (…) that the two are neither the same nor similar.

E. PRACTICAL ASPECTS OF DESIGN LAW

1. Business Aspects: Transferability/Licensing

3.119   As for any other type of patents and IP rights, design patent's applications and registrations can be transferred, licensed and pledged by their respective owner.

(a) Transfer of design patent rights and technology transfer

3.120   Applicants for or owners of a patent can transfer or assign their priority applications, pending applications or granted patents to any assignee under the China Patent Law.[180] This includes of course design patents. To be valid and opposable to third parties in good faith, an assignment must be in written form and registered with the CNIPA. The said contract shall be published by the patent administrative department of the State Council. The assignment of the right to apply for the patent or the patent right shall come into force as of the date of registration.[181]

(b) License of design patent rights

3.121   The holder of a registered design patent can license to any third party the right to use and exploit such patent by means of a written contract.[182] Therefore, only third parties with a written license from the right holder can use the patented design, while use without such a license is an act of infringement.

3.122   Within three months from the day of entry into force of the license contract, the same must be filed with the Patent Administration Department of the State Council.[183] The license contract to be recorded must be in writing and a standard prepared by the CNIPA is available online for everybody to be used for the purpose of the recordation.[184] The review of the application by CNIPA

---

180   China Patent Law 2020, art 10.1.
181   China Patent Law 2020, art 10.2.
182   China Patent Law 2020, art 12.
183   Implementing Regulations of the China Patent Law 2014, art 14.2.
184   中华人民共和国国家知识产权局令 - 第62号 (Order of the State Intellectual Property Office of the People's Republic of China, no 62/2011, art 4). http://gkml.samr.gov.cn/nsjg/bgt/202106/t20210625 _331510.html accessed on May 15, 2023.

must be completed within seven days from receipt of the request and the complete documents[185] and the approved license of publication will be published in the Patent Gazette.[186] The recording can be extended if the contract is renewed but a request must be filed within a certain time limit.[187]

3.123 The recording or lack thereof will not affect the existence and the validity of a contract. The contract exists and is executable in the terms agreed by the parties in the contract itself. The recording of the patent with the CNIPA serves a different purpose, that is the creation of a presumption of publicity of the contractual agreement. Furthermore, a recorded license will constitute important evidence and reference in case of determination of damages for infringement of a design patent, if the damage calculation method chosen by the court or the parties is that of the royalty factor. Compulsory licensing in China does not apply to design patents.[188] A new system of open licensing has been recently introduced by the latest amendment of the China Patent Law.[189] It allows a design right holder to make an open offer of licensing through publication and advertising of such offer through the CNIPA. The norms on open licensing aim at incentivizing exploitation of design patents.

2. Specific Interesting Application of Design Patents

(a) Auto parts

3.124 The introduction of partial design protection seems to also bring more clarity to the protection of spare parts by design patents. Under the previous version of the China Patent Law, spare parts found protection if they could be sold and used separately from the rest of the product. With the latest amendment of the China Patent Law and the introduction of partial designs, we can expect even greater protection for auto spare parts. Specific spare parts designs can now be filed as design patents without the concern of whether they can be used or sold separately from the rest of the vehicle. The only concern will be that of determining their scope of protection and degree of functionality.

(b) Design patents and the metaverse

3.125 Is design protection eligible for metaverses? Is a digital product a product 'fit for industrial use' as required by the law to obtain design protection? While

---

185 Order of the State Intellectual Property Office of the People's Republic of China, No. 62/2011, art 11.
186 Order of the State Intellectual Property Office of the People's Republic of China, No. 62/2011, art 14.
187 Order of the State Intellectual Property Office of the People's Republic of China, No. 62/2011, art 16.
188 China Patent Law 2020, art 53.
189 China Patent Law 2020, art 50.

Singapore had included the design for non-physical products/virtual products in the scope of products protectable by a design patent since 2017,[190] in April 2020 Japan's 'Craftsmanship Law'[191] expanded the design protection to include projected graphic images and other designs used by virtual reality (VR) technology, South Korea has also recently done so in 2021,[192] China has not implemented any specific regulations in this respect. One of the objections to registrability of a design patent for metaverse products is whether they can be considered 'industrial products', as required by the China Patent Law. The current practice seems to relegate such digital/virtual goods to the realm of copyright protection. Nonetheless, there have been applications filed for 'metaverse' focused designs. Some have already been successfully registered. For example, one application was filed for as 'Smart Street Lamp (Metaverse)' instead of directly naming them as metaverse street lamp.[193] The applicant was obviously aware that using the words 'metaverse' or 'virtual' would have likely led to a rejection. By using 'Smart' the application passed the formal test for registration. It remains to be seen whether at the time of enforcement, such designs will be indeed allowed to protect the use of the Street lamp in a game or metaverse context. A 'smart' product is a data-processing object, which has several interactive functions. A smart product combines the hardware and software interfaces. However, the physical element is key to the definition of 'Smart'.

3.126 Based on the actual system and how design protection is applied in China, it is doubtful that such designs, even if defined as 'smart' will meet the requirements for enforcement in the metaverse context. It is doubtful that at present, a design patent in China will be suitable to protect non-physical/virtual products in the metaverse. If we take the example of design protection of GUIs, the closest thing to a metaverse we can think of in the actual design world, these are protectable only with the carrier of the design, which must be a 'physical product'. GUIs are only eligible for protection if they are attached to display panel terminals such as computer screens. However, there is an ongoing debate in China about this issue and there is legal literature, strongly supporting statutory changes to the China Patent Law and the Patent Examination Guidelines

---

190 Registered Designs (Amendment) Act (no 29 of 2017) 2017, art 2(c) https://sso.agc.gov.sg/Acts-Supp/29-2017/Published/20170615170000?DocDate=20170615170000 accessed on May 15, 2023.
191 Design Act 2020, art 2.1 https://wipolex.wipo.int/en/text/581568 accessed on May 15, 2023.
192 Industrial Design Protection Act 2020 https://wipolex.wipo.int/en/legislation/details/20927 accessed on May 15, 2023.
193 Huang Bin, 构建元宇宙虚拟世界之虚拟现实法律问题探析 (An Analysis of Virtual Reality Legal Issues Constructing Metaverse Virtual World), Baidu Academics, April 29, 2022 https://baijiahao.baidu.com/s?id=1731405871933873692&wfr=spider&for=pc accessed on May 15, 2023.

in favour of expanding design protection to non-physical products.[194] The near future will surely bring changes to the design system in China in relation to Metaverse.

F. CONCLUSION

In the past decades, China has continuously updated and improved the statutory and regulatory framework to offer effective protection to industrial designs. Partly, this has been the result of external pressure, especially from the US and the EU since China's accession to the WTO and the TRIPS agreement back in 2001 and the demand by foreign right holders. Partly, this has also been the result of the emergence of a pure Chinese design industry. From furniture to clothing and home goods and more recently to the metaverse and the gaming industry, Chinese people are rediscovering their traditions and history, increasing awareness among designers and product consumers. The result is that protection of designs is now simple and inexpensive, while enforcement is fast and efficient. The accession of China to the Hague Convention on international design is the proof that Chine is striving to offer the best international protection standards. Recent amendments allow administrative injunctions for design patents along pre-lawsuit injunctions and the possibility of speedy administrative enforcement proceedings, and also enable right holders to quickly stop infringements without too many formalities and without the high costs of civil litigation.[195] At the same time, civil litigation is a reliable tool for more complex design infringement cases. Despite this, foreigners tend to neglect design registrations in China. They often realize this was a mistake only after their creations have been copied. Without a design patent, the new and original ornamental features of a design product will be left at the mercy of infringers. Copyright, or unfair competition are far from ideal alternatives to stop these violations. Education about the creation and protection of design assets becomes therefore important. Foreign right holders need to know more about design protection in China to eliminate

3.127

---

194 Shun Diao, '虚拟现实科技对我国外观设计制度的挑战与应对' (The Challenge and Response of Virtual Reality Technology to my country's Design System) 2020 Electronic Intellectual Property Center of the Ministry of Industry and Information Technology https://www.163.com/dy/article/FNAPUONR05149FJG.html accessed on May 15, 2023.
195 Paolo Beconcini, 'Light Administrative Injunctions for Designs in China: Status-check on the 2021 Shenzhen AMR Reform', 2022 Squire Patton Boggs Global IP & Technology Blog https://www.iptechblog.com/2022/02/light-administrative-injunctions-for-designs-in-china-status-check-on-the-2021-shenzhen-amr-reform/ accessed on May 15, 2023.

pre-conceived ideas about Chinese IP laws and their enforcement. We hope that this chapter will be a helpful tool for that purpose.

4

INDUSTRIAL DESIGN LAW IN FRANCE

Catherine Mateu

A. SUBSTANTIVE	4.002	2. Litigation	4.058
1. Legal Framework	4.003	3. Remedies	4.064
2. Rights Granted, Ownership, Term	4.008	4. Customs Measures	4.068
3. Conditions for Protection	4.012	D. PRACTICAL ASPECTS OF DESIGN LAW	4.070
(a) The appearance of the product	4.016	1. A Few Figures	4.070
(b) Novelty	4.021	2. Business Aspects of Design Law	4.072
(c) Individual character	4.027	(a) Exploitation of designs	4.073
(d) Public policy and morality	4.032	(b) Scope of the right	4.078
(e) Lack of functionality	4.034	(c) Limits of the right	4.083
(f) Interconnectability	4.035	E. IMPORTANT JUDGMENTS RECENTLY ISSUED IN THE DESIGNS SPHERE	4.091
(g) Harm to prior copyrights, designs and distinctive rights	4.036	1. Comments, Analysis, Evaluation	4.101
(h) Repair clause	4.037	2. Current Legal Framework	4.104
B. PROSECUTION	4.038	(a) In France	4.104
1. Duration	4.044	(b) In Europe	4.106
2. Priority	4.047	F. THE EU LEGISLATION REFORM PROJECT	4.115
3. Grounds for Refusal	4.048		
4. International Option	4.051	G. FUTURE OUTLOOK RELATED TO 3D PRINTING	4.120
C. DISPUTES	4.052		
1. Invalidity Actions	4.052		

In France, design rights emerged in the 19th century when silk manufacturers living in Lyon, a French town, claimed protection for the designs of their silks. They were behind the first law on the subject, the 1806 law, which was inspired by the royal privileges granted in the 18th century to silk manufacturers from Lyon. Case law then extended the scope and the legislator consecrated these achievements in the 1909 law, which is now codified. Design law was then revitalized in the 20th century under the impetus of European law. Community designs were created and national design rules were harmonized at European level. Under French law and practice, designs may be also protected by copyright law and tort law which prohibits unfair competition and parasitic conduct. **4.001**

A. SUBSTANTIVE

4.002 Design law is a temporary property right relating to the appearance of a product and is, in principle, dependent on registration. However, unregistered designs are also protected under certain conditions.

1. Legal Framework

4.003 The legal framework for designs is now well-established and divided into French and European legislation. For instance, French designs are under the authority of the National Institute of Intellectual Property ('**INPI**'), and Community designs are under the authority of the European Union Intellectual Property Office ('**EUIPO**'). Moreover, the relevant legislations in the French jurisdiction are both the French Intellectual Property Code ('**IPC**'), book V, and EU regulations such as Regulation (EC) No. 6/2002 that established the Community design and was modified by Regulation (EC) 1891/2006.

4.004 Designs can also be protected by other IP laws such as copyrights, trademarks, and patents, similarly codified in the IPC and by EU Regulations. The question that arose, and was deeply discussed, was, whether it was possible to cumulate protections. As far as copyright protection is concerned, the French have indeed argued strongly in favour of keeping the dual protection.

4.005 A two-and-three-dimensional product could be protected quite easily by both design law and copyright. However, at the end of the 20th century, European texts encouraged a break with this double protection. Design law evolved towards an autonomous right in relation to copyright. Following a French application, cumulation with copyright remains possible,[1] but it is not systematic.[2] In other words, partial cumulation is allowed, and total cumulation is not always admitted. A distributive application of the criteria is therefore necessary: conditions of originality specific to copyright for obtaining copyright protection and conditions of novelty and specific character in order to obtain design protection. As we will see below, originality is not a condition for the protection of designs. Thus, some designs are protected by design law without being protected by copyright if they are not original. In this case, they do not

---

[1] Criminal Chamber of the Supreme Court, June 27, 2018, Parisac Sarl v. C (Christophe), case n° 2016-86478, PIBD 2018, 1102, IIID-640, regarding handbags.
[2] Appeals Court of Paris, Pole 5, chamber 1, November 16, 2021, Sonia Rykiel Création et Diffusion de Modèles SA v Fashion Retail SA (Espagne); Industria de Diseno Textil (Inditex, Espagne) SA; Tempe SA (Espagne); et al., case n°2018/20990, PIBD 2022, 1175, IIID-8, handbags design was held protectible by design law (novelty and individual character acknowledged) but not by copyright law (lack of originality).

benefit from the long-term protection of copyright, which lasts 70 years after the death of the author.

Cumulative protection with patent law is also possible if the conditions of protection of both rights are met. The same applies to trademark laws. For example, a shape can be protected by means of a three-dimensional trademark, and design law if that shape meets the conditions laid down by trademark (notably of distinctiveness) and design law (notably of novelty).[3]   **4.006**

The difference in coverage will mostly remain in the duration of the protection. Under French law, a design is protected for a maximum period of 25 years. Patents are protected for a maximum of 20 years. Original works are protected by copyright as detailed above. Finally, trademarks are protected indefinitely but must be renewed every ten years. From a business perspective, filing, mandatory for registered designs, patents and trademarks, confers a date certain, helpful when it comes to prove the existence of a right.   **4.007**

2. Rights Granted, Ownership, Term

As a property right, design right reserves exclusivity to its holder and allows exclusive exploitation. It is also a right to prohibit, which offers the holder to bring an infringement action against unauthorized exploitation.   **4.008**

The duration of the design right is limited, to a maximum of 25 years from the filing date of the application for national or Community registered designs. This right is renewable every five years up to a total of 25 years. Unregistered Community designs are only protected for three years from their public disclosure date. From a practical perspective, rightsholders may want to have public disclosures recorded by public notaries or bailiffs so that they can establish a date of disclosure to claim rights for unregistered designs.   **4.009**

As it depends, in principle, on a filing, the design right is granted to the first applicant, i.e., the person who has completed the necessary filing formalities. The right itself is evidenced by a title. However, unregistered Community designs can also be protected under certain conditions, as explained below.   **4.010**

Under French copyright law, the entity that discloses the design is assumed to be the rightsholder. When designs are created by employees, ownership to the employer will depend on whether the work was performed collectively under   **4.011**

---

3   Paris Court of First Instance, January 22, 2008, Beauté Prestige International SA / Tissus Manal SARL, case n°2006/14593, regarding a perfume bottle.

the employer's direction[4] or exclusively by an individual. In the latter case, the assignment of rights is subject to specifying the particular rights assigned. While design rights belong to creators, French designs assumes, unless proven to the contrary, that the applicant is the beneficiary.[5] Community designs created by an employee in the course of its employment shall belong to the employer unless specified to the contrary by the national legislation or by contract.[6]

3. Conditions for Protection

4.012 A design can be protected if three cumulative conditions are met: it relates to the appearance of a product, it is new, and it has an individual character.

4.013 The legislator has also provided for various exclusions from protection, namely failure to comply with public policy and morality, characteristics of the appearance of the product imposed exclusively by its technical function, and the shape of the product imposed by the need to connect it or assemble it with another product.

4.014 A design can also be invalidated because of prior art, if the design lacks novelty or individual character.

4.015 Furthermore, Directive 98/71 left it to the Member States to choose whether to exclude spare parts' protection by design law. However, as of January 1, 2023, France has introduced the repair clause exception to design law.

(a) The appearance of the product

4.016 Under French and European laws, a design refers to the appearance of the whole or a part of a product resulting from the features of 'the lines, contours, colors, shape, texture and/ or materials.'[7] These characteristics may be those of the product itself or its ornamentation.

4.017 In other words, any industrial or craft object, including parts designed to be assembled into a complex product, packaging, displays, graphic symbols, and typefaces, can be assimilated into a design.

---

[4] Supreme Court, Social Chamber, September 22, 2015, G (Pierrette G) / Lalique SA; Lalique Parfums SAS; D, case n°2013-18803, PIBD 2015, 1039, IIID-800.
[5] Article L.511-9 of the IPC.
[6] Article 14 of Reg. n°6/2002.
[7] Article 511-1 of the IPC and Article 3 of EU Regulation No. 6/2002.

Therefore, as they relate to the appearance of a product, design rights concern **4.018**
creations of form. Although the difference has no legal impact, a distinction
is made in France between designs protected by two-dimensional shapes, and
models protected by three-dimensional shapes. For instance, the product may
be an armchair, a lamp, or a piece of jewellery.

On this note computer programs are not considered designs and cannot be **4.019**
protected. Similarly, designs contrary to public order or morality and designs
whose characteristics are exclusively imposed by the technical function of
a product are excluded from protection.

Furthermore, invisible parts of a complex product do not benefit from design **4.020**
protection.[8] Only the part visible during normal use of the product can be
protected.

(b) Novelty

Determination of validity is based on a comparative examination between the **4.021**
design applied for and any products, disclosed before the filing date of the
former or the priority date if any. The design is new if no identical design has
been disclosed by that date.

The IPC provides that 'a design shall be considered new if, on the date of **4.022**
filing of the application for registration or the date of the priority claimed,
no identical design has been disclosed. Designs are considered identical when
their characteristics differ only in insignificant details'.[9]

In other words, designs are considered identical when their features differ **4.023**
only in insignificant details. The subjective personality of the designer is not
sought here, as the condition of novelty is quite distinct from the condition of
originality, overall visual impression, or personal creative effort, which applies
in copyright law.

The identity between two designs is retained when their characteristics differ **4.024**
only in insignificant details, i.e., details that will not be immediately perceptible and which will therefore not produce even slight differences between the
said drawings or designs.[10]

---

8   Article 4, RDMC; Article 3, dir. 98/71; Article L.511-5 of the IPC.
9   Article L.511-3 of the IPC.
10 EU Trib., June 6, 2013, T-68/11, ref. Erich Kastenholz/ OHMI.

4.025 Thus, a subsequent design filed by a rightsholder may be held invalid because of lack of novelty, even if such subsequent design is slightly different from the prior design.[11]

4.026 Disclosure that precludes novelty is assessed taking into account whether it could reasonably have become known in the normal course of business to the circles specialized in the sector concerned, operating within the community.[12] Thus, a disclosure in a trade show in China may be considered to invalidate a design.[13]

(c) Individual character

4.027 A design can only be protected if it has an individual character.[14] This condition entered French law in 2001 through Directive 98/71. It was added to the condition of novelty.

4.028 The inherent or individual character is assessed over time, like novelty, by comparing the design at issue with designs disclosed before the filing date or at the priority date. The individual character is based on the subjective difference between the design concerned and previously disclosed designs.

4.029 The design must give rise to an overall visual impression that is different from that of the designs previously disclosed.[15] The difference sought here is subjective, as it is based on an impression made by the observer or informed user. It is, therefore, necessary to prove the disclosure of a prior design, to compare the designs, and then assess through them the degree of difference in their appearance. In practice, the question that must be asked to evaluate this difference in visual impression is whether the informed user is overwhelmed by an impression of 'déjà vu' or whether he perceives the distinctiveness of each design.

4.030 The standard by which visual impression is measured is that of the informed user, a fictional reference character. He or she does not possess average attention but is particularly vigilant, either because of personal experience or extensive knowledge of the sector under consideration. In design, the notion

---

11 Appeals Court of Paris, Pole 5, Chamber 1, November 16, 2021 (n 2).
12 Article 7 of the CDR n°6/2002 and L.511-6 of the IPC.
13 Paris Appeals Court, Pole 5 chamber 2, October 18, 2019, Maisons du Monde France SAS v Billiet Vanlaere BVT SA (Belgique); Save Willy Sarl (Belgique); Saint Herblain Distribution SAS, case n°2018/09091, PIBD 2020, 1132, IIID-101.
14 Article L.511-2 of the IPC and Article 4, RDMC and Article 3, dir. 98/71.
15 Article 6, CDIR and Article 4, Directive 98/71.

of 'informed observer' is, in fact, an intermediate notion between, the average consumer, applicable in trademark law, who is not required to have any specific knowledge on one hand and, on the other hand, the average consumer, applicable in the field of design law, who is not required to have specific knowledge.

4.031 For instance, a thermic hair brush was held not to have individual character because the overall visual impression of the brushes was identical even if some small differences related to decorative characteristics could be found.[16]

(d) Public policy and morality

4.032 Designs that are contrary to public policy or morality can have their registration refused, by the INPI and the EUIPO.[17]

4.033 In the French legislative landscape, these designs often take the appearance of official symbols, representing the attributes of the country. For example, French courts have ruled that an image that clearly represents Marianne, the emblem of France[18] is contrary to public policy.

(e) Lack of functionality

4.034 There is abundant case law regarding validity of designs because of alleged functionality. In particular, regarding the way such functionality can be assessed, questioning whether a design is not functional because there are various shapes that can generate the same result or, whether a design is functional because its shape cannot be distinguished from its function.[19] Thus, a design on floating devices that included Velcro stripes was invalidated because such bands were held to be exclusively imposed by their function.[20]

(f) Interconnectability

4.035 Interconnectable products can only be protected under design law if, they remain visible once they are incorporated, and their visible shape is novel and has an individual character.[21]

16　Paris Appeals Court, Pole 5, 2nd chamber, June 19, 2020, Olivia Garden (Belgique) v Coiffidis SAS, case n° 2018/20559, PIBD 2020, 1143, IIID-8.
17　Article 9, RDMC; Article 8, dir. 98/71; Article L.511-7, CPI.
18　Paris Appeals Court, Pole 5, 2nd chamber, October 13, 2017, Association Expressions de France v. INPI case n° 2016/23487.
19　Article L.511-8 of the IPC.
20　Paris Appeals Court, Pole 5, 2nd chamber, June 18, 2021, Clee Sasu / Sensas SA; C, case n°2019/20119.
21　Article L.511-5 of the IPC and Supreme Court, Commercial Chamber March 10, 2010, Proconect SA; Ametek Inc. (États-Unis) v Albright France Sarl; Prestolite (Royaume-Uni) case n°08-17167, PIBD.

(g) Harm to prior copyrights, designs and distinctive rights

4.036 A French design can also be held invalid because it infringes prior third-party copyrights, design rights or distinctive rights.[22] A French design right can thus be declared invalid if it infringes a prior right, be it a copyright, a design right or the reproduction of a distinctive sign.

(h) Repair clause

4.037 In the car industry, for products intended to restore a vehicle to its initial appearance, the French legislator has introduced the repair clause which came into force in French law on January 1, 2023 and which significantly limits intellectual property rights for these goods.[23] This new legislation creates an additional exception to copyright.[24] It also creates an exception to design rights with regard to glass in the car industry and to all products that are manufactured by the spare parts manufacturer.[25]

B. PROSECUTION

4.038 An application for design protection can be filed following the national, Community, or international path. The national and international paths permit obtaining one or more national designs. Whereas, the Community path allows one to obtain a Community design, which is a unitary title valid throughout the European Union.

4.039 The national design takes effect in the territory of one State only. For example, a French design will produce its effects in France. This is the application of the principle of territoriality. More specifically, designs registered in France cover the following territories: Metropolitan France and Overseas Territories.

4.040 The application must be filed with a national registration office: in France, with the INPI. It can also be filed with the clerk of the commercial court. Since October 16, 2019, applications for the registration of designs are only made electronically. The application may be filed by a legal or natural person, by a single person or by several persons, by a French person or a foreigner who is a beneficiary of the Paris Convention or a national of a Member State of the World Trade Organization (and under certain conditions for other foreign-

---

22 Article L.512-4 of the IPC. Supreme Court Commercial Chamber, March 3, 2015, MARK & STYL SARL (Suisse) / PSL FRANCE SARL ; PSL Ltd (Chine), case n°/2013/25969, PIBD 2015, 1026, IIID-332.
23 Article L.513-1 of the IPC and Article L.513-6 of the IPC.
24 New Article L.122-5 of the IPC.
25 New Article L.513-6 of the IPC.

ers). The application may be made by the applicant himself or by a qualified representative, such as an industrial property attorney. The appointment of an agent is, however, mandatory when the design is filed in the name of a third party or if the applicant is not domiciled or headquartered in France. A power of attorney does not require notarization or legalization in France. Any natural or legal person can own a design in France.

4.041 An application may concern several designs. However, the reproductions, i.e., photographs, drawings, or samples, which will be attached to the application, shall define the aesthetic characteristics of the design in a precise manner. Indeed, it is necessary to submit a representation showing different angles or states. It is also recommended to show the design in a neutral environment, generally alone with a uniform background with no decorative elements.

4.042 Designs must be registered for the goods or products that belong to their category, also known as 'class.' In France, the classes are organized according to the international 'Locarno classification' that comprises 32 classes.

4.043 Fees must be paid on the day of filing and vary according to the number of designs filed. The charge to apply for a single design is €39, and €52 extra to protect the design for a ten-year period. The cost increases by €23 per additional black and white reproduction and €47 per color reproduction.

1. Duration

4.044 Once the file has been published online, INPI will examine the admissibility and material regularity of the application then publish the design in the BOPI, which is the Official Bulletin of Intellectual Property. Approximately three to four months after filing, a notice of publication, which is equivalent to a certificate of registration, is sent to the applicant.

4.045 An applicant may request an adjournment. It allows the publication to be postponed for three years. At the end of the three years, the publication of all the designs registered in the application is automatically performed.

4.046 A design right lasts for five years from the date of filing and is renewable five times, i.e., up to 25 years.[26] The design must be renewed within the six months preceding the last day of the anniversary month of the filing against payment of a fee of €52. In France, before the 2001 reform, protection lasted for 25

---

26 Except for products of the car industry that will be under the repair clause regime as of January 1, 2023, which will have a limited ten-year protection, new Article L.513-1 of the IPC.

years, with a possible extension of up to 50 years. Designs whose protection was extended before October 1, 2001, are protected until the expiry of the period.[27] The registration is effective from the date of filing of the application. If the design is also protected by copyright because of its originality, it benefits from the protection of copyrighted works. This protection lasts for the lifetime of the author and continues for 70 years after the author's death.[28]

2. Priority

4.047 France, as does the EU, provides a grace period of 12 months before the filing date of the application for registration. Disclosure during this period shall not destroy novelty, if the design has been disclosed by the applicant or a third party on the basis of information provided or acts performed by the applicant; or if the design has been disclosed as a result of abusive conduct against the applicant. Priority gives the applicant or successor in title the right to register the design subsequent to the application in a country that recognizes this right. It has the effect of guaranteeing novelty, in that the date taken into account for registration will be that of the first registration and not the date of the subsequent registration under priority.

3. Grounds for Refusal

4.048 The INPI examines the form of the application and checks that the national design complies with public policy and morality. If the file contains an irregularity, the applicant is then notified by mail by the INPI. Within the deadlines indicated in the mail, the applicant has the possibility to regularize his application.

4.049 There is a right to appeal the INPIs' decisions before a Court of Appeal within one month from the decision.

4.050 However, it is not possible to oppose the application of a design.

4. International Option

4.051 The international path makes it possible to obtain several national registrations by making a single application: it is a centralized single filing procedure. The French applicant files with the registration office, the INPI, which forwards the application to the International Bureau of the World Intellectual Property

---

27 Article L.513-1 of the IPC.
28 Article L.123-1 of the IPC.

Office. This international channel is organized by the Hague Agreement, of which France is a member.

C. DISPUTES

1. Invalidity Actions

4.052 An application for invalidity can be made before the courts, either by way of principal claim or by way of counterclaim. A distinction is also made here between absolute and relative grounds for invalidity. The grounds for invalidity are provided in the IPC.[29]

4.053 There are four absolute grounds for invalidity: (1) designs not relating to the appearance of a product; (2) lack of novelty; (3) lack of specific or individual character; and (4) unlawfulness, in particular failure to respect public policy or morality or the exclusively functional character of the design. Relative grounds for invalidity, on the other hand, are invoked in the case of prior copyright or distinctive signs, or if the holder of the design protection is not the creator of the design.

4.054 Absolute grounds of invalidity can be invoked by any person who is not the holder of the design right and who shows a legitimate interest for its invalidity action, such as needing to use the design for business. Whereas, relative grounds for action can only be invoked by the person entitled to the right being opposed.

4.055 Since the enactment of the French law, known as the PACTE law of May 22, 2019, the action for invalidity of a design is not time-barred.[30] Before this date, the common law limitation period of five years provided by the Civil Code was used. This provision of the PACTE Act has opened up more actions for invalidity.[31] It should also be noted that there is no administrative procedure for invalidity of designs, unlike trademark law, for which such procedure was put in place by order of November 13, 2019.

4.056 In the event of an invalidation action, there are several grounds for defense. First, the defendant may challenge the plaintiff's standing, as well as the

---

29 Article L.512-4 of the IPC.
30 Article L.521-3-2 of the IPC.
31 Paris Judicial Court, February 8, 2022, F v Akis Technology Sarl; O, case n°2019/14142, PIBD 2022, 1183, IIID-8.

admissibility of the evidence. Second, on the merits, the defendant can underline that the design is new and has an individual character and emphasize that the plaintiff's evidence is not sufficient. In such assessment, firstly the differences between the design and the prior art are taken into account, then those perceptible to the informed user and finally the overall impression of them.

4.057 A finding of invalidity can be appealed before the Court of Appeal. An appeal must be filed with the registry, accompanied by a statement of grounds.

2. Litigation

4.058 Claims relating to designs, even if there is also an issue of unfair competition, are exclusively brought before specialized judicial courts. Those claims can only be brought by lawyers admitted to practice before the courts. Civil actions for design infringements are time-barred after five years from the day on which the rightholder knew or should have known the last fact allowing him to exercise a claim.

4.059 With respect to the evidence to be presented at trial, an infringement proceeding often begins with a seizure. If the plaintiff discloses relevant evidence, seizure orders may immediately be granted by the President of the Paris Court. Seizures are performed by bailiffs, who have the power to investigate, describe or seize allegedly infringing goods and documents linked to those goods, in accordance with the authorization given by the judge. In some cases, it is necessary for the bailiff to be assisted by an expert, such as a technician, a computer specialist, or an accountant. In France, a seizure can be conducted without proof, or the commencement of proof of an infringement.[32] After the seizure is carried out, the plaintiff must not exceed the limit of 31 calendar days or 20 business days from the seizure to deliver a complaint to the defendant; otherwise, it will be deemed invalid. Moreover, the plaintiff must also try to resolve the dispute amicably before delivering the complaint.[33]

4.060 No costs are involved when filing a proceeding before the court. A party must, however, pay attorney fees and the bailiff fees if their services have been used. Standard procedures require the writing of a brief for the plaintiff and another for the defendant, and the defendant is the last one to respond. In practice, more briefs are usually filed, for instance in France the number generally

---

[32] Paris Civil Court of Appeal, May 26th, 2017, Telekom Slovenije (Slovénie) v Générale de Téléphone SA n°15/10204.
[33] Decree No. 2015-282, March 11th, 2015.

varies from three to four. These briefs include a statement of the facts and proceedings, a discussion of the claims and arguments, and an operative part summarizing the claims. It is also possible to add pleas in law, presenting them in a formally distinct manner.[34]

4.061 Regular proceedings on the merits take between a year to 18 months to reach the stage of oral pleadings and obtain a judgment. At the early stage design cases are merely written proceedings that, subsequently, end up in oral pleadings. Except in criminal law cases, no witnesses or cross-examination are used in France. To speed up matters, attorneys may agree to a 'participative proceeding' which is a procedural contract by which the attorneys for each party may jointly set their deadlines, as well as the conditions to disclose their evidence.

4.062 Prior to trials, if plaintiffs establish a strong argument in favour of infringement, notably, if defendant fails to seriously dispute the plaintiff's infringement claim, preliminary injunctions may be granted.[35] Also, preliminary injunctions may be granted during case management proceedings. Plaintiffs successful on the merits are usually granted injunctive relief. More precisely, under French law, injunctive relief is granted on the basis of penalties per day of delay or per infringement, with the benefit of immediate execution (there is no suspension of the injunction even if there is an appeal). Infringement proceedings can be stayed pending resolution of validity in another court.

4.063 Besides civil proceedings, criminal prosecution of design matters is also possible. Indeed, criminal law proceedings can be initiated either by customs, the public prosecutor, or by the rightholder. Contrary to civil actions, the plaintiff must prove a willfulness to infringe. Here, the sanctions also differ. In criminal proceedings, five years imprisonment or fines up to €500,000 may be imposed. Other sanctions, such as suspension of access to online communications services, in case of wrongdoings committed by means of an online communications service, may be applied on a case-by-case basis.

3. Remedies

4.064 Sanctions in design cases may be civil or criminal. In civil cases, it is possible to obtain damages, as well as prohibition, confiscation, destruction, and judicial publication. For instance, it is possible to enjoin infringement based on

---

34 Article 768 of the French Code of Civil Procedure.
35 Supreme Court, December 19th, 2013, No. 12/29499.

penalties per day of delay or per infringing conduct. Furthermore, a court may issue publication orders both online and on paper, as well as recall of infringing products. The other remedy often granted is monetary compensation. In criminal proceedings, infringement is punishable by fines or imprisonment.

4.065 Damages are generally assessed on the ruling of the merits that decides on infringement or validity. Occasionally, in some matters, the court may order provisional damages and then either order the communication or production of evidence to be able to assess the actual loss or appoint an expert to calculate the loss that will be then assessed by the court. Damages are assessed according to EU Directive 2004/48/EC that was transposed into French law by Article L.521–7 of the IPC. In practice, damages are assessed by taking into account the economic losses the party has suffered, the unfair profits made by the infringer, and the moral consequences caused to the rightholder. Less frequently, courts may set the damages as a lump sum on the basis of elements such as the royalties or fees which would have been due if the infringer had requested authorization to use the intellectual property right in question.

4.066 Then, finally, the losing party must pay the cost of the attorney and the legal expenses to the prevailing party.

4.067 First instance decisions relating to designs can be appealed according to the French rules of Civil Procedure. The appeal must be filed within one month from the notification of the decision, and a two-month extension to this deadline is granted to parties living outside France. After the filing of the appeal, the appellant must present its grounds of appeal within three months. The appellee must reply within the same three months' time frame. Appeal declarations must specify their scope. In France, and since the procedural reform of January 1, 2020, an appeal is not possible when the decision of the first instance is based on a claim that amounts to less than €5,000, so the decision of the first instance is final.

4. Customs Measures

4.068 The most important custom measure in the field of designs is the possibility to seize and prevent the importation of infringing products.

4.069 Indeed, France applies EU Regulation 608/2013, which harmonizes and sets the conditions for seizures by customs authorities of infringing goods entering the EU. In order to seize the goods, either customs act on their own account or they receive a request to perform a custom control. As soon as customs have seized the goods, the design right holder has ten working days to start proceedings to claim the infringement of its intellectual property right. In some cases, such as when the products are perishable, the time frame can be reduced.

D. PRACTICAL ASPECTS OF DESIGN LAW

1. A Few Figures

4.070 In France, the number of design registrations listed each year by the INPI is relatively stable and lower than that of trademarks or patents. Indeed, the Institute's figures indicate that, since 2012, about 5,351 designs have been registered annually with INPI, compared to 83,816 registrations for trademarks and 15,986 for patents.

4.071 It should be noted that, in 2020, amidst the health crisis, the INPI announced a 3.7 percent increase in design registrations and this number remained stable in 2021. This attests to the importance of designs within intellectual property.

2. Business Aspects of Design Law

4.072 Product appearance is of strategic importance. More than just expressing a company's identity or highlighting its capacity for innovation, it is the result of financial investments whose aim is to contribute to a company's commercial success and a product's sustainability. Indeed, the aesthetic aspect of a product not only distinguishes it from the competition, but also induces the consumer, who, facing the choice between several products of the same quality, will choose the most appealing one.

(a) Exploitation of designs

4.073 Pursuant to Article L. 513–2 of the IPC, registration confers on its holder an exclusive right to the object depicted in the application, more specifically, a property right, which can be freely transferred or granted by the holder.

4.074 The transfer is treated as a sale, even if it concerns only part of the registered design, since it entails the substitution of the transferee in the rights of the owner of the registration. As such, it may also constitute a capital contribution.

4.075 The license, on the other hand, is a form of leasing property, since it only confers on the licensee a more or less extensive right of exploitation. It may or may not be exclusive, which, in the former case, does not prevent the licensor from retaining a right of exploitation for its benefit.

4.076 The validity of an agreement is not contingent on formal criteria, such as a written form. However, a written document is necessary to comply with the publicity organized by the Designs Register and for opposability to third parties (Article R. 512–15 and L.513–3 of the IPC).

4.077 Community designs are considered national rights and the law of the holder's domicile applies,[36] based on the information provided to the register; if any. It should, however, be noted that a minimum set of rules is harmonized by the Regulation and must prevail over national laws. For instance, Article 28, provides how the registration of the transfer of a registered Community design conditions the transferee's capacity to exercise the rights received.

(b) Scope of the right

4.078 The scope of protection conferred by a national or Community design is relatively broad. Articles L.513–5 of IPC and 10.1 of Regulation (EC) No. 6/2002 both provide that it includes 'any design, which does not produce on the informed user a different overall impression.' The monopoly applies not only to identical creations, but also to those sufficiently similar, so that the informed observer cannot distinguish them. Article 9.2 of Directive No. 98/71 and Article 10.2 of Regulation (EC) No. 6/2002 further specify, that the assessment must take into account the degree of freedom of the designer in the development of the design.

4.079 French courts have adjudicated and are currently handling many cases relating to design infringements in all the fields of the industry.

4.080 Moreover, the protection granted does not merely apply in the presence of a slavish copy: it extends beyond the product included in the application for registration, since design law does not recognize the principle of specialty. In national design law, even similar shapes developed independently are infringing. Therefore, and as already mentioned, the traditional criterion of similarity cannot be used to assess counterfeiting, unlike the assessment of liability for unfair competition in trademark law. As stated by the French Supreme Court,[37] it is the lack of overall difference between two designs, and not the risk of confusion, that must be sought. As implied by the prior reference to the fictitious character, that is the informed observer, the assessment must be as objective

---

36 Article 27 of Regulation (EC) No. 6/2002.
37 Commercial Chamber, Court of Cassation, March 26th, 2008, No. 06-22.013.

as possible and the comparison based on the combination of the dominant characteristics of the models, to the exclusion of purely functional features.[38]

The design right contains a set of economic prerogatives. Article L.513–4 of the IPC indeed provides that the manufacture, offering, putting on the market, importing, exporting, trans-shipping, use, or possession, for any of the purposes stated above, of a product incorporating a registered design are reserved to the rightholder. The latter is, in its capacity as owner, free to authorize a third party to exercise the enlisted acts. **4.081**

Because this provision defines, in the negative, the extent of the owner's economic rights by drawing up a chronological inventory of the various acts of exploitation, from the producer to the user, passing through the marketing phases, it suggests one should favour a global appreciation of the exclusive right and the cause of the infringement. The recent addition of 'trans-shipping' to the article seems to fit the logic of strengthening the fight against counterfeiting. With law No. 2014–315 of March 11, 2014, it is now possible to seize goods that simply transit through the European Union, meaning goods neither come from nor are destined to Member States. **4.082**

(c) Limits of the right

In addition to its limited duration and the obligations related to the renewal of the title, the exclusive right on designs is not absolute. **4.083**

The texts provide for a series of exceptions to the scope of protection that aim to meet particular needs or to reconcile the protection of the exclusive right with certain fundamental freedoms. **4.084**

As stated in Article L.513–6, acts performed privately and for non-commercial purposes, acts performed for experimental purposes, and acts of reproduction for illustration or teaching, do not require the holder's authorization. In the latter case, the implementation of the acts is conditioned on mentioning the registration and the name of the owner of the rights, their conformity with fair trade practices, the absence of prejudice to the normal exploitation of the design, and, of course, the nature of their purposes. While the educational aim of the provision is relatively easy to understand, the illustrative purpose requires clarification. The Court of Justice thus specified in a 2017 judgment that this autonomous concept is to be interpreted as '[serving] as a basis for explanations or comments specific to the person seeking to rely on that limita- **4.085**

---

38   Paris, Court of Appeal, November 24th, 2020, No. 18/23477.

tion'.[39] The scope of this article is nevertheless not broad, and its primary merit is to avoid the controversies in the field of copyright relating to the application of Article L. 122–5 of the IPC.

4.086 Furthermore, Article L.513–7 of the IPC provides a specific exception for acts performed with designs that apply to equipment of foreign ships and aircraft and to spare parts and accessories imported for their repair, during their temporary presence on the French territory. It thus enshrines the specificity in international law of the status of foreign ships or aircraft temporarily stationed on national soil, while reiterating the crucial question of the protection of repair parts.

4.087 Concerning this matter, the 'Climate' law[40] introduced a 'repair clause' into French law, which came into force on January 1, 2023, and only applies to parts of motor vehicles or a trailer within the meaning of Article L. 110–1 of the Highway Code. With regard to design law, a series of measures are introduced in Book V of the IPC. First of all, the manufacturer of the spare part, benefits from an exception for acts aimed at restoring the initial appearance of a vehicle or trailer, against the design owner. For any other entity, the exception for repair purposes, which can be opposed to the design owner, is valid only for parts related to glazing. Finally, for all parts used to restore a vehicle or trailer to its original appearance, the maximum protection period is reduced from 25 to ten years.

4.088 In France, an exception to the rights of owners is also provided for the free use of the appearance and texture of oral medicines for which the patent has expired.

4.089 The Community regulation of December 12, 2001, has retained another exception. A right of bona fide prior personal use is thus granted to the benefit of the person, who used, or made serious and effective preparations to use, a design falling within the scope of a registered Community design.[41] Although its interest is, in reality, limited, for instance, the beneficiary is not in a position to grant a license and, the beneficiary, as a prior creator, may request the nullity of the registration. This mechanism seems fair in a system where the acquisition of rights depends on the deposit.

---

39 CJEU, September 27th, 2017, joined cases C-24/16 and C-25/16, Nintendo Co. Ltd v. BigBen Interactive GmbH and BigBen Interactive Sa.
40 L. No. 2021-1104, August 22, 2021.
41 Article 22 of Regulation (EC) No. 6/2002.

Lastly, Book V of the IPC comprises a provision regarding the system of exhaustion in the customs territory of the Union or the European Economic Area. This jurisprudential concept, which has its source in German law, has been taken up by the Community legal texts relating to trademarks and designs so as to reconcile the protection of intellectual property rights with the free movement of goods. Now set out in Article L.513–8 of the code, it means that the rightholder, who has authorized the marketing of a product in the European territory, cannot prohibit any marketing of this product in the same territory, including parallel imports into its own State. The assignee or licensee may operate throughout Europe. However, a product lawfully manufactured in a Member State without protection constitutes an infringement if exported to territories that have recognized an intellectual property right.

4.090

E. IMPORTANT JUDGMENTS RECENTLY ISSUED IN THE DESIGNS SPHERE

The Court of Justice of the European Union (CJEU) issued a ruling on September 12, 2019, in the case of *Cofemel v. G-Star*. Referred to by the Portuguese Supreme Court for a preliminary ruling on the protection of designs by copyright, the CJEU answered, that the grant of protection, under copyright, to an object already protected as a design 'can only be envisaged in certain situations'. Cumulation of the regimes does therefore not occur automatically. Further, it states that Article 2(a) of Directive 2001/29/EC of the European Parliament and of the Council of May 22, 2001, on the harmonization of certain aspects of copyright and related rights in the information society 'must be interpreted as precluding national legislation from conferring copyright protection on designs [...] on the ground that, over and above their utilitarian purpose, they generate a distinctive and aesthetically significant visual effect'.

4.091

In substance, the Court explains that because copyright and design laws have different objectives, they are each intended to protect a certain type of creation under different regimes. Protection by design law has an economically utilitarian character, aiming at the profitability of an investment over a limited period. In contrast, copyright, of a longer duration, applies to a work that the European jurisprudence defines as an intellectual creation reflecting the personality of its author by manifesting its free and creative choices.

4.092

On March 24, 2021, in case T-5151/19, an important decision was issued regarding the protection of the well-known Lego bricks at the EU level.

4.093

4.094 The judgment first underlined that, although Article 8 of Regulation (EC) No. 6/2002 does not confer any rights on the features of a product's appearance solely dictated by its technical function, but there is an exception. This same article provides that 'a Community design shall under the conditions set out in Articles 5 and 6 subsist in a design serving the purpose of allowing the multiple assembly or connection of mutually interchangeable products within a modular system.' Because the mechanical fittings of modular products may constitute an essential element of the innovative characteristics and present a significant marketing asset, they should be protected. Thus, the EUPIO made a legal error by neglecting to verify that the conditions for the exception's application were met.

4.095 Then the General Court of the European Union ruled on the identification of the product's features exclusively imposed by its technical function. If at least one of the product's characteristics is not exclusively imposed by its technical function but for instances solely serves its visual appearance, the design cannot be annulled. In this instance, the Court considered that because the EUIPO did not identify all the characteristics of the products, especially those purely aesthetical, it had disregarded the aforementioned regulation.

4.096 In another case (No 18/05368), the Paris Court of Appeal confirmed a first instance judgment on June 29, 2021, notably regarding the counterfeiting of a Community design.

4.097 When comparing the registered design of a ring with an earlier model, the Court found that the design at issue and the previous one presented no relevant differences apart from the use of different materials. It was thus judged that the change in material of the products could not suffice to avoid the infringement of another party's design rights.

4.098 The aforementioned CJEU judgment also recalled the classic definition of originality, also referred to as the imprint of the author's personality. According to the Court, originality is present when the author has been able to express its creative abilities during the creation of the work by making free and creative choices.

4.099 In a decision (No 20/04501) rendered on June 15, 2022, regarding the protection of embroidery designs under copyright and design law, the Paris Court of Appeal emphasized the difference between the two regimes of protection. Finding that the appellant did not demonstrate a particular creative effort in developing the disputed designs compared to earlier designs, the Court held that these designs could not benefit from copyright protection. It dismissed the DUBOS company's claims in this regard.

On the other hand, the overall comparison between the design as claimed and the previously disclosed design opposed to it, both taken as a whole, differed significantly. The contested design could therefore be considered new. With respect to the examination of the individual character, the Court held that the designs in question being applied to household linen, higher degree of designer freedom had to be considered since functional constraints did not limit them. The appellant company, S.A.S. DUBOS AS, was therefore entitled to claim three-year protection for the unregistered Community design on the three designs at issue. **4.100**

1. Comments, Analysis, Evaluation

Design law, already essential to the commercial development of companies, is particularly in the spotlight nowadays. **4.101**

The European Commission and the EUIPO indeed rolled out in early 2022 the new European SME Fund, designed to support SMEs in the post-Covid-19 recovery and their ecological and digital transitions over the next three years. The support, limited by the planned allocation, includes reimbursement of 75 per cent of the fees charged by intellectual property offices (including national intellectual property offices, the EUIPO, and the Benelux Intellectual Property Office) for trademark registration and design registration and reimbursement of 50 per cent of the fees charged by the World Intellectual Property Organization for obtaining international trademark protection and design protection. **4.102**

These measures raise questions about the current state of the law and the means to update it. This new fund ran from January 23, 2023 to December 8, 2023. **4.103**

2. Current Legal Framework

(a) In France

Concerning French practices that have recently become apparent, changes in French procedural law have prompted an immediacy in the enforcement of most first instance decisions, even if an appeal is lodged. As a way to speed up proceedings, the assessment of the validity of rights in infringement proceedings may take place at the case management stage. **4.104**

4.105 As mentioned earlier, amendments, entered into force on January 1, 2023, have been drafted by the legislator and accepted with regard to the spare parts market. There is now a 'repair clause,' approved on August 22, 2021, providing an exception to design protection that applies to both acts regarding glazing and to acts performed by the OEM producer. The legislator also amended Article L. 513–1 of the IPC by introducing an additional paragraph reducing maximum term of protection of the parts listed in the provision mentioned above to ten years for which the law applies classically.

(b) In Europe

4.106 Lately, though, more precisely since January 2021, we have been able to observe the effects of Brexit, whose multiple implications make it still a very relevant question, affecting particularly UK national unregistered designs.

4.107 The UK left the EU on February 1, 2020, following the Withdrawal Agreement concluded between both parties. With the ending on December 31, 2020, of the transition period provided for in the above-mentioned agreement, the UK's exit from the EU has impacted the effects of Community designs in the UK. Moreover, during this period. EU law remained applicable in the UK. Indeed, the EU-UK-Trade and Cooperation Agreement, applied since January 1, 2021, affects neither the applicability of the Withdrawal Agreement nor how the EUIPO handles the circumstances of cessation of applicability of the EUTM and RCD Regulations to the UK.

4.108 Some of the main provisions of the Withdrawal Agreement are listed below.

4.109 On one hand, titles registered after the UK's exit obviously have no effect in the EU territory.

4.110 On the other hand, unregistered Community designs disclosed to the public in the manner provided under EU law are only valid and effective in the EU Member States.

4.111 The Exit Agreement also provides that holders of registered Community designs, whose registration or protection date from the end of the transition period, that is December 31, 2020, have a comparable national industrial property right registered and enforceable in the UK. This is without the UK Intellectual Property Office having to re-examine them and while benefiting from the filing or priority date of the European title.

For Community design applications still pending at the end of the transition period, the applicant had nine months from the end of the transition period, that is September 30, 2021, to file the same design in the UK. Their national rights are also retroactive to the filing or priority date of the European title. **4.112**

It is provided that a decision to cancel the European industrial property right in a procedure (administrative or judicial), still pending to the last day of the transitional period, also extends to the corresponding national right in the UK. The decision takes effect on the date of cancellation of the European right unless the basis for the cancellation of the European right does not exist in English law. In this case, the UK is under no obligation to cancel the corresponding British right. **4.113**

Article 56 of the Agreement requires the UK to take measures to ensure that natural or legal persons who have obtained protection before the end of the transition period for internationally registered designs designating the EU under the Hague system are granted design protection in the UK in respect of those international registrations. **4.114**

F. THE EU LEGISLATION REFORM PROJECT

Currently, the EU design rights framework is about 20 years old. Prior to that, the ECJ was responsible for its most significant updates. However, the usually relatively discreet European legislator, is in the process of undertaking this task. **4.115**

In a 2020 IP Action Plan, the European Commission announced that a system review would be performed in 2021. On Thursday, November 11, 2021, the European Parliament issued a resolution on an intellectual property action plan to support recovery and resilience in the European Union. In all likelihood, significant changes in design law are expected in the years to come. **4.116**

Concerning the revision of the EU legislation on design protection, in particular, the Parliament stresses that the current design protection system at the EU level should be revised, or more exactly modernized, so as to 'better support the transition to the digital, sustainable and green economy.' In this view, the registration procedure should also be updated to allow easier grant of protection to new forms of design, such as graphical user interfaces, virtual and animated designs, fonts and icons, and those relevant following new developments and technologies. **4.117**

4.118 It is also underlined that, as a way to prevent design infringing goods from entering the customs territory, there should be an alignment of the EU design protection system with that of trademarks. Indeed, contrary to rights attached to design, those attached to trademarks are enforceable against infringing goods transiting through the EU.

4.119 The Parliament globally calls for harmonization in the Member States, whether it is about the application and invalidation procedures or design protection for parts used for the repair of complex products by including a 'repair clause' in future texts. The idea being to ascertain greater legal certainty, the legislator aims for uniform design protection throughout the single market, suggesting an alignment between the Design Directive and the Community Design Regulation be performed by the Commission.

G. FUTURE OUTLOOK RELATED TO 3D PRINTING

4.120 The discussion of 3D printing during the design law reform currently underway in the EU is much awaited. This innovation raises questions about all intellectual property rights, copyright, patent, trademark, and design.

4.121 3D printing is an additive technique that allows, via a digital model, the fabrication of a three-dimensional solid object of virtually any shape. The process starts with the scanning of an original object or the writing of a code on a Computer-Aided Design (CAD) file, creating a design model or blueprint stored on a digital file, which then works as guidance for the subsequent printing. The design is 'sliced' into cross-sections, sent to the 3D printer, and manufactured by the addition of layers, all using the raw materials selected among an extensive range of choices.

4.122 Design rights present potentially the most significant challenge to commercial 3D printing of everyday objects. Whether registered or not, valid or not, manufacturing a product incorporating the protected design is illegal if done by a third party for commercial purposes, even in good faith.

4.123 However, the rapid development of this technology raises questions since it is increasingly accessible to the general public. Today one can indeed find 3D printers for less than €1,000, and this technology is increasingly being used, as it offers a quick and low-cost solution to making personalized solid objects for both prototyping and distributed manufacturing. The issue is that the infringement of design rights disappears as soon as the end-user carries out the 3D printing for personal and non-commercial use.

Given the unlimited possibilities for illegally copying designs made possible by 3D printers, the question arises of introducing a fair compensation mechanism. In contrast to copyright law, such a compensation mechanism does not exist in the context of design law. **4.124**

In France the question arose as to whether the private copying exception could be applied, in which case the private copying levy should be extended to 3D printing materials. **4.125**

5

INDUSTRIAL DESIGN LAW IN ITALY

Marco F. Francetti and Matteo Mozzi

A. PROTECTION OF INDUSTRIAL DESIGN	5.001	H. EXHAUSTION OF RIGHTS	5.051
B. THE LEGAL FRAMEWORK	5.005	I. PROTECTION UNDER COPYRIGHT LAW	5.053
C. REQUIREMENTS FOR PROTECTION	5.011	J. ENFORCEMENT OF RIGHTS	5.065
D. THE EXCLUSION OF PROTECTION DUE TO TECHNICAL CHARACTERISTICS	5.026	K. TECHNICAL EXPERTISE	5.097
E. REGISTRATION PROCEDURE	5.030	L. COMPENSATION FOR DAMAGES AND OTHER SANCTIONS	5.101
F. THE RIGHTS CONFERRED BY THE REGISTRATION	5.041	M. CUSTOMS ENFORCEMENT	5.108
G. NULLITY OF THE REGISTRATION	5.048	N. ADMINISTRATIVE DATA	5.119

A. PROTECTION OF INDUSTRIAL DESIGN

5.001 The protection of industrial design, a definition which can be applied (in a non-technical sense) to the shape and/or ornamentation of commodities that have no technical functions. However, such definition has significantly changed in the recent legal practice in Italy. At present, design law, tends to be given higher consideration based on the ground that industrial design has become an important form of cultural expression, independently of the fact that it also represents an important marketing tool and that the visual appearance of a product plays a very important role in the consumers' choice.

5.002 This has contributed to the proliferation of the legal tools on which the protection of industrial design may be based, ranging from the more traditional design registration to, under certain conditions, copyright protection, not to mention the possibility of concurring legal titles that include trademark rights and claims under the unfair competition law.

5.003 Traditionally, the Italian practice, was quite reluctant to recognize the protection of industrial design on grounds other than the 'traditional' design registration ('*modello ornamentale*'), like for example, under copyright law. The influence exercised on the Italian law and practice by the European Regulations has changed this more traditional approach, opening spaces for additional and alternative forms of protection.[1]

Furthermore, recent case law, like the *Cofemel* decision[2] (which will be considered later) may also have an impact on the design protection in Italy. In fact, *Cofemel* seems to be moving towards the grant of a more easily accessible copyright protection for industrial design. However, to implement the teaching of such a decision the Italian Law will have to be amended to remove the requirement of the '*artistic value*', to allow for copyright protection.

5.004

B. THE LEGAL FRAMEWORK

Preliminarily it appears necessary to list the legal provisions which deal with the protection of industrial design, which can be found in different legal sources.

5.005

The first provision Article 2593 of the Italian Civil Code which regulates ornamental models and designs and expressly states that 'Whoever has obtained a registration for a new design or model which has individual character, has the exclusive right to implement it and to prevent third parties from using it, without its consent, in accordance with the provisions of the special laws.'

5.006

Specialized laws mean, in particular, the Industrial Property Code (IP Code),[3] Article 31.1 states that:

5.007

> Registration as designs and models may be granted to the appearance of the whole or a part of a product resulting, in particular, from the features of the lines, contours, shape, texture or materials of the product itself or of its ornamentation, provided that the same are new and have an individual character.

---

1 In this respect, an important role was played by Art. 17 by the EU Design Directive which states that: Design protected by a design right registered in or in respect of a Member State in accordance with this Directive shall also be eligible for protection under the law of copyright of that State as from the date on which the design was created or fixed in any form. The extent to which, and the conditions under which such a protection is conferred, including the level of originality required, shall be determined by each Member State.
2 EUCJ of September 12, 2019, in case C-683/17 – *Cofemel - Sociedade de Vestuário SA v. G-Star Raw CV*.
3 Industrial Property Code: Legislative Decree no. 30 of February 10, 2005, as lastly amended by Legislative Decree no. 16 of March 11, 2020 and by Legislative Decree no. 34 of May 11, 2020.

5.008 Another important provision is Article 2 of the Italian Copyright Law[4] which provides that: 'In particular are protected: … (10) the work of industrial design having a creative character and artistic value.'

5.009 With regard to trademark protection, Article 9 of the IP Code[5] provides that:

> May not be registered as a trademark signs which consist exclusively of:
>
> (a) the shape, or other feature, which results from the nature itself of the product;
> (b) the shape, or other feature, which is necessary to obtain a technical result;
> (c) the shape, or other feature, which gives substantial value to the product.

5.010 As a final rule which, under certain conditions, may be enforced to protect works of industrial design, the legislative framework on unfair competition provided in Article 2598 of the Civil Code states that:

> Subject to the provisions concerning the protection of distinctive signs and patent rights, acts of unfair competition are performed by whoever:
>
> (1) uses names or distinctive signs which are likely to create confusion with the names or distinctive signs legitimately used by others, or slavishly imitates the products of a competitor, or performs, by any other means, acts which are likely to create confusion with the products and activities of a competitor;
> (2) spreads news and comments, with respect to the products and activities of a competitor, which are likely to discredit them, or treats as their own the beneficial qualities of the products or of the enterprise of a competitor;
> (3) avails themselves directly or indirectly of any other means which do not conform with the principles of correct behavior in the trade and are likely to injure another's business.

C. REQUIREMENTS FOR PROTECTION

5.011 Article 31 of the IP Code provides that the appearance of the whole or a part of a product resulting, in particular, from the features, the lines, contours, colours, shape, texture or materials of the product itself, may be registered as designs and models on condition that it is new and has an individual character.

5.012 As seen above, according to Article 31 of the IP Code, novelty and individual character are the necessary requisites to obtain a valid design registration.

---

[4] Law no. 633 of April 22, 1941, as amended by Art. 22 of the Legislative Decree no. 95 of February 2, 2001, repealed by Art. 246.1 of the Legislative Decree no. 30 of February 10, 2005.
[5] As amended by Art. 2.1 of the Legislative Decree no. 15 of February 20, 2019.

On the requirements of novelty and individual character, the Supreme Court has stated that: **5.013**

> For the registration of an ornamental design, simple objective novelty, namely a simple marginal differentiation from what is already existing, is not sufficient, but rather the formal innovation introduced towards the existing forms already applied to the same products, with diffusion and industrial exploitation, must be the expression of a new ornamental idea, characterized by elements that are able to convey the sensation of a new aesthetic of the product.[6]

Novelty is generally intended to mean the lack of prior divulgation of a design before filing of the registration, namely it refers to the identity or quasi-identity of the newly applied-for design, with what is already known to the public. The concept of identity expands beyond exact identity between designs, to include designs with features that differ only in immaterial details.[7] **5.014**

To determine whether a design has been made publicly available, Article 34 of the IP Code states that the design shall be deemed to have been made available to the public, following registration or otherwise, or exhibited, used in trade, or otherwise disclosed, except where these events could not reasonably have become known to qualified users in the involved industrial field operating within the European Community, before the filing date of the application for registration or, if priority is claimed, before the date of priority. **5.015**

According to Article 34.3 of the IP Code, a design is not regarded as having been made available to the public when it was disclosed by the designer or by his successor in title within 12 months preceding the filing date or, when priority is claimed, within 12 months preceding the priority date. **5.016**

The same applies in cases where the design was made available to the public due to an abuse directly or indirectly committed against the designer or his successors. **5.017**

A legislative modification recently enforced, added Article 34-*bis*,[8] providing for the temporary protection of designs and models that are displayed during national and international fairs, so as to date their protection back to the date of their exhibition, implementing the provisions of Article 11 of the Paris Convention of 1883. **5.018**

---

6   Supreme Court, January, 21, 2009, no. 1570.
7   See Art. 32 of the IP Code and art. 4 of the Directive 98/71/EC.
8   Law n. 102 of July 24, 2023, in force from August 23, 2023.

5.019 Obviously, the novelty requirement is judged in a relative sense, namely by referring to the merceological sector which the design belongs to, taking into account the reasonable knowledge of specialized insiders, during the normal course of their commercial activity.

5.020 On the other side, individual character is recognized when the overall impression on the informed user ('*utilizzatore informato*') differs from the overall impression produced on such a user by any design which has been made available to the public before the date of filing of the application for registration or, if priority is claimed, the date of priority.[9]

5.021 As indicated, the evaluation of individual character is made from the perspective of the 'informed user', a novel concept placed midway between the 'person skilled in the art' found in patent law and the 'average consumer', found in the trademark law. The 'informed user' can be considered as one that has a level of attention that is higher than the average consumer, as they are able to notice differences that would usually not be noticed by the average buyer. According to national case law, the informed user is a person who has a deep knowledge of the relevant field, who can appreciate differences that are not easily visible to the general consumer, but must not be confused with the person skilled in the art, who has an excessive knowledge of the field.

5.022 It is important to consider that the evaluation of the individual character must be carried out by taking into consideration the degree of freedom of the designer in developing the design, as provided by Article 33.2 of the IP Code and by referring to Article 33 that states that the design has an individual character if its overall impression differs from the overall impression it produces on the 'informed user' by any design or model that has been made available to the public prior to the date of filing of the application for registration, or prior to the date of priority, if claimed. The freedom of the designer is obviously linked to the crowding of the relevant sector to which the design refers, as well as to the possible functional limitations, in the sense that, the more crowded the sector the less freedom the designer enjoys and, in this case, even a small variation of the design could be considered as sufficient to recognize the existence of individual character.

5.023 In addition, Article 33-*bis* of the IP Code states that a design cannot be registered if it does not comply with the public policy or the morality, specifying however that it cannot be considered as contrary to the public policy or the

---

[9] See Art. 33 of the IP Code and Art. 5 of the Directive 98/71/EC.

morality, simply because it is in contrast with a legal or administrative provision. Furthermore, a design cannot be registered if it represents an improper use of one of the elements listed in Article 6-*ter* of the Paris Convention or of any other signs, emblems or coats of arms which have a particular public interest to the State.

These requirements must be assessed as of the date on which the application was filed or the priority is claimed. and the assessment is subject to an absolute standard, namely that the applied-for design is considered to be challenged by all the designs publicly made available to the public before the relevant date. **5.024**

After the registration, designs are protected for a five-year term, which is renewable for up to a maximum period of 25 years. **5.025**

D. THE EXCLUSION OF PROTECTION DUE TO TECHNICAL CHARACTERISTICS

Article 36 of the IP Code prohibits the registration of designs that consist of: (i) the features of the appearance of a product that are uniquely dictated by a technical function, and (ii) the features of the appearance of a product that must necessarily be reproduced in their exact form and dimensions in order to allow the product in which the design is incorporated or to which it is applied to be mechanically connected to or placed in or around or in contact with another product, so that either product may perform its function. **5.026**

In any case registration is permitted, provided that they comply with the novelty and the individual character, with respect to designs having the purpose of allowing the assembly or the connection of multiple interchangeable products within a modular system, which means that the reproduction of the parties of a product which are necessarily required for the mechanical connection to other parties of a modular system is in general allowed, being on the contrary permitted the registration if the connection may be reached by means of a different shape. **5.027**

With respect to the protection of spare parts, Article 241 of the IP Code provides for a transitional rule based on the provisions of the EU Directive 71/1998 and, as a consequence, exclusive design rights on a component of a complex product (partial design right) may not be enforced to prevent the manufacture and trade of said components, when intended to restore the original appearance of the complex product. **5.028**

5.029 The case law has made an interesting distinction between accessories and spare parts (mainly in the automotive world) stating, in most cases that, while products aimed at restoring the original aspect of a complex products can freely circulate in the market,[10] accessories (i.e., products intended to modify or improve the original aspect of a product) may be protected as registered models/designs and the registrant may therefore enjoy the exclusive protection granted by the registration.[11]

E. REGISTRATION PROCEDURE

5.030 Registration of a design (Art. 38.1 of the IP Code) confers exclusive rights and extends over the whole Italian territory. The national law does not provide any kind of protection for 'unregistered designs', unlike Council Regulation 6/200.2.[12]

5.031 According to Article 38.2, the right to the registration shall vest in the designer or his successors in title; Article 38.3 provides for special rules in case the design has been created by an employee or by an independent contractor (i.e., a freelance designer)[13] who shall, in any case, always maintain the moral right to be regarded as the author and may be entitled to a special economic reward, according to the circumstances, generally to be understood as financial compensation.

5.032 For registration, it is necessary to file an application, in Italian and with an Italian translation of any documents filed in foreign language, with the Italian Patent and Trademark Office (*Ufficio Italiano Brevetti e Marchi*). The application must contain (Art. 167 of the IP Code):

(i) the name of the applicant and of their legal representative, of his attorney, if any;
(ii) an indication of the design's title and of the features of the product which protection is sought;

5.033 The application must be accompanied by:

---

10 Court of Bologna – May 5, 2011, Giurisprudenza Annotata Diritto Industriale no. 5728.
11 Court of Turin – June 25, 2009; Giurisprudenza Annotata di Diritto Industriale, no. 5441.
12 Art. 19.2 of the Council Regulation 6/2022 provides for the protection of unregistered Community designs, while a similar provision is not contained in the Industrial Property Code with regard to designs created in Italy.
13 In case of a design created by an employee, the same provisions (and the same case law) provided by Art. 66 of the Intellectual Property Code with regard to inventions of the employees are applied.

(i)   a graphical reproduction of the design, or a sample of the products;
(ii) a description of the design, if necessary;
(iii) a copy of the power of attorney appointing the legal representative, if any;
(iv) priority documents, if a priority is claimed.

With a single application, a request for a multiple registration may be filed, on condition that it refers to products belonging to the same class of the international classification of designs and models provided for by the Locarno Agreement of October 10, 1968. **5.034**

The Italian Patent and Trademark Office will undertake an examination to ascertain if the application complies with the formal requirements, if the design complies with the legal provisions and that the drawings/samples attached thereto allow one to determine the scope of protection sought, giving the applicant a deadline to reply to any possible objections. In case the applicant does not reply or where the reply does not overcome the objections, the application shall be rejected. In cases where no objections are made, or the reply received is adequate, the application will proceed to registration. **5.035**

As an alternative, Italian applicants may also elect to file an application for International Registration according to The Hague Agreement of 1960 (as implemented in Italy by the Law no. 744 of October 24, 1980). The application may be extended to multiple objects belonging to the same class of the international classification. **5.036**

In this case the application may be filed either directly with the international Office (WIPO) or with the Italian administration ('*Ufficio Italiano Brevetti e Marchi*'). The application must contain: **5.037**

(i)   one or more photos or other representation of the design;
(ii) the receipt confirming the payment of the fees;
(iii) an indication of the object on which the design is intended to be applied;
(iv) documents proving the existence of a priority, if it is claimed.

The application may also contain: **5.038**

(i)   a short description of the characterizing features of the design;
(ii) identification of the author of the design;
(iii) samples of the objects in which the design is incorporated.

The application is published in the Office's Bulletin containing the reproduction of the design, the date of application, the name of the applicant and the designated States for which coverage is required. **5.039**

5.040 For an International Design Registration, the minimum term of protection is ten years, including a five-year initial term and, if renewed, another five-year term. That said, if the legislation of a contracting State provides for a term of protection that is longer than ten years – either with or without the obligation to renew – the international registration will be protected for the same duration. Renewals may be filed every five years with payment of the requisite fees; in the event renewal is not required for all the contracting States in which the design is valid, the renewal must indicate the State(s) for which the renewal is required.

F. THE RIGHTS CONFERRED BY THE REGISTRATION

5.041 According to Article 41 of the IP Code, the registration of a design or model shall confer on its holder the exclusive right to use it and to prevent any third party from using it, without its consent.

5.042 In particular, the following are listed as acts of use by Article 41.2 IP Code:

(i) manufacturing;
(ii) offering for sale;
(iii) putting on the market;
(iv) importing;
(v) exporting;
(vi) using a product in which the design or model is incorporated or to which it is applied;
(vii) holding of such a product for those purposes which constitute in particular use of the design or model.

5.043 The exclusive rights conferred by the registration of a design or model prevents any unauthorized third party from exercising any of the above listed actions whenever they concern any design or model that does not create a different overall impression (i.e., is identical or similar) on the informed user and, to determine the extension of protection, it is necessary to consider the degree of the author's freedom in realizing the design or model (*see above*).

5.044 From the above, it follows that, to evaluate the infringement of the design or model, the same criteria as used to determine the existence of the individual character will be taken into account.

5.045 According to the case law, in evaluating the interference of designs subsequently used by third parties with a registered design, the same criterion of the overall impression on the informed user must be referred to, in order to determine the existence of the individual character requisite.[14]

Furthermore, the evaluation of infringement of a design must not be carried out in an analytic way, but referring to the overall impression which the products exert on the informed user.[15]   **5.046**

Finally, when evaluating the infringement of a design in case of a crowded sector, a minimal differentiation may be sufficient to exclude infringement.[16]   **5.047**

G. NULLITY OF THE REGISTRATION

A design registration may only be declared null and void by a decision of a Court. This may occur, according to Article 43 of the IP Code, when the design: **5.048**

(i) is barred from registration under the IP Code, according to Articles 31 (object of the registration), 32 (novelty), 33 (individual character), 34 (disclosure), 35 (complex product), 36 (technical function);
(ii) is in contrast with the public policy or the principles of morality (Art. 33-*bis*);
(iii) is in conflict with a prior design that has been made available to the public after the date of the filing of the application or, if priority is claimed, after the priority date, whose exclusive right runs from a prior date due to Community, national or international registration or due to an application that has been filed for the same;
(iv) represents a violation of a distinctive sign or of a work protected by copyright;
(v) represents an improper use of one of the elements listed in Article 6-*ter* of the Paris Convention or of any other signs, emblems or coats of arms in which the State holds a particular public interest (Art. 33-*bis*);
(vi) is held by a person or entity that was not entitled to obtain the design registration, and the author has not made use of the right to claim the ownership according to Article 118 of the IP Code.

It is also possible to obtain a declaration of partial nullity, according to Article 39.4 of the IP Code.   **5.049**

---

14   Court of Turin – IP Specialized Section, January 12, 2018.
15   Court of Milan – IP Specialized Section, November 22, 2017.
16   Court of Venice – IP Specializes Section, August 10, 2015 (the register design concerned a jewel).

5.050 A nullity action may be filed by any person or entity that has a legitimate interest in obtaining the declaration, except when the claim is based on prior rights or on the improper use of one of the elements listed in in Article 6-*ter* of the Paris Convention or of any other signs, emblems or coats of arms in which the State holds a particular public interest: in these cases only the owner of the prior right or the person/entity having such public interest, are entitled to file the nullity claim.

H. EXHAUSTION OF RIGHTS

5.051 Article 5 of the IP Code provides that the exclusive rights that are bestowed by an industrial property right expire when the products protected thereby have been placed on the market by the holder or with their consent in the Italian territory, or in the territory of a Member State of the European Union or of the European Economic Area.

5.052 This limitation does not apply when the holder has legitimate reasons to oppose the downstream trade of the products, in particular when status of the products has been modified or when the products are altered after they are placed on the market.

I. PROTECTION UNDER COPYRIGHT LAW

5.053 Whether industrial designs should enjoy copyright protection, which covers the form of expression of creative works from the moment when they are created and without any registration formalities, has long been discussed in Italian law. In particular, this debate has centred around the element of 'artistic value', which, according to the law, is a condition precedent for a work of industrial design to also be protected by copyright.[17] The search to identify 'artistic value' in an object of industrial design has often been seen to conflict with the fact that objects of design are, by their nature, subject to production in industrial quantities for sale on the market.

5.054 Copyright protection is, obviously, an extremely interesting prospect for the holder of a design right, since there are no registration formalities, and therefore no related costs to be incurred. Furthermore, the protection it not subject

---

17 Art. 2 of the Italian Copyright Law which provides that: 'In particular are protected: ... (10) the work of industrial design having a creative character and artistic value'.

to renewal, as it originates from the simple creation of the work,[18] and has a duration of to 70 years after the death of the author, as provided for by Article 25 of the Copyright Law as well as, with specific reference to industrial design works, by Article 44 of the IP Code.[19]

Finally, because Italy is a party to the Bern Convention,[20] copyright protection – for a work of industrial design or otherwise – can be invoked in all of the contracting States to the Convention. **5.055**

Traditionally, and until an amendment was introduced to the Copyright Law by Italian Legislative Decree no. 95 of February 2, 2001 to implement EU Directive 98/71/EC on the legal protection of designs, a work of industrial design was not entitled to copyright protection under Italian law. This position was based on the consideration that where the only function of the shape is to provide a particular aesthetic or ornamental quality to a product, it remains closely linked to the purpose of the product itself and may only be protected as an ornamental design, by obtaining a design registration. Notwithstanding this strict interpretation, some authors and court decisions recognized the protection of aesthetically separable features of a mass product under the provisions of the Copyright Law, if these features were not subservient to the industrial or utilitarian nature of the product, namely if it was theoretically possible to imagine the work as an aesthetic project, separated from its function ('*scindibilità concettuale*'). **5.056**

In more recent times, the Supreme Court did not exclude protection of works of industrial design from copyright protection merely because they were intended for mass production, but stated that the artistic value of such works may be derived from objective elements, such as the recognition by cultural and institutional environments of the work's aesthetic and artistic qualities, exhibition of the work in fairs and museums, publication of the work in specialized magazines, that the product has acquired a market value that is independent of its function, as well as the fact that the work may have been created by an artist. In doing so, the Supreme Court added that Article 2(10) of the Copyright Law, which provides that copyright protection may be granted to works of **5.057**

---

18   Art. 56 of the Italian Copyright Law provides that 'The original title of purchase of the copyright consists of the creation of the work, as peculiar expression of the intellectual work.'
19   Art. 44 of the IP Code states that 'The rights of economic exploitation of designs and models protected according to art. 2.1, no. 10 of the law no. 633 of April 22. 1941, last for the entire life of the author and up to the seventieth calendar year after their death or the date of the last of the co-authors.'
20   Bern Convention of the Protection of Literary and Artistic Works of September 9, 1886, as implemented by Law no. 399 of June 20, 1978.

industrial design on condition that they have an artistic value, is not in conflict with the Bern Convention.[21]

5.058 Following this path, some lower courts have also recently stated that, even if the artistic value of an industrial design is not excluded by the simple fact that the work is produced on an industrial scale, it must however be proved that the design has some features that surpass its mere functionality. Such proof may include publication of the work of design in specialized magazines, sale on the art market, or the fact that it has achieved a value that overcomes that which would be connected to its peculiar function.[22]

5.059 These decisions have opened the door to broader protection of works of industrial design on the grounds of copyright law, even if it remains necessary for the holder of the design to prove, based on objective and reasonable criteria, the existence of a certain degree of 'artistic value'.

5.060 It will now be interesting to see the impact of the recent CJEU decision in *Cofemel – Sociedade de Vestuaria SA vs. G-Star Raw CV* (September 12, 2019 in Case C-683/2017) on the Italian legal framework, and, specifically, whether it will push Italian courts to move further in the direction of offering copyright protection to works of industrial design that is broader, and easier to obtain.

5.061 In the *Cofemel* decision, the Court specified that an EU Member State cannot require a higher level of originality for works of industrial design to obtain copyright protection. This position is different from the majority stance of Italian case law, which limits copyright protection only to those industrial designs which can be regarded as real works of art.

5.062 Based on the CJEU decision, copyright protection may ultimately be extended to designs that fall within the notion of 'work' that represents a precise and objective form of expression and is sufficiently original, in the sense that it must be the author's own intellectual creation, expressing their own personality and their free and creative choices, these criteria being necessary and sufficient, without the need for the holder of the design to prove that it presents an additional aesthetic or artistic level, since this evaluation would be excessively subjective.

---

21   Supreme Court, March 23, 2017, no. 7477.
22   Court of Milan – IP Specialized Section – November 22, 2017. On the same grounds, a very recent decision of the IP Specialized Section of the Court of Venice (May 13, 2020) granted protection to the famous *Moon Boot* après-ski shoes.

It will now be interesting to see how Italian courts will react to the *Cofamel* **5.063** decision, which, of course must be taken into consideration when evaluating if copyright protection can be granted to works of industrial design, without referring to the element of 'artistic value', provided by the letter of the law and, traditionally, required by previous case law.

In this respect, a recent decision rendered in preliminary injunction pro- **5.064** ceedings, by the IP Specialized Court of Venice is extremely interesting.[23] In that case, the judge, expressly referring to the *Cofemel* decision by the CJEU, granted copyright protection to a work of industrial design (a chandelier) on the grounds that, to meet the originality requirement, it is sufficient that the work reflects the personality of the creator, being the result of their free and creative choices, without the additional need to evaluate the 'artistic value' of the work.

J. ENFORCEMENT OF RIGHTS

In Italy, intellectual property matters are heard by a specific section of the **5.065** court, referred to as the Specialized IP Courts. These specialized IP Courts initially established in 12 districts and then increased to 21 in 2012 establishing roughly one for each Court of Appeal district. The Specialized IP Courts have jurisdiction on industrial property and copyright cases, as well as on antitrust cases, unfair competition matters, unless they bear no relation at all to IP rights,[24] company law and matter regarding public contracts.

The judges of the Specialized IP Courts are civil judges that specialize in IP, **5.066** but they do not have a technical background. To compensate for this lack of technical background, the judges can – and almost always do – appoint technical experts to assist the court when a case involves technical issues.

Article 120 of the IP Code states that actions concerning an Italian IP right **5.067** that has already been granted or is in the process of being granted must be filed with the Italian Judicial Authority, regardless of the parties' citizenship, domicile or residence of the place where the defendant is resident or domiciled and, if such places are unknown or the defendant has no residence domicile or abode, with the Judicial Authority of the place where the plaintiff is resident

---

23 Court of Venice, July 5, 2021 – case 2052/2021 Am s.r.l. + Officina Murano s.r.l. vs. New Murano Gallery s.r.l. + New Murano Gallery Production s.r.l.
24 For example, the Court of Rome (December 19, 2003) stated the simple subtraction of employees does not fall within the jurisdiction of the Specialized IP Sections, having no interference with any IP rights.

or domiciled. It is important to note, however, that special rules apply to litigation involving foreign subjects.

5.068 In this respect new rules were introduced by Legislative Decree no. 145 of 2013,[25] which established the exclusive jurisdiction of the IP Specialized Courts of Bari, Cagliari, Catania, Genoa, Milan, Naples, Rome, Turin, Venice, Trento and Bolzano, as the sole competent courts when a party involved (either as plaintiff as well as defendant) is a company whose registered office is located abroad. The exclusive jurisdiction also applies in joint cases against multiple defendants and extends to related matters.

5.069 Finally, Article 120.6 of the IP Code provides an additional jurisdiction criteria states that actions based on the alleged infringing of the plaintiff's rights can also be filed with the Judicial Authority having a Specialized IP Court in whose district the facts allegedly took place ('*locus commissi delicti*').

5.070 Within proceedings for design infringement, registered designs enjoy a presumption of validity and, as a consequence, while the burden to prove an infringement falls on the right holder, the burden of proof to challenge the validity of the design falls on the person or entity that challenges the existence of the right.

5.071 Under special circumstances and following an adequate (i.e., serious indicia about the foundation of its claims) request filed by the plaintiff, the Judicial Authority may order the defendant to disclose documents or to reveal information about the origin or the channels of distribution of the infringing products or any person or entity involved in the production or trade of the infringing products.[26] In issuing such an order, the judge shall take appropriate measures to safeguard confidential information and may derive elements of proof form the answers given by the parties or from the unjustified refusal to comply with the disclosure order.

5.072 A right holder seeking to enforce their IP rights, including those relating to designs and models, in Italy may choose between two different kinds of proceedings: interlocutory proceedings and actions on the merits.

---

25   Legislative Decree no. 145 of December 23, 2013, converted into Law no. 9 of 2014.
26   According to Art. 121.2 of the IP Code, the Court may order the other party to provide documents, elements or information that confirm the indicia and to provide the elements for the identification of the persons involved in the production and distribution of the goods or serviced that constitute an infringement of the IP rights.

5.073 Interlocutory proceedings are governed by the general provisions contained in Article 669-*bis* to Article 669-*quaterdecies* of the Code of Civil Procedure. In cases of special urgency, when the delay may cause the IP right holder irreparable harm ('*periculum in mora*'), and provided that *prima facie* evidence exists to show that a valid right has been infringed ('*fumus boni iuris*'), the right holder may start an action for interim relief, including a preliminary injunction.

5.074 The request for an interlocutory order may be filed – as occurs in most cases – before the filing of an action on the merits ('*ante causam*'), as well as during the action on the merits. When there is no action on the merits pending and, in certain cases involving urgency and/or risks associated with providing prior notice, the order may be granted without previously hearing the respondent ('*ex parte*'), according to Article 669-*sexies*. 2 of the Code of Civil Procedure. In this case, the judge must order the parties to appear in court no later than 15 days after the issuance of the order, to confirm, modify or withdraw the interlocutory order.

5.075 If required during the action on the merits, the request for an interlocutory order must be filed with the judge already in charge of the matter, who will discuss the request at the hearing in the presence of both, within the scope of the pending action.

5.076 When granting an interlocutory order, the judge may require the plaintiff to post a bond as a guarantee for any possible damages that may arise as a consequence of the enforcement of the order, according to Aricle 669-*undecies* of the Code of Civil Procedure.

5.077 The decision to grant or reject the interlocutory order may be appealed within 15 days from the date on which it was issued or communicated. The appeal will be discussed in front of a panel of three judges, which does not include the judge who issued the decision under appeal. The filing of the appeal does not automatically suspend the execution of the appealed decision but, if requested, the president of the panel may suspend enforcement, if necessary ordering the original plaintiff to post a bond.

5.078 The IP code provides for a range of provisional and urgency measures, such as judicial description, seizures and injunctions and, when a design or model is involved, they are usually granted within a few weeks from the filing of the relevant application.

5.079 The practice of judicial description is governed by Articles 129–130 of the IP Code, and the goal of these measures is to collect and preserve evidence of the alleged infringement, and in most cases the order is granted *ex parte*. It may be requested either in connection with or as an alternative to seizure, an involves the participation of a judicial officer engaged to describe the object(s) allegedly infringing the right, the means used for their production and other evidence that may be relevant to the alleged violation of the right, which may also be extended to objects belonging to third parties that are used in commercial activity.[27]

5.080 The description order is carried out by a court bailiff, if necessary with the assistance of a technical expert appointed by the judge, who must use any appropriate measure to protect confidential information belonging to the party against which the precautionary measure is carried out.

5.081 Articles 129 and 130 of the IP Code also provides for seizures, the function of which is either to collect evidence, including samples of the infringing objects, or to prevent the accused infringer from continuing the illicit activity, by removing the infringing objects. The court bailiff presides over the enforcement of the seizure order, which also may be extended to goods belonging to third parties that are used in commercial activity.

5.082 Until recently, Article 129(3) contained a provision to the effect that infringing products displayed in exhibitions and trade fairs could not be seized, but only described, unless there was an accompanying violation of criminal law provisions. This exception has been abolished,[28] and therefore it is now also possible to seize infringing products that are displayed during trade fairs and exhibitions.

5.083 Article 131 of the IP Code provides for the remedy of an injunction, stating that a right owner may ask for an injunction enjoining the target from manufacturing, trading and using any means that infringe the asserted right, and ordering the target or any third party that is using such means in a commercial activity to withdrawal the infringing products from trade. These orders can be granted either together or separately, and do not need to be confirmed by a subsequent decision on the merits to be valid and enforceable. These meas-

---

27 The judicial description ('*descrizione*') is a preliminary order aimed to collect the evidence of the alleged infringement by describing the infringing products, collecting photographs, designs, samples and, if available, sale and advertising documents. It is carried out by the Court bailiff upon order of the judge.

28 Art. 129.3 has been abolished according to the reform provided by the Law no. 102 of July 24, 2023.

ures are enforced by a court bailiff, who will serve a certified copy of the order on the infringer.

To strengthen their effectiveness, injunctions are often ordered together with a penalty, to be applied in case of delays in complying with the order, or in case of any violations of the order that occur subsequently. **5.084**

Conversely, and unlike the procedure that is applicable to injunctions, description and seizure orders must be confirmed by filing an action on the merits within the deadline provided by the judge who granted the preliminary measure. If no deadline has been expressly indicated, the action on the merits must be filed (by serving a writ of summons on the other party) within 20 working days or 31 calendar days, whichever is longer, counting from the day on which the order has been issued by Court or has been served on the parties (Art. 131–1-*bis* IP Code). **5.085**

An action on the merits may be filed independently, or following a request for an interlocutory order (as described above) either to confirm the order or seek additional relief, including compensation for damages suffered. Indeed, an action on the merits is the only judicial framework in which the right holder can submit a request for compensation for the damages that have occurred as a consequence of the infringement of their rights. **5.086**

The framework for an action on the merits[29] is set forth by the general provisions of the Code of Civil Procedure, together with the special provisions set forth in the IP Code. The plaintiff initiates an action on the merits by serving a writ of summons on the alleged infringer, informing them that they are called to appear in court on a scheduled date, which must be no earlier than 120 days after the date of service (150 days if the defendant resides abroad). **5.087**

The writ of summons must contain, the indication of the court, as well as the name and all relevant data of the plaintiff and of the defendant, a complete exposition of the facts and of the legal arguments on which the claim is based, as well as the evidence filed in support of the action. Eventually the demands addressed to the court. **5.088**

After the writ of summons has been served on the defendant, it is filed with the court, entered into the docket and a judge is appointed as judge *rapporteur*, **5.089**

---

29 A recent reform of the Code of Civil Procedure has been introduced by the Legislative Decree no. 149 of October 10 2022 and it applies to all the cases filed after June 30, 2023.

which will be in charge of directing the course of the action and the collection of evidence, before reporting the matter to a panel of three judges (the judge *rapporteur* and two colleagues) which will render the decision. The judge *rapporteur* will then set a date for the first hearing and inform the parties accordingly.

5.090 The defendant is then required to file its answer and statement of defence either on the date of the first hearing (as scheduled by the examining judge), or if the defendant intends to summon other parties or file a counterclaim (for instance, requesting a declaration of invalidity of the enforced design), no later than 70 days before the date of the first hearing.

5.091 The judge *rapporteur* will then set deadlines for the parties to file a series of three briefs: to restate their claims, to file additional evidence in support of their claims, and to file a rebuttal to the evidence filed by the other party or parties (scheduled as 40, 20 and ten days before the date of the first hearing). On the day of the first hearing, the judge is required to explore whether a settlement between the parties is possible and, if not, will decide on issues of admissibility of the evidence filed by the parties. Please note that the hearings may be done with remote video connections or replaced by written briefs. Once this procedural phase has been completed, and if there are no technical issues the case is transferred to the three-judge panel for a decision.

5.092 The decision may be appealed within 30 days from its service on the losing party upon request of the winning party, or within six months from the date on which the decision was filed with the office of the court. A party may appeal by serving a writ of appeal on the other party. If no appeal is filed, the decision will become final and can no longer be challenged.

5.093 Generally speaking, the appeal does not review the case in its entirety, but reconsiders the decision of the first instance court within the limits of the challenges filed by the parties. The parties are prohibited from introducing new evidence on appeal, unless they can prove they were unable to produce the evidence during the first instance trial for reasons beyond their control.

5.094 According to the Code of Civil Procedure, first instance decisions are immediately enforceable in Italy and the appeal does not automatically stay the enforceability of the first instance decision, which instead may be ordered by the Court of Appeal, upon a justified request made by the appealing party.

5.095 Following the decision of the Court of Appeal, it is possible for the parties to appeal further to the Italian Supreme Court (*Corte di Cassazione*). This appeal must be filed within 60 days from service of the Court of Appeal decision on the losing party, completed by the court bailiff upon request of the other party, or within six months from the date on which it was filed with the office of the court. The content of the appeal is limited, and may not request the review of questions of fact.

5.096 The Supreme Court has discretion to accept the appeal. In the event it rejects the appeal, the second instance decision will become final. If the Supreme Court accepts the appeal, it has the option to either decide the case on the merits, or to remand the case to a different Court of Appeal for a further evaluation of the merits. In the latter case, the appealing party will have to file the case with the Court of Appeal within three months from the filing of the decision with the office of the Supreme Court.

K. TECHNICAL EXPERTISE

5.097 As mentioned above, the judges of the IP Specialized Courts do not have a technical background. They do, however, have the option to appoint an expert to support the court with regards to various aspects of a case.

5.098 In design litigation, it is unlikely for a judge to decide to order a technical expertise phase (for contrast, it is a common feature of patent litigation). That said, it is possible, and in this event, the presiding judge in charge of the matter may appoint a technical expert ('*Consulente Tecnico d'Ufficio*') to examine documents and evidence filed by the parties and to make technical evaluations.

5.099 When the judge appoints a technical expert to evaluate an aspect of design validity or infringement, the expert will usually be chosen from a list of available registered patent attorneys. After selecting the expert, the expert will be called to swear an oath, after which the judge will entrust them with a technical question and formally instruct the expert to: (i) undertake the necessary investigations, in cooperation with the technical experts that may be appointed by the parties; (ii) to prepare a preliminary report, to be discussed with the parties' technical experts; and (iii) to prepare a final report, replying to the questions he or she was entrusted with. The expert's final report is usually then discussed at a hearing that is scheduled after it is filed.

5.100 The role of the technical expertise phase is highly relevant in IP litigation in Italy, especially in patent infringement matters. The technical expert's opinion, if properly supported by sufficient analysis, is usually followed by the court in rendering its decision. Of course, judges are not bound by the conclusions of the technical expert, and may even decide to perform a new technical expertise or to disregard the expert's opinion entirely but, in this case, the judges would be required to explain why they disagreed with the conclusions of the technical expert.

L. COMPENSATION FOR DAMAGES AND OTHER SANCTIONS

5.101 Compensation for damages may only be ordered by a decision rendered following an action on the merits. Similarly, a decision in an action on the merits is required to confirm certain interlocutory orders, such as description and seizure, as well as other final measures, such as an order to withdraw from trade, destruction of the infringing goods or the transfer of ownership of the goods to the right holder.

5.102 With regards to publication of an extract of the decision in one or more newspapers / magazines or on the website of the infringer, while this form of relief is more typically issued at the end of an action on the merits, it can be granted at the end of preliminary injunction proceedings under special circumstances.

5.103 The compensation for damages is governed by Article 125 of the IP Code which states that the amount of compensation is calculated pursuant to Articles 1223,[30] 1226,[31] and 1227[32] of the Civil Code by considering all the relevant aspects, including the negative economic consequences, loss of profits, the benefits obtained by the infringer and, if appropriate, moral damages caused to the right owner. The decision on the compensation of damages may award a global amount and, in this case, the loss of profits may not be less than the royalty fees that the infringer would have been bound to pay if they had obtained a license from the right owner.[33] In any case, the right owner may ask for the restitution of the profits realized by the infringer as an alternative to

---

[30] Art. 1223 of the Civil Code states that the reimbursement must cover both the loss suffered as well as the loss of profits as they are a direct consequence of the unlawful act.

[31] Art. 1226 of the Civil Code authorizes the liquidation on an equitable basis when it is impossible to proving the precise amount of the damage.

[32] Art. 1227 of the Civil Code states that the amount of the damage can be reduced when the creditor contributed to create the damage.

[33] According to the majority of the case law, in order to allow an effective compensation, the standard royalty amounts is usually increased (Court of Milan, January 31, 2011).

the reimbursement of the loss of profits or in the measure exceeding the latter amount.

It is important to note that, according to Article 2598 of the Civil Code, the right to compensation for damages is subject to a statute of limitation, in the sense that the rights to obtain compensation for damages arising from unlawful acts is prescribed five years from the date on which the act occurred. However, such prescription must be pleaded by the defendant as a defence, since the Court cannot take notice of it *ex officio*. **5.104**

Other civil penalties are provided by Article 124 of the IP Code which states that with the decision ascertaining the infringement, the court may issue an injunction from manufacturing, trading and using items infringing the IP right, as well as the withdrawal of said items from trade, setting an amount for each violation or subsequently ascertained non-compliance or any delay in complying with the order. **5.105**

The decision may also order the destruction of the infringing items at the infringer's expenses and that the infringing products and the specific means univocally devoted to their manufacture are assigned to the right holder, without prejudice to the right to compensation of damages. **5.106**

Finally, as anticipated above, according to Article 126 or the IP Code, with the decision issued at the end of interlocutory proceedings or (and more frequently) at the end of an action on the merits, the court may order the publication of the decision either in full or – more frequently – in summery or excerpt from limited to the conclusions, in one or more newspapers and/or on the infringer's website, at the losing party's expense. **5.107**

M. CUSTOMS ENFORCEMENT

EU Regulation No. 608/2013[34] concerning customs enforcement of intellectual property rights enables the competent Customs Authorities to enforce IP rights regarding goods, which, in accordance with European Union customs legislation, are subject to customs supervision or customs control, and to carry out adequate controls on such goods with a view to preventing operations in violation of laws governing intellectual property rights. **5.108**

---

34 Regulation (EU) No 608/2013 of the European Parliament and of the Council of 12 June 2013 concerning customs enforcement of intellectual property rights and repealing Council Regulation (EC) No 1383/2003.

5.109 Article 3 of EU Regulation No. 608/2013 enables right holders and, under certain conditions, holders of exclusive licenses covering the entire territory of two or more Member States, to apply for a national or Union application, consisting of a request made to the competent customs department for customs authorities to take action with respect to goods suspected of infringing an IP right.

5.110 Article 2 of EU Regulation No. 608/2013 provides in the definition of IP rights, among others, design rights, also including: (a) a Community design as provided for in Council Regulation (EC) 6/2002 of 12 December 2001 on Community designs; (b) a design registered in a Member State, or, in the case of Belgium, Luxembourg or the Netherlands, at the Benelux Office for Intellectual Property; (c) a design registered under international arrangements which has effect in a Member State or in the Union.

5.111 According to Article 17 of EU Regulation No. 608/2013, where the customs authorities identify goods suspected of infringing an intellectual property right for which a surveillance application has been granted, they shall suspend the release of the goods or detain them. Before suspending the release of or detaining the goods, the customs authorities may ask the right holder, or their representative, to provide them with any relevant information with respect to the goods, providing them information about the actual or estimated quantity of goods, their actual or presumed nature and images thereof, as appropriate.

5.112 The initial suspension of the goods is ten working days and may be extended by a maximum of an additional ten working days if necessary. In the case of perishable goods, the term is three working days. Within these deadlines, the right holder must assess whether or not the suspect goods infringe their IP rights and submit to the customs office a written declaration confirming the infringement. Where no written declaration is submitted, the customs office may release the goods.

5.113 According to the Regulation, the right holder must initiate legal proceedings within ten working days of the beginning of the suspension term (three working days in case of perishable goods), to determine whether an intellectual property right has been infringed. Under Italian law, given that the infringement of intellectual property rights is a criminal offence, when an Italian customs office receives the right holder's declaration confirming the infringement, the judicial authorities are notified and criminal proceedings are started automatically.

Customs authorities may also suspend the release of goods suspected of infringing an intellectual property right even in absence of a surveillance application filed by a right holder, except in the case of perishable goods. **5.114**

The EU Directorate General for Taxation and Customs Union (TAXUD) and the EUIPO jointly publish an annual report describing the results of the enforcement of intellectual property rights (IPRs) carried out by the customs authorities at the EU border and within the EU internal market. The most recent edition provides statistics relating to the detentions of IPR-infringing goods and other related information for the year 2020.[35] **5.115**

The report indicated that number of detentions of goods suspected of infringing an IP right by customs authorities at the EU border decreased significantly in 2020 compared to the previous year (from circa 90,000 in 2019 to circa 70,000 in 2020). **5.116**

The 2020 report also indicated that where infringed IPRs have been recorded, trademarks predominated as the most infringed IPR in detentions at the EU border (in over 72 per cent of the articles detained where at least one IPR was infringed, that right was a trade mark). **5.117**

With regard to design rights (over 27 per cent of the items detained constituted an infringement of a design). Instances of design infringement is clearly increasing with an almost 9 per cent increase over the data reported for 2019. In addition to the overwhelming preponderance of trademark infringement across subcategories, it is also remarkable that designs were mainly infringed by goods belonging to the subcategories of Clothing Accessories (87 per cent of the 'fake items detained' in this subcategory) and Audio/Video Apparatus (69 per cent). **5.118**

N. ADMINISTRATIVE DATA

Unfortunately, there is no data available in Italy concerning the number of court cases involving designs/models, nor the rate of success of the enforcement of design rights. The only available data refers to the number of cases handled by the IP Specialized Court of Milan, which has jurisdiction over industrial property and copyright cases, as well as antitrust cases, unfair com- **5.119**

---

[35] Available at: https:// euipo .europa .eu/ tunnel -web/ secure/ webdav/ guest/ document _library/ observatory/ documents/ reports/ 2021 _EU _enforcement _intellectual _property _rights/ 2021 _EU _enforcement _intellectual_property_rights%20_FullR_en.pdf.

petition matters (unless they bear no relation at all to IP rights), company law and public contracts, for the relevant territory.

5.120 The number of cases handled by the IP Specialized Court of Milan has progressively increased from 2018. Measuring the number of cases on the docket at December 31 of each year, the court reports that the number of cases was: 784 in 2018, 984 in 2019, 1,197 in 2020 and 1,256 in 2021. Strictly speaking, however, not all of these cases refer to IP matters.

5.121 With respect to IP right filings, the data available from the Italian Patent and Trademark Office's website show that, even despite the COVID-19 pandemic the number of filings has remained constant during the last five years: 1,182 applications were filed in 2017, 1,139 in 2019, 1,272 in 2020 and 1,184 in 2021. This demonstrates that the interest of the Italian population continues to be concerned in this type of protection, which appears particularly suitable for the design industry, one of the most important sectors for the Italian economy.

5.122 In this regard, it should be taken into account that, rather than filing an Italian design application before the Italian Patent and Trademark Office, an applicant could obtain a valid design registration in Italy via the EUIPO route (filing a Community design application) or via the WIPO route (filing an International design application designating EU).

6

INDUSTRIAL DESIGN LAW IN INDIA

Shwetasree Majumder and Eva Bishwal

A. SUBSTANTIVE AND PROCEDURAL LAW	6.001	a known design	6.044
1. Brief Overview of Industrial Design Protection in India and Applicable Legislations	6.001	Comprises contains scandalous or obscene material	6.047
2. Scheme of the Act	6.006	4. Other IP laws that Protect the Two- and Three-dimensional Appearance of Products	6.048
(a) What is a design?	6.006	(a) Trademarks	6.048
(b) What is an article?	6.009	(b) Copyrights	6.054
(c) Functionality	6.012	(c) Patents	6.058
(d) Industrial process or means	6.015	5. Disputes	6.060
(e) What is 'new' and 'original'?	6.016	(a) Cancellation	6.061
(f) Grace period for 'exhibitions'	6.022	(i) Prior-registered designs	6.062
(g) Reciprocity arrangement and priority	6.024	(ii) Prior publication	6.063
(h) Classification of articles	6.025	Publication in prior documents	6.065
(i) Rights granted and term	6.026	Publication by prior use	6.066
(j) Lapsed design	6.029	(iii) Not new or original	6.067
3. Procedure	6.030	(iv) Not registerable under this Act	6.068
(a) Registration	6.030	(v) Not a design defined under section 2 (d)	6.069
(i) Summary of steps	6.030	(b) Piracy	6.070
(ii) Formality	6.038	B. PRACTICAL ASPECTS OF DESIGN LAW	6.073
(iii) Substantive examination	6.040	1. Licensing of Design Rights	6.073
New or original	6.041	2. Assignment	6.076
Has been disclosed to the public in India or in any other country	6.043	C. EVALUATION, ANALYSIS, COMMENTS	6.078
Is not significantly distinguishable from			

A. SUBSTANTIVE AND PROCEDURAL LAW

1. Brief Overview of Industrial Design Protection in India and Applicable Legislations

6.001 In India, industrial design rights are recognised only if they stand registered under the statute. The first statute providing protection for designs was enacted in 1872 by the British Indian government called the Patterns and Designs Protection Act. It provided protection to inventors of 'new patterns and designs' and the exclusive privilege of making, selling, and using the same in India. This was followed by the enactment of the Invention and Designs Act, 1888 which was enacted to consolidate the laws relating to protection of designs and comply with British India's obligations as a signatory to the Paris Convention for the Protection of Industrial Property, 1883.[1] In the United Kingdom the Patents and Designs Act was enacted in 1907. It became the basis of the Indian Patents and Designs Act, 1911 which brought the Indian patent administration under the management of the Controller of Patents for the first time. Its foundation lay in the Patents and Designs Act, 1907 of the United Kingdom.[2] After India's Independence, it was felt that the Indian Patents & Designs Act, 1911 was not fulfilling its objective. Various committees were constituted to review and update the patent laws – the first the Justice Bakshi Tek Chand Committee in 1949 and thereafter the Justice N. Rajagopala Ayyangar Committee in 1957.

6.002 As a culmination of all of the Committees' recommendations, Patents and Designs laws were bifurcated in 1970 with the enactment of the Patents Act, which repealed the provisions relating to patents in the Indian Patents and Designs Act, 1911. The provisions relating to designs in the Indian Patents and Designs Act, 1911, were allowed to continue under the new title Designs Act, 1911 ('the 1911 Act') with some consequential amendments.

6.003 India joined the WTO as a member State in 1995. Consequently, the Patents & Designs Act, 1911 was repealed and the Designs Act, 2000 ('the Act') was enacted, to make the Designs law in India TRIPS compliant. The definition

---

1 Prof. Krishna Swami Ponnuswami, *"Design Protection in India: The Designs Act, 1911"*, Paper presented at WIPO National Workshop on Intellectual Property Teaching, University of Delhi, 1991, p. 3.
2 Virendra Kumar Ahuja, *"Design Protection in India: A Critique"*, (Nov. 6, 2021, 11:48 PM), https://www.ebc-india.com/lawyer/articles/94v2a3.htm accessed 4 June 2024.

of 'design' in the Act is more or less the same as that of the 1911 Act with the following exceptions:

i. Novelty was now required to be determined on a global basis.
ii. The classification system was no longer based on material characteristics of the article, but followed the Locarno Classification system.[3]

6.004 The object of the Act is to protect 'new' or 'original' designs which are created to be applied to an article manufactured by an industrial process, such that once the design is removed from the article, it ceases to exist.[4]

6.005 The Act and Rules provide for filing of a Design Application in any of the four Patent Offices i.e., Patent Office Delhi, Mumbai, Chennai or Kolkata. However, the prosecution of a Design Application is carried out only at the Patent Office, Kolkata until the present day.

2. Scheme of the Act

(a) What is a design?

6.006 A 'design' is defined under the Act in section 2 (d)[5] as meaning features of shape, configuration, pattern, ornament or composition of lines or colours which are applied to any 'article' which are judged solely by the eye. The application of a design to the article may be two-dimensional or three-dimensional or in both forms and should be done by any industrial process or means. The definition of design specifically excludes the following from its purview:

i. any mode or principle of construction or anything which is in substance a mere mechanical device;

---

3   Classification of Designs was brought in through the Design Rules 2001 (amended in 2008).
4   (Nov. 6, 2021, 10:11 PM), https://ipindia.gov.in/faq-designs.htm accessed 4 June 2024.
5   Section 2 (d) of the Designs Act, 2000:
    'design' means only the features of shape, configuration, pattern, ornament or composition of lines or colours applied to any article whether in two dimensional or three dimensional or in both forms, by any industrial process or means, whether manual, mechanical or chemical, separate or combined, which in the finished article appeal to and are judged solely by the eye; but does not include any mode or principle of construction or anything which is in substance a mere mechanical device, and does not include any trademark as defined in clause (v) of sub-section (1) of section 2 of the Trade and Merchandise Marks Act, 1958 or property mark as defined in section 479 of the Indian Penal Code or any artistic work as defined in clause (c) of section 2 of the Copyright Act, 1957.

ii. any trademark as defined in clause (v) of sub-section (1) of section 2 of the Trade and Merchandise Marks Act, 1958[6] or property mark as defined in section 479 of the Indian Penal Code;[7]

iii. any artistic work as defined in clause (c) of section 2 of the Copyright Act, 1957.

6.007 An artistic work has, in turn, been defined in section 2 (c) of the Copyright Act as:

- a painting, a sculpture, a drawing (including a diagram, map, chart or plan), an engraving or a photograph, whether or not any such work possesses artistic quality;
- a work of architecture; and
- any other work of artistic craftsmanship.

6.008 The Manual of Designs Practice and Procedure[8] issued by the Indian IP Office provides an illustrative list of non-registrable designs as under:

- book jackets, calendars, certificates, forms and documents;
- dress-making patterns, greeting cards, leaflets, maps and plan cards;
- post cards, stamps and medals;

---

6 Section 2 (1) (v) of the Trade and Merchandise Act, 1958:
'trade mark' means a registered trade mark or a mark used in relation to goods for the purpose of indicating or so as to indicate a connection in the course of trade between the goods and some person having the right as proprietor to use the mark; and (ii) in relation to the other provisions of this Act, a mark used or proposed to be used in relation to goods for the purpose of indicating or so as to indicate a connection in the course of trade between the goods and some person having the right, either as proprietor or as registered user, to use the mark whether with or without any indication of the identity of that person, and includes a certification trade mark registered as such under the provisions of Chapter VIII.
This provision was repealed by section 2 (1) (zb) of the Trade Marks Act, 1999:
'trade mark' means a mark capable of being represented graphically and which is capable of distinguishing the goods or services of one person from those of others and may include shape of goods, their packaging and combination of colours; and –
(i) in relation to Chapter XII (other than section 107), a registered trade mark or a mark used in relation to goods or services for the purpose of indicating or so as to indicate a connection in the course of trade between the goods or services, as the case may be, and some person having the right as proprietor to use the mark; and
(ii) in relation to other provisions of this Act, a mark used or proposed to be used in relation to goods or services for the purpose of indicating or so as to indicate a connection in the course of trade between the goods or services, as the case may be, and some person having the right, either as proprietor or by way of permitted user, to use the mark whether with or without any indication of the identity of that person, and includes a certification trade mark or collective mark.

7 Section 479 of the Indian Penal Code, 1860: Property mark – A mark used for denoting that movable property belongs to a particular person is called a property mark.

8 (May 5, 2022, 3:46 PM), https:// ipindia .gov .in/ writereaddata/ Portal/ I POGuidelin esManuals/ 1 _30 _1_manual-designs-practice-and-procedure.pdf accessed 4 June 2024.

- labels,[9] tokens, cards and cartoons.

(b) What is an article?

An 'article' has been defined under section 2 (a)[10] of the Act to mean any product that is capable of being manufactured and is either artificial or partly artificial and partly natural. For example, posters, wall papers, tapestries, etc. which are printed through an industrial process will be protected under the Act, however, a painting which is created by hand will not qualify as an article. The term 'industrial process' under the Act has been understood to mean a process of mechanised production that makes multiple replications of the article possible. **6.009**

The definition of an article also includes any part of an article capable of being made and sold separately. For example, a diffuser of a bulb, the head of a doll or the cap of a bottle. **6.010**

The Delhi High Court, while ruling on whether the handle of a toothbrush constituted a 'part of an article' and could be the subject matter of an infringement comparison when the toothbrush as a whole was a registered design, held that since the handle was a non-detachable part of an article that is not 'capable of being made and sold separately' it would not fall within the definition in section 2(a).[11] As the entire toothbrush is made from a single mould, the applicable design registration could not be interpreted to cover the handle if the neck had already been held to be functional in a previous proceeding. **6.011**

(c) Functionality

As is clear from the definition, a design which is purely functional in nature would not be entitled to protection under the Act. A design is understood to **6.012**

---

9   In *Hindustan Lever Ltd. v Nirma Pvt. Ltd.* AIR 1992 Bom 195, it was held that label put on a carton to be used as container for the goods can never amount to design within the meaning of s. 2 (5) of the Designs Act, 1911. Section 2 (5) of the Designs Act, 1911:
    'design' means only the features of shape, configuration, pattern or ornament applied to any article by any industrial process or means, whether manual, mechanical or chemical, separate or combined, which in the finished article appeal to and are judged solely by the eye ; but does not include any mode or principle of construction or anything which is in substance a mere mechanical device, and does not include any 2[trade mark as defined in clause (v) of sub-section (1) of section 2 of the Trade and Merchandise Marks Act, 1958 or property mark as defined in section 479 of the Indian Penal Code.
10 Section 2 (a) of the Designs Act, 2000: '"article" means any article of manufacture and any substance, artificial, or partly artificial and partly natural and includes any part of an article capable of being made and sold separately;…'.
11 Ibid.

be functional when it is the only mode/option of making the article which is based on the functional requirements of the product.[12]

6.013 For a defence of functionality to succeed, according to the Delhi High Court,[13] it is not enough to say that the form has some relevance to the function. If a particular function can be achieved through a number of different forms, then a defence of functionality must fail. For the defence of functionality to succeed, it is essential for the defendant to establish that the design applied for, is the only mode/option which was possible considering the functional requirements of the products. Even otherwise, assuming that the shape also performs a certain function, that, by itself, is not determinative of the fact that the design is functional, if that is not the only shape in which the function could be performed.

6.014 In *Escorts Construction Equipment Ltd. v Action Construction Equipment Pvt. Ltd.*[14] the Court noted that the primary object of the Act is to protect shape and not the function or functional shape. In the said instance, in addition to the industrial drawing of the entire crane, the plaintiff also claimed copyright in the boom and slider assembly, the lower structure assembly, the main frame – axle assembly, the differential housing, etc. The Court observed that these parts of the crane are made in a particular shape so as to interrelate with others mechanically. These parts of the crane are not made to appeal to the eye but solely to make the crane work or function. Most of the key components of the crane were not visible, and had only to pass the test of being able to perform their function. They would be judged by performance and not by appearance. Consequently, these components were found to be incapable of being registered as designs.

(d) Industrial process or means

6.015 A design which cannot be repeated is not registrable. Thus, an article made of naturally occurring substances like rocks, etc. cannot be the subject of a design registration as it will be impossible to replicate it through industrial means and two pieces of the same article are likely to look different.

---

12 *Apollo Tyres v Pioneer Trading Corporation and Ors*, 2017 (72) PTC 253 (Del); *Dart Industries Inc. and Ors v Polyset Plastics Pvt. Ltd. and Ors.* 2018(75)PTC495(Del).
13 Ibid.
14 1999 PTC 36 (Del).

(e) What is 'new' and 'original'?

6.016 Section 4 of the of the Act[15] provides that a design must be 'new' and 'original'. It should not have been published anywhere and it should not have been made known to the public. It should have been invented for the first time and should not have been reproduced by anyone.[16] This section is couched in negative terms and does not explain what is 'new' and 'original'. The Supreme Court in the case of *Bharat Glass Tube Ltd. v Gopal Glass Works Ltd.('Bharat Glass')*[17] held that the burden to show that a design is not 'new' or 'original' lies on the defendant/complainant and that the defendant/complainant must show that the design has been published in tangible form or is in use in products.

6.017 The Supreme Court held[18] that specifications, drawings and/or demonstrations in connection with registration of a design do not *per se* constitute publications which prohibit future registration of that design. Had publication of design specifications by a registering authority (particularly a registering authority in a foreign country), in itself, amounted to prior publication, that would hit all future applications in India for registration of designs. If that were so, the subsistence of prior registrations in India would not separately have been made a ground for cancellation of a registered design.

6.018 The Court also noted that the legislative intent was clear that a design published anywhere in the world would constitute prior art for cancellation purposes, but a prior registration *per se* would not constitute prior art unless it was an Indian registration. This essentially means that the burden of proof of what constitutes a 'prior publication' (i.e., the publication must have clear views of the article, the design must be 'substantially similar' and the two articles must be identical) would need to be discharged equally for all prior publications, but if it is a prior Indian registration, then relying on the registration is sufficient without any additional burden.

6.019 Therefore the Court concluded that in order to destroy the novelty of a design registration, prior disclosure, whether by publication or use or any other way, must be of the pattern, shape and/or configuration applied to the same article.

---

15 Section 4 of the Designs Act:
   A design which (a) is not new or original; or b) has been disclosed to the public anywhere in India or in any other country by publication in tangible form or by use or in any other way prior to the filing date, or where applicable, the priority date of the application for registration; or (c) is not significantly distinguishable from known designs or combination of known designs; or (d) comprises or contains scandalous or obscene matter shall not be registered.
16 *Bharat Glass Tube Ltd v Gopal Glass Works Ltd.*, 2008 (37) PTC 1 (SC).
17 Ibid.
18 *Supra* no. 13.

6.020 This position was further upheld by the full bench of the Delhi High Court in *Reckitt Benckiser India Ltd. v Wyeth Ltd.* ('*Reckitt Benckiser*')[19] where the Court noted that records of design office in a Convention country may or may not amount to prior publication depending on 'the complete clarity, available to the eye, of the design found in the public record so that it can be said to be understood for being applied to a specific article'.

6.021 Generally, there is no grace period for filing of a design application once the design has been published.

(f) Grace period for 'exhibitions'

6.022 In section 21, the Act[20] exempts the pre-condition of non-publication in the case of specific exhibitions to which the provision of the Act may extend from time to time through gazette notification of the Central Government. The design or the article to which the design is applied or the description of the design if exhibited in such exhibition or elsewhere during or after the exhibitions without the privity or consent of the proprietor, will not bar the design from being registered. The application for design in such case must be made within six months of the exhibition and the exhibitor must give previous notice in the prescribed form for the exemption under this provision to apply.

6.023 The ten-year term of a design registration can be extended to 15 years by the proprietor by making a request in the prescribed manner and format to the Controller.[21]

---

19 2013 (54) PTC 90 (Del).
20 Section 21 of the Designs Act, 2000:
   The exhibition of a design, or of any article to which a design is applied, at an industrial or other exhibition to which the provisions of this section have been extended by the Central Government by notification in the Official Gazette, or the publication of a description of the design, during or after the period of the holding of the exhibition, or the exhibition of the design or the article or the publication of a description of the design by any person else-where during or after the period of the holding of the exhibition, without the privity or consent of the proprietor, shall not prevent the design from being registered or invalidate the registration thereof:
   Provided that- (a) the exhibitor exhibiting the design or article, or publishing a description of the design, gives to the Controller previous notice in the prescribed form; and (b) the application for registration is made within six months from the date of first exhibiting the design or article or publishing a description of the design.
21 Section 11 (2) of the Designs Act, 2000:
   If, before the expiration of the said ten years, application for the extension of the period of copyright is made to the Controller in the prescribed manner, the Controller shall, on payment of the prescribed fee, extend the period of copy-right for a second period of five years from the expiration of the original period of ten years.

(g) Reciprocity arrangement and priority

6.024 The Act provides for special priority benefit for applicants who have applied in the UK or any other Convention countries or group of countries or countries which are members of inter-governmental organisations under section 44.[22] These countries or group of countries or inter-governmental organisations have been explained in Explanation 1.[23]

(h) Classification of articles

6.025 Section 6 (1) of the Act[24] provides that a design must be registered in respect of any or all prescribed classes of articles. India follows the Locarno Classification, which ensures that design searches are systematic, and obviates substantial reclassification work when documents are exchanged both at national and international level.[25]

(i) Rights granted and term

6.026 As per section 11 of the Act,[26] the proprietor of a design has copyright over the design for ten years from the date of registration. This means that for ten years from the date of registration, the design will be construed as an artistic work which will enjoy the economic rights available to an artistic work under the Copyright Act. The same is provided in section 14 (c) of the Copyright Act[27]

---

22   Section 44 (1) of the Designs Act, 2000:
     Any person who has applied for protection for any design in the United Kingdom or any of other convention countries or group of countries or countries which are members of inter-governmental organisations, or his legal representative or assignee shall, either alone or jointly with any other person, be entitled to claim that the registration of the said design under this Act shall be in priority to other applicants and shall have the same date as the date of the application in the United or any of such other convention countries or group of countries or countries which are members of inter-governmental organisations, as the case may be…
23   Explanation- (1) to Section 44 of the Designs Act, 2000:
     For the purposes of this section, the expression 'convention countries', 'group of countries' or 'inter-governmental organisation' means, respectively, such countries, group of countries or inter-governmental organisation to which the Paris Convention for Protection of Industrial Property, 1883 as revised at Stockholm in 1967 and as amended in 1979 or the Final Act, embodying the results of the Uruguay Round of Multilateral Trade Negotiations, provided for the establishment of World Trade Organisation applies.
24   Section 6 (1) of the Designs Act, 2000: 'A design may be registered in respect of any or all of the articles comprised in a prescribed class of articles.'
25   (Nov. 26, 2021, 5:10 PM), https://www.wipo.int/classifications/locarno/en/faq.html.
26   Section 11 (1) of the Designs Act, 2000: 'When a design is registered, the registered proprietor of the design shall, subject to the provisions of this Act, have copyright in the design during ten years from the date of registration.'
27   Section 14 (c) of the Copyright Act, 1957: in the case of an artistic work,— For the purposes of this Act, "copyright" means the exclusive right subject to the provisions of this Act, to do or authorise the doing of any of the following acts in respect of a work or any substantial part thereof, namely:—
     [(i) to reproduce the work in any material form including—
     (A) the storing of it in any medium by electronic or other means; or(B) depiction in three-dimensions of a two-dimensional work; or (C) depiction in two-dimensions of a three-dimensional work;]
     (ii) to communicate the work to the public;

and includes the right to reproduce the work in any material form, including storing it in electronic or other medium, to reproduce it in two-dimensional and three-dimensional forms, to communicate the work to the public and to include the work in any cinematograph film. In the context of designs, the relevant economic right is the exclusive right to industrially reproduce and manufacture articles to which the design has been applied to.

6.027 Upon the expiry of the ten-year period, the term of the design can be renewed for a maximum of an additional five years by making payment of the prescribed renewal fee.

6.028 The term 'copyright in a design' is used consistently throughout the Act, although design rights are understood to be separate from copyrights. The overlap becomes apparent in the context of section 15 (2) of the Copyright Act which contains a carve out to the effect that if copyright is sought over an artistic work applied to an article capable of design registration, then the said copyright will extinguish once 50 copies of the article are made using an industrial process. This provision is discussed in detail in section 4.2 below.

(j) Lapsed design

6.029 A design ceases to have effect upon the expiry of ten years from the date of registration of the design if the renewal fee has not been paid. However, a proprietor can restore the design by making an application for restoration within one year from the date of lapse of the design. If between the lapse date and the restoration date certain third parties have taken steps to avail themselves of the benefit of the design, the restoration might be subject to conditions prescribed by the Controller as they deem fit to protect such third parties.

3. Procedure

(a) Registration

(i) Summary of steps

6.030 Design applications filed in India are classified as 'Ordinary Applications' or 'Priority Applications'. The latter has to be filed within six months from the date of filing in a Convention country, before the Controller of Designs, Office

---

(iii) to issue copies of the work to the public not being copies already in circulation;
(iv) to include the work in any cinematograph film;
(v) to make any adaptation of the work;
(vi) to do in relation to adaptation of the work any of the acts specified in relation to the work in sub-clauses (i) to (iv);

of the Controller General of Patents, Designs and Trademarks, Ministry of Commerce and Industry, Government of India.

6.031 The 'representation sheets', which are required to contain exact representations of the article for which registration is sought, may be in the form of drawings, photographs, tracings including computer graphics or specimens of the design. In rare cases, the Controller may require a specimen of the article to be submitted. The figure(s) are to be placed in an upright position on the sheet with the views marked clearly (i.e., perspective view, front view, side view, etc.). Sectional views are not permitted. If design is to be applied to articles of a set, the representation is required to depict various arrangements in which the design is to be applied to such articles. If the representation contains a surface pattern which repeats, the representation sheet should show the complete pattern, and a sufficient portion of the repeating pattern in length and width.

6.032 No descriptive matter or matter denoting the components by reference letters/ numerals should be included, nor dimensions or engineering symbols.

6.033 Where trademarks, words, letters or numerals are not the essence of the design, they should be removed from the representations or specimens. Where they are essential to the design, a disclaimer shall be given in the representation sheet disclaiming any right to their exclusive use.

6.034 A statement of novelty and disclaimer (if any) in respect of mechanical action, trademark, word, letter, numerals should be endorsed on each representation sheet.

6.035 Dotted lines may be used in the representation sheet to indicate those elements of the article for which no protection is sought. For instance, an ornamentation or surface pattern on an article can be registered. In such a case, the representation should contain a solid line drawing for the claimed ornamentation or surface pattern, and a dotted line for rest of the article. When the colour combination is the essence of a design as applied to an article, the same should be clearly depicted in the representation. Colouring may be used, on a black and white drawing, to highlight only those features of the design for which protection is sought. In such cases, the novelty statement should clearly indicate that the claim is restricted only to the portions depicted by colouring and the colours so given are not part of the design.

6.036 A proprietor of a design may be:

a. an author of design,

DESIGN LAW

b. a person who has acquired the design,
c. a person for whom the design has been developed by the author, or
d. a person on whom the design has devolved.

6.037 All applications need to be filed with an 'address for service' in India, which in the case of foreign applicants, may be the address of the agent in India. Separate applications are required to be filed for designs sought to be registered in multiple classes.

(ii) Formality

6.038 Once the application is filed, the Examiner determines whether:

a. the application is in the prescribed format;
b. the prescribed fee has been paid;
c. the name, address, and nationality of the applicant is mentioned;
d. the address for service is given in the application form;
e. declaration of proprietorship is given in the application form;
f. the representation sheet is in the prescribed manner;
g. power of attorney is filed;
h. in case of reciprocity application, whether it was filed within the prescribed time along with the priority document or whether the latter was filed within the extendible period of three months along with the prescribed form and fees.

6.039 Once the formalities are complied with, the application proceeds for substantive examination.

(iii) Substantive examination

6.040 Substantive examination is thereafter carried out under Sections 2 (d),[28] 2 (g),[29] 4,[30] and 5(1)[31] to determine whether the design under consideration is:

a. a design under the Act;
b. new or original;

---

28 *Supra* n. 5.
29 Section 2 (g) of the Designs Act, 2000: '"original", in relation to a design, means originating from the author of such design and includes the cases which though old in themselves yet are new in their application'.
30 *Supra* n. 15.
31 Section 5 (1) of the Designs Act, 2000:
   Application for registration of designs. — (1) The Controller may, on the application of any person claiming to be the proprietor of any new or original design not previously published in any country and which is not contrary to public order or morality, register the design under this Act: Provided that the Controller shall before such registration refer the application for examination, by an examiner appointed under sub-section (2) of section 3, as to whether such design is capable of being registered under this Act and the rules made thereunder and consider the report of the examiner on such reference.

c. prejudicial to public order or morality;
d. prejudicial to the security of India.

New or original
6.041 The words 'new' and 'original' for a design mean a design which is invented or created for the first time and was unknown before. The words can also refer to a new application of an existing design.[32]

6.042 The Examiner conducts a novelty search in the available databases to ascertain the novelty of the design under consideration. Search is conducted class-wise or article wise to ascertain whether the applied design is significantly different from the previously registered, used or published designs. If it is found that the design is not new, the Examiner mentions the fact along with the citations in his report to the Controller.[33]

Has been disclosed to the public in India or in any other country
6.043 As discussed above in section 2.4, disclosure means disclosure in tangible form or in use in the product. The types of evidence acceptable in court in support of a claim of disclosure are – physical third-party products available in the market, patent and design applications and registrations published in Indian or foreign jurisdictions, any other form of literature such as books, journals, advertisement and promotional material etc. However, such evidence should clearly disclose the application of the design to the specific article.

Is not significantly distinguishable from a known design
6.044 Under sections 6(3) and (6) of the 2000 Act, if it is found upon examination that the design under consideration is already registered by the same applicant in another class and the applicant has not disclosed that fact in the application form, the Examiner shall raise an objection only with an objective to pre-date the application, and not on the ground of novelty. In such cases, the objection is communicated along with the citation of such prior registered design and the applicant is asked to amend the application. The term of the copyright of the design under consideration shall be co-terminus with the term of previously registered design.

6.045 If it is found that the applied design is already registered by another person in respect of some other article, the design under consideration may be registered only if the applicant becomes registered proprietor of the already registered

---

32 Virendra Kumar Ahuja, *Law Relating to Intellectual Property Rights*, LexisNexis, ISBN 978-81-8038-989-4, p 226.
33 *Supra* n. 6.

design. The term of the copyright of the design under consideration shall be co-terminus with the term of previously registered design.

6.046 However, if it is found that the design has been previously registered by another person in respect of a different article, or the design to which the application relates consists of a design previously registered by other person in respect of the same or some other article with modifications or variations not sufficient to alter the character or substantially to affect the identity, and if during the pendency of the application, the applicant becomes the proprietor of the previously registered design, the application shall not be refused on the ground:

a. that the design is not new or original only because it was previously registered, or
b. that design has been previously published in India or in any other country, only because the design has been applied to an article in respect of which a design has been registered.

Comprises contains scandalous or obscene material

6.047 The terms 'scandalous' and 'obscene' have not been defined under Indian laws but find mention across a wide range of statutes. It is thus left open to judicial pronouncements to determine what qualifies as 'scandalous' and 'obscene' from time to time, basis individual perception set against the evolving morality of the times.

4. Other IP laws that Protect the Two- and Three-dimensional Appearance of Products

(a) Trademarks

6.048 Trademarks are protected in India under The Trademarks Act, 1999 and also under common law. The statute recognises the existence of protectable but unregistered trademark rights under the law of passing off (a species of unfair competition).[34] Much like the Designs Act, 2000, the Trademarks Act, 1999 covers shapes, packaging, combination of colours, and combination of shapes, patterns and ornament of goods.[35] The statutory definition of a trademark does

---

34 Section 27 (2) of the Trademarks Act, 1999: '(2) Nothing in this Act shall be deemed to affect rights of action against any person for passing off goods or services as the goods of another person or as services provided by another person, or the remedies in respect thereof.'
35 Section 2 (m) of the Trademarks Act, 1999: '"mark" includes a device, brand, heading, label, ticket, name, signature, word, letter, numeral, shape of goods, packaging or combination of colours or any combination thereof;…'.

not provide for exclusions, unlike the definition of a design, which expressly excludes subject matter that qualifies as a trademark. Unlike designs, trademarks are afforded perpetual protection as the registration can be renewed every ten years.[36] Hence for subject matter such as 'shape of goods', 'product packaging', the preference is to seek design protection in the first instance and trademark protection once the shape attains distinctiveness.

6.049 The law recognises that a design can acquire trademark function by virtue of long use and acquired distinctiveness,[37] and the proprietor of a design can apply for registration of a trademark after the expiry of the term of the design protection.[38] However, there is no embargo on applying for trademark protection during the subsistence of a design registration as long as the latter is surrendered at the time trademark protection is sought to be claimed.

6.050 However, despite the statutory demarcation created in respect of the scope of protection that can be claimed under trademark law and designs law, courts in India have been known to permit a claim for passing off in respect of an article which enjoys registered design protection.

6.051 The Full Bench of the Delhi High Court in *Mohan Lal and Ors v Sona Paints and Ors* ('*Mohan Lal*')[39] ruled that a passing off action is maintainable along with a claim for design infringement, however, the plaintiff must demonstrate that the component over which trademark protection was sought, was 'something which is extra' and was 'added on to the goods to denote origin' and to that end was not the identical subject matter as that for which design protection was claimed. It also held that an action for passing off and design infringement are independent causes of action and cannot be combined. Therefore, a plaintiff had to file separate suits for design infringement and passing off.

Section 2 (zb) of the Trademarks Act, 1999: '"trademark" means a mark capable of being represented graphically and which is capable of distinguishing the goods or services of one person from those of others and may include shape of goods, their packaging and combination of colours;...'.

36 Section 25 (1) and (2) of the Trademarks Act, 1999:
   (1) The registration of a trademark, after the commencement of this Act, shall be for a period of ten years, but may be renewed from time to time in accordance with the provisions of this section.
   (2) The Registrar shall, on application made by the registered proprietor of a trademark in the prescribed manner and within the prescribed period and subject to payment of the prescribed fee, renew the registration of the trademark for a period of ten years from the date of expiration of the original registration or of the last renewal of registration, as the case may be (which date is in this section referred to as the expiration of the last registration).

37 *Smithkline Beecham plc. and Ors v Hindustan Lever Ltd. and Ors* 2000 (20) PTC 83 (Del).
38 *Mohan Lal and Ors v Sona Paints and Hardwares and Ors* 2013 (55) PTC 61 (Del).
39 Ibid.

6.052 The latter position was overruled by a five-Judge Bench in the case of *Carlsberg Breweries A/S v Som Distilleries and Breweries Ltd.* (*'Carlsberg'*)[40] which held that if both the causes of action arise against the same entity and in respect of the same article, a composite suit can be filed claiming relief for both design infringement and passing off.[41]

6.053 The decisions in *Mohan Lal* and *Carlsberg* were interpreted by a Single Judge of the Delhi High Court in the case of *Crocs Inc. U.S.A. vs Aqualite India Ltd.*[42] which held that a registered design cannot be protected as trademark, and only the features other than those registered as a design can be protected as trademark. The Judge further clarified that what is covered in the design registration has to be expressly excluded from a passing off claim. After such an exclusion, if what remained was not significant, then a passing off claim would not stand. The Judge additionally observed that this would hold good not only during the period of registration as a design but even thereafter. The reasoning was that, since the Act provides for a duration of 15 years of protection, a proprietor cannot be allowed to evergreen this protection by obtaining a trademark registration which will last in perpetuity. The matter went to appeal and the Appeal Court held that while legal position laid down by the Single Judge is correct, protectability of a registered design when used as a trademark cannot be denied.[43] The Appeal Court clarified that the position laid down in *Mohan Lal (supra)* and *Carlsberg (supra)* did not exclude a product embodying a registered design from trademark protection.

(b) Copyrights

6.054 Indian Copyright law protects an artistic work, which are defined to clearly overlap with the definition of designs. Consequently, the definition of design under the Designs Act includes features of a product including shape, configuration, pattern, ornament, composition of lines or colours and expressly excludes artistic work defined under section 2 (c) of the Copyright Act.[44] This implies that the owner of a design foregoes copyright in the same once the

---

40 2019 (77) PTC 1 (Del).
41 Order I Rule 3 of the Code of Civil Procedure, 1908:
    3. Who may be joined as defendants. —All persons may be joined in one suit as defendants where— (a) any right to relief in respect of, or arising out of, the same act or transaction or series of acts or transactions is alleged to exist against such persons, whether jointly, severally or in the alternative; and
    (b) if separate suits were brought against such persons, any common question of law or fact would arise.
42 2019 (78) PTC 100 (Del).
43 *Crocs Inc. USA v Aqualite India Ltd.*, 2019 (79) PTC 75 (Del).
44 Section 2 (c) of the Copyright Act, 1957: "'artistic work' means — (i) a painting, a sculpture, a drawing (including a diagram, map, chart or plan), an engraving or a photograph, whether or not any such work possesses artistic quality; (ii) a work of architecture; and (iii) any other work of artistic craftsmanship; …'.

design is registered. Given that the term of copyright is 60 years from the death of the author and the term of a registered design is 15 years, the former provides a longer horizon of protection.

6.055 While it is apparent that two-dimensional images of products only qualify for copyright protection, the ambiguity in the catch-all phrase 'any other work of artistic craftsmanship' under section 2 (c) (iii) of the Copyright Act fails to provide clarity on the specific type of three-dimensional products that would qualify for copyright protection but would be disqualified for design protection. The practical approach therefore has been to seek copyright protection for blueprints/ drawings of objects, and design protection for the objects themselves. In the case of architectural works or sculptures, however, given that they are specifically identified in section 2 (c) (ii) and (i) respectively, copyright protection is sought for the objects themselves and not just their drawings.

6.056 Section 15 (2) of the Copyright Act states that copyright in an unregistered design applied to an article shall cease as soon as the article has been reproduced more than 50 times by an industrial process.

6.057 This overlap between designs and copyright was discussed in great detail by a two-Judge Bench of the Delhi High Court in *Microfibers Inc. v Girdhar & Co. and Another*[45] where the Court observed that there is a clear distinction between an original artistic work, and the design derived from it for industrial application on an article and this position is clarified by the use of the expression 'only' before the words 'the features of shape, configuration, pattern, ornament or composition of lines or colours' in the definition of 'design' in the Designs Act, 2000. The Court observed that the Designs Act, 2000 intended a shorter term for copyright when from the copyright a design is created which is applied for commercial purposes. The Court also rejected 'intention' of the creator as the determinative criteria and upheld that the nature of reproduction would determine whether a work or article would be a subject matter of copyright or designs. The Court also held that while artistic work such as painting or drawing may be used as the basis for designing an object through an industrial process for the purpose of commerce, nevertheless, the original artistic work would enjoy full copyright protection. This distinction assumes critical significance for the fashion industry where a designer can claim copyright protection over an innovatively cut and draped garment only until the garment is manufactured 50 times. Once the legal fiction of the 50th article is reached, the garment loses copyright protection (as it was capable of design registration but

---

45   2009 (40) PTC (Del).

DESIGN LAW

Table 6.1   Comparison of visual features protected by design law and functional features protected by patent law

	Patents Act, 1970	Designs Act, 2000
Common elements covered by the definition	Three-dimensional features of shape and configuration	
Subject matter	New functional and mechanical inventions	Visually appealing features
Duration of protection	20 years from the date of filing*	Limited protection for 15 years**

*Notes:** Section 53 (1) of the Patents Act, 1970: 'Subject to the provisions of this Act, the term of every patent granted, after the commencement of the Patents (Amendment) Act, 2002, and the term of every patent which has not expired and has not ceased to have effect, on the date of such commencement, under this Act, shall be twenty years from the date of filing of the application for the patent. Section 53 (1) of the Patents Act, 1970: Subject to the provisions of this Act, the term of every patent granted, after the commencement of the Patents (Amendment) Act, 2002, and the term of every patent which has not expired and has not ceased to have effect, on the date of such commencement, under this Act, shall be twenty years from the date of filing of the application for the patent.' ** Section 11 of the Act, 2000: Copyright on registration.— (1) When a design is registered, the registered proprietor of the design shall, subject to the provisions of this Act, have copyright in the design during ten years from the date of registration.
Source: Author.

not so registered in the first place).[46] If the garment has a pattern on it which has a standalone identity in the form of an artwork that can be reproduced on paper, then the artistic copyright over the pattern outlives the legal fiction, as the latter only applies to the finished articles and not the artistic works on them. Consequently, claims for copyright infringement can continue to be made in respect of patterns on garments, basis the underlying two-dimensional artistic work even after the threshold of 50 reproductions has been crossed.

(c) Patents

6.058 The Indian Patents Act, 1970 protects new 'inventions' which are products or processes involving inventive steps and capable of industrial application.[47] Therefore, the focus in the case of a patent if on the functional and/or mechanical features of the invention. In case of design, the focus is on features which 'appeal to and are judged solely by the eye' which excludes 'a mode or principle of construction or anything which is in substance a mere mechanical device'. Since both designs and patents relate to three dimensional features of shape and configuration, the distinction is not always clear. The visually appealing aspects of a product form part of design protection and the mechanical and functional invention are protected under patent law. The differences between the two kinds of protections are shown in Table 6.1 below.

---

46 *Dart Industries Inc. v Techno Plast and Ors* 2016 (67) PTC 457; *Ritika Pvt Ltd v Biba Apparels Pvt. Ltd.* MANU/DE/0784/2016.
47 Section 2 (1) (j) of the Patents Act, 1970: '"invention" means a new product or process involving an inventive step and capable of industrial application; …'.

The nature of protection and the rights conferred are similar for both patent **6.059**
and designs, i.e., they are statutory in nature and confer exclusive rights for
industrial manufacture and sale. Design rights and patent rights can co-exist
for an article.

5. Disputes

The two types of disputes that a proprietor or user of a design may face are **6.060**
cancellation actions and piracy actions:

(a) Cancellation

Under section 19 of the Act,[48] 'any person' can file a petition for cancellation **6.061**
before the Controller of Designs (the nodal administrative authority for
registration and regulation of designs in India). There are five grounds for
cancellation of a design:

(i) Prior-registered designs

Under section 19 (1) (a),[49] if a prior-registered design in India shows that it is **6.062**
substantially similar to the design being challenge, it is liable to be cancelled.
This provision is restricted to registrations in India and drawings and details
in foreign registrations, by themselves, cannot amount to prior publication.[50]
Here, section 44 (1) of the Act becomes relevant which does not broaden the
scope of section 19 (1) (a) to include designs in convention countries, making
the legislative intent about restricting the embargo of prior registration to
Indian registrations alone.[51] Substantially similar publications are sufficient to
invalidate a design and they need not be identical to the design.[52]

(ii) Prior publication

A prior published design is a design which is available in the public domain or **6.063**
is known to the public. Publication does not mean that every member of the

---

48   Section 19 of the Designs Act, 2000:
     (1) Any person interested may present a petition for the cancellation of the registration of a design at any time after the registration of the design, to the Controller on any of the following grounds, namely:–
     (a) that the design has been previously registered in India; or (b) that it has been published in India or in any other country prior to the date of registration; or (c) that the design is not a new or original design; or (d) that the design is not registrable under this Act; or (e) it is not a design as defined under clause (d) of section 2.
     (2) An appeal shall lie from any order of the Controller under this section to the High Court, and the Controller may at any time refer any such petition to the High Court, and the High Court shall decide any petition so referred.
49   Ibid.
50   *Supra* n. 16.
51   *Supra* n. 19.
52   *Faber- Castell Aktiengesellschaf and Anr v Pikpoen Pvt. Ltd.* 2003 (27) PTC 538 (Bom).

public should know of the design as long as it was in the public domain.[53] The legislative intent of the Act is such that prior registration is to be considered only with respect to India, whereas prior publication has to be considered on global basis.[54] If a design has been published in India or anywhere in the world prior to the filing date, or wherever applicable the priority date, the same cannot be registerable. What is publication is a question of fact and it should be determined according to the evidence led. A document can qualify as prior art only if:

a. it is a published document dated prior to the plaintiff's design registration;
b. it contains the same article. If the plaintiff's design is for a bottle, and the document shows a vase or a bag or a bulb, it would not qualify as prior art;
c. The article must be viewable for the Court to come to a conclusion that it is the same article as to defeat the plaintiff's claim of priority. For example, if the document shows a pattern applied to glass sheets, the prior art documents should also show the same or similar pattern being glass sheets[55]
d. A mosaic of several prior documents cannot be cited to attack novelty.[56]

6.064 Prior publication is of two kinds:

Publication in prior documents

6.065 This is publication in the form of documents such as journals, magazines, books, advertisements, brochures, patent specifications, trademarks, etc. While comparing a subject design against a prior published document, the visual effect and appeal of the drawings and images need to be adjudged.[57] The moment a person with ordinary prudence sees the prior documents, he should be able to say 'Oh! I have seen (this) before'.[58]

Publication by prior use

6.066 Publication by prior use is publication in the form of disclosure of articles to which a design is applied to the public. Such publication is said to have taken place if the article has been disclosed to even a single member of the public.[59] However, as the Court notes in *Reckitt Benckiser*,[60] prior publication must be of the pattern, shape and/or configuration applied to the same article, since

---

53 *Add Print (India) Enterprises Pvt. Ltd. v Mohan Impressions Pvt. Ltd.* 2013 (53) PTC 485 (Mad).
54 *Supra* n. 54.
55 *Supra* n. 19.
56 Ibid.
57 Ibid.
58 *Supra* no. 32 at p 244.
59 *The Wimco Ltd. v Meena Match Industries* AIR 1983 Del 537.
60 *Supra* n. 19.

a particular pattern of surface ornamentation could be applied to wide range of different articles.

(iii) Not new or original

A new and original design means that a new design should come into existence which is not a mere trade variation of an earlier design. Minor changes which do not add to an older design significantly cannot be used to monopolise a proprietor's old design.[61] **6.067**

(iv) Not registerable under this Act

If a design is not a design, i.e., it is prohibited under section 4,[62] it is liable to be cancelled. **6.068**

(v) Not a design defined under section 2 (d)

A design that does not fall within the definition of section 2 (d), such as for example, a part of an article, or something that cannot be made through an industrial process. **6.069**

(b) Piracy

Section 22 of the Act[63] provides the statutory remedy of piracy for the proprietor of a design. The Section explains piracy as the act of applying or causing **6.070**

---

61 *GlaxoSmithKline Consumer Healthcare GmbH& Co. vs Anchor Health and Beautycare Pvt. Ltd.*, 2004 (29) PTC 72 (Del).
62 Section 4 of the Designs Act, 2000:
   Prohibition of registration of certain designs. —A design which—
   (a) is not new or original; or
   (b) has been disclosed to the public anywhere in India or in any other country by publication in tangible form or by use or in any other way prior to the filing date, or where applicable, the priority date of the application for registration; or
   (c) is not significantly distinguishable from known designs or combination of known designs; or
   (d) comprises or contains scandalous or obscene matter, shall not be registered.
63 Section 22 of the Designs Act, 2000:
   (1) During the existence of copyright in any design it shall not be lawful for any person (a) for the purpose of sale to apply or cause to be applied to any article in any class of articles in which the design is registered, the design or any fraudulent or obvious imitation thereof, except with the license or written consent of the registered proprietor, or to do anything with a view to enable the design to be so applied; or (b) to import for the purposes of sale, without the consent of the registered proprietor, any article belonging to the class in which the design has been registered, and having applied to it the design or any fraudulent or obvious imitation thereof, or (c) knowing that the design or any fraudulent or obvious imitation thereof has been applied to any article in any class of articles in which the design is registered without the consent of the registered proprietor, to publish or expose or cause to be published or exposed for sale that article.
   (2) If any person acts in contravention of this section, he shall be liable for every contravention – (a) to pay to the registered proprietor of the design a sum not exceeding twenty-five thousand rupees recoverable as a contract debt, or (b) if the proprietor elects to bring a suit for the recovery of damages for any such contravention, and for an injunction against the repetition thereof, to pay such damages as may be awarded and to be restrained by injunction accordingly:
   Provided that the total sum recoverable in respect of any one design under clause (a) shall not exceed fifty thousand rupees:

to be applied a registered design or a 'fraudulent or obvious imitation' of a registered design and publish and/or sell and/or import for sale the said article. 'Fraudulent and obvious imitation' means overall similarity or substantial similarity where overall look and feel of the rival articles is seen to ascertains similarity and the identity on all points.[64]

6.071 For a case where an action for piracy has been without a claim made for damages, the Section caps the monetary compensation at INR 25,000. In case a claim of damages has been made in such action, the damages that can be awarded is capped at INR 50,000.

6.072 Under Section 22 (3), in a suit for piracy, the Defendant can invoke all grounds for cancellation under Section 19 as a ground of defence. Section 22 (3) contemplates the limited scope of a Defendant raising a defence of grounds of cancellation and does not empower the Court to invalidate the Plaintiff's design.[65] However, the actual cancellation/ removal of the design from the register is ultimately a ministerial act which will logically follow once the Court has arrived at the finding that a design is invalid/ liable to be cancelled.

B. PRACTICAL ASPECTS OF DESIGN LAW

1. Licensing of Design Rights

6.073 Copyright in registered designs being critical economic assets is commonly licensed in India amongst business enterprises and is a vital source of revenue. In case of license agreement executed in India, Indian law is applicable, unless the parties have opted for some other governing law.

Provided further that no suit or any other proceeding for relief under this subsection shall be instituted in any court below the court of District Judge.
(3) In any suit or any other proceeding for relief under subsection (2), ever ground on which the registration of a design may be cancelled under section 19 shall be available as a ground of defence.
(4) Notwithstanding anything contained in the second proviso to sub-Section (2), where any ground or which the registration of a design may be cancelled under section 19 has been availed of as a ground of defence and sub-section (3) in any suit or other proceeding for relief under sub-section (2), the suit or such other proceedings shall be transferred by the Court in which the suit or such other proceeding is pending, to the High Court for decision.
(5) When the court makes a decree in a suit under sub-section (2), it shall send a copy of the decree to the Controller, who shall cause an entry thereof to be made in the register of designs.

64 *Dabur India Ltd. V Amit Jain* 2009 (39) PTC 104 (Del) (DB); *Dart Industries and Anr. v Polyset Plastics Pvt. Ltd. and Ors* 2018 (75) PTC 495 (Del); *Alert India v Naveen Plastic* 1997 (17) PTC 15 (Del); *J.N. Electricals v President Electrical* (1980) ILR 1 Delhi 215.
65 *Microlube India Ltd. v Rakesh Kumar Trading and Ors* 2012 (50) PTC 161 (Del).

6.074 A license agreement should be in writing. It should identify the parties and the design being licensed. Most importantly, the agreement should define the scope of the license, i.e., the article to be applied to, the purpose and manner of reproduction of the design, territory of distribution, etc. The agreement must specify the consideration as agreements without consideration are invalid under Indian law. The consideration may be in the form of a monetary figure which is either a lump sum or royalties, or other consideration (such as a cross-license or strategic advice, distribution of the products, etc.). While fixing the remuneration, the value of the design, and its profitability must be factored in. It is also critical that the contract has a confidentiality term to protect the licensor's confidential commercial/non-commercial information.

6.075 When a licensee or mortgagee seeks to come on record in respect of a registered design, the instrument from which they derive their title must be filed in the prescribed form before the Controller of Designs in the IP Office. The Controller's satisfaction as to the proof of title is a condition precedent to its recordation.

2. Assignment

6.076 Assignment of designs is governed by Section 30 of the Designs Act, 2000 read with Rules 32–35 of the Designs Rules. An assignment is required to be in writing and contain all the terms and conditions governing the rights and obligations of the parties. It must be filed in the prescribed form before the Controller of Designs in the IP Office within six months from the date of execution of the instrument or within such further period not exceeding six months in the aggregate as the Controller on the application made in the prescribed manner allow. The Controller's satisfaction as to the validity of the assignment is a condition precedent to its recordation.

6.077 An assignment or license that is not duly recorded before the Controller of Designs will not be admitted in evidence in a court of law.

C. EVALUATION, ANALYSIS, COMMENTS

6.078 One of the greatest challenges of implementation of the Indian law of designs is the ease with which registration is granted. Registrations are granted for ever-so-slight modifications of existing designs (which is then found to be an infringement of the original design when the parties end up in litigation). The thresholds for similarity need to be uniform at the Registry and the Courts to avoid situations such as those reported in *Pentel Kabushiki Kaisha v M/s Arora Stationers*,[66] *Vega Auto Accessories Pvt Ltd v S.K. Jain*[67] and *Whirlpool of India Ltd. v Videocon Industries Ltd*,[68] each of which was a case where the defendant was the subsequent registrant of a design that was substantially similar to the plaintiff's prior registered design and was found to have infringed it.

6.079 The absence of properly maintained online records (with all the views of an article) make it impossible to search for and obtain prior publications in a manner that conforms to the thresholds laid down by the Supreme Court in *Bharat Glass*.[69]

6.080 The lack of clarity as to subject matter covered in the overlap of designs with trademarks and copyrights has led to a number of conflicting judgments on the subject. For example, the shape of an article is capable of being both a trademark and a design and consequently the Designs Office often objects to a design application for the shape of an article on the basis that it qualifies as a trademark and is therefore excluded from the definition of a design. Similarly design applications for parts of buildings and other architectural works that serve as embellishments on buildings are objected on the basis that they are artistic works that fall within the scope of the Copyright Act and are therefore excluded. A clear demarcation of the contours of design registrability would serve as a guide both for applicants and the Designs Office.

6.081 The possibilities that new technology throws up are endless! In light of Indian law firmly according protection to designs which 'though old in themselves… are new in their application', it is possible for a pre-existing product fabricated through traditional tools and/or methods of industrial manufacture to become registrable all over again as a 3D printed product. The emphasis, as the Supreme Court notes in *Bharat Glass*,[70] is 'the visual image conveyed by the manufactured article'. Hence, the Court notes, 'the visual effect and/or appeal of a pattern embossed into glass sheets by use of embossing rollers could be different from the visual effect of the same pattern etched into glass sheets manually'. Using this principle, it is apparent that the mere use of a different technology to achieve the same aesthetic result could make the new product design-eligible under Indian law. This perspective significantly narrows the exclusivity enjoyed by articles that currently hold design registrations or

---

66 (2019) 79 PTC 42 (Del).
67 (2018) 75 PTC 59 (Del).
68 2014 (60) PTC 155 (Bom).
69 *Supra* n. 16.
70 Ibid.

expands the possibilities of new registrations being granted, depending on which way you look at it.

7

INDUSTRIAL DESIGN LAW IN JAPAN

Taketo Nasu

A. DESCRIPTIVE PART	7.001	
1. Substantive	7.001	
(a) Brief overview of industrial design protection in the jurisdiction	7.001	
(i) Design	7.002	
(ii) Trademark	7.007	
(iii) Copyright	7.008	
(iv) Unfair competition	7.009	
(b) Legal framework for registered and non-registered industrial design in effect in Japan	7.010	
(i) Industrially applicable	7.012	
(ii) Novel	7.013	
(iii) Not easily creatable	7.015	
(iv) Not identical or similar to a part of design in earlier applications	7.016	
(v) First-to-file rule	7.017	
(vi) Unregistrable items	7.019	
2. Registration Procedure	7.020	
(a) National registration	7.020	
(i) Enjoyment of rights	7.020	
(ii) Application procedure	7.022	
(iii) Appeal trial	7.028	
(iv) Post registration	7.030	
(v) Remedies in cases of inconsistent views, etc.	7.034	
(vi) Priority claim	7.036	
(b) International registration	7.037	
3. Disputes	7.040	
(a) Prosecution	7.040	
(i) Grounds for invalidity	7.040	
(ii) Procedure – invalidation trial	7.042	
(iii) Procedure – action against trial decision	7.045	
(b) Litigation	7.048	
(i) Scope of protection	7.048	
(ii) Finding infringement in view of the specific scope of protection	7.051	
(iii) Defences	7.052	
(iv) Enforcement (injunction, damages)	7.057	
(c) Other dispute resolution	7.063	
(i) Customs measures	7.063	
(ii) Criminal penalty	7.064	
4. Significant Judicial Decisions in the Jurisdiction	7.065	
(a) *Flexible and Elastic Hose* case	7.065	
(b) *Carabiner* case	7.066	
B. PRACTICAL ASPECTS OF DESIGN LAW	7.067	
1. Statistics/Trends	7.067	
(a) Number of filings	7.067	
(b) Number of court cases	7.068	
(c) Rate of success; etc.	7.069	
2. Business Aspects	7.070	
(a) Transferability	7.070	
(b) Licensing	7.072	
3. Specific Interesting Applications or Case Studies	7.075	
C. COMMENTS, ANALYSIS, EVALUATION	7.076	
1. Comments on Present Legal Framework (Legislation and Case Law)	7.076	
2. Design Law Reform *de lege ferenda*	7.077	
3. Future Outlook in Light of New Technologies	7.078	

A. DESCRIPTIVE PART

1. Substantive

(a) Brief overview of industrial design protection in the jurisdiction

The legislation applicable for the protection of industrial design are, Design Act,[1] Trademark Act,[2] Copyright Act[3] and Unfair Competition Prevention Act.[4] The subject industrial design must be registered to seek protection under Design Act or Trademark Act, while registration is not required under Copyright Act or Unfair Competition Prevention Act to seek protection.

7.001

(i) Design

The Design Act applies to protection of registered industrial designs. The term 'design' is defined therein as the shape, patterns or colours, or any combination thereof ('**shape, etc.**'), of: an article (including a part of an article), a building (including a part of a building), or a graphic image (limited to those provided for use in the operation of the device or those displayed as a result of the device performing its function, and including a part of a graphic image), which creates a visual aesthetic impression.[5]

7.002

Protectable industrial designs are not limited to the shape, etc. of an article, building or a graphic design as a whole, rather the shape, etc. of a part of a design can also be registered.

7.003

In general, an application for design registration must be filed for each design as provided by an Ordinance of the Ministry of Economy, Trade and Industry ('**Ordinance**').[6] Exceptionally, a design for two or more articles, buildings or graphic images used together, which are specifically designated by the Ordinance ('**Set of Articles**') may be filed as one design and a design registration can be obtained where such Set of Articles provide a sense of unit as a whole.[7] In addition, designs for articles, buildings or graphic images that constitute equipment and decorations inside a store, office and the other facilities ('**Interior**') may be filed as one design, and a design registration can

7.004

---

1   Act No. 125 of 1959; last amended by Act No. 42 of 2021.
2   Act No. 127 of 1959; last amended by Act No. 42 of 2021.
3   Act No. 48 of 1970; last amended by Act No. 52 of 2021.
4   Act No. 47 of 1993; last amended by Act No. 33 of 2018.
5   Article 2, Paragraph 1 of Design Act.
6   Article 7 of Design Act.
7   Article 8 of Design Act.

be obtained where the Interior creates a coordinated aesthetic impression as a whole.[8]

7.005 Where two or more applications for design registration have been filed for identical or similar designs on different dates, only the applicant who filed the application for design registration on the earlier date may be entitled to obtain a design registration for the design ('**Principal Design**').[9] However, an applicant for design registration may obtain design registration of a design that is similar to another design ('**Related Design**') selected from the applicant's own designs for which either an application for design registration has been filed or design registration has been granted. In order to obtain design registration of the Related Design, the applicant must apply for design registration of the Related Design on or after the filing date of the application for design registration of the Principal Design and before a lapse of ten years from the date of filing of the application for design registration of the Principal Design. Design registration on the Principal Design should remain valid as of the time of the registration establishing the rights of the Related Design.[10] Furthermore, a design only similar to the Related Design to be registered can also be registered, whereby the Related Design shall be deemed to be the Principal Design. The same shall apply to a design that is similar only to the Related Design for which the design registration above may be granted and to a design that is similar only to the further-removed Related Design linked to the Related Design.[11]

7.006 The registered design must be published in the design gazette if the registration of design has been made.[12] However, an applicant for design registration may request that the design be kept secret for a period designated in the request of no more than three years from the date of the registration establishing the design right.[13]

(ii) Trademark

7.007 The Trademark Act not only applies to protection of registered marks, as industrial designs of two- and three-dimensional appearance of products can also be registered as a trademark. However, the trademark that consists solely

---

8 Article 8-2 of Design Act.
9 Article 9, Paragraph 1 of Design Act.
10 Article 10, Paragraph 1 of Design Act.
11 Article 10, Paragraph 4 of Design Act.
12 Article 20, Paragraph 3 of Design Act.
13 Article 14, Paragraph 1 of Design Act.

of a mark indicating the appearance in a common manner can in general[14] not be registered.[15] Therefore, it is often difficult to register the appearance of goods as a trademark, unless such appearance is too unique to discern its intended purpose or the function of the goods from its appearance.

(iii) Copyright

7.008 The Copyright Act applies to protect copyrightable artwork and registration is not required to acquire rights. There are two types of art works: pure art and applied art. Commentators have construed pure art to be copyrightable, while applied art is generally not copyrightable, but rather protectable as industrial design under the Design Act. However, the Intellectual Property High Court has recently indicated different views. In one case,[16] the Court examined the copyrightability of applied art in the same manner as that of pure art. In another case, the Court recognized copyrightability of applied art where the work is of an artistic nature that can be subject to artistic appreciation, separately from the practical function of the product.[17]

(iv) Unfair competition

7.009 The configuration of goods can be protected without registration under the Unfair Competition Prevention Act. The acts of transferring, leasing, displaying for the purpose of transfer or lease, exporting or importing goods that imitate the configuration of another person's goods (excluding that which is indispensable to its functioning) constitute unfair competition.[18] The configuration of goods can be protected from imitation for three years from the date such goods were first sold in Japan.[19]

(b) Legal framework for registered and non-registered industrial design in effect in Japan

7.010 As mentioned in the preceding section (a), registration is required to protect industrial design under the Design Act, while non-registered design can be protected as copyrightable artwork or under unfair competition law. A creator

---

14 According to Article 3, Paragraph 2 of Trademark Act, the trademark falling under Item 3 of Article 3, Paragraph 1 thereof can be registered if, as a result of the use of the trademark, consumers are able to recognize the goods or services as those pertaining to a business of a particular person.
15 Article 3, Paragraph 1, Item 3 of Trademark Act.
16 IP High Court, Heisei 26-nen (ne) 10063, decide on April 14,2015, 2267 Hanrei Jiho 91. The English translation of the judgement is available at: https://www.ip.courts.go.jp/eng/hanrei/Important_IP_Judgment_by_Category/Copyright/Copyrighted_Work/index.html accessed 4 June 2024 (*TRIPP TRAPP* Case).
17 IP High Court, Heisei 25-nen (ne) 10068, decided on August 28, 2014, 2238 Hanrei Jiho 91. The English translation of the judgment is available at: https://www.ip.courts.go.jp/eng/hanrei/Important_IP_Judgment_by_Category/Copyright/Copyrighted_Work/index.html accessed 4 June 2024 (*Fashion Show* Case).
18 Article 2, Paragraph 1, Item 3 of Unfair Competition Prevention Act.
19 Article 19, Paragraph 1, Item 5(a) of Unfair Competition Prevention Act.

of a design that is industrially available may be entitled to obtain registration[20] by filing an application for design registration.[21] A design right is established by grant of a registration,[22] upon payment of the registration fee for the first year.[23] The term of a design right (excluding the design right of a Related Design) expires after a period of 25 years from the date of the application for design registration,[24] while the term of a design right of a Related Design expires after a period of 25 years from the date of the application for registration of its Principal Design.[25]

7.011 In addition to constituting a 'design' as defined by the Design Act,[26] an application for design registration must also satisfy the following requirements:

(i) Industrially applicable

7.012 First, the design should be industrially applicable.[27] This means that the design of an article, building or graphic image must be identically reproducible multiple times. Therefore, the design of a natural object and a pure artwork for the purpose of a single production are not 'industrially available'.

(ii) Novel

7.013 A design is not deemed to be novel if it is: (a) publicly known in Japan or a foreign country, prior to the filing of the application for design registration;[28] (b) described in a distributed publication or made publicly available through an electric telecommunication line in Japan or a foreign country, prior to the filing of the application for design registration;[29] or (c) similar to those prescribed in the preceding two items.[30]

7.014 Exceptionally, an applicant for design registration can enjoy a one-year grace period in case the design falls under the aforementioned section (a) or (b),

---

20 Article 3, Paragraph 1 of Design Act.
21 Article 6, Paragraph 1 of Design Act.
22 Article 20, Paragraph 1 of Design Act.
23 Article 20, Paragraph 2 of Design Act.
24 Article 21, Paragraph 1 of Design Act, applicable to the applications filed on or after April 1, 2020. The term of a design right shall be 20 years from the date of registration of establishment for the applications filed on April 1, 2007 to March 31, 2020, and 15 years from the date thereof for the applications filed on or before March 31, 2007.
25 Article 21, Paragraph 2 of Design Act, applicable to the applications filed on or after April 1, 2020. The term of a design right shall be 20 years from the date of registration of establishment of its Principal Design for the applications filed on April 1, 2007 to March 31, 2020, and 15 years from the date thereof for the applications filed on or before March 31, 2007.
26 Article 2, Paragraph 1 of Design Act.
27 Article 3, Paragraph 1 of Design Act.
28 Article 3, Paragraph 1, Item 1 of Design Act.
29 Article 3, Paragraph 1, Item 2 of Design Act.
30 Article 3, Paragraph 1, Item 3 of Design Act.

in case it occurred against the will of the person having the right to obtain a design registration,[31] or as a result of an act of the person having the right to obtain a design registration (excluding those which have fallen under the aforementioned (a) or (b) by being published in a gazette relating to an invention, utility model, design or trademark).[32]

(iii) Not easily creatable
Even if the design satisfies the novelty requirement, a design registration is not granted for a design if, prior to the filing of the application for design registration, a person ordinarily skilled in the art of the design would have been able to easily create the design based on the shape, etc. or graphic images that were publicly known, described in a distributed publication or made publicly available through an electric telecommunication line in Japan or a foreign country.[33] **7.015**

(iv) Not identical or similar to a part of design in earlier applications
Where a design is identical – or similar to part of a design described in the statement of the application and drawing, photograph, model or specimen attached to an earlier application for design registration but which was published after the filing of the subsequent application in the design gazette ('**earlier application**'), a design registration may not be granted for such a design.[34] However, this does not apply where the applicant of the later application and the applicant of the earlier application are the same person, and the application was filed before the date on which the design gazette was issued, in which the earlier application was published.[35] **7.016**

(v) First-to-file rule
Where two or more applications for design registration have been filed for identical or similar designs on different dates, only the applicant who filed on the earliest date may be entitled to obtain a design registration for the design.[36] **7.017**

Where two or more applications for design registration have been filed for identical or similar designs on the same day, only one applicant, selected by consultation among the applicants, is entitled to obtain a design registration for the design. If no agreement is reached by consultation or any consultations **7.018**

---

31 Article 4, Paragraph 1 of Design Act.
32 Article 4, Paragraph 2 of Design Act.
33 Article 3, Paragraph 2 of Design Act.
34 Article 3-2 of Design Act.
35 Article 3-2 *proviso* of Design Act.
36 Article 9, Paragraph 1 of Design Act.

are unable to be held, none of the applicants is entitled to obtain a design registration for the design.[37]

(vi) Unregistrable items

7.019 The following designs may not be registered:

- a design that risks impairing public policy,[38]
- a design which is liable to create confusion with an article, building or graphic image pertaining to another person's business,[39] or
- a design solely consisting of a shape that is indispensable for ensuring the functions of the article or a shape that is indispensable for use of the building, or a design solely consisting of a display that is indispensable for use of the graphic image.[40]

2. Registration Procedure

(a) National registration

(i) Enjoyment of rights

7.020 Those who have their domicile or residence in Japan can enjoy protection of a registered design under the Design Act, regardless of their nationality. A foreign national not domiciled or residing in Japan (in case of a legal entity, without a business office in Japan) can enjoy the same in the following instances: First, if the country of the foreign national allows Japanese nationals the enjoyment of design rights or other rights relating to design registrations based on the same conditions as for its own nationals. Second, if the country of the foreign national has decided to allow Japanese nationals the enjoyment of design rights or other rights relating to design registrations based on the same conditions as for its own nationals, so long as Japan allows nationals of that country the enjoyment of design rights or other rights relating to design registrations. Third, in case so provided by a treaty.[41]

7.021 Moreover, an overseas resident (in cases of a legal entity, without a business office in Japan) may only undertake procedures or file an action objecting to a disposition reached by an administrative agency pursuant to the provisions of

---

37 Article 9, Paragraph 2 of Design Act.
38 Article 5, Item 1 of Design Act.
39 Article 5, Item 2 of Design Act.
40 Article 5, Item 3 of Design Act.
41 Pursuant to Article 68, Paragraph 3 of Design Act, Article 25 of the Patent Act will be applied *mutatis mutandis*.

the Design Act or an order based on the Design Act, through a design administrator that is domiciled or resident in Japan and that acts as the person's agent in respect of the design, unless otherwise provided for by Cabinet Order.[42]

(ii) Application procedure

First, a person requesting a design registration must file with the Commissioner of the Patent Office an application and a drawing depicting the design for which registration is requested.[43] The application must include the following items:

- the name, and domicile or residence of the applicant for the design registration;[44]
- the name and domicile or residence of the creator of the design;[45] and
- the article to the design, or the usage of the building or graphic image to the design.[46]

7.022

In lieu of the aforementioned drawing, the applicant may submit a photograph, model or specimen representing the design for which the registration is requested, the applicant must indicate in the application which among the photograph, model and specimen is submitted.[47]

7.023

When an application for design registration is filed, the Commissioner of the Patent Office will examine the formal requirements of the application and drawings. In cases where the Commissioner finds any amendable incomplete matters, the Commissioner will order an amendment,[48] and dismiss the procedures if the applicant fails to make the amendment within the period of time specified by the Commissioner.[49] In cases of unamendable matters, the Commissioner must notify the applicant and give an opportunity to submit a written explanation within an adequate specified time to dismiss the procedures.[50]

7.024

---

42   Pursuant to Article 68, Paragraph 2 of Design Act, Article 8 of the Patent Act will be applied *mutatis mutandis*.
43   Article 6, Paragraph 1 of Design Act.
44   Article 6, Paragraph 1, Item 1 of Design Act.
45   Article 6, Paragraph 1, Item 2 of Design Act.
46   Article 6, Paragraph 1, Item 3 of Design Act.
47   Article 6, Paragraph 2 of Design Act.
48   Pursuant to Article 68, Paragraph 2 of Design Act, Article 17, Paragraph 3 of Patent Act will be applied *mutatis mutandis*.
49   Pursuant to Article 68, Paragraph 2 of Design Act, Article 18, Paragraph 1 of Patent Act will be applied *mutatis mutandis*.
50   Pursuant to Article 68, Paragraph 2 of Design Act, Article 18-2 of Patent Act will be applied *mutatis mutandis*.

7.025 The applications for design registration which satisfy formal requirements will be subject to substantive examination.[51] The examiner will examine whether the applications for design registration present any of the reasons for refusal provided for in Article 17 of the Design Act. In practice, the examination consists of several steps. First the design is recognized, following a comprehensive consideration of the description of the application and drawings, based on the normal knowledge of a person skilled in the field to which the design pertains. Moreover, the requirements of industrial availability,[52] one application per design,[53] design for a set of articles,[54] design for interior,[55] etc., will usually be examined during this recognition step. Second, prior art is researched and compared with the design in the application. Finally, reasons for refusal are examined. For example, requirements of novelty,[56] not easily creatable,[57] first-to-file rule,[58] etc., will be examined by comparing the recognized design with prior art.

7.026 Where no reason is found to refuse application for design registration, the examiner must issue a decision to the effect that a design registration is to be granted.[59] Where reasons for refusal are found, the examiner must notify the applicant of the grounds thereof and give the applicant the opportunity to submit a written opinion within an adequate specified period of time before deciding to reject the application.[60] In order to cure the grounds for refusal, the applicant must submit a written opinion, as well as an amendment to the description in the application or drawing, photograph, model or specimen attached to the application.[61] In cases where the amendment changes the substance of the original description, the examiner must dismiss the amendment by a ruling.[62] An amendment that has not changed the substance of the original application or the written opinion, if any was submitted, will be taken into account when the examiner reconsiders whether any reasons for refusal still exist. The examiner must issue a decision of grant or refusal in writing that includes the grounds for grant/refusal.[63] Once an examiner's decision is

---

51 Article 16 of Design Act.
52 Article 3, Paragraph 1 of Design Act.
53 Article 7 of Design Act.
54 Article 8 of Design Act.
55 Article 8-2 of Design Act.
56 Article 3, Paragraph 1, Items 1 to 3 of Design Act.
57 Article 3, Paragraph 2 of Design Act.
58 Article 9 of Design Act.
59 Article 18 of Design Act.
60 Pursuant to Article 19 of Design Act, Article 50 of Patent Act will be applied *mutatis mutandis*.
61 Article 60-24 of Design Act.
62 Article 17-2 of Design Act.
63 Pursuant to Article 19 of Design Act, Article 52, Paragraph 1 of Patent Act will be applied *mutatis mutandis*.

rendered, the Commissioner of the Patent Office must serve a certified copy of the decision on the applicant.[64]

7.027 Where the examiner has granted the application, the applicant must pay the registration fee for the first year within 30 days from the date on which a certified copy of the examiner's decision has been served.[65] The design right must be registered when the registration fee for the first year has been paid,[66] then a design right becomes effective upon registration.[67] The application for design registration will be dismissed if the applicant fails to pay the registration fee within the aforementioned period of the time.[68]

(iii) Appeal trial

7.028 Where the examiner has refused to grant the application, the applicant may file a request for an appeal against examiner's refusal within three months from the date the certified copy of the examiner's decision has been served.[69] An appeal trial is conducted by a panel consisting of three or five trial examiners[70] designated by the Commissioner of the Patent Office.[71] The procedure followed during the examination also applies to the appeal of the examiner's refusal.[72] The applicant may make amendments to the description in the application or drawing, photograph, model or specimen attached to the application during an appeal trial,[73] but the amendment will be dismissed if it has changed the substance of the description.[74]

7.029 Where a panel of trial examiners finds the ground for refusal appropriate, it renders a decision dismissing the appeal. Where a panel finds the refusal inappropriate, it will either render a decision rescinding the examiner's refusal and order a further examination[75] or examine other possible grounds for refusal supporting dismissal of the application.[76] If a panel finds that grounds for refusal are not contained in the examiner's decision, it must notify the appli-

---

64   Pursuant to Article 19 of Design Act, Article 52, Paragraph 2 of Patent Act will be applied *mutatis mutandis*.
65   Article 42, Paragraph 1 and Article 43, Paragraph 1 of Design Act.
66   Article 20, Paragraph 2 of Design Act.
67   Article 20, Paragraph 1 of Design Act.
68   Pursuant to Article 68, Paragraph 2 of Design Act, Article 18, Paragraph 1 of Patent Act will be applied *mutatis mutandis*.
69   Article 46, Paragraph 1 of Design Act.
70   Pursuant to Article 52 of Design Act, Article 136, Paragraph 1 of Patent Act will be applied *mutatis mutandis*.
71   Pursuant to Article 52 of Design Act, Article 137, Paragraph 1 of Patent Act will be applied *mutatis mutandis*.
72   Pursuant to Article 52 of Design Act, Article 158 of Patent Act will be applied *mutatis mutandis*.
73   Article 60-24 of Design Act.
74   Pursuant to Article 50, Paragraph 1 of Design Act, Article 17-2 thereof will be applied *mutatis mutandis*.
75   Pursuant to Article 52 of Design Act, Article 160, Paragraph 1 of Patent Act will be applied *mutatis mutandis*.
76   Pursuant to Article 52 of Design Act, Article 150, Paragraph 1 and Article 153, Paragraph 1 of Patent Act will be applied *mutatis mutandis*.

cant of such grounds and give the applicant an opportunity to submit a written opinion within an adequate specified period of time.[77] If a panel does not find grounds for refusal, it will render a decision that a trial appeal be affirmed.[78] A design right is granted when the applicant pays the registration fee for the first year within 30 days from the date on which a certified copy of the appeal trial decision has been served[79] and the design right is registered.[80]

(iv) Post registration

7.030 Where a design right has been registered, the design gazette must publish the following information: (a) the name, and the domicile or residence of the holder of the design right; (b) the number and the filing date of the application for the design registration; (c) the registration number and the date of registration of establishment; (d) the contents of the application and drawing, photograph, model or specimen attached to the application; and (e) other necessary matters.[81]

7.031 As an exception to the above, the contents of the application and drawing, photograph, model or specimen attached to a design application for which secrecy has been requested under Article 14, Paragraph 1 of the Design Act, will not be published for the designated period, but will be published without delay after the lapse of such period.[82]

7.032 The registration fee must be paid each and every year to continue the validity of a registered design right. The annual registration fee is 16,900 Japanese Yen.[83] The registration fees for each year from the second and subsequent years must be paid by the end of the previous year.[84] Where a holder of a design right is unable to pay the registration fees within the aforementioned time limit, the holder thereof may make a late payment of the registration fees within six months following the expiration of the time limit.[85] In case of a late payment, the right holder shall, in addition to the annual registration fee, pay a surcharge in the same amount as the annual registration fee.[86]

---

77 Pursuant to Article 50, Paragraph 3 of Design Act, Article 50 of Patent Act will be applied *mutatis mutandis*.
78 Pursuant to Article 50, Paragraph 2 of Design Act, Article 18 thereof will be applied *mutatis mutandis*.
79 Article 42, Paragraph 1 and Article 43, Paragraph 1 of Design Act.
80 Article 20, Paragraphs 1 and 2 of Design Act.
81 Article 20, Paragraph 3 of Design Act.
82 Article 20, Paragraph 4 of Design Act.
83 Article 42, Paragraph 1 of Design Act, applicable to the application filed on or after April 1, 2022. The annual registration fees for the first, second and third year is reduced to 8,500 Japanese Yen each for the application filed on or before March 31, 2022.
84 Article 43, Paragraph 2 of Design Act.
85 Article 44, Paragraph 1 of Design Act.
86 Article 44, Paragraph 2 of Design Act.

As mentioned in Section 1(a)(i), an applicant for registration of a Principal 7.033
Design may obtain registration of a Related Design, if the filing date of the
application for the Related Design is on or after the filing date of the application for the Principal Design and before a lapse of ten years from the date of
filing of the application for Principal Design, as long as the Principal Design
registration is valid.[87]

(v) Remedies in cases of inconsistent views, etc.
Amendments to the description of design may be made only while the case is 7.034
pending in examination, appeal trial or retrial.[88] Where the amendment has
been dismissed by a ruling, the applicant may file, within three months from
the date on which the certified copy of the examiner's decision of dismissal
has been served, either (a) a request for an appeal trial against dismissal of
request for amendment[89] or (b) a new application for design registration for the
amended design, that is deemed to have been filed at the time when the written
amendment of proceedings for the amendment was submitted.[90] Where, after
the registration establishing a design right, it is found that an amendment
made to any description of design in the application or to the drawing, photograph model or specimen attached to the application has changed the gist
thereof, the application for design registration is deemed to have been filed at
the time of submission of the written amendment of proceedings therefor.[91]

In general, an application for design registration must be filed for each design 7.035
as provided by the Ordinance,[92] and an application that fails to comply with
this requirement will constitute a ground for refusal.[93] Still, an applicant can
satisfy this requirement by extracting one or more new applications for design
registration out of a single application for design registration containing two
or more designs, while examination, appeal trial or retrial of the application for
design registration is pending.[94]

(vi) Priority claim
As a nation of the Union of the Paris Convention, an applicant for design 7.036
registration in Japan may make a priority claim if the application satisfies all

---

87   Article 10, Paragraph 1 of Design Act.
88   Article 60-24 of Design Act.
89   Article 47, Paragraph 1 of Design Act.
90   Article 47, Paragraph 1*proviso* and Article 17-3, Paragraph1 of Design Act.
91   Article 9-2 of Design Act.
92   Article 7 of Design Act.
93   Article 17, Item 3 of Design Act.
94   Article 10-2, Paragraph 1 of Design Act.

requirements provided for in the Paris Convention.[95] Also, as a member state of the World Trade Organization ('**WTO**'), Japanese nationals or nationals of a nation of the Union of the Paris Convention may make a priority claim based on the application filed in a member state of the WTO, and nationals of a member state of the WTO may make a priority claim based on the application filed in a nation of the Union of the Paris Convention.[96] A priority claim may be made based on the application in a country that is neither a nation of the Union of the Paris Convention nor a member state of the WTO, if such country allows Japanese nationals to make a priority claim under the same conditions as in Japan.[97] Even after lapse of the period during which priority claims may be filed (six months), it is possible to file a design application priority claim within two months following the lapse, if reasonable grounds for failing to file the application within the six-month period exist.[98]

(b) International registration

7.037 Japan joined the Geneva Act of the Hague Agreement concerning the International Registration of Industrial Designs ('**Geneva Act**') in 2015. Accordingly, the Design Act has a series of special provisions to implement the Geneva Act into national law.[99]

7.038 A Japanese national or a foreign national domiciled or resident (or a legal entity with a business office) in Japan may file an international application as provided in Article 1 (vii) of the Geneva Act through the Commissioner of the Patent Office[100] as well as directly with the International Bureau prescribed in Article 1 (xxviii) of the Geneva Act ('**International Bureau**'). An international application designating Japan as a designated Contracting Party prescribed in Article 1 (xix) of the Geneva Act, where publication of an international registration prescribed in Article 1 (vi) of Geneva Act ('**international registration**') pertaining to the international application has been made under Article 10 (3)(a) of the Geneva Act, is deemed to be an application for design registration filed on an international registration date prescribed in Article 10

---

95 Pursuant to Article 15, Paragraph 1 of Design Act, Article 42 of Patent Act will be applied *mutatis mutandis*, where only the procedural matters are provided for.
96 Pursuant to Article 15, Paragraph 1 of Design Act, Article 42-3, Paragraph 1 of Patent Act will be applied *mutatis mutandis*.
97 Pursuant to Article 15, Paragraph 1 of Design Act, Article 42-3, Paragraph 2 of Patent Act will be applied *mutatis mutandis*.
98 Pursuant to Article 15, Article 42-2 and Article 42-3, Paragraph 3 of Patent Act will be applied *mutatis mutandis*.
99 Chapter 6-2 of Design Act, from Article 60-3 to Article 60-23.
100 Article 60-3 of Design Act.

(2) of the Geneva Act.[101] In line with the one application per design rule,[102] an international application including two or more designs is deemed to be an application for design registration filed for each design that is the subject of an international registration,[103] where a domestic application number is additionally given to each design.

In lieu of the registration fees provided for in Article 42 of the Design Act, an applicant for international applications for design registration must pay, as the individual designation fee under Article 7, paragraph (2) of the Geneva Act, the amounts equivalent to those provided for in the Cabinet Order not exceeding 100,500 Japanese Yen per case to the International Bureau[104] in accordance with Article 5, paragraph (1)(vi) of the Geneva Act. Consequently, international design right is registered without the payment of registration fee for the first year, but only when the decision or appeal decision is rendered to the effect that the design is to be registered.[105] 7.039

3. Disputes

(a) Prosecution

(i) Grounds for invalidity

The grounds for invalidity, provided for in Article 48, Paragraph 1 of the Design Act, are almost the same as those for a refusal provided for in Article 17, Paragraph 1 of the Design Act. For example, a registered design lacking novelty or easily creatable based on the prior art has grounds for invalidity. 7.040

However, while violation of some application rules may be a ground for refusal, it may not be a ground for invalidity, because the design registration based on the respective application will not directly cause substantive harm to third parties' interests. For example, a design registration based on an application for multiple designs in violation of Article 7 of the Design Act, is treated as a valid registration of one design, just like a design registration for a set of articles.[106] For the same reason, a design registration based on an application for the design for a set of articles or an interior lacking a sense of unity as a whole, that respectively violates Article 8 or Article 8-2, can remain valid. A design registration based on an application for a Related Design which is not 7.041

---

101 Article 60-6, Paragraph 1 of Design Act.
102 Article 7 of Design Act.
103 Article 60-6, Paragraph 2 of Design Act.
104 Article 60-21, Paragraphs 1 and 3 of Design Act.
105 Article 60-13 of Design Act.
106 See Article 8 of Design Act.

similar to the Principal Design, that violates Article 10 of the Design Act, can also remain valid, because a design not similar to the Principal Design can be registered as a single design.

(ii) Procedure – invalidation trial

7.042 Unlike the patent system, the Design Act does not provide an opportunity to file an opposition to a granted design registration during a limited period after the publication in a gazette.[107] For this reason, any person may file a request for invalidation of a design registration in general. Exceptionally, a claimant shall be limited to a person with the right to obtain registration where the request is filed on the ground that an application for design registration was not filed by all joint creators of the subject design and that an application therefore was filed by a person without the right to obtain design registration.[108] A joint trial is available where two or more persons file a request for invalidation for the same design right.[109]

7.043 A request for invalidation of a design registration may be filed during the validity of the registration and even when the design right has lapsed.[110] An invalidation trial is conducted by a panel consisting of three or five trial examiners[111] designated by the Commissioner of the Patent Office.[112]

7.044 Once a request for invalidation has been filed, the presiding trial examiner must serve a copy of the written request to the respondent and give the respondent (the holder of design right) an opportunity to submit a written answer within an adequate period of time specified by the presiding trial examiner.[113] A copy of the written answer must be served to the claimant by the presiding trial examiner.[114] Further exchange of written arguments may be conducted if the panel considers it necessary to further listen to the parties' position. The presiding trial examiner may also interrogate the parties regarding the trial[115] to clarify their written allegation. Post the stage of written arguments, the panel determines the issues in dispute and conducts oral proceedings.[116] When a case reaches the point at which a decision can be rendered, the presiding trial

---

107 See Article 113 of Patent Act.
108 Article 48, Paragraph 2 of Design Act.
109 Pursuant to Article 52 of Design Act, Article 132, Paragraph 1 of Patent Act will be applied *mutatis mutandis*.
110 Article 48, Paragraph 3 of Design Act.
111 Pursuant to Article 52 of Design Act, Article 136, Paragraph 1 of Patent Act will be applied *mutatis mutandis*.
112 Pursuant to Article 52 of Design Act, Article 137, Paragraph 1 of Patent Act will be applied *mutatis mutandis*.
113 Pursuant to Article 52 of Design Act, Article 134, Paragraph 1 of Patent Act will be applied *mutatis mutandis*.
114 Pursuant to Article 52 of Design Act, Article 134, Paragraph 3 of Patent Act will be applied *mutatis mutandis*.
115 Pursuant to Article 52 of Design Act, Article 134, Paragraph 4 of Patent Act will be applied *mutatis mutandis*.
116 Pursuant to Article 52 of Design Act, Article 145, Paragraph 1 of Patent Act will be applied *mutatis mutandis*.

examiner must notify the parties of the conclusion of the proceedings.[117] The decision must be rendered in writing.[118] Where a decision to invalidate a design registration has become final and binding, it is deemed as if the design right never existed.[119]

(iii) Procedure – action against trial decision

An action challenging an invalidation decision may be filed with the Intellectual Property High Court as a special branch of the Tokyo High Court.[120] Such action may not be filed later than 30 days from the date a certified copy of the invalidation decision has been served.[121] This 30-day time frame is unalterable.[122] However, the presiding trial examiner will usually grant time in addition to the 30-day period for persons in a distant location or an area with transportation difficulties, typically a party located in a country overseas.[123] 7.045

If the court finds grounds supporting the challenge against the invalidation decision, it must rescind the invalidation trial decision.[124] Once the court's decision rescinding an invalidation trial decision has become final and binding, the trial examiners must carry out further proceedings and issue a trial decision.[125] In such further proceedings, the trial examiners may not repeat a trial decision on the same grounds as those rescinded in the judgment. According to the Administrative Case Litigation Act,[126] which governs actions against government decisions, including invalidation trial decisions by trial examiners of the Patent Office, such judgment is binding on the trial examiners who originally decided the case.[127] 7.046

The party dissatisfied with the judgment may file a final appeal, or a petition for the acceptance of a final appeal, with the Supreme Court in accordance 7.047

---

117 Pursuant to Article 52 of Design Act, Article 156, Paragraph 1 of Patent Act will be applied *mutatis mutandis*.
118 Pursuant to Article 52 of Design Act, Article 157, Paragraph 2 of Patent Act will be applied *mutatis mutandis*.
119 Article 49 of Design Act.
120 Article 59, Paragraph 1 of Design Act.
121 Pursuant to Article 59, Paragraph 2 of Design Act, Article 178, Paragraph 3 of Patent Act will be applied *mutatis mutandis*.
122 Pursuant to Article 59, Paragraph 2 of Design Act, Article 178, Paragraph 4 of Patent Act will be applied *mutatis mutandis*.
123 Pursuant to Article 59, Paragraph 2 of Design Act, Article 178, Paragraph 5 of Patent Act will be applied *mutatis mutandis*.
124 Pursuant to Article 59, Paragraph 2 of Design Act, Article 181, Paragraph 1 of Patent Act will be applied *mutatis mutandis*.
125 Pursuant to Article 59, Paragraph 2 of Design Act, Article 181, Paragraph 2 of Patent Act will be applied *mutatis mutandis*.
126 Act No. 139 of 1962; last amended by Act No. 89 of 2016.
127 Article 33, Paragraph 1 of Administrative Case Litigation Act.

with Code of Civil Procedure,[128] which provides for an unalterable time frame of two weeks from the date when the written document was served.[129] The grounds for a final appeal are statutorily limited to those provided under Article 312 of Code of Civil Procedure. Upon petition, the Supreme Court, as the final appellate court, may rule to accept a case if it recognizes that a prior judgment is in conflict with judicial precedents or involves matters of material importance in the construction of laws and regulations.[130] If a ruling of acceptance is issued, a final appeal is deemed to have been filed in a timely manner.[131]

(b) Litigation

(i) Scope of protection

7.048 A holder of a design right has the exclusive right to implement the registered design and designs similar thereto during trade.[132] The scope of a registered design must be determined based on the design depicted in the application, as well as in the drawing or represented in the photograph, model, or specimen attached to the application.[133]

7.049 The term 'implement' is defined in Article 2, Paragraph 2 of Design Act, which enumerates the following acts:

– manufacturing, using, transferring, leasing, exporting or importing (including acts of a person in a foreign country having another person import; the same applies hereinafter), or offering to transfer or lease (including displaying for the purpose of transferring or leasing; the same applies hereinafter) an article embodying the design;
– constructing, using, transferring or leasing, or offering to transfer or lease a building embodying the design;
– creating or using the graphic image embodying the design (including a computer program or anything equivalent (refers to a computer program or anything equivalent provided in Article 2, Paragraph 4 of Patent Act; the same applies hereinafter) that has a function to display the graphic image; the same applies hereinafter), or providing or offering to provide it through a telecommunications line (this includes displaying it in order to provide it); and

---

128 Act No. 109 of 1996; last amended by Act No. 24 of 2021.
129 Pursuant to Article 313 of Code of Civil Procedure, Article 285 thereof will be applied *mutatis mutandis*.
130 Article 318, Paragraph 1 of Code of Civil Procedure.
131 Article 318, Paragraph 4 of Code of Civil Procedure.
132 Article 23 of Design Act.
133 Article 24, Paragraph 1 of Design Act.

- transferring, leasing, exporting or importing, or offering to transfer or lease a recording medium on which the graphic image embodying the design has been recorded or a device that incorporates the graphic image embodying the design ('**recording medium or device holding a graphic image**').

In addition to the acts that fall into the definition of 'implement', the following acts are deemed to constitute an infringement of a design right:

7.050

- any of the following acts that a person does in the course of trade in connection with an article, computer program or anything equivalent, or recording medium or device containing a computer program or anything equivalent, that is used exclusively in the manufacturing of the article embodying the registered design or a design similar thereto: (a) the act of manufacturing, transferring, leasing, importing, or offering to transfer or lease an article or recording medium or device containing a computer program or anything equivalent that is used exclusively in the manufacturing of such an article, or (b) the act of creating a computer program or anything equivalent that is used exclusively in the manufacturing of such an article, or of providing it or offering to provide it through a telecommunications line;[134]
- any of the following acts that a person does in the course of trade in connection with an article, computer program or anything equivalent, or recording medium or device containing a computer program or anything equivalent, that is used in the manufacturing of the article embodying the registered design or a design similar thereto (excluding cases in which these are widely distributed within Japan), and that is indispensable to the aesthetically pleasing visual presentation that the registered design or design similar thereto creates, while knowing that the design is a registered design or a design similar thereto and that the article or computer program or anything equivalent or the recording medium or device containing a computer program or anything equivalent, is used for the working of the design: (a) the act of manufacturing, transferring, leasing, or importing, or offering to transfer or lease any article or the recording medium or device containing a computer program or anything equivalent that is used in the manufacturing of such an article, or (b) the act of creating any computer program or anything equivalent that is used in the manufacturing of such an article, or providing it or offering to provide it through a telecommunications line;[135]

---

[134] Article 38, Item 1 of Design Act.
[135] Article 38, Item 2 of Design Act.

- the act of possessing an article that uses a registered design or a design similar thereto for the purpose of transferring, leasing or exporting it in the course of trade;[136]
- any of the following acts that a person does in the course of trade in connection with an article, computer program or anything equivalent, or recording medium or device containing a computer program or anything equivalent, which is used exclusively in the construction of a building embodying a registered design or a design similar thereto: (a) the act of manufacturing, transferring, leasing, or importing, or offering to transfer or lease an article or recording medium or device containing a computer program or anything equivalent that is used exclusively in the construction of such a building, or (b) the act of creating a computer program or anything equivalent that is used exclusively in the construction of such a building, or of providing or offering to provide it through a telecommunications line;[137]
- any of the following acts that a person does in the course of trade in connection with an article, computer program or anything equivalent, or recording medium or device containing a computer program or anything equivalent, that is used in the construction of a building embodying the registered design or a design similar thereto (excluding cases in which these are widely distributed within Japan), and that is indispensable to the aesthetically pleasing visual presentation that the registered design or design similar thereto creates, while knowing that the design is a registered design or a design similar thereto and that the article, computer program or equivalent thing, or recording medium or device containing the computer program or equivalent thing is used in the working of the design: (a) the act of manufacturing, transferring, leasing, or importing, or offering to transfer or lease an article or recording medium or device containing a computer program or anything equivalent that is used in the construction of such a building, or (b) the act of creating a computer program or anything equivalent that is used in the construction of such a building, or of providing it or offering to provide it through a telecommunications line;[138]
- the act of owning a building embodying a registered design or a design similar thereto for the purpose of transferring or leasing it during trade;[139]
- any of the following acts that a person does in the course of trade in connection with an article, graphic image, recording medium or device holding an ordinary graphic image, computer program or anything equivalent, or

---

[136] Article 38, Item 3 of Design Act.
[137] Article 38, Item 4 of Design Act.
[138] Article 38, Item 5 of Design Act.
[139] Article 38, Item 6 of Design Act.

recording medium or device containing a computer program or anything equivalent, that is used exclusively in the creation of the graphic image embodying the registered design or a design similar thereto: (a) the act of manufacturing, transferring, leasing, or importing, or offering to transfer or lease an article, recording medium or device holding an ordinary graphic image, or recording medium or device containing a computer program or anything equivalent, that is used in the creation of such a graphic image, or (b) the act of creating a graphic image or computer program or anything equivalent that is used exclusively in the creation of such a graphic image, or providing it or offering to provide it through a telecommunications line;[140]

– any of the following acts that a person does in the course of trade in connection with an article, graphic image, recording medium or device holding an ordinary graphic image, computer program or anything equivalent, or recording medium or device containing a computer program or anything equivalent, that is used in the creation of the graphic image embodying a registered design or a design similar thereto (excluding cases in which these are widely distributed within Japan), and that is indispensable to the aesthetically pleasing visual presentation that the design creates, while knowing that the design is a registered design or a design similar thereto and that the article, graphic image, recording medium or device holding the ordinary graphic image, computer program or equivalent thing, or recording medium or device containing the computer program or equivalent thing, is used in the working of the design: (a) the act of manufacturing, transferring, leasing, or importing, or offering to transfer or lease an article, recording medium or device holding an ordinary graphic image, or recording medium or device containing a computer program or anything equivalent, that is used exclusively in the creation of such an image, or (b) the act of creating any graphic image or computer program or anything equivalent that is used in the creation of such an image, or of providing it or offering to provide it through a telecommunications line;[141] and

– the act of holding a graphic image embodying a registered design or a design similar thereto for the purpose of providing it through a telecommunications line during trade, or the act of possessing a recording medium or device holding a graphic image embodying a registered design or a design similar thereto for the purpose of transferring, leasing, or exporting it in the course of trade.[142]

---

140 Article 38, Item 7 of Design Act.
141 Article 38, Item 8 of Design Act.
142 Article 38, Item 9 of Design Act.

(ii) Finding infringement in view of the specific scope of protection

7.051 Whether a registered design is similar to another design must be determined based upon the aesthetic impression that the designs would create through the eye of their consumers.[143] In finding infringement, two points are taken into consideration by the court, first, while not specifically provided in the statute, consideration is unquestionably given to whether use and function of an article, building or graphic image embodying the registered design, are identical or similar to those of the accused design.[144] Next, if such use and function are found to be identical or similar, then consideration is given to whether shape, patterns or colours, or any combination thereof of the registered design are identical or similar to that of the accused design. It is commonly recognized that identicalness or similarity should be judged by observing the design as a whole, taking into consideration the nature, intended use and manner of use of the design, as well as the presence or absence of new creative parts not found in publicly known designs. The part of the design that is most likely to attract the attention of traders and consumers should be considered as the essential part of the design. Emphasis should be placed on observing whether the registered design and the accused design share the same configuration in the essential part of the design.[145]

(iii) Defences

7.052 First, a design right may not be enforced against (a) the implementation of the design for experimental or research purposes, (b) vessels or aircraft merely passing through Japan, or machines, apparatus, equipment or other products used in them, and (c) products present in Japan prior to the filing of the design application.[146]

7.053 Second, an exhaustion defence may be asserted against a claim for infringement of a design right, similar to that of a patent right.

7.054 Third, an accused infringer may allege that a design right is unenforceable on the ground that it would be invalidated through an invalidation trial, even if such an invalidation trial has not been filed yet.[147]

---

143 Article 24, Paragraph 2 of Design Act.
144 See, e.g., IP High Court, Heisei 17-nen (ne) 10079, decided on October 31, 2005. The English translation of the judgment available at: https://www.ip.courts.go.jp/eng/hanrei/Important_IP_Judgment_by_Category/Design/Similarity/index.html accessed 4 June 2024 (*Dust Mask* Case).
145 See, e.g., IP Court judgment, Heisei 28-nen (ne) 10001, decided on July 13, 2016, 2325 Hanrei Jiho 94.
146 Pursuant to Article 36 of Design Act, Article 69, Paragraphs 1 and 2 of Patent Act will be applied *mutatis mutandis*.
147 Pursuant to Article 41 of Design Act, Article 104-3 of Patent Act will be applied *mutatis mutandis*.

Fourth, if an accused infringer, without knowledge of a design in a pending application, (a) created a design identical with or similar to the design in the pending application or (b) learned of the design from a person that created a design identical with or similar to the design therein, and has been implementing the design or a design similar thereto or preparing to implement the design or a design similar thereto in Japan at the time of filing of the pending application, such accused infringer is entitled to a non-exclusive license to the design right, only to the extent of the design and the purpose of the business being implemented or prepared.[148]

7.055

Fifth, if an accused infringer, without knowledge of a design in a pending application, (a) created a design identical with or similar to the design in the pending application or (b) learned of the design from a person that created a design identical with or similar to the design therein, and has been implementing the design or a design similar thereto or preparing to implement the design or a design similar thereto in Japan at the time of registration of establishment of design right for the design in the pending application, such accused infringer may allege a non-exclusive license on the design right, only to the extent of the design and the purpose of the business being implemented or prepared. In such case, the accused infringer must satisfy the following conditions: (a) the accused infringer had filed an application for registration of the design or design similar thereto prior to the date of filing of the successful application and has been implementing or preparing to implement the design in the application, and (b) the design in the application filed by the accused infringer falls under any of items of Article 3, Paragraph 1 of the Design Act and an examiner's decision or appeal trial decision rejecting the application has become final and binding.[149]

7.056

(iv) Enforcement (injunction, damages)
Injunctive relief consists of a demand to stop or prevent the infringement[150] and a demand of measures necessary for the prevention of infringement including the disposal of articles, etc., and the removal of the facilities used for the act of infringement. The acts provided for in Article 2, Paragraph 2 of the Design Act are subject to injunction if such acts are conducted during trade. A holder of a design right can also seek an injunction against the acts enumerated in Article 38 of the Design Act.[151] The latter demand (disposal and

7.057

---

148   Article 29 of Design Act.
149   Article 29-2 of Design Act.
150   Article 37, Paragraph 1 of Design Act.
151   See '(i) Scope of protection' above in detail.

removal) may not be claimed alone but must always be claimed together with the former demand (stop or prevention).[152] Neither wilfulness nor negligence of the infringer is required to seek an injunction. Regarding a design for which secrecy is requested,[153] the holder of design rights may not demand an injunction unless prior warning has been given by presenting documents stating the matters listed in the items of Article 20, paragraph 3 of Design Act, which are certified by the Commissioner of the Japan Patent Office.[154]

7.058 Compensation for damages caused by infringement may be sought pursuant to Article 709 of Civil Act[155] for which a right holder shall demonstrate the following requirements:

- wilfulness or negligence of infringer,
- infringing act(s),
- amount of damage, and
- cause-and-effect relationship between infringing act(s) and damage.

7.059 In order to reduce the burden of proof, Article 40 of the Design Act, provides that an infringer of a design right is presumed negligent in the commission of the act of infringement, except in a case of infringement of a design for which secrecy is requested. In addition to this, Article 39 of the Design Act, provides that a certain monetary amount may be deemed or presumed to be the damage that a holder of a design right was incurred.

7.060 In summary, a holder of design right may choose any of the following three measures to demonstrate the amount of damage:

7.061 Where the infringer has transferred articles that constitute an act of infringement, the amount of damages sustained by the holder of design rights may be established to be the total amounts of: (a) the amount arrived at when the amount of profit per unit for the products that the holder of the design rights would have been able to sell if the infringement had not taken place is multiplied by that part of the quantity of articles that the infringer has transferred ('**quantity transferred**') which does not exceed the quantity covered by the right holder's ability to implement the design ('**implementable quantity**') (if there are circumstances that render the holder of design rights unable to sell a quantity of products equivalent to all or part of the implementable quantity,

---

152 Article 37, Paragraph 2 of Design Act.
153 See Article 14, Paragraph 1 of Design Act.
154 Article 37, Paragraph 3 of Design Act.
155 Act No. 89 of 1896; last amended by Act Nos. 24 and 37 of 2021.

the implementable quantity less the quantity not sellable due to those circumstances ('**specified quantity**')) and (b) if applicable, an amount equivalent to the amount of money that is to be received in exchange for the implementation of the registered design under the design right, for any quantity exceeding the implementable quantity which is part of the quantity transferred, or for any specified quantity which is part of the quantity transferred (except in the case where it is not found that the holder of design rights would have been able to establish an exclusive license or grant a non-exclusive license under the holder's design rights);[156]

7.062 Alternatively, if the infringer has profited from the infringement, the amount of that profit can be presumed to be the value of damage incurred by the holder of design rights;[157] or even if neither of the above measures are applicable, the holder of design rights can still seek the equivalent amount of money the holder of design rights would have been entitled to receive for the implementation of the registered design or a design similar thereto.[158]

(c) Other dispute resolution

(i) Customs measures

7.063 Pursuant to the Customs Act,[159] it is prohibited to export or import cargo where the goods infringe intellectual property rights including design rights,[160] and the Director General of Customs may confiscate and dispose of such cargo.[161] Prior to such confiscation or disposal, the Director General of Customs must implement procedures to verify whether the cargo in question constitutes infringement of design rights ('**verification procedures**').[162] A design right holder may submit to any of the Directors General of Customs evidence necessary to establish facts that prima facie support their belief that the cargo, infringes its design right, and may file a petition with any of the Directors General of Customs to implement verification procedures for any such cargo.[163]

(ii) Criminal penalty

7.064 A person that infringes a design right (excluding one who has committed acts which are deemed to constitute infringement of a design right pursuant to

---

156 Article 39, Paragraph 1 of Design Act.
157 Article 39, Paragraph 2 of Design Act.
158 Article 39, Paragraph 3 of Design Act.
159 Act No. 61 of 1954; last amended by Act No. 12 of 2021.
160 Article 69-2, Paragraph 1, Item 3 and Article 69-11, Paragraph 1, Item 9 of Customs Act.
161 Article 69-2, Paragraph 2 and Article 69-11, Paragraph 2 of Customs Act.
162 Articles 69-3 and 69-12 of Customs Act.
163 Articles 69-4 and 69-13 of Customs Act.

Article 38 of Design Act) is punished by imprisonment for a term not exceeding ten years, a fine not exceeding 10 million yen, or both.[164] A person that has committed acts which are deemed to constitute infringement of a design right pursuant to the provisions of Article 38 of the Design Act is punished by imprisonment for a term not exceeding five years, a fine not exceeding five million yen, or both.[165] Pursuant to the Criminal Code,[166] an intent to commit infringement is required to criminally punish an infringer, and infringement by negligence is not punishable.[167]

4. Significant Judicial Decisions in the Jurisdiction

(a) *Flexible and Elastic Hose* case[168]

7.065 In this case, the Supreme Court addressed the relationship and applicability of the registration requirement provided for in Article 3, Paragraph 1 (novelty) and Paragraph 2 (lack of easiness of creation) of Design Act. It held that the effect of a design right covers designs similar to the registered design, namely, designs that convey beauty that is similar to that of the registered design to general traders and consumers with regard to articles that are identical or similar to the article pertaining to the registered design (Article 23 of the Design Act). In connection with this, with regard to the design of such articles, Article 3, Paragraph 1, Item 3 focuses on whether or not the beauty is similar from the perspective of general traders and consumers. On the other hand, Article 3, Paragraph 2, removed the limitation of identicalness or similarity of articles, and based on a motif widely known in society, focuses on whether the idea of a design possesses novelty or creativity from the perspective of a person ordinarily skilled in the art of the design. It can be understood that the two provisions are based on different points of view. Therefore, even with regard to designs relating to identical or similar articles, the determination of the similarity referred to in Paragraph 1, Item 3 of Article 3 is made by whether or not the effects of designs are similar, and the determination of the easiness of creation referred to in Paragraph 2 of the same Article is made by whether or not a person ordinarily skilled in the art of the design would have been able

---

164 Article 69 of Design Act.
165 Article 69-2 of Design Act.
166 Act No. 45 of 1907; last amended by Act. No.72 of 2018.
167 See Article 38, Paragraph 1 of Penal Code, which provides that an act performed without the intent to commit a crime is not punishable; provided, however, that the same does not apply unless otherwise specially provided for by law.
168 Supreme Court, Showa 45-nen (gyo-tsu) 45, decided on March 19, 1974, Vol. 28, 2 Minshu 308. The English translation of the judgment is available at: https://www.ip.courts.go.jp/eng/hanrei/Important_IP _Judgment_by_Category/Design/Requirements_for_Registration/index.html accessed 4 June 2024 (*Flexible and Elastic Hose* Case).

to easily create one of the designs based on shape, patterns, colours, etc., of another design, do not necessarily correspond with each other. There may be a case where one design is similar to another design and also falls under a design that can be easily created as referred to in Paragraph 2 of Article 3, and there may also be a case where one design cannot be said to be similar to another design because the effects of the design differ from each other, but the easiness of creation referred to in Paragraph 2 of Article 3 can be acknowledged. In the former case, the information in parentheses in Paragraph 2 of Article 3 stipulates that it is necessary to refuse the registration by applying only a provision of Paragraph 1, Item 3 of Article 3.

(b) *Carabiner* case[169]

7.066 Here the Court clarified that similarity of articles should be determined before considering whether a registered design is similar to an accused design. An application for design registration must be prepared in the form prescribed by the Ordinance.[170] The application provides a section titled 'Article to Which the Design Is Applied' to comply with Article 6, Paragraph 1, Item 3 of the Design Act,[171] and also provides the 'Explanation of the Article to Which the Design Is Applied' section to explain the purpose and manner of use of the applied design. The Court held that the statements in the 'Explanation of the Article to Which the Design Is Applied' section of the design application are intended to help understand an article, such as that stated in the 'Article to Which the Design Is Applied' section. Thus the scope of articles to which the registered design is applied should be defined by the class of article as stated in the 'Article to Which the Design Is Applied' section. In this case, the appellant (plaintiff in the first instance) holds the design right entitled 'Carabiner', where the design of a heart-shaped carabiner was registered and 'Carabiner' was clearly stated as the class of article in the 'Articles to Which the Design Is Applied' section. The product sold by the appellee (defendant in the first instance) is named 'heart carabiner key chain', which is a heart-shaped key holder. The Court held that the key holder should be significantly different from the article to which the registered design is applied in terms of the purpose and manner of use and would not be confused with the latter. Therefore, the appellee's products cannot be deemed to be included within the

---

169 IP High Court, Heisei 17-nen (ne) 10079, decided on October 31, 2005. The English translation of the judgment is available at: https://www.ip.courts.go.jp/eng/hanrei/Important_IP_Judgment_by_Category/Design/Similarity/index.html accessed 4 June 2024 (*Carabiner* Case).
170 Article 2, Paragraph 1 of the Regulations for the Enforcement of the Design Act.
171 Article 6, Paragraph 1 of the Act enumerates items to be stated in an application, among which 'the article embodying the design' was set forth in Item 3 when the case was litigated.

scope of rights for the registered design and shall not be subject to the effects of the design right.

B. PRACTICAL ASPECTS OF DESIGN LAW

1. Statistics/Trends

(a) Number of filings

7.067 The JPO Status Report 2023 (Table 7.1 below)[172] shows the number of design applications during the recent seven years (2016–2022) as follows:

Table 7.1   The JPO Status Report 2023

Year	Number of international applications*	Number of national applications**	Total number of applications
2016	2,083	28,796	30,879
2017	2,216	29,745	31,961
2018	2,261	29,145	31,406
2019	2,072	29,417	31,489
2020	2,986	28,812	31,798
2021	3,303	29,222	32,525
2022	3,353	28,358	31,711

Notes: * The number of international applications for design registration under the Geneva Act of the Hague Agreement concerning the International Registration of Industrial Designs that designate Japan as a designated contracting party and that have been recorded as an international registration and published by the International Bureau. ** The number of applications for design registration excluding the number of international applications therefor under the Geneva Act.
Source: 'General Situation of Civil and Administrative Cases Concerning Intellectual Property in the Year 2016/2017/2018/2019/2020/2021' Hoso Jiho, Vols. 69–74, No. 10.

(b) Number of court cases

7.068 The Administrative Affairs Bureau of the Supreme Court publishes the annual statistics of intellectual property cases pending before the court in October of the following year.[173] According to these statistics (see Tables 7.2, 7.3 and 7.4 below), the number of design right case appears limited, compared to the number of applications for design registration before the JPO:[174]

---

172   Available at https://www.jpo.go.jp/e/resources/report/statusreport/2023/index.html accessed 4 June 2024.
173   Available at Hoso Jiho (Lawyers Association Journal), a monthly booklet published by Hoso Kai (Lawyers Association).
174   'General Situation of Civil and Administrative Cases Concerning Intellectual Property in the Year 2016/2017/2018/2019/2020/2021' Hoso Jiho, Vols. 69 to 74, No. 10.

Table 7.2   Number of civil cases involving design rights before the District Court

Year	Number of newly filed cases	Number of concluded cases
2016	21	9
2017	9	23
2018	15	9
2019	11	11
2020	7	11
2021	9	9

Source: 'General Situation of Civil and Administrative Cases Concerning Intellectual Property in the Year 2016/2017/2018/2019/2020/2021' Hoso Jiho, Vols. 69 to 74, No. 10.

Table 7.3   Number of civil cases involving design rights before the High Court

Year	Number of newly filed cases	Number of concluded cases
2016	0	4
2017	3	3
2018	2	1
2019	3	2
2020	4	4
2021	6	2

Source: 'General Situation of Civil and Administrative Cases Concerning Intellectual Property in the Year 2016/2017/2018/2019/2020/2021' Hoso Jiho, Vols. 69–74, No. 10.

Table 7.4   Number of actions against the JPO's trial decision involving design rights before the intellectual property high court

Year	Number of newly filed cases	Number of concluded cases
2016	26	17
2017	10	15
2018	9	9
2019	1	6
2020	1	0
2021	5	2

Source: 'General Situation of Civil and Administrative Cases Concerning Intellectual Property in the Year 2016/2017/2018/2019/2020/2021' Hoso Jiho, Vols. 69–74, No. 10.

(c)   Rate of success; etc.

7.069 The Supreme Court does not disclose the success rate in cases where design rights are involved. It only discloses such rate in intellectual property cases as a whole, as well as patent infringement cases before Tokyo and Osaka District Courts.[175]

---

[175] Only the Tokyo District Court and the Osaka District Court have exclusive jurisdiction as courts in the first instance in patent infringement cases. See Article 6, Paragraph 1 of Code of Civil Procedure.

2. Business Aspects

(a) Transferability

7.070 Due to its nature as a property right, it is undisputed that a design right is transferrable, not only by general succession (inheritance, merger, etc.), but also by limited succession (sale and purchase, gift, etc.). Transfer other than general succession shall not take effect between a transferor and a transferee until such transfer is duly recorded in the design gazette.[176] In cases of transfer by general succession, transfer shall take immediate effect without registration. Still, notification of general succession must be filed with the Commissioner of the Japan Patent Office without delay.[177]

7.071 There are two exceptions to transferability. One is the case of jointly owned design right, where a joint owner may not transfer his/her own share without the consent of all other joint owners.[178] The other is rights to Related Design(s), which may not independently be transferred from those to a Principal Design.[179] This is because the scope of design right of a Principal Design and that of the Related Design(s) overlap one another so only the lump sum transfer is acceptable. Even in a case where the rights to a Principal Design have been extinguished the rights to Related Designs associated with the Principal Design may not independently transferred.[180] This rule does not apply to instances where the respective rights have expired.

(b) Licensing

7.072 The Design Act provides for two types of licenses: one is *Sen'yo Jisshi-Ken*[181] (exclusive license), and the other is *Tsujo Jisshi-Ken*[182] (non-exclusive license).

7.073 A holder of design rights may establish a *Sen'yo Jisshi-Ken* on their design rights,[183] and a holder of *Sen'yo Jisshi-Ken* has an exclusive right to implement the registered design or designs similar thereto in the course of trade to the extent so established.[184] This means that even the holder of the design rights is precluded from implementing the registered design or designs similar thereto in the course of trade within the scope of *Sen'yo Jisshi-Ken* established by the

---

176 Pursuant to Article 36, Article 98, Paragraph 1, Item 1 of Patent Act will be applied *mutatis mutandis*.
177 Pursuant to Article 36, Article 98, Paragraph 2 of Patent Act will be applied *mutatis mutandis*.
178 Pursuant to Article 36, Article 73, Paragraph 1 of Patent Act will be applied *mutatis mutandis*.
179 Article 22, Paragraph 1 of Design Act.
180 Article 22, Paragraph 2 of Design Act.
181 It literally means an exclusive right of implementation.
182 It literally means an ordinary right of implementation.
183 Article 27, Paragraph 1 of Design Act.
184 Article 27, Paragraph 2 of Design Act.

holder him/herself.¹⁸⁵ Establishment of *Sen'yo Jisshi-Ken* will not take effect between a right holder and a licensee until the license is duly registered.¹⁸⁶ Establishment of *Sen'yo Jisshi-Ken* without due registration is treated as an effective *Tsujo Jisshi-Ken* with a stipulation that a license shall not be granted to any other third parties.¹⁸⁷

Conversely, the *Tsujo Jisshi-Ken* is a flexible licensing mechanism. Due to its non-exclusive nature, a right holder may grant *Tsujo Jisshi-Ken* to multiple licensees. Furthermore, the right holder him/herself may implement the registered design or designs similar thereto in the course of trade, regardless of the scope of *Tsujo Jisshi-Ken* granted. No registration is required for a *Tsujo Jisshi-Ken* to take effect or be perfected.¹⁸⁸ 7.074

3. Specific Interesting Applications or Case Studies

Until the enactment of Act No. 3 of 2019, design registration was available only for the shape, patterns or colours, or any combination thereof of articles. This amended the Design Act to enable design registration of shapes, etc., of buildings, a graphic image (limited to those provided for use in the operation of the device or those displayed as a result of the device performing its function and including a part of a graphic image) and interiors. Since April 1, 2020, the date the amended Design Act came into force, design registration of these new items has gradually increased. The Japan Patent Office discloses some registered cases of graphic image, building and interior at: https://www.jpo.go.jp/e/system/laws/rule/guideline/design/case-examples/graphic-image/2019.html accessed 4 June 2024. 7.075

C. COMMENTS, ANALYSIS, EVALUATION

1. Comments on Present Legal Framework (Legislation and Case Law)

An extensive amendment to the Design Act was made by Act No. 3 of 2019, and a further amendment is not expected in the near future. No judicial prece- 7.076

---

185 Article 23*proviso* of Design Act.
186 Pursuant to Article 27, Paragraph 4, Article 98, Paragraph 1, Item 2 of Patent Act will be applied *mutatis mutandis*.
187 Osaka District Court, Showa 57-nen (wa) 7035, decided on December 20, 1984, Vol. 16, 3 Mutai-Saishu 803.
188 Pursuant to Article 28, Paragraph 3 of Design Act, Article 99 of Patent Act will be applied *mutatis mutandis*.

dents as to infringement of design rights of graphic image, building or interior have been found since the amendment came into force in April 1, 2020.

2. Design Law Reform *de lege ferenda*

7.077 It has been argued that pictograms and typefaces should be protected by design rights, but recent amendments did not cover these items. They may have a limited scope of copyrightability.[189] However, it is apparent that both pictograms and typefaces are created and used for practical purposes. Now that design registration becomes available for designs not associated solely with articles, it seems to be a good time to argue again that pictograms and typefaces should be protected as practical industrial design.

3. Future Outlook in Light of New Technologies

7.078 Before the amendment by Act No. 3 of 2019, Article 7 of Design Act required that an application for design registration be 'corresponding to an article in the classes of articles' as provided by Order of the Ministry of Economy, Trade and Industry. However, it becomes difficult to update the classes of articles in a timely manner every time new articles have been produced and marketed by new technologies. Consequently, amended Article 7 abolished the requirement of 'corresponding to an article in the classes of articles' even in a case of an application for design registration of design associated with articles.

---

[189] cf. Osaka District Court, Heisei 25-nen (wa) 1074, decided on September 24, 2015, 2348 Hanrei Jiho 62 (pictograms), and Supreme Court, Heisei 10-nen (ju) 332, decided on September 7, 2000, Vol. 54, 7 Minshu 2481, 1703 Hanrei Jiho 123, 1046 Hanrei Times 101 (typefaces). The English translation of the judgment in typefaces case is available at: https://www.ip.courts.go.jp/eng/hanrei/Important_IP_Judgment_by_Category/Copyright/Copyrighted_Work/index.html (*Printing Fonts* Case) accessed 4 June 2024.

8

DESIGN PROTECTION IN THE NORDIC COUNTRIES (DENMARK, FINLAND AND SWEDEN)

Teemu Matikainen, Jens Schovsbo and Marcus Norrgård

A. DESCRIPTIVE PART	8.001	countries	8.018
1. Substantive	8.001	2. Procedural Aspects	8.030
(a) Brief history of industrial design protection in the Nordic countries	8.001	3. Disputes	8.037
		(a) Grounds for invalidity	8.037
		(b) Litigation	8.040
(b) Overview of the current situation	8.010	4. Significant Judicial Decisions in the Jurisdiction	8.049
(c) A closer look at the (national) design right system in the Nordic		B. PRACTICAL ASPECTS OF DESIGN LAW	8.057
		C. COMMENTS, ANALYSIS, EVALUATION	8.064

A. DESCRIPTIVE PART

1. Substantive

(a) Brief history of industrial design protection in the Nordic countries

8.001 Even though the 'Nordic' countries are members of the European Union and as such, subject to its Design Directive (DDir)[1] and Design Regulation (CDReg),[2] national design law remains in place on national level. Given its history and its characteristics, Nordic design provides an interesting counterpart to other national design law systems.

8.002 The term 'Nordic design' is often associated with furniture, lamps, crockery, silverware, etc. which have been designed in a way which combines beauty,

---

1 Directive 98/71/EC of 13 October 1998 on the legal protection of designs [1998] OJ L289/28.
2 Council Regulation (EC) 6/2002 of 12 December 2001 on Community designs [2002] OJ L3/1.

simplicity and functionality. Think of Arne Jacobsen's or Wegner's chairs or Alvar Aalto's vases. This kind of design can also often be an attractive target for imitations. It is then perhaps no surprise that Denmark, Finland and Sweden (hereinafter 'the Nordic countries')[3] early on identified a need for specific Acts in order to protect designs and designers. In Sweden, the legislation had already provided design protection for silk fabrics as early as 1753.[4] This was followed by the Design Act of 1899, which only protected ornaments within the metal industry.[5] Denmark had its first Design Act in 1905. Despite a seemingly broad scope of the 1905 Design Act, products which were shaped primarily to be fit for their purpose and without added elements (ornaments, etc.) would often not be protected.[6] At the time in Finland, a bill was drafted in 1904 to protect designs.[7] It was passed by the parliament, but in the unstable political conditions of the time, it was not ratified by the Russian emperor.[8]

8.003 Beginning with the first half of the 20th century designers could also acquire protection based on copyright law and the law on unfair competition (the latter provided protection against so-called slavish imitation). However, in the case of copyright there was some scepticism whether works of applied art could be considered as 'artistic' and thus gain copyright protection.[9] Also, the protection of the shape of products against slavish imitation under unfair competition law was in practice difficult to achieve.[10]

8.004 In 1960, the Swedish government invited other Nordic governments to take part in a joint legislative committee in order to develop a system for the protection of designs which could be implemented in the Nordic countries by similar national Acts. The work by the joint legislative committee culminated

---

3   In this chapter, we refer to Denmark, Finland and Sweden using the term 'Nordic countries'. It should be noted that Norway and Iceland are also included in the Nordic countries, but the legal situation in these two countries is excluded from this chapter.
4   Apparently this legislation took inspiration from France. Marianne Levin, *Lärobok i immaterialrätt : upphovsrätt, patenträtt, mönsterrätt, känneteckensrätt i Sverige, EU och internationellt* (12th edn, Norstedts Juridik 2019) 349–50 (only in Swedish).
5   See Jens Schovsbo and Morten Rosenmeier, 'The Copyright/Design Interface in Scandinavia' in Estelle Derclaye (ed.), *The Copyright/Design Interface – Past, Present and Future* (Cambridge University Press 2018).
6   See Jens Schovsbo, 'Design Protection in the Nordic countries: Welcome to the smörgåsbord' (2020) Nordiskt Immateriellt Rättsskydd 323, 325 and Jens Schovsbo 'Design Protection in the Nordic Countries: The Past, the Present and Maybe the Future', 323–43 in Tsukasa Aso, Christoph Rademacher, Jonathan Dobinson (eds.), *History of Design and Design Law* (Springer 2022).
7   Lainvalmistelukunnan ehdotus laiksi kaavojen ja mallien suojelemisesta ynnä perustelmat (Keisarillisen senaatin kirjapaino 1907) (only in Finnish).
8   Pirkko-Liisa Haarmann, *Immateriaalioikeus* (5th edn, Talentum 2014) 265 (only in Finnish). Finland was an autonomous Grand Duchy in the Russian Empire 1809–1917. Finland declared itself independent on 6 December 1917.
9   Schovsbo (2020) (n 6) 324–25, Schovsbo (2022) (n 6) and Haarmann (n 8) 266.
10 Schovsbo (2020) (n 6) 325, Schovsbo (2022) (n 6) and Haarmann (n 8) 266.

in a report which was published by the committee in 1966 and as a result, Denmark, Finland, Sweden and Norway adopted similar national Design Acts in the 1970s.[11]

A key driver of this legal initiative was the inclusion of Article 5*quinquies* in the Paris Convention in Lisbon in 1958. It required that 'Industrial designs shall be protected in all the countries of the Union.' Even though the obligations created by this Article are vague and do not necessarily require protection of designs by *sui generis* legislation, it was found that for example the Swedish Design Act needed updating, and at the time Finland did not even have a Design Act.[12] 8.005

Moreover, the Nordic legislators had a specific idea about what they wanted with the reform: 8.006

> Along with growing wealth consumers will demand that products – industrially made or craft-made – are not only suited for their purpose but have also an attractive outer form. This goes in particular for personal articles for everyday use such as apparel and furniture but the demand for good design has also increased considerably in relation to tools, industrial machines, transport and so forth. In order to meet such demands it seems fair to encourage innovation in craft-based and industrial design.[13]

Looking more closely at the 1970s Acts,[14] they defined the object of protection as 'a model for a commodity's appearance or for an ornament' (sec. 1(1)). The definition was neutral, i.e., the protection was simply available for the appearance of the products regardless of whether the appearance was deter- 8.007

---

11   At the time, similar co-operation and development took place also in other areas of IPR such as copyright, trade mark and patent law.
12   Schovsbo (2020) (n 6) 326, Schovsbo (2022) (n 6) 324 ff. Another failed attempt in Finland took place in the 1930s. Once again a bill was drafted but opinions from various stakeholders were so divided and to some extent even against it so that the introduction of the Act became impossible. The Finnish Government Bill No. 113/1970 to the Parliament concerning the Finnish Design Act [Hallituksen esitys 113/1970 Eduskunnalle mallioikeuslaiksi] 2 (only in Finnish).
13   Parliamentary Report No. 417/1966 concerning a new Danish Act on designs prepared by the commission which was formed by the Ministry of Trade on 5 February 1960 in collaboration with similar Finnish, Norwegian and Swedish commissions ('The Design Law Report')) [Betænkning 417/1966 vedrørende en ny dansk lov om mønstre udarbejdet af den af handelsministeriet den 5.2.1960 nedsatte kommission i samarbejde med tilsvarende finske, norske og svenske kommissioner ('mønsterlovsbetænkningen')] 34 (only in Danish); translation by Jens Schovsbo and Stina Teilmann-Lock, 'We wanted more Arne Jacobsen but all we got was Boxes: Experiences from the Protection of Designs in Scandinavia from 1970 till the Directive' (2016) 47(4) *International Review of Industrial Property and Competition Law* 418, 420.
14   Denmark (Design Act ([Lov om mønstre]) No. 218 of 27 May 1970), Finland (Design Act [Mönsterrättslag] No. 221/1971 of 12 March 1971), and Sweden (Design Act [Mönsterskyddslag] 1970:485). English language versions are available on the World Intellectual Property Organization (WIPO) website. See, for instance, the Danish Designs Act at 'Denmark – The Danish Designs Act (Act No. 218 of May 27, 1970)', WIPO website www.wipo.int/wipolex/en/details.jsp?id=1121 accessed 21 February 2022.

mined by aesthetic or functional considerations. The function itself could not be protected by the Design Act.[15] To be registrable, a design should 'differ essentially' from what was known prior to the priority date (sec. 2(1)). Novelty was assessed in a similar way as in patent law, and included 'everything made available to the public by depiction, by exhibition, offer for sale, or in any other way' (sec. 2(2)). The extent of the exclusive right was similar to patent law: also third parties acting in good faith without prior knowledge of the design could be enjoined from using the design (sec. 5).[16] Design was not protected in 'the abstract' but only against the use of a similar design in relation to goods which incorporated the design or goods of a similar kind.[17] A narrow list of limitations included prior use and repair of aircrafts (sec. 6–7). A very narrowly defined compulsory licensing rule was also provided for in cases where a third party had 'very particular reasons' and had no knowledge of the application and, furthermore, had not reasonably been able to acquire such knowledge (sec. 28).

8.008 The 1970s Acts were based on the so-called 'patent approach' to design protection in the sense that protection required an application and registration. The registration authority (national patent and trade mark office) conducted an examination ex officio. This included the requirements of novelty and 'essential difference'. However, in practice, the search was limited to design registrations in force, applications and previous registrations which had been cancelled within the past a few years. To compensate for this relatively scarce examination of novelty and 'essential difference', the application had to be accompanied by a declaration signed by the applicant that the design, as far as the applicant was aware, had not become known prior to the application (or priority) date in such a way that prevents registration of the design (sec. 10(3)).[18] If the application met the formal and substantive requirements, the application was published and the public was given an opportunity to file oppositions (sec. 18). The opposition period was two months and if no opposition was filed within that period, the design could be registered for up to 15 years (sec. 24).

8.009 Unfortunately, the 1970s Acts were not quite the success that the legislators had hoped for. Many designers rejected the design right system and instead relied on copyright law (which expanded its reach at the time) and to some

---

15　Schovsbo (2020) (n 6) 327 and Schovsbo (2022) (n 6) 327.
16　Schovsbo (2020) (n 6) 327 and Schovsbo (2022) (n 6) 327.
17　Schovsbo (2020) (n 6) 327 and Schovsbo (2022) (n 6) 326 f.
18　If the applicant intentionally gave false declaration, this was punishable under the provisions of the Criminal Code. See, for instance, the Finnish Government Bill (n 12) 14.

extent on the law of unfair competition.[19] Especially copyright was often seen as a more 'worthy' kind of protection as it did not require registration and it set the designers on par with 'other artists'.[20] Furthermore, the registration process of design rights had its inner weaknesses: the limited examination of the requirements for registration meant that, although registration was granted, it was still vulnerable to attacks based on matters which were not examined by the registration authority.[21]

(b) Overview of the current situation

8.010 Denmark joined the EU (then known as the European Communities) in 1973 and Finland and Sweden in 1995. The Design Acts of the 1970s remained in place until the two-tiered EU-harmonised design system took over in the early 2000s. Nowadays, the EU-harmonised design system established by the DDir, and the CDReg applies to these countries. DDir has been implemented in these countries by the following national legislation:

- The Consolidate Designs Act (Consolidate Act No. 89 of January 29, 2019) (Denmark);[22]
- Registered Designs Act (Act No. 221 of March 12, 1971, as amended up to Act No. 551 of April 26, 2019) (Finland);[23]
- Design Protection Act (1970:485) (as amended up to Act (2020:542) (Sweden).[24]

19　For Denmark, see Schovsbo and Teilmann-Lock (n 13).
20　Schovsbo (2020) (n 6) 328 and Schovsbo (2022) (n 6) 328.
21　Schovsbo (2020) (n 6) 328 and Schovsbo (2022) (n 6) 328.
22　Bekendtgørelse af designloven (LBK nr 89 af 29/1/2019). An English version is available at 'Denmark – The Consolidate Designs Act (Consolidate Act No. 89 of January 29, 2019)', WIPO website https://wipolex.wipo.int/en/legislation/details/18694 accessed 21 February 2022.
23　Mallioikeuslaki 12.3.1971/221 (26.4.2019/551). An almost up-to-date English version is available at 'Finland – Registered Designs Act (Act No. 221 of March 12, 1971, as amended up to Act No. 718 of August 25, 2016)', WIPO website https://wipolex.wipo.int/en/legislation/details/17864 accessed 21 February 2022. In Finland, a relevant piece of legislation is also the Registered Designs Decree (Decree No. 252/71 of 2 April 1971)(583/2013) (Mallioikeusasetus 2.4.1971/252 (583/2013)). An English version is available at 'Registered Designs Decree (Decree No. 252/71 of 2 April 1971 as amended by Decree No. 583 of 18 July 2013)', The Finnish Patent and Registration Office website https://prh.fi/en/mallioikeudet/lainsaadantoa/mallioikeusasetus.html accessed 21 February 2022.
24　Mönsterskyddslag (1970:485) (i ändrad lydelse upp till Lag (2020:542)). An almost up-to-date English version is available at 'Sweden – Design Protection Act (1970:485) (as amended up to Act (2018:1656))', WIPO website https://wipolex.wipo.int/en/legislation/details/18531 accessed on 21 February 2022. In Sweden, a relevant piece of legislation is also the Design Protection Regulation (1970:486)(2018:376) (Mönsterskyddsförordning (1970:486)(2018:376)). An almost up-to-date English version is available at 'Sweden – Design Protection Regulation (1970:486) (as amended up to Regulation (2017:1059))', WIPO website https://wipolex.wipo.int/en/legislation/details/17754 accessed 21 February 2022.

8.011 As we can see, a new Act has been enacted in Denmark. In Finland and Sweden, the old Acts of the 1970s are still in force, but in significantly amended forms. Despite all this, part of the 'spirit' of the 1970s Acts lives on to some extent since the Nordic legal model was part of the inspiration for the so-called 'Design Approach' which constitutes the backbone of the EU design system.[25]

8.012 Particularly the entry into force of CDReg has meant a significant change for the Nordic countries. CDReg and its combination of a registered community design right (RCD) and an unregistered community design right (UCD) offers a very attractive alternative to the national design systems. This system is administrated by the European Intellectual Property Office (EUIPO) in Alicante, Spain. We will see later how RCD in particular has led to a significant decrease in the number of national design right application filings (see section B. Practical aspects of design law).

8.013 Looking for a moment beyond the Design Acts, copyright law and unfair competition law offer protection for product appearances too. In their current form, copyright law and unfair competition law thus supplement design protection and may even offer very useful alternatives to it.

8.014 For copyright, the CJEU has ruled that 'originality' constitutes the sole criterion for copyright protection for all types of works within the EU.[26] Following this case law, courts in the EU countries have to grant copyright protection even to works of applied art which are:

(i) the result of the author's free and creative choices;
(ii) not determined by technical constraints or by following rules;
(iii) stamped with the author's 'personal touch'; and
(iv) expressed in a manner which makes it identifiable with sufficient precision and objectivity.[27]

---

25 Annette Kur and Marianne Levin, 'The Design Approach Revisited: Background and Meaning' in Annette Kur, Marianne Levin and Jens Schovsbo (eds), *The EU Design Approach – A Global Appraisal* (Edward Elgar 2018). See also Annette Kur, 'The EU Design Approach – what is left and what is right? (2020) Nordiskt Immateriellt Rättsskydd 230 ff.

26 In particular C-5/08 *Infopaq International A/S v Danske Dagblades Forening* [2009] ECLI:EU:C:2009:465; C-145/10 *Eva-Maria Painer v Standard Verlags GmbH and Others* [2011] ECLI:EU:C:2011:798; C-310/17 *Levola Hengelo BV v Smilde Foods BV* [2018] ECLI:EU:C:2018:899; C-683/17 *Cofemel – Sociedade de Vestuário SA v G-Star Raw CV* [2019] ECLI:EU:C:2019:721; and C-833/18 *SI and Brompton Bicycle Ltd v Chedech / Get2Get* [2020] ECLI:EU:C:2020:461.

27 The points are deduced from the case law mentioned in note 26, see Schovsbo (2022) (n 6) 331 ff.

8.015 For example, the Danish Supreme Court recently relied on CJEU's judgment in *Cofemel*. Even though the Court denied copyright in fancy rubber boots due to lack of originality, it also made it clear that fashion items as such may acquire copyright protection according to the same principles as other types of works.[28] This in turn may open copyright's doors to fashion items such as clothing, footwear and accessories which have hitherto not been protected by copyright law in Denmark. In this way it would seem that copyright's reach has in fact expanded because of the development in EU case law and now covers even more of design law's traditional fields.[29] Because of this the overlap between design and copyright law has increased in Denmark. In Finland, however, it has in principle been possible for any design object to be protected by copyright also before *Cofemel*. Thus, *Cofemel* did not bring any fundamental changes to the situation in Finland.

8.016 Unlike copyright law, unfair competition law is largely unharmonised in the Nordic countries when it comes to the relationship between commercial actors. In Denmark, product appearances enjoy protection under unfair competition law against slavish imitation, which is applied generously by the courts, even without any clear risk of confusion.[30] In Finland and Sweden the shape of products is protected under unfair competition law against slavish imitation which, in turn, requires a risk of confusion.[31] In addition, in Finland and Sweden, protection is nowadays also provided in some exceptional cases against so-called 'reputation parasitism' (Finnish: *'maineen norkkiminen'*, Swedish: *'renommésnyltning'*) which refers to the exploitation of a competitor's goodwill in marketing without a requirement of risk of confusion.[32] Finally, as

---

28 Judgment reported in Ugeskrift for Retsvæsen 2020, 2817. See also Jens Schovsbo, 'Danish Supreme Court denies copyright in rubber boots' (2020) 15(9) *Journal of Intellectual Property Law & Practice* 679.

29 See on Denmark Schovsbo (2022) (n 6).

30 In Denmark, there is no specific rule on slavish imitation. Instead, the Danish courts often rely on the 'general clause' of unfair competition found in sec. 3 of the Marketing Practices Act (Markedsføringsloven, LBK nr 1216 af 25/09/2013): 'Traders subject to this Act shall exercise good marketing practice with reference to consumers, other traders and public interests.' See also Schovsbo (2020) (n 6) 336 and Schovsbo (2022) (n 6).

31 In Finland, the protection is based on the general clause on unfair competition found in sec. 1(1) of the Unfair Business Practices Act (Laki sopimattomasta menettelystä, 22.12.1978/1061, 10.8.2018/596): 'Good business practice may not be violated nor may practices that are otherwise unfair to other entrepreneurs be used in business.' In Sweden, there is a specific provision on slavish imitation. According to sec. 14 of the Marketing Act (Marknadsföringslag, 2008:486 i ändrad lydelse upp till Lag 2020:542) '[a] trader may not, in the course of marketing, use copies that are misleading in that they can easily be confused with another trader's known and distinctive products. This does not, however, apply to copies the design of which is primarily intended to render the product functional'.

32 In Finland, also the protection against 'reputation parasitism' is based on the general clause of unfair competition (sec. 1(1) of the Unfair Business Practices Act). In Sweden, this protection is based on the general clause of unfair competition, which is provided for in sec. 5 of the Marketing Act: 'Marketing shall be consistent with good marketing practice.' See also sec. 6 of the Act: 'Marketing that contravenes good marketing practice under Section 5 is to be regarded as unfair if it appreciably affects or probably affects the recipient's

regards the protection under unfair competition law, it should be noted that this protection is not limited in time but is available as long as the product appearance has 'commercial value'. Consequently, this protection may be had even after the expiration of any design rights in the product. This is particularly significant in relation to UCDs which are limited to three years from the date on which the design was first made available to the public within the EU (CDReg Article 11(1)).[33]

8.017 In recent decades, trade mark law has also opened its doors to the protection of product appearances with certain requirements: most importantly, the product appearance must have inherent or acquired distinctiveness and it cannot be technically or aesthetically functional.[34] Unlike copyright and design protection, trade mark protection is not limited in time but lasts as long as the product appearance that makes up the trade mark is used. This feature in particular makes trade mark protection a highly attractive alternative and supplement to protection by design law. It should also be noted that for well-known marks trade mark law offers protection not only against consumer confusion (or likelihood of it), but also against taking unfair advantage of or misappropriating the repute of the trade mark.[35] Finally, it is significant that in Denmark, Finland and Sweden trade marks may be established not only by registration, but also through use alone.[36]

(c) A closer look at the (national) design right system in the Nordic countries

8.018 The present national Design Acts of Denmark, Finland and Sweden are based closely on the DDir. Using the Finnish Design Act as illustration, its sec. 1 provides that the creator of a design (the designer), or their successor in title, may in accordance with this Act by registration obtain an exclusive right to

---

ability to make a well-founded transaction decision.' Concerning the 'reputation parasitism', Finnish case law has so far largely followed that of Sweden. For example, in judgment of 4 April 2012 in case MAO:121/12 (Granströms Båtvarv), the Finnish Market Court explicitly refers to Swedish case law.

33   See also Schovsbo (2020) (n 6) 337 and 341–42.
34   See Art. 4 of the Directive 2015/2436 of 16 December 2015 to approximate the laws of the Member States relating to trade marks [2015] OJ L336/1. Denmark, Finland and Sweden have implemented these requirements in their national trade mark legislation. For Denmark, see sec. 3 and 13–14 of the Consolidate Trade Marks Act (Bekendtgørelse af varemærkeloven, LBK nr 88 af 29/01/2019). For Finland, see sec. 11–12 of the Trade Marks Act (Tavaramerkkilaki, 26.4.2019/544). For Sweden, see Chapter 1, sec. 5 and 9 of the Trademarks Act (Varumärkeslag, 2010:1877 i ändrad lydelse upp till Lag 2021:561. See also Art. 7 of the Regulation 2017/1001 of 14 June 2017 on the European Union trade mark [2017] OJ L154/1.
35   See Art. 10 of the Trade Mark Directive. For Denmark, see sec. 4 of the Consolidate Trade Marks Act. For Finland, see sec. 5 of the Trade Marks Act. For Sweden, see Chapter 1, sec. 10 of the Trademarks Act. See also Art. 9 of the European Union trade mark Regulation.
36   For Denmark, see sec. 3 of the Consolidate Trade Marks Act. For Finland, see sec. 4 of the Trade Marks Act. For Sweden, see Chapter 1, sec. 7 of the Trademarks Act.

the design ('design right').³⁷ It is worth noticing that the Danish, Finnish and Swedish Design Acts do not have any provisions regarding unregistered designs. Thus, to obtain a design right under national law in Denmark, Finland and Sweden registration with the national authority is mandatory.

8.019 Again using the Finnish Design Act as illustration, the basic concepts ('design', 'product' and 'complex product') are defined in sec. 1a in accordance with the DDir.³⁸ The conditions for protection (novelty and individual character) are defined in sec. 3, also in accordance with the DDir.³⁹ For component parts of complex products, the special conditions ('visibility during normal use') have been incorporated in sec. 2 in accordance with the DDir.⁴⁰

8.020 It is important to note that the Danish, Finnish and Swedish Design Acts *do not* have the so-called 'repair clause' which excludes spare parts from design protection. However, the protection for 'must match' parts (notably 'crash parts' of automobiles such as fenders) is limited to a maximum of 15 years (the maximum period under the national Designs Acts adopted in the 1970s). This reflects the so-called 'freeze plus' compromise included in the DDir (Art. 14) according to which the Members States may uphold the protection offered to spare parts but may not increase the existing level of protection at the time of the adoption of the directive.

8.021 As follows from the DDir, the novelty requirement in all of these Nordic countries is global and objective but with an exception for 'remote' designs and a 12-month grace period.⁴¹ Also, as required by the DDir, design protection is not available for designs which are contrary to *ordre public* or morality or which make use of prior rights such as another person's trade mark, work protected by copyright or earlier design.⁴² Furthermore, and again as required by the DDir, design protection may not be obtained in respect of features which are solely dictated by the technical function of the product or 'must fit' aspects.⁴³

---

37 For Denmark, see sec. 1 of the Danish Design Act and for Sweden, sec. 1a of the Swedish Design Act.
38 For Denmark, see sec. 2 of the Danish Design Act and for Sweden, sec. 1 of the Swedish Design Act.
39 For Finland and Sweden, see sec. 2 of the respective Design Acts.
40 For Denmark, see sec. 4 of the Danish Design Act and for Sweden, sec. 2a of the Swedish Design Act.
41 For Denmark, see sec. 5-6 of the Danish Design Act. For Finland and Sweden, see sec. 3-3a of the respective Design Acts.
42 For Denmark, see sec. 7 of the Danish Design Act. For Finland, see sec. 4-4a of the Finnish Design Act and for Sweden, sec. 4 of the Swedish Design Act.
43 For Denmark, see sec. 8 of the Danish Design Act. For Finland, see sec. 4b of the Finnish Design Act and for Sweden, sec. 4a of the Swedish Design Act.

8.022 The rights conferred by the design right and the limitations thereto are provided for in accordance with the DDir. The right to a design means that no person other than the design right owner is entitled to use the design without his or her consent, for example, by the making, offering, putting on the market, importing, exporting or use of a product which does not produce on the informed user a different overall impression.[44] Exclusivity covers also 'accidental copying' done by third parties, that is, they do not need to have prior knowledge of the design in order to infringe. A narrow list of limitations includes acts done for private or experimental purposes or for making quotations. Furthermore, design rights shall not be exercised against equipment on board ships or aircraft registered in another country that are only temporarily in the territory of protection; parts needed for repair of such ships or aircraft may be imported and used for that purpose.[45]

8.023 The principle of regional exhaustion applies in Danish, Finnish and Swedish Design law. As follows from DDir, the right to prevent further circulation of products incorporating the design is exhausted if the goods were put on the market in the EEA by the rights holder or with his consent.[46]

8.024 Unlike the CDReg (Article 22), DDir does not provide for a prior use right. However, Member States are free to adopt a provision to that effect if they wish to do so. As was mentioned above, the Nordic countries did have such a provision in the 1970s Acts, but only Finland decided to maintain it in its Design Act. According to this rule (sec. 6), any third party who, at the time the application for registration is made (or, if priority was claimed, at the relevant priority date), has in the course of trade been using a design in Finland, may notwithstanding another's right to the design continue such use while retaining its general character, provided that such use did not entail a *manifest abuse* with respect to the applicant for registration or to his or her predecessor in title. Under similar conditions, any person who has taken substantial steps to use the design in the course of trade in this country shall have the same right of use. Of course, these kinds of situations are extremely rare. The aforementioned term 'manifest abuse' means, for example, stealing the design or breaching confidentiality undertakings.[47] This prior use right can only be transferred to

---

44   For Denmark, see sec. 9 of the Danish Design Act. For Finland, see sec. 5-5a of the Finnish Design Act and for Sweden, sec. 5 of the Swedish Design Act.
45   For Denmark, see sec. 10-11 of the Danish Design Act. For Finland, see sec. 5b of the Finnish Design Act and for Sweden, sec. 7-7a of the Swedish Design Act.
46   For Denmark, see sec. 12 of the Danish Design Act. For Finland, see sec. 5c of the Finnish Design Act and for Sweden, sec. 7b of the Swedish Design Act.
47   The Finnish Government Bill (n 12) 13.

other parties together with the business in which it has arisen or in which the design was to be used.

Similarly, the above-mentioned very narrowly defined compulsory licensing provision that was included in the 1970s Acts, is still maintained only in Finland (sec. 28–30 of the Finnish Design Act).[48] This type of compulsory license shall be issued by the Court, which shall also decide the extent to which the design may be used and determine the compensation and other terms of the license. When a substantial change in circumstances so demands, the Court may, if so requested by the person concerned, revoke the license or stipulate new terms.

8.025

Unlike CDReg (Art. 14), DDir does not contain provisions on who has the right in the design. The rights under the Danish, Finnish and Swedish Design Acts arise with the 'designer' (physical person) who has created the design or his or her successor in title.[49] All rights are vested with the designer, unless they have been assigned by way of contract.[50]

8.026

The Danish, Finnish and Swedish Design Acts contain no specific rules on 'employees' designs' (and CDReg Art. 14(3) does not apply by extension, see below).[51] Therefore, and in principle, any transfer of the design right from the designer to their employer must be based on contract. In many cases, an employment contract stipulates a transfer of the design rights to the employer. However, even in the absence of an explicit contract to that effect, there is a general perception that design rights are transferred to the employer by an implied license to the extent that this is 'usual' in the light of the employment.[52] In order to avoid possible problems of interpretation, at least the basic provisions on the conditions, scope and compensation for the transfer of design rights should be included in the employment contracts. It should be remem-

8.027

---

48   Competition law may be relied upon to provide for compulsory licenses, cf. CJEU in C-238/87 *AB Volvo v Erik Veng (UK) Ltd* [1988] ECLI:EU:C:1988:477 and C-53/87 *CICRA et al. v Renault* [1988] ECLI:EU:C:1988:472.
49   For Denmark, see sec. 1 of the Danish Design Act. For Finland, see sec. 1 of the Finnish Design Act and for Sweden, sec. 1a of the Swedish Design Act.
50   As per the CJEU in C-32/08 *Fundación Española para la Innovación de la Artesanía (FEIA) v Cul de Sac Espacio Creativo SL and Acierta Product & Position SA* [2009] ECLI:EU:C:2009:418. The same principles apply regarding these Nordic Design Acts, see Schovsbo (2022) (n 6) 330 f.
51   See Schovsbo (2022) (n 6) 330 f.
52   Schovsbo (2022) (n 6) 330 f. and Jens Schovsbo and Niels Holm Svendsen, *Designret – Designloven med kommentarer* (2nd edn, DJØF Publishing 2013) 93–96 (Denmark, the source available only in Danish); Haarmann (n 8) 271–72 and Rainer Oesch, 'Muotoilutyön sopimukset' in Rainer Oesch, Marja-Leena Rinkineva, Heli Hietamies and Karri Puustinen, *Mallioikeus: muotoilun suoja* (Talentum 2005) 216 ff (Finland, both sources available only in Finnish); Levin (n 4) 375 ff (Sweden, the source available only in Swedish).

bered that for designs which are also protected under copyright law as works of art, the designer could also rely on the copyright protection against the employer.[53] Still, even here a transfer of copyright would normally be deemed to follow implicitly from the employment relationship.[54]

8.028 Unlike the national Design Acts, CDReg Article 14(3) contains a clear 'work for hire'-rule. According to that rule, where a design is developed by an employee in the execution of his duties or following the instructions given by his employer, the right to the Community design shall vest in the employer, unless otherwise agreed or specified under national law. Since Danish, Finnish or Swedish law has not provided for anything in this regard, Article 14(3) covers RCDs and UCDs by designers employed in these countries. As in particular RCDs constitute nowadays the vast majority of protected designs, cf. below, Article 14(3) is in fact the 'main rule' in Danish, Finnish and Swedish design law.[55] However, the effects of Article 14(3) are to some extent limited. Firstly, for designs which are also protected by copyright law, it follows from CDReg, rec. 32 that the individual EU Member States are free to apply the rules and principles of their national copyright law. As a result, designers (in this case 'authors') may invoke copyright to try to control the employer's use of their design. Secondly, as *lex specialis* Article 14(3) does not apply to designs which are protected solely by the Design Act. Thirdly and lastly, the CJEU has ruled in FEIA that Article 14(3) should be construed narrowly and only applies to traditional employment relationships where the designer works under the instruction of the employer.[56] Therefore, Article 14(3) does not affect the rights to designs made by freelancers etc. In those cases, contract law and its general principles (and copyright if the design meets the requirement of an original work of art) apply.

8.029 The maximum protection period for national design rights in Denmark, Finland and Sweden is 25 years, that is, five periods of five years (as was mentioned above, for 'spare parts' the maximum is 15 years).[57]

---

53 This is due to the fact that the Nordic countries follow the principle of cumulation, see Schovsbo and Rosenmeier (n 5).
54 Most likely, the court would find the transfer of copyright to be narrower than the transfer for design rights. Hence, it matters even in employment situations whether the products are protected both by design and copyright law, see Schovsbo (2022) (n 6) 330 f.
55 On Denmark see Schovsbo (2022) (n 6) 330 f.
56 FEIA (n 50), para 50.
57 For Denmark, see sec. 23 of the Danish Design Act. For Finland and Sweden, see sec. 24 of the respective Design Act.

2. Procedural Aspects

For Denmark, applications for design protection are filed with the Danish Patent and Trademark Office (DKPTO).[58] The responsible authority in Finland is the Finnish Patent and Registration Office (PRH), and in Sweden the Swedish Intellectual Property Office (PRV). The amount of the filing fee varies between these countries. In Denmark, the basic filing fee for registration of one design is the lowest: 1,200 DKK (approximately €160). In Finland, the amount is the highest: €250. Sweden is in the middle: 2,000 SEK (approximately €190). In addition, in Finland and Sweden applicants are encouraged to use the registration authority's own electronic system when filing the application because for paper or email application an additional fee is charged. The filing fee must be paid when the application is submitted. More information on possible additional fees, such as multiple registration fees for each additional design, can be found in English on the website of each registration authority.[59] **8.030**

The design application must meet the formality requirements set forth in the Nordic Design Acts, e.g., information about the applicant(s) and, if applicable, representative; representation(s) or a specimen of the design; an indication of the product and class(es) for the design.[60] In the application, the applicant may also request priority and/or deferred publication, i.e., that the application be kept secret for a maximum period of six months form the filing date (or the priority date).[61] Unlike Denmark and Sweden, Finland requires foreign applicants to appoint representatives.[62] **8.031**

DKPTO, PRH and PRV will examine whether the application meets the aforementioned formalities. In addition, the offices examine ex officio e.g., **8.032**

---

58 In addition to the registration of designs under the Danish Design Act, the DKPTO also offers an informal system called 'DesDoc®', which merely records the design for a very low fee (approximately €75). The DesDoc system may be used, for instance, to support claims for protection of the design as an UCD, see Schovsbo (2022) (n 6) 330 and more at https://desdoc.dkpto.dk/, accessed 21 February 2022.
59 https:// www .dkpto .org/ (Denmark), https:// prh .fi/ en/ index .html (Finland), https:// www .prv .se/ en/ (Sweden) accessed 21 February 2022.
60 For Denmark, see sec. 13 of the Danish Design Act. For Finland and Sweden, see sec. 10 of the respective Design Act. See also sec. 2 of the Finnish Registered Designs Decree and sec. 2 of the Swedish Design Protection Regulation.
61 For Denmark, see sec. 18 of the Danish Design Act. For Finland, see sec. 18 of the Finnish Design Act and for Sweden, sec. 19 of the Swedish Design Act.
62 See sec. 12 of the Finnish Design Act: 'An applicant who is not domiciled in Finland shall have an agent resident in the European Economic Area who is authorised to represent the applicant in matters concerning the application.'

whether the application actually concerns a design, as opposed for example to a patent and whether the design is contrary to *ordre public* or morality.[63]

8.033 The EUIPO does not examine novelty and individual character ex officio in the case of RCD applications. The same approach is also in Denmark and Sweden: DKPTO and PRV do not check novelty and individual character ex officio when they examine national design right applications. Finland, however, is an exception in this respect. PRH examines both novelty and individual character ex officio. It is thus possible to claim that this makes the Finnish registration stronger (as to validity) than its RCD, Danish or Swedish counterparts. However, as Alhonnoro has pointed out, this alleged strength of the Finnish design registration is 'a misconception'.[64] This is because PRH only examines design applications against prior designs *included in the Finnish design register* (both national Finnish registrations and international registrations designating Finland).[65] This very limited examination of novelty and individual character makes it therefore possible, for example, to obtain a national design registration that is identical to a prior RCD since RCDs are not taken into account by the PRH in the ex officio examination.[66]

8.034 Finland and Sweden provide nowadays for a post-registration opposition procedure.[67] If the design passes official examination, possibly after amendments following communications between the PRH/PRV and the applicant, the Office will publish the design as registered. Third parties may then file with the PRH/PRV oppositions against the registration within two months of publication claiming, for example, lack of novelty, lack of individual character, functionality or a prior right. There are certain restrictions with regard to who is competent to file an opposition. In case of prior rights, it is the holders of the respective rights. In a situation where registration has been applied for by a person not entitled to it, opposition may be lodged by anyone who considers him or herself to be entitled to the design. In case of improper use of an official emblem, symbol or similar, or something liable to be confused with them, only

---

63 For Denmark, see sec. 17 of the Danish Design Act. For Finland and Sweden, see sec. 14 of the respective Design Acts. See also sec. 13 of the Finnish Registered Designs Decree and sec. 13 of the Swedish Design Protection Regulation.
64 Marjut Alhonnoro, 'Is there still a need for national design protection? A view from industry' (2020) Nordiskt Immateriellt Rättsskydd 302, 306.
65 Sec. 13(2) of the Finnish Registered Designs Decree.
66 Alhonnoro (n 64) 306.
67 See sec. 18-20 of the respective Design Acts. There is no post-registration opposition period for designs in Denmark where instead anyone may request for the cancellation of a design at any point in time, cf. below point 3.

a person or entity concerned by the use may file opposition.[68] Appeals against decisions taken by the PRH/PRV can be lodged with the Market Court (Finland)/the Patent and Market Court (Sweden).

8.035 A national design registration may be renewed at the earliest three months (Denmark) or one year (Finland and Sweden) before and at the latest within six months from the expiration of the current period of registration.[69] The renewal fee is higher if renewal is requested after the registration period has expired.[70]

8.036 Industrial designs can also be registered internationally, in a similar fashion as patents and trade marks. The Hague Agreement Concerning the International Registration of Industrial Designs (Hague Agreement) offers the possibility to obtain design protection for industrial designs on an international level in several Contracting Parties by a single application filed with the World Intellectual Property Organization. Finland and Denmark are Contracting Parties to the Hague Agreement. Sweden is not a Contracting Party. However, since the EU (including Sweden) is a Contracting Party, protection can also be obtained in Sweden based on an international application.

3. Disputes

(a) Grounds for invalidity

8.037 It is possible to request an entire or partial cancellation of a (national) design registration, which has been registered contrary to the provisions of the Nordic Design Acts.[71] The grounds for invalidity are based on the DDir and mirror the requirements of design registration, e.g., lack of novelty and/or individual character, functionality, design being contrary to *ordre public* or morality or design is making use of prior rights. There are certain restrictions with regard to who is competent to bring an action for invalidity. In case of a prior right, it is the right holder. Where registration has been granted to a person who is not the rightful owner of the design, an action to cancel the registration must

---

68 See sec. 18a of the respective Design Acts.
69 For Denmark, see sec. 24 of the Danish Design Act. For Finland and Sweden, see sec. 25 of the respective Design Acts.
70 Information on renewal fees can be found in English on the website of each registration authority https://www.dkpto.org/ (Denmark), https://prh.fi/en/index.html (Finland), https://www.prv.se/en/ (Sweden); accessed 21 February 2022.
71 For Denmark, see Part 5 of the Danish Design Act. For Finland, see Chapter 5 of the Finnish Design Act and for Sweden, sec. 31 and the following provisions of the Swedish Design Act.

be brought by the person who claims to be entitled to the design.[72] In case of improper use of an official emblem, symbol or similar, or something liable to be confused with them, a request for cancellation can be requested by the person or entity concerned by the use. Like a RCD, a registered national design can be declared invalid even after the design right has lapsed or has been surrendered.

8.038 In Denmark, a request for invalidity may be filed with the DKPTO.[73] Alternatively, it is possible to institute cancellation proceedings before the Maritime and Commercial Court in first instance. In Finland and Sweden (after the post-registration opposition timeframe has lapsed, see above) invalidity may be sought in the form of a cancellation action before the Market Court (Finland) or the Patent and Market Court (Sweden) in first instance.

8.039 In the case of RCDs, cancellation of the registration on the basis of invalidity is sought from EUIPO. In the case of UCDs, however, a declaration of invalidity may be instituted before the Maritime and Commercial Court (Denmark), the Market Court (Finland) and the Patent and Market Court (Sweden) acting as a Community design court (Arts 80–81 CDReg).

(b) Litigation

8.040 Unauthorised use of designs is normally addressed through infringement proceedings before the courts – in the first instance (normally) the Maritime and Commercial Court (Denmark),[74] the Market Court (Finland) and the Patent and Market Court (Sweden). In some cases, and before any court proceedings, an infringement may be halted by sending a cease-and-desist letter detailing the rights of the design's owner or licensee to an alleged infringer (and possible connected parties). Too strongly worded cease-and-desist letters can, however, lead to problems for the sender.[75]

---

72 As regards this scenario: if a design has been registered for someone other than the eligible person, there is of course no need to cancel the registration. The right holder can instead have the design right transferred to him/her.
73 Decisions rendered by the DKPTO may be appealed to the Board of Appeals within two months.
74 See the Danish Administration of Justice Act [Retsplejeloven, LBK nr 1835 af 15/09/2021938 sec. 225–227 (the Maritime and Commercial Court has exclusive competence for EU-rights and is often called to decide cases on national designs too).
75 See, for instance, the judgment of 29 September 2005 of the Finnish Supreme Court in KKO 2005:105 (Fiskars). In that case, Fiskars Oyj sent a cease-and-desist letter to the retailers of the competing product and forbidding actions infringing the registered design. The Finnish Supreme Court held that the cease-and-desist letter violated good business practice (sec. 1 and 2 of the Unfair Business Practices Act) because it was: strict and commanding in tone; it was sent to the retailers, not to the producer; the recipients of the letter may have believed that the industrial design was violated and the prohibition is legally binding, which it was not; the marketing prohibition was unfounded and affected damagingly the demand of the product and defendant's business.

8.041 It is nowadays common in these Nordic countries to request interim injunctions as part of the infringement proceedings.[76] Interim injunctions are granted only if the court finds it likely that the plaintiff will ultimately succeed in the final court proceedings and there are no doubts or concerns regarding the request. A bank guarantee or similar is usually required before a preliminary injunction can be granted. Interim injunctions are granted promptly. The granted interim injunction will remain in force until the main case has been decided or until the court revokes it. A granted interim injunction can not only put an end to the infringement (at least temporarily), but also work as a leverage for a speedy settlement in which case there is no need for the final court proceedings in the main case.

8.042 It is possible to request a court order ordering the alleged infringer or a third party to provide information in order to use it as evidence of the infringement. The courts may also grant an order for seizure of documents, etc., so as to provide the plaintiff with access to evidence.[77]

8.043 Whether a design (national or RCD) is infringed is assessed in light of the same standards that are in use in the assessment of individual character in the registration phase. Of pivotal importance is the overall impression produced on an informed user, with the degree of freedom of the designer in developing the design having to be taken into consideration. The Finnish Supreme Court Judgment from 2007 in KKO 2007:103, described in the following sub-section, provides an example of how this assessment has been executed by the national courts. In the case of UCDs, the scope of protection is narrower and limited only to imitations, i.e. the infringer must have been probably familiar with the design (Art. 19(2) CDReg).

8.044 There are various defences to an infringement claim. A defendant may, for instance, argue that the design of the right holder is not valid (on the grounds of novelty, individual character, functionality etc.) and bring a counterclaim to this effect.[78] A defendant may also argue in favour of non-infringement, e.g., that the contested design is not sufficiently similar to the protected design.

---

76 For Denmark, see Chapter 40 of the Danish Administration of Justice Act. For Finland, see Chapter 7 of the Code of Judicial Procedure [Oikeudenkäymiskaari, 1.1.1734/4, 1.7.2021/642](Finland) and for Sweden, sec. 35b of the Swedish Design Act and Chapter 15, sec. 3 of the Code of Judicial Procedure [Rättegångsbalk (1942:740) (i ändrad lydelse upp till Lag (2021:1107)].

77 For Denmark, see Chapter 29a and 57a and of the Danish Administration of Justice Act. For Finland, see the Act Concerning the Safeguarding of Evidence in Cases of Intellectual Property Disputes [Laki todistelun turvaamisesta teollis- ja tekijänoikeuksia koskevissa riita-asioissa, 7.4.2000/344, 1.5.2019/550]. For Sweden, see sec. 35c and the following provisions of the Swedish Design Act.

78 Counterclaims can be made in the case of national design rights, RCDs or UCDs.

A defendant may also rely on the number of aforementioned limitations and exceptions to protection, e.g., private use, citations and exhaustion of rights.

8.045 If in the final court proceedings an infringement is found, a court may order the infringer to cease the unauthorised use of the design(s); pay a penalty in case that order is not met; pay reasonable compensation to the injured party for the use of the design and damages for the further injury which the infringement has caused; pay for the distribution of information regarding the judgment.[79] The provisions in the Nordic Design Acts as regards to liability reflect those found in the EU Directive on Enforcement of IP Rights.[80]

8.046 In Denmark, judgments from the Maritime and Commercial Court can be appealed to the Court of Appeal or (if the case has general interest (*'principiel interesse'*)) directly to the Supreme Court. In Sweden, the Patent and Market Court of Appeal (PMCA) hears appeals from the Patent and Market Court. PMCA has the possibility, under special circumstances, to refer a matter to the Supreme Court. The Supreme Court will then decide whether or not to grant leave to appeal. In Finland, decisions of the Market Court can be appealed to the Supreme Court, if it grants leave to appeal.

8.047 Criminal proceedings are also available when design rights are infringed. In criminal actions, the courts will impose a fine or a prison sentence, provided that the infringement was intentional and clear.[81] In practice, the criminal proceedings are not very common and generally take place only in clear cases of counterfeiting and piracy.

8.048 As for border measures, EU Regulation concerning customs enforcement of Intellectual Property Rights is in force in Denmark, Finland and Sweden.[82] The Customs Regulation defines which procedures the customs authority must follow if it during a customs control or an inspection discovers goods, which are suspected of violating intellectual property rights, inter alia, design rights. It is noteworthy that violations based on unfair competition law, e.g. slavish imitation, are not enforceable under the Customs Regulation.

---

79 For Denmark, see Part 7 of the Danish Design Act. For Finland, see Chapter 7 of the Finnish Design Act and for Sweden, sec. 35 and the following provisions of the Swedish Design Act.
80 Corrigendum to Directive 2004/48/EC of 29 April 2004 on the enforcement of intellectual property rights (OJ L157/45) [2004] OJ L195/16.
81 For Denmark, see sec. 36 of the Danish Design Act. For Finland, see sec. 35b of the Finnish Design Act and for Sweden, sec. 35 of the Swedish Design Act.
82 Regulation (EU) No 608/2013 of 12 June 2013 concerning customs enforcement of intellectual property rights and repealing Council Regulation (EC) No 1383/2003 [2013] OJ L181/15.

4. Significant Judicial Decisions in the Jurisdiction

The amount of case law and particularly the amount of significant judgments has been rather moderate in the area of design law in the Nordic countries. The following judgments, which are all from the period after the entry of the EU-harmonised design system, are examples of this case law. At the end of this section, a few general comments are made on the case law in these Nordic countries. **8.049**

In Denmark, the Danish Supreme Court had in 2015 an opportunity to interpret the repair clause in CDReg Article 110. Whereas the solution on the national level with regard to protection of spare parts is largely left to the individual national legislatures (the implementation of Art. 14 DDir into the Nordic Design Acts was explained above), Article 110 CDReg provides that, until entry into force of a final Community-wide solution, 'protection as a Community design shall not exist for a design which constitutes a component part of a complex product used within the meaning of Article 19(1) for the purpose of the repair of that complex product so as to restore its original appearance'. According to the Danish Supreme Court, this rule was limited to must match-parts (for instance, body parts of cars whose shape depend on the appearance of the car) and did not apply to parts like wheel trims.[83] As a result, independent producers of spare parts to cars could not invoke the repair clause in order to manufacture wheel trims which were protected as RCDs. It was rather remarkable that the Supreme Court came to this conclusion without referring a question to the CJEU on the interpretation of Article 110. This interpretation by the Danish Supreme Court was later rejected by the CJEU in *Acacia* even though the CJEU ruling leaves a rather limited scope for the repair clause.[84] **8.050**

In Finland, the Finnish Supreme Court had to assess in 2007 whether the defendant's anti-slip device for shoes infringed the right holder's (national) design right.[85] The main features of the registered design were the following: studs in the tread placed under the heel, an ankle strap in the front side and the upper part holding the heel in the back side with an opening that leaves a part of the heel exposed. **8.051**

---

83 Judgment of the Supreme Court reported in Ugeskrift for Retsvæsen U 2015.2011, see Schovsbo (2022) (n 6) 337 f.
84 C-397/16 *Acacia Srl v Pneusgarda Srl and Audi AG and Acacia Srl and Rolando D'Amato v Dr. Ing. h.c.F. Porsche AG* [2017] ECLI:EU:C:2017:992. Requests for a preliminary ruling came from the Corte d'appello di Milano and the Bundesgerichtshof.
85 Judgment of 31 December 2007 in KKO 2007:103.

8.052 On the one hand, the Court held that in the development of the design, the designer's freedom is linked to certain basic shapes due to practical aspects related to the use of the anti-slip device, to the extent that even small differences from the protected design may in themselves be sufficient to give a different overall impression. Indeed, there were some differences between the registered design and the allegedly infringing product. The main difference was the different shape of the upper part in the back holding the heel: in the registered design it was horizontal, while in the defendant's anti-slip device it was formed obliquely upwards.[86] However, the Court held that this and other differences between the registered design and the defendant's product were very small and concerned details. The result was that according to the Court the defendant's product did not produce on the informed user a different overall impression. Consequently, there was an infringement. The judgment is significant in the sense that it provides an example of a situation where an infringement is still found, even if the designer's freedom is restricted due to practical aspects related to the use of the product.

8.053 The second judgment of the Finnish Supreme Court to be mentioned here concerned criminal liability for violation of, inter alia, RCDs.[87] It had the following premise. In 2013, A and B had imported to Finland 1,000 steam mops and 1,320 choppers that were copies of C Inc.'s mops and D GmbH's choppers. This infringed C's and D's trademark and design rights according to Community trade mark regulation (CTMR, still applicable in the case at hand) and CDReg. As a result, A and B were charged with intellectual property offences under the Criminal Code of Finland. The problem was that Chapter 49, Section 2 of the Criminal Code of Finland did not mention the breach of CTMR and CDReg as grounds for an intellectual property offence. The wording of the provision only covered a violation of national intellectual property rights (trade mark, design, etc.). The District Court of Helsinki considered that CTMR and CDReg are comparable to the Finnish Trademark Act and Registered Designs Act, so it regarded a violation of CTMR and CDReg as falling within the scope of the criminal provision. On appeal the Court of Appeal of Helsinki overruled the judgment and dismissed the charges on the grounds that the CTMR and CDReg did not contain any criminal provisions and therefore a Community Trade Mark (CTM) and a RCD could not be considered comparable to the national rights in relation to criminal sanc-

---

86 Unfortunately, a high-resolution figure of the defendant's product was not available. Low-resolution figures can be found in the Judgment KKO 2007:103 (in Finnish) at https://finlex.fi/fi/oikeus/kko/kko/2007/20070103 accessed 21 February 2022.
87 Judgment of 26 April 2018 in KKO 2018:36.

tions. Also, and most importantly, taking into account the principle of legality, the Court of Appeal held that it was not possible to interpret Chapter 49, Section 2 of the Criminal Code to cover a violation of CTMR and CDReg. This was upheld by the Finnish Supreme Court in its judgment in 2018. The judgment is a significant one in the sense that it was a very visible instruction to the Finnish legislator to fix the deficiency in the Criminal Code. The said provision has since been amended to cover a violation of CTMR (nowadays EUTMR) and CDReg.

In Sweden, Göta Court of Appeal's judgment in 2013 was about whether a registered national design right for a chimney hood should be declared invalid.[88] The plaintiff argued, inter alia, that the design was solely dictated by technical function. **8.054**

In its judgment, the Court explained that there are two competing tests for deciding whether a design is solely dictated by technical function: 'no aesthetic considerations-test' (also known as the 'causality theory') or 'multiplicity of forms approach'. The first asks whether there were only technical considerations contributing to the design of the product. If the answer is affirmative, the design is solely dictated by technical function. The second test asks if the technical function can be achieved with any other form. If the answer is negative, the design is solely dictated by technical function. These two tests can lead to different results when applied to the same case. The Court decided that the second test ('multiplicity of forms approach') was the proper test to be applied in Sweden.[89] When assessing the functionality of the registered design (chimney hood), the Court explained that there are restrictions to how a chimney hood can be designed so that it can fulfil its function. However, according to the Court, the designer still has 'possibility of variation in the design which is not insignificant'. Consequently, while the design of the chimney hood was largely dictated by technical function, the design was not *solely* dictated by technical function. Features such as the lock, rail and groove of a chimney hood were features which were not *solely* dictated by technical function. The Court therefore ruled that the design was not invalid. In addition, the Court even stated that the outcome would have been the same had the Court applied the 'no aesthetic considerations-test'. The judgment was appealed to the Swedish Supreme Court by the invalidity applicant. The Supreme Court granted leave to appeal, but the appeal was subsequently with- **8.055**

---

88   Judgment of 16 May 2013 in T 1519-12.
89   The same line of thought was present in an earlier Judgment of 8 June 2010 in T 3469-09 (Drawbar) by the Court of Appeal for Western Sweden.

drawn by the appellant. Of course, nowadays this judgment by the Göta Court of Appeal must be read in the light of CJEU's judgment in *Doceram*,[90] which concerned interpretation of the corresponding Article 8(1) CDReg according to which a Community design shall not subsist in features of appearance of a product which are solely dictated by its technical function. In that judgment, the CJEU decided in favour of the 'no aesthetic consideration-test' and explicitly rejected the 'multiplicity of forms approach'.[91]

8.056 In general, the following can be said about the Danish, Finnish and Swedish case law on design rights. The Courts have closely followed the established principles enshrined in the DDir and CDReg and developed by the EU Courts and EUIPO.[92] On some issues, of course, it may have taken some time before a 'correct' interpretation was adopted. For instance, the Danish courts for some time stuck to the pre-harmonisation principles and did not focus that much on the identification of the 'informed user' but engaged themselves in a broad overall assessment.[93] In its recent case law, however, the Maritime and Commercial Court has conducted an assessment based on the 'informed user' – standard and thus seems to have abandoned the previous practice.[94] Finally, it can be noted that in some cases, the national judgments from these Nordic countries are also based on a rather careful analysis of the *raison d'être* and the general objectives of design right.[95]

---

90 C-395/16 *DOCERAM GmbH v CeramTec GmbH* [2018] ECLI:EU:C:2018:172.
91 See also Jens Schovsbo and Graeme Dinwoodie, 'Design Protection for Products that are 'dictated by function" in Annette Kur, Marianne Levin and Jens Schovsbo (eds), *The EU Design Approach – A Global Appraisal* (Edward Elgar 2018) 142, 146–53; Kur (n 25) 237–38 and Jason J Du Mont and Mark D Janis, 'Trends in Functionality Jurisprudence: U.S. and E.U. Design Law' in Henning Hartwig (ed), *Research Handbook on Design Law* (Edward Elgar 2021) 30, 49–61. Very recently, the Finnish Market Court referred to Doceram and declared invalid a design for eaves because it was found that only technical considerations contributed to the design of the product. Judgment of 29 September 2021 in MAO:214/ 21.
92 See also Estelle Derclaye, 'EU Design Law: Transitioning Towards Coherence? 15 Years of National Case Law' in Niklas Bruun, Graeme Dinwoodie, Marianne Levin and Ansgar Ohly (eds), *Transition and Coherence in Intellectual Property law* (Cambridge University Press 2021) 61.
93 Schovsbo (2022) (n 6) 335 ff. and see also Jens Schovsbo, Morten Rosenmeier and Clement Salung Petersen, *Immaterialret* (6th edn, DJØF Publishing 2021), 425 ff (only in Danish).
94 See, for instance, Judgment from the Maritime and Commercial Court of 30 March 2021, BS-9628/2020-SHR and for more Schovsbo (2022) (n 6) 334 ff.
95 For instance, the Finnish Supreme Administrative Court Judgment of 13 November 2012 in KHO 2012:94. For a case comment on the Judgment, see Pessi Honkasalo and Verna Vesanen, 'There's Many a Slip 'twixt Cup and Lip: On Overall Impression, Nature of the Product and Freedom of the Designer' (2013) 35(4) *European Intellectual Property Review* 236.

B. PRACTICAL ASPECTS OF DESIGN LAW

Nordic designers are not using their national design system nearly as much as they used to. Ever since the entry into force of the RCD system (2003), the number of direct applications (i.e., excluding international application via the Hague system) to the national offices has declined in Denmark, Finland and Sweden. As we can see from the statistics in Table 8.1 below, the high number of direct applications in the past is nowadays just a distant memory: 8.057

Table 8.1   The number of direct national design right applications in Denmark, Finland and Sweden (1980–2020)

	1980	1990	2000	2005	2010	2015	2020
Denmark	1,089	1,466	1,399	364	190	136	140
Finland	925	1,030	962	201	187	182	97
Sweden	2,643	2,751	2,340	774	585	536	241

Source: WIPO Statistics Database at https://www3.wipo.int/ipstats/ accessed 21 February 2022.

It is clear that nowadays many Nordic designers prefer the RCD system. In 2020, Danish applicants applied for 1,904 RCDs. For Finland and Sweden the numbers were, respectively, 1,058 and 1,613.[96] These numbers are eclipsing the present day numbers of direct national design right applications by more than ten times in Denmark and Finland and by eight times for Sweden. 8.058

As was mentioned above, the national filing fees vary between these Nordic countries (of one design: approximately €160 in Denmark; €190 in Sweden and €250 in Finland). Compared to the filing fee of the RCD (€350 of one design), these national filing fees appear relatively pricy in comparison to what you get (national right v. EU-wide right). Still, many Small and Medium Sized Enterprises (SMEs) use the national Design systems. Reasons for this vary, but perhaps lack of knowledge and understanding of the Community Design system (RCDs and also UCDs) is a factor.[97] Also, it should be mentioned here that in the case of Denmark, a need for protection in Greenland requires the use of the national system under the Danish Design Act.[98] 8.059

---

[96]   See for all countries the statistics at https://euipo.europa.eu/tunnel-web/secure/webdav/guest/document_library/contentPdfs/about_euipo/the_office/statistics-of-community-designs_en.pdf accessed 21 February 2022.

[97]   Torben Engholm Kristensen, 'National Designs – Against the Wind' (2020) *Nordiskt Immateriellt Rättsskydd* 246, 247 (on Denmark) and Alhonnoro (n 64) 307 (on Finland). Cf. Oliver Church, Estelle Derclaye and Gilles Stupfler, 'Design Litigation in the EU Member States: are Overlaps with Other Intellectual Property Rights And Unfair Competition Problematic and are SMEs Benefitting from the EU Design Legal Framework?' (2021) 46(1) *European Law Review* 37, 57 ff.

[98]   Greenland is a part of the Kingdom of Denmark (and is covered by the Design Act by Royal Decree No. 656 of 11 June 2010) but not a member of the EU, see Schovsbo (2022) (n 6) 334.

8.060 The speed of the national design registration process in Denmark, Finland or Sweden is not able to compete with the RCD registration process handled by the EUIPO. While the EUIPO boasts that it will examine and register most RCD applications within a couple days,[99] the process is considerably slower in the Nordic countries. The examination of a Danish design application takes approximately a month,[100] while in Sweden the same is around three months[101] and in Finland over four months on average.[102]

8.061 In recent years, popular designs in the Danish, Finnish and Swedish national design systems, when taking into account both direct applications and international applications via the Hague system, have been furniture (Locarno class 6) and spare parts for vehicles (Locarno subclass 12–16).[103] The popularity of the latter is clearly a consequence of the lack of the so-called 'repair clause' in the Danish, Finnish and Swedish Design Acts.[104]

8.062 With regard to court cases, Estelle Derclaye has recorded that between 28 October 2001 (the date of entry into force of the DDir) and 31 August 2017 the following number of court cases involving national or EU designs had been heard in the Nordic countries: Denmark: 35; Finland: 24; and Sweden 23.[105] As regards Denmark, a very interesting feature in these court cases is that in most of them, the plaintiff relied also on other protection systems than only design right system. Out of the Danish cases there were 14 cases in which copyright was used in addition to design rights and as many as 25 cases in which unfair competition was used in addition to design rights.[106] In the end, the additional claims based on copyright were more often rejected than accept-

---

99 See EUIPO website at https://euipo.europa.eu/ohimportal/en/rcd-registration-process accessed 21 February 2022.
100 See DKPTO website at https://www.dkpto.org/apply/apply-designs accessed 21 February 2022.
101 See PRV website at https://www.prv.se/en/designs/prepare-for-the-design-application/processing-of-design-applications/ accessed 21 February 2022.
102 See PRH website at https://www.prh.fi/en/mallioikeudet/for_applicants/application_process_at_the_prh.html accessed 21 February 2022. See also Alhonnoro (n 64), 303.
103 Source: WIPO Statistics Database at https://www3.wipo.int/ipstats/ and EUIPN Design View Database at https://www.tmdn.org/tmdsview-web/welcome#/dsview accessed 21 February 2022.
104 For example, Scania CV AB (a major Swedish company in the automotive industry) has been active in obtaining national design rights in these kinds of spare parts.
105 Derclaye (n 92) 57–59. The dataset encompasses only decisions handed down on substantive aspects of design law (Arts 1–13 and 15 of the DDir and the corresponding articles in the CDReg), i.e., purely procedural or criminal proceedings are excluded. For more information based on the same dataset, see Oliver Church, Estelle Derclaye and Gilles Stupfler, 'An Empirical Analysis of the Design Case Law of the EU Member States' (2019) 50(6) *International Review of Intellectual Property and Competition Law* 685 and Church, Derclaye and Stupfler (2021) (n 97).
106 See Schovsbo (2022) (n 6) (figures generously provided by Professor Estelle Derclay from the dataset described in Church, Derclaye and Stupfler (2019) (n 105), (2021) (n 100) and Derclaye (n 92)).

ed.¹⁰⁷ In comparison, the additional claims based on unfair competition law have been more successful.¹⁰⁸ In Finland and Sweden, additional claims based on other protection systems such as copyright and/or unfair competition have been much less common in litigation. Even taking into account the Finnish and Swedish case law of recent years, there have not been many cases where plaintiffs have relied on other protection systems in addition to design rights.¹⁰⁹

As regards ownership changes and design rights transfers involving design rights, the Danish, Finnish and Swedish Acts provide no formal requirements for transfers or licences. A transfer or licence can be established in writing, orally or be implied by the parties' behaviour. The parties are, of course, advised to use written agreements for clarity and evidentiary purposes. In the case of the transfer of the right to a design or a license, it is possible to request, in return for a prescribed fee, that a note to that effect is entered in the Register of Designs.¹¹⁰   **8.063**

C. COMMENTS, ANALYSIS, EVALUATION

As Denmark, Finland and Sweden are EU Member States, the laws governing design protection in these countries have largely been harmonised with and are similar to those in the rest of the EU. However, there are a few differences – most notably, the Danish, Finnish and Swedish Design Acts do not contain the so-called 'repair clause' which excludes spare parts from design protection. However, the protection for these 'must-match' parts is limited to a maximum of 15 years. According to some commentators, the recent introduction of the 'repair clause' into German law is expected to have 'a knock-on effect on the group of EU countries that have so far opposed the introduction of repair clauses'.¹¹¹ It remains to be seen whether this will be the case in Denmark,   **8.064**

---

107 Church, Derclaye and Stupfler (2021) (n 97) 45.
108 Ibid., 49–50 and also Schovsbo (2020) (n 6) 337 and Schovsbo (2022) (n 6) 333 ff.
109 As for Finland, we only found the Market Court judgment of 16 February 2015 in MAO:110/15. Both the plaintiff and the defendant were selling camouflage hunting clothing with a design depicting a winter forest landscape. In addition to the alleged infringement of RCD, the plaintiff's claims were based on unfair competition (in the form of slavish imitation) and even on trade mark rights. In the end, the Court dismissed all the infringement claims. As for Sweden, see Stockholm District Court judgment of 25 February 2009 in T 27373-06 in which the plaintiff alleged that the pacifier sold by the defendant infringed its national design right and copyright. The Court dismissed both claims. See also Stockholm District Court judgment of 16 December 2009 in T 10454-08 in which it was found by the Court that the defendant had infringed the plaintiff's UCD and copyright when it had been selling boots almost identical to that of the plaintiff.
110 For Denmark, see sec. 51 of the Danish Design Act. For Finland and Sweden, see sec. 27 of the respective Design Acts.
111 Dana Beldiman, Constantin Blanke-Roeser and Anna Tischner, 'Spare Parts and Design Protection – Different Approaches to a Common Problem. Recent Developments from the EU and US Perspective' (2020) 69(7) *GRUR International* 673, 678.

Finland and Sweden. The outcome is difficult to predict. Given that the 'repair clause' has raised criticism and possible problems in Germany,[112] it is perhaps unlikely that the equivalent will be introduced, at least on a voluntary basis, in the Nordic countries. Therefore, a lot depends on the upcoming EU Design reform and possible amendments to the DDir.

8.065 As was explained and described above, the number of judicial decisions has been rather moderate in the area of design law in Denmark, Finland and Sweden. Overall, the courts have closely followed the established principles enshrined in the DDir and CDReg and developed by the EU Courts and EUIPO. It has certainly been a welcome development that Denmark, Finland and Sweden have nowadays a specialist IP courts: the Maritime and Commercial Court (Denmark); the Market Court (Finland) and the Patent and Market Court (Sweden). It is therefore expected that the above described trend will continue in the future. Furthermore, we think that the Nordic IP courts are well placed to develop into internationally renowned IP courts, whose rulings, inter alia, in design matters will also be read and referenced in other European countries.

8.066 Two further observations are worth highlighting. The first concerns the existence of national design systems alongside the CDReg. The second concerns the overlap of rights.[113]

8.067 The EU design system consists of a combination of national protection via the national design systems and EU-wide protection via the CDReg. More than 30 years ago, it was projected in the Green Paper that national design systems might 'slowly fade out' once an effective EU-system with a combination of registered and unregistered design rights and cumulation with copyright had been put in place.[114] At that time, it was however concluded that 'no effort should be displayed in the near future to abolish existing national design protection systems'.[115]

8.068 Since Article 5*quinquies* in the Paris Convention does not seem to imply an obligation to uphold a national design systems alongside the CDReg, it has been suggested by Schovsbo that it is time to re-evaluate the existence of national design systems alongside the CDReg.[116] As it was demonstrated

---

112 Ibid 685.
113 See also Schovsbo (2022) (n 6).
114 Green Paper on the legal protection of industrial design, Brussels, June 1991, III/F/5131191- EN, available at http://aei.pitt.edu/1785/1/design_gp_1.pdf accessed 21 February 2022, 132 ff.
115 Ibid., 134.
116 See Schovsbo (2020) (n 6) 342–43 and Schovsbo (2022) (n 6) 339 ff.

above, Nordic designers have largely moved on to apply for RCDs instead of the national design rights provided by their national design right system. Of course, some drop in numbers was expected after the entry of CDReg, but taking into account the recent statistics on direct national design right applications we have to start asking where lies the critical threshold in the sense that maintaining the national design system is still justified. Is it worth keeping up the national system (e.g., from an economic standpoint) if the amount of annual direct applications lie, let's say, around 100 or even below as is currently the case in Finland?[117] If the so-called 'repair clause' (or something similar) is introduced in the updated DDir and it becomes compulsory for the Member States to adopt it,[118] this further reduces the number of national applications. Another disadvantage of the national design systems is that the registration process in Denmark, Finland and Sweden is compared to RCDs rather slow and relatively pricy compared to what you get in return.

On the other hand, it has been pointed out that there are reasons to justify the existence of national systems. Perhaps most importantly, some national designers (mostly SMEs) may be timid in reaching for EU-wide protection provided by the CDReg.[119] For them, the national protection is a safer option and it brings a greater feeling of accessibility. From the Nordic perspective, the registration authority for the RCDs (EUIPO) may seem to be far away. As a consequence, the lack of a national option could mean that valuable designs would be left unprotected.[120]

8.069

This is a reasonable argument in support of maintaining the national design protection systems.[121] However, is this something that could be solved by increasing the knowledge on the instruments that provide EU-wide protection (RCDs and UCDs) and bringing the EUIPO closer to the users?[122] In the end, we think that in the coming EU Design review it is necessary to adopt a clear and common-sense approach according to which EU States would remain free in deciding whether or not to operate national design protection systems next to the CDReg.

8.070

---

117 In 2021, the number of direct national applications in Finland was again less than one hundred (95). Source: PRH website at https://prh.fi/fi/mallioikeudet/tilastoja/mallien_rekisterointihakemukset_ja_haetut_mallit.html accessed 21 February 2022.
118 As it was hinted at in the Commission Staff Working Document Evaluation of EU legislation on design protection {SWD(2020) 265 final}, Brussels, 6 November 2020, available at https://eur-lex.europa.eu/legal-content/EN/TXT/PDF/?uri=CELEX:52020SC0264&rid=3 accessed 21 February 2022, 68–69.
119 Schovsbo (2020) (n 6) 337 and Schovsbo (2022) (n 6) 340.
120 Kristensen (n 97) 247 and Alhonnoro (n 64), 307.
121 See for more arguments, Schovsbo (2020) (n 6) 337, 343 and Schovsbo (2022) (n 6) 339 f.
122 Alhonnoro (n 64), 308.

8.071 The other observation deals with the overlap of rights. Design law remains in an awkward position especially in the company of copyright law and unfair competition. From the Danish, Finnish and Swedish perspective, the copyright law and unfair competition law are attractive alternatives or supplements to protection by design law.

8.072 Of course, an overlap of rights itself is not an evil. However, the consequences of an overlap can bring unwanted problems. The CJEU's judgment in *Cofemel* has made it more difficult for national courts and legislators to police the border between copyright law and design law.[123] The border between unfair competition law and design law is an even greater problem due to the unharmonised nature of unfair competition law as regards the relationship between commercial actors. More specifically, the problem is that right holders may try to avoid specific limitations and exceptions carved into one system by claiming protection under another system which does not have similar limitations and exceptions. By way of example, if spare parts can gain protection via copyright or unfair competition then the limitations in design law in this respect are being undermined.[124] Another example is that designers rely on alternative protection after the lapse of the three-year term of protection for UCDs. This would undermine the carefully crafted approach in design law to grant short-term protection based on the use of the design and a longer protection based on registration. In view of the foregoing, a reform of the EU Design system should try to adopt a clearer approach to deal with the overlap of rights.[125]

---

123 See, for instance, Schovsbo 2020 (n 6) 340-341.
124 Schovsbo 2020 (n 6) 340-342.
125 See for possible solutions, for instance, Ansgar Ohly, "Buy me because I'm cool': the 'marketing approach' and the overlap between design, trade mark and unfair competition law' in Annette Kur, Marianne Levin and Jens Schovsbo (eds), *The EU Design Approach – A Global Appraisal* (Edward Elgar 2018) 108, 140-141. See also Schovsbo 2020 (n 6), 341-342 and Kur (n 25) 244.

9

DESIGN PATENT LAW IN THE UNITED STATES

Elizabeth Ferrill, Kelly Horn, William Neer and Troy Viger

A. DESCRIPTIVE PART 9.001	(v) Defences to infringement 9.059
1. Substantive Aspects of U.S. Design Patent Law 9.001	(vi) Remedies for infringement 9.063
(a) Sources of design patent law 9.003	4. Significant Judicial Decisions in the United States 9.071
(b) Protectable subject matter 9.006	(a) *Egyptian Goddess, Inc. v. Swisa, Inc.*, 543 F.3d 665 (Fed. Cir. 2008) (en banc) 9.071
(c) Design disclosure requirements 9.008	
(d) Novelty (anticipation) 9.011	
(e) Obviousness (inventive step) 9.013	(b) *International Seaway Trading Corp. v. Walgreens Corp.*, 589 F.3d 1233 (Fed. Cir. 2009) 9.072
(f) Additional considerations 9.014	
(g) Related IP laws and comparison to design protection 9.017	
(i) Utility patents 9.018	(c) *In re SurgiSil, L.L.P.*, 14 F.4th 1380 (Fed. Cir. 2021) 9.074
(ii) Copyright 9.019	(d) *In re Maatita*, 900 F.3d 1369 (Fed. Cir. 2018) 9.078
(iii) Trademarks/trade dress 9.021	(e) *In re Daniels*, 144 F.3d 1452 (Fed. Cir. 1998) 9.081
(iv) Unfair Competition Prevention Acts 9.023	
2. Procedural 9.024	(f) *In re Owens*, 710 F.3d 1362 (Fed. Cir. 2013) 9.084
(a) Registration procedure 9.024	
(b) Overview 9.025	(g) *Hoop v. Hoop*, 279 F.3d 1004 (Fed. Cir. 2002) 9.088
(c) Application requirements 9.027	
(d) Priority 9.035	(h) *Pacific Coast Marine Windshields Ltd. v. Malibu Boats, LLC*, 739 F.3d 694 (Fed. Cir. 2014) 9.089
(e) Expedited examination 9.036	
(f) Amendments 9.037	
(g) International registration 9.038	(i) *Samsung Electronics Co. v. Apple Inc.*, 137 S. Ct. 429 (2016) 9.091
3. Disputes 9.039	
(a) Prosecution 9.039	(j) *Columbia Sportswear N. Am., Inc. v. Seirus Innovative Accessories, Inc.*, 80 F.4th 1363 (Fed. Cir. 2023) 9.092
(i) Administrative body 9.039	
(ii) Legal grounds 9.041	
(iii) Challenges 9.043	B. PRACTICAL ASPECTS OF DESIGN LAW 9.095
(iv) Timing 9.046	1. Statistics/Trends 9.095
(v) Fees 9.047	2. Business Aspects: Transferability/Licensing 9.104
(b) Litigation 9.048	
(i) Related enforcement proceedings to prosecution 9.048	3. Case Studies 9.107
	C. COMMENTS, ANALYSIS, AND EVALUATION 9.116
(ii) Infringement 9.049	
(iii) Direct infringement 9.053	1. Comments on Present Legal Framework (Legislation and Case
(iv) Indirect infringement 9.057	

Law)	9.116	Amendment Is Required (e.g., Inconsistencies, Gaps, and Insufficiencies), and How They Should Be Corrected	9.122
(a) Design patent enforcement in district court	9.116		
(b) Design patent enforcement at the International Trade Commission	9.117	(a) Damages for design patent infringement	9.122
2. Design Law Reform De Lege Ferenda	9.119	(b) Multi-component products under the total profits rule	9.124
(a) Conflict between product life cycle and design patent pendency at the USPTO	9.119	4. Future Outlook in Light of New Technologies	9.128
3. Areas in Which Improvement/			

A. DESCRIPTIVE PART

1. Substantive Aspects of U.S. Design Patent Law

9.001 In the United States (U.S.), design patents protect 'any new, original and ornamental design for an article of manufacture.'[1] Design patents expire 15 years after the date of grant.[2] Design patents give the owner the right to exclude others from practicing the patented design. In other words, any person or entity—who without authorization—'makes, uses, offers to sell, or sells any patented invention' (or a colorable imitation thereof) in the U.S. or imports said invention into the U.S. will be liable as an infringer, entitling the patentee to damages and injunctive relief.[3]

9.002 This section first details the sources of design protection before delving into patentability requirements, such as novelty, obviousness, and more. Then, it discusses other forms of intellectual property ('IP') protection that may also protect ornamental designs.

(a) Sources of design patent law

9.003 The Patent Act is the statutory law that governs design patents. Although the original Patent Act only established protection for inventions using utility patents, since the mid-1800s, design patents have been available for design protection. Sections 171–173 of 35 U.S.C. created design patents in the U.S.[4] Other provisions of the Patent Act covering utility patents, however, gener-

---

1   35 U.S.C. § 171(a).
2   35 U.S.C. § 173.
3   35 U.S.C. § 271(a).
4   35 U.S.C. §§ 171–173.

ally apply to design patents with a few exceptions.⁵ For example, the validity requirements of 35 U.S.C. §§ 102 (novelty or anticipation), 103 (obviousness or inventive step), and 112 (enablement, written description, definiteness), among many others, apply to design patents, while the right of priority, the term of a design patent, the existence of certain damages, and the utility requirement of § 101 are different.⁶

There are a few additional sources of law that govern or impact design patents. The U.S. Patent and Trademark Office ('USPTO') is responsible for examining and issuing design patents. The agency implements rules that further define the patentability of a design, which can be found in title 37 of the Code of Federal Regulations ('C.F.R.').⁷ The USPTO also outlines guidelines for the examination process in various sections of the Manual of Patent Examining Procedure ('MPEP'). Rules in the C.F.R. can have the weight of law, whereas the MPEP does not.⁸   9.004

The Federal District Courts, Court of Appeals for the Federal Circuit, and the Supreme Court of the United States interpret design patent laws and decide issues of validity and infringement.⁹ There are also a few adjudicative bodies at agencies that can resolve some design patent issues as well. These courts and adjudications are discussed in detail in the 'Disputes' section below.   9.005

(b) Protectable subject matter

As noted above, design patents in the U.S. protect 'any new, original and ornamental design for an article of manufacture.'¹⁰ This could include the shape or configuration of an article, the surface ornamentation of an article, or a combination of both.¹¹ An article is a type of product, such as a chair, for example.   9.006

---

5   35 U.S.C. § 171(b) ('The provisions of this title relating to patents for inventions shall apply to patents for designs, except as otherwise provided.').
6   See 35 U.S.C. §§ 172 ('The right of priority provided for by subsections (a) through (d) of section 119 shall be six months in the case of designs. The right of priority provided for by section 119(e) shall not apply to designs.'), 173 ('Patents for designs shall be granted for the term of 15 years from the date of grant.'), 289 ('Additional remedy for infringement of design patent'); *In re Finch*, 535 F.2d 70, 71–72 (C.C.P.A. 1976) (holding that § 101 does not apply to design patents).
7   See 37 C.F.R. §§ 1.3, 1.63, 1.76, 1.84, 1.121, 1.152–1.155.
8   See, e.g., *Cuozzo Speed Techs., LLC v. Lee*, 579 U.S. 261, 276 (2016) (holding that the USPTO's claim construction rule was proper and should be given deference); *Cleveland Clinic Found. v. True Health Diagnostics LLC*, 760 F. App'x 1013, 1020–21 (Fed. Cir. 2019) (holding that USPTO guidance should not be afforded deference).
9   U.S. Const. art. III § 2; 28 U.S.C. §§ 1295, 1331, 1338(a).
10 35 U.S.C. § 171(a).
11 MPEP § 1504.01; see also *In re Schnell*, 46 F.2d 203, 206 (C.C.P.A. 1931); *Ex parte* Donaldson, 26 U.S.P.Q.2d 1250, 1251 (B.P.A.I. 1992); *Gorham Mfg. Co. v. White*, 81 U.S. 511, 524 (1871).

The design is limited to the article recited in its claims[12] and must be tied to an article—meaning it cannot be just a design by itself or a design per se as in other countries.[13] A design patent, however, does not need to claim the entire article, nor does the claimed design need to be visible during the entire use of the article.[14] For example, design patents can protect graphical user interfaces or icons as 'surface ornamentation[s]' on a display screen.[15]

9.007 The underlying article of manufacture to which the claimed design is applied must serve a function, but the function of the underlying article must not be confused with 'functionality' of the design.[16] A design patent cannot claim a design that is purely functional, meaning a design that is 'dictated by' its function and completely lacking in ornamentality.[17] When a claimed design contains both functional elements and elements that have ornamental aspects, the scope of the claimed design must be construed to identify the functional elements.[18]

(c) Design disclosure requirements

9.008 Design patents essentially contain two parts: a claim and a specification. The claim recites a variation of the phrase: 'the ornamental design for [*an article*] as shown and described.'[19] The specification contains the visual depiction of the claimed design as well as any written description required to clearly define the design and enable a designer of ordinary skill in the art to make or re-create the design under § 112.[20] The visual depiction represents the design in drawing or photograph forms, but one cannot mix the two forms.[21] There is no limit or requirement to the number of views of the design, but the design must be 'sufficiently' disclosed.[22] Sufficiency of disclosure will depend on the complexity of the design;[23] however, design applications will generally include the following

---

12 *In re SurgiSil, L.L.P.*, 14 F.4th 1380, 1382 (Fed. Cir. 2021).
13 MPEP § 1502 (citing *Ex parte* Cady, 1916 C.D. 62, 232 O.G. 621 (Comm'r Pat. 1916)).
14 *In re Webb*, 916 F.2d 1553, 1557–58 (Fed. Cir. 1990) (holding that designs can be visible at the 'beginning after completion of manufacture or assembly and ending with the ultimate destruction, loss, or disappearance of the article').
15 *See* MPEP § 1504.01(a).I.A.
16 *Hupp v. Siroflex of Am., Inc.*, 122 F.3d 1456, 1460 (Fed. Cir. 1997).
17 *Sport Dimension, Inc. v. Coleman Co.*, 820 F.3d 1316, 1320 (Fed. Cir. 2016).
18 Ibid., at 1320–21.
19 Design Patent Application Guide, USPTO, https:// www .uspto .gov/ patents/ basics/ types -patent -applications/design-patent-application-guide#single (last visited Jan. 3, 2022).
20 35 U.S.C. § 112; see also MPEP § 1504.04.I (detailing the sufficiency of a design patent's specification).
21 MPEP § 1504.02.
22 Ibid.
23 *In re Maatita*, 900 F.3d 1369, 1377–78 (holding that a single drawing was sufficient to satisfy the enablement and definiteness requirements of § 112).

views: one or two perspective (to clearly depict a three-dimensional design), front elevation, rear elevation, left side, right side, top plan, and bottom plan. Occasionally, applicants will include exploded views, alternate configurations (e.g., open and closed), or cross-sectional views.

9.009 When the claimed design is depicted in drawings, the type of line defines the claim scope. A solid line shows claimed portions of the design, whereas broken lines (e.g., dash-dash or dot-dash) may depict unclaimed subject matter, such as environment, boundaries, or fold lines.[24] Broken lines cannot be used to show hidden or unseen features within a view.[25] And the applicant must explain what the broken lines mean in the specification.[26] Surface shading may be used to more clearly convey the shape and contours of the claimed design.[27]

9.010 The procedural aspects of design patent prosecution are further detailed below.

(d) Novelty (anticipation)

9.011 To be protectable, a design must be novel. It cannot have been 'patented, described in a printed publication, or in public use, on sale, or otherwise available to the public before the effective filing date' of the claimed design.[28] It further cannot have been described in an application for a patent that has or is deemed to have been published.[29] An effective filing date is the earliest date that the application can claim priority. Because design patents cannot claim priority to a provisional application, this date will either be the actual filing date or the filing date of an international design application. Section 172 (and an international treaty) limits the time design patents can claim priority to six months.[30] Not every disclosure of a design before the effective filing date, however, will bar patent protection of a design. If the disclosure was made or authorized by the inventor less than one year before the effective filing date, then it will not bar protection.[31] This allows for inventor-originated advertising, promotion, and/or sale of the claimed design within one year before filing for protection.

---

24   37 C.F.R. § 1.84.
25   MPEP § 1503.02.
26   See, e.g., *Apple, Inc. v. Samsung Elecs. Co.*, 678 F.3d 1314, 1317 (Fed. Cir. 2012); *In re Owens*, 710 F.3d 1362, 1367 n.1 (Fed. Cir. 2013).
27   37 C.F.R. § 1.84(m).
28   35 U.S.C. § 102(a)(1).
29   Ibid. at § 102(a)(2). Applications are deemed to be published if filed under 35 U.S.C. § 122(b), which includes published international applications designating the U.S.
30   See 35 U.S.C. § 172 ('The right of priority provided for by subsections (a) through (d) of section 119 shall be six months in the case of designs. The right of priority provided for by section 119(e) shall not apply to designs.').
31   35 U.S.C. § 102(b)(1).

9.012 When a design is not novel because it existed before the effective filing date, it is said to be 'anticipated' by prior art. Novelty, or anticipation, is determined through the eyes of an 'ordinary observer'—the typical purchaser of the goods at issue, who 'view[s] the differences between the patented design and the accused product in the context of the prior art.'[32] The test for anticipation is the same as the test for design patent infringement: the 'ordinary observer test.'[33] In the ordinary observer test, the inquiry is whether in the eye of the ordinary observer, who is familiar with the prior art, given such attention as the purchaser usually gives, the claimed design and the accused design are 'substantially the same' such that the ordinary observer would be deceived into purchasing one design supposing it to be the other design.[34]

(e) Obviousness (inventive step)

9.013 Under § 103, designs must also be 'non-obvious' to obtain protection.[35] A design is obvious if, before the effective filing date of the application, 'the differences between the claimed invention and the prior art are such that the claimed invention as a whole would have been obvious ... to a person having ordinary skill in the art.'[36] This is similar to the 'inventive step' requirement of other countries. A designer of ordinary skill, rather than an ordinary observer, is the perspective used to determine obviousness.[37] While novelty asks whether one prior art reference is similar to the claimed design, obviousness generally asks whether a designer of ordinary skill in the art would have combined multiple references to achieve the claimed design.[38] To evaluate obviousness, first determine the scope of analogous art and then visually compare the appearance of the prior art with that of the design claim at issue.[39] Analogous prior art is within the scope of the claimed design when they are within the same field of endeavor, which is a factual inquiry decided on a case-by-case basis.[40] This factor is not dispositive, and designs outside the claimed design's field of endeavor may still be analogous art.[41] The visual similarity of the designs is

---

32 *Egyptian Goddess, Inc. v. Swisa, Inc.*, 543 F.3d 665, 676 (Fed. Cir. 2008) (en banc).
33 *Int'l Seaway Trading Corp. v. Walgreens Corp.*, 589 F.3d 1233, 1240-41 (Fed. Cir. 2009).
34 Ibid., at 1239.
35 35 U.S.C. § 103.
36 35 U.S.C. § 103; see also *High Point Design LLC v. Buyers Direct, Inc.*, 730 F.3d 1301, 1313 (Fed. Cir. 2013).
37 35 U.S.C. § 103; see also *High Point Design LLC*, 730 F.3d at 1313 ('The use of an "ordinary observer" standard to assess the potential obviousness of a design patent runs contrary to the precedent of this court and our predecessor court, under which the obviousness of a design patent must, instead, be assessed from the viewpoint of an ordinary designer.').
38 *LKQ Corp. v. GM Glob. Tech. Operations LLC*, 102 F.4th 1280, 1298 (Fed. Cir. 2024).
39 Ibid. at 1295–298.
40 Ibid. at 1297–298.
41 Ibid. at 1298.

evaluated from the perspective of a designer with ordinary abilities in the type of articles at issue and does not have a threshold requirement.[42] Secondary considerations may also be applied in the obviousness analysis, such as commercial success, long-felt but unsolved needs, and failure of others.[43]

(f) Additional considerations

9.014 In addition to the standard requirements (novelty, nonobviousness, and sufficient disclosures), there are other considerations that affect a design's patentability.

9.015 A design not only has to be 'new' but also must be 'original' to be patentable.[44] The purpose of the originality requirement is unclear; however, the MPEP instructs that a design that 'simulates an existing object or person' will not satisfy the originality requirement.[45]

9.016 Designs are only allowed to be patented once and must contain patentably distinct subject matter from related applications.[46] Allowing multiple patents with different expiration dates to cover the same design could improperly extend the term of the design's protection.[47] During prosecution, an examiner may reject an application for double-patenting when she finds that a second application is an obvious variant of a first-filed patent or application. To overcome such a rejection, an applicant may file a terminal disclaimer that limits the term of the second application to the first's term—this also assumes that the same entity owns both designs.[48]

(g) Related IP laws and comparison to design protection

9.017 U.S. law offers additional IP protection for the two- and three-dimensional appearance of products that can, at times, overlap with design patent protection. Such protection can include utility patents, copyrights, trademarks or trade dress, and unfair competition prevention. Although nonregistered (or

---

42 Ibid. at 1298–299.
43 *Campbell Soup Co. v. Gamon Plus, Inc.*, 10 F.4th 1268, 1276–77 (Fed. Cir. 2021) (providing an example of commercial success as applied to obviousness of design patents).
44 35 U.S.C. § 171.
45 MPEP § 1504.01(d); see *Int'l Seaway Trading*, 589 F.3d at 1238:
    The purpose of incorporating an originality requirement is unclear; it likely was designed to incorporate the copyright concept of originality—requiring that the work be original with the author, although this concept did not find its way into the language of the Copyright Act until 1909. In any event, the courts have not construed the word 'original' as requiring that design patents be treated differently than utility patents.' (citation omitted).
46 *See* MPEP § 1504.06.II.
47 Ibid.
48 *In re Geiger*, 425 F.2d 1276, 1279–80 (C.C.P.A. 1970); *see also* MPEP § 804.02.II.

unregistered) design protection exists in other countries, the U.S. does not offer such protection.

(i) Utility patents

9.018 Utility patents protect inventions rather than designs. That being said, both utility and design patents may protect the same article. For example, a utility patent could cover the way an article functions or is used while a design patent would be limited to the appearance of the article.[49] Utility patents have terms of twenty (20) years from the earliest effective filing date.[50]

(ii) Copyright

9.019 Copyright law protects the original expression of an idea, including pictorial, graphic, sculptural, and architectural works.[51] A work is 'copyrighted' at the moment it is fixed to a tangible medium of expression. Although it is not mandatory to register a copyright, registration is required to enforce a copyright.[52] During registration, the work is examined for originality (i.e., the work is both independently created by the author and contains a minimal degree of creativity).[53] Copyright protection lasts for the life of the author plus seventy (70) years for works created by a natural person, or 120 years from creation or ninety-five (95) years from publication, whichever is shorter, for 'work[s] made for hire.'[54] Thus, copyright protection lasts significantly longer than design patent protection and has a lower bar to acquire protection.

9.020 Copyright protection may coexist with design patent protection to the extent that the expression is ornamental. However, copyright protection does not apply to functional aspects of a product. If a work is a 'useful article'—i.e., one that is not merely aesthetic in nature but has an intrinsic utilitarian purpose—then only certain nonfunctional aspects of the design may be subject to protection.[55] To determine whether an aesthetic element of a useful article is protectable, the element must (1) 'be perceived as a two- or three-dimensional work of art separate from the useful article' and (2) 'qualify as a protectable pictorial, graphic, or sculptural work—either on its own or fixed in some other tangible medium of expression—if it were imagined separately from the useful

---

49   See 35 U.S.C. §§ 101, 171.
50   35 U.S.C. § 154.
51   See 17 U.S.C. § 102.
52   *Fourth Est. Pub. Benefit Corp. v. Wall-Street.com, LLC*, 139 S. Ct. 881, 889 (2019).
53   See *Feist Publ'ns, Inc. v. Rural Tel. Serv. Co.*, 499 U.S. 340, 345 (1991).
54   17 U.S.C. § 302.
55   *Star Athletica, L.L.C. v. Varsity Brands, Inc.*, 137 S. Ct. 1002, 1007 (2017).

article into which it is incorporated.'[56] Therefore, it is much harder to copyright an ornamental aspect of a product than it is to obtain design protection for it.

(iii) Trademarks/trade dress

9.021 Trademarks identify the source of goods and/or services in commerce.[57] 'Trade dress' is a trademark composed of a product's shape or packaging. Thus, design patent rights may also coexist with trade dress rights.[58] Trademarks are registerable at the USPTO and have indefinitely renewable terms of twenty (20) years from the date of issue, provided that the owner continues to use the trademark in commerce.[59]

9.022 Trade dress must be nonfunctional and distinctive.[60] Product packaging trade dress can be inherently distinctive, which makes it protectable upon first use.[61] Product design trade dress, on the other hand, requires a showing of 'secondary meaning.'[62] This takes time as consumers have to associate the design with the source of the product to be afforded protection. To register a trade dress under this category requires evidence of extensive commercial use, advertising, and sales to prove that consumers 'look for' the particular product shape or design when making purchasing decisions.[63] Proof of continuous and exclusive use of a trade dress for five years is generally acceptable proof of secondary meaning. Design patents are an option to protect the design during this five-year period.

(iv) Unfair Competition Prevention Acts

9.023 Unfair competition laws protect against deceptive business practices that can harm consumers and other businesses. These laws encompass broad concepts, such as torts for false advertising, right of publicity, and even trade secrets. Many of these causes of action are irrelevant to designs. Unfair competition laws can, however, protect against the unauthorized use of source-identifying product packaging or configurations that cause consumer confusion.

---

56 Ibid.
57 15 U.S.C. § 1127.
58 See *TrafFix Devices, Inc. v. Mktg. Displays, Inc.*, 532 U.S. 23, 29–30 (2001) (holding claimed subject matter of utility patent creates 'strong evidentiary inference of functionality' in the trade dress context).
59 15 U.S.C. § 1052; 37 C.F.R. § 2.181.
60 15 U.S.C. § 1052.
61 15 U.S.C. § 1052.
62 *Converse, Inc. v. ITC*, 909 F.3d 1110, 1116–17 (Fed. Cir. 2018).
63 Ibid.; see also *Two Pesos, Inc. v. Taco Cabana, Inc.*, 505 U.S. 763, 769 (1992).

2. Procedural

(a) Registration procedure

9.024 The U.S. has a patent examination system. This means that each design application is not only reviewed for filing formalities but is also reviewed for substantive requirements. The USPTO is the federal agency responsible for examining design patent applications and issuing design patents. Technology Center 2900, one of the nine technology centers, solely examines design patent applications.

(b) Overview

9.025 Ornamentality, novelty, nonobviousness, enablement, and definiteness are statutory requirements to obtain a design patent. If a patent examiner determines that the design patent application does not satisfy any one of these requirements, the examiner will reject the application and issue a 'nonfinal' office action. The applicant may respond to the office action by way of amendment to the claim or by providing convincing arguments that the rejection should be withdrawn to obtain a notice of allowability. The applicant may have to amend the specification or figures if the applicant is rejected under 35 U.S.C. §§ 102, 103, or 112, or may make substantive arguments if rejected under §§ 171, 102, 103, or 112.[64] The USPTO may issue a 'final' rejection if it maintains its rejections or finds new problems with the application. The applicant then may respond and decide whether to only submit arguments, appeal to the Patent Trial and Appeal Board ('PTAB'), or file for a continued prosecution application.

9.026 The applicant has three months to respond, and this deadline may be extended in one-month increments for a total of six months with the payment of extra fees.[65] The USPTO may issue an *Ex parte Quayle* if it determines the claims should be allowed but the application fails to satisfy formal requirements.[66] The USPTO will then issue a notice of allowance and set a three-month deadline to pay an issue fee.[67]

(c) Application requirements

9.027 The process for obtaining a design patent begins with filing an application. To obtain a filing date, a design application must contain (1) a design application

---

[64] Sydney English and Elizabeth D. Ferrill, *Comparative Global Design Law* ch. 8, at 4 (2020).
[65] Ibid.
[66] MPEP § 714.14; English and Ferrill, ibid., at 5.
[67] MPEP §§ 607, 714.14; English and Ferrill, ibid.

transmittal form, (2) a fee transmittal form, (3) an application data sheet, (4) a specification, (5) drawings or photographs, and (6) an executed oath or declaration.[68]

The specification of an application includes a title that identifies the article of manufacture in which the design is embodied.[69] The specification can also include a preamble, which would include a description of the nature and the intended use of the article.[70] The specification must also include a single claim and a description of the figures.[71] The description describes the relationship between the figures and defines drafting techniques. The specification may also reference an appendix to help avoid a new matter rejection. **9.028**

Drawings represent the design and contain enough views to completely disclose the design.[72] An application data sheet ('ADS') includes the title, international and foreign application information, applicant information, assignee information, and other information. **9.029**

An inventor or assignee can file an application electronically using the electronic filing system ('Patent Center'), which is available 24 hours a day, seven days per week. Alternatively, the application may be filed by paper using Priority Mail Express from the U.S. Postal Service for an additional fee. **9.030**

In the U.S., the applicant for a design application must identify the inventor or inventors.[73] An inventor is a human who 'conceived the invention.'[74] Anyone who contributes to the claimed design will be considered an inventor. This is true regardless of whether they physically worked together, contributed disproportionately,[75] or were unaware of each other. To establish joint inventorship, there must be a 'quantum of collaboration or connection.'[76] Each inventor must apply for the patent or be named in the application for an assignee-applicant and must execute an oath or declaration.[77] **9.031**

---

68   MPEP § 1503.01; 37 C.F.R. § 1.154.
69   MPEP § 1503.01; English and Ferrill, *supra* note 64, at 2.
70   MPEP § 1503.01; English and Ferrill, ibid.
71   MPEP § 1503.01; English and Ferrill, ibid.
72   MPEP § 1503.02; English and Ferrill, ibid., at 3.
73   MPEP § 2109; English and Ferrill, ibid.
74   MPEP § 2109; English and Ferrill, ibid.
75   MPEP § 2109.01; 35 U.S.C. § 116(a). Co-inventors also need not contribute to every claim of the patent. English and Ferrill, ibid.
76   MPEP § 2109.01; Kimberly-Clark Corp. v. Procter & Gamble Distrib. Co., 973 F.2d 911, 916–17 (Fed. Cir. 1992); English and Ferrill, ibid., at 3.
77   37 C.F.R. §§ 1.53(f), 1.63; English and Ferrill, ibid., at 3.

9.032 The applicant may be either one or all of the named inventors or a party that has been assigned the rights in the application. Each applicant's name, residence, and country of citizenship must be provided.[78]

9.033 The named inventors are initially vested with ownership of the application, but the rights are assignable, which must be signed and in writing, to a different entity (including individuals or corporations).[79] An applicant may convey ownership at the time of filing, during prosecution, or after the patent has issued. An entity must obtain assignments from every inventor to own the entire interest in the application.[80] Assignments should be recorded but are not required.[81]

9.034 Under 35 U.S.C. § 173, patents issued from design applications filed on or after May 13, 2015, shall be granted for the term of 15 years.[82]

(d) Priority

9.035 An applicant may claim priority to a nonprovisional U.S. utility patent application or a prior U.S. design patent application, provided that the application is still pending, or by claiming priority to a prior-filed foreign application for the same design within six months of the earliest foreign filing for that design.[83] A design application may not claim priority to a U.S. provisional application. The applicant may claim priority at any time during prosecution. The applicant must perfect a priority claim by completing the relevant section on the ADS and by filing a certified copy of the priority application. For the USPTO to recognize the priority claim, the applicant must file a copy of the certified priority document before the notice of allowance is issued.

(e) Expedited examination

9.036 In the U.S., design patent applications do not publish before issuance. An applicant may request to expedite the examination of a design application. To do so, the applicant must file a complete application with drawings and an information disclosure statement ('IDS').[84] Additionally, the applicant must perform a pre-examination search and file a petition, which includes a fee

---

78 37 C.F.R. § 1.76(b)(1); 35 U.S.C. § 115; English and Ferrill, ibid.
79 35 U.S.C. § 261; English and Ferrill, ibid.
80 MPEP § 301.IV; English and Ferrill, ibid.
81 35 U.S.C. § 261; English and Ferrill, ibid. An unrecorded assignment will not have superior rights to a subsequent transaction for the same patent if the third-party purchaser did not have knowledge of the assignment.
82 Pre-AIA 35 U.S.C. § 173. However, applications filed before May 13, 2015, shall be granted for the term of 14 years. Ibid.
83 35 U.S.C. §§ 119(a)–(d), 172; *see also* MPEP § 1504.10.
84 English and Ferrill, *supra* note 64, at 4.

and a statement that the search was performed in a specified field or fields of search.[85]

(f) Amendments

9.037 To file an amendment to an application, no 'new matter' may be added.[86] New matter is any change or amendment to the application that is not supported by the initial filing. Generally, existing solid lines may be changed to broken lines, and vice versa. A broken boundary line may be added so long as 'it is clear from the design specification that the boundary of the claimed design is a straight broken line connecting the ends of existing full lines defining the claimed design.'[87] Any amendment, whether narrowing or broadening the design, must be supported by the initial filing.[88]

(g) International registration

9.038 The U.S. joined the Hague Agreement Concerning the International Registration of Industrial Designs.[89] Since 2015, the U.S. may receive indirect filings by way of international applications. The USPTO examines Hague applications designating the U.S. the same way it examines U.S. design applications. However, Hague applications are published prior to issuance, unlike the U.S. Thus, a patentee may recover pre-grant reasonable royalties (also known as provisional rights) following a finding of infringement under certain circumstances.[90] The Hague international registration is not self-executing in the U.S.

3. Disputes

(a) Prosecution

(i) Administrative body
9.039 The PTAB is an administrative body of the USPTO consisting of administrative patent judges ('APJs').[91] The PTAB is responsible for deciding issues of patentability and, as such, hears applicants' appeals regarding final rejections and appeals of re-examinations, and conducts derivation proceedings, *inter*

---

85 Ibid.
86 MPEP § 1504.04; English and Ferrill, ibid., at 4.
87 MPEP § 1503.02.III; English and Ferrill, ibid.
88 In re Daniels, 144 F.3d 1452, 1456–57 (Fed. Cir. 1998); English and Ferrill, ibid.
89 *See* Hague Agreement Concerning the International Registration of Industrial Designs, USPTO, https://www.uspto.gov/patent/initiatives/hague-agreement-concerning-international-registration-industrial-designs (last visited Dec. 29, 2021).
90 *See* 35 U.S.C. § 154(d).
91 35 U.S.C. § 6(a).

partes reviews ('IPRs'), and post-grant reviews ('PGRs') that challenge the patentability of issued design patents.[92] These hearings are generally held before a panel of three APJs; IPRs and PGRs are discussed further below.

9.040 As a member of the PTAB, the USPTO Director is also responsible for certificates of correction to correct typographical errors and reissues for patents whose specification, drawings, or scope are substantively defective.[93]

(ii) Legal grounds

9.041 An IPR may only be brought under two statutory grounds—anticipation (under 35 U.S.C. § 102) and obviousness (under 35 U.S.C. § 103) based on patents and/or printed publications.[94]

9.042 Alternatively, PGRs may be brought under any statutory grounds to challenge a patent's validity, excluding a failure to disclose the best mode. As such, in addition to patents and/or printed publications, a PGR may incorporate other evidence of public exposure, including public use and sales activities.

(iii) Challenges

9.043 Any third party may file a petition instituting an IPR.[95] An IPR may not be filed if more than one year has passed since the petitioner was served a complaint alleging infringement of the patent, the petitioner has filed a civil action challenging the patent's validity, or the petitioner is estopped.[96]

9.044 Any third party may also file a petition instituting a PGR if it is filed before the petitioner has filed a civil action challenging the validity of the design patent or the petitioner is precluded.[97]

9.045 A petitioner will be estopped from initiating a proceeding before the USPTO, a district court, or the International Trade Commission on any ground that 'the petitioner raised or reasonably could have raised' during the IPR or PGR.[98]

(iv) Timing

9.046 If the patent is filed on or after March 16, 2013, then the patent is covered by section 3(n)(1) of the Leahy-Smith America Invents Act ('AIA').[99] The IPR

---

92 35 U.S.C. § 6(b)(1)–(4).
93 35 U.S.C. §§ 251, 255.
94 37 C.F.R. § 42.104.
95 37 C.F.R. § 42.101.
96 *Id.*
97 37 C.F.R. § 42.201.
98 35 U.S.C. §§ 315(e), 325(e); English and Ferrill, *supra* note 64, at 12.
99 English and Ferrill, ibid.

must be filed nine months after the grant of the design patent.[100] If the patent is filed before March 16, 2013, then the IPR petition may be filed at any time. But if a PGR is filed, then the IPR petition may only be filed after the termination date of the PGR.[101]

(v) Fees

A fee of $19,000 USD must accompany an IPR petition, and $20,000 USD for a PGR petition, before a petition will be accorded a filing date.[102] At the time of filing, the petitioner must also pay the post-institution fees of 22,500 USD and 27,500 USD, respectively,[103] but this fee will be refunded if the petition is not instituted.[104] The USPTO updates these fees on an almost annual basis.[105]

9.047

(b) Litigation

(i) Related enforcement proceedings to prosecution

When a patentee initiates an infringement action in district court, it is up to the district court's discretion whether to stay the co-pending district court litigation. However, a district court must stay infringement litigation that is initiated by a party who has previously initiated an IPR or PGR.[106] This stay may be lifted at the request of the patent owner if the patent owner files an infringement action or counterclaim against the petitioner or if the petitioner moves to dismiss the civil action.[107]

9.048

(ii) Infringement

Under 35 U.S.C. § 271, any person or entity—who without authorization—'makes, uses, offers to sell, or sells any patented invention' in the U.S. or imports said invention into the U.S. will be liable as an infringer, entitling the patentee to damages and injunctive relief.[108] Section 289 discusses the unauthorized use for sale or manufacture of patented subject matter, and a patentee may be awarded the infringer's total profits.[109] Section 289 applies only to the

9.049

---

100 35 U.S.C. § 311(c)(1).
101 37 C.F.R. § 42.102; 35 U.S.C. § 321.
102 37 C.F.R. § 42.15(a)(1), (b)(1). Only one patent may be challenged in each petition. Multiple petitions may be filed on a single patent.
103 37 C.F.R. § 42.15(a)(2), (b)(2).
104 *See* Frequently Asked Questions, PTAB E2E (July 11, 2016), https://www.uspto.gov/sites/default/files/documents/PTAB%20E2E%20Frequently%20Asked%20Questions%20July%2011%202016.pdf (last visited June 4, 2024).
105 English and Ferrill, *supra* note 64, at 16. Current fees can be found on the USPTO's website at https://www.uspto.gov/learning-and-resources/fees-and-payment/uspto-fee-schedule#Patent%20Petition%20Fee (last visited June 4, 2024).
106 35 U.S.C. §§ 315(a)(2), 325(a)(2).
107 35 U.S.C. §§ 315(a)(2), 325(a)(2).
108 35 U.S.C. § 271; English and Ferrill, *supra* note 64, at 16.
109 35 U.S.C. § 289; English and Ferrill, ibid.

infringement of designs.¹¹⁰ A plaintiff must prove by a preponderance of the evidence that the defendant infringes a design patent.¹¹¹ The issue is a question of fact.

9.050 Determining design patent infringement involves two steps. First, the court determines the scope of the claims.¹¹² The second determination is whether the claims encompass the accused product.¹¹³

9.051 In construing the scope of the design, 'the claimed ornamental features of all figures of a design' must be considered.¹¹⁴ The court considers the language of the claim and the figures of the patent. The written description is considered to see if it disclaims, characterizes, or limits any design features.¹¹⁵ Elements in solid lines define the claimed design and elements in broken lines depict unclaimed subject matter.¹¹⁶

9.052 Prosecution history estoppel and functionality may also limit the scope of the claimed design. Canceling a design in response to a restriction requirement, if not filed in a divisional application, may narrow the resulting patented claim.¹¹⁷ Arguments made during the prosecution of the application may also limit the scope of the claim.¹¹⁸ Functional aspects of the design may also limit the scope of the claimed design, which 'must be limited to the ornamental aspects of the design, and does not extend to 'the broader general design concept.'¹¹⁹ Finally, prior art may limit the scope of the claimed design.¹²⁰

(iii) Direct infringement

9.053 After claim construction, the claim 'must be compared to the accused design to determine whether there has been infringement.'¹²¹ In 2008, the Federal

---

110 See generally 35 U.S.C. § 289.
111 See *Richardson v. Stanley Works, Inc.*, 597 F.3d 1288, 1295 (Fed. Cir. 2010); see also *L.A. Gear, Inc. v. Thom McAn Shoe Co.*, 988 F.2d 1117, 1124 (Fed. Cir. 1993).
112 See *Markman v. Westview Instruments, Inc.*, 52 F.3d 967, 976–79 (Fed. Cir. 1995) (en banc), *aff'd*, 517 U.S. 370 (1996).
113 Ibid. at 976.
114 *Contessa Food Prods., Inc. v. Conagra, Inc.*, 282 F.3d 1370, 1379 (Fed. Cir. 2002); English and Ferrill, *supra* note 64, at 16.
115 English and Ferrill, ibid.
116 See *Contessa Food Prods.*, 282 F.3d at 1378, abrogated on other grounds *by Egyptian Goddess*, 543 F.3d 665; English and Ferrill, *supra* note 64.
117 *See Pac. Coast Marine Windshields Ltd. v. Malibu Boats, LLC*, 739 F.3d 694, 703–04 (Fed. Cir. 2014).
118 See *Goodyear Tire & Rubber Co. v. Hercules Tire & Rubber Co.*, 162 F.3d 1113, 1116 (Fed. Cir. 1998), abrogated on other grounds by *Egyptian Goddess*, 543 F.3d 665.
119 *Ethicon Endo-Surgery, Inc. v. Covidien, Inc.*, 796 F.3d 1312, 1333 (Fed. Cir. 2015) (citation omitted). But functional elements of a design may have ornamental aspects that are included in the construction.
120 *Egyptian Goddess*, 543 F.3d at 680.
121 *Elmer v. ICC Fabricating, Inc.*, 67 F.3d 1571, 1577 (Fed. Cir. 1995).

Circuit modified the ordinary observer test to determine whether designs are substantially the same 'in light of the prior art.'[122] The ordinary observer analysis 'is not limited to those features visible at the point of sale, but instead must encompass all ornamental features visible at any time during normal use of the product.'[123]

Under the ordinary observer test, courts focus on the 'actual product that is presented for purchase, and the ordinary purchaser of *that* product.'[124] The 'purchaser' may be the end consumer.[125]

9.054

Courts look at two points in their analysis of infringement. First, '[w]here the claimed and accused designs are 'sufficiently distinct' and 'plainly dissimilar,' the patentee fails to meet its burden of proving infringement as a matter of law.'[126] However, '[i]f the claimed and accused designs are not plainly dissimilar,' then courts compare the most relevant prior art to the claimed design and the accused product.[127] The goal of this comparison is 'to identify differences that are not noticeable in the abstract but would be significant to the hypothetical ordinary observer familiar with the prior art.'[128]

9.055

'Once the accused product has been found to infringe, any defendant who manufactured, offered to sell, sold, or imported the accused product in the United States will be considered a direct infringer.'[129]

9.056

(iv) Indirect infringement

In the U.S., patent law also recognizes indirect infringement of design patents.[130] There are two types of indirect infringement: (1) inducement to infringement,

9.057

---

122 *Egyptian Goddess*, 543 F.3d at 677; See also *Columbia Sportswear N. Am., Inc. v. Seirus Innovative Accessories, Inc.*, 80 F.4th 1363, 1377 (Fed. Cir. 2023).
123 *Contessa Food Prods.*, 282 F.3d at 1381.
124 *Goodyear Tire*, 162 F.3d at 1117 (emphasis added).
125 *Arminak & Assocs., Inc. v. Saint-Gobain Calmar, Inc.*, 501 F.3d 1314, 1323 (Fed. Cir. 2007):
We agree, therefore, with the district court that the ordinary observer of the sprayer shroud designs at issue in this case is the industrial purchaser or contract buyer of sprayer shrouds for businesses that assemble the retail product from the component parts of the retail product bottle, the cap, the sprayer tube, the liquid, the label, and the trigger sprayer device atop the cap, so as to create a single product sold to the retail consumer. Here, the patented design is only the shroud of the sprayer device.
abrogated on other grounds by Egyptian Goddess, 543 F.3d 665; English and Ferrill, *supra* note 64, at 17.
126 *Ethicon Endo-Surgery*, 796 F.3d at 1335 (quoting Egyptian Goddess, 543 F.3d at 678); English and Ferrill, ibid.
127 *Ethicon Endo-Surgery*, 796 F.3d at 1335; English and Ferrill, *supra* note 64, at 17.
128 *Ethicon Endo-Surgery*, ibid.; English and Ferrill, ibid., at 17–18.
129 35 U.S.C. § 271(a); English and Ferrill, ibid., at 18.
130 See, e.g., *Wing Shing Prods. (BVI), Ltd. v. Simatelex Manufactory Co.*, 479 F. Supp. 2d 388, 407–08 (S.D.N.Y. 2007).

and (2) contributory infringement.[131] Inducement occurs when there has been (1) direct infringement and (2) the alleged inducer knowingly induced infringement with (3) a specific intent to encourage another's infringement.[132]

9.058 Whoever induces the infringement of a patent will be considered an indirect infringer.[133] Inducement occurs when (1) there has been direct infringement and the alleged inducer (2) knowingly induced infringement with (3) a specific intent to encourage another's infringement.[134] Contributory infringement occurs when (1) there has been direct infringement; (2) the alleged contributor knew its components were designed for a combination that was both patented and infringing; (3) the component has no substantial non-infringing uses; and (4) the component is a material part of the invention.[135] This type of infringement, unlike inducement, requires that the contributory acts occur within the U.S.[136]

(v) Defences to infringement

9.059 A defendant may allege non-infringement and a number of other defences.[137] The defendant may argue that the patent is invalid based on a failure to meet all of the requirements of Title 35, including novelty, nonobviousness, lack of written description, enablement, or definiteness.

9.060 Inequitable conduct is a defence and occurs when an applicant misrepresents or omits material information during the prosecution of the claimed design with an intent to deceive the USPTO.[138] A defendant must show that (1) the applicant intended to deceive the USPTO, and (2) the information withheld was material to the issuance of the patent.[139]

9.061 Patent exhaustion, or the 'first sale doctrine,' shields future purchasers of a patented design from infringement claims after the patentee authorized the sale of the design.[140] Once a patentee first sells the article, the patentee will be con-

---

131 35 U.S.C. § 271(b), (c).
132 See, e.g., *Wing Shing Prods.*, 479 F. Supp. 2d at 407–08.
133 35 U.S.C. § 271(b).
134 See, e.g., *Wing Shing Prods.*, 479 F. Supp. 2d at 407–08. Mere knowledge of infringement will not amount to inducement—inducement requires action by taking affirmative steps. See *ZUP, LLC v. Nash Mfg., Inc.*, 229 F. Supp. 3d 430, 454 (E.D. Va. 2017), *aff'd*, 896 F.3d 1365 (Fed. Cir. 2018).
135 *See Progme Corp. v. Comcast Cable Commc'ns LLC*, No. 17-1488, 2017 WL 5070723, at *9 (E.D. Pa. Nov. 3, 2017).
136 35 U.S.C. § 271(c).
137 English and Ferrill, *supra* note 64, at 18.
138 *Therasense, Inc. v. Becton, Dickinson & Co.*, 649 F.3d 1276, 1287 (Fed. Cir. 2011) (en banc).
139 Ibid. at 1287–88.
140 See *Quanta Comput., Inc. v. LG Elecs., Inc.*, 553 U.S. 617, 625 (2008).

sidered to have exhausted its patent rights.[141] Thus, any subsequent purchases of the same article will not be infringement.[142]

9.062 The statute of limitations is six years to bring a patent infringement claim.[143] In this regard, a patentee's recovery for damages will not extend to infringing activity occurring more than six years prior to the filing of the complaint.[144]

(vi) Remedies for infringement

9.063 A design patent owner may elect for infringer's profits under § 289 or a reasonable royalty under § 284.[145] Under § 289, a design patentee may recover the infringer's total profit on the 'article of manufacture' to which the claimed design has been applied—a remedy not afforded to utility patents.[146]

9.064 A patentee may recover compensatory damages in the amount of a reasonable royalty.[147] Courts consider 'not only of the amount that a willing licensee would have paid for the patent license but also of the amount that a willing licensor would have accepted.'[148]

9.065 However, double recovery for the same infringement is prohibited under 35 U.S.C. § 289.[149] While the infringer's profits are typically sought by the rights holder, in some cases, it may make sense to seek a reasonable royalty, if, for instance, the product accused of infringement is sold with little to no profit.

---

141 Ibid.
142 See ibid. at 638 ('The authorized sale of an article that substantially embodies a patent exhausts the patent holder's rights and prevents the patent holder from invoking patent law to control postsale use of the article.').
143 35 U.S.C. § 286; see also *SCA Hygiene Prods. Aktiebolag v. First Quality Baby Prods., LLC*, 137 S. Ct. 954, 961 (2017).
144 35 U.S.C. § 286.
145 Catalina, 295 F.3d at 1291, *Catalina Lighting, Inc. v. Lamps Plus, Inc.*, 295 F.3d 1277, 1291 (Fed. Cir. 2002); 35 U.S.C. §§ 284, 289.
146 35 U.S.C. § 289.
147 35 U.S.C. § 284; English and Ferrill, *supra* note 64, at 19–20.
148 *Georgia-Pacific Corp. v. U.S. Plywood Corp.*, 318 F. Supp. 1116, 1121 (S.D.N.Y. 1970), *modified and aff'd sub nom. Georgia-Pacific Corp. v. U.S. Plywood-Champion Papers, Inc.*, 446 F.2d 295 (2d Cir. 1971). When a patentee cannot prove lost profits, it can elect to recover a reasonable royalty. *SmithKline Diagnostics, Inc. v. Helena Lab'ys Corp.*, 926 F.2d 1161, 1164 (Fed. Cir. 1991). Compensatory damages are the difference between the patentee's present pecuniary condition and where the patentee would have been absent the infringement of the lost profits. See *Grain Processing Corp. v. Am. Maize-Prods. Co.*, 185 F.3d 1341, 1350 (Fed. Cir. 1999); English and Ferrill, *supra* note 64, at 20. Courts have calculated lost profits in a variety of ways, including loss of market share, price erosion, increased promotional expenses, and lost sales. Lost profits are not typically sought in design patent cases, because there is almost always, by definition, a non-infringing alternative design, and that is one of the main factors in the calculation of lost profits.
149 See also *Catalina Lighting*, 295 F.3d at 1291; 35 U.S.C. § 289.

9.066 Section 284 also authorizes enhanced damages—up to three times the damages award.[150] Generally, courts award enhanced damages in 'exceptional cases,' including those that involve willful infringement.[151] Enhanced damages have not been applied to awards under § 289.[152]

9.067 A patentee may also receive injunctive relief or an order prohibiting the infringing activities.[153] Courts focus on four factors in determining whether to grant a permanent injunction: (1) whether the patentee has suffered an irreparable injury; (2) whether remedies available at law are inadequate to compensate for that injury; (3) the balance of hardships between the patentee and defendant and whether a remedy in equity is warranted; and (4) whether public interest would not be disserved by a permanent injunction.[154]

9.068 A patentee may also obtain a preliminary injunction before or at the time of filing the complaint.[155] In determining whether a preliminary injunction is decided, a court considers the following factors: (1) the patentee's likelihood of success on the merits of the underlying litigation, (2) whether irreparable harm is likely if the injunction is not granted, (3) the balance of hardships between the patentee and defendant, and (4) public interest.[156]

9.069 There is no statute that imposes criminal penalties for patent infringement under U.S. law.

9.070 Typically, in the U.S., each party is responsible for its own attorney fees. However, a district court may award attorney fees to the prevailing party in exceptional cases.[157] As with enhanced damages, attorney fees may be awarded in exceptional cases that could include those of willful infringement.[158]

---

150 35 U.S.C. § 284; English and Ferrill, *supra* note 64, at 20.
151 See *Halo Elecs., Inc. v. Pulse Elecs., Inc.*, 579 U.S. 93, 105 (2016); English and Ferrill, ibid.
152 English and Ferrill, ibid.
153 See *eBay Inc. v. MercExchange, L.L.C.*, 547 U.S. 388, 391–92 (2006).
154 Ibid., at 391.
155 English and Ferrill, *supra* note 64, at 20.
156 See *Oakley, Inc. v. Sunglass Hut Int'l*, 316 F.3d 1331, 1338–39 (Fed. Cir. 2003).
157 35 U.S.C. § 285.
158 See *Octane Fitness, LLC v. ICON Health & Fitness, Inc.*, 572 U.S. 545, 555 (2014) ('But a case presenting either subjective bad faith or exceptionally meritless claims may sufficiently set itself apart from mine-run cases to warrant a fee award.').

4. Significant Judicial Decisions in the United States

(a) *Egyptian Goddess, Inc. v. Swisa, Inc.*, 543 F.3d 665 (Fed. Cir. 2008) (en banc)

In *Egyptian Goddess*, Swisa sold a nail buffer that Egyptian Goddess thought was similar to its patented design (U.S. Design Patent No. D467,389). The district court granted Swisa's summary judgment of noninfringement based on the novelty test. Prior to *Egyptian Goddess*, courts applied a two-prong test to determine whether infringement occurred in a design patent case. The first prong—the ordinary observer test—was satisfied when 'two designs are substantially the same, if the resemblance is such as to deceive such an observer, inducing him to purchase one supposing it to be the other, the first one patented is infringed by the other.'[159] The second prong—the point of novelty test—was met if the accused design 'appropriate[d] the novelty of the claimed design in order to be deemed infringing.'[160] The Federal Circuit, sitting en banc, struck down the second prong, holding only that the ordinary observer test would be used as the test for infringement. However, the court modified the test, requiring infringement to be determined 'in light of the prior art' by 'applying the ordinary observer test through the eyes of an observer familiar with the prior art.'[161]

9.071

(b) *International Seaway Trading Corp. v. Walgreens Corp.*, 589 F.3d 1233 (Fed. Cir. 2009)

In *International Seaway*, International Seaway Trading Corporation filed suit against Walgreens Corporation and Touchsport Footwear USA, Inc., claiming infringement of Seaway's design patents. The district court found the claim of each asserted patent was invalid under 35 U.S.C. § 102 as anticipated by a design patent assigned to Crocs, Inc. The district court used the ordinary observer test to determine design patent invalidity. Further, when comparing the designs of the patents-in-suit to Crocs's design patents, the district court only examined the 'portions of the product that are visible during normal use, regardless of whether those portions are visible during the point of sale.'[162]

9.072

On appeal, the Federal Circuit affirmed-in-part, vacated-in-part, and remanded. The Federal Circuit affirmed that, like *Egyptian Goddess*, the ordinary observer test was the sole test for design patent invalidity under 35 U.S.C.

9.073

---

159 *Gorham*, 81 U.S. at 528.
160 *Egyptian Goddess*, 543 F.3d at 670.
161 Ibid., at 677.
162 *Int'l Seaway*, 589 F.3d at 1237 (quoting *Int'l Seaway Trading Corp. v. Walgreens Corp.*, 599 F. Supp. 2d 1307, 1315 (S.D. Fla. 2009)).

§ 102 and struck down the point of novelty test for determining anticipation. However, the Federal Circuit agreed that the district court misapplied the ordinary observer test, as the 'precedent makes clear that all of the ornamental features illustrated in the figures must be considered in evaluating design patent infringement.'[163] The district court erred in only examining the portions of the products visible during normal use.

(c) *In re SurgiSil, L.L.P.*, 14 F.4th 1380 (Fed. Cir. 2021)

9.074 In *In re SurgiSil*, SurgiSil's design patent application claimed an 'ornamental design for a lip implant as shown and described.'[164] An image of SurgiSil's lip implant is reproduced in Figure 9.1 below.

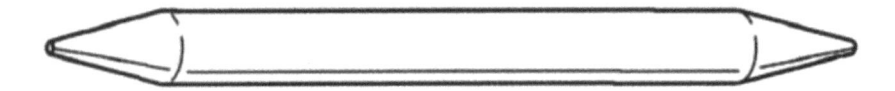

Source: *In re SurgiSil, L.L.P.*, 14 F.4th 1380 (Fed. Cir. 2021).

Figure 9.1   Drawing of SurgiSil lip implant

9.075 The examiner rejected the design as anticipated by a Blick art tool called a stump. An image of Blick's stump is reproduced in Figure 9.2 below.

Source: *In re SurgiSil, L.L.P.*, 14 F.4th 1380 (Fed. Cir. 2021).

Figure 9.2   Drawing of Blick art tool 'Stump'

9.076 The PTAB affirmed the rejection, finding the differences in shape between the claimed design and Blick's design to be minor, reasoning 'it is appropriate to ignore the identification of the article of manufacture in the claim language.'[165]

9.077 The Federal Circuit disagreed and reversed the PTAB's decision, holding that a 'design claim is limited to the article of manufacture identified in the claim; it does not broadly cover a design in the abstract.'[166] Rather, a claim is 'limited

---

163   Ibid,. at 1241 (citing *Contessa Food Prods.*, 282 F.3d at 1378).
164   *In re SurgiSil*, 14 F.4th at 1381 (citation omitted).
165   Ibid. (citation omitted).
166   Ibid. at 1382.

to the particular article of manufacture identified in the claim,'[167] as a '[d]esign is inseparable from the article to which it is applied and cannot exist alone.'[168]

(d) *In re Maatita*, 900 F.3d 1369 (Fed. Cir. 2018)

9.078 In *In re Maatita*, Ron Maatita filed a design patent application containing a two-dimensional plan-view drawing of an athletic shoe bottom. An image of the shoe bottom is reproduced in Figure 9.3 below.

FIG. 1

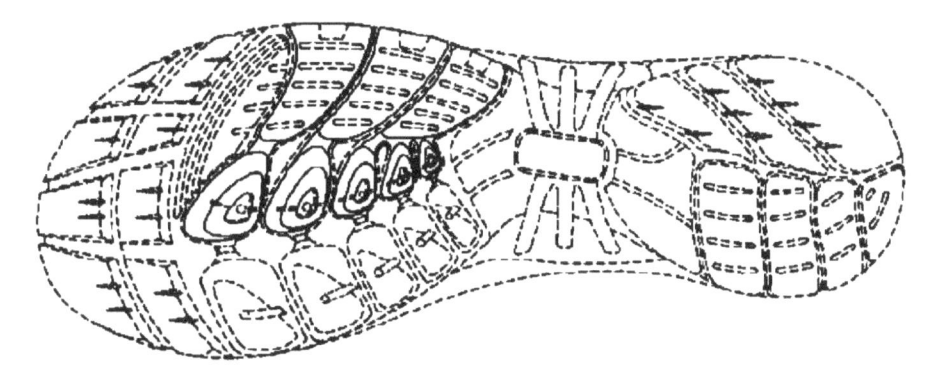

Source: *In re Maatita*, 900 F.3d 1369 (Fed. Cir. 2018).

Figure 9.3   Drawing of shoe bottom

9.079 During prosecution, the examiner rejected the claim under 35 U.S.C. § 112 for lack of enablement and definiteness as the two-dimensional view did not convey the depth and contour of the shoe bottom. Maatita appealed the examiner's rejection to the PTAB. The PTAB affirmed the examiner's rejection.

9.080 On appeal, the Federal Circuit found the proper inquiry for an indefiniteness challenge is whether one skilled in the art, viewing the design as an ordinary observer, would understand the scope of the design with reasonable certainty based on the claim and the visual disclosure.[169] Thus, from the perspective of a potential infringer, it would not be left in doubt as to how to determine infringement. Therefore, a single two-dimensional plan-view drawing of a three-dimensional object may be sufficient for disclosure under 35 U.S.C. § 112.

---

167   Ibid. (citing *Curver Luxenbourg, SARL v. Home Expressions Inc.*, 938 F.3d 1334, 1336 (Fed. Cir. 2019)).
168   Ibid. (alteration in original) (quoting MPEP § 1502).
169   *In re Maatita*, 900 F.3d at 1376–77.

(e) *In re Daniels*, 144 F.3d 1452 (Fed. Cir. 1998)

9.081 In *In re Daniels*, Scott Daniels filed a design patent application for a 'leecher'—a device for trapping leeches claiming priority to a previously filed parent application. The drawings originally showed the leecher decorated on each side with a pattern of leaves, but during prosecution, the design was later changed to remove the leaf pattern from the drawings. The leecher with the leaf ornamentation and the leecher without the leaf ornamentation are reproduced in Figure 9.4 below.

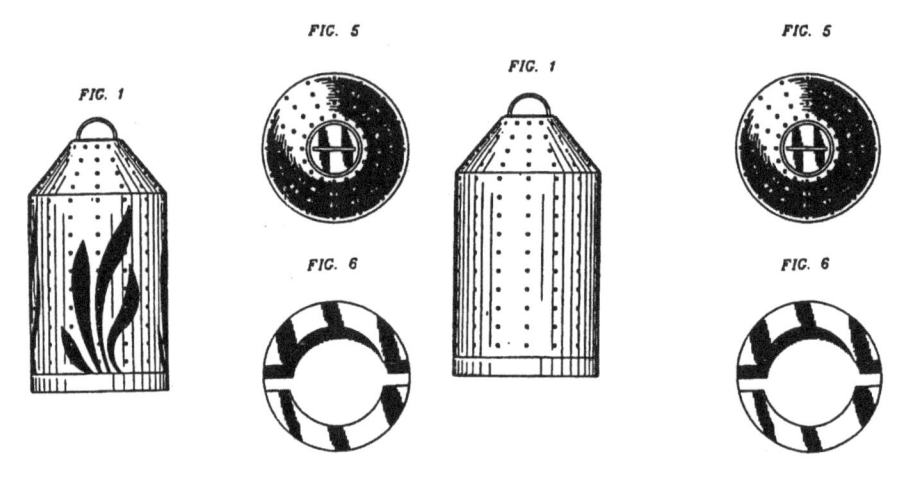

Source: In re Daniels, 144 F.3d 1452 (Fed. Cir. 1998).

Figure 9.4   *Drawing of 'leecher' with and without leaf*

9.082 Daniels appealed the rejection. The Board of Patent Appeals and Interferences ('BPAI') determined that the deletion of the leaf pattern defeated compliance with the written description requirement of 35 U.S.C. § 112.[170] Thus, the BPAI found the design patent application was not entitled to the benefit of the filing date of the earlier co-pending parent design application and was unpatentable for obviousness in view of an intervening publication.[171]

9.083 On appeal, the Federal Circuit reversed the BPAI's decision, holding that Daniels was entitled to the parent application's filing date, as the leecher design without the leaf pattern was fully disclosed in the previously filed application. Under 35 U.S.C. § 120, design and utility patents are entitled to claim

---

170 *In re Daniels*, 144 F.3d at 1453–54.
171 Ibid. at 1455.

DESIGN PATENT LAW IN THE UNITED STATES

priority if the later-claimed subject matter is described in the earlier application in compliance with 35 U.S.C. § 112.

(f) *In re Owens*, 710 F.3d 1362 (Fed. Cir. 2013)

In *In re Owens*, applicant Timothy S. Owens filed U.S. Design Patent Application No. 29/219,709 ('the '709 application'), claiming the design for a bottle related to mouthwashes and rinses. An image of the Bottle is reproduced in Figure 9.5 below.   **9.084**

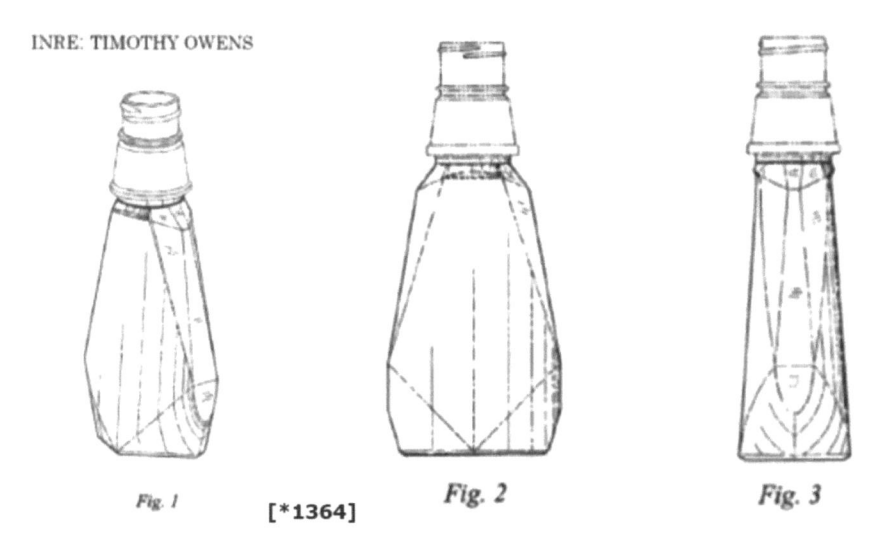

Source: In re Owens, 710 F.3d 1362 (Fed. Cir. 2013).

Figure 9.5   *Drawings of the mouthwash bottle of the '709 application*

Owens later filed U.S. Design Patent Application No. 29/253,172 ('the '172 application') as a continuation application claiming the benefit of the '709 application under 35 U.S.C. § 120. In the '172 application, Owens claimed specific design elements on the top and side portions of the original bottle, adding a broken line bisecting the pentagonal front panel. An image of the Bottle is reproduced in Figure 9.6 below.   **9.085**

The '709 application disclosed no boundary that corresponded to the added broken line. Thus, the examiner rejected Owens's continuation application as containing new matter and not meeting written description requirements. The BPAI affirmed.   **9.086**

On appeal, the Federal Circuit clarified the broken line at issue was an 'unclaimed boundary' line—when an unclaimed boundary line 'divides a pre-   **9.087**

Figure 9.6   *Drawings of the mouthwash bottle of the '172 application*

viously claimed area, it indicates that the applicant has disclaimed the portion beyond the boundary while claiming the area within it.'[172] Owens argued that because all portions of front panel were 'clearly visible' in the '709 application, the amendment made in the continuation satisfied the written description test.[173] The Federal Circuit disagreed, clarifying that the written description test turns on 'whether the original disclosure 'clearly allow[s] persons of ordinary skill in the art to recognize that [the inventor] invented what is *claimed*.'[174] Nothing in the parent application's disclosure suggested 'anything uniquely patentable about the top portion of the bottle's front panel.'[175] Unclaimed boundary lines typically should satisfy the written description requirement 'only if they make explicit a boundary that *already exists*, but was unclaimed, in the original disclosure.'[176]

(g)   Hoop v. Hoop, 279 F.3d 1004 (Fed. Cir. 2002)

9.088   In *Hoop v. Hoop*, Jeffrey and Stephen Hoop ('the Hoop brothers') conceived a design for eagle-shaped motorcycle fairing guards. Lacking drawing and casting experience, the Hoop brothers hired Mark and Lisa Hoop to create detailed drawings and three-dimensional models for a patent application. The design patent application issued as U.S. Design Patent No. D428,831. Several months after the Hoop brothers filed their patent application, Mark and Lisa

---

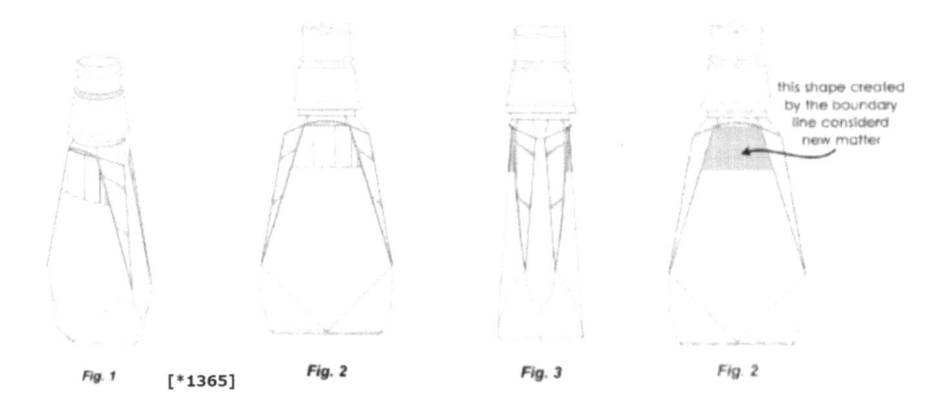

172   *In re Owens*, 710 F.3d at 1367.
173   Ibid. at 1367.
174   Ibid. at 1368 (alterations in original) (quoting *Ariad Pharms., Inc. v. Eli Lilly & Co.*, 598 F.3d 1336, 1351 (Fed. Cir. 2010) (en banc)).
175   Ibid. at 1368.
176   Ibid. at 1369 (emphasis added).

Hoop filed an identical design patent application, which issued as U.S. Design Patent No. D431,211. During reexamination, the examiner rejected Mark and Lisa Hoop's patent as anticipated by the Hoop brothers' patent. The district court found that the Hoop brothers were the true inventors, as the Hoop brothers conceived the invention and Mark and Lisa Hoop merely assisted the brothers in perfecting the invention. The court issued a preliminary injunction against Mark and Lisa Hoop. On appeal, the Federal Circuit affirmed the district court and confirmed that the same standard of inventorship applies to utility and design patents. Thus, an inventor is the 'person or persons who conceived the patented invention.'[177] Further, an inventor may use the services and aid of others to perfect an invention without forfeiting their right to a patent. One does not become a joint inventor by merely assisting the inventor after the conception of the claimed invention.

(h) *Pacific Coast Marine Windshields Ltd. v. Malibu Boats, LLC*, 739 F.3d 694 (Fed. Cir. 2014)

In *Pacific Coast Marine Windshields*, Darren Bach, owner and chief executive officer of Pacific Coast Marine Windshields Limited ('Pacific Coast'), filed a design patent application for an ornamental boat windshield design and assigned all rights to Pacific Coast. During examination, the examiner issued a restriction requirement identifying five distinct groups of designs as windshields. The applicant elected a design with four vent holes and the amended application issued as U.S. Design Patent No. D555,070. Pacific Coast later brought suit against Malibu Boats, alleging infringement for a windshield design with three vent holes. The district court granted Malibu Boats' motion for summary judgment of noninfringement, finding that prosecution history estoppel barred the infringement claim. Pacific Coast appealed to the Federal Circuit. **9.089**

Whether the doctrine of prosecution history estoppel applied to design patents was one of first impression. Prosecution history estoppel occurs where subject matter is surrendered during prosecution, and the doctrine 'prevents the patentee from "recaptur[ing] in an infringement action the very subject matter surrendered as a condition of receiving the patent."'[178] Prosecution history estoppel limits the patentee's ability to recover under the doctrine of equivalents, but it does not limit literal infringement. Unlike utility patents, design patent infringement does not require literal identicality; instead, it requires **9.090**

---

177 *Hoop*, 279 F.3d at 1007 (quoting *C.R. Bard, Inc. v. M3 Sys., Inc.*, 157 F.3d 1340, 1352 (Fed. Cir. 1998)).
178 *Pac. Coast Marine Windshields*, 739 F.3d at 701 (alteration in original) (quoting *Festo Corp. v. Shoketsu Kinzoku Kogyo Kabushiki Co.*, 535 U.S. 722, 734 (2002)).

sufficient similarity. Despite this difference, the Federal Circuit concluded that the principles of prosecution history estoppel apply to design patents as well as utility patents. In the matter of restriction requirements, a surrender resulting from a restriction requirement invokes the doctrine where the surrender was necessary 'to secure the patent.'[179]

(i) *Samsung Electronics Co. v. Apple Inc.*, 137 S. Ct. 429 (2016)

9.091 In *Samsung Electronics*, Apple was awarded $399 million in damages for Samsung's design patent infringement of Apple's various design patents related to its smartphones. The Federal Circuit affirmed the design patent infringement damages award, declining to limit the damages, reasoning a consumer could not purchase the infringing components separately from the smartphones. The Supreme Court granted certiorari and reversed and remanded the decision. To calculate a damages award under 35 U.S.C. § 289, it involves two steps: (1) 'identify the "article of manufacture" to which the infringed design has been applied'; and (2) 'calculate the infringer's total profit made on that article of manufacture.'[180] The Supreme Court clarified what constitutes an 'article of manufacture,' determining it is 'simply a thing made by hand or machine' that is broad enough to encompass both a product sold to a consumer and a component of that product.[181]

(j) *Columbia Sportswear N. Am., Inc. v. Seirus Innovative Accessories, Inc.*, 80 F.4th 1363 (Fed. Cir. 2023)

9.092 In *Columbia Sportswear*, Columbia accused Seirus of infringing its ornamental design for 'Heat Reflective Material.' The district court granted Columbia summary judgment on the infringement claim and a jury awarded Columbia $3,018,174 in damages. Seirus appealed to the Federal Circuit, which vacated the summary judgment of infringement and remanded for further proceedings. On remand, the jury found that Seirus did not infringe and Columbia appealed back to the Federal Circuit.

9.093 In the second appeal, the Federal Circuit vacated the non-infringement judgment, challenging the way that the district court handled Seirus's comparison prior art. The court acknowledged that the scope of comparison prior art is an 'open question of law.'[182] To resolve this question, the court held that 'to

---

179 Ibid. at 704 (quoting *Festo*, 535 U.S. at 736).
180 Samsung Elecs., 137 S. Ct. at 434.
181 *Id.* at 435.
182 Columbia Sportswear N. Am., Inc. v. Seirus Innovative Accessories, Inc., 80 F.4th 1363, 1378 (Fed. Cir. 2023).

qualify as comparison prior art, [a] prior-art design must be applied to the article of manufacture identified in the claim.'[183] This rule is meant to align the scope of comparison prior art with that of anticipatory prior art, and to aid in infringement analysis by preventing consideration of any prior art designs which are not applied to the same article of manufacture as the claimed and accused designs.

The Federal Circuit also held that the district court did not err by declining to instruct the jury that consumer confusion as to source is irrelevant for design-patent infringement. Seirus's allegedly infringing design features its logo throughout, a fact which the district court was appropriately within its discretion to treat as relevant if not dispositive. 'The takeaway is: just because consumers might not be confused about an accused product's source, that alone would not preclude an ordinary observer from deeming the claimed and accused designs similar enough to constitute design-patent infringement. At the same time, however, just because a logo's potential to eliminate confusion as to source is irrelevant to design-patent infringement, its potential to render an accused design dissimilar to the patented one—maybe even enough to establish non-infringement as a matter of law—should not be discounted.'[184]

9.094

B. PRACTICAL ASPECTS OF DESIGN LAW

1. Statistics/Trends

In recent years, the amount of design patent applications being filed at the USPTO has been increasing (as shown in Table 9.1 below).[185]

9.095

Even though the number of design patent applications being filed is increasing each year, when compared to the total number of patent applications being filed, design patent filings as a percentage of total patent filings is remaining nearly the same. From 2000 to 2020, for example, the percent of design patents out of total patent filings (utility, design, and plant) has been between 5–7.5 per cent.[186]

9.096

---

183 *Id.*
184 *Id.* at 1383.
185 USPTO, U.S. Patent Statistics Chart Calendar Years 1963 - 2020, https://www.uspto.gov/web/offices/ac/ido/oeip/taf/us_stat.htm (last accessed Feb. 14, 2022); USPTO, Design Data August 2023, https://www.uspto.gov/dashboard/patents/design.html#design-unexamined-trend-bar-data-table (last accessed Oct. 18 2023).
186 Ibid.

Table 9.1 U.S. design patent applications filed (USPTO, U.S. patent statistics chart calendar years 1963–2020, USPTO, design data August 2023)

Year	U.S. Design Patent Applications Filed
2014	35,378
2015	39,097
2016	42,571
2017	43,340
2018	45,083
2019	46,847
2020	47,838
2021	54,201
2022	54,476

Source: https://www.uspto.gov/web/offices/ac/ido/oeip/taf/us_stat.htm (last accessed Feb. 14, 2022); https://www.uspto.gov/dashboard/patents/design.html#design-unexamined-trend-bar-data-table (last accessed Oct. 18 2023).

9.097 Currently, there are 79,696 new design patent applications in the pipeline that are awaiting a First Office Action by the patent examiner. These applications will be examined by one of 315 design examiners.[187]

9.098 The traditional total pendency of a design patent application, meaning the average number of months from the design application filing date to the date the application has reached final disposition (e.g., issued as a patent or abandoned), is 21 months. The total pendency has been stable over the past two years (fluctuating between 20.4 months and 21.4 months since December 2021 and August 2023).

9.099 To accelerate examination, the USPTO offers an expedited examination process (sometimes called the 'Rocket Docket') where design applicants have an expedited path to examination. Applicants may take advantage of this process by filing a request for expedited examination with a fee for the expedited examination, an information disclosure statement, a statement that a pre-examination search was conducted, and a statement as to the field of the search.[188] By using this procedure, an application may be placed in front of a design examiner within 2.3 months (based on the average for all expedited applications that have received a first action during fiscal year 2023). The expedited process affords the applicant rapid design patent protection that may be especially important where marketplace conditions are such that new designs

---

187 USPTO, Design Data September 2023, https:// www .uspto .gov/ dashboard/ patents/ design .html (last accessed Nov. 22, 2023).
188 MPEP 1504.30(a).

on articles are typically in vogue for limited periods of time. All processing is expedited—including appeals—from the date the request is granted.[189]

By the time the application is in front of the design examiner, the allowance rate is fairly high at 86.4 per cent cumulative for fiscal year 2022. The allowance rate is calculated by dividing the number of design applications allowed by the number of design applications disposed in the current fiscal year. The allowance rate includes the abandonments for requests for continued prosecution applications ('CPAs') in the disposals. 9.100

Nike, Inc., Samsung Electronics Co., Ltd., Apple, Inc., LG Corporation, and Alphabet Inc. are among the top five organizations that received the most design patent grants in 2021. 9.101

Since 2008 at least 200 design patent infringement cases have been filed each year, with 2016 being the year with the most lawsuits, totaling at least 307.[190] Jury trials during this time period on average lasted three years and three months, whereas bench trials (before a judge) lasted close to one year, 11 months.[191] Cases settle, however, on average about seven months after the lawsuit is filed.[192] In this period, damages were awarded in around 114 cases[193]—the highest award coming from the *Apple v. Samsung* case. Around 30 cases granted a temporary restraining order, around 44 granted a preliminary injunction, around 22 awarded enhanced damages, and around 71 awarded attorney fees.[194] 9.102

According to a recent study, district court litigation has largely favoured the patentee over the past ten years. Since 2011 courts usually found design patent infringement in over 50 per cent of cases.[195] Moreover, between 2015 and 2020, courts found infringement over 80 per cent of the time.[196] This study reported 246 cases that involved a validity or enforceability determination; 203 of those cases contained validity determinations where 88.4 per cent of the patents involved were found to be valid;[197] 103 of those cases contained 9.103

---

189 USPTO, Design Data September 2023, https://www.uspto.gov/dashboard/patents/design.html (last accessed Nov. 22, 2023).
190 English and Ferrill, *supra* note 64, at 20–22.
191 Ibid.
192 Ibid.
193 Ibid.
194 Ibid.
195 Sarah Burstein and Saurabh Vishnubhakat, *The Truth About Design Patents*, Tex. A&M, Research Paper No. 22-08, at 65–66.
196 Ibid. at 66.
197 Ibid. at 61.

enforceability determinations where 99.5 per cent of the patents involved were found to be enforceable.[198]

2. Business Aspects: Transferability/Licensing

9.104 Ownership of a design patent gives the patent owner the right to exclude others from making, using, offering for sale, selling, or importing into the U.S. the invention claimed in the design patent. Ownership of the design patent does not furnish the owner with the right to make, use, offer for sale, sell, or import the claimed invention because there may be other legal considerations precluding the same.

9.105 In some instances, for example, when an inventor may not be able to make or sell products or designs, patent licensing may allow the inventor to profit from the rights to his or her invention. For instance, a design patent owner may license its patent to others (one or more licensees) in exchange for a royalty payment using a license agreement. The terms of the license agreement allow the licensee to use or sell the design patent for a limited period of time (the maximum being 15 years from the date that the USPTO granted the design patent application). The license agreement may be drafted to indicate it is either an exclusive license (the licensee may use or sell the patented invention for a limited period of time) or a nonexclusive license.

9.106 Instead of licensing, the patent owner may transfer the patent to another in a contractual agreement. 'Assignment,' in general, is the act of transferring to another the ownership of one's property, i.e., the interest and rights to the property. An assignment of a design patent, or design patent application, is the transfer to another of a party's entire ownership interest or a percentage of that party's ownership interest in the design patent or design application. In order for an assignment to take place, the transfer to another must include the entirety of the bundle of rights that is associated with the ownership interest, i.e., all of the bundle of rights that are inherent in the right, title, and interest in the patent or patent application. As compared to assignment of patent rights, the licensing of a patent transfers a bundle of rights that is less than the entire ownership interest, e.g., rights that may be limited as to time, geographical area, or field of use. By licensing or selling (assigning) a patent, a patent owner may turn its patent into an asset capable of generating income.

---

198 Ibid.

3. Case Studies

Some typical design patent case studies include (1) patents used to combat counterfeits or copycat products (e.g., handbags, kitchen items, and baby products, where most of the design is claimed); (2) replacement or consumable products (e.g., auto parts and consumables like coffee cups for coffee machines); and (3) design aesthetic (e.g., design patents directed to specific design features that may be used on multiple products (like the lululemon yoga pant waist bands)). **9.107**

In a case involving allegedly copycat products, *Jack Schwartz Shoes v. Skechers U.S.A.*, Plaintiff sought summary judgment on its claim that Defendant's 6905 shoe infringed Plaintiff's U.S. Design Patent No. D435,332 ('the '332 patent').[199] **9.108**

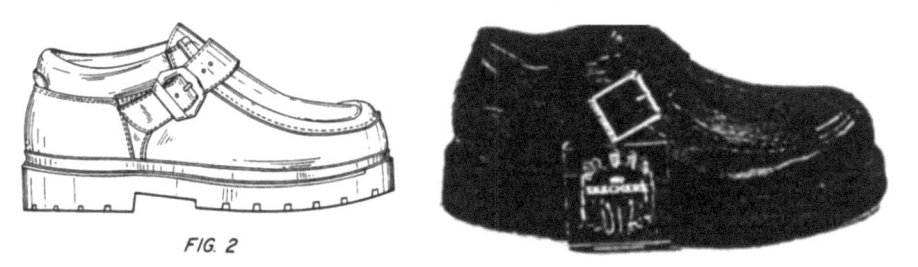

Source: Jack Schwartz Shoes v. Skechers U.S.A., 2002 U.S. Dist. LEXIS 25699, at *1–5 (S.D.N.Y. Sep. 9, 2002).

Figure 9.7   *Drawing of Fig. 2 in Design Patent No. D435,332*

Plaintiff claimed that defendant's 6905 shoe appropriated the design protected by its '332 patent, which included a low-cut wallabee design with a buckle and a strap.[200] The court opined that to determine infringement, a two-part test is used. First, 'if, in the eye of an ordinary observer, giving such attention as a purchaser usually gives, two designs are substantially the same, if the resemblance is such as to deceive such an observer, inducing him to purchase one supposing it to be the other.'[201] Second, the court must determine whether the similarity in the two designs is attributable to the 'novelty which distinguishes the patented design from the prior art.'[202] The court determined that it is beyond dispute that the designs of the two shoes are substantially the same, **9.109**

---

199 *Jack Schwartz Shoes v. Skechers U.S.A.*, 2002 U.S. Dist. LEXIS 25699, at *1–5 (S.D.N.Y. Sep. 9, 2002).
200 Ibid. at 8–9.
201 Ibid. at 32 (citing '*Gorham Co. v. White*, 81 U.S. 511, 528, 20 L. Ed. 731 (1871); see also *Contessa Food Prods., Inc. v. Conagra, Inc.*, 282 F.3d 1370, 1377 (Fed. Cir. 2002)').
202 Ibid.

so as to confuse the ordinary observer, and that the similarity of the shoes is attributable to the '332 patent's point of novelty.[203] Ultimately, the court concluded that plaintiff's patent was infringed by defendant's 6905 shoe design.

9.110 In a replacement/consumable products case, *Daimler AG v. A-Z Wheels LLC*, plaintiff Daimler AG alleged that defendants infringed U.S. Design Patent No. D542,211 ('the '211 patent'), which was an ornamental design for a front face of a vehicle wheel commonly seen on their Mercedes Benz vehicles.[204]

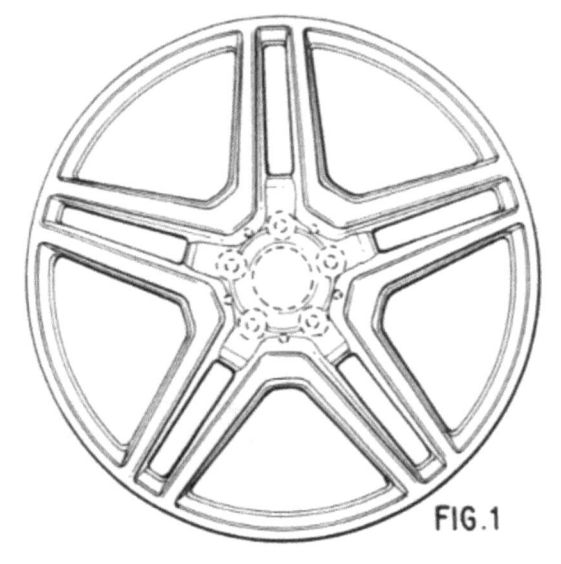

Source: Daimler AG v. A-Z Wheels LLC, 334 F. Supp. 3d 1087 (2018).

Figure 9.8   *Drawing of Fig. 1 of the D542,211 patent*

9.111 When addressing the legal standard, the court opined that a determination of design patent infringement involves a two-step analysis. First, the claim must be properly construed to determine its meaning and scope. Secondly, the properly construed claim must be compared to the accused design to determine whether there has been infringement.[205] In addressing the second factor, defendants argued that there were a number of significant differences between the accused and protected designs (e.g., plaintiff's design 'has a sharp drop from the outer, upper rim to the lower, inner rim,' but defendants' design 'has a sloping decline from the outer, upper rim of the wheel that suddenly

---

203   Ibid. at 34–48.
204   See generally *Daimler AG v. A-Z Wheels LLC*, 334 F. Supp. 3d 1087 (2018).
205   Ibid. at 1102 (citing *Elmer*, 67 F.3d at 1577).

Source: Daimler AG v. A-Z Wheels LLC, 334 F. Supp. 3d 1087 (2018).

Figure 9.9 Product sold by Defendants on eBay with part number MBZ-610–19-MB

drops to the lower, inner rim of the wheel.' Defendants' design has spokes that 'are completely smooth along their sides, meeting with the outer rim in such a way that the bottom of the spokes appear to be resting on the top of the lower, inner rim of the wheel,' but plaintiff's design has spokes that 'are not completely smooth along their sides, and appear to have edges or layers to their appearance.' The spokes on defendants' design 'rest[] upon' the 'rim below the bottom of the lower, inner rim,' but the spokes of plaintiff's design 'merge with the rim below the bottom of the lower, inner rim.').[206]

9.112 The court described that the proper test for infringement of a design patent is whether the ordinary observer, "giving such attention as a purchaser usually gives' and viewing any differences between the patented design and the accused product 'in the context of the prior art,' finds that the devices bear such resemblance as to deceive the observer, inducing him or her 'to purchase one supposing it to be the other."[207] Based on the analysis of the figures, the court found plaintiff's patented design and defendants' accused product were substantially similar.[208] In the second tier of the *Egyptian Goddess* test, the court

---

206   Ibid. at 1102–05.
207   Ibid. at 1103.
208   Ibid. at 1104.

analysed the design as a whole and compared it to the prior art. In the end, the court found that the accused device and the claimed design were substantially similar.²⁰⁹ An ordinary observer would be deceived and could be induced to purchase defendants' product over plaintiff's.²¹⁰ There are no sharp distinguishing features between the two designs against the context of the prior art.²¹¹ Plaintiff had therefore met its burden in proving design patent infringement.

9.113 In a case involving design rights and trade dress rights, Apple asserted several patents against multiple Samsung devices.²¹² Three of Apple's design patents claimed the 'ornamental design of an electronic device,' and the final design patent claimed 'the ornamental design for a graphical user interface for a display screen or portion thereof.'²¹³ Samsung's accused products included various phones and tablets.

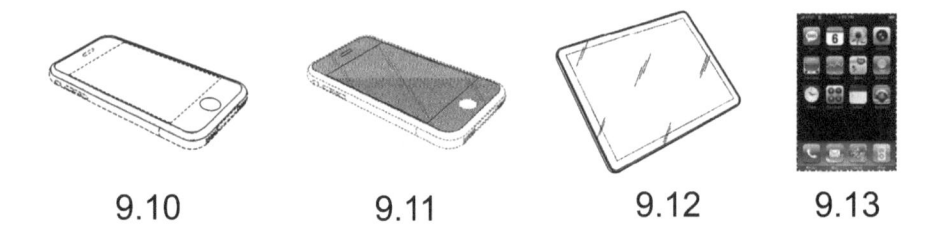

9.10   9.11   9.12   9.13

Figure 9.10   Drawing of Fig. 1 of Design Patent D593,087
Source: US Patent No. US D593,087 S.

Figure 9.11   Drawing of Fig. 1 of Design Patent D618,677
Source: US Patent No. D618,677.

Figure 9.12   Drawing of Fig. 1 of Design Patent D504,889
Source: US Patent No. US D504,889 S.

Figure 9.13   Drawing of Fig. 1 of Design Patent D604,305
Source: US Patent No. D604,305.

---

209   Ibid. at 1104–05.
210   Ibid.
211   Ibid.
212   *See Samsung Elecs.*, 137 S. Ct. at 434; *Apple, Inc. v. Samsung Elecs. Co.*, 786 F.3d 983 (Fed. Cir. 2015); *Apple, Inc. v. Samsung Elecs. Co.*, No. 11-CV-01846-LHK, 2011 WL 7036077, at *24 (N.D. Cal. Dec. 2, 2011), aff'd in part, vacated in part, remanded, 678 F.3d 1314 (Fed. Cir. 2012).
213   *Apple, Inc. v. Samsung Elecs. Co.*, 920 F. Supp. 2d 1079, 1090 (N.D. Cal. 2013); *Apple, Inc. v. Samsung Elecs. Co.*, No. 11-CV-01846-LHK, 2011 WL 7036077, at *2 (N.D. Cal. Dec. 2, 2011).

9.114 After trial, a jury ultimately found that most of Samsung's products infringed the D'087 patent, D'677 patent, and D'305 patent.[214] Both the trial court and the Federal Circuit agreed that the jury's verdict was reasonable and that the jury instructions were sound.[215] As the Federal Circuit summarized, 'if, in the eye of an ordinary observer, giving such attention as a purchaser usually gives, two designs are *substantially the same*, if the resemblance is such as to deceive such an observer, inducing him to purchase one supposing it to be the other, the first one patented is infringed by the other.'[216] It noted that the verdict was also supported by witness testimony regarding 'the *similar overall visual impressions* of the accused products to the asserted design patents such that an ordinary observer would likely be deceived.'[217] With this understanding of infringement, the trial court awarded, and the Federal Circuit affirmed, damages based on the idea that damages depend the end product sold to consumer, not merely based on an infringing component of the product.[218]

9.115 The Supreme Court had a slightly different opinion, holding that damages in design patent cases can be based on an end product or a component of that product.[219] The Court agreed that 'a design patent is infringed 'if, in the eye of an ordinary observer, giving such attention as a purchaser usually gives, two designs are substantially the same."[220] However, the Court declined to create a test 'identifying the relevant article of manufacture at the first step of the § 289 damages inquiry and to parse the record to apply that test in this case.'[221]

C. COMMENTS, ANALYSIS, AND EVALUATION

1. Comments on Present Legal Framework (Legislation and Case Law)

(a) Design patent enforcement in district court

9.116 A design patent owner who accuses a third party of infringement of its design patent can file a complaint for design patent infringement to seek damages

---

214 *Apple Inc. v. Samsung Elecs. Co.*, 786 F.3d 983, 996–97 (Fed. Cir. 2015); *Apple, Inc. v. Samsung Elecs. Co.*, 920 F. Supp. 2d 1079, 1090 (N.D. Cal. 2013).
215 *Apple Inc. v. Samsung Elecs. Co.*, 786 F.3d 983, 998–1000 (Fed. Cir. 2015); *Apple, Inc. v. Samsung Elecs. Co.*, 920 F. Supp. 2d 1079, 1090–91 (N.D. Cal. 2013).
216 *Apple Inc. v. Samsung Elecs. Co.*, 786 F.3d 983, 999 (Fed. Cir. 2015) (internal citations omitted).
217 Ibid. at 1000.
218 Samsung Elecs., 137 S. Ct. at 434; *see also supra* Section A.4.j.
219 Ibid. at 434; *see also supra* Section A.4.j.
220 Ibid. at 432.
221 Ibid. at 436.

and/or injunctive relief in an appropriate U.S. district court because such courts 'have original jurisdiction of any civil action arising under any Act of Congress relating to patents.'[222] Interestingly, the vast majority of patent cases filed in district courts in the U.S. are utility patent cases.[223] Only a small fraction of cases (just over 4 per cent) assert only a design patent, and an even smaller number assert a mix of design and utility patents (just under 2 per cent).[224] However, 'the percent increase in design-patent cases is much higher than that of utility-patent cases' in the U.S. district courts, suggesting that activity enforcing U.S. design patent rights is increasing.[225] The most popular district court in which to enforce a U.S. design patent is the Central District of California, followed by the Northern District of Illinois, which has about one-third the number of cases as the Central District of California.[226]

(b) Design patent enforcement at the International Trade Commission

9.117 A design patent owner can alternatively or additionally pursue relief through Section 337 of the Tariff Act of 1930 ('Section 337'), which prohibits '[t]he importation into the United States, the sale for importation, or the sale within the United States after importation by the owner, importer, or consignee, of articles that—(i) infringe a valid and enforceable United States patent.'[227] The U.S. International Trade Commission ('ITC') is thus tasked with protecting the U.S. border from importing products that infringe a valid U.S. patent, including U.S. utility and design patents. To pursue this remedy, a design patent owner files a complaint with the ITC, which, if instituted, may result in a finding that imported accused goods violate the design patent and should be excluded from entering the U.S. As such, the sole remedy available at the ITC for design patent infringement is an exclusion order preventing goods from being imported and/or a cease and desist order preventing existing U.S. inventory from being sold. Damages are not available in this forum.

9.118 Nonetheless, this forum can be attractive for design patent owners because by law, the ITC must complete an instituted investigation 'at the earliest practicable time,' which provides relative speed compared to many district courts on

---

222 28 U.S.C. § 1338(a).
223 David L. Schwartz and Xaviere Giroud, An Empirical Study of Design Patent Litigation, 72 *Ala. L. Rev.* 417, 443 (2020).
224 Ibid.
225 Ibid. at 444.
226 Ibid. at 445. The increase in filings in the Northern District of Illinois is recent and largely related to an increase in design patent case filings against Internet sellers.
227 19 U.S.C. § 1337(a)(1)(B).

slower time frames.²²⁸ This forum may also become more attractive for different types of products as new technologies emerge. For example, while batteries are typically thought to be buried inside products and, thus, less important for design patent protection, with the recent rise of electric cars, this may no longer be the case. In early 2021, the ITC instituted an investigation based on three design patents directed to ornamental features of batteries.²²⁹

2. Design Law Reform De Lege Ferenda

(a) Conflict between product life cycle and design patent pendency at the USPTO

9.119 Commentators have noted that some of the industries that might benefit most from design patent protection have product life cycles that are not commensurate with the timing of the U.S. patent examination process.²³⁰ For example, the fashion industry has a short product life cycle with high innovation levels.²³¹ One key problem commentators have noted with the U.S. design patent examination system is that 'the time for all patent applications at the USPTO to be granted is exceedingly long and slow.'²³²

9.120 As of September 2023, the pendency of design patent applications, as measured by the average number of months from the design application filing date to the date the application has reached a final disposition, is 21 months.²³³ This time period accounts for the post-filing activities associated with patent prosecution in the U.S., including the examination process, through which a patent examiner at the USPTO examines the application to ensure compliance with the requirements of title 35 of the U.S. Code. During this process, the examiner may reject the claim in the application if the claim is not directed to patent-eligible subject matter, or fails to meet the novelty, nonobviousness, or definiteness requirements. The examiner will then issue an Office Action outlining the deficiencies of the application, if any, and the applicant has the opportunity to respond, pointing out any errors in the Office Action and/or making appropriate amendments to address the objections and/or rejections

---

228 19 U.S.C. § 1337(b)(1).
229 Notice of Institution of Investigation, In the Matter of Certain Batteries and Products Containing Same, Inv. No. 337-TA-1244 (Jan. 29, 2021).
230 See, e.g., Harold C. Wegner, 'The New Industrial Design Law, a TRIPS Trap?', Patentlyo Blog (Nov. 15, 2012), http://patentlyo.com/media/docs/2012/11/wegnerindustrialdesignsnov12.pdf; Tiffany Mahmood, Design Law in the United States as Compared to the European Community Design System: What Do We Need to Fix?, 24 *Fordham Intell. Prop. Media & Ent. L.J.* 555, 580 (2014).
231 Mahmood at 581–82, ibid.
232 Ibid. at 582.
233 USPTO, Design Data September 2023, https://www.uspto.gov/dashboard/patents/design.html (last visited Nov. 22, 2023).

set forth by the examiner. Upon receipt of the applicant's response, the examiner will reconsider the application and, if all issues have been resolved, allow the application to issue as a design patent. Commentators have suggested that this substantive process is out of pace with the requirements of fast-paced industries seeking design patent protection.[234] For example, Wegner notes that 'a design examination law is fundamentally unsuited to the many aspects of industrial designs which have a very short life cycle that will expire long before an examined design can be patented.'[235]

9.121 This examination-based system in the U.S. differs from the registration system in the European Union because an examiner is assigned to consider and review the U.S. application, as explained above—it is not merely registered. Thus, some commentators have suggested adopting a 'registration system' similar to other countries in the international community.[236] One commentator has suggested that to address any concerns that no substantive examination would occur, third parties could be given the opportunity to intervene to invalidate the registration.[237] Under this proposed system, a third-party intervention would effectively result in an action before the USPTO or a court such that substantive examination occurs only in contested cases.[238]

3. Areas in Which Improvement/Amendment Is Required (e.g., Inconsistencies, Gaps, and Insufficiencies), and How They Should Be Corrected

(a) Damages for design patent infringement

9.122 A prevailing plaintiff in an action for utility patent infringement can optionally recover a reasonable royalty or its lost profits due to the defendant's infringement.[239] These same types of compensatory damages are available for design patent infringement as well, pursuant to 35 U.S.C. § 171(b), which extends the utility patent infringement remedies to the design patent context.[240] However, prevailing plaintiffs in design patent infringement cases can also optionally seek damages under the total profits rule, which is exclusively available in the design patent context:

---

234 Mahmood at 581–82, *supra* note 234.
235 See Wegner at 6, *supra* note 234.
236 Ibid. at 7.
237 Mahmood at 582, *supra* note 234.
238 Ibid.
239 35 U.S.C. § 284.
240 35 U.S.C. § 171(b) ('Applicability of This Title.--The provisions of this title relating to patents for inventions shall apply to patents for designs, except as otherwise provided.').

§ 289. Additional remedy for infringement of design patent
Whoever during the term of a patent for a design, without license of the owner, (1) applies the patented design, or any colorable imitation thereof, to any article of manufacture for the purpose of sale, or (2) sells or exposes for sale any article of manufacture to which such design or colorable imitation has been applied shall be liable to the owner to the extent of his total profit, but not less than $250, recoverable in any United States district court having jurisdiction of the parties.
Nothing in this section shall prevent, lessen, or impeach any other remedy which an owner of an infringed patent has under the provisions of this title, but he shall not twice recover the profit made from the infringement.[241]

9.123 This rule provides a third option as an available remedy for design patent infringement, namely, the entire profits gained by the infringer through sale of the article of manufacture to which the design is applied.[242] This is often referred to as the total profits rule because the infringer is liable 'to the extent of his total profit,'[243] and the Supreme Court has clarified that '[t]otal,' of course, means all.'[244] However, if the prevailing plaintiff asserts a utility patent and a design patent covering the same product and elects to seek damages under § 289 for the design patent infringement, it cannot recover additional damages for the same infringing product based on § 284.[245]

(b) Multi-component products under the total profits rule

9.124 As noted above, § 289 relates to the 'total profit[s]' for the sale of an 'article of manufacture' to which the patented design is applied.[246] One question that has arisen is what constitutes the 'article of manufacture' for purposes of computing the 'total profit[s]' when the product to which the design is affixed includes multiple components. In the now-overturned *Apple v. Samsung* decision (discussed above), the Federal Circuit, the U.S. court that has exclusive jurisdiction over patent law appeals, held that the 'article of manufacture' referred to the entire product on sale even if the design is affixed to only part of it, and the product comprises multiple components.[247] Under that ruling, even though Apple's design patents covered only the screen and a portion of the housing of its smartphone, Samsung was nevertheless liable for its profits on the entire smartphone.[248]

---

241 35 U.S.C. § 289.
242 Ibid.
243 Ibid.
244 *Samsung Elecs.*, 137 S. Ct. at 434 (citing AMERICAN HERITAGE DICTIONARY 1836 (5th ed. 2011)).
245 See, e.g., *Catalina*, 295 F.3d at 1291–92.
246 35 U.S.C. § 289.
247 *Apple Inc. v. Samsung Elecs. Co.*, 786 F.3d 983, 1002 (Fed. Cir. 2015), *rev'd and remanded*, 137 S. Ct. 429 (2016).
248 Ibid.

9.125 In an important case for design patent law, the U.S. Supreme Court agreed to review that decision to address 'whether in the case of a multicomponent product, the relevant 'article of manufacture' must always be the end product sold to the consumer or whether it can also be a component of that product.'[249] After finding that '[a]n article of manufacture ... is simply a thing made by hand or machine,' the Supreme Court reasoned that the term 'is broad enough to encompass both a product sold to a consumer as well as a component of that product,' whether sold separately or not.[250] However, the Supreme Court declined to resolve the factual question of whether the 'article of manufacture' in that particular case was the smartphone or a component of it.[251] Accordingly, under present U.S. law, the Supreme Court resolved the question of whether the 'article of manufacture' under § 289 could be a component of a product (it can) but left open for the lower courts the question of how to determine what the 'article of manufacture' is on a case-by-case basis.

9.126 Thus, an ambiguity remains under U.S. law as to what test to use to properly identify the 'article of manufacture' for purposes of determining damages under § 289 for multi-component products. In the case between Samsung and Apple, the district court applied a four-part test for determining the 'article of manufacture,' modeled after the test suggested by the Department of Justice in an amicus curiae brief when the case was pending before the U.S. Supreme Court.[252] That district court considered the following four factors:

(1) '[T]he scope of the design claimed in the plaintiff's patent, including the drawing and written description';
(2) '[T]he relative prominence of the design within the product as a whole';
(3) '[W]hether the design is conceptually distinct from the product as a whole'; and
(4) '[T]he physical relationship between the patented design and the rest of the product,' including whether 'the design pertains to a component that a user or seller can physically separate from the product as a whole,' and whether 'the design is embodied in a component that is manufactured separately from the rest of the product, or if the component can be sold separately.'[253]

---

249 *Samsung Elecs.*, 137 S. Ct. at 434.
250 Ibid. at 435.
251 Ibod. at 434–36.
252 *Apple Inc. v. Samsung Elecs. Co.*, No. 11-CV-01846-LHK, 2017 WL 4776443, at *7–8, *11 (N.D. Cal. Oct. 22, 2017).
253 Ibid. at *11 (alterations in original).

Other district courts have taken a similar approach,[254] but neither the Federal Circuit nor the U.S. Supreme Court has definitively provided clarification with respect to how to determine the 'article of manufacture' for purposes of computing damages under § 289.   9.127

4. Future Outlook in Light of New Technologies

U.S. law provides that '[w]hoever invents any new, original and ornamental design for an *article* of manufacture may obtain a patent therefor.'[255] The USPTO has interpreted this phrase to extend design patent protection to (1) designs of 'an ornament, impression, print, or picture applied to or embodied in an *article of manufacture* (surface indicia)'; (2) designs 'for the shape or configuration of an *article of manufacture*'; and (3) combinations thereof.[256] That is, a design must be applied to or embodied in an article of manufacture to be eligible for design patent protection.[257] A mere picture or ornamentation does not qualify.[258]   9.128

As new technologies have emerged, the definition of what constitutes an 'article of manufacture' has evolved too. For example, as the prevalence of graphical user interfaces having computer-generated icons has grown, the USPTO has expanded its guidance for design patent applicants and USPTO examiners to determine whether this new technology meets the 'article of manufacture' requirement. According to the USPTO guidance, computer-generated icons, taken alone, are merely '[two]-dimensional images' that amount to nothing more than unpatentable surface ornamentation.[259] This doctrine has its roots in *Ex parte Strijland*, where the applicant presented a design for a computer-generated icon without showing the display, and the BPAI found that it was unpatentable because '[s]howing the design applied to an article is a threshold requirement for design protection.'[260] However, 'if an application claims a computer-generated icon shown on a computer screen, monitor, other display panel, or a portion thereof, the claim complies with the 'article of manufacture' requirement.'[261] The guidance also evolved to account for   9.129

---

254 *Columbia Sportswear N. Am., Inc. v. Seirus Innovative Accessories, Inc.*, No. 3:17-cv-01781-HZ, 2017 WL 5494999, at *1 (S.D. Cal. Nov. 16, 2017); *Nordock, Inc. v. Sys., Inc.*, No. 11-CV-118, 2017 WL 5633114, at *5 (E.D. Wis. Nov. 21, 2017).
255 35 U.S.C. § 171(a) (emphasis added).
256 MPEP § 1504.01 (emphases added).
257 Ibid.
258 Ibid.
259 Ibid. § 1504.01(a).I.
260 *Ex parte Strijland*, 26 U.S.P.Q.2d 1259 (B.P.A.I. 1992).
261 MPEP § 1504.01(a).I.

changing computer-generated icons, specifically allowing 'images that change in appearance during viewing' to be design patent eligible, while clarifying that it is only the beginning and end images that qualify for protection, not the intermediaries.[262]

9.130 Recently, the USPTO issued a notice seeking 'public input on whether its interpretation of the *article of manufacture* requirement in the United States Code should be revised to protect digital designs that encompass new and emerging technologies.'[263] The new and emerging technologies referenced in this call for comments include 'projections, holographic imagery, or virtual/ augmented reality [that] do not require a physical display screen or other tangible article to be viewable.'[264] At least one commentator has suggested that the term 'article of manufacture' should be construed broadly to encompass this new technology and make it eligible for design patent protection.[265] Okolie suggests that augmented and virtual realities could be 'likened to those for GUIs, [and] their claims may be represented as a transitional or animated virtual design on a disclaimed display screen.'[266] Okloie, however, does note that one complication might be 'whether the relevant article of manufacture is the entire augmented or virtual reality system or some component thereof,'[267] raising potential concerns over how to compute damages under § 289 and the Supreme Court's interpretation of it in the *Samsung v. Apple* case discussed above.

---

262   MPEP § 1504.01(a).IV.
263   USPTO, The Article of Manufacture Requirement, 85 Fed. Reg. 83,063, 83,063 (Dec. 21, 2020).
264   Ibid. at 83,064.
265   Sonia Okolie, 'Determining the Article of Manufacture in Augmented Reality and Virtual Reality Design Patents', 48 AIPLA Q.J. 95, 115–16 (2020).
266   Ibid. at 118 (footnote omitted).
267   Ibid. at 117.

10

DESIGN LAW AT THE CROSSROADS – A POST-BREXIT REVIEW OF DESIGN PROTECTION IN THE UK

Jane Cornwell and Lynne Chave

A.	OVERVIEW	10.001	D. OTHER IP RIGHTS PROTECTING DESIGNS	10.064
B.	UK REGISTERED DESIGNS	10.004	1. Copyright	10.065
	1. Introduction	10.004	2. Registered Trade Marks and Passing Off	10.068
	2. Requirements for Valid UK Design Registration	10.007	E. PROCEDURE AND ENFORCEMENT	10.070
	(a) 'Design'	10.007	1. UK Design Registration Procedure	10.070
	(b) Novelty and individual character	10.011	(a) Introduction	10.070
	(c) Exclusions from protection	10.023	(b) Filing basics	10.071
	3. Ownership, Duration and Post-grant Invalidation	10.027	(c) Examination	10.075
	4. Infringement and Defences	10.031	(d) Publication, registration and post-grant matters	10.077
C.	UK UNREGISTERED DESIGN RIGHTS	10.035	2. Enforcement of Design Rights	10.079
	1. UK Unregistered Design Right	10.035	(a) Introduction	10.079
	(a) Introduction	10.035	(b) Choice of forum	10.080
	(b) Qualification	10.039	(c) Pre-action communications, 'threats' and standing to sue	10.083
	(c) Protectable UKUDR 'designs'	10.041	(d) The English courts' approach to design cases	10.085
	(d) Exclusions from UKUDR	10.045	(e) Remedies	10.088
	(e) Originality	10.050	(f) Criminal enforcement	10.093
	(f) Ownership and duration	10.053	F. CONCLUSION	10.095
	(g) Infringement and defences	10.055		
	2. New Post-Brexit Forms of UK Unregistered Design	10.059		

A. OVERVIEW

10.001 The UK has a long history of design protection, first introducing unregistered design rights in 1787 and design registration in 1839.[1] There have been many developments since then. Currently, the primary mechanisms for protecting designs are through UK design registration and various forms of unregistered right, the most longstanding of which is UK unregistered design right.[2] Designs may also be protected via registered trade marks, passing off and copyright; there is, in particular, a complex relationship in UK law between designs and copyright.

10.002 At the time of writing, UK design law stands at a crossroads, triggered in large part by Brexit. As the chapter will explain, UK design law has evolved over time: the early years of the 21st century marked a particular period of significant change under the influence of EU design law. In 2001, UK registered design law was harmonised by the EU Designs Directive.[3] The registered and unregistered Community design also took effect in the UK for many years.[4] Now that the UK has left the EU, however, the position has changed. Although UK registered design legislation is currently still aligned with the Directive, post-Brexit the UK may amend this.[5] In addition, since the end of the Brexit transition period,[6] registered and unregistered Community designs no longer cover the UK. The loss of these EU-level design rights has brought some forced simplification to the UK design regime, in that all design protection in the UK now exists only under national law. However, as will be discussed further below, Brexit also prompted the creation of two further forms of domestic unregistered design right, bringing (at the time of writing in late 2023) the total number of different forms of unregistered design protection in UK law to three. The UK Intellectual Property Office ('UKIPO') is currently conducting a review of UK design law, noting the 'new flexibilities

---

1 B Sherman and L Bently, *The Making of Modern Intellectual Property Law* (Cambridge University Press, 1999), 61–94; M Howe, J St Ville and A Chantrielle, *Russell-Clarke & Howe on Industrial Designs* (10th ed, Sweet & Maxwell, 2022), Chapter 1.
2 For more in-depth discussion, see: Howe et al, *Russell-Clarke & Howe* (n 1); D Musker, *Navigating Design Law* (CIPA, 2021).
3 Directive 98/71/EC on the legal protection of designs [1998] OJ L289/28 ('DD').
4 Under Council Regulation (EC) 6/2002 on Community designs [2002] OJ L3/1 ('CDR').
5 Within the constraints of its international IP treaty obligations, including the post-Brexit EU-UK Trade and Cooperation Agreement [2021] OJ L149/10, which contains some (relatively high-level) design provisions: see Arts 245-249.
6 At 11pm GMT on 31 December 2020: European Union (Withdrawal Agreement) Act 2020, s1 and s39(1). See further: UKIPO, 'Intellectual property and the transition period', 31 January 2020 www.gov.uk/government/news/intellectual-property-and-the-transition-period accessed 2 August 2023.

and opportunities' to define the domestic design regime post-Brexit.[7] Overall, the multiplicity of forms of design protection in the UK has resulted in a 'law of labyrinthine complexity';[8] the existence of so many parallel but substantively different forms of protection has been repeatedly flagged as a point of concern, including in the current UKIPO review.[9]

10.003 Section B reviews UK registered design law. Section C considers UK unregistered design protection in its various forms, and Section D outlines how other intellectual property rights may protect designs. Section E considers procedural matters relating to filing and enforcement. The implications of Brexit and current UKIPO design law review will be noted as relevant.

B. UK REGISTERED DESIGNS

1. Introduction

10.004 UK registered design law is governed by the Registered Designs Act 1949 ('RDA 1949'). The RDA 1949 was comprehensively overhauled in 2001 to implement the EU Designs Directive, significantly liberalising registrability.[10]

10.005 As regards Brexit, a significant practical consequence is that the UK designs register is now populated with a very large number of 're-registered designs', based on registered Community designs ('RCDs') which were in force at the time, but which ceased to provide protection in the UK once Brexit took effect. Pursuant to the terms of the EU-UK Withdrawal Agreement, new 're-registered designs' were automatically added to the UK designs register at no cost to the holder.[11] These received the same filing, priority and registration dates and remaining term of protection as the original RCDs.[12] These

---

7   UKIPO, 'Call for views on designs', 25 January 2022 www.gov.uk/government/consultations/reviewing-the-designs-framework-call-for-views/call-for-views-on-designs accessed 2 August 2023.
8   Howe et al, *Russell-Clarke & Howe* (n 1), para 1-002.
9   UKIPO, 'Call for views on designs' (n 7); UKIPO, 'Call for views on designs: Government response', 12 July 2022 www.gov.uk/government/consultations/reviewing-the-designs-framework-call-for-views/outcome/call-for-views-on-designs-government-response accessed 2 August 2023.
10 Current law applies to all UK design registrations resulting from an application filed on or after 9 December 2001. Infringement of earlier-filed designs is also governed by current law, but validity by the old version of the RDA 1949. For more on pre-harmonisation UK registered design law, see: Howe et al, *Russell-Clarke & Howe* (n 1), Chapter 3; Musker (n 2), 119–30.
11 With an opt-out for rightholders who did not wish such rights: RDA 1949, Schedule 1A, para 3.
12 RDA 1949, s12A and Schedule 1A. Similar steps were taken for international design registrations designating the EU: RDA 1949, Schedule 1B. For pending RCD applications and international (EU) applications, holders had until 30 September 2021 to reapply in the UK (paying the usual fee) to maintain the filing and priority dates of their original filing. See generally: Agreement on the Withdrawal of the United Kingdom

're-registered designs' now stand independently as UK design registrations under the RDA 1949: they must be assigned, licensed, challenged and renewed separately from the RCDs on which they were based.[13]

10.006 Substantively, Brexit has had no immediate impact on the RDA 1949. As noted above, the UKIPO is considering design reform, although for registered designs its consultation so far has focused mostly on procedural matters and it remains to be seen whether the UKIPO will consider any of the more substantive reform proposals recently made by the European Commission for the DD and CDR.[14] Before Brexit, much of the case law relevant to UK registered designs involved registered and unregistered Community designs, which were governed by the same core principles.[15] The UK was part of the harmonised EU design regime for nearly 20 years, and European Court of Justice ('ECJ') and General Court ('GC') rulings are generally well consolidated within UK case law.[16] Since Brexit, ECJ decisions pre-dating the end of the transition period still bind the lower UK courts, but can be departed from by UK appellate courts; UK courts can no longer make ECJ preliminary references and have discretion on whether to have regard to ECJ rulings decided after the end of the transition period.[17] It is unclear how much impact this will have, at least in the short term: not only do relatively few registered design cases make it to appeal in the UK (see further Section E.2.(a) below), but early post-Brexit UK copyright case law suggests that UK judges may be reluctant to engage in immediate wholesale change.[18] Given constraints of space, this chapter will focus on key UK cases, with brief mention of selected ECJ authorities (many of which are discussed in fuller detail elsewhere in this volume).

---

of Great Britain and Northern Ireland from the European Union and the European Atomic Energy Community [2019] OJ C384I/1, Arts 54–56 and 59.

13   The RDA 1949 contains provisions addressing continuity of pre-existing licences, security interests, consents and other documentary references to relevant RCDs: RDA 1949, Schedule 1A, paras 6–8. There are also rules governing pending proceedings and the enforceability of existing RCD-based injunctions: RDA 1949, Schedule 1A, paras 9 and 10. See also RDA 1949, Schedule 1B for equivalent provisions for international (EU) filings.

14   On which see further: A Kur, T Endrich-Laimböck and M Huckschlag 'Substantive Law Aspects of the "Design Package"' (2023) 72 *GRUR International* 557. At the time of writing, the Council of the EU has adopted just its positions on the proposed amendments to the DD and CDR: see Council of the European Union, 'Intellectual property: Council adopts two positions on designs protection legislation', 25 September 2023 https://www.consilium.europa.eu/en/press/press-releases/2023/09/25/intellectual-property-council-adopts-two-positions-on-designs-protection-legislation/ accessed 2 August 2023.

15   See further section C.2 below.

16   And the UKIPO's 'Registered Designs Examination Practice', 2 November 2021, www.gov.uk/government/publications/registered-designs-examination-practice accessed 2 August 2023.

17   European Union (Withdrawal) Act 2018, s6.

18   *TuneIn Inc v Warner Music UK Ltd and Sony Music Entertainment UK Ltd* [2021] EWCA Civ 441.

2. Requirements for Valid UK Design Registration

(a) 'Design'

A registrable 'design' consists of:[19]

10.007

the appearance of the whole or a part of a product resulting from the features of, in particular, the lines, contours, colours, shape, texture or materials of the product or its ornamentation.

Designs can be two- or three-dimensional, and can relate to part of a product. The focus is on what can be perceived visually.[20] In line with the 'design approach' underpinning EU harmonisation,[21] there is no requirement that a design must be aesthetic or ornamental. A 'product' is:[22]

10.008

any industrial or handicraft item other than a computer program; and, in particular, includes packaging, get-up, graphic symbols, typographic type-faces and parts intended to be assembled into a complex product.

This definition encompasses the full spectrum of products from the artisanal to the industrially-produced, including intangible products, such as digital icons. It also includes 'complex products' and their component parts,[23] and may include a set of items where these can be treated as single design for a single product.[24] What is protected is the design as such: scope of protection is not restricted to use for any particular product.

10.009

Determining which design features a registration actually protects in any given case requires interpretation of the registration, particularly the design representations.[25] The design representations are to be interpreted objectively: this is a matter for the court rather than the 'informed user' or experts.[26] This task has at times proved controversial, particularly when distinguishing between design drawings which claim a three-dimensional 'shape-only' design and those in which the absence of any surface decoration should be taken as claim-

10.010

---

19 RDA 1949, s1(2).
20 *Gimex International Groupe Import Export v Chill Bag Company Ltd and Others* [2012] ECDR 25, [25].
21 A Kur, 'The Green Paper's "Design approach": what's wrong with it?' (1993) 15 EIPR 374.
22 RDA 1949, s1(3).
23 A 'complex product' is 'composed of at least two replaceable component parts permitting disassembly and reassembly of the product': RDA 1949, s1(3).
24 *GBL UK Trading Ltd v H&S Alliance Ltd* [2022] RPC 3.
25 *Magmatic Ltd v PMS International Group Plc* [2016] ECDR 15, [30].
26 *Sealed Air Ltd v Sharp Interpack Ltd* [2013] EWPCC 23, [18]-[21]; *Rothy's Inc v Giesswein Walkwaren AG* [2021] FSR 18, [55].

ing a specifically 'unadorned' shape.[27] UK courts have interpreted line drawings both ways, depending on the facts.[28] In the controversial *Magmatic* ruling, involving the well-known 'Trunki' ride-on suitcase, the UK Supreme Court ('UKSC') also appeared to endorse an approach in which greyscale CAD drawings – previously thought of as typical of 'shape only' designs – were instead interpreted as claiming an unadorned shape.[29] Unhelpfully, beyond confirming that absence of ornamentation can in principle be a feature of a design, the UKSC declined to give definitive guidance on how this should be represented, or to refer the issue to the ECJ.[30] This is not the only interpretation challenge: UK courts also interpret dotted/dashed lines according to the facts of the case, rather than necessarily adopting the typically-understood drafting convention that dotted/dashed features are not part of the claimed design.[31]

(b) Novelty and individual character

10.011 A UK design is validly registered if it is 'new' and has 'individual character'.[32] These are cumulative requirements.[33] An additional rule applies to component parts of complex products: the component part, once incorporated, must remain visible during normal use of the complex product and the visible features of the component must be new and have individual character.[34] As discussed below (see Section E.1.(c)), neither novelty nor individual character is examined pre-registration: compliance will only be tested in a post-grant invalidation challenge.

---

27 This has been most acute in cases dealing RCDs, for which (in contrast with UK registrations – see Section E.1.(b)) written disclaimers are not permitted and any optional written description cannot affect scope of protection: CDR, Art 36(6).

28 *Procter & Gamble Co v Reckitt Benckiser (UK) Ltd* [2008] ECDR 3, [40] (shape only); *Samsung Electronics (UK) Ltd v Apple Inc* [2013] ECDR 2, [18] (unadorned shape).

29 At first instance, Magmatic's RCD was held to be for shape only. On appeal, alongside certain tonal contrasts in Magmatic's greyscale CAD images (which were, perhaps wrongly, not taken into account at first instance), the English Court of Appeal also took into consideration the absence of surface decoration in the representations as a feature of the RCD, and thus a point of contrast with the alleged infringement: *Magmatic Ltd v PMS International Ltd* [2014] ECDR 20, [41] and [47]. On appeal to the UKSC, Lord Neuberger preferred to 'leave... open' whether absence of ornamentation was actually a feature of Magmatic's design, but the appeal court's conclusions were nonetheless upheld: *Magmatic Ltd* (UKSC, n 25), [50]. See further: D Stone, 'Trunki – How did things go so wrong?' (2016) 11 JIPLP 662.

30 *Magmatic* (UKSC, n 25), [50] and [59]. The UKSC did comment that a line drawing is much more likely to be interpreted as claiming 'shape only' than a CAD image: ibid, [46]. It has since also been noted that only in a 'very unusual case indeed' would a line drawing be taken to claim an absence of surface decoration: *Lutec (UK) Ltd v Cascade Holdings Ltd* [2022] FSR 6, [24].

31 *Samsung Electronics (UK) Ltd v Apple Inc* [2013] ECDR 1, [11], and on appeal at *Samsung* (EWCA, n 28), [21]–[24]; *Kohler Mira Ltd v Bristan Group Ltd* [2014] FSR 1, [22]-[23] and [52]. See criticism of this approach in D Stone, 'Transparency over the use of dotted lines?' (2013) 8 JIPLP 437.

32 RDA 1949, s1B(1).

33 *Procter & Gamble Co v Reckitt Benckiser (UK) Ltd* [2007] ECDR 4, [25].

34 RDA 1949, s1B(8).

A design will lack novelty if an identical design, or one 'whose features differ **10.012**
only in immaterial details' has been made available to the public before the filing
or, if relevant, priority date.[35] Given the additional, more onerous requirement
of individual character, unsurprisingly novelty has received little judicial attention. The English Court of Appeal has suggested that, although central to the
assessment of individual character, the perception of the 'informed user' is not
relevant for novelty purposes.[36] The fullest articulation in UK case law of what
constitute 'immaterial details' can be found in *Shnuggle v Munchkin*:[37]

> 'Immaterial details' means 'only minor and trivial in nature, not affecting overall appear-
> ance'. This is an objective test. The design must be considered as a whole. It will be new
> if some part of it differs from any earlier design in some material respect, even if some
> or all of the design features, if considered individually, would not be.

'Individual character' has received much greater consideration from the UK **10.013**
courts. A design has 'individual character' if:[38]

> the overall impression it produces on the informed user differs from the overall impres-
> sion produced on such a user by any design which has been made available to the public
> before the relevant date.

This mirrors the test for infringement: 'overall impression' will be assessed on **10.014**
the same basis for validity and infringement, and case law is interchangeable –
indeed, most UK cases deal with infringement disputes.[39]

The perspective of the 'informed user' is critical. The English courts **10.015**
have stressed that the informed user is 'notional' and a 'construct'.[40] The
most-commonly cited approach to characterizing the informed user is that
of Birss J at first instance in *Samsung v Apple*,[41] the Apple 'iPad' litigation, in
which Birss J emphasised how important properly adopting the perspective of

---

35   RDA 1949, s1B(2).
36   *Green Lane Products Ltd v PMS International Group plc* [2008] ECDR 15, [41], although note some disagree-
     ment: Howe et al, *Russell-Clarke & Howe* (n 1), para 2-047.
37   *Shnuggle Ltd v Munchkin Inc* [2020] FSR 22, [26].
38   RDA 1949, s1B(3).
39   An early ruling suggesting a difference between validity and infringement was rapidly reversed: *Dyson Ltd v
     Vax Ltd* [2012] FSR 4, [34], correcting *Procter & Gamble* (EWCA, n 28) on this point.
40   See, e.g., *Woodhouse UK plc v Architectural Lighting Systems (trading as Acquila Design)* [2006] ECDR 11,
     [49]–[51].
41   *Samsung* (EWHC, n 31).

the informed user had been to his ultimate conclusion.[42] Among key points, the informed user:

- is a user of the relevant product, not a designer, technical expert, manufacturer or seller;
- is particularly observant (unlike the average consumer of trade mark law);
- has knowledge of the design corpus and of design features normally included in designs existing in the sector; and
- is interested in the relevant products, showing a relatively high degree of attention when using them.[43]

10.016   The informed user is not necessarily always the end-user: a trade user involved in selecting or buying the product may be the appropriate perspective in some cases.[44]

10.017   When assessing individual character, the 'degree of freedom of the author in creating the design' must be taken into consideration.[45] This focuses on objective design constraints.[46] There is some lingering uncertainty as to exactly what type of constraint will be relevant, particularly whether this extends to economic considerations such as price.[47] However, design trends are not relevant.[48] Design freedom may be indicated by large departure from the existing design corpus,[49] and by a wide variety of subsequently-produced designs.[50] Similarities between designs attributable to design constraints are to be given little significance in the comparison of overall impression: the informed user's attention is more focused on design features where there is more scope for variation.[51]

---

42   *Samsung* (EWHC, n 31), [189].
43   *Samsung* (EWHC, n 31), [34]–[35], drawing from C-281/10 *PepsiCo Inc v Grupo Promer Mon-Graphic SA* ECLI:EU:C:2011:679, T-9/07 *Grupo Promer Mon Graphic SA v OHIM* ECLI:EU:T:2010:96 and T-153/08 *Shenzhen Taiden Industrial Co Ltd v OHIM* ECLI:EU:T:2010:248. Approved on appeal: *Samsung* (EWCA, n 28), [10]-[11].
44   See, e.g., *Louver-Lite Ltd v Harris Parts Ltd (t/a Harris Engineering)* [2012] EWPCC 53, [24]–[32].
45   RDA 1949, s1B(4).
46   *Procter & Gamble* (EWCA, n 28), [31].
47   Arnold J adopted this broader approach in *Dyson Ltd v Vax Ltd* [2010] ECDR 18, [34], repeated in his later judgments in *Magmatic Ltd v PMS International Ltd* [2013] ECC 29, [47] and *Whitby Specialist Vehicles Ltd v Yorkshire Specialist Vehicles Ltd* [2015] ECDR 11, [24]. Arnold J drew support from the apparent endorsement of his ruling in *Dyson* by the Court of Appeal. However, doubts have been raised by the parties (although not decided) in other cases: *Samsung* (EWHC, n 31), [41]; *Scomadi Ltd v RA Engineering Co Ltd* [2018] FSR 14, [80].
48   *Cantel Medical (UK) Ltd v Arc Medical Design Ltd* [2018] EWHC 345 (Pat), [176], citing T-357/12 *Sachi Premium-Outdoor Furniture Lda v OHIM* ECLI:EU:T:2014:55.
49   *Procter & Gamble* (EWCA, n 28), [57].
50   *Dyson* (EWHC, n 47), [37].
51   *Dyson* (EWHC, n 47), [38]; *Cantel Medical* (n 48), [173]–[174].

10.018 The UK courts have also acknowledged the further guidance on assessing individual character in the recitals to the Designs Directive and Community Design Regulation, in particular that this should take into account the nature of the product to which the design is applied, the industrial sector to which it belongs and whether the overall impression on the informed user clearly differs from the 'existing design corpus'.[52] Although some cases have equated the 'design corpus' with the entirety of the prior art,[53] the better view (it is suggested here) is as HHJ Birss explained in *Gimex*: taking into account the design corpus to assess overall impression is analogous to the exercise of approaching the patent prior art in light of the skilled person's common general knowledge, with the 'design corpus' in registered design law informing the informed user's 'design awareness', since '[a]cquiring their design awareness by the experience of using the products concerned is what characterises the informed user'.[54] Where features are common in the design corpus, they should be given little or no weight in the assessment of overall impression.[55]

10.019 Various judicial formulations have been offered on how to approach the determination of 'overall impression',[56] the most recent (and currently most-cited) being that in *Cantel Medical* where HHJ Hacon noted:[57]

The court must:

(1) Decide the sector to which the products in which the designs are intended to be incorporated or to which they are intended to be applied belong;
(2) Identify the informed user and having done so decide
   (a) the degree of the informed user's awareness of the prior art and
   (b) the level of attention paid by the informed user in the comparison, direct if possible, of the designs;
(3) Decide the designer's degree of freedom in developing his design;
(4) Assess the outcome of the comparison between the RCD and the contested design, taking into account
   (a) the sector in question,
   (b) the designer's degree of freedom, and

---

52 *Procter & Gamble* (EWCA, n 28), [17], noting that this guidance is also relevant to infringement. See CDR Recital 14, and DD Recital 13.
53 *L'Oreal SA v RN Ventures Ltd* [2018] ECDR 14, [146]-[152]; *Rothy's* (n 26), [80].
54 *Gimex* (n 20), [44]–[46], approved by Arnold J in *Magmatic* (EWHC, n 47), [46] (not criticised on appeal). For a contrary view, see D Stone, *European Union Design Law – A Practitioner's Guide* (2nd edn, Oxford University Press, 2016), para 10.76.
55 *Cantel Medical* (n 48), [170].
56 See, e.g., *Samsung* (EWHC, n 31), [53]–[56], cited frequently in subsequent cases.
57 *Cantel Medical* (n 48), [181]–[182], building on the four-stage test articulated in T-525/13 *H&M Hennes & Mauritz BV & Co KG v OHIM* ECLI:EU:T:2015:617.

(c) the overall impressions produced by the designs on the informed user, who will have in mind any earlier design which has been made available to the public.

To this I would add:

(5) Features of the designs which are solely dictated by technical function are to be ignored in the comparison.

(6) The informed user may in some cases discriminate between elements of the respective designs, attaching different degrees of importance to similarities or differences. This can depend on the practical significance of the relevant part of the product, the extent to which it would be seen in use, or on other matters.

10.020 Features dictated by technical function are discounted in their entirety.[58] Greater or lesser significance may also be attached to similarities or differences between designs depending on factors such as the practical relevance of the relevant part of the product, or other reasons affecting the degree to which appearance would matter to the informed user.[59] The assessment will be in light of how the design is used:[60] the informed user is taken as likely to pay more attention to parts of the design that are visible when using the product.[61]

10.021 Overall, the approach of the UK courts is that the comparison of designs must be done 'with a reasonable degree of care', at the level of generality which would be taken by the informed user.[62] At least insofar as the expression is used in English, recent case law has rejected as too high-level the language of 'déjà vu' used by the GC to describe the overall impression test.[63] UK courts have typically approached determination of overall impression through a mixture of 'feature analysis' and stepping back to consider overall impression as a whole,[64] as exemplified in *Dyson* and *Samsung*. In *Dyson*, the judge worked in detail through the points of similarity and difference relied upon by the parties before, as he put it, '[s]tanding back from the details and considering the overall impressions of the respective designs' (on which, among other points, he noted the 'smooth, curving and elegant' nature of the registered design compared to the 'rugged, angular and industrial, even somewhat brutal' style of the alleged infringement).[65] In *Samsung v Apple*, after detailed review of similarities and differences HHJ Birss concluded that the allegedly infringing

---

58 *Cantel Medical* (n 48), [168].
59 Ibid., [177]–[179].
60 *Lutec* (n 30), [32], citing T-22/13 *Senz Technologies v OHIM* ECLI:EU:T:2015:310.
61 *Rothy's* (n 26), [93(d)], citing *Shenzhen* (n 43).
62 *Procter & Gamble* (EWCA, n 28), [35(v) and (vii)].
63 *Original Beauty Technology Co Ltd v G4K Fashion Ltd* [2021] FSR 20, [124]–[127].
64 *PulseOn OY v Garmin (Europe) Ltd* [2019] ECDR 8, [19].
65 *Dyson* (EWHC, n 47), [92]–[93]; upheld on appeal *Dyson* (EWCA, n 39), [31]–[32].

Samsung products lacked the same 'understated and extreme simplicity' as Apple's design and were, as he pithily put it, 'not as cool'.[66]

10.022 For both novelty and individual character, the comparison is with one single prior art design at a time, not an amalgam of features from multiple earlier designs.[67] The default position is that the prior art includes any design made available to the public anywhere in the world before the filing or (if relevant) priority date: '[a]ll prior designs for anything are capable of being relevant'.[68] It is not necessary to show that the informed user would actually know of any particular piece of prior art;[69] the informed user 'only comes in once the prior art to be considered is identified'.[70] There are statutory carve-outs for confidential disclosures,[71] disclosures resulting from an abuse,[72] and a 12-month grace period for disclosure by (or in consequence of information or action from) the designer or their successor in title.[73] A disclosure will also not form part of the prior art if that disclosure:[74]

> could not reasonably have become known before the relevant date in the normal course of business to persons carrying on business in the geographical area comprising the United Kingdom and the European Economic Area and specialising in the sector concerned.

The English Court of Appeal has held that this only removes from the prior art disclosures which were obscure in their own sector.[75] The ECJ has also considered this carve-out, concluding that it excludes events that are difficult to verify and that occur in a third country, and does not make distinctions between business sectors within the EU.[76]

---

66 *Samsung* (EWHC, n 31), [190]; upheld on appeal *Samsung* (EWCA, n 28).
67 *Whitby Specialist Vehicles* (n 47), [25] and *PulseOn* (n 64), [14], both citing C-345/13 *Karen Millen Fashions Ltd v Dunnes Stores* ECLI:EU:C:2014:2013.
68 *Gimex* (n 20), [42]. See also RDA 1949, s1B(5).
69 *L'Oreal SA* (n 53), [150]–[151], citing C-361/15 P *Easy Sanitary Solutions v Group Nivelles* ECLI:EU:C:2017:720.
70 *Green Lane* (n 36), [41].
71 RDA 1949, s1B(6)(b).
72 RDA 1949, s1B(6)(e).
73 RDA 1949, s1B(6)(c) and (d), held in *Marks and Spencer v Aldi* to cover disclosure by the designer of any design, not merely the exact design applied for: *Marks and Spencer Plc v Aldi Stores Limited* [2023] FSR 17, [65]-[67].
74 RDA 1949, s1B(6)(a). This is an adjusted post-Brexit version of DD Art 6(1) and CDR Art 7(1), which refer to disclosures which could not have become known 'in the Community'. For more on these provisions, see L Brancusi, 'Prior art in EU design law and its worldwide implications – taking advantage of flexibilities or being obstructed by ambiguities', Chapter 16, this volume.
75 *Green Lane* (n 36).
76 *Easy Sanitary Solutions* (n 69).

(c) Exclusions from protection

10.023 There are three exclusions from protection for UK registered designs.[77]

10.024 First, no rights subsist in features of appearance of a product 'which are solely dictated by the product's technical function'.[78] This is assessed on a feature-by-feature basis: whether a design is validly registered depends on whether there are any features with novelty and individual character left after the exclusion has been applied. Interpretation of this exclusion has proved notoriously controversial. In the UK, after initially adopting the 'multiplicity-of-forms' approach (focused on the availability of design alternatives),[79] in *Dyson* the 'causality' approach (focused on the reasons for the choice of design feature) was preferred.[80] The causality approach has since also been favoured by the ECJ in *DOCERAM*, focusing on whether technical reasons underlie the choice of the feature's appearance.[81]

10.025 Second, rights in a UK registered design also do not subsist in 'features of appearance of a product which must necessarily be reproduced in their exact form and dimensions so as to permit the product in which the design is incorporated or to which it is applied to be mechanically connected to, or placed in, around or against, another product so that either product may perform its function'.[82] This exclusion does not apply to a design 'serving the purpose of allowing multiple assembly or connection of mutually interchangeable products within a modular system'.[83]

10.026 Finally, rights will not subsist in a design which is contrary to public policy or to accepted principles of morality.[84] This exclusion has received little judicial attention. In pre-harmonisation UK case law, it was ruled that distaste among a section of the public was insufficient;[85] that case drew analogy with the equiv-

---

77 For discussion of the equivalent provisions in the DD and CDR, see H Hartwig, 'Design prosecution before the EUIPO and the Court of Justice of the EU', Chapter 11, this volume.
78 RDA 1949, s1C(1).
79 *Landor & Hawa International Ltd v Azure Designs Ltd* [2006] ECDR 31, [30]–[43].
80 *Dyson* (EWHC, n 47), [23]–[31]; endorsed by the Court of Appeal in *Samsung* (EWCA, n 28), [31]. This had been the preferred approach to a similarly-worded exclusion in pre-harmonisation UK registered design law: *AMP Inc v Utilux Pty Ltd* [1971] FSR 572.
81 C-395/16 *DOCERAM GmbH v CeramTec GmbH* ECLI:EU:C:2018:172. The UK courts had adopted the 'reasonable observer' test developed by the EUIPO: *Cantel Medical* (n 48), [166], applying *Linder Recycling Tech GmbH v Franssons Verkstäder AB* (R 690/2007-3). However, the 'reasonable observer' test was rejected in *DOCERAM*.
82 RDA 1949, s1C(2).
83 RDA 1949, s1C(3).
84 RDA 1949, s1D.
85 *Masterman's Design* [1991] RPC 89.

alent provision in registered trade mark law, and it remains to be seen whether a UK court considering this exclusion further would be influenced by recent ECJ developments in trade mark matters.[86]

3. Ownership, Duration and Post-grant Invalidation

10.027 The author of a design is its first owner, unless created by an employee in the course of their employment.[87] The 'author' of a design is the person who creates it.[88] Entitlement may be raised during examination (see Section E.1.(c)), and grant of a registration to a person not entitled is a ground for invalidation (see below) or rectification of the register.[89]

10.028 Fortuitously, given the increasingly pressing debate around ownership of IP in AI outputs, the RDA 1949 already contains provision on computer-generated designs. This identifies the author of a design generated by computer in circumstances such that there is no human author as 'the person by whom the arrangements necessary for the creation of the design are made'.[90] There was general agreement in the UKIPO's recent consultation that this provision is adequate, and that AI should not be recognised as the author or owner of a computer-generated design.[91] This is consistent with views received in an earlier UKIPO consultation on AI and IP.[92]

10.029 A UK design registration lasts in the first instance for five years and can be renewed, on payment of relevant fees, for four more five-year periods up to a maximum of 25 years.[93] Registrations and applications can be transferred and given in security; a UK registration can also be licensed.[94] Such transactions must be recorded on the register.[95]

---

86   C-240/18 P *Constantin Film Produktion GmbH v EUIPO* ECLI:EU:C:2020:118.
87   RDA 1949, ss2(1) and 2(1B). The first owner of a design produced on commission used to be the commissioning party, but this was reformed in 2014 to bring UK law into line with the CDR: now, the designer is the first owner of a commissioned UK registered design.
88   RDA 1949, s2(3).
89   RDA 1949, ss11ZA(2), 20(1) and 20(1A)(c).
90   RDA 1949, s2(4).
91   UKIPO, 'Government response' (n 9), [30].
92   UKIPO, 'Government response to call for views on artificial intelligence and intellectual property', 23 March 2021 www.gov.uk/government/consultations/artificial-intelligence-and-intellectual-property-call-for-views/government-response-to-call-for-views-on-artificial-intelligence-and-intellectual-property#designs accessed 2 August 2023. In both consultations, the UKIPO indicated that it would keep the position under review.
93   RDA 1949, s8.
94   RDA 1949, s15B.
95   RDA 1949, s19.

10.030 Post-grant, a UK registration may be declared invalid on various grounds, including that:[96] it is not a 'design';[97] it lacks novelty or individual character, or falls within one of the exclusions from protection;[98] the design is not new or does not have individual character when compared to a design which was made available to the public on or after the filing or (if relevant) priority date of the registered design, but which is protected as from a prior date;[99] the registered proprietor is not the proprietor of the design;[100] or the design incorporates another's earlier trade mark or copyright work.[101]

4. Infringement and Defences

10.031 Subject to any limitation attaching to the registration (for example, under a disclaimer – see Section E.1.(b) below),[102] a UK registered design gives the proprietor the exclusive right to use the design and any design which does not produce on the informed user a different overall impression.[103] This right is infringed by doing, without consent, anything falling within the proprietor's exclusive right.[104] This is an absolute monopoly right – it does not depend on copying. Since it is the design as such which is protected, the nature of the infringer's product is irrelevant. As 'overall impression' is the same for infringement and validity, the principles discussed in Section B.2.(b), above will apply, including that the designer's degree of freedom in creating the protected design must be taken into consideration.[105]

10.032 A particular point of controversy on UK registered design infringement is low rightholder success rates before the UK courts, particularly on appeal. Concern has been expressed that the scope of protection afforded to Community and UK registered designs 'has been so curtailed by the UK courts that it is no use litigating: even if the design is found to be valid, it will not be found to

---

96 These grounds are exhaustive: see *PepsiCo* (n 43). Some grounds are only actionable by specific persons: RDA 1949, s11ZB.
97 RDA 1949, s11ZA(1)(a).
98 RDA 1949, s11ZA(1)(b).
99 RDA 1949, s11ZA(1A).
100 RDA 1949, s11ZA(2).
101 RDA 1949, s11ZA(3) and (4).
102 RDA 1949, s7(4).
103 RDA 1949, s7(1).
104 RDA 1949, s7A(1).
105 RDA 1949, s7(3).

be infringed'.¹⁰⁶ Some judges have struck an explicitly narrow approach: for example, HHJ Birss noted in *Samsung*: ¹⁰⁷

> How similar does the alleged infringement have to be to infringe? Community design rights are not simply concerned with anti-counterfeiting. One could imagine a design registration system which was intended only to allow for protection against counterfeits. In that system only identical or nearly identical products would infringe. The test of 'different overall impression' is clearly wider than that. The scope of protection of a Community registered design clearly can include products which can be distinguished to some degree from the registration. On the other hand the fact that the informed user is particularly observant and the fact that designs will often be considered side by side are both clearly intended to narrow the scope of design protection. Although no doubt minute scrutiny by the informed user is not the right approach, attention to detail matters.

10.033 There have been relatively few registered design appeals to date (as at the time of writing in late 2023, five to the English Court of Appeal and one to the UKSC). However, it is notable that all of those appeals resulted in non-infringement. The Court of Appeal has conceded that the overall impression test is 'inherently rather imprecise' and leaves 'a considerable margin for the judgment of the tribunal',¹⁰⁸ but was nevertheless willing to reverse the first instance judge in the two appealed disputes in which the registered design had initially been found to be infringed.¹⁰⁹ Although it has also repeatedly confirmed that a strikingly novel design enjoys a greater scope of protection than one which is only incrementally different to the prior art,¹¹⁰ the Court of Appeal also has a track record of finding such designs not infringed, even with this 'broad' protection.¹¹¹ Most appeals have involved designs for essentially new product types, which may have been a concern; some appeal judgments have expressed explicit caution about the policy ramifications of conferring unduly broad protection, including that fear of potential liability might discourage innovation and investment, and the potential foreclosure of markets to competitors.¹¹² While empirical data on UK design litigation suggests an overall higher rightholder success rate once decisions at all levels are taken into account,¹¹³ and commentary has noted that rightholders enjoy a better

---

106 E Derclaye, 'CUDR and CRDR post-Brexit from a UK and EU perspective—Will all unregistered design rights become history?' (2018) 13 JIPLP 325, 328.
107 *Samsung* (EWHC, n 31), [58].
108 *Procter & Gamble* (EWCA, n 28), [34].
109 *Procter & Gamble* (EWCA, n 28); *Magmatic* (EWCA, n 29).
110 *Procter & Gamble* (EWCA, n 28), [35(iii)].
111 Stone, 'How did things go so wrong?' (n 29), 679, suggesting that this is a 'worrying' trend.
112 *Procter & Gamble* (EWCA, n 28), [54]; *Samsung* (EWCA, n 28), [54].
113 Although even then, for some categories of infringement claim, the success rate was low: Oliver Church, Estelle Derclaye and Gilles Stupfler, 'An Empirical Analysis of the Design Case Law of the EU Member

success rate in the lower-level Intellectual Property Enterprise Court, it has also been observed that, even in such successful cases, scope of protection is often narrow.[114]

10.034 In terms of defences, the principal provisions cover: acts done privately and for purposes which are not commercial;[115] acts done for experimental purposes;[116] and acts of reproduction for teaching purposes or for the purposes of making citations.[117] These defences have made little appearance in UK case law.[118] There is a repair defence, permitting use of the design for the purpose of the repair of a complex product so as to restore its original appearance.[119] The equivalent defence for Community designs did receive detailed consideration from Arnold J in *BMW v Round & Metal*, in which he notably took the opposite approach to that later taken by the ECJ in *Acacia*:[120] this area may be one to watch in terms of potential future UK departure from ECJ authority in relation to UK domestic law going forward. There is also a prior use defence,[121] and (for the time being, while the UK Government continues to assess its long-term position on exhaustion of IP rights) rights in a UK registered design will not be infringed by any act relating to a product has been put on the market in the UK or European Economic Area by the registered proprietor or with his consent.[122]

States' (2019) 50 IIC 685, 704, recording findings of infringement before the UK courts in 85.7 per cent of CUDR cases and 71.4 per cent of UK registered design cases, but only 41.6 per cent of RCD cases. The authors express caution about drawing statistical conclusions from their data given the low number of cases.

114 A Borthwick, 'The scope of registered design protection following *Magmatic v PMS International*' (2015) 37 EIPR 180, 185. Recent examples of success at IPEC include: *Marks and Spencer* (n 73); *Fairfax & Favor Ltd v The House of Bruar Ltd* [2022] ECDR 12; *Lutec* (n 30); *Rothy's* (n 26).
115 RDA 1949, s7A(2)(a).
116 RDA 1949, s7A(2)(b).
117 The act of reproduction must be compatible with fair trade practice, not unduly prejudice the normal exploitation of the design and mention the source: RDA 1949, ss7A(2)(c) and (3).
118 The citations defence has been considered by the ECJ in Joined Cases C-24/16 and C-25/16 *Nintendo Co Ltd v BigBen Interactive GmbH* ECLI:EU:C:2017:724.
119 RDA 1949, s7A(5).
120 *Bayerische Motoren Werke Aktiengesellschaft v Round & Metal Ltd* [2012] ECC 28; Joined Cases C-397/16 and C-435/16 *Acacia Srl v Pneusgarda Srl, Audi AG; Acacia Srl, Rolando D'Amato v Dr Ing hcF Porsche AG* ECLI:EU:C:2017:992, discussed in J Cornwell, 'Nintendo v BigBen and Acacia v Audi; Acacia v Porsche: Design exceptions at the CJEU' (2019) 14 JIPLP 51.
121 RDA 1949, s7B.
122 RDA 1949, s7A(4). The EU does not reciprocally recognise the placing of goods in the market in the UK as exhausting IP rights under EU law. The UKIPO has consulted on options for a long-term UK law position on exhaustion of IP rights, but without reaching a conclusion: UKIPO, 'UK's future exhaustion of intellectual property rights regime', 18 January 2022, www.gov.uk/government/consultations/uks-future-exhaustion-of-intellectual-property-rights-regime accessed 2 August 2023.

C. UK UNREGISTERED DESIGN RIGHTS

1. UK Unregistered Design Right

(a) Introduction

The UK has long sought to channel industrial designs away from copyright and towards registered design protection. However, for a period in the 20th century, UK legislation inadvertently led to a perverse result. As copyright subsisted in design drawings irrespective of artistic merit, 'industrial copyright' in blueprints and schematics for industrial designs could be indirectly infringed by copying the industrial articles shown in such drawings, even when those articles themselves were not entitled to copyright protection.[123] At the same time, legislation intended to restrict copyright in the industrial sphere applied only where the relevant subject matter was also a registrable design. As designs were only registrable at that time if (among other matters) they satisfied a requirement of 'eye appeal', the somewhat anomalous upshot was that utilitarian designs were protected by 'industrial copyright' in their design drawings for a much longer period than designs which met the requirements for registration.[124]

10.035

The legislative response, the Copyright, Designs and Patents Act 1988 ('CDPA 1988'), involved various moves to largely remove industrial design from copyright's reach (discussed further below). Alongside this (and to compensate for loss of copyright protection), the CDPA 1988 introduced UK unregistered design right ('UKUDR') as a form of limited design protection intended particularly for functional designs. UKUDR has been invoked (successfully or otherwise) in many cases involving this sort of design – from pig fenders and slurry separators to contact lenses and medical devices.[125] However, UKUDR has also proved its broader usefulness: its scope is not limited to utilitarian designs, and it has been successfully relied upon in cases involving aesthetic designs including clothing and footwear.[126]

10.036

---

123 See Laddie J in *Ocular Sciences Ltd v Aspect Vision Care Ltd* [1997] RPC 289, 421.
124 See further: Howe et al, *Russell-Clarke & Howe* (n 1), paras 1-043–1-053; P Johnson, 'Design Right – From Investment to Creativity for 'Industrial Copyright' in E Bonadio and P Goold (eds) *The Cambridge Handbook of Investment-Driven Intellectual Property* (Cambridge University Press, 2023).
125 *C&H Engineering v F Klucznik & Sons Ltd (No.1)* [1992] FSR 421; *Farmers Build Ltd (In Liquidation) v Carier Bulk Materials Handling Ltd* [2000] ECDR 42; *Ocular Sciences* (n 123); *Cantel Medical* (n 48).
126 For recent examples, see: *G-Star Raw CV v Rhodi Ltd and others* [2015] EWHC 216 (Ch); *Original Beauty* (n 63); *Fairfax & Favor* (n 114). See also Johnson, 'Design Right – From Investment to Creativity' (n 124).

10.037 Although EU harmonisation never affected UKUDR, questions were raised as to the continued need for UKUDR once unregistered Community design right ('CUDR') was introduced in the early 2000s. However, after consultation in 2013, the UKIPO concluded that UKUDR should be retained, particularly given its usefulness for SMEs without design registrations, and its ability to fill gaps in other forms of protection.[127] Confirming its continuing (if, perhaps, at times overlooked) importance in the UK design law landscape, more recent empirical work has established that UKUDR is in fact relied upon significantly more frequently in decided UK design cases than any other form of design right.[128] Commentary has also lauded UKUDR as a versatile and well-used right.[129] UKUDR may be pleaded alongside registered design infringement, and has succeeded in cases where registered design claims have failed.[130]

10.038 UKUDR remains governed by the CDPA 1988, with some amendments introduced in 2014 noted briefly below. Other than some adjustments to qualification requirements, Brexit has had no impact on UKUDR. That said, the UKIPO's recent design review has again raised the possibility of reform.

(b) Qualification

10.039 A design must meet certain qualification requirements to be eligible for UKUDR.[131] These were to some degree simplified as part of the amendments to the CDPA 1988 introduced in 2014. Qualification depends upon whether the designer or (as relevant) their employer is a 'qualifying person', or on whether first marketing of articles made to the design is by a qualifying person and takes place in the UK or another relevant country as designated from time to time.[132] For individuals, a 'qualifying person' must be habitually resident in a 'qualifying country'; a legal person must be formed under the law of a part of the UK or another qualifying country or have a place of business there at which substantial business activity is carried on.[133]

---

127 UKIPO, 'The Consultation on the Reform of the UK Designs Legal Framework Government Response—April 2013' (April 2013), 13.
128 Church et al, 'An Empirical Analysis' (n 113), 698, recording that UKUDR was relied upon in 53.2 per cent of decided UK design cases, compared to 19.5 per cent for UK registered designs, 16.9 per cent for RCDs and 10.4 per cent for CUDR.
129 S Ashby and C Smith, 'Unregistered design law: the good, the bad, and the ugly' (2018) 13 JIPLP 315.
130 Including (albeit on relatively minor design elements) in the 'Trunki' litigation: *Magmatic* (EWHC, n 47) (the conclusion on UKUDR was not appealed).
131 CDPA 1988, s213(5).
132 CDPA 1988, ss213(5), 217–220.
133 CDPA 1988, s217(1).

10.040 As a *sui generis* right, UKUDR is not governed by international treaties:[134] the principle of national treatment and arrangements for reciprocal protection for copyright do not apply. The list of 'qualifying countries' relevant to the qualifying status of the designer or their employer is short, and (beyond the UK) is mostly focused on British overseas territories and Crown dependencies.[135] It has always omitted major jurisdictions, including the USA, Japan and Korea, and, since Brexit, also no longer includes any EU Member States. Since Brexit, qualification by place of first marketing also now only covers the UK.[136]

(c) Protectable UKUDR 'designs'

10.041 UKUDR does not subsist unless and until the design has been recorded in a design document or an article has been made to the design.[137] For UKUDR purposes, 'design' means:

> the design of the shape or configuration (whether internal or external) of the whole or part of an article.[138]

10.042 Although UKUDR was introduced to primarily provide protection for functional designs, this definition is neutral in terms of functionality or aesthetics. UKUDR can subsist in 'articles' of all kinds, including component parts.[139] The definition focuses on 'shape' and 'configuration'. Coupled with the exclusion of surface decoration from protection (Section C.1.(d) below), it is clear that UKUDR protects only three-dimensional forms.[140] This is an important point of contrast with UK registered designs, which can protect two-dimensional designs and surface decoration of three-dimensional products. Another important point of distinction is that UKUDR can subsist in elements of shape or configuration which are wholly internal to the relevant article, unlike UK registered designs which cannot protect features of component parts of complex products not visible in normal use (see Section B.2.(b)).

---

134 E Derclaye, 'Protection of Designs on the Basis of Use' in H Hartwig (ed) *Research Handbook on Design Law* (Edward Elgar, 2021), 239.
135 Plus Hong Kong and New Zealand: CDPA 1988, s 217(3) and the Design Right (Reciprocal Protection) (No 2) Order (SI 1989/1294).
136 CDPA 1988, s220(1)(b) allows for extension to other countries by statutory order, but no such order is in place.
137 CDPA 1988, s213(6). On 'design document', see CDPA 1988, s263(1).
138 CDPA 1988, s213(2).
139 See e.g.: *Farmers Build* (n 125); *Dyson Ltd v Qualtex (UK) Ltd* [2006] RPC 31.
140 Perhaps surprisingly for such a central concept, there are unresolved issues as to the exact meaning of 'configuration' in UKUDR, particularly as to how far this encompasses more abstract notions of the relative arrangement of different parts or elements: see *Mackie Designs Inc v Behringer Specialised Studio Equipment (UK) Ltd* [1999] RPC 717 (accepting that a circuit diagram could constitute relevant 'configuration' of an article), subsequently doubted in *Lambretta Clothing Co Ltd v Teddy Smith (UK) Ltd* [2005] RPC 6, [26]–[27].

10.043 Referring as it does to the shape or configuration of 'the whole or part of' an article, the UKUDR definition of 'design' is inherently flexible: a UKUDR rightholder can rely on whatever part or parts of their article they see fit, specifying this only at the point of making a claim. There is no requirement that a protectable 'part' must be an independent item of commerce, or separately created or manufactured. Thus, many different UKUDR 'designs' may subsist in any one article – possibilities include claiming for the article as a whole and/or for a range of different 'parts', separately or in differently-constituted combinations. A recent case, *Shnuggle v Munchkin*, about the design of baby baths, provides an example (albeit ultimately unsuccessful) of multiple overlapping UKUDR 'designs' pleaded in relation to one article.[141]

10.044 Originally, the definition of 'design' at section 213(2) CDPA 1988 provided that UKUDR could subsist in 'any aspect of' the shape or configuration of the whole or part of an article. 'Aspects' of a design only had to be 'discernible' or 'recognisable'; they did not need to be visually significant and could be points of detail, even invisible to the naked eye,[142] thereby setting 'a very low threshold which is hardly a threshold at all'.[143] This allowed UKUDR rightholders to 'crop' their claims to fit the alleged infringement, enhancing prospects of success by homing in on the most similar elements of shape or configuration even if only a small part of the alleged infringement overall. Such concerns led to the deletion of the words 'any aspect of' from the definition of 'design' in 2014.[144] However, it is still possible to claim UKUDR in 'part' of an article, without any statutory indication of how small such a 'part' might be – leading to some doubt as to the overall impact of the 2014 amendment. After some suggestion that this amendment has served to rule out 'disembodied features' rather than 'concrete parts',[145] the point was considered more recently in *Schnuggle v Munchkin*, where it was held that a protectable 'part' of an article is 'an actual, but not abstract part which can be identified as such and which

---

141 *Shnuggle* (n 37).
142 See e.g., *Ocular Sciences* (n 123), a case concerning contact lenses. See also *A Fulton v Totes Isotoner (UK) Ltd* [2004] RPC 16, [31]; *Qualtex* (n 139), [22]–[23]; *Virgin Atlantic Airways Ltd v Premium Aircraft Interiors Group Ltd* [2009] ECDR 11, [26].
143 *Shnuggle* (n 37), [83].
144 Intellectual Property Act 2014, s1(1); UKIPO, 'The Consultation on the Reform of the UK Designs Legal Framework' (n 127), 13-14.
145 *Neptune (Europe) Ltd v Devol Kitchens Ltd* [2017] ECDR 25, [44]. The rather brief discussion gave the following illustration: 'aspects of the design of a teapot could include the combination of the end portion of the spout and the top portion of the lid, which are disembodied from each other and from the spout and lid. They are not parts of the design': ibid, [44].

is not a trivial feature'.¹⁴⁶ At the time of writing, there is yet to be a UKUDR ruling where this amendment has made a difference in practice.

(d) Exclusions from UKUDR

There are four exclusions from UKUDR protection. **10.045**

First, consistent with its focus on three-dimensional forms (and the overall **10.046** legislative aim of avoiding overlap with copyright), UKUDR does not subsist in surface decoration.¹⁴⁷ Surface decoration is not limited to purely flat ornamentation.¹⁴⁸ Conversely, the fact that a feature is three-dimensional does not necessarily mean that it is saved: 'surface decoration' can include three-dimensional elements – what matters is whether the relevant feature can 'fairly be described as a decorated surface'.¹⁴⁹ Surface features which have significant function are not surface decoration.¹⁵⁰

UKUDR will also not subsist in a method or principle of construction.¹⁵¹ This **10.047** has been applied to exclude overbroad claims seeking to protect concepts or ideas capable of multiple embodiments.¹⁵² It also excludes designs which are the unavoidable result of the application of a particular production method or process, as illustrated by *Bailey v Haines*, a case in which a claim to UKUDR in a design of knitted micromesh failed as that design was the inevitable product of using a particular knitting method.¹⁵³

Finally, there are 'must-fit' and 'must-match' exclusions.¹⁵⁴ These have **10.048** broad parallels with the interconnections exclusion and repair defence in UK registered design law, but there are important differences and the UKUDR provisions must be interpreted and applied on their own terms. The UKUDR 'must-fit' provision excludes features of shape or configuration of an article which enable the article to be connected to, or placed in, around or against, another article so that either article may perform its function.¹⁵⁵ This does not

---

146 *Shnuggle* (n 37), [92]; see further J Cornwell, '*Shnuggle v Munchkin*: don't throw the baby out with the bathwater!' (2020) 42 EIPR 255.
147 CDPA 1988, s213(3)(c).
148 See, e.g., *Mark Wilkinson Furniture Ltd v Woodcraft Designs (Radcliffe) Ltd* [1998] FSR 63 (excluding certain three-dimensional decorative features of kitchen unit designs).
149 *Qualtex* (n 139), [81].
150 Ibid., [83].
151 CDPA 1988, s213(3)(a).
152 *Rolawn Ltd v Turfmech Machinery Ltd* [2008] ECDR 13, [81]; *Red Spider Technology v Omega Completions Technology* [2010] EWHC 59 (Ch), [124].
153 *Bailey (t/a Elite Anglian Products) v Haynes (t/a RAGS)* [2007] FSR 10.
154 CDPA 1988, s213(3)(b).
155 CDPA 1988, s213(3)(b)(i).

require the features in question to be the only way to achieve this; however, there does need to be 'a degree of precision' in the relationship between the articles, and the excluded features must be such as to 'enable' the relevant placement of the articles in question.[156] The UKUDR 'must-match' provision excludes features which are dependent upon the appearance of another article of which the article in which UKUDR is claimed is intended by the designer to form an integral part.[157] The key question here is when a design will be considered 'dependent' on the appearance of another article, the English courts focusing on whether there is a 'real need to copy a feature of shape or configuration because of some design consideration of the whole article'.[158]

10.049 Importantly, and consistent with the underlying objective for introducing UKUDR, there is no exclusion from UKUDR for purely functional designs – this is a major point contrast with UK registered designs.

(e) Originality

10.050 The threshold requirement for protection in UKUDR is another important – and markedly less demanding – point of difference to UK registered designs. UKUDR subsists in an 'original' design.[159] Determining originality is a two-step process: first, whether the design is original in the copyright sense; and second, whether it is 'commonplace in a qualifying country in the design field in question at the time of its creation'.[160]

10.051 On the first step, the need for the design to be original 'in the copyright sense' had been seen as embodying the traditionally low English law 'skill, labour and judgment' threshold for copyright originality.[161] However, more recent UKUDR decisions have debated (without definitively answering) whether the EU copyright standard of the 'author's own intellectual creation' should now be adopted.[162] This has yet to be resolved, although it is suggested here that

---

156 *Ocular Sciences* (n 123), 424; *A Fulton Co Ltd v Grant Barnett & Co Ltd* [2001] RPC 16, [75]; *Action Storage Systems Ltd v G-Force Europe.com Ltd* [2017] FSR 18 (IPEC), [68]; *Cantel Medical* (n 48), [224]–[226] and [233]–[234].
157 CDPA 1988, s213(3)(b)(ii).
158 *Qualtex* (n 139), [64].
159 CDPA 1988, s213(1).
160 CDPA 1988, s213(4); *Farmers Build Ltd* (n 125), 64. The linking of the commonplace requirement to 'a qualifying country' was introduced by Intellectual Property Act 2014, ss1(3) and (4).
161 *Farmers Build* (n 125), 65, noting that the key issue on this limb of the test should be that the design in which UKUDR is claimed should not have been slavishly copied from an earlier design.
162 As articulated by the ECJ in C-5/08 *Infopaq International A/S v Danske Dagblades Forening* ECLI:EU:C:2009:465 and subsequent cases. See further: *Whitby Specialist Vehicles* (n 47), [43]; *Raft Ltd v Freestyle of Newhaven Ltd and Others* [2016] EWHC 1711 (IPEC), [9]; *Action Storage* (n 156), [19]–[22]; *Shnuggle* (n 37), [93]–[95].

(given the ECJ's copyright case law on originality and technical functionality) this change would be inappropriate for UK legislation intended to protect functional designs.[163]

10.052 On the second step, it is the design that must not be commonplace, not the relevant 'article'. The fact that a design lacks novelty (which would be fatal to registered design protection) does not mean it must be considered commonplace for UKUDR purposes.[164] *Action Storage* provides a useful summary of the key principles for the assessment of 'commonplace-ness'.[165] 'Commonplace-ness' has been articulated in various ways – for example, that a design is commonplace if it is current in the thinking of designers in the field at the time the design was created, or if it is 'trite, trivial, common-or-garden, hackneyed or of the type which would excite no particular attention in those in the relevant design field'.[166] This should be assessed from the perspective of the type of person to whom the design is intended to appeal, rather than a design expert.[167]

(f) Ownership and duration

10.053 Unless a design qualifies for UKUDR as a result of first marketing, the first owner of UKUDR is the designer or (as relevant) the designer's employer.[168] The designer is the person who creates the design.[169] As for UK registered designs, the designer of a computer-generated design (i.e., a design generated by a computer in circumstances where there is no human designer) is the person 'by whom the arrangements necessary for the creation of the design are undertaken'.[170] UKUDR can be assigned or licensed.[171]

10.054 UKUDR is shorter in duration than UK registered designs, lasting for a maximum of 15 years from the end of the calendar year in which the design was first recorded in a design document or in which an article was made to

---

163 See further J Cornwell, 'Preserving the traditional English approach to originality in UK UDR' (2021) 43 EIPR 483 (arguing against a change of approach).
164 *Grant Barnett* (n 156), [51]–[52].
165 *Action Storage* (n 156), [37].
166 Ibid., citing *Lambretta* (n 140) and *Ocular Sciences* (n 123).
167 *Scholes Windows Ltd v Magnet Ltd* [2002] FSR 10, [48]–[49]; *Albert Packaging Ltd v Nampak Cartons & Healthcare Lt*d [2011] FSR 32, [31].
168 CDPA 1988, ss215(1) and (3). If a design qualifies through first marketing, the owner is the person who first marketed the design: CDPA 1988, s215(4). As for UK registered designs (see n 87 above), since 2014 ownership of designs produced on commission vests with the designer.
169 CDPA 1988, s214(1).
170 CPDA 1988, ss214(2) and 263(1). See Section B.3 above in relation to UKIPO consultation on AI-generated outputs.
171 CDPA 1988, s222.

the design, whichever occurs first.[172] If articles made to the design are made available for sale or hire anywhere in the world by or with the licence of the rightholder within five years of the end of that calendar year, the duration of UKUDR is reduced to a maximum of ten years.[173] The effective period of protection is reduced yet further by the entitlement of third parties to a licence of right within the last five years of UKUDR protection.[174]

(g) Infringement and defences

10.055 Unlike for UK registered designs, UKUDR infringement is dependent on copying. A UKUDR rightholder has the exclusive right to reproduce the design for commercial purposes by making articles to that design, or by making a design document recording the design for the purpose of enabling such articles to be made.[175] UKUDR is infringed by any person who, without consent, does or authorises another to do anything within that exclusive right.[176]

10.056 Reproduction of a design by making articles to the design means copying the design 'so as to produce articles exactly or substantially to that design'.[177] Reproduction may be direct or indirect.[178] The infringing articles do not need to be of the same type as those of the UKUDR rightholder.[179] As in copyright cases, in the absence of direct evidence of copying, the court may infer copying; however, in the UKUDR context, this inference must be moderated by recognition that similarities may arise as a result of common functional considerations rather than copying.[180] Whether an allegedly infringing design is reproduced 'substantially to the design' is not the same as the 'substantial part' infringement test in UK copyright law.[181] In copyright, the central question is whether a substantial part of the infringed work has been reproduced, irrespective of how much additional matter might also be present in the alleged infringement; in UKUDR, the assessment is whether the allegedly infringement design is, as a whole, substantially the same as the UKUDR-protected design.[182]

---

172 CDPA 1988, s216(1)(a).
173 CDPA 1988, s216(1)(b).
174 CDPA 1988, s237.
175 CDPA 1988, s226(1).
176 CDPA 1988, s226(3).
177 CDPA 1988, s226(2).
178 CDPA 1988, s226(4).
179 *Electronic Techniques (Anglia) Ltd v Critchley Components Ltd* [1997] FSR 401 at 418.
180 *Farmers Build* (n 125), 64.
181 *Neptune* (n 145), [53].
182 *L Woolley Jewellers Ltd v A and A Jewellery Ltd* [2003] FSR 15.

The CPDA 1988 also contains provision for UKUDR secondary infringement committed by importing or dealing with infringing articles.[183] In such cases, infringement is dependent on knowledge.

10.057

Until the 2014, there were no statutory defences to UKUDR infringement. However, the Intellectual Property Act 2014 introduced a new set of exceptions mirroring the exceptions to registered design infringement discussed at Section B.4 above.[184] To keep UKUDR and copyright apart, in those (generally limited) cases where UKUDR and copyright co-exist in the same article (for example, for a three-dimensional design which meets the requirements of UKUDR and is also a copyright artistic work), the only infringement action lies in copyright: it is not infringement of UKUDR to do anything which is an infringement of copyright in the relevant work.[185]

10.058

2. New Post-Brexit Forms of UK Unregistered Design

Before the introduction of CUDR, the UK was the only EU Member State with a system of unregistered design protection.[186] From 2003, CUDR also took effect in the UK alongside UKUDR. As noted at Section B.1 above, CUDR was governed by the same core principles as harmonised national registered design law and RCDs (definition of 'design', novelty and individual character, exclusions, scope of protection and defences), with key differences lying in how CUDR came into subsistence, much shorter three-year duration, and infringing acts dependent on copying.[187] Like RCDs, however, from the end of the Brexit transition period CUDR ceased to cover the UK.

10.059

To avoid loss of protection for CUDR holders, under the terms of the UK-EU Withdrawal Agreement, holders of rights in CUDR in existence before the end of the transition period were to become holders of an equivalent right in the UK, affording the same level of protection and lasting for at least the remaining period of protection due to the original CUDR.[188] This obligation was implemented in the UK by the creation of the 'continuing unregistered Community design' ('UK CUD').[189] For such designs, UK CUD provides pro-

10.060

---

183 CDPA 1988, s227.
184 CDPA 1988, ss244A and 244B.
185 CDPA 1988, s236.
186 Derclaye, 'Protection of designs' (n 134), 233, noting the availability of protection via unfair competition in other jurisdictions.
187 CDR, Arts 11 and 19(2).
188 Withdrawal Agreement (n 12), Art 57.
189 The UKIPO has also referred to this new right (more briefly) as the 'continuing unregistered design': UKIPO, 'Changes to unregistered designs', 30 January 2020 www.gov.uk/guidance/changes-to-unregistered

tection in the UK from the end of the transition period on essentially the same terms as the Community Design Regulation, adapted in scope to the UK only and lasting for three years from the date upon which the design was first made available in the EU. Although a fully-fledged new form of design right, given that UK CUD is available only for designs already protected by CUDR at end of the transition period, its impact on the overall UK design law landscape will be short-lived: all designs protected by UK CUD will have expired by the end of 2023.

10.061 However, the implications of Brexit for UK unregistered designs do not stop there. Although commentators disagreed on the impact of losing CUDR[190] (with its much shorter term than UKUDR, and more demanding requirements of novelty and individual character), it did offer some advantages, particularly protection for two-dimensional designs and surface decoration. Recognising this, the UK created another new form of UK unregistered design right, called the 'supplementary unregistered design' ('UK SUD'),[191] intended as a replacement for CUDR going forward. UK SUD protects designs first made available to the public from after the end of the Brexit transition period onwards. Its substantive provisions are, again, essentially the same as for CUDR, adapted to the UK only. UK SUD lasts for three years from the date when the design is first made available to the public in the UK.

10.062 While UK SUD will have greater impact than its short-lived sibling, UK CUD, it is open to debate whether the introduction of the UK SUD was the best long-term response to the loss of CUDR, particularly given the ever-present concerns about the overall complexity of UK law. Seeking views on the simplification of the UK design system, the most common suggestion received in the UKIPO's recent consultation was the creation of a new, single form of unregistered design combining the 'best elements' of UKUDR and UK SUD.[192] The UKIPO intends to investigate options.

10.063 In the meantime, there is an immediate challenge facing businesses looking to protect their designs in the UK via UK SUD and in the EU via CUDR. It is

---

-designs accessed 2 August 2023. UK CUD is implemented in a rather complex way, by enacting a series of amendments to the CDR which is kept in force in the UK for this purpose: Designs and International Trade Marks (Amendment etc) (EU Exit) Regulations 2019/638, reg 4 and Schedule 2.

190 Contrast Derclaye, 'CUDR and CRDR post-Brexit' (n 106) with Ashby and Smith, 'Unregistered Design Law' (n 129).

191 In another complex move, this is done by a set of amendments to the CDR which sit alongside and in parallel to those creating UK CUD: Designs and International Trade Marks (Amendment etc) (EU Exit) Regulations 2019/638, reg 3 and Schedule 1.

192 UKIPO, 'Government response' (n 9), [19].

generally understood that a design must be first disclosed within the territory of the EU to be entitled to CUDR.[193] At the same time, UK SUD requires first disclosure of the design in the UK.[194] This poses a major dilemma: disclosure in the UK may protect the design in the UK by UK SUD, but will not give rise to CUDR and will be novelty-destroying for CUDR purposes; conversely, disclosure in the EU may give rise to CUDR, but will preclude protection in the UK via UK SUD. Designers may feel compelled to disclose their designs first in the EU to secure CUDR given the relative sizes of the respective markets, and concern has been expressed about impacts on major events such as London Fashion Week or the London Design Fair.[195] There may be some sign that the European Commission intends to soften the disclosure rule for CUDR in its proposed reforms of the Community Design Regulation, although this unclear at the time of writing.[196] In its consultation, the UKIPO has acknowledged stakeholder concerns and is considering the position further.[197]

D. OTHER IP RIGHTS PROTECTING DESIGNS

10.064 In addition to the forms of design protection discussed above, the three-dimensional appearance of a product or a two-dimensional design may also be protected in the UK by copyright, registered trade mark law, or passing off.

1. Copyright

10.065 As noted above, alongside the creation of UKUDR, it was a core objective of the CDPA 1988 to minimise copyright protection for industrial designs. The CPDA 1988 pursued this objective in three ways. First, a closed definition of 'artistic works' restricted copyright in three-dimensional product forms to 'sculptures' and 'works of artistic craftsmanship' only.[198] Secondly, tackling the problem of 'industrial copyright' outlined at Section C.1.(a) above, the CPDA

---

193 CDR, Arts 11 and 110a(5). See further A Kur, 'Finally back to TRIPS-compliance? EU design law and the criterion of publication 'within EU territory'' (2023) 18 JIPLP 11, and Derclaye, 'Protection of Designs' (n 134), although note the contrary arguments in Musker (n 2), 178–80. A preliminary reference on this issue in *Beverly Hills Teddy Bear Co v PMS International Group Plc* [2020] FSR 11 was discontinued before the ECJ could rule, as the parties settled.
194 Or a qualifying country or a qualifying territory: Designs and International Trade Marks (Amendment etc.) (EU Exit) Regulations 2019/638, Schedule 1, para 10.
195 Derclaye, 'CUDR and CRDR post-Brexit' (n 106), 328; UKIPO, 'Government response' (n 9), [25].
196 See further Kur, 'Finally back to TRIPS-compliance?' (n 193).
197 UKIPO, 'Government response' (n 9), [24]–[27].
198 CDPA 1988, s4. On 'sculpture', see *Lucasfilm Ltd v Ainsworth* [2011] ECDR 21; on 'works of artistic craftsmanship', see *George Hensher Ltd v Restawile Upholstery (Lancs) Ltd* [1976] AC 64.

1988 provided a defence to claims of copyright infringement in design drawings where a three-dimensional article was copied (directly or indirectly) from the design drawing, with an exception only if the design drawing was for a design which itself constituted an artistic work.[199] Finally, if a copyright-protected artistic work was exploited by making articles constituting copies of the work using an industrial process and by marketing those articles, the CDPA 1988 allowed third parties also to copy the work by making articles of any description after the end of 25 years from the rightholder's first marketing of those articles.[200] This effectively cut down the term of copyright protection for industrially-exploited copyright works to the same as the maximum for registered designs.

10.066 However, EU copyright developments have increasingly challenged the UK's position. First, following the ECJ's decision in *Flos*,[201] the UK repealed its rules on industrially-exploited copyright works in 2016, concerned (perhaps wrongly) that these rules were incompatible with EU law.[202] Industrially-exploited copyright artistic works are now enforceable in UK law for the full copyright period of life of the author plus 70 years. The UKIPO consulted in 2021 on the impact of this repeal;[203] post-Brexit, there have been calls for the UK to reinstate the 25-year limit on the enforceability of copyright in such works.[204]

10.067 In addition, although the CPDA 1988 itself remains otherwise unaltered (and the defence to copyright infringement in design drawings remains), EU copyright case law has challenged the UK's closed-list approach to protectable copyright works. In current ECJ case law, the only requirement for a protectable copyright 'work' is that it is an original expression identifiable with sufficient precision and objectivity: EU copyright law therefore now seemingly allows any original three-dimensional product form to be a copyright 'work', including utilitarian items not typically thought of as artistic works in UK terms.[205] This seems to place UK statute at odds with EU law. The implications are uncertain: this ECJ case law was not clearly examined in UK rulings

---

199 CDPA 1988, s51; see further Howe et al, *Russell-Clarke & Howe* (n 1), paras 5-083–5-098.
200 CDPA 1988, s52 (now repealed); see further Howe et al, *Russell-Clarke & Howe* (n 1), paras 5-099–5-100.
201 C-169/08 *Flos SpA v Semeraro Casa e Famiglia SpA*, ECLI:EU:C:2011:29.
202 L Bently, 'The return of industrial copyright?' (2012) 34 EIPR 654.
203 UKIPO, 'Repeal of section 52 CDPA and related amendments: Call for views', 7 January 2022 www.gov.uk/government/consultations/repeal-of-section-52-cdpa-and-related-amendments-call-for-views accessed 2 August 2023.
204 See, e.g., L Porangaba, 'Copyright (in design) post-Brexit: Should section 52 of CDPA 1988 be reinstated?' (2022) 44 EIPR 1.
205 C-310/17 *Levola Hengelo BV v Smilde Foods BV* ECLI:EU:C:2018:899; see further also C-683/17 *Cofemel – Sociedade de Vestuário SA v G-Star Raw CV* ECLI:EU:C:2019:721; C-833/18 *SI and Brompton Bicycle v Chedech/Get2Get*, ECLI:EU:C:2020:416.

pre-Brexit and, while post-Brexit UK cases have attempted to reconcile the two positions through more flexible interpretation of the UK's categories of artistic work, the case law has also flagged the need for the point to be resolved at some stage 'by Parliament or the higher courts'.[206] The UKIPO's design consultation has noted the desirability of a clearer distinction between design law and copyright.[207]

2. Registered Trade Marks and Passing Off

In contrast to the apparently increasing role for copyright in relation to industrial designs, the position in relation to registered trade marks remains more cautious. Of course, two-dimensional designs in the form of logos are a conventional form of trade mark and are readily registrable. However, the UK has always exhibited a conservative approach to the registrability of three-dimensional product and packaging shapes. These only became registrable as trade marks in the UK under the Trade Marks Act 1994, introduced to implement the first EU Trade Marks Directive:[208] prior to that, even the readily recognisable *Coca-Cola* bottle was refused registration.[209] Even after EU harmonisation of registered trade mark law, whilst the definition of a registrable trade mark explicitly includes the shape of goods and packaging,[210] UK courts have remained wary in their approach to shape marks with a generally strict approach in particular to the assessment of inherent and acquired distinctiveness.[211] Other objections, such as those which deny registration in the case of natural, technical and value-adding shapes, are also relevant.[212]

10.068

Although there is no general tort of 'unfair competition' in UK law,[213] it may be possible to bring proceedings in appropriate cases under the law of 'passing off'. *Reckitt v Borden* (generally known as the *Jif Lemon* case, as it related to a dispute over lemon-shaped packaging) established the 'classical trinity' of requirements for a passing off claim: goodwill, misrepresentation and damage.[214] However, claimants may face an uphill task in satisfying the court that goodwill

10.069

---

206 *Waterrower (UK) Ltd v Liking Ltd (t/a Topiom)* [2023] ECDR 1, [77]; see also *Response Clothing Ltd v Edinburgh Woollen Mill Ltd* [2020] ECDR 11.
207 UKIPO, 'Call for views on designs' (n 7).
208 First Council Directive 89/104/EEC of 241/12/1988.
209 *In re Coca-Cola Co* [1986] 1 WLR 695.
210 TMA 1994, s1(1).
211 Under TMA 1994, ss3(1)(b) and proviso thereto. See e.g.: *Société des Produits Nestlé SA v Cadbury UK Ltd* [2017] ETMR 31; *London Taxi Corp Ltd (t/a London Taxi Co) v Frazer-Nash Research Ltd* [2018] ETMR 7; *Jaguar Land Rover Ltd v Ineos Industries Holdings Ltd* [2020] ETMR 56.
212 TMA 1994, s3(2).
213 *L'Oreal SA v Bellure NV* [2008] ETMR 1, [135]-[161].
214 *Reckitt & Colman Products Ltd v Borden Inc* [1990] RPC 341.

has attached to their product's design as opposed to other, conventional trade marks on the goods.[215] Furthermore, even if goodwill is demonstrated, there will only be actionable passing off where there is 'misrepresentation'; simply demonstrating that the defendant has 'rid[den] on the [claimant's] coat-tails' is not enough.[216] Nevertheless, passing off cases involving product designs have succeeded, both as stand-alone complaints and alongside design infringement claims. For example, in *Numatic v Qualtex*, the manufacturer of the successful, anthropomorphic *Henry* vacuum cleaner successfully relied upon passing off to prevent launch of a look-a-like product after design protection had expired.[217] In *Freddy v Hugz*, a dispute involving shapeware jeans that also involved a parallel claim in UKUDR, the judge accepted that the claimant had goodwill in a combination of design features, and also found misrepresentation by the selling of the defendant's 'rip off' copies.[218]

E. PROCEDURE AND ENFORCEMENT

1. UK Design Registration Procedure

(a) Introduction

10.070 Linked to Brexit, UK design filings have been rapidly increasing. For much of the latter part of the 20th century filings sat between 5,000 and 10,000 per annum,[219] but the introduction of the RCD in 2003 saw annual UK filings drop as many applicants preferred EU-wide protection. However, the UKIPO reports a 'dramatic increase' in filings since 2015, the number of UK applications growing by over 1000% between 2015 and 2021 to more than 70,000 in 2021.[220] The UK joined the Hague system for the international registration of designs in 2018[221] and international filings account for some of this growth: the UKIPO reports that 14,973 international applications designated the UK

---

215 *George East Housewares Ltd v Fackelmann GMBH & Co KG* [2017] ETMR 4.
216 *Original Beauty* (n 63), [500]–[501].
217 *Numatic International Ltd v Qualtex UK Ltd* [2010] RPC 25.
218 *Freddy SPA v Hugz Clothing Ltd* [2021] ECDR 8.
219 L Bently, 'The Design/Copyright Conflict in the United Kingdom: A History' in E Derclaye (ed), *The Design/Copyright Interface* (Cambridge University Press, 2018), 205, Figure 6.2.
220 UKIPO, 'Facts and figures: patents, trade marks, designs and hearings: 2022' www.gov.uk/government/statistics/facts-and-figures-patents-trade-marks-designs-and-hearings-2022 accessed 2 August 2023. There was a slight drop to around 67,000 filings in 2022.
221 See further UKIPO, 'Guidance - Hague agreement for the International registration of industrial designs', 25 May 2018 www.gov.uk/government/publications/hague-system-design-protection-for-applicants/hague-agreement-for-the-international-registration-of-industrial-designs accessed 2 August 2023, and comments on the UK's participation in the Hague system at R Mirko Stutz, 'International Design Law Policies: Present and Future' in H Hartwig (ed), *Research Handbook on Design Law* (Edward Elgar, 2021), 420.

in 2022.²²² WIPO records the UKIPO as receiving the third-largest share of global design filings in 2021, more than twice as many as received in 2020 and pushing the UKIPO up four positions in WIPO's world rankings within a year.²²³

(b) Filing basics

10.071 UK design applicants may file in hard copy or electronically, with reduced fees for e-filings; multiple designs may be filed in a single application, also with fee savings.²²⁴ Multiple designs in a single filing are treated as independent designs; unlike the current position for RCDs,²²⁵ designs included in a single UK filing need not fall within the same Locarno class.

10.072 The mandatory requirements for a UK application are that it must (i) identify the applicant; (ii) include a design representation (or specimen); (iii) provide an indication of the product; and (iv) be accompanied by the prescribed official fee.²²⁶ If a specimen is filed, it must be subsequently supplemented by design representations suitable for publication.²²⁷ The applicant must also provide an address for service in the UK.²²⁸ The applicant is not required to designate a Locarno class, as classification is carried out by the UKIPO.²²⁹

10.073 Looking further at some of these mandatory elements, although UK applicants are required to provide an indication of the product to which the design is intended to be applied or incorporated, as for RCDs, this has no effect on scope of protection.²³⁰ However, the applicant's choice of design representations is critical. In the wake of the UKSC ruling in *Magmatic* (see Section B.2.(a) above),²³¹ the UKIPO issued detailed guidance on the likely implications of different format choices, and advising how use of disclaimers (see Section E.1.(b)) and/or filing multiple designs may mitigate against some of

---

222 UKIP', 'Facts and figures' (n 220).
223 WIPO, 'WIPO IP Facts and Figures 2022', 21–22 www.wipo.int/edocs/pubdocs/en/wipo-pub-943-2022-en-wipo-ip-facts-and-figures-2022.pdf accessed 2 August 2023.
224 UKIPO, 'Design forms and fees', 31 July 2023 www.gov.uk/government/publications/design-forms-and-fees/design-forms-and-fees accessed 2 August 2023. There is no limit on the number of multiple designs in a paper filing; for e-filings, this is capped at 50: UKIPO, 'Examination Practice' (n 16), para 7.02.
225 At the time of writing, the European Commission has proposed to remove the 'unity of class' requirement for multiple RCD filings, see Kur, 'Substantive Law Aspects' (n 14).
226 Registered Designs Rules 2006, SI 2006/1974 ('RDR'), r 4(1) and 5(2).
227 RDR 2006, r 9(1); UKIPO, 'Examination Practice' (n 16), para 7.08.
228 RDR 2006, r 42(1)(a), 42(4) and 43.
229 UKIPO, 'Examination Practice' (n 16), para 15.04.
230 RDR 2006, r 5(2) and 5(5).
231 *Magmatic Ltd* (UKSC, n 25).

the uncertainty surrounding around how representations will be interpreted.[232] An applicant may choose how many views are required for each design,[233] but mixed forms of representation should be avoided as these may be treated as different designs and require division of the application.[234] The UKIPO accepts magnified views, representations depicting 'transformable' designs and designs in different stages of use, 'exploded' (i.e., disassembled) views, partial and sectional views, and sequential 'snapshots' for designs consisting of animated sequences, including graphical user interfaces.[235] The UKIPO's recent consultation has acknowledged the need to keep pace with technological developments, including on the range of acceptable file formats; however, respondents also emphasised the importance for multi-territorial filings of international harmonisation of representation requirements.[236]

10.074 In terms of 'optional' elements, a UK application may include a priority claim,[237] a disclaimer and/or a written description.[238] Disclaimers may be visual or written,[239] although note the risks mentioned at Section B.2.(a) above on how visual disclaimers (particularly dashed lines) may be interpreted by UK courts. The option of including a written disclaimer is a point of contrast to RCD practice, where written disclaimers are not permitted. Where a UK applicant opts to include a written description, there is some uncertainty over its status: unlike for RCD descriptions (which explicitly do not affect scope of protection), the UK Registered Designs Rules 2006 do not indicate whether the description affects scope of protection or not.[240] There has been some (tentative) judicial criticism of the proposition that the description should be irrelevant, noting a 'real possibility that members of the public consulting the UK design register could be misled if they are given a steer by the description in a registration when seeking to resolve an ambiguity in the image shown'.[241]

---

232 UKIPO DPN 01/16, 'Use of representations in design applications', 1 June 2016, [15] and [16].
233 An e-filing may contain up to 12 representations per design, with no upper limit for paper filings: UKIPO, 'Examination Practice' (n 16), para 11.01.
234 Ibid., para 11.04.
235 Ibid., paras 11.25-11.35.
236 UKIPO, 'Government response' (n 9), [29].
237 RDA 1949, s14. The UKIPO does not accept priority claims based on utility models: UKIPO, 'Examination Practice' (n 16), para 10.06.
238 RDR 2006, r 4(5) and r 6.
239 UKIPO, 'Examination Practice' (n 16), paras 12.01–12.14.
240 Possibly as a result of accidental deletion of earlier rule 17A of the Registered Designs Rules 1995, which had stipulated that the description did not limit scope of protection: Musker, *Navigating Design Law* (n 2), 79.
241 *Marks and Spencer* (n 73), [16].

(c) Examination

At the examination stage, a UK design application may be refused only on very limited grounds: non-compliance with filing formalities, or if it appears to the examiner that the applicant is not entitled to file the application, that what is applied for does not conform to the definition of a 'design', that the design falls within the technical functionality, interconnections or public policy/morality exclusions, or includes a protected national or international emblem.[242] The UKIPO stopped examining for novelty and individual character in 2006, bringing its practice in line with the EUIPO.[243] However, the UKIPO's recent consultation has asked whether mandatory search and examination should be reintroduced, to a mixed response: some respondents favoured increased examination to improve legal certainty and prevent 'anti-competitive' filings of existing third-party designs, while others questioned the adequacy of search tools and increase to the time and expense of securing registration.[244] Other suggestions raised by the UKIPO to tackle invalid and abusive filings include an Australian-style system requiring a novelty search before a design registration may be enforced, or some form of 'bad faith' objection.[245] At the time of writing, the UKIPO plans to consult further.

10.075

In the meantime, applicants wanting support with design clearance can request a UKIPO search of the UK design register, although this is not comprehensive.[246] The UKIPO consultation acknowledges the need for far better search tools for designs: on the UKIPO website, these fall far short of what is available for trade marks.[247]

10.076

(d) Publication, registration and post-grant matters

Publication of a UK design registration can be deferred by up to 12 months from the filing date,[248] a shorter period than for RCDs for which publication

10.077

---

242 RDA 1949, s 3A.
243 UKIPO, DPN '1/06 'Ending examination on novelty grounds', 20 November 2007. See also, H Pudley and K Starks, 'Registered designs: modernisation of system' (2007) 18(1) Ent LR 2007 N8-9, noting that the previous system was 'arbitrary'.
244 UKIPO, 'Government response' (n 9), [10]–[17]. Re-introducing examination was also considered in 2013 but rejected, still at that time influenced by procedural alignment with the EUIPO: UKIPO, 'The Consultation on the Reform of the UK Designs Legal Framework' (n 127), [93]–[97].
245 UKIPO, 'Government response' (n 9), [14]–[15].
246 For example, it does not include international registrations designating the UK. A search request is made using Form DF21.
247 UKIPO, 'Government response' (n 9), [13]. Online searches of the UK designs register are only possible by registration number and applicant name, via www.gov.uk/search-registered-design accessed 2 August 2023.
248 DPN 02/22, 'Application forms, deferring publication, and time periods for replying to objections' 2 November 2022 www.gov.uk/government/publications/designs-practice-notice-dpn-0222-application-forms-deferring-publication-and-time-periods-for-replying-to-objections accessed 2 August 2023.

can be deferred for up to 30 months.[249] Otherwise, UK designs are published automatically as soon as possible after grant. If no objections are raised, this might be within a few weeks.[250] In rare cases, the UKIPO may prescribe that a design is kept secret, if publication of the design would be 'prejudicial to the defence of the realm'.[251]

10.078 As noted above (Section B.3), once a design has been registered, it remains in force for an initial period of five years, renewable in five-year periods up to a maximum of 25 years. Fees increase for each five-year period.[252] There are statutory provisions dealing with late renewal.[253] Post-grant invalidity challenges can be brought at the UKIPO and before the UK courts.

2. Enforcement of Design Rights

(a) Introduction

10.079 Enforcement of intellectual property rights (including designs) in the UK generally requires action in the civil courts (see Section E.2.(f) below on criminal enforcement). Empirical research into the IP caseloads of both the English and Scottish courts has shown that designs are the least litigated of the principal IP rights.[254]

(b) Choice of forum

10.080 Although intellectual property legislation applies UK-wide, the UK is comprised of three separate jurisdictions: England and Wales, Scotland, and Northern Ireland. While all are bound by decisions of the UKSC, each has its own first instance and appellate courts. The allocation of jurisdiction between different parts of the UK is governed by the Civil Jurisdiction and Judgments Act 1982. The relevant courts will have jurisdiction in design infringement litigation if the defendant is domiciled there or if that is where the harmful event has occurred or may occur.[255] If there is concurrent jurisdiction and a dispute

---

249 From the filing or priority date: CDR, Art 50(1).
250 'The Patent Office Annual Report and Accounts 2022/23' 13 July 2023, at 23 noting achievement against the target of examining domestic and international designs in under ten days, www.gov.uk/government/publications/ipo-annual-report-and-accounts-2022-to-2023 accessed 2 August 2023.
251 RDA 1949, s5.
252 UKIPO, 'Design forms and fees' (n 224).
253 RDA 1949, ss8(3), 8(4) and 8A.
254 C Helmers, Y Lefouili and L McDonagh, 'Evaluation of the Reforms of the Intellectual Property Enterprise Court 2010–2013' (2015), Tables 1 and 2 https://openaccess.city.ac.uk/id/eprint/12600/1/Evaluation_of_the_Reforms_of_the_Intellectual_Property_Enterprise_Court_2010-2013.pdf accessed 2 August 2023; J Cornwell, 'Intellectual Property Litigation at the Court of Session: A First Empirical Investigation' (2017) 21 Edin LR 192, 201.
255 Civil Jurisdiction and Judgments Act 1982, s16 and Schedule 4.

arises as to where the case should be heard, the doctrine of *forum non conveniens* will apply.²⁵⁶

10.081 Most UK design cases are litigated in England and Wales, where UK registered design claims must be initiated in the High Court, either in the Patents Court or the Intellectual Property Enterprise Court ('IPEC').²⁵⁷ IPEC is a specialist list which deals with claims up to a value of £500,000 and adopts more streamlined procedures and costs caps.²⁵⁸ Within England and Wales, the High Court also has exclusive jurisdiction over UK CUD and UK SUD claims.²⁵⁹ UKUDR claims may be started in the Chancery Division of the High Court, IPEC, or certain County Courts.²⁶⁰ IPEC also has a 'small claims track', intended to be suitable for unrepresented claimants, which can hear UKUDR, UK CUD and UK SUD claims (but not UK registered design claims) worth up to £10,000.²⁶¹ The recent UKIPO designs consultation asked whether UK registered designs should be introduced into the small claims track, but to a mixed response.²⁶²

10.082 In Scotland, IP litigation is typically conducted in the Outer House of the Court of Session, with appeals lying to the Inner House.²⁶³ Northern Ireland also has its own High Court and Court of Appeal.²⁶⁴ Further appeal from all parts of the UK lies to the UKSC, either with permission from that court or from the UKSC itself. The UKSC (and its predecessor, the UK House of Lords) has only heard one design case, the *Magmatic* litigation noted above, in over 50 years.²⁶⁵

---

256 See e.g.: *Vetco Gray UK Ltd v FMC Technologies Inc* [2007] EWHC 540 (Pat) (a patent case); *The University Court of The University of St Andrews v Student Gowns Ltd* [2020] ETMR 17 (a trade mark case).
257 Civil Procedure Rules, Part 63, rule 63.2.
258 See further www.judiciary.uk/courts-and-tribunals/business-and-property-courts/business-list-general-chancery/intellectual-property-list/intellectual-property-enterprise-court-ipec/work/ accessed 2 August 2023.
259 Designs and International Trade Marks (Amendment etc) (EU Exit) Regulations 2019/638, Schedule 1, para 33 and Schedule 2, para 29.
260 Civil Procedure Rules, Part 63, rule 63.13.
261 See further HM Courts & Tribunals Service, 'Guide to the Intellectual Property Enterprise Court small claims track', July 2023 www.gov.uk/government/publications/intellectual-property-enterprise-court-a-guide-to-small-claims accessed 2 August 2023.
262 UKIPO, 'Government response' (n 9), [39].
263 There is some limited concurrent jurisdiction with the Scottish Sheriff Courts in some intellectual property matters, but details fall outwith the scope of this chapter.
264 See further www.judiciaryni.uk/ accessed 2 August 2023.
265 Before *Magmatic*, the last design case heard by the UKSC/House of Lords was *Amp v Utilux* (n 80). The Supreme Court was established in 2009, replacing the judicial role previously undertaken by the House of Lords.

(c) Pre-action communications, 'threats' and standing to sue

10.083 Across all jurisdictions within the UK, litigants are encouraged to resolve their claims via pre-action communication. However, despite this push towards pre-action correspondence and settlement, would-be IP litigants must be aware of the risk of liability in UK law for the making of 'unjustified threats'. Potential liability attaches to the making of threats of infringement proceedings in relation to all forms of design protection in UK law.[266] The law is complex and beyond the scope of this chapter: some communications are permissible and it is a defence to show that the relevant acts did indeed constitute infringement, but the risks are substantial – actionable threats may be implicit as well as explicit, need not be in writing, may be sued upon by any 'person aggrieved' (not just the recipient of the threat), and carry liability for remedies including injunction and damages.[267] Legal advice should always be sought.

10.084 In terms of standing to sue, for all UK registered designs and UKUDR, each of the proprietor and any exclusive licensee can sue for infringement.[268] For UK SUD and UK CUD, an exclusive licensee may sue if the proprietor, having been given notice, does not bring proceedings in an appropriate period; a non-exclusive licensee may also bring UK CUD or UK SUD proceedings with the rightholder's consent.[269]

(d) The English courts' approach to design cases

10.085 Focusing in particular on the English courts, there are specific procedural rules for all intellectual property matters in Part 63 of the Civil Procedure Rules and its associated Practice Direction.[270] The English courts have taken a particularly robust perspective on managing evidence in design cases, particularly in relation to registered designs. Emphasising that in registered design cases '[w]hat really matters is what the court can see with its own eyes',[271] the Court of Appeal has also observed:[272]

---

266 For registered designs, see RDA 1949, ss26–26E. For UKUDR, see CDPA 1988, ss253–253E. For UK CUD and UK SUD, see Community Design Regulations 2005 (SI 2005/2339), regs 2–2F, as modified by the Designs and International Trade Marks (Amendment etc) (EU Exit) Regulations 2019/638, Schedule 1, paras 59–61 and Schedule 2, paras 54–56.
267 See more fully Howe et al, *Russell-Clarke & Howe* (n 1), Chapter 7.
268 RDA 1949, ss 24A(1) and 24F; CDPA 1988, ss229(1) and 234. Both must be parties to the proceedings: RDA, s24F(4); CDPA, s235(1).
269 CDR, Art 32(3), as modified by the Designs and International Trade Marks (Amendment etc) (EU Exit) Regulations 2019/638, Schedule 1, para 27 and Schedule 2, para 25.
270 See further www.justice.gov.uk/courts/procedure-rules/civil/rules accessed 2 August 2023.
271 *Dyson* (EWCA, n 39), [8].
272 *Procter & Gamble* (EWCA, n 28), [3].

The most important things in a case about registered designs are:

(i)   The registered design;
(ii) The accused object;
(iii) The prior art.

And the most important thing about each of those is what they look like. Of course parties and judges have to try to put into words why they say a design has 'individual character' or what the 'overall impression produced on an informed user' is. But 'it takes longer to say than to see'… And words themselves are often insufficiently precise on their own.

Only 'very limited' evidence will be admissible in registered design cases, most likely technical evidence in relation to design constraints.[273] Permission is required to adduce expert evidence and the ambit of that evidence should be pre-defined precisely.[274] Expert evidence has tended to be led only on functionality and design constraints, and to educate the court on the relevant design corpus.[275] Expert evidence should not be led on whether the registered design and alleged infringement produces the same or a different overall impression on the informed user in cases concerning consumer products.[276] It has also been cautioned that during an 'elongated trial over-burdened with expert evidence on issues which are actually for determination by the court', there is a real risk that the tribunal becomes over-familiar with the designs: this could cause the court to become 'too expert – too close to the sectoral expert who notices every difference', thereby distorting the determination of overall impression.[277] The Court of Appeal has noted that '[b]y and large it should be possible to decide a registered design case in a few hours'.[278] This seems, perhaps, ambitious; however, some cases have indeed been dealt with this quickly,[279] and even larger and more high-profile disputes have been dealt with relatively speedily.[280]

10.086

In UKUDR cases, the English courts have developed an approach first established in *Action Storage*, whereby the claimant uses a chart to identify the significant features of the claimed UKUDR design and the extent to which

10.087

---

273 *Spin Master Ltd v PMS International Ltd* [2018] ECDR 22, [6].
274 Ibid.
275 The courts have taken a strict line where expert evidence exceeds the set remit: see for example *Rothy's* (n 26), [27]–[37].
276 *Spin Master* (n 273), [27].
277 *Rothy's* (n 26), [96].
278 *Procter & Gamble* (EWCA, n 28), [4].
279 In *Lutec* (n 30), the trial was completed in just over an hour, the judge (at [47]) praised the parties' 'efficient and proportionate approach'.
280 The *Samsung v Apple* trial was completed in two days: *Samsung* (n 31), [5].

these also appear in the defendant's design.²⁸¹ The defendant then adopts the claimant's list, either agreeing or revising the list of features before admitting or denying whether they appear in the alleged infringement, and then identifying whether they are original and non-commonplace, or are excluded from design protection.

(e) Remedies

10.088 Full consideration of the remedies available to IP rightholders in the UK falls beyond the scope of this chapter.²⁸² Although some EU harmonisation of civil procedure and remedies was effected by the IP Enforcement Directive ('IPED'),²⁸³ most of the IPED's requirements were already met in the UK jurisdictions. As a result, although there have been some EU law-led developments,²⁸⁴ remedies have largely remained a matter of domestic law.

10.089 As for other IP infringements, a design rightholder's priorities are likely to be an injunction against future infringement (including an interim injunction, in appropriate cases), and a financial remedy in the form of damages or an account of the infringer's profits.²⁸⁵ In addition, rightholders may seek remedies such as delivery up or disposal of infringing items, or a publicity order requiring the losing party to disseminate of information on the outcome of the dispute (for example, via a notice on their website).²⁸⁶

10.090 There are, however, some particular points of note to flag in relation to remedies in design cases. First, in cases involving UK registered designs and UKUDR, an 'innocent infringer' will not be required to pay damages.²⁸⁷ The defendant must establish that at the time of infringement they were not aware, and had no reasonable grounds for supposing, that the infringed rights existed. This is hard to show in practice: the courts expect businesses to undertake

---

281 *Action Storage* (n 156), [109]–[113].
282 For a comprehensive discussion, see Howe et al, *Russell-Clarke & Howe* (n 1), Chapter 6, Section 5.
283 Directive 2004/48/EC on the enforcement of intellectual property rights [2004] OJ L157/45.
284 In particular (for present purposes), there has been some controversy around the impact of Art 13 IPED on the UK approach to damages claims in light of its implementation into UK law by The Intellectual Property (Enforcement etc) Regulations 2006 (SI 1028/1006), reg 3. See further: Howe et al, *Russell-Clarke & Howe* (n 1), paras 6-070–6-076.
285 If proceedings are brought in IPEC, damages are capped at £500,000 (or £10,000 under the small claims track): see Section E.2.(b) above.
286 A particularly high-profile example of a publicity order (granted, in that instance, against the losing design rightholder) can be found in the *Samsung v Apple* litigation: see in particular, *Samsung Electronics (UK) Ltd v Apple Inc* [2013] FSR 9 and [2013] FSR 10.
287 RDA 1949, s24B; CDPA 1988, s233. An account of profits can, however, still be pursued. There was no 'innocent infringement' defence in UK law in relation to Community designs; post-Brexit, the position in relation to UK CUD and UK SUD is perhaps not entirely clear: see Howe et al, *Russell-Clarke & Howe* (n 1), para 6-077.

clearance searches, and to be aware that new products that they encounter are likely to be protected against copying by unregistered design rights.[288]

Second, in UKUDR cases (but not UK registered designs, UK CUD or UK SUD), the rightholder may be entitled to 'additional damages', which operate as an uplift on standard damages in cases of flagrant infringement.[289] In a recent UKUDR case, the judge held that the defendant's 'couldn't care less' attitude justified additional damages worth £300,000 (an uplift of 200 per cent on the standard award), noting that one of the purposes of additional damages is to 'send the general message that infringement does not pay'.[290] 10.091

Third, in UKUDR cases it is also important to be aware of the impact of the defendant undertaking to take a licence of right (see Section C.1.(f) above). A defendant facing an infringement claim is well-advised to consider this option: it can be done without admission of liability and, in the event of a finding of infringement, prevents the grant of an injunction or an order for delivery up, as well as restricting financial liability.[291] 10.092

(f) Criminal enforcement

As a result of statutory provisions introduced in 2014, certain design infringements may be subject to criminal sanctions. It is a criminal offence if, in the course of a business and without consent, a person intentionally copies a registered design so as to make a product exactly to the design or with features that differ only in immaterial details, knowing or having reason to believe, that the design is a registered design.[292] It is also an offence for a person, in the course of a business and without consent, knowingly to offer, market, import, export, use or stock such a product.[293] It is a defence to show that the offender reasonably believed that the registration in question was invalid, that they did not infringe the right, or that they reasonably believed that they did not infringe.[294] These offences carry a maximum sentence of ten years' imprisonment and/or a fine.[295] 10.093

---

288 See e.g., *Kohler Mira Ltd v Bristan Group Ltd (No2)* [2015] FSR 9, [13]–[18].
289 CDPA 1988, s.229(3). Although additional damages cannot be claimed in other cases involving other forms of design right, it remains unclear as to whether an award of damages under The Intellectual Property (Enforcement etc) Regulations 2006 (SI 1028/1006), reg 3 could address some of the same considerations: see n 284 above.
290 *Original Beauty* (n 63), [509] and [511(vi)]; *Original Beauty Technology Co Ltd v G4K Fashion Ltd* [2022] ECDR 18 [141].
291 CDPA 1988, s239.
292 RDA 1949, s35ZA(1).
293 RDA 1949, s35ZA(3).
294 RDA 1949, ss35ZA(4) and (5).
295 RDA 1949, s35ZA(8).

DESIGN LAW

10.094 There are no corresponding criminal offences in relation unregistered designs, although lobbying for this continues. In its recent consultation, the UKIPO noted that 'no firm evidence' was provided by stakeholders to support claims as to either the deterrent effect of criminalisation or potential problems for businesses if criminal sanctions were extended.[296]

F. CONCLUSION

10.095 This chapter has outlined the various ways in which UK law protects designs, addressing UK registered design protection, UKUDR and the new forms of UK unregistered design right (the UK continuing unregistered Community design, and the UK supplementary unregistered design) introduced post-Brexit. The chapter has also outlined the way in which designs may be protected via other intellectual property rights, noting the UK's longstanding (but increasingly tested) aim to minimise the role for copyright in the field of industrial design and attitudes to protection of designs via registered trade mark law and passing off. This chapter has also summarised key points relating to the application process for UK registered designs and various aspects of design enforcement.

10.096 As this chapter has sought to highlight, UK design law currently stands at something of a crossroads. Although the UK has been registering designs since the mid-19th century, and was the first jurisdiction in Europe to introduce a bespoke domestic unregistered design right under the CDPA 1988, the impetus since the early 2000s has consistently been to adapt long-established UK ways to fall in line with EU design law and EUIPO practice. With Brexit finally taking effect at the start of 2021, discussion has begun to re-open on what shape post-Brexit UK design law should take. This chapter has sought to highlight key areas which await the outcome of the UKIPO's ongoing design law review.

10.097 In that review, an overriding consideration must surely be the complexity of the state of protection for designs in UK law. The issues arising from IP overlaps are well-known and are discussed in relation to design law in more detail in Chapter 15 of this book.[297] With UK registered design protection sitting alongside (at the time of writing) three forms of unregistered design protection, plus (to a greater or lesser degree) the possibility of protecting designs *via* copyright, registered trade marks and passing off, UK law presents perhaps

---

296 UKIPO, 'Government response' (n 9), [41].
297 Shubha Ghosh, 'Redesigning design protection: the problem of overlap', Chapter 15, this volume.

a particularly egregious case study in overlap and complexity in relation to designs. The UKIPO's review of UK design protection must surely take at least some steps to address and simplify the position, particularly given repeatedly expressed concerns expressed about the uncertainties and challenges posed for designers and businesses in seeking to navigate the UK regime.

11

DESIGN PROSECUTION BEFORE THE EUIPO AND THE COURT OF JUSTICE OF THE EU

Henning Hartwig

A. INTRODUCTION TO THE COMMUNITY DESIGN SYSTEM 11.001	3. Exception in Case of Modular System 11.083
B. FACTS, EVIDENCE, AND ARGUMENTS 11.006	4. Visible During Normal Use 11.088
1. EUIPO Case Law and Practice 11.009	H. CONFLICT BETWEEN EARLIER TRADEMARK AND LATER COMMUNITY DESIGN 11.095
2. General Court and CJEU 11.011	
C. DISCLOSURE OF PRIOR ART 11.016	1. Trademark Standards 11.096
1. Relevant Prior Art 11.018	2. Distinctive Sign (Earlier Mark) 11.098
2. Disclosure of Obscure Prior Art 11.023	3. Genuine Use of the Earlier Mark 11.100
3. Disclosure of Own Prior Art 11.026	4. Use of the Earlier Mark in the Later Design as a Mark 11.101
4. Disclosure of Confidential Prior Art 11.028	
5. Disclosure of Prior Art as a Consequence of an Abuse 11.031	5. Use of the Earlier Mark in the Later Design for Similar or Identical Goods and Services 11.102
6. Burden of Submission and Proof in a Case of Unauthorised Disclosure 11.035	6. Similarity of Signs 11.106
D. NOVELTY OF THE COMMUNITY DESIGN 11.038	7. Likelihood of Confusion 11.107
E. INDIVIDUAL CHARACTER OF THE COMMUNITY DESIGN 11.045	8. Maintenance of the Later Design in an Amended Form? 11.108
1. Degree of Freedom of the Designer 11.051	I. CONFLICT BETWEEN EARLIER COPYRIGHT AND LATER COMMUNITY DESIGN 11.112
2. Informed User 11.053	1. Copyright Standards 11.113
3. Overall Impression 11.057	2. Work Protected Under National Copyright Law 11.115
F. LACK OF CONSISTENCY OF THE COMMUNITY DESIGN 11.061	3. Unauthorised Use of the Work 11.118
1. Lack of Unity in Invalidity Proceedings 11.066	J. CONFLICT BETWEEN EARLIER DESIGN AND LATER COMMUNITY DESIGN 11.121
2. Lack of Unity in Registration Proceedings 11.070	1. Design Infringement Standards 11.122
G. OTHER GROUNDS OF INHERENT INVALIDITY OF THE COMMUNITY DESIGN 11.073	2. Degree of Freedom of the Designer of the Earlier Design 11.124
1. Features of Community Design Solely Dictated by Technical Function 11.074	3. Scope of Protection of the Earlier Design 11.130
2. Features of Community Design Necessarily Reproduced to Permit Interconnectivity 11.080	4. Infringing Use of the Earlier Design by the Later Community Design 11.131
	K. CONCLUSIONS 11.133

A. INTRODUCTION TO THE COMMUNITY DESIGN SYSTEM

Design law in the European Union ('EU') consists of the Designs Directive (98/71/EC), harmonising the national design laws of the current 27 EU Member States to some substantive extent, and the Community Designs Regulation (6/2002), which protects *eo ipso* registered and unregistered Community designs. Registered Community designs ('RCD') are administered by the European Union Intellectual Property Office ('EUIPO').

11.001

Key requirements for establishing design protection are 'novelty' and 'individual character' as provided in Article 5 and Article 6 Community Designs Regulation ('CDR') and the parallel provisions of the Designs Directive. To establish novelty, a design must vary in more than just immaterial details from any prior design. Whether a design has individual character depends on whether or not it creates the same overall impression on the informed user as an earlier design.

11.002

According to the General Court of the EU ('General Court'), this notional informed user is a person who is particularly observant and who has some knowledge of the prior state of the art. The status of 'user' implies that such person uses the product in which the design is incorporated, in accordance with the purpose for which the product is intended. The qualifier 'informed' suggests in addition that, without being a designer or a technical expert, the user knows the various designs which exist in the relevant sector, possesses a certain degree of knowledge with respect to the features which those designs normally include and, as a result of his or her interest in the relevant products, shows a relatively high degree of attention when he or she uses them.

11.003

At EU level, rights in designs can be acquired not only through registration but also through mere disclosure. Unregistered Community designs are protected for three years from the date on which the design is first made available to the public within the territory of the EU, pursuant to Article 11 and Article 110a CDR. Such protection does not require any kind of use; the design must simply be disclosed in such a way that, in the normal course of business, the disclosing event could reasonably have become known to the circles specialized in the relevant sector, operating within the EU. A first disclosure outside the EU does not create any unregistered Community design rights.[1] Evidently, such

11.004

---

1 See *Bakery Press,* German Federal Supreme Court, 9 October 2008, I ZR 126/06, para 17; Maierski, in: Zentek/Gerstein (ed.), *German Designs Act,* 2022, A II para 207; Eichmann/Jestaedt, in: Eichmann/Jestaedt/Fink/Meiser (ed.), *German Designs Act/Community Designs Regulation,* 2019, 6th edition, Article 11 para 9; Ruhl, in: Ruhl/Tolkmitt (ed.), *Community Designs Regulation,* 2019, 3rd edition, Article

rights, in the absence of any registration, are not administered by the EUIPO. However, provided that a design is filed with the EUIPO (or any national office of an EU Member State) and publication of the subsequent registration constitutes first disclosure of the design, such publication – automatically and simultaneously – establishes protection as an unregistered Community design for three years, which will co-exist with the registered design right. Similarly, a design first disclosed in the EU resulting in an unregistered Community design may also be submitted for registration at the EUIPO and will result in a registered Community design, if filed within the grace period of one year.

11.005 This chapter will address manifold issues related to the prosecution of Community designs before the EUIPO and, if the registration or cancellation proceedings do not end before the EUIPO, before the General Court and the Court of Justice of the EU ('CJEU'), both having their seat in Luxembourg. Issues related to unregistered Community designs will not be covered by this contribution.[2]

B. FACTS, EVIDENCE, AND ARGUMENTS

11.006 As a rule, in Community design matters, issues of validity are primarily decided by the Invalidity Division and the – solely competent[3] – Third Board of Appeal of the EUIPO (the number of invalidity counterclaims before Community design courts is insignificant in comparison), with the possibility of an appeal to the General Court and, as a final instance, on points of law to the CJEU.

11.007 Since the implementation of the Community design system, stakeholders from the EU and abroad have kept the EUIPO and the Luxembourg courts continuously if not increasingly busy. Consequently, there is already a rich body of case law providing helpful guidance on how to challenge and defend validity of

---

11 para 17; STONE, *EU Design Law*, 2016, 2nd edition, para 18.13; SCHAAP/VAN DEN BERG/GEORGE, in: HASSELBLATT (ed.), *Community Designs Regulation*, 2015, Article 11 para 11. – With respect to the ongoing EU Design Law reform, also in that context, see below note 167.

2 On the important 'Ferrari' saga and the question of whether and under what circumstances the making available to the public of images of a product, such as the publication of photographs of a car, entails the making available to the public of a design of a part of that product ('parallel partial protection') see HARTWIG, *'Ferrari' and the level of intellectual abstraction in European design law* [2022] JIPLP 791; HARTWIG, *Offenbarung, Schutzgegenstand und Eingriffsprüfung beim nicht eingetragenen Gemeinschaftsgeschmacksmuster. Zugleich Besprechung von OLG Düsseldorf 'Front Kit II'* [2023] GRUR 937.

3 The Third Board of Appeal is EUIPO's only Board of Appeal (of overall five Boards of Appeal) having authority to hear cases on appeal in Community design matters (irrespective of whether the underlying ground for invalidity is based on a prior design, trademark, or copyright); see https://euipo.europa.eu/tunnel-web/secure/webdav/guest/document_library/contentPdfs/law_and_practice/presidium_boards_appeal/Decision2021-17_en.pdf accessed 31 December 2023.

a Community design under the different scenarios, including fascinating conflicts between a prior trademark or copyright and a later Community design.

What is common to both the EUIPO practice and the case law of the EU courts in Luxembourg is a clear and welcome distinction between facts, evidence, and arguments. Such distinction – self-evident as it may appear at first sight – flows from Article 63 CDR, pursuant to which in proceedings relating to a declaration of invalidity, the EUIPO shall be restricted 'in this examination to the facts, evidence and arguments provided by the parties and the relief sought' and may disregard facts or evidence which are not submitted in due time by the parties concerned. **11.008**

1. EUIPO Case Law and Practice

By the end of December 2023, the Invalidity Division had decided approx. 4,450 cases and the Board of Appeal approx. 1,700 cases, related to the application for a declaration of invalidity of a Community design (including cases related to the invalidation of multiple Community designs). It is remarkable that in the decade from 2004 to 2014 (status: 31 December 2014), on average, about one-third of the decisions of the Board of Appeal in Community design matters have been annulled by the General Court,[4] starting, to the best of our knowledge, with the first decision of the Third Board of Appeal from 21 September 2004.[5] In contrast, of the 21 invalidity decisions of the Board under appeal decided by the General Court in 2015 and 2016, only three were annulled and three others were removed from the registry (without any decision on the merits), while 15 decisions have been confirmed, meaning that the number of successful appeals decreased from one in three to one in seven.[6] Since then, on average, 80–85 per cent of the decisions of the Board of Appeal appealed to the General Court have been confirmed, according to unpublished EUIPO sources. **11.009**

Issues of disclosure – which are governed by Article 7 CDR[7] and are most important for assessing novelty (Article 5 CDR) and individual character (Article 6 CDR) of a Community design but also when determining its scope **11.010**

---

4   See HARTWIG, *Reciprocity in design law: another brick in the wall* [2015] JIPLP 465, 466 note 1.
5   *Stenman [Safety locks for bicycles]*, EUIPO (Board of Appeal), 21 September 2004, R 351/2004-3.
6   See HARTWIG, *The 'Legal Review on Industrial Design Protection in Europe': A closer look* [2018] JIPLP 332, 333 note 7.
7   A parallel provision can be found in Article 6 Designs Directive.

of protection[8] – have reached the General Court only to a limited extent.[9] Nonetheless, determining the relevant design corpus and separating obscure from non-obscure prior art are among the most important and complicated tasks in design law. Therefore, guidance from the Third Board of Appeal is most helpful and welcome, particularly when considering that the EUIPO's Guidelines[10] are not binding[11] as confirmed by the Second Board of Appeal (as regards the EUIPO's Guidelines for examination of EU trademarks').[12]

2. General Court and CJEU

11.011 Since the Third Board of Appeal is required, under Article 60 (1) CDR, to undertake a full review of the facts and law assessed by the Invalidity Division the question has been discussed whether the General Court, in return, would have jurisdiction to conduct a full review of the legality of the Board of Appeal's decisions, including both the assessment of the facts submitted in the EUIPO proceedings and all relevant legal issues. Eventually, the CJEU, under Article 61 (2) CDR, answered this question in the affirmative.

11.012 Accordingly:

(...) the General Court has exclusive jurisdiction to find the facts, save where a substantive inaccuracy in its findings is apparent from the documents submitted to it, and to appraise those facts. That appraisal of the facts thus does not, save where the clear sense

---

8 See, for instance, Dusseldorf Appeal Court, 25 November 2014, I-20 U 193/13; Frankfurt Appeal Court, 17 November 2014, 6 W 96/14.
9 See, for instance, Case T-68/10 *Sphere Time* ECLI:EU:T:2011:269, paras 22 *et seq.* – Pursuant to Case T-15/13 *Group Nivelles v EUIPO and Easy Sanitary Solutions* ECLI:EU:T:2015:281, para 122, it is clear '(...) that the "sector concerned", within the meaning of Article 7(1) of Regulation No 6/2002, is not limited to that of the product in which the contested design is intended to be incorporated or applied.'
10 See EUIPO, Guidelines for Examination of Registered Community Designs (status: 31 March 2023; see Decision No EX-23-2 on 24 March 2023).
11 See also EUIPO Guidelines for Examination of Registered Community Designs, Examination of applications for registered Community designs (see note 10), para 1.1:
The purpose of the Guidelines is to ensure consistency among the decisions taken by the Operations Department and to ensure a coherent practice in file handling. These Guidelines are merely a set of consolidated rules setting out the line of conduct that the Office itself proposes to adopt, which means that, to the extent that those rules comply with the legal provisions of a higher authority, they constitute a self-imposed restriction on the Office, in that it must comply with the rules that it has itself laid down. However, these Guidelines cannot derogate from the CDR, the CDIR or the CDFR, and it is solely in the light of those regulations that they should be interpreted and applied.
12 See, by analogy, *ING-DiBa v Banca Monte*, EUIPO (Board of Appeal), 26 November 2015, Joined cases R 113/2015-2 and R 174/2015-2, para 89: '(...) these Guidelines are not binding legal acts for the purpose of interpreting such provisions of EU law. The Boards of Appeal are therefore not required to apply the Guidelines.' – These findings were confirmed by Case T-84/16 *Banca Monte v EUIPO/ING-DiBa* ECLI:EU:T:2017:661, para 68.

of the evidence has been distorted, constitute a point of law which is subject, as such, to review by the Court of Justice in an appeal (…).

11.013 The CJEU, however, accepted that the General Court may, in appropriate cases, restrict its review of decisions in industrial design matters, by way of an exception, to an examination of manifest errors of assessment, particularly where the EUIPO is called upon to perform highly technical assessments.[13] Such 'special cases' where the General Court deferred to the expertise of the EUIPO have not arisen so far.

11.014 Since finding validity of a design and, more particularly, assessing the overall impression of two conflicting designs is a question of fact, falling, in general, into the General Court's exclusive jurisdiction,[14] the approach of this Court is fundamental both to the understanding of European design law and to the assessment of the quality of the daily work of the Board of Appeal. Previously, when reviewing pertinent case law, it seemed that the decided cases consisted of separate pieces of a puzzle, rather than being a coherent whole.[15] More recently, however, the General Court proceeded to create 'specialised Chambers', including six Chambers exclusively dealing with intellectual property matters (i.e., actions brought against decisions of Boards of Appeal of the EUIPO and the Community Plant Varieties Office),[16] resulting in more consistency, efficiency, and speediness as it is fair to expect.[17]

11.015 As a final remark, the General Court is not *per se* allowed to take itself a decision which the Board of Appeal ought to have or could have taken. Rather, exercise of the power to alter decisions is limited to situations in which the General Court, after reviewing the assessment made by the Board of Appeal, is in a position to determine, on the basis of the matters of fact and of law as established, what decision the Board of Appeal was required to take. In return, where the Board of Appeal has not established all the elements of fact and of law to enable the Court to determine the decision it was required to take, the conditions for alteration are not satisfied.[18]

---

13   See Joined Cases C-101/11 P and C-102/11 P *Neuman* ECLI:EU:C:2012:641, paras 41 and 66; see also HARTWIG, IIC 2013, 249 *et seq.*
14   See HARTWIG, IIC 2013, 249, 252.
15   See HARTWIG, *Community design law: further guidance from the General Court of the European Union* [2013] JIPLP 862 *et seq.*
16   See https://curia.europa.eu/jcms/upload/docs/application/pdf/2019-09/cp190111en.pdf accessed 31 December 2023.
17   However, recent case law of the General Court in design matters caused concerns with respect to quality, terminology, and consistency. – For details see HARTWIG, *A critical review of recent design case law by the General Court of the European Union*, QMJIP 12 [2022] 553 *et seq.*
18   See Case T-515/19 *Lego* ECLI:EU:T:2021:155, para 118 *et seq.*

C. DISCLOSURE OF PRIOR ART

11.016 While Article 7 CDR is titled 'disclosure' and the term 'disclosure' or 'disclose' is frequently used in that provision, neither the nature nor the specific content nor the possible subject of such a disclosure is specified in the text.

11.017 Overall, the language of Article 7 (1) CDR suggests that the act of disclosure as such – exemplified by the wording 'published following registration or otherwise, or exhibited, used in trade or otherwise disclosed' – is a *question of fact*. However, while the exception ('where these events could not reasonably have become known in the normal course of business to the circles specialised in the sector concerned, operating within the Community') to that act would seem to include aspects of legal analysis and evaluation ('reasonably' and 'normal course of business'), i.e., a balancing of interests which must avoid subjectivity as much as possible, relevance of disclosure (lack of obscurity) is nonetheless limited to factual evidence and beyond the legal review by the CJEU.[19]

1. Relevant Prior Art

11.018 Overall, pursuant to Article 7 (1) CDR, disclosure is related to a specific prior design ('a design'), a specific prior date ('before the date referred to'), a specific act ('these events') and a specific addressee ('circles specialised in the sector concerned, operating within the Community'). The only limits set to a proper disclosure under Article 7 (1) CDR are those mentioned at the end of that provision, allowing courts or tribunals to find that a specific act of disclosure was obscure and, therefore, '(…) could not reasonably have become known in the normal course of business to the circles specialised in the sector concerned, operating within the Community (…).'[20]

11.019 Overall, it follows from the nature and content of disclosure that one needs to distinguish between what is submitted (the subject of disclosure[21]) and how to demonstrate that this subject was disclosed (proof of disclosure[22]). To

---

19 Case C-479/12 *Gautzsch v Münchener Boulevard Möbel Joseph Duna* ECLI:EU:C:2014:75, para 34. – For details how to test under the scheme of Article 7 (1) CDR *see*, by way of example, *Activa v Targa [Grilling apparatus]*, EUIPO (Board of Appeal), 4 October 2021, R 1651/2020-3, paras 22 *et seq.*
20 For the test of obscurity *see* below at C 2.
21 See also *Linak v ChangZhou Kaidi [Electrically operated lifting column, in particular for tables]*, EUIPO (Board of Appeal), 21 March 2017, R 1412/2015-3, para 22, considering each prior design as a 'different subject matter' and finding the '(…) reliance on additional earlier designs and/or rights inadmissible when submitted at a later procedural stage (…).'
22 For details see HARTWIG, *Disclosure on the Internet under Community Design Law*, in EUIPO (ed.), *20 years of the Boards of Appeal at EUIPO – Celebrating the Past, Looking Forward to the Future*, Liber Amicorum (2017) 188 *et seq.*

that extent, one needs to discriminate accordingly, i.e., formally identifying the specific prior art (usually classified as D1, D2, D3 etc.[23]) which has been introduced (assertion of facts) on the one hand and substantively qualifying or dismissing the supportive documentation as reliable and adequate (submission of evidence) on the other,[24] including invoices and documents showing the asserted prior design.[25]

11.020 By way of example, interestingly, with respect to printouts of offers on *Amazon*, the German Federal Patent Court found that Amazon offers are inherently subject to concerns with respect to their probative value; without further supporting evidence, they are not suitable for proving, with sufficient certainty, the date of a sales offer which is claimed to be prior to the date of filing a design. In this respect, it would be up to the nullity claimant to provide further evidence of disclosure, e.g., submission of sales invoices dated before the date of application or witness evidence.[26] This coincides with what the Dusseldorf Appeal Court held before, namely that if an alleged disclosure, by way of printouts of offers on Amazon, is disputed in a substantiated manner, it is up to the party bearing the corresponding burden of proof to explain and demonstrate the relevance of these printouts in more detail. This is especially true against the background that it is generally known that offers on Amazon can be changed, for example the product descriptions and product photos on Amazon Marketplace can be changed, without changing the offer date at the same time.[27] Similarly, the General Court found that when assessing the probative value of a document, the likelihood and credibility of its information must be examined, concluding that since the online encyclopedia *Wikipedia*

---

23   *Actona v Inter Link [Coffee tables]*, EUIPO (Board of Appeal), 5 February 2015, R 1496/2013-3, paras 4 *et seq.*
24   See, for instance, *Actona v Inter Link [Coffee tables]*, EUIPO (Board of Appeal), 5 February 2015, R 1496/2013-3, para 5.
25   *Cutelarias Cristema v Francisco do Carmo Silva Mota [Hatchets]*, EUIPO (Board of Appeal), 18 May 2021, R 2019/2020-3, paras 17 *et seq.*
26   See *Wheel Cap*, German Federal Patent Court, 18 February 2021, 30 W (pat) 806/18.
27   See *Bathing Shoe*, Dusseldorf Appeal Court, 25 April 2019, I-20 U 103/18. – Contrary to this, *Lafner v Abart [Adornment]*, EUIPO (Board of Appeal), 19 November 2020, R 1213/2019-3, para 31, concluded with respect to the so-called 'Amazon Standard Identification Number' ('ASIN') that:
   (…) although the date of creation of the ASIN cannot be changed, it is independent from the product publication date mentioned on Amazon and is therefore not necessarily identical to it. As the ASIN is issued in the first time of the preparation of the product information, that also means that publication of a product can take place no earlier than which the ASIN can be published but not before the creation date of the ASIN. As a consequence of this, ASIN only allows for the determination of the earliest possible time at which a product illustration corresponding to the ASIN was published on the Amazon platform, rather than stating the date of actual publication.

can be changed at any time by any Internet user, images shown there must be assumed to have extremely limited evidential value.[28]

11.021 Different from the other factual parameters (what, when, how, to whom), the place of disclosure (where) is not mentioned in Article 7 (1) CDR. Also, the provision does not distinguish between digital and non-digital acts of disclosure. It follows from that lack of specification that there are, in general, no limits to the place of disclosure, meaning that *any disclosure anywhere in the world*, as a rule, would and should be relevant (concept of absolute world-wide novelty[29]).

11.022 More specifically, it is common ground that disclosure is not limited to companies or individuals being established or domiciled in the European Union.[30] Rather, pursuant to Article 7 (1) CDR, disclosure is related to the 'circles specialised in the sector concerned, operating within the Community'.[31] This notion is construed broadly, according to the CJEU, with the consequence that the law '(...) lays down no restrictions relating to the nature of the activity of natural or legal persons who may be considered to form part of the circles specialised in the sector concerned.'[32] Finally, the 'sector concerned' – another vague term – may either consist of the sector of the challenged Community design (to be determined according to the indication of product which, however, does not affect its scope of protection 'as such'; *cf.* Article 36 (6) CDR) or of the sector of the prior art. It has been submitted – also by the General Court in the proceedings *'Group Nivelles'*[33] – that the 'sector concerned' should include the sector to which the prior design belongs.[34] This position was also taken by the CJEU.[35]

---

28 Case T-192/18 *Rietze v EUIPO and Volkswagen* ECLI:EU:T:2019:379, para 59; Case T-191/18 *Rietze/EUIPO and Volkswagen* ECLI:EU:T:2019:378, para 57.
29 Case C-479/12 *Gautzsch v Münchener Boulevard Möbel Joseph Duna* ECLI:EU:C:2014:75, para 33.
30 See also, ibid., para 36.
31 The same notion is used in Article 11 (2) CDR with respect to the standard for establishing an unregistered Community design right.
32 Case C-479/12 *Gautzsch v Münchener Boulevard Möbel Joseph Duna* ECLI:EU:C:2014:75, para 27.
33 Case T-15/13 *Group Nivelles v EUIPO and Easy Sanitary Solutions* ECLI:EU:T:2015:281, para 116:
    (...) a Community design cannot be regarded as being novel (...) if an identical design has been made available to the public before the dates specified in that provision, even if that earlier design is intended to be incorporated into a different product or to be applied to a different product. In the contrary situation, the subsequent registration of that design as a Community design intended to be incorporated in a different product from that made available to the public or to be applied to that other product, would (...) allow the holder of that subsequent registration to prevent its use even for the product that was made available to the public earlier. Such a result would be paradoxical.
34 For details see HARTWIG, GRUR [2016] 882 *et seq.*
35 Joined Cases C-361/15 P and C-405/15 P *Easy Sanitary v EUIPO/Group Nivelles* ECLI:EU:C:2017:720, paras 96 and 103 ('not limited to the product in which the contested design is intended to be incorporated or applied'). – Such a concept of allowing cross-sectoral prior art, which impacts both the test for infringement

2. Disclosure of Obscure Prior Art

When establishing disclosure of a prior design, an overall assessment must be made taking into account all the relevant circumstances of the particular case. Disclosure cannot be proved by means of probabilities or suppositions but must be demonstrated by solid and objective evidence. Such evidence must be considered in its entirety. While some elements of the evidence considered on their own may be insufficient to demonstrate the disclosure of a prior design, the fact remains that, when combined or in conjunction with other documents or information, they can contribute to the proof of disclosure.[36]

11.023

Individual cases show the application of these principles. For example, the publication of photographs on the design holder's *Facebook* page (even when proven by two 'certified reports') was not considered an event that could have reasonably become known in the normal course of business to the relevant circles of designers, manufactures and traders.[37] Interestingly, in the UK case *Ahmet Erol v Sumaira Javaid*, the issue was not whether a disclosure on Facebook was obscure but reliable. Michael Howe QC found that where the prior art is a photograph on Facebook, which appears as part of a screen shot which bears on its face a specific date, for discounting this evidence positive evidence is required to demonstrate that the date on the screen shot has been forged; a contention that it would have been technically possible to forge the date is not sufficient.[38]

11.024

In terms of burden of submission and proof, it is common ground that while the applicant requesting a declaration of invalidity must show evidence under Article 7 (1) CDR, the holder of the contested Community design, in return, must produce evidence that the asserted prior art 'could not reasonably have become known in the normal course of business to the circles specialised in the

11.025

---

and validity, clearly differs from, particularly, the US design patent system where the subject matter is determined by and limited to the title of the design patent and protection, overall, is provided only with respect to a 'design for an article of manufacture' (35 U.S.C. 171), with a clear nexus between the design and the product, and protection is limited to designs likely to be confused by average consumers. Consequently, the scope of USD677,946 (title: 'Pattern for a chair') does not include a basket; see *Curver Luxembourg, SARL, v Home Expressions, Inc.*, 938 F.3d 1334 (Fed. Cir. 2019). Likewise, an 'art tool made of tightly spiral-wound, soft gray paper' is no proper prior art when challenging US29/491,550 (title: 'Ornamental design for a lip implant'); see *In re: SurgiSil, L.L.P. et al.*, No. 2020-1940 (Fed. Cir. Oct. 4, 2021).

36 *Xeltys v Cavius [Smoke alarms (part of-)]*, EUIPO (Board of Appeal), 13 July 2016, R 277/2016-3, para 19.
37 Ibid., para 20.
38 *Ahmet Erol v Sumaira Javaid*, 18 May 2017, O-253-17, paras 41 *et seq*. – For more details see HARTWIG, *Disclosure on the Internet under Community Design Law*, in EUIPO (ed.), *20 years of the Boards of Appeal at EUIPO – Celebrating the Past, Looking Forward to the Future*, Liber Amicorum (2017), 188 *et seq*.

sector concerned, operating within the Community', *i.e.*, that disclosure was obscure.[39]

3. Disclosure of Own Prior Art

11.026 Pursuant to Article 7 (2) CDR, a disclosure shall be ignored if a design for which protection is claimed under a registered Community design has been made available to the public by the designer, his successor in title, or a third person 'as a result of information provided or action taken by the designer or his successor in title' and 'during the 12-month period preceding the date of filing of the application or, if a priority is claimed, the date of priority'. This complex and entangled scenario, also known as *'grace period'*, enables stakeholders to test their product, or a variant thereof, on the market (in Europe or abroad) before spending costs (low as they may be) for registering a Community design. Thus, the 'standard situation' covered by the grace period is to protect a Community design from challenges to its validity based on a prior own publication of the same or a similar design.

11.027 There are, however, two reasons which may speak against relying on the grace period and suggest seeking early registration of a Community design instead. *Firstly*, grace periods are not universally recognised, and any protection sought outside Europe may become unavailable because of the prior disclosure of the design by the designer himself or on his behalf (if the only market of interest is the EU, this argument of course does not apply). *Secondly*, the grace period does – in any event – not provide protection or shelter when a third party developed and disclosed a similar design (second design) independently before the filing date of the first Community design. This second design may then be a ground of invalidity. Thus, the grace period does not provide protection when an independently developed design is made available to the public ('intermediate publication') prior to the filing date, or priority date if any, of the Community design. The grace period protects only against the designer's own publication or a publication made on his behalf. In these situations, the publication of the second design in the period between publication of the first design, for which the grace period applies, and the filing date (or priority date if any) constitutes relevant prior art.[40]

---

39 See Case T-651/16 *Crocs v EUIPO and Gifi* ECLI:EU:T:2018:137, paras 47 *et seq.*; *Ur & Penn v Bell & Ross [Watches]*, EUIPO (Board of Appeal), 27 October 2009, R 1267/2008-3, paras 35 *et seq.*; CASTROL *v NORMANPLAST [Cans]*, EUIPO (Board of Appeal), 7 July 2008, R 1516/2007-3, para 9.

40 For more details see HARTWIG, *From idea to design: protection under the 'Grace Period' in Europe* [2013] WIPR (May/June) 46. – From an international perspective see VOLKEN, *Requirements for Design Protection: Global Commonalities*, in HARTWIG (ed.), Research Handbook on Design Law, 2021, 28 *et seq.*

4. Disclosure of Confidential Prior Art

11.028 Pursuant to Article 7 (1) CDR, a design shall not be deemed to have been made available to the public for the sole reason that it has been 'disclosed to a third person under explicit or implicit conditions of confidentiality'.

11.029 This exception from the rule of a broad notion of disclosure is not limited to prior art originating from the holder of the later Community design under attack but includes prior art from any source – provided the conditions of disclosure were confidential. So, there is overlap with the exemption under the grace period regime but only to some extent.

11.030 Case law on the construction and application of the confidential prior art defence is rare to the best of our knowledge. In 2014, the CJEU had to decide on the scope of Article 7 (1) CDR but the underlying fact pattern was explicitly limited to the situation where the design was 'disclosed to third parties without any explicit or implicit conditions of confidentiality' so that the Court did not need to discuss the reach of this vague legal concept. The least one can say is that the *burden of submission and proof* that the disclosure was confidential should rest on the holder (comparable to the obscurity defence).

5. Disclosure of Prior Art as a Consequence of an Abuse

11.031 We have seen that the grace period does not provide protection when an independently developed design is made available to the public ('intermediate publication') prior to the filing date, or priority date if any, of the Community design. Even where the intermediate publication is of a design copied by a third party from the previously published design, the grace period also does not apply, unless the Community design proprietor can claim that the intermediate publication is the consequence of an 'abuse in relation to the designer or his successor in title'; Article 7 (3) CDR.

11.032 However, Article 7 (3) CDR does not seem to apply as the mere copying does not amount to an 'abuse'. Such abuse would require some action on behalf of the person publishing the copied design which is against accepted morals or practices, such as theft, illicit access to data, unauthorised disclosure by employees of the designer or the successor in title, etc.

11.033 The result would be that a person having published a design copied from the first design can defeat a later Community design registration. That appears inequitable. It has been suggested therefore that the intervening publication of a copy of the original design should fall under Article 7 (2) lit a CDR, as having been derived from or being based on information made available by the original designer. The intervening publication would then also fall within the one-year grace period and would not constitute prior art.[41]

11.034 One should consider this result to be appropriate; but there remains a certain risk that tribunals will interpret Article 7 (2) lit a CDR differently and require some active participation by the original designer in the publication of his design. Consequently, filing an application for registration as early as possible will help to minimise the number of prior designs potentially detrimental to the validity of the Community design.

6. Burden of Submission and Proof in a Case of Unauthorised Disclosure

11.035 Different from other jurisdictions, European design law does not use the term 'unauthorized disclosure' but, rather, distinguishes between a disclosure under 'explicit or implicit conditions of confidentiality' (above at C 4) and disclosure following an 'abuse in relation to the designer or his successor in title' (above at C 5). Under both scenarios, the subject matter of the disclosure is not intended to become 'public', and, in that sense, disclosure would be 'unauthorized'.

11.036 Also, under both scenarios, 'unauthorized disclosure' would be a defence raised by the holder of the Community design when being confronted with an attack on the validity of the design (either in proceedings started before the EUIPO or by way of a counterclaim for a declaration of invalidity of a Community design raised in connection with an infringement action before a national Community design court). In both situations, the burden of submission and proof would rest on the holder to show that disclosure was 'unauthorized'.

11.037 In this respect, the General Court confirmed that the burden of proving facts establishing confidentiality, under Article 7 (1) Sentence 2 CDR, lies with the holder of the contested Community design.[42] Also, the Board of Appeal found that it is up to the holder of the contested Community design to show that there has been commercial behaviour on the part of the other party which any trader would describe as an abuse, fraudulent or dishonest.[43]

---

41 For more details see HARTWIG, *From idea to design: protection under the 'Grace Period' in Europe* [2013] WIPR (May/June) 46.
42 Case T-748/18 *Glimarpol v EUIPO/Metar* ECLI:EU:T:2020:321, para 25.
43 *THD Acoustic v HARRON [MP3 players and recorders]*, EUIPO (Board of Appeal), 25 July 2009, R 552/2008-3, paras 24 *et seq.*

D. NOVELTY OF THE COMMUNITY DESIGN

Testing the novelty of a Community design follows a rather straightforward, two-step procedure. What matters is whether the Community design is new over any other prior design which has been disclosed in a relevant matter and introduced by the parties. Novelty is defined in Article 5 (1) CDR as absence of identity ('considered to be new if no identical design has been made available to the public'). According to Article 5 (2) CDR, two designs shall be deemed to be identical (placed side by side[44]) if their features differ only in immaterial details. Hence, eventually one vague legal term ('identity') is replaced by another ('immaterial details'). **11.038**

Fortunately, tribunals have made some efforts to shape the contours of the novelty test under the Community design regime. Accordingly, two designs are considered identical if their features differ only in details that are not immediately recognisable and therefore do not cause any differences, not even minor ones, between these designs. Conversely, when assessing the novelty of a design, it must be checked whether there are differences between the conflicting designs that are not insignificant, even if those differences are minor.[45] For example, where the contested design does not show a bottom view the examination of identity of the conflicting designs cannot be based on differences flowing from the bottom view.[46] Also, the assessment of the novelty of a design must be conducted in relation to one or more specific, individualised, defined and identified designs from among all the designs which have been made available to the public previously.[47] If the overall impression of a design is determined by the combination of several different features, there is only a lack of novelty if the complete synopsis of all combined elements can be taken from one single specific prior design revealed in the existing design corpus, according to the Dusseldorf Appeal Court.[48] **11.039**

As regards the determination of 'immaterial differences', it is settled case law of the Board of Appeal that differences must be considered as immaterial where differences were 'hardly perceivable' when the two designs are viewed side by **11.040**

---

44 Case T-41/14 *Argo v EUIPO and Clapbanner* ECLI:EU:T:2015:53, para 23.
45 Case T-228/16 *Haverkamp v EUIPO and Sissel* ECLI:EU:T:2018:369, para 22.
46 Ibid., para 40.
47 Case T-532/18 *Aroma Essence v EUIPO and Refan Bulgaria* ECLI:EU:T:2019:609, para 29.
48 *Bathing Shoe*, Dusseldorf Appeal Court, 25 April 2019, I-20 U 103/18.

side; to detect these differences, one would have to compare the two designs 'very closely'.[49] The Board of Appeal also stated:[50]

> The concept of 'immaterial details' must be interpreted restrictively if the identity requirement of Article 5 (1) CDR is not to be deprived of meaning. Design differences cannot in principle be classed as 'immaterial detail'. An 'immaterial' detail is one that is not intrinsic to the design as such but extraneous or accessory thereto. An immaterial detail might be, for example, the presence of a sign stamped on a design, such as a product code or quality mark. In such a way that, if the two designs differ only by the presence of that sign – and it is clear that the stamp does not form part of the design –, they must be considered, despite this difference, identical in accordance with Article 5 (2) CDR.

11.041 More particularly, the Board of Appeal found that a 'slight difference in the depth of the indentation' which appeared slightly deeper in the Community design was an immaterial detail.[51] Other examples of an immaterial detail are a 'slight variation in the shade of the colour pattern'[52] or absence of the manufacturer's trademark.[53] Similarly, pursuant to the General Court,[54]

> (…) two designs are to be deemed to be identical if their features differ only in immaterial details, that is to say, details that are not immediately perceptible and that would not therefore produce differences, even slight, between those designs. *A contrario*, for the purpose of assessing the novelty of a design, it is necessary to assess whether there are any, even slight, non-immaterial differences between the designs at issue.

11.042 Adding more background, according to the Board of Appeal, while Article 6 CDR ('individual character') refers to the notion of the 'informed user', Article 5 CDR ('novelty') does not specify such a referenced person. The EUIPO, therefore, '(…) simply has to decide whether two designs are identical'.[55]

11.043 In terms of comparison, the concept of individual character under Article 6 CDR requires a Community design to create a different overall impression than any other prior design. If this is the case, the Community design must also be regarded as new because the novelty filter is more fine-meshed than

---

49 *Roll4you v Kesselman [Cigarette paper]*, EUIPO (Board of Appeal), 19 July 2017, R 691/2016-3, para 48; *Haverkamp v Sissel [Pebble beach surface pattern]*, EUIPO (Board of Appeal), 26 February 2016, R 2619/2014-3, para 30; *Greiner Packaging v Vrhovski [Plastic spoon, foldable]*, EUIPO (Board of Appeal), 1 October 2013, R 505/2012-3, para 24.
50 *Vasco v ANTRAX [Radiators for heating]*, EUIPO (Board of Appeal), 2 November 2010, R 1451/2009-03, para 32.
51 *Essity v The Procter & Gamble [Part of sanitary napkin]*, EUIPO (Board of Appeal), 25 October 2011, R 978/2010-3, paras 20 *et seq*.
52 *Blažek Glass v Šindelářová [Nail files]*, EUIPO (Board of Appeal), 28 July 2009, R 921/2008-3, para 25.
53 *CENTREX v ISOGONA [Coffee pot]*, EUIPO (Board of Appeal), 8 November 2006, R 216/2005-3, para 26.
54 Case T-68/11 *Kastenholz v EUIPO/Qwatchme* ECLI:EU:T:2013:298, para 37.
55 *Normann v Paton Calvert [Colanders]*, EUIPO (Board of Appeal), 11 August 2009, R 887/2008-3, para 17.

the individual character filter, meaning that where two designs differ in their overall impression they *eo ipso* differ *a fortiori* in more than only 'immaterial details'.[56] This is the reason why, in many cases, the contested design is tested immediately and only under Article 6 CDR: If the design lacks individual character it is irrelevant for the outcome whether the design is nonetheless new, but if the design has individual character it is, *argumentum a fortiori*, also new. There remains only a third scenario where the design already lacks novelty (and, consequently, *argumentum a fortiori*, also lacks individual character) so that the tribunal may start, for reasons of judicial economy and efficiency, with the test under Article 5 CDR.

Finally, the CJEU correctly found that:[57]

11.044

> (...) a Community design cannot be regarded as being new, within the meaning of Article 5 (1) CDR, if an identical design has been made available to the public before the dates specified in that provision, even if that earlier design was intended to be incorporated into a different product or to be applied to a different product. The fact that the protection granted to a design is not limited only to the products in which it is intended to be incorporated or to which it is intended to be applied must therefore mean that the assessment of the novelty of a design must also not be limited to those products alone. Otherwise, (...) the subsequent registration of a Community design, which would be obtained despite the earlier disclosure of an identical design intended to be incorporated in a different product or to be applied to such different product, would allow the holder of that subsequent registration to prohibit the use of that same design for the product that was the subject of the earlier disclosure, which would be an absurd result.

E. INDIVIDUAL CHARACTER OF THE COMMUNITY DESIGN

Pursuant to Article 6 CDR, a design lacks individual character if the overall impression it produces on the informed user does not differ from the overall impression produced on such a user by a design which has been made available to the public before. In assessing individual character, the degree of freedom of the designer in developing the design shall be taken into account.

11.045

---

56 *Furniture*, Hamburg Appeal Court, 11 January 2018, 5 U 98/16. – See also *Normann v Paton Calvert [Colanders]*, EUIPO (Board of Appeal), 11 August 2009, R 887/2008-3, para 16: 'Obviously, if two designs are identical, except in immaterial details, they will produce the same overall impression on the informed user. It is equally obvious that if two designs produce a different overall impression on the informed user, they cannot be identical.' – See also Case T-684/20 *Legero v EUIPO/Rieker* ECLI:EU:T:2021:912, paras 113 *et seq*.

57 Joined Cases C-361/15 P and C-405/15 P *Easy Sanitary v EUIPO/Group Nivelles* ECLI:EU:C:2017:720, para 96.

11.046 Pursuant to established case law, the contested RCD is the point of reference when assessing novelty and individual character in the comparison with any earlier design. Novelty and, particularly, the individual character of any Community design, therefore, must be assessed solely on the basis of the features disclosed in the contested RCD.[58] In return, what is not shown in the contested RCD cannot be submitted as a basis for comparing the conflicting designs.[59]

11.047 Consequently, where the contested RCD shows more features than the earlier design, the comparison is not limited to what is shown in both designs but extends to all features claimed by the contested RCD.[60] Thus, where the contested RCD, by way of two-dimensional representation of an animated GUI, consists of a sequence of various different views (without being overall inconsistent) and only one of these views produces the same overall impression as the prior design, the overall impression of the RCD must be considered as being different from that of the prior design.[61] Overall,[62]

> (…) when determining the earlier and later design's subject matter it seems appropriate to take the claimed design as the logical starting and reference point both in validity and infringement proceedings; that is, for both the prior art and the accused design. The underlying idea is that the accused infringer cannot avoid infringement simply by adding matter to the claimed design, particularly in the case of partial designs. In return, the owner of the claimed design cannot avoid invalidity simply by omitting matter from the prior design (colour, for example). Consequently, prior art and accused design are treated equally and reciprocally in view of the claimed design; that is, both subjects are adjusted to the claimed design.

11.048 When assessing the earlier design, pursuant to established case law, only features visible during normal use must be considered and the 'visible elements of the earlier design must be identified correctly'.[63] In fact, the criterion of visibil-

---

58 Case T-9/15 *[Beverage] cans* ECLI:EU:T:2017:386, para 87; Case T-90/16 *Electronic wristbands* ECLI:EU:T:2017:464, para 65.
59 Case T-286/16 *Toilet seats [part of -]* ECLI:EU:T:2017:411, paras 42, 43 and 47.
60 Case T-767/17 *Lights* ECLI:EU:T:2019:67, paras 47, 51 and 53.
61 *King.com v TeamLava [Animated Icons]*, EUIPO (Board of Appeal), 1 December 2016, R 1951/2015-3, para 51. – This case is different from Case T-84/21 *Doll's heads* ECLI:EU:T:2021:844, para 53, where the contested RCD with seven views consisted of a three-dimensional representation of a doll's head without any hair, including a bottom view (showing a hole at the base of the head) and a top view (showing the shape of a skull), all of these views relating to the same doll's head and, as a whole, producing the same overall impression as the prior design (consisting of one view of a doll's head only).
62 HARTWIG, *Reciprocity in European Design Law*, in HARTWIG (ed.), *Research Handbook on Design Law*, 2021, 136.
63 Case T-39/13 *Skirting boards* ECLI:EU:T:2014:852, para 53.

ity applies to both the later Community design as established under Article 4 (2) lit a CDR and the earlier design.⁶⁴

11.049 The same is true in case of disclaimed features. Pursuant to established case law, features of a contested Community design that are disclaimed are disregarded for the purposes of comparing the designs. This, particularly, applies to features represented with broken lines making clear that protection is not sought in respect of such features.⁶⁵ Consequently, features disclaimed in the prior design must also be ignored.⁶⁶

11.050 The fact that the criterion of visibility applies to both the earlier design and the later Community design and that their appearance must be treated equally in order to compare 'like with like', has been confirmed, again, by the General Court⁶⁷ and, in addition, by the CJEU:⁶⁸

> In that regard, it should be noted that, according to Article 3 lit a CDR, a design is defined as being 'the appearance of the whole or a part of a product resulting from the features of, in particular, the lines, contours, colours, shape, texture and/or materials of the product itself and/or its ornamentation'. It follows that, in the context of the system set out by Regulation No 6/2002, appearance is the decisive factor of a design.
>
> Consequently, the fact that a characteristic of a design is visible is an essential feature of that protection. It is stated in Recital 12 CDR that the protection of designs should not be extended to those component parts which are not visible during normal use of a product, nor to those features of such part which are not visible when the part is mounted and that those characteristics should not, for those reasons, be taken into consideration for the purpose of assessing whether other features of the design fulfil the requirements for protection.
>
> It follows from the foregoing that (...) it is essential that the departments of EUIPO have an image of the earlier design that makes it possible to see the appearance of the product in which the design is incorporated and to identify the earlier design precisely and with certainty, so that they may (...) assess the novelty and individual character of the contested design and carry out a comparison of the designs at issue as part of that assessment. It is a prerequisite of an examination whether the contested design does in fact lack novelty or individual character that a specific and defined earlier design is available.

---

64   Ibid., paras 51 and 52.
65   Case T-68/10 *Watches* ECLI:EU:T:2011:269, para 64.
66   Case T-39/13 *Skirting boards* ECLI:EU:T:2014:852, paras 51 and 52; Case T-90/16 *Electronic wristbands* ECLI:EU:T:2017:464, para 57.
67   Case T-767/17 *Lights* ECLI:EU:T:2019:67, para 38.
68   Joined Cases C-361/15 P and C-405/15 P *Easy Sanitary v EUIPO/Group Nivelles* ECLI:EU:C:2017:720, paras 62 *et seq.*

1. Degree of Freedom of the Designer

11.051 According to the General Court, the greater the designer's freedom in developing the challenged design, the less likely it is that minor differences between the designs at issue will be sufficient to produce a different overall impression on an informed user. Conversely, the more the designer's freedom in developing the challenged design is restricted, the more likely minor differences between the designs at issue will be sufficient to produce a different overall impression on an informed user[69] (*concept of reciprocity*).[70]

11.052 As the degree of freedom of the designer in developing the contested RCD matters, related evidence must date from the period prior to the filing date.[71]

2. Informed User

11.053 Thanks to well-established case law of, particularly, the General Court, the notion and concept of the informed user has become firmly established and sufficiently specified. Accordingly:[72]

> the status of 'user' implies that the person concerned uses the product in which the design is incorporated, in accordance with the purpose for which that product is intended. The qualifier 'informed' suggests in addition that, without being a designer or a technical expert, the user knows the various designs which exist in the sector concerned, possesses a certain degree of knowledge with regard to the features which those designs normally include, and, as a result of his interest in the products concerned, shows a relatively high degree of attention when he uses them.
>
> The concept of the informed user must be understood as lying somewhere between that of the average consumer, applicable in trade mark matters, who need not have any specific knowledge and who, as a rule, makes no direct comparison between the trade marks at issue, and the sectoral expert, who has detailed technical expertise. Thus, the concept of the informed user may be understood as referring not to a user of average

---

[69] Case T-560/18 *Atos v EUIPO and Andreas Fahl* ECLI:EU:T:2019:767, para 47. – See also *Writing Utensil*, German Federal Supreme Court, 24 March 2011, I ZR 211/08, para 32.

[70] See HARTWIG, *The Concept of Reciprocity in European Design Law* [2010] JIPLP 186-191. – Others have suggested notions such as 'synchronicity' or 'concept of congruency'; see THIELE/SCHNEIDER, *Musterschutzgesetz* (Verlag Österreich 2018) Section 4 para 48. However, the situation covered by the concept of reciprocity is characterised by a flexible 'the more the less' that strives for a balance, and not by a mere static duplication. – Likewise, the expression 'symmetry' does not fit (against, for the copyright law, RITSCHER, *Weichenstellung beim urheberrechtlichen Schutz von Gebrauchsobjekten* [2020] sic! 545, 551) because it indicates less interaction and more synchronization.

[71] Case T-767/17 *Eglo v EUIPO and Briloner* ECLI:EU:T:2019:67, para 26.

[72] See, *pars pro toto*, Case T-192/18 *Rietze v EUIPO and Volkswagen* ECLI:EU:T:2019:379, paras 28 *et seq.*

attention but to a particularly observant one, either because of his personal experience or his extensive knowledge of the sector in question.

Finally, the Court has held that the very nature of the informed user means that, when possible, he will make a direct comparison between the earlier design and the contested design.

11.054 The informed user can include both end users and commercial sellers.[73] The informed user devotes only limited attention to components which are completely banal and common to all specimens of the type of products in question, concentrating on arbitrary or non-standard characteristics.[74]

11.055 Apart from that, the General Court found that:[75]

(…) in order to ascertain the products in which a design is intended to be incorporated or to which it is intended to be applied, the relevant indication in the application for registration should be taken into account.

(…) where necessary, the design itself, in so far as it makes clear the nature of the product, its intended purpose or its function, should also be taken into account. Taking into account the design itself may, indeed, enable the product to be placed within a broader category of goods, such as that indicated at the time of registration.

However, although it is common ground that the contested design is intended to be applied to motor vehicles, the mere fact that the applicant describes the products to which the contested design is intended to be applied as 'sports cars' or 'luxury cars' is not sufficient, without further clarification, to establish that such a design, which represents the design of the 991 series 'Porsche 911', makes it possible to identify a particular category of motor car distinguishable from motor cars in general by their nature, intended purpose or function.

Indeed, on the one hand, there is no such specific category in the existing international classification for industrial designs (…) and, on the other, the applicant itself applied for and obtained registration of the contested design for products in Class 12–08 corresponding to the following description: 'Motor cars, buses and lorries'.

Under those circumstances, nor can the applicant profitably criticise the Board of Appeal for finding that the notion of informed user related to a 'hypothetical person', since that legal concept, created precisely for the purposes of analysing whether a design has individual character under Article 6 of Regulation No 6/2002, can only be defined in general terms, as a reference to a person with standard characteristics, and not on a case by case basis in relation to a particular design.

In that respect, in order to refute the applicant's arguments alleging that it had not specifically analysed the informed user (…), the Board of Appeal did indeed confine

---

73 Case T-367/17 *Linak v EUIPO and ChangZhou Kaidi* ECLI:EU:T:2018:694, para 30.
74 Case T-767/17 *Eglo v EUIPO and Briloner* ECLI:EU:T:2019:67, para 43.
75 Case T-209/18 *Porsche v EUIPO and Autec* ECLI:EU:T:2019:377, paras 33 *et seq.* – The case concerned a conflict between RCD No 198387-0001 (indication of products 'Cars'; Locarno-Class 12-08) on the one hand and, *inter alia*, prior German design No M9705639-0001 (indication of products 'Rear spoiler for a motor vehicle'; Locarno-Class 12-16) and German design No 49906704-0001 (indication of products 'Motor vehicle, especially sports car'; Locarno-Class 12-08) on the other.

itself to the definition given by the case-law referred to above, and therefore did not explain why the fact that certain designs have been present on the market for decades means that users of those designs, as in the case of the 'Porsche 911', cannot be regarded as paying particular attention and, as the applicant contends, having above-average knowledge.

Nevertheless, that circumstance cannot cause the contested decision to be vitiated by an insufficient statement of reasons, since (…) in the present case it was necessary to look at the category of product rather than the specific products in question, and that it was therefore appropriate to have regard to the informed user of motor cars in general, instead of the informed user of a 'Porsche 911'.

Even if the applicant does not concur with that view, the fact is nevertheless that, on that point, the Board of Appeal presented its reasoning clearly and unambiguously, informing the applicant, to the requisite legal standard, of the grounds for the measure taken.

The Board of Appeal was therefore also entitled, without thereby erring in law or procedure, when assessing the notion of the informed user of the products for which the designs at issue were intended, not to take into account opinion surveys carried out of the target public for sports cars, assuming that the applicant actually intended to rely on such surveys in support of its thesis. In any event, if the applicant did intend to criticise the Board of Appeal for not having such surveys carried out, such a complaint would be irrelevant, since the level of attention of the average user, defined in general terms, cannot be verified empirically.

11.056 In contrast, the German Federal Patent Court held that the design and conception of a radiator grille regularly serve to demonstrate a certain independence of the corresponding car brand in times of similar design languages and concepts, leading to the fact that this part is regularly not fundamentally changed in the context of a facelift or renewal (but rather often only in details). This is due to corresponding market and consumer expectations and the importance of the appearance of a radiator grille for the 'face' of a passenger car, having impact on the level of attention of an informed user. The informed user is aware that car manufacturers, over the years, often give a facelift to their series, also with respect to the design, before a new model is put onto the market. As a result, generally, the informed user will meet radiator grilles and other components where aspects of design have a special importance or are of particular interest with special attention, which is why, with respect to such parts, he is more sensitive to the differences in the existing models that result, for example, from a model update.[76]

---

[76] *Radiator Grille*, German Federal Patent Court, 11 July 2019, 30 W (pat) 812/16. – This appears to be doubtful because user expectations are not proper criteria when finding validity or infringement in design law.

3. Overall Impression

According to established case law[77] **11.057**

the assessment as to whether a design has individual character must be conducted in relation to one or more specific, individualised, defined and identified designs from among all the designs which have been made available to the public previously. Consequently, in order for a design to be considered to have individual character, the overall impression which that design must produce on the informed user must be different from that produced on such a user not by a combination of features taken in isolation and drawn from a number of earlier designs, but by one or more earlier designs, taken individually.

The individual character of a design results from an overall impression of difference, or lack of 'déjà vu', from the point of view of an informed user, in relation to any previous presence in the design corpus, without taking account of any differences that are insufficiently significant to affect that overall impression, even though they may be more than insignificant details, but taking account of differences that are sufficiently marked so as to produce dissimilar overall impressions.

In the assessment of the individual character of a design in relation to any previous presence in the design corpus, account must be taken of the nature of the product to which the design is applied or into which it is incorporated, and, inter alia, the industrial sector to which it belongs, the degree of freedom of the designer in developing the design, whether there is saturation of the state of the art, which, whilst it cannot be regarded as limiting the freedom of the designer, could be capable of making the informed user more attentive to the differences between the designs under comparison, and also the manner in which the product at issue is used, in particular on the basis of the handling to which it is normally subject on that occasion.

(…) In addition, it should be borne in mind that it is possible that, when comparing designs, the impression produced by each of them may be dominated by certain features of the goods or the parts of the goods concerned. However, in order to determine whether a given feature dominates a product, or a part thereof, it is necessary to assess the greater or lesser influence which the various features of the product or the part at issue have on the appearance of that product or that part.

Also:[78] **11.058**

(…) the comparison of the overall impressions produced by the designs must be synthetic and may not be limited to an analytic comparison of a list of similarities and differences.

(…) Furthermore, that comparison must relate solely to the elements actually protected, without taking account of the features excluded from the protection. Accordingly, that comparison must relate to the designs as registered, and the applicant for a declaration of invalidity cannot be required to provide a graphic representation of

---

77 See, for instance, Case T-219/18 *Piaggio v EUIPO and Zhejiang Zhongneng* ECLI:EU:T:2019:681, paras 46 et seq.
78 See Case T-209/18 *Porsche v EUIPO and Autec* ECLI:EU:T:2019:377, paras 71, 73 and 76.

the design relied upon that is comparable to the representation in the application for registration of the contested design.

(...) it is however only appropriate to take into account the goods actually marketed, even for illustrative purposes when making that comparison, to the extent that the goods correspond to the designs as registered.

11.059 In that respect, one may not rely on articles in the specialist press or opinions of design award juries given that it is necessary to assess the overall impression from the perspective of an informed user who, although being aware of various designs and having specific knowledge enabling him to pay a relatively high level of attention, is neither a technical expert nor a design specialist.[79]

11.060 Pursuant to the CJEU, in *'Ferrari'*, whether the appearance of a part or a component part of a product satisfies the condition of individual character, '(...) it is necessary that the part or component part in question constitute a visible section of the product or complex product, clearly defined by particular lines, contours, colours, shapes or texture.'[80]

F. LACK OF CONSISTENCY OF THE COMMUNITY DESIGN

11.061 Under Article 25 (1) lit a CDR, a Community design may be declared invalid '(...) if the design does not correspond to the definition under Article 3 lit a CDR.' This provision stipulates that 'design' means the '(...) appearance of the whole or a part of a product resulting from the features of, in particular, the lines, contours, colours, shape, texture and/or materials of the product itself and/or its ornamentation (...).'

11.062 It has been decided[81] that where the different views of the specific design are visually inconsistent the subject matter of the design is directly impacted in that not 'a design' exists, more precisely not 'only one design'. For instance, the Board of Appeal[82] found, in 2017, that examination under Article 3 lit a CDR is:

(...) restricted to the question of whether the representation of the contested Community design shows the appearance of a product, a product part or its ornamentation. The basis of this examination is the design as reproduced in the representation filed. In this case, account is also to be taken of discrepancies and inconsistencies in the

---

79   See Case T-209/18 *Porsche v EUIPO and Autec* ECLI:EU:T:2019:377, para 95.
80   Case C-123/20 *Ferrari v Mansory* ECLI:EU:C:2021:889, para 52.
81   *Sports Helmet*, German Federal Supreme Court, 20 December 2018, I ZB 25/18, paras 17 *et seq*.
82   *Caresyntax v EIZO [Computer screens]*, EUIPO (Board of Appeal), 17 February 2017, R 755/2016-3, para 22.

views filed, which may lead to the conclusion that the representation shows different products and therefore more than one design.

11.063 The same, in principle, applies where the design covers an animated icon or graphical user interface where all views need to be visually related, which means that they must have features in common. Hence, lack of consistency would apply where the views fail to provide a clear perception of movement/progression.[83]

11.064 Flowing from such incongruity, the Board of Appeal[84] held that while:

> (...) a design represented by incongruent views is to be rejected pursuant to Article 47 CDR in conjunction with Article 11 CDIR unless duly remedied, the Office is not entitled to remedy such deficiencies once the Community design is registered and published. (...) Once registered, the issue of whether the registration occurred in compliance with Article 47 CDR can only be raised in an application for a declaration of invalidity in accordance with Article 25 (1) lit a and b CDR.

11.065 In other words: Lack of consistency is a ground for invalidity. While there is no case law yet from the Luxembourg courts or the Board of Appeal confirming that conclusion the Board of Appeal issued two *obiter dicta*, supporting the concept that presence of 'a design' requires presence of 'one design' and, thus, presence of consistency.[85]

1. Lack of Unity in Invalidity Proceedings

11.066 It took quite a while before the Board of Appeal of the EUIPO addressed the question of whether an inconsistent design could or would be invalid for the first time in 2008. The Board of Appeal found to the contrary, arguing that the function of Article 3 CDR was that of determining, through a general definition, what can be subject to legal protection under the terms of the CDR, and 'certainly not that of indicating how many designs may be protected by a single application (...).' Consequently, the purpose of Article 25 (1) lit a CDR was

---

83   On virtual designs see HARTWIG, *Animated designs revisited* IELR 7 [2024] 3; DURKIN, *Design Protection for Graphical User Interfaces*, in HARTWIG, *Research Handbook on Design Law*, 2021, 345; SARLANGUE, *Registered Community designs in the video game industry* IELR 4 [2021] 87.
84   *WebTuner [Adapter]*, EUIPO (Board of Appeal), 3 December 2013, R 1332/2013-3, para 16.
85   Case T-9/15 *Ball v EUIPO and Crown* ECLI:EU:T:2017:386, para 57, is another *obiter dictum*:
    Moreover, it should be noted that the refusal by the Board of Appeal to define the subject matter of the protection afforded by the contested design as a group of cans did not lead to an unlawful questioning of the validity of the contested design (...) the Board of Appeal, while considering that the contested design failed to satisfy the conditions set out in Article 3 lit a CDR, in so far as it did not constitute a unitary object, correctly stated that, to the extent that the intervener had not put forward the ground for invalidity of Article 25 (1) lit a CDR, that fact (namely, the failure to satisfy the conditions set out in Article 3 lit a CDR) could not justify the invalidity of the contested design.

to preclude protection as a Community design for anything which cannot be visibly perceived, or which does not represent a material object. The fact that a Community design application includes one or more designs, therefore, had nothing to do with the legal 'definition' of designs contained in Article 3 CDR.[86]

11.067 Nine years later, in 2017, the same tribunal found to the contrary, holding that, under Article 3 lit a CDR, account had also to be taken of discrepancies and inconsistencies in the views filed, which may lead to the conclusion that the representations show different products and, thus, more than one design.[87]

11.068 Later in 2017, the General Court of the EU, by way of an *obiter dictum*, concluded that the Board of Appeal, while considering that the contested design failed to satisfy the conditions set out in Article 3 lit a CDR, in so far as it did not constitute a unitary object, correctly stated that, to the extent that the intervener had not put forward the ground for invalidity of Article 25 (1) lit a CDR, that fact (namely, the failure to satisfy the conditions set out in Article 3 lit a CDR) could not justify the invalidation of the contested design.[88]

11.069 Against this unclear background, practitioners were interested to see, in late 2018, that the German Federal Supreme Court was going to address the issue whether lack of unity would be a ground of finding invalidity in cancellation proceedings. In Summer 2019, the written grounds of the two parallel cases – *'Sports Helmet'* and *'Sports Glasses'* – were released, providing both clear and uncomfortable guidance for right holders. According to the German Federal Supreme Court, where several views of a design filed by way of a single application show different embodiments of a product (here: sports helmet) with different features of the appearance of this product (here: different strap, with or without tab, different colours, colour contrasts, decors), these views do not visibly reproduce the appearance of the whole of 'a' product. In such a case, the design does not disclose a single subject matter, in the sense of Section 1 No. 1 German Designs Act, and, therefore, is invalid pursuant to Section 33 (1) No. 1 German Designs Act.[89] If the design holder claims design protection for the representations that do not show the 'same' design, it is not permissible to determine a unitary subject matter based on the intersection of the

---

86 *Vasco [Radiators for heating]*, Board of Appeal (EUIPO), 17 March 2008, R 592/2007-3, paras 14 *et seq.*
87 *Caresyntax v EIZO [Computer screens]*, Board of Appeal (EUIPO), 17 February 2017, R 755/2016-3, para 22.
88 Case T-9/15 *Ball Beverage v EUIPO/Crown Hellas* ECLI:EU:T:2017:386, para 57.
89 Section 1 No. 1 and Section 33 (1) No. 1 German Designs Act correspond to Article 3 lit a and Article 25 (1) lit a CDR.

features common to all views.⁹⁰ In the parallel *'Sports Glasses'* case, the court clarified that the same consequence applies where the application of a design is accompanied by a black-and-white photograph showing the design with a representation of a colour contrast in grayscale, with the consequence that the resulting light-dark contrast, independent from any specific colour, is part of the subject matter. Accordingly, a design does not disclose a unitary subject matter – a single design – and is invalid if its application is accompanied by black-and-white photographs in which colour contrasts are displayed once in a light-dark combination and once, conversely, in a dark-light combination.⁹¹

2. Lack of Unity in Registration Proceedings

Following the EUIPO's Guidelines for Examination of Registered Community Designs, '(…) where the use of different visual formats leads to an inconsistency of views showing more than one design, the examiner will issue a deficiency letter (…).'⁹² However, these Guidelines do not bind any user or applicant.⁹³ **11.070**

Also, pursuant to Article 11 (1) and (2) Community Designs Implementing Regulation ('CDIR'), where the Office finds that the design for which protection is sought does not correspond to the definition of design provided in Article 3 lit a CDR, the Office '(…) shall specify a time limit within which the applicant may submit his/her observations, withdraw the application or amend it by submitting an amended representation of the design, provided that the identity of the design is retained.' **11.071**

Given that the EUIPO Guidelines '(…) cannot derogate from the CDR, the CDIR or the CDFR, and it is solely in the light of those regulations that they should be interpreted and applied (…)',⁹⁴ it is suggested that the Office should accept and allow without reservation a replacement of views prior to registration provided that 'the identity of the design is retained', i.e., that where differences between the 'original' and the 'corrected' view would amount to **11.072**

---

90 *Sports Helmet*, German Federal Supreme Court, 20 December 2018, I ZB 25/18, para 17.
91 Ibid., para 35. These standards have been recently confirmed; see *Cutting Board*, German Federal Supreme Court, 24 March 2022, I ZR 16/21, para 18, finding that, in essence, disregarding those features not shown in all views and reducing the subject matter to those features shown in all views would be the *mere result of a conceptual construction and only exist in the mind of the beholder*.
92 EUIPO Guidelines for Examination of Registered Community Designs, Examination of applications for registered Community designs (note 10), para 5.2.1.
93 See above note 11.
94 EUIPO Guidelines for Examination of Registered Community Designs, Examination of applications for registered Community designs (note 10), para 1.1.

'immaterial details', as that same term is used in the context of novelty examination in Article 5 (2) CDR.[95]

G. OTHER GROUNDS OF INHERENT INVALIDITY OF THE COMMUNITY DESIGN

11.073 Other, perhaps somewhat more remote grounds of invalidity are discussed and to be decided under the buzzwords 'technical function', 'interoperability', 'modular system' and 'visibility' – with an interesting overlap and interlock between each of these grounds.

1. Features of Community Design Solely Dictated by Technical Function

11.074 Pursuant to Article 8 (1) CDR, a Community design shall not subsist in features of appearance of a product which are solely dictated by its technical function.

11.075 In that regard, it follows from established case law that – in a negative sense – Article 8 (1) CDR excludes protection for features of appearance of a product where considerations other than the need for that product to fulfil its technical function, particularly those related to the visual aspect, have not played any role in the choice of those features, even if other designs fulfilling the same function exist.[96] In other words – in a positive sense – when determining whether the features of appearance of a product are solely dictated by its technical function, it must be established that that technical function is the only factor which determined those features, the existence of alternative designs not being decisive in that regard.[97] According to the CJEU, assessment as to whether the features of appearance of a product fall within Article 8 (1) CDR must be made in the light of all the objective circumstances relevant to each individual case. That assessment must be made, particularly, having regard to the design at issue, the objective circumstances indicative of the reasons which dictated the choice of features of appearance of the product concerned, or information on its use or the existence of alternative designs which fulfil the same technical

---

95 For details see HARTWIG, *Evaluation of EU Legislation on Design Protection* [2022] JIPLP, 107, 112 *et seq.* – See also EUIPO Guidelines for Examination of Registered Community Designs, Examination of applications for registered Community designs (note 10), para 4.3: 'Maintenance in an amended form will, therefore, be limited to cases in which the removed or disclaimed features are so insignificant in view of their size or importance that they are likely to pass unnoticed.'
96 Case T-515/19 *Lego* ECLI:EU:T:2021:155, para 93.
97 Case C-395/16 *Doceram* ECLI:EU:C:2018:172, para 32.

function, provided that those circumstances, data, or information as to the existence of alternative designs are supported by reliable evidence.⁹⁸

11.076 It follows that a design must be declared invalid if all the features of its appearance are solely dictated by the technical function of the product concerned by that design, i.e., if at least one of the features of appearance of the product concerned by a contested design is not solely dictated by the technical function of that product, the design at issue cannot be declared invalid under Article 8 (1) CDR.⁹⁹

11.077 According to the General Court, the assessment of a Community design, under Article 8 (1) CDR, comprises the following steps: it is necessary, in the first place, to determine the technical function of the product concerned, in the second place, to analyse the features of appearance of that product, and, in the third place, to examine, in the light of all the relevant objective circumstances, whether those features are solely dictated by the technical function of the product concerned. In other words, it must be examined whether the need to fulfil that technical function is the only factor that determined the choice by the designer of those features, with considerations of another nature, particularly those related to the visual aspect of that product, having played no role in the choice of those features.¹⁰⁰

11.078 When an applicant for a declaration of invalidity refers to the ground of invalidity under Article 8 (1) CDR, it is for him to provide evidence to demonstrate that the exclusion from protection under Article 8 (1) CDR applies.¹⁰¹ Particularly, it is for the applicant to demonstrate and for EUIPO to find that all the features of appearance of the product concerned by the contested design are solely dictated by the technical function of that product.¹⁰² Consequently, where the EUIPO does not identify all the features of appearance of the product concerned by the contested design and, *a fortiori*, does not establish that all of those features are solely dictated by the technical function of that product, Article 8 (1) CDR must be found infringed.¹⁰³

---

98 Ibid., paras 36 and 37.
99 Case T-515/19 *Lego* ECLI:EU:T:2021:155, para 96. – See also *Paper Dispenser*, German Federal Supreme Court [2022] 53 IIC 278, 285 para 32.
100 Case T-515/19 *Lego* ECLI:EU:T:2021:155, para 98.
101 Ibid., para 99.
102 Ibid., para 109.
103 Ibid., para 114.

11.079 Apart from that, the CJEU ruled as follows:[104]

1. Article 8 (1) of Council Regulation (EC) No 6/2002 of 12 December 2001 on Community designs must be interpreted as meaning that the assessment as to whether the features of appearance of a product are dictated solely by its technical function, within the meaning of that provision, must be made having regard to all of the objective circumstances relevant to each case, inter alia those dictating the choice of features of appearance, the existence of alternative designs which fulfil the same technical function, and the fact that the proprietor of the design in question also holds design rights for numerous alternative designs, although that latter fact is not decisive for the application of that provision.

2. Article 8 (1) of Regulation No 6/2002 must be interpreted as meaning that, in the assessment as to whether the appearance of a product is dictated solely by its technical function, the fact that the design of that product allows for a multicolour appearance cannot be taken into account in the case where that multicolour appearance is not apparent from the registration of the design concerned.

2. Features of Community Design Necessarily Reproduced to Permit Interconnectivity

11.080 Pursuant to Article 8 (2) CDR, a Community design shall not subsist in features of appearance of a product which must necessarily be reproduced in their exact form and dimensions to permit the product in which the design is incorporated or to which it is applied to be mechanically connected to or placed in, around or against another product so that either product may perform its function.

11.081 Starting with the relation between Article 8 (1) and Article 8 (2) CDR, features of appearance of the product concerned by a design, according to the General Court, may fall within both Article 8 (1) and Article 8 (2) CDR since they may both be solely dictated by the technical function of that product, i.e., to allow the connection and disconnection of that product, and constitute features of interconnection. However, not all features of interconnection for the purposes of Article 8 (2) CDR are necessarily solely dictated by the technical function of the product concerned by a design since the interconnection of that product may not be the only factor which determined the appearance of those features;

---

104 Case C-684/21 *Papierfabriek Doetinchem BV v Sprick GmbH Bielefelder Papier- und Wellpappenwerk & Co.* ECLI:EU:C:2023:141, paras 23 and 32.

rather, features of interconnection for the purposes of Article 8 (2) CDR may be designed in such a way that visual considerations have played a role and, for that reason, those features do not fall within Article 8 (1) CDR so that, consequently, Article 8 (2) CDR covers a broader category of features of interconnection than Article 8 (1) CDR. In fact, if all features of interconnection were solely dictated by a technical function, there would have been no need for the legislature to provide for the application of Article 8 (2) CDR. It follows that Article 8 (2) CDR covers all features of interconnection, some of which do not fall within the scope of Article 8 (1) CDR, namely those for the appearance of which considerations other than technical considerations existed.[105]

In light of that, there is a certain overlap between the features referred to in Article 8 (1) and Article 8 (2) CDR, with the result that the same feature of appearance of the product concerned by a design may be covered by the description of the features referred to in both Article 8 (1) and in Article 8 (2) CDR; these are features of appearance of the product concerned by a design permitting the connection of that product to another product for which that function is the only factor which determined their appearance.[106] Against this background, where a feature of appearance falls within both Article 8 (1) and Article 8 (2) CDR, it must be possible to apply both those provisions.[107]

11.082

3. Exception in Case of Modular System

Pursuant to Article 8 (3) CDR, and notwithstanding Article 8 (2) CDR, a Community design shall subsist in a design serving the purpose of allowing the multiple assembly or connection of mutually interchangeable products within a modular system (to the extent that the design fulfils the requirements as to novelty and individual character). Hence, according to the General Court, Article 8 (3) CDR is an exception to Article 8 (2) CDR which makes it possible to protect designs covering products which form part of a modular system despite their possible features of interconnection.[108]

11.083

In this respect, it is for the proprietor of the contested design to rely on the benefit of Article 8 (3) CDR.[109] Interestingly, no provision of Regulation No 6/2002 precludes that benefit from being relied on, for the first time,

11.084

---

105 Case T-515/19 *Lego* ECLI:EU:T:2021:155, paras 61 *et seq.*
106 Ibid., para 68.
107 Ibid., para 74.
108 Ibid., para 38.
109 Ibid., para 39.

before the Board of Appeal.¹¹⁰ Hence, the Board of Appeal cannot be deprived of that jurisdiction merely because the proprietor of the contested design has chosen to claim the benefit of Article 8 (3) CDR, for the first time, at the stage of appeal proceedings.¹¹¹

11.085 More specifically, when determining whether Article 8 (3) CDR is applicable to the contested design, it is necessary to assess whether that design, in the light of its features, is covered by other provisions of that article, in order, if necessary, to examine whether those other provisions preclude the application of Article 8 (3) CDR.¹¹² Thus, it is necessary to assess whether the features identified are covered by that provision or by Article 8 (2) CDR.¹¹³ However, there is also some overlap with Article 8 (1) CDR, namely if and to the extent that the features of appearance of the product concerned by a design are determined exclusively by the function allowing assembly and disassembly, i.e., where, for instance, the possibility of assembling the product concerned by the contested design with other building blocks and dismantling them is the only factor which determined those features.¹¹⁴ Furthermore, where – in order to fulfil the function of assembly and disassembly of the product concerned by the contested design – the features of appearance of that design must be reproduced in the exact dimensions in order to permit their connection, they also fall within Article 8 (2) CDR.¹¹⁵

11.086 Overall, the benefit of Article 8 (3) CDR is not limited to some of the features referred to in Article 8 (2) CDR, namely those which do not fall within Article 8 (1) CDR.¹¹⁶ Rather, it is possible to rely on Article 8 (3) CDR for the benefit of all the features referred to in Article 8 (2) CDR.¹¹⁷

11.087 It follows that where the EUIPO, when examining an application for a declaration of invalidity based on Article 8 (1) CDR, finds that the features of appearance of the product concerned by the contested design fall within both Article 8 (1) and Article 8 (2) CDR, and where the proprietor of the contested design relies on the benefit of Article 8 (3) CDR, it must examine whether those features are capable of benefiting from the protection of modular systems

---

110 Ibid., para 47.
111 Ibid., para 49.
112 Ibid., para 53.
113 Ibid., para 56.
114 Ibid., para 59.
115 Ibid., para 60.
116 Ibid., para 76.
117 Ibid., para 77.

4. Visible During Normal Use

According to Article 4 (2) CDR, a: **11.088**

> (...) design applied to or incorporated in a product which constitutes a component part of a complex product shall only be considered to be new and to have individual character: (a) if the component part, once it has been incorporated into the complex product, remains visible during normal use of the latter; and (b) to the extent that those visible features of the component part fulfil in themselves the requirements as to novelty and individual character.

Pursuant to Article 4 (3) CDR, 'normal use' shall mean use by the end user, excluding maintenance, servicing or repair work. **11.089**

On July 1, 2021, the German Federal Supreme Court issued a court order,[119] referring questions to the CJEU for a preliminary ruling pursuant to Article 267 TFEU. The case is related to the component part of a complex product, namely the bottom view of a saddle for bicycles or motorcycles, and, more precisely, the interpretation of the term 'visible' within the meaning of Article 3 (3) Designs Directive and the criteria for assessing the 'normal use' of a complex product.[120] The questions read as follows: **11.090**

1. Is a component part incorporating a design a 'visible' component within the meaning of Article 3 (3) of Directive 98/71/EC if it is objectively possible to recognise the design when the component is mounted, or should visibility be assessed under certain conditions of use or from a certain observer perspective?
2. If the answer to Question 1 is that visibility under certain conditions of use or from a certain observer perspective is the decisive factor:
(a) When assessing the 'normal use' of a complex product by the end user within the meaning of Article 3 (3) and (4) of Directive 98/71/EC, is it the use intended by the manufacturer of the component part or complex product that is relevant, or the customary use of the complex product by the end user?
(b) What are the criteria for assessing whether the use of a complex product by the end user constitutes a 'normal use' within the meaning of Article 3 (3) and (4) of Directive 98/71/EC?

---

118 Ibid., para 80. On 30 May 2022, the Board of Appeal dismissed the appeal of the invalidity applicant; *Building blocks from a toy building set*, Board of Appeal (EUIPO), 30 May 2022, R 1524/2021-3. On 24 January 2024, this decision was confirmed by the General Court (T-537/22).
119 *Saddle bottom view I*, German Federal Supreme Court, 1 July 2021, I ZB 31/20.
120 Article 3 (3) and (4) Designs Directive correspond to Article 4 (2) and (3) CDR.

11.091 Interestingly, on 16 July 2021, EUIPO's Board of Appeal addressed a similar scenario, i.e., whether consumables shall be regarded as component parts of complex products. In summary, the tribunal sided with the right holder, finding that consumables are not component parts of complex products so that the requirement of visibility in normal use set out in Article 4 (2) CDR does not apply and must not be met.[121]

11.092 On 16 February 2023, in the *'Monz'* matter, the CJEU finally ruled as follows:[122]

> Article 3 (3) and (4) of Directive 98/71/EC (...) must be interpreted as meaning that the requirement of 'visibility', laid down in that provision, that is to be met in order for a design applied to or incorporated in a product which constitutes a component part of a complex product to be eligible to benefit from the legal protection of designs, must be assessed in the light of a situation of normal use of that complex product, so that the component part concerned, once it has been incorporated into that product, remains visible during such use. To that end, the visibility of a component part of a complex product during its 'normal use' by the end user must be assessed from the perspective of that user as well as from the perspective of an external observer, and that normal use must cover acts performed during the principal use of a complex product as well as acts which must customarily be carried out by the end user in connection with such use, with the exception of maintenance, servicing and repair work.

11.093 While the findings in *'Monz'* overall appear to be rather owner-friendly, proceeding from a broad notion of 'visible use',[123] the question nonetheless remains – given that visibility must be assessed from the perspective of the end user as well as from the perspective of an external observer and given that this is a matter of fact, not of law – what to do where the outcome of the factual assessment from the perspective of the end user differs from the outcome of the factual assessment from the perspective of an external observer?

Interestingly, when the German Federal Supreme Court, based on the guidance from the CJEU, revisited the matter a few months later,[124] the German court did not address that issue. Instead, the court held:[125]

> So far, the Federal Patent Court has only assumed visibility in case of acts associated with the transport or storage of a bicycle in favour of the design owner and now will

---

121 *Hypertherm v B & Bartoni [Welding torches (part of -)]*, EUIPO (Board of Appeal), 16 July 2021, R 2843/2019-3, para 31 (the decision has been appealed, with the appeal having been dismissed on 22 March 2023; see Case T-617/21 *B & Bartoni* ECLI:EU:T:2023:152).
122 Case C-472/21 *Monz Handelsgesellschaft International mbH & Co. KG v Büchel GmbH & Co. Fahrzeugtechnik KG* ECLI:EU:C:2023:105, para 56.
123 *Saddle bottom view II*, German Federal Supreme Court, 15 June 2023, I ZB 31/20, para 23.
124 *Saddle bottom view II*, German Federal Supreme Court, 15 June 2023, I ZB 31/20.
125 Ibid., paras 30–33.

have to make findings in this regard. *If necessary, it will also have to examine other acts put forward by the parties.*

The *applicant must demonstrate and prove* that the design does not remain visible during normal use after the component part has been incorporated into the complex object. The design holder, as the party not bearing the onus of proof, must contest this negative fact in a substantiated manner within the scope of what is reasonable for it, setting out the circumstances that speak in favour of the contrary positive fact. The party with the burden of proof must then disprove the circumstances in favour of the positive fact.

The Federal Patent Court has limited its assessment (...) to the bottom view of a bicycle saddle, without addressing any *possible use related to the bottom view of a motorcycle saddle*. Since the design holder has indicated 'motorcycle saddles' as an additional product, the Federal Patent Court will have to extend its examination to this as well, if necessary.

To the extent that the Federal Patent Court affirms the visibility of the design, it will have to decide whether the visible features of the component part itself meet the requirements of novelty and individual character. So far, the Federal Patent Court has assumed this without a conclusive examination of the merits.

11.094 These conclusions appear doubtful because, under established law and practice, the indication of the product shall not impact or affect the subject matter or scope of protection of the design.[126] Consequently, the saddle of a home trainer or a tricycle, in principle, must also be considered.

H. CONFLICT BETWEEN EARLIER TRADEMARK AND LATER COMMUNITY DESIGN

11.095 Under Article 25 (1) lit e CDR, a Community design may be declared invalid '(...) if a distinctive sign is used in a subsequent design, and Community law or the law of the Member State governing that sign confers on the right holder of the sign the right to prohibit such use.'[127]

1. Trademark Standards

11.096 The key for solving a conflict between an earlier mark and a later design, as a rule, is provided by the principles of the laws protecting distinctive signs (not: design law). Consequently, given that the trademark is 'a distinctive sign' according to Article 25 (1) lit e CDR, any potential conflict between prior

---

126 Article 36 (6) CDR; Case T-9/15 *Ball Beverage v EUIPO and Crown Hellas* ECLI:EU:T:2017:386, para 56.
127 For an exhaustive analysis see VON MÜHLENDAHL, *Three-Dimensional Trade Marks and Designs: Comparison and Conflict*, in HARTWIG (ed.), *Research Handbook on Design Law*, 2021, 441. – With respect to the reverse conflict between an earlier design and a later trademark see Case T-169/19 *Style & Taste v EUIPO and Polo/Lauren* ECLI:EU:T:2021:318.

trademark rights and later Community design rights must be dealt with on the basis of six issues, namely whether (i) there is a 'distinctive sign', (ii) whether there is genuine use of the earlier mark (if such use is challenged by the holder of the Community design), (iii) whether use of the sign in the Community design amounts to use in relation to goods or services ('use as a mark'), (iv) whether use of the sign in the Community design relates to the goods or services for which the prior mark is protected or to similar goods ('similarity of goods'), (v) whether the design is identical with or similar to the prior mark ('similarity of signs'), and (vi) whether, unless the goods and signs are identical, there exists likelihood of confusion.[128]

11.097 This order of analysis largely corresponds to daily practice of national trademark infringement courts in Europe, resulting from 'classic' defences raised in court proceedings for trademark infringement. Although, overall, regular case law, to a large extent, involves claims for the infringement of a word or figurative mark, rather than a shape mark,[129] the analysis under Article 25 (1) lit e CDR is not limited to the conflict between a (two-dimensional) word or figurative mark and a two-dimensional design. Rather, the principles applied under Article 25 (1) lit e CDR certainly also comprise three-dimensional trademarks and designs.

2. Distinctive Sign (Earlier Mark)

11.098 It has been held that any sign registered as a trademark, which has effect in any Member State, is presumed to be a 'distinctive sign' in the sense of Article 25 (1) lit e CDR.[130] In other words: The trademark registration on its own is sufficient to fulfil the qualification of Article 25 (1) lit e CDR. This approach appears to be correct because sufficient distinctiveness of the mark has already been established by the EUIPO or the respective trademark office of the Member State as a legal precondition of its registrability. In any event, the registration should confer a presumption of distinctiveness, even if in an individual case the respective trademark office did not carry out an examination as to distinctiveness or made a mistake.

---

128 Claims for trademark infringement based on a well-known mark shall not be covered hereafter.
129 Establishing protection for shape marks (configuration or packaging) has become even more burdensome if not nearly impossible over time, with only a few marks eventually proceeding to registration. – See, by way of example, protection afforded to the 'Volkswagen Type 2' shape (*Volkswagen v European Flipper*, EUIPO (Board of Appeal), 15 December 2021, R 609/2021-2) but refused with respect to the 'Moon Boot' design (see Case T-483/20 *Tecnica v EUIPO and Zeitneu* ECLI:EU:T:2022:11).
130 *Hee Jung Kim v Zellweger*, EUIPO (Invalidity Division), 1 March 2006, ICD 1477, para 11; published in: HARTWIG, *Design Protection in Europe*, Vol. 1 (Carl Heymanns 2007) 213.

Following established European trademark law and practice, a global assessment of the likelihood of confusion requires the assessment of relevant factors, including the scope of protection of the prior trademark in terms of (above-average, average or below-average) distinctiveness. Consequently, findings on the particular strength, i.e., degree of distinctiveness of the specific mark at hand – beyond the *mere presumption of distinctiveness qua registration post-examination* – appear to be necessary. Naturally, such findings largely depend on the facts and evidence the parties submit in the proceedings.

11.099

3. Genuine Use of the Earlier Mark

It is common ground that when an earlier registered trademark is asserted as a ground of invalidity of a later design, the holder of the contested design may request proof of use of the earlier mark as if it were a trademark opposition or invalidation case, and if the proof is not delivered, the invalidity request must be rejected. That said, in the *'Ferrero'* case, the absence of such a challenge was remarkable as the earlier mark, which is a 'classic' black and white line drawing showing a transparent container without any content and any labelling, is, if at all, hardly marketed in that specific appearance (but, rather, labelled and filled). Where genuine use of the earlier mark is challenged tribunals must decide whether use of a concrete product (in the *'Ferrero'* case: the 'Tic-Tac' container) amounts to use of an abstract mark shown in black and white.[131]

11.100

4. Use of the Earlier Mark in the Later Design as a Mark

It has been submitted that use of a sign in a Community design amounts to use 'in the course of trade' in the sense of Article 9 (2) EUTMR since the purpose of registering a design is its use for commercial purposes.[132] This appears to be in line with Article 20 (1) lit a CDR, according to which the rights conferred by a Community design shall not be exercised in respect of acts done privately and for non-commercial purposes. It appears to be impossible that the purpose of registering a design is done privately and for non-commercial purposes. In other words: 'Acts done privately and for non-commercial purposes' in the sense of Article 20 (1) lit a CDR apparently do not include the act of registering.

11.101

---

[131] For more details see HARTWIG, *Conflicts between Earlier 3D Marks and Later Designs under European Law – Some Remarks on the CJEU Ferrero/BMB Case* [2020] JIPLP 516.
[132] HARTWIG/TRAUB, in: HARTWIG, *Design Protection in Europe*, Vol. 1 (Carl Heymanns 2007) 223.

5. Use of the Earlier Mark in the Later Design for Similar or Identical Goods and Services

11.102 The fourth step in assessing a trademark conflict with a later sign is to examine whether the use of the earlier mark in the Community design relates to the goods and services of the mark.

11.103 In the 'Midas' case, for instance, the Invalidity Division found that the earlier mark was 'used in the design of a logo which intrinsically relates to any type of goods and services.' Particularly, it was the 'commercial purpose of a logo to be affixed to goods or to the packaging thereof or to be used on business papers and in advertising.'[133] These findings remind us on the fact that the conflict between an earlier mark and a later Community design raises questions especially with respect to the relationship of the goods and services for which the trademark is *registered* on the one hand and the potential *use* of the Community design on the other hand.

11.104 To start with, the Invalidity Division did not refer to the indication of goods of the contested Community design but to the 'design of a logo', i.e., to the graphical appearance of a logo.[134] As such – according to the decision – the Community design could be used for all goods and services since it is the nature of a logo to be affixed to goods or to the packaging thereof or to be used on business papers and in advertising. Consequently, the decision focused on the *abstract and potential use* of the design in question, concluding that the graphical appearance of the design may be used in connection with any of the goods or services, including the goods for which the prior trademark is registered. The Invalidity Division was correct in concluding that the graphical appearance of a logo may be used for 'electric washing machines', 'electric flat irons', 'cooling apparatus' or alike. From a trademark perspective, any logo is potentially used in connection with any kind of goods and services. Hence, the graphical appearance of a logo is always in conflict with the specification of goods and services of a prior trademark.

11.105 That said, the Invalidity Division's approach may be considered overly broad or even 'too extensive'. In fact, under European trademark law, the test is to look precisely at the *concrete use* of a later sign (in infringement proceedings) or at the specific goods and services for which a later mark seeks protection (in

---

133 *Hee Jung Kim v Zellweger*, EUIPO (Invalidity Division), 1 March 2006, ICD 1477, para 17; published in: HARTWIG, *Design Protection in Europe*, Vol. 1 (Carl Heymanns 2007) 214.
134 *Hee Jung Kim v Zellweger*, EUIPO (Invalidity Division), 1 March 2006, ICD 1477, para 16; published in: HARTWIG, *Design Protection in Europe*, Vol. 1 (Carl Heymanns 2007) 213.

opposition proceedings). However, the graphical appearance of a logo (not: 'sticker', etc.) may be used in conjunction with any kind of goods and services. Therefore, all goods and services for which the prior mark was granted protection in the *'Midas'* case were affected by the registration of the graphical appearance of the later design.[135]

6. Similarity of Signs

In the *'Midas'* case, the Invalidity Division held that the incorporation of the five letters 'm', 'i', 'd', 'a' and 's' into the later Community design constitutes use of a sign *identical* to the earlier mark. It has been submitted that this analysis is questionable.[136] While the prior mark consisted only of the word 'MIDAS' (written in a standard type of letters with no figurative elements), the contested Community design showed an additional figurative element above the letter 'i' and the subtitle 'Everything we touch is safer'. Consequently, the conflicting signs were not identical according to European case law but arguably *similar*. Therefore, the Invalidity Division should have found similarity of signs.

11.106

7. Likelihood of Confusion

As a rule, following established European trademark law and practice, a global assessment of the likelihood of confusion implies some interdependence between all the relevant factors discussed above, and, particularly, a sufficient similarity between the marks and goods or services involved.[137] Furthermore, in accordance with CJEU jurisprudence, the more distinctive, i.e., stronger the earlier mark, the greater the risk of confusion.[138]

11.107

8. Maintenance of the Later Design in an Amended Form?

Should confusing similarity between the earlier mark and the later Community design be found the question remains whether registration of the latter may be maintained at least in part or whether it must be declared invalid *in toto*.[139] This issue can be analysed under two different aspects, namely, *firstly*, whether the

11.108

---

135 For more details see HARTWIG/TRAUB, in: HARTWIG, *Design Protection in Europe*, Vol. 1 (Carl Heymanns 2007) 216 *et seq.*
136 HARTWIG/TRAUB, in: HARTWIG, *Design Protection in Europe*, Vol. 1 (Carl Heymanns 2007) 216.
137 Case C-39/97 *Canon* ECLI:EU:C:1998:442, para 17.
138 Ibid., para 18.
139 Would the use of the earlier mark within the later Community design be challenged in classic infringement proceedings, the trademark infringement court would prohibit use only as regards the specific goods covered by the earlier mark (and similar goods).

later design may be limited to specific goods, and, *secondly*, whether the later design may be limited as regards the representation of the design.

11.109 To begin with the second option, a limitation of the representation of Community design, in general, is possible, according to Article 25 (6) CDR. Pursuant to Article 25 (6) Sentence 1 CDR, '(…) a registered Community Design which has been declared invalid pursuant to paragraph (1) lit b, lit e, lit f or lit g may be maintained in an amended form, if in that form it complies with the requirements for protection and the identity of the design is retained.' According to Article 25 (6) Sentence 2 CDR, '(…) maintenance in an amended form may include registration accompanied by a partial disclaimer by the holder of the registered Community Design or entry in the register of a court decision or a decision by the Office declaring the partial invalidity of the registered Community Design.'

11.110 With respect to the first option, i.e., whether invalidation of a later Community design – in conflict with a prior mark registered for specific goods – may or must be limited only to these goods, it must be recalled that, under Article 36 (6) CDR, the indication of products 'shall not affect the scope of protection of the design as such'. Hence, any limitation of the Community design's indication of products would be without any legal effect.

11.111 Therefore, as a result, in accordance with the wording of Article 25 (1) lit e CDR, a Community design must always be declared invalid *in toto* if a distinctive sign is used in the design and the trademark owner is entitled to prohibit such use (even if the trademark is registered only for a single, although still similar good). This may lead to discrepancies between invalidity and infringement proceedings, but these must be accepted – at least so long as the law does not provide a clear solution to this conflict.[140]

I. CONFLICT BETWEEN EARLIER COPYRIGHT AND LATER COMMUNITY DESIGN

11.112 Under Article 25 (1) lit f CDR, a Community design may be declared invalid '(…) if the design constitutes an unauthorised use of a work protected under the copyright law of a Member State.' This ground of invalidity appears to be

---

[140] For more details see von Mühlendahl, *Three-Dimensional Trade Marks and Designs: Comparison and Conflict*, in Hartwig (ed.), Research Handbook on Design Law, 2021, 477 *et seq.*; Pomares Caballero, in: Hartwig, *Design Protection in Europe*, Vol. 4 (Carl Heymanns 2012) 289 *et seq.*; Hartwig/Traub, in: Hartwig, *Design Protection in Europe*, Vol. 1 (Carl Heymanns 2007) 219 *et seq.*

both clear *prima facie* and a rare[141] and a burdensome alternative to applicants seeking invalidation of later Community design, for the reasons explained in the following.

1. Copyright Standards

In formal terms, under European law, there is no copyright register (unlike the United States Copyright Office, for instance) which would allow applicants for a declaration of invalidity to show at least the subject matter of their copyright claim. More significantly, in substantive terms, European copyright law is harmonised only to some extent, resulting in significant discrepancies with respect to the degree of originality, which is required, under the national copyright law of the specific Member State, to establish a copyright claim, or, even more important, the scope of protection which is attributed to the specific work under the national copyright law.

11.113

In fact, Article 25 (1) lit f CDR results in a straightforward but nevertheless sophisticated two-step examination, requiring both the showing of sufficient originality (i.e., acquisition of a copyright claim) and the establishing of a claim for copyright infringement (i.e., unauthorised reproduction of the work protected).

11.114

2. Work Protected Under National Copyright Law

In this respect, the General Court emphasised[142] that '(…) in accordance with the international agreements on copyright to which Germany is a party, copyright protection extends to the configuration or to the features of the work and not to ideas.'

11.115

The Court also opined[143] that it is not for the author of an expert report on the claimed work to make a '(…) legal assessment of the extent of the protection conferred by copyright and on the existence of an infringement of that right.' Rather, the applicant must provide information '(…) as to the scope of copyright protection under the national law, in particular as to whether copyright protection prohibits the unauthorised reproduction of the idea underlying

11.116

---

141   See, by way of exception, Case T-68/11 *Kastenholz v EUIPO/Qwatchme* ECLI:EU:T:2013:298; Joined Cases T-566/11 and T-567/11 *Viejo Valle v EUIPO/Coquet* ECLI:EU:T:2013:549.
142   Case T-68/11 *Kastenholz v EUIPO/Qwatchme* ECLI:EU:T:2013:298, para 81.
143   Ibid., para 77.

the earlier works of art and is not limited to protecting the configuration or features of those works.'[144]

11.117 Proceeding from these general requirements, the General Court found, in a case related to the design of crockery, that it was '(…) apparent from the French case law in the file and cited by the Board of Appeal' that, under French copyright law, '(…) an item of crockery may, both by its shape and by its decoration, constitute a work protected by copyright, provided that one or other of those aspects is the result of a creative activity and that it is of an originality that attests to the designer's personality.'[145] Hence, according to the Court, '(…) there was nothing in principle to prevent the Board of Appeal accepting the decoration of the intervener's items of crockery as a work whose unauthorised use was at issue.'[146] That included the Board of Appeal's statements on the 'irrelevance of an artistic appreciation' of the work and on the 'applicability of copyright law to industrial goods'.[147]

3. Unauthorised Use of the Work

11.118 This step – finding copyright infringement by use of the later Community design – also needs to proceed from the construction and application of national copyright law. In this respect, the General Court held that the outcome of such analysis does not:

> (…) have to be determined on the basis of a global comparison between two designs in which a constraint on the designer's freedom as a result of technical or legal constraints, which moreover have not been established in the present case, may make the informed user more attentive to details and better able to recognise the individual character of the disputed design.[148]

11.119 Therefore, according to the General Court, it is:

> (…) not appropriate to compare the designs at issue as a whole, but only to determine whether the work protected by copyright was used in the later designs, that is to determine whether the presence of that work could be noted in those designs, with the result that, in that context, the differences relied on by the applicant, such as the shape of the cup or the design of its handle or the shape of the bowl of the soup dish, were irrelevant.[149]

---

144 Ibid., para 80.
145 Joined Cases T-566/11 and T-567/11 *Viejo Valle v EUIPO/Coquet* ECLI:EU:T:2013:549, para 79.
146 Ibid., para 80.
147 Ibid., para 90.
148 Ibid., para 98.
149 Ibid., para 100.

Rather, it suffices that: 11.120

> (...) the decoration of the disputed designs greatly resembles the decoration of the intervener's items of crockery, both as concerns the identical nature of the covered surfaces and as concerns the concentric nature, regularity and narrowness of the grooves. The greater thickness and the more pronounced character of the grooves, claimed by the applicant, are not sufficient to obscure that similarity.[150]

J. CONFLICT BETWEEN EARLIER DESIGN AND LATER COMMUNITY DESIGN

Pursuant to Article 25 (1) lit d CDR, a later registered Community design   11.121
must be declared invalid if it is 'in conflict' with a design having an earlier filing date but having been published after the filing date of the contested later Community design.

1. Design Infringement Standards

It has been submitted that, in the event of a conflict between an earlier design[151]   11.122
and a later Community design, the term 'in conflict' in Article 25 (1) lit d CDR necessarily means that the later Community design falls within the scope of protection of the earlier design. Thus, 'in conflict' is a synonym for 'infringement' within the meaning of Article 10 CDR even though this term is not explicitly used in Article 25 (1) lit d CDR.[152]

Proceeding from that preposition, and considering that the earlier design could   11.123
be either a Community design or a national design or a prior international design registration extended to the EU and/or to any of its 27 Member States, the relevant standard, in each of these situations, is either Article 10 CDR (where the earlier design is a Community design or an international design registration extended to the EU) or Article 9 Designs Directive (where the earlier design is either a national design or a prior international design registration extended to any of the 27 Member States of the EU). However, given that both provisions are virtually identical there is no need for further distinction,

---

150 Ibid., para 101.
151 Under Article 25 (1) lit d CDR, the earlier design could be either (also) a Community design or a national design registered in one of the 27 Member States of the EU or a prior international design registration extended to the EU and/or to any of its 27 Member States. What matters is that the earlier design was filed earlier but published after the date of filing of the later Community design application.
152 For details see HARTWIG, *Community design infringement test before the General Court – an unfortunate setback*, QMJIP 12 [2022] 158 *et seq.*

so that we shall proceed from the construction and application of Article 10 CDR.

2. Degree of Freedom of the Designer of the Earlier Design

11.124 Proceeding from the position that the degree of freedom of the designer of the earlier design is crucial, the finding of such degree of freedom – in view of the existing design corpus – must be synchronised when testing validity and infringement. If both validity and infringement are in dispute (by way of a counterclaim in proceedings on the merits[153]) the degree of freedom must be the same and neither party can claim a different standard under such circumstances.

11.125 However, under Article 25 (1) lit d CDR, the holder of the later design is not allowed to argue invalidity of the earlier design because that provision is limited to the testing of infringement.[154] Thus, the holder of the later design, in order to escape from infringement, must argue that the degree of freedom of the designer of the earlier design was limited. This is true because, according to the German Federal Supreme Court,[155] there exists an:

> (...) interaction between the designer's freedom and the design's scope of protection. A great concentration of designs and, thus, only little freedom of the designer will lead to a narrow scope of protection of the design so that minor differences in appearance may produce a different overall impression on the informed user. In contrast, a low concentration of designs and, therefore, a great freedom of the designer will lead to a broad scope of protection of the design so that even major differences in appearance may not produce a different overall impression on the informed user.

11.126 In addition, the German Federal Supreme Court found[156] that:

> the scope of protection of a design also depends on its departure from the existing design corpus. (...) The larger the distance between the claimed design and the prior art the broader the scope of protection of the claimed design.

---

153 Article 85 (1) Sentence 2 CDR.
154 For details on how to construe Article 25 (1) lit d CDR and, particularly, on how not to confuse with Article 6 CDR see HARTWIG, *Community design infringement test before the General Court – an unfortunate setback*, QMJIP 12 [2022] 158 *et seq.*
155 *Pram II*, German Federal Supreme Court, 12 July 2012, I ZR 102/11, para 31; *Milla*, German Federal Supreme Court, 23 February 2012, I ZR 68/11, para 19; *Pram I*, German Federal Supreme Court, 28 September 2011, I ZR 23/10, para 24; *ICE*, German Federal Supreme Court, 7 April 2011, I ZR 56/09, para 35; *Writing Utensils*, German Federal Supreme Court, 24 March 2011, I ZR 211/08, para 42; *Table Mat*, German Federal Supreme Court, 19 May 2010, I ZR 71/08, para 17.
156 *Ballerina*, German Federal Supreme Court, 11 January 2018, I ZR 187/16, para 21; *Pram II*, German Federal Supreme Court, 12 July 2012, I ZR 102/11, para 32.

Likewise, for instance, the England and Wales High Court of Justice (Chancery Division) held:[157] **11.127**

> Article 9 (2) Designs Directive indicates that, other things being equal, a registered design should receive a broader scope of protection where the designer had a greater degree of freedom and a narrower scope of protection where the designer had a lesser degree of freedom. (…) Recital (13) Designs Directive indicates that, other things being equal, a registered design should receive a broader scope of protection where the registered design is markedly different to the design corpus and a narrower scope of protection where it differs only slightly from the design corpus.

This understanding of reciprocity between prior art and scope of protection has become common ground over the past years.[158] In this respect, the England and Wales High Court of Justice concluded correctly:[159] **11.128**

> In the light of the decision of the CJEU in Easy Sanitary, it is not necessary, in my view, for it to be established that the informed user would know of an item of prior art for it to be considered as part of the design corpus. To introduce such a requirement, which is not contained in the Regulation, would apply a different test to overall impression for the purposes of validity and scope of protection, and would add unnecessary complications to registered design claims, which should require very little evidence to determine.

These findings, which ostensibly refer to the overall-impression-test under Article 6 (1) and Article 10 (1) CDR, clearly support reciprocity also when assessing the degree of freedom of the designer under Article 6 (2) and Article 10 (2) CDR. In both situations, the degree of freedom of the designer must not be considered as being the degree of freedom of the designer *theoretically remaining* to any designer in view of the relevant prior art ('abstract degree of freedom'). Rather, what is decisive is the degree of freedom of the designer of the earlier design *effectively used*, i.e., as manifested in the specific departure from the specific prior art ('specific departure from the design corpus'). **11.129**

3. Scope of Protection of the Earlier Design

Turning back to Article 25 (1) lit d CDR, the holder of the later Community design would have to demonstrate – in order to prevail with a claim for non-infringement – that the abstract degree of freedom of any designer (at the time when filing the earlier design) was limited and, in addition, that **11.130**

---

157 *Whitby Specialist Vehicles Ltd v Yorkshire Vehicles Ltd and Ors* [2014] EWHC 4242 (Pat), paras 26 *et seq.*
158 This concept, in general, also applies, e.g., in the United States where differences between the claimed and accused design are considered in light of the claimed design's scope which, in return, depends on the prior art ('context in which this comparison is made may be supplied by the background prior art, which may provide a frame of reference'); *Wine Enthusiast v Vinotemp International*, 317 F.Supp.3d 795, 801 (S.D.N.Y. 2018).
159 *L'Oréal v RN Ventures* [2018] EWHC 173 (Pat) para 152.

the designer of the specific earlier design did not make use of the remaining freedom in so far as he failed to establish a significant departure from any prior design introduced in the specific proceedings by any of the parties when developing the earlier design. Succeeding in this two-step exercise, the holder of the later Community design would be allowed to submit that already minor differences in appearance between the earlier and the later design produce a different overall impression on the informed user, resulting in absence of infringement and, thus, validity of the contested later design.

4. Infringing Use of the Earlier Design by the Later Community Design

11.131 As explained before, any success, under Article 25 (1) lit d CDR, largely depends on whether only major differences between the earlier design and the later Community design would allow finding non-infringement (based on a broad scope of protection of the earlier design) or whether already minor differences in appearance may produce a different overall impression on the informed user (proceeding from a narrow scope of protection of the earlier design).

11.132 Either way, identifying features and weighing differences when comparing two designs is a complicated and burdensome, multi-step endeavour:[160]

  i. starting with the subject matter of the earlier design, identifying the characteristic features of appearance which amount to the overall impression as shown in the registration of the earlier design[161]
  ii. identifying the characteristic features of appearance which amount to the overall impression as shown in the registration of the later Community design[162]
  iii. identifying similarities and differences between both designs[163]
  iv. weighing similarities against the relevant prior art and the technical function of the underlying product, i.e., considering existing similarities as less important over other similarities neither known from prior art nor dictated by technical function,[164] overall weighing similarities and differences according to whether, from the point of view of the informed user,

---

160 See also HARTWIG/TRAUB, in: HARTWIG, *Design Protection in Europe*, Vol. 2 (Carl Heymanns 2008) 278 *et seq.*
161 *ICE*, German Federal Supreme Court, 7 April 2011, I ZR 56/09, para 36.
162 Ibid.
163 Ibid.
164 *Pram II*, German Federal Supreme Court, 12 July 2012, I ZR 102/11, paras 60 and 62.

they are of primary importance for the overall impression or whether they take a back seat[165]

v. finding whether remaining differences are 'major' or 'minor' over the existing similarities.[166]

K. CONCLUSIONS

11.133 Community design law and practice, in summary, is in relatively good shape these days and certainly needs no tinkering. Case law from the EUIPO – Invalidity Division and Board of Appeal – and, as a quasi-final instance, from the General Court is appreciated for providing clear and balanced guidance on how to anticipate and decide conflicts with respect to validity or infringement of a Community design right. If legislative steps must be taken, they should be set carefully, limited to a minimum of revision, and should by no means touch upon secure and precious foundations; there is no need for substantive improvement *de lege lata*. Overall, EU design law and practice should develop organically via judicial interpretation, through the EUIPO and the EU courts.[167]

11.134 In fact, the importance and impact of the General Court with respect to Community design matters is expected to increase even more considering that since 1 May 2019, under Article 58a (1) Statute of the CJEU, an appeal

---

165 *Meda Gate*, German Federal Supreme Court, 24 January 2019, I ZR 164/17, para 31; *Wristwatch*, German Federal Supreme Court, 28 January 2016, I ZR 40/14, para 35.

166 *Pram II*, German Federal Supreme Court, 12 July 2012, I ZR 102/11, para 71:
   Features 1, 3 and 4 to 6 are of above-average importance for the overall impression of the claimed design while the other features contribute to the overall impression only to an average extent. Since of the features characterizing the overall impression of the claimed design to an above-average extent, only Feature 6 has been copied almost identically while Features 1 and 5 show only similarities and Features 3 and 4 have not been copied, quasi-identity, in case of Features 2 and 7, does not suffice, based on the findings made by the Appeal Court, for finding infringement of the scope of protection of the claimed design.

167 See also HARTWIG, *The 'Legal Review on Industrial Design Protection in Europe': A closer look* [2018] JIPLP 332; HARTWIG, *Evaluation of EU Legislation on Design Protection* [2022] JIPLP 107. – With respect to the ongoing EU design law reform see https://data.consilium.europa.eu/doc/document/ST-16992-2023-INIT/en/pdf and https://www.consilium.europa.eu/en/press/press-releases/2023/12/05/council-and-parliament-strike-provisional-deal-on-design-protection-package/ accessed 31 December 2023; see also the detailed comments submitted by the Committee for Design Law of the German Association for the Protection of Intellectual Property, 125 [2023] GRUR 387, particularly as to the – welcome – possibility of rectifying deficiencies of the representation of the design before/after registration and the codification of visual disclaimer, as well as further comments by HARTWIG, *The EU Commission's proposal to codify visual disclaimers – a great leap for EU design law* [2023] JIPLP 432; see also the report by WAGNER, 125 [2023] GRUR 1174 on the 11th 'GRUR meets Brussels' workshop on 13 June 2023, providing a perfect platform for practitioners, academics, stakeholders and representatives of the EU legislator to discuss the long-awaited reform package on the EU designs, particularly the European Commission's 'Proposal to recast Directive 98/71/EC on the legal protection of designs' ('DD Proposal') and a 'Proposal to amend Council Regulation (EC) 6/2002 on Community designs and repeal Fees Regulation (EC) 2246/2002' ('CDR Proposal').

brought against a decision of the General Court concerning a decision of an independent Board of Appeal of EUIPO is not to proceed unless the CJEU first decides that it should be allowed to do so. In accordance with Article 58a (3), an appeal is to be allowed to proceed, in accordance with the detailed rules set out in the Rules of Procedure of the CJEU, where it raises an issue that is *significant with respect to the unity, consistency or development of EU law.*

11.135 Consequently, according to the CJEU, a request that an appeal be allowed to proceed must, in any event, set out clearly and in detail the grounds on which the appeal is based, identify with equal clarity and detail the issue of law raised by each ground of appeal, specify whether that issue is significant with respect to the unity, consistency or development of EU law, and set out the specific reasons why that issue is significant according to that criterion. As regards, particularly, the grounds of appeal, the request that an appeal be allowed to proceed must specify the provision of EU law or the case law that has been infringed by the judgment or order under appeal, explain succinctly the nature of the error of law allegedly committed by the General Court, and indicate to what extent that error had an effect on the outcome of the judgment or order under appeal.[168] Moreover, even where the Appellant specified the paragraphs of the judgment under appeal and those of the ruling of the CJEU alleged to have been misapplied and the rulings of the General Court alleged to have been disregarded, this does not suffice where the Appellant does not provide sufficient information regarding the similarity of the situations referred to in those rulings to make it possible to establish the existence of the contradictions relied on.[169]

11.136 The CJEU also repeatedly reminded us that assessing the individual character of a design, which results from an overall impression of difference, produced on the informed user, in relation to any previous presence in the design corpus, is a factual analysis. However, a claim alleging that the General Court erred in its assessment of the facts cannot state that the appeal raises an issue that is significant with respect to the unity, consistency, or development of EU law.[170]

11.137 This case law serves as a welcome reminder that utmost attention should be given to preparing all relevant facts, evidence, and arguments already and *in toto* in proceedings before the EUIPO. While the General Court may re-assess questions of facts (and of law, of course), under the new, strict practice of the

---

168 Case C-199/20 P *Gamma-A v EUIPO/Zivju* ECLI:EU:C:2020:662, para 11.
169 Case C-358/23 P *Tinnus v EUIPO/Mystic* ECLI:EU:C:2023:809, para 22.
170 Case C-199/20 P *Gamma-A v EUIPO/Zivju* ECLI:EU:C:2020:662, para 19.

CJEU, cases coming from the EUIPO will hardly be reviewed by the CJEU as it will be extremely difficult for the appellant to meet the standards.[171] In fact, until to date (status: 31 December 2023), in *only one of the overall 27 cases in Community design matters*[172] *and in five of 133 cases in EU trademark matters* reaching the CJEU from the General Court, the CJEU allowed an appeal to proceed.

As a final remark, *de facto* the CJEU's strict gatekeeper policy deprived stakeholders of a full, final instance on questions of law, including a full hearing (as practiced, in many cases, before 1 May 2019). This unfortunate situation should be reason enough for the EUIPO, and particularly the Boards of Appeal, to consider becoming more liberal in allowing oral hearings[173] (also in times of virtual meetings being the new gold standard).[174]

11.138

---

171 See, *pars pro toto*, Case C-199/20 P *Gamma-A v EUIPO/Zivju* ECLI:EU:C:2020:662.
172 See C-382/21 P *EUIPO v KaiKai* ECLI:EU:C:2021:1050. In that case, the Court of Justice allowed an appeal to proceed brought by the EUIPO and directed against a decision of the General Court, stating that priority for a Community design would depend on the nature of the right from which priority was claimed, allowing therefore 12 months for the priority claim rather than six months (against the explicit wording of Article 41 CDR). See, with some critical comments on the General Court decision, Massa, *La Tentation de Paris – Libre opinion sur la possible distorsion du droit et du délai de priorité dans l'arrêt* KaiKai *du TUE*, 82 PI (2022) 5 *et seq*.
173 By the end of 2023, the Third Board of Appeal of the EUIPO had held no oral hearings in design cases; so far, a total of five hearings have been held in trademark cases.
174 The EPO recently and repeatedly found hearings by videoconference to be acceptable; Case G 1/21 *Videoconference* ECLI:EP:BA:2021:G000121.20210716, para 42 (no violation of the right to be heard), paras 53f and 61 (necessary characteristics of an oral hearing are ensured) and para 78 (practice following numerous other EPC contracting states); Case T 2125/16 *Doherty Amplifier* ECLI:EP:BA:2021:T212516.20210916, paras 59 and 60 (permissible if everyone can follow without interruption and without technical difficulties). Overall, the EPO still seems to be reluctant to schedule an online hearing where there is no specific exceptional situation with difficulties in participating in an on-site hearing. However, finding that a video conference is equivalent to an on-site hearing and, thus, a video conference is covered by Article 116 EPC, it makes no sense, in view of the same legal basis, to require virtual meetings to be held only in exceptional cases, such as the pandemic; see Case G 1/21 *Videoconference* ECLI:EP:BA:2021:G000121.20210716, paras 49 *et seq*.

PART II

INTERNATIONAL TREATIES AND JURISDICTION

12

THE FUNCTIONING OF THE AFRICAN REGIONAL INTELLECTUAL PROPERTY ORGANISATION (ARIPO) FOR INDUSTRIAL DESIGN REGISTRATION: REALITIES AND POSSIBILITIES

Chijioke Okorie[1]

A.	INTRODUCTION	12.001	5. Appeals	12.028
B.	THE LEGAL FRAMEWORK OF ARIPO'S INDUSTRIAL DESIGN SYSTEM	12.006	C. THE HARARE PROTOCOL: REALITIES AND FILING TRENDS	12.029
	1. The Registration Procedure at ARIPO	12.009	D. FUTURE POSSIBILITIES: ARIPO AND THE AFRICAN CONTINENTAL FREE TRADE AREA AGREEMENT	12.031
	2. The Formal Examination	12.013		
	3. 'Opposition' by Member States	12.017	E. CONCLUSION	12.036
	4. Substantive Examination	12.021		

A. INTRODUCTION

The African Regional Intellectual Property Organisation's (ARIPO) system **12.001** as it works in practice and across all intellectual property rights, has its legal basis in the Lusaka Agreement of December 9, 1976.[2] For the protection and registration of industrial designs specifically, this is governed by the Harare Protocol on Patents and Industrial Designs (Harare Protocol). The Harare Protocol was adopted on December 10, 1982 and since then has been amended about 15 times with the latest amendment being on December 8, 2021.

---

1   I am grateful to the various industrial design attorneys and IP firms who helped with introductions to various persons and/or shared their ARIPO filing experiences with me especially Danie Dohmen, Marius Schneider, Sara Moyo and, Nicky Garnett. All laws stated are correct as at June 2023.

2   See https://www.aripo.org/wp-content/uploads/2018/12/Lusaka-Agreement1.pdf accessed 5 December 2022.

12.002 The Harare Protocol is accompanied by the Regulations for implementing the Protocol on Patents and Industrial Designs (Harare Protocol Regulations) which entered into force on April 25, 1984 and has been amended about 14 times since then. Since its adoption in the 1980s, 11 countries joined the Harare Protocol in the 1980s, two countries in the 1990s, two countries in the 2000s, three countries in the 2010s and two countries (so far) in the 2020s.[3] ARIPO operates the industrial designs registration regime for the 20 Contracting States who are parties to the Harare Protocol.[4]

12.003 The Harare Protocol and the Harare Protocol Regulations provide for matters such as the procedure for applying for the registration of an industrial design, formal and substantive requirements to be met prior to the registration of an industrial design, duration of protection for registered industrial designs, as well as the mechanism for appeals against the decision of ARIPO regarding an industrial design application. During its 11th Extraordinary Session held in August 2021 and its 45th Ordinary Session held in December 2021, ARIPO's Administrative Council adopted the amendments to the Harare Protocol as well as its Implementing Regulations. For industrial designs, these amendments inter alia provided applicants with an opportunity to respond to rejection notices issued by Member States; extended the duration of ARIPO registered designs from ten to 15 years and included pandemics, natural disaster, war and civil disorder as circumstances under which the Director General can extend time limits under the Protocol.[5]

12.004 In 2019, the African Union's (AU) African Continental Free Trade Area (AfCFTA) Agreement officially entered into force with the submission (at that time) of the 22nd ratification instrument.[6] The AfCFTA Agreement requires Member States to inter alia, commit to cooperating on intellectual property rights.[7] The cooperation on intellectual property rights is in the form of a Protocol on intellectual property which is expected to include formulating provisions that address the existence of sub-regional intellectual property

---

3   Seychelles became a party to the Protocol in October, 2021 while Cape Verde joined in July 2022. See https://www.aripo.org/accession-of-the-republic-of-seychelles-to-the-harare-protocol/ accessed 10 October 2022.
4   The 20 Contracting States are Botswana, Cape Verde, Kingdom of Eswatini, The Gambia, Ghana, Kenya, Kingdom of Lesotho, Liberia, Malawi, Mozambique, Namibia, Rwanda, Sao Tome and Principe, Seychelles, Sierra Leone, Sudan, Tanzania, Uganda, Zambia and Zimbabwe.
5   Notice to all applicants on the amendments to the Harare Protocol, https://www.aripo.org/wp-content/uploads/2021/12/Notification-of-Amendments-to-Harare-Protocol-2021.pdf accessed 24 September 2022.
6   See https://au.int/en/treaties/agreement-establishing-african-continental-free-trade-area accessed 24 September 2022.
7   Other commitments relate to eliminating tariffs and non-tariff barriers to trade in goods and liberalising trade in services and establishing a dispute settlement system (Phase 1 negotiations) and; cooperating on investment, competition policy, customs matters, and all other trade-related areas (Phase 2 negotiations).

organisations on the continent including ARIPO; provisions that take cognisance of the fact that innovation in Africa occurs mostly in the informal sector; and provisions that take advantage of flexibilities available in the Agreement on Trade-Related Aspects of Intellectual Property (TRIPS flexibilities) to strike the right balance between development goals, innovation and trade.[8]

12.005 This chapter focuses on the functioning of ARIPO under the Harare Protocol and the Harare Protocol Regulations as they relate to the registration of industrial designs. The chapter explains the industrial design system in ARIPO, evaluates the performance of ARIPO under the Harare Protocol and the Harare Protocol Regulations and in the light of the Intellectual Property Protocol under the AfCFTA Agreement,[9] explores some future possibilities for ARIPO's industrial design system. In doing this, this chapter relies on a desktop review of the legal developments at ARIPO and comparison of those developments with ARIPO's trends and statistics. These trends and statistics were largely supported by design and patent attorneys and firms who shared with the author their experience on ARIPO's design system and procedures.

B. THE LEGAL FRAMEWORK OF ARIPO'S INDUSTRIAL DESIGN SYSTEM

12.006 The Harare Protocol accords with the objective of ARIPO to establish common services as may be needed to coordinate intellectual property protection affecting its members.[10] It seeks to create and does create a mechanism where protection may be obtained in Contracting States by a single procedure for the grant of patents, registration of utility models and of industrial designs.[11] Members retain their national design statutes and regulations as well as their operational intellectual property offices. This is unlike the unitary industrial designs protection system applicable under the *Organisation Africaine de la Propriété Intellectuelle* (OAPI), where the Bangui Agreement defines industrial designs, delineates the eligibility criteria for protection of designs, the scope

---

8 Caroline B. Ncube, 'Intellectual Property and the African Continental Free Trade Area: Lessons and Recommendations for the IP Protocol' (2022) 21(2) *Journal of International Trade Law and Policy* 105–21. See also, Adewopo, Adebambo, Desmond Oriakhogba, and Chijioke Okorie. 'Negotiating the Intellectual Property Protocol under the Agreement Establishing the African Continental Free Trade Area: Priorities and Opportunities for Nigeria' (2022) 15(1) *Law and Development Review* 33-62.
9 An official copy of the adopted IP Protocol has not been released by the African Union (AU). For a copy of the decision to adopt the IP Protocol, see https://au.int/sites/default/files/decisions/42725-Assembly_AU_Dec_839_-_865_XXXVI_E.pdf accessed 5 June 2024.
10 Preamble to the Harare Protocol.
11 Preamble to the Harare Protocol.

of the exclusive rights of the design right holders, duration of protection, registration and examination procedures and rules on enforcement of design rights.[12] Furthermore, while the Harare Protocol adheres only to the Paris Convention for the Protection of Industrial Property Rights 1883, OAPI's Bangui Agreement adheres to both the Paris Convention and the Hague Agreement Concerning the International Registration of Industrial Designs (Hague Agreement).[13]

12.007 The Harare Protocol has nine sections in all. While sections 1, 2, and 5–9 cover matters pertaining to patents, utility models and industrial designs, section 4 specifically deals with industrial designs. ARIPO keeps an Industrial Designs Register where all industrial designs registered under the Harare Protocol are recorded.[14] This register may be inspected by any person upon payment of the prescribed fee.[15] ARIPO is also required by the Harare Protocol Regulations to publish, at least monthly, a journal (ARIPO Journal) to publish matters provided for in the Harare Protocol and the Harare Protocol Regulations.[16] For industrial designs, these matters include a reference to the registration of the design, the number of the design, the name and address of the owner of the design, the name and address of the originator/creator, the filing date of the application, the most illustrative reproduction of the design, and the Contracting State or States for which the design is registered.[17] No person is allowed to inspect or obtain extracts from files on yet-to-be-published applications without the written consent of the applicant.[18] However, bibliographic data such as name and address of applicant, application number, filing and priority dates, title of industrial design, may be provided on request.[19]

12.008 ARIPO accepts applications for and may register an assignment and/or a licence regarding a registered industrial design if prescribed fees have been paid and relevant documents satisfying it that a transfer has taken place are produced.[20]

---

12 This is the same across the various intellectual property rights.
13 Some anglophone African countries are party to the Hague Agreement. These are Rwanda; Namibia; Ghana; Egypt; Botswana. See https://www.wipo.int/export/sites/www/treaties/en/docs/pdf/hague.pdf accessed 24 September 2022.
14 See Rule 2(1) of the Harare Protocol Regulations.
15 Rule 3(1).
16 Rule 2(4).
17 Rule 20bis.
18 Rule 3(2)(a).
19 Rule 3(2)(b).
20 Rule 22bis.

1. The Registration Procedure at ARIPO

12.009 Under section 1 of the Harare Protocol, ARIPO is empowered to register industrial designs ('ARIPO industrial designs') and to administer such designs on behalf of Contracting States. Such ARIPO industrial designs shall have the same effect and be subject to the same conditions as a national industrial design registered by the Contracting States.[21] Industrial designs filed at ARIPO are classified according to the Locarno Classification.[22]

12.010 ARIPO allows both electronic and paper applications but offers a 20 per cent discount on fees for electronic applications.[23] Applications for the registration of an industrial design must contain a request for registration; a reproduction of the industrial design proposed to be registered and a designation of the Contracting States in respect of which the industrial design is requested to be registered.[24] Such applications may be filed by applicants themselves or through an authorised representative either with ARIPO or, where the national laws of a Contracting State permit or mandate, the industrial property office of that Contracting State.[25] When filed with the industrial property office of a Contracting State, that office must conduct a formal examination of the application and ensure that the application fulfils the requirements of the Regulations.[26] The industrial property offices in these countries have one month from the date of receiving the application for registration to transmit such application to ARIPO.[27] If filed with ARIPO, applicants are entitled to request for the registration of an ARIPO industrial design to cover one or more Contracting States upon payment of a designation fee.[28]

12.011 The Harare Protocol allows industrial design applications to be lodged in any language but such applications must be translated into English within two months of filing.[29] Filings under the national law of the Contracting State where it was due are recognised as giving rise to a right of priority. Multiple priorities may be claimed in respect of ARIPO industrial design application regardless of whether they originated from different countries.[30] Applicants

---

21   See section 1(3).
22   See https://www.wipo.int/classifications/locarno/locpub/en/fr/ accessed 15 October 2022.
23   Rule 5bis.
24   Rule 9. See also, section 4(1) of the Harare Protocol.
25   See Rule 10.
26   See Rule 13.
27   See section 2(5) of the Harare Protocol.
28   See section 1bis.
29   See section 2(6).
30   See section 2(8)(c).

who have filed a prior application in any Paris Convention or World Trade Organisation member state are allowed to claim priority in respect of such application within ten months of filing their ARIPO Industrial Design application.[31] The declaration of priority is to be made either on filing the ARIPO application or within the ten months from the earliest priority date claimed. Applicants are allowed to correct their declaration of priority within ten months from the earliest priority date claimed.

12.012 The examination and/consideration of the application starts once the application for registration is filed.

2. The Formal Examination

12.013 Here, ARIPO checks filed applications to confirm that the formal requirements have been satisfied. Section 4(2) of the Harare Protocol provides that:

(a) The Office shall examine whether the formal requirements for applications have been complied with and, if so, shall accord the appropriate filing date to the application.

(b) If the Office finds that the application does not comply with the formal requirements, it shall notify the applicant accordingly, inviting him to comply with the requirements within the prescribed period. If the applicant does not comply with the requirements within the said period, the Office shall refuse the application.

12.014 These formal requirements relate to whether the application on the face of it contains a request for registration filed on the appropriate form in English language or with English translation, whether the applicant submitted an appropriate reproduction of the design proposed to be registered and whether the prescribed fees have been paid. The requisite forms and the requirements for the reproduction of the design to be registered are available in the Harare Protocol Regulations and the Administrative Instructions under the Regulations for implementing the Protocol on Patents and Industrial Designs[32] respectively. Applicants are given time to comply with any formal requirements they have missed failing which their application is refused.[33]

12.015 Where an applicant for or proprietor of an ARIPO industrial design is unable to adhere to a time limit despite taking due care, they may request

---

31 See Rule 8 of the Harare Protocol Regulations.
32 See Instructions 60-71.
33 See section 4(2)(b); Rule 15 of the Harare Protocol Regulations.

a re-establishment of their rights and their request shall be granted provided they meet any requirements laid down in the Harare Protocol Regulations.[34] In reality, ARIPO's online system automatically updates the time limit and the relevant right.

The Harare Protocol does not differentiate between aesthetic and functional designs in definition and in duration of protection and section 4(6) provides for 15 years from the filing date as the duration of registration of an industrial design. However, for designated States with a shorter term of protection, the duration is in accordance with their respective national design laws. The duration was extended in the latest amendments to the Harare Protocol and does not have retrospective effect.[35] ARIPO industrial designs are still subject to provisions relating to compulsory licences or public interest uses in the relevant laws of each designated State.[36]   12.016

3. 'Opposition' by Member States

Where an application complies with the formal requirements, ARIPO will notify each designated State of the fact and each such designated State has six months from the date of notification to indicate in writing whether the design, if registered, will have no effect in its territory either because the design is not new, or, due to the nature of the design, it cannot be registered under its laws or that the design is a textile design and is the subject of a special register.[37] Since substantive examination is left to the Contracting Parties and they may communicate that a design would have no effect in their country, this process essentially serves as opposition.   12.017

This procedure may be considered as part of the registration procedure because until the expiration of the six-month duration indicated for the procedure, it will not be possible for ARIPO to effect the registration of the design.[38] Furthermore, this 'opposition procedure' is the *de facto* procedural framework for some substantive examination of design because one of the grounds for   12.018

---

34 See section 5bis.
35 Section 4(6) of the Harare Protocol provides inter alia, '…Where an industrial design was registered before the commencement of the amendment of this Section, the registration period shall be as provided before this amendment.'
36 See section 4(7).
37 See section 4(3)(a).
38 Section 4(4) of the Harare Protocol provides that: '*After the expiration of the said 6 months*, the Office shall effect the registration of the industrial design, which shall have effect in those designated States which have not made the communication referred to in Sub-section (3). The Office shall publish the registration' [italics mine for emphasis].

'rejection' by any designated State is that the design is not new. By extension, Member States that have no system for substantive examination of designs are unlikely to oppose registration except where their national design laws indicate that certain articles are not registrable in the first place. Under the national design statutes of most Member States, there are no provisions and/or procedures for actual substantive examination of designs. However, in Botswana for instance, there are provisions for the Registrar of the relevant industrial property office to refuse an application on the grounds that the design is contrary to public order or morality.[39]

12.019 Applicants are allowed to amend and/or argue the communication from the designated State that the design registration will have no effect in its territory and the designated State may respond to such amendments or arguments. Should the designated State refuse the application despite the applicant's amendments and/or arguments, applicants are allowed to request that the application be treated in the designated State as an application according to the national law of that State.[40] It may be more straightforward to allow applicants to, instead or in addition, withdraw the designation of that particular State given that section 1bis(3) permits withdrawal of designation at any time subject to payment of a prescribed fee. However, the Protocol does not offer such option.

12.020 At the end of the six months given to the designated State to oppose or communicate their rejection, ARIPO shall go ahead and effect the registration of the industrial design to have effect in non-opposing designated States.[41]

4. Substantive Examination

12.021 Currently, ARIPO does not have a system for substantive examination of designs and Member States are left to do so should they desire. Rule 18*quater* of the Harare Protocol Regulations provides that: 'substantive examination of industrial designs shall be conducted in accordance with the national laws of each designated State'. It seems from the wording of the remainder of Rule 18quater that it is linked to section 4(3) of the Protocol which allows Contracting Parties to make written communications to ARIPO if an industrial design registration will have no effect in its territory.[42]

---

39 See section 45(4) of Botswana's Industrial Property Act 2010.
40 See section 4(3)(d) of the Harare Protocol.
41 See section 4(4).
42 Rule 18*quater* (2) makes reference to and links to the provisions of section 4(3).

12.022 Substantive examinations consist of the examination and/or consideration of novelty of the design, originality of the design, morality of the designs and registrability of the designs.[43] Novelty is linked to the state of the art or prior art where designs submitted for registration are evaluated vis-à-vis existing, registered designs to ensure that the submitted design is not already part of the existing registered designs.[44] Novelty considerations therefore require that industrial property offices have a searchable database. Neither ARIPO nor its Member States currently have such a searchable database. There are however plans under the Intellectual Property Rights Action for Africa program funded by the EUIPO to integrate the EUIPO's DesignView – a centralised access point to registered designs information held by participating National IP Offices – into national and regional IP offices in Africa.[45]

12.023 As stated earlier, ARIPO (unlike OAPI) does not determine what designs are unregistrable or under what grounds they may be registrable. Instead, the individual national statutes of its Member States determine such matters. Accordingly, questions of the morality of designs and/or registrability of designs proposed to be registered are determined by national laws. In Botswana for instance, section 45(4) of its Industrial Property Act 2010 provides that 'a design which is contrary to public order shall not be registered'. This is similar to section 93(4) of Namibia's Industrial Property Act No. 1 of 2012 and section 2(4) of Ghana's Industrial Designs Act, 2003.[46] Neither 'public order' nor 'morality' is defined in these statutes.

12.024 Botswana's Industrial Property Act 2010 does not also allow the registration of designs that 'consist entirely of features dictated solely by functional or technical considerations'. However, in determining this, it will take into account the degree of freedom the designer had in developing the design.[47] Again, this is somewhat similar to the provisions of section 93(3) of Namibia's Industrial Property Act 2012.[48] Ghana's Industrial Designs Act 2003 does not delineate such grounds for unregistrability of a design. Though South Africa is not an ARIPO Member State, it may be noted that its Designs Act 1993 provides for registration of both aesthetic and functional designs. Functional designs are

---

43 It could also consist of disclosure and considerations of origin requirements. See paragraph D.
44 Cita Citrawinda Noerhadi, 'The Weak Aspects of the Industrial Design Protection System in Indonesia' (2013 3) *Indon. L. Rev* 115.
45 See https://internationalipcooperation.eu/en/afripi accessed 16 September 2022.
46 See also, section 86(4) of Kenya's Industrial Property Act, 2001, https://www.aripo.org/wp-content/uploads/2018/12/Kenya-Industrial-Property-Act-2001.pdf accessed 15 September 2022.
47 Ibid., section 45(5).
48 See also, section 84(2) of Kenya's Industrial Property Act, 2001.

DESIGN LAW

defined in somewhat similar terms as the prohibition in Botswana's Industrial Property Act 2010 and in Namibia's Industrial Property Act 2012. Section 1(xi) of the Designs Act 2003 in South Africa defines 'functional designs' to mean:

> any design applied to any article, whether for the pattern or the shape or the configuration thereof, or for any two or more of those purposes, and by whatever means it is applied, **having features which are necessitated by the function which the article to which the design is applied, is to perform**, and includes an integrated circuit topography, a mask work and a series of mask works" [bold for emphasis].

12.025 The duration of protection for such functional designs is ten years from the filing date and 15 years for aesthetic designs.[49]

12.026 As stated earlier, the Harare Protocol does not differentiate between aesthetic and functional designs and section 4(6) provides for 15 years from the filing date as the duration of registration of an industrial design. In practical terms, countries that indicate different durations for aesthetic and functional designs or that do not protect functional designs at all, may need to use the 'opposition procedure' to indicate such, where it is the case.

12.027 In essence, the procedures stipulated by the industrial design statutes of the respective Contracting States may supersede ARIPO's at the application stage.

5. Appeals

12.028 If ARIPO refuses an application, applicants may request that their application be treated in any designated State, as an application according to the national law of that State.[50] Applicants have three months from the date of the refusal notification to make this request. ARIPO's decisions may be appealed to the Board of Appeal established under section 4bis of the Harare Protocol.[51]

C. THE HARARE PROTOCOL: REALITIES AND FILING TRENDS

12.029 Attorneys who frequently make filings and/or apply for design registration on behalf of clients using the Harare Protocol opine that ARIPO's online filing system works efficiently and effectively. Applications for industrial designs registration are processed within a predictable time frame and in accordance

---

49 See section 22.
50 See section 4(5).
51 See Regulation 15bis(2).

with the provisions and requirements stipulated in the Harare Protocol, the Regulations and the ARIPO Administrative Instructions. In addition, the monthly Journal reports are available to the public in digital format shortly after publication. The general consensus amongst users who shared their experience with the author is that ARIPO is user-centric, accessible and open to suggestions. The online services are excellent allowing access to the system at all times (24/7) and the information is accurate and up to date. There is also consensus that ARIPO's service delivery and communication is effective and easy, facilitated by a social media presence (Facebook), a well-administered website, workshops, Administrative Council sessions, etc. There is widespread preference for ARIPO filings as opposed to national filing for most ARIPO member states, given that it is both time and cost effective and also because most national industrial property offices of Member States are not digitised. ARIPO's fees are designated in US Dollars and may prove more straightforward to pay than the local currency for applicants who are non-African entities.

For most of the attorneys who shared their experience, the majority of their clients using the Harare Protocol are in the telecommunications sector (for mobile apparatus), mining sector (for protective gear) and those producing ornamental household materials. These sectors also feature in the top ten classes for industrial design applications filed in 2022 as reported in the Working Documents for the 46th Session of ARIPO's Administrative Council held in November 2022. The Working Documents indicated Classes 9, 15, 13, 23, 25, 12, 14, 2, 32, and 7 of the Locarno Classification. 12.030

D. FUTURE POSSIBILITIES: ARIPO AND THE AFRICAN CONTINENTAL FREE TRADE AREA AGREEMENT

As stated in the introductory part of this chapter, the cooperation on intellectual property rights under the AfCFTA Agreement is in the form of a Protocol on intellectual property (IP Protocol). However, while it was reported that the AfCFTA IP Protocol was adopted by the AU Assembly during its 36th Ordinary Session held in February 2023, the AU is yet to release an (official) copy.[52] In 2019, the UN Economic Commission for Africa (UNECA) launched a report on Assessing Regional Integration in Africa (ARIA) IX. ARIA is an annual report that provides in-depth assessment of 12.031

---

52 See https:// uneca .org/ stories/ %28blog %29 -deepening -the -afcfta -celebrating -the -adoption -of -new -protocols-on-investment%2C accessed 17 April 2023.

steps and policies towards regional integration in Africa.[53] The ARIA IX was jointly published by the UNECA, UNCTAD, African Union and African Development Bank and inter alia made suggestions on the approach and principles to guide negotiations on the Protocol on IP. Relevant to ARIPO's design system, the Report argued that neither the OAPI's unitary system for regional cooperation on intellectual property rights, the development of one substantive law for members of a regional economic community nor ARIPO's regional filing systems for patents, trademark and industrial designs would be suitable for the IP Protocol given the overall objectives of the AfCFTA.[54] These objectives are: sustainable and inclusive socioeconomic development, gender equality and structural transformation; competitiveness of the economies of States parties within the continent and the global market; industrial development through diversification and regional value chain development, agricultural development and food security.[55] The key argument here is that unitary systems may not be appropriate for the IP Protocol for several reasons including the fact that it would be too ambitious and impractical to harmonise IP laws for the 55 African countries with 'significant cultural, geographical and economic differences'.[56] National regimes that work within a regional filing system may be more appropriate as it obviates the impracticalities of harmonisation for a unitary system. However, it must be noted that while ARIPO's regional filing system model has the advantage of a one-stop filing system, it may, according to the Report, attract more filing outside Africa than within Africa. This is already the case as indicated in the Working Documents for the 46th Session of ARIPO's Administrative Council held in November 2022. The Working Documents indicated China, India, Germany, the US and UK as amongst the top ten countries of origin for industrial design applications filed in 2022.

12.032 It seems from a general interpretation of the functioning of ARIPO per the Harare Protocol that a regional filing system that covers 55 AU member States would be quite attractive for those wishing to conduct business in the continent or desiring an Africa-wide protection. However, if the filing patterns are anything to go from, it may still be non-African entities who would benefit the most from such a regional filing system. In terms of revenue from filing fees though, the relevant national IP offices may benefit. Rule 12 of the Harare

---

53 See https:// archive .uneca .org/ publications/ assessing -regional -integration -africa -aria -ix accessed 15 September 2022.
54 Ibid., 126.
55 Ibid.
56 Ibid.

Protocol Regulations indicate a fee distribution arrangement between ARIPO and Contracting States.[57]

AfCFTA may result in increased filings and number of designated States for several reasons. First, because AfCFTA's aim is to liberalise trade across Africa, design rights owners are likely to have increased apprehension of infringement which would in turn motivate them to widen the protection locations of their designs. Currently, the majority of design filings are from outside Africa and many of the filings originating from the African continent are from countries that are not party to the Harare Protocol. **12.033**

The recommendation from many quarters is to not create new IP institutions under the AfCFTA seeing as ARIPO and OAPI already exist and are competently receiving and processing applications for IP registration.[58] What that means for the motivation for countries who are not party to either institution to join is an entirely different matter. **12.034**

Another relevant issue for the IP Protocol relates to substantive examination consisting of disclosure of origin requirements in design registration applications.[59] As proposed by the African Group at the WIPO General Assembly, such disclosure of origin requirements envisages disclosure of traditional cultural expressions such as such as designs, carvings, paintings, artefacts, etc. and traditional knowledge (e.g., distinctive wearing techniques) used in designs creation.[60] As argued elsewhere, even though there are strong oppositions against this proposal, the opportunity offered by the IP Protocol could make this an Africa-wide requirement, which would feature more prominently in substantive examination procedures. **12.035**

E. CONCLUSION

In the light of the foregoing chapter which has briefly examined the functioning of ARIPO as it relates to industrial designs under its Harare Protocol, it is evident that ARIPO functions effectively and the number of industrial designs applications is expected to grow. Furthermore, ARIPO's functioning which **12.036**

---

57 For application fees, it is 5 per cent to the Contracting State and 95 per cent to ARIPO and for the designation fee and the annual maintenance fee, it is 50 per cent for each entity.
58 Ncube (n 6); ARIA IX (n 49).
59 Adewopo, Oriakhogba and Okorie (n 6).
60 Margo A. Bagley, 'Illegal Designs? Enhancing Cultural and Genetic Resource Protection Through Design Law,' (2017) Centre for Int'l Governance Innovation, Paper No. 155, December 2017.

allows a regional one-stop filing shop while recognising national regimes, offers a workable roadmap for future harmonisation of registered IP rights in Africa, particularly with respect to the IP Protocol within the AfCFTA Agreement.

13

THE DRAFT DESIGN LAW TREATY'S FORBIDDEN WORDS

Margo A. Bagley[1]

A. INTRODUCTION	13.001	EXPERIMENTATION IN DESIGN LAW	13.017
B. THE AFRICAN GROUP DISCLOSURE OF ORIGIN PROPOSAL	13.007	D. THE DRAFT DESIGN LAW TREATY AND THE WIPO IGC	13.026
C. THE NEED FOR POLICY SPACE AND		E. CONCLUSION	13.032

A. INTRODUCTION

13.001 It really is quite puzzling. How could the inclusion of just eight words[2] halt meaningful negotiations on a draft treaty for eight years, after similar words brought negotiations on a different treaty to a standstill 20-plus years earlier? I call these words 'forbidden words' in the realm of international intellectual property as they have not, despite valiant effort on the part of many, been included in any major multilateral intellectual property agreement to date. But that may be about to change. The words are: traditional knowledge, traditional cultural expressions, and biological/genetic resources.

13.002 The draft Design Law Treaty (DLT) developed in the World Intellectual Property Organization's (WIPO) Standing Committee on Trademarks, Industrial Designs, and Geographical Indications (SCT), is principally directed

---

1 I served as Friend of the Chair in the WIPO IGC from 2018–2022 and as a technical expert to Mozambique in WIPO matters from 2014 to 2018 and to the African Union in WIPO matters from 2018 to the present; however, the views expressed in this chapter are my own. This chapter borrows from Margo A. Bagley, *Illegal Designs? Enhancing Cultural and Genetic Resources Protection through Design Law*, Ctr. For Int'l Governance Innovation (2017) and from Margo A. Bagley, '"Ask Me No Questions": The Struggle for Disclosure of Cultural and Genetic Resource Utilization in Design', 20 *Vand. J. Ent. & Tech. L.* 975 (2018) [hereinafter Ask Me No Questions].

2 Traditional Knowledge, Traditional Cultural Expressions, and Biological/Genetic Resources.

toward making the cross-border acquisition and protection of industrial design rights more efficient and effective for users, such as corporations, who obtain such rights.[3] Like the WIPO Patent Law Treaty (PLT), the DLT is styled as a formalities treaty.[4] As such, it focuses on minimizing administrative requirements that countries can impose on design applicants.

13.003 Article 3 of the proposed DLT is the heart of the treaty and prescribes a 'closed' list of elements or information that countries can require of applicants seeking to protect designs in DLT member states.[5] Put differently, it sets out the *maximum* content that can be required in a design application by a contracting party to the DLT.[6] For example, it allows countries to require applicants to provide their name and address, a registration request, correspondence information, representation of the design, and an indication of the product(s) incorporating the design.[7]

13.004 One item absent from the original draft DLT text was any language allowing countries to require applicants to disclose the origin of traditional knowledge, traditional cultural expressions, or genetic resources used in the subject design. But with an evolving awareness of the different ways in which cultural and genetic resources can be misappropriated with the assistance of the intellectual property (IP) system, some developing countries have considered whether disclosure of origin requirements are appropriate in the design context and, in some cases, are already instituting them.[8] Thus, it is not completely surprising that in November 2014, the African Group (AG) inserted an additional item into Article 3's closed list that ultimately brought negotiations on the DLT to an impasse. The provision would allow, but not compel, countries to require the disclosure of the origin of traditional cultural expressions, traditional

---

3   WIPO Secretariat, *Relationship Between the Hague System for the International Registration of Industrial Designs and the Draft Design Law Treaty*, ¶¶ 3–5, WIPO Doc. SCT/29/4 (Mar. 27, 2013) [hereinafter *Relationship Between the Hague System and the Draft DLT*].
4   Ibid. ¶ 4 ('The aim of the draft DLT is to establish a dynamic and predictable legal framework for the simplification and harmonization of industrial design formalities and procedures set by national/regional offices.'). However, it does have some concerning provisions that seem substantive in effect. See Bagley, Ask Me No Questions, at 995.
5   WIPO Secretariat, *Industrial Design Law and Practice – Draft Articles*, Annex at 6–8, WIPO Doc. SCT/33/2 (Jan. 16, 2015) [hereinafter *Industrial Design Law and Practice I*].
6   *See Relationship Between the Hague System and the Draft DLT*, *supra* note 3, ¶ 4 ('The draft DLT does not create a single set of standard requirements, but rather a maximum set of requirements to be applied by the Offices of Contracting Parties.').
7   *See* WIPO Secretariat, *Industrial Design Law and Practice – Draft Articles*, Annex at 6, WIPO Doc. SCT/35/2 (Feb. 25, 2016) [hereinafter *Industrial Design Law and Practice II*].
8   *See generally* World Intellectual Prop. Org., Disclosure Requirements Table (2017), https://perma.cc/G4MV-EEEX.

knowledge, or biological or genetic resources used in creating a design.⁹ Interestingly, a proposal to include a disclosure of origin requirement in relation to some of these same elements in the draft Patent Law Treaty, brought that negotiation to a standstill, and progress was only resumed when the WIPO Director General promised to create a new WIPO Committee where questions relating to these issues could be discussed and (hopefully) addressed.¹⁰

13.005 What are these terms and why do they matter? While there are no definitive definitions for the terms, a recent WIPO publication describes traditional knowledge as being generally understood to encompass 'the know-how, skills, innovations and practices developed by indigenous peoples and local communities' and traditional cultural expressions as generally referring to 'the tangible and intangible forms in which traditional knowledge and cultures are expressed.'¹¹ Genetic resources are defined in the Convention on Biological Diversity (CBD) as 'genetic material [defined as 'material of plant, animal, microbial or other origin containing functional units of heredity'] of actual or potential value'.¹²

13.006 This short chapter provides a snapshot of the controversy over the African Group proposal, reasons why it may have caused such a kerfuffle, and what it took to break the impasse. It concludes that the two WIPO Diplomatic Conferences in 2024 promise a fascinating exploration of the continuing struggle for these forbidden words to gain a long-sought place in the lexicon of international intellectual property agreements.

---

9   Catherine Saez, *WIPO New Proposal on Disclosure Requirement in Design Applications*, Intell. Prop. Watch (Nov. 25, 2014), https://perma.cc/2M82-MEC4.
10 *See* WIPO, *Report Adopted by the Assembly*, WO/GA/26/10 (Oct. 10, 2000). *See also* Nuno Pires de Carvalho, 'Sisyphus Redivivus? The Work of WIPO on Genetic Resources and Traditional Knowledge', in *Routledge Handbook of Biodiversity and the Law*, (Charles McManis and Burton Ong (eds), 2017) (describing this history and its continuing impact on the IGC negotiations). See also Ruth L. Okediji, 'A Tiered Approach to Rights in Traditional Knowledge', 58 *Washburn L.J.* 271 (2019).
11 *See* Begoña Venero Aguirre and Hai-Yuean Tualima, 'World Intellectual Prop. Org., *Protect and Promote Your Culture: A Practical Guide to Intellectual Property for Indigenous Peoples and Local Communities*' 9 (2017), https://perma.cc/AT59-JULK. The term 'traditional' in both phrases relates not to the age of the subject matter—new traditional knowledge and new traditional cultural expressions are constantly being created—rather, it refers to the manner and communal context in which the cultural resources are created. *See* Matthias Leistner, 'Analysis of Different Areas of Indigenous Resources: Traditional Knowledge', *in Indigenous Heritage and Intellectual Property* 49, 56 (Silke von Lewinski ed., 2004). Exact definitions for traditional or Indigenous knowledge and new traditional cultural expressions differ and are the subject of heated discussion in the WIPO IGC, but these phrasings will be used for the purposes of this chapter.
12 Convention on Biological Diversity, art. 2, June 5, 1992, 1760 U.N.T.S. 79.

B. THE AFRICAN GROUP DISCLOSURE OF ORIGIN PROPOSAL

13.007 Design protection encompasses a wide swath of eligible subject matter, ranging from automobiles and salad bowls to zip fasteners. The design right covers the ornamental appearance of a useful article. For example, design protection in the United States applies to 'an ornamental design' for 'an article of manufacture', while the European Union applies design protection to the 'appearance' of an 'industrial or handicraft item', and China limits such protection to new designs for the shape or pattern of products that 'are rich in an aesthetic appeal and are fit for industrial application'. Regardless of jurisdiction, design protection generally is available for designs not solely dictated by the function of the product in which the design subsists or to which it is applied. Such protection does not, however, extend to the way the product works, which is the province of utility patents.

13.008 Admittedly, a requirement that an applicant disclose the origin of traditional cultural expressions, traditional knowledge, or biological or genetic resources used in creating a design or invention in an IP application is a relatively new development in national or regional systems for the protection of any type of IP right.[13] Yet, as a recent WIPO study confirms, disclosure of origin requirements are proliferating—particularly in relation to utility patents and genetic resources.[14]

13.009 The African Group proponents deemed this amendment necessary because protectable designs can be based on and use all three types of subject matter. This is because cultural and genetic resources, namely traditional cultural expressions (e.g., designs, artifacts, carvings, and paintings), traditional knowledge (e.g., distinctive weaving or painting techniques), and biological or

---

13 See, e.g., Alison L. Hoare and Richard G. Tarasofsky, 'Asking and Telling: Can "Disclosure of Origin" Requirements in Patent Applications Make a Difference?' (2007) 19 *J. World Intell. Prop.* 149, 156:
  To date, [disclosure or origin requirements] have had limited impact ... because they have not been in place very long[and] ... they only refer to national patent applications. ... Consequently, there have been very few patent applications in which disclosure has been made.
  Since that time, the international community saw the enactment of the Nagoya Protocol and Swakopmund Protocol, as well as domestic laws requiring disclosure. *See* Nagoya Protocol on Access to Genetic Resources and the Fair and Equitable Sharing of Benefits Arising from Their Utilization, Oct. 29, 2010 [hereinafter Nagoya Protocol], https://perma.cc/6VVN-M5UD; Swakopmund Protocol on the Protection of Traditional Knowledge and Expressions of Folklore, Aug. 9, 2010 [hereinafter Swakopmund Protocol], https://perma.cc/VGX5-UEWU.
14 *See* World Intellectual Prop. Org., Key Questions on Patent Disclosure Requirements for Genetic Resources and Traditional Knowledge 8 (2017), https://perma.cc/R4CC-W668: 'At the time this study was published, more than 30 countries—including both developed and developing countries—had implemented such requirements through national or regional laws.'

genetic resources (e.g., DNA, enzymes, fibers, and microorganisms), can be used to create protectable designs.

The African Group offered an improved version of the amendment during the 34th session of the WIPO SCT in November 2015 that is now reflected in the current draft articles:

13.010

> Article 3 – Application
>
> (1) [Contents of Application; Fee] (a) A Contracting Party may require that an application contain some, or all, of the following indications or elements:
>   (i) a request for registration; ... [(ix)a disclosure of the origin or source of traditional cultural expressions, traditional knowledge or biological/genetic resources utilized or incorporated in the industrial design;]
>   (x) any further indication or element prescribed in the Regulations.[15]

To be clear, the African Group proposal was and is intended to be permissive, giving countries the right, but not the obligation, to require disclosure of origin.[16] The African Group proposal is important for several reasons, including that:

13.011

- It strengthens complementarity and mutual supportiveness of the traditional cultural expressions, traditional knowledge, and biological or genetic resources international regime complex[17] that involves scientific, cultural, and natural resources;
- It enables countries to advance coherent policy goals across IP, biodiversity, cultural, human rights, and trade regimes;
- It can facilitate member state compliance with access and benefit sharing (ABS) obligations under national, regional, and international laws and agreements by increasing transparency in domestic design protection systems; and

---

15 *Industrial Design Law and Practice II*, *supra* note 7, Annex at 6 (emphasis added); *see also* Standing Comm. on the Law of Trademarks, Indus. Designs & Geographic Indications, *Report*, Annex I at 3, WIPO Doc. SCT/34/8 (Apr. 25, 2016) [hereinafter *SCT Report I*].

16 For a discussion of the WIPO IGC disclosure of origin issue, see contributions in *Protecting Traditional Knowledge: The WIPO Intergovernmental Committee on Intellectual Property and Genetic Resources, Traditional Knowledge and Folklore* (Daniel F. Robinson et al. eds., 2017)[hereinafter Protecting Traditional Knowledge]; specifically Margo A. Bagley, 'Of Disclosure 'Straws' and IP System 'Camels': Patents, Innovation, and the Disclosure of Origin Requirement', *in Protecting Traditional Knowledge* at 98; Georges Bauer, Cyrill Michael Berger and Martin Girsberger, 'Disclosure Requirements: Switzerland's Perspective', *in Protecting Traditional Knowledge*, at 244; Dominic Keating, 'The WIPO IGC: A U.S. Perspective', *in Protecting Traditional Knowledge*, at 265; and Dominic Muyldermans, 'Genetic Resources, Traditional Knowledge and Disclosure Obligations: Some Observations from the Life Science Industry', *in Protecting Traditional Knowledge*, at 230.

17 *See* Kal Raustiala and David G. Victor, 'The Regime Complex for Plant Genetic Resources', (2004) 58 *Int'l Org.* 277, 279 (introducing the concept of regime complexes).

- It provides domestic policy space for beneficial legal experimentation.[18]

13.012 The timing of the introduction of the amendment is a reflection of the new and unprecedented nature of the issue in the design context as well as advances in law, science, and digital technologies which are creating evolving scenarios that may have been unimaginable when efforts to harmonize aspects of design law via the DLT began.[19]

13.013 For example, as work on the DLT was beginning in 2008, the objectives were to 'identify possible areas of convergence on industrial design law and practice in WIPO SCT Members, highlighting particular issues to be addressed in that context and taking into account existing international instruments.'[20] The international instruments considered at that time included the Paris Convention for the Protection of Industrial Property, the PLT, the Singapore Treaty on the Law of Trademarks, and TRIPS.[21] However, since that time, the Nagoya Protocol to the CBD was adopted in 2010 and came into force in 2014, requiring compliance with ABS obligations in relation to genetic resources and associated traditional knowledge.[22] Also, the regional Swakopmund Protocol came into effect in 2015 and requires 19 African countries to provide a variety of protections for traditional knowledge and traditional cultural expressions that would require disclosure of source or origin in design applications.[23] As the DLT is still in the negotiating phase, consideration of the interplay between the DLT and the obligations contained in these agreements seemed quite appropriate and, for countries party to the Swakopmund Treaty, a necessity.[24]

---

18 *See* Standing Comm. on the Law of Trademarks, Indus. Designs & Geographical Indications, *Report*, ¶ 13, WIPO Doc. SCT/35/8 (Oct. 19, 2016) [hereinafter *SCT Report II*]; *SCT Report I, supra* note 15, ¶¶ 21, 29, 56, 57; Saez, *supra* note 9.
19 Peter K. Yu, 'Currents and Crosscurrents in the International Intellectual Property Regime', (2004) 38 *Loy. L.A. L. Rev.* 323, 434–35.
20 WIPO Secretariat, *Possible Areas of Convergence in Industrial Design Law and Practice*, ¶1, WIPO Doc. SCT/21/4 (May 15, 2009) [hereinafter *Possible Areas of Convergence*].
21 Ibid. ¶ 3.
22 *See* Nagoya Protocol, *supra* note 13, art. 15(1).
23 *See* Swakopmund Protocol, *supra* note 13, § 1.1.
24 *See* Vienna Convention on the Law of Treaties, Art. 18 (1969) ('A State is obliged to refrain from acts which would defeat the object and purpose of a treaty when: (a) it has signed the treaty or has exchanged instruments constituting the treaty subject to ratification, acceptance or approval').

Countries opposed to the African Group amendment to Article 3 launched 13.014
a vigorous and sustained objection to the proposal based, ostensibly, on four
primary concerns:

- The African Group proposal was introduced very late in the DLT negotiation process when the agreement was largely finalized in anticipation of a diplomatic conference, and the only outstanding issue was believed to be technical assistance.
- Disclosure of origin requirements are not common core features of industrial design systems and do not belong in a formalities treaty, or at most could be accommodated by interpretation of the draft regulations to the DLT.[25]
- A disclosure of origin requirement could introduce detrimental uncertainty for designers, and create a chilling effect on filings by serving as a basis for rejection or invalidation of applications using vague criteria.
- The origin of genetic resources, in particular, are widely considered irrelevant to the registrability of a design.[26]

While these may be valid concerns, it seems unlikely that any of these articulated reasons fully constitute the basis for the exceptionally strong resistance to the provision. This is because, as discussed below, many of the countries opposed to the African Group proposal have deemed acceptable alternative language which is argued to have the same effect of allowing countries to require disclosure of such information, but which lacks the key words of traditional knowledge, traditional cultural expressions, and biological/genetic resources. 13.015

Thus despite these objections, the African Group—supported to varying 13.016
degrees and at different times by the delegations of Iran, India, Saudi Arabia,

---

25 Catherine Saez, *Another Setback for Design Law Treaty at WIPO; GIs in Contention*, Intell. Prop. Watch (Nov. 27, 2014), https://perma.cc/C843-RN9G; *see also* WIPO Secretariat, *Industrial Design Law and Practice – Draft Regulations*, Annex at 2–4, WIPO Doc. SCT/31/3 (Jan. 20, 2014) (listing draft Rule 2's requirements under Article 3 of the draft DLT). Draft Rule 2(1)(x) states that parties can also require applicants to provide 'an indication of any prior application or registration, or other information, of which the applicant is aware, that could have an effect on the eligibility for registration of the industrial design.' Ibid. Annex at 3. This language seems to open up the closed list of Article 3. However, member states disagree on whether it is broad enough to include a formal or substantive disclosure of origin requirement. *See SCT Report I*, *supra* note 15, ¶¶ 29, 31. Moreover, Article 23(4) of the draft DLT states '[i]n the case of conflict between the provisions of this Treaty and those of the Regulations, the former shall prevail.' *Industrial Design Law and Practice II*, *supra* note 7, Annex at 37. Consequently, the African Group expressed its discomfort with relying for disclosure of origin policy space on a regulation that appears to be in facial noncompliance with an article of the agreement. See, e.g., *SCT Report I*, *supra* note 15, ¶ 52.
26 *See SCT Report II*, *supra* note 18, ¶¶ 13–14, 23, 28, 32, 34, 36; *SCT Report I*, *supra* note 15, Annex at 2.

and several members of the Asia-Pacific group of countries[27]—remained steadfast in its demand for disclosure of origin policy space in the draft DLT and inclusion of the forbidden words.

C. THE NEED FOR POLICY SPACE AND EXPERIMENTATION IN DESIGN LAW

13.017 Design protection is becoming more attractive to businesses worldwide, with increasing numbers of design applications filed each year through systems that are largely formalities based, with no substantive examination of the design's entitlement to protection. Thus, there are increasing opportunities for misappropriation of cultural and genetic resources through the design system. For many developing countries grappling with challenges arising from more traditional forms of IP such as patents and copyrights,[28] the nuances of possible issues pertaining to design protection simply may not have been apparent earlier in the DLT negotiations.

13.018 For this same reason, few countries are currently requiring disclosure of origin in relation to design protection, but it is an emerging practice. At least 20 African countries, including South Africa and the 19 countries that comprise the African Regional Intellectual Property Organization (ARIPO),[29] are all likely to need the policy space to require disclosure of origin—at least for traditional knowledge and traditional cultural expressions incorporated into designs.

13.019 On May 11, 2015, the ARIPO Swakopmund Protocol entered into force.[30] It provides holders of traditional knowledge and expressions of folklore, also known as traditional cultural expressions, with certain rights and protections in relation to their cultural resources. In particular, Section 10, relating to traditional knowledge, specifies that '[a]ny person using traditional knowledge

---

27 *SCT Report II*, *supra* note 18, ¶¶ 16, 19, 20, 30, 40; *SCT Report I*, *supra* note 15, ¶¶ 42, 46.
28 *See* Boatema Boateng, *The Copyright Thing Doesn't Work Here* 168 (2011).
29 *See Membership/Member States*, Afr. Regional Intell. Prop. Org., https://perma.cc/YKD2-G47B (last visited Aug. 1, 2022). ARIPO is a regional IP organization for a number of English-speaking African countries. *See About Us*, Afr. Regional Intell. Prop. Org., https://perma.cc/EV6C-R2PC (last visited Aug. 1, 2022).
30 *Entry into Force of the ARIPO Swakopmund Protocol on the Protection of Traditional Knowledge and Expressions of Folklore*, Afr. Regional Intell. Prop. Org., https://perma.cc/YL6Z-4VPF (last visited Aug. 1, 2022). To date, Botswana, Zimbabwe, the Gambia, Rwanda, Liberia, Malawi, Zambia, and Namibia have deposited instruments of ratification, but implementing legislation is in varying stages of completion in each country. *SCT Report I*, *supra* note 15, ¶ 29; *Zambia Ratifies the Swakopmund Protocol*, Afr. Regional Intell. Prop. Org., http://www.aripo.org/news-events-publications/news/item/79-zambia-ratifies-the-swakopmund-protocol (last visited Apr. 5, 2018).

beyond its traditional context shall acknowledge its holders, *indicate its source* and, where possible, *its origin*, and use such knowledge in a manner that respects the cultural values of its holders.'[31]

Likewise, Section 19, relating to expressions of folklore (another name for traditional cultural expressions) mandates the following:

13.020

> 19.2. In respect of expressions of folklore of particular cultural or spiritual value or significance to a community, the Contracting States *shall provide adequate and effective legal and practical measures to ensure that the relevant community can prevent the following acts* from taking place without its free and Prior Informed Consent:
>
> [(a)]...iv. *the acquisition or exercise of intellectual property rights over the expressions of folklore* or adaptations thereof; ...
>
> 19.3. In respect of the use and exploitation of other expressions of folklore, the Contracting States *shall provide adequate and effective legal and practical measures to ensure that*:
> [((a) *the relevant community is identified as the source* of any work or other production adapted from the expressions of folklore[.][32]

These provisions require ARIPO Members to, among other things, ensure proper acknowledgement and source identification of cultural resource holders and enable such holders to prevent the acquisition of IP rights over those resources and adaptations thereof.[33] A disclosure of origin requirement for industrial design applications appears to be a necessary element for complying with these provisions of the Protocol, and the draft DLT without the African Group amendment would prevent parties to the Protocol from employing such a requirement. Thus, while a disclosure of origin requirement is not a common core feature of design regimes, that seems to be an insufficient reason for denying countries the right to employ these requirements to meet treaty and domestic policy objectives and obligations. Arguably, for those ARIPO countries it could be a violation of regional and national law.

13.021

---

31 Swakopmund Protocol, *supra* note 13, § 10 (emphasis added).
32 Ibid. §§ 19.2, 19.3 (emphasis added).
33 The South African Protection, Promotion, Development and Management of Indigenous Knowledge Systems Bill 2016, in conjunction with the Intellectual Property Laws Amendment Act 2013, provides for disclosure of Indigenous knowledge, Indigenous cultural expressions, and Indigenous knowledge associated with natural resources. *See* Intellectual Property Laws Amendment Act of 2013 §§ 28B(4)(b), 43B(6)(b), 53B(3)(b) (S. Afr.), http://www.wipo.int/wipolex/en/text.jsp?file_id=315146 [https://perma.cc/C28S-9GGH]; Protection, Promotion, Development and Management of Indigenous Knowledge Bill, B 6B—2016 § 13(2)(b)(iii) (S. Afr.), http://pmg-assets.s3-website-eu-west-1.amazonaws.com/B6B-2016.pdf [https://perma.cc/DG5T-MFHK].

13.022 According to the WIPO Secretariat, 'the draft DLT aims at simplifying and harmonizing industrial design formalities and procedures set by national/regional offices, so as to reduce discrepancies among future Contracting Parties'.[34] Harmonization historically was seen as an unexceptional goal because territoriality is inefficient and imposes numerous costs on inventors and creators.[35] However, harmonization also has its downside, and there is growing criticism of its negative impacts, including the way it constrains the policy choices of sovereign nations facing diverse societal needs. Moreover, harmonization in international IP agreements does not equate to harmonization in domestic implementing legislation, and low and middle income countries (LMICs) may lack the sophisticated interpretive tools high-income countries use to creatively and favorably implement treaties in national law. This, paradoxically, can result in more stringent IP protection standards in the very countries most in need of flexibility.[36]

13.023 Another drawback of harmonization is its negative impact on legal experimentation and domestic policy preferences.[37] There are many aspects of calibrating cultural and genetic resource laws that would benefit from legal experimentation across jurisdictions, including whether a disclosure of origin requirement should be employed at all and, if so, in what form and to what ends. Countries should not be prevented from engaging in such experimentation or from adopting justifiably distinctive approaches in their domestic design regimes—especially in light of the historical lack of comparative design law harmonization. The original closed list approach of Article 3 of the draft DLT would prevent such experimentation.

13.024 The African Group proposal also appears to be a reasonable tool to facilitate policy coherence.[38] African Group members and many other biodiverse

---

34 *Relationship Between the Hague System and the Draft DLT*, supra note 3, ¶ 19.
35 *See* Edward Lee, 'The Global Trade Mark, 35 *U. Pa. J. Int'l L.* 917, 933 (2014); Peter K. Yu, The International Enclosure Movement', (2007) 82 *Ind. L.J.* 827, 901.
36 An example of this phenomenon is the revised Bangui Agreement, which prevents AIPO Members from utilizing flexibilities in the Doha Declaration without first going through a judicial procedure in national civil courts. *See* Carolyn Deere, *The Implementation Game: The TRIPS Agreement and the Global Politics of Intellectual Property Reform in Developing Countries* 276 (2009); *see also* Ruth L. Okediji, 'Reframing International Copyright Limitations and Exceptions as Development Policy', *in Copyright Law in an Age of Limitations and Exceptions* 429, 448–50 (Ruth L. Okediji ed., 2017).
37 Lisa Larrimore Ouellette, 'Patent Experimentalism', (2015) 101 *Va. L. Rev.* 65, 67–68 (2015); *see also* Yu, *supra* note 35, at 832 ('[T]he one-size-fits-all templates [in TRIPS and other] agreements have drastically reduced the policy space available to less-developed countries.').
38 *See, e.g.*, Jean-Frédéric Morin and Mathilde Gauquelin, Trade Agreements as Vectors for the Nagoya Protocol's Implementation 1 (2016); *see also* Nuno Pires de Carvalho, *Sisyphus Redivivus? The Work of WIPO on Genetic Resources and Traditional Knowledge*, *in Routledge Handbook of Biodiversity and the* Law 337, 339–40 (Charles R. McManis & Burton Ong eds., 2018).

countries in the global South are party to the CBD and one or more other treaties, such as the Nagoya Protocol, the Food and Agriculture Organization's International Treaty on Plant Genetic Resources for Food and Agriculture, and, in some cases, regional agreements such as the Swakopmund Protocol or the Andean Decision. These countries are also in the process of modifying their domestic laws to better protect biodiversity and valuable cultural and natural resources from misappropriation. It would be illogical, and would create incoherent internal policy positions, for these countries to agree not to require disclosure of origin in design applications just when they are modifying their laws to facilitate transparency, acknowledgment of rights, and improved stewardship of cultural resources.

13.025 The issue of inserting disclosure of origin provisions into formalities treaties is not new to WIPO. Such concerns were first raised in the WIPO Standing Committee on Patents (SCP) in 1999, when a group of Latin American Members proposed inserting a disclosure of origin requirement into the draft PLT.[39] This turn of events precipitated a political compromise in which matters relating to genetic resources and traditional knowledge would be addressed in WIPO—but in a new forum, the IGC, and not in the SCP.[40] This allowed the 2000 Diplomatic Conference on the PLT to proceed to a successful conclusion, producing a treaty devoid of any mention of genetic resources or traditional knowledge. In light of this history; the myriad developments relating to genetic resources and traditional knowledge outside of WIPO, such as the Nagoya Protocol; and the painfully slow progress of the IGC, it is unsurprising that the African Group has remained adamant in its demand for disclosure of origin policy space to be explicitly retained, through incorporation of the forbidden words in the draft DLT.[41]

D. THE DRAFT DESIGN LAW TREATY AND THE WIPO IGC

13.026 The WIPO IGC's first meeting was in 2001, and while there has been much talk in successive meetings, real progress largely began with the start of

---

39   *See* Florian Rabitz, *The Global Governance of Genetic Resources: Institutional Change and Structural Constraints* 96 (2017).
40   *See* Ruth L. Okediji, 'Legal Innovation in International Intellectual Property Relations: Revisiting Twenty-One Years of the TRIPS Agreement', (2014)36 *U. Pa. J. Int'l L.* 191, 217–18, 218 n.114.
41   Ahmed Abdel-Latif, 'Genetic Resources, Patents and Benefit Sharing: State of Play and Challenges Facing Multilateral Discussion, *in Intellectual Property in the Pharmaceutical Industry* 59, 63 (Jacque de Werra ed., 2012).

text-based negotiations in 2009.[42] The current mandate of the WIPO IGC is to continue to engage in text-based negotiations leading to one or more international legal instruments.[43] Recent negotiations have yielded three draft texts: a genetic resources text that would include provisions such as a requirement that inventors seeking patent protection disclose the origin of tangible genetic resources and associated traditional knowledge used in developing a claimed invention, as well as two texts—for traditional knowledge and traditional cultural expressions—that would include, among other things, a suite of moral and economic rights for certain categories of traditional knowledge and traditional cultural expressions.[44]

13.027 Failure to achieve progress in narrowing gaps in what is widely seen as the least contentious of the three agreements, relating only to a genetic resources and associated traditional knowledge disclosure requirement, not any new IP rights, led IGC Chair Mr. Ian Goss of Australia,[45] to develop his own text, a Chair's text, based on his wide-ranging consultations with Member States to understand and develop compromises for their concerns.[46] His text, issued in 2019, was well-received by many delegations, including the African Group and incorporates a formal disclosure of origin or source requirement for tangible genetic resources and associated traditional knowledge. As proposed, the disclosure requirement would be mandatory, but would not be linked to ABS compliance nor be penalized by revocation; providing an improvement for patent applicants over some existing national regimes which would, it is hoped, join the treaty and adopt the Chair's text approach.

13.028 Returning to the draft DLT, during the 2019 WIPO General Assemblies, the following compromise language was proposed to replace the AG proposal:

---

42 *WIPO Traditional Knowledge Committee Pushes Toward Text-Based Talks*, Int'l Ctr. for Trade & Sustainable Dev. (Dec. 16, 2009), https://perma.cc/BD6X-HR3J.
43 Assemblies of Member States of WIPO, Agenda Item 17: Matters Concerning the Intergovernmental Committee on Intellectual Property and Genetic Resources, Traditional Knowledge and Folklore (2015), http://www.wipo.int/export/sites/www/tk/en/igc/pdf/igc_mandate_1617.pdf [https://perma.cc/9USA-K9BV].
44 *See* WIPO Secretariat, *The Protection of Traditional Cultural Expressions: Draft Articles*, Annex, WIPO Doc. WIPO/GRTKF/IC/28/6 (June 2, 2014); WIPO Secretariat, *The Protection of Traditional Knowledge: Draft Articles*, Annex, WIPO Doc. WIPO/GRTKF/IC/28/5 (June 2, 2014); Communication from Canada et al., *Joint Recommendation on Genetic Resources and Associated Traditional Knowledge*, Annex, WIPO Doc. WIPO/GRTKF/IC/28/7 (May 9, 2014).
45 Mr. Goss served as Chair of the IGC from 2016 to early 2022.
46 *See* WIPO IGC, Chair's Text of a Draft International Legal Instrument Relating to Intellectual Property, Genetic Resources and Traditional Knowledge Associated with Genetic Resources, WIPO/GRTKF/IC/43/5 (May 3, 2022).

*Article 1*bis – *General Principles*

(1) *[No Regulation of Substantive Industrial Design Law]* Nothing in this Treaty or the Regulations is intended to be construed as prescribing anything that would limit the freedom of a Contracting Party to prescribe such requirements of the applicable substantive law relating to industrial designs as it desires.

(2) *[Relation to Other Treaties]* Nothing in this Treaty shall derogate from any obligation that Contracting Parties have to each other under any other treaties.

Article 3 – Application

(1) *[Contents of Application; Fee]* (a) A Contracting Party may require that an application contain some, or all, of the following indications or elements: [...]

(ix) an indication of any prior application or registration, or of other information[1], of which the applicant is aware, that is relevant to the eligibility for registration of the industrial design; [...]

Footnote 1. Other information could include, among other things, information relating to traditional knowledge and traditional cultural expressions.[47]

Considering the fact that this language allows countries to require all kinds of information, both substantively and formally, in design applications, it begs the question as to why the formulation of the African Group is problematic. The answer seemingly is that the African Group proposal contains the forbidden words in the text of the agreement. As could be expected, the African Group rejected this compromise, refusing to settle for the forbidden words being relegated to a footnote.[48] **13.029**

The intervention of the pandemic in 2020 continued the lack of progress on advancing the draft DLT to a Diplomatic Conference at both 2020 and 2021 WIPO General Assemblies.[49] Moreover, in 2021, the United States actually proposed moving the draft DLT discussions back to the SCT from the General Assemblies in order that progress could hopefully be made.[50] However, that move did not prove necessary. **13.030**

---

47 WIPO General Assembly 51st Session Report, Doc. WO/GA/51/18, paragraphs 150-151 (Dec. 2019).
48 See ibid., paras 150–153 (Dec. 2019):
    The Delegation [of Uganda for the African Group] added that, as it believed that all Member States' interests should be reflected in an instrument on an equal footing, the African Group wished to see its position duly and unambiguously reflected in the main text and not in a footnote. For that reason, the Delegation informed the Plenary that the African Group was unable to join the consensus at the present stage but remained open for further discussions, building on the fruitful deliberations held so far.
49 WIPO General Assemblies, Matters Concerning the Convening of a Diplomatic Conference for the Adoption of a Design Law Treaty (DLT), WO/GA/54/8, (Sept. 2021) (providing a helpful chronology of the draft DLT).
50 See WIPO SCT 45th Session, Proposal by the Delegation of the United States of America regarding the Agenda for the Forty-fifth Session of the Standing Committee on the Law of Trademarks, Industrial Designs and Geographical Indications, Doc. SCT/45/4 (Mar. 2022).

13.031 On July 21, 2022, the African Group's steadfast persistence paid off in a surprising and momentous way. During a meeting of the WIPO General Assemblies, Member States agreed, by consensus,[51] to advance both the draft Design Law Treaty (with the African Group proposal and the 2019 compromise language) and an International Legal Instrument Relating to Intellectual Property, Genetic Resources and Traditional Knowledge Associated with Genetic Resources based on the IGC Chair's text, to Diplomatic Conferences no later than 2024.[52] This result clearly involved some level of horse-trading, with the African Group keen to see progress in the IGC after more than 20 years of discussions, and high-income countries wanting the DLT and its broader and more harmonized provisions.

E. CONCLUSION

13.032 Much work remains to be done over the next several months to bring both agreements to fruition as treaties, as there are still areas of significant disagreement on provisions in both texts. A series of expert meetings to refine textual proposals, and preparatory sessions to define the operational terms of the Diplomatic Conferences, are taking place over the next several months, the outcomes of which should provide insights into the likelihood of success for each agreement. Nevertheless, prospects have never been higher for the forbidden words to emerge from the shadows and take their place in the lexicon of international intellectual property agreements.

---

51 Of course, consensus is not unanimity; some countries chose to register their disagreement for the record but indicated they would not block consensus.

52 See Assemblies of the Member States of WIPO, 63rd Series of Meetings, Summary Report, Doc. A/63/9 para. 27 (Jul. 2022).

14

MULTISTATE INFRINGEMENT OF DESIGN RIGHTS: JURISDICTION AND APPLICABLE LAW – THE EUROPEAN APPROACH

Alexander von Mühlendahl

A. INTRODUCTION	14.001	
B. EUROPEAN UNION	14.004	
1. IP Rights in the EU	14.004	
2. Enforcement of IP Rights in the EU	14.006	
3. Infringement of National Design Rights	14.010	
(a) Design right protected in a single Member State	14.010	
(b) Multiple parallel national design rights	14.019	
(c) Applicable law to the infringement of national design rights	14.024	
4. Unitary IP Rights	14.025	
(a) Competent courts	14.026	
(b) Jurisdiction	14.030	
(i) Subject-matter jurisdiction	14.031	
(ii) International jurisdiction	14.034	
(aa) Community Design Courts with EU-wide jurisdiction	14.035	
(bb) Community Design Courts with limited jurisdiction	14.038	
(iii) Multiple defendants – involuntary joinder of several parties	14.040	
(iv) Jurisdictions for provisional measures and remedies	14.043	
(c) Defences	14.044	
(d) Applicable law	14.045	
(e) Related actions	14.053	
C. THE EUROPEAN UNION AND THE LUGANO CONVENTION	14.057	
D. SOLUTIONS AT THE INTERNATIONAL LEVEL	14.063	
1. Hague Conference on Private International Law	14.063	
2. Academic Studies and Proposals	14.065	
(a) CLIP Principles	14.067	
(i) Jurisdiction	14.069	
(ii) Applicable law	14.070	
(b) Kyoto Guidelines	14.072	
(i) Jurisdiction	14.074	
(ii) Applicable law	14.077	

A. INTRODUCTION

14.001 This chapter deals with jurisdiction and applicable law in situations where more than one country is involved in the alleged infringement of design rights.¹ When the design right alleged to be infringed is protected in the same country where the alleged infringement took place and where the plaintiff and the defendant are domiciled, generally no issues of jurisdiction and applicable law arise. We will see however that the situation is different where the design right is valid in more than one country, as is the case with unitary design rights protected throughout the European Union (EU), and we will deal with this situation separately. The generalizing statement is also not correct in countries where more than one court is competent to decide design infringement cases – as is the case in most countries. In these situations the choice of the proper forum, under the applicable rules determining venue, is often of great practical significance, as the recurrent disputes in the United States (US) about venue for patent infringement cases in more or less inconvenient locations, such as the US District Court for the Western District of Texas, demonstrate.² We merely mention the special situation in the US, which may – and actually does – also occur in any other country with more than one competent infringement court, but we will not deal with it in any detail.

14.002 As a general proposition, design rights, as any other intellectual property (IP) right, are infringed only by acts committed in the territory where they are protected. Nevertheless, certain acts carried out outside but directed at or having effects in the territory of protection may amount to direct or indirect infringement or to contributory acts like aiding and abetting or incitement. While the issues arising in this context are controversial and of special interest, this chapter is limited to procedural issues and will not deal with these or any other issue of substantive law (validity or infringement of design rights).

14.003 As the situation in the EU is 'consolidated' significantly and as there is a complete set of rules for all intra-EU litigation, both regarding jurisdiction and applicable law, it appears appropriate to look primarily at the way the EU has solved the issues arising within it, before turning to less developed situations elsewhere.

---

1 This chapter, as does the whole volume, deals with design rights. However, most issues regarding jurisdiction and applicable law are not specific to design law, and therefore examples and arguments will be drawn also from other fields of intellectual property law. There is an abundance of academic literature on the EU's intellectual property system in general and the protection of designs in particular. For a recent publication presenting current issues of design law, not limited to the EU, we refer to H. Hartwig (ed.), *Research Handbook on Design Law*, Edward Elgar 2021. One of the chapters in the Research Handbook, Kur, 'Enforcing Design Rights throughout Europe', p. 283, is somewhat different in scope than the present contribution.
2 See the *writ of mandamus* issued on 2 August 2021 by the Court of Appeals for the Federal Circuit in *In re Hulu*, LLC, Case 2021-142.

B. EUROPEAN UNION

1. IP Rights in the EU

14.004 In the EU, with its 27 Member States, the competence for legislating in the field of intellectual property is shared between the institutions of the EU and the Member States. In accordance with Article 118 of the Treaty on the Functioning of the European Union (TFEU),[3] the EU is competent for establishing EU-wide unitary titles of intellectual property and provide for the appropriate administrative institutions.[4] This competence has been exercised in the field of trademarks[5] and designs,[6] with the European Union Intellectual Property Office (EUIPO) in Alicante (Spain) being the administrative authority for trademarks and designs. There also exist EU-wide unitary plant variety rights,[7] administered by the Community Plant Variety Office in Angers (France).

14.005 In addition, the EU is competent for adopting measures to harmonize or 'approximate' national legislation in all areas relevant for the functioning of the internal market (Article 114 TFEU). On the basis of this provision (or predecessors in earlier EU treaties), Directives to 'approximate' the laws of the Member States have been adopted in the field of copyrights and neighbouring rights, integrated circuits, patents, trademarks,[8] designs,[9] databases, business and trade secrets, and unfair commercial practices (unfair competition).

---

3   The text of the TFEU is widely available. Here is a link to the consolidated version available from EUR-Lex (EUR-Lex is the online gateway to EU law; it provides the official and most comprehensive access to EU legal documents and is available in all of the EU's 24 official languages and is updated daily): https://eur-lex.europa.eu/LexUriServ/LexUriServ.do?uri=CELEX:12012E/TXT:en:PDF accessed 7 June 2024.
4   Article 118 reads as follows:
    In the context of the establishment and functioning of the internal market, the European Parliament and the Council, acting in accordance with the ordinary legislative procedure, shall establish measures for the creation of European intellectual property rights to provide uniform protection of intellectual property rights throughout the Union and for the setting up of centralised Union-wide authorisation, coordination and supervision arrangements. The Council, acting in accordance with a special legislative procedure, shall by means of regulations establish language arrangements for the European intellectual property rights. The Council shall act unanimously after consulting the European Parliament.
5   Regulation (EU) 2017/1001 of the European Parliament and of the Council of 14 June 2017 on the European Union trade mark (OJ 2017 L 154 p. 1).
6   Council Regulation (EC) No 6/2002 of 12 December 2001 on Community designs (OJ 2002 L 3 p. 1) (Community Designs Regulation – CDR).
7   Council Regulation (EC) No 2100/94 of 27 July 1994 on Community plant variety rights (OJ 1994 L 227 p. 1).
8   Directive (EU) 2015/2436 of the European Parliament and of the Council of 16 December 2015 to approximate the laws of the Member States relating to trade marks (OJ 2015 L 336 p. 1).
9   Directive 98/71/EC of the European Parliament and of the Council of 13 October 1998 on the legal protection of designs (OJ 1998 L 289 p. 28).

Directives require the Member States to adopt legislation which complies with the mandates of the Directive. In the field of design protection this has been done on the basis of the 2003 Designs Directive. That Directive has led to uniform rules regarding availability of protection, requirements, in particular novelty and individual character, exclusive rights and their limits, but Member States are free to adopt their own rules regarding the registration procedure as well as the way in which the validity of registered design may be challenged. Thus, designs are currently protected in accordance with the Designs Directive by the applicable legislation in each Member State.[10]

2. Enforcement of IP Rights in the EU

14.006 Infringements of IP rights may result in criminal penalties. Administrative remedies may also be available, such as the intervention of customs authorities when infringing goods cross frontiers. Arbitration may also be available. Interesting as these means of enforcement may be, the present chapter deals only with 'civil' enforcement, i.e., the enforcement by means of actions brought before courts with 'civil' or 'ordinary' jurisdiction, with the most common remedies or sanctions being injunctive relief and damages.

14.007 In some of the EU Member States these courts may be called 'commercial' or 'mercantile' courts, in others, such as in Germany, the 'civil' courts may have 'commercial' chambers, which may have lay judges as part of the panel of judges hearing infringement cases. Whatever the specific situation in the Member States may be, all have in common that infringements of IP rights, and thus including infringement of design rights, are dealt with, together with other torts, by the courts as part of their competence for civil and commercial disputes. EU law neither prescribes nor proscribes the organization of the courts, which belongs to the exclusive competence of the Member States.

14.008 However, EU law regulates the 'international' jurisdiction of the courts in civil and commercial matters, EU law prescribes the substantive law applicable in cases of infringement of IP rights, and EU law contains rules and standards as regards sanctions and remedies available in cases of infringements of IP rights.

14.009 Jurisdiction (as well as the enforcement of judgments) in cases having trans-border elements brought before courts with civil or commercial jurisdic-

---

10 The three Benelux countries – Belgium, The Netherlands, Luxembourg – have united their IP legislation in the field of designs and trademarks. Benelux designs and trademarks are administered by the Benelux Office of Intellectual Property (BOIP) and are valid throughout the territories of the three countries.

tion is governed by an EU law, Regulation 1215/2012 on jurisdiction and the recognition and enforcement of judgments in civil and commercial matters.[11] The EU has its own legislation governing conflicts of law (international private law), and for non-contractual obligations, including torts and thus the infringement of IP rights, the Regulation Rome II[12] determines the applicable law. We will see hereafter how these various EU laws interact in cases of IP rights infringements.

3. Infringement of National Design Rights

(a) Design right protected in a single Member State

When a national design right protected in one of the EU Member States is (alleged to be) infringed by acts committed in the same Member State, and the claimant (owner of the design right) and the defendant are both domiciled in the same Member State, jurisdiction of the courts is a matter purely for the national law of that Member State, and the law applicable to these acts of infringement is the law protecting designs in that Member State. Thus, no issues of international procedural or substantive law arise. 14.010

Jurisdictional issues are limited to intra-Member State issues, and only in those Member States where more than one court is competent to hear design infringement cases. This is the case, inter alia, in Germany, in Italy, and in Portugal. In these countries the national law governing civil procedure determines whether and on which basis the claimant can choose the court where he wishes to bring the action. In Germany, a jurisdiction with which the author is familiar, the claimant can choose between the court in whose district the defendant is domiciled, and any court in whose district acts of infringement have been committed or are threatened. 14.011

Issues of international procedural law arise when the defendant charged with the infringing acts (e.g., sales of infringing goods via the Internet) is domiciled in a Member State other than that where the infringement is committed. In these situations, under the rules of the Brussels I Regulation, the claimant, 14.012

---

11 Regulation (EU) No 1215/2012 of the European Parliament and of the Council of 12 December 2012 on jurisdiction and the recognition and enforcement of judgments in civil and commercial matters (recast), OJ 2012 L 351 p. 1, also referred to as the Brussels I Regulation, or Brussels Ia Regulation. This is the successor to Council Regulation (EC) No 44/2001 of 22 December 2000 on jurisdiction and the recognition and enforcement of judgments in civil and commercial matters, which in turn replaced an international agreement among the EU Member States from 1968, the so-called Brussels Convention on Jurisdiction and the Enforcement of Judgments in Civil and Commercial Matters.
12 Regulation (EC) No 864/2007 of the European Parliament and of the Council of 11 July 2007 on the law applicable to non-contractual obligations (Rome II) (OJ 2007 L 199 p. 40).

located in the Member State where the design right is protected and alleged to be infringed, may bring the infringement action in the Member State where the defendant is domiciled.[13] Thus, taking Germany as an example and postulating a defendant in France, the infringement action may be brought in the competent court in Paris.

14.013 Under the Brussels I Regulation, the claimant may also choose to bring the action in the Member State before the court where the infringement is taking place or is threatened to take place – in the language of the Brussels I Regulation[14] – 'before the courts for the place where the harmful event occurred or may occur.' This is the same jurisdictional rule that applies in the purely national case. The jurisdiction in the place of the wrong (*loci delicti commissi*) has received a broad interpretation by the Court of Justice of the European Union (CJEU): when trans-border torts are at issue, that is to say acts having their origin in one Member State but causing the damage in another Member State, the claimant can choose between the court of the Member State where the act had its origin and the court of the Member State where the infringement has its direct effect.[15] This rule applies to all torts, such as those committed by newspaper or Internet publications, and also to IP rights infringements. Regarding the 'origin' of Internet infringements of IP rights– such as offering for sale infringing goods – under the case law of the CJEU the location of the 'starting point' is where the defendant responsible for putting the infringing offer on the Internet has its establishment; and the 'effect' occurs in the Member State where the IP rights is protected.[16]

14.014 When both the claimant and the defendant are not domiciled in the Member State where the design right is protected, under the rules of the Brussels I Regulation just described, the infringement action may be brought in the

---

13 This follows from Article 4 of the Brussels I Regulation, which reads as follows:
   1. Subject to this Regulation, persons domiciled in a Member State shall, whatever their nationality, be sued in the courts of that Member State.
   2. Persons who are not nationals of the Member State in which they are domiciled shall be governed by the rules of jurisdiction applicable to nationals of that Member State.
14 Article 7 No. 2 of the Brussels I Regulation reads as follows:
   A person domiciled in a Member State may be sued in another Member State: …
   (2) in matters relating to tort, delict or quasi-delict, in the courts for the place where the harmful event occurred or may occur; (…).
15 This case law began with a famous judgment of 30.11.1976, Case 21/76, *Handelskwekerij G. J. Bier BV v. Mines de potasse d'Alsace SA*, where the starting point was the release of saline outflow from salt mines into the Rhine in France and the damage from the salty waters occurred when tomato plantations were irrigated in The Netherlands.
16 CJEU 19.4.2012, Case C-523/10, *Wintersteiger AG v. Products 4U Sondermaschinenbau GmbH* (a trademark infringement case).

Member State where the defendant is domiciled and in the courts of the Member State or Member States where acts of infringement have their starting point as well as in the Member State where the design right is protected.

14.015 The rules explained above might have the result that many actions are brought not in the country where the design right is protected but in the country of the defendant's domicile. This is however not really the case. Rather, claimants generally prefer to bring the infringement action in the Member State where the right is protected, even if the jurisdiction is then based on place of the infringement and the choice of forum is actually limited to the very court of the place of infringement.

14.016 The reasons are several. The first reason is that the courts in the country of protection are more familiar with the rules and principles applicable when national IP rights are infringed. An additional reason is that as regards the validity of the allegedly infringed design right, pursuant to Article 24 No. 4 of the Brussels I Regulation only the courts of the Member State where the right is registered are competent to decide whether the right is valid or not.[17] According to the case law of the CJEU, the exclusive competence of the courts of the Member State where the IP right is registered has the effect that not only direct actions contesting the validity of a registered IP right may be brought only in that Member State, but also that if a plea or defence with the argument of invalidity is raised in a Member State which is not the Member State of registration, the court loses its jurisdiction also for the infringement action.[18] Thus, in our previous example, when assuming that a defendant domiciled in France is sued in France for the infringement of German design right, and the defendant then claims that the asserted design right is invalid, the French court is no longer competent to deal with the infringement. It still

---

17   Article 24 (4) of the Brussels I Regulation reads as follows:
The following courts of a Member State shall have exclusive jurisdiction, regardless of the domicile of the parties: (…)
(4) in proceedings concerned with the registration or validity of patents, trade marks, designs, or other similar rights required to be deposited or registered, irrespective of whether the issue is raised by way of an action or as a defence, the courts of the Member State in which the deposit or registration has been applied for, has taken place or is under the terms of an instrument of the Union or an international convention deemed to have taken place. Without prejudice to the jurisdiction of the European Patent Office under the Convention on the Grant of European Patents, signed at Munich on 5 October 1973, the courts of each Member State shall have exclusive jurisdiction in proceedings concerned with the registration or validity of any European patent granted for that Member State; (…).

18   CJEU 13.7.2006, C-4/03, *Gesellschaft für Antriebstechnik mbH & Co. KG v. Lamellen und Kupplungsbau Beteiligungs KG*. This rule does not apply to actions seeking preliminary or provisional measures because the absence of validity of the asserted right cannot be raised in such proceedings; CJEU 12.7.2012, C-616/10, *Solvay SA v. Honeywell Fluorine Products Europe BV*.

is not entirely clear whether the French court merely has to stay the infringement action until the issue of validity is decided, or whether merely by raising the defence the French court will lose its competence for the infringement action. In any event, a prudent claimant is unlikely to venture into a 'foreign' jurisdiction for the infringement of a domestic IP right.

14.017 The Brussels I Regulation provides another powerful tool for claimants: When infringing acts are committed by two or more infringers domiciled in one or more Member States other than the forum state, the claimant, pursuant to Article 8 No. 1 of the Brussels I Regulation, may join other parties, such as suppliers or traders, challenged with the same infringing acts as the principal defendant and domiciled in different Member States as (involuntary) co-defendants.[19] The requirement for such joinder is that the risk of contradictory judgments would exist if the infringement actions would be pursued separately. Under the case law of the CJEU, this requires that the facts and the law are the same in relation to each defendant.[20]

14.018 The possibility of involuntary joinder[21] may be of little relevance when the case is essentially limited to the infringement of a single national IP right and the case is brought in the jurisdiction where that right is protected. Still, even in such a situation the involuntary joinder of a foreign party participating in the infringing activity, for example as supplier, may be useful. But in the practice of proprietors of IP rights, the involuntary joinder is more often used when the infringement of the same IP right in several Member States by different infringers is involved, the situations we turn to next.

(b) Multiple parallel national design rights

14.019 In the EU, IP rights, including design rights, may be protected in more than one Member State and often are actually protected in many or even in all Member States. For example, copyright protection arises without any administrative intervention by the creation of the work, without any formalities. Consequently, works are protected in principle everywhere in the EU. Patent rights may be obtained in one or more EU countries either directly,

---

19 Article 8 (1) reads as follows:
   A person domiciled in a Member State may also be sued:
   1. where he is one of a number of defendants, in the courts for the place where any one of them is domiciled, provided the claims are so closely connected that it is expedient to hear and determine them together to avoid the risk of irreconcilable judgments resulting from separate proceedings; (…).
20 CJEU 13.7.2006, C-539/03, *Roche Nederland BV v. Primus* (infringement of parallel European patents).
21 Voluntary joinder is possible under general rules; in such a situation the party supporting the claimant or the defendant would voluntarily submit to the jurisdiction of the court.

mostly based on a first filing in one of the Member States or via the Patent Cooperation Treaty, or via the European Patent, valid in one or more EU Member States, granted by the European Patent Office. Trademark protection is available in all or some Member States in addition to the EU trademark obtained through registration at the EUIPO. This situation also applies to design rights, even though simultaneous protection of designs in many Member States is not as frequent (or advisable) as in the field of trademarks. The rapid and user-friendly registration procedure for EU designs obviates the need for parallel national design rights. Nevertheless, there is an (unknown) number of designs protected in two or more EU Member States.

14.020 When IP rights protected in more than one Member State are infringed by the same or by unrelated infringers in some or all of these States, the Brussels I Regulation provides at least a partial answer when the issue of jurisdiction arises. When the potential defendant is domiciled in the EU, an infringement action, seeking relief or sanctions for all infringements wherever in the EU committed, may be brought in the Member State of the defendant's domicile.[22]

14.021 Where the same act of infringement is committed by other defendants – such as by suppliers and retailers – the involuntary joinder pursuant to Article 8(1) of the Brussels Regulation is available. Involuntary joinder requires that without the joinder the risk would exist that contradictory judgments result if each of the defendants would be sued in another jurisdiction. This requires, according to the case law of the CJEU, that the factual situation giving rise to the claim of infringement and the applicable legal rules are the same. When the infringement of design rights is the issue, it appears that the applicable legal rules are (more or less) the 'same', as the law on the protection of designs and the rights conferred is the same in all EU Member States.

14.022 Whether the factual situation is the same would seem to depend on the circumstances in each case – but the condition would seem to be present if the infringing product is the same. For example, the CJEU held that the unauthorized publication of a photograph by several newspapers independent from each other established in different Member States, alleging in all cases the infringement of the copyright in the same photograph, in principle satisfied the criteria of 'same law' and 'same facts'.[23] The CJEU considered the 'same legal situation' satisfied because the question of whether photographs are entitled to copyright protection was determined by the EU's copyright Directives.

---

22 Article 4 Brussels I Regulation.
23 CJEU 1.12.2011, C-145/10, *Painer v. Standard VerlagsGmbH*.

In an earlier decision, subject to much criticism in the legal writings, the CJEU had held that where an infringement of patents granted by the European Patent Office and validated for a number of Member States was pursued in one Member State, with the defendants in other Member States joined as involuntary defendants, the requirement of the 'same legal rules' was not met.[24] As a consequence of that rather unfortunate judgment in the field of patents infringement actions country-by-country are required where the infringer (or the patentee) does not agree to abide by the judgment in one of the several competent jurisdictions. We consider, however, that the *Roche Nederland* case law applying to patents does not apply to EU harmonized law, such as it exists in the field of trademarks, designs, and (to some extent) copyright.

14.023 Even though the possibility of involuntary joinder exists, and this 'tool' facilitates actions against multiple infringers in multiple Member States, we have not seen such actions in the field of design rights. One of the reasons, and likely the principal reason for such an absence is the ability of defendants to 'defeat' jurisdiction in a single court by merely defending themselves with the claim or argument that the asserted design right is not valid. As a consequence of this situation, infringements of IP rights subject to grant or registration, such as patents, trademarks, and designs, are generally pursued country-by country and not in the single jurisdiction of the defendant's domicile for more than one Member State.

(c) Applicable law to the infringement of national design rights

14.024 When a court in an EU Member State is competent to decide upon an alleged infringement of a design right – or any other IP right – protected in another Member State, the question arises which law the court must apply. Under the EU's conflict of law rules, as incorporated in the Rome II Regulation, the court must apply the law of the country where the IP right is protected (*lex protectionis*).[25] This is in line with the generally recognized principle of territoriality, which means that IP rights are available and valid and protected (only) in accordance with the laws of the country where protection is claimed (subject

---

24   CJEU 13.7.2006, C-539/03, *Roche Nederland BV v. Primus*.
25   Article 8 Rome II Regulation reads as follows:
     Article 8 - Infringement of intellectual property rights
     1. The law applicable to a non-contractual obligation arising from an infringement of an intellectual property right shall be the law of the country for which protection is claimed.
     2. In the case of a non-contractual obligation arising from an infringement of a unitary Community intellectual property right, the law applicable shall, for any question that is not governed by the relevant Community instrument, be the law of the country in which the act of infringement was committed.
     3. The law applicable under this Article may not be derogated from by an agreement pursuant to Article 14.

to any international obligations of the country of protection). This principle applies to all issues of 'substantive' law, including conditions of protection (validity) and scope of protection (infringement). The applicable procedural law is the one of the *forum* court.

4. Unitary IP Rights

As explained earlier, in the EU unitary IP rights exist for trademarks, plant varieties, and for designs. Trademarks and designs are administered at the EUIPO, which is competent for the grant, administration and also for decisions challenging the validity of the granted right. When such rights – and in the present context we focus on design rights – are infringed, the EU legislation – in the present context the Regulation on the protection of Community designs – contains specific rules on the competent courts, the jurisdiction of these courts, as well as the law applicable to such infringements. **14.025**

(a) Competent courts

In the EU, the CJEU and its first instance, the General Court of the EU, with their seat in Luxembourg, are exclusively competent for controlling the legality of decisions of the EU institutions and any other agency or office established by EU legislation. In addition, the CJEU is competent for giving 'preliminary rulings concerning the interpretation of the EU treaties and the validity and interpretation of acts of the institutions, bodies, offices or agencies of the Union'.[26] However, in the EU there are no EU courts with general jurisdiction, comparable to the District Courts and Courts of Appeal in the USA, which exist alongside the state courts and have circumscribed jurisdiction, primarily when a 'federal issue' arises or when there is diversity of citizenship, or to the federal courts in Canada, which exist alongside the courts in the Canadian provinces. **14.026**

In the EU the courts established in the 27 Member States are competent in all civil and criminal cases, regardless of whether the case arises under national law or EU law. National courts must apply EU law, and in cases of conflict EU law prevails over national law. When questions of interpretation of EU law arise, national courts must refer the question to the CJEU for a preliminary ruling. **14.027**

When the EU's trademark legislation was adopted in 1993, it was clear that actions for the infringement of EU trademarks would be heard before national courts. In view of the large number of potentially competent national courts **14.028**

---

26 Article 267 TFEU.

the EU legislature included an obligation in the trademark legislation for the Member States to 'designate in their territories as limited a number as possible of national courts and tribunals of first and second instance (...).'[27] The same mandate is included in the Community Designs Regulation.[28]

14.029 Thus, we have in all 27 Member States courts with the name 'EU Trademark Court' and 'Community Design Court', with the mandate 'as limited a number as possible' having been implemented in the Member States according to their own rules governing the organization of the judiciary. Most Member States have designated a single court for trademark and design cases, but in some Member States the number is quite significant. This applies, for example, in Germany, where there is at least one such court for each of the 16 states (*Länder*).[29] Italy has designated more than 20 courts of first and second instance. A complete list of these courts is published in the EU's Official Journal.[30]

(b) Jurisdiction

14.030 The EU Trademark Regulation and, following the model of that Regulation, the Community Designs Regulation provide for the exclusive subject-matter jurisdiction of the EU Trademark Courts and Community Design Courts as well as for the 'personal' jurisdiction, denominated 'international jurisdiction.'

(i) Subject-matter jurisdiction

14.031 According to Article 81 CDR, the Community Design Courts have exclusive jurisdiction for infringement actions, for declaratory actions of non-infringement, for actions for a declaration of invalidity of an unregistered community design, and for counterclaims in an infringement action seeking a declaration of invalidity of the allegedly infringed Community design.

14.032 For all other actions relating to or connected with a Community design, such as disputes concerning license agreements, or ownership disputes, all national civil courts have jurisdiction which would be competent for such disputes if arising in connection with a national design right. International jurisdiction in such cases follows the general rules of the Brussels I Regulation. Residual jurisdiction, i.e., in cases where no national court is competent (e.g., ownership

---

27 The provision was originally found in Article 95 of Regulation 40/94 and is currently found in Article 123 of Regulation 2017/1001.
28 Article 80 (1) CDR.
29 Only Berlin and Brandenburg have agreed that a single court (the competent court in Berlin) shall have jurisdiction for cases arising in either Berlin or in Brandenburg.
30 OJ C 327, 5.10.2020, p.6.

dispute concerning a Community design between two US entities without a presence in the EU), exists for the courts of the Member State where the EUIPO is located, i.e., for the courts in Spain.[31]

14.033 What may appear surprising in this list of situations where the national EU design courts have jurisdiction is the competence of these courts to declare the asserted design invalid, with effect *erga omnes*. Thus, national courts applying EU law may deny validity to a right granted by an EU institution, even though the validity of the right granted may be challenged before the same institution. However, comparative law shows that it is quite frequently the situation in EU Member States and in many other countries, such as the US, that courts with civil jurisdiction are entitled to declare the asserted right invalid. A differentiated situation exists in Germany for trademarks, where an action for declaration of invalidity based on absolute grounds must be brought before the German Patent and Trademark Office (GPTO), whereas the civil courts are competent, parallel to the GPTO, for revocation and invalidity actions based on other than absolute grounds. In German design law, the parallel competence is entirely shared between the GPTO for administrative invalidation actions and the civil courts for counterclaims for a declaration of invalidity in infringement actions.

(ii) International jurisdiction

14.034 With a view to ensuring that for all infringements there is at least one court that has EU-wide jurisdiction, the EU legislature has added a number of specific jurisdictional rules which extend jurisdiction of the Community Design Courts beyond the rules of the Brussels I Regulation. As was pointed out above, the Brussels I Regulation does not apply when the defendant is not domiciled in an EU Member State; in these situations, the respective national law applies when an action against a third-country defendant is brought. In order to fill this 'gap' and add additional bases of 'personal' or 'international' jurisdiction, the Community Design Regulation, again following the model of the EU Trademark Regulation, provides for jurisdiction of courts with EU-wide competence and for courts with jurisdiction limited to the territory of the Member State where they are located.[32]

---

31 Article 93 CDR.
32 Articles 79 and 82 CDR. Article 79 CDR in substance means that the Brussels I Regulation applies subject to the special provisions in the CDR.

(aa) Community Design Courts with EU-wide jurisdiction

14.035 Actions for which Community Design Courts are exclusively competent may be brought according to the following 'cascade', where the next category applies only if the previous categories are not applicable:

(1) before the courts of the Member State where the defendant is domiciled;
(2) if (1) does not apply, before the courts of the Member State where the defendant has an establishment;
(3) if neither (1) nor (2) applies, before the courts of the Member State where the claimant is domiciled;
(4) if neither (1) nor (2) nor (3) applies, before the courts of the Member State where the claimant has an establishment;
(5) if neither (1), (2), (3) nor (4) applies, before the Community Design Court of Spain, as the Member State where the EUIPO has its seat.

14.036 In addition, a Community design court not falling within the previous cases becomes competent pursuant to a prorogation agreement of the parties or by appearing before a Community Design Court without challenging its jurisdiction. Such a challenge to the jurisdiction of the court must be brought at the first opportunity and prior to a defence on the merits.[33]

14.037 The Community Design Courts falling in the above categories have plenary competence for all acts of infringement, regardless of where committed, and can issue orders and sanctions applying throughout the EU. Case law has established that a claimant is not required to seek pan-European relief, but may limit the sanctions (injunctive relief, damages, etc.) to one or several Member States only.[34] Whether such a limited action is beneficial to the claimant requires careful analysis of benefits and drawbacks of such an action.

(bb) Community Design Courts with limited jurisdiction

14.038 Pursuant to Article 81 (5) CDR, all actions for which Community Design Courts have exclusive competence, with exception of declaratory actions of non-infringement and declaratory actions of invalidity of a non-registered Community designs, may, at the election of the claimant, also be brought in the courts of the Member States 'in which the act of infringement has been committed or threatened.' The *forum delicti commissi* is available in parallel to the *fori* described above with plenary jurisdiction. The principal difference to the pan-European competence of the first category of courts is that at the

---

[33] German Federal Supreme Court, judgment of June 2, 2016, I ZR 226/14, para. 25 and 27.
[34] CJEU 12.4.2011, C-235/09, *DHL Express France SAS v. Chronopost SA*, para. 48.

forum delicti commissi only acts of infringement committed or threatened in that Member State may be pursued.

According to the case law of the CJEU, 'acts committed or threatened' must be interpreted autonomously and, different from the broad interpretation of what is now Article 7 No. 1 of Brussels I Regulation established by the *Bier* judgment of 1976,[35] these terms refer only to the Member State where the infringing acts were committed, not also to the Member State where the act produced its effects.[36] The strict application of the *Coty* judgment obviously limits the choice of *fora* for a claimant whose rights are infringed by the presence of infringing goods in several Member States when the goods have their origin in only one Member State. It was therefore with some relief that the CJEU, in a later judgment involving trademark infringement,[37] concluded that in a case where infringing goods were advertised on a webpage operated by a person located in Spain, addressed in English *inter alia* to customers in the United Kingdom, the EU Trademark Court in the United Kingdom did have jurisdiction under the principle of *forum delicti commissi*. 14.039

(iii) Multiple defendants – involuntary joinder of several parties
We have seen earlier that, under the rules of the Brussels I Regulation and specifically pursuant to Article 8 No. 1 of that Regulation, a claimant may join other persons domiciled in different Member States as involuntary defendants in an infringement action brought against one of them, provided that the required degree of connectivity exists, i.e., same facts and the same law must be applicable to the alleged infringing acts. We have also seen that in practice such actions in cases of multiple infringements of parallel IP rights valid in several Member States are of little practical relevance because the defendant, merely by raising the plea that the design rights are invalid, would force the infringement court to deny jurisdiction over the foreign defendants accused of having infringed the foreign design right. 14.040

According to Article 79 (3) (c) CDR, provisions in the Brussels I Regulation which require a domicile in the EU are applicable as well where the party is not domiciled but has an establishment in the EU. This enlarges the scope for the application of the involuntary joinder under Article 8 No. 1 of the Brussels I Regulation. Also, the defence of invalidity of the asserted IP right which puts an effective break on joining defendants when the infringement of 14.041

---

35   See above at note 15.
36   CJEU, 5.6.2014, C-360/12, *Coty Germany GmbH v. First Note Perfumes NV*.
37   CJEU, 5.9.2019, C-172/18, *AMS Neve Ltd v. Heritage Audio SL*.

parallel national rights is concerned is not a problem when the enforcement of EU-wide protected designs is involved. Therefore the 'weapon' of involuntary joinders is particularly effective, provided that the claimant can allege that all of the defendants can be accused of infringement of the same design or designs by the same infringing acts. Where the principal action is pending before a Community Design Court having pan-European competence as described above, any joined defendant is similarly liable for all acts of infringement anywhere, and the Community Design Court has the same pan-European jurisdiction over the 'foreign' defendant or defendants as it has over the local defendant.[38]

14.042 When the principal action is pending before a Community Design Court with jurisdiction under the *forum delicti commissi*, joinder of defendants domiciled in other Member States would also be available although these other defendants would be liable only for acts also committed in the forum state.

(iv) Jurisdictions for provisional measures and remedies

14.043 A claimant requesting provisional remedies in cases of Community design infringement, such as the securing of evidence, or a preliminary injunction, may request such measures not only before a Community Design Court competent under the rules previously explained, but also before any other national court with jurisdiction for preliminary measures in cases of infringement of national design rights.[39] However, only Community Design Courts having pan-European jurisdiction may adopt such preliminary measures with effect to all Member States.[40] Thus, claimants have additional *fora* available for quick relief when infringements are ongoing or threatened.

(c) Defences

14.044 In infringement actions, the defendant may raise all defences capable of defeating the infringement claim, such as private use, absence of overall similarity, exhaustion, or prior use. However, the claim or defence or plea of absence of validity of the allegedly infringed registered Community design is not admissible, except in preliminary proceedings. Rather, a defendant wishing to challenge the validity of the allegedly infringed registered Community design may either assert invalidity by way of a counterclaim,[41] or bring a separate action

---

38 CJEU, 27.9.2017, Joined Cases C-24/16 and C-25/16, *Nintendo Co. v. BigBen Interactive GmbH*. The author's law firm represents Nintendo in the ongoing litigation with BigBen.
39 Article 90 (1) CDR.
40 Article 90 (3) CDR.
41 Articles 85 and 86 CDR.

for declaration of invalidity against the design holder before the EUIPO.[42] As regards a claim of infringement of an unregistered Community design, the defendant may either bring a counterclaim requesting the declaration of invalidity of that design, or may raise invalidity by way of a plea.[43]

(d) Applicable law

14.045 It is essential for the operation of unitary IP rights, protected throughout the EU, that the rules applicable to validity and infringement, as well as the limitations of the exclusive right, such as private use or exhaustion, are the same throughout the EU and are applied regardless of the court or the Member State where the issue arises. Thus, it is clear that EU law applies to the extent that a particular issue is actually subject to an EU regulation. This is expressly (and actually unnecessarily) expressed in Article 88 (1) CDR.

14.046 To the extent that the EU law does not have any provisions, the Community Design Regulation, in Article 88 (2) CDR, instructs the Community Design Court to apply its (substantive) national law, including its private international law. In addition, as regards sanctions to be adopted in an infringement action where the Community Design Court finds for infringement, the Community Design Regulation provides, in Article 89 CDR, for injunctive relief (Article 89 (1)(a) CDR), the seizure of infringing products (Article 89 (1)(b) CDR), and of materials and implements predominantly used to manufacture the infringing goods (Article 89 (1)(c) CDR). As regards additional sanctions, such as, in particular, damages or accounting, or publication of judgments, or the costs of litigation, Article 89 (1)(d) CDR directs the Community design court to adopt 'any order imposing other sanctions appropriate under the circumstances which are provided by the law of the Member State in which the acts of infringement or threatened infringement are committed, including its private international law.'

14.047 If one compares the language of Article 88 (2) CDR – the court shall apply its national law, including its private international law – with Article 89 (1)(d) – the court may impose sanctions which are provided by the law of the Member State in which acts of infringement are committed, including its private international law – we notice significant differences. In the first instance, the law to be applied is the law of the forum, including its conflict of laws rules, whereas in the second instance it is the law of the Member State where acts of infringement have been committed – and these are not necessarily the same

---

42 Article 52 CDR.
43 Article 85 (2) CDR.

Member States. It thus came as a surprise when the CJEU, in a case relating to sanctions for the infringement of an unregistered Community design, concluded that damages are not 'sanctions', and thus the national law of the forum (Article 88 (2) CDR) applies, whereas accounting and destruction of goods would fall under the notion of 'sanctions,' and thus be governed by Article 89 (1) (d) CDR.[44] While in either case private international law applies, and thus the applicable law is in both cases determined pursuant to Article 8 (2) of the Rome II Regulation, the classification of 'damages' as not falling into the category of sanctions is puzzling, especially in view of the Enforcement Directive which specifically lists recovery of damages among the sanctions for infringement of IP rights which the Member States must provide.

14.048 As regards the application of Article 81 (1) (d) CDR – or the parallel provision in Article 130 (2) EUTMR – there was debate in the academic literature and partially also in the case law whether the infringement court, in a case of multi-state infringement of a Community design (or an EU trademark), must apply, for the sanctions not provided in the CDR or the EUTMR, the law of each Member State separately where infringing goods are on the market (so-called 'mosaic theory'), or whether, and under which approach, the law of a single Member State must be applied.[45] The answer requires an interpretation of Article 8 (2) of the Rome II Regulation, which reads as follows:

> In the case of a non-contractual obligation arising from an infringement of a unitary Community intellectual property right, the law applicable shall, for any question that is not governed by the relevant Community instrument, be the law of the country in which the act of infringement was committed.

14.049 As should be apparent from the previous discussion, and notably the interpretation by the CJEU of Article 82 (5) CDR identifying the *forum delicti commissi* by reference to the 'Member State in which acts of infringement have been committed or threatened',[46] an interpretation of Article 8 (2) Rome II Regulation in the same sense as Article 82 (5) CDR appeared more than likely. Fortunately for proprietors of Community designs, and by implication also of EU trademarks, the CJEU, in the *Nintendo* judgment previously referred to,[47] held that the interpretation of the jurisdictional provision in Article 82 (5) CDR does not apply to the interpretation of Article 8 (2) of the Rome II

---

44 CJEU, 13.2.2014, C-479/12, *H. Gautzsch Großhandel GmbH & Co. KG v. Münchener Boulevard Möbel Joseph Duna GmbH.*
45 See the discussion and the references supplied Kur, *supra* n. 1, at 299–301.
46 See *supra* note 35.
47 See *supra* note 37.

Regulation. Rather, according to the *Nintendo* judgment, the following interpretation is correct (emphasis added):

> In the light of all the foregoing considerations, the answer to the third question is that Article 8 (2) of Regulation No 864/2007 must be interpreted as meaning that the 'country in which the act of infringement was committed' within the meaning of that provision refers to the country where the event giving rise to the damage occurred. Where the same defendant is accused of various acts of infringement committed in various Member States, the correct approach for identifying the event giving rise to the damage is not to refer to each alleged act of infringement, but to make an overall assessment of that defendant's conduct in order to determine the place where the initial act of infringement at the origin of that conduct was committed or threatened by it.

This provides a very favourable solution for claimants in multi-state infringement cases where the 'initial act' takes places in the EU. The *Nintendo* judgment, however, does not provide an answer to the question of the law to be applied when there is no 'initial act' in the EU, but the infringing goods are made abroad and then distributed in the EU, and there is no central distribution hub in the EU. 14.050

The *Nintendo* judgment involved a case of a multi-state infringement, and therefore it remained unclear whether the same rule should be applied when the infringement action is brought in the Member State where acts of infringement have been committed, i.e., jurisdiction is based on Article 82 (5) CDR.[48] This issue was been presented to the CJEU in a reference for a preliminary ruling, again from the Düsseldorf Higher Regional Court, in a case where the claimant, BMW, brought a Community design infringement case against an Italian defendant in Germany. In his Opinion of October 28, 2021, the Advocate General, M. Szpunar, had proposed to follow the *Nintendo* precedent and thus apply Italian law. The CJEU however ruled that in such a case the Community design court should apply its own law, i.e., the forum law, holding as follows: 14.051

> Article 88 (2) and Article 89 (1)(d) of Council Regulation (EC) No 6/2002 of 12 December 2001 of Community designs, and Article 8 (2) of Regulation (EC) No 864/2007 of the European Parliament and of the Council of 11 July 2007 on the law applicable to non-contractual obligations (Rome II) must be interpreted as meaning that the Community Design Courts before which an action for infringement pursuant to Article 82 (5) of Regulation No 6/2002 is brought concerning acts of infringement committed or threatened within a single Member State must examine the claims supplementary to that action, seeking the award of damages, the submission of information, documents and accounts and the handing over of the infringing products with

---

48 CJEU 3.3.2022, C-421/20, *Acacia Srl v. Bayerische Motoren Werke Aktiengesellschaft.*

a view to their being destroyed, on the basis of the law of the Member State in which the acts allegedly infringing the Community design relied upon are committed or are threatened, which is the same, in the circumstances of an action brought pursuant to that Article 82 (5), as the law of the Member State in which those courts are situated.

14.052 This outcome, somewhat doubtful as regards principles, is certainly welcome news for claimants bringing infringement actions in the Member State where infringements have been committed, rather than at the defendant's domicile.[49]

(e) Related actions

14.053 'Related actions' are proceedings concerning the same design in different *fora*. The *fora* are on the one side infringement courts in different Member States dealing with the infringement of the same design and possibly also counterclaims for a declaration of invalidity. The different *fora* may also be infringement courts and the EUIPO, as both are competent for validity judgments, the first limited to counterclaims in infringement actions, the second competent for direct actions.

14.054 The Community Design Regulation specifically provides, in Article 91 CDR, for the second type of related actions, i.e., for situations where the validity of a Community design is at issue. When an application for a declaration of invalidity is pending before the EUIPO, or a counterclaim is pending before a Community Design Court, an infringement court thereafter seized with an action for infringement is required to stay the action until the earlier action is completed, unless there are special reasons for continuing the infringement action, regardless of whether the parties are the same or not. Conversely, an earlier counterclaim precludes a later direct application before the EUIPO, subject to the same 'special reasons'. In essence, the first invalidity action 'blocks' a subsequent invalidity action (which appears self-evident), but in addition also 'blocks' a later infringement action. For a potential defendant, this arsenal provides an opportunity for – in any event significantly – delaying an infringement suit merely by requesting a declaration of invalidity before EUIPO – this is the so-called 'Alicante Torpedo.'

14.055 For the first kind of 'related actions,' infringement actions in different Member States, the answer is provided by the Brussels I Regulation. Where an infringement action is pending in a Community Design Court, a second action between the same parties and relating to the same cause of action

---

49 For a favourable review of the *Acacia* judgment, see Kur, Internationale Zuständigkeit und anwendbares Recht bei Verletzung von unionsweiten Rechten- Zugleich eine Anmerkung zu EuGH C-421/20 – Acacia/BMW, MarkenR 2022, 201.

(subject-matter) is inadmissible as soon as the jurisdiction of the court first seized is established.[50] Where the actions are merely related, the second court may stay the action, but is not obliged to do so.[51]

Finally, the Community Design Regulation also provides for the situation where actions are brought in different Member States, one action on the basis of a Community design, the other action on the basis of the same design protected under national law, between the same parties and for the same cause of action. In these situations, the later-seized court must deny its jurisdiction once the jurisdiction of the first-seized court is established.[52] This provision **14.056**

---

50 This follows from Article 29 Brussels I Regulation, which reads as follows:
Article 29
1. Without prejudice to Article 31(2), where proceedings involving the same cause of action and between the same parties are brought in the courts of different Member States, any court other than the court first seized shall of its own motion stay its proceedings until such time as the jurisdiction of the court first seized is established.
2. In cases referred to in paragraph 1, upon request by a court seised of the dispute, any other court seised shall without delay inform the former court of the date when it was seised in accordance with Article 32.
3. Where the jurisdiction of the court first seised is established, any court other than the court first seised shall decline jurisdiction in favour of that court.
51 This follows from Article 30 Brussels I Regulation, which reads as follows:
Article 30
1. Where related actions are pending in the courts of different Member States, any court other than the court first seised may stay its proceedings.
2. Where the action in the court first seised is pending at first instance, any other court may also, on the application of one of the parties, decline jurisdiction if the court first seised has jurisdiction over the actions in question and its law permits the consolidation thereof.
3. For the purposes of this Article, actions are deemed to be related where they are so closely connected that it is expedient to hear and determine them together to avoid the risk of irreconcilable judgments resulting from separate proceedings.
52 This follows from Article 95 CDR, which reads as follows:
Article 95 - Parallel actions on the basis of Community designs and national design rights
1. Where actions for infringement or for threatened infringement involving the same cause of action and between the same parties are brought before the courts of different Member States, one seized on the basis of a Community design and the other seized on the basis of a national design right providing simultaneous protection, the court other than the court first seized shall of its own motion decline jurisdiction in favour of that court. The court which would be required to decline jurisdiction may stay its proceedings if the jurisdiction of the other court is contested.
2. The Community design court hearing an action for infringement or threatened infringement on the basis of a Community design shall reject the action if a final judgment on the merits has been given on the same cause of action and between the same parties on the basis of a design right providing simultaneous protection.
3. The court hearing an action for infringement or for threatened infringement on the basis of a national design right shall reject the action if a final judgment on the merits has been given on the same cause of action and between the same parties on the basis of a Community design providing simultaneous protection.
4. Paragraphs 1, 2 and 3 shall not apply in respect of provisional measures, including protective measures.

only applies if indeed the action, on the basis of the Community design, covers the same territory as the action based on the national design.[53]

C. THE EUROPEAN UNION AND THE LUGANO CONVENTION

14.057 The situation regarding multi-state infringements of design rights in the European Union is characterized by a complete set of rules for determining jurisdiction of the courts[54] and the applicable law. The situation in the 'rest of the world' is essentially characterized by the absence of international treaty obligations and thus by each country applying its own law.

14.058 There is a small exception to this general statement because the EU and its Member States are members of an international agreement on jurisdiction and enforcement of judgments in civil and commercial matter with Switzerland, Norway, and Iceland. This agreement, called Lugano II Convention (because it is successor to the Lugano Agreement of 1988), was signed in 2007 and entered into force between the EU and Norway on 1 January 2010, between the EU and Switzerland on 1 January 2011, and between the EU and Iceland on 1 May 2011, in accordance with Article 69(5) of the Convention.[55]

14.059 The Convention essentially mirrors the intra-EU regulation found today in Regulation 1215/2012, previously explained. Thus, for the pursuits of infringement of national design rights in any of the members of the Lugano II Convention, what has been explained above for intra-EU cases applies as well, *mutatis mutandis*. Infringement actions based on the infringement of a national design right protected in any of the Lugano countries may be brought in accordance with the general principles either in the country where the defendant is domiciled (and these courts in the country have pan-Lugano

---

53 CJEU 19.10.2017, C-231/16, *Merck KGaA v. Merck & Co. Inc.*, n. 44:
    In view of the foregoing considerations, the answer to the first and second questions is that Article 109(1)(a) of Regulation No 207/2009 must be interpreted as meaning that the condition laid down in that provision as to the existence of the 'same cause of action' is satisfied where actions for infringement between the same parties, on the basis of a national trade mark and an EU trade mark respectively, are brought before the courts of different Member States, only in so far as those actions relate to an alleged infringement of a national trade mark and an identical EU trade mark in the territory of the same Member States.
54 With the exception of jurisdiction over non-EU domiciled defendants in cases of infringements of national IP rights; in these situations, each Member State applies its own law on jurisdiction, without recourse to the Brussels I Regulation.
55 The text of the Convention is widely available. For a source of the consolidated version of the Convention, see the website of EUR-Lex, at https://eur-lex.europa.eu/legal-content/EN/TXT/?uri=celex%3A02009A0610%2801%29-20160411 accessed 6 June 2024.

jurisdiction), or in the country where the design right is infringed, with jurisdiction then limited to the territory of that country.

14.060 If the defendant in such an infringement action should raise invalidity as a defence, the infringement court loses its competence because of the exclusive jurisdiction of the authorities of the country having granted the design right, in accordance with Article 22 of the Lugano II Convention.[56] This provision mirrors the corresponding provision in Article 24 of Regulation 1215/2012, referred to above.[57] The Lugano II Convention also has provisions on involuntary joinder, corresponding to Article 8 of Regulation 1215/2012.[58]

14.061 The courts in Switzerland, Norway, and Iceland are, in principle, also competent for dealing with infringements of Community designs, as such infringement actions belong to 'civil and commercial matters.' Thus, when the action is brought in the non-EU Lugano II country where the defendant is domiciled, that court has pan-European jurisdiction, including all EU Member States, the only territory in which unitary EU rights are protected and may be infringed. Jurisdiction in a non-EU Lugano II country on the basis of 'place of the wrong' is irrelevant because the unitary EU design right cannot be infringed in Switzerland, Norway, or Iceland.

14.062 If the defendant in an infringement proceeding based on an EU design right should wish to attack or contest the validity of that design, i.e., if invalidity is raised as a defence, the jurisdiction of the non-EU Lugano country would end. This is because the non-EU Lugano countries have no jurisdiction to judge the validity of an EU design right, and a defendant cannot bring a counterclaim for a declaration of invalidity of the asserted EU design right because, again, the courts in non-EU Lugano countries lack competence for judging the validity of EU design rights. Because the defence of invalidity practically 'ousts' the infringement court in a non-EU Lugano country from jurisdiction, it is in practice very unlikely that such an action will be brought in Switzerland, Norway or Iceland.

---

56 Article 22 in relevant parts reads as follows:
    The following courts shall have exclusive jurisdiction, regardless of domicile: (…)
    4. In proceedings concerned with the registration or validity of patents, trade marks, designs, or other similar rights required to be deposited or registered, irrespective of whether the issue is raised by way of an action or as a defence, the courts of the State bound by this Convention in which the deposit or registration has been applied for, has taken place or is, under the terms of a Community instrument or an international convention, deemed to have taken place. (…).
57 See text at note 17, above.
58 Article 6 No. 1 of the Lugano II Convention.

D. SOLUTIONS AT THE INTERNATIONAL LEVEL

1. Hague Conference on Private International Law

14.063 The Hague Conference on Private International Law (HCCH) was established in the late 19th century. The agreement establishing the HCCH as an international organization, signed in 1951, entered into force in 1955.[59] Since its inception, over 40 Conventions and instruments have been adopted under the auspices of the HCCH. Of these, a selected number, known as the core Conventions and instruments, are prioritized based on their recent adoption, popularity, or practical relevance.[60]

14.064 Long-standing efforts to obtain binding agreements at the international level of rules for determining jurisdiction and corresponding recognition and enforcement of judgments have so far not led to results. While a broad-based approach was pursued since the early 1990s,[61] the negotiations resulted in 2019 in the Convention on the Recognition and Enforcement of Judgments in Civil or Commercial Matters.[62] This Convention, which so far has not entered into force, has been ratified by six countries (Costa Rica, Israel, Russian Federation, Ukraine, Uruguay, USA). The EU is set to become a member as well.[63] The Convention expressly does not apply to intellectual property. Among the studies undertaken in the field of IP protection, a 2019 publication by Bennett and Granata, titled 'When Private International Law Meets Intellectual Property Law' is particularly noteworthy.[64]

---

59 The HCCH has 90 contracting states and the EU as members.
60 This is the language on the website of the HCCH. These are the following Conventions: 1961 Form of Wills Convention, 1961 Apostille Convention, 1965 Service Convention, 1970 Divorce Convention, 1970 Evidence Convention, 1980 Child Abduction Convention, 1980 Access to Justice Convention, 1985 Trusts Convention, 1993 Adoption Convention, 1996 Child Protection Convention, 2000 Protection of Adults Convention, 2006 Securities Convention, 2005 Choice of Court Convention, 2007 Child Support Convention, 2007 Maintenance Obligations Protocol, 2015 Principles on Choice of Law in International Commercial Contracts, 2019 Judgments Convention.
61 Details are available from the website of the HCCH.
62 The Convention has been negotiated in English and French. Translations into other languages, including German, are available from the HCCH website.
63 See Draft Recommendation of the Legal Affairs Committee of the European Parliament on the draft Council decision concerning the accession of the European Union to the Convention (13404/2021 – C9-0465/2021 – 2021/0208 (NLE), dated 3 May 2022, available from the website of the European Parliament.
64 This publication is a joint HCCH-WIPO publication. It is available for free download in English and French; see https://www.wipo.int/publications/en/details.jsp?id=4465 accessed 6 June 2024.

2. Academic Studies and Proposals

14.065 Scholars and scientific or non-governmental organisations active in international and comparative law studies have always been intrigued by the intricacies of the law applicable to IP rights, and especially the consequences of the principle of territoriality, and the issues arising in multi-state infringements of IP rights, notably the issue of jurisdiction of states other than those where the IP right is valid and protected. We have seen that in the EU we actually do have a complete set of rules on applicable law and jurisdiction and recognition and enforcement of judgments, whereas no such binding rules exist elsewhere.

14.066 The failure to obtain a binding international agreement has encouraged groups of legal scholars to develop, adopt, publish, and propagate rules on applicable law and jurisdiction of universal scope as 'soft law', i.e., guidelines for how reasonable courts should approach these issues, in the absence of binding multilateral or bilateral agreements. These guidelines have built on recent codifications of conflict of law rules in major jurisdictions, such as the EU and Switzerland, but also on efforts undertaken elsewhere, such as in Asian countries or also the intra-US conflict of law rules and the Full Faith and Credit Clause of the US Constitution.[65] Two recent broad-based approaches with largely overlapping approaches and proposals merit special consideration: the CLIP Principles and the Kyoto Guidelines of the International Law Association (ILA).

(a) CLIP Principles

14.067 'CLIP' stands for Conflict of Laws in Intellectual Property. The CLIP Principles were developed over a number of years by 'The European Max Planck Group on Conflict of Laws in Intellectual Property (CLIP)' made up of scholars in the fields of intellectual property and private international law. The group was established in 2004 and has regularly met to discuss issues of intellectual property, private international law and jurisdiction.

14.068 The Group has prepared Principles on Conflict of Laws in Intellectual Property (Principles). These Principles cover international jurisdiction, the applicable law, and recognition and enforcement of foreign judgments in the field of intellectual property.[66] The Final Text of the Principles was published

---

[65] Article IV Sec. 1: Full Faith and Credit shall be given in each State to the public Acts, Records, and judicial Proceedings of every other State. And the Congress may by general Laws prescribe the Manner in which such Acts, Records and Proceedings shall be proved, and the Effect thereof.
[66] https://www.ip.mpg.de/en/research/research-news/principles-on-conflict-of-laws-in-intellectual-property-clip.html accessed 6 June 2024.

with the date December 1, 2011.⁶⁷ The Principles are published by Oxford University Press with extensive commentaries by members of the group of scholars.⁶⁸

(i) Jurisdiction

14.069 As regards jurisdiction, the Principles propose that a defendant may always be sued in the country of his or her habitual residence (which corresponds to domicile in EU law).⁶⁹ In addition, again similar to EU law, a defendant may also be sued in the country where acts of infringement have been committed or threatened.⁷⁰ Beyond the EU law, the Principles also deal with the extent of jurisdiction of the infringement court in cases where there are acts of infringement in other countries.⁷¹ The Principles also propose jurisdiction over non-resident defendants on the basis of connexity, comparable to Article 8 No. 1 of the Brussels I Regulation.⁷² The Principles also provide for the exclusive jurisdiction of the tribunals of the country where the IP right has been granted.⁷³ However, contrary to EU law, the infringement court remains competent when the issue of validity is not raised as a principal claim or a counterclaim but only as an *inter partes* issue; and a decision of the court concerning an invalidity defence has effects only between the parties.⁷⁴

(ii) Applicable law

14.070 As regards the law or laws to be applied by the courts, the Principles follow established tradition by stipulating that, as regards substantive law of IP rights, the *lex protectionis* applies⁷⁵ whereas the forum law applies to procedural matters.⁷⁶

14.071 Overall, the CLIP Principles are a modern set of rules which build on the rules and experiences gained in the EU but add and clarify points and issues for which EU law provides no or insufficient or unsatisfactory answers.

---

67   https://www.ip.mpg.de/fileadmin/ipmpg/content/clip/Final_Text_1_December_2011.pdf accessed 6 June 2024.
68   Conflict of Laws in Intellectual Property: The Clip Principles and Commentary, 2013. For a German-language summary, see Kur, Die Ergebnisse des CLIP-Projekts – zugleich eine Einführung in die deutsche Fassung der Principles on Conflict of Laws in Intellectual Property, GRUR Int. 2012, 857.
69   CLIP Principles, Article 2:101.
70   CLIP Principles, Article 2:202.
71   CLIP Principles, Article 2:203.
72   CLIP Principles, Article 2:206.
73   CLIP Principles, Article 2:401 (1)
74   CLIP Principles, Article 2:401 (2).
75   Article 3:102: Lex protectionis
     The law applicable to existence, validity, registration, scope and duration of an intellectual property right and all other matters concerning the right as such is the law of the State for which protection is sought.
76   CLIP Principles, Article 3:101.

(b) Kyoto Guidelines

14.072 The ILA's Guidelines on Intellectual Property and Private International Law ('Kyoto Guidelines') are the product of a decade of work by a group of international scholars:

> The Kyoto Guidelines are the outcome of an international cooperation of a group of 35 scholars from 20 jurisdictions lasting for ten years under the auspices of ILA. The Kyoto Guidelines have been approved by the plenary of the ILA 79th Biennial Conference, held (online) in Kyoto on December 13, 2020. The Kyoto Guidelines provide soft-law principles on the private international law aspects of intellectual property, which may guide the interpretation and reform of national legislation and international instruments, and may be useful as source of inspiration for courts, arbitrators and further research in the field.
>
> The ILA Committee on 'Intellectual Property and Private International Law' was created in November 2010. Its aim was to examine the legal framework concerning civil and commercial matters involving intellectual property rights that are connected to more than one State and to address the issues that had emerged after the adoption of several legislative proposals in this field in different regions of the world. The work of the Committee was built upon the earlier projects conducted by the Hague Conference of Private International Law as well as several academic initiatives intended to develop common standards on jurisdiction, choice of law and recognition and enforcement of judgments in intellectual property matters.[77]

14.073 The scope of the Kyoto Guidelines is universal whereas the CLIP Principles clearly have a European orientation. Nevertheless, the proposals are not so different in substance.

(i) Jurisdiction

14.074 Kyoto Guideline No. 3 ('Defendant's Forum'), provides that defendants should be subject to – territorially unlimited – jurisdiction of the courts in the country where they have their habitual residence. This would mean that for the infringement of multiple parallel IP rights the courts of the residence of the defendant would, in principle, have competence to adjudge these conflicts for all those jurisdictions. This is indeed the same situation as that in the EU (and beyond the EU in the Lugano countries) under Article 4 of Regulation 1215/2012.

14.075 Kyoto Guideline No. 5 ('Infringements') provides for jurisdiction of the courts in the country where the defendant acted, and also for the jurisdiction of the

---

[77] This text is taken from the Editorial, by Toshiyuki Kono, Axel Metzger and Pedro de Miguel Asensio, accompanying the publication of the Guidelines together with extensive commentaries in a special number of jipitec, the (2021) 12(1) *Journal of Intellectual Property, Information Technology and Electronic Commerce Law*, devoted exclusively to the Kyoto Guidelines.

courts where damage was suffered.⁷⁸ This is a reflection of the case law of the CJEU in the famous *Bier* case where it was held that a claimant may choose to bring the action (in addition to the defendant's domicile) in the EU Member State where the defendant acted or in the Member State where the damage occurred. The Kyoto Guidelines specify that in the first situation the territorial competence of the court is not limited, whereas in the second situation the court may only judge infringements in the territory where the damage was suffered. Kyoto Guideline No. 7 ('Consolidation') provides for joinder of defendants in connexity situations, similar to Article 8 No. 1 of Regulation 1215/2012.

14.076 Kyoto Guideline No. 11 ('Validity Claims and Related Disputes') provides for the exclusive jurisdiction of the country having granted the IP right when the issue of validity is the main object of the action. In other situations, such as when invalidity is raised a defence, the court would retain jurisdiction, but the resulting decision would be valid only *inter partes*. Thus, the Kyoto Guidelines also accept the ability of a 'foreign' court' to decide on the validity of an allegedly infringed IP right as a preliminary issue, such as when invalidity is raised by means of a defensive plea, thus departing from the strict separation currently found in Article 24 of Regulation 1215/2012 and in Article 22 of the Lugano II Convention.

(ii) Applicable law

14.077 Kyoto Guideline No. 19 provides, just as do the CLIP Principles and the EU's Rome II Regulation, that the substantive law applicable to IP rights should be the law of the country for which protection is sought.⁷⁹ Here again, the Kyoto Guidelines accept the territoriality principle, for all IP rights covered by the Guidelines.

---

78   5. Infringements – In a case of an alleged infringement a person may be sued:
   (a) In the courts of the States where the alleged infringer has acted to initiate or further the alleged infringement; the courts' jurisdiction to award remedies arising from those acts shall be territorially unlimited; or
   (b) In the courts of the States where the infringement may have caused direct substantial harm unless it could not be anticipated that the infringement would cause that harm there; the courts' jurisdiction shall be territorially limited to the State in which the court is situated.
79   19. Existence, Scope and Transferability (lex loci protectionis) – The law applicable to determine the existence, validity, registration, duration, transferability, and scope of an intellectual property right, and all other matters concerning the right as such, is the law of the State for which protection is sought.

PART III

PRESENT-DAY AND FUTURE TRENDS IN DESIGN LAW

15

REDESIGNING DESIGN PROTECTION: THE PROBLEM OF OVERLAP

Shubha Ghosh

A. INTRODUCTION	15.001	REGIMES	15.043
B. MEANING OF DESIGN	15.010	1. Design Patent in US with Some	
1. Industrial Design	15.018	Comparison with Japanese Design	
2. Ornamental Design	15.028	Registration	15.043
3. Functional Design	15.042	2. The Problem of Overlap	15.049
C. CRITICAL CONCERNS OF OVERLAPPING		D. CONCLUSION	15.052

A. INTRODUCTION

15.001 This Chapter discusses what United States (US) design patent law teaches about the problem of overlap in the protection of design. Unlike many jurisdictions, the US does not have a standalone *sui generis* regime for the protection of design. Instead, design protection consists of design patent and aspects of copyright and trademark laws. This constellation of regimes creates the possibility of overprotection for design and the concomitant need for limitations within and across each regime. By looking at US design patent law and comparing that regime with that of design protection in other countries, we can hone in on the problem of overlap and launch a research program for reforming design patent law.

15.002 Design law is, according to two prominent scholars, an undervalued branch of intellectual property.[1] Lacking the muscularity of technological innovation, the subject of utility patent law, and the elegance of grace of artistic creations, the

---

[1] Brad Sherman and Lionel Bently, *The Making of Modern Intellectual Property Law* 163 (1999). For a fuller history, pre-TRIPS, see J.H. Reichman, 'Design Protection and the New Technologies: The United States Experience in a Transnational Perspective', *19 U. Balt. L. Rev.* 6, 153 (1989).

subject of copyright law, legal protection for design has become peripheral in the scheme of intellectual property laws. This denigration is surprising given the centrality of design law in the development of intellectual property law historically. Design has been, historically, a focal point for countries launching intellectual property statutes. Given the historical importance of design, it is perhaps not surprising that design law is gaining some prominence as companies focus more on the aesthetic appeal of new products in the marketplace and the interface between user and object (such as graphical user interfaces for computer applications or the look and feel of an electronic appliance). Design often blurs into the useful aspects of a new product providing consumers with sleeker and visually or tactilely appealing products. As design has regained prominence, issues of the lines among specific areas of intellectual property also come centre stage as practitioners and policymakers rethink the boundaries among utility patent, copyright, and design.

This Chapter engages in these issues through a comparative study of design protection in Japan and the US. The study is comparative in two senses. First, at the heart of the analysis is a comparative study of different areas of intellectual property (design patent and design registration) as to their respective policies, subject matter, and doctrinal boundaries. This dimension of comparison emphasizes how intellectual property protects design as one element of a product complementing innovative functionality and creative expression. Attorneys advising clients seeking to commercialize new products must consider the full set of intellectual property rights contained in distinctive, novel, useful, original, and aesthetically appealing forms of innovation. Policymakers need, however, to untangle the web of intellectual property protection to avoid issues of multiple protection and possible multiple recoveries for infringement. Equally salient for policymakers is offering guidance for companies and attorneys, confused by the complex set of intellectual property rights implicated in a new product. 15.003

This complexity is exacerbated by different laws and processes across countries, which leads to the second point of comparison and provides another foundation for this study: understanding how different member states legislate to protect design within a set of intellectual property laws. Japan and the US, given their importance to the world economy, provide a good basis for comparison in assessing and understanding how to protect design. Japan has a *sui generis* design registration system that is within the jurisdiction of the Japan Patent Office (JPO). The country also has addressed design issues within copyright law and to a lesser extent within trademark law. Given this panoply of protection, Japanese courts have addressed boundary issues, particularly the 15.004

boundary between copyright and design registration, in order to avoid confusing and duplicative double protection. As I will demonstrate, the doctrinal line between applied art and fine art serves as a demarcation between design and copyright, the line has been shifting and is not all that clear. For example, a high court in Japan has ruled on the protection of the design of chopsticks as a work of fine art when the chopsticks included seemingly artistic features that also aided in teaching children how to use the sticks.[2] A similar issue of protection arose with respect to a high chair that had aesthetically pleasing features but integrated into the look and feel of the functional, otherwise non-artistic chair.[3] Doctrinal push and pull in Japan offers an example for the US, where the line between applied art and fine art has largely been extinguished, with attendant problems for practitioners and policymakers.

15.005 While many jurisdictions have adopted *sui generis* protection for design similar to design registration in Japan, as mentioned above, the US has declined to do so. Instead, design is protected through specialized rules within design patent and aspects of copyright and trademark laws. This kaleidoscope of legal protection has led to controversies over the proper scope of the various legal doctrines. After percolating for several decades, these issues have come to the attention of the current Supreme Court during the 2016–2017 term: *Samsung v. Apple*,[4] which addresses remedies for design patent infringement and *Star Athletica v. Varsity Brands*,[5] which deals with the standard for copyright protection for product designs. This Chapter examines the continuing controversies sparked by these two cases by looking more closely at US design patent law.

15.006 With a multiplicity of legal regimes come questions of the boundaries demarcating the scope of protection. These boundary questions are necessary in order to avoid possible double recovery by intellectual property plaintiffs and predictability by creators engaged in the design industries. Justice Thomas opened his majority opinion in Star Athletica with a clear statement of problem: 'Congress has provided copyright protection for original works of art, but not for industrial design.'[6] His language echoes the Supreme Court's ruling in *Mazer v. Stein*: 'We do hold that the patentability of the statuettes, fitted as lamps or unfitted, does not bar copyright as works of art. Neither the

---

2   Edison's Chopsticks Case (October 13, 2016, Intellectual Property High Court).
3   TRIPP TRAPP Case (April 14, 2015, Intellectual Property High Court).
4   *Samsung Electronics, Ltd. v. Apple, Inc.*, 137 Sup. Ct. 429 (2016).
5   *Star Athletica, L.L.C. v. Varsity Brands, Inc.*, 137 S. Ct. 1002 (2017).
6   Ibid. at 1007.

Copyright Statute nor any other says that because a thing is patentable it may not be copyrighted.'7

As I elaborate, protection for industrial design lies in design patent and trademark law. To complicate matters, industrial design is ornamental and can serve as a work of art, although one that is integrated with a product, such as decorative cutlery, clothing, or appliances. These complications lead to the problem addressed by the Court in its *Apple v. Samsung* decision: if the industrial design of a product is infringed, are damages measured by the full value of the product or the value of design component?[8] The Court ruled that component was the property measure of damages, saving Samsung from having to compensate Apple for every iPhone whose design was infringed. How this valuation is to occur is a technical matter, but the need for separating value of the design from the value of the product highlights the complexity of design protection in the US.

15.007

Simply stated, generalizing from Japanese and US law on design, the various types of design protection reduce to straightforward propositions. Copyright protects elements of design that can stand alone of the product. Design patent protects elements of design that are integrated, or inseparable, from the product. Trademark law protects design elements of a product that have secondary meaning as a source identifier among consumers. While these three regimes of design law suggest three borders that the law must police, there is an implicit fourth border between ornamental features and functional features, which are not protected by design law. These functional features are protected by utility patents if the features meet the statutory requirements. As the Apple decision indicates, there is even a fifth boundary, that between the design and the product, the latter protected under personal property law. Imagining the visual map of these legal regimes can be dizzying. But it can also pose a challenge, both entertaining and intellectually engaging. I take up that challenge in this Chapter by focusing on the borders among copyright, design patent, trademark, and utility patent.

15.008

In undertaking this challenge, I focus on the problem of overlap as it relates to the underlying policies for design protection. The mistake is focusing on one legal rule, the useful article doctrine in this case, to police multiple boundaries. The argument of this Chapter proceeds along the following roadmap. Section B sets forth different definitions of design for purposes of discussion. Section

15.009

---

7   *Mazer v. Stein*, 347 U.S. 201, 217 (1954).
8   See *Samsung Electronics, Ltd. v. Apple, Inc* (n.4).

C presents some data on overlapping protection of design in Japan and the US. Section D concludes.

B. MEANING OF DESIGN

15.010 The word design, in English, is used colloquially in several ways. One speaks of the design of an automobile engine or the design of a bridge. One also speaks of the design of a suit or the design of a house. Design can mean pattern, as in the colours, shapes, and figures printed on clothing or on wallpaper or in a tapestry. Not all these uses of design correspond to the legal meaning of design. Design protection can mean suitable for design registration. Design protection can mean original aesthetic creations of art suitable for copyright protection. Finally, design can mean how a particular work functions, not just simply how it looks, and therefore the potential subject of a utility patent. For the purposes of legal analysis, specifically under intellectual property law, design can either mean the way a product looks (the suit, the house, the clothing, the wallpaper, the tapestry, in the examples above) or the way a product functions (the engine, the bridge, in the examples above). Which definition one means has implications for the type of intellectual property law that is relevant for protection. The way a product looks leads to protection for industrial or ornamental design; the way a product functions leads to utility patent law.

15.011 The Agreement on Trade Related Aspects of Intellectual Property Law (TRIPS) imposes requirements on member states for enacting appropriate design protection legislation through Article 25 and Article 26, sections on 'Industrial Design'. Article 25 imposes the following 'Requirements for Protection':

1. Members shall provide for the protection of independently created industrial designs that are new or original. Members may provide that designs are not new or original if they do not significantly differ from known designs or combinations of known design features. Members may provide that such protection shall not extend to designs dictated essentially by technical or functional considerations.
2. Each Member shall ensure that requirements for securing protection for textile designs, in particular in regard to any cost, examination or publication, do not unreasonably impair the opportunity to seek and obtain

such protection. Members shall be free to meet this obligation through industrial design law or through copyright law.⁹

15.012 This Article expressly refers to industrial design and textile design. In addition, the Article makes references to limitations based on technical or functional considerations. A member state must protect independently created industrial design that is either new or original, meaning it must significantly differ from known designs or combinations of known designs. By reference to the terms new or original, the language invokes patent and copyright concepts. The requirement of excluding from protection designs that 'do not significantly differ from known designs or combinations of known design' parallels requirements of novelty and inventive step under patent law, where prior art is relevant for determining protection. Industrial design protection is a hybrid of patent and copyright law, borrowing prior art notions from the former and independent creation notions from the latter. Furthermore, technical and functional characteristics are not protected under industrial design protection law, implying a boundary between industrial design protection and utility patent law.

15.013 Textile design is distinct from industrial design. The term refers to patterns or other features of textiles, such as rugs, clothing, or tapestry. Article 25 requires protection that is not burdensome in terms of costs or procedural requirements. This suggests textile design rights should be obtained through a process less burdensome than that for utility patent prosecution. The provision allows member states to meet this requirement through either a *sui generis* industrial design law that addresses textile designs or through copyright law. The reference to copyright law is illustrative of the closeness of textile design protection to protection for artistic expression. Article 9.2 of the TRIPS Agreement states that copyright shall extend to 'expression', broadly stated, and not to ideas, procedures, methods of operation, or mathematical concepts as such.¹⁰ The latter exclusions indicate the copyright protection (and textile designs to the extent they are protected under copyright) shall not extend to functional subject matter. Article 9.1 of TRIPS incorporates some provisions of the Berne Convention, which through its Article 2 protects 'literary and artistic works' under copyright. What Article 25.2 imposes is a requirement for protection of textile designs that parallels the protection under copyright law for artistic creations.

---

9   TRIPS, Article 25.
10 TRIPS, Article 9.2.

15.014 The drafters of the TRIPS Agreement elaborate on the parameters of protection for industrial design in Article 26, which states:

1. The owner of a protected industrial design shall have the right to prevent third parties not having the owner's consent from making, selling or importing articles bearing or embodying a design which is a copy, or substantially a copy, of the protected design, when such acts are undertaken for commercial purposes.
2. Members may provide limited exceptions to the protection of industrial designs, provided that such exceptions do not unreasonably conflict with the normal exploitation of protected industrial designs and do not unreasonably prejudice the legitimate interests of the owner of the protected design, taking account of the legitimate interests of third parties.
3. The duration of protection available shall amount to at least ten years.[11]

15.015 Whatever form industrial design protection takes in a particular country, the legislation should provide protection against making, selling, or importing an article that bears or embodies a design that copies the protected design. The right to exclude pertains to making, selling, or importing for commercial purposes, allowing for non-commercial uses of design. The Article allows member states to include other exceptions that do not conflict with normal exploitation of the design or unreasonably prejudice the legitimate interests of the owner, taking into account third party interest. Furthermore, the duration of protection is ten years, at a minimum. Design registration in Japan provides 25 years of protection[12] while design patent protection in the US extends to 14 years. When copyright protection extends to certain designs (such as textile design),[13] it lasts for life of the author plus 70 years.

15.016 The TRIPS Agreement sets forth the foundational requirements for design protection. Framed in terms of industrial design and textile design, terms that are undefined in the Agreement, the Agreement formulates a design protection regime that borrows from patent law and copyright law with its own minimum duration requirement. Member states can work within these parameters to implement various types of design protections. *Sui generis* provisions are allowed. Design, particularly textile design, can be protected under copyright. Industrial design, in theory, is also possible under copyright law as an original

---

11 TRIPS, Article 26.
12 Japan Design Act, Article 21 Para 1.
13 While textile designs are generally protected, in at least one case the court did not recognize the copyrightability of textile design (Saganishiki Double-layered Obi case, Kyoto District Court decided on June 15, 1989, 1327 Hanrei Jiho 123).

creation although the standard for originality is more analogous to patent's requirement based on prior art rather than copyright's requirement based on individual creative expression. Furthermore, industrial design protection can be implemented under a utility patent system. However, textile design cannot be protected through a patent system because of Article 25.2's requirement for either a copyright or *sui generis* system.

Japan and the US comply with the TRIPS requirement. Japan has a *sui generis* design registration system that would apply to all industrial design, including textile design. Japan also offers copyright protection for designs that are works of fine art. The US, with its panoply of patent, copyright, and trademark, also complies with Articles 25 and 26. The design patent system extends to textile designs and offers a less stringent set of procedural requirements than those for utility patents. Furthermore, copyright extends to textile designs as protection for separable ornamental features of a textile work. This background allows us to now consider the various definitions of regime more closely and connect the different meanings of design to the statutory definitions under both Japanese and US laws.

15.017

1. Industrial Design

Industrial design refers to the appearance of mass-produced and mass-marketed products. These can include electronic goods, appliances, simple consumer goods like pens and pencils, clothing and shoes, or even mass-produced houses. As we have seen, the TRIPS Agreement refers explicitly to industrial design and includes within its purview textile design. Two points are critical to industrial design. First, the design is integrated with the product and does not stand independently of the marketed commodity. The design, in other words, is part of the look and feel of the product and contributes to consumer demand and desire to purchase the product in question. Second, the design does not have an independent aesthetic appeal apart from the product as used by a consumer. While museums might display the product in question, the design is not created for museum display but for commercial distribution and marketing. In this way, industrial design differs from fine arts where the skill, craftsmanship, and artistic judgment serves to create a work that has purely aesthetic appeal. A work of fine art is meant to be displayed; a work of industrial design is meant to be used by consumers and to generate commercial appeal.

15.018

Design registration in Japan applies to works of industrial design. Article 2 of the Design Act protects the shape, patterns or colours, or any combination thereof of an article or a part of an article, of a building (including a part of

15.019

a building), as well as a graphic image (limited to those provided for use in the operation of the device or those displayed as a result of the device performing its function, and including a part of a graphic image)'.[14] The language of the statute limits design to the visual and excludes designs based on scent, touch, or sensory impression other than sight. Article 1 of the Design Act states that the purpose of the statute is to promote industrial development, and this industrial purpose is reflected in the requirements of Article 3 which provides that:

> 'design' shall be produced repetitively on a large scale through industrial production process (either mechanically or hand-crafted) on condition that; (i) it is 'Design' as the object of protection of design rights; (ii) the purpose and the state of use of the article is clear; and (iii) the shape of the item is concretely expressed.[15]

15.020 To meet the goals of industrial development, Article 3 also requires that:

> the design or similar design shall not be publicly known in Japan or a foreign country, prior to the filing of the application for design registration, in other words, the design has novelty; that the design shall not be the one that is found to be easily created by a person ordinary skilled in the artbased on the shape, patterns or colors, or any combination thereof, or graphic images, that were publicly known, described in a distributed publication, or made publicly available through an electric telecommunication line in Japan or a foreign country, even if it has novelty; and that the design is not identical with or similar to part of a design in a prior application.[16]

15.021 The statute provides the following elaboration on novelty:

> Where a design in an application for design registration is identical with or similar to part of a design in prior application and registration, it shall not be registered. Because the design in a later application is not found to be a creation of a new design. However, this shall not apply where the applicant of the said application and the applicant of the earlier application are the same person and the said application was filed before the date when the design bulletin in which the earlier application was published.[17]

15.022 Design registration protects novel shapes, patterns, or colours that are applied to an article that is industrially produced. Excluded from design registration, however, are:

> (i) a design which is liable to injure public order or morality; (ii) a design which is liable to create confusion with an article pertaining to another person's business; or (iii) a design solely consisting of a shape that is indispensable for securing functions of the

---

14   Design Act of Japan, Article 2.
15   Design Act of Japan, Article 3.
16   Ibid.
17   Design Act of Japan, Article 3 bis.

article or for use of the building, or solely consisting of an indication indispensable for use of a graphic image.[18]

15.023 Section C below will provide further discussion, especially of the third exception from design registration.

15.024 By contrast, the US protects industrial design through design patent and trademark law. The procedures for protection are more straightforward than under design registration protection in Japan. Section 171 of the Patent Act states that '[w]hoever invents any new, original and ornamental design for an article of manufacture may obtain a patent therefor, subject to the conditions and requirements of this title'.[19] A US design patent extends to a new, original, and ornamental design for an article of manufacture. Even though the statute refers to 'ornamental design', protection extends to such design for an 'article of manufacture'. Therefore, a design patent does not exist separate from the article that is mass-produced and distributed. Therefore, design patent protection is distinguishable from the ornamental design discussed in the next section which falls under copyright protection for creative works. Furthermore, a design patent is granted based on the criteria for a utility patent; as Section 171 states, a design patent is 'subject to the conditions and requirements of this title', meaning the Patent Act. Therefore, a design must be novel and nonobvious as well as disclosed in order a patent to be granted. Novelty and nonobviousness are based on a consideration of prior art, namely previous designs that are publicly disclosed anywhere in the world. Finally, the design is published for anyone to search and review once the design patent is granted.

15.025 Trademark law also protects product design in the US as trade dress. Trademarks provide protection for:

> any word, name, symbol, or device, or any combination thereof—(1) used by a person, or (2) which a person has a bona fide intention to use in commerce and applies to register on the principal register established by this chapter, to identify and distinguish his or her goods, including a unique product, from those manufactured or sold by others and to indicate the source of the goods, even if that source is unknown.[20]

15.026 The term 'device' covers trade dress, or the look and feel, or design of a product. The Supreme Court has made a distinction between two types of trade dress: 'product packaging' and 'product design'. This language is unfortunately confusing, but product packaging refers to elements of trade dress that help

---

18   Design Act of Japan, Article 5.
19   35 USC § 171.
20   15 USC § 1127.

consumers to identify the source of a product and product design refers to elements of trade dress that are features of the product that serve a function other than source identification. As the Court stated: 'product design almost invariably serves purposes other than source identification not only renders inherent distinctiveness problematic'.[21] Both product packaging and product design are examples of industrial design, as defined in this subsection. For the purposes of trademark law, however, the key difference is that trademark protection for product design requires a showing that consumers actually associate a feature of a product with its source, what is referred to as acquired distinctiveness. Industrial design that is product packaging can be protected as a trademark either upon a showing of acquired distinctiveness or inherent distinctiveness.

15.027 As I discuss below, Japan law offers minimal protection for design under its trademark law. The US provides broader protection for industrial design through either design patent or trademark protection for trade dress. Section C will discuss the relationship between patent and trademark law in greater detail.

2. Ornamental Design

15.028 Ornamental design is aesthetic design of a product that can exist independently of the product as a work of art. An example would be a salt shaker in the shape of an animal. The shape can exist as a sculpture separate from its particular application as a shaker. One can imagine a painting, such as Van Gogh's sunflowers, that is placed as decoration on a T-shirt. Although the image has some industrial application for the sale of the T-shirt, the image can also exist separately on a campus.

15.029 Ornamental design is the subject of copyright law, protectible if independently created and original. If the design cannot be separated from the product, it is a case of industrial design. Consider the example of an automobile. The body of a car has aesthetic features that are associated with the car. Such design features are examples of industrial design. The hood ornament of the car—such as the jaguar figure on the Jaguar car—can exist separately as a sculpture. The jaguar figure is an example of ornamental design.

15.030 Both Japan and US law covers ornamental design through copyright law. We will discuss some aspects of the law in this subsection and in more detail in Section C. A key difference between design copyright in Japan and the US is

---

21 *Wal-Mart Stores, Inc. v. Samara Bros.*, 529 U.S. 205, 213 (2000).

the distinction between fine art and applied art. Japanese law grants copyright protection to ornamental design if the design is fine art. If the design is applied art, then design registration would be appropriate. However, US design copyright law does not recognize the distinction between fine and applied art. In the US, as I discuss in more detail below, design copyright rests on the doctrine of separability. As US copyright law has evolved on the issues of design since 1954, I will discuss US law first before presenting the details of Japanese copyright law and design, which is of more recent vintage.

Contemporary design copyright law in the US originates with the Supreme Court's 1954 decision, *Mazer v. Stein*. At issue in the case was the legality of copyright registration for a lamp that had a statue of a dancer as a base. The registration was challenged on the grounds that copyright did not extend to useful articles like a lamp. The Court ruled that copyright was appropriate: **15.031**

> It is clear Congress intended the scope of the copyright statute to include more than the traditional fine arts. Herbert Putnam, Esq., then Librarian of Congress and active in the movement to amend the copyright laws, told the joint meeting of the House and Senate Committees:
>
>> The term 'works of art' is deliberately intended as a broader specification than 'works of the fine arts' in the present statute with the idea that there is subject-matter (for instance, of applied design, not yet within the province of design patents), which may properly be entitled to protection under the copyright law.
>
> The successive acts, the legislative history of the 1909 Act and the practice of the Copyright Office unite to show that 'works of art' and 'reproductions of works of art' are terms that were intended by Congress to include the authority to copyright these statuettes. Individual perception of the beautiful is too varied a power to permit a narrow or rigid concept of art.[22]

In recognizing copyright protection for aesthetic features of useful articles, the US Supreme Court erased the distinction between fine and applied arts. Copyright protection could extend to works of art broadly, regardless of whether they were works of craftsman, fine artists, or industrial designer. **15.032**

Congress enacted the holding of *Mazer v. Stein* in the Copyright Act of 1976 through the definition of 'pictorial, graphic, sculptural works.' For copyright purposes, design is a picture, a drawing, or a sculpture. The definition of 'pictorial, graphic, sculptural work' is as follows: **15.033**

---

22 *Mazer v. Stein*, 347 U.S. 201, 213–14, 74 S. Ct. 460, 468 (1954).

'Pictorial, graphic, and sculptural works' include two-dimensional and three-dimensional works of fine, graphic, and applied art, photographs, prints and art reproductions, maps, globes, charts, diagrams, models, and technical drawings, including architectural plans. Such works shall include works of artistic craftsmanship insofar as their form but not their mechanical or utilitarian aspects are concerned; *the design of a useful article, as defined in this section, shall be considered a pictorial, graphic, or sculptural work only if, and only to the extent that, such design incorporates pictorial, graphic, or sculptural features that can be identified separately from, and are capable of existing independently of, the utilitarian aspects of the article.* [emphasis added][23]

15.034 In turn, a useful article is defined as: 'an article having an intrinsic utilitarian function that is not merely to portray the appearance of the article or to convey information. An article that is normally a part of a useful article is considered a "useful article"'.[24]

15.035 In assessing copyright protection for design under US law, the judge must first identify the useful article (whether a lamp, a clock, or a shirt) and then identify pictorial, graphic, or sculptural features of the work. If these features can be identified separately from the useful article, then they are eligible for copyright protection. Section C below provides further examples and analysis.

15.036 Japanese copyright law also provides protection for design. Professor Kimiaki Suzuki of the Tokyo University of Science, Graduate School of Innovation Studies, reports the following.[25] Recently in Japan, increasing attention has been focused on intellectual property in the fashion business. The book on this topic written by Masayoshi Sumida and Masaya Seki, *Fashion Law* (2017), discusses the case cited as a case representing the current situation in the US (Chapter 8, etc.).

15.037 In Japan, the drafters, courts, and scholars discuss the aesthetic level of elements of a design as an issue of whether 'the design can be the object of aesthetic appreciation as a complete work of art separately from the aspect of utility' only for the purpose of determining whether the design of a useful article (applied art) is a work under the Copyright Act. The separability test is not applied to the design after it is determined to be not copyrightable.

15.038 The Copyright System Council proposed as follows to solve the difficulty in taking measures to adjust the Copyright Act and the Design Act:

---

23 17 USC § 101.
24 Ibid.
25 Written responses to questions by author from Professor Kimiaki Suzuki, November 24, 2017 (on file with the author).

Designs to be used as design drawings, shapes of mass-produced products or patterns of useful articles should basically be protected under the Design Act and other industrial property right regimes, without providing for any special measures under the Copyright Act; however, they should be treated as artistic works if they have the nature of pure art.

In the drafting process, the term 'work of artistic craftsmanship' under Article 2(2) of the Copyright Act was understood as referring to artistic crafts made as one-of-a-kind items. However, the provision actually enacted reads 'As used in this Act, an "artistic work" includes a work of artistic craftsmanship,' which does not clearly state whether objects of applied art other than works of artistic craftsmanship are included in the scope of artistic work. **15.039**

Basically, applied art must be protected by a design right. In order to be eligible for protection as a copyrightable work, applied art must involve aesthetic creativity at a level where it can equate fine art. Applied art that deserves protection is limited to works of artistic craftsmanship which are specially mentioned as being included in the scope of artistic work. **15.040**

Section C below presents further discussion of both the separability doctrine in the US and the demarcation between works of applied and fine art in Japan as well as a comparison of the two jurisdictions. **15.041**

3. Functional Design

Functional design covers features of a product that affect how the product works or functions. Examples would include the pedals on a bicycle, the engine in an automobile, the screen on a smartphone or computer, or the buttons on a shirt. Such design features are covered by utility patent law (or protection for utility models in Japan). Utility patent law protects new and innovative inventions that have a practical utility in solving an industrial problem. The details of utility patent law are beyond the scope of this Chapter. What is relevant is that, in general, functional design is not protected by design law. As I discuss below, functional features are not protected under design registration, design patent, copyright, or trademark law. Section C discusses what doctrines courts have developed to channel functional design to utility patent law and exclude it from design law protection. **15.042**

C. CRITICAL CONCERNS OF OVERLAPPING REGIMES

1. Design Patent in US with Some Comparison with Japanese Design Registration

15.043 As discussed in Section A, the US Supreme Court has addressed an important issue of calculating damages for infringement of a design patent. In *Samsung v. Apple*, damages for infringement for design of the face of a smartphone were calculated on the value of the entire smartphone as opposed to the value of the face protected by a design patent. The Federal Circuit, the intermediate appellate court, adopted this approach to calculating damages based on the statutory language allowing recovery for profits from the 'article of manufacture,' the product to which the design was applied. The Supreme Court confronted the issue of what constitutes an article of manufacture as follows:

> Arriving at a damages award under § 289 thus involves two steps. First, identify the 'article of manufacture' to which the infringed design has been applied. Second, calculate the infringer's total profit made on that article of manufacture.
>
> This case requires us to address a threshold matter: the scope of the term 'article of manufacture.' The only question we resolve today is whether, in the case of a multicomponent product, the relevant 'article of manufacture' must always be the end product sold to the consumer or whether it can also be a component of that product. Under the former interpretation, a patent holder will always be entitled to the infringer's total profit from the end product. Under the latter interpretation, a patent holder will sometimes be entitled to the infringer's total profit from a component of the end product. ...
>
> So understood, the term 'article of manufacture' is broad enough to encompass both a product sold to a consumer as well as a component of that product. A component of a product, no less than the product itself, is a thing made by hand or machine. That a component may be integrated into a larger product, in other words, does not put it outside the category of articles of manufacture. ...
>
> The Federal Circuit's narrower reading of 'article of manufacture' cannot be squared with the text of § 289. The Federal Circuit found that components of the infringing smartphones could not be the relevant article of manufacture because consumers could not purchase those components separately from the smartphones. See [lower court opinion] (declining to limit a § 289 award to a component of the smartphone because '[t]he innards of Samsung's smartphones were not sold separately from their shells as distinct articles of manufacture to ordinary purchasers'); see also *Nordock, Inc. v. Systems Inc.*, 803 F.3d 1344, 1355 (C.A.Fed.2015) (declining to limit a § 289 award to a design for a ' 'lip and hinge plate' ' because it was 'welded together' with a leveler and 'there was no evidence' it was sold 'separate[ly] from the leveler as a complete unit'). But, for the reasons given above, the term 'article of manufacture' is broad enough to embrace both a product sold to a consumer and a component of that product, whether sold separately or not. Thus, reading 'article of manufacture' in § 289 to cover only an end product sold to a consumer gives too narrow a meaning to the phrase. ...

Although the Supreme Court held that an article of manufacture could be a smaller component of a larger product, the Court left open the question of how to define the relevant article of manufacture, returning the issue to the lower court for further clarification. **15.044**

In October, 2017, the Northern District of California, which had original jurisdiction over the dispute, provided a four factor test with which to identify the relevant article of manufacture. The lower court adopted the following four factors from the US' brief: **15.045**

- '[T]he scope of the design claimed in the plaintiff's patent, including the drawing and written description';
- '[T]he relative prominence of the design within the product as a whole';
- '[W]hether the design is conceptually distinct from the product as a whole'; and
- '[T]he physical relationship between the patented design and the rest of the product,' including whether 'the design pertains to a component that a user or seller can physically separate from the product as a whole,' and whether 'the design is embodied in a component that is manufactured separately from the rest of the product, or if the component can be sold separately.'

As the US explained the first factor, 'the scope of the design claimed in the plaintiff's patent ... provides insight into which portions of the underlying product the design is intended to cover, and how the design relates to the product as a whole.' [internal citation omitted] Furthermore, the remaining factors should help a factfinder assess competing contentions where one party argues that the relevant article of manufacture is the entire product as sold and the other party argues that the relevant article of manufacture is some lesser part of the product. Each factor helps the factfinder think through whether the patented design has been applied to the product as a whole or merely a part of the product. **15.046**

Under Japanese design law, by contrast, the question of apportioning damages for the infringement of design which is a component of a larger product is based on the contribution ratio. The court must determine how the design contributes to the total value of the product, based on the market demand, the price of the product, and the manufacturing cost. Japanese law also permits protection of only a component of a product through the notion of a partial design through which the applicant can designate a specific portion of a product as subject to design protection. **15.047**

15.048 A comparison of registration of design in Japan and the US illustrates to what extent there is overlap across different intellectual property regimes for design. First, Table 15.1 below presents aggregate data on design patent and utility patent allowance rates. The figures for Japan are based on 2016 data and for US, on 2017 data. While the utility patent application rates are closely similar in Japan and the US, the allowance rate for design registration in Japan is higher than the allowance rate for design patent applications in the US. There are disparities between the success of domestic national and foreign nationals in grant rates between the two countries. While the grant rates between domestic and foreign applicants are close to parity in the US, there is disparity in Japan. This difference reflects the attractiveness of the respective markets for commercializing designs and utility patents in the two countries. Table 15.2 below sets forth the top five recipients of design registrations in Japan and design patents in the US in 2016. In the US, the top five are electronics or software companies with one shoe company in the list. In Japan, the top five consist of three electronics companies and two furniture companies. The data on recipients of grants will be analysed in more detail in the next section where information on overlapping protection across copyright and patent in the US is analysed.

Table 15.1   Breakdown of patent and design applications and grants in 2017

	JAPAN	USA
Design application allowance rate	82%	66% (based on 2017)
Patent application allowance rate	55%	51%
National origin/Foreign Grants Design Patents	83/17	55/45
National/Foreign Utility patent grants	79/21	48/52

Source: Shubha Ghosh, Design Protection Law & Policy: A Comparative Perspective Japan and US, Institute for Intellectual Property Working Paper (June 2018).

Table 15.2   Top recipients of design patents, 2017

	JAPAN	USA
538/1428	Panasonic Corp	Samsung Electronics
445/455	Mitsubishi Electric Corp	LG Electronics
368/318	Okamura Corp	Microsoft
289/171	LIXIL Corp	Nike Inc
281/49	Sharp Corp	Sony Corp

Source: Shubha Ghosh, Design Protection Law & Policy: A Comparative Perspective Japan and US, Institute for Intellectual Property Working Paper (June 2018).

2. The Problem of Overlap

One concern is whether companies seeking design protection obtain multiple protection under copyright and patent. Alternatively, companies may pick and choose among the various regimes. One way to examine this prediction is to study design patent grants and copyright registrations by companies in the US.

15.049

I conducted this study by identifying design patent grants and copyright registrations in the US for two product sectors: furniture and jewellery (see Tables 15.3 and 15.4 below). I found that the top five design patent owners and copyright registrants did not overlap. Looking deeper I found no companies that had both design patents and copyright registrations. This finding would support the thesis that companies choose among the regimes. However, one caveat is that registration is not a requirement for copyright protection. Therefore, many of the designs protected under patent law may already be protected under copyright. Nonetheless, the fact that companies with design patents do not seem to be filing copyright registrations suggests that firms do engage to some extent in the selection of regimes. Even if copyright protection does not require registration, one wonders why companies register their copyright. Firms engaging in intellectual property management do not seem to be pursuing design patents and copyright registrations. Furthermore, firms seeking copyright registrations do not seek design patents. My suspicion is that a similar pattern is true for Japan.[26] Finally, I will look to see more closely the pattern of utility patent grants for companies that already have design patents. A preliminary inquiry found little overlap.

15.050

One might expect that companies seeking design protection might choose the legal regime that is the most protective, however measured. But such a choice does not seem to be occurring. Design patents and copyright registrations are being used. An individual company, however, seems to be choosing between the two perhaps based on a range of choices including the level of protection, costs, and market conditions. Looking at that economic decision requires some deeper consideration of internal firm management as to intellectual property strategy. Several hypotheses are worth considering in future research. First, counsel might be making decisions based on their familiarity and experience with legal regimes. Patent lawyers gravitate towards design patent; copyright attorneys, towards copyright. Identifying counsel involved in obtaining the patents and registrations may help to test this hypothesis.

15.051

---

26 Although, in Japan, the configuration of goods can be protected by the Unfair Competition Prevention Act for three years from the date of first sale in Japan without design registration.

Second, decision-making about design patent may be based on fixed categories of industrial design and ornamental design. Decision-makers within the firm may have a predetermined idea about the design their firm creates, filtering design into categories of industrial and creative works. These prior categories map on to patent and copyright. It would be useful to examine and test this psychological explanation, which may also have a cultural dimension.

Table 15.3   Overlapping design protection in furniture

FURNITURE/Top 5 1975–2017 USA	Design Patent Owners	Design Patent Inventors	Copyright owners
960 granted design patents	American Signature (44)	David Thompson (37)	Ganz (248)
	Baronet (37)	Alan Juneau (21)	Banker & Brisebois (105)
100 copyright registrations	Sugatsune (32)	Sidney Lenger (16)	Ken Su (40)
	Steelcase Dev (27)	Slear (16)	Atico Intl (19)
	Krueger Intl (22)	Du Blois/Paus (13)	John-Richard (18)

Source: Shubha Ghosh, Design Protection Law & Policy: A Comparative Perspective Japan and US, Institute for Intellectual Property Working Paper (June 2018).

Table 15.4   Overlapping design protection in jewellery

Jewellery/Top 5 1973–2017 USA	Design Patent Owners	Design Patent Inventors
862 granted design patents	National Pak Limited (11)	David Rozenwasser (15)
	SILO (10)	Steven Wolf (14)
461 no assignment	Sandberg & Sikorski (10)	Ka Fa Hinsen Au (13)
	Continental Jewelry (9)	Chia Team (10); James Mohundro (10)
		Vicky Chan (9); Danny Lai (9)
	Nakagawa Corp (9) Rozenwasser (9)	

Source: Shubha Ghosh, Design Protection Law & Policy: A Comparative Perspective Japan and US, Institute for Intellectual Property Working Paper (June 2018).

D. CONCLUSION

15.052 The word design is used in many ways. This overlapping meaning corresponds to overlapping rights across intellectual property regimes. Some evidence suggests that in practice companies may select which intellectual property regime to use. More empirical work is needed, and is in progress, on understanding design intellectual property practice by industry and type of work. This Chapter, however, presents preliminary work and the conceptual problems in demarcating the potentially confounding overlap in intellectual property protection for design.

16

PRIOR ART IN EU DESIGN LAW AND ITS WORLDWIDE IMPLICATIONS – TAKING ADVANTAGE OF FLEXIBILITIES OR BEING OBSTRUCTED BY AMBIGUITIES

Lavinia Brancusi[1]

A. INTRODUCTION 16.001	(a) EU concepts of 'design' and 'product' 16.044
B. DEFINING PRIOR ART IN THE EU DESIGN LAW 16.005	(b) Earlier disclosure and IPRs 16.048
1. Setting the Scene 16.006	2. Comparing a Contested Design with an Earlier Disclosure 16.051
(a) EU prior art matching the model of relative novelty 16.007	(a) The significance of the representation of 'design features' vis-à-vis wording 16.052
(b) Presumptive knowledge of disclosure established by administrative or judicial body 16.011	(b) Relevant subject-matter for the comparison of two designs when testing novelty or individual character 16.057
2. What Constitutes Disclosure, What Does Not? 16.015	(c) Subject-matter of self-disclosure and grace period 16.062
(a) Rules of disclosure 16.017	D. THE INTERSECTION BETWEEN EU PRIOR ART AND FOREIGN STANDARDS – REMARKS FROM GLOBAL PERSPECTIVE 16.065
(b) The safeguard clause – the general exception 16.023	
(c) First disclosure of an unregistered Community design 16.028	1. Divergent Standards of Prior Art – Absolute Novelty and Different Models of Grace Period 16.067
3. Additional Normative Exceptions 16.032	
(a) Confidential disclosure 16.033	
(b) Disclosure within 'grace period' 16.034	2. Divergent Notions of a Protectable Design 16.073
(c) Abusive disclosure 16.039	
C. ISSUES OF THE SUBJECT-MATTER DISCLOSED UNDER THE EU DESIGN LAW 16.042	3. Concluding Remarks 16.080
1. The Subject-matter of a Relevant Piece of Prior Art 16.043	

---

1 Special thanks are addressed to Professor Dana Beldiman for the invitation to contribute and editorial help.

A. INTRODUCTION

16.001 This chapter explores the definition and use of prior art in the EU design law with the aim of emphasizing the specifics that connect and intersect similar issues in non-EU law. It discusses the rules and exceptions that set the boundaries of relevant disclosures in the EU design law and the relationship between the scope of EU and non-EU prior art. It focuses on divergences between EU and non-EU design law regarding the model of examination, the subject-matter of a design, the novelty standard, the definition of disclosure and the exception of grace period. In quest for global harmonized standards, many interpretative issues of the EU prior art discussed by this chapter should be further clarified by the EU judiciary, so as to encourage their possible transposition to other non-EU laws.

16.002 Design protection is an area of law with significant local particularities. International conventions cover substantive rules in a limited way,[2] dealing mostly with formalities to facilitate registration worldwide.[3] In the European Union (EU), design law has been subject to a two-level harmonization. First, EU Member States implemented a set of unified standards of substantive law provided by the Directive 98/71/EC(DD).[4] The effect is that national design rights of the EU Member States share many aspects. In the second move, Regulation (EC) No 6/2002[5] (RCD) created EU-effective uniform design rights[6], that is Community Registered Designs (CRD)[7] and Unregistered

---

2   Agreement on Trade-Related Aspects of Intellectual Property Rights (hereinafter TRIPS), as amended on 23 January 2017 - https://www.wto.org/english/docs_e/legal_e/31bis_trips_01_e.htm (last visited 7 June 2024).
3   Paris Convention for the Protection of Industrial Property of 1883, currently governed by the World Intellectual Property Organization (WIPO), counts the highest number of signatories https://www.wipo.int/treaties/en/ip/paris/ (last visited 7 June 2024). In the case of designs this act introduces a six-month right of priority which allows an applicant to submit a subsequent filing in another country as if it has been filed on the same day as the first application. Hague Agreement concerning the International Registration of Industrial Design (1925) is a formalities treaty also governed by WIPO https://www.wipo.int/treaties/en/registration/hague/ (last visited 7 June 2024). This act allows multiple registrations in designated countries upon one international filing submitted in front of the WIPO, which deals with formal examination. Substantive control is conducted by each country individually.
4   Council Directive 98/71/EC of 13 October 1998 on the legal protection of designs, OJ L 289, 28.10.1998, p. 28–35.
5   Council Regulation (EC) No 6/2002 of 12 December 2001 on Community designs, OJ L 3, 5.1.2002, p. 1–24. For a consolidated version see https://euipo.europa.eu/ohimportal/en/community-design-legal-texts (last visited 7 June 2024).
6   For ease of reading, the terms 'EU designs' and 'EU design law' have been used below to encompass both national designs of EU Member States and Community registered and unregistered designs, unless there has been the need to individually address a given category of designs.
7   They are filed at the European Union Intellectual Property Office (EUIPO) – previously Office for Harmonization in the Internal Market (OHIM) – situated in Alicante, Spain.

Community Designs (UCD).⁸ Currently, the EU design law is being revised; on November 28, 2022, the Commission adopted two proposals for an amended Directive (see COM (2022) 667 final, **'Proposed Directive'**)⁹ and amended Regulation (see COM (2022) 666 final, **'Proposed Regulation'**).¹⁰ These acts were passed to the European Parliament and the Council to be adopted in the near future.

Although EU design protection appears to be an autonomous and self-sufficient regime, however in matters of substantive law it may interact with foreign design systems. The scope of prior art represents the tangency point. A standard requirement of any design law is that the design must be new.¹¹ Novelty is measured against that which had been previously known, or, to put it in legal terms, that which had been made publicly available. These disclosures constitute the state of 'prior art'. If the comparison of a design with an earlier item does not satisfy the conditions of protection, such as novelty or individual character under the EU design law – the validity of the tested design is compromised. The design faces either refusal of registration, where applications are subject to substantive examination, or a possible invalidity claim, submitted in an ex-post examination.¹² Furthermore, in addition to the lack of uniformity relating to substantive law, design law across globe also varies in determining the state of art. 16.003

This chapter explores the definition and use of prior art in the EU design law with the aim of emphasizing the specifics that connect and intersect similar issues in non-EU law. Following an introduction in Part A, Part B addresses the EU legal framework of prior art, including the main rules and exceptions that set the boundaries of relevant disclosures. In Part C, for purposes of comparing a design with a prior art, the key-concepts of 'design' and 'product' are analysed under the EU law. Part D adopts an overall approach and discusses the interaction between the EU and non-EU prior art (parts D.1 and D.2). 16.004

---

8   A three-year protection is conferred – without registration – upon the first making publicly available, and subject to general conditions of protection (see art. 11 RCD).
9   https://eur-lex.europa.eu/legal-content/EN/TXT/?uri=CELEX:52022PC0667 (last visited 7 June 2024).
10 https://eur-lex.europa.eu/legal-content/EN/TXT/?uri=CELEX:52022PC0666 (last visited 7 June 2024).
11 TRIPS introduced mandatory protection of industrial designs that are 'independently created', giving signatories the choice between two requirements of protection: novelty or originality, or both. See Nuno Pires de Carvalho, *The TRIPS Regime of Trademarks and Designs* (4th ed., Wolters Kluwer 2019) 427–29.
12 For concise overview, Annette Kur, 'The Design Approach and the Procedural Practice – Mismatch or Smooth Transition' in Annette Kur, Marianne Levin, Jens Schovsbo (eds), *The EU Design Approach. A Global Appraisal* (Elgar 2018) 17; Annette Kur, 'From Law in Books to Enforcement in Court: Jurisdiction, Applicable Law and Sanctions', in ibid 194–95; Catherine Seville, *EU Intellectual Property Law and Policy* (2nd ed, Elgar 2016) 225.

Finally, Part D.3, articulates the differences between various design systems to channel the efforts aimed at greater global coherence.

B. DEFINING PRIOR ART IN THE EU DESIGN LAW

16.005 The present section starts by outlining the historical background of the model of relative novelty adopted by the EU design law that determines the identification of prior art (part B.1). Next, its main part tackles the intricacies of relevant disclosure (part B.2). Finally, the normative exceptions to disclosure are explored, with emphasis on the lack of guidance pertaining to certain unharmonized concepts of the EU design law (part B.3).

1. Setting the Scene

16.006 The EU design regime was meant to be a brand new, *sui generis* system of protection, adapted to meet the modern design-market needs. It drew from efficient legislations of certain Member States and avoided the extremes of patent or copyright model of protection.[13] The issue of how prior art is defined has an impact on the assessment of novelty and individual character, which constitute the basic conditions of a EU design.[14] The present part looks at the rationale of allowing certain relativism in the assessment of prior art in the EU design law, whilst giving an overview of the problems resulting therefrom.

(a) EU prior art matching the model of relative novelty

16.007 Both the Directive under Art. 6(1) and Regulation under Art. 7(1) define prior art as comprising any 'design' made publicly available before the relevant priority date, through publishing, following registration or otherwise, exhibitions, use in trade, or any other kind of disclosure. Although this general definition prima facie matches the absolute worldwide novelty model, typical for patent protection, the European legislator sought standards better suited for design activities.[15] Absolute novelty would have meant that any disclosure anywhere

---

13 Annette Kur, 'The Green Paper's Design Approach. What's wrong with it?' (1993) 10 EIPR 374.
14 See Art. 3 DD or Art. 4 RCD. For concise presentation William Cornish, David Llewelyn, Tanya Aplin, *Intellectual Property* (8th ed., Sweet & Maxwell 2013) 598–600.
15 Annette Kur, Marianne Levin, 'The Design Approach revisited: background and meaning', in Kur, Levin, Schovsbo (n 11) 14; Annette Kur, 'The Max-Planck Draft for EU Design Law', in *The Green Paper on Legal Protection of Industrial Design* (E. Story-Scientia 1993) 17. As emphasized by Professor Kur, designs usually do not bring real innovation, but enrichment of design corpus i.e., products' appearance.

in the world, even of limited scope, such as one single copy of a document lodged at a library, would have destroyed novelty.[16]

Instead, the Official Commentary to the Proposal of Directive emphasized the aim to protect the design industry from the risk of invalidating a design right based on prior art 'found in remote places or museums', 'somewhere in the world where the European industry could not possibly have been aware of it.[17] A so-called 'safeguard clause' was, therefore, introduced to Art. 6(1) DD and Art. 7(1) RCD to exclude from the state of prior art disclosures which 'could not reasonably have become known in the normal course of business to the circles specialised in the sector concerned, operating within the Community'. This kind of exception was previously known under German and Benelux law as the means of softening the effects of applying the requirement of objective novelty.[18] Objective novelty was tested against earlier disclosed items regardless of whether the designer knew of them, whereas subjective novelty referred to a standard defined by the individual knowledge of the creator of the design. German practice understood disclosure in the context of events known to interested business circles ('im Verkehr') which could have taken place in Germany or a country of a similar level of civilisation.[19] Benelux law also limited relevant disclosure to the knowledge of national industrial or commercial interested circles, with an additional time-limitation of prior art going back up to 50 years before the priority date.[20] Because of these similarities, the EU disclosure model implemented a 'relative' standard, which applies to both novelty and individual character.[21]

16.008

In addition to the safeguard clause, the state of prior art does not include a situation in which a design is disclosed under explicit or implicit confidentiality (Art. 6(1) DD and Art. 7(1) RCD in fine). Additional normative exceptions

16.009

---

16   Derk Visser, Laurence Lai, Peter de Lange, Kaisa Suominen, *Visser's Annotated European Patent Convention* (Wolters Kluwer 2021) 88–89.
17   Official Commentary of Proposal of Directive (Art. 6) in Mario Franzosi (ed.) *European Design Protection, Commentary to the Directive and Regulation Proposals* (Hague-London-Boston 1995) 79.
18   Green Paper explicitly referred to German and Benelux solutions, consult Green Paper on the Legal protection of Industrial Design, Commission of the European Communities, Brussels June 1991, III/F/5131/91-EN cf. http://aei.pitt.edu/1785/1/design_gp_1.pdf (last visited 6 October 2023), para 2.3.7 p. 18.
19   Marie-Angèle Perot-Morel, '*Les Principes de Protection des Dessins et Modèles dans les Pays du Marché Commun*' (Mouton 1968) 238-39 with reference to pre-1960 jurisprudence. The seminal *Rüschenhaube* case concerned a frilled bonnet which was previously advertised in the US and deemed to have come to the attention of German interested business circles, BGH of 8 May 1968, I ZR 67/65, GRUR 1969, 90–91.
20   Jaap Spoor, 'The Novelty Requirement in Design Protection Law: Benelux Experience' (1996) 24 *AIPLA Quarterly Journal* 725, 733; Perot-Morel, ibid. 257–59.
21   Charles-Henry Massa, Alain Strowel, 'Community Design: Cinderella Revamped' (2003) 2 EIPR 68, 73; Herman Speyart, 'The Grand Design' (1997) 10 EIPR 603, 607.

address disclosure that belongs to the 'grace period' and abusive disclosure (Art. 6(2) and (3) DD and Art. 7(2) and (3) RCD, correspondingly). These situations are closely examined in B.3 below.

16.010 Additional discrepancies over the definition of prior art may exist across national design laws of EU Member States. They stem from slightly different implementations of the Design Directive. A design study commissioned by the European Commission noted that the concept of disclosure is generally uniform within EU laws, yet displays small variations in respect to the geographical scope.[22] For instance, Polish law formulates the safeguard clause without any limitation to operating within the Community.[23] To note, elaboration of prior art provisions under individual EU national laws is beyond the scope of this work.

(b) Presumptive knowledge of disclosure established by administrative or judicial body

16.011 Disclosure constitutes a preliminary step of any invalidity proceedings because it defines the state of prior art which comprises earlier designs to be compared with the contested one. Any proof of prior designs must comply with the standard of disclosure set out in Art. 6 DD and Art. 7 RCD. The applicant for a declaration of invalidity bears the burden of proof to establish the compliance with disclosure,[24] irrespective whether the invalidity is subject to administrative or judicial proceedings.[25] The design right holder, then, has the obligation to challenge such evidence. One of the general defences taken is the exception of disclosure being done in the grace period.

16.012 The EUIPO Guidelines clearly provide that if an earlier design does not meet the requirement of relevant disclosure, the absence of novelty and individual character cannot be established, and the declaration of invalidity fails upon

---

22 Uma Suthersanen et al., 'Legal Review on the Industrial Design Protection in Europe' (MARKT 2014/083/D), Final Report 15 April 2016, 78–79.
23 Art. 103(2) of Polish Industrial Property Law of June 30, 2000 'Prawo własności przemysłowej' (consolidated version Dz.U. 2023 item 1170) reads: 'Wzoru nie uważa się za udostępniony publicznie, w rozumieniu ust. 1, jeżeli nie mógł dotrzeć do wiadomości osób zajmujących się zawodowo dziedziną, której wzór dotyczy'. Such a missing may be held an improper implementation of the Directive, subject to future amendments.
24 Lionel Bently, Bred Sherman, Dev Gangjee and Philip Johnson, *Intellectual Property Law* (5th ed., OUP 2018) 766.
25 A Community design right can be invalidated either in front of the EUIPO (under Art. 52 RCD), or in front of a Community design court, usually by means of a counterclaim filed during proceedings for infringement (under Arts 85–86 RCD). National design rights are invalidated according to national rules of proceedings, be they administrative or judicial, which are not harmonized by the DD.

these causes.²⁶ This is because the comparison between the contested design and the alleged earlier design cannot be performed. If there are multiple proofs of prior designs, the right holder has to refute the presumption of disclosure in relation to each of them.

Interpreting the notion of being made publicly available is essentially based on presumptive knowledge. This is in fact legal fiction. When reading the definition of making publicly available together with the safeguard clause, the assessment does not rely on actual disclosure, but on the assumption that a given event could have reasonably come to the attention of the public concerned.²⁷ The test is held to be objective – however, that which what represents, or not, relevant disclosure, remains a question of fact.²⁸ The legal evaluation of these facts belongs to the autonomous competence of administrative body or judicial court. **16.013**

Assessing the evidence goes together with interpreting a set of normative concepts that define disclosure and its exceptions. As to the latter, because the safeguard clause contains multiple ambivalent, or even ambiguous terms, the outcome may lack legal certainty. There are various ways of understanding the degree of required knowledge captured by the word 'reasonably'. That which belongs, or not, to the 'normal course of business' may also be disputed. It is equally important to define the composition of the 'specialized circles' in correlation with the 'sector concerned'. Doubts concerning the type of a product in relation to which the 'sector' and 'specialists' should be defined remain valid up to this day. Finally, the query about any geographical limitation to the state of prior art requires clarification of the meaning of 'operating within Community'. It may be stated that these aspects of interpretation belong to the realm of 'points of law', that is, legal assessment which may be subject to review by the highest court of law.²⁹ Differently, assessing the value of the evidence presented – for instance, whether exhibiting an item at a fair could **16.014**

---

26   EUIPO Guidelines for Examination of design invalidity application, hereinafter Invalidity Guidelines, https://guidelines.euipo.europa.eu/1937338/1786993/designs-guidelines/examination-of-design-invalidity-applications (last visited 7 June 2024), para 5.7.1.1.
27   David Musker, 'Commentary to Art. 7 CDR' in Charles Gielen, Verena von Bomhard (eds.), *Concise European Trade Mark and Design Law* (2nd ed., Wolters Kluwer 2016) 645.
28   David Stone, *European Union Design Law* (2nd ed., OUP 2016) 163, 177.
29   As to proceeding before EUIPO, this role is performed by the Court of Justice of the European Union (CJEU), cf. Art. 267 of the Consolidated version of the Treaty on the Functioning of the European Union [2012] OJ C 326/ 47. In the case of EU national registrations, the highest instance may be an administrative court (if invalidity is handled by a corresponding patent office), or the supreme (civil) court (if invalidity is handled by regular or specialized courts). The CJEU's ruling in C-281/10 P *PepsiCo v. Grupo Promer*, EU:C:2011:679 was the first judgement to discuss the admissible grounds of appeal concerning legal *versus* factual findings, there in the context of the normative definitions of 'informed user' and 'designer freedom'.

have reasonably come to the knowledge of the pre-defined circle of specialists of the pre-defined product sector – remains within the competence of the administrative body or court of the *meritum* and cannot be easily appealed. For example, an appeal is admissible in case of distortion of evidence.[30]

2. What Constitutes Disclosure, What Does Not?

16.015 The EU disclosure standards do not contain clear-cut notions and guidance. On the contrary, there are multiple difficulties, some of legal interpretation and some resulting from the discretion of authorities. This section examines these issues more closely.

16.016 Worldwide disclosure is the principle set forth by the EU law and refers to 'any design made publicly available' before the priority date. However, as intended by the Green Paper,[31] obscure disclosures should not affect the validity of EU designs. For this reason, the safeguard clause contains the conditions under which a piece of prior art can be removed from the scope of 'relevant' prior art. Distinct rules concern the geographical scope of disclosure of an unregistered Community design. Each of these aspects is discussed below.

(a) Rules of disclosure

16.017 Timing represents the most important feature of disclosure. For disclosure to be included within the scope of prior art, the date must be prior to filing of an application for registration of the contested design, or to the date of priority, if such is claimed.[32] A six-month priority right may result either from an earlier application for a design right or utility model according to Paris Convention,[33] or from the date of disclosing a product at an officially recognized international exhibition.[34]

16.018 EUIPO Guidelines indicate that the date of making publicly available is dispositive, rather than the date of actual knowledge of the specialized circles.[35] This matches the legal fiction set by the standard of what 'could have reason-

---

30 General Court (previously Court of the First Instance) represents the last instance to assess factual findings, in an appeal from a decision of the Board of Appeal of EUIPO (hereinafter BoA). For another design case discussing the scope of GC's exclusive jurisdiction vis-à-vis facts, see C-101/11 P and C-102/11 P *Neumann, Galdeano del Sel v. Baena Grupo*, EU:C:2012:641.
31 See (n 18).
32 The effect of the priority right is that the date of priority counts as the date of filing for a registered Community design, for the purposes of prior art as well as for novelty and individual character (see Art. 43 RCD).
33 Art. 41(1) RCD.
34 Art. 44(1) RCD.
35 Guidelines (n 25) para 5.7.1.2.

ably become known'. Even if a disclosure took place at a certain point in time before the filing or the priority date, the fact may be assumed by corroborating several documents (facts), although the exact date of disclosure cannot be established.[36]

16.019 EU design law contains no time-limitation for discarding disclosures going back too far. The significance of a piece of prior art depends on whether it is deemed to have been known to the specialist circles of that particular field. The patterns of Greek antique pottery used for modern crockery may constitute such an example. From a neighbouring context, doubts may be raised by the use, and often misappropriation, of designs embedding ethnical or traditional cultural expression, or belonging to cultural heritage. It has occurred that modern fashion designers use, mostly without permission, African indigenous patterns and, next, and apply to register quasi-identical or similar designs.[37] Currently WIPO is holding negotiations around the adoption of Design Law Treaty (DLT), intended as a formalities treaty, which would require any design registration to include a declaration indicating 'the origin or source of traditional cultural expression, traditional knowledge or biological or genetic resources utilized or incorporate in the industrial design'.[38] For the moment, the EU design law does not ask for any information concerning the origin or source of inspiration of the design for which protection is sought.

16.020 The EU legislator adopted an open-ended catalogue of sources of disclosure.[39] It comprises, first, official publications of intellectual property offices from anywhere in the world.[40] What counts are publications which contain graphic documentation enabling view of the piece of prior art. In the cases from the pre-digital age, if an official bulletin contained only a word description, and the access to the graphic representation was given only upon request, then the requirement of public availability was not fulfilled.[41] The wording of Art. 6(1)

---

36   Guidelines (n 25), referring T-74/18 *Visi/one v. EasyFix*, EU:T:2019:417, 34 (disclosure upon catalogue files and annexes) and T-68/10 *Sphere Time v. Punch*, EU:T:2011:269, 31-2 (date established upon shipping invoices and counting the time for transport). Another example: a copyright notice of 2008 is sufficient evidence of the publication of a book in that year (which disclosed pieces of prior art) before the filing date of the contested design – BoA R-1948/2015-3, 34.
37   Margo Bagley, 'Designing Disclosure: Disclosure of Cultural and Genetic Resource Utilisation in Design Protection Regimes', in Susy Frankel (ed.), *The Object and Purpose of Intellectual Property* (Elgar 2019) 110, 117–25.
38   The proposal of disclosing the origin was advanced by the African group. Bagley, ibid., 128–39. For recent update on WIPO works, https://www.wipo.int/edocs/mdocs/govbody/en/a_62/a_62_2_prov_1.pdf (last visited 7 June 2024).
39   See the wording: 'any other kind of disclosure'.
40   Guidelines (n 25) 5.7.1.2. iii). R2300/2018-3; R0019/2018-3 – official publications.
41   R 442/2011-3; R 1482/2009-3.

DD and 7(1) RCD refers to the item from prior art as 'design'. However, it is a generally accepted rule that prior art may comprise *any* subject-matter of an IP right shown by official publications, irrespective of the nature and nomenclature of that right (such as trade mark, patent, utility model, design patent – emphasis added). Part C discusses the same in detail.

16.021 A design may be disclosed during exhibitions, fairs, show-rooms, or other kind of presentation.[42] A typical disclosure represents use in trade, when products incorporating, or having the design applied on, are offered, sold, stocked, imported, and so on. In other words, when the designs reach their commercial addressees, such as distributors, wholesalers, end-consumers.[43] The piece of prior art may be placed in trade as an individual item or be a part of a bigger product. For instance, if the design at issue is a doll, then prior art may encompass both a real doll or a photo of the doll, as featured on a packaging. Disclosure does not require production or commercialization of a product. The mere publication in a catalogue as offer for sale may be sufficient to consider a design to have been made publicly available.[44] This is because the EU design law speaks about disclosing a design (*per se*), understood as an intangible asset that corresponds to the appearance of a product, and not about disclosing a real object. It may be argued that design may be disclosed merely through digital files (such as CAD), such an issue is important for the enforcement of design rights via 3D printing technology.[45]

16.022 Lastly, today the Internet represents a commonly used source of disclosure. This prompted the EUIPO to adopt a set of specific guidelines, as part of convergence projects, that is 'Common Practice CP10 – Criteria for assessing disclosure of designs on the internet', which have been followed by national IP patent offices.[46] The document indicates that disclosure may originate from various sources, such as websites, apps, sharing files, electronic mails. Pieces of evidence, such as printouts, screenshots, images, videos, must necessarily display the appearance of the product. These proofs may be combined with information from metadata, URLs, hyperlinks, statements in writing, sworn

---

42 R 0070/2019-3; R1575/2016-3; R 1426/2015-3 – trade fair exhibitions.
43 R 2272/2018-3; R 0339/2018-3; R 1577/2016-3 – sales/online sales.
44 Stone (n 28), approvingly, mn. 10.22.
45 The most important element of a 3D-printing process constitutes the digital design file, which may be legally, or unlawfully obtained, an issue relevant for finding the infringement of design rights or copyright, more Dinusha Mendis, 'The Rise of 3d Printing and its Implications for Intellectual Property Law – Learning Lessons from the Past?' (2013) 35(3) EIPR 155, 163; Eli Greenbaum, 'Three-dimensional Printing and Open Source Hardware' (2013) 2(2) *NYU Journal of Intellectual Property and Entertainment Law* 257, 270.
46 https://euipo.europa.eu/tunnel-web/secure/webdav/guest/document_library/News/cp10/CP10_en.pdf (last visited 7 June 2024).

or affirmed.⁴⁷ Worldwide accessibility of Internet sources is rather presumed, while restricted access would be subject to ad hoc examination, resulting in various outcomes. According to the EUIPO's practice, password or payment requirements do not preclude disclosure, however limited access of employees to an internal database may be excepted from disclosure.⁴⁸ Most importantly, any Internet disclosure must objectively place the date at a certain moment in the past.⁴⁹

(b) The safeguard clause – the general exception

The safeguard clause operates with a fictional standard of knowledge of a disclosure (more precisely, the absence of it). The EU design law contains several unspecified terms which may be given flexible interpretation. This may be a good, or a bad thing, depending on whether the authority judges the facts and gathered evidence accurately and properly interprets the law. The following remarks address some of the doubts which have arisen during the EU practice in this regard.   **16.023**

The first issue is defining the composition of the specialized circle. It is rather undisputed that it should comprise people involved in creating, developing the design or manufacturing the products.⁵⁰ Additionally, the seminal CJEU judgement in *Gautzsch* answered a set number of queries resulting from requests for a preliminary ruling which involved, inter alia, the interpretation of prior art.⁵¹ The judgment held that distributing the image of a design to 'traders' could not be excluded from the scope of disclosure.⁵² However, the concept of 'specialist circles' does not include the 'informed user' – who remains relevant for assessing individual character and scope of protection of a design – or any other kind of users, such as consumers who may display some sort of design awareness, and yet, no specific expertise.⁵³ The EU design   **16.024**

---

47   EUIPO CP10, ibid., paras 2.2. and 2.4, p. 6-30.
48   Guidelines (n 26) para 5.7.1.5. in fine. Hennig Hartwig 'Disclosure on the Internet under Community Design Law', in *20 Years of the Boards of Appeal at EUIPO. LIBER AMICORUM* (EUIPO 2017) 188, 198 discussed the cases when publication of photos on Facebook personal page or posting an image on individual private blogs did not amount to disclosure.
49   Hartwig, ibid., 196, referring to EUIPO's distinction between the date of uploading information to the website and the date of printing an Internet page.
50   Green Paper (n 18) identified the relevant circle as comprising 'specialists, designers, merchants and manufactures', para 5.5.5.2.
51   C-479/12 *Gautzsch Großhandel v. Münchener Boulevard* ..., EU:C:2014:75. The case dealt with an unregistered design of canopied gazebo. However, for the purposes of defining relevant disclosure, *Gautzsch* guidance applies equally to registered designs, as the scope of Art. 7 RCD covers both types of design.
52   Ibid., 25–29.
53   Along similar lines Oliver Ruhl, *Gemeinschaftsgeschmackmuster. Kommentar* (2nd ed., Carl Heymanns Verlag 2010) 189. Differently, Musker in Gielen, Bomhard (n 27) 645.

practice has consequently refrained from applying a quantitative threshold. A sufficient reason constituted the *Gautzsch* guidance according to which disclosure to a single undertaking supported the presumption of being publicly available.[54] Scholars contend that the very concept of circles (used in plural) should not mean a broader group of persons than a single entity.[55]

16.025 Geography is the second dimension of the presumptive knowledge. The only restriction set by the EU design law is that business circles must operate within the EU. There is no geographical limitation as to where disclosure actually took place in the world. It is only significant that such events could have been reasonably become known in the normal course of business to the specialized circles operating within the EU. The CJEU in *Gautzsch* was also asked to explain whether certain events met the requirements of being in the 'normal course of business'. The events submitted to the CJEU's attention were: disclosure to third parties without any explicit or implicit conditions of confidentiality, making available to one undertaking in the sector, and presentation in the showrooms of an undertaking in China. The CJEU refrained from giving a clear-cut answer, indicating that it might go both ways.[56] This is a factual assessment which belongs to the competence of the court or administrative body that examines specific circumstances of each individual case.

16.026 The type of product and the specifics of industry sector play the central role in determining what information should be presumed to be material in terms of the knowledge of specialized circles. For instance, Asian or US disclosures should matter in the case of technical devices, while ethnic, traditional knowledge can be significant for fashion (including textiles), furniture, ceramics, decorative items in general.[57] The EUIPO in the *Crocs* case, a decision confirmed later by the GC, drew up a list of factors to determine the scope of presumptive knowledge.[58] Some of these factors related to the specialized circles (composition, qualifications, customer behaviour, activities, attendance of design presentations), while others to the nature or type of the design (characteristics, interdependency with other products, industrial sector, degree of technicality).[59] As concerns the clogs, disclosure at a US international nautical

---

54　C-479/12, 31; T-651/16 *Crocs v. Gift Diffusion*, EU:T:2018:137, 73.
55　Stone (n 28) mn. 10.62.
56　The court gave a positive answer in paras 33–35 of C-479/12, whilst formulating the conclusions of the second operative part of the sentence in the negative.
57　Massa, Strowel (n 21) 73.
58　BoA R-853/2014-3, paras 53–87.
59　T-651/16 *Crocs v. Euipo & Gift Diffusion* EU:T:2018:137, paras 56–73. See also T-153/08 *Shenzhen v. Bosch* EU:T:2010:248 (communication devices) – access to specialized publications and press.

show, sales in several US states and on websites originating from Florida and Colorado, but technically accessible worldwide, were deemed to catch the attention of EU professionals from the footwear industry.[60]

Above all, the knowledge of the specialist circles depends on the 'sector concerned' which, in turn, depends on the product's nature. It is an important issue to establish the relevant sector if the prior art was applied to a different product than the contested design. Is the prior art field limited to a specific kind of product? The UK pre-Brexit jurisprudence took the position that all prior designs could be relevant, irrespective of the type of product applied to.[61] There were various doctrinal schools of thought on the matter.[62] Finally, the CJEU confirmed in the *inter partes* decision in the case *Group Nivelles* that 'the 'sector concerned', within the meaning of Art. 7(1) of that regulation, was not limited to that of the product in which the contested design was intended to be incorporated or applied'.[63] This approach prevents re-monopolization of prior art,[64] as the same or similar design filed later with a different product indication could easily be the object of invalidity claims. The CJEU interpreted the rationale of the safeguard clause to be a means to protect disclosure against events that occurred in third countries and difficult to verify.[65] The intention of the CJEU was not to discriminate amongst various business sectors within the EU or to exclude the possibility that events of one business sector could be reasonably known to the specialists of another.[66] Prior to the *Group Nivelles* judgment, scholars doubted whether the extension of relevant prior art to any product sector was confined to the assessment of novelty, or it equally applied to the assessment of individual character.[67] The CJEU rightly confirmed that in the case of a disclosure fulfilling the standards of Art. 7(1) RCD, it can be used for the purposes of examining both novelty and individual character,

16.027

---

60 T-651/16, paras 61–68.
61 *Green Lane v. PMS International* [2008] EWCA Civ 358 (spiky balls for laundry v. massage aids); *Gimex International v. The Chillbag Company*, [2012] EWPCC 31 (ice bucket bag v. carrying wine bottles). Approvingly, Helmut Eichmann, '§2 Geschmacksmusterrecht' in Helmut Eichmann, Anette Kur (eds), *Designrecht. Praxishandbuch* (Nomos 2009), 62–63.
62 David Musker, *Community Design law. Principles & Practice* (Sweet & Maxwell London 2002) mn. 1-062 advocated for linking with the sector of the earlier design, while Stone (n 28), mn. 10-42 favoured the sector of the contested design.
63 C-361/15 P and C-405/15 P *Easy Sanitary Solution v. Group Nivelles*, EU:C:2017:720, para 103 with reference to GC judgement T-15/13, EU:T:2015:281, para 122.
64 Musker (n 62) mn. 1-044, discussing the example of a cartoon character printed in a magazine and later used for another type of product.
65 C-361/15 P and C-405/15 P, para 102.
66 Ibid.
67 Suthersanen (n 22) 70; Musker (n 27) 645 in fine.

regardless of whether the informed user knew the piece of prior art or not.[68] In other words, the presumptive knowledge of an informed user is not a legal requirement provided by Art. 7 RCD. The EUIPO has already dealt with products of different categories. For instance, a design for an animated icon was compared and invalidated based on prior designs which showed confectionary items.[69] The EUIPO ruled that the informed user and the scope of designer's freedom should be established with respect to the contested design, here the digital icon, and not with regard to the designs from prior art.

(c) First disclosure of an unregistered Community design

16.028 The unregistered Community design ('**UCD**') is an autonomous design regime effective throughout the EU that follows the same conditions of protection as registered designs. However, a UCD features lesser extent of rights[70] and does not provide a presumption of validity.[71] The main characteristic is its short term of protection.[72] Pursuant to Art. 11(1) RCD, a UCD is protected for three years from the date on which the design was first made publicly available within the Community. The provision of Art. 11(2) RCD explains the notion of being publicly available 'for the purpose of paragraph 1' by using terms identical to that of Art. 7(1) RCD.

16.029 In practice a query arose, whether a design disclosed for the first time outside the EU could initiate the term of protection of a UCD. Such an interpretation would result from the application of Art. 11(2) RCD which refers only to the knowledge of the specialist circles operating within the EU. By contrast,

---

68 C-361/15 P and C-405/15 P, paras 96–133. The CJEU widely analysed the impact of prior art in the context of the scope of protection of a design (Art. 10 RCD) and extent of a design right (Art. 19 RCD) – which under RCD are both independent from the indication of a product (Art. 36(6) RCD). This means that, for example, a design of a bottle is protected 'as such', regardless of whether the design is incorporated in a bottle or printed on a T-shirt or in a book.
69 BoA, R-1948/2015-3, 39–53.
70 Art. 19(2) RCD reads:
   An unregistered Community design shall, however, confer on its holder the right to prevent the acts referred to in paragraph 1 only if the contested use results from copying the protected design. The contested use shall not be deemed to result from copying the protected design if it results from an independent work of creation by a designer who may be reasonably thought not to be familiar with the design made available to the public by the holder.
71 Art. 85(2) RCD reads:
   In proceedings in respect of an infringement action or an action for threatened infringement of an unregistered Community design, the Community design court shall treat the Community design as valid if the right holder produces proof that the conditions laid down in Article 11 have been met and indicates what constitutes the individual character of his Community design. However, the defendant may contest its validity by way of a plea or with a counterclaim for a declaration of invalidity.
72 Critically, Anna Tischner, 'The Role of Unregistered Rights – A European Perspective on Design Protection' (2018) 13(4) JIPL&P 303. For an overall study, Victor Saez, 'The Unregistered Community Design' (2002) 12 EIPR 585.

because the term of protection starts from the date of making the UCD publicly available within the EU, this may imply that disclosure also must necessarily occur within the EU.

The problem originated from the German case *Thane*, which involved an abdominal muscle trainer and which was publicly advertised in the USA, before being made available in the EU. The owner sought to claim a UCD based on the USA disclosure.[73] The German court held that not only could a disclosure outside EU not form the basis of a UCD, but that the event also had reached the attention of specialist circles in the normal course of business as belonging to the state of prior art. For these reasons, the USA disclosure destroyed the novelty of the identical design marketed later within the EU.[74] This judicial view was later confirmed by the Hamburg court in a similar case concerning an electric biscuit-maker. The design was first published in China as a patent and design and later delivered to a British company, from which moment protection as UCD was sought.[75] The German Federal Supreme Court upheld the judgment by introducing a new argument to the discussion: the amendment of 2006 to the RCD text added Art. 110a (5) RCD, which provided that a design disclosed outside the Community does not enjoy protection as a UCD.[76] The rule of Art. 110a RCD was specifically adopted in view of the accession to the EU of new countries from Central and Eastern Europe. However, the German court considered that it also embedded the general terms of geographical disclosure for UCDs. Clearly, such a disclosure outside the EU belonged to the state of art and served to challenge the validity of a UCD disclosed later within the EU. Legal scholarship has confirmed this approach.[77]

16.030

In the near future, significant changes may occur with the proposal for the amended Regulation to delete the aforementioned Art. 110a (5) RCD second sentence.[78] Professor Kur welcomed this change by extensively explaining why

16.031

---

73   LG Frankfurt am Main 3/12 O 5/04 (*Ab Swing-Hometrainer*), (English version) *Thane International Group's Application*, [2006] ECDR 8, 71.
74   Ibid., mn. 11-5, p. 74–75. Critically about the disharmony of interpreting differently Art. 7(1) RCD and Art. 11(1) and (2) RCD see Richard Plaistowe, Mark Heritage, 'Europe versus The World: Does Unregistered Community Design Right Only Protect Designs First Made Available in Europe' (2007) 29(5) EIPR 187.
75   Hanseatisches Oberlandgericht 5 U 96/05 *Gebäckpresse design*, commented by Mareike Hunfeld, 'Chinese Pre-publication Precludes European Community Unregistered Design' (2007) 2(7) JIPL&P 441, 442.
76   BGH I ZR 126/06, GRUR 2009, 79.
77   Uma Suthersanen, *Design Law: European Union and United States of America* (2nd ed., Sweet & Maxwell 2016), 157–58; Alexander Tsoutsanis, in: Charles Gielen, Verena von Bomhard (eds.), *Concise European Trade Mark and Design Law* (2nd ed., Wolters Kluwer 2016), 652–53; Ruhl (n 50) 299–300; Eichmann in (n 61), mn 204, p. 123 inclining to the view that an Internet disclosure of an unregistered design right might suffice to be a disclosure within the EU.
78   Amendment no 126 of the Proposed Regulation.

the current regulation represented a 'less favourable treatment', a discrimination of entities operating outside the EU, which amounted to a breach of the 'principle of national treatment' set forth in Art. 3(1) TRIPS, and even of the 'non-discrimination' rule embedded by Art. 18 of the Treaty on the Functioning of the European Union.[79] However, this amendment would not remove all doubts as to the moment of commencement of a UCD protection. For these reasons Professor Kur suggests either removing the terms 'within the Community' from the terms of Art. 11(1) and/or Art. 11(2) RCD, or anchoring the commencement of the UCD's protection to the event of the 'first marketing in the EU'.[80] The latter should be correlated with applying the terms of the exceptions to disclosure grace period set in Art. 7(2) and 7(3) RCD[81] also to a UCD, a matter that would require explicit legislative intervention (see below).

3. Additional Normative Exceptions

16.032 The following section discusses three categories of exceptions to disclosure that are set forth in the text of DD and RCD. Unlike some countries (Japan, South Korea, Brazil, Mexico), the EU design law does not require an applicant to submit a declaration related to disclosures made before filing, irrespective of when the applicant learnt about it.[82] This is because at the stage of registration there is no substantial *ex ante* control over the conditions of protection of the design applied for. However, during an *ex post* control when the validity of a design is objected based on an earlier disclosure, the design holder bears the burden to refute such a disclosure, by arguing, for instance, that it falls within the normative exceptions.

(a) Confidential disclosure

16.033 Pursuant to Art. 6(1) DD and Art. 7(1) RCD, an exception to what is deemed to be made available to the public constitutes a disclosure made to a third person under explicit or implicit conditions of confidentiality. EU design law does not provide any further guidance. There are no time limits to this type of disclosure. The notion of 'explicit' may refer to what has been clearly established between two parties. It certainly encompasses any written clauses, yet it should also extend to confidentiality requirements made during oral

---

79 Annette Kur, 'Finally Back to TRIPS-compliance? EU Design Law and the Criterion of Publication 'within EU territory'' (2023) 18(1) JIPL&P 11, 13–14.
80 Ibid., 17.
81 Ibid., 16.
82 Elizabeth Ferrill, Jeanette Roorda, 'Amazing Grace Period for Registered Designs and Design Patents: A Sweet Sound or a Funeral Toll' (2016) 11(10) JIPL&P 762, 769.

negotiations. The concept of 'implicit' is more vague, as it may refer to what is sought to be confidential given the circumstances and the customary means of establishing it, considering the usual practices, the type of contract discussed, the relationship between the parties, the industry sector.[83] Legal scholarship rightly notices that confidentiality remains a matter of national law.[84] Because of the lack of harmonization of confidentiality standards, the interpretation of conditions of explicit or implied confidentiality may raise doubts and lead to unpredictable practice.

(b) Disclosure within 'grace period'

16.034 Pursuant to Art. 7(2) RCD or 6(2) DD a disclosure is not taken into consideration as a part of the state of prior art with regard to a design for which the protection is claimed under a registered design (Community or national, accordingly), if the disclosure simultaneously fulfils two conditions:

(a) it is undertaken by the designer, his successor in title, or a third person, as a result of information provided or action taken by those two persons;
(b) it occurred within the 12-month period preceding the filing of the application or the priority date.

16.035 These legal provisions constitute autonomous rules of designs known colloquially under the concept of 'grace period', though the EU legislator emphasized its difference from the analogue concept in patent law.[85] The purpose of the design grace period was to enable designers to test their products on the market before deciding on the type of protection to be sought, that is, filing for a CRD or subsisting on a UCD.[86]

16.036 The law explicitly stipulates that disclosures during the grace period can only apply to registered designs, thus not to unregistered ones.

---

83   Along similar lines, Claus Barrett Christiansen, 'Commentaries to Art. 7' in Gordian Hasselblatt (ed), *Community Design Regulation. Article-by-Article Commentary* (2nd ed., Beck, Hart, Nomos 2018) mn. 30, 137.
84   Bently (n 24) 768.
85   Official Commentary to the Proposal of Regulation in Franzosi (n 17), 78. Here to note is that grace period is still not a standard among national patent legislations (examples of countries retaining a grace period include: USA, Canada, Japan, South Korea, Australia, Brazil, Mexico, Singapore, Estonia, Russian Federation), while discussions about introducing such a regulation to the European Patent Convention have been conducted for more than 20 years. For an earlier, worldwide evaluation of grace period standards consult Joseph Strauss, 'Grace Period and the European and International Patent Law: Analysis of Key Legal And Socio-economic Aspects', IIC studies vol. 20 (Beck 2001).
86   Official Commentary, ibid., 78, and also Recital 20 RCD. Green Paper (n 18) para 4.3.4. acknowledged the importance of testing designs in the market for industries that develop a large number of designs, such as fashion.

16.037 Legal doctrine unanimously warns against an erroneous view of considering that grace period moves the filing date or priority date back in time to the first disclosure.[87] That is not its effect. The grace period only allows the act of disclosure undertaken by the designer, his successor in title, or a third person that used the initial self-disclosure or information coming from the designer or successor, to be discarded from the relevant prior art.[88] However, another disclosure undertaken independently by a third person beyond the conditions of Art. 7(2)(a) RCD or 6(2)(a) DD[89] would constitute prior art and may challenge the validity of the design registered later within the grace period. For this reason, waiting too long to file a design application after an initial disclosure within the grace period may entail risks with regard to the status of other designs, either independently disclosed or filed. Speaking about such risks, the comparison between the design filed later corresponding to the one from grace period and a design filed earlier that constitutes an independent disclosure is a significant issue. It may be noted that the identical or immaterial differences between these two designs would mean lack of novelty, whilst similar overall impression in the eyes of the informed user would mean lack of individual character of a design filed later.[90]

16.038 Another issue of whether a design filed for registration may be different from the one disclosed earlier and still support a claim for grace period, is examined in Section C below.

---

87 Bently (n 24), 769; Christiansen (n 83), mn 33, 137; Stone (n 28), 185–88 and 191, extensively.

88 There are some doubts about the exact extent of actions taken by third parties and their relationship with the designer. A legitimate query is what the terms of 'resulting of information provided or action taken by the designer or legitimate successor' should mean. Bently (n 24), 769, consider that it addresses a disclosure authorized by the designers (e.g., publication of advertisers or exhibitions by retailers), because other kinds of unauthorized actions would fall under the concept of an 'abuse', which makes the object of the separate legal provision of Art. 7(3) RCD or 6(3) DD (see below (c)). Practitioners, however, argue that invoking Art. 7(3) RCD is generally more onerous, as the plaintiff would have to prove the abusive nature of a behaviour, see The Bird and Bird IP Team, 'Fashion-related IP decisions round-up 2020' (2021) 16(6) JIPL&P 595, 624 discussing the ruling of the OG Düsseldorf court I 20 U 103/18 concerning a slide sandal disclosed by third parties during grace period.

89 Art. 7(2)(a) RCD and Art. 6(2)(a) DD indicate: 'by the designer, his successor in title, or a third person as a result of information provided or action taken by the designer or his successor in title'.

90 The issue is more complex – first disclosure of a design invoking grace period should be theoretically relevant for a later independently filed design, which may be invalidated, if it does not differ in immaterial details or overall impression. However, hypothetically, there may be cases when a design filed independently invokes an earlier priority date before the disclosure of a design in grace period – for instance, a national application filed upon Paris Convention which was published later than the disclosure concerning grace period. Consequently, the design in grace period could not be invoked as a basis for invalidating the design filed later. Simultaneously, a design based on national application – being earlier – constitutes prior art and may be invoked to invalidate the registered design corresponding to that one in grace period.

(c) Abusive disclosure

The last exception pertains to an abusive disclosure in relation to the designer or his legal successor and is set forth in Art. 7(3) RCD or Art. 6(3) DD. The legal provision focuses on the mere fact of disclosure and does not indicate who may commit such an abuse. It is also not clear whether the person who discloses the design is also the one who had previously come into its possession by abuse. Therefore, the group of persons involved in abusive disclosure remains large. It may encompass persons or entities linked by business, having contractual relationship with the designer or its legal successors. It may also comprise competitors who came into the possession of the design by their own acts or by effect of theft (commissioned or by unknown perpetrators). **16.039**

Another source of doubt is how to explain the explicit reference of Art. 7(3) RCD to Art. 7(2) RCD, namely, whether the 12-month period preceding the date of filing or the priority date, should also include abusive disclosures. It is true that Recital 20 of RCD discussed the rationale of introducing the exceptions of grace period and abusive disclosure, by stating that the relevant events for both cases should take place during the period of 12 months. This approach has found sufficient support in the scholarship.[91] Different arguments contended that it was very likely that the person conducting an abusive disclosure would try to keep it secret, and the design holder would learn about it too late to be able to legally invoke the exception.[92] Although such an hypothesis seems to be detrimental to the design holder, explicit guidance on this issue will be most welcome. Because of reference to Art. 7(2) RCD or Art. 6(2) DD, abusive disclosure does not cover a UCD.[93] **16.040**

Last, but not least, significant doubts concern the very notion of an abuse. An earlier commentator suggested a broad understanding of misconduct, encompassing not only theft, industrial espionage, breach of confidence and all sorts of fraudulent, negligent acts, conduct in bad faith, but also an act performed in good faith, if it negatively affected the rights of the entitled person.[94] It may be stated, that good faith does not fit the notion of the 'abuse', which implies some kind of faulty conduct. The assessment is thought to be on a case-by-case basis, and a certain degree of subjectivity is unavoidable. In general terms, an abuse tends to be a civil law concept, known especially in legislations that operate with the institution of an 'abuse of right' (Fr. *'abus en droit'*). Civil law **16.041**

---

91 Bently (n 24), 769; Cornish (n 14), 599.
92 Christiansen, (n 83), mn. 39, 138; Stone (n 28), 189.
93 Stone (n 28), 190; Ruhl (n 53), mn. 59, 207.
94 Franzosi (n 17), 81.

in the EU is still not extensively harmonized,[95] which may result in different understanding of the circumstances of an abusive conduct. The CJEU has not yet had the occasion to explain its meaning.

C. ISSUES OF THE SUBJECT-MATTER DISCLOSED UNDER THE EU DESIGN LAW

16.042 Accepting worldwide disclosures for the purposes of EU prior art does not mean that, regardless of the nature of the product, any disclosed item can be compared as such with a challenged EU design for testing the validity of the latter. This is a critical issue, as foreign laws may understand the concept of a design differently (see Part D.2), whereas the appearance of a product may be protected by various IPRs. Part C first examines possible subject-matter of earlier disclosures from the vantage point of EU design law (Part C.1) then tackles the issues of comparing CRD/UCD disclosures (Part C.2). One element looks into the specificities of how a design is represented or described. Another section examines the relation between a design and disclosures of partial products or of combinations of features. The final significant issue deals with a mismatch between a design filed and the earlier self-disclosure during the grace period.

1. The Subject-matter of a Relevant Piece of Prior Art

16.043 The general rule of disclosure of Art. 7(1) RCD or Art. 6(1) DD[96] describes the piece of prior art by using the term 'design'. Does it mean that only design rights may be invoked as prior art? The answer is 'No'. The EUIPO Guidelines consistently have held that irrespective of the kind of right the piece of prior art (has) enjoyed,[97] what matters is that the subject-matter of the earlier right matches the EU normative definition of a 'design', set forth in Art. 3(a) RCD and Art. 1(a) DD.

---

95 There are incidentally certain topics harmonized, especially with regard to B2C contractual relationship.
96 Art. 7(1) RCD reads:
   For the purpose of applying Articles 5 and 6, a design shall be deemed to have been made available to the public if it has been published following registration or otherwise, or exhibited, used in trade or otherwise disclosed, before the date referred to in Articles 5(1)(a) and 6(1)(a) or in Articles 5(1)(b) and 6(1)(b), as the case may be, except where these events could not reasonably have become known in the normal course of business to the circles specialised in the sector concerned, operating within the Community.(…)
   Art. 6(1) DD is formulated in a similar way.
97 Guidelines (n 25) para 5.7.1.2 ii).

(a) EU concepts of 'design' and 'product'

The EU design law adopts a broad definition of a design, understood as the 'appearance' of the whole or a part of a 'product' determined by an open-ended[98] category of features: lines, contours, colours, shape, texture and/or materials of the product itself and/or its ornamentation. The proposed amendments explicitly include movement, transition or 'any other sort of animation of those features' (Art. 2(3) Proposed Directive and Art. 3(1) Proposed Regulation). The practice has imposed the interpretation that only design features perceived by the eye may be taken into consideration. However, dissenting scholarship argued in favour of other senses, for instance touch would include the weight of a product as a design attribute.[99] The prime importance of visual features would seem a little outdated with respect to the evolution of modern design, new technologies, and the growth of digital environment. For instance, the audio layer of an app would not currently enjoy EU design protection. However, the Proposed Amendments do not touch upon this issue. It may be assumed that the key objective consists in ensuring precise understanding of the subject-matter of a design defined by other than visual means, and ultimately, the legal certainty needed by all market figures. Future technology used by registrars may solve such difficulties, so, law may also be updated.

16.044

As designs refer to what the product looks like, the notion of 'product' represents the important corollary. The EU design law, again, chose a wide definition, that is 'any industrial or handicraft item', and employs an open-ended catalogue with normative examples (Art. 3(b) RCD and 1(b) DD).[100] It includes parts intended to be assembled into a complex product, packaging, get-up, graphic symbols and typographic typefaces, while excluding computer programs as such. Significantly, a product by this definition need not be a three-dimensional object.[101] Graphic symbols, such as logos or graphic compositions, and get-up – which de facto means an arrangement or layout – do not have tangible nature, and still, they are products within the meaning of the EU law. This approach facilitates the protection of graphical user interfaces and other kind of virtual designs in the EU. The new law explicitly confirms that a design may take a digital form, whilst listing 'spatial arrangement of items intended to form, in particular, an interior environment', and 'graphical

16.045

---

98   Legal text uses the wording 'in particular'. Gordian Hasselblatt, 'Commentaries to Art. 3', in (n 83), 40–46, with examples.
99   Musker (n 62), para 1-018.
100 The provision reads: 'product' means any industrial or handicraft item, including inter alia parts intended to be assembled into a complex product, packaging, get-up, graphic symbols and typographic typefaces, but excluding computer programs. Consult Hasselblatt, in (n 83) 47–60 with examples.
101 Anette Kur, 'No Logo', (2004) 2 IIC 184; critically Cornish (n 14) mn. 15-15, 597.

user interfaces' under Art. 2(4) Proposed Directive and Art. 3(2) Proposed Regulation. Using an example, the appearance of a hotel room may constitute a design, where the product represents the very arrangement (layout) of elements shown in the room – thus, not the objects themselves – but the design represents that specific view i.e., the appearance of the hotel room.

16.046 Another important aspect of the EU law is that protection of partial designs is possible in different ways. A partial design may be a certain part of a product (a knife handle), an autonomous part of a product comprising two or more elements (a pot lid), a component/spare part of what the EU law defines as a 'complex product' (a mower engine).[102] A recent CJEU preliminary ruling explained that a 'part of a product' should be understood according to the usual meaning in the everyday language, that is as a 'section' of the 'whole' product.[103] The CJEU laid down additional requirements. To attract design protection, the appearance of that section must be 'visible' and clearly defined by 'particular lines, contours, shapes or texture', which would make that part capable of producing an overall impression that cannot be 'completely lost in the product as a whole'.[104] Until now, the visibility requirement was explicitly confined to 'parts of a complex product'. To ensure greater legal certainty with regard the 'visibility requirement' the new law introduces a new provision for registered designs which stipulates that 'design protection is conferred only on those features of appearance which are shown visibly in the application for registration'.[105] The provision of Art. 18(a) of the Proposed Regulation appears to be a general provision that would apply to any kind of design, thus, not restricted to 'parts of a product' or 'parts of a complex product'.

16.047 Under the EU law, there are not many things within the meaning of a 'product' whose appearance cannot be protected as a 'design' such as living organisms[106] or ideas/concepts, or methods of use.[107]

---

102 There is a specific definition of a 'complex product' and additional requirements pertain to component parts of a complex product (that is visibility during normal use). For global analysis, Dana Beldiman, Constantin Blanke-Roeser, *An International Perspective on Design Protection of Visible Spare Parts* (Springer 2017).
103 C-123/20 *Ferrari SpA v. Mansory Design Holding GmbH*, EU:C:2021:889, para 49.
104 C-123/20, ibid., para 50 and the operative part of the judgment.
105 Art. 18(a) Proposed Regulation and Explanatory Memorandum, p. 8.
106 EU design has yet to cope with issues arising from the use of synthetically created biotechnological materials for designs with parts of the appearance mimicking real life. An example would be a textile showing leather grown from mushrooms, cf. Bagley (2019), 115. Such a design currently risks the objections of 'not being a design', or of being without novelty/individual character.
107 Guidelines (n 26) para 5.1.

(b) Earlier disclosure and IPRs

A worldwide disclosure under Art. 7 RCD[108] of anything that fits the EU definition of a 'design' of a 'product' belongs to the state of prior art. Such a disclosure may constitute the subject-matter of various IPRs. Considering the EUIPO practice, which relies on various EU and non-EU official publications, the following applications, or granted rights were invoked as relevant prior art: **16.048**

- design[109]
- utility model[110]
- patent[111]
- design patent[112]
- trade mark[113]
- copyright[114]
- distinctive sign protected via unfair competition (technically, it is not covered by a right)[115]

As discussed in Part B.2, it is evident that an earlier disclosure does not need to be protected by an IPR in order to serve as basis for challenging the novelty or individual character of an EU design. It suffices that the piece of prior art constitutes the appearance of a product, within the meaning of EU law, which was made available to the public in the circumstances and by the means provided under Art. 7 RCD,[116] for example by trading real products.[117] **16.049**

It is important to emphasize that any disclosed piece of prior art within the meaning of Art. 7 RCD and Art. 6 DD is material only for the examination of novelty and individual character under Arts 5–6 RCD,[118] when such a ground has been explicitly indicated (that is, ticked) in a request for invalidity or in a counterclaim, and supported by relevant evidence and arguments. However, **16.050**

---

108 Art. 6 DD, see fn 96 above.
109 BoA dec. in cases R 1827/2019-3; R 1243/2017-3; R 0414/2018-3; T-41/14 *Argo v. Clapbanner* EU:T:2015:53; T-83/11 & T-84/11 *Antrax v. Heating Company*, EU:T:2012:592.
110 BoA dec. in cases R 1928/2018-3 (German utility model); R 1586/2017-3 (Polish utility model).
111 BoA dec. in cases R 931/2018-3 (Taiwanese patent); R 1008/2018-3 (European Patent application); R0151/2017-3 9 (European patent).
112 BoA dec. in cases R 1283/2018-3; R 1060/2017-3 (US design patents); T-11/08 *Kwang Yang v. Honda Giken*, EU:T:2011:447; T-22/13 and T-23/13 *Senz v. Impliva*, EU:T:2015:310 (US design patents).
113 T-666/11 *Danuta Budziewska v. Puma SE*, EU:T:2013:584; T-148/08 *Beifa v. Schwan Stabilo*, EU:T:2010:190, and T-608/11 *Beifa v. Schwan Stabilo*, EU:T:2013:334 (earlier German trade marks).
114 T-68/11 *Erich Kastenholz v. Qwatchme*, EU:T:2013:298 (German copyright to a painting).
115 Guidelines (n 26) para 5.9.1.
116 Art. 6 DD.
117 T-368/17 *Linak v. ChangZhou*, EU:T:2018:695 (offer of lifting columns on webpages).
118 See Arts 4 and 5 DD.

if the disclosure represents a distinctive sign or a work protected by copyright, there are additional legal grounds upon which the validity of a design may be challenged by use of the earlier disclosure in a way entirely different from testing novelty and individual character.[119] In the case of a distinctive sign, pursuant to Art. 25(1)(e) RCD or Art. 11(2)(a) DD, the right holder must prove that the right conferred on the distinctive sign – stemming from a EU trade mark or a national law of a EU country – prohibits the use of that sign in a subsequent design. In other words, the design infringes the trade mark right or use of the design gives rise to claims under an unfair competition regime.[120] In the case of a work protected under the copyright of a EU member state, its right holder must show that the design represents an unauthorized use of that work.[121] These distinct legal grounds are not presumed and need to be explicitly invoked and substantiated in the application for invalidity, or the counterclaim.[122]

2. Comparing a Contested Design with an Earlier Disclosure

16.051 Testing the validity of a design with respect to an earlier disclosure is essentially a matter of comparison, whether it is verifying novelty or individual character, or applying different criteria of assessment that pertain to other invalidity grounds, set forth in Art. 25(1) RCD or Art. 11(1) and (2) DD. The purpose of this part is to focus on several basic issues that matter when using worldwide disclosures as a comparison item vis-à-vis a contested CRD or UCD, but without going into details of each validity test. For ease of reading, a piece of prior art, irrespective of its form of protection, if any, is referred to below as 'a design'.

(a) The significance of the representation of 'design features' vis-à-vis wording

16.052 The requirement that relevant design features constituting the subject-matter of an EU design are to be identified visually translates into the corresponding

---

119 Seville (n 12) 232–46 discussing grounds of invalidity.
120 In the case of an earlier trade mark, the examination follows the criteria of assessing the infringement of a trade mark. As practice has mostly dealt with trade marks without reputation, the similarity of goods/services and similarity of signs constituted the core issues, see cases T-55/12 *Su-Shan Chen v. AM Denmark*, EU:T:2013:219; BoA R 609/2006-3 (logo Midas), commented at an earlier stage by Daren Smith, (2006) 1(8) JIPL&P 509. More Magdalena Kolasa, 'The Scope and Limits of Protection for Distinctive Signs against the Community Design', MIPLC Studies vol. 17 (Nomos 2012).
121 Consult Art. 25(1)(f) RCD or Art. 11(2)(b) DD. The person challenging a design must prove their legal title to the work, that the work is protected by copyright and that use of the design constitutes an infringement of the copyright, see T-566/11 and T-567/11 *Viejo Valle v. Établissements Coquet*, EU:T:2013:549 (French copyright to crockery items).
122 C-101/11 P and C-102/11 P, *Neuman v. Baena*, paras 71–73.

requirement that any piece from prior art need also to be visually defined. If an earlier national design protects sound or taste properties, these features cannot be currently opposed to a CRD or UCD.

It is also significant how the design is represented – by means of photos, drawings, videos – and not how the design is described or claimed by words.[123] This is because the description, principally, does not define the scope of protection of an EU design. Both DD and RCD read that 'the scope of protection of a design right shall include *any design* which does not produce on the informed user a different overall impression'.[124] Additionally, with respect to CRD, the provision of Art. 36(6) RCD explicitly indicates that a description 'shall not affect the scope of protection of the design as such'. 16.053

Therefore, the subject-matter of an EU design is established upon graphic representation, which should be self-contained and consistent, especially if multiple views of the same object are enclosed.[125] This requirement aims at ensuring legal certainty, as people consulting public design registers should be able to easily understand what is protected.[126] For these reasons, under the RCD, description is not a mandatory part of an application for registration.[127] 16.054

In the case of CRD, the legal provision of Art. 1(1) of Implementing Regulation 2245/2002 ('**CDIR**') indicates the required content of a request for registration. Description is not a part of it. Any statements, disclaimers, or other explanatory texts or wording are not accepted in an application to elaborate on what is disclosed by the views. In 2016 the EUIPO introduced the guidance named 'CP6 – Convergence Project on the Graphic representation of a design',[128] which explains in detail what is allowed, and what is not, in making 16.055

---

123 Similarly, Stone (n 28) mn. 10.16. Discussing the need of word description in case of ambivalent graphic representation see Anna Tischner, 'Lost in Communication: A Few Thoughts on the Object and Purpose of the EU Design Protection' in Frankel (n 37), 154.
124 See Art. 10(1) RCD and Art. 9(1) DD, emphasis added. Theoretically, under the EU Directive the protection conferred by a design should be independent from the product classification filed by the applicant. This matter is ultimately decided by member states. For instance, Polish Industrial Property Act is clearly inconsistent with the standard of DD, as Art. 105(5) stipulates that a (Polish) design right shall be limited to the kind of products, in respect of which the protection has been applied for. Amendment is still much awaited.
125 EUIPO Guidelines conc. *Examination of applications for registered Community designs*, chapter 5, at https://guidelines.euipo.europa.eu/2058424/1785654/designs-guidelines/examination-of-applications-for-registered-community-designs (last visited 7 June 2024).
126 Annette Kur, 'The Design Approach and Procedural Practice…', in (n 12), 179, discussing the risks of strategic claiming over mere representation.
127 National design legislations dealt with this issue distinctly by the time of implementation of the Directive.
128 For official information, see https://euipo.europa.eu/ohimportal/en/news/-/action/view/2922696 (last visited 8 June 2024). To access the document, see https://euipo.europa.eu/tunnel-web/secure/webdav/

an accurate submission of a design application. Even when a description is optionally attached to the application, it is not published in the Community Designs Bulletin and does not form part of a certificate of registration.[129] The register only indicates that such a description was filed[130] and may be accessed only upon request.

16.056 In conclusion, if the subject-matter of a piece of prior art is defined by non-visual design features or by word description (such as, claims) according to the local legislation, in addition to the features visible from the representation, these aspects cannot be taken into account when comparing this antecedent with the contested EU design.

(b) Relevant subject-matter for the comparison of two designs when testing novelty or individual character

16.057 This section applies to the examination of novelty and individual character – the basic conditions of protection under EU law. Novelty requires comparison of the designs side-by-side and feature-by-feature in order to assess whether they are different in more than immaterial details.[131] Individual character requires a global assessment from the perspective of the informed user, who firstly selects the features capable of conferring the overall impression of a design, and, taking into account the degree of designer's freedom, next assesses synthetically whether the compared designs have the same overall impression.[132]

16.058 The EUIPO has adopted the rule that the contested CRD represents 'the point of reference' when compared with an earlier disclosure.[133] This means, for instance, that if the challenged design constitutes only part of a product, or only certain views (for example, the front side of a product), whereas the piece from prior art represents the entire product, and/or discloses extra views, all these additions should be disregarded from the assessment.[134] By contrast, if the design at hand comprises more features than the piece from prior art, then

---

guest/ document _library/ contentPdfs/ about _euipo/ who _we _are/ common _communication/ common _communication_7/ common_communication7_en.pdf (last visited 7 June 2024). For instance, this document discusses the use of 'visual disclaimers', such as broken lines, blurring, colour shading, boundaries (para 3.1.4).

129 See Art. 14 (1) and (2) CDIR.
130 See Art. 14(1)(d) CDIR.
131 Marianne Levin, 'The Harmonising Decisions from Luxembourg' in (n 12) 55–56; Gordian Hasselblatt, 'Commentaries to Art. 5' in (n 83), 82–87 with examples.
132 Levin (n 12) 57–62; Joanna Bruckner-Hofmann, 'Commentaries to Art. 6' in (n 12) 91–129 with examples.
133 Guidelines (n 26) para 5.7.2.
134 T-9/15 *Ball Beverages v. Crown Hellas*, EU:T:2017:386 (beverage cans without printed text compared to earlier cans with wording/graphics).

the subject-matter of the contested design is held relevant in its entirety, unless certain exceptions apply. The latter refers to normative exceptions which disregard upfront certain type of features from the scope of protection, such as features of parts of a complex product which are not 'visible during normal use', or features solely dictated by a product's technical function.

National courts that resolve matters involving infringement of CRD or UCD or a national design may adopt their own rules of establishing the 'terms of comparison' – in other words, in deciding what to compare. While it is beyond the scope of this section, it may be noted that the leading UK jurisprudence initially used the 'yard stick of comparison' determined by the contested design as filed, which meant that any additional features shown by the infringing product were disregarded.[135] Next, the well-known *Apple v. Samsung* litigation brought the change that gave a decisive role to features displayed by the Samsung tablet which did not have a visible equivalent in the subject-matter of the Apple design.[136] Later on, UK *Trunki* case confirmed this new, disputable, approach of taking into account additions vis-à-vis the contested design.[137]

16.059

The CJEU ruling in *Karen Miller* answered requests for a preliminary ruling regarding the manner of assessing the individual character of a design as compared to combinations of prior art features.[138] The CJEU held that a design cannot be compared – in its overall impression – to a mix or combination of features isolated and put together from several distinct items of prior art. Instead, the individual character of a design has to be assessed with regard to individual designs, taken one-by-one and as separate combinations of features.[139] The Court also indicated that this approach does not contradict the provision of Art. 25(1) of TRIPS which correlates the conditions of novelty and originality to the requirement of significant difference 'from known designs or combination of known design features'.[140] Moreover, this provision has an optional character,[141] thus, the EU legislator is free to choose a different standard for the novelty and individual character of designs with respect to combinations of known features from prior art.

16.060

---

135 *Procter &Gamble v. Reckitt Benckiser*, [2006] EWHC 3154 (Ch).
136 *Samsung v. Apple*, [2012] EWHC 1882 (Pat).
137 *Magmatic v. PMS International* [2014] EWCA 181 and [2016] UKSC 12 by contrast to [2013] EWHC 1925, commented by Alexander Borthwick, 'The Scope of Registered Design Protection Following Magmatic v. PMS International', (2015) EIPR 180; David Stone, '*Trunki*–How Did Things Go So Wrong?' (2016) 11(9) JIPL&P 662.
138 C-345/13 *Karen Millen v. Dunnes Stores*, EU:C:2014:2013.
139 C-345/13, 23–35.
140 C-345/13, 34.
141 'Members may provide…' (see Art. 25(1), 2nd sentence of TRIPS). Consult Carvalho (n 10), 425–34.

16.061 The final essential aspect of any proper comparison, also required by the EUIPO, is that an earlier design should be identified and reproduced in its entirety with accuracy.[142] A disclosure cannot display a product ambiguously, otherwise it is impossible to compare the appearances of the products at issue. Consequently, the person challenging the validity of a design must produce evidence enabling a complete representation of the piece from the prior art. EUIPO is not entitled to combine various components of one or more earlier designs in order to obtain a complete view of a disclosure.[143] In joint cases C-361/15 P and C-405/15 featuring the design of a shower drainage channel, EUIPO erroneously combined proofs of illustration showing a cover plate and catalogues showing collectors and siphons in order to get to a complete representation of the disclosure (that is a drainage device for liquid waste).

(c) Subject-matter of self-disclosure and grace period

16.062 A normal consequence of a successful product is long market life, whilst subsequent upgrades aim at retaining the original image of the product. However, seeking design protection for newer products may be obstructed by self-disclosure of older models, which destroy novelty or individual character. A high-profile case concerned invalidation of the design marked '991' from the series '*Porsche 911*' regarding the earlier design marked '997' of the same line.[144] Between the two models too much time lapsed so as to invoke any exception to disclosure, such as a grace period. The GC and EUIPO rejected the arguments concerning a restricted designer's freedom due to a 'design trend' dictated by the iconic prototype of *Porsche 911* and consumers' expectations of a reduced modification of the original version.[145] The consequence was that the differences between the two models were found insufficient to change the same overall impression which was dominated by the shape of bodywork, windows and doors. As a result, the later design failed for the lack of individual character.[146]

16.063 This case redirects attention to the extent of acceptable differences between a design filed for registration and an earlier self-disclosure in respect of which the grace period is invoked to exclude the latter from the prior art. *De lege lata*, the legal provisions of Art. 7(2) RCD and Art. 6(2) DD define the subject-matter of an item disclosed within grace period as 'a design for which

---

142 Invalidity (n 26) para 5.7.1.2. ii).
143 C-361/15 P and C-405/15 P *Easy Sanitary… v. Group Nivelles*, 67–77.
144 T-209/18 *Porsche AG v. Autec*, EU:T:2019:377.
145 T-209/18, 56–61.
146 T-209/18, 94.

protection is claimed'. The EUIPO, with the support of the legal doctrine, has accepted that these terms do not mean identity between the compared designs.[147] An earlier disclosure within the grace period can be either identical, as defined by Art. 5(2) RCD and Art. 4(2) DD, or a design that does not produce a different overall impression in the eyes of the informed user, as defined by Art. 6(2) RCD and Art. 5(2) DD.[148] *De lege ferenda*, this approach will become embedded in the new law.[149] New provisions will read that:

> A disclosure shall not be taken into consideration for the purpose of applying Articles 5 and 6 if the disclosed design, which is identical with or does not differ in its overall impression from the design for which protection is claimed under a registered EU design, has been made available to the public.

16.064 This addition certainly fits the practical purpose of the grace period, that is, testing a prototype on the market prior to registration. It enables the initial product to be slightly modified according to the needs which have become apparent in use, while the path to design registration remains open.

D. THE INTERSECTION BETWEEN EU PRIOR ART AND FOREIGN STANDARDS – REMARKS FROM GLOBAL PERSPECTIVE

16.065 The state of the art requirement of EU design law is based on the principle of worldwide disclosure, albeit subject to significant exceptions. The status of any EU design right depends on what lies within and outside the frontiers of the EU. On the contrary, EU designs may also affect the legal status of designs protected by non-EU laws. The relationship between EU and non-EU designs is determined by how non-EU design laws set the parameters of eligible designs upon relevant prior art. This area, though, is subject to much divergence. In search for uniformity, it seems meaningful that the International Association for the Protection of Intellectual Property known as AIPPI chose the topic 'Industrial designs and the role of prior art' to be one of the key-topics of 2021, marked under query 'Q278'. This was examined based on the reports

---

147 Bently (n 24) 769 in fine; Musker (n 27) 646; Stone (n 28) mn. 10.110–113, noticing that the representation of a design as filed (diagrammatic drawing, CAD, etc.) usually slightly differs from the real look of products as marketed during grace period.
148 Guidelines (n 26) para 5.7.1.4. referring BoA R 658/2010-3.
149 See Art. 6(2) of the Proposed Directive and Art. 7(2) of the Proposed Regulation.

filed by respondents from 40 countries and led to adoption of a 'Resolution'.[150] Some of the national reports provided information for the analysis below.[151]

16.066 The following section starts with emphasizing specifics of several non-EU design laws concerning prior art (Part D.1) as well as the normative concepts of a design and a product (Part D.2). However, an in-depth analysis of the registration framework of selected non-EU laws is beyond the scope of this chapter. The remarks below rather aim at accentuating some issues that the author considers useful for the final comparative evaluation with EU law (Part D.3).

1. Divergent Standards of Prior Art – Absolute Novelty and Different Models of Grace Period

16.067 Many economically developed countries apply substantive examination at the registration stage. This means that registrars conduct prior art searches upon which the eligibility of filed designs is assessed. A visible weakness of this model is that it delays grant of the design right. Its advantage lies in increasing the legal certainty through the quality of examination of registration. It is a common understanding that designs examined *ex ante* are likely to be less prone to future invalidation.

16.068 Japan adopts a patent approach to designs by using 'the first to file system', and applies a substantive examination of applications based on the requirements of novelty and creative difficulty.[152] In China, designs are governed by patent regulations,[153] which also cover inventions and utility models. Designs are subject to a simple formal examination, though a design owner may request from the registration authority a detailed evaluation report. The registrar would check whether the requirements of protection, novelty, distinctiveness, no conflict with prior rights, have been fulfilled.[154] Australian law enables registration of designs on the basis of a 'formalities check' with regard to the minimum

---

150 https://aippi.soutron.net/Portal/Default/en-GB/DownloadImageFile.ashx?objectId=8760&ownerType=0&ownerId=4156 (last visited 8 June 2024).
151 https://aippi.soutron.net/Portal/Default/en-GB/SearchResults (last visited 8 June 2024) – search upon the entry 'q278'.
152 Tsukasa Aso, Christoph Rademacher, 'Noteworthy Features of Japanese Design Law from the Perspective of European Law', in Christoph Rademacher and Tsukasa Aso (eds), *Japanese Design Law and Practice* (Wolters Kluwer 2021) 353–58.
153 *Patent Law* of the People's Republic of China (as amended upon the decision of 17 October 2020) https://www.wipo.int/wipolex/en/text/585084 (last visited 8 June 2024). The fourth amendment to this act came into force June 1, 2021 and fostered China's recent accession to the Hague system, https://www.wipo.int/hague/en/news/2022/news_0005.html (last visited 6 October 2023).
154 Peter Ganea, 'Patents, Utility Models and Designs' in Christopher Heath (ed.) *Intellectual Property Law in China* (2nd ed., Wolters Kluwer 2021) 19-20.

filing requirements.¹⁵⁵ However, a substantive examination of the design upon the requirements of novelty and distinctiveness may be requested later by the design owner in order to have the design 'certified' by the IP Australia. The latter is compulsory for enforcing the design against infringement.¹⁵⁶

India also conducts substantive examination of the main conditions of novelty and originality, as well as over other statutory requirements.¹⁵⁷ US legal provisions stipulate that a design patent may be conferred for any new, non-obvious and ornamental design for an article of manufacture, whilst there is no legal definition of the concept of a 'design'.¹⁵⁸ Following the patent model of protection, a US design patent application is subject to substantive examination. However, there is scholarship arguing that the system is too lax and that too few applications are rejected.¹⁵⁹ **16.069**

In terms of disclosure, the most of non-EU design laws opt for the model of absolute novelty, which does not contain a general exception to disclosures similar to the EU safeguard clause. As mentioned in Part B, absolute novelty usually means that any piece from the prior art may be invoked for checking whether a design fulfils the conditions of protection required in a given jurisdiction. To soften the effect of worldwide standard of prior art, non-EU laws comprise specific exceptions to disclosure, such as grace period. The multitude of local particularities is shown by the following examples. **16.070**

Japanese law applies a worldwide standard of novelty, with a one-year grace period, in case of abusive disclosure or disclosure resulted from the actions of/information provided by the designer.¹⁶⁰ The grace period applies to identical and similar disclosures, however, Japanese law requires a declaration of disclosure from an applicant who wishes to invoke grace period, unless an abuse took place.¹⁶¹ A similar standard of absolute worldwide novelty exists in Chinese **16.071**

---

155 See Australian *Designs Act 2003* at https://www.wipo.int/wipolex/en/legislation/details/19653 (last visited 8 June 2024) and Australian *Design Regulations 2004* https://wipolex-res.wipo.int/edocs/lexdocs/laws/en/au/au186en.pdf (last visited 8 June 2024), with the latest 2021 amendments at https://www.legislation.gov.au/Details/C2021A00100 (last visited 8 June 2024).
156 More in Chapter 1 pertaining to Australian law authored by Stuart Irvine and Carl Harrap. Consult also Tyrone Berger, *Australian Design Law and Practice* (Thomson Reuters 2022), mn 2.10, p. 14–15.
157 The Indian *Designs Act No 16* of 25/05/2000 https://wipolex.wipo.int/en/text/128103 (last visited 8 June 2024); Amrita Majumdar, India Study 2021 AIPPI Q278 https://aippi.soutron.net/Portal/Default/en-GB/SearchResults (last visited 8 June 2024).
158 35 U.S. Code § 171 Patents for Designs (a)–(b). Graeme Dinwoodie, Mark Janis, *Trade Dress and Design Law* (Aspen Publishers 2010), 305-308; Suthersanen (n 77), 209–11.
159 Sarah Burstein, 'Is Design Patent Examination Too Lax?' (2018) 33 *Berkeley Technology Law Journal* 607, 611.
160 Aso, Rademacher (n 152) 353–58.
161 Etsuko Yoshida, 'Requirements for Design Protection', in Aso, Rademacher ibid., 83–84.

law. The six-month grace period has a more restricted scope than it is in the EU, there self-disclosure is confined to international exhibitions sponsored by the Chinese government or academic technological conferences.[162] The Indian grace period provision is also restrictive. It refers to a disclosure without the proprietor's consent during or following an exhibition, which enables the filing of an application within six months of the date of first exhibiting a design or an article or publishing a description of a design.[163] Another interesting example comes with the latest amendments to Australian law which introduced the 12-month grace period for designs filed or with a priority date on or after 10 March 2022. It encompasses only disclosures made after 10 March 2022 and that resulting from acts of the owner of a design, his legal predecessor, the designer, or other party that derived or obtained the design therefrom, who published or authorized the publication of the design.[164] The owner of a design who wishes to invoke the benefit of the grace period must submit to the IP Australia a declaration in which the prior use or publication of the design at issue is explained.[165] Notably, the grace period does not cover official publications by the IP Australia or foreign design offices, including WIPO and EUIPO. In US law, prior art widely comprises everything that has been made worldwide publicly available by various means, such as publication, use, sale, before the effective filing date.[166] There is a one-year grace period relating to this date which covers disclosures made by the inventor or a third party in relation to the subject-matter disclosed directly or indirectly by the inventor.[167]

16.072 The aforementioned examples are informative of how differently the non-EU laws decide on numerous aspects of the grace period exception: the duration; the persons from whom the initial disclosure of a design originated; the circumstances of the disclosure covered by an exception, and those disregarded that remain relevant for defining prior art; the possible formalities required when relying on grace period. Additional differences between the EU and non-EU design laws with impact on prior art relate to the issue of protectable subject-matter of a design (as discussed below).

---

162 More in Chapter 3 pertaining to Chinese law authored by Paolo Beconcini.
163 Art. 21 of Indian *Designs Act* (n 157).
164 Berger (n 156) mn 5.150, p. 69.
165 Ibid., p. 70.
166 See 35 U.S.C. § 102(a)(1). The adoption in 2011 of 'Leahy-Smith America Invents Act' had a direct impact on the scope of prior art for the purpose of design patents. https://www.uspto.gov/sites/default/files/aia_implementation/20110916-pub-l112-29.pdf (last visited 8 June 2024). The Act changed the system from 'first-to-invent', to 'first inventor-to-file'. Prior art comprises also antecedents filed before, but published after the filing date of the design at issue, which constitute the so-called 'secret prior art', with additional provisions introducing exceptions to this kind of disclosure, consult 35 U.S.C. § 102(b)((1) and (2).
167 See 35 U.S.C. § 102(b)(1).

2. Divergent Notions of a Protectable Design

Across the globe, there is no uniform understanding of a design right's subject-matter. As discussed in Part C.1, EU law broadly defines the notions of a 'design' and a 'product'. This enables the registration of two- and three-dimensional visual features of, both, tangible and intangible items. By contrast, numerous non-EU laws adopt more restricted approach to eligible designs. This divergence of standards has significant effects for the identification of the scope of relevant prior art. There may be EU designs that will not obtain similar protection under a non-EU design law that enshrines more restricted subject-matter. Further, such an unacceptable EU design cannot also constitute relevant prior art for the purpose of the non-EU law that disregards it as a relevant design. However, even if the features of an item cannot be protected under non-EU law, publication or use in trade may constitute a piece of relevant prior art for the purpose of EU law, if the item relates to the 'appearance of a product' within the meaning of EU law.

16.073

The following examples demonstrate that the inhibition to protect certain types of designs resides, basically, in the traditional understanding that an article should have tangible nature and be separately manufactured or sold. This is an issue that stands against an increased use of digital technology nowadays.

16.074

Australian law, although recently amended, maintains the requirement that a product must be manufactured or handmade. Furthermore, parts or portions of a product that cannot be separately made or extracted (without altering the bigger product) from a bigger product do not match the definition of a product.[168] The consequence is that virtual designs, graphic symbols or logos, get-up or arrangements of variable features, as well as certain categories of partial designs, cannot be currently protected.[169] Studies have argued in favour of further extending the scope of protectable designs to meet the needs of an innovative economy.[170]

16.075

Brazilian law defines a design as an ornamental plastic form of an object or an arrangement of lines and colours that may be applied to a product, whilst the basic conditions of protection are novelty, originality and suitability for

16.076

---

168 Irvine, Harrap (n 156).
169 Guidance conferred by the IP Australia at https://www.ipaustralia.gov.au/designs/understanding-designs/what-design-right (last visited 8 June 2024).
170 Michael Campbell, Lana Halperin, 'Redesigning Designs: The Future of Design Protection in Australia' (2020) 121 *Journal of IPSANZ* 9, 13–14; Berger (n 156) mn. 8.30, 109–11.

industrial manufacture.¹⁷¹ The latter requirement leads to the situation that two-dimensional patterns or ornamentation match this definition only if they can be applied to a product; purely artistic works do not, however, fulfil the requirement of being manufactured on industrial scale.¹⁷²

16.077 Another interesting example is Japanese law which defines a 'design' as the shape, pattern or colours, or any combination thereof, of an article or part of it, including shapes of buildings and graphical user interfaces, which creates an aesthetic impression.¹⁷³ However, additional specifications indicate that 'articles' are only movable, tangible objects – thus, not fixtures or land – capable of being distributed on the market as independent items. This means that two-dimensional graphic symbols, typefaces or mere arrangements, such as of a garden or a playground, do not fit this definition, either because of intangibility, or because of the exclusions pertaining to land and fixtures. Graphical user interfaces (GUI), exceptionally, may be protected independently from an article, if used in the operation or as a result of a device performing its function.¹⁷⁴ In a similar way, Chinese design law protects GUI, only if they serve for a physically human-machine interaction.¹⁷⁵

16.078 Indian law also protects designs in relation to articles of manufacture artificial, natural, or combined, including parts capable of being made and sold separately, which implies that intangible items, such as virtual designs, do not meet this standard.¹⁷⁶ Additional exceptions from the eligible subject-matter comprise mere mechanical devices, modes or methods of construction, trademarks and artistic works. The latter precludes the cumulation of rights during the term of design protection.

16.079 Last, but not the least, as US law does not confer a normative definition on what a 'design' may cover,¹⁷⁷ its meaning is explained by the Guidelines of the US Patent and Trademark Office. The subject-matter constitutes the design determined by visual characteristics, that is, the appearance, which is embodied

---

171 Art. 95 of *Lei no 9.279 de 14/05/1996 (Lei da Propriedade Industrial alterada pela Lei no 14.200 de 2/09/2021)* at: https://www.wipo.int/wipolex/en/text/583827 (last visited 8 June 2024).
172 Cristiane Manzueto, 'Brazil' in: *Designs Laws and Regulations* (ICLG 2022) at: https://iclg.com/practice-areas/designs-laws-and-regulations/brazil (last visited 8 June 2024).
173 Tsukasa Aso, 'Purpose of the Design Law System and the Definition of 'Design' under the Design Act', in Rademacher, Aso (eds) (n 152) 19–31.
174 Ibid., 27.
175 Ganea (n 154) 41.
176 Art. 2 of the Indian *Designs Act* (n 157).
177 35 U.S.C. § 171(a)–(b).

or applied to an article, thus, not the article itself.[178] A classification of eligible designs comprises the following categories: configuration or shape of an article, surface ornamentation applied to an article, or the combination of two.[179] This means that under US law a design cannot exist without an article, and that it must be 'a definite preconceived thing'. As compared to EU law, there is no protection of design concepts, patterns of ornamentation without surface of an article, graphic symbols, icons without the underlying object.[180] Another notable difference is that the application for a US design patent must comprise drawings and written claims, whilst the EU design law only gives relevance to the representation of a design. This may pose difficulty to the use of the centralized Hague system or the paths of Paris Convention priority right, when asking for an EU design right on the basis of a US filing, or vice versa.

3. Concluding Remarks

16.080 The specificity of the EU model of disclosure lies in the standard of relative novelty determined by the boundaries of the 'safeguard clause'. As discussed in Part B.2.(b), the safeguard clause of presumptive knowledge confined to circles specialized in the normal course of business aims at insulating against obscure disclosures that extend beyond time or territorial restrictions. This appears to be a valuable tool for business entities who do not have financial resources to undertake thorough prior art searches. However, all stakeholders require legal certainty as a major guarantee. Difficulties stem from the necessity to interpret the set of undefined concepts, such as 'normal course of business' or 'circles specialized', which are provided to define the presumptive knowledge covered by the safeguard clause. The issue is not about semantics, but about reliability and practical value. What may appear as legal ambiguity may beneficially confer the degree of flexibility and enable the safeguard clause to serve its purpose, namely, to produce sensible judgements. The EU safeguard clause has the character of an exception and requires careful, if not, restrictive interpretation.[181] For the reason that the CJEU cannot replace national courts in assessing facts and tends to avoid imparting clear-cut guidance to the referrals, the doubts that result from undefined concepts of the safeguard clause remain

---

178 https://www.uspto.gov/web/offices/pac/mpep/s1502.html (last visited 8 June 2024), para 1502.
179 Chris Carani, Dunstan Barnes, 'United States' in Chris Carani (ed.) *Design Rights. Functionality and Scope of Protection* (2nd ed, Wolters Kluwer 2022), 3–8; Suthersanen (n 77), 212–13.
180 https://www.uspto.gov/web/offices/pac/mpep/s1504.html#d0e152415 (last visited 8 June 2024), para 15.44 and 1504.01(a). For an overview with the EU law, Lena Schickl, 'Protection of Industrial Design in the United States and in the EU: Different Concepts or Different Labels?' (2013) 16(1–2) *Journal of World Intellectual Property* 15.
181 According to the Latin principle that exceptiones non sunt *extendendae*.

to be elucidated by coordinated work of the EUIPO and national courts with an aim to develop common standards of assessment.[182]

16.081 Is flexibility useful for softening the standard of absolute novelty applied by other non-EU laws? In other words, should a similar safeguard clause be implemented globally by non-EU laws? Interestingly, this was not the position expressed by the final resolution of AIPPI 2021 on 'Industrial designs and the role of prior art'. The resolution upheld the system of worldwide disclosure, however, it failed to mention a provision modelled upon the EU 'safeguard clause'.[183] The author contemplates that the current range of interpretative issues of the EU safeguard clause does not appear to encourage its transposition by other non-EU laws. The EU design practice has still much work to do on its own turf in order to develop more clear and consistent case-law, which can only later serve as a model.

16.082 The EU design law has also opted for the absence of substantive examination of design applications, viewed as an incentive to the development of design activities. A granted design right represents an economic asset, the commercialization of which may serve to attract further funding – an essential target of any start-up. Adopting a more stringent standard of protection, like that applied in patent law, would not necessarily foster the economic purpose of designs, to facilitate launch and marketing of new products. A query may arise whether the fact of increasing the number of design registrations reflects the fact that more innovative products, or at least, products of better quality are being offered. This is the point where the EU design area is in high need of dedicated market studies to measure the efficiency of design protection. From a theoretical standpoint, it seems difficult to predict which system of design protection, that is with or without substantive examination of the filing, better serves pre-defined economic goals.

16.083 Non-EU laws differ in many aspects in terms of registration framework, and more specifically the model of examination, novelty standard, and definition of prior art. As to the latter, it may be noted that, although the exception pertaining to the grace period could play an essential role in restricting the scope of prior art, it is still the subject of too many differences among the design laws worldwide. First, grace period is still not enshrined in all design

---

182 The Design Study of 2016 (n 22) 81–82 reached similar conclusions; however, it gave more confidence in the interpretative capabilities of the CJEU.
183 See res. 4) first sentence p. 2 of the Resolution at: https:// aippi .soutron .net/ Portal/ Default/ en -GB/ DownloadImageFile.ashx?objectId=8760&ownerType=0&ownerId=4156 (last visited 8 June 2024).

laws. Second, even if there is such a provision, it takes various time limits and spectrum of acts. For example, in China or India the extent of events accepted under the umbrella of grace period is so limited that it severely diminishes the practical usefulness for foreign applicants. It seems that the 12-month period preceding the filing or priority date would represent the optimal solution for a global standard. However, further clarification is required as regards the subject-matter disclosed, the type of acts disclosed, and subjective qualification of the behaviour, especially in terms of possible interaction with rules relating to abusive disclosure.

Specifically, most non-EU laws that comprise exceptions to disclosure also consider that abusive disclosure should be disregarded from the scope of prior art. However, as discussed in Part B.3, the notion of 'abuse' under EU law raises issues of interpretation in terms of subjective appreciation of the behaviour and access to the original source. For instance, an issue refers to whether the information enabling the abusive disclosure should originate only from the designer, design holder, its successors, or it may stem from any third party, regardless of the means of disclosure about the design. The standard suggested by the AIPPI 2021 Resolution appears to be a good solution. The grace period would include disclosures resulting from a 'wrongful or illegitimate act in relation to the designer, applicant or owner'.[184] These terms seem to be sufficiently broad and neutral to overcome any limitation otherwise implied by linking an abusive behaviour to a faulty conduct and damage.   16.084

Most of the countries are also parties to Paris Convention and thus a priority right from an EU country application would be accepted elsewhere. However, the variable status of grace period provisions undermines early disclosures, which, as safe as they may be for the purposes of an EU design, can block the subsequent filing in a non-EU country.   16.085

With regard to the relationship between the appearance of a product and the scope of EU and non-EU prior art, the following may constitute the essential take-away findings.   16.086

On one hand, for a design protected by an EU right or a national right of EU member states, any appearance of a product, irrespective of its form of protection, made previously available to the public according to the EU disclosure rules or applicable exceptions, constitutes prior art. This includes items which may not qualify for design protection under non-EU laws either   16.087

---

184 See res. 6) in fine p. 2 of the Resolution, ibid.

because they are not protectable subject-matter, or because they do not meet the requirements of protection. Such items, once made publicly available, may be used to challenge the validity of subsequently filed EU designs. By the time the amendments to the EU design law come into force, attention should be paid to the fact that self-disclosure of an unregistered design must occur within EU borders, otherwise it risks undermining the validity of a subsequently filed design.

16.088 On the other hand, non-EU laws generally have narrower definitions of a 'design', 'design features' and 'product' than the EU design law, with a tighter and more tangible link required between a design and a product. Particularities related to the representation of a design, such as drawing requirements, use of disclaimers, or specification via word description may render the use of one application to request protection in another country difficult. These issues demonstrate that adopting similar standards pertaining to the subject-matter of a protectable design would, indeed, facilitate global trade and business strategies based on multiple registrations. Currently, there is a set of earlier EU designs that cannot constitute relevant prior art for the purpose of non-EU law, simply because such items would have never been accepted as protectable subject-matter of a design in that particular country. It should also be borne in mind that the standard of worldwide disclosure which is linked to absolute novelty covers many more earlier designs and products made publicly available than the EU standard of relative novelty. A caveat applies that if non-EU law describes the means of making publicly available differently than EU law does, then, for instance, the mere advertisement or sale of items in a shop within the EU cannot constitute relevant disclosure for the purpose of that non-EU law.

16.089 The mosaic of design laws can at first glance be discouraging for global business strategies Consummate lawyers would find it attractive, as it fosters creative solutions. However, practical needs are more vital than speculative thinking. Globalization places the need for efforts of finding common legal rules to assist business development beyond doubt. The matter is particularly important for small- and medium-sized enterprises, if funds do not allow vast IP portfolio. The golden mean is balancing simple and clear, that is predictable, access to registration with enhanced legal certainty. Such approach appears to be the right direction of future works on the international stage towards global harmonization of design standards.

17

THE CONCEPT OF AESTHETIC CREATIVE FREEDOM IN DESIGN, COPYRIGHT, AND TRADEMARK LAW – A EUROPEAN PERSPECTIVE

Henning Hartwig[1]

A. INTRODUCTION	17.001	(b) Technical limits	17.050
B. THE LEGAL CONCEPT OF AESTHETIC CREATIVE FREEDOM	17.002	(c) Statutory limits	17.057
		2. Limits to Aesthetic Creative Freedom in Copyright Law	17.064
C. AESTHETIC CREATIVE FREEDOM IN DESIGN, COPYRIGHT, AND TRADEMARK LAW	17.007	(a) Aesthetic limits	17.064
		(b) Technical limits	17.067
1. Aesthetic Creative Freedom in Design Law	17.008	(c) Statutory limits	17.074
2. Aesthetic Creative Freedom in Copyright Law	17.014	3. Limits to Aesthetic Creative Freedom in Trademark Law	17.076
3. Aesthetic Creative Freedom in Trademark Law	17.044	(a) Aesthetic limits	17.076
		(b) Technical limits	17.078
D. LIMITS TO AESTHETIC CREATIVE FREEDOM IN DESIGN, COPYRIGHT, AND TRADEMARK LAW	17.046	(c) Statutory limits	17.085
		E. COMPARABLE STANDARDS UNDER DESIGN, COPYRIGHT, AND TRADEMARK LAW?	17.088
1. Limits to Aesthetic Creative Freedom in Design Law	17.047	1. Commonalities	17.089
(a) Aesthetic limits	17.047	2. Differences	17.092
		3. Too Much Cumulation?	17.096

---

[1] Updated and extended version of a German text previously published; see HARTWIG, *Grenzen ästhetischer Gestaltungsfreiheit* [2021] MarkenR 349–362. Aspects of trade dress law are not covered hereafter. The author would like to thank Burga Lenz, trainee lawyer (Munich, Germany), for carefully reading and improving earlier versions of the manuscript.

A. INTRODUCTION

17.001 At first glance, this topic may not seem very familiar, as the concept of 'aesthetic creative freedom' in European design, copyright, and trademark law can be found neither in law nor practice. However, the concept of the 'degree of freedom of the designer in developing the design'[2] or, as repeatedly used by the German Federal Supreme Court,[3] the term 'creative leeway' or 'creative room for manoeuvre' is commonly known. Such terms are used not only in design but particularly in copyright law.[4] The concept of 'aesthetic design' is also repeatedly referred to in, for instance, German practice.[5] In light of most recent case law, the following questions seem worth being addressed below: Are there limits to aesthetic creative freedom and, if so, where do they lie? Do any such limits differ depending on the underlying intellectual property right? Might there be even more commonalities than differences? In short: Where do design and copyright law, on the one hand, and design and trademark law, on the other, meet?[6]

B. THE LEGAL CONCEPT OF AESTHETIC CREATIVE FREEDOM

17.002 From a theoretical perspective, and considering substantive law, it seems appropriate to interpret the term 'aesthetic creative freedom' as a legal concept.[7] This appears to make sense given that, for instance, German public planning approval law refers to 'limits to plan-related creative freedom'.[8]

---

2   *Cf.* Article 6 (2), 10 (2) Council Regulation (EC) No 6/2002 of 12 December 2001 on Community designs [2002] OJ L 3, 1 ('CDR'); Article 5 (2), 9 (2) Directive 98/71/EC of the European Parliament and of the Council of 13 October 1998 on the legal protection of designs [1998] OJ L 289, 28 ('Designs Directive'). On the freedom of the designer under Community design law overall HARTWIG, *Gestaltungsfreiheit im Gemeinschaftsgeschmacksmusterrecht* [2020] GRUR 1260–1267.

3   *E.g.*, *Writing Utensil*, German Federal Supreme Court, 24 March 2011, I ZR 211/08, para 32; *Pram II*, German Federal Supreme Court, 12 July 2012, I ZR 102/11, para 32.

4   *E.g.*, Case C-683/17 *Cofemel v G-Star* ECLI:EU:C:2019:721, para 31 ('no room for creative freedom'); *Birthday Train*, German Federal Supreme Court, 13 November 2013, I ZR 143/12, para 41.

5   *E.g.*, *Climbing Spider*, German Federal Supreme Court, 12 May 2011, I ZR 53/10, para 31.

6   *Cf.* also VON MÜHLENDAHL, *Three-Dimensional Trademarks and Designs: Comparison and Conflict*, in: HARTWIG (ed), *Research Handbook on Design Law* (Edward Elgar Publishing 2021), 441–481.

7   See also *Meda Gate*, German Federal Supreme Court, 24 January 2019, I ZR 164/17, para 32:
    It is essentially up to the trial court to determine whether the overall impression of the conflicting designs is the same. Upon appeal on points of law, it is only necessary to examine whether the trial court used an appropriate legal concept as a basis, did not violate empirical principles or laws of thought and did not disregard any essential circumstances.

8   *Cf.* IBLER, *Die Schranken planerischer Gestaltungsfreiheit im Planfeststellungsrecht*, 1988 (also Dissertation University of Göttingen 1987).

17.003 Against this background, the concept of creative freedom is not synonymous with 'aesthetic freedom' (nor 'creative' with 'aesthetic') and the concept of 'aesthetic creative freedom' by no means tautological.[9] This also follows *argumentum e contrario* from European design law, according to which the 'degree of freedom of the designer in developing the design' must be taken into account.[10]

17.004 If 'creative freedom' were simply to be understood as the freedom of the designer of the design, there would have been no need for the specification. Moreover, the term 'designer of a design' suggests that there may also be other designers, for example the designer of two-dimensional construction drawings or architectural plans, which neither concern the appearance of a product, i.e., an industrial or handicraft item, nor packaging, get-up, graphic symbols, or typographic typefaces,[11] but are merely blueprints for the appearance of a finished product.

17.005 Moreover, the term 'aesthetic'[12] is not to be equated with 'artistic'; in this respect, the German Supreme Court clearly differentiates between 'artistic work' and the 'aesthetic effect of the design' based on it.[13] The fact that, according to recent case law, an 'aesthetic effect'[14] or an 'aesthetic surplus'[15] is no longer necessary does not change this conclusion.

17.006 Is the suggested concept of aesthetic creative freedom thus merely a synonym for the parameter of the 'degree of freedom of the designer in developing the design'?[16] No – because, in the present context, 'functional creative freedom'

---

9   *Cf.* above n 5.
10 *Cf.* Article 6 (2), 10 (2) CDR; Article 5 (2), 9 (2) Designs Directive.
11 *Cf.* Article 3 lit b CDR; Article 1 lit b Designs Directive.
12 *Cf.*, to that extent, also GÜVEN, *Eliminating 'Aesthetics' from Copyright Law: The Aftermath of 'Cofemel'*, [2022] GRUR Int. 213.
13 *Birthday Train*, German Federal Supreme Court, 13 November 2013, I ZR 143/12, para 41. – See also Case C-683/17 *Cofemel v G-Star* ECLI:EU:C:2019:721, para 31:
    On the other hand, when the realisation of a subject matter has been dictated by technical considerations, rules or other constraints, which have left no room for creative freedom, that subject matter cannot be regarded as possessing the originality required for it to constitute a work.
14 See also Case C-683/17 *Cofemel v G-Star* ECLI:EU:C:2019:721, para 54:
    Nonetheless, the fact remains that the circumstance that a design may generate an aesthetic effect does not, in itself, make it possible to determine whether that design constitutes an intellectual creation reflecting the freedom of choice and personality of its author, thereby meeting the requirement of originality (...).
    Thus, the concept of 'artistic value', as stated in Article 2 (10) Italian Copyright Act, is no longer allowed. However, recent case law speaks a different language; *cf.* PEROTTI, 'The Court of Milan on the impact of 'Cofemel' on the copyright protection of industrial designs in Italy. A new CJEU referral on the horizon?' (IPlens, 22 June 2021) https://iplens.org/2021/06/22/the-court-of-milan-on-the-impact-of-Cofemel-on-the-copyright-protection-of-industrial-designs-in-italy-a-new-cjeu-referral-on-the-horizon/ accessed 31 December 2023.
15 *Paper Dispenser*, German Federal Supreme Court [2022] IIC 278, 281 para 12.
16 *Cf.* Article 6 (2) CDR.

of the designer might also be possible.[17] Hence, 'aesthetic creative freedom' is to be understood more narrowly, allowing for the 'choice of a product's shape as the result of a free and creative decision' (on this phrasing borrowed from CJEU jurisprudence see C 2 below). This 'choice of shape' (not: 'choice of function') can be limited by a variety of constraints, namely aesthetic (i.e., 'departure' from existing design corpus), technical ('dictated by function') as well as statutory (i.e., 'standards').[18]

C. AESTHETIC CREATIVE FREEDOM IN DESIGN, COPYRIGHT, AND TRADEMARK LAW

17.007 Over time, the progression of case law has led to a remarkable overlap and cross-fertilisation with respect to how aesthetic creative freedom is variously understood in design, copyright, and trademark law. Nevertheless, remaining differences are considerable and justify cumulative protection, i.e., where protection is sought not only under design law but, for example, also under trademark law, clearly different requirements will need to be met.

1. Aesthetic Creative Freedom in Design Law

17.008 Under harmonised European design law, the German Federal Supreme Court has found, with respect to the establishment of rights (validity), as follows:[19]

> (…) [A] design shall be considered to have individual character if its overall impression produced on the informed user differs from the overall impression produced on such a user by any design which has been disclosed before the date of filing the application. In this assessment, the degree of freedom of the designer in developing his design shall be taken into consideration. As a consequence of a great concentration of designs and only little freedom of the designer, already minor differences in appearance may produce a different overall impression on the informed user. In contrast, a low concentration of designs and, therefore, a great freedom of the designer may not produce a different overall impression on the informed user, even in case of major differences in appearance (…).

---

17   See also US trade dress law, differentiating between 'utilitarian functionality' and 'aesthetic functionality'; *cf.*, e.g., *Rubik's Brand Limited v Flambeau, Inc., et al*, No. 17CV6559PGGKHP, 2021 WL 363704 (S.D.N.Y. 31 Jan 2021); BELDIMAN, *Protecting the Form but Not the Function: Is U.S. Law Ready for a New Model High Tech?*, (2004) *Santa Clara Computer & High Tech. L.J.* 529–75.

18   In January 1933, days only before Nazism ultimately took over Germany, the Imperial Court ('Reichsgericht' as it was called in those days) confirmed that, under German copyright law, a distinction must be made between the 'utilitarian purpose of design' and the 'aesthetic surplus'; *Door Opener*, 14 January 1933, I 149/32: 'The realm of aesthetics and art only begins where the more detailed form must be developed beyond the circumstances dedicated to the purpose.'

19   For example, *Writing Utensil*, German Federal Supreme Court, 24 March 2011, I ZR 211/08, para 32.

In this respect, 'concentration of designs' is to be understood – qualitatively or materially – in the sense of an existing *variety of designs* (similar or non-similar to each other).[20]

17.009

Pursuant to Article 10 (2) CDR, in 'assessing the scope of protection (of a design), the degree of freedom of the designer in developing his design shall be taken into consideration'. Starting from that proposition, the German Federal Supreme Court confirmed[21] that there exists an:

17.010

> (...) interaction between the designer's freedom and the design's scope of protection. A great concentration of designs and only little freedom of the designer can lead to a narrow scope of protection of the design so that minor differences in appearance may produce a different overall impression on the informed user. In contrast, a low concentration of designs and, therefore, a great freedom of the designer can lead to a broad scope of protection of the design so that even major differences in appearance may not produce a different overall impression on the informed user (...). The scope of protection of the claimed design is also determined by its departure from the existing design corpus. The greater the distance between the claimed design and the prior art, the greater the scope of protection of the claimed design. (...) for assessing the scope of protection of the claimed design, one must take into account the extent to which the designer actually used the freedom of design available to him. The scope of protection of the claimed design, therefore, is determined by the concentration of designs, on the one hand (...), and the utilisation of the freedom of design by the designer and the departure from the prior art thus achieved, on the other.

According to the German Federal Supreme Court, this *'doctrine of departure'* applies to the assessment of infringement (more precisely: when determining the scope of protection) but not – at least not explicitly – when testing validity.[22]

17.011

---

20 *Cf.* in detail HARTWIG, *Musterdichte und Mustervielfalt im Geschmacksmusterrecht* [2015] GRUR 845–851, submitting in detail that and why a great concentration of designs corresponds to a low variety/multiplicity of designs/forms and *vice versa*. See also HARTWIG, *Reciprocity in European Design Law*, in: HARTWIG (ed), *Research Handbook on Design Law* (Edward Elgar Publishing 2021) 119, 121–124.
21 *E.g.*, *Pram II*, German Federal Supreme Court, 12 July 2012, I ZR 102/11, paras 31–32.
22 According to the General Court of the EU, the following test applies when assessing individual character of a design (Case T-209/18 *Porsche/EUIPO and Autec* ECLI:EU:T:2019:377, paras 45–46):
   (...) the greater the designer's freedom in developing a design, the less likely it is that minor differences between the designs at issue will be sufficient to produce different overall impressions on an informed user. Conversely, the more limited the designer's freedom in developing a design, in particular by the constraints referred to above, the more likely it is that minor differences between the designs at issue will be sufficient to produce different overall impressions on that category of user. Therefore, if the designer enjoys a high degree of freedom in developing a design, that reinforces the conclusion that the designs which do not display significant differences will produce the same overall impression on an informed user (...).
   The Court also stressed that the decisive factor is that the designer actually uses the available freedom, *e.g.*, Case T-10/08 *Kwang Yang Motor Co. Ltd. v Honda Giken Kogyo Kabushiki Kaisha* ECLI:EU:T:2011:446, para 36: '(...) the designer of the internal combustion engine is free to choose the shape of the components of that engine and their position'; Case T-90/16 *Thomas Murphy/EUIPO and Nike Innovate CV* ECLI:EU:T:2017:464, para 46: '(...) it could still be designed and situated on the product in various ways,

17.012 In fact, since the Community Designs Regulation ('CDR') came into force on 6 March 2002, the German Federal Supreme Court has had the opportunity to rule on the requirements for examining the individual character of a design only twice.[23] All other proceedings before the German Federal Supreme Court dealt either with the former version of the German Designs Act, issues of inconsistent subject matter, the solely-dictated-by-function-defence, issues of disclosure, ownership, the repair-clause-defence, prior use or questions of infringement.[24] The reason for this is that, according to the Supreme Court, individual character and scope of protection – quasi in breach of the concept of reciprocity[25] – do not necessarily (have to) correspond.[26] Proceeding from that case law, correctly read, there is no 'scope' of individual character (different from the 'scope' of protection).[27] Therefore, one cannot conclude the scope of protection (i.e., large, medium, or small) from the mere presence (or absence) of individual character (which requires a finding of 'yes' or 'no'). This marks a significant divergence from current copyright law and the former German design law (see C 2 below).

17.013 However, the degree of freedom of design, which has an impact both when assessing individual character and scope of protection, cannot be determined differently in proceedings in which both validity and infringement are at stake. As a result, even though there is no direct symmetry between the requirements for protection and the scope of protection, if the use of a small degree of creative freedom is deemed sufficient to find validity (which is often doubtful), the scope of protection would in any case be limited. In principle, however, the *abstract degree of freedom of design* is rather broad (or at least average) because of the great variety or multiplicity of designs, which is why it essentially comes down to the specific departure of the individual design from the existing

---

and numerous configurations of that button were possible'. As a result, finding presence or absence of individual character also depends on the existing abstract freedom of the designer (resulting from a large, medium, or small variety/multiplicity of earlier forms) on the one hand and its concrete use (manifested in a corresponding departure from the prior art) on the other hand while – as it happens when assessing scope of protection – a correspondingly large departure must be required in case of a broad abstract freedom of the designer.

23 *Cf. Writing Utensil*, German Federal Supreme Court, 24 March 2011, I ZR 211/08, para 32, where the court, however, did not establish the 'doctrine of departure' as it later did when determining the scope of protection (*Writing Utensil*, para 42).
24 For details see HARTWIG, *Grenzen ästhetischer Gestaltungsfreiheit* [2021] MarkenR 349, 350.
25 For a recent summary see HARTWIG, *Reciprocity in European Design Law*, in: HARTWIG (ed), *Research Handbook on Design Law* (Edward Elgar Publishing 2021) 119–168.
26 *Table Mat*, German Federal Supreme Court, 19 May 2010, I ZR 71/08, para 14.
27 See also, *e.g.*, BRÜCKNER-HOFMANN, in: HARTWIG, *Design Protection in Europe*, Vol. 4 (Carl Heymanns 2012) 115.

design corpus (both in case of assessing individual character and the scope of protection).[28]

2. Aesthetic Creative Freedom in Copyright Law

According to the CJEU, the following applies under European copyright law (when finding whether protection subsists):[29] 17.014

> (...) Articles 2 to 5 of Directive 2001/29 must be interpreted as meaning that the copyright protection provided for therein applies to a product whose shape is, at least in part, necessary to obtain a technical result, where that product is an original work resulting from intellectual creation, in that, through that shape, its author expresses his creative ability in an original manner by making free and creative choices in such a way that that shape reflects his personality, which it is for the national court to verify, bearing in mind all the relevant aspects of the dispute in the main proceedings.

A prerequisite for a finding of sufficient originality ('original work') is therefore that the author has made – 'through that shape' – 'free and creative choices', i.e., has taken advantage of an existing aesthetic freedom of choice. 17.015

The test according to *'Cofemel'* is, in essence, not merely two-staged but rather complex. The decisive factor for the establishment of copyright protection is that the subject matter in question constitutes the 'author's own intellectual creation' ('originality') (1) and that the corresponding 'elements' 'express such a creation' ('requirement of precision and objectivity') (2).[30] 17.016

With respect to (1), it is required that the object '(...) reflects the personality of its author, as an expression of his free and creative choices'[31] (1.1) so that the realisation of the object is not '(...) dictated by technical considerations, rules 17.017

---

28 *E.g.*, *Wristwatch*, German Federal Supreme Court, 28 January 2016, I ZR 40/14, para 32; *Pram II*, German Federal Supreme Court, 12 July 2012, I ZR 102/11, para 45; *Milla*, German Federal Supreme Court, 23 February 2012, I ZR 68/11, para 21; *Table Mat*, German Federal Supreme Court, 19 May 2010, I ZR 71/08, para 19. – Case law shows that, over the years, the degree of freedom was found either broad or average, but never (or extremely seldom) narrow; see Case T-684/20 *Legero/EUIPO and Rieker* ECLI:EU:T:2021:912, para 73:
  The EU judge finds the degree of freedom of the designer as broad or very broad if different designs are conceivable for a product, if the product can be produced in a variety of shapes, colours, or materials, where the description of the product in question is very broad and does not contain any information about its nature or functionality, or when the functional constraints related to the presence of certain essential elements do not affect, to a significant extent, the shape and general appearance of the product, which can have different shapes and can be designed in different ways.
29 Case C-833/18 *Brompton v Chedech/Get2Get* ECLI:EU:C:2020:461, para 38; *cf.* also Case C-683/17 *Cofemel v G-Star* ECLI:EU:C:2019:721, para 30.
30 Case C-683/17 *Cofemel v G-Star* ECLI:EU:C:2019:721, paras 29 and 32.
31 Case C-683/17 *Cofemel v G-Star* ECLI:EU:C:2019:721, para 30.

or other constraints, which have left no room for creative freedom' (1.2).[32] Also – this is the essence of *Cofemel* – '(...) the fact (...) that a design may generate an aesthetic effect does not, in itself, make it possible to determine whether that design constitutes an intellectual creation reflecting the freedom of choice and personality of its author' (1.3).[33]

17.018 With respect to (2), the 'existence of a subject matter that is identifiable with sufficient precision and objectivity' is required,[34] i.e., the subject matter protected must be 'clearly and precisely' identifiable (2.1) and it must have been 'expressed in an objective manner'[35] (2.2). A 'factor of aesthetic originality' is not relevant in this respect which is another result of *Cofemel* (2.3);[36] an 'aesthetic effect', which is the 'product of an intrinsically subjective sensation of beauty experienced by each individual who may look at that design', does not permit 'a subject matter to be characterised as existing and identifiable with sufficient precision and objectivity'.[37]

17.019 This understanding of law – the test whether there is 'room for creative freedom'[38] on the one hand and the creation of a 'subject matter (...) characterised as existing and identifiable with sufficient precision and objectivity'[39] on the other – coincides with German case law (in the context of finding subsistence of copyright):[40]

> The Court of Appeal has clearly assumed that it is neither submitted nor evident based on which individual features of appearance, that go beyond the technical idea and its implementation, the climbing spider made by the claimant may have acquired copyright protection. It took the view that the claimant did not use the existing room for an aesthetic design, which was relatively small *a priori*.

17.020 A short time later, the German Supreme Court confirmed its opinion[41] (again at the level of finding subsistence of copyright):

> Even if there are no stricter requirements – on the level of finding originality – with respect to works of applied art in comparison with works of fine art, it must be taken into account, when assessing whether such a work reaches the level of originality

---

32 Case C-683/17 *Cofemel v G-Star* ECLI:EU:C:2019:721, para 31.
33 Case C-683/17 *Cofemel v G-Star* ECLI:EU:C:2019:721, para 54.
34 Case C-683/17 *Cofemel v G-Star* ECLI:EU:C:2019:721, para 32.
35 Case C-683/17 *Cofemel v G-Star* ECLI:EU:C:2019:721, para 33.
36 Case C-683/17 *Cofemel v G-Star* ECLI:EU:C:2019:721, para 49.
37 Case C-683/17 *Cofemel v G-Star* ECLI:EU:C:2019:721, para 53.
38 Case C-683/17 *Cofemel v G-Star* ECLI:EU:C:2019:721, para 31.
39 Case C-683/17 *Cofemel v G-Star* ECLI:EU:C:2019:721, para 53; see also para 32.
40 *Climbing Spider*, German Federal Supreme Court, 12 May 2011, I ZR 53/10, para 31.
41 *Birthday Train*, German Federal Supreme Court, 13 November 2013, I ZR 143/12, para 41.

required for copyright protection, that the aesthetic effect of the design can only justify copyright protection if it is not due to the intended purpose of use but is based on an artistic effort (…). An author's own intellectual creation requires that there is room to manoeuvre which is used by the author to express his creative mind in an inventive way (…).

17.021 Although the Supreme Court has not yet opined on the 'precision and objectivity' requirement in the copyright context, it has done so under trademark[42] and design law.[43]

17.022 In the context of copyright infringement, the standard is as follows:[44]

When examining whether there is a derivative work, it is first necessary to decide in detail which objective features determine the creative individuality of the original used. The decisive criterion in this respect is an overall comparison with the prior designs, for which the overall impression of the original and the features of appearance on which it is based are the starting point. The result of this overall comparison also determines the degree of individuality on which the scope of protection depends.

---

42 *E.g.*, *Variable Figurative Mark*, German Federal Supreme Court, 6 February 2013, I ZB 85/11, para 21 ('subject matter of the application must be sufficiently clear, unambiguous and self-contained, thus not merely abstract, but concretely defined').

43 *E.g.*, *Sports Helmet*, German Federal Supreme Court, 20 December 2018, I ZB 25/18, para 19: '(…) third parties, and in particular competitors, must be able to see directly and unambiguously, for reasons of legal certainty, from the representation of the design (…) what the holder claims protection for (…).'

44 *Dog Figure*, German Federal Supreme Court, 8 July 2004, I ZR 25/02 [at III 5 a]. – So far, to the best of the author's knowledge, there is no detailed CJEU case law establishing standards for assessing scope of protection and finding infringement. Rather, the CJEU only stated that '(…) nothing in Directive 2001/29 or in any other directive applicable in this field supports the view that the extent of such protection should depend on possible differences in the degree of creative freedom in the production of various categories of works' (Case C-145/10 *Painer v Standard* ECLI:EU:C:2011:798, para 97) and that, with respect to a portrait photograph, protection '(…) cannot be inferior to that enjoyed by other works, including other photographic works' (para 98). – These findings are in line with '*Infopaq/DDF*' where the CJEU emphasised that a 'high level of protection' must be ensured for the benefit of the author (Case C-5/08 *Infopaq v Danske Dagblades Forening* ECLI:EU:C:2009:465, para 40), that the '(…) acts covered by the right of reproduction be construed broadly' (para 41), and that protection 'must be given a broad interpretation' (para 43). In this respect, according to the CJEU, the question is whether '(…) the elements (…) reproduced are the expression of the intellectual creation of their author' which is for the national court to determine (para 51).

17.023 In contrast to design law, thus, under copyright law, a low level of individuality/originality – reciprocally – results in a correspondingly narrow scope of protection.[45] In this regard, according to the German Supreme Court,[46]

> (…) the law under the Community Designs Regulation differs from the law applied in Germany before the implementation of Directive 98/71/EC on the legal protection of designs. Accordingly, the degree of individuality to be determined by an overall comparison with the existing design corpus was decisive for the scope of protection of the claimed design (…).

17.024 In fact, the German Federal Supreme Court, with respect to the former German Designs Act, recently confirmed:[47]

> Assessing individuality and its degree – unlike assessing novelty – must not to be carried out by an individual comparison of the claimed design with each single prior design but by an overall comparison with the design corpus in the sector concerned. The overall impression must be based on the establishment of the overall impression of the claimed design and the features of appearance on which that overall impression is based (…).

17.025 This dichotomy between *'one-to-one comparison'* (design law)[48] and *'overall comparison'* (copyright law) as established under German law and practice is fundamental when comparing both regimes and discussing their possible overlap/overreach (see below E). Interestingly, it seems that Danish[49] and Swiss[50] copyright law and practice likewise endorse the overall-comparison-concept.

17.026 With a view to establishing copyright protection and the criterion of the overall comparison, the *'Cofemel'* decision does not change the fact that it is left to national law to determine the degree of freedom of design in each individual case, the specific exploitation/use of which is decisive. In this respect, the

---

45 The extent to which this well-established German case law withstands scrutiny by the CJEU may appear to be open; see Case C-683/17 *Cofemel v G-Star* ECLI:EU:C:2019:721, para 35: 'Where a subject matter (…) constitutes a work, it must, as such, qualify for copyright protection, in accordance with Directive 2001/29, and it must be added that the extent of that protection does not depend on the degree of creative freedom exercised by its author, and that that protection is therefore not inferior to that to which any work falling within the scope of that directive is entitled.' However, the CJEU only dealt with this issue as *obiter dictum*. It would also seem inconsistent to consider the 'degree of creative freedom' when determining subsistence but not when determining scope of protection (see also further below in this subchapter).
46 *Table Mat*, German Federal Court of Justice, 19 May 2010, I ZR 71/08, para 15.
47 *Wristwatch*, German Federal Court of Justice, 28 January 2016, I ZR 40/14, para 21.
48 E.g., *Stretch-Limousine*, German Federal Court of Justice, 22 April 2010, I ZR 89/08, para 33.
49 *Ilse Jacobsen Rubber Boots*, Danish Supreme Court, 10 June 2020, BS-7741/2019-HJR, [2021] IIC 228, 233 ('combination of elements from traditional long leather boots with a natural rubber boot').
50 *Barbecue grill*, Aargau Commercial Court, 3 August 2021, HOR.2019.16 (at 4.2.1: 'so-called mosaic examination according to which the design corpus is dissected into single elements to be compared is inadmissible'). – The decision was confirmed by *Barbecue grill*, Swiss Federal Supreme Court, 17 June 2022, 4A_472/2021 and 4A_482/2021.

CJEU merely requires that – in the positive sense – the subject matter must reflect the personality of its author by expressing his free and creative choices[51] or – negatively – that the realisation of the subject matter has not been dictated by technical considerations, rules or other constraints, which have left no room for creative freedom.[52] How creative freedom is to be determined – beyond these limits (see D 2 below) – is up to the Member States[53] ('aesthetic considerations' may well be important but not any 'aesthetic effect').[54]

In other words: Standards for finding copyright infringement remain within the confines of national jurisprudence. Accordingly, the German Federal Supreme Court recently held:[55]

17.027

> There is no need to refer the matter to the Court of Justice of the European Union pursuant to Article 267 (3) TFEU. It follows from the foregoing that, in the case at hand, no question of interpretation of EU law relevant to this judgment arises which either has not already been clarified by the case law of the CJEU or which cannot be answered beyond doubt (...). There is no reasonable doubt that the statement of the CJEU that the scope of protection of a work of applied art is not inferior to that of other works covered by Directive 2001/29/EC (...) refers solely to the legal standard that applies equally to all categories of works and does not conflict with the determination of the specific scope of copyright protection of a work, which must be carried out in each individual case, taking into account the level of originality. The CJEU has clarified, in the decisions 'Infopaq International' (...) and 'Pelham et al.' (...), the principles according to which the scope of protection of copyright exploitation rights is determined. In view of the Appeal Court's assessment of the overall impression of the cabinet lamps, the question does not arise, in the case at hand (...), whether it is compatible with Article 2 lit a Directive 2001/29/EC if the national court, when examining a reproduction, only considers the creative individual features that *eo ipso* establish copyright protection and, conversely, does not take the overall impression into account.

---

51   Case C-683/17 *Cofemel v G-Star* ECLI:EU:C:2019:721, para 30.
52   Case C-683/17 *Cofemel v G-Star* ECLI:EU:C:2019:721, para 31.
53   As far as can be seen, this is also the approach taken by lower German courts when applying *Cofemel* or *Brompton*, proceeding from an unchanged practice of overall comparison; see, e.g., *Porsche 911*, Stuttgart Appeal Court, 20 November 2020, 5 U 125/19 [under II C 5 e cc (1)] being confirmed, to that extent, by *Porsche 911*, German Federal Supreme Court, 7 April 2022, I ZR 222/20, para 31; *Beetle*, Braunschweig Appeal Court, 10 March 2022, 2 U 47/19 [under B 1 f cc (4)]; *Magnetic Jewellery*, Frankfurt Appeal Court, 15 September 2020, 11 U 76/19 [under I 1 d]; *Lego Mini Figure*, Dusseldorf District Court, 8 December 2022, 14c O 46/21 [at B I 2 e]; *USM Haller*, Dusseldorf District Court, 14 July 2020, 14c O 57/19 [at C I 2 b]. – Italian case law, however, has not yet really divested itself of the 'artistic value' criterion (n 14 above).
54   Case C-683/17 *Cofemel v G-Star* ECLI:EU:C:2019:721, paras 53 and 54.
55   *Cabinet Lamp*, German Federal Supreme Court, 15 December 2022, I ZR 173/21, para 37 (referring to *Porsche 911*, German Federal Supreme Court, 17 April 2022, I ZR 222/20, para 100).

17.028 And: In '*Porsche 911*', the German Federal Supreme Court provided for a detailed scheme how to test copyright infringement:[56]

1. What are the objective features determining the creative originality of the earlier work?
2. Are the creative features of the earlier work copied by the later design (and to what extent)?
3. Does the overall impression produced by the earlier work match with the overall impression produced by the later design, taking all copied creative features into account?
   3.1 Mere reproduction?
   3.2 Derivative work?
   3.3 Other transformation of the earlier work?
4. Does the overall impression produced by the earlier work differ from the overall impression produced by the later design, taking all copied creative features into account?
   4.1 No reproduction/adoption of earlier work
   4.2 Free/fair use (later design also protected under copyright law)

17.029 On 21 September 2023, 17 months after '*Porsche 911*', the Swedish Patent and Market Court of Appeal issued a court order,[57] referring questions to the CJEU for a preliminary ruling pursuant to Article 267 TFEU concerning the interpretation of Directive 2001/29/EC. The questions read as follows:

1. In the assessment of whether a subject-matter of applied art merits the far-reaching protection of copyright as a work within the meaning of Articles 2 to 4 of Directive 2001/29/EC, how should the examination be carried out – and which factors must or should be taken into account – in the question of whether the subject-matter reflects the author's personality by giving expression to his or her free and creative choices? In that regard, the question is in particular whether the examination of originality should focus on factors surrounding the creative process and the author's explanation of the actual choices that he or she made in the creation of the subject-matter or on factors relating to the subject-matter itself and the end result of the creative process and whether the subject-matter itself gives expression to artistic effect.

---

56   *Porsche 911*, German Federal Supreme Court, 17 April 2022, I ZR 222/20, para 57.
57   *Mio and Others v Galleri Mikael & Thomas Asplund Aktiebolag*, Swedish Patent and Market Court of Appeal, 21 September 2023, PMT 13496-22 https://curia.europa.eu/juris/showPdf.jsf?text=&docid=279261&pageIndex=0&doclang=EN&mode=lst&dir=&occ=first&part=1&cid=1227963 accessed 31 December 2023. – The matter is now pending before the CJEU; C-580/23.

2. For the answer to Question 1 and the question of whether a subject-matter of applied art reflects the author's personality by giving expression to his or her free and creative choices, what is the significance of the facts that
   (a) the subject-matter consists of elements that are found in common designs?
   (b) the subject-matter builds on and constitutes a variation of an earlier known design or an ongoing design trend?
   (c) identical or similar subject-matter has been created before or – independently and without knowing whether the subject-matter of applied art for which protection as a work is claimed – after the creation of the subject-matter in question?
3. How should the assessment of similarity be carried out – and what similarity is required – in the examination of whether an allegedly infringing subject-matter of applied art is covered by a work's scope of protection and infringes the exclusive right to the work which, according to Articles 2 to 4 of Directive 2001/29/EC, must be conferred on the author? In that regard, the question is in particular whether the examination should focus on whether the work is recognisable in the allegedly infringing subject-matter or on whether the allegedly infringing subject-matter creates the same overall impression as the work, or what else the examination should focus on.
4. For the answer to Question 3 and the question of whether an allegedly infringing subject-matter of applied art is covered by a work's scope of protection and infringes the exclusive right to the work, what is the significance of
   (a) the degree of originality of the work for the scope of the work's protection?
   (b) the fact that the work and the allegedly infringing subject-matter of applied art consist of elements found in common designs or build on and constitute variations of earlier known designs or an ongoing design trend?
   (c) the fact that other identical or similar subject-matter has been created before or – independently and without knowledge of the work – after the creation of the work?

17.030 This referral, inspiring as it may appear on the outside,[58] seems to mix or even confuse established principles of law and practice for finding copyright infringement, including CJEU and German case law:

---

58 The recent request for a preliminary ruling is likely to make history. In any event, the German Federal Supreme Court, in view of that referral, suspended the 'USM Haller' proceedings (I ZR 96/22) and sub-

17.031 *First*, to the extent that the Court concluded that it was unclear '(…) how what the CJEU has stated regarding the originality of a work – that the work must express the free and creative choice of the author – should be interpreted and applied (…)' and, more specifically, '(…) how the concrete assessment should be made – and which factors should or should be taken into account – in the question of whether a work of applied art reflects the personality of the author, by expressing his free and creative choice (…)'[59], the Court, in the author's opinion, ignores the fact that the CJEU, in *'Brompton'*, found that:[60]

> (…) copyright protection (…) applies to a product whose shape is, at least in part, necessary to obtain a technical result, where that product is an original work resulting from intellectual creation, in that, through that shape, its author expresses his creative ability in an original manner by making free and creative choices in such a way that that shape reflects his personality, *which it is for the national court to verify, bearing in mind all the relevant aspects of the dispute in the main proceedings.*

17.032 Interestingly, even the Swedish Patent and Market Court of Appeal concedes that such understanding would focus on whether '(….) the author has had room and has in fact made various choices in the creation of the work, that these choices are not governed by technical considerations, rules or requirements and that the choices are in some way reflected and expressed in the work'.[61] However, the Court errs when concluding that such a '(…) far-reaching interpretation would (…) mean that the assessment should be based on the creation process itself and the choices made by the author in this process'.[62] Contrary to that understanding, the underlying assessment is not based on the choices made by the author in the 'creation process' but, quite the opposite, the *result of that process, which is reflected in the work itself – and only in the work – and its departure from the existing design corpus.*[63] Consequently, the Court errs when

---

mitted three questions to the CJEU concerning the interpretation of the term 'works'; *USM Haller*, German Federal Supreme Court, 21 December 2023, I ZR 96/22 https://www.bundesgerichtshof.de/SharedDocs/ Pressemitteilungen/EN/2023/2023210.html?nn=10690868 accessed 31 December 2023.

59 *Mio and Others v Galleri Mikael & Thomas Asplund Aktiebolag*, Swedish Patent and Market Court of Appeal, 21 September 2023, PMT 13496-22, para 25 (since the translation and 'summary of the request for a preliminary ruling' provided by the CJEU differs from the text of the original in that the original makes repeated, albeit sometimes inaccurate reference to German case law while this reference is no longer contained in the translation and summary provided by the CJEU this author hereafter proceeds from an English translation of the original).

60 Case C-833/18 *Brompton v Chedech/Get2Get* ECLI:EU:C:2020:461, para 38 (emphasis added).

61 *Mio and Others v Galleri Mikael & Thomas Asplund Aktiebolag*, Swedish Patent and Market Court of Appeal, 21 September 2023, PMT 13496-22, para 26.

62 *Mio and Others v Galleri Mikael & Thomas Asplund Aktiebolag*, Swedish Patent and Market Court of Appeal, 21 September 2023, PMT 13496-22, para 26.

63 See above C 1 regarding design law and below E 1. – See also *Mio and Others v Galleri Mikael & Thomas Asplund Aktiebolag*, Swedish Patent and Market Court of Appeal, 21 September 2023, PMT 13496-22, para 31 ('assessment as to whether the work of applied art reflects the personality of the author, by expressing his

finding that – proceeding, wrongly, from the process of creation, not the result – this would '(…) mean that, in principle, all the choices made by the creator during the creation and which were not guided by technical considerations, rules or requirements, would be considered free and creative'.[64] No, again quite to the contrary, the test is whether the author actually used the existing room to make free and creative choices – which, when considering the result of that process, is shown by the degree of departure from the existing design corpus and, thus, the level of originality.[65]

Second, to the extent that the Swedish Patent and Market Court of Appeal found that – again, wrongly, proceeding from the process of creation, not the result – such an approach would result in that the '(…) question of whether the work exhibits sufficient originality would thus become a *question of evidence* rather than a question of law (…)'[66] this finding is indeed in line with 'Brompton' as shown above.[67]

17.033

Third, as far as the Court concludes that proceeding from the question of whether the work exhibits sufficient originality as a question of evidence would mean '(…) that fairly low demands are placed on the creative and free choices that the author must have made and that a work of applied art must express (…)'[68] this is, again, incorrect. Rather, all (i.e., the level of originality and, consequently, the scope of protection) depends on the degree of departure from the existing design corpus as expressed in the specific work. In other words: The larger the degree of departure, the greater the level of originality and, consequently, the scope of protection.[69] As a result, there is no '(…) risk leading to the granting of copyright protection to works that possibly do not deserve to be qualified as works (…)'.[70]

17.034

---

    free and creative choices, should be based on the work itself'). In other words: The work follows/is the result of the choices made, which is demonstrated by the degree of departure from the existing design corpus and, thus, the level of originality (being either low, average, or high).

64 *Mio and Others v Galleri Mikael & Thomas Asplund Aktiebolag*, Swedish Patent and Market Court of Appeal, 21 September 2023, PMT 13496-22, para 26.

65 See above C 1 regarding design law and below E 1.

66 *Mio and Others v Galleri Mikael & Thomas Asplund Aktiebolag*, Swedish Patent and Market Court of Appeal, 21 September 2023, PMT 13496-22, para 27 (emphasis added).

67 Case C-833/18 *Brompton v Chedech/Get2Get* ECLI:EU:C:2020:461, para 38.

68 *Mio and Others v Galleri Mikael & Thomas Asplund Aktiebolag*, Swedish Patent and Market Court of Appeal, 21 September 2023, PMT 13496-22, para 28.

69 See also above C 1 and below E 1.

70 Contrary to *Mio and Others v Galleri Mikael & Thomas Asplund Aktiebolag*, Swedish Patent and Market Court of Appeal, 21 September 2023, PMT 13496-22, para 28. – Whether a work has been created 'with an artistic purpose' does not matter either; see also *Mio and Others v Galleri Mikael & Thomas Asplund Aktiebolag*, Swedish Patent and Market Court of Appeal, 21 September 2023, PMT 13496-22, para 32 ('artistic quality of the work irrelevant'). Rather, since the assessment of whether the work should be granted protection is

17.035 *Fourth*, to the extent that the Swedish Patent and Market Court of Appeal, proceeding from its – incorrect – understanding above, is concerned about the 'low standard of originality' which would allow 'relatively simple works, which in many cases can be very commercially valuable' to receive the 'generous protection offered by copyright'[71] the Court confuses the – legal – standard of establishing originality (as explained above[72]) with the – factual – question of how to assess the degree of departure (demonstrating the level of originality and, consequently, the scope of protection). For the same reason, there is no reason to suspect a 'risk undermining the importance of the less generous protection for designs' and to proceed from an 'excessively low requirement of originality'[73] as also shown below.[74]

17.036 *Fifth*, to the extent that the Swedish Patent and Market Court of Appeal contemplates '(...) whether it is of any significance in the assessment that identical or similar works have been created before or – independently and without knowledge of the work – after the creation of the work in question (...)'[75] it follows from established law and practice that what happens after the date of creation of the work will neither impact the level of originality nor, hence, the scope of protection.[76]

17.037 Another issue, *sixth*, is indeed whether, and to what extent, it matters '(...) that the work of applied art consists of elements found in the general stock of designs or that the work builds on and constitutes a simple variation of

---

based on the work itself (being the result of the choices the author actually made in creating the work) it is important that the work itself constitutes an artistic achievement and expresses an artistic effort (see, e.g., *Access right of the architect*, German Federal Supreme Court, 29 April 2021, I ZR 193/20, para 57; *Birthday Train*, German Federal Supreme Court, 13 November 2013, I ZR 143/12, para 41).

71 *Mio and Others v Galleri Mikael & Thomas Asplund Aktiebolag*, Swedish Patent and Market Court of Appeal, 21 September 2023, PMT 13496-22, para 29.
72 See above at the beginning of C 2.
73 *Mio and Others v Galleri Mikael & Thomas Asplund Aktiebolag*, Swedish Patent and Market Court of Appeal, 21 September 2023, PMT 13496-22, para 30.
74 See below E 3.
75 *Mio and Others v Galleri Mikael & Thomas Asplund Aktiebolag*, Swedish Patent and Market Court of Appeal, 21 September 2023, PMT 13496-22, para 34.
76 Case C-833/18 *Brompton v Chedech/Get2Get* ECLI:EU:C:2020:461, para 37: '(...) in order to assess whether the folding bicycle at issue in the main proceedings is an original creation and is thus protected by copyright, it is for the referring court to take account of all the relevant aspects of the present case, as they existed when that subject matter was designed, irrespective of the factors external to and subsequent to the creation of the product'. – See also *Tubular Steel Chair I*, German Federal Supreme Court, 27 February 1961, I ZR 127/59 [at III 4]. – Different opinion: *Thun*, Italian Supreme Court, 14 October 2022, 30331/2022, finding that the display of a product in an exhibition can be one of the factors to be considered for recognizing its artistic value and eligibility for copyright protection.

previously known models (...)'.⁷⁷ According to the Swedish Patent and Market Court of Appeal, it is 'not clear or established' how EU law should be interpreted where a work of applied art consists of 'elements from the general stock of designs', whether it is sufficient that those elements '(...) have been used and combined in such a way that the end result deserves copyright protection as works of art (...)', and whether 'the scope for artistic creation based on already known formal elements' should be 'more limited' so that '(...) simple variations on previously known models as a starting point are unlikely to be able to express the artistic achievement required to qualify for protection as a work (...)'.⁷⁸

17.038 Revisiting, *seventh*, the copyright infringement test, the Swedish Patent and Market Court of Appeal contemplates – quite in a *Tour d'Horizon* – '(...) the precise manner in which the assessment should be made when determining whether an allegedly infringing work of applied art falls within the scope of protection of the work (...)', what, more specifically, '(...) similarity is required for the allegedly infringing work to be considered to infringe the work (...)', '(...) how the assessment should be made and what exactly is required for the work to be recognisable in the allegedly infringing work (...)', and/or whether '(...) the question is whether or not the work gives a different overall impression from the work or what else the test should focus on'.⁷⁹

17.039 The Swedish Patent and Market Court of Appeal, finally and *eighth*, returns to the issue of assessing the scope of protection under copyright law, finding that, on the one hand, the CJEU had '(...) pointed out that the scope of that protection does not depend on the degree of creative freedom enjoyed by its author (...)'⁸⁰ but, on the other, submits that it is unclear whether that case law refers to the 'importance of originality for the scope of protection of the work' or whether it constitutes a '(...) finding that copyright works of different kinds

---

77 *Mio and Others v Galleri Mikael & Thomas Asplund Aktiebolag*, Swedish Patent and Market Court of Appeal, 21 September 2023, PMT 13496-22, para 35.
78 *Mio and Others v Galleri Mikael & Thomas Asplund Aktiebolag*, Swedish Patent and Market Court of Appeal, 21 September 2023, PMT 13496-22, paras 35–36.
79 *Mio and Others v Galleri Mikael & Thomas Asplund Aktiebolag*, Swedish Patent and Market Court of Appeal, 21 September 2023, PMT 13496-22 paras 37–40.
80 *Mio and Others v Galleri Mikael & Thomas Asplund Aktiebolag*, Swedish Patent and Market Court of Appeal, 21 September 2023, PMT 13496-22, para 44 (referring to Case C-683/17 *Cofemel v G-Star* ECLI:EU:C:2019:721, para 35).

(…) must be assessed and protected in the same way.'[81] Interestingly, *'Cofemel'* reads as follows:[82]

> Where a subject matter (…) constitutes a work, it must, as such, qualify for copyright protection (…), and it must be added that the *extent of that protection does not depend on the degree of creative freedom exercised by its author*, and that that protection is therefore not inferior to that to which any work falling within the scope of that directive is entitled.

17.040 However, revisiting *'Painer'*, it seems that *'Cofemel'* is an unfortunate reduction of what the CJEU found in *'Painer'* which reads as follows:[83]

> Moreover, nothing in Directive 2001/29 or in any other directive applicable in this field supports the view that the *extent of such protection should depend on possible differences in the degree of creative freedom in the production of various categories of works*.
>
> Therefore, as regards a *portrait photograph*, the protection conferred by Article 2(a) of Directive 2001/29 cannot be inferior to that enjoyed by *other works*, including other photographic works.
>
> In the light of the foregoing, (…) a portrait photograph can (…) be protected by copyright if, which it is for the national court to determine in each case, such photograph is an intellectual creation of the author reflecting his personality and expressing his free and creative choices in the production of that photograph. *Since it has been determined that the portrait photograph in question is a work*, its protection is not inferior to that enjoyed by any other work, including other photographic works.

17.041 Consequently, *first*, the CJEU, in *'Painer'*, proceeded from the assumption that for finding whether a work is protected by copyright it is for the national court to determine in each case whether the work is an intellectual creation of the author reflecting his personality and expressing his free and creative choices in the production of the work. Once, *second*, it has been determined that copyright subsists in a specific work, the question of scope of protection comes into play. The extent of such protection, *third*, does not depend on possible differences in the degree of creative freedom in the production of various categories of works. For that reason, *fourth*, the protection of a specific category of work is not inferior to that enjoyed by any other category of work.[84] Thus, *fifth*, proceeding – correctly – from *'Painer'*, nothing supports the view that the

---

81 *Mio and Others v Galleri Mikael & Thomas Asplund Aktiebolag*, Swedish Patent and Market Court of Appeal, 21 September 2023, PMT 13496-22, para 44.
82 Case C-683/17 *Cofemel v G-Star* ECLI:EU:C:2019:721, para 35 (referring to Case C-145/10 *Painer* EU:C:2011:798, paras 97–99; *emphasis* added).
83 Case C-145/10 *Painer* EU:C:2011:798, paras 97–99 (*emphasis* added).
84 Unclear *Barbecue grill*, Swiss Federal Supreme Court, 17 June 2022, 4A_472/2021 and 4A_482/2021 [at 5.3], finding that, on the one hand, the requirements for individuality are the same for all categories of works but, on the other, the criterion of individuality is 'relative to the respective category of work'.

scope of protection should not depend on or follow from the degree of creative freedom exercised by the author.

In fact, to the contrary, it has been established law and practice – prior and after 'Cofemel' – that the scope of protection correlates with the level of originality which, in return, corresponds with the degree of departure from the existing design corpus, i.e., the 'degree of creative freedom exercised by the author'.[85] In that context, the Swedish Patent and Market Court of Appeal correctly points out that a '(…) system where the degree of originality is important for the scope of protection appears (…) to be appropriate. The more original (…) a work is, the greater the scope of protection it should have.'[86] This concept of interaction or reciprocity is also endorsed by German case law as demonstrated above.[87]

17.042

The *concept of reciprocity* – as the Swedish Patent and Market Court of Appeal correctly found (although not using this term) – also exists and prevails in European trademark law[88] and design law. However, different from trademark and copyright law, there is no reciprocity between validity and scope of protection in Community design law as explained elsewhere.[89]

17.043

3. Aesthetic Creative Freedom in Trademark Law

Under harmonised EU trademark law, according to the CJEU (and again starting with the establishment of trademark rights), the finding of distinctiveness must be based on whether the shape for which registration as a trademark is sought (shape of the goods themselves or their packaging) *departs significantly* from the norm or customs of the sector, taking into account the extent to which the specific shape differs from other designs as they normally appear

17.044

---

85 See above n 82.
86 *Mio and Others v Galleri Mikael & Thomas Asplund Aktiebolag*, Swedish Patent and Market Court of Appeal, 21 September 2023, PMT 13496-22, para 46 (referring to Swedish case law, e.g., [1994] Nytt Juridiskt Arkiv 74 https://lagen.nu/dom/nja/1994s74 accessed 31 December 2023).
87 See at the beginning of C 2 and, e.g., n 44. Thus, the Swedish Patent and Market Court of Appeal errs when submitting that *'Birthday Train'* would suggest the 'opposite'. Indeed, *Birthday Train*, German Federal Supreme Court, 13 November 2013, I ZR 143/12, para 41, clearly endorses the concept of reciprocity.
88 *Mio and Others v Galleri Mikael & Thomas Asplund Aktiebolag*, Swedish Patent and Market Court of Appeal, 21 September 2023, PMT 13496-22, para 45 (referring to Case C-251/95 *Sabel v Puma* EU:C:1997:528, para 24 and to Case C-342/97 *Lloyd Schuhfabrik Meyer vs Klijsen Handel* ECLI:EU:C:1999:323, para 20).
89 See above C 1. In fact, *Mio and Others v Galleri Mikael & Thomas Asplund Aktiebolag*, Swedish Patent and Market Court of Appeal, 21 September 2023, PMT 13496-22, para 45, mixes reciprocity between scope of protection and infringement with reciprocity between validity and scope of protection. Also, there is no degree of individual character (different from the level of originality and the degree of distinctiveness).

on the market concerned ('variety of forms'-test).⁹⁰ Comparable to design and copyright law, the question of sufficient distinctiveness is therefore also about how the abstract freedom of design was exercised.

17.045 In cases of examining infringement, the defendant typically argues that the claimed mark has been diluted by tolerating use of third-party marks. In this respect, the decisive criterion is whether the third-party mark is similar to the claimed mark or its specific elements.⁹¹ Third-party marks which maintain the same or even greater distance from the claimed mark than the contested sign, therefore, will have no dilutive effect;⁹² only third-party marks that are closer are deemed critical and detrimental to distinctiveness.⁹³ As far as the similarity of goods or services is concerned, only third-party marks for the same or very similar goods, services or sectors may be considered detrimental.⁹⁴ Thus, again, departure is the key parameter in this context.⁹⁵ In principle, the following applies:⁹⁶

> Normative considerations should therefore also be taken into account here, namely the lesser worthiness of protection for a mark neglected to a certain extent, whose owner has not prevented the encroachment of similar signs (…). (…) With regard to prior third-party marks, however, the lesser worthiness of protection must be based on a different normative approach and can only be derived from the fact that a narrower scope of protection was accepted from the outset by choosing a sign situated in a crowded field.⁹⁷

---

90   See Case C-783/18 P *EUIPO/Wajos* ECLI:EU:C:2019:1073, paras 24 and 29; Case T-489/20 *Eos v EUIPO* ECLI:EU:T:2021:547, paras 43 and 83 ('great variety of packaging forms'); Case T-488/20 *Guerlain/EUIPO* ECLI:EU:T:2021:443, paras 18 and 50; Case T-862/19 *Brasserie St Avold v EUIPO* ECLI:EU:T:2020:561, para 38; *Device of a gummy bear*, EUIPO (Board of Appeal), 11 October 2023, R 872/2023-4, para 26; *Blake [Outer portion of a tyre]*, EUIPO (Board of Appeal), 29 August 2022, R 197/2021-5, para 43 ('significant variety of appearances of treads').

91   INGERL/ROHNKE/NORDEMANN, *Markengesetz*, 4th ed (C. H. Beck 2023) Section 14 para 652 with further references.

92   *Raupentin*, German Federal Supreme Court, 2 April 1971, I ZB 3/70 [under IV 2].

93   STRÖBELE/HACKER/THIERING, *Markengesetz*, 13th ed (Carl Heymanns 2021) Section 9 para 187, with further references in n 457.

94   *Bogner B/Barbie B*, German Federal Supreme Court, 2 February 2012, I ZR 50/11, para 40.

95   INGERL/ROHNKE/NORDEMANN, *Markengesetz*, 4th ed (C. H. Beck 2023) Section 14 para 655, explicitly referring to a 'theory of departure'.

96   INGERL/ROHNKE/NORDEMANN, *Markengesetz*, 4th ed (C. H. Beck 2023) Section 14 para 651.

97   The notion 'crowded field' is particularly specific to design law; *cf.* MUSKER, *Easier to see than to say: catching the elusive spirit of design in a net of words*, in: HARTWIG (ed), *Research Handbook on Design Law* (Edward Elgar Publishing 2021), 77, 105; MUSKER, *The Wisdom of the Crowd(ed Art): Difference, Density and Saturation in European Union Design Law*, in EUIPO (ed.), *20 Years of the Boards of Appeal at EUIPO – Celebrating the Past, Looking Forward to the Future*, Liber Amicorum (2017) 211.

D. LIMITS TO AESTHETIC CREATIVE FREEDOM IN DESIGN, COPYRIGHT, AND TRADEMARK LAW

As a rule, case law places possible limits to aesthetic creative freedom into three categories, namely aesthetic limits (i.e., 'variety of forms' or – more generally – 'departure' from prior art), technical limits (particularly 'patent defence'), and statutory limits ('standards'). These categories can be found – in various specifications – in design, copyright, and trademark law and, although their 'labelling' may differ, the basic 'tone' is quite similar, and overall efforts towards consistency are being made. **17.046**

1. Limits to Aesthetic Creative Freedom in Design Law

(a) Aesthetic limits

According to the German Federal Supreme Court,[98] '(…) a great concentration of designs and, thus, only little freedom of the designer will lead to a narrow scope of protection of the design so that minor differences in appearance may produce a different overall impression on the informed user (…)'. **17.047**

Absence of variety of forms, thus, sets limits to the designer's aesthetic creative freedom; what others did not achieve cannot be demanded from the designer of the design challenged in invalidity proceedings or claimed in infringement proceedings either, naturally resulting in an only minor departure from the prior art. However, this scenario of little or no variety or multiplicity of forms or designs is extremely unrealistic; on the contrary, it should be quite easy to introduce a large volume of dissimilar prior designs – with the result that aesthetic limits to aesthetic creative freedom tend not to exist in design law.[99] **17.048**

Moreover, the question whether a design follows a general design trend is irrelevant when assessing individual character; accordingly, the degree of the designer's creative freedom cannot depend on whether such a design trend exists.[100] Nor can consumer expectations constitute a statutory constraint that necessarily limits the degree of freedom of a designer; the fact that a general design trend is capable of meeting the expectations of relevant consumers cannot be regarded as a factor which restricts the designer's freedom since that freedom enables the designer to discover new shapes and new lines or even to innovate in the context of an existing figurative trend. Consequently, 'potential **17.049**

---

98 *E.g., Pram II*, German Federal Supreme Court, 12 July 2012, I ZR 102/11, para 31.
99 *Cf.* also HARTWIG, *Musterdichte und Mustervielfalt im Geschmacksmusterrecht* [2015] GRUR 845, 850.
100 Case T-767/17 *Eglo/EUIPO and Briloner* ECLI:EU:T:2019:67, para 29.

market expectations' shall not be taken into account in order to determine the designer's degree of aesthetic creative freedom.[101]

(b) Technical limits

17.050 According to the General Court,[102] the designer's degree of aesthetic creative freedom in developing the design, under Article 6 (2) CDR, is '(…) established, inter alia, by the constraints of the features imposed by the technical function of the product or an element thereof (…). Those constraints result in a standardisation of certain features, which will thus be common to the designs applied to the product concerned'.

17.051 However, to the best of the author's knowledge, there is not a single example, according to the relevant case law available, of concrete (not: abstract) features that have become 'common' due to their *technical standardisation*. For example, in case of bicycle baskets, the designer's creative freedom is limited by technical specifications only to the extent that the baskets must be fastened to the bicycle and be able to hold objects without them falling out while cycling. However, the designer can choose between a wide variety of colours, materials (e.g., plastic, metal, rattan, or fabric) and shapes (round, oval or square) of the basket.[103] Likewise, in case of so-called toilet rim blocks, the freedom of the designer is limited with regard to the material used, which is dictated by the chemical substances used, as well as the size and shape, which must allow the toilet rim blocks to be placed in the holder provided for this purpose, but not with regard to the colouring and the specific design.[104] Also in case of paint spray guns, creative freedom has been deemed considerable.[105]

17.052 Apart from that, in the decision *'Paper dispenser'*, the German Federal Supreme Court (proceeding from the CJEU's decision *'Doceram'*[106]) brought the degree of differentiation to a higher level thanks to the much more complex factual and legal setting (the findings of the German Federal Supreme Court can be subdivided into 'topic of evidence', 'subject matter of evidence', 'standard of evidence', 'means of evidence', 'burden of proof', and 'assessment of evi-

---

101 Case T-209/18 *Porsche/EUIPO and Autec* ECLI:EU:T:2019:377, paras 57, 59 and 61.
102 Case T-9/07 *Grupo Promer v EUIPO/PepsiCo* ECLI:EU:T:2010:96, para 67; Case T-560/18 *Atos/EUIPO and Andreas Fahl* ECLI:EU:T:2019:767, para 46; Case T-684 *Legero v EUIPO/Rieker* ECLI:EU:T:2021:912, para 70.
103 Case T-760/16 *Basil/EUIPO and Artex* ECLI:EU:T:2018:277, para 81.
104 Case T-296/17 *Buck-Chemie/EUIPO and Henkel* ECLI:EU:T:2018:823, paras 44–48.
105 Case T-651/17 *Hours/EUIPO and Zhejiang Auarita* ECLI:EU:T:2018:855, paras 33–35.
106 Recently Du Mont/Janis, *Trends in Functionality Jurisprudence: U.S. and E.U. Design Law*, in: Hartwig (ed), *Research Handbook on Design Law* (Edward Elgar Publishing 2021) 30, 49.

dence').[107] In this respect, the Supreme Court clarified that Article 8 (1) CDR – in the context of establishing protection – only applies if '(...) all features of appearance of the product relevant to its overall impression are solely dictated by its technical function'.[108] The Supreme Court also clarified that '(...) an 'aesthetic surplus' cannot be taken as a basis, for the simple reason that aesthetic content is not one of the requirements for protection of a Community design'.[109] Furthermore, the Supreme Court emphasised that, in the context of Article 8 (1) CDR, it is always about the question of being *solely* dictated by the technical function; a finding that certain features of appearance of the product are determined by its technical function is therefore not sufficient.[110] With respect to the relationship between design and patent protection, the Court found that '(...) the fact that a technical property right has been applied for or granted in respect of a product does not preclude the protectability of such product as a design'. On the contrary, the individual features of appearance of the design must be compared specifically with the claims, description, and drawings of the first publication of the patent application.[111] According to the Supreme Court, claims, description, and drawings of the first publication of a patent application – as 'objective circumstances' – are in principle suitable for providing information about which features realise the underlying technical teaching and, therefore, are at least partly technically dictated.[112] However, '(...) the absence of considerations on the visual appearance of the product in the first publication of the patent application does not in itself allow the conclusion that a feature of appearance is solely dictated by technical function, nor does the presence of considerations on its technical function'.[113] Finally, the Supreme Court clarified that the existence of alternative designs with which the same technical function can be fulfilled is a circumstance that can be taken into account in the context of the overall assessment to be carried out in accordance with Article 8 (1) CDR, i.e., the existence of alternative designs alone is not sufficient to exclude the application of Article 8 (1) CDR. Accordingly, the lower Court of Appeal should not have disregarded the circumstance that the claimant was the owner of a number of design registrations for alternative forms that enabled the same technical function to be executed as in case of the

---

107 See for details HARTWIG, *Ausschließlich technische Bedingtheit im Gemeinschaftsgeschmacksmusterrecht* [2021] GRUR 685-690.
108 *Paper Dispenser*, German Federal Supreme Court, 7 October 2020, I ZR 137/19, para 9 and *cf.* para 32.
109 *Paper Dispenser*, German Federal Supreme Court, 7 October 2020, I ZR 137/19, para 12 and *cf.* para 36.
110 *Paper Dispenser*, German Federal Supreme Court, 7 October 2020, I ZR 137/19, para 31.
111 *Paper Dispenser*, German Federal Supreme Court, 7 October 2020, I ZR 137/19, para 24.
112 *Paper Dispenser*, German Federal Supreme Court, 7 October 2020, I ZR 137/19, para 25.
113 *Paper Dispenser*, German Federal Supreme Court, 7 October 2020, I ZR 137/19, para 28.

product according to the claimed design.[114] Competing products were also to be included in the overall assessment.[115]

17.053 How are these findings to be understood when determining technical limits to aesthetic creative freedom, given that Article 8 (1) CDR, unlike Article 6 (2) or Article 10 (2) CDR, contains no element of creative freedom? Do the 'patent defence' or the 'alternative forms'-test also apply when assessing individual character or scope of protection?

17.054 It is true that Article 8 (1) CDR – when examining susceptibility to protection – only applies if all features of appearance relevant to the overall impression of the product are solely dictated by its technical function.[116] It is also true – when finding infringement under Article 10 (1) CDR – that 'similarities of the designs in features determined by technical function have a rather minor significance for the overall impression produced on the informed user' (this does not apply, however, to 'differences in the features that fulfil a technical function').[117]

17.055 In short: When evaluating the respective features of appearance, features dictated by the technical function of the product (not necessarily: features solely dictated by its technical function) must be weighted accordingly. However, this does not preclude considerations based on the 'patent defence' or 'alternative forms or designs' from being fruitful in this respect. This means that the corresponding findings of the German Supreme Court in the decision 'Paper dispenser' on Article 8 (1) CDR (requirement for protection) apply equally to Article 6 (2) CDR (requirement for protection), Article 10 (2) CDR (scope of protection), and Article 10 (1) CDR (infringement), with the fundamental difference that features dictated by the technical function of the product must not be ignored but merely weighted accordingly.[118]

17.056 Hence, in the present context, the question of the existence of possible technical limits to aesthetic creative freedom – especially under the category of a 'patent defence' but also with respect to any alternative forms – must be answered in the affirmative.

---

114 *Paper Dispenser*, German Federal Supreme Court, 7 October 2020, I ZR 137/19, para 39 (confirmed by Case C-684/21 *Papierfabriek Doetinchem BV v Sprick GmbH Bielefelder Papier- und Wellpappenwerk & Co.* ECLI:EU:C:2023:141, para 23).
115 *Paper Dispenser*, German Federal Supreme Court, 7 October 2020, I ZR 137/19, para 40.
116 *Paper Dispenser*, German Federal Supreme Court, 7 October 2020, I ZR 137/19, paras 9 and 32.
117 *Pram II*, German Federal Supreme Court, 12 July 2012, I ZR 102/11, para 60.
118 In that sense, from a US design patent perspective, also SAIDMAN, *A Primer on Design Patent Functionality*, (2021) *Berkeley Technology Law Journal* 147–167.

(c) Statutory limits

17.057 According to the General Court,[119] the degree of freedom of the designer in developing the design, under Article 6 (2) CDR, is '(...) established, inter alia, by the constraints of the features imposed (...) by statutory requirements applicable to the product. Those constraints result in a standardisation of certain features, which will thus be common to the designs applied to the product concerned.'

17.058 However,[120]

> (...) consumer expectations such as those the applicant claims, namely that [consumers] will find the 'creative idea' or the prototype of the original design of the 'Porsche 911' in subsequent series, cannot constitute a statutory constraint that necessarily limits the degree of freedom of a car designer, since those expectations relate to neither the nature nor the purpose of such a product, in which the contested design is incorporated, nor to the industrial sector to which that product belongs. In contrast, (...) those expectations relate only to the fact that the design of the 'Porsche 911' is 'iconic', that is to say, to consumers' supposed wish to remain loyal to it over time, which does not mean that, independently of aesthetic or commercial considerations, its designer is necessarily obliged to meet those expectations in order to ensure the functioning of the product to which the design in question is intended to be applied.

17.059 In this respect, it is not the degree of freedom of the designer of the 991 series 'Porsche 911' that must be determined, but that of a designer of motor cars in general.[121]

17.060 Insofar as the General Court, in *'Grupo Promer'*, took the view that the freedom of the designer could also be limited by the fact that the 'items' involved '(...) had to be inexpensive, safe for children and fit to be added to the products which they promote',[122] this argument of 'market acceptance' has been abandoned.[123] As far as the argument of 'standardisation' is concerned, it has been submitted elsewhere[124] that there are hardly any examples of concrete (not: abstract) features of appearance in law and practice that had become 'common' due to a possible statutory *standardisation*.[125] Particularly in the case of *'Grupo Promer'*, the General Court's findings lack any concrete reference to a specific

---

119 Case T-9/07 *Grupo Promer v EUIPO/PepsiCo* ECLI:EU:T:2010:96, para 67; Case T-560/18 *Atos/EUIPO and Andreas Fahl* ECLI:EU:T:2019:767, para 46.
120 Case T-209/18 *Porsche/EUIPO and Autec* ECLI:EU:T:2019:377, paras 57–58.
121 Case T-209/18 *Porsche/EUIPO and Autec* ECLI:EU:T:2019:377, para 54.
122 Case T-9/07 *Grupo Promer v EUIPO/PepsiCo* ECLI:EU:T:2010:96, para 70.
123 See D 1 a above.
124 See HARTWIG, *Gestaltungsfreiheit im Gemeinschaftsgeschmacksmusterrecht* [2020] GRUR 1260, 1264.
125 In *'Grupo Promer'*, for example, the General Court found that the '(...) designer's freedom was also limited [insofar] as those items had to be inexpensive, safe for children and fit to be added to the products which they

design feature. Moreover, in case of different product categories or industrial sectors being involved – e.g., the prior art comes from the toy industry whereas the contested design is from the automotive sector – any possible 'standardisation of certain features' would extend to both categories.

17.061 No further clarification is to be expected from the CJEU given that finding validity of a design and, more particularly, assessing the overall impression of two conflicting designs, including the question whether 'similar dimensions of the designs at issue were (…) the result of a constraint on the designer's freedom' because such 'elements of similarity' were 'necessary if the goods at issue are to fulfil their function',[126] is a question of fact, falling, in general, into the General Court's exclusive jurisdiction.[127] More specifically,[128]

> (…) the General Court has exclusive jurisdiction to find the facts, save where a substantive inaccuracy in its findings is apparent from the documents submitted to it, and to appraise those facts. That appraisal of the facts thus does not, save where the clear sense of the evidence has been distorted, constitute a point of law which is subject, as such, to review by the Court of Justice in an appeal (…).

17.062 The CJEU, however, accepted that the General Court may, in appropriate cases, restrict its review of decisions in industrial design matters, by way of an exception, to an examination of manifest errors of assessment, particularly where the EUIPO is called upon to perform highly technical assessments.[129] Such 'special cases' where the General Court deferred to the expertise of the EUIPO have not arisen so far.

17.063 Overall, it seems that the formula 'constraints of the features imposed by statutory requirements applicable to the product → degree of creative freedom → standardisation of certain features' is a theorem without any discernible practical benefit. On the contrary, statutory limits to aesthetic creative freedom do not tend to exist in European design law.

---

promote (…)'; see Case T-9/07 *Grupo Promer v EUIPO/PepsiCo* ECLI:EU:T:2010:96, para 70. However, these findings are made without any concrete reference to a specific feature of appearance.
126 Case C-281/10 P *PepsiCo v EUIPO/Grupo Promer* ECLI:EU:C:2011:679, paras 43-45.
127 See HARTWIG, *Case Comment on Herbert Neuman v EUIPO/José Manuel Baena* [2013] IIC 249, 252.
128 See Joined Cases C-101/11 P and C-102/11 P *Neuman* ECLI:EU:C:2012:641, para 66; *see also* HARTWIG, *Case Comment on Herbert Neuman v EUIPO/José Manuel Baena* [2013] IIC 249-254.
129 See Joined Cases C-101/11 P and C-102/11 P *Neuman* ECLI:EU:C:2012:641, para 41; *see also* HARTWIG, *Case Comment on Herbert Neuman v EUIPO/José Manuel Baena* [2013] IIC 249-254.

2. Limits to Aesthetic Creative Freedom in Copyright Law

(a) Aesthetic limits

17.064 An author's own intellectual creation presupposes that there is a room to manoeuvre which is used by the author to express his creative ability in an original manner (see C 2 above). Where the realisation of the subject matter is dictated by 'technical considerations, rules or other constraints', there is 'no room for creative freedom'[130] (see D 2 (b) and (c) below). This clearly does not include aesthetic limits.

17.065 Nevertheless, it is at least conceivable in theory that a creator is operating in a 'crowded field' characterised by a large number of similar forms (this would correspond to a 'low variety of designs' under design law; see C 1 above). However, as already emphasised in the context of design law (see D 1 a above), such a scenario is extremely unrealistic; law and practice show that, in the applicable overall comparison with the prior designs – the findings impact the degree of individuality on which the scope of protection depends (see C 2 above) – forms that are not merely similar are typically submitted and examined. On the contrary, the submission of less similar or even significantly different designs has been interpreted as evidence of a broad aesthetic creative freedom.[131]

17.066 Thus, as in design law, aesthetic limits to aesthetic creative freedom tend not to exist in copyright law either.

(b) Technical limits

17.067 In case of articles of daily use, which, according to the German Federal Supreme Court,[132]

> (…) must have features of appearance dictated by the article's intended use, the scope for artistic creativity is usually restricted. That is why, particularly, the question arises as to whether the article has been artistically designed beyond its form prescribed by the function and whether this design reaches a level of originality that justifies copyright protection (…).

17.068 Although the Supreme Court refers here to 'intended use' and 'function', it avoids – unlike in the *'Climbing Spider'* case – defining or limiting such use or

---

130 Case C-683/17 *Cofemel v G-Star* ECLI:EU:C:2019:721, para 31.
131 *Crib*, Dusseldorf District Court, 17 September 2019, 14c O 225/17 [under A I 1 b].
132 *Birthday Train*, German Federal Supreme Court, 13 November 2013, I ZR 143/12, para 41.

function in a technical sense or context.¹³³ This clarification was provided by the CJEU shortly afterwards:¹³⁴

> (…) if a subject matter is to be capable of being regarded as original, it is both necessary and sufficient that the subject matter reflects the personality of its author, as an expression of his free and creative choices (…). On the other hand, when the realisation of a subject matter has been dictated by technical considerations, rules, or other constraints, which have left no room for creative freedom, that subject matter cannot be regarded as possessing the originality required for it to constitute a work (…).

17.069 In this context, the CJEU also found:¹³⁵

> (…) in so far as only the originality of the product concerned needs to be assessed, even though the existence of other possible shapes which can achieve the same technical result makes it possible to establish that there is a possibility of choice, it is not decisive in assessing the factors which influenced the choice made by the creator.

17.070 The CJEU, thus, confirmed the principle (see C 2 above) that the question of granting copyright protection depends on whether there is aesthetic creative freedom and whether the author has made use of it accordingly. The extent to which third parties have previously used (or not) such freedom is therefore irrelevant.

17.071 A decision of the Stuttgart Appeal Court fits almost seamlessly into this picture:¹³⁶

> According to general experience, numerous technical specifications matter when designing a motor vehicle; this applies primarily to the stability of the vehicle in terms of structure and material selection, *e.g.*, with respect to torsional and bending stiffness of the regularly self-supporting body, aerodynamics ('air drag coefficient'), the functionality of visible parts (*e.g.*, retractable side windows), the ease of production and repair, optical conditions (*e.g.*, position of lights, angle of inclination for a distortion- and glare-free windscreen) but also to passive elements such as accident or impact protection for third parties, etc. The creative freedom of a designer is, thus, limited from the

---

133 *Climbing Spider*, German Federal Supreme Court, 12 May 2011, I ZR 53/10, para 25:
In case of articles of daily use that must meet specific technical requirements and show features of appearance dictated by technical function, possibilities of an artistic-aesthetic design are not excluded but usually restricted (…). In case of such designs, the question therefore arises to a particular extent as to whether the selected form is dictated by technical function due to the intended use (…). Therefore, in case of such works of applied art, it must be submitted precisely and clearly to what extent the article of daily use is artistically designed beyond its shape dictated by the function (…).
On the relationship between technology and function, *cf.* recently VON MÜHLENDAHL, *Three-Dimensional Trademarks and Designs: Comparison and Conflict*, in: HARTWIG (ed), *Research Handbook on Design Law* (Edward Elgar Publishing 2021), 449–456.
134 Case C-683/17 *Cofemel v G-Star* ECLI:EU:C:2019:721, paras 30 and 31.
135 Case C-833/18 *Brompton v Chedech/Get2Get* ECLI:EU:C:2020:461, para 35.
136 *Porsche 911*, Stuttgart Appeal Court, 20 November 2020, 5 U 125/19 [under II C 5 e bb].

outset since the technicality of usability always remains dominant even with generous modification of the prototype of a car (...). Nevertheless, it should be noted that, with respect to the design of the exterior of a passenger car, there is sufficient room for creative modification of the individual necessary elements of a vehicle body, so that there is room for artistic creation. This is well known to everyone from the countless different designs of vehicle bodies over the last 100 years.

17.072 This decision is remarkable not only because, in the context of the question of the limits to aesthetic creative freedom in copyright law, it does not contain any reference to 'Cofemel' and in particular 'Brompton' and instead cites the German Federal Patent Court in detail, although that court had decided solely on the question of registrability of a 3D mark (specifically: the silhouette of the Porsche 911).[137] Rather, the findings of the Stuttgart Appeal Court are significant, according to which, despite the fact that the '(...) technicality of usability always remains dominant even with generous modification of the prototype of a car (...)', '(...) there is sufficient room for creative modification of the individual necessary elements of a vehicle body (...)' with respect to the 'design of the exterior of a passenger car' (against the background of 'countless different designs of vehicle bodies over the last 100 years').[138]

17.073 Thus, it seems, there is a lack of concrete (not: abstract) features of appearance for which technical limits to aesthetic creative freedom might have existed. Once again, any rule proceeding from the assumption that technical constraints would not allow room for exercising aesthetic creative freedom appears to be a rule with no practical benefit. Rather, the decision of the Stuttgart Appeal Court demonstrates that a large variety of forms ('countless different designs') is incontrovertible proof of great aesthetic creative freedom ('sufficient room for creative modification of the individual necessary elements of a vehicle body') – which should then also be used.[139]

(c)   Statutory limits

According to the CJEU,[140] **17.074**

> (...) if a subject matter is to be capable of being regarded as original, it is both necessary and sufficient that the subject matter reflects the personality of its author, as an expression of his free and creative choices. (...) On the other hand, when the realisation

---

137 *Car Body*, German Federal Patent Court, 13 October 2004, 28 W (pat) 98/00 [under II 1].
138 *Porsche 911*, Stuttgart Appeal Court, 20 November 2020, 5 U 125/19 [under II C 5 e bb].
139 In the specific case, the Stuttgart Appeal Court found that the body of the Porsche 356 is protected as a work of applied art but dismissed claims for reasonable participation in the economic success of the Porsche 911 of the 991 series, under Section 32a German Copyright Act, due to a different overall impression; *cf. Porsche 911*, Stuttgart Appeal Court, 20 November 2020, 5 U 125/19 [under II C 6].
140 Case C-683/17 *Cofemel v G-Star* ECLI:EU:C:2019:721, paras 30 and 31.

of a subject matter has been dictated by technical considerations, rules, or other constraints, which have left no room for creative freedom, that subject matter cannot be regarded as possessing the originality required for it to constitute a work (…).

17.075 However, what has already been submitted with respect to the area of design law (see D 1 (c) above) also applies to copyright law, namely that pertinent law and practice in essence provides for no examples of concrete (not: abstract) features of appearance that would not have allowed room for exercising aesthetic creative freedom due to *rules or other constraints*. Again, it seems, the corresponding phrase is more of an academic theorem without any practical benefits. In other words, statutory limits to aesthetic creative freedom do not tend to exist in copyright law (as in design law).

3. Limits to Aesthetic Creative Freedom in Trademark Law

(a) Aesthetic limits

17.076 When comparing signs under trademark law (at the level of infringement), only similarities in those features matter that serve as an indication of origin of the respective trademark. In this respect, the protection of 3D trademarks applies against impairment of the trademark's function as an indication of origin and not against 'copying of aesthetic design ideas'. As a result, similarities in features alone, which prove to be ineligible for protection when their distinctive character is examined incidentally, cannot as such establish any similarity of signs relevant to finding likelihood of confusion.[141]

17.077 Comparable to the situation under design law (see D 1 a above), general design trends are therefore irrelevant in determining any aesthetic limits in trademark law. However, while in design law the designer's freedom in developing the design tends to be limitless from an aesthetic point of view (in particular because prior designs may be introduced also from other sectors)[142] and potential market expectations also do not play a role (see D 1 a above), in trademark law, given the requirement 'similarity of goods', there are certainly aesthetic limits to creative freedom in this respect.

(b) Technical limits

17.078 As stated before (see D 3 b above), the German Federal Patent Court addressed the question of technical limits to aesthetic creative freedom in trademark law in the year 2004. In the end, the court answered in the negative

---

141 INGERL/ROHNKE, *Markengesetz*, 3rd ed (C. H. Beck 2010) Section 14 para 988 with further references.
142 See HARTWIG, *Relevanter Formenschatz im Gemeinschaftsgeschmacksmusterrecht* [2017] GRUR 1212-1215.

because the specific 'shape of a motor vehicle' (i.e., the silhouette of a Porsche 911) – despite numerous technical specifications that set limits on the designer's freedom – had other features going beyond a mere technical design which neither resulted from the nature of the goods themselves nor were necessary to obtain a technical result nor gave substantial value to the goods, which is why the grounds for exclusion under Section 3 (2) German Trademarks Act did not apply.[143]

In 2019, the General Court decided slightly different by finding:[144]   **17.079**

> (…) when the shape of a product merely incorporates the technical solution developed by the manufacturer of that product and patented by it, protection of that shape as a trademark once the patent has expired would considerably and permanently reduce the opportunity for other undertakings to use that technical solution. In the system of intellectual property rights developed in the European Union, technical solutions are capable of being granted protection only for a limited period, so that subsequently they may be freely used by all economic operators. (…) The technical functionality may be assessed, inter alia, by taking account of the documents relating to previous patents describing the functional elements of the shape concerned (…). (…) if the prohibition under Article 7 (1) lit e (ii) Regulation No 40/94 only applied to shapes the graphic representation of which reveals all the characteristics allowing a product to perform its technical function, it could easily be circumvented. It would be sufficient to omit, in the graphic representation, a characteristic without which that technical function could not be achieved, notwithstanding the fact that that function requires the presence of all the essential characteristics displayed in the sign at issue. If this were the case, the provision referred to above would not safeguard the public interest in competitors being able to use technical solutions which are not, or no longer, protected by a patent.

In this respect, the General Court confirms the absolute ground for refusal under Article 7 (1) lit e (ii) Regulation (EC) No 40/94, which is now Regulation (EU) 2017/1001, pursuant to which 'signs which consist exclusively of the shape, or another characteristic, of goods which is necessary to obtain a technical result' are excluded from trademark protection, and refers to the essential characteristics of the 3D mark in question (specifically: the black-and-white representation of the well-known *'Rubik's Cube'*), namely 'to   **17.080**

---

143 *Car Body*, German Federal Patent Court, 13 October 2004, 28 W (pat) 98/00 [under II 1]. – The further step taken by the Stuttgart Appeal Court 16 years later – namely that, with respect to the body of a passenger car, in the light of 'countless different designs of vehicle bodies over the last 100 years', there was 'sufficient room for creative modification of the individual necessary elements of a vehicle body' – is not yet present to the same degree in *'Car Body'*.
144 Case T-601/17 *Rubik's Cube* ECLI:EU:T:2019:765, paras 44, 52 and 97. – On 23 April 2020, the CJEU rejected the proprietor's application for leave to appeal under Article 170b Rules of Procedure of the Court of Justice, on the grounds that it had not been shown that the questions raised were relevant to the unity, coherence or development of EU law (C-936/19 P). – *Cf.* previously also Case C-30/15 P *Rubik's cube* ECLI:EU:C:2016:849; Case T-450/09 *Rubik's Cube* ECLI:EU:T:2014:983.

the overall cube shape, on the one hand, and to the black lines and little squares on each face of the cube, on the other'.[145]

17.081 Based on those characteristics, the Court held, firstly, that:[146]

(...) as regards the analysis of the functionality of the essential characteristics of the contested mark, as a preliminary point it is important to note that the Board of Appeal was fully entitled to consider (...) that it had to be carried out in the light of the actual goods concerned and the intended technical result of those goods (...).

17.082 Secondly, the Court held:[147]

The applicant's argument based on the existence of alternative geometrical shapes capable of achieving the same intended technical result as that of the actual goods concerned cannot succeed. While it is true that a three-dimensional puzzle with a rotating capability can appear in shapes other than that of a cube, it is, however, irrelevant, as is apparent from the case law, as regards the examination of the functionality of the essential characteristics of a shape, whether or not there are other shapes which could achieve the same technical result (...). It should be emphasised in that context that the registration as a trademark of a shape is likely to allow the proprietor of that trademark to prevent other undertakings not only from using the same shape, but also from using similar shapes. A significant number of alternative shapes might therefore become unusable for that proprietor's competitors (...).

17.083 Finally, and thirdly, the Court ruled:[148]

(...) the fact that the rotating capability of the vertical and horizontal lattices of the 'Rubik's Cube' resulted from a mechanism internal to the cube, that is, an element which was not visible in the graphic representation of the contested mark, did not prevent the Board of Appeal from being able to have regard to that rotating capability in its analysis of the functionality of the essential characteristics of that mark.

17.084 As a result – in view of *'Rubik's Cube'* – there are remarkably large commonalities when determining possible limits to aesthetic creative freedom under trademark and design law.

---

145 Case T-601/17 *Rubik's Cube* ECLI:EU:T:2019:765, para 70.
146 Case T-601/17 *Rubik's Cube* ECLI:EU:T:2019:765, para 84. That position is consistent with the findings of *'Paper Dispenser'*; see D 1 b above.
147 Case T-601/17 *Rubik's Cube* ECLI:EU:T:2019:765, para 90. Those observations are in line with the *'Doceram'* under Community design law (D 1 b above) to which the General Court, however, does not refer in the present case.
148 Case T-601/17 *Rubik's Cube* ECLI:EU:T:2019:765, para 96. In *'Paper Dispenser'* [2022] IIC 278, the German Federal Supreme Court repeatedly refers to the 'visual appearance' of the product (paras 12 and 28), the 'visual appearance of individual features of appearance' (para 28) and whether the 'relevant feature of appearance is visually dictated' (para 28). This supports the assumption that the Supreme Court would have decided differently under design law, in dealing with the *Rubik's Cube*, since the General Court essentially based its decision on non-visible features.

(c) Statutory limits

17.085 Is there a concept under trademark law – comparable to design law (see D 1 c above) – that creative freedom is dictated by requirements resulting from statutory requirements applicable to the specific product, establishing a standardisation of certain features, which then become common features of the products concerned?

17.086 As far as can be seen, this principle does not apply directly in trademark law; the first decision of the General Court, in the field of design law, in which such concept was established dates from 2010 and contains no references, for example to trademark law.[149] However, as a rule, trademark law is[150]

> (...) intended to prevent the protection conferred by the trademark right from being extended, beyond signs which serve to distinguish a product or service from those offered by competitors, so as to form an obstacle preventing competitors from freely offering for sale products incorporating such technical solutions or functional characteristics in competition with the proprietor of the trademark.

17.087 Insofar as technical solutions have been established or specified by a certain DIN standard, for example, one could speak of a 'standardisation of certain features' and, thus, of corresponding statutory limits to aesthetic creative freedom. However, there are practically no examples in trademark law and practice of concrete (not: abstract) features of appearance that had become common due to a possible *statutory standardisation* (see D 1 (c) above).

E. COMPARABLE STANDARDS UNDER DESIGN, COPYRIGHT, AND TRADEMARK LAW?

17.088 As a starting point, it should be common sense that the regime of design, copyright and trademark law is based on the principles of autonomy, coexistence, and cumulation. The CJEU, only recently, confirmed this consensus with respect to the relationship between design and copyright law on the one hand[151] and design and trademark law on the other.[152]

---

149 Case T-9/07 *Grupo Promer v EUIPO/PepsiCo* ECLI:EU:T:2010:96, para 67.
150 Case C-299/99 *Koninklijke Philips Electronics NV/Remington Consumer Products Ltd* ECLI:EU:C:2002:377, para 78.
151 Case C-683/17 *Cofemel v G-Star* ECLI:EU:C:2019:721, para 43: 'Against that background, the EU legislature opted for a system in which the protection reserved for designs and the protection ensured by copyright are not mutually exclusive.'
152 See also Case C-237/19 *Gömböc v Szellemi Tulajdon Nemzeti Hivatala* ECLI:EU:C:2020:296, paras 53–54:
    It is apparent from the above that the fact that the appearance of a product is protected as a design does not prevent a sign consisting of the shape of that product from benefiting from protection under trademark law,

1. Commonalities

17.089 Revisiting pertinent case law shows a remarkable overlap, including inspiration, in the relationship between European design, copyright, and trademark law, both in substance and approach, likely not found in any other jurisdiction. This applies, particularly, to the determination of aesthetic creative freedom itself as well as to any aesthetic, technical, and statutory limits (see D above). There is also mutual consent that, in principle, protection can already be granted based on sketches, drafts, etc., i.e., the right holder can proceed against a specific product already on this abstract basis.[153]

17.090 Above all, especially when determining the scope of protection, it is not the sheer quantity of prior designs that is important but – in terms of their individual overall impression – their specific quality ('variety or multiplicity of designs and forms'). This applies not only to design[154] and copyright[155] but also particularly to trademark law[156] (with the caveat that parallel third-party signs matter because of the flexible standard that applies in this respect).[157]

17.091 Only against this background of variety of forms, the overarching 'doctrine of departure' makes sense after all, i.e., what matters – whether in the context of design, copyright, or trademark law – is whether the designer (of a design), author (of a work) or applicant (of a trademark) used the existing creative freedom accordingly and established a corresponding departure as a result. This departure is what is commonly referred to in copyright law as the 'level of originality'.[158] In other words, *use of existing aesthetic creative freedom* establishes

---

provided that the conditions for registration of that sign as a trademark are satisfied. It also follows that the rules of EU law concerning the registration of designs and those applicable to the registration of trademarks are independent, without any hierarchy existing as between those rules.

153 For copyright law: *Fun Glasses*, Dusseldorf Appeal Court, 1 September 2020, I-20 U 27/19 [under B I 1].
154 See above C 1 and D 1 (a).
155 See above C 2 and D 2 (a).
156 See above C 3 and D 3 (a).
157 This applies, particularly, to the fundamental consideration of a possible weakening of the distinctiveness of the claimed trademark; *cf.* in detail INGERL/ROHNKE/NORDEMANN, *Markengesetz*, 4th ed (C. H. Beck 2023) Section 14 paras 525, 651ff with further references. Trademark law does not refer to 'scope of protection' (or a corresponding infringement) but rather to 'likelihood of confusion', resulting from sufficient similarity between goods and signs in case of corresponding distinctive character. However, the latter may increase – following own economic activities ('strengthening') – or decrease – due to third-party activities ('weakening') – overall resulting in a flexible scope of protection under trademark law.
158 Article 17 Sentence 2 Designs Directive.

individual character (design law),¹⁵⁹ distinctiveness (trademark law),¹⁶⁰ and level of creativity/originality (copyright law).¹⁶¹

2. Differences

17.092 Significant differences exist (beyond the characteristics already discussed above) in particular insofar as, under design and copyright law, with regard to the *date of determining aesthetic creative freedom*, a 'static' scope of protection applies (reference: date of filing, priority, or creation),¹⁶² while trademark law is based on a 'flexible' scope of protection.¹⁶³ Another difference is that a trademark – if it is to serve as a ground for invalidity pursuant to Article 25 (1) lit e CDR – must have been sufficiently used where five years have passed since the trademark was registered,¹⁶⁴ whereas this does not apply to a request for a declaration of invalidity based on an earlier design under Article 25 (1) lit b CDR (lack of novelty/individual character).

17.093 In contrast to design law, which, despite the lack of substantive examination before registration, is based on the *presumption of validity* of the registered Community design,¹⁶⁵ in copyright law the burden of submission and proof rests on the person claiming that a specific subject matter enjoys copyright protection. This includes, particularly, submissions on the prior art and the departure of the claimed subject matter from the prior art as well as – similarly

---

159 See C 1 above.

160 See C 3 above.

161 See C 2 above. Interestingly, the Swedish Patent and Market Court recently found that the Swedish designer and architect Bruno Mathsson, when developing the cushion of the 'Jetson Chair', has made his own free and creative choices, thus granting copyright protection also for the cushion as such ('partial copyright protection'); *Jetson Chair*, Swedish Patent and Market Court, 2 November 2022, PMT 16530-21 https://www.domstol.se/nyheter/2022/11/fatoljdyna-har-upphovsratt/ accessed 31 December 2023. Intentions of the creator are irrelevant for assessing whether copyright subsists in a particular work; what matters is whether the work – the result – expresses the choice made by and the intention of the author; contrary *WaterRower (UK) Ltd v Liking Ltd (T/A Topiom)* [2022] EWHC 2084 (IPEC) 5 August 2022, para 44 ('intention of the creator at least relevant to whether or not a work of craftsmanship is artistic').

162 For Community design law: *Ballerina*, German Federal Supreme Court, 11 January 2018, I ZR 187/16, para 26; *Table Mat*, German Federal Supreme Court, 19 May 2010, I ZR 71/08, para 18; for copyright law: Case C-833/18 *Brompton v Chedech/Get2Get* ECLI:EU:C:2020:461, para 37; *Le Corbusier*, German Federal Supreme Court, 10 December 1986, I ZR 15/85 [under II 1 a]. Hence, it does not matter whether the *'Climbing Spider'* – *pars pro toto* – can be found in an art museum or on a children's playground; any subsequent reception, for example by art critics or inclusion in the Museum of Modern Art, is irrelevant. On the different national approaches to copyright law SUTHERSANEN, *Cross-border Copyright Protection in Europe*, in: HARTWIG (ed), *Research Handbook on Design Law* (Edward Elgar Publishing 2021), 482-506.

163 See above n 157.

164 See Case T-148/08 *Beifa Group v OHIM* ECLI:EU:T:2010:190, paras 63-67.

165 *Cf.* Article 85 (1) CDR (there is no equivalent in the Designs Directive); Section 39 German Designs Act.

to the institution of the unregistered Community design[166] – the identification of the specific features of appearance from which copyright protection allegedly results.[167]

17.094 While in copyright law, when assessing infringement, the degree of similarities (not: differences) must be taken into account because the public usually focuses more on the similarities than on differences[168] (similar to trademark law),[169] the infringement test under Article 10 (1) CDR must take into account both similarities and differences between the claimed and the accused design.[170]

17.095 Finally, although design and copyright law are both inherently subject to the *concept of reciprocity*, an exception applies to design law: In design law, the degree of individual character and the scope of protection are not reciprocal[171] or 'inversely proportional',[172] which is a difference to copyright law.[173]

3. Too Much Cumulation?

17.096 The main difference between trademark and design law on the one hand and copyright law on the other with regard to the content of aesthetic creative

---

166 See Case C-345/13 *Karen Millen v Dunnes* ECLI:EU:C:2014:2013, para 47:
   In those circumstances, the answer to the second question is that Article 85 (2) Regulation No 6/2002 must be interpreted as meaning that, in order for a Community design court to treat an unregistered Community design as valid, the right holder of that design is not required to prove that it has individual character within the meaning of Article 6 of that regulation, but need only indicate what constitutes the individual character of that design, that is to say, indicates what, in his view, are the element or elements of the design concerned which give it its individual character.
167 *E.g.*, *Saint Gottfried*, German Federal Supreme Court, 19 March 2008, I ZR 166/05, para 19; *Porsche 911*, Stuttgart Appeal Court, 20 November 2020, 5 U 125/19 [under II C 5 c].
168 *Porsche 911*, German Federal Supreme Court, 7 April 2022, I ZR 222/20, para 57:
   First, it is necessary to assess in detail which objective features determine the creative originality of the earlier work. Next, by comparing the conflicting designs, it must be determined whether and, if so, to what extent own creative features of the earlier work have been copied by the later design. Ultimately, what matters is a comparison of the respective overall impression of the designs in the context of which all creative features adopted must be taken into account in an overall view. Where the overall impression of the earlier work and the later design corresponds, the latter is a reproduction of the earlier work. In such a case, it must be further examined whether the accused design nonetheless shows such significant changes that it must not be regarded as a mere reproduction but as a derivative work or other transformation of the earlier work.
169 *IPS/ISP*, German Federal Supreme Court, 5 March 2015, I ZR 161/13, para 23.
170 *E.g.*, *Wristwatch*, German Federal Supreme Court, 28 January 2016, I ZR 40/14, para 35.
171 See for details HARTWIG, *Reciprocity in European Design Law*, in: HARTWIG (ed), *Research Handbook on Design Law* (Edward Elgar Publishing 2021) 119–168.
172 In 2021, the General Court coined and started using the notion 'rule of inverse proportionality', which, to the limited extent used by the Court, corresponds to the (much broader) 'concept of reciprocity' established in 2010; see HARTWIG, *The Concept of Reciprocity in European Design Law* [2010] JIPLP 186-191 on the one hand, and Cases T-684/20 *Legero v EUIPO/Rieker* ECLI:EU:T:2021:912, para 72, T-193/20 *Eternit v EUIPO/Eternit* ECLI:EU:T:2021:782, para 60 on the other.
173 See C 2 and D 2 above.

freedom ('variety of forms') and the determination of how it is individually used ('doctrine of departure') is that, when assessing the establishment of protection, copyright law has always been based on an *overall comparison* of the prior designs introduced in the proceedings,[174] while trademark and design law proceed from a *one-to-one comparison*.[175] As far as the overall comparison under copyright law is concerned, this specific difference is not only based on established national case law but is also in line with the CJEU's concept of 'work', constituting an 'autonomous concept of EU law which must be interpreted and applied uniformly'.[176]

For as much as the CJEU confirms that copyright protection requires that the concrete '(...) product is an original work resulting from intellectual creation, in that, through that shape, its author expresses his creative ability in an original manner by making free and creative choices in such a way that that shape reflects his personality, (...)' the CJEU emphasised as much that it is '(...) for the national court to verify, bearing in mind all the relevant aspects of the dispute in the main proceedings' whether that is the case.[177] In this respect, the CJEU also refers to Article 17 Sentence 2 Designs Directive or Article 96 (2) Sentence 2 CDR,[178] according to which 'the extent to which, and the conditions under which, such a protection is conferred, including the level of originality required, shall be determined by each Member State.' However, 'level of originality' is to be understood as nothing other than the concrete use of an 'abstract aesthetic creative freedom' (see C 2 above), which is why its determination (according to German law and practice: by means of an overall comparison) is likely to be unassailable under EU law. The decisive factor in this respect is, of course, that the features relevant to the overall impression of the work must first be determined before examining whether the combination

17.097

---

174 *Dog Figure*, German Federal Supreme Court, 8 July 2004, I ZR 25/02 [at III 5 a]:
When testing whether the accused design is a derivative work it is first necessary to assess in detail which objective features determine the creative individuality of the earlier work. The decisive factor in this regard is an overall comparison with the existing design corpus, proceeding from the overall impression of the earlier work and the features of appearance on which it is based. The result of this overall comparison also determines the degree of individuality on which the scope of protection depends.

175 *E.g.*, *Stretch-Limousine*, German Federal Supreme Court, 22 April 2010, I ZR 89/08, para 33 (for Community design law); for trademark law, e.g., STRÖBELE/HACKER/THIERING, *Markengesetz*, 13th ed, 2021, Section 9 para 183.

176 Case C-683/17 *Cofemel v G-Star* ECLI:EU:C:2019:721, para 29; *Porsche 911*, German Federal Supreme Court, 7 April 2022, I ZR 222/20, para 29.

177 Case C-833/18 *Brompton v Chedech/Get2Get* ECLI:EU:C:2020:461, para 38; see also *Marcel Breuer II*, German Federal Supreme Court, 5 November 2015, I ZR 91/11, para 27.

178 Case C-683/17 *Cofemel v G-Star* ECLI:EU:C:2019:721, para 44.

of these features conveys an overall impression that stands out from any prior designs as a whole (not merely individually).[179]

17.098 However, since it is much easier to keep departure from a single prior design than from the design corpus in total,[180] it is clearly much more demanding to establish not only protection under design law ('individual character') but also under copyright law ('originality') for the same subject matter. German copyright law and practice, thus, complies with the strict requirements established by the CJEU.[181]

17.099 It is rather unlikely that protection under trademark law on the one hand and under design or copyright law on the other could become unduly cumulated ('overreach') since the prerequisites, purpose and legal consequences of the respective legal tools are too different. For instance, the attempt to establish trademark protection for 3D objects as far as the form of the goods themselves or their packaging are concerned has been met with increasing resistance for years, either because registration has already been refused or because 3D trademarks initially registered were subsequently cancelled.[182]

17.100 In fact, there have been decisions in cases of collision between trademark and design rights on the one hand[183] and design rights and copyright on the other.[184] However, case law granting protection under two or even three different fields of law or finding infringement of parallel IP rights presumably remains extremely rare.[185]

---

179 *Cf.* above n 174.
180 BULLING, *Das neue deutsche Geschmacksmustergesetz mit Anmerkungen zum Gemeinschaftsgeschmacksmuster*, [2004] Mitt. 254, 256.
181 *Cf. Porsche 911*, German Federal Supreme Court, 7 April 2022, I ZR 222/20, para 29; Case C-683/17 *Cofemel v G-Star* ECLI:EU:C:2019:721, para 52: 'It follows that, although the protection of designs and the protection associated with copyright may, under EU law, be granted cumulatively to the same subject matter, that concurrent protection can be envisaged only in certain situations.'
182 On the fundamental differences between design and trademark law VON MÜHLENDAHL, *Three-Dimensional Trademarks and Designs: Comparison and Conflict*, in: HARTWIG (ed), *Research Handbook on Design Law* (Edward Elgar Publishing 2021), 441-481.
183 For details see VON MÜHLENDAHL, *Three-Dimensional Trademarks and Designs: Comparison and Conflict*, in: HARTWIG (ed), *Research Handbook on Design Law* (Edward Elgar Publishing 2021), 441–481.
184 *E.g.*, Case T-68/11 *Kastenholz v EUIPO/Qwatchme* ECLI:EU:T:2013:298.
185 See also recently *Savic NV v Plana D.O.O.*, Brussels District Court, 19 October 2023, A/22/02872, dismissing claims for infringement based on RCD No. 2090365-0001 and No. 2472472-0002, copyright, and national trade dress law. From a US perspective see *Jason Scott Collection, Inc., v Trendily Furniture, LLC*, No. 21-16978, US App. (9th Cir. 2023), awarding damages under both copyright and trademark laws due to 'fundamentally different measures'. Copyright damages were based on the defendants' retrospective gross profits from the infringement while trade dress damages were based on the plaintiff's prospective lost profits; https://law.justia.com/cases/federal/appellate-courts/ca9/21-16978/21-16978-2023-05-30.html accessed 31 December 2023.

Insofar as Italian courts, in the *'Piaggio'* case, found claims against one and the same accused design based on claims for infringement under trademark, copyright and trade dress law,[186] it must be noted that the Italian trademark No. 1556520 (3D), which claims priority from EUTM No. 11686482 (3D), differs, in its abstract representation, from the specific design of the famous 'Vespa' scooter from 1946, for which Italian courts had granted copyright protection. In other words, the *subject matter of protection* according to the different IP rights was not identical at all so that for this reason alone there was no 'dual protection'[187] (whether claims under copyright law, in the *'Piaggio'* case, have been construed too broadly regarding their specific scope of protection by the Italian courts when finding infringement is a different question). Moreover, it should be common ground that trademark and copyright law can and should coexist based on their own reasoning, aim and legislative basis; cumulative protection is legitimate if and insofar as the respective requirements are met.[188]

17.101

In the *'Piaggio'* case, there was also no overlap let alone 'overreach' between design and copyright law at any time; on the contrary, design rights were not even asserted by the parties against each other.

17.102

As far as the relationship between trademark and design law is concerned, the EUIPO explicitly stated, in its decision of 21 December 2020, that – in the absence of the same overall impression and, hence, likelihood of confusion – EUTM No. 11686482 (3D) cannot be cancelled based on RCD No. 1783655–0002 (which corresponds, in its shape, to the accused design challenged before the Italian courts); see Article 53 (2) lit d CTMR; now: Article 60 (2) lit d EUTMR.[189] In this context, the EUIPO relied on a decision of the General Court of 24 November 2019, according to which, under Article 25 (1) lit e CDR, there was no conflict between the two IP rights involved due to the absence of likelihood of confusion under trademark law.[190] Thus, revisiting

17.103

---

186 *Zhejiang Zhongneng v Piaggio*, Turin District Court, 17 March 2017, Sentenza No. 1900/2017 RG No. 13811/2014; *Zhejiang Zhongneng v Piaggio*, Turin Appeal Court, 12 December 2018, Sentenza No. 677/2019 RG No. 1628/2017. With respect to the decision of the Italian Supreme Court, 28 November 2023, Sentenza 19136/2019 RG No. 33100/2023, see https://ipkitten.blogspot.com/2023/12/the-vespa-appearance-italian-supreme.html accessed 31 December 2023.
187 See Case C-683/17 *Cofemel v G-Star* ECLI:EU:C:2019:721, para 52, which explicitly refers to whether or under what circumstances protection should be granted 'cumulatively to the same subject matter'.
188 The concerns in *'Cofemel'* are explicitly only directed against excessive cumulation of protection based on design and copyright law; Case C-683/17 *Cofemel v G-Star* ECLI:EU:C:2019:721, para 52.
189 *Zhejiang Zhongneng v Piaggio*, Cancellation Division (EUIPO), 21 December 2020, 9295 C. On 29 November 2023, the General Court found that the EUIPO's Board of Appeal had erred in holding that EUTM No. 11686482 (3D) was invalid due to lack of distinctiveness; Case T-19/22 *Piaggio v EUIPO/Zhejiang Zhongneng* ECLI:EU:T:2023:763.
190 Case T-219/18 *Piaggio v EUIPO/Zhejiang Zhongneng* ECLI:EU:T:2019:681, paras 65–92.

the *'Piaggio'* case, there can hardly be any question of overlap or 'overreach' between trademark and design law; on the contrary, in the absence of any conflict, EUTM No. 11686482 (3D) and RCD No. 1783655–0002 peacefully coexist.[191]

17.104 One final question seems to remain: What if an object or its design is 'converted' or 'transformed' from one product category or industrial sector to another (*'transformed design'*)?[192] How, then, is aesthetic creative freedom to be determined in such a case – for example, taking into account prior forms or designs from both 'worlds' as is the case under Community design law?[193] It would seem reasonable to apply this concept also to copyright law[194] so that the mere transfer of a design to another product category is no circumstance that would allow for copyright protection.[195] After all, aesthetic limits to aesthetic creative freedom do not result from a specific product category as the sheer number of transformed designs – relevant case law on this topic has grown

---

191 See also Case C-237/19 *Gömböc v Szellemi Tulajdon Nemzeti Hivatala* ECLI:EU:C:2020:296, paras 50–54: In this regard, it should be borne in mind that the objective of the ground for refusal of registration provided for in Article 3 (1) lit e (iii) of Directive 2008/95, like that of the ground for refusal of registration provided for in Article 3 (1) lit e (ii) of that directive (…) is, indeed, to prevent the exclusive and permanent right that a trade mark confers from serving to extend indefinitely the life of other rights in respect of which the EU legislature has sought to impose time limits (…). However, such an objective does not mean that EU intellectual property law prevents the coexistence of several forms of legal protection. As regards the protection of designs, Article 16 Directive 98/71 provides that that directive 'shall be without prejudice to any provisions of [European Union] law or of the law of the Member State concerned relating to unregistered design rights, trademarks or other distinctive signs, patents and utility models'. It is apparent from the above that the fact that the appearance of a product is protected as a design does not prevent a sign consisting of the shape of that product from benefiting from protection under trademark law, provided that the conditions for registration of that sign as a trademark are satisfied. It also follows that the rules of EU law concerning the registration of designs and those applicable to the registration of trade marks are independent, without any hierarchy existing as between those rules.
192 Here, this notion means the transfer of shape/appearance from one sector/industry (e.g., furniture) to another (*e.g.*, automotive).
193 See HARTWIG, *Relevanter Formenschatz im Gemeinschaftsgeschmacksmusterrecht* [2017] GRUR 1212–1215. Under trademark law, this constellation is only conceivable, if at all, in the case of a well-known trademark.
194 *Crib*, Dusseldorf District Court, 17 September 2019, 14c O 225/17 [under A I 1 b bb (6)].
195 It seems that under Swiss copyright law different standards apply; *Barbecue grill*, Swiss Federal Supreme Court, 17 June 2022, 4A_472/2021 and 4A_482/2021 [at 6.1.2]: 'A certain surprise effect arises not least from the fact that it is not obvious at first glance that the 'fire ring' is a grill. The unbiased observer does not initially recognize a grill with a special (different) shape, but rather an artistic object, which, upon closer inspection, reveals itself to be a grill.' – See also, for the Canadian perspective, *Pyrrha Design Inc. v Plum and Posey Inc.*, 2019 FC 129, para 109: 'Copyright subsists in each individual Pyrrha Design to the extent that Pyrrha took the imagery of a wax seal and expressed it in metal in a specific way.' This decision was confirmed by *Pyrrha Design Inc. v Plum and Posey Inc.*, 2022 FCA 7, holding that the Federal Court (FC) did not err in its analysis on the issues of originality and infringement of jewelry designs.

again in recent times[196] – impressively proves.[197] Otherwise, if transformed designs would *eo ipso* establish IP rights this would lead to 'absurd'[198] or 'paradoxical'[199] results.

In a quite comparable context, the *United States District Court, D. Colorado* addressed this issue already in 2005 when denying copyright protection for a golden bracelet in the form of traditional barbed wire, *inter alia* on the following grounds:[200]

17.105

> (…) if a court were to grant copyright in an arrangement that is visually but not conceptually distinguishable from barbed-wire, it would risk giving Plaintiff a monopoly over the idea itself. Arguably it would be impossible for other artists to create barbed-wire style jewellery (no matter how visually distinguishable) without infringing on Plaintiff's copyrighted arrangement.

This, too, namely that transformed designs do not in themselves constitute copyright protection, i.e., previously known designs from cross-product or product-independent sectors must in principle be taken into account when determining aesthetic creative freedom, tends to restrict protection for works of fine arts, including works of architecture and applied art. Consequently, there is no risk of an excessive cumulation of parallel IP rights.[201]

17.106

---

196 HARTWIG, *What you see is what you get* [2016] GRUR 882, 884; HARTWIG, *Gestaltungsfreiheit im Gemeinschaftsgeschmacksmusterrecht* [2020] GRUR 1260, 1267 n 85.
197 A number of disputes between Porsche and Autec/Rietze (German toy car makers) shows that challenges to Community designs registered under the title 'Passenger cars' come from the toy industry. This makes sense because if the Porsche designs would remain unchallenged these rights would block Autec/Rietze from unauthorized use in the toy sector.
198 Joined Cases C-361/15 P and C-405/15 P *Easy Sanitary v EUIPO/Group Nivelles* ECLI:EU:C:2017:720, para 96.
199 Case T-15/13 *Group Nivelles/EUIPO and Easy Sanitary Solutions* ECLI:EU:T:2015:281, para 116.
200 *Todd v. Montana Silversmiths, Inc.*, 379 F. Supp. 2d 1110 (D. Colo. 2005).
201 From a US perspective see BURSTEIN, *Uncreative Designs*, 73 Duke L.J. (Forthcoming), Suffolk University Law School Research Paper No. 20-22, 76: 'Contrary to the conventional wisdom, the copyright requirement of originality is not 'lower' than the substantive requirement for design patentability. It's just different.'

18

FASHION AND DESIGN LAW

Ulrika Wennersten, Laurent Manderieux and Patricia Covarrubia

A. GLOBAL PERSPECTIVE ON THE PROTECTION OF FASHION BY DESIGN LAW 18.001	5. Infringement in the Fashion Industry 18.041
1. Introduction 18.001	C. CONTEMPORARY ISSUES IN THE FASHION INDUSTRY 18.052
B. THE PROTECTION OF FASHION BY EU DESIGN LAW 18.011	1. Artificial Intelligence, Fashion and Design Law 18.052
1. Fashion and the Concept of Design 18.011	2. 3D and 4D Printing in Fashion and Design Law 18.057
2. Community and National Registered Design 18.016	3. Fashion and Traditional Knowledge 18.061
(a) Novelty and individual character 18.021	4. Fashion, Design Law, and Circular Economy 18.066
(b) Grounds for refusal 18.028	5. Overlapping IP Protections for Fashion in EU Law 18.075
3. Unregistered Community Designs 18.032	
4. Ownership of Design in the Fashion Industry 18.038	

A. GLOBAL PERSPECTIVE ON THE PROTECTION OF FASHION BY DESIGN LAW

1. Introduction

18.001 The fashion industry plays a central role in society and history and accounts for around 2 percent of the world's Gross Domestic Product (GDP). The global apparel market is valued at 3 trillion US dollars.[1] Fashion is highly important for the European Economy. Over five million people are employed in the fashion industry value chain, and over one million in the high-end industries.[2]

---

1 Global Fashion Industry Statistics – International Apparel, see https://fashionunited.com/global-fashion-industry-statistics accessed 16 January 2024.
2 Fashion and high-end industries in the EU, https://fashionunited.com/global-fashion-industry-statistics/2016042011023 accessed 16 January 2024.

Protection for fashion is essential for the industry, and the EU has legislated to ensure protection. Creativity is the driving force of fashion. The creator wants to influence and inspire – be a trendsetter, but not be copied; sometimes described as the Paradox of Fashion.[3] There is also complexity in fashion, as it can be culture, craftsmanship, and cultural heritage.

18.002 The global nature of manufacturing and trade in fashion contrasts with legal rules that are national or regional and territorial.

18.003 The Paris Convention was adopted 1883, with the aim to harmonise intellectual property protection worldwide.[4] The Convention, administered by WIPO, is structured around a few key principles, one of which is the principle of national treatment, and another is the principle of minimum protection. Regarding design protection, the Paris Convention contains only a few articles. Article 5 quinquies states that 'industrial designs' shall be protected in all the countries of the Union, but the Convention does not impose any requirements as to the form of such protection. There is also no definition of design. The Paris Convention also contains an article on priority of designs. The rules on priority are found in Article 4.C and state that the priority right is six months for industrial design from the first application.

18.004 The Berne Convention for the Protection of Literary and Artistic Works[5] from 1886 is also relevant for certain fashion designs. According to Article 2(7) of the Berne Convention, Member States may determine the scope of application of industrial design laws and the conditions for such protection. At the same time, that provision also does not preclude the cumulation of those two protections.[6] Furthermore, Article 2(7) provides that works which are protected in their country of origin solely as designs may, in another country of the Union, claim only the protection afforded in that country to designs. If there is no such special protection for designs in the other EU country, the work will be protected as a work of art if the conditions for protection are met.

---

3   Katonomics 5: Economics of IP: The Paradox of Fashion, http://ipkitten.blogspot.com/2011/12/katonomics-5-economics-of-ip-paradox-of.html accessed 16 January 2024, and The Piracy Paradox: Innovation and Intellectual Property in Fashion Design, Virginia Law Review, Vol. 92, p. 1687, 2006, UCLA School of Law Research Paper No. 06-04.
4   WIPO, Paris Convention for the Protection of Industrial Property, https://www.wipo.int/treaties/en/ip/paris accessed 16 January 2024.
5   WIPO, Berne Convention for the Protection of Literary and Artistic Works, https://www.wipo.int/treaties/en/ip/berne/ accessed 16 January 2024.
6   C-683/17, *Cofemel*, EU:C:2019:721, para. 42.

18.005 In 1925, an agreement on the international registration of designs was concluded in The Hague. It established the possibility for designers to obtain design protection through a single international application in countries that have ratified or acceded to one of the treaties on which the system is based. The Hague system is essentially based on three different treaties. The first two are the 1934 London Treaty and the 1960 Hague Treaty. The third treaty, which entered into force on 23 December 2003, is the 1999 Act of the Hague Convention on the International Registration of Industrial Designs, known as the Geneva Act. The Geneva Act is adapted both to countries with mandatory novelty searches and to countries without such searches, allowing more countries to join the Hague Convention. The Geneva Act can also be signed by intergovernmental organisations that have a regional office for the registration of designs. The EU joined in 2008, establishing a link between the Community design system and the international registration system under the Geneva Act. As a result, designers can designate the Union through an international application and obtain protection there for their designs under the Community Design Regulation, but they can also designate the territories that are party to the Geneva Act. It is therefore possible to obtain protection both inside and outside the EU through an international application. A registration with the WIPO International Bureau has the same effect as a national registration. However, the detailed content of the protection is determined by the national legislation of each of the countries or organisations mentioned in the application. The system thus contains only one registration procedure and is a so-called closed system, which means that it can only be used by applicants from countries that have joined the system.[7]

18.006 The Locarno Agreement was concluded in 1968 and creates an international classification system for designs. The convention is administered by WIPO. The classification consists of an alphabetical list of products divided into classes and subclasses, which is used in the registration of designs.[8] The Locarno Agreement classification is applied by many national Patent and Registration Offices. European Union Intellectual Property Office (EUIPO) has developed a sophisticated system for classifying products called Eurolocarno, which is based on the Locarno Agreement classification.[9]

---

[7] WIPO, Guide to the Hague system, https://www.wipo.int/hague/en/guide/introduction.html accessed 15 July 2024.

[8] WIPO, Summary of the Locarno Agreement Establishing an International Classification for Industrial Designs (1968), https://www.wipo.int/treaties/en/classification/locarno/summary_locarno.html accessed 16 January 2024.

[9] EUIPO, Locarno Classification (designs), https:// euipo .europa .eu/ ohimportal/ en/ locarno -classification accessed 16 January 2024.

The Agreement on Trade-Related Aspects of Intellectual Property Rights **18.007**
(TRIPS)[10] from 1996 contains a few provisions on design protection. Article 25 provides for the protection of independently created designs that are 'new or original'. Member states can provide that designs are not new or original if the designs do not significantly differ from previous designs or combination of previous designs. Article 25 reflects the fact that countries protect design differently. Some countries give a copyright-like design protection and other countries use a patent-like system.[11] However, EU has rejected both and follows instead a 'design approach'.[12] Member states can also decide if the protection should extend to designs dictated essentially by technical or functional considerations. When it comes to textile design Article 25.2 states that member states shall ensure that requirements for securing protection do not unreasonable impair the opportunity to seek and obtain protection, especially when it comes to cost, examination and publication. Article 26 sets out the scope of protection and states that 'the owner of a protected design shall have the right to prevent third parties not having the owner´s consent from making, selling and importing articles bearing or embodying a design which is a copy, or substantially a copy, of the protected design, when such acts are undertaken for commercial purposes'. The same article also states that limited exceptions to design protection are permitted under the three-step test. The duration of design protection shall amount to at least ten years.

Within the EU, two legal instruments have been adopted that regulate design **18.008**
protection in the Union.[13] One is the Directive 98/71/EC of the European Parliament and of the Council of 13 October 1998 on the legal protection of designs (Design Directive (DDir)), which aims to harmonise member states' laws on design protection. The directive is not a full harmonisation directive, harmonisation was limited to the rules that were considered to have the greatest impact on the functioning of the internal market. It was left to each nation to determine the rules on penalties, liability, application and enforcement (see Recital 5). Although harmonised rules on sanctions were later introduced via

---

10   World Trade Organization, Overview: the TRIPS Agreement, https://www.wto.org/english/tratop_e/trips_e/intel2_e.htm accessed 16 January 2024.
11   Susy Frankel and Daniel J. Gervais, *Advanced Introduction to International Intellectual Property* (Edward Elgar 2016) 83.
12   Anette Kur, 'The Green Paper's "Design approach" – what is wrong with it?', (1993) EIPR 15(10) 374.
13   Both instruments are currently undergoing a revision, see Proposal for a Regulation of the European Parliament and of the Council amending Council Regulation (EC) No 6/2002 on Community designs and repealing Commission Regulation (EC) No 2246/2002, https://eur-lex.europa.eu/procedure/EN/2022_391 accessed 25 January 2024, and Proposal for a Directive of the European Parliament and the Council on the legal protection of designs (recast), COM/2022/667 final, https://www.europarl.europa.eu/doceo/document/A-9-2023-0317_EN.html accessed 25 January 2024.

the Directive 2004/48/EC of the European Parliament and of the Council of 29 April 2004 on the enforcement of intellectual property rights (IPRED Directive). Member states also retained 'the freedom to determine the procedures for the registration, renewal, and cancellation of design rights, as well as the rules governing the effects of such cancellation' (see Recital 6). The purpose of the Directive was thus to harmonise the requirements for qualification, the scope of protection, the term of protection, the presumption of validity and the exclusive right.

18.009 The second legal instrument governing design protection is the Council Regulation (EC) No 6/2002 of 12 December 2001 on Community Designs (Design Regulation (CDReg)). The Regulation establishes an EU legal system for the protection of designs and is directly applicable in the Member States. It states that Community designs can be protected either as unregistered or registered designs.

18.010 The fashion sector produces large numbers of 'collections' a year, with a relatively short market life. It creates a demand for automatic, efficient, short-term IP protection that could hinder copying without the burden of registration. The Community Design Regulation answers that demand as it provides both for unregistered and registered design protection.[14] The unregistered design gives the fashion designer three-year protection from the design first being made available to the public and protects against copying the protected design. However, sometimes there is a need for broader protection covering designs that produce the same overall impression on the informed user. For iconic fashion products, such as the Hermés Birkin Bag, the industry often values the advantages of registration as this gives broader and longer-term protection.

B. THE PROTECTION OF FASHION BY EU DESIGN LAW

1. Fashion and the Concept of Design

18.011 A design is the visual appearance of a product or part of a product. A *product* is an 'industrial or handicraft item', including, inter alia, parts intended to be assembled into a complex product, packaging, get-up, graphic symbols, and typographic typefaces, but excluding computer programs.[15] EUIPO does not examine whether the product claimed is actually made or used, or can be made

---

[14] Annette Kur and Marianne Levin, 'The Design Approach Revisited: Background and Meaning' in Annette Kur, Marianne Levin and Jens Scovsbo, *The EU Design Approach: A Global Appraisal* (Edward Elgar 2018) 20.
[15] Article 3b CDReg.

or used, in an industrial or handicraft manner.[16] As most of the goods in the fashion industry are industrial or handcraft items, such as garments, shoes, bags, jewellery, etc.

18.012 A *complex product* is 'a product which is composed of multiple components which can be replaced permitting disassembly and re-assembly of the product'.[17] A complex product could for example be a bag. However, a complex product can only be protected if the component part, once it has been incorporated into the complex product, remains visible during normal use and these visible features of the component part meets the requirement novelty and individual character (see below).[18]

18.013 A *design* is defined as 'the appearance of the whole or a part of a product resulting from the features of, in particular, the lines, contours, colours, shape, texture and/or materials of the product itself and/or its ornamentation'.[19] The design must be manifested in physical form and therefore design rights do not protect thoughts or design concepts. The definition also excludes ideas and styles e.g., a garment made with the patchwork technique.[20] However, it must form part of the product's visual appearance.[21] It means that the design must be perceptible to the eye, with or without aids can be protected. However, the design need not be aesthetically pleasing, beautiful, or creative.[22]

18.014 According to the definition, appearance results from features. The words 'in particular' shows that this list of features is not exhaustive.[23] Lines and contours probably has its ordinary meaning.[24] A colour per se cannot constitute a design. However, a combination of two colours forming a graphic symbol, for example, can be protected by design rights. Furthermore, a more complex combination of colours, such as a pattern on a garment can be protected by design rights. If an application is drawn in black and white, it protects the use of the design in any colour. If the image is coloured the protection only extends to that specific colour.[25] Texture is interesting in relation to the fashion

---

16 EUIPO Design Guidelines, section 4.1.
17 Article 3c CDReg.
18 Article 4.2 CDReg.
19 Article 3.8 CDReg and Article 1a DDir.
20 *Gal v Yves St Laurent* CA Paris, 18 September 2002 cited by Estelle Derclaye, 'Are Fashion Designers Better Protected in Europe Than in the United Kingdom: A Comparative Analysis of the Recent Case Law in France, Italy and the United Kingdom' (2010) 13(3) *Journal of World Intellectual Property* 315.
21 Directive, Recital 11 reads 'in whole or in part, which are shown *visibly* in an application' [emphasis added].
22 Lionel Bently and others, *Intellectual Property* (6th edn, OUP 2020) 751.
23 David Stone, *European Union Design Law. A Practitioner's Guide* (2nd edn, OUP) 50.
24 Ibid.
25 Ibid., 51.

industry. In the Green Paper texture was said to protect how the product feels.[26] However, the Directive and the Regulation only protect the product's appearance. In other words, how the product is perceived visually. This means that only how the texture is perceived by the eyes is relevant, not how it feels.[27] It is the same with material as with texture. The material must be a feature of the product that can be seen by the eyes. There is a proposal to change the definitions after the word texture to 'materials of the product itself and/or its decoration, including the movement, transition or any other sort of animation of those features'.[28]

18.015 Design, in the context of fashion, pertains to the appearance of products such as garments, shoes, jewellery, and other related articles, including wearable technologies.[29] This can even extend to specific fabrics, like the knitted fabric made from recycled plastic used in a ballerina shoe.[30]

2. Community and National Registered Design

18.016 The design law in the European Union (EU) is primarily governed by the two Community instruments listed above: the CDReg,[31] and the DDir.[32] These legal frameworks, which are substantially identical, aim to protect the 'aesthetic' and 'ornamental' aspects of both 2D and 3D designs. They grant an exclusive right to use a design and prohibit third parties from using it without consent.[33]

---

26 Green Paper on the Legal Protection of Industrial Design. (Working document of the services of the Commission. III/F/5131/91-EN, June 1991) 61.
27 Stone (n 22) 52.
28 Proposal for a regulation of the European Parliament and of the council amending Council Regulation (EC) No 6/2002 Community designs and repealing Commission Regulation (EC) No 2246/2002.
29 Wearable technology worth was $34 billion in 2020. See Gionanni Ziccardi, 'Wearable Technologies and Smart Clothes in the Fashion Business: Some Issues Concerning Cybersecurity and Data Protection' (2020) 9((2) MDPI 12.
30 *Rothy's Inc v Giesswein Walkwaren AG* [2020] EWHC 3391 (IPEC), 16 December 2020, Case No IP 2019-000084.
31 Council Regulation (EC) No6/2002 of 12 of December 2001 on Community Designs, 2002 OJ (L3). The regulation is currently undergoing a revision, see Proposal for a Regulation of the European Parliament and of the Council (n 12).
32 Directive 98/71/EC of the European Parliament and of the Council of 13 October 1998 on the Legal Protection of Designs, 1998 OJ (L289). The Directive is currently undergoing revision, see and Proposal for a Directive of the European Parliament and the Council on the legal protection of designs (recast), COM/2022/667 final, https:// www .europarl .europa .eu/ doceo/ document/ A -9 -2023 -0317 _EN .html, accessed 25 January 2024.
33 Joanna Buchalska, 'Fashion Law: A New Approach' (2016) 7 *Queen Mary Law Journal* 13, 22.

18.017 It is important to note that the EU is a member of the Hague Agreement. This agreement establishes an international system that allows industrial designs to be protected in multiple countries (or regions) with minimal formalities.

18.018 Fashion designs can be registered under the Community Design system, which offers protection across all EU member states with a single registration (RCD). This gives owners the power to enforce their rights uniformly across the EU as it has been evaluated by Church and others, who examined over 1,000 design cases across the EU member states.[34] They found that in the first 15 years since the EU design law was enforced, it has been effective. Designs were more likely to be found infringed (63.5 per cent of the cases studied) than not infringed (36.5 per cent of the cases studied).[35]

18.019 The Community Design registration in the EU has some unique characteristics. Unlike some of the national registrations, it is subject only to formal examination by the EUIPO, and there is no opposition period. This makes the registration process relatively quick, with approvals even possible on the same day.[36] Another peculiarity is that a single application can include up to 99 designs, provided they belong to the same Locarno class.[37] However, design protection is not limited to designs within these classes.[38] A characteristic that is distinctive is that the Community legislation allows for the 'cumulative doctrine',[39] which means copyright and design protection can be combined – a practice previously disallowed by some EU member states.[40] This cumulation is also possible between registered and unregistered designs, as well as other intellectual property rights such as patents and trade marks.[41] However, if a design has entered the public domain due to the term of protection expiring, it cannot be registered or protected under design law as it would not meet the novelty requirement.[42] The initial term of protection for registered designs is five years from the date of filing, and this can be renewed up to 25 years, provided renewal fees are paid every five years.[43]

---

34 Oliver Church, Estelle Derclaye and Gilles Stupfler, 'An Empirical Analysis of the Design Case Law of the EU Member States' (2019) 50 *Int Rev Intellectual Property Competition Law* 685, 686.
35 Ibid.
36 Rosie Burbidge, *European Fashion Law: A Practical Guide From Start-up to Global Success* (EE 2019) 87.
37 The Locarno classification is a system for classifying industrial designs established by the Locarno Agreement (1968), administered by the World Intellectual Property Organization.
38 Burbidge (n 35), 92.
39 Article 16 DDir.
40 Derclaye (n 19), 317.
41 Buchalska (n 32), 22.
42 Derclaye (n 19), 333.
43 Article 12 CDReg and Article 10 DDir.

18.020 The next section of the text evaluates the requirements for registration.

(a) Novelty and individual character

18.021 The registration of a design requires it to be novel and possess an individual character.[44] This includes 'complex products',[45] where each part that is to be individually protected must also meet these criteria.[46] These aspects are typically addressed during invalidity proceedings or counterclaim in infringement proceedings, rather than during the application process.[47]

18.022 These criteria apply to the design which must be visible during the normal use of the product, at least some of the time[48] noting that internal features can be protected too if they can be represented. However, if a design is not visible at the time of purchase, it cannot be considered for determining individual character.[49] This suggests that the inside of a garment is protected.[50]

18.023 Starting with the criterion of novelty, it is defined as a design being 'new if no identical design has been available to the public'[51] before the date of filing the application for registration or the date of priority.[52] For instance, if a pattern is applied to a different item of clothing but remains the same, it lacks novelty.[53] The Directive expands on the phrase 'available to the public' by explaining 'disclosure' for assessing 'novelty and individual character'. Disclosure is understood as publication, exhibition, or use before the filing of the application for registration or the priority date[54] and must occur within the EU.[55] Some disclosures, such as those made by the designer or during the grace period (one year following the date of disclosure to the public), are not considered. For example, in Germany, the publication of a slide shoe image by the designer before regis-

---

44 Article 4 RCDReg.
45 Complex products are defined under Article 3(c) Regulation as 'a product which is composed of multiple components which can be replaced permitting disassembly and re-assembly of the product'.
46 Derclaye (n 19), 317.
47 Bently and others (n 21), 745.
48 Article 4.1(a)(b) CDReg; Article 3 DDir.
49 *Biscuits Poult v Banketbakkerij Merva* Case T-494/12 EU:T2014757. See further Krystian Maciaszek, 'Poland: Are the Designs Within an Ice-cream to be Registered as an Industrial Design' (2012) EIPR 656.
50 Bently notes that the inside of a luggage may be protected, in Bently and others (n 21), 752.
51 Article 5.1 CDReg.
52 Article 5.1(b) CDReg.
53 Spanish Supreme Court, *Original Buff, SA v The owner of the Spanish industrial design No 514810-01 and No 514810-02*, decision No 608/2021, 16 September 2021.
54 Article 7 CDReg and Article 6 DDir.
55 Marie-Astrid Huemer, Revision of Directive 98/71/EC on the legal protection of designs and of Regulation(EC) No 6/2002 on Community designs (European Parliamentary Research Unit, Briefing Implementation Appraisal, May 2020) https:// www .europarl .europa .eu/ RegData/ etudes/ BRIE/ 2022/ 730318/EPRS_BRI(2022)730318_EN.pdf accessed 30 September 2023.

tration (within the grace period), which was subsequently published by a third party, was not considered to render the registered design void.[56]

18.024 The validity of a design also depends on its individual character, which is defined as the 'overall impression it produces on the informed user' and how it differs from any design made available to the public[57] before the design for which protection is claimed.[58] The 'degree of freedom of the designer in developing the design' is also considered.[59] For instance, in a crowded sector, even slight differences can show individual character.[60]

18.025 The overall impression is also linked to the 'representation' in the application for registration. For example, in Germany, the contrasting colour scheme used in the application for a ski goggles design determined the scope of protection of the design.[61]

18.026 European courts have interpreted the term literally. In the *Karen Millen* case,[62] the CJEU disagreed with the argument that the garment lacked individual character due to several earlier items in clothing. They noted that individual character depends on the 'overall impression' that the design has on the 'informed user'. If a single earlier design does not have the same overall impression, the design has an individual character. Moreover, the court ruled that the right holder of a design *does not need to prove* that it has individual character but just *needs to indicate* what constitutes individual character of that design, that is, what are the element(s) of the design which give its individual character. Italian courts have interpreted the notion of individual character by using a test that includes identifying the relevant sector, the prior art in the sector, the informed user, and comparing the prior art with the design at issue.[63]

18.027 Finally, novelty and individual character are accompanied by another term, that of 'informed user' which is significant in the Community legal framework. While the term changes linguistically in France to 'informed observer', Derclaye notes that the wording difference is not substantial.[64] French courts define the concept as 'a user not with average attention but with special vigi-

---

56   Higher Regional Court of Dusserldorf, judgement dated 24 April 2019 – I-20 U 103/18.
57   Article 6.1 CDReg.
58   Article 6.1(b) CDReg.
59   Article 10.2 CDReg and Article 5.2 DDir.
60   Derclaye (n 19), 336.
61   BGH judgement dated 20 December 2018 – I ZB 26/18.
62   *Karen Millen Fashion Ltd v Dunnes Stores* C-345/13 EU:C:2014:2013.
63   Derclaye (n 19), 337.
64   Ibid., 331.

lance' due to their personal experiences and knowledge in the sector.[65] In Italy, the understanding of 'informed user' is similar. In *Casa Daminani*, the court refers to the informed user as someone 'familiar with and having knowledge in the field',[66] and as a person 'whose attention is markedly superior to the average'.[67] Suthersanen suggests that an 'informed user' could be a user, a designer, or a collector.[68] She also notes that the term 'informed user' differs from 'person skilled in the art' used in patent law or 'average consumer' used in trade mark law.[69] In *PepsiCo Inc v Grupo Promer Mon Graphic SA*, the CJEU interprets the informed user as 'a particularly observant one, either because of his personal experience or his extensive knowledge of the sector in question'.[70]

(b) Grounds for refusal

18.028 There are certain limitations on design registration, resulting in some designs being excluded. For instance, a design cannot be registered if it is dictated solely by its technical function or if it is contrary to public order and morality. In the case of technical function, a design is excluded if it is dictated solely by its technical function[71] or those of interconnections, unless its interconnections allow for the 'multiple assembly or connection of mutually interchangeable products within a modular system'.[72] The exception is applicable when the aesthetic configurations are inseparable from the functional characteristics which are needed for the product.[73] Recital 10 of the Regulation notes that technological innovation should not be 'hampered by granting design protection to features dictated solely by a technical function'. All EU member states, including the UK, have adopted this ground of refusal, and the Court of Justice has ruled on the matter asserting that 'Community design does not subsist in features of appearance of a product which are solely dictated by its technical function'.[74]

18.029 The reason for this is the existence of two theories around the EU: the 'multiplicity of forms' and the 'causality (or causative)' theory.[75] The former implies

---

65 Ibid., 333.
66 Ibid., 335.
67 Ibid., 336.
68 Uma Suthersamen, *Design Law in Europe* (Sweet and Maxwell 2000) 39.
69 *Procter & Gamble Company v Reckitt Benckiser (UK) Ltd* [2007] EWCA Civ 936.
70 Ibid., [53].
71 Article 8.1 CDReg; Article 7.1 DDir.
72 Article 8.3 CDReg.
73 Derclaye (n 19), 333.
74 See Case C-395/16 *DOCERAM GmbH v CeramTec GmbH*, and Case C-684/21 *Papierfabriek Doetinchem BV v Sprick GmbH Bielefelder Papier- und Wellpappenwerk & Co.*
75 Due to the scope of this chapter, the theories are not studied.

that if a technical function can be achieved through the use of alternative forms, the particular feature of the design is not determined 'solely' by its technical function and thus, not constrained by the function.[76] The latter theory is based on the intention of the designer and thus, alternative forms are not considered. In other words, the design is chosen because of its technical function rather than the aesthetic consideration.[77] However, in *DOCERAM*, the CJEU seems to have followed the causality theory, arguing that technical function is the only factor which determines, and that the existence of alternative designs is not decisive. Yet, the court continues to suggest that information as to the existence of alternative designs should be part of the criteria when analysing the ground. On one hand, courts within the EU, including the UK, have granted protection when a variety of shapes can fulfil the same function. For instance, his Honour Judge Fysh QC noted in *Landor & Hawa International Ltd* that the word 'solely dictated by' meant driven without option.[78] And on the other hand, French courts observe that when a product design has a functional character, but the design comes from 'aesthetic research and a creative effort' like a reversible Hermés' bag, it is capable of being protected.[79]

18.030 Another ground of refusal is that of being contrary to morality and or public policy[80] which aligns with other areas in intellectual property such as trade mark law and patent. The test applied is whether 'the moral principles of rights-thinking members of the public would think it very wrong for the law to grant protection'.[81] This test can be used during the application process or as a ground for invalidity.[82]

18.031 Designs can be registered either at the EU level or at the national level and because the design law is harmonised among EU member states, the system is similar among them except for the timeframe for registration as well as the examination phase between registries which may vary slightly.[83]

3. Unregistered Community Designs

18.032 In addition to the protection provided by registered designs, the EU also protects unregistered designs through the provision of the Unregistered

---

76 See AG in Case C-395/16 *DOCERAM GmbH v CeramTec GmbH*.
77 Ibid.
78 *Landor & Hawa International Ltd v Azure Designs Ltd* [2006] EWCA 1285.
79 Derclaye (n 19), 333.
80 Article 9 CDReg.
81 Bently and others (n 21) 765.
82 Article 25(1)(b) CDReg.
83 Burbidge (n 35), 87.

Community Design (UCD). This protection lasts for three years from the date the design is first made available to the public. It is intended to provide short-term protection for industries with a short shelf-life due to their seasonal nature, such as the clothing industry,[84] or to provide temporary protection while designers/proprietors consider registration.[85]

18.033 Buchalska observes that this right is based on British legislation, which was created to 'fill in the gap between copyrights and design protection for artistic craftsmanship'.[86] In an empirical research study by Church and others, it was found that unregistered designs were of great utility in the fashion industry.[87] Moreover, Bently observes that the 'textile and fashion industries have tended to rely more on unregistered design right'.[88]

18.034 Unregistered design right is flexible, and no formal application is needed. Therefore, the right is automatically granted upon publication and can protect the whole or part of a product,[89] including its shape, texture, and even surface decoration, including 2D features. To qualify for protection, a design must meet the same criteria as a registered design, that is, it must be novel (new) and have individual character.

18.035 In the case of *Ferrari SpA v Mansory Design Holding GmbH*, the CJEU noted the extent of unregistered design protection. Following the publication of an image of the entire product (a photograph of the Ferrari FXX K), parts of the products were protected under unregistered design due to the appearance of the parts being clearly identifiable.[90]

18.036 In this era of the fast fashion industry, where trends are changing rapidly, obtaining unregistered design protection is beneficial to the industry. The scope of protection is generally narrower than that of registered design, which provides a more comprehensive and secure form of protection. For instance, a proprietor of a registered design can object to the use of a design even if such design is independently created by a third party. This is not the case for unregistered design, as infringement only occurs when the design has been

---

84   Abbe Brown and others, *Contemporary Intellectual Property Law* (5th edn, OUP 2019) 360.
85   Bently and others (n 21) 737.
86   Buchalska (n 32), 23.
87   Church, Derclaye and Stupfler (n 33), 686.
88   Bently and others (n 21) 742.
89   Burbidge (n 35), 84.
90   C-123/20 *Ferrari SpA v Mansory Design Holding GmbH*, ECLI:EU:C:2021:889.

copied.⁹¹ Moreover, infringement is assessed by the similarities rather than the differences,⁹² focusing on the overall impression.⁹³

Both registered and unregistered design protections encourage creativity within the fashion industry in the EU. It is left to designers and the industry to choose the form of protection that best suits their needs.

4. Ownership of Design in the Fashion Industry

The Design Directive contains no provisions on who is entitled to a registered design or ownership. This is left to the member states' national laws. However, the Regulation states that design vests in the designer or his or her successor in title.⁹⁴ In the case *FEIA*, the CJEU stated that the terms 'designer' and 'successor in title' should be given a uniform interpretation within the Community legal order, but the court did not define the terms.⁹⁵ According to Stone, a designer is likely to be the person who designs the design.⁹⁶ Hence, the starting point is that the fashion designer, the creator, is the initial owner of the Community design. However, if two or more designers have cooperated to jointly develop the design, the right to the Community design shall vest in them jointly.⁹⁷

In many cases, a fashion design is developed by employees in executing their duties or following the instructions given by their employer. In those cases, the right to the Community design vests in the employer, unless otherwise agreed or specified under national law.⁹⁸ The term employee refers, according to CJEU, to the person who works under the instructions of an 'employer' when developing a Community design in the context of an employment relationship'.⁹⁹

In the case of a company commissioning a fashion design, the CJEU has stated in the case *FEIA*, that Article 14.3 CDReg only applies to employees and that commissioned design falls under Article 14.1 CDReg, with the result that

---

91 Bently and others (n 21) 742.
92 Paris Court of Appeal, 23 March 2021, no 18/28435 *APM Monaco v Swarosvski Crystal Online*.
93 Paris Court of Appeal, 25 June 2021, no 19/05464 as noted in The Bird & Bird IP Team, 'Round-up of fashion-related IP decision 2021' (2022) 17(3) JIPLP 260, 285.
94 Article 14.1 CDReg.
95 C-32/08, *FEIA*, EU:C:2009:418, paras 66 and 68.
96 Stone (n 22) 125.
97 Article 14.2 CDReg.
98 Article 14.3 CDReg.
99 C-32/08, *FEIA*, EU:C:2009:418, para 49.

the ownership vests in the designer.[100] If the Commissioner wishes to obtain ownership of the fashion design, he or she is advised to agree with the designer in a written contract on the right to the design.

5. Infringement in the Fashion Industry

18.041 A *registered design* gives its holder the exclusive right to use it and to prevent any third party not having his consent from using it.[101] The right holder can hinder any use of a fashion design that does not produce on the informed user a different overall impression.[102] When assessing this, 'the degree of freedom of the designer in developing his design shall be taken into consideration'.[103]

18.042 Design law protects the visual appearance of any product or part of a product. This means that in an infringement action, a company cannot argue that they have used another technique to achieve the same result, because it is the end result, i.e., the visual appearance of the product, that is protected.

18.043 An unregistered Community design gives its holder the right to prevent the same acts as a registered design but only if the contested use results from copying the protected design, and the article states that 'the contested use shall not be deemed to result from copying the protected design if it results from an independent work of creation by a designer who may be reasonably thought not to be familiar with the design made available to the public'.[104] Registration is needed if the designer or his successor wants a more prolonged and broader protection. Even if novelty is required to register, it is still possible to register the design due to the 12-month grace period provided for in Article 7.2 CDReg. The purpose of the grace period is to allow the designer or his successor in title to test the products in which the design is embodied in the marketplace before deciding if registration is desirable.[105] The grace period means that disclosures of the design by the designer or his successor in title, during a period of 12 months prior to the date of the filing of the application for a registered Community design should not be prejudicial in assessing the novelty or the individual character of the design in question.

---

100   Ibid., paras 51–55.
101   The word use covers, e.g., 'the making, offering, putting on the market, importing, exporting or using of a product in which the design is incorporated or to which it is applied, or stocking such a product for those purposes', Article 19.1 CDReg.
102   Article 10.1 CDReg and Article 9.1 DDir.
103   Article 10.2 CDReg and Article 9.2 DDir.
104   Article 19.2 CDReg.
105   Recital 20 CDReg.

18.044 In the case *Gautzsch Großhandel GmbH*, which dealt with an unregistered design of a gazebo, the CJEU stated that it is the holder of the unregistered design that bears the burden of proving that the contested use results from copying that design.[106] The court continues by stating that:

> [...] if a Community design court finds that the fact of requiring that holder to prove that the contested use results from copying that design is likely to make it impossible or excessively difficult for such evidence to be produced, that court is required, in order to ensure observance of the principle of effectiveness, to use all procedures available to it under national law to counter that difficulty, including, where appropriate, rules of national law which provide for the burden of proof to be adjusted or lightened.[107]

18.045 It is quite common in infringement actions that the defendant tries to attack the validity of the design right. Article 85.1 CDReg states that the Community design court shall treat the registered Community design as valid. However, the validity can be challenged in a counterclaim for a declaration of invalidity. If invalidity of a Community design is submitted in a plea otherwise than by way of counterclaim it shall be admissible in so far as the defendant claims that the Community design could be declared invalid on account of an earlier national design right, Article 85.1 CDReg.

18.046 When it comes to unregistered design Article 85.2 CDReg states that the:

> Community design court shall treat the Community design as valid if the right holder produces proof that the conditions laid down in Article 11 have been met and indicates what constitutes the individual character of his Community design. However, the defendant may contest its validity by way of a plea or with a counterclaim for a declaration of invalidity.

18.047 In the case *Karen Millen*, the CJEU clarified that in order for a Community design court to treat an unregistered Community design as valid under Article 85.2 CDReg, the right holder is not required to prove that the design has individual character within the meaning of Article 6 CDReg, but need only indicate what constitutes the individual character of that design, that is to say, indicates what, in his view, are the element or elements of the design concerned which give it its individual character.[108]

18.048 When a limitation is applicable, there is no infringement. This is the case if the acts are done privately and for non-commercial purposes. For example, if

---

106 C-479/12, *Gautzsch Großhandel GmbH* EU:C:2014:75, para 41.
107 Ibid., para 44.
108 C-345/13, *Karen Millen*, EU:C:2014:2013, para 47.

someone makes a dress for her own use using a protected design as a model. It is not an infringement either if the acts are done for experimental purposes.[109]

18.049 Another limitation is that acts of reproduction for the purpose of making citations or of teaching are not infringing if the acts are 'compatible with fair trade practice and do not unduly prejudice the normal exploitation of the design, and that mention is made of the source', Article 20.1 c CDReg and 13.1c DDir.

18.050 In the case *Nintendo*, the CJEU interpreted that *making citation* could include uses of images of goods corresponding to design protected goods when lawfully offering for sale goods intended to be used as accessories to the protected design, in order to explain or demonstrate the joint use of the goods thus offered for sale and the design protected goods.[110]

18.051 Exhaustion of rights limits the right holder's rights. Once the product, in which a design included within the scope of protection of the Community design is incorporated or to which it is applied, has been put on the market in the Community by the holder of the Community design or with his consent.[111]

C. CONTEMPORARY ISSUES IN THE FASHION INDUSTRY

1. Artificial Intelligence, Fashion and Design Law

18.052 Artificial intelligence (AI) is fast developing in all parts of the world. The EU fashion industry is no exception to this trend, that permits speeding up and often further refining creations of fashion products. Clearly, protection of such works obey the traditional dichotomy that the most common tools for protecting fashion are copyright and design law. Indeed, in Europe, since the adoption in 2001 of EU legislation protecting registered industrial designs, and to a lesser extent unregistered industrial designs, a new momentum has been gained during the last 20 years, favouring double protection of new fashion products as much as possible, combined with strong EU trademark protection. Indeed, the immense possibilities offered by AI in fashion creations immediately raises the question of possible protection or not of creative processes resulting from AI-created fashion, and if so, of their ownership. Design law, just as copyright, is neutral with respect to the creative process. The criterion of novelty/ original shape for AI fashion creations can be considered for admit-

---

109 Article 20.1 a–b CDReg and Article 13.1a–b DDir.
110 The joined cases C-24/16 and C-25/1, *Nintendo*, EU:C:2017:724, para 86.
111 Article 21 CDReg and Article 15 DDir.

ting or not appropriation on them through registered Community Designs / Unregistered Community Design rights. The EU jurisdiction therefore offers vast possibilities of testing legal analysis for this matter compared to other jurisdictions, including the US.[112]

18.053 First of all, the product must have a new appearance. The criterion of novelty (a comparison with the opposable prior art identified) permits AI to play its role as a creative tool and AI databases permit to identify new appearances, i.e., 'not not' new appearances. Identically, the shape of the product plays a key role. An AI tool is based on the use of statistical models, and it is always possible for new products to be derivatives of existing ones thanks to a trained algorithm. This is ideal for fashion, as it is a constantly evolving sector.

18.054 However, it may be necessary to take into consideration the influence of the analysis grid developed by European Union courts:[113] indeed, they attribute a key role to the freedom of the designer creator in the assessment of individual character for the assessment of the specific character: account is taken of the freedom left to the creator in the creation of the design or model, in full accordance with Community Designs Regulation 6/2002 that states:

> Article 6: Individual character
> A design shall be considered to have individual character if the overall impression it produces on the informed user differs from the overall impression produced on such a user by any design which has been made available to the public:
> (a) in the case of an unregistered Community design, before the date on which the design for which protection is claimed has first been made available to the public;
> (b) in the case of a registered Community design, before the date of filing the application for registration or, if a priority is claimed, the date of priority.
>
> In assessing individual character, the degree of freedom of the designer in developing the design shall be taken into consideration.

18.055 Based on this provision, academic circles may allege that compared designs or models presenting no significant differences produce the same overall impression on the informed user, and therefore trained algorithms cannot normally provide a 'new' appearance or shape in the sense of EU Law, since the greater the freedom of the designer in developing a design is, the less minor differences between the compared designs are sufficient to produce a different overall

---

112 Cf. Francesca Montalvo Witzburg, 'Protection Fashion: A Comparative Analysis of Fashion Design Protection in the US and Europe' (2014), AELJ Blog 51, *Cardozo Entertainment Law Journal*.
113 Cf. Case C-683/17 *in re. Cofemel*, and Chapter X. *Artificial Intelligence and EU Design Law*, Section C. 3, of the current Book.

impression on the informed user. Elements connected to commercial success of the product are not to be considered and the criteria related to a process of creating the design or model, or recognition that the product would have as well as the contribution of the design or model to the sector concerned, do not seem to be among those taken into account by EU courts for the purposes of appreciation of the individual character of an industrial design.

18.056 This approach, rooted in the freedom of the designer creator, would confirm that an intellectual good could only be the product of the voluntary intellectual activity of the human being. Thus, for AI, the autonomy of the machine could be limited by taking into account 'machine training' work by the creator. The creator (or the creators, in case of 'data mills') intervenes in any case at least during the settings of the AI machine/process and may also intervene during choices among the multiple designs proposals generated by artificial intelligence. Design law, which is not centred on the designer creator, but is centred on the creation, certainly opens the door to fully automated production. However, it does not detach it from the human designer creator. This means that the designer creator is necessarily to be considered in this case as the natural person who intellectually contributes to the creation of the appearance of the product. If the freedom of the designer creator must be appreciated, the appearance produced without any human intervention would hardly be appropriable by UCD/RCD law. Any alternative reading of this criterion in the EU seems excluded under current legislation and EU case law. It should be noted that such a legal approach, connected to designs law, would also comply well with current moral rights aspects[114] that may exist on fashion copyrighted creations under EU laws.[115]

2. 3D and 4D Printing in Fashion and Design Law

18.057 Over the last decade, 3D printing has become established in the fashion and textile industry. It is used not only for decorative elements but also for shoes, garments, and even textiles, with the advantage of enhancing structures and functionalisation.[116] Consequently, a product manufactured by 3D combines

---

114 Cf. Heidi Härkönen, Chapter 36, in forthcoming E Rosati and I. Calboli (eds) *Routledge Handbook on Fashion Law* (Routledge tbp. 2024).
115 Cf. Chapter X. Artificial Intelligence and EU Design Law, Sections D.2 and E, of the current Book, that also draws a general picture on possible future options in the relationship between AI and Design Law that is applicable also to the Fashion world.
116 Marjeta Čuk and others, '3D Printing and Functionalization of Textiles' in *Proceedings of the 10th International Symposium GRID 2020*, 499; LaPorchia C Davis and others, 'Collaboration of 3D Technology and Fashion Innovations: A Creative Accessory Development Assessment' (2020) 7(2–3) *Fashion, Style & Popular Culture* 179.

the advantages of both technologies and materials, influencing the 'quality and durability of the final product'.[117]

For instance, since 2008, Iris van Herpen has incorporated 3D technology into both her Haute Couture and women's ready-to-wear clothing designs. TIME Magazine named van Herpen's 3D-printed dresses one of the 50 Best Inventions of 2011, and she continues to push a complex connection between nature, architecture, science, and more crucially, the 'traditional craftsmanship and future-facing technology'.[118] In September 2023, Coperni debuted a 3D-printed CD-player bag as part of the Spring 2024 collection, which has already caused a stir.[119]

18.058

Aside from this, many scholars see the potential of 3D printing, be it for reducing production time, as well as costs related to inventory, warehousing, packaging, and transportation,[120] and finally, for sustainable fashion and thus, minimising waste.[121] Currently, 3D fashion is using biodegradable materials and brands like Nike, Adidas, and New Balance are using recycled plastics from the oceans.[122]

18.059

One of the most recent technological advancements is 4D printing, which is used in wearables and smart clothes. Rocha notes that the difference between 3D and 4D is the use of 'intelligent materials' which are programmed to adjust to the changing needs of the user, e.g., hydrogel, polymers with memory shape (PMF), and liquid crystal elastomers (LCE).[123] In a world where garments and shoes adapt to users and change with movement and temperature changes, among others, there is much to discuss as such technological advances raise concerns in the fashion world, such as personal data protection and counter-

18.060

---

117 Ibid.
118 The House of Iris Van Herpen, 'State-of-the-art' https://www.irisvanherpen.com/state-of-the-art accessed 15 November 2023.
119 Fashionista, 'Coperni offered its subversive take on 'corporate' casual for Spring 2024' (Fashionista 29 September 2023) https://fashionista.com/2023/09/coperni-spring-2024-collection#gid=ci02ca9df4c000271a &pid=coperni-spring-2024-1 accessed 15 November 2023.
120 Alyson Vanderploeg, Seung-Eun Lee and Michael Mamp, 'The Application of 3D Printing Technology in the Fashion Industry' (2016) 10(2) *International Journal of Fashion Design, Technology and Education* 170; Anna Perry, '3D-printed Apparel and 3D-printer: Exploring Advantages, Concerns, and Purchases' (2018) 11(1) *International Journal of Fashion Design, Technology and Education* 95.
121 A Pasricha and R Greeninger, 'Exploration of 3D Printing to Create Zero-Waste Sustainable Fashion Notions and Jewelry' (2018) 5(1) *Fashion and Textiles* 1.
122 Ibid.
123 Maria Victória Rocha, 'Fashion: From 3D Printing to Digital Fashion' in Ashutosh Sharma(ed), *Advances in 3D Printing* (IntechOpen 2023).

feiting and eroding the authenticity of garments.[124] The latter prompts the relevance of protecting designs in the fashion industry.[125] Rocha writes about the importance of respecting intellectual property rights but also observes the matter of enforcement 'when the CAD files and its online sharing and 3D printing are done for strictly private uses.'[126]

3. Fashion and Traditional Knowledge

18.061 The intersection of fashion with Traditional Knowledge (TK) and Traditional Cultural Expressions (TCEs) within the realm of design law involves considerations that extend beyond the umbrella of intellectual property due to conflicting ideologies.[127] This is because TK and TCEs involve designs, motifs, and patterns which are often deeply rooted in the heritage, identity, and in some instances, religious beliefs of specific communities. While there are various legal mechanisms for protecting designs, addressing the cultural and ethical dimensions of incorporating traditional elements in fashion is equally important. A major concern is to distinguish between what is inspiration and what is appropriation. Generally, in fashion, inspiration is allowed[128] as designers regularly look for inspiration from earlier styles, artworks, travels, or nature.[129]

18.062 Cultural appropriation in fashion has recently received much attention in the media. This could be due to globalisation or the growth of the internet (and consequently sharing without boundaries), or both. However, Pozzo asserts that this phenomenon is not new.[130] She recalls that the world of textiles, which has travelled since ancient times, brought with it styles and shapes. Providing examples, she mentions how inspired by the Orient, Poiret (a French couturier) set aside the women's corset for comfort, creating harem trousers and tunics during the mid-20th century. Similarly, in Japan, the kimonos changed to colourful designs influenced by European art and design.[131]

---

124 Mark K Brewer, 'Fashion Law: More Than Wigs, Gowns, and Intellectual Property' (2017) 54(4) *San Diego Law Review* 739, 761.
125 Ibid. See 3D printing study; there are technical issues and questions around the scope of existing design limitations when applied to 3D printing especially carried out by intermediaries or hosted/uploaded/downloaded from public platforms. The Intellectual Property implications of the development of industrial 3D printing - Publications Office of the EU (europa.eu).
126 Ibid.
127 Elizabeth Oyange Ngando, 'Fashion as Property in Traditional Culture: A Maasai Case Study' (2018) 13(11) JIPLP 878.
128 Buchalska (n 32), 26.
129 Susan Scafidi, 'Intellectual Property and Fashion Design' in Peter K Yu (ed), *Intellectual Property and Information Wealth* (2006).
130 Barbara Pozzo, 'Fashion Between Inspiration and Appropriation' (2020) 9(5) Laws 1.
131 Ibid., 4.

Therefore, taking inspiration is not a new phenomenon in the fashion market and thus, using textiles, images, and patterns from other cultures have been seen as 'transcultural creativity'.[132]

18.063 The intersection of fashion with TK and TCEs can be a delicate balance between appreciation of cultural diversity and inappropriate use of cultural and religious symbols. For instance, Yves Saint Laurent's Spring-Summer 1967 collection dedicated to Africa and Dior's Fall-Winter 1988–89 collection showing Indian influence are seen as cultural appreciation. However, Lisa Blue's swimsuit depicting Hindu goddess Lakshmi and Karlie Kloss's native American style headdress during the 2012 Victoria's Secret fashion show were viewed as degrading cultural or religious items.[133]

18.064 Misappropriation of TK occurs when elements of a particular culture are used by individuals outside that culture without consent and understanding. This extends beyond moral and economic rights, as the use of designs can become offensive to the culture of the people involved in the creation of such designs.[134] Examples include accusations against Williamson for copying traditional Ethiopian pattern dresses during the London Fashion Week 2007,[135] Nike's design of shoes based on the traditional 'mola' patterns of the Guna people,[136] and SHEIN's launch of a piece identical to a garment designed by the Mayan communities of Yucatan, Campeche, and Quintana Roo.[137] These instances demonstrate that copying works made by local communities can diminish and devalue their culture, raising not only economic and moral rights issues, but also ethical concerns.

18.065 While WIPO is exploring the legal framework to protect TK and TCEs among other aspects,[138] the Convention on Biological Diversity 1993 (aka the Biodiversity Convention), and the Nagoya Protocol 2010, already address the

---

132 Ibid., 6.
133 Ibid., 6–7.
134 See Brewer (n 123), 763.
135 Pozzo (n 129), 8.
136 The Guna people noted that the objection was not about the commercialisation of the design, but that it was done 'without consulting [them] first'. Patricia Covarrubia, 'The Guna People to Nike: Just Don't Do It' (*IPTango*, 27 May 2019) https://iptango.blogspot.com/2019/05/the-guna-people-to-nike-just-dont-do-it.html accessed 30 September 2023.
137 Its design would have not be possible without knowledge 'transmitted from generation to generation, product of the collective creativity of the Mayan people'. Patricia Covarrubia, ' Mexico: Cultural (mis) Appropriation' (*IPTango*, 29 July 2022) https://iptango.blogspot.com/2022/07/mexico-cultural-mis-appropriation.html accessed 30 September 2023.
138 WIPO Intergovernmental Committee on Intellectual Property and Genetic Resources, Traditional Knowledge and Folklore (IGC).

fair and equitable sharing of benefits from the use of TK and the importance of 'informed consent'. However, these two latest international agreements focus on genetic resources, they reflect a broader recognition of the importance of respecting traditional knowledge and resources, and thus, preventing the unauthorised use and exploitation of traditional designs by external entities. In the meantime, many regions and countries already recognise tangible cultural expressions such as textiles, jewellery, costumes, and needlework.[139] Besides, traditional communities may have their own customary laws and practices for protecting their cultural designs. These may involve community-level agreements, licensing arrangements, or other mechanisms to ensure that the use of traditional designs aligns with community values. However, it seems that these instruments have not reached the expected goal due to the principle of territoriality and therefore, developing compliance with corporate social responsibility is a present aim. Certainly, designers should consider engaging in respectful collaborations with communities and seeking permission when incorporating traditional designs into fashion garments.

4. Fashion, Design Law, and Circular Economy

18.066 The term the circular economy does not seem to have a uniform definition.[140] Furthermore, the term is sometimes used as an umbrella term, including the sharing economy.[141] However, the circular economy is about creating a system where the flows do not burden our environment, which means that waste and pollution are eliminated. Products and materials can then be circulated endlessly as new natural resources do not need to be used.[142]

18.067 The circular economy is often discussed as the opposite of the linear economy. The linear economy developed during industrialism and is usually described as being based on the idea of a 'take, make and dispose' society.[143] It should

---

139 Swakopmund Protocol on the Protection of Traditional Knowledge and Expressions of Folklore withing the framework of the African Regional Intellectual Property Organization (ARIPO); Kenyan Protection of Traditional Knowledge and Cultural Expressions Act 2016 No 33 of 2016 ; Panama Law No. 20 of June 26, 2000.

140 Julian Kirchherr, Denise Reike, Marko Hekkert, 'Conceptualizing the Circular Economy: An Analysis of 114 Definitions, (2017) 127 *Resources, Conservation and Recycling* 221–232, https://doi.org/10.1016/j.resconrec.2017.09.005, https://www.sciencedirect.com/science/article/pii/S0921344917302835 accessed 25 January 2024.

141 Marvin Henry, Daan Schraven, Nancy Bocken, Koen Frenken, Marko Hekkert, Julian Kirchherr, 'The Battle of the Buzzwords: A Comparative Review of the Circular Economy and the Sharing Economy Concepts', (2021) 83 *Environmental Innovation and Societal Transitions* 1–21.

142 Ellen Macarthur Foundation, What is a Circular Economy?, https://ellenmacarthurfoundation.org/topics/circular-economy-introduction/overview accessed 25 January 2024.

143 Sariatli, Furkan, 'Linear Economy Versus Circular Economy: A Comparative and Analyzer Study for Optimization of Economy for Sustainability' (2017) *Visegrad Journal on Bioeconomy and Sustainable Development*. 6. 10.1515/vjbsd-2017-0005 accessed 25 January 2024.

be noted that even though intellectual property law existed before the Second Industrial Revolution, the two world conventions – the Berne and Paris Conventions – came into being during this period. Thus, the intellectual property system was essentially designed in an era of a linear economy, which has affected the design of the exclusive rights' structure, as well as the limitations and exceptions designed to balance the system. Hence, a transition from a linear economy to a circular economy requires a review of intellectual property law and its functioning.[144]

18.068 Being able to repair and have access to spare parts and reuse products will be of great importance in this transition.[145]

18.069 The problem with the right to repair and access to spare parts is not new in design law. It was discussed when the directive and regulation were negotiated. Spare parts are component parts used to repair a complex product to restore its original appearance (must-match parts). When the Design Directive was negotiated, no agreement was reached on must-match parts, only on must-fit parts.[146] As a result, spare parts (must-match parts) were left outside the Directive. Therefore, Article 14 DDir states that 'Member States shall maintain in force their existing legal provisions relating to the use of the design of a component part used for the purpose of the repair of a complex product so as to restore its original appearance and shall introduce changes to those provisions only if the purpose is to liberalise the market for such parts' (the freeze plus clause).[147] In the CDReg a 'repair clause' was introduced in Article 110(1) which limits the Community design right in cases that concern the component parts of a complex product used for repairing that product so as to restore its original appearance.[148] In the European Commission proposal for a revisited Regulation and Directive on design, a repair clause is introduced codifying the CJEU ruling in the case *Acacia*.[149]

---

144 Cf. Ulrika Wennersten, 'Många immaterialrättsliga utmaningar i den cirkulära ekonomin – Spaning på två nya affärsmodeller (Many challenges for intellectual property in the circular economy) – A focus on two new business models)' NIR 1/2023 p. 132 ff.
145 Cf. European Commisson, EU Strategy for Sustainable and Circular Textiles, COM (2022) 141 final.
146 Jens Scovsbo and Graeme B. Dinwoodie, 'Design Protection for Products that are "dictated by function"' in Annette Kur, Marianne Levin and Jens Scovsbo, *The EU Design Approach: A Global Appraisal* (Edward Elgar 2018) 155 ff.
147 Ibid.
148 Anna Tischner and Katarzyna Stasiuk. 2023. 'Spare Parts, Repairs, Trade Marks and Consumer Understanding', IIC 54:30, https://doi.org/10.1007/s40319-022-01274-8.
149 C-397/16, *Acacia*, EU:C:2017:992 cf. Proposal for a directive of the European Parliament and of the Council on the legal protection of designs (recast) of 28.11.2022, COM(2022) 667 final and Proposal for a Regulation of the European Parliament and of the Council amending Council Regulation (EC) No 6/2002 on Community designs and repealing Commission Regulation (EC) No 2246/2002, COM/2022/666 final.

18.070 Different forms of product reuse will increase in the new economy.[150] Traditional reuse is second hand, where the consumer buys used goods. Another type of reuse is renting or borrowing goods instead of buying them. A new business model based on the latter kind of reuse is Libraries of Things (LoTs), where you rent or borrow things other than books.[151] LoTs can be libraries where people borrow clothes, shoes, and accessories. The idea behind these libraries is easy to understand when it has been found, for example, that a drill is used on average for less than an hour by the buyer, even perhaps as little as 13 minutes.[152]

18.071 If a design right protects the product, the exhaustion rule in Articles 15 DDir and 21 CDreg restricts the exclusive rights stipulated in Articles 12 DDir and 19 CDReg. The exclusive right is formulated to give the right owner the exclusive right 'to use it and to prevent any third party not having his consent from using it'. Use covers 'making, offering, putting on the market, importing, exporting or using of a product in which the design is incorporated or to which it is applied, or stocking such a product for those purposes'. The concept of offering includes offering a product not only for sale but also for rent or loan.

18.072 Traditional second hand is not infringing as the genuine product's design right is exhausted. The exhaustion rule means that the right holder cannot prevent the exploitation of the protected product if it has been put on the market in the Community by the designer or the holder of the Community design or with his/her consent. The same applies to LoTs, as genuine products are rented or borrowed. It should be noted that the right to the physical, unmodified product placed on the market is exhausted.

18.073 Creative reuse (redesign, upcycling, remake) is a form of recycling that reuses materials or products and adds value through a creative process. In many cases, only the recycled material is used. For example, old towels, curtains, and rugs

---

150 Cf. Tanja Pihlajarinne, 'Repairing and Re-using from an exclusive Rights Perspective: Towards Sustainable Lifespan as Part of a New Normal?' in Ole Andreas Rognstad and Ingrid Ørstavik, *Intellectual Property and Sustainable Markets* (Edward Elgar 2021) 89 ff. This article focuses on trademark and patent law. See also Maria Elena Aldescu and Fernanda Donaire Passoni, 2023. *Fashion, Intellectual property (IP) & Sustainability – Best practices, interactions, and strategies*, 4IP Council, https://www.4ipcouncil.com/research/fashion-intellectual-property-ip-and-sustainability-best-practices-interactions-and-strategies accessed 25 January 2024.
151 Denise Baden, Ken Peattie, and Adekunle Oke. 2020. 'Access Over Ownership: Case Studies of Libraries of Things', *Sustainability* 12, no. 17: 7180. https://doi.org/10.3390/su12177180, accessed 25 January 2024.
152 Ellen Macarthur Foundation, How Tool Sharing Could Become a Public Utility: Toronto Tool Library and Makerspace, https://ellenmacarthurfoundation.org/circular-examples/how-tool-sharing-could-become-a-public-utility accessed 25 January 2024.

can become new clothes.¹⁵³ In other cases, genuine goods are re-designed creatively. Here, it is often genuine products or product parts of famous brands that are used to create new products or redesigned by a specific actor.¹⁵⁴ Like the business model mentioned above, the admissibility of this model is mainly based on the applicability of the principle of exhaustion.

18.074 If a product exhausted by design right is redesigned, upcycled, or remade, it has been established above that it is the physical, unmodified product put into circulation on the market in the Community that is exhausted. This has been confirmed by the Bundesgerichtshof in an infringement case concerning a community design. In that case, a genuine Daimler car had been modified by lengthening the vehicle by adding a centre section. In this case, the alleged infringer claimed exhaustion, but the court noted that exhaustion refers only to the goods placed on the market and not to any of the characteristics of those goods. Furthermore, the court stated that the converted car was clearly different from the standard version placed on the market and that exhaustion did not apply.¹⁵⁵ However, if the converted product produces a different overall impression on the informed user it will fall outside the scope of protection of the design and it will not be an infringement.¹⁵⁶

5. Overlapping IP Protections for Fashion in EU Law

18.075 Fashion can also be protected by other intellectual property protections and EU intellectual property law prevents the coexistence of several forms of legal protection.¹⁵⁷ Fashion can be protected by copyright as a work of applied art – probably not an ordinary T-shirt, but definitely haute couture. Fashion that falls between these two categories can be protected if the subject matter is a work and the work meets the originality requirement. To be a work, two cumulative conditions must be satisfied. First, the subject matter concerned must be original in the sense that it is the author's own intellectual creation.¹⁵⁸ That means that the creator must have been able to express his or her creative abilities by making free and creative choices.¹⁵⁹ By making these different choices the work will have a 'personal touch' and reflect the author's personality.¹⁶⁰ Second, only something which is the expression of the author's own intel-

---

153 Cf Hôtel, https://www.hotelvetements.com/blogs/infos/our-story accessed 2024-01-16.
154 Cf Shiver + Duke, which made accessories of old Chanel buttons, accessed 2024-01-16.
155 I-ZR 89/08 Verlängerte Limousinen [2010] GRUR Int 12/2010 (Bundesgerichtshof, 22 April 2010) 1072.
156 Cf. Wennersten, (n 143), 132 ff.
157 C-237/19, *Gömböc*, EU:C:2020:296, para 50.
158 C-310/17, *Levola Hengelo*, EU:C:2018:899, para 36.
159 C-145/10, *Painer*, EU:C:2011:798, para 89.
160 Ibid., paras 88 and 92.

lectual creation may be classified as a 'work'.¹⁶¹ The subject matter must also be expressed in 'a manner which makes it identifiable with sufficient precision and objectivity, even though that expression is not necessarily in permanent form'.¹⁶² When creating fashion pieces, it will not be unusual that technical considerations or constraints dictate the creation, as the fashion piece must fit the body. If the shape of the garment is solely dictated by its technical function and there has not been 'any room for creative freedom or the room was so limited that the idea and its expression become indissociable that garment cannot be protected by copyright'.¹⁶³

18.076 A patent is probably not the first thing one would consider when protecting fashion. However, technical innovations (e.g., new fabrics/textiles) can attract consumers and business partners. Inventions are the solution to a technical problem. As an example of invention in the fashion industry, the Swedish company BOOB's patented nursing collection¹⁶⁴ can be mentioned as well as the Spanish entrepreneur who developed Piñatex®, a patented alternative to leather made from pineapple leaf fibres. The patented textile was commercialised through Ananas Anam.¹⁶⁵ The requirements to obtain a patent for an invention are novelty, inventive step, and industrial application.¹⁶⁶ However, it should be noted that aesthetic creations are not regarded as inventions.¹⁶⁷

18.077 Fashion can also be protected by trademark law. Trademark law protects signs. It can be 'words, including personal names, or designs, letters, numerals, colours, the shape of goods or of the packaging of goods, or sounds, provided that such signs are capable of distinguishing the goods or services of one undertaking from those of other undertakings, and being represented on the Register of European Union trade marks'.¹⁶⁸ It is obvious that fashion brands can be protected as word marks or figurative marks, for example Gucci as a word mark or a swoosh for Nike. Unconventional marks are quite common in the fashion sector. Pattern mark, which are marks consisting exclusively of a set of elements that are repeated regularly, are often used in relation to

---

161 C-310/17, *Levola Hengelo*, EU:C:2018:899, para 37.
162 Ibid., para 40.
163 C-833/18, *Brompton Bicycle*, EU:C:2020:461, paras 31 and 33.
164 EPO, EP1127499 B1.
165 EPO, https://www.epo.org/en/news-events/european-inventor-award/meet-the-finalists/carmen-hijosa accessed 2024-01-16.
166 Article 52.1 European Patent Convention (EPC).
167 Article 52.2b EPC.
168 Article 4 Regulation (EU) 2017/1001 of the European Parliament and of the Council of 14 June 2017 on the European Union trade mark.

clothing articles, leather goods, jewellery.¹⁶⁹ For example Burberry Limited has a pattern mark for its print and DAKS Simpson, producing luxury clothing and accessories for both men and women, has a trademark for a combination of colours in a check pattern.¹⁷⁰

18.078 Article 3 in the Trade mark Directive states that signs which consist exclusively of '(i) the shape, or another characteristic, which results from the nature of the goods themselves, or (ii) the shape, or another characteristic, of the goods which is necessary to obtain a technical result, or (iii) the shape, or another characteristic, which gives substantial value to the goods' cannot be registered or if registered are liable to be declared invalid.¹⁷¹ The various grounds for refusal of registration listed in the article must, according to CJEU, be interpreted in the light of the public interest underlying each of them.¹⁷² The CJEU has also stated that the grounds pursue the same objective and that the first indent must be interpreted in a way that is consistent with the aims of the other two indents.¹⁷³

18.079 In the *Louboutin red-sole* case the CJEU ruled that a sign consisting of a colour applied to the sole of a high-heeled shoe, is not covered by the prohibition of the registration of shapes, since the mark does not consist 'exclusively of a shape'.¹⁷⁴

18.080 According to the *Hauk* case, the concept of a 'shape which results from the nature of the goods themselves' means that shapes with essential characteristics inherent to the generic function or functions of such goods must, in principle, be denied registration. It would otherwise be difficult for competing undertakings as this essential characteristic is something the consumers are looking for in the products, given that they are intended to perform an identical or similar function.¹⁷⁵

18.081 The sign is also, as mentioned above, unregistrable if it is established that the essential functional features of that shape are attributable only to the technical result. The fact that there may be alternative shapes, with another design,

---

169 Article 3(3)(e) EUTMIR and Trademark Guidelines, Chapter 3, Chapter 3 Non-distinctive trade marks (Article 7(1)(b) EUTMR), Section 12 Pattern Marks.
170 *Burberry Limited*, EUTM No 017911858 and *DAKS Simpson Limited*, EUTM No 008134405.
171 Article 7(1)(e)(i–iii) EUTMR.
172 C-205/13, *Hauk*, EU:C:2014:2233, para 17.
173 Ibid., para 20.
174 C-163/16, *Louboutin*, EU:C:2018:423, para 27.
175 C 205/13, *Hauk*, EU:C:2014:2233, paras 25–26.

capable of achieving the same technical result does not in itself mean that this provision is not applicable.[176]

18.082 The objective of the ground for refusal of registration provided for in Article 3 (ii) and (iii) is intended to prevent the exclusive and permanent right that a trade mark confers from serving to extend indefinitely the life of other rights in respect of which the EU legislature has sought to impose time limits.[177]

18.083 Article 3 (iii) is not limited purely to products having only artistic or ornamental value as this would, according to CJEU, otherwise, risk that products with essential functional characteristics and a significant aesthetic element will not be covered.[178] Hence, that provision is also applicable to a sign which consists exclusively of the shape of a product with several characteristics each of which may give that product substantial value.[179]

18.084 However, it follows from the *Gömböc* case that this ground for refusal of registration must not be applied systematically to a sign protected by design law or where the sign consists exclusively of the shape of a decorative item.[180]

---

176 C-48/09 P, *Lego*, EU:C:2010:516, paras 53–58. Cf. C-299/99, *Philips*, EU:C:2002:377, para 84.
177 C-237/19, *Gömböc*, EU:C:2020:296, para 50.
178 C 205/13, *Hauk*, EU:C:2014:2233, para 32.
179 Ibid., para 36.
180 C-237/19, *Gömböc*, EU:C:2020:296, para 62.

PART IV

THE WAY FORWARD – A LOOK AT THE FUTURE

19

ARTIFICIAL INTELLIGENCE AND EU DESIGN LAW

Mikko Antikainen and Heidi Härkönen

A. INTRODUCTION	19.001
B. DESIGN AND DESIGN LAW IN THE DIGITAL AGE	19.007
1. The Roots of the Design Regime and the Digital Revolution of Design	19.007
2. Virtual/Digital Designs According to EU Design Law	19.011
C. AI-DRIVEN DESIGN IN THE IP REGIME	19.022
1. AI and IP in General	19.022
2. AI-generated Output as Artistic Works: The Conflict with Copyright	19.026
3. AI and EU Design Law: The Issues of 'Designership' and Design Development	19.030
(a) 'Designership'	19.034
(b) The concept of 'design development' in EU design law	19.045
(c) Practical implications	19.059
D. TAILORING EU DESIGN LAW FOR THE DIGITAL AGE?	19.068
1. Design-based Approach in the Age of AI	19.068
2. Issues to Consider in Terms of Protecting Purely AI-generated Designs	19.079
E. CONCLUSIONS	19.083

A. INTRODUCTION

19.001 The relationship between intellectual property (IP) law and industrial designs and products of applied art has never been straightforward. It is even less so now that the digital revolution, including the development of artificial intelligence (AI) adds complications to it. AI's non-human 'creativity' requires us to reconsider some of the traditional IP rules and doctrines, as this technological advancement inevitably changes our views on creativity in general and its worthiness of protection. 'AI artists' and 'AI designers' – i.e., artists and designers who delegate (a part of) their creative work to AI – distance creativity from humanity, which eventually disrupts the normative justification of IP laws. Although the problems of AI technology have attracted academic interest especially from the perspective of copyright and patent law, design law is often forgotten in this discussion. This is unfortunate, because EU design law could solve some of the problems caused by the increasing use of AI.

In general, AI programs can be incorporated to design processes as tools or even as independent designers. When AI is used as a tool to assist a human designer in their design development, the output is generally referred to as 'AI-assisted'. 'AI-generated designs' then refers to designs that AI programs have independently developed, while the involved human designer has merely 'pushed a button'. The term 'AI-driven design' includes both of the above and refers to design processes where AI plays a significant, but not necessarily a dominant role. It is noted that the line between AI-assisted and AI-generated output is not always clear, as will be discussed later in this Chapter. Thus, in certain situations the terms 'AI-assisted' and 'AI-generated' may overlap. **19.002**

Typically, AI programs utilise generative adversarial networks (GANs). The use of GANs refers to 'a process of taking a dataset of images, and outputting images that are visually similar but generated by the model'.[1] One domain where AI-generated designs are increasingly used is the 'metaverse'. Metaverse is a parallel universe beyond the physical world, which expands people's lives to the virtual reality.[2] The term metaverse is quite broad and vague. It does not refer to any one specific type of technology, but rather to a broad shift in how we use and interact with technology in general.[3] In this chapter, the terms 'metaverse' and 'metaverses' are used to describe various virtual platforms, such as social media networks, video games and other digital environments where users can interact with each other and, inter alia, use various virtual designs.[4] **19.003**

In legal literature, the increasing role that AI plays in design development has been identified as the biggest challenge for the European Union (EU) design regime to address, especially from the perspectives of ownership and authorship of such designs.[5] IP scholarship seems to somewhat agree that **19.004**

---

1 Leanne Luce, *Artificial Intelligence for Fashion* (Apress Media LLC 2019), 125–126.
2 John David N. Dionisio, William G. Burns III & Richard Gilbert, '3D Virtual Worlds and the Metaverse: Current Status and Future Possibilities' (2013) 45 *ACM Computing Surveys*, 1–38.
3 Erick Ravenscraft 'What is the Metaverse, Exactly?' WIRED (15 June 2023) https://www.wired.com/story/what-is-the-metaverse/ accessed 15 August 2023.
4 In this chapter, the terms 'virtual design' and 'digital design' are used as synonyms to describe designs that are used predominantly in metaverses. This is because some creative sectors, such as the fashion world, commonly refer to 'digital fashion designs' whereas in the sphere of others, such as the gaming industry, the term 'virtual design' is more common.
5 Anna Tischner, 'Design Rights and Designer's Rights in the EU' in Henning Hartwig (ed) *Research Handbook on Design Law* (Edward Elgar Publishing 2021), 206.

digitalisation and AI bring forth fundamental doctrinal issues.[6] The new creative environments and new types of 'creators' challenge our ideals of what kind of creativity, and more importantly, creativity by *whom* or *what* is worth protecting. The implications that generative AI has on creative sectors have been noted (to some extent) by the legislator as well, since the European Commission has proposed the first EU regulatory framework for AI (EU AI Act).[7]

19.005 This Chapter delves into the afore-described theme by assessing the design law framework of AI-generated designs, paying special attention to those created mainly for virtual use in metaverses. More specifically, we ask (i) is it possible for EU design law to provide protection for computer-generated designs, and (ii) how should the EU design regime respond to the challenges brought forth by digitalisation and AI. The Chapter does not aim to solve the question whether AI-generated designs *should* be protected by design law; the focus is on whether the current law permits this and to what extent. This Chapter contributes to the broader scholarly debate on possibilities to protect machine-initiated innovations, inventions, and creations by IP rights.[8]

19.006 The Chapter is structured as follows: first, we briefly describe the digital creative environments and the interaction between human and machine in

---

6   E.g., Eleonora Rosati, 'The Monkey Selfie Case and the Concept of Authorship: An EU Perspective' (2017) 12 *Journal of Intellectual Property Law & Practice* (JIPLP) 12, 973; P. Bernt Hugenholtz and João Pedro Quintais, 'Copyright and Artificial Creation: Does EU Copyright Law Protect AI-Assisted Output?' 52 IIC Vol 9; Mikko Antikainen, *Surviving Technological Change: Towards More Coherent Regulation of Digital Creativity Through EU Copyright and Design Law* (Phd Thesis, Hanken School of Economics, 2021); Mikko Antikainen, 'Differences in Immaterial Details: Dimensional Conversion and Its Implications for Protecting Digital Designs Under EU Design Law' (2021) 52 IIC, 137; Guadamuz, Andres 'Do Androids Dream of Electric Copyright? Comparative Analysis of Originality in Artificial Intelligence Generated Works' in Jyh-An Lee, Reto Hilty and Kung-Chung Liu (eds) *Artificial Intelligence and Intellectual Property* (Oxford University Press 2021); Heidi Härkönen 'Fashion Piracy and Artificial Intelligence–Does The New Creative Environment Come With New Copyright Issues?' (2020) 15 JIPLP 3; Heidi Härkönen and Natalia Särmäkari, 'Copyright and Digital Fashion Designers: The Democratization of Authorship?' (2023) 18 JIPLP 1, 42–57; Jane C. Ginsburg, 'People Not Machines: Authorship and What it Means in the Berne Convention' (2018) 49 IIC 131–135; Mikko Antikainen and Daniël Jongsma, 'The Art of CAD: Copyrightability of Digital Design Files' in Rosa Maria Ballardini, Marcus Norrgård and Jouni Partanen (eds) *3D Printing, Intellectual Property and Innovation—Insights from Law and Technology* (Wolters Kluwer 2017).
7   Amendments adopted by the European Parliament on 14 June 2023 on the proposal for a regulation of the European Parliament and of the Council on laying down harmonised rules on artificial intelligence (Artificial Intelligence Act) and amending certain Union legislative acts (COM(2021)0206 – C9- 0146/2021 – 2021/0106(COD)), Strasbourg, 14 June 2023. The proposed EU AI Act does not offer much clarification for the issues of AI 'designership' or AI's role in design development. Thus, the EU AI Act is not further discussed in this Chapter.
8   See above footnote 6 and Michael S. Carolan, 'Constructing the "pure" Inventor: Individual, Collective, and Corporate Authorship Within Patent Law' (2008) 27 *New Genetics and Society* 4.

design work. Next, we outline the IP framework for such design, pinpointing the main conflicts between IP protection and AI-generated output. This is followed by the analysis of the concepts of 'designership' and 'design development' in EU design law, and whether they permit inclusion of AI-generated output in the scope of protection. Then we move to evaluating whether the EU design regime can respond to the challenges brought forth by the digital revolution, especially in the age of AI.

B. DESIGN AND DESIGN LAW IN THE DIGITAL AGE

1. The Roots of the Design Regime and the Digital Revolution of Design

19.007 In the copyright realm, countries of the Berne Convention for the Protection of Literary and Artistic Works (as amended on September 28, 1979) (Berne Convention) have not been able to reach an agreement on what 'design' actually is – something technical, aesthetic, or both – and this reflects in the convention, which leaves it up to the countries of the union to decide how to protect works of applied art (designs) in their national laws.[9] The EU, which is a member of the Berne Convention had, more than 30 years ago, addressed the importance for a Community-wide design protection regime. The EU Member States' fragmentation to versatile national protection regimes was seen as a threat to the European design industries.[10] These concerns led to the development of the EU design regime, consisting of the Community Design Regulation (6/2002, CDR)[11] and the Design Directive (98/71/EC, DD).[12] After a few decades of the initiation of a Community-wide design, the importance of creating a single market in IP-relevant sectors has only grown. This is especially due to the rapid digitalisation which has enhanced the swift movement of designs (both physical and digital) from one Member State to another.

19.008 Compared to the era when the EU design regime was introduced, designers' work is increasingly digital – both in terms of the creative process and its output. Algorithmic designing and AI offer multiple advantages for design-

---

9   Stina Teilmann-Lock, 'Industrial Property or Artistic Property? Design, Intellectual Property Law and the PH Lamp' (2016) 30(4) *Journal of Design History* 411; The Berne Convention for the Protection of Literary and Artistic Works (as amended on 28 September 1979) Art. 2 (7).
10 Commission of the European Communities (1991), Green Paper on the legal protection of industrial design ('Green Paper'), III/F/5131/91/EN, 2–3.
11 Council Regulation (EC) No 6/2002 of 12 December 2001 on Community designs [2002] OJ L 3, 1.
12 Directive 98/71EC of the European Parliament and of the Council of 13 October 1998 on the legal protection of designs [1998] OJ L 289, 28.

ers in different creative sectors. They can, for instance, improve and speed up the design process, permit user engagement, and help to personalise designs.[13] AI programs permit the rapid production of massive amounts of new designs. Advanced AI technologies may develop designs independently or with a minimal human intervention,[14] although for the time being most 'AI-designers' are merely tools used by human designers.[15] The latter means that most AI-driven design is still 'AI-assisted', although design-specific generative AI programs are constantly developing. Distinguishing between the contributions of a human designer (perhaps made with a little help of the AI) and the independent contribution of the AI-program can be extremely difficult.[16] In some creative sectors, the interplay between a human designer and a machine designer still requires a significant contribution from the human designer to result in a working product. For instance, an AI-driven physical fashion design (that seeks at least some kind of a commercial success) still requires curating from a human designer. This is because in 'data-driven generative hybrid design', as characterised by fashion researcher Natalia Särmäkari, the designers' role is to 'curate and monitor aesthetic quality based on their tacit knowledge'.[17] In other words, a fashion design independently generated by AI has the risk of appearing 'too weird' for a consumer for cultural, societal, or modesty reasons, for instance.

19.009 In addition, acquiring the proper fit and functionality in the physical world requires human curating. When commenting on the first-ever AI Fashion Week which was held in April 2023, the Business of Fashion (BoF) noted that although AI Fashion Week offered a convincing showcase for AI-generated fashion, it might be difficult to turn the designs into real clothes. By using an AI-generated belt as an example, BoF noted that although an AI program generated an image of a belt, the fact that the belt was portrayed as a single strip of leather with random hole patterns (rather than by two overlapping ends that join with a buckle) strongly suggests that AI did not understand how a belt actually works.[18] Producing this AI-generated belt to a physical item

---

13   Tischner (n 5), 176.
14   Andres Guadamuz, 'Artificial Intelligence and Copyright' (2017) *WIPO Magazine*, 17.
15   Natalia Särmäkari, *'From a Tool to a Culture. Authorship and Professionalism of Fashion 4.0 Designers in Contemporary Digital Environments'* (PhD thesis, Aalto University School of Arts, Design and Architecture, 2022).
16   Tischner (n 5), 176; Guadamuz (n 6), 176.
17   Särmäkari (n 15), 87–89, 101.
18   Marc Bain, 'AI Is Really Good at Designing Knitwear (Belts, Not So Much)' Business of Fashion 26 April 2023 https://www.businessoffashion.com/articles/technology/ai-is-really-good-at-designing-knitwear-belts-not-so-much/?utm_source=newsletter_technology&utm_medium=email&utm_campaign=Technology_260423&utm_content=intro accessed 27 April 2023.

thus requires human curation. However, if an AI-generated design is exclusively digital, most of these issues that require human curating are omitted, because the metaverse is not bound by the same rules that govern the physical world. Thus, in the sphere of e.g., digital fashion,[19] video games, and various virtual realities, encountering designs that are independently generated by AI-programs is more likely.

Knowing the level and amount of human contribution reflected in the final design is essential, because (as will be elaborated later) according to current understanding, they determine whether the design will qualify for either one of the most important IP rights that protect industrial designs and works of applied art in the EU: design right and copyright.[20] Thus, knowledge of the nature of the designer behind a product is essential.[21] The question of the source of a design might not arise immediately after the design is created or registered. Instead, as noted by Anna Tischner, the issue is likely to arise incidentally in invalidation or infringement proceedings.[22]   19.010

2. Virtual/Digital Designs According to EU Design Law

An important issue to consider in the context of design law and AI-generated designs is the question of virtual designs and how those fit into the current EU design legislation, because designs generated by AI programs typically exist and are used mainly in the digital form.[23] Virtual designs in video games and other metaverses are increasingly depicting works of applied art such as cars, sneakers, handbags, and other fashion items,[24] all of which are commonly seen as subject matters protected by design law. Although in practice, design protection has increasingly shifted from protecting three-dimensional physical   19.011

---

19 'Digital fashion' refers to garments and accessories that are designed using fashion-specific 3D software, producing digital 3D prototypes and samples for physical collections or digital-only clothing. Digital-only fashion designs can be worn in, e.g., photographs or videos and in various virtual spaces, such as video games Härkönen and Särmäkari (n 6).
20 Tischner (n 5), 176.
21 See ibid., 175.
22 Ibid., 177.
23 Hasan Kadir Yilmaztekin: *Artificial Intelligence, Design Law and Fashion* (Routledge 2023), 29; Andy Ramos 'The Metaverse, NFT and IP Rights: To Regulate or not to Regulate?' *WIPO Magazine* (June 2022) https:// www.wipo.int/wipo_magazine/en/2022/02/article_0002.html accessed 15 August 2023.
24 Emmanuelle Sarlangue 'Registered Community designs in the video game industry: a neglected yet potent tool' (2021) 4 *Interactive Entertainment Law Review* 87, 94; Monika Górska and Lena Marcinoska-Boulangé 'When 3-D Objects in Video Games Pose IP Challenges' *International Bar Association the global voice of the legal profession* 12 August 2021 https://www.ibanet.org/ip-july-2021-3d-object-video-games-ip accessed 4 August 2023; Madeleine Schulz, 'Ralph Lauren Partners with Fortnite to Create First Phygital Fashion Collection' *Vogue Business* 23 October 2022 https:// www .voguebusiness .com/ technology/ ralph -lauren -partners-with-fortnite-to-create-first-phygital-fashion-collection accessed 28 June 2023.

designs to protecting virtual designs,[25] design law has still some challenges adapting to the digital world. First, the question whether virtual designs are protected by design law in the first place is a quite fundamental issue.[26] The current EU design law does not explicitly mention virtual or digital designs. According to the CDR article 3(a), 'design' means: '[T]he appearance of the whole or a part of a product resulting from the features of, in particular, the lines, contours, colours, shape, texture and/or materials of the product itself and/or its ornamentation.'

19.012 As visible in Article 3(a), another essential part of a 'design' is the concept of 'product'. This concept is further defined in CDR Article 3(b) as 'any industrial or handicraft item, including inter alia parts intended to be assembled into a complex product, packaging, get-up, graphic symbols and typographic typefaces, but excluding computer programs'.

19.013 Although computer programs are excluded in CDR Article 3(b), this is not detrimental for the protection of digital and virtual designs, as it is generally seen that most of them fall outside this exclusion.[27] However, although the concept of a 'product' is defined broadly in CDR Article 3(b) it still appears to some extent problematic for the protection of virtual designs. Arguably, the term 'product' itself (in addition to 'industrial or handicraft item') may be seen to refer exclusively to physical products.[28] Taking such a purist view would lead to the exclusion of all digital-only designs from the scope of design protection. However, the CDR Article 3(b) including 'graphic symbols' as products implies that there is no clear distinction between physical and immaterial in design law.[29] Although digital designs are today generally seen as protected,[30]

---

25 Rainer Filitz et al, 'Digital Design Protection in Europe: Law, Trends, and Emerging Issues' Centre for European Economic Research Discussion Paper No. 17-007 (January 2017) 9; Sarlangue (n 24), 87; Antikainen, Differences in Immaterial Details (n 6).
26 It should be noted that there are several requirements for protection such: firstly, there must be a design that is novel and has individual character. The design should not be contrary to the morality. However, due to the limited length of this chapter, only certain aspects related to (AI-generated) virtual designs are considered.
27 David Musker, 'The Design Directive' (The Chartered Institute of Patent Agents 2001), 18; Lionel Bently and Brad Sherman, *Intellectual Property Law* (3rd edn. Oxford University Press 2014), 710; Antikainen, Differences in Immaterial Details (n 6), 142; See also, Case C-393/09, *Bezpečnostní softwarová asociace — Svaz softwarové ochrany v Ministerstvo kultury* ECLI:EU:C:2010:816.
28 Mark McKenna and Lucas Osborn 'Trade mark Protection for Digital Goods' in Tanya Aplin (ed), *Research Handbook on Intellectual Property and Digital Technologies* (Edward Elgar Cheltenham 2020), 395; Bently and Sherman (n 27), 710; Thomas Margoni, 'Not for Designers: On the Inadequacies of EU Design Law and How to Fix It' (2013) 4 *Journal of Intellectual Property, Information Technology and Electronic Commerce Law*, 232; Viola Elam ' CAD Files and European Design Law' (2016) 7 JIPITEC, 145, 151.
29 Sarlangue (n 24), 88; Bently and Sherman (n 27), 709; Antikainen, Differences in Immaterial Details (n 6), 147.
30 For example, the EUIPO has long accepted registrations of virtual designs, such as GUIs and animated designs under class 14.04 of the Locarno Agreement. Antikainen, Differences in immaterial details (n 6),

there is still, some uncertainty regarding their legal situation, which is why further clarification is welcome. This uncertainty has produced diverging views regarding whether digital designs are actually protected due to the lack of physical products,[31] what is the scope of protection for digital designs, and whether it covers using 3D designs in 2D form or vice versa,[32] and how digital designs representing physical objects or animated designs should be registered.[33] In essence, in EU design law there is still a somewhat stark distinction between physical and digital designs, which is the root cause for many of the problems mentioned above.

Based on the ambiguities described above, some form of clarification is clearly needed for the design law to address the symptoms of digitalisation. Fortunately, the European Commission is proposing a revised Regulation[34] and Directive on industrial designs,[35] which address many of the challenges described above and aims to lift EU design law into the digital age, although they do not directly assess the issue of AI-driven design. The new proposal acknowledges that to encourage innovation and the creation of new product designs in the digital age, there is an increasing need for accessible, future-proofed, effective, and consistent protection of design right.[36] In other words, design protection should be fit for the purposes of the digital age.[37]   **19.014**

In relation to virtual and digital designs, the most important change is that the uncertainties regarding designs eligible for protection will be removed. This   **19.015**

---

148. See also Annette Kur, 'Protection of Graphical User Interfaces Under European Design Legislation' (2003) 34(1) IIC, 50.
31 See, e.g., McKenna and Osborn (n 28), 395; Bently and Sherman (n 27), 710; Margoni (n 28), 232; Elam (n 28), 151; Dinusha Mendis 'Fit for Purpose? 3D Printing and the Implications for Design Law: Opportunities and Challenges' in Aplin (n 28), 445, 451.
32 Antikainen, Differences in Immaterial Details (n 6), 147–51; Sarlangue (n 24), 99; For challenges regarding 3D printing and design law, see e.g., Mendis, ibid., 445.
33 At the moment of writing this chapter, the registration needs to be done with a series of seven images representing the different stages of the animation. The application procedure is governed by the CDR and the Community Design Implementing Regulation (Commission Regulation (EC) No. 2245/2002 of 21 October 2002 implementing Council Regulation (EC) No. 6/2002 on Community designs [2002] *OJ L* 341/28 (17 December 2002) (CDIR) article 1(2).
34 Proposal for a Regulation of the European Parliament and of the Council on the legal protection of designs amending Council Regulation (EC) No 6/2002 on Community designs and repealing Commission Regulation (EC) No 2246/2002. Brussels 28 November 2022, COM(2022) 666 final, 2022/0391 (COD).
35 Proposal for a Directive of the European Parliament and of the Council on the legal protection of designs (recast), Brussels, 28 November.2022, COM(2022) 667 final, 2022/0392(COD).
36 European Commission staff working document impact assessment report accompanying the documents to the proposal for a regulation of the European Parliament and of the Council amending Council Regulation (EC) No 6/2002 on Community designs and repealing Commission Regulation (EC) No 2246/2002 and the proposal for a Directive of the European Parliament and of the Council on the legal protection of designs (recast), 28 November 2022, 4.
37 Ibid., 4.

will be done by broadening the definition of design and the concept of product. For example, the revised design regulation Article 3(1) states that:

> 'design' means the appearance of the whole or a part of a product resulting from the features, in particular, the lines, contours, colours, shape, texture, materials of the product itself and/or its decoration, *including the movement, transition or any other sort of animation of those features* (emphasis added).[38]

19.016 This clearly establishes animated and moving designs, which are common features for virtual designs, as protected subject matter.

19.017 The design law reform also seems to remove the stark distinction between physical and digital products, which has caused uncertainty. Although the concept of 'product' remains the core component in the definition of design, Article 3(2) of the revised design regulation expands this definition by stating that

> 'product' means any industrial or handicraft item other than computer programs regardless of whether it is *embodied in a physical object or materializes in a digital form*, including:
>
> (a) packaging, sets of articles, get-up, spatial arrangement of items indented to form, in particular, an interior environment and parts intended to be assembled into a complex products;
> (b) *graphic works or symbols, logos, surface patterns, typographic typefaces, and graphic user interfaces* (emphasis added).[39]

19.018 The revised definition of 'product' greatly improves the situation for virtual designs. At the directive level, it is no longer unclear whether a 'product' only refers to physical designs, as the definition also includes designs in digital forms. Importantly, the addition of the word 'including' suggests that the list is non-exhaustive and open for new types of designs. This makes design law more future-oriented and adaptative for new types of designs and overall, more responsive to changes happening in the creative sectors. It can be easily argued that this new definition includes 3D models and virtual designs used in metaverses.

19.019 The new revised EU design legislation also expands the scope of protection to accommodate different ways of using digital designs. The revised design regulation Article 19(2)d also allows prohibiting, 'creating, downloading, copying and sharing or distributing to others any medium or software recording the

---

38 Similarly in the proposed design directive Art. 2(3).
39 Similarly in the proposed design directive Art. 2(4).

design for the purpose of enabling a product referred to in point (a) to be made'.

19.020 This improves the overall situation for digital designs, especially in the case of 3D printable CAD files containing registered designs,[40] as sharing such file would be infringing regardless of whether the design is visually represented. Even before the reform, EU design law already gives broad exclusive rights and allows preventing any third party from using the design.[41] Thus, the liabilities of a metaverse company do not only cover AI-generated virtual designs that are included by the company itself, but also designs that are uploaded, created, and used by the users of such metaverse.[42]

19.021 It can thus be concluded that the typical form of AI-generated designs (i.e., digital/virtual) is not an obstacle for design protection in the EU, especially once the design law reform has been completed. The protection of virtual/digital designs is (in most cases) a prerequisite for protecting AI-generated designs, but it is only one step forward in the analysis of EU design law's capability to protect such designs. The next Section inspects the effects that AI's contribution in the development of designs has to the designs' possibilities to qualify for protection under EU law, and whether such protection would align with the foundations of EU design law.[43]

C. AI-DRIVEN DESIGN IN THE IP REGIME

1. AI and IP in General

19.022 AI designers have proven to be successful in fields that used to belong exclusively to human designers, and AI programs are even awarded for merits previously granted for humans. For instance, in 2019, the AI fashion designer DeepVogue won the second prize in the China International Fashion Design Innovation Competition in Shanghai.[44] In some creative sectors, such as fashion, digitalisation and AI-generated designs have not been unanimously cherished. It has been noted that the increasing use of AI is likely to increase

---

40 See Recital 11 of the revised regulation and recital 28 of the proposed directive.
41 CDR Art. 19(1).
42 Sarlangue (n 24), 94; Yilmaztekin (n 23), 61.
43 A further interesting question is whether this would also mean that this kind of use covers using designs to train AI systems. Due to the limited length of this chapter, this issue remains for further research to be solved.
44 Yilmaztekin (n 23), 33.

design piracy, creating even more tension in the notoriously complex relationship between fashion and IP.[45]

19.023 When digitalisation changes the creative environments in virtually all creative sectors, the development of generative AI challenges the principle that human effort is necessary for the creation of intangible goods. As a result, it is inevitable that the justification of the protection of such intangible assets requires some reconsideration. Especially in the civil law jurisdictions (including most EU Member States), the most dominant IP law justification theories are very anthropocentric, meaning that creative human effort is required to yield protection. AI-generated 'creativity' inevitably clashes with such anthropocentric justification theories and decreases the deontological justification of IP rights. A common denominator for the deontological theories is that IP protection is awarded to *humans* – not, for instance, animals or machines (and awarding such rights to legal persons, such as companies, is limited to a certain degree). Of all the IP rights, the copyright regime has the highest degree of anthropocentrism.

19.024 Anthropocentrism is also visible in the European Parliament's Report on IP rights for the development of AI technologies. The European Parliament recommends a 'human-centred approach to AI' and notes that the use of AI technologies must not come at the expense of the interests of human creators.[46] Thus, when assessing the proper IP approach to AI, the interests of human designers and artists must be taken into consideration.[47]

19.025 The more anthropocentric the IP right we have at hand, the more difficult it is to justify that it ought to cover AI-generated output that lack any human creative contribution. This is the case especially in the continental copyright regime (the 'author's right regime'), where the anthropocentric justification theories have particular importance.[48] However, as argued by Reto Hilty, Jörg Hoffmann and Stefan Scheuerer, although the anthropocentric IP justification theories require that protection must be granted if there is sufficient human input, these theories do not necessarily *prohibit* the protection of intangible

---

45 Heidi Härkönen, 'Fashion Piracy and Artificial Intelligence (n 6), 3.
46 European Parliament: Report on intellectual property rights for the development of artificial intelligence technologies (2020/2015(INI)) Committee on Legal Affairs, 2 October 2020, paras. D, E, 6.
47 See also Heidi Härkönen, 'The Impact of Artificial Intelligence on the Fashion Sector: A Moral Rights' Perspective' forthcoming in Eleonora Rosati and Irene Calboli (eds), *Routledge Handbook of Fashion Law* (Routledge, 2024) https://ssrn.com/abstract=4573087 accessed 8 November 2023.
48 Reto M. Hilty; Jörg Hoffmann & Stefan Scheuerer, 'Intellectual Property Justification for Artificial Intelligence' in Jyh-An Lee, Reto Hilty and Kung-Chung Liu (eds) *Artificial Intelligence and Intellectual Property* (Oxford University Press 2021), 51–52.

subject matter that is generated without such human input.⁴⁹ Because these theories stem from times when advanced AI programs did not exist, they cannot be interpreted as deliberately preclusive for such new technologies.⁵⁰ Correspondingly, the less an IP right is concerned with protecting the human behind a creation, the more chances there are that this IP right could be used to protect non-human 'creativity'. As copyright and design right are the most important IP rights to protect industrial deigns, works of applied art and models, we will next compare these two IP rights and their justification theories from the perspective of AI.

2. AI-generated Output as Artistic Works: The Conflict with Copyright

19.026 To be able to understand the effects and complications AI-driven design causes in the sphere of design law, it is worthwhile first to have a brief look at the same phenomenon in the copyright realm. Making comparisons between copyright and design law not only provides depth and broader perspective to the topic but is also relevant in the practical sense. Due to the European Union Court of Justice (CJEU) judgement *Cofemel*,⁵¹ it is now certain that Member States may no longer discriminate against works of applied art and industrial designs in their national copyright regimes. In practice, this means that many industrial designs that have been primarily protected by design rights can now also be protected by copyright.⁵² In other words, digital designers and undertakings that produce AI-generated designs must often consider both copyright and design protection of their products.

19.027 The Berne Convention does not explicitly require an author of a copyright-protected work to be a human being, however, its wording and historical context strongly suggest that the terms 'author' and 'authorship' refer to a natural person.⁵³ For instance, the term of protection is tied to the author's life (Art. 7(1)) – which AI does not have. Thus, a work protected by the Berne

---

49 Ibid., 56–57.
50 Ibid., 57.
51 Case C-683/17 *Cofemel — Sociedade de Vestuário SA v G-Star Raw CV* [2019] ECLI:EU:C:2019:721.
52 Heidi Härkönen, 'Fashion and Copyright: Protection as a Tool to Foster Sustainable Development' (PhD thesis, University of Lapland Faculty of Law, 2021) 59, 68–72; Annette Kur 'Twenty Years in Design Law – What Has Changed?' on Hayleigh Bosher and Eleonora Rosati (eds) *Development and Directions in Intellectual Property Law: 20 Years of The IPKat* (Oxford University Press, 2023) 145, 156.
53 Hugenholtz and Quintais (n 6), 1190, 1195; Sam Ricketson, 'The 1992 Horace S. Manges Lecture - People or Machines: The Bern Convention and the Changing Concept of Authorship' (1991) 16 *Columbia-VLA Journal of Law & the Arts* 1, 11, 21–22.

Convention must not be generated by an AI program.[54] Moreover, the highly anthropocentric *personality theory* has a strong significance in the author's right regime. This theory views the act of creation as an expression of author's personality.[55] Therefore, by protecting the work, copyright is indirectly protecting the personhood of the author of said work. This is visible also in the scope of protection: author's personal, non-pecuniary interests are protected in the form of moral rights. An AI program, however, does not have a 'personhood' or 'personality' that need to be protected, which is why the personality theory justification conflicts with any attempts to grant copyright protection to AI-generated output.

19.028 The personality theory's importance in the EU copyright regime is visible in judgments by the CJEU, such as *Painer* (2011). In this judgement, the CJEU noted that a copyright-protected work must be its 'author's own intellectual creation',[56] meaning that the author should stamp the work with their 'personal touch', resulting to the work 'reflecting their personality'.[57] These criteria form the European standard of originality, which any subject matter searching for copyright protection must fulfil. Although the issue in *Painer* was not per se about the person or personhood of the author of a copyright-protected work, the judgment's clarifications to the EU standard of originality indirectly relate to issues concerning authorship. The European standard of originality can be seen as another obstacle for copyright protection of AI-generated subject matter, as *Painer* so strongly highlights the importance of the author's personhood. The European originality standard is thus deeply connected to a natural person and their creativity.[58] As a result, it is difficult to see how subject matter independently generated by AI would meet the criteria for copyright protection.[59]

---

54 Ricketson (n 53), 11.
55 Hilty et al (n 48), 52–53.
56 The 'author's own intellectual creation' requirement of copyright law originally derives from the CJEU judgement C-5/08 *Infopaq International A/S v Danske Dagblades Forening*, [2009] ECLI:EU:C:2009:465, para. 37, where the CJEU extended the standard of originality of certain types of works (databases, software, and photographs) to apply to all other categories of works.
57 The European Union Court of Justice Case C-145/10 *Eva-Maria Painer v. Standard VergkagsGnbH* [2011] ECLI:EU:C:2011:798, paras 88, 92. There are other judgments from the CJEU concerning the standard of originality as well, however, since they do not diverge from the message of *Painer*, they shall be excluded from this chapter that focuses on the design law regime.
58 Guadamuz (n 6), 175.
59 European Parliament: Report on intellectual property rights for the development of artificial intelligence technologies (n 46), para. 16; Guadamuz (n 6), 161. Some scholars have explored whether it would be possible to circumvent the European originality requirement to accept AI-generated subject matter in the scope of copyright protection (see e.g., Hugenholtz and Quintais (n 6), 1190–216; Anette Alén-Savikko; Rosa Ballardini and Taina Pihlajarinne, 'Tekoälyn tuotokset ja omaperäisyysvaatimus – kohti koneorien-

19.029 In sum, both the roots of copyright, as well as the contemporary European copyright regime, are very much focused on the personhood of the author, which indirectly leads to the requirement of human authorship. This, combined with the above-described human-centric standard of originality, make the European copyright regime unsuitable for protecting AI-generated output. The originality standard also limits the possibilities to protect AI-assisted designs by copyright: if the human designer gives the control of most creative choices to the AI program they are using as a tool, it is unlikely that the result meets the standard of originality. For those types of products that (if human-created) can typically enjoy both copyright and design protection, such as works of applied art, industrial designs, and models, it is therefore worthwhile to turn towards design law and assess, whether this IP right could be a more suitable tool to protect AI-generated output.

3. AI and EU Design Law: The Issues of 'Designership' and Design Development

19.030 Design is a tricky category of IP. It does not neatly fit under the category of artistic property, nor under industrial property, and has been vacillating between the legal categories.[60] Although in this day and age, 'design law' is its own branch of IP, its status remains unsettled in several ways.[61] In the era of digital revolution and technological advancement, this arguably indeterminate status is not necessarily a disadvantage of design law. Instead, it might give design law the flexibility that, for instance, copyright law lacks when it comes to protecting new forms of creativity, such as AI-driven design.

19.031 Although design law has a much lower degree of anthropocentrism than copyright law, it cannot be concluded that it would provide a perfect match for AI-generated output, or even for AI-assisted output that have been designed without sufficient human interaction. Unlike within the sphere of copyright, the design regime's conflicts with non-human creativity are more subtle. It appears that in several ways, EU design law indirectly requires that the designer of a protected subject matter must be a natural person.[62]

19.032 It has been noted in legal scholarship (for instance, by Hasan Kadir Yilmaztekin) that under the current legislation, AI design programs are not likely to be

---

   toitunutta tekijänoikeutta?' [Automated Content Production and Originality in Copyright Law – Towards a Machine-oriented Regime?] (2018) 116 *Lakimies* 7–8, 975–995.
60   Annette Kur 'The Green paper's 'Design Approach' – What's wrong with it?' [1993] 10 EIPR, 374, 376.
61   Teilmann-Lock (n 9), 408.
62   Tischner (n 5), 176.

considered as owners of their designs.⁶³ This is unsurprising, as only natural persons or subjects with legal personhood can be considered as rightsholders. However, a more important – and a more complicated question is whether *anyone* owns rights to AI-generated designs or are they predominantly in the public domain.

19.033 Before delving more deeply to the requirements for 'designership' in EU design law, it must be noted that these requirements might just stem from the fact that the design regime predates the AI era.⁶⁴ Although the question of computer-generated designs has been raised, for example, in the Green Paper (1991),⁶⁵ technological development was not foreseen in the extent to which it materialised. Regardless, the aims and goals of EU design law do not seem to completely preclude AI-designership. As this Chapter will illustrate, when considering whether AI-generated designs could be protected under EU design law, attention ought to be paid to the act of *developing* a design. Determining the meaning of 'developing', and whether AI can commit this act, is therefore essential.

(a) 'Designership'

19.034 The essence and function of a 'designer' has not been a popular topic among researchers, perhaps because it has always been assumed that there is a human behind every design. Unlike the concept of 'authorship, which is in the centre of the continental copyright tradition and thus widely discussed in legal literature, 'designership' has remained in the shadow of IP scholarship.⁶⁶ This is no wonder, since these two IP rights have such differentiating views when it comes to the importance of the person who created the (potentially) protected subject matter. Whereas copyright is very keen on the relationship between an author and their work, design law focuses on the *designs*, rather than the designers themselves.⁶⁷ Instead, design law aims to pay as little attention to the person behind the design and their qualities as possible.

19.035 Odd enough, the notion of a 'designer' has remained in the shadow not only in legal scholarship, but also in the European legislative pieces concerning design protection.⁶⁸ EU design law – both the CDR and the DD – lacks a clear defi-

---

63 Ibid.; Yilmaztekin (n 23), 71.
64 See also Hilty et al. (n 48), 57.
65 Green Paper (n 10), para. 5.6.2.
66 A notable exception being, e.g., Tischner (n 5).
67 Ibid. 170–171; Bently and Sherman (n 27) 720.
68 See, e.g., Kur, 'The Green Paper's 'Design Approach' – What's wrong with it? (n 60), 376.

nition of a designer.[69] Copyright and patent laws also refrain from determining the concepts of 'author' or 'inventor'. However, these concepts are widely discussed in legal scholarship,[70] whereas the same cannot be said about designers.

Thomas Margoni has argued that overall, EU design law is not particularly designer friendly.[71] The design regime remains silent on *who* and/or *what* qualifies as a designer. Margoni views the lack of definition of a designer as a reflection of the fact that the CDR has been created and implemented with industry and market interests in mind – not designers. This argument is supported with the notion that the CDR gives plenty of attention to the concept of 'design' as an industrial product, while the concept of a 'designer' as an individual who undertakes productive and innovative activities remains is unclear.[72] However, even though designers are not enshrined in EU design law, this does not mean that the regime would completely lack the kind anthropocentrism that can be viewed as an obstacle for protecting AI-generated designs. Yilmaztekin argues that the entire EU design regime is 'human centric'.[73] Without forgetting Margoni's point of the focus of design law being on designs rather than designers, Yilmaztekin's conclusion seems correct when one takes a closer look at the text adopted in the CDR and the DD. First of all, anthropocentrism in the CDR is visible in the fact that the right to a community design (both registered or unregistered) shall vest in the designer or their successor in title (CDR Art. 14(1)), without, however, determining who qualifies as a designer.[74] In Tischner's view this article establishes that the right to a design is attached to the individual who developed the design, and that the right to the design is conferred on its creator.[75] This is called the 'designer doctrine'.[76] This starting point of EU design law can be viewed as anthropocentric, inter alia, because the doctrine suggests that a designer is a living person, as their design rights can be inherited. The Green Paper also reminds that the basic principle in the

19.036

---

69   Margoni (n 28), 225, 237.
70   See e.g., Martha Woodmansee, *The Author, Art, and the Market: Rereading the History of Aesthetics* (Columbia University Press 1994); Lionel Bently, 'Copyright and the Death of the Author in Literature and Law' (1994) 57 MLR; Tuomas Mattila, 'Yhteistyö tekijänoikeudessa' [Collaboration in copyright law—A study of original copyright holders in creative processes based on cooperation and communality] (PhD thesis, University of Helsinki Faculty of Law. Suomalainen Lakimiesyhdistys, A-series, No 345, 2022); Carolan (n 8).
71   Margoni (n 28), 237.
72   Ibid., 233, 226. Margoni furthermore claims that the absence of a clear legal definition of the word 'designer', as well as the EU legislative pieces' recitals' multiple references to industrial needs, are 'warning signs', pointing out that Individual designers are only mentioned in the preamble to the CDR Recitals 7 and 24 (ibid., 227).
73   Yilmaztekin (n 23), 71; Similarly, Tischner (n 5), 176.
74   Margoni (n 28), 233.
75   Tischner (n 5), 174.
76   Ibid.

national design laws of EU Member States is that the right originates in the person of the designer.[77] However (as will be elaborated later), the anthropocentrism of design law is not as strict as in the continental copyright regime.

19.037 Although designers are generally the first owners of the rights to designs they developed in accordance with the CDR Article 14(1), they can surrender their design rights to third parties. The starting point thus appears very similar to that of the copyright regime, where authors are the first owners of copyrights to their works (although there may be certain exceptions in Member States' national laws). It is, however, what follows in the CDR Article 14 that makes EU design law much more liberal and less anthropocentric compared to the continental copyright regime when it comes to first owners of designs. Article 14(3) includes an exception from the designer doctrine: according to this article, 'where a design is developed by an employee in the execution of [their] duties or following the instructions given by [their] employer, the right to the Community design shall vest in the employer, unless otherwise agreed or specified under national law'.[78]

19.038 CDR Article 14(3) hints that a designer is someone who can be employed, and make contractual arrangements – in other words, a designer in EU design law has a legal personality, which AI does not have. However, when considering the importance of the person of the designer in terms of qualifying for protection, it is worth noting that Article 14(3) effectively blurs the link between a designer and their creative output. This would suggest that the personhood and personal interests of the designer are not that important in EU design law.[79] As visible in Article 14(3), the starting point of European design law is that employees' designs belong to their employer *unless* the national law states otherwise, or the employer and the employee have agreed otherwise.[80] The contrast between the CDR Article 14(3) and the continental copyright regime is thus striking. Author's right regime jurisdictions typically do not have such provisions that resemble the common law copyright regime's work-for-hire doctrine.[81] One of the underlying reasons for the reluctance to assign the rights to employees' works to employers by default is that the author's right regime

---

77 Green paper (n 10), para. 7.1.2.
78 A similar provision is included in the proposed design directive's Art. e 11(3).
79 See also Kur, The Green Paper's 'Design Approach' – What's wrong with it? (n 60), 377.
80 This has been said to reflect the need to balance the sometimes-conflicting interests between designers and producers/investors (see Tischner (n 5), 174).
81 This is, however, not a rule and for the time being, this aspect of copyright is not harmonised in the EU. See also Directive 2009/24/EC of the European Parliament and of the Council of 23 April 2009 on the legal protection of computer programs art. 2(3): when it comes to computer programs created by employees, the employer is generally viewed as the rightsholder.

views the relationship between an author and their work as something very special and quite intimate, even. Because a copyright-protected work – the author's own intellectual creation – is considered to include its author's personal touch / personal stamp / even a piece of their personality, the automatic assignment of such work to anyone else than the author themselves seems inherently wrongful, and ought to be left for the author themselves to freely decide. Considering above, this comparison between copyright law and design law helps to understand how the design law approach to designs developed in the course of employment is an indication of the weakness of the link between a designer and their design.

The absence of any moral rights provisions in the design regime further suggests that the relationship between a designer and their design is something completely different than its equivalent in the copyright regime. In copyright literature, it has been considered that the existence of moral rights is perhaps the strongest display of the civil law jurisdictions' intention to preserve the special relationship with an author and their work.[82] EU design law contains a provision that slightly resembles the right of attribution in copyright law, however, they are not quite the same. According to CDR Article 18, '[t]he designer shall have the right […] to be cited as such before the Office and in the register. If the design is the result of teamwork, the citation of the team may replace the citation of the individual designers'.   **19.039**

Tischner rightfully notes that the wording in Article 18 is incorrect and confusing. The right to be cited before the Office and in the register is not really a 'right': nothing happens if one does not comply with it.[83] Moreover, this 'right' can be waived completely, whereas waiving the author's right of attribution would be generally questionable in the continental copyright regime. In some Member States, any such agreement would be considered null and void. To conclude, unlike moral rights in the sphere of copyright, Article 18 is a powerless provision.[84] The fact that including the name of the designer in the application is not mandatory under the CDR demonstrates that the design regime does not view the link between a designer and their design particularly strong. The provision, however, does not give us hints whether AI could be mentioned as the designer. Yilmaztekin supposes that some IP offices or courts could even welcome AI programs as designers.[85] This does not sound far-fetched, as the   **19.040**

---

82 Florian De Rouck, 'Moral Rights and AI Environments: The Unique Bond Between Intelligent Agents and Their Creations' (2019) 14 *Journal of Intellectual Property Law & Practice* 4, 299–304, 303.
83 Tischner (n 5), 172.
84 Ibid.
85 Yilmaztekin (n 23), 64–65.

CDR Article 18 already permits to replace the name of the individual designer with the name of a designer team.[86]

19.041 Yet another indication of the weakness of the link between a designer and their design relates to the citation exception in CDR Article 20(c). According to this article, 'acts of reproduction for the purpose of making citations or of teaching, provided that such acts are compatible with fair trade practice and do not unduly prejudice the normal exploitation of the design, *and that mention is made of the source*' (emphasis added).

19.042 This raises the question of who or what is the source? In the quotation exception in copyright, the source to be credited would clearly be the author of the cited work. However, in design law, the answer is not as straightforward, as design law accepts 'corporate designership' in the CDR Article 14(3). It is therefore unclear whether the source to be credited would be the designer, the manufacturer, or the proprietor.[87]

19.043 Due to the notions above, the following can be concluded: As opposed to copyright protection, which is essentially founded on the intimate bond between an author and their work, design law views the connection between a designer and their design as a more distant relationship.[88] Fostering this relationship through IP law is thus less of an importance. Especially in commercial design where trends dominate the appearance of designs (such as in the fashion sector), plenty of external demands and requirements may come in between of a designer and their creation, dictating the direction of the design development, and distancing the design from its designer's personality. Such external constraints might be, inter alia, the market, the laws of physics, users' needs, and trends.[89] All this suggests that the most important thing in design law is the *design* and what it consists of, not the designer and their personality.

19.044 To highlight the distance between the designer and their design, Margoni draws attention to the choice of words in EU design law that suggests that there is a weak link between the designer and their design: a designer does not 'create' a design, they 'develop' it.[90] Viewing the designer as a 'developer', rather than as a 'creator', is very different to the perspective of copyright law, where

---

86 See also Tischner (n 5), 171.
87 Margoni (n 28), 233.
88 Yilmaztekin (n 23), 63; See also Kur, The Green Paper's 'Design Approach' – What's wrong with it? (n 60), 376.
89 Yilmaztekin (n 23); See also Härkönen and Särmäkari (n 6), 51.
90 Margoni (n 28), 233; CDR Arts 6(2), 10(2), 14(2), 14(3).

authors 'create' works and 'express [their] creative abilities'.[91] Considering that this 'development' is something that determinates the relationship between the designer and their design in EU design law, it is necessary to assess, what does 'developing' mean in the context of design law, and how does it relate to 'creation' in copyright law?

(b) The concept of 'design development' in EU design law

19.045 A protected design must be new and have individual character.[92] Both of these criteria are objective requirements in a sense that they do not consider subjective thoughts or motives of the designer but mainly concentrate on the characteristics of the design that it produces to an outsider observer.[93] For example, a registered design is new if no identical design, or design features of which only differ in immaterial details, has been made available to the public before the date of application.[94] It is not enough that the design is new to the designer (subjective novelty): it must be new in a sense that it is not identical when compared to existing design corpus and differences in the design material and contribute to the overall appearance (objective novelty).[95] It is, however, not clear from whose perspective the difference should be immaterial: the designer, the design expert, the consumer, the informed user or the relevant circles.[96] The General Court (GC) has suggested that it should be addressed from an objective point of view and should not include the informed user.[97]

19.046 In addition to novelty, a design must also have individual character. A design has individual character if it produces a different overall impression to an informed user.[98] Thus whether, a design produces a different overall impression is not examined through the eyes of designer but through a fictional char-

---

91   See e.g., Case C-145/10 *Painer* (n 57) paras 89, 92.
92   CDR Art 4(1).
93   This is also called the 'reasonable observer test'. Estelle Derclaye 'Doceram, Cofemel and Brompton: How Does the Current and Future CJEU Case Law Affect Digital Designs?' in: Barbara Pasa E (ed), *Il design, l'innovazione tecnologica e digitale, Un dialogo interdisciplinare per un ripensamento delle tutele – Design, Technological and Digital Innovation. Interdisciplinary Proposals for Reshaping Legal Protection* (ESI Press, Naples, 5. Forthcoming 2020) https://ssrn.com/abstract=3507802 accessed 14 August 2023; Bently and Sherman (n 27), 718.
94   CDR Art 5(2); While the design is compared with existing designs this objective test is in contrast to copyright's originality test, which is a subjective test and focuses on the relationship between the creator and the creation. Bently and Sherman (n 27), 722.
95   Yilmaztekin (n 23) 53.
96   Bently and Sherman (n 27), 734; Yilmaztekin (n 23), 53.
97   Case T-68/11 *Erich Kastenholz v. OHIM* [2013] EU:T:2013:298, General Court, para. 40; See also Bently and Sherman (n 27), 734.
98   It is important to note that individual character mirrors the test used to determine the scope of protection and thus, the test of infringement.

acter[99] (the informed user) who is neither an expert in the sector nor average consumer but instead particular observant user, based on personal experience or extensive knowledge in the field.[100] Most importantly, it is typically seen that the informed user is not concerned with the inner motivations of the designer or how the design features were formed, but only with the kind of overall impression that the appearance of the design gives. As Bently and Sherman note, what matters is whether the informed user buys, considers, or appreciates the design for its individual character.[101]

19.047 Consequently, the law and corresponding academic literature regarding the requirements of protection rarely concentrate on the actions of the designer and what kind of contribution is required from them,[102] highlighting the law's design-oriented approach.[103] However, regardless of the link between the designer and the design being weak (as pointed out above), there still seems to be a connection and we cannot completely disregard the designer's perspective. As AI system can today easily generate designs that are objectively new and produce different overall impression to an informed user, the connection between a design and its designer – even though it is weak – has at least some significance.[104]

19.048 In fact, when AI-generated designs are considered, the main issue is not necessarily whether the designer is a human being but rather,[105] *what kind of contribution is required from the designer* and *how to evaluate what kind of contribution is sufficient.*[106] For example, in the realm of copyright, in addition to the requirement of human authorship, the author needs to contribute something original to the work. In other words, in the EU, a work protected by copyright

---

99   Case T-209/18 *Dr. Ing h c F Porsche AG v. EUIPO* [2019] ECLI:EU:T:2019:377. General Court, para. 37 (noting that informed user is a 'hypothetical person').
100 See e.g., Case C-281/10 P, *PepsiCo v. Grupo Promer Mon Graphic* [2011] ECLI:EU:C:2011:679, para. 53.
101 Bently and Sherman (n 27), 740.
102 Yilmaztekin, e.g., sees that AI-generated fashion designs are no different from human-generated designs if those fulfil the requirements of protection being a design, novelty, and individual character but does not consider what kind of interaction, if any, is required from the human designer. See Yilmaztekin (n 23), 57.
103 Annette Kur and Marianne Levin 'The Design Approach Revisited: Background and Meaning' in Annette Kur, Marianne Levin and Jens Schovsbo (eds.), *The EU Design Approach – A Global Appraisal* (Edward Elgar 2018)
104 Yilmaztekin (n 23), 57. This is because AI system can easily generate designs that are new in a sense that those have not existed or become public before and which have individual character in a sense that they produce different overall impression to the informed user.
105 In most cases when AI-generated designs are considered, there is almost always some degree of human interaction.
106 This issue was also raised by the stakeholders in the European Commission impact assessment report. See European Commission staff working document impact assessment report (n 36), 66.

must be its 'author's own intellectual creation'.¹⁰⁷ Copyright protection thus requires the act of *creativity*.¹⁰⁸ This becomes especially relevant when the work is created by using an AI program. Although in EU copyright law, the required level of creativity (or originality, to be specific) is not considered to be very high,¹⁰⁹ 'just pushing the button' is typically not considered enough to make a work original. In EU design law, however, there is no such delineating qualitative criterion.¹¹⁰ EU design law's only corresponding term for the copyright term 'creativity' to describe the act that is necessary for protection is *developing*. The verb 'develop' appears several times in the EU design law. For example, in Article 6(2) of the CDR when assessing individual character 'the degree of freedom of the designer in *developing* the design shall be taken into consideration' (emphasis added).¹¹¹ Although the concept of development is closely tied to a design's protection status and to the actions of the designer, it is not defined in the law. Thus, there is an obvious uncertainty regarding what kind of acts it should include. Like in copyright law, it can be asked whether just 'pushing a button' can make somebody a designer in the meaning of design law?

The act of development can be seen to include some form of intellectual effort from a natural person.¹¹² Tischner notes that the definition of a 'design' in the CDR indirectly reveals the person of a designer. The designer is the person who *develops* the design, who gives the *product* its *specific appearance*, which is new and has individual character.¹¹³ According to Tischner, this act of design development is based on the *intellectual effort* of one or more individuals, which would lead to the logical consequence that only natural persons may be designers in the light of CDR.¹¹⁴ The act of development also needs to

19.049

---

107 Case C-5/08 *Infopaq* (n 56), para. 37.
108 Under patent law, contribution needs to be *inventive*.
109 Petér Mezei and Heidi Härkönen, 'Monopolising Trash: A Critical Analysis of Upcycling under Finnish and EU Copyright Law' (2023) 18 JIPLP 5, 363; João Pedro Quintais, 'Generative AI, Copyright and the AI Act' *Kluwer Copyright Blog* 9 May 2023 https://copyrightblog.kluweriplaw.com/2023/05/09/generative-ai-copyright-and-the-ai-act/ accessed 17 August 2023.
110 Tischner (n 5), 182.
111 For example, the term 'develop' is also present in Arts 10 and 14 and in the recitals 7 and 14 of the preamble to the CDR.
112 For example, in the Green Paper the Commission considered whether there should be explicit requirement that 'the design must be the result of the designer's intellectual effort', because this would stress the role of human intervention and that the protected design must not be a copy of an already existing design. However, this was not seen necessary while the same can be derived from the general principles in the field of IPR and could lead to practical difficulties in its application. Green paper (n 10), paras 5.6.1.2, 5.6.1.4.
113 Tischner (n 5), 176. It could be argued that intellectual effort could be seen that there needs to be some form of will, intention, purpose or aim in addition to free will to make these choices. Machines do not have these qualities.
114 Tischner (n 5), 176.

contain some form of choices which affect the appearance or the visual aspects of the product[115] and which have some purpose or aim to solve a certain design problem.[116]

19.050 Design law also requires that the designer has some degree of freedom when developing the design so they can express themselves.[117] Although the term 'express themselves' points more towards the terminology of copyright and is generally not used in design law, Bently and Sherman, for example, see that, 'When evaluating a design, the informed user will focus on those aspects of the design (if any) where the designer was able to **express themselves** and, in doing so, imbue the design with "individual character"' (emphasis added).

19.051 Thus, if there is no design freedom, the designer cannot express themselves.[118] When developing the appearance of a product, the designer can face various constraints,[119] including limitations related to the product's need to perform a particular function and statutory requirements applicable to the product.[120] Importantly, in design law the effect of the designer's limited freedom is different compared to copyright. In design law, if the designer's freedom is very limited, even relatively small differences in the design itself can be sufficient to create a different overall impression to an informed user.[121] In copyright law, on the other hand, if the author's creative freedom is very limited, it is harder to express originality and personal choices. Thus, if the designer can develop small but novel differences in a very populated or restricted design field with the help of an AI, the results could more easily get protection compared to copyright law.

19.052 A designer's freedom is often limited because of a product's functional purpose. Although protection is not possible for designs which are solely dictated by their technical function, there has been uncertainty about how this dictating

---

115 Case C-395/16, *Doceram GmBH v. Ceramtec GmBH* [2018] ECLI:EU:C:2018:172, paras 26, 31 and 37.
116 Tischner (n 5), 180. According to Kur, a good designer's primary task is to develop an optimal combination of form and function. She views this activity in many cases identical with the process of resolving a technical problem (Kur, The Green Paper's 'Design Approach' – What's wrong with it? (n 60), 376).
117 CDR Art. 6(2); Bently and Sherman (n 27), 742.
118 Ibid., 742; Kur, however, mentions that although one reason for design protection might have been the protection the designer's personal expression, there are other more significant aspects which contribute to the need of protecting designs (Kur, The Green Paper's 'Design Approach' – What's wrong with it? (n 60), 376).
119 CDR Art. 6(2).
120 For example, Case T-9/07, *Grupo Promer Mon Graphic Sa v OHIM* [2010] ECLI:EU:T:2010:96, General Court, para. 67; Bently and Sherman (n 27), 741.
121 Conversely, the greater the freedom in developing the design is, the less likely it is that minor differences will be sufficient to produce a different overall impression on an informed user. Case T-10/08, *Kwang Yang Motor v OHIM*, [2011] ECLI:EU:T:2011:446, General Court, para. 33; Bently and Sherman (n 27), 742.

role should be determined. The CJEU *Doceram* judgment (2018) concerned this issue, and while doing so, the CJEU at least vaguely touches upon the act of development and its meaning. In *Doceram*, the CJEU had the opportunity to some extent to clarify what 'dictated by the technical function' means, at the same time rejecting *multiplicity of form theory* over *causality theory*.[122] In the causality theory, the main factor is whether the design's function other than the technical one was decisive for the designer when developing the design.[123] The possibility for alternative designs (which is the focus of multiplicity of forms theory) is irrelevant.[124] In Advocate General (AG) Saugmandsgaard Øe's opinion concerning *Doceram* it was stated that 'it is necessary to identify the reason why the feature in question was chosen by the designer of the product'.[125] Similarly, the CJEU points out by referring to AG's opinion that in the assessment it is necessary to take into account, '[...] *the objective circumstances indicative of the reasons which dictated the choice of features of appearance of the product concerned*, or information on its use or the existence of alternative designs which fulfil the same technical function [...]' (emphasis added).[126]

19.053 Interestingly, while the AG refers to the 'subjective intention'[127] of the designer, the CJEU refers to 'objective circumstances',[128] which again highlights the more design-neutral approach rather than the designer's own motives or personality.[129] The choice of wording by the CJEU distances the assessment from the motives behind the designer and concentrates on the objective circumstances. However, the CJEU also states that unlike Article 6(1) and Article 10(1) CDR, the assessment under Article 8(1) CDR does not require the perception of an 'objective observer'.[130] This highlights the challenge of whether we can use a purely design-based or design-neutral approach

---

122 Case C-395/16 *Doceram* (n 115); Derclaye (n 93). However, Suthersanen argues more nuanced reading of the decision. See Uma Suthersanen 'Excluding Designs (and Shape Marks): Where Is the EU Court of Justice Going?' (2019) 50 IIC, 157.
123 Jens Schovsbo and Graeme B. Dinwoodie 'Design Protection for Products that are "Dictated by function"' in Kur, Levin and Schovsbo (n 103), 148.
124 Ibid., 150.
125 Case C-395/16, *Doceram GmBH v. Ceramtec GmBH*,[2018] ECLI:EU:C:2018:172, Opinion of AG Saugmandsgaard Øe, para. 21.
126 Case C-395/16 *Doceram* (n 115), para. 37.
127 Case C-395/16 *Doceram*. Opinion of AG Saugmandsgaard Øe (n 125), para. 67.
128 Case C-395/16 *Doceram*, (n 115), para. 37.
129 Schovsbo and Dinwoodie (n 123), 9; Derclaye, e.g., sees that designer's intention is not an appropriate criterion although pointing out inconsistency in the OHIM decisions after *Doceram* in this regard. See, Derclaye (n 93), 4; Uma Suthersanen and March D. Mimler 'An Autonomous EU Functionality Doctrine for Shape Exclusion' (2020) 69 GRUR International, 567, 570, also point out to the uncertainty.
130 Case C-395/16 *Doceram* (n 115), para. 35. Art. 6(1) and Art. (10)(1) expressly provide that, for the purpose of their application, the assessment must be based on the overall impression produced by a design on an 'informed user'. See also Derclaye (n 93), 4.

when considering what kind of contribution is required from the designer and the design itself.

19.054 In *Doceram*, the CJEU also notes that a design can be excluded from protection if the technical function of the product was the only factor determining the designer's design choices and if other 'considerations of another nature, in particular those related to its visual aspect, have not played a role in the choice of that feature'.[131] It is, however, unclear what these other considerations of another nature could actually be. Could they include, for example, aesthetic appeal or aesthetic choices?[132] The AG's opinion is that the designer's freedom and their creative contribution can play a role in the EU's autonomous functionality doctrine,[133] but the CJEU chose to remain silent about this.[134] In the end, the designer should have the freedom to make choices when developing the design. These choices should not be solely dictated by the technical function nor require aesthetic quality[135] but should rather affect the visual aspects of the design.[136]

19.055 In relation to the acts that result in protected subject matter, another possible difference between copyright and design law is the question of whether the designer's choices need to express their personality or have creative character in the first place. For example, Bently and Sherman point out that although the requirement of individual character might suggest that some form of 'personality' is necessary, this is not what is required by the definition. Instead, the requirement of individual character merely focuses on the impression made by the design.[137] Thus, when evaluating whether the design has individual character, the informed user is not concerned with, for example, the motivations of the designer,[138] how the design features were formed, behaviour of the design or whether the design is a poor-quality imitation.[139] Rather, the informed

---

131 Case C-395/16 *Doceram* (n 115), para. 26. See also, Noam Shemtov 'Software and Graphic User Interfaces' in Aplin (n 28), 24; Suthersanen, Excluding Designs (and Shape Marks) (n 122), 158.
132 Ibid.
133 Case C-395/16, *Doceram*, Opinion of AG Saugmandsgaard Øe (n 125), para. 71.
134 Suthersanen and. Mimler (n 129), 570.
135 Recital 10 of the preamble to the CDR. The design law neither give any requirements for aesthetic merit, artistic creativity or eye appeal. See, Case R 690/2007-3 *Linder Recyclingtech GmbH v. Franssons Verkstäder AB* [2009] Decision of the Third Board of Appeal, para. 34; Case C-395/16 *Doceram* (n 115), para. 23 stating that: 'Thus, as the Advocate General observed, in point 27 of his Opinion, it is not essential for the appearance of the product in question to have an aesthetic aspect to be protected under that regulation.'; Kur and Levin (n 103), 15.
136 Case C-395/16 *Doceram* (n 115), para. 26.
137 Bently and Sherman (n 27), 739.
138 Case R 1003/2005-3 *Pepsico v. Grupo Promer Mon-Graphic* [2006] Decision of the Third Board of Appeal, para. 23.
139 Bently and Sherman (n 27), 739.

user will focus on whether the designer has been able to *express themselves in a manner which gives the design individual character*.[140]

Another issue to consider is whether the designer's choices must be creative by nature, and whether the designer needs to make a creative contribution when developing the design. For example, the concept of creativity used to be a part of some national design systems of EU Member States,[141] but also a part of the initial definitions of protectable designs when the EU design regime was being crafted.[142] Today, creativity or creative acts are not explicitly required or mentioned in the CDR nor in the DD. Similarly, the CJEU seems to avoid using the term creativity.[143] However, while the CJEU chose to support the causality theory in *Doceram*, it seems to hint that at least some creative effort could be required from the designer.[144] For example, in the *Doceram* case, the Landgericht Düsseldorf (Regional Court of Düsseldorf), which originated the question to the CJEU, points out (by referring to the causality theory) that if the design's appearance is dictated solely by the need to achieve a technical solution and that the aesthetic consideration are entirely irrelevant, 'there is *no creative effort* worthy of protection as a design' (emphasis added).[145] Similarly, the AG's opinion suggests on several points that the designer's freedom and their creative contribution can play a role in the EU's autonomous functionality doctrine.[146] 19.056

Regardless of the CJEU choosing the causality theory in *Doceram*, it does not make any reference to creativity and only focuses on assessing the designer's choice, which leaves the definite answer to this issue open.[147] Also Tischner argues that the designer's choices need to be creative.[148] However, according 19.057

---

140 Ibid., 742.
141 For example, in Italy see, Estelle Derclaye *The Copyright/Design Interface – Past, Present and Future* (Cambridge University Press 2018), 280 and 290.
142 According to the initial definitions, design was the symbiosis of three elements: (i) functional improvement or technical innovation in the product;(ii) *creative* contribution of an aesthetic nature by the designer; and (iii) investment by the manufacturer to develop the two preceding elements. See: Uma Suthersanen 'Function, Art and Fashion: Do we need the EU Design Law?' (2011) School of Law Legal Studies Research Paper No. 88/2011. Queen Mary University of London, 7; Suthersanen and Mimler (n 129), 570; Green Paper (n 10), paras 5.4.1–5.4.3.
143 Suthersanen and Mimler (n 129), 570.
144 Case C-395/16 *Doceram* (n 115), para. 15.
145 Ibid., para. 15; For example, Suthersanen has speculated whether the Court with the *Doceram* decision is on a journey towards a harmonised exclusion clause in relation to three-dimensional objects (which may even extent, in terms of 'creative choices'. See, Suthersanen, Excluding Designs (and Shape Marks) (n 122), 160.
146 Case C-395/16, *Doceram*, Opinion of AG Saugmandsgaard Øe (n 125), paras 33,35, 47, 60, 71; Suthersanen and Mimler (n 129), 570.
147 Case C-395/16 *Doceram* (n 115), paras 26, 31, 37; Suthersanen and Mimler (n 129), 570.
148 Similarly, Yilmaztekin sees the designer as someone who can decide to develop a design by making creative choices, e.g., concerning style ornaments or length of fashion design. Yilmaztekin (n 23), 67.

to her, the creative choices reflected in the product's appearance and sufficient under the design regime are not the same as the authorial contribution relevant for copyright law, resulting in an 'author's own intellectual creation'.[149] The connection between a designer and their design is weak, and creativity in design law can also be described as having a more 'market-oriented perspective'.[150] For example, according to the Third Board of Appeal, a designer is often only concerned about making a good design: namely that the design must perform its function and it should be pleasant to look at.[151] As will be pointed out later, requiring even a minimum level of creativity from the designer could help to avoid overextending the scope of protected designs in the case of AI-generated designs.

19.058 To some extent, AI-driven design can be compared to co-creating or joint development of designs with other (human) designers. Also in this matter, it is necessary to determine whether a designer's contribution is sufficient for the status of a co-designer.[152] A design process can include several designers, engineers and, for example, marketing professionals, but not everyone's input to the design leads to the development of a design.[153] For example, it can be argued that contributing mere labour or minor contributions to details that are insignificant to the product's appearance do not necessarily mean that the person becomes a designer in the sense of the CDR article 14(1).[154] Similarly, formulating a design brief, or carrying out necessary probes, performing experiments or undertaking market research as such can be seen not to contribute to the appearance of the design, nor to constitute a substantial or considerable input.[155] However, for example Tischner sees that because design law uses more objective criteria of distinguishing contribution in determining joint designership than does copyright law, it is not reasonable to require each input to be creative in the sense of being new and individual to form joint development of the design.[156] In the case of AI-assisted designs, it can be argued that the designer's contribution should have some amount of creativity to amount to protection. Otherwise, the result of such human-machine interaction would

---

149 Tischner (n 5), 177. See also Bently and Sherman (n 27), 743.
150 Yilmaztekin (n 23) 170; See also, Kur and Levin (n 103), 7–8.
151 Case R 690/2007-3 *Linder Recyclingtech GmbH v. Franssons Verkstäder AB* (n 135), paras 33 and 35; Similarly, Suthersanen Excluding Designs (and Shape Marks), (n 122), 157.
152 For example, Tischner highlights the intention to share a designership, Tischner (n 5), 180.
153 Ibid., 181.
154 Ibid., 182.
155 Neither does managerial or entrepreneurial support, nor organising manufacture of the final product incorporating the design. See ibid., 182.
156 According to Tischner, this would discriminate contributors of elements without which the design would not exist, but which are neither novel nor contribute to individual character (ibid).

be an almost purely AI-generated, lacking the sufficient act of 'design development' from the human designer.

(c) Practical implications

The effects of interpreting design law in the manner described in the previous subsections can be examined through some practical situations, in which a designer co-develops virtual design with an AI tool for the metaverse. **19.059**

As explained above, the fact that a design is created for the metaverse in most cases should not be an issue for EU design law, especially after the design reform. Virtual designs such as GUIs, icons, animations but also digital designs representing physical objects are generally seen as protected, if they are new and have individual character.[157] Thus, for example a virtual design representing a fashion design such as a sneaker can be protected even though it is created and used in the metaverse. **19.060**

However, if such virtual designs are 'co-designed' with AI, the issue becomes more complex. When co-designing with AI, there are several ways for the designer to affect and interact with the process. At the simplest level, an AI can generate a flood of random generated digital designs representing, for example, different kind vases.[158] It could be argued that if a designer just chooses from a pool of AI-generated options a design which they consider new and have individual character, this choice could be some form of 'intellectual effort' (although very limited). It could be argued that by making such choice, the designer exercises some form of curating[159] and decides whether the design could be functional[160] or solves some design problem. However, in this scenario, the designer does not commit acts of development for the design itself nor contribute to the design process by giving instructions to the AI. Thus, the designer does not affect the visual appearance of the design, but their contribution could be characterised as *discovering* a new design. In this case, the designer's choices neither represent any freedom of design expected by design law nor contain any creative effort in a way that the designer could express themselves. Thus, designs generated in this manner would not be protected. **19.061**

---

157 Although the scope of protection in the metaverse is a subject of debate, it is excluded from the scope of this Chapter.
158 For example, Derek Philip Au has trained the AI systems to generate 'fake' vases which combine and imitate existing vase designs. Derek Au, 'This vessel does not exist' *Derekau.net*, (6 June 2019) https://www.derekau.net/blog/2019/06/07/this-vessel-does-not-exist accessed 16 August 2023.
159 Särmäkari (n 15), 87–89, 101.
160 As mentioned above, AI might not understand e.g., how a belt buckle works (Bain (n 18)).

19.062 There is also the possibility for the designer to continue the development further after the design is generated by the AI. In this situation, AI is functioning more as a tool to generate new ideas or concepts for the designer, who develops them further into a final product. This scenario represents a more traditional design development process in which the designer gets inspiration from existing shapes and forms. In this scenario, it would be hard to argue against design protection based on the lack of human development or choice if the resulting design is new and has individual character. However, it can be asked how substantial the acts of development need to be for the protection to arise. Regardless, those finalising design development acts can be assessed in more traditional manners, as changes at this point are made by a human. This represents more a joint development of a design, and it could be argued that if the designer's actions do not contribute to the appearance or visual aspects in any meaningful manner, then the design should not get design protection.

19.063 A more challenging situation arises when the designer interacts more closely with the AI tool before the final design is produced. In such a case, the designer can determine both the kind of designs that AI will generate and the appearance of those designs. It should be noted that the designer does not necessarily control exactly what kind of designs the AI will generate but rather the direction of style or function of the generated designs. For one, the designer can determine the design problem that the developed design should solve and direct the AI tool accordingly to generate the desired designs. This can be done, for example, by requesting certain types of designs, including request prompts, training the AI with certain kinds of designs, or by choosing the AI training material for certain types of designs. This part of the process can be very labour intensive and require many trials and errors to get the AI to produce the desired designs. The designer can also determine what kind of material, colour or surface the AI should produce, in addition to styles or combinations of styles that the AI should imitate.

19.064 To give an example, AI can be tasked to combine a 19th-century fashion style with modern sneakers. The designer can also guide the AI tool to produce new shapes or forms to designs which are partly dictated by their technical functions, while avoiding mundane or ordinary shapes. None of such actions would be traditionally considered to contribute to originality in copyright law, but they could be seen as parts of the development process for the appearance of new and individual design. It could be argued that there is intellectual effort and that the choices affect the appearance and visual aspects of the product, as well as that they can aim to solve a certain design problem. The designer also has much more room for expression and freedom to make creative choices.

The designer functions more as the originator of the idea and desired shape, while the AI is the tool to iterate and develop the desired design further.

19.065 However, due to the lack of any official definition regarding the term 'development', the quality and quantity of the actions required from the designer are unclear. Some further clarification is still needed regarding whether the act of development can contain, for example, personal or aesthetic intentions or creative choices. There is also the question of how the acts of development and designer freedom should be seen from the perspective of an informed user in the case of co-development with an AI. Although design law aims to be objective, many of the described designer choices are not evident just by looking and comparing the design with prior art. In the end, it seems that specially in the case of AI-generated designs, it is difficult to purely rely on design-based approach: there still needs to be some (small) contribution from the designer.

19.066 The final issue to be considered is what kind of actions EU design law requires for the design to obtain protection when the requirements of novelty and individual character are fulfilled. To acquire protection, the design either needs to be registered through EUIPO to acquire registered Community design protection or made available to the public to acquire unregistered Community design (URCD). This is an essential difference compared to copyright, which does not require any registration procedures but rises automatically when the work is created. For registered Community designs, the registration functions as design publication and informs about protected subject matter. Registration can also be seen as a barrier to prevent flood of AI-generated designs to get protection while it takes effort and monetary investment from the applicant.

19.067 In the case of URCDs however, the appearance demonstrated by the product itself forms the basis of the design identification when it is made available to the public.[161] Many see that the creation and publication of the design through a video game or online is enough to trigger URCD.[162] Thus, disclosing output of AI-driven design in the metaverse could satisfy the requirements of URCD, provided that the design is new and has an individual character.[163] The publication in the metaverse would also trigger a 12-month grace period, during which a design holder can apply for a registered design protection.[164] In URCD, however, there is no apparent registration cost and effort barrier pre-

---

161 Anna Tischner 'The Role of Unregistered Rights – a European Perspective on Design Protection' (2018) 13 JIPLP, 303, 309; CDR Art. 11.
162 Elam (n 28), 154; Antikainen, Differences in Immaterial Details (n 6), 152; Sarlangue (n 24), 91.
163 CDR Art. 4.
164 CDR Art. 7(2).

venting the protection of a flood of AI-driven design output.[165] If the required contribution or the acts of development from the designer are non-existent, almost all AI-generated novel designs included in the metaverse would be automatically eligible for URCD protection. It can be asked whether this could lead to overprotection of designs which potentially blocks competition and prevents creation of new designs through monopolising certain styles and shapes. However, in URCD, infringement requires the act of *copying* (i.e., incidental similarities do not constitute an infringement),[166] which makes it more difficult for the rightsholder to monopolise certain design styles. Moreover, the term of protection is only for three years, which also diminishes some worries regarding overprotection. Regardless of the aforementioned factors diminishing many of the concerns regarding overprotection, a more sensible approach would be to interpret design development to require a contribution from the human designer – the contribution can be small, but it should be meaningful. This would permit the protection of most AI-driven design where AI is used as a tool, while preventing a flood of purely AI-generated designs entering the scope of design protection.

D. TAILORING EU DESIGN LAW FOR THE DIGITAL AGE?

1. Design-based Approach in the Age of AI

19.068 Regardless of the text of EU design legislation assuming that the designer of a protected design is a human being, it is worth noting that the normative justification of design law does not carry quite the same baggage as copyright, which connects protection to the personhood of the author. It is the public's perception that matters in design law.[167] Moreover, as argued above, many of the views that object to the protection of AI-driven design due to the lack of human designership can be revoked with the notion that there is, in most cases, basically a human using the AI program, and this human is committing the necessary act of 'development'. It is thus worthwhile to inspect whether design law could be tailored to suit the realities of creative sectors that are increasingly incorporating AI in their creative processes and whether the possibility for protection would benefit the public.

---

165 One factor that prevents protection could be that including the design in the metaverse would not be seen as disclosing, because the design has not reasonably become known to the circles specialised in the sector concerned operating within the Community (CDR Art. 11).
166 CDR Art. 19(2).
167 Tischner (n 5), 171.

19.069 Design protection has never been justified by the necessity of protecting the designers' non-pecuniary interests, such as moral rights in the copyright regime.[168] Instead, the roots of design law are in commercial interests. Although the Green Paper notes that the basic principle is that design right originates in the person of the designer, still the right can be assigned or transferred in its entirety, and a fair balance must be struck between the possible different respective interests of designers and producers (investors).[169] According to the Green Paper, the reason for this is that EU design protection must be attractive for industries, thus revealing that the system is commercialised by nature.[170]

19.070 The market-oriented history of design protection is also visible in the recent developments of design law in the EU. The European Commission's proposal for the revised CDR and DD stresses the importance of design protection for companies. It describes well-designed products as important competitive advantages for producers, and highlights that investing in design tends to lead to profits and faster growth. This is in line with the notion of design law having a role as a marketing instrument.[171] In its proposal, the Commission also sees that accessible, modern, effective, and consistent legal protection of designs is important to encourage innovation of new product design also in the digital age.[172]

19.071 As noted above in Section C.3.(a), the role of an individual designer in design law is rather irrelevant. This is evident not only in the legislative history but also in the text adopted in the CDR and DD. Article 14 of the CDR has been adapted to the realities of the design sector: design development can take place in various personal and organisational relationships, e.g., by an independent designer, a commissioned freelance designer, an employed designer or a team of designers. This is reflected in Article 14, as the rights to a Community design may vest in (one or more) natural person(s), their successor in title, or in a legal person, like an employer.[173] Hence, compared to continental copyright, there seems to be more flexibility in terms of *what* sparks a design right. Regardless of the starting point in Article 14(1) being that the designer is also the first rightsholder, an exception that overrules this designer-friendly

---

168 Ibid.
169 This materialised in the CDR Art. 14(3). See Tischner (n 5), 174.
170 Green Paper (n 10), para. 7.1.1.
171 Kur, The Green Paper's 'Design Approach' – What's wrong with it? (n 60), 376–77; Annette Kur 'Unite De L'Art is here to stay – Cofemel and its Consequences' (2019) Max Planck Institute for Innovation & Competition Research Paper No. 19–16, 9; Tischner (n 5), 171.68.
172 Proposal for amending CDR and the proposal for a Directive on the legal protection of designs (recast) (n 34), 4.
173 Tischner (n 5), 175.

premise follows immediately in terms of designs created in the course of employment. Design law has no problem with vesting the original right of ownership for employers (CDR Art. 14(3)). This is a premise that the continental copyright struggles with, and often causes problems in sectors where works of authorship are typically created in employment relationships. In this sense, there is a much smaller conflict between design law and the realities of the creative labour market.

19.072 Design law's starting point, where the initial ownership of a design is granted to a legal person, could also be seen as a flexibility of the system. It appears that, in general, design law is a more elastic IP right than copyright, mainly due to their diverging backgrounds and normative justifications. Indeed, design law's tendency to disregard the persons behind the products gives it flexibility which permits it to rather easily comply with certain changes in creative environments, especially in the field of industrial art and where creativity is strongly commercialised. Such flexibility could also extend to AI-driven design: because design law does not have to follow neither the copyright nor the patent law route but can follow its own design based approach, this leaves design law more room to find its own path when AI is concerned.[174] In practice, this could mean for instance that the result of an AI-driven design process could be protected if there is sufficient human contribution in the design development, even if this human contribution was not per se *creative* or *inventive*.

19.073 The absence of a moral rights regime in EU design law is yet another indicator of it being suitable for a type of creativity that aims to serve commercial 'needs' rather than personal ones, making it an even less problematic IP right to protect AI-generated output.[175] The only provision in EU law which acknowledges the designer-person's possible need for attribution is the de facto powerless provision in CDR Article 18, which seemingly provides the designer with the right to be cited as such before the Office and in the register. It indeed seems that the commercial motives behind the legislation are so strong that they overpower the designers. In EU design law, the interests of big companies and corporations have been given more weight than the interests of designers. Margoni has furthermore argued that modern, digitally-based individual or small-sized, 3D printing, open designers and their needs are also largely neglected by EU design legislation.[176]

---

174 Kur, The Green Paper's 'Design Approach' – What's wrong with it? (n 60), 376.
175 However, as Member States may grant their designers stronger 'moral rights' protection than the CDR Art. 18, the national laws in those Member States might become an obstacle.
176 Margoni (n 28), 226.

19.074 In practice, design law's negligence towards designers is visible in the attention given to the concept of 'design as an industrial product' at the expense of the 'figure of the designers as individuals undertaking productive and innovative activities'.[177] The goal of design law is to protect the design as a *design*. The subject matter of protection is a product appearance that is new and has individual character. Design law is thus not about protecting individual creativity, nor is the main rationale to prevent consumer confusion or deception (such as in trademark law). Although one of the EU design regime's aims is to promote designers' innovative contribution,[178] its focus is quite strictly on designs themselves. The lack of attention towards designers makes this IP right strikingly different compared to copyright, which arguably focuses as much on authors as on their works. In design law, the quality of the intellectual / creative effort does not matter; the focus is on the result. Whereas copyright, for instance, is quite process-oriented in the sense that the author's de facto free and creative choices in the making of the work are very relevant, design law is result-oriented. The journey does not matter, because design law mainly cares about the destination.

19.075 To sum up, the designer and their (non-pecuniary) interests do not play a strong role when it comes to the justification of design protection in the EU. At first glance, the history of EU design law does not seem to object to the protection of AI-generated output, either. According to the Green Paper,

> The question 'computer generated designs' is sometimes evoked. The Commission considers that the requirement that a design be the result of a human activity covers this type of designs and in the same time gives an answer to the question of the entitlement to the right on such designs. It should be admitted that the generation of a design by computer is just one untraditional method of operating which should entitle the person using the computer to this effect and choosing the design generated among the possible multiplicity of solutions given by the computer, to obtain protection if the design fulfils the objective requirement of distinctive character.[179]

19.076 The Green Paper sees no problem with protecting computer-generated designs if they fulfil the objective requirements for protection. However, during the drafting of the Green Paper, AI technology was still in its infancy and computer-generated output still required plenty of human interference. Thus, it cannot be assumed that the term 'computer generated' was meant to cover designs generated AI without any human intervention. This conclusion gets further support from the notion that the Green Paper seems to presume

---

177 Ibid., 233.
178 Recital 7 of the preamble to the CDR.
179 Green Paper (n 10), para. 5.6.2. (direct quote).

that a human designer has at least some kind of a role in the design process: they curate the process, and/or make choices among the solutions given by the computer. The Green Paper thus appears to mainly comment on a situation where a human designer uses a computer program as a tool. Although the text in the Green Paper seems to generally have a positive approach to computer-generated designs, it cannot be read as a clear permission to protect AI-generated designs that have been developed without any human interference at all.

19.077 Although the design regime is not very interested in designers, has rather market-oriented objectives, and no problem with viewing a legal person as the initial rightsholder of a protected design, one cannot conclude that there are no major obstacles for considering AI-generated designs in the scope of protection. As the analysis of the act of 'design development' the previous section illustrates, human intervention still has a vital role for a design to receive protection under EU design law. Although the link between a human designer and their design is weak, the complete lack of such link leads to the no-protection zone. However, the concept of design development is much more flexible compared to the EU originality standard, which would make design law a useful tool to protect AI-driven design in the contemporary, increasingly digitised processes of design production.

19.078 As explained above in Section C.3.(b), many of the choices that can be considered to contribute to the development of design would not be normally considered to contribute to originality in the copyright realm. This allows plenty of designs co-developed with the help of an AI program to be protected through design law, at the same time denying protection from designs which the designer just happens to 'discover' from a flood of AI-generated output while not actually contributing to the appearance of the design.

2. Issues to Consider in Terms of Protecting Purely AI-generated Designs

19.079 Lastly, we must consider whether we *want* to reserve the design regime strictly for human creativity, as the question of whether design law *could* protect purely AI-generated output is of course different than the question of whether it *should* do that. This is an important (and surely, a difficult) policy decision. Although this chapter has focused on the first question and does not aim to solve the latter, it is necessary to briefly point out certain factors that ought to be considered when making any related policy decisions regarding the inclusion of purely AI-generated designs in the scope of protection.

19.080 For decades, IP scholarship and legislative reforms have aimed at solving challenges brought forth by technological advancement and digitalisation, without reaching a consensus regarding the question of the necessity of human creativity.[180] But is there – and *should* there be – a political will to protect AI-generated designs? In EU design law, this essentially means whether the concept of 'design development' should always include a human contribution that is significant for the design's appearance.

19.081 When searching for the answer to this question, the focus should not be solely on design law's commercial function as a protector of investments and as a marketing tool. Although EU design law appears to see designers as rather irrelevant (despite requiring them to be human), this does not lead to the conclusion that human designers and their position ought not to be taken into consideration when tailoring design law to the changing, increasingly digital creative market. It all comes down to the role of anthropocentrism in IP law, which varies between different IP rights. As Hilty et al. note, although the deontological IP justification theories do not necessarily prohibit protecting AI-generated output, they may exclude protection regimes for AI if such protection would result in negative consequences vis-à-vis human creators.[181] Yilmaztekin suggests that failure to protect AI-generated 'creations' would discourage businesses from using AI to generate new IP, even in cases where AI would be more effective than a person.[182] Tischner, however, notes that granting exclusive rights to purely AI-generated design might hinder creativity, because it is in the designer community's interests to have free access to the public domain material that results from machine-made choices and standard tools applied in design development.[183] IP protection of purely AI-generated design products could also be considered unfair for human designers especially.[184] Also, the European Parliament notes that the development of AI ought not to come at the expense of the interests of human creators.[185] It is thus clear that the perspective of the designer community must be taken into consideration, at least to some degree.

19.082 However, as designers are not at the centre of the design regime, the designer community's interests arguably weigh a lot less compared to the interests of

---

180 Teilmann-Lock (n 9), 411.
181 Hilty et al. (n 48), 57.
182 Yilmaztekin (n 23), 128.
183 Tischner (n 5), 177.
184 Härkönen, 'The Impact of Artificial Intelligence on the Fashion Sector: A Moral Rights' Perspective' (n 47).
185 European Parliament: Report on intellectual property rights for the development of artificial intelligence technologies (n 46), paras. D, E, 6.

authors in considerations regarding copyright and AI. It would not be sensible to bend the rules of copyright law to cover AI-generated output where human intellectual creation is absent without effectively destroying the purpose and credibility of this IP right. Thus, *if* there is a political will to include AI-generated output to the scope of IP protection to incentivise investment in AI technologies, design protection would be a more viable option than copyright. This perhaps would not completely annihilate the purpose and aims of design law. However, it would run counter to the assumption in Green Paper that there is a human behind every design, as well as to the anthropocentrism that is a distinctive feature of the IP regime (despite it being less obvious in the design regime). Thus, any aims to including non-human design development in the scope of design protection would require significant changes in the foundations of the EU design regime.

E. CONCLUSIONS

19.083 This chapter has shed light on the scarcely researched theme of AI-driven design and design law. It has also contributed to the broader academic debate on the conflict between European design law and technological change. Unsurprisingly, at the time EU design law was drafted, the legislator had not been prepared for the development of AI technologies and the digital design realm, as AI programs' capacity was not foreseen to the extent to which it has now materialised.

19.084 Regardless of the technological advancement coming as a surprise, the conflict between design law and the challenges brought forth by digitalisation is not impossible – nor even that difficult – to solve. Especially the issue of protecting digital/virtual designs becomes less and less complicated due to the EU design law reform, making it a viable and useful tool to protect virtual designs especially in the metaverse. This is often a prerequisite for protecting AI-driven design, as such designs exist primarily in metaverses and other virtual realms.

19.085 Today, AI programs can generate designs that seem to fulfil the requirements of novelty and individual character. However, this does not necessarily mean that such designs would qualify for protection under EU design law, because the act of 'design development' that leads to protection requires human interference. Moreover, EU design law indirectly requires human designership. This is the case regardless of the regime being extremely market-oriented and fostering commercial interests while leaving individual designers in the shadows. Although one of the purposes of EU design law is to promote the development of new designs through protecting novel innovative designs,[186] it would be wrong to assume that this equals to protecting *all* possible designs, especially those generated independently by AI.

19.086 Although the connection between the designer and their design is not in the centre of design law in the same way as copyright fosters the author-work relationship, the importance of this connection materialises in the act of design development. This chapter has illustrated the importance of design development and its meaning when assessing whether the result of an AI-driven design process is protected or not. As noted, the meaning of design development is still rather unclear, which makes it difficult to draw the line between AI-assisted protected designs and unprotected, AI-generated designs. This chapter has made suggestions and recommendations regarding the interpretation of this important concept, but even further research on this concept would be welcome. There is also a need for some clarification regarding what actions the development of designs must contain, as well as how the acts of development and the designer's freedom should be viewed from the perspective of an informed user in the case of AI-generated designs.

19.087 The chapter has furthermore noted that the design-based approach combined with the interpretations of the concept of 'design' allows design law to be more flexible compared to copyright when AI-driven design is considered. This enables accepting many AI-assisted designs in the scope of protected subject matter under EU design law. However, the design-based approach does not mean that purely or almost completely AI-generated designs would be protected by the current law. Because the act of design development must still have at least some human interference, we cannot completely abandon a *designer*-based approach. In the end, the question is not so much whether a design resulting from human-machine interaction is *purely* generated with AI, but to *what extent*. Thus, just pushing a button would not make a person a designer, but their actions need to contribute to the visual aspects and overall impression of the design. This would prevent overextending design protection to include all novel AI-generated designs that are generated without human interaction, especially in the case of URCDs.

19.088 Although it is justified to exclude purely AI-generated designs from the scope of IP protection, one should not be too hostile towards the protection of *all* AI-driven design. The realities of the design-intensive sectors cannot be denied: AI programs are increasingly important everyday tools and assistants

---

186   Recital 7 of the preamble to the CDR.

for humans. It is likely that the design industries still have the interest and the need to protect their products regardless of the changes in creative environments. This may add political pressure to protect AI-driven design. In the best case, welcoming designs that result from human-machine co-development to the scope of design protection might remove some of the pressure put on the crown jewel of protecting actual *creativity* – copyright.[187] This would also help to maintain a clear boundary between copyright and design law, especially now that these IP rights are increasingly overlapping when it comes to protecting industrial designs and works of applied art.

---

[187] It is, however, noted that during the history of the EU design regime, attempts to guide industrial design away from copyright have not succeeded (see e.g., Jens Schovsbo and Stina Teilmann-Lock, 'We Wanted More Arne Jacobsen Chairs but All We Got Was Boxes – Experiences from the Protection of Designs in Scandinavia from 1970 till the Directive' (2016) 47 IIC; Case C-683/17 *Cofemel — Sociedade de Vestuário SA v G-Star Raw CV* [2019] ECLI:EU:C:2019:721).

20

DESIGNING FOR THE EUROPEAN GREEN DEAL – A SUPPLEMENTARY PROTECTION REGIME FOR CIRCULAR DESIGNS IN THE EU

Dana Beldiman, Stina Teilmann-Lock and Anna Tischner[1]

A. INTRODUCTION	20.001	LAW MODEL	20.036
B. BACKGROUND – THE CIRCULAR ECONOMY'S DESIGN MANDATES	20.007	1. Introduction	20.036
		2. Access and Incentive	20.041
1. Circularity in the Design Industry	20.008	(a) Two models	20.043
2. Circular Business Models for Design: Gerrard Street and Skagarak	20.013	(i) Compensatory liability regime	20.044
C. DESIGN LAW IN LIGHT OF CIRCULAR DESIGN POLICY GOALS	20.017	(ii) The unregistered design regime	20.050
1. Design Law Policies in a Linear Economy	20.017	(b) The envisioned circular design protection regime	20.055
2. Design Law in a Circular Economy	20.023	(c) Does the proposed model provide an adequate balance between early and broad access and incentive to be attractive to circular designers?	20.059
D. THE OBJECT OF PROTECTION	20.028		
1. Trapped by the Concept of a Product's Appearance	20.029		
2. Is There a Way Ahead?	20.032		
E. CONSIDERATIONS FOR A NEW DESIGN		F. CONCLUSION	20.065

A. INTRODUCTION

20.001 This chapter examines the existing industrial design regime in light of the principles of the circular economy embodied in the EU's EcoDesign legislation. It is in line with the growing volume of scholarly literature that deals with

---

[1] The research and proofreading of this chapter have also been supported by a grant from the Faculty of Law and Administration under the Strategic Programme Excellence Initiative at Jagiellonian University.

the intersection of IP laws and social considerations, including those related to the environment and climate.[2]

20.002 The concept of circularity is rooted in social and environmental policy. Circularity refers to modifying human behaviour in the contexts of production and consumption for the sake of closing, slowing or narrowing resource loops. This implies a shift towards products that are designed for longevity, repair and reuse and the elimination of waste and carbon emissions. These ultimately social goals are part of political aims to adapt to and mitigate the effects of the climate crisis for the benefit of humanity at large. In this context, we venture to inquire whether a purely economic regulation, such as design law, can accommodate these social goals and what modifications and rebalancing of interests may be required to do so.

20.003 We investigate ways in which design law may play a proactive role in moving towards a circular economy. In particular, we outline a possible regime of protection to incentivize circularity in the design industry, supplementing the existing design regime.

20.004 We focus on two essential aspects of the *sui generis* EU design law: whether the definition of the 'object of protection' is sufficiently capacious to include circular features and whether social considerations may justify a rebalancing in favour of enhanced access. Finally, we outline a possible supplementary circular design protection regime tailored to the needs of the circular economy.

20.005 The main doctrinal sources of the supplementary regime that we are proposing include recent contributions to the scholarly debate on liability rules, in combination with principles borrowed from the European unregistered design system. Part and parcel of the transition to a circular economy is the innovation of circular business models.[3] As we will argue, a variety of business models for circular designs that already show a way forward may be reinforced by the

---

[2] For recent contributions, see e.g., R M Ballardini, J Kaisto and J Similä, 'Developing Novel Property Concepts in Private Law to Foster the Circular Economy' (2021) 279 no 123747 *Journal of Cleaner Production*; E Eppinger, A Jain, P Vimalnath, A Gurtoo, F Tietze and R Hernandez Chea, 'Sustainability Transitions in Manufacturing: The Role of Intellectual Property' (2021) 49 *Current Opinion in Environmental Sustainability* 118–126; A Perzanowski, *The Right to Repair: Reclaiming the Things We Own* (Cambridge University Press 2022); O A Rognstad and I B Ørstavik, *Intellectual Property and Sustainable Markets* (Edward Elgar Publishing 2021); L Wiseman and K Kariyawasam, 'Revisiting the Repair Defence in the Designs Act (2003) in Light of the Right to Repair Movement and the Circular Economy' (2020) 31(2) *Australian Intellectual Property Journal* 133–46.

[3] In the chapter, we refer to *circular business models for design* as the plans that companies have for generating revenue in a circular economy and to *circular designs* as key offerings of circular design businesses.

supplementary protection regime mentioned above, without requiring major changes in European design law.

Although we recognize that this chapter may raise as many questions as it answers, our hope is that it will contribute to accelerating the scholarly debate on the role that design law – and intellectual property law in general – plays in the circular economy and the 'green transition'. The planetary environmental crisis makes it high time to have this conversation. Hopefully, the debate will gain traction and qualify our thinking and solution-making even more with respect to what we envision as a circular turn in design law. **20.006**

B. BACKGROUND – THE CIRCULAR ECONOMY'S DESIGN MANDATES

In response to the increasing threat to the environment posed by exponentially growing amounts of waste and the global spread of pollution, the EU legislator has issued new mandates which embody the principles of the circular economy. The EU Circular Economy Action Plan,[4] one of the main building blocks of the European Green Deal,[5] provides for the optimization of product design for long-term use, emphasizing criteria such as durability, easy replacement of parts, modularity, repairability and recyclability. Its overall goal is to extend the life cycle of products and to reuse all parts of a product, thereby managing resource loops. This regulation addresses the fact, as noted by the European Commission (EC), that '[p]roduct design does not sufficiently take into account environmental impacts over the life cycle, including *circularity* aspects' [emphasis added], resulting in frequent replacement of products and increased energy and resource use in producing and distributing new products and disposing of old ones.[6] **20.007**

1. Circularity in the Design Industry

A linear economy has been the backbone of production and consumption in developed parts of the world since the beginning of the industrial revolution. **20.008**

---

[4] Communication from the Commission to the European Parliament, the Council, the European Economic and Social Committee and the Committee of Regions of 11 March 2020 COM/2020/98 final, https://ec.europa.eu/environment/pdf/circular-economy/new_circular_economy_action_plan.pdf accessed 9 June 2024.
[5] Communication from the Commission on The European Green Deal COM/2019/640.
[6] European Commission, 'EcoDesign for Sustainable Products Regulation, Executive Summary of the Impact Assessment' (30 March 2022) https://ec.europa.eu/environment/publications/proposal-ecodesign-sustainable-products-regulation_en accessed 9 June 2024.

Often referred to as a 'take-make-use-dispose' model, the linear economy entails cycles of extracting resources, manufacturing them into products and selling them to consumers, who eventually discard them and turn the products into waste. This constitutes a threat to the planetary ecosystem and to social welfare, and it demands a change. The circular economy seeks to address the effects of waste and pollution. It is founded on the principles of circulating materials and products with minimal value loss and of regenerating ecosystems.[7] The key aspects of product design that responds to the needs of the circular economy – such as the durability, reusability and repairability of products – are listed in the EC's Regulation for Ecodesign for Sustainable Products.[8] These principles have been translated into strategic frameworks for narrowing, slowing and closing resource loops so as to manage environmental impact.

20.009 Circular designs come in different forms. Present-day designers are trained to address 'wicked problems', i.e., higher-level problems that involve multiple stakeholders and climate change and other environmental problems.[9] As such, in circular designs, designers address social, technological, economic and other issues systemically. Designs include ways in which sourcing, engineering and consumption of resources operate with long or multiple life cycles and with product end-of-life schemes.

20.010 As such, specific circular designs often take the shape of 'design for x'.[10] This can be *design for long life*, which entails developing products that are durable,

---

7   For an introduction to the circular economy, see https:// elle nmacarthur foundation .org/ topics/ circular -economy -introduction/ overview accessed 9 June 2024; see also S K Ghosh, *Circular Economy: Global Perspective* (Springer Singapore 2019). For more on the evolution of the principles of the circular economy in the scholarly literature, see P L Simmonds, *Waste Products and Undeveloped Substances: Or, Hints for Enterprise in Neglected Fields* (R. Hardwicke 1862); R B Fuller, *Operating Manual for Spaceship Earth* (Simon and Schuster 1969); W McDonough and M Braungart, *Cradle to Cradle: Remaking the Way We Make Things* (Farrar, Straus and Giroux 2010); W Stahel, *The Performance Economy* (Palgrave Macmillan 2010).

8   In Art. 5 of the Regulation (EU) 2024/1781 of the European Parliament and of the Council of 13 June 2024 establishing a framework for the setting of ecodesign requirements for sustainable products, amending Directive (EU) 2020/1828 and Regulation (EU) 2023/1542 and repealing Directive 2009/125/EC, OJ L, 2024/1781, the following aspects of product design are listed as requiring improvement: (a) durability; (b) reliability; (c) reusability; (d) upgradability; (e) reparability; (f) possibility of maintenance and refurbishment; (g) presence of substances of concern; (h) energy use or energy efficiency; (i) use and water efficiency; (j) resource use and resource efficiency; (k) recycled content; (l) the possibility of remanufacturing; (m) recyclability; (n) the possibility of the recovery of materials; (o) environmental impacts, including carbon footprint and environmental footprint; (p) expected generation of waste.

9   H W J Rittel and M M Webber, 'Dilemmas in a General Theory of Planning' (1973) 4(2) *Policy Sciences* 155–169.

10 In brief, 'design for x' is a methodology used by designers that involves systematically applying a set of technical guidelines in the design process for the sake of optimizing a specific aspect of the design product to achieve the defined objective, 'x'. See M D Bovea and V Pérez-Belis, 'Identifying Design Guidelines to

meaning that they do not easily break, that their appeal and functionalities do not become obsolete, that they can possibly be upgraded, that they can easily be maintained and repaired and, more generally, that they have particular design features which ensure longevity by taking into account their shifting status and condition throughout their life spans.[11] *Design for resource and energy efficiency* is another example of a common design strategy for slowing or narrowing resource loops; it entails designing for more holistic and minimalistic approaches to the uses of raw materials whilst taking into consideration supply chains and the afterlife of products and resources for the sake of improving environmental performance.[12] By the same token, additive manufacturing (3D printing) and modularity on diverse levels of product architecture may contribute to resource efficiency.[13]

20.011 Designs for closing resource loops include, for example, *design for disassembly, design for remanufacturing, design for bio-based loops* and *design for recycling*. These all involve plans for reusing products, components or materials in multiple life cycles, allowing waste to become the input for new processes.[14] The key

---

Meet the Circular Economy Principles: A Case Study on Electric and Electronic Equipment' (2018) 228 *Journal of Environmental Management* 483–494; C Sassanelli, A Urbinati, P Rosa, D Chiaroni and S Terzi, 'Addressing Circular Economy Through Design for X Approaches: A Systematic Literature Review' (2020) 120 no 103245 *Computers in Industry*.

11 M F Aguiar, J A Mesa, D Jugend, M A P Pinheiro and P P D C Fiorini, 'Circular Product Design: Strategies, Challenges and Relationships with New Product Development' (2021) 33(2) *Management of Environmental Quality: An International Journal* 300–329; C Bakker, F Wang, J Huisman and M den Hollander, 'Products That Go Round: Exploring Product Life Extension Through Design' (2014) 69 *Journal of Cleaner Production* 10–16; M D Bovea and V Pérez-Belis, 'Identifying Design Guidelines to Meet the Circular Economy Principles: A Case Study on Electric and Electronic Equipment' (2018) 228 *Journal of Environmental Management* 483–494; A Perzanowski, *The Right to Repair: Reclaiming the Things We Own* (Cambridge University Press 2022) 246–253.

12 S Pauliuk, N Heeren, P Berrill, T Fishman, A Nistad, Q Tu, P Wolfram and E G Hertwich, 'Global Scenarios of Resource and Emission Savings from Material Efficiency in Residential Buildings and Cars' (2021) 12(1) no 5097 *Nature Communications*; P van Loon, D Diener and S Harris, 'Circular Products and Business Models and Environmental Impact Reductions: Current Knowledge and Knowledge Gaps' (2021) 288 no 125627 *Journal of Cleaner Production*.

13 M Sauerwein, E Doubrovski, R Balkenende and C Bakker, 'Exploring the Potential of Additive Manufacturing for Product Design in a Circular Economy' (2019) 226 *Journal of Cleaner Production* 1138–1149; K Schischke, M Proske, N F Nissen and K D Lang, 'Modular Products: Smartphone Design from a Circular Economy Perspective' (2017) *2016 Electronics Goes Green 2016+* 1–8. Modularity can be on different levels, including material modularity, add-on modularity, platform modularity, mix and match modularity and repair modularity.

14 M F Aguiar, J A Mesa, D Jugend, M A P Pinheiro and P P D C Fiorini, 'Circular Product Design: Strategies, Challenges and Relationships with New Product Development' (2021) 33(2) *Management of Environmental Quality: An International Journal* 300–329; F M A Asif, M Roci, M Lieder, A Rashid, A Mihelič and S Kotnik, 'A Methodological Approach to Design Products for Multiple Lifecycles in the Context of Circular Manufacturing Systems' (2021) 296 no 126534 *Journal of Cleaner Production*; H Desing, G Braun and R Hischier, 'Resource Pressure – A Circular Design Method' (2021) 164 no 105179 *Resources, Conservation and Recycling*; A Mestre and T Cooper, 'Circular Product Design: A Multiple Loops Life Cycle Design Approach for the Circular Economy' (2017) 20 supp 1 *Design Journal* 1620–1635; M Virtanen, K Manskinen and S

elements of many design strategies for closing resource loops include resource sharing,[15] standardization and minimization of components.[16] Addressing user behaviour is crucial for closing, narrowing and slowing resource loops. It is not a given that end users will handle products in the ways intended by designers or manufacturers. Accordingly, for a product to be circular, its design must be informed by the cultural and social practices of users, so as to prevent products from immaturely reaching their end of life by falling into aesthetic, emotional, technological or functional obsolescence.[17]

20.012 Hand in hand with developing design strategies, companies build business models which allow them to capture economic value from circular designs. As noted above, for a business model to be circular, it must contribute to narrowing, slowing or closing resource loops. Thus, examples of circular business models include *product long-life models* that base their monetization strategy on the willingness of consumers to pay premium prices for long-lasting products. In a nutshell, higher prices make up for lower sales of products that need not be replaced (as often).[18] In a similar vein, there are circular business models for *extending product and resource value* based on exploiting the residual value of products and resources and recirculating them, sourcing materials that would otherwise have become waste. Furthermore, *access-based* business models revolve around clients paying for the use of a function, performance or service rather than for private ownership of a good. Revenues come from subscriptions, for example, *pay-per-use* or *pay-per-result*.[19] The brief description of two existing businesses below will help illustrate some of these principles.

Eerola, 'Circular Material Library: An Innovative Tool to Design Circular Economy' (2017) 20 supp 1 *Design Journal* 1611–1619.

15 M Palmié, J Boehm, C K Lekkas, V Parida, J Wincent and O Gassmann, 'Circular Business Model Implementation: Design Choices, Orchestration Strategies, and Transition Pathways for Resource-Sharing Solutions' (2021) 280(2) no 124399 *Journal of Cleaner Production*.

16 K Anastasiades, J Goffin, M Rinke, M Buyle, A Audenaert and J Blom, 'Standardisation: An Essential Enabler for the Circular Reuse of Construction Components? A Trajectory for a Cleaner European Construction Industry' 298 no 126864 (2021) *Journal of Cleaner Production*.

17 R S Atlason, D Giacalone and K Parajuly, 'Product Design in the Circular Economy: Users' Perception of End-Of-Life Scenarios for Electrical and Electronic Appliances' (2017) 168 *Journal of Cleaner Production* 1059–1069; J Daae, L Chamberlin and C Boks, 'Dimensions of Behaviour Change in the Context of Designing for a Circular Economy' (2018) 21(4) *Design Journal* 521–541; V Lofthouse and S Prendeville, 'Human-Centred Design of Products And Services for the Circular Economy: A Review' (2018) 21(4) *Design Journal* 451–476; T Wastling, F Charnley and M Moreno, 'Design for Circular Behaviour: Considering Users in a Circular Economy' (2018) 10(6) *Sustainability* 1743.

18 Bakker et al. (n 11).

19 Access-based models are not circular by default, but they have great potential for it by administering sourcing and production at the one end, and facilitating green behaviour among consumers, at the other. See e.g., S d C Fernandes, D C A Pigosso, T C McAloone and H Rozenfeld, 'Towards Product-Service System Oriented to Circular Economy: A Systematic Review of Value Proposition Design Approaches' (2020) 257 no 120507

2. Circular Business Models for Design: Gerrard Street and Skagarak

Gerrard Street[20] is a Dutch consumer electronics company specializing in wireless headphones designed by graduates of Technical University Delft. The company's move towards a circular business model encompasses several elements. Their headphones are fully modular, implying that they are designed to ensure full disassembly: if any part is broken, it can be replaced independently, and the company guarantees the delivery of replacement components. Moreover, Gerrard Street offers maintenance service and retrieval of old parts, which will be reused. Customers are offered a subscription model as an alternative to purchasing; the subscription provides upgrades and downgrades, free service and repairs, as well as free parts and delivery thereof. In terms of resource management, Gerrard Street takes charge of reusing, repurposing or recycling the components, aiming to move towards zero waste.

20.013

Skagarak,[21] established in Denmark in 1976, is a design company known for its high-end solid wood furniture designed by a range of distinguished designers. As in the case of Gerrard Street, the company's steps towards a circular business model encompass several elements. The company offer their customers spare parts (slats, armrests, screws, fabrics, poles and more), and they have a care team that gives free advice on maintenance and repairs. Skagarak offers 'Reclassics', which is a scheme for buying back, restoring and re-selling pre-owned furniture. Furthermore, the company provides a rental service for outdoor furniture. Between rentals, the furniture is renovated and restored. On the production side, the designers commissioned by Skagarak commit to designing for circularity, and the materials have recognized sustainability certifications and are sourced according to codes of conduct defined by UN bodies and the OECD.

20.014

As illustrated by the examples of circular design business models, it is possible for value in design to be generated and captured in ways other than creating an attractive product, the value of which is to be realized only at the moment of sale (as envisioned in the existing European design regime[22]). Notably,

20.015

Journal of Cleaner Production; M D P Pieroni, C A N Marques, R N Moraes, H Rozenfeld and A R Ometto, 'PSS Design Process Models: Are They Sustainability-Oriented?' (2017) 64 *Procedia CIRP* 67–72.
20   https://gerrardstreet.nl/en accessed 9 June 2024.
21   https://www.skagerak.com/us accessed 9 June 2024.
22   Directive 98/71/EC of the European Parliament and of the Council of 13 October 1998 on the legal protection of designs (DD) [1998] OJ L 289/28 and Council Regulation (EC) No 6/2002 of 12 December 2001 on Community designs (CDR) [2002] OJ L 3/1.

a design's value creation can be tied to its use and performance over an extended life cycle. Note that this goes beyond the (old European) Bauhaus ideal that form follows function. Now form follows a social function, more specifically, a function that enables design circularity by means of change, redesign and more: design affords the products' recirculation. The recirculation of resources is attainable by design that facilitates reuse, repair, recycling, redesign, remanufacture and recovery. A product's life cycle can be orchestrated and managed by the design company, which is perhaps also the manufacturer, serving as a point of connection between the systems of production and consumption.

20.016 As nations adopt laws that empower consumers and grant them the 'right to repair', we find that the original designer or manufacturer has an increasingly limited legal right to demand participation in the product's extended life cycle, and thus the designer must work to ensure that they are best positioned to enjoy the revenue stream generated by the product's extended life cycle. Importantly, the value proposition of circular design businesses, as in our examples, is closely tied to the provision of seamless circular consumption for customers, who can be assured that the company will be best positioned to manage the extended life cycles of their design products. In other words, design companies like Gerrard Street and Skagarak are seeking to provide not only 'traditional design value' with products well-designed for their users, but equally what we might label 'circularity value by design'. Both types of value are key parts of the business offerings of these companies and all others that wish to function in the emerging circular economy. In a nutshell, 'traditional design value' is a measure of value derived from the syntheses of form and function, aesthetics and utility. 'Circularity value by design' is a measure of the ease and style with which a product can create added social benefits for users and society from design-afforded durability, redesign, remanufacturing, recycling, reuse and repair.

C. DESIGN LAW IN LIGHT OF CIRCULAR DESIGN POLICY GOALS

1. Design Law Policies in a Linear Economy

20.017 Turning to the policy aspect of design law, in a linear economy the task assigned to the framers of modern European design law at the time it was drafted[23] was to regulate 'saturated markets, where demand is no longer driven

---

23 Given that European design law has become a model for other jurisdictions, this objective may also be found in other regional and national design legislations. See T Aso, C Rademacher and J Dobinson (eds), *History of Design and Design Law: An International and Interdisciplinary Perspective* (Springer 2022).

by the urge to satisfy basic needs, and where the commodities offered are largely interchangeable in their functional aspects'.[24] The EU design law was a response to the needs of the last decades of the 20th century, characterized in Europe by overproduction and exuberant consumerism. Customers are provided with ever newer designs featuring small changes intended for a short market life.[25] In acknowledgement of the environmental crisis and the new policy goals mandated by the circular economy, we suggest that the original objective of European design law is no longer apposite, as society is now confronted with new challenges.

20.018 To understand the fundamental changes that circular business models impose upon design law, a step back into the history of the existing design law is required. Design laws are economic instruments intended to incentivize the production and marketing of design products. Little is required of the designs themselves. Their primary role is to be visually attractive with the goal of enhancing sales. At the time that design law was harmonized in the EU, design was perceived mainly as a marketing tool in accordance with the saying 'good design sells'. The drafters paid particular attention to the economic value associated with a product's appearance, as this aspect of design did not benefit from adequate and uniform IP law protection in Europe at that time.[26]

20.019 Consequently, the primary aim of this model is to stimulate creativity in designs and new product development and to reward investment in the creative effort to produce the individual face of products on the market.[27] Design protection, adapted to the linear economy model of the time, was expected to contribute to the economic well-being of the EU, which derives from continuous market growth. Design creativity and innovation were promoted as drivers of market growth.

---

24 A Kur and M Levin, 'The Design Approach Revisited: Background and Meaning' in A Kur, M Levin and J Schovsbo (eds), *The EU Design Approach: A Global Appraisal* (Edward Elgar Publishing Ltd. 2018) 7.
25 Explanatory Memorandum to Proposal for a Regulation on the Community Design (1993), COM/93/342 final COD 463, OJ C 29, 31 January 1994, paras 3.1–3.2. See A Kur and M Levin (n 24).
26 Green Paper on Legal Protection of Industrial Design (Brussels, June 1991) III/F/5131/91-EN, para 2.1.2; Explanatory Memorandum to Proposal for a Regulation on the Community Design COM/93/342 final COD 463, OJ C 29, 31 January 1994, para 3.2 https://eur-lex.europa.eu/legal-content/EN/TXT/PDF/?uri=CELEX:51993PC0342&from=EN accessed 9 June 2024. The process of Europeanizing design law had a complex rationale: it was also intended to solve some internal problems of intellectual property protection in the EU (i.e., no harmonized standards of copyright protection of works of applied art and unharmonized unfair competition law).
27 Recital 7 CDR: Enhanced protection for industrial design not only promotes the contribution of individual designers to the sum of Community excellence in the field, but also encourages innovation and development of new products and investment in their production. This protection was seen to be of particular importance for entrepreneurs, especially SMEs.

20.020 The efforts to create a *sui generis* form of design protection have been strongly linked to the desire to offer protection that addresses the unique nature and role of creativity in the field of design, as well as the needs of the main stakeholders, following its own purpose and playing a special role in the economy and society.[28] The starting point for its creation was the very role played by design at that time and the desire to offer a regime that would address the needs of designers and design-dependent industries. The European tailor-made design regime represents a remarkable example of a *sui generis* approach reflecting 'the operation of specific subject matter in practice as well as the intentions of those who invest therein'.[29] Well-functioning design protection was perceived as beneficial to designers (rewarding their creative contribution), investors (incentivizing the investment and offering a limited market monopoly) and their competitors (interested in a reasonably defined sphere of access to design features), as well as, indirectly, purchasers of products (design users).

20.021 Nowadays, the role of the design audience is shifting: design users have ceased to be passive consumers of goods; their needs, experiences and opinions have begun to play a co-creative role; and their modes of consumption are having a direct impact on the environment. The problems of the 21st century are widening the group whose interests matter in the context of adequate design protection. In addition to the interests of investors, entrepreneurs and designers, to get their due share of creativity and investment, the interests of the users and the common good are coming into play.

20.022 The rationale underlying the design regime is that the results of intellectual effort in that area deserve special protection, not because they are personal, original or because they advance technological development, but mainly because they make products individual (special) and attractive in the eyes of buyers (users).[30] The designer's creative contribution is relevant insofar as it leads to the creation of a product with an individual character that is noticeable and meaningful to informed users. The role of design, in this view, is to fuel consumer appetites and consumption. Products designed for this purpose are not created to last. All of this prompts the following question: if 20th-century EU design law is primarily focussed on adding more 'stuff' to the world,[31] is this the kind of design the world still needs in the 21st century?

---

28 In the early 19th century, the interests of investors in emerging and booming industries (especially the textile industry in the UK and France) prevailed.
29 A Kur and M Levin (n 24). Ansgar Ohly aptly calls the 'design approach' moving from the dichotomy of patent and copyright approaches a Copernican turn (Ibid., 110).
30 A Kur, 'The Green Paper's "Design Approach" – What's Wrong with it?' (1993) 10 *EIPR* 377.
31 J Silbey and M P McKenna, 'Investigating Design' (2022) 84 *U Pitt L Rev* 146.

2. Design Law in a Circular Economy

Indeed, only 30 years after adopting the EU design law packet, the rationale underlying the design regime is being questioned again for several reasons. As discussed above, designers are widely abandoning the linear approach and the take-make-use-dispose paradigm. Recent years have seen a turn in business towards a circular economy and circular design, motivated by calls to address global challenges, including climate change, increasing amounts of plastic and other types of waste, the pollution of both land and oceans, deforestation and the loss of biodiversity.

20.023

As mentioned above, in a circular economy new demands are placed upon product design: to contribute to the environmental goal of slowing and closing resource loops and designing out waste and pollution.[32] Design is a tool that can play a unique role in this respect, as 'the ultimate job of design is to transform man's environment and tools and, by extension, man himself'.[33] Design matters far beyond a marketing role as a driver of sales charts. It is not reducible to a trivial activity concerned with superficial market differentiation: as phrased by designers themselves, design 'is about envisioning change'.[34] The communicative function of design, essential for the EU design regime, takes on new meaning: design can educate and transform consumer attitudes and thus change the world. This adds a social/environmental aspect to the current, solely economic role of product design and creates a new economic reality, which raises new questions.

20.024

The New European Bauhaus,[35] an initiative announced by the President of the European Commission,[36] rewards design that connects the European Green Deal to our living spaces and experiences with enriching, sustainable, inclusive design (respectively, inspired by art/culture and responding to needs beyond functionality; in harmony with nature, the environment and our planet; and encouraging a dialogue across cultures, disciplines, genders and ages).[37] It was inspired by Bauhaus, a 20th-century movement that significantly influenced the social and economic transition to an industrial society. Given that the

20.025

---

32 https://ellenmacarthurfoundation.org/topics/circular-economy-introduction/overview accessed 9 June 2024.
33 V Papanek, *Design for the Real World: Human Ecology and Social Change* (Thames & Hudson 1984) 28. For a discussion of design as a human capability to transform our environment, see also J Heskett, *Design and the Creation of Value* (Bloomsbury Publishing 2017) 52–53.
34 cf J Heskett (n 33) 135.
35 https://new-european-bauhaus.europa.eu/index_en accessed 9 June 2024.
36 Ursula von der Leyen, 'New European Bauhaus' https://ec.europa.eu/commission/presscorner/detail/en/AC_20_1916 accessed 15 October 2020.
37 https://new-european-bauhaus.europa.eu/index_en accessed 9 June 2024.

rationale of intellectual property law has always been to promote the public good, it is appropriate to ask whether European design law is fit for promoting design that meets the requirements of a circular economy. Can IP laws, which are intended to have a purely economic effect, operate to incentivize a social component as well? Can design law stimulate the production of designs which respond to the needs of the circular economy? If so, how should a purely economy-orientated law be modified to incorporate such goals?

20.026 The question is whether design law, as it was adopted in the 20th century, has the capacity to respond adequately to this broader perspective of issues to be addressed by design today and in the future. Does the current regime provide sufficient incentive for design creativity to fulfil this momentous role? Undeniably, 'incentives are needed to induce people to produce particular objects beneficial to society'.[38] This is the first time that public interest orientation has entered the design field with such impetus. What does this mean for the design regime? With these questions in mind, a critical examination of some of the aspects of existing design law is in order. We aim to assess to what extent they respond to the circular economy's mandates and how they can be adapted in the event they do not.

20.027 In an attempt to answer these questions, two proposals are outlined below in order to address some of the concerns with the existing design law. We explore expanding the current definition of the 'object of protection', and then an unregistered design alternative, aimed at accelerating market penetration of circular designs.

D. THE OBJECT OF PROTECTION

20.028 EU design law protects the appearance of the whole or a part of a product to the extent that it is new and has an individual character.[39] The subject matter of design protection was defined so as to cover a wide range of design outcomes, both material objects and visual signals. In practice, however, conceiving of the visual, external aspect of a product as a configuration of features such as shape, line, colour, texture, ornamentation/decoration, etc. significantly limits the potential for circular design protection.[40]

---

38   P Aduser, *The Myth of Patents Justification* (Springer 2013) 121.
39   Art 1(a) DD; Art 3 CDR.
40   See product definition in Art 2(b) DD and Art 3(b) CDR.

1. Trapped by the Concept of a Product's Appearance

20.029 The European regime has adopted a neutral definition of design, one which does not require aesthetic appeal or quality. It encompasses both eye-catching and functional features of a product's appearance.[41] Although design is generally about identifying, approaching and solving a problem, EU design protection covers only its visually perceptible outputs;[42] it is focussed on how a product looks and not on how it works.[43] Underlying ideas and concepts are not protected. This concept of protected design does not cover the idea of solving a design problem, but the incorporation and physical manifestation of such an idea in the individual form of a product's appearance.

20.030 A further limitation of the object of protection under existing EU design law is an implied requirement of visibility, in the sense of restricting protection to those aspects that are visible in the application for design registration.[44] As a result, protection extends to those features of the product's appearance that can be represented in a way that is suitable for visual perception. In other words, 'what you see is what you get', both in terms of registration and scope of protection. The rationale for visibility as a criterion is part and parcel of the concern with optimizing a product's outer appearance for marketability

---

[41] The neutrality of the definition of design is seen as a cornerstone of EU design legislation (G Dinwoodie, 'Federalized Functionalism: The Future of Design Protection in the European Union' (1996) 24 *American Intellectual Property Law Association Quarterly Journal* 648; J Schovsbo and S Teilmann-Lock, 'We Wanted More Arne Jacobsen Chairs but All We Got Was Boxes – Experiences from the Protection of Designs in Scandinavia from 1970 till the Directive' (2016) *IIC* 418).

[42] Features of the lines, contours, colours, shape, texture, materials and ornamentation.

[43] cf Explanatory memorandum for a proposal for a Regulation of the European Parliament and of the Council amending Council Regulation (EC) No 6/2002 on Community designs and repealing Commission Regulation (EC) No 2246/2002 (2022), COM(2022) 666 final, para 1 and Explanatory memorandum for a proposal for a Directive of the European Parliament and of the Council on the legal protection of designs (recast), COM/2022/667 final: 'Industrial design is what makes a product appealing. Visual appeal is one of the key factors that influence consumer's choice of one product over another.'

[44] Recital 11 DD. In the case of unregistered Community designs, features of appearance that are clear from its first disclosure, respectively (see judgment of CJEU of 28 October 2021 in C-123/20, *Ferrari SpA v Mansory Design Holding GmbH and WH*, EU:C:2021:889, paras 38–40). Under the EU design regime, the explicit criterion of visibility applies only to component parts under a complex product under Art 3(3) DD and Art 4(2) CDR. The notion of 'a component part of a complex product' which must remain visible during the normal use of the complex product in order to be protected by the design right was originally tailored to solve the problems generated by the complex products with aftermarkets where design protection could create a captive market in spare parts. See Explanatory Memorandum to Proposed Regulation of 3 December 1993 (COM/93/342 final-COD 463, para 9.3). Compare, however, the GC's incorrect view in the judgment of 9 September 2014 in T-494/12 *Biscuits Poult SAS v OHIM*, EU:T:2014:757, paras 25, 29–30. The ambiguities that this requirement generated led the EU legislator to regulate it explicitly in Art 15 (and Recitals 17–18) of the proposal for a directive and Art 18a (and Recital 10) of the proposal for a regulation (fn 43), which provide that protection is conferred for design features that are shown visibly in an application. Such features do not need to be visible at any particular time or in any particular situation, with the only exception of component parts that should be visible during the normal use of a complex product.

purposes. However, with respect to circular designs, defining the outer surface of a product – that which lends itself to visual representation – is inadequate as the object of protection. A product's visible form falls short of defining (the value of) circular design. In particular, limiting protection to what is visually representable implies that features intrinsic to the circularity of a design – including material composition, recyclability, repairability and remanufacturing features – remain unprotectable.[45] Crucially, design law would, in many cases, simply fail to protect what is valuable in a circular design.

20.031 Another restraint, closely related to the requirement of visibility, is the manner in which the object of EU design protection is communicated to third parties in the design register. Design is best communicated by images since it predominantly affects sight.[46] The EU design regime relies solely on the communication of visual information: designs are represented through pictures alone (visual claims).[47] A description is optional and does not affect the scope of protection. Applicants for design registration usually omit the description as an irrelevant element that does not affect the scope of protection.[48] As it stands, under existing EU law, the only circular features covered by the concept of design are those that meet the product's appearance requirement, for instance, a material (or texture) – as long as it can be presented graphically and perceived visually.[49] Features related to the use of the design, such as its longevity, its

---

45 As an example, see Re-Chair made from recycled espresso coffee capsules designed by Antonio Citterio (Kartell), https://www.kartell.com/se/en/ktse/corporate/kartell-loves-the-planet accessed 9 June 2024. Its outer appearance is protected as RCD 003405364-0004.

46 For more, see A Tischner, 'Lost in Communication: A Few Thoughts on the Object and Purpose of the EU Design Protection' in S Frankel (ed) *The Object and Purpose of Intellectual Property* (Edward Elgar Publishing 2019) 159 ff.

47 Art 36 (1) and (6) CDR.

48 cf 'Green Paper on Legal Protection of Industrial Design' (1991), III/F/5131/91-EN, para 8.6.7. The role of description has evolved in the lawmaking process of the EU design law, and the provision for describing a picture was originally prescribed by the Max Planck Institute ('Max Planck Institute Proposal: On the Way to a European Law of Designs' (1991) IIC 4, art 39(3)) ('a description explaining the representation may be included'). Only with regard to the class indication did the Proposal explicitly state that 'the classification does not affect the scope of protection'. Almost the same regulation was included in the 'Proposal for a European Parliament and Council Regulation on the Community Design presented by the Commission' ((1993) COM/93/342 final, COD 463, 39), regarding the description as an optional element of the application. The official commentary of the Proposal of Regulation of 1993 provided 'that such texts may be helpful in order to identify the specific features of the appearance of the product which constitute the essence of the design and which might not show up very well in a picture or drawing'. However, in the 'Regulation Proposal' ((1999) COM/99/310 final), the description as an optional element explaining the representation was subjected to the principle that it does not affect the scope of protection of the design. This principle is maintained under Art 36(3) and (6) CDR; the draft proposals for amendments to DD and CDR (fn 42) do not provide for any changes in this respect.

49 cf Recital 11 DD. In *Rothy's Inc v Giesswein Walkwaren AG* [2020] EWHC 3391 (IPEC), a case regarding the design of a shoe of knitted yarn made from recycled plastic, the judge concluded that it was clear from

efficient use of resources or its recyclability, do not receive protection under existing design law.

2. Is There a Way Ahead?

As mentioned above, current EU design law, as reflected in the definition of the object of design, incentivizes the optimization of a product's appearance for purposes of commercialization.[50] By extension, the value of product design is realized at the moment of sale.[51] However, as we have seen, in a circular economy, design value is realized as a function of considerations, such as the type and source of materials, their carbon footprint, options for reuse and assessing whether the infrastructure supporting circularity is reasonably available.[52] Value is measured in terms of use and of life cycle(s), as design for circularity essentially encompasses an entire economic system. A design protection regime aimed at incentivizing design that is responsive to the transition to a circular economy must recognize and take into account these aspects when defining the object of protection.

20.032

In summary, it is virtually impossible to encapsulate all the design features that contribute to its circularity within the concept of the product's appearance, which is visible in the application form. The broader and more complex needs of circularity require features that burst the framework of the 'object of protection' definition under existing EU law, in particular as the visibility limitation is concerned. This is so because a circular design must also fulfil a social function linked to changes in patterns of consumption and reduction of waste in the context of the climate crisis. Thus, circularity-driven features, such as biodegradable materials, easily accessible and replaceable parts and many others, are the very features that need to be incentivized. This would require foregoing the visibility requirement. Communicating solely by way of images (design visualization) may be a significant drawback in the context of

20.033

---

the representation that the RCD indicated a knitted/meshwork fabric; the origin of the materials remained unprotected.

50 A protectable design is defined as 'the appearance of the whole or a part of a product resulting from the features of, in particular, the lines, contours, colours, shape, texture and/or materials of the product itself and/or its ornamentation' (Art 3 (a) CDR). Designs which are solely based on technical considerations and designs of interconnections as well as component parts not visible in normal use of the product do not qualify for protection (Arts 8 and 4(2) CDR).

51 Today's design regime is based on a 'design-as-marketing' paradigm, even though designers and design educators abandoned this approach in the 1970s. See Stina Teilmann-Lock, 'The Design Approach in a Design Historical Perspective' in Annette Kur, Marianne Levin and Jens Schovsbo (eds), *The EU Design Approach: A Global Appraisal* (Edward Elgar Publishing 2018) 28–48.

52 For example, designing a recyclable shampoo bottle does not resolve the problem unless facilities exist for collecting, cleaning, refilling, etc.

circular design, as many of its key features can only be captured verbally. Visual language is too limited a tool to communicate the value of a circular design. A verbal description of features that make design circular seems indispensable.

20.034 In light of this, the question arises whether it is possible to broaden the design definition so as to include non-visible circular qualities without undermining the rationale of existing design law. This would bring the concept of an object of protection closer to a utility model.[53] Here, however, we hit the slippery slope of non-harmonized protection of utility models and the multiplicity of approaches to defining utility models in Europe and worldwide. Perhaps it is circular design and the inadequacy of the current design regime that will become the impetus for a return to work on European utility model law.

20.035 The alternative would be to establish a subset of circular designs within the existing EU design regime, as explained in further detail below.[54] In this scenario, the role of the register would change. In addition to communicating the object of protection, it would disseminate information about the design's circular features to other economic operators and users. This format might contribute to the climate change discourse, stimulate consumer interest and inspire future circular products.[55]

E. CONSIDERATIONS FOR A NEW DESIGN LAW MODEL

1. Introduction

20.036 As a response to the questions regarding the adequacy of the present design regime for the circular economy, the following examines a design law alternative intended to accelerate innovation and dissemination of 'green' or 'sustainable' design ideas, aimed at accelerating market penetration of new design products.

20.037 Currently, the climate crisis, and more generally the environmental crisis, is at the forefront of global public discourse. One of its messages is that of urgency: hardly a day goes by in which humanity is not reminded that the world is sitting on a ticking time bomb in terms of climate change and the need

---

[53] The potential overlap between design and utility model law in the context of product circularity is beyond the scope of this chapter, but may have important ramifications on the structure of a design law that responds to the needs of circularity.
[54] See section 2(a)(ii).
[55] For more on the complex role of the patent register, see Or Cohen-Sasson, 'The Patent Medium: Toward a Network Paradigm of the Patent Medium' (2022) 32 *Fordham Intell. Prop. Media & Ent. L.J.* 857.

for pervasive and rapid innovation of products to help adapt to and mitigate the effects of climate change.[56] Indeed, investment is gaining traction, as is research and development of such products.[57]

In designing a legal framework meant to support a rapid transition to circularity, the factors of urgency and timing cannot be ignored. Existing design law is not directly concerned with increasing the speed of dissemination or with widespread access. On the contrary, both dissemination and access are restricted by intellectual property rights, as the control of design information tends to be concentrated within a single entity. During the relatively long exclusivity period, designs tend to be disseminated primarily in furtherance of the originator's economic interests. There is relatively little spontaneous diffusion by third-party use, improvement or commercialization.[58] Any exceptions, such as for experimental use, are limited in scope.[59] Due to lack of access to existing designs and an inability to experiment and 'tinker',[60] the exchange of ideas may be stifled. The risk, accordingly, is that innovation will proceed at an unnecessarily slow pace.

20.038

Seen from the perspective of the needs of the circular economy, current design laws tend to result in underprotection and undersupply. Designs which respond to the requirements of the circular economy are left unprotected and without the benefit of the incentive provided by IP laws, because they do not fit into the definition of the object of protection under existing law. Undersupply occurs because in a key period of transition to circularity, when the market penetration of such designs is critical for increasing acceptance and commercialization of the new standards, the current rules limit the diffusion of designs. In short, design law as currently legislated does not sufficiently cater for the needs of the circular economy.

20.039

---

56 'Climate Change 2023, Report by the Intergovernmental Panel on Climate Change (2023)' https://www.ipcc.ch/report/ar6/syr/downloads/report/IPCC_AR6_SYR_SPM.pdf accessed 9 June 2024.
57 Malahat Ghoreishi and Ari Happonen, 'New promises AI brings into circular economy accelerated product design: A review on supporting literature' (E3S Web of Conferences 2020, 158, 06002); see also World Bank, 'Accelerating Innovation and Technology Diffusion' (2009) https://doi.org/10.1596/978-0-8213-7987-5_ch7 accessed 9 June 2024.
58 See Yochai Benkler, 'Law, Innovation and Collaboration in Networked Economy and Society' (2017) 13 *Ann. Rev. L. & Soc. Sci.* However, commentators are registering a shift in this trend; see Eric von Hippel, *Free Innovation* (MIT Press 2016).
59 Except possibly to the extent that Art 20(1)(b) CDR legitimizes acts done for experimental purposes.
60 Pamela Samuelson, 'Freedom to Tinker' (15 June 2016) https://ssrn.com/abstract=2800362 accessed 9 June 2024; see also Yochai Benkler, 'When von Hippel Innovation Met the Networked Environment: Recognizing Decentralized Innovation' in Dieter Harhof and Karim Lakhani (eds), *Revolutionizing Innovation Users, Communities, and Open Innovation* (MIT Press 2016) 195.

20.040 Instead, the circular economy would be better served by a mechanism that allows broad and early diffusion of design ideas, making them accessible to third parties – including competitors. Such diffusion would tend to stimulate the broad circulation and adoption of new design ideas within design communities. Innovation would thereby be accelerated and result in widespread commercialization,[61] as well as increased market penetration of circularity-compliant products. The question then arises whether design law can be tailored in a manner that satisfies these desiderata.

2. Access and Incentive

20.041 In light of the above, a design law allowing broad and early access to designs would seemingly be the answer, as it would accelerate innovation and favour the rapid diffusion of circular designs. Nonetheless, this strategy is not without its downsides. Broad access creates opportunities to second comers, but usually risks undermining the originator's incentive.[62] It effectively 'punishes' originators of circular designs by giving them 'less' legal protection and depriving them of the incentive to design.

20.042 However, in the context of circularity, ensuring that incentives exist is just as important as ensuring access. Rapid development of a range of products that meet circularity requirements is as critical as ensuring a sufficient supply of participating designers. The task of a design regime is therefore to achieve a correct access–incentive balance for circular designs by allowing the greatest quantum of access by second comers whilst maintaining the designer's incentive.[63]

---

61   World Bank, 'Accelerating Innovation and Technology Diffusion' https://doi.org/10.1596/978-0-8213-7987-5_ch7 accessed 9 June 2024.

62   In general, giving an originator a high degree of control over the market operates as an incentive, whereas creating opportunities for competitor access risks undermining it. 'How to enable entrepreneurs to appropriate the fruits of their investments in cumulative and sequential innovation without impeding follow-on innovation and without creating barriers to entry has become one of the great unsolved puzzles that the law and economics of intellectual property rights needs to address as the new millennium gets underway' (Jerome H Reichman, 'Of Green Tulips and Legal Kudzu: Repackaging Rights in Subpatentable Innovation' (2000) 53 *Vanderbilt Law Review* 1743–1798.

63   Of course, mechanisms to achieve this goal already exist and have been extensively discussed in the literature. The first thought goes to limitations and exceptions of design laws. Generally, however, these are quite limited in EU design law (see Art 20 CDR and Art 13 DD). Alternatively, one might contemplate creating early access by means of compulsory licences (CL), as under Art 31 TRIPS and the national laws implementing it. A CL would require that a public interest of significant magnitude be demonstrated. More than likely, the climate crisis would qualify. However, the CL mechanism is geared more towards one-time calamities, as opposed to an urgent, yet continuous need to infuse new ideas and designs. Furthermore, seeking a CL is procedurally complicated, and resulting delays and transaction costs might easily deter a second comer. Finally, the spectre of a CL might operate as an overall disincentive to designers. Nonetheless, the possible

(a) Two models

20.043 Taking into account the goals and priorities discussed above, we will next consider a regime tailored to the needs of circular design. The intention is to supplement, rather than replace, the existing design regime by offering an additional 'green' or 'sustainable' option of design protection meant to incentivize circularity in the design industry. The proposed regime is rooted in two main doctrinal sources: (1) scholarly literature relating to entitlements in the form of liability rules[64] and (2) the existing unregistered design regime.[65] The former is geared towards facilitated access, whilst the latter serves as a benchmark to measure the proposal in terms of realism and practical feasibility. A more detailed elaboration of the theoretical underpinnings of both sources follows.

(i) Compensatory liability regime

20.044 Existing design law seeks to solve the fundamental challenge of monetizing intangible assets by resorting to a legal entitlement in the form of a property rule.[66] Most countries' design laws are based on property rules, by which rightsholders are granted entitlements in the form of exclusive property rights. This regime offers remedial options by way of injunctions and damages to prevent unauthorized use.[67]

---

use of the CL as an instrument for relief should not be completely disregarded. Absent any other reform, a licence tailored to certain critical products might accelerate the diffusion of design products.

64 Guido Calabresi and A Douglas Melamed, 'Property Rules, Liability Rules, and Inalienability: One View of the Cathedral' (1972), 85(6) *Harvard Law Review*, 1089–1128; Mark A Lemley and Philip J Weiser, 'Should Property or Liability Rules Govern Information?' (2007) 85 *Tex L Rev* 783; Robert Merges, 'Of Property Rules, Coase, and Intellectual Property' (1994) 94 *Colum L Rev* 2655; Jerome H Reichman, 'Database Protection in a Global Economy' (2002) 2–3 Vol XVI *Revue internationale de droit économique* 455–504; Tracy Lewis and J H Reichman, 'Alternatives to Patents: Law and Economics of a Multipurpose Liability Rule' (paper presented to Ecoinformation Lecture Series, Duke University School of Law 2004); Dana Beldiman, 'Avoiding the "Anticommons": A Mixed Liability and Property Rule Approach to Prevent Underuse of Patented Resources in R&D Involving Microbiological Materials' (2012) *International Journal of the Commons*. In addition to the unregistered design, liability rules have been adopted in several areas of law, including utility models and the protection of printed circuits, and have been proposed as an alternative mechanism to relieve the effect of restrictive IP rights (Shamnad Basheer, 'The End of Exclusivity: Towards a Compensatory Patent Commons'; Reichman, Jerome H. and Santos Rutschman, Ana, Protecting Sub-Patentable Innovation: The Case for Codified Liability Rules (August 6, 2023). *UC Davis Law Review*, 2024, Duke Law School Public Law & Legal Theory Series No. 2023-43, available at SSRN: https://ssrn.com/abstract=4532824

65 Regulation on Community Designs No 6/2002 ('CDR') Arts 11 and 19(2); UK Unregistered Design Right (UDR) Intellectual Property Act 2014, c 18, Part 1.

66 A property rule grants an entitlement to the effect 'that someone who wishes to remove the entitlement from its holder must buy it from him in a voluntary transaction in which the value of the entitlement is agreed upon by the seller' (Guido Calabresi and A Douglas Melamed (n 64)).

67 '[T]he founding vision of intellectual property viewed owners of governmentally conferred rights—in patent and copyright—as the beneficiaries of a government license and as entitled only to remedies sufficient to encourage innovation' (Mark A Lemley and Philip J Weiser (n 64)). 35 USC s. 289 provides for damages for infringement of design patents in the USA.

20.045 As an alternative to the property rule regime, the law recognizes a different approach, known as a 'liability rule'. This form of entitlement is theoretically grounded in the seminal work of Calabresi and Melamed.[68] The features of the liability rule are discussed below, and its pros and cons are examined relative to the incentive–access balance.

20.046 Unlike a property regime, a liability regime does not grant originators a property right. Instead, rightsholders receive an entitlement to collect compensation for third-party use of the invention or design at issue.[69] In other words, under this view, a second comer 'may infringe first, and a tribunal will determine the appropriate compensation in an *ex post* proceeding'.[70]

20.047 In a circular economy context, a liability regime presents the advantage that it facilitates access. Second comers are not required to await the expiration of an exclusivity period or, alternatively, to seek a licence which is granted at the originator's discretion. Instead, second comers enjoy *de facto* and *de jure* access once the design is published. This feature tends to promote dissemination of designs and allows second comers to make, distribute and improve designs as soon as they become public.[71]

20.048 On the downside, a second comer's freedom under a liability rule diminishes originators' incentive to innovate. The presence of competitors in the market limits originators to charging market-determined, rather than monopoly, prices. Liability rules entitle originators to collect royalties for a third party's use of the design at issue. However, the originator has the burden of enforcing and collecting. Transaction costs for tracking down infringers and prosecuting legal actions may put originators between a rock and a hard place: either enforce their exclusivity and incur unspecified transaction costs or lower their prices in the face of competition.[72] Originators may therefore have a hard time recouping their investment under a liability rule regime.

---

68 'Whenever someone may destroy the initial entitlement if he is willing to pay an objectively determined value for it, an entitlement is protected by a liability rule.' Guido Calabresi and A Douglas Melamed (n 64).
69 Jerome Reichman and Tracy Lewis, 'Using Liability Rules to Stimulate Local Innovation in Developing Countries: Application to Traditional Knowledge' in Keith E Maskus and Jerome H Reichman (eds), *International Public Goods and Transfer of Technology Under a Globalized Intellectual Property Regime* (2005) 337–366.
70 Robert Merges (n 64).
71 In general, such a rule, if properly crafted, would solve the problem of incentive and access with fewer social costs and without impoverishing the public domain (Jerome H Reichman (n 62)).
72 Studies have found that the design community considers design protection law to be expensive and unpredictable (see the psychometric survey analysed in Chapter 5 of A Carter-Silk and M Lewiston, 'UK IPO Report: The Development of Design Law: Past and Future' (2012) 8; see also Anna Tischner, 'The Role

20.049 One way to somewhat equalize this imbalance is to allow originators a certain amount of lead time over potential competitors. This would give originators the opportunity to recoup their investment and make a small profit, thereby incentivizing designers. Similarly, the burden of collecting compensation by means of enforcement action can be alleviated by using technology.[73]

(ii) The unregistered design regime

20.050 The second doctrinal source for the model proposed here is the unregistered design regime (UDR), a form of design protection that is in effect in selected jurisdictions, including the EU[74] and the UK.[75] Conceptually, it derives from the liability rule described above.[76] Unlike registered design, a UDR, as its name indicates, requires no registration. In the EU, once a design has been made public, a designer enjoys a period of exclusivity of 36 months, after which the design becomes part of the public domain. Within that term, a designer is given the right to enjoin unauthorized use and to be compensated by such users in a court proceeding.[77] Substantive law standards for both the protectability and scope of protection of an unregistered design are substantially the same as those of the registered design regime.[78]

20.051 The UK national unregistered design right prevents third parties from copying the shape and configuration of man-made articles. It lasts for ten years after the first marketing of articles to which the design has been applied; however, during the second five-year term, competitors are entitled to copy the design, provided they pay royalties under a licence of right.[79] The UK unregistered design right only protects the three-dimensional aspects of the design (func-

---

of Unregistered Rights-a European Perspective on Design Protection' (2018) 13(4) *Journal of Intellectual Property Law & Practice* 303.

73 See text accompanying n 82.
74 See Arts 11 and 19(2) CDR, modelled on the informal seasonal protection against pure misappropriation of garment designs provided by German unfair competition law. See also A Kur, 'Protection for Fashion: The European Experience' in R C Dreyfuss et al (eds), *Intellectual Property at the Edge* (2014) 187; Anna Tischner (n 72) 305.
75 Copyright Designs and Patents Act 1988 ('CDPA 1988'), Art 213 et seq.
76 The concept of a liability regime derives from the seminal article by Calabresi and Malamud (n 64), and was proposed by Prof Reichman in various settings, including Jerome H Reichman (n 62); and Jerome H Reichman, 'A Compensatory Liability Regime to Promote the Exchange of Microbial Genetic Resources for Research and Benefit Sharing' in Paul F Uhlir (ed), Designing the Microbial Research Commons: Proceedings of an International Symposium (2011) 43–53.
77 The claimant is obliged to prove the date from which the design is protected (disclosure) and the right to the design (entitlement), as well as to identify the design at issue (object of protection) and prove that an alleged infringer copied the design (copying). The unregistered Community design right owner does not benefit from the presumption of ownership. The plaintiff has the burden of identifying the design at issue.
78 Arts 3–13 CDR.
79 Section 237 CDPA1988.

tional and aesthetic), and does not cover such matters as surface patterns, ornamentation or colour.[80]

20.052 The advantage of the UDR is the absence of registration formalities and the early access to the design by third parties. The challenge lies in the originator's ability to collect revenue from design users. As the designs have been made public, they are available for copying by third parties. Law-abiding second comers may approach the originator for a licence. As for those who do not, the burden is on the originator to enforce their rights in court. Successful enforcement theoretically provides originators with revenue, in the form of court-ordered royalties or other compensation. Still, the uncertainty and transaction costs associated with enforcement may diminish the originator's revenue.

20.053 In short, a UDR includes several features that favour early diffusion and thereby support circularity. On the other hand, designers receive limited support from the IP system. It is only when it comes to enforcement, i.e., at the 'tail end', that designers can rely on legislated norms. Consequently, UDR's popularity has been limited, often serving as secondary mechanism to save costs or as a fallback protection mechanism.

20.054 Designers might find more attractive a regime that maintains a UDR's ease of dissemination as well as its procedural simplicity, whilst ideally also mitigating the drawbacks of not owning property rights. The following will present a proposed model that attempts to meet these requirements in an effort to support the promotion of circular designs.

(b) The envisioned circular design protection regime

20.055 We propose a model that would increase designers' incentive by providing support at the 'front end' (commercialization). Designers would have the opportunity to register ('record') their designs in a centralized electronic repository associated with an online platform from which users may 'purchase' licences to a design. Smart contracts would enable users to obtain non-exclusive licences on customized terms via the platform.[81] The designer would set their own royalty rate. Upon successful purchase, the licensee would receive in an

---

80 These deficiencies can likely be worked around in the proposed new model discussed below.
81 Inspiration can be drawn from existing mechanisms. For example, the UK IPO maintains a searchable database of patents that are endorsed 'licence of right', i.e., the patent holder has agreed to licence their patent to anyone, effectively turning it into claims for remuneration. https://www.gov.uk/guidance/licensing-intellectual-property accessed 9 June 2024.

electronic format the design record, which would contain the entire design file and all other information necessary to a potential user.[82]

20.056 In this way, a successful designer can potentially collect streams of royalty income from multiple licensees. Furthermore, designers are largely relieved of transaction costs and time required by marketing, licensing and tracking royalties. On the enforcement side, the proposed model would operate in much the same way as an unregistered design. Should a third party use the design without a licence, or should a user fail to comply with the licensing conditions, a design owner would have the right to sue for compensation in court. The standards would generally seek to follow those for registered and unregistered design laws.

20.057 In summary, we propose a simple architecture in the form of a 'take and pay' model[83] intended for circular designs. From a legal perspective it can be seen as a regulated framework for contractual licences, operating on the assumption that an entitlement exists. Rather than relying on an issuing authority to validate the design based on pre-established standards, the value of the design is determined by its attractiveness to potential licensees/users. In turn, this is based on the users' assessment of the design's effectiveness and marketability. Legal standards relating to validity and scope of protection only come into play in the event of a dispute. Compared to the UDR, the proposed model offers the 'front end' benefit of marketing and licensing support via a centralized, electronic licensing mechanism.

20.058 Next, we will consider whether this model provides sufficient benefits to circular designers, so as to outweigh the absence of property rights associated with it.

(c) Does the proposed model provide an adequate balance between early and broad access and incentive to be attractive to circular designers?

20.059 As outlined above, the goal of the proposed regime is to promote the development and commercialization of circular designs. The urgency associated with the need to mitigate and adapt to climate change demands rapid dissemination

---

82   The online record would include the information relevant to a licensee, including the identity of the designer, the date of publication, a description and rendition of the design and its circular features – such as materials and configuration – which allow for reuse, repurpose, repair and the like. The platform might be supported by e.g., blockchain technology and could be maintained by an organixation such as WIPO or EUIPO (e.g. WIPO Green https://www3.wipo.int/wipogreen/en/faqs.html accessed 9 June 2024). Technologies of this type are already in use in various contexts. For instance, Github and similar repositories allow design information to be transferred. Alternatively, a negotiation/bidding mechanism can be built into the system.
83   Jerome Reichman and Tracy Lewis (n 69).

of new designs. This in turn requires facilitated access to existing designs. At the same time, it is important not to disincentivize originators monetarily.

20.060 From an access standpoint, the proposed model presents numerous benefits. It would make available circular designs to third parties from the day of recordation. The system of non-exclusive licences would generate competition among manufacturers. Products would penetrate the market more rapidly and would likely accelerate the phasing out of old designs with greater carbon footprints. The widespread commercial availability of circularity-compliant products would help speed up changes in public consumption patterns in a more sustainable direction. Finally, the non-exclusive licensing model would prevent bottlenecks resulting from single-source supply and prevent single actors from capturing secondary product markets. Combined, these elements would result in a significant beneficial impact on issues of societal and environmental interest.

20.061 Of course, for these access benefits to be achieved, the regime must offer sufficient incentive to designers to actually make use of it.[84] We argue that the proposed electronic platform presents advantages that can make the system attractive, certainly to aspiring designers. Let's consider the benefits a designer can derive from it. Firstly, the platform effectively constitutes a centralized method of advertising and distribution, largely obviating the costs associated with marketing and intermediaries. Secondly, a successful designer can potentially receive multiple streams of income from multiple licensees. Thirdly, designers are free to set their own market-based royalty rates. Fourthly, designers are not obligated to forego a registered design option.[85] Finally, using the centralized platform may prove attractive to licensees, as it tends to reduce the information asymmetry between designers and users of the design. Specifically, it provides background information on the designer, as well as the design and its use (including detailed CAD files and a tracking system of the number of licences issued and available, which can help prospective users develop nuanced business strategies).

---

84 Ultimately, as with any IP right, business success is contingent on the market. Therefore, a word about the market for circular, sustainably orientated products is in order. Currently, the market for these products is still emerging. Most circularity-compliant products are initially likely to have a 'green premium', i.e., a higher price than their functional non-green equivalent. Whether this market can take off based on the consumers' willingness to pay a green premium out of a sense of social responsibility or whether legislative intervention is required is still uncertain.

85 Even assuming design protection is obtained, a designer would be free to take advantage of the centralized platform for distribution purposes if the design qualifies as 'circular'. In this case, the platform's contractual provisions would prevail over the exclusivity of the design patent.

20.062 Combined, these benefits may well outweigh the disadvantages associated with the absence of an IP right. The proposed model may thus become quite attractive, initially mainly to emerging, technologically savvy designers who are also advocates of the circular economy and whose goal is in part to 'make a difference'. Furthermore, if such a platform were to be installed as a pilot project, it would be a useful test case through which to assess the attractiveness of the model, once sufficient use data have been collected.

20.063 Understandably, concerns over the use of a liability rule-based model might be raised as a matter of principle. These would be mainly based on the fact that under the proposed model, designers would receive no property right and would instead be limited to a right of compensation for unauthorized use. In IP law circles it is widely believed that the absence of a property right tends to reduce a designer's incentive to create.[86] It might also be argued that it interferes with a designer's freedom to license or to withhold a licence, or that alternatively, the proposed model comes close to a compulsory licence.[87]

20.064 These are all valid concerns, supported by strong arguments. Ultimately, however, no metric exists to determine the sufficiency of access or incentive or the balance between them. Time will tell whether the proposed modifications are effective once data have been gathered to allow for evidence-based analysis. In the meantime, IP law must follow the times and explore whether technological means can help reach the desired policy outcome.

F. CONCLUSION

20.065 This chapter delves into a fundamental issue which confronts all IP regimes: the potential flexibility of IP rules when weighed against urgent social and environmental concerns of significant global impact. Naturally, the answer to this question should be in the affirmative because, after all, the intellectual property law system is supposed to serve society, not the other way round.

---

86   Richard A Epstein, 'A Clear View of the Cathedral: The Dominance of Property Rules' (1997) 106 *Yale Law Journal* 2091.

87   The authors take the position that the proposed model differs fundamentally from a compulsory licence. However, as a counterargument, social concerns have at times required the imposition of statutory licences on IP owners, such as Art. 31 TRIPS, most notably, and the various licences in the pharmaceutical industry granted under it, the US mechanical licence for sound recordings, etc, or in the design field, the UK licence as of right, the Chinese statutory licences, etc. These licences are generally intended to correct an imbalance caused by IP rights and to respond to a greater societal goal. Even if that were not the case, would the environmental concern not justify the flexibility of IP laws designed to further this significant human goal?

20.066 In this chapter we address two pivotal and likely controversial issues. Firstly, we consider the appropriate scope of the 'object of protection' of a circular design law, primarily questioning the focus on the visibility of a product's outer appearance as a response to the circular economy's emphasis on new, ecologically orientated materials. Secondly, we propose the use of a liability-type rule, associated with a centralized platform for licensing and distributing designs. This constitutes a novel approach to ensuring broad and timely access to circular designs, aimed at maintaining a practically achievable balance between access and designers' incentive.

20.067 Of course, this rough, conceptual framework must be populated with the other constituent elements required by a circular design law.[88] These may or may not require significant changes, and this remains a task for future research. Ultimately, the final contours of a circular design law must be determined by considering the framework systemically, whilst adjusting each element so as to maintain a realistic access–incentive balance that responds to the needs of the circular economy.

20.068 Considered from a broader perspective, the ongoing reform of design law in the EU has overlooked the critical examination of the rationale underlying design protection in the context of circular economy mandates.[89] The disconnect between the world of designers and the world of the legal protection of design is becoming increasingly apparent. The so-called design approach featuring EU design legislation is worth continuing in the sense that it is necessary to reflect on the essence and value of creativity in this field, which in the 21st century requires going beyond purely economic motivation and switching to sustainable, long-lasting products designed to be durable and repairable.[90] The proposed model, meant to incentivize circularity in design industries whilst facilitating access to socially desirable designs, is an attempt to find an adequate response to today's challenges without substantially deconstructing

---

88   These elements may include the treatment of functional designs, including a possible overlap with utility model laws, royalty structures, smart contracts in the context of licensing designs, treatment of design improvements in the context of centralized electronic platforms for the distribution of designs, etc.

89   The declared goal of the ongoing EU design law reform is to ensure that the design protection regime better supports the transition to the digital and green economy. See Communication from the Commission to the European Parliament, the Council, the European Economic and Social Committee and the Committee of Regions of 25 November 2020, Making the most of the EU's innovative potential: An intellectual property action plan to support the EU's recovery and resilience, COM/2020/760 final. Disappointingly, however, a review of the proposed changes shows that the reformers have not addressed the problem adequately, limiting themselves in this context to the nonetheless important issue of repairs and access to spare parts.

90   See the Proposal for a directive on common rules promoting the repair of goods and amending Regulation (EU) 2017/2394, Directives (EU) 2019/771 and (EU) 2020/1828 https://commission.europa.eu/system/files/2023-03/COM_2023_155_1_EN_ACT_part1_v6.pdf accessed 9 June 2024.

the existing principles of design protection. Nevertheless, the problem of adequate incentive/access mechanisms in the context of circular design raises fundamental questions as to whether the *sui generis* EU design regime serves a valid purpose.

INDEX

abusive disclosure 16.039–16.041
access-based business models 20.012
access–incentive balance 20.036–20.064
    for circular designers 20.059–20.064
    compensatory liability regime model 20.044–20.049
    envisioned circular design protection regime 20.055–20.058
    unregistered design regime model 20.050–20.054
accused infringer 7.054–7.056
Administrative Case Litigation Act 7.046
administrative data 5.119–5.122
administrative enforcement 3.108–3.110
administrative patent judges (APJs) 9.039
adoption and implementation timeline I.078
aesthetic creative freedom 17.001–17.106
    copyright law 17.014–17.043
        aesthetic limits 17.064–17.066
        commonalities 17.089–17.091
        cumulative effects 17.096–17.106
        differences 17.092–17.095
        statutory limits 17.074–17.075
        technical limits 17.067–17.073
    design law 17.008–17.013
        aesthetic limits 17.047–17.049
        commonalities 17.089–17.091
        cumulative effects 17.096–17.106
        differences 17.092–17.095
        statutory limits 17.057–17.063
        technical limits 17.050–17.056
    legal concept 17.002–17.006
    trademark law 17.044–17.045
        aesthetic limits 17.076–17.077
        commonalities 17.089–17.091
        cumulative effects 17.096–17.106
        differences 17.092–17.095
        statutory limits 17.085–17.087
        technical limits 17.078–17.084
aesthetic design concept 17.001
aesthetic effect 17.005
aesthetic freedom 17.003
aesthetic surplus 17.005
African Continental Free Trade Area (AfCFTA) Agreement 12.004, 12.005, 12.031–12.035
African Group Disclosure of Origin Proposal 13.007–13.016
African Regional Intellectual Property Organisation (ARIPO) I.054, 12.001–12.036
    AfCFTA Agreement 12.004, 12.005, 12.031–12.035
    Harare Protocol 12.001–12.007, 12.009, 12.011, 12.013–12.016, 12.021, 12.029–12.030
    legal framework 12.006–12.028
        appeals 12.028
        formal examination 12.013–12.016
        opposition by Member States 12.017–12.020
        registration procedure 12.009–12.012
        substantive examination 12.021–12.027
    overview of 12.001–12.005
Agreement of Trade-Related Aspects of Intellectual Property Rights (TRIPS) 1.019, 12.004, 15.011, 15.013, 15.014, 15.016–15.018, 18.007
AI-assisted designs 19.002, 19.008, 19.029, 19.058, 19.087
AI-driven designs 19.002, 19.008, 19.022–19.067
AI-generated belt 19.009

AI-generated designs 19.002, 19.003, 19.005,
    19.009, 19.011, 19.020–19.022,
    19.026, 19.032, 19.036,
    19.048, 19.057, 19.065–19.067,
    19.076, 19.077, 19.079–19.082,
    19.086–19.088
alternative application mechanisms
    2.021–2.022
amendments
    Australian industrial design protection
        1.155–1.159
    Canadian design law 2.139–2.142
    United States Design Patent Law
        9.122–9.127
Antikainen, Mikko I.063
appeal of refusal 2.029–2.030
appeal trial 7.028–7.029
application data sheet (ADS) 9.029
application refusal 2.027–2.030
    appeal of refusal 2.029–2.030
    grounds of objection 2.027
    response 2.028
article of manufacture 9.128–9.130,
    15.043–15.046
    requirement I.049
artificial intelligence (AI) I.052,
    19.001–19.088
    as artistic works 19.026–19.029
        author/authorship 19.027
        Berne Convention 19.027
        European standard of originality
            19.028
        personality theory 19.027–19.028
    artists 19.001
    conflict with copyright 19.026–19.029
    design-based approach 19.068–19.078
    designers 19.001, 19.008
    designership/design development
        19.030–19.067
        causality theory 19.052
        design development 19.045–19.058
        designership 19.034–19.044
        multiplicity of form theory 19.052
        objective novelty 19.045
        objective observer 19.053
        practical implications
            19.059–19.067

subjective intention 19.053
subjective novelty 19.045
design regime roots 19.007–19.010
digital designs 19.011–19.021
digital revolution design 19.007–19.010
fashion industry design law
    18.052–18.056
in general 19.022–19.025
non-human creativity 19.001
protecting purely AI-generated designs
    19.079–19.082
virtual designs 19.011–19.021
artistic craftsmanship work 15.039
artistic value 5.053, 5.064
artistic work 15.039
attenuated visibility I.042–I.044
Australian Copyright Act (1968) 1.006
Australian Designs Act 1.001, 1.016, I.042
Australian Government's Advisory Council
    on Intellectual Property 1.039
Australian industrial design protection
    1.001–1.276
    amendments applications 1.155–1.159
    certificate of examination 1.053–1.055
    compulsory licences 1.249–1.251
    consumer protection laws 1.014–1.015
    copyright protection 1.005–1.010
    Court cases 1.240–1.245
    de lege ferenda law reform 1.252–1.276
        incremental improvement
            protection 1.273–1.276
        partial designs 1.263–1.272
        virtual/non-physical designs
            1.255–1.262
    design 1.021–1.040
    design filings, registrations, and
        certifications 1.238–1.239
    disputes 1.185–1.200
    divisional design applications
        1.108–1.112
    entitlement 1.090–1.098
        rights of co-owners 1.096–1.098
    examination and certification procedures
        1.046–1.054
    exclusions 1.059
    familiar person 1.086–1.089
    filing date applications 1.103–1.104

grace period 1.046–1.058
infringement 1.063, 1.186–1.200
    innocent 1.193–1.195
    proceedings 1.186–1.190
    remedies 1.191–1.192
    unjustified threats 1.196–1.200
infringement exemptions 1.067–1.078
    prior use 1.067–1.071
    spare parts 1.072–1.078
infringing conduct 1.063–1.066
invalidity disputes 1.185
judicial decisions 1.201–1.237
    Apple Inc [2017] ADO 6 1.227–1.228
    Astrazeneca AB [2007] ADO 4 1.216–1.218
    GM Global Technology Operations LLC v S.S.S. Auto Parts Pty Ltd [2019] FCA 97 1.229–1.237
    Keller v LED Technologies Pty Ltd [2010] FCAFC 55 1.219–1.221, 1.224
    LED Technologies Pty Ltd v Elecspess Pty Ltd [2008] FCA 1941 1.222–1.223
    LED Technologies Pty Ltd v Roadvision Pty Ltd [2012] FCAFC 3 1.209–1.210
    Microsoft Corporation [2008] ADO 2 1.225–1.226
    Multisteps Pty Ltd v Source and Sell Pty Ltd [2013] FCA 743 1.214–1.215
    Review 2 Pty Ltd v Redberry Enterprise Pty Ltd [2008] FCA 1588 1.201–1.208
    World of Technologies (Aust) Pty Ltd v Tempo (Aust) Pty Ltd [2007] FCA 114 1.211–1.213
minimum filing requirements 1.103–1.104
multi-design applications 1.105–1.107
notification responses and amendment 1.049–1.052
ownership 1.090–1.098

rights of co-owners 1.096–1.098
post-registration rights and renewal 1.042–1.045
prior art 1.041–1.045
prior disclosures 1.046–1.058
    before 10 March 2022 1.052–1.053
    corresponding design 1.054–1.058
    on/after 10 March 2022 1.047–1.051
priority date applications 1.113–1.118
product design 1.023–1.029
publication applications 1.126–1.128
register correction amendments 1.166–1.167
registered designs 1.001–1.003
    amendments 1.060–1.165
    assignment of 1.246–1.248
registration procedures 1.029–1.041
    common design 1.039–1.041
    formalities 1.034–1.037
    notifications under section 41 and amendment 1.032–1.033
    refused designs 1.038
registration request applications 1.123–1.125
rights granted 1.060–1.062
sources of law 1.016–1.020
Statement of Newness and Distinctiveness 1.119–1.122
substantial similarity in overall impression 1.079–1.085
terms 1.099–1.100
time extensions 1.179–1.184
trademark protection 1.011–1.013
validity challenges 1.168–1.178
    information 1.170–1.172
    requesting examination 1.168–1.169
    revocation proceedings before the Commissioner 1.173–1.174
    revocation/rectification proceedings before the Court 1.175–1.178
visual design features 1.030–1.040
Australian Trade Marks Act (1995) 1.011
author/authorship 19.027

Bagley, Margo I.055

INDEX

Bangui Agreement 12.006
Beldiman, Dana I.064
Benelux Designs Convention 1.115
Berne Convention 5.055, 5.057, 15.013, 18.004, 19.007, 19.027
border control appeal 2.075–2.077
Botswana's Industrial Property Act 12.024
Brancusi, Lavinia I.059
Brussels I Regulation 14.012–14.014, 14.016, 14.017, 14.020, 14.032, 14.034, 14.039–14.041, 14.055, 14.069
burden of submission and proof 11.035–11.037

Canadian design law 2.001–2.154
    additional grounds defences 2.070
    administration 2.005
    application refusal 2.027–2.030
        appeal of refusal 2.029–2.030
        grounds of objection 2.027
        response 2.028
    border control appeal 2.075–2.077
    design applications filed/registrations granted 2.124
    design protection 2.006–2.026
        alternative application mechanisms 2.021–2.022
        application procedure 2.012–2.013
        articles 2.015
        deferred publication 2.026
        examination period 2.019
        formalities 2.023
        geographic scope 2.017
        grace period 2.016
        ownership rights 2.018
        priority 2.024–2.025
        representation 2.014
        required information 2.011
        subject matter 2.006–2.010
        typical costs 2.020
    enforcement 2.051–2.067
        criminal liability 2.066
        expedited proceedings 2.061–2.063
        infringement 2.052–2.054
        injunctive relief 2.059
        jurisdiction 2.051
        limitation period 2.065
        procedures 2.055–2.058
        representation 2.064
        stays 2.060
        unauthorised threats 2.067
    Hague Agreement 2.080–2.107
    invalidity 2.047–2.050
        grounds 2.047
        procedures 2.048–2.050
    legislation 2.001–2.004
    legislative reform 2.125–2.154
        amendments 2.139–2.142
        application requirements 2.133
        fees 2.148
        final comment 2.154
        history 2.125–2.127
        multiple design application 2.134–2.138
        novelty provision 2.128–2.132
        other issues 2.149–2.153
        policy and practice changes 2.143–2.147
    non-infringement defences 2.068–2.069
    protection strategies 2.108–2.123
    recovery of costs 2.074
    registrable transactions 2.040–2.046
        assignments 2.040
        licenses 2.042–2.045
        security interests 2.046
    registration 2.032–2.039
        effects 2.032–2.035
        renewal 2.038–2.039
        term 2.036–2.037
    relief/remedies 2.071–2.073
    third-party oppositions 2.031
Canadian Intellectual Property Office (CIPO) 2.005, 2.029, 2.097, 2.099
causality theory 8.055, 18.029, 19.052
causative test I.020, I.021
certificate of examination 1.053–1.055
China National Intellectual Property Administration (CNIPA) 3.050, 3.093, 3.095
Chinese Amended Patent Law (2020) I.035
Chinese design protection 3.001–3.127
    administrative enforcement 3.108–3.110
    business aspects 3.119–3.123
    civil enforcement 3.098–3.107

INDEX

civil claims 3.102
common defences 3.107
damages 3.104–3.106
remedies 3.103–3.106
designer freedom 3.039–3.042,
  3.112–3.118
disputes 3.090–3.110
eligibility requirements 3.005–3.021
  disclosure by use 3.011–3.012
  distinctiveness 3.014–3.018
  fit for industrial use 3.019–3.020
  good faith 3.021
  grace period 3.013
  novelty 3.007–3.013
  publication disclosure 3.008–3.010
functionality 3.043–3.044
identity/similarity comparison
  3.030–3.038
  evaluation process 3.031–3.035
  infringement 3.036–3.038
  observation method 3.031–3.035
  scope of protection 3.036–3.038
infringement 3.096–3.097
international registration 3.087–3.089
invalidation rights 3.090–3.095
judicial decisions 3.111–3.118
national registration 3.049–3.086
  application procedure 3.056–3.061
  drawings 3.062–3.068
  examination procedure 3.080–3.083
  granting authority 3.050
  partial designs 3.069–3.079
  priority 3.051–3.055
  publication 3.084–3.086
  registration 3.084–3.086
  renewal 3.084–3.086
object of comparison 3.025–3.027
ordinary user test 3.028–3.029
ownership 3.045–3.048
  co-ownership 3.048
  service inventions 3.046–3.047
patent applications 3.124–3.126
  auto parts 3.124
  designing patents 3.125–3.126
  metaverse 3.125–3.126
patent rights 3.120–3.123
  license 3.121–3.123

transfer 3.120
technology transfer 3.120
circular designers 20.059–20.064
circular economy design approach
  20.001–20.068
  access and incentive balance
    20.036–20.064
    for circular designers 20.059–20.064
    compensatory liability regime model
      20.044–20.049
    envisioned circular design
      protection regime
      20.055–20.058
    unregistered design regime model
      20.050–20.054
  access-based business models 20.012
  business models 20.013–20.016
  in design industry 20.008–20.012
  fashion industry design law
    18.066–18.074
  Gerrard Street and Skagarak models
    20.013–20.016
  linear economy policies vs.
    20.017–20.022
  new design law model 20.036–20.064
  object of protection 20.028–20.035
  policy goals 20.023–20.027
  product long-life models 20.012
  product's appearance concept
    20.029–20.031
circularity
  definition of 20.002
  design industry 20.008–20.012
  value by design 20.016
climate crisis 20.037
climate law 4.087
Code of Federal Regulations (C.F.R.). 9.004
community design courts 14.035–14.039
Community Design Courts 14.035–14.039
  EU-wide jurisdiction 14.035–14.037
  limited jurisdiction 14.038–14.039
Community Design Regulation (CDReg)
  I.029, 4.119, 10.018, 10.060, 10.063,
  14.034, 14.046, 14.054, 14.056,
  18.005, 18.010, 19.007
Community Designs Implementing
  Regulation (CDIR) 11.071, 11.072

community trade mark regulation (CTMR) 8.053
compensation
    for damages 5.101–5.107
    liability regime model 20.044–20.049
    for other sanctions 5.101–5.107
competent courts 14.026–14.029
complex product 1.024, 16.046, 18.012
compulsory licences 1.249–1.251
concept of reciprocity 11.051
confidential disclosure 16.033
confidential prior art disclosure 11.028–11.030
Conflict of Laws in Intellectual Property (CLIP) principles 14.067–14.071
    applicable law 14.070–14.071
    jurisdiction 14.069
consumer protection laws 1.014–1.015
Convention on Biological Diversity (CBD) 13.005, 18.065
co-ownership 3.048
Copyright Act I.014, 1.006, 2.001, 2.002, 6.006, 6.007, 6.026, 6.028, 6.054–6.056, 6.080, 7.001, 7.008, 15.033, 15.037–15.039
Copyright, Designs and Patents Act 1988 (CDPA) I.026, 10.036, 10.038, 10.039, 10.044, 10.065, 10.067, 10.096
copyright infringement 17.022, 17.028
copyright law
    aesthetic creative freedom 17.014–17.043
        aesthetic limits 17.064–17.066
        commonalities 17.089–17.091
        cumulative effects 17.096–17.106
        differences 17.092–17.095
        statutory limits 17.074–17.075
        technical limits 17.067–17.073
    Italian design protection 5.053–5.064
copyright protection 1.005–1.010
    curtailing effect I.014–I.016
    expansion of I.008–I.013
    Italian industrial design law 5.053–5.064
corporate designership 19.042
corresponding designs 1.006, 1.054–1.058

Court of Justice of the European Union (CJEU) 4.091
Covarrubia, Patricia I.061
creative freedom 17.003
    functional 17.006
creative leeway 17.001
creative reuse 18.073
criminal enforcement 10.093–10.094
criminal liability 2.066
criminal penalty 7.064
cultural heritage I.077
cumulation
    aesthetic creative freedom 17.096–17.106
    concept I.010
    of rights I.013
cumulative doctrine 18.019
cumulative protection I.006–I.016
customs measures 7.063
Customs Regulation 8.048

damages 3.104–3.106, 4.065, 9.122–9.123
Danish Patent and Trademark Office (DKPTO) 8.030
data-driven generative hybrid design 19.008
defences I.073
    Chinese design protection 3.107
    Japanese industrial design approach 7.052–7.056
    non-infringement 2.068–2.069
    UK design law approach 10.031–10.034, 10.055–10.058
    unitary IP rights 14.044
    United States Design Patent Law 9.059–9.062
deferred publication 2.026
de lege ferenda law reform
    Australian industrial design protection 1.252–1.276
        incremental improvement protection 1.273–1.276
        partial designs 1.263–1.272
        virtual/non-physical designs 1.255–1.262
    Japanese industrial design approach 7.077

INDEX

design (cont.)
  United States Design Patent Law
    9.119–9.121
Denmark design protection *see* Nordic
    countries design protection
design
  aesthetic creative freedom
    17.008–17.013
    aesthetic limits 17.047–17.049
    commonalities 17.089–17.091
    cumulative effects 17.096–17.106
    differences 17.092–17.095
    statutory limits 17.057–17.063
    technical limits 17.050–17.056
  definition of I.068, 18.013
  development 19.045–19.058
  functional 15.042
  industrial 15.018–15.027
  laws *see specific countries*
  ornamental 15.028–15.041
  regulation I.068–I.073
    defenses I.073
    definitions I.068–I.069
    digital infringement I.072
    repair clause I.071
    visibility I.070
Design Directive I.074–I.077
  cultural heritage I.077
  national level unregistered designs I.075
  repair clause transition period I.076
designer freedom 3.039–3.042, 3.112–3.118
designership 19.034–19.044
  corporate 19.042
Design Law Treaty (DLT) 13.001–13.032
  African Group Disclosure of Origin
    Proposal 13.007–13.016
  experimentation 13.017–13.025
  policy space 13.017–13.025
  WIPO 13.026–13.031
digital designs 19.011–19.021
digital infringement I.072
digital revolution designs 19.007–19.010
direct infringement 9.053–9.056
dispute(s)
  Australian industrial design protection
    1.185–1.200
  Chinese design protection 3.090–3.110
  French design law approach 4.052–4.069
    customs measures 4.068–4.069
    invalidity 4.052–4.057
    litigation 4.058–4.063
    remedies 4.064–4.067
  Indian design law approach 6.060–6.069
    not a design defined under section 2
      (d) 6.069
    not new/original 6.067
    not registerable under this Act
      6.068
    piracy 6.070–6.072
    prior document publications 6.065
    prior publication 6.063–6.064
    prior-registered designs 6.062
    publication by prior use 6.066
  Japanese industrial design approach
    action against trial decision
      procedures 7.045–7.047
    criminal penalty 7.064
    customs measures 7.063
    defences 7.052–7.056
    enforcement 7.057
    grounds for invalidity 7.040–7.041
    infringement 7.051
    invalidation trial procedures
      7.042–7.044
    scope of protection 7.048–7.050
  jurisdictional I.056
  Nordic countries design protection
    8.037–8.048
    grounds for invalidity 8.037–8.039
    litigation 8.040–8.048
  United States Design Patent Law
    9.039–9.070
    administrative body 9.039–9.040
    challenges 9.043–9.045
    defences to infringement
      9.059–9.062
    direct infringement 9.053–9.056
    fees 9.047
    indirect infringement 9.057–9.058
    infringement 9.049–9.052
    legal grounds 9.041–9.042
    related enforcement proceedings
      9.048
    remedies for infringement
      9.063–9.070

INDEX

timing 9.046
Distillers Test 1.163–1.164
distinctive rights 4.036
divisional design applications 1.108–1.112

enforcement
    Canadian design protection 2.051–2.067
        criminal liability 2.066
        expedited proceedings 2.061–2.063
        infringement 2.052–2.054
        injunctive relief 2.059
        jurisdiction 2.051
        limitation period 2.065
        procedures 2.055–2.058
        representation 2.064
        stays 2.060
        unauthorised threats 2.067
    Chinese design protection
        administrative 3.108–3.110
        civil 3.098–3.107
    Italian industrial design law
        customs 5.108–5.118
        of rights 5.065–5.096
    Japanese industrial design approach 7.057
    UK design law approach 10.079–10.094
        choice of forum 10.080–10.082
        criminal enforcement 10.093–10.094
        English courts approach 10.085–10.087
        pre-action communications 10.083–10.084
        remedies 10.088–10.092
        standing to sue 10.083–10.084
        threats 10.083–10.084
    United States Design Patent Law 9.048
English courts approach 10.085–10.087
enjoyment of rights 7.020–7.021
entitlement 1.090–1.098
environmental crisis 20.037
envisioned circular design protection regime 20.055–20.058
erga omnes effect 14.033
European Court of Justice (ECJ) 10.006
European Green Deal *see* circular economy design approach

European standard of originality 19.028
European Union community design 11.001–11.138
    brief overview of 11.001–11.005
    CJEU 11.011–11.015
    conflict with earlier copyright 11.112–11.120
        National Copyright Law 11.115–11.117
        standards 11.113–11.114
        unauthorised use 11.118–11.120
    conflict with earlier design 11.121–11.132
        degree of freedom designer 11.124–11.129
        infringement standards 11.122–11.123
        infringing usage 11.131–11.132
        scope of protection 11.130
    conflict with earlier trademark 11.095–11.111
        benefits 11.101
        distinctive sign 11.098–11.099
        genuine use 11.100
        likelihood of confusion 11.107
        maintenance 11.108–11.111
        similar/identical goods and services 11.102–11.105
        similarity of signs 11.106
        standards 11.096–11.097
    EUIPO case law and practice 11.009–11.010
    General Court 11.011–11.015
    individual character 11.045–11.060
        degree of freedom designer 11.051–11.052
        impressions 11.057–11.060
        informed user 11.053–11.056
    inherent invalidity 11.073–11.094
        interconnectivity permits 11.080–11.082
        modular system exceptions 11.083–11.087
        technical function 11.074–11.079
        visibility 11.088–11.094
    lack of consistency 11.061–11.072
    lack of unity

invalidity proceedings
  11.066–11.069
registration proceedings
  11.070–11.072
novelty 11.038–11.044
prior art disclosure 11.016–11.037
  burden of submission and proof
    11.035–11.037
  confidential prior art disclosure
    11.028–11.030
  as consequence of abuse
    11.031–11.034
  obscure prior art disclosure
    11.023–11.025
  own prior art disclosure
    11.026–11.027
  relevant prior art 11.018–11.022
  unauthorized disclosure
    11.035–11.037
European Union design law prior art
  16.001–16.089
  contested design vs. earlier disclosure
    16.051–16.064
    grace period 16.062–16.064
    relevant subject-matter comparison
      16.057–16.061
    self-disclosure 16.062–16.064
    significance of representation
      16.052–16.056
    testing novelty/individual character
      16.057–16.061
  disclosure
    abusive 16.039–16.041
    administrative/judicial body
      16.011–16.014
    confidential 16.033
    within grace period 16.034–16.038
    presumptive knowledge
      16.011–16.014
    rules of 16.017–16.022
    safeguard clause 16.023–16.027
    unregistered Community design
      16.028–16.031
  model of relative novelty 16.007–16.010
  standards from global perspective
    16.065–16.089
    absolute novelty 16.067–16.072

grace period models 16.067–16.072
protectable design 16.073–16.079
subject-matter disclosure
  earlier disclosure 16.048–16.050
  EU concepts of design/product
    16.044–16.047
  IPRs 16.048–16.050
  relevant piece 16.043
European Union design law reform
  adoption and implementation timeline
    I.078
  Design Directive I.074–I.077
  design regulation I.068–I.073
European Union Design Package I.050
European Union design rights 14.001–14.077
  CLIP principles 14.067–14.071
    applicable law 14.070–14.071
    jurisdiction 14.069
  Hague Conference on Private
    International Law 14.063–14.064
  infringement 14.010–14.024
    applicable law 14.024
    multiple parallel national design
      rights 14.019–14.023
    single Member State 14.010–14.018
  IP rights 14.004–14.005
    enforcement 14.006–14.009
  Kyoto guidelines 14.072–14.077
    applicable law 14.077
    jurisdiction 14.074–14.076
  Lugano Convention 14.057–14.062
  national design rights 14.010–14.024
  unitary IP rights 14.025–14.056
    applicable law 14.045–14.052
    Community Design Courts
      14.035–14.039
    competent courts 14.026–14.029
    defences 14.044
    international jurisdiction
      14.034–14.039
    multiple defendants 14.040–14.042
    provisional measures and remedies
      14.043
    related actions 14.053–14.056
    subject-matter jurisdiction
      14.031–14.033

European Union Intellectual Property
    Office (EUIPO) 4.003, 11.001,
    11.004–11.005, 11.008–11.010
European Union Trade Marks Directive
    10.068
exploitation of designs 4.073–4.077

familiar person 1.086–1.089
fashion industry design law 18.001–18.084
    contemporary issues 18.052–18.084
        3D printing 18.057–18.060
        4D printing 18.057–18.060
        artificial intelligence 18.052–18.056
        circular economy 18.066–18.074
        overlapping IP protections
            18.075–18.084
        traditional knowledge
            18.061–18.065
    design concept 18.011–18.015
    global perspectives 18.001–18.010
    infringement 18.041–18.051
    ownership 18.038–18.040
    registered Community designs
        18.016–18.031
        grounds for refusal 18.028–18.031
        individual character 18.021–18.027
        novelty 18.021–18.027
    unregistered Community designs
        18.032–18.037
Federal Court of Canada 2.051
fees 2.085–2.087, 2.148, 9.047
Finland design protection *see* Nordic
    countries design protection
first-to-file rule 7.017–7.018
fit for industrial use 3.019–3.020
fonts 1.225–1.228
4D printing 18.057–18.060
fraudulent/obvious imitation 6.070
freedom designer 11.051–11.052,
    11.124–11.129
French design law approach 4.002–4.125
    business approach 4.072–4.090
        exploitation of designs 4.073–4.077
        limits of rights 4.083–4.090
        scope of rights 4.078–4.082
    disputes 4.052–4.069
        customs measures 4.068–4.069

    invalidity 4.052–4.057
    litigation 4.058–4.063
    remedies 4.064–4.067
judgments 4.091–4.100
legal framework 4.003–4.007,
    4.104–4.114
    in Europe 4.106–4.114
    in France 4.104–4.105
legislation reform project 4.115–4.119
ownership 4.008–4.011
prosecution approach 4.038–4.051
    duration 4.044–4.046
    grounds for refusal 4.048–4.050
    international option 4.051
    priority 4.047
protection conditions 4.012–4.037
    distinctive rights 4.036
    functionality 4.034
    harm to prior copyrights/designs
        4.036
    individual character 4.027–4.031
    interconnectability 4.035
    morality 4.032–4.033
    novelty 4.021–4.026
    product appearance 4.016–4.020
    public policy 4.032–4.033
    repair clause 4.037
rights granted 4.008–4.011
term 4.008–4.011
3D printing 4.120–4.125
functional creative freedom 17.006
functional design 15.042
functionality I.017–I.026
    causative test I.020, I.021
    Chinese design protection 3.043–3.044
    French design law approach 4.034
    Indian industrial design law 6.012–6.014
    multiplicity of forms approach I.019,
        I.021, I.023
    no alternative design approach I.022
    ornamentality requirement I.024
    primarily I.024
    purely I.024
    technical I.025, I.026

generative adversarial networks (GANs)
    19.003

INDEX

genetic resources 13.005
Geneva Act 7.037–7.039, 18.005
German Federal Supreme Court
    11.069, 11.090, 11.093, 11.125,
    11.126, 16.030, 17.001, 17.008,
    17.010–17.012, 17.024, 17.027,
    17.028, 17.047, 17.052, 17.067
Gerrard Street and Skagarak business model
    20.013–20.016
Ghana's Industrial Designs Act 12.024
Ghosh, Shubha I.058
good faith 3.021
Goss, Ian 13.027
grace period
    Australian industrial design protection
        1.046–1.058
    Canadian design law 2.016
    Chinese design protection 3.013
    European Union design law prior art
        16.062–16.064
    Indian industrial design law 6.022–6.023
graphical user interface (GUI) I.049
    in Australian design 1.225–1.228
green transition 20.006
grounds for refusal 4.048–4.050,
    18.028–18.031

Hague Agreement 1.020, 1.115,
    2.080–2.107, 3.087, 5.036, 8.036,
    9.038, 12.006
    Canadian applicants international
        protection 2.080–2.094
        application procedures 2.081–2.084
        examination 2.088–2.090
        fees 2.085–2.087
        publications 2.092–2.094
        registration 2.091
    Canadian applicants treatment
        2.095–2.107
        basic procedures 2.095–2.096
        design unity 2.098–2.099
        examination 2.097
        grant 2.101
        novelty 2.100
        term and renewal 2.102–2.105
        transfers 2.106–2.107

Hague Conference on Private International
    Law (HCCH) 14.063–14.064
Hague Treaty 18.005
Harare Protocol 12.001–12.007, 12.009,
    12.011, 12.013–12.016, 12.021,
    12.029–12.030, I.054
Härkönen, Heidi I.063
harmonization 13.022–13.023
Hartwig, Henning I.057, I.060

identity/similarity comparison 3.030–3.038
    evaluation process 3.031–3.035
    infringement 3.036–3.038
    observation method 3.031–3.035
    scope of protection 3.036–3.038
implementable quantity 7.061
Indian Copyright law 6.054–6.057
Indian industrial design law 6.001–6.081
    article definition of 6.009–6.011
    assignment 6.076–6.077
    cancellation disputes 6.060–6.069
        not a design defined under section 2
            (d) 6.069
        not new/original 6.067
        not registerable under this Act
            6.068
        prior document publications 6.065
        prior publication 6.063–6.064
        prior-registered designs 6.062
        publication by prior use 6.066
    classification of articles 6.025
    design 6.006–6.008
        artistic work 6.007
        definition of 6.006
        non-registrable designs 6.008
    evaluation/analysis/comments
        6.078–6.081
    fraudulent/obvious imitation 6.070
    functionality 6.012–6.014
    grace period 6.022–6.023
    industrial process/means 6.009, 6.015
    lapsed design 6.029
    legislations 6.001–6.005
    licensing of design rights 6.073–6.075
    new/original designs 6.016–6.021
    piracy disputes 6.070–6.072
    priority 6.024

prior publication 6.018
reciprocity arrangement 6.024
registration procedures 6.030–6.047
    formality 6.038–6.039
    ordinary applications/priority
        applications 6.030
    representation sheets 6.031–6.035
    scandalous/obscene material 6.047
    substantive examination
        6.040–6.047
    summary of steps 6.030–6.037
rights granted 6.026–6.028
term 6.026–6.028
two/three-dimensional product
    appearances 6.048–6.059
    copyrights 6.054–6.057
    patents 6.058–6.059
    trademarks 6.048–6.053
Indian Patents Act 6.058–6.059
Indian Patents and Designs Act 6.001, 6.002
indirect infringement 9.057–9.058
individual character 4.027–4.031,
    10.011–10.022, 11.045–11.060
    contested design *vs.* earlier disclosure
        16.057–16.061
    degree of freedom designer
        11.051–11.052
    fashion industry design law
        18.021–18.027
    impressions 11.057–11.060
    informed user 11.053–11.056
inducement 9.057, 9.058
industrial design 15.018–15.027
Industrial Design Office Practice Manual
    2.127, 2.134, 2.137, 2.144, 2.147
information disclosure statement (IDS) 9.036
informed consent 18.065
informed consumer 2.053
informed observer 18.027
informed user 5.020–5.022, 8.056, 10.010,
    10.015, 11.053–11.056, 16.024,
    18.027
    in Australian design 1.214–1.218
infringement 1.063, 1.186–1.200, 7.051,
    9.049–9.052
    Canadian design law 2.052–2.054
    Chinese design protection 3.096–3.097

    copyright 17.022, 17.028
    defences to 9.059–9.062
    direct 9.053–9.056
    EU design rights 14.010–14.024
        applicable law 14.024
        multiple parallel national design
            rights 14.019–14.023
        single Member State 14.010–14.018
    exemptions 1.067–1.078
        prior use 1.067–1.071
        spare parts 1.072–1.078
    fashion industry design law
        18.041–18.051
    indirect 9.057–9.058
    innocent 1.193–1.195
    proceedings 1.186–1.190
    remedies 1.191–1.192, 9.063–9.070
    UK design law approach 10.031–10.034,
        10.055–10.058
    unauthorised threats 2.067
    unjustified threats 1.196–1.200
injunctive relief 2.059, 7.057
innocent infringement 1.193–1.195
innocent infringer 10.090
intellectual property (IP) 19.022–19.025
Intellectual Property Enforcement Directive
    (IPED) 10.088
Intellectual Property Enterprise Court
    (IPEC) 10.081
intellectual property rights (IPRs) 5.115,
    5.117
    enforcement 14.006–14.009
    in EU 14.004–14.005
    unitary 14.025–14.056
        applicable law 14.045–14.052
        Community Design Courts
            14.035–14.039
        competent courts 14.026–14.029
        defences 14.044
        international jurisdiction
            14.034–14.039
        multiple defendants 14.040–14.042
        provisional measures and remedies
            14.043
        related actions 14.053–14.056
        subject-matter jurisdiction
            14.031–14.033

INDEX

interlocutory injunctions 2.059
international jurisdiction 14.034–14.039
International Law Association (ILA) 14.066
International Trade Commission
 9.117–9.118
inter partes reviews (IPRs) 9.039, 9.041,
 9.043
invalidation
 proceedings 2.049–2.050
 rights 3.090–3.095
 trial procedures 7.042–7.044
 UK design law approach 10.027–10.030
invalidity 1.185, 2.047–2.050, 7.040–7.041,
 8.037–8.039
 EU community design 11.066–11.069
involuntary joinder 14.018, 14.021, 14.023,
 14.040–14.042
Italian Civil Code 5.006
Italian Copyright Law 5.008
Italian industrial design law 5.001–5.122
 administrative data 5.119–5.122
 compensation
  for damages 5.101–5.107
  for other sanctions 5.101–5.107
 enforcement
  customs 5.108–5.118
  of rights 5.065–5.096
 exhaustion of rights 5.051–5.052
 legal framework 5.005–5.010
 protection 5.001–5.004
  copyright law 5.053–5.064
  exclusion of 5.026–5.029
  requirements 5.011–5.025
  technical characteristics
   5.026–5.029
 registration
  nullity of 5.048–5.050
  procedures 5.030–5.040
  rights conferred 5.041–5.047
 technical expertise 5.097–5.100
Italian Judicial Authority 5.067
Italian Patent and Trademark Office 5.032,
 5.035, 5.122

Japanese industrial design approach
 7.001–7.078
 business aspects approach 7.070–7.074

  licensing 7.072–7.074
  transferability 7.070–7.071
 de lege ferenda law reform 7.077
 judicial decisions 7.065–7.066
  Carabiner case 7.066
  Flexible and Elastic Hose case 7.065
 jurisdiction protection 7.001–7.009
  copyright 7.008
  design 7.002–7.006
  trademark 7.007
  unfair competition 7.009
 legal framework 7.010–7.019
  first-to-file rule 7.017–7.018
  industrially applicable 7.012
  not easily creatable 7.015
  not identical/similar of design 7.016
  novelty 7.013–7.014
  unregistrable items 7.019
 litigation disputes 7.048–7.062
  defences 7.052–7.056
  enforcement 7.057
  infringement 7.051
  scope of protection 7.048–7.050
 new technologies 7.078
 number of court cases 7.068
 number of filings 7.067
 other disputes
  criminal penalty 7.064
  customs measures 7.063
 present legal framework comments 7.076
 prosecution disputes 7.040–7.047
  action against trial decision
   procedures 7.045–7.047
  grounds for invalidity 7.040–7.041
  invalidation trial procedures
   7.042–7.044
 rate of sucess 7.069
 registration procedure 7.020–7.039
  appeal trial 7.028–7.029
  application procedure 7.022–7.027
  enjoyment of rights 7.020–7.021
  international registration
   7.037–7.039
  post registration 7.030
  priority claim 7.036
  remedies 7.034–7.035
 specific applications/case studies 7.075

Japan's Craftsmanship Law I.047, 3.125
joint ownership 3.048
judicial decisions
    Australian industrial design protection
        1.201–1.237
    Chinese industrial design protection
        3.111–3.118
    French design law approach 4.091–4.100
    Japanese industrial design approach
        7.065–7.066
    Nordic countries design protection
        8.049–8.056
    United States Design Patent Law
        9.071–9.094
jurisdictional disputes I.056
Justice Bakshi Tek Chand Committee 6.001
Justice N. Rajagopala Ayyangar Committee
    6.001

Kyoto guidelines 14.072–14.077
    applicable law 14.077
    jurisdiction 14.074–14.076

lapsed design 6.029
Leahy-Smith America Invents Act (AIA)
    9.046
legal framework I.050–I.051
    ARIPO 12.006–12.028
    French design law approach
        4.003–4.007, 4.104–4.114
    Italian industrial design law 5.005–5.010
    Japanese industrial design approach
        7.010–7.019
legislation
    Canadian design law approach
        2.001–2.004
    French design law approach 4.115–4.119
    Indian industrial design law 6.001–6.005
liability rules 20.045, 20.048
Libraries of Things (LoTs) 18.070
licensing
    Canadian design protection 2.042–2.045
    Chinese design protection 3.121–3.123
    Indian industrial design law 6.073–6.075
    Japanese industrial design approach
        7.072–7.074

United States Design Patent Law
    9.104–9.106
likelihood of confusion 11.107
linear economy design law policies
    20.017–20.022
litigation
    French design law approach 4.058–4.063
    Japanese industrial design approach
        7.048–7.062
    Nordic countries design protection
        8.040–8.048
    United States Design Patent Law
        9.048–9.070
Locarno Agreement 1.106, 1.131, 1.134,
    1.141, 5.034, 18.006
London Treaty 18.005
Lugano Convention 14.057–14.062
Lusaka Agreement 12.001

Manderieux, Laurent I.061
manifest abuse 8.024
Manual of Patent Examining Procedure
    (MPEP) 9.004
Margoni, Thomas 19.036
metaverse 3.125–3.126, 19.003
model of relative novelty 16.007–16.010
modular system exceptions 11.083–11.087
morality 4.032–4.033
multi-design applications 1.105–1.107,
    2.134–2.138
multiple parallel national design rights
    14.019–14.023
multiplicity of forms approach I.019, I.021,
    I.023, 8.055, 10.024
multiplicity of form theory 19.052

Nagoya Protocol 18.065
Namibia's Industrial Property Act 12.024
National Copyright Law 11.115–11.117
no alternative design approach I.022
non-infringement defences 2.068–2.069
non-physical designs 1.255–1.262
Nordic countries design protection
    8.001–8.072
    comments/analysis/evaluation
        8.064–8.072
    disputes 8.037–8.048

grounds for invalidity 8.037–8.039
litigation 8.040–8.048
judicial decisions 8.049–8.056
   causality theory 8.055
   informed user 8.056
   multiplicity of forms approach 8.055
practical aspects 8.057–8.063
procedural aspects 8.030–8.036
substantive aspects 8.001–8.029
   current situation 8.010–8.017
   essential difference 8.008
   history details 8.001–8.009
   manifest abuse 8.024
   national design right system 8.018–8.029
   patent approach 8.008
   regional exhaustion principle 8.023
   repair clause 8.020, 8.064
   reputation parasitism 8.016

objective novelty 19.045
object of protection I.041
obviousness 9.013
Okorie, Chijokie I.054
ordinary observer test 9.053, 9.054
ordinary user test 3.028–3.029
originality 4.098, 10.050–10.052
   European standard of 19.028
ornamental design 15.028–15.041
   artistic craftsmanship work 15.039
   artistic work 15.039
   useful article 15.034
ornamentality requirement I.024
overlapping design protection 15.001–15.052
   article of manufacture 15.043–15.046
   fashion industry 18.075–18.084
   functional design 15.042
   industrial design 15.018–15.027
   Japanese design registration 15.043–15.048
   ornamental design 15.028–15.041
      artistic craftsmanship work 15.039
      artistic work 15.039
      useful article 15.034
   textile design 15.013

TRIPS Agreement 15.011, 15.013, 15.014, 15.016–15.018
US design registration 15.043–15.048
ownership
   Australian industrial design protection 1.090–1.098
   Canadian design protection 2.018
      transfers of 2.106–2.107
   Chinese design protection 3.045–3.048
      co-ownership 3.048
      service inventions 3.046–3.047
   fashion industry design law 18.038–18.040
   French design law approach 4.008–4.011
   UK design law approach 10.027–10.030, 10.053–10.054

PACTE Act 4.055
Paris Convention 1.019, 1.113, 1.116, 2.010, 2.083, 4.040, 5.018, 5.023, 5.050, 6.001, 7.036, 8.005, 8.068, 12.006, 12.011, 13.013, 16.017, 16.079, 16.085, 18.003, 18.067
partial designs 1.263–1.272
participative proceedings 4.061
Patent and Market Court of Appeal (PMCA) 8.046
patent applications 3.124–3.126
patent defence 17.046, 17.053, 17.055, 17.056
Patent Law Treaty (PLT) 13.002, 13.004
Patent Trial and Appeal Board (PTAB) 9.025, 9.039, 9.040, 9.076, 9.077, 9.079
Patterns and Designs Protection Act 6.001
personality theory 19.027–19.028
planetary environmental crisis 20.006
policy coherence 13.024
post-grant reviews (PGRs) 9.039, 9.042
primarily functional I.024
prior art design 1.041–1.045
prior art disclosure 11.016–11.037
   burden of submission and proof 11.035–11.037
   confidential 11.028–11.030
   as consequence of abuse 11.031–11.034
   European Union design law

abusive 16.039–16.041
administrative/judicial body
 16.011–16.014
confidential 16.033
within grace period 16.034–16.038
model of relative novelty
 16.007–16.010
presumptive knowledge
 16.011–16.014
rules of 16.017–16.022
safeguard clause 16.023–16.027
unregistered Community design
 16.028–16.031
obscure 11.023–11.025
own 11.026–11.027
relevant prior art 11.018–11.022
unauthorized disclosure 11.035–11.037
prior art EU *vs.* foreign standards
 16.065–16.089
absolute novelty 16.067–16.072
grace period models 16.067–16.072
protectable design 16.073–16.079
prior disclosures 1.046–1.058
before 10 March 2022 1.052–1.053
corresponding design 1.054–1.058
on/after 10 March 2022 1.047–1.051
prior use infringement exemption
 1.067–1.071
product, definition of I.069
product design 1.023–1.029
product long-life models 20.012
protectable industrial designs 7.003
protectable subject matter 9.006–9.007
protectable UKUDR designs 10.041–10.044
publications 10.077–10.078
 applications 1.126–1.128
 deferred 2.026
 disclosure 3.008–3.010
 prior 6.018, 6.063–6.064
 prior document 6.065
 prior-registered designs 6.062
 by prior use 6.066
public policy 4.032–4.033
purely functional I.024

quantity transferred 7.061

reciprocity concept 11.051, 17.043, 17.095
recovery of costs 2.074
refused designs 1.038
regional exhaustion principle 8.023
registered Community designs (RCDs)
 8.012, 8.028, 10.005
fashion industry design law
 18.016–18.031
grounds for refusal 18.028–18.031
individual character 18.021–18.027
novelty 18.021–18.027
registered designs 1.001–1.003
amendments 1.060–1.165
assignment of 1.246–1.248
UK design law approach 10.004–10.034
defences 10.031–10.034
design details 10.007–10.010
duration 10.027–10.030
exclusions 10.023–10.026
individual character 10.011–10.022
infringement 10.031–10.034
novelty 10.011–10.022
ownership 10.027–10.030
post-grant invalidation
 10.027–10.030
requirements 10.007
Registered Designs Act (1949) I.048
registered trade marks 10.068–10.069
registrable transactions 2.040–2.046
assignments 2.040
licenses 2.042–2.045
security interests 2.046
registration procedures
ARIPO 12.009–12.012
in Australia 1.029–1.041
common design 1.039–1.041
formalities 1.034–1.037
notifications under section 41 and
 amendment 1.032–1.033
refused designs 1.038
in Canada 2.032–2.039
effects 2.032–2.035
renewal 2.038–2.039
term 2.036–2.037
Indian industrial design law 6.030–6.047
formality 6.038–6.039

ordinary applications/priority
    applications 6.030
representation sheets 6.031–6.035
scandalous/obscene material 6.047
substantive examination
    6.040–6.047
summary of steps 6.030–6.037
Italian industrial design law
    nullity of 5.048–5.050
    procedures 5.030–5.040
    rights conferred 5.041–5.047
Japanese industrial design approach
    7.020–7.039
    appeal trial 7.028–7.029
    application procedure 7.022–7.027
    enjoyment of rights 7.020–7.021
    international registration
        7.037–7.039
    post registration 7.030
    priority claim 7.036
    remedies 7.034–7.035
UK design law approach 10.070–10.078
    examination 10.075–10.076
    filing basics 10.071–10.074
    post-grant matters 10.077–10.078
    publications 10.077–10.078
United States Design Patent Law 9.024
relevant entity 1.049
remedies/relief 2.071–2.073, 3.103–3.106,
    7.034–7.035, 9.063–9.070,
    10.088–10.092
    infringement 1.191–1.192
repair clause 4.037, 8.020, 8.064, 18.069
    design regulation I.071
    in EU I.029–I.032
    jurisdictions without I.034–I.037
    in other jurisdictions I.033
    transition period I.076
representation 2.014, 2.064
reputation parasitism 8.016
rights of co-owners 1.096–1.098
right to repair I.027–I.037
Rome II Regulation 14.024, 14.047–14.049,
    14.077

safeguard clause 16.008, 16.023–16.027,
    16.080

Särmäkari, Natalia 19.008
self-disclosure 16.062–16.064
service inventions 3.046–3.047
similar/identical goods and services
    11.102–11.105
similarity of signs 11.106
Singapore Registered Designs Act I.047
soft law 14.066
spare parts I.027–I.037
    infringement exemptions 1.072–1.078
specified quantity 7.061
Statement of Newness and Distinctiveness
    1.119–1.122, 1.128, 1.268
statutory standardisation 17.060, 17.087
stays 2.060
subjective novelty 19.045
subject matter 2.006–2.010
subject-matter disclosure
    earlier disclosure 16.048–16.050
    EU concepts of design/product
        16.044–16.047
    IPRs 16.048–16.050
    relevant piece 16.043
subject-matter jurisdiction 14.031–14.033
substantial similarity 1.079–1.085,
    1.201–1.213
Swakopmund Protocol 13.019
Sweden design protection *see* Nordic
    countries design protection

'take-make-use-dispose' model 20.008
TAXUD 5.115
technical functionality I.025, I.026
technologies 7.078, 9.128–9.130, I.046–I.052
    artificial intelligence I.052
    challenges I.046–I.048
    legal reform I.050–I.051
    workarounds I.049
technology transfer 3.120
Teilman-Lock, Stina I.064
term 1.099–1.100, 2.036–2.037, 2.102–2.105,
    4.008–4.011, 6.026–6.028
textile design 15.013
third-party oppositions 2.031
3D printing 4.120–4.125, 18.057–18.060
timeline 9.046
    adoption and implementation I.078

Tischner, Anna 19.010, I.064
total profits rule 9.124–9.127
trade dress 9.021–9.022
Trademark Act 2.001, 2.003, 2.067, 2.123, 6.048, 7.001, 7.007, 8.053, 17.078
trademark law
    aesthetic creative freedom 17.044–17.045
        aesthetic limits 17.076–17.077
        commonalities 17.089–17.091
        cumulative effects 17.096–17.106
        differences 17.092–17.095
        statutory limits 17.085–17.087
        technical limits 17.078–17.084
    protection 1.011–1.013
traditional cultural expressions (TCEs) 18.061
traditional knowledge 18.061–18.065
transfers of ownership 2.106–2.107
transformed designs 17.104
Treaty Establishing the European Community 1.115

UK continuing unregistered Community design (UK CUD) 10.060, 10.084, 10.091
UK design law approach 10.001–10.097
    enforcement 10.079–10.094
        choice of forum 10.080–10.082
        criminal enforcement 10.093–10.094
        English courts approach 10.085–10.087
        pre-action communications 10.083–10.084
        remedies 10.088–10.092
        standing to sue 10.083–10.084
        threats 10.083–10.084
    IP rights 10.064–10.069
        copyright 10.065–10.067
        registered trade marks 10.068–10.069
    registered designs 10.004–10.034
        defences 10.031–10.034
        design details 10.007–10.010
        duration 10.027–10.030
        exclusions 10.023–10.026
        individual character 10.011–10.022
        infringement 10.031–10.034
        novelty 10.011–10.022
        ownership 10.027–10.030
        post-grant invalidation 10.027–10.030
        requirements 10.007
        registration procedure 10.070–10.078
            examination 10.075–10.076
            filing basics 10.071–10.074
            post-grant matters 10.077–10.078
            publications 10.077–10.078
    unregistered design rights 10.035–10.063
        defences 10.055–10.058
        duration 10.053–10.054
        exclusions 10.045–10.049
        infringement 10.055–10.058
        originality 10.050–10.052
        ownership 10.053–10.054
        post-Brexit forms 10.059–10.063
        protectable UKUDR designs 10.041–10.044
        qualification 10.039–10.040
UK Intellectual Property Office (UKIPO) 10.002, 10.006, 10.028, 10.037, 10.038, 10.062, 10.066, 10.067, 10.070, 10.073, 10.075–10.078, 10.081, 10.094, 10.096, 10.097
UK supplementary unregistered design (UK SUD) 10.061–10.063, 10.081, 10.084
UK Supreme Court (UKSC) 10.010, 10.033, 10.073, 10.080, 10.082
UK unregistered design right (UKUDR) I.026, I.044
    exclusions 10.045–10.049
    protectable designs 10.041–10.044
    see also UK design law approach
unauthorised threats infringement 2.067
unauthorized disclosure 11.035–11.037
UN Economic Commission for Africa (UNECA) 12.031
unfair competition 7.009
Unfair Competition Prevention Act 7.001, 7.009, 9.023
unitary IP rights 14.025–14.056
    applicable law 14.045–14.052

INDEX

Community Design Courts
    14.035–14.039
competent courts 14.026–14.029
defences 14.044
international jurisdiction 14.034–14.039
multiple defendants 14.040–14.042
provisional measures and remedies
    14.043
related actions 14.053–14.056
subject-matter jurisdiction
    14.031–14.033
United States Copyright Office 11.113
United States Design Patent Law
    9.001–9.130
business aspects 9.104–9.106
case study approach 9.107–9.115
de lege ferenda law reform 9.119–9.121
improvement/amendment areas
    9.122–9.127
    damages for design patent
        infringement 9.122–9.123
    multi-component products
        9.124–9.127
judicial decisions 9.071–9.094
    *Columbia Sportswear N. Am., Inc. v.
        Seirus Innovative Accessories,
        Inc.*, 80 F.4th 1363 (Fed.
        Cir. 2023) 9.092–9.094
    *Egyptian Goddess, Inc. v. Swisa,
        Inc.*, 543 F.3d 665 (Fed. Cir.
        2008) (en banc) 9.071
    Hoop v. Hoop, 279 F.3d 1004 (Fed.
        Cir. 2002) 9.088
    *International Seaway Trading Corp.
        v. Walgreens Corp.*, 589
        F.3d 1233 (Fed. Cir. 2009)
        9.072–9.073
    *Pacific Coast Marine Windshields
        Ltd. v. Malibu Boats, LLC*,
        739 F.3d 694 (Fed. Cir.
        2014) 9.089–9.090
    In re Daniels, 144 F.3d 1452 (Fed.
        Cir. 1998) 9.081–9.083
    In re Maatita, 900 F.3d 1369 (Fed.
        Cir. 2018) 9.078–9.080
    In re Owens, 710 F.3d 1362 (Fed.
        Cir. 2013) 9.084–9.087

In re SurgiSil, L.L.P., 14 F.4th 1380
    (Fed. Cir. 2021) 9.074–9.077
Samsung Electronics Co. v. Apple Inc.,
    137 S. Ct. 429 (2016) 9.091
litigation disputes 9.048–9.070
    defences to infringement
        9.059–9.062
    direct infringement 9.053–9.056
    indirect infringement 9.057–9.058
    infringement 9.049–9.052
    related enforcement proceedings
        9.048
    remedies for infringement
        9.063–9.070
new technologies 9.128–9.130
present legal framework comments
    9.116–9.118
    district court 9.116
    International Trade Commission
        9.117–9.118
procedural aspects 9.024–9.038
    amendments 9.037
    application requirements
        9.027–9.034
    expedited examination 9.036
    international registration 9.038
    priority 9.035
    registration procedure 9.024
product life cycle *vs.* design patent
    pendency 9.119–9.121
prosecution disputes 9.039–9.047
    administrative body 9.039–9.040
    challenges 9.043–9.045
    fees 9.047
    legal grounds 9.041–9.042
    timing 9.046
statistics/trends 9.095–9.103
substantive aspects 9.001–9.023
    additional considerations
        9.014–9.016
    copyrights 9.019–9.020
    disclosure requirements
        9.008–9.010
    novelty 9.011–9.012
    obviousness 9.013
    protectable subject matter
        9.006–9.007

696

related IP laws 9.017–9.023
sources 9.003–9.005
trademarks/trade dress 9.021–9.022
Unfair Competition Prevention
Acts 9.023
utility patents 9.018
United States Patent Code I.051
unjustified threat infringements 1.196–1.200
unregistered Community designs (URCDs)
I.061, 8.012, 8.028, 16.028–16.031,
18.032–18.037,
unregistered designs I.075
regime model 20.050–20.054
useful article 15.034
US Patent and Trademark Office (USPTO)
9.004, 9.026, 9.060, 9.119–9.121,
I.051
utility patents 9.018

van Herpen, Iris 18.058

virtual designs 1.255–1.262, 19.011–19.021,
19.060
visibility I.038–I.045
attenuated I.042–I.044
concept of I.038
design regulation I.070
EU community design inherent
invalidity 11.088–11.094
EU present and proposed law
I.039–I.041
jurisdictions I.045
von Mühlendahl, Alexander I.056

Wennersten, Ulrika I.061
World Intellectual Property Organization's
(WIPO) 2.022, 2.097, 4.102, 8.036,
13.002
WIPO IGC 13.026–13.031
World Trade Organization (WTO) 1.019,
1.113, 4.040, 7.036